D0480350

Platter's
by
Diners Club
INTERNATIONAL

2016
SOUTH AFRICAN

WINE
GUIDE

36TH EDITION

Available on the
App Store

GET IT ON
Google play

John Platter SA Wine Guide (Pty) Ltd
www.wineonaplatter.com

PUBLISHER

Jean-Pierre Rossouw

EDITOR

Philip van Zyl

ASSOCIATE EDITORS

Joanne Gibson, Tim James, Cathy van Zyl

TASTERS

Angela Lloyd; Master of Wine Cathy van Zyl; Cape Wine Masters Winnie Bowman, Greg de Bruyn, Tim James, Christine Rudman and Meryl Weaver; David Biggs, David Clarke (2014 edition), Christian Eedes (2014 edition), Joanne Gibson, Higgo Jacobs, Cathy Marston, Fiona McDonald, Ingrid Motteux, Khuselo Mputa (2010 edition), Gregory Mutambe, Jörg Pfützner, James Pietersen (2014 edition) & Dave Swingler.

COPYWRITERS

Greg de Bruyn, Joanne Gibson, Tim James, Angela Lloyd, Cathy Marston, Fiona McDonald, Christine Rudman, Wendy Toerien, Cathy van Zyl & Meryl Weaver

COORDINATORS

Ina de Villiers (information) & Christina Harvett (wine & tasting)

DATABASE & QR CODES

Sean de Kock, Ben van Rensburg (Modern Web Presence)

TYPESETTING & MAPS

Gawie du Toit

ADVERTISING

Highbury Safika Media ▪ Tel +27 (0)21-416-0141

SALES & ADMINISTRATION

Christine Parent ▪ Tel: +27 (0)28-316-3049 ▪ Fax: +27 (0)28-316-1048 ▪ Email: office@wineonaplatter.com

© John Platter SA Wine Guide (Pty) Ltd 2016
PO Box 537, Hermanus 7200
Tel: +27 (0)28-316-3049 ▪ Fax: +27 (0)28-316-1048
Email: office@wineonaplatter.com

Wineonaplatter.com

Facebook.com/wineonaplatter

Twitter.com/wineonaplatter ▪ @wineonaplatter

All rights reserved. All rights attached in and to this book are, unless the context clearly indicates otherwise, the property of John Platter SA Wine Guide (Proprietary) Limited. They are protected under local and international laws and treaties. No part of this book may be reproduced, adapted or transmitted in any form or by any means (including, but not limited to, photocopying, recording, or by any information storage and retrieval system) without express written permission from the author/publisher.

All reasonable care has been taken in the preparation of this book, but the publishers and authors accept no liability whatsoever for any consequences, or loss, damages, whatsoever and howsoever incurred, or suffered resulting or arising from the use of the book or any information contained therein.

We receive numerous requests for lifting rights and, when these are for non-commercial, non-profit activities, we will assess and oblige same in writing at our sole discretion. Those wishing to quote from the book for commercial and advertising purposes, however, should make prior written arrangements with the publisher, who, permission is granted, will request a donation be made to a suitable education programme.

ISBN 978-0-9870046-5-9

Contents

A Warm Welcome from Diners Club

Welcome to the new annual edition of the Platter's by Diners Club Wine Guide – your essential handbook to all that's happening in our exciting world of wine, and your primer to where to go and what to taste.

Every year, our fabulous wine producers work extremely hard to bring us these vinous delights to enjoy at home or when we are out and about – and we salute their dedicated work. And every year, the Platter's team spends long months assessing all the new vintage wines, to write the detailed notes and descriptions that you will find here.

And in the end wine is all about relaxation and reward, and Diners Club is glad we can help make your leisure time ever more pleasurable.

Here's to a great 2016.

Chris Sweeney

Chris Sweeney
Director, Diners Club South Africa

A Word from Standard Bank

It is with great pleasure that Standard Bank, as the proud holder of the Diners Club franchise across Africa, welcomes you to the annual 2016 Platter's by Diners Club Wine Guide.

The 36th edition of the complete guide is the benchmark of what South Africa has to offer. Filled with information on around 8,000 wines, the guide ensures that consumers are informed and producers are well represented. The publication is inclusive and represents the unique diversity of what the winelands have to offer, from grape to glass.

South Africa's wine industry has a rich history and continues to move forward – at mid-year 2015 there was a 7% total year-on-year increase in domestic wine sales. Exports of packaged wines, wines that are proudly branded South Africa, also saw a 3% increase. Our wines are now enjoyed throughout the world, and we're also very excited by their strong sales growth within Africa itself.

We will always be there to help our wine industry face the challenges of the modern wine market, and wish all producers well in 2016.

Cheers!

Schlebusch

Peter Schlebusch
Chief Executive Officer, Personal and Business Banking, Standard Bank Group

Editor's Note

The most significant change for this, our 36th edition, may be invisible to the reader but is worth noting here, as it links into an ongoing process of levelling the playing field for the now 8,000 wine labels featured in the guide.

This particular tweak concerns the wines at the top end of the quality scale, and the process by which they are entered into the second round of judging aimed at awarding the guide's highest rating of five stars.

Previously wines were nominated by individual tasters but this time all wines mooted by individual judges as 'outstanding', i.e. potentially worthy of 4½ stars (90–94 points on the 100-point scale) were entered for the second review automatically. As expected this resulted in a significantly higher number of 'candidates' (close to 650) and accordingly two judging days were set aside versus the traditional one. The tasting itself was done blind (without sight of the label), as in previous years, and our tasters worked in small groups alongside expert palates from outside the team.

What on paper looked to be a spectacular tasting turned out to be that and more, team members, seasoned as they are, indicating they had felt part of something truly special. The wines which emerged from the review with ratings of 95-100 points were awarded the maximum five stars. The top scorers in this elite group were then subjected to a further evaluation to determine the Wines of the Year. This year, for the first time, a third category was introduced, namely Dessert Wine of the Year, joining the Red and White.

Long-standing aim and approach

The bottlings which were rated 94 points and thus did not make the five star cut, clearly are extremely fine in their own right and that fact is duly recognised in their being accorded the lofty status of the year's Highly Recommended wines.

Amid the fine-tuning, our long-standing aim and approach remain that of tasting, rating and describing as many as possible South African-made wines available during the currency of the book, both locally and overseas.

The rankings reflected in the book are the result of a process beginning towards the end of June, when we mobilise our team of tasters.

The results of their work are reflected in the A–Z section, along with news about the wineries and winemakers (and distilleries and distillers), general information about products, vinification facilities, vineyards, amenities available to visitors and more. (Scores for all wines in the A–Z are also listed separately for convenience in the section named This Year's Ratings Summarised on page 548.)

For visitors in search of wine-route information, we've incorporated GPS coordinates for as many as possible of the wineries open to the public at set hours or by appointment. The maps have again been fully updated, along with the quick-lookup tables which furnish key visitor information about the wineries of a particular area, such as whether or not they are open on weekends and public holidays, offer meals or refreshments, specifically cater for children, or are friendly to individuals with reduced mobility.

Hidden Gems

Our wine ranking system remains the same as last year. We cover the full spectrum, from wines we consider 'somewhat less than ordinary' (and award 0 stars, equivalent to 50–59 on the 100-point scale) to 'superlative South African classics', worthy of a full 5 stars (95-100 points). Wines rated ★★★★ or higher are usually listed first in each entry. Vintages deviating from the general rating are individually starred in the text. Very good/promising wines and more modest examples (★★★★☆ or fewer) are included in the 'run-on' listings at the end of entries.

Good-value wines are highlighted with the ⊘ icon for easy identification. Interesting, attractive, unusual, unique or otherwise particularly noteworthy Hidden Gems are flagged with this icon: ⊕. See also How to Use the Guide on page 18.

Because of deadlines, many wines in the guide are tasted freshly bottled or as works-in-progress; any considered unrateable as a result are noted as such in the text. It's worth mentioning that we taste from the end of June to end-August. Except for the bottlings assessed for five stars, all wines are tasted 'sighted' (with labels exposed) and the name of the producer known.

Sighted tasting has been the preferred approach since the inception of the guide. The reason is that we wish to remain true to the essence of this project – that of being a wine guide and not a wine competition. Platter's 'reason for being' is to inform winelovers about wines and wineries. To best do this, our tasters are encouraged to learn as much as possible about their allocated wines and wineries, and winemakers are asked to provide background information along with the tasting samples.

Tracking wines' form over time

Understanding what producers intend to achieve is far more difficult when wines are assessed blind, because then perforce you are assessing only the organoleptic qualities of what's in the glass. Since we understand the intention of the winery, we can assess how successfully the intent manifests in the glass. The more we know about the sites, the soils, the winemaking and the philosophy of the winery, the better we can assess the final product in terms of character, style and quality – and tell you about it. Our scores are the considered opinion of wine experts who understand the responsibility of adducing a star rating to a product as changeable as wine.

Another reason for sighted tasting is that the guide aspires responsibly to track the performance of the wines under review over successive vintages, to consider them against one another and to highlight those vintages which are particularly successful (and ones that are less so). This is why, for the better scoring wines, there is a 'general' or 'track record' rating in the left margin plus a 'vintage-specific' rating, if applicable, in brackets beside the particular vintage in the wine description.

Because of the subjective element associated with wine assessment, we strongly recommend you view our rankings as adjuncts to the tasting notes rather than as oracular pronouncements. And we continue to urge you, in the words of a local winery's marketing slogan, to 'trust your taste'.

Enthusiastic team

Wines featured in this edition were assessed by a team whose professionalism and unflagging enthusiasm we gratefully acknowledge. Their initials appear below the wines they tasted, as follows: Angela Lloyd (AL); Master of Wine Cathy

van Zyl (CvZ); Cape Wine Masters Winnie Bowman (WB), Greg de Bruyn (GdB), Tim James (TJ), Christine Rudman (CR) and Meryl Weaver (MW); also David Biggs (DB), Joanne Gibson (JG), Higgo Jacobs (HJ), Cathy Marston (CM), Fiona McDonald (FM), Ingrid Motteux (IM), Gregory Mutambe (GM), Jörg Pfützner (JPf) and Dave Swingler (DS). For potted biographies of the tasters, see page 15.

Warm thanks to the rest of the splendid team, specially to associate editors Cathy van Zyl, Tim James (also proofreader) and Joanne Gibson; copywriters Greg de Bruyn, Joanne Gibson, Tim James, Angela Lloyd, Cathy Marston, Fiona McDonald, Christine Rudman, Wendy Toerien, Cathy van Zyl and Meryl Weaver; information coordinator Ina de Villiers; wine coordinator Christina Harvett and assistants Bronwyn Tod, Jessica Paterson, Joanne Williams, Marga Vermaak, MF Schoeman, Nolubabalo Mashiya, Stephan Steyn and Tristan Jaftha; map and typesetting guru Gawie du Toit; Highbury Safika Media for advertising sales; Christine Parent for book sales and administration; Lara Philp and Johan Rademan of Vineyard Connection for the use of their excellent facilities; Angela Lloyd for indexing; Lauren de Kock for fact-checking; Mark Whyte and XtraSmile Couriers; Danie Pretorius and the Brandy Foundation; Ben van Rensburg (Modern Web Presence) for the QR code; and the ever-helpful SAWIS. Special thanks to Sean de Kock for 24 x 7 help with the database, intranet and website.

Most of all, loving thanks to Cathy, wife and associate editor, who outdid herself this year, juggling a day job, mothering, mentoring, fire-fighting and numerous other roles, plus Platter's, with inimitable grace, humour and efficiency; and to son Luke, proud and deserved possessor of a Private Pilot Licence (and a terrestrial one too).

Certainly not least, sincere thanks to South Africa's wine producers and negociants, without whose support the book could not be produced.

Finally, an invitation to join us on the web, Facebook and Twitter (see page 2 for details), and to look for our apps on the App Store and Google Play.

Philip van Zyl

Winery & Wines of the Year

Winery of the Year

Mullineux & Leeu Family Wines

Husband-and-wife winemaking teams have done extraordinarily well in gathering five star ratings in this edition: three for David and Nadia Sadie and another three for Gordon and Nadia Newton Johnson. True, both pairs were just pipped by the singular Frans K Smit (who won four maximum ratings for Spier).

The benefits of connubial winemaking triumphed most resoundingly, however, for Andrea and Chris Mullineux: they were awarded a total of 25 stars for their five most winning wines, and two of those five star winners ranked so high in the opinions of our assembled tasters that they were named, respectively, Red Wine and Dessert Wine of the Year. (All of these are named on the next pages.)

So, repeating their success of just two editions ago, Mullineux & Leeu Family Wines gets the most prestigious accolade we can offer, and is our Winery of the Year.

In fact, in 2014, the '& Leeu' bit was not in the name. It followed the formation of a new business partnership with Analjit Singh of India (Peter Dart remains a partner too), and the start of an important new phase in the development of Mullineux winegrowing. Above all, it has meant the acquisition of a splendid Swartland farm, Roundstone, on the slopes of the Kasteelberg between Malmesbury and Riebeek-Kasteel.

The Mullineux pair have been working with Roundstone fruit since they established their own winery in 2007. It has provided a key component for their blended Syrah (Red Wine of the Year in 2013), and is the source of their Schist Syrah – one of the single-soil-type wines they make in exceptional vintages from both shiraz and chenin blanc. They were, in fact, pioneers in showing that single-variety, and single-source, shiraz wines could work as successfully in Swartland as the blends (of varieties and/or scattered vineyards) that had already become famous.

Together with ace viticulturist Rosa 'Old Vines' Kruger, they have begun a significant medium-term planting programme at Roundstone, but will continue to source fruit elsewhere too, especially from other shale and schist soils of Kasteelberg and the granite-based Perdeberg. On their vineyards they use no weedkillers, insecticides or systemic fungicides; mulch and compost they make themselves – with the help of their herd of free-ranging Nguni cattle.

An approach that is equally reticent when it comes to artificial additives is found in their winemaking – only a small of amount of sulphur is added; definitely no yeasts, acid, tannins, enzymes or fining and filtering agents. This more natural philosophy had already characterised their work at Tulbagh Mountain Vineyards, now Fable (where Chris had been cellarmaster, more latterly assisted by Andrea, as their professional and personal lives started to happily merge).

Also dating from that time and place is their innovative concept of a solera-type system for making a sweet wine, whereby each year some wine, from dried grapes, that is not suited to their Straw Wine gets added to the solera. Occasionally, when the time is right, some is drawn off: as it was for the first time last year for the brilliant Olerasay, our Dessert Wine of the Year.

In short, this is a great and dynamic wine partnership, as well as a personal one. Their commitment to building Swartland as a source of remarkable wines (through, for example, the annual Swartland Revolution festival and the Swartland Independent Producers organisation) is intense and valuable for the whole region. They work together closely as well as tending to specialise: Chris takes primary responsibility for the vineyards, and California-born and -trained, Cape Winemakers Guild member Andrea for the cellar (where she's assisted by Tremayne Smith). They are now living on Roundstone, with their two children and two dogs.

Red, White and Dessert Wines of the Year

Five Stars & Red Wine of the Year

Mullineux Iron Syrah 2013

Co-owners and winemakers Chris and Andrea Mullineux craft three varietal shirazes/syrahs for their Terroir Specific range. The grapes for our Red Wine of the Year 2016 are sourced from a single parcel of organically farmed dryland bushvines on rolling hills with iron-rich soils west of Malmesbury in Swartland. Iron Syrah is more firmly structured than its stablemate from the schist terroir, more approachable in youth than the occasional release from granite soils. Expect complexity and sleek muscularity when you open the bottle.

Five Stars & White Wine of the Year

Warwick The White Lady Chardonnay 2014

Stellenbosch's Warwick has built its enviable reputation mostly on red wines, perhaps most notably its single-variety Cabernet Franc and Bordeaux-style red Trilogy. The estate's first wines were crafted by Norma Ratcliffe, who has passed the baton to the next generation but remains actively involved. A relatively new addition to the portfolio, The White Lady 2014 Chardonnay is fermented with wild yeasts and matured in 33% new French wood for 10 months. Its lime seam, stony minerality and resonant length make for an exceptional package.

Five Stars & Dessert Wine of the Year

Mullineux Olerasay Straw Wine NV

The latest addition to the star-studded Mullineux & Leeu line-up is a chenin blanc straw wine from vintages 2008-2014, fractionally blended solera-tyle, as the playful name — and the inspired 'triangular' packaging — suggest. The process has resulted in a wine that rewards all the senses, from its hue to its billowing bouquet, complex flavours and rich but uncloying mouthfeel. Though the Olerasay is pretty irresistible, there is a compelling reason to pace oneself when tempted to draw the cork: the next bottling is due in 'five to ten years'!

Wines of the Year

Five Stars

Cabernet Franc
- [ ] Chamonix 2013

Cabernet Sauvignon
- [ ] Delaire Graff Laurence Graff Reserve 2012
- [ ] Guardian Peak Lapa 2013
- [ ] Kleine Zalze Vineyard Selection 2012

Cinsaut
- [ ] AA Badenhorst Ramnasgras 2014

Grenache Noir
- [ ] David & Nadia Sadie 2014

Pinotage
- [ ] Beeslaar 2013
- [ ] Rijk's Reserve 2011
- [ ] Spier 21 Gables 2013
- [ ] Windmeul Reserve 2014

Pinot Noir
- [ ] Bouchard Finlayson Galpin Peak 2013
- [ ] Newton Johnson Family Vineyards 2014

Shiraz/Syrah
- [ ] Bellingham Basket Press Syrah 2013
- [ ] Eagles' Nest Shiraz 2012
- [ ] Leeuwenkuil Heritage Syrah 2013
- [ ] Reyneke Syrah 2013
- [ ] Richard Kershaw Elgin Clonal Selections Syrah 2013

Red Blends
- [ ] AA Badenhorst Red 2013
- [ ] Delaire Graff Botmaskop 2013
- [ ] Ernie Els CWG Auction Reserve 2013
- [ ] Fleur du Cap Laszlo 2012
- [ ] Haskell IV 2010
- [ ] Kaapzicht Steytler Vision 2012
- [ ] Luddite Saboteur 2012
- [ ] Meerlust Rubicon 2010
- [ ] Miles Mossop Max 2012
- [ ] Mulderbosch Faithful Hound 2013
- [ ] Mvemve Raats MR de Compostella 2013
- [ ] Nico van der Merwe Mas Nicolas Cape 2013
- [ ] Savage Wines CWG Auction Reserve Follow the Line 2013
- [ ] Spier CWG Auction Reserve Frans K Smit 2011
- [ ] The Winery of Good Hope Black Rock 2013
- [ ] Vondeling Erica 2012
- [ ] Vuurberg Reserve 2012

Chardonnay
- [ ] Buitenverwachting 2014
- [ ] Dorrance Cuvée Anaïs 2014
- [ ] GlenWood Grand Duc 2013
- [ ] Graham Beck Lonehill 2014
- [ ] Haskell Anvil 2014
- [ ] MVH Signature 2014
- [ ] Newton Johnson Family Vineyards 2014
- [ ] Paul Cluver Seven Flags 2014
- [ ] Sterhuis Barrel Selection 2013
- [ ] Sumaridge 2013

Chenin Blanc
- [ ] Botanica Mary Delany 2014
- [ ] David & Nadia Sadie Hoë-Steen 2014
- [ ] Eenzaamheid 2013
- [ ] Kaapzicht The 1947 2014
- [ ] Keermont Riverside 2014
- [ ] Ken Forrester Old Vine Reserve 2014
- [ ] Mullineux Granite 2014

Roussanne
- [ ] Bellingham Whole Bunch 2015

Sauvignon Blanc
- [ ] Cederberg David Nieuwoudt Ghost Corner 2014
- [ ] Nederburg The Young Airhawk 2014
- [ ] Neil Ellis Groenekloof 2015
- [ ] Spier 21 Gables 2014

Semillon
- [ ] Constantia Uitsig 2014
- [ ] Mullineux CWG Auction Reserve The Gris 2014

Viognier
- [ ] The Foundry 2014

White Blends
- [ ] Bloemendal Kanonberg 2014
- [ ] Cape Point CWG Auction Reserve White 2014
- [ ] Constantia Glen Two 2014
- [ ] Constantia Uitsig Natura Vista 2014
- [ ] David & Nadia Sadie Aristargos 2014
- [ ] Mullineux White Blend 2014
- [ ] Newton Johnson Resonance 2014
- [ ] Nitida Coronata Integration 2014
- [ ] Oak Valley Mountain Reserve White Blend 201
- [ ] Sadie 'T Voetpad 2014
- [ ] Spier Creative Block 2 2014
- [ ] Waterkloof Circle of Life White 2013

Five Stars (continued)

Méthode Cap Classique
- ☐ Anura Brut 2011
- ☐ Cederberg Blanc de Blancs Brut 2010

Dessert Wine, Unfortified
- ☐ Miles Mossop Kika Noble Late Harvest 2014
- ☐ Nederburg Winemaster's Reserve Noble Late Harvest 2014
- ☐ Klein Constantia Vin de Constance Natural Sweet 2011

Dessert Wine, Fortified
- ☐ La Couronne Muscadel NV
- ☐ Boplaas Heritage White Muscadel 2012

Port-Style
- ☐ Boplaas Cape Vintage Reserve 2012

- ☐ De Krans Cape Vintage Reserve 2013

Brandy/Husk Spirit
- ☐ Boplaas Potstill 20 Years
- ☐ Dalla Cia 10 Year Old Cabernet Sauvignon-Merlot Husk Spirit
- ☐ KWV 10 Year Old Vintage
- ☐ KWV 12 Year Old Barrel Select
- ☐ KWV 15 Year Old Alambic
- ☐ KWV 20 Year Old
- ☐ KWV Nexus
- ☐ Oude Meester Souverein
- ☐ Van Ryn 12 Year Distillers Reserve
- ☐ Van Ryn 15 Year Fine Cask Reserve
- ☐ Van Ryn 20 Year Collectors Reserve
- ☐ Van Ryn Au.Ra

Highly Recommended

Cabernet Franc
- ☐ Holden Manz Reserve 2013
- ☐ Warwick 2012

Cabernet Sauvignon
- ☐ Camberley The 5th Element 2011
- ☐ Cederberg Five Generations 2013
- ☐ Le Riche Reserve 2012
- ☐ Meerlust 2012
- ☐ Nederburg II Centuries 2011
- ☐ Webersburg 2013

Cinsaut
- ☐ Adoro Naudé Old Vines 2014
- ☐ Mount Abora Saffraan 2014

Grenache Noir
- ☐ Sadie Soldaat 2014

Merlot
- ☐ Bein 2014

Pinotage
- ☐ Diemersfontein Carpe Diem 2013

Pinot Noir
- ☐ Bouchard Finlayson Tête de Cuvée Galpin Peak 2012
- ☐ Chamonix Reserve 2014
- ☐ Creation Reserve 2014
- ☐ Elgin Vintners 2012
- ☐ Paul Cluver Seven Flags 2013

Red Blends
- ☐ Bartho Eksteen Groepsdruk 2013
- ☐ Bergsig Icarus Red 2012

- ☐ Chamonix Troika 2013
- ☐ Constantia Glen Five 2011
- ☐ De Toren Z 2013
- ☐ Ernie Els Signature 2012
- ☐ Hartenberg The Mackenzie 2012
- ☐ Hermanuspietersfontein Die Martha 2012
- ☐ Jordan Cobblers Hill 2012
- ☐ Ken Forrester Renegade 2011
- ☐ Klein Constantia Estate Red Blend 2013
- ☐ Longridge Ekliptika 2013
- ☐ Meinert Synchronicity 2011
- ☐ Mitre's Edge Sholto 2012
- ☐ Nederburg The Motorcycle Marvel 2013
- ☐ Oak Valley The Oak Valley Blend 2009
- ☐ Rall Red 2013
- ☐ Remhoogte Sir Thomas Cullinan 2012
- ☐ Ridgeback His Master's Choice 2012
- ☐ Saronsberg Full Circle 2013
- ☐ Tokara Director's Reserve Red 2012
- ☐ Van Biljon Cinq 2013

Shiraz/Syrah
- ☐ Beau Constantia Stella 2012
- ☐ Groot Constantia Shiraz 2013
- ☐ La Motte Syrah 2013
- ☐ Luddite Shiraz 2011
- ☐ Mont Destin Destiny Shiraz 2011
- ☐ Mullineux Schist Syrah 2013
- ☐ Mullineux Syrah 2013
- ☐ The Winery of Good Hope Radford Dale Syrah 2013

Highly recommended *(continued)*

Tinta Barocca
☐ Sadie Treinspoor 2014

Touriga Nacional
☐ Sijnn 2013

Chardonnay
☐ Chamonix Reserve 2014
☐ De Grendel Op Die Berg 2014
☐ DeMorgenzon Reserve 2014
☐ De Wetshof The Site 2014
☐ Jordan Nine Yards 2014
☐ Richard Kershaw Elgin Clonal Selections 2014

Chenin Blanc
☐ Adoro Naudé Old Vines 2013
☐ Beaumont Hope Marguerite 2014
☐ Bergsig Reserve 2014
☐ Botanica 'Untitled No 1' 2014
☐ David & Nadia Sadie Skaliekop 2014
☐ DeMorgenzon Special Cuvée 2013
☐ Donkiesbaai Steen 2014
☐ Doran 2013
☐ Jean Daneel Signature 2014
☐ Mulderbosch Block W 2014
☐ Mullineux Quartz 2014
☐ Nederburg The Anchorman 2014
☐ Sadie Mev. Kirsten 2014

Grenache Blanc
☐ The Foundry 2014

Marsanne
☐ Bellingham Whole Bunch 2014

Sauvignon Blanc
☐ Cape Point Reserve 2014
☐ Cederberg David Nieuwoudt Ghost Corner Wild Ferment 2014

☐ De Grendel Koetshuis 2015
☐ Flagstone Free Run 2013
☐ Klein Constantia Organic 2014
☐ Nederburg II Centuries 2014
☐ Uva Mira Sing-a-Wing 2014

Semillon
☐ Bloemendal 2014
☐ Sadie Kokerboom 2014

White Blends
☐ Delaire Graff White Reserve 2013
☐ Miles Mossop Saskia 2013
☐ Sadie Palladius 2013

Méthode Cap Classique
☐ Charles Fox Cipher 2011
☐ Graham Beck Blanc de Blancs Brut 2010
☐ Graham Beck Brut Zero 2009
☐ Saltare Brut Blanc de Blancs NV
☐ Silverthorn CWG Auction Reserve Big Dog 2010
☐ Silverthorn The Green Man 2012
☐ The House of GM&Ahrens Vintage Cuvée 2011
☐ Villiera Monro Brut 2009
☐ Woolworths Vintage Reserve Brut 2009

Dessert Wine, Unfortified
☐ Boschendal Vin d'Or Noble Late Harvest 2013
☐ Donkiesbaai Hooiwijn Vin de Paille 2014
☐ Groot Constantia Grand Constance Natural Sweet 2012

Port-style
☐ Boplaas Cape Tawny Vintners Reserve Bin 1880 NV
☐ De Krans Cape Tawny Limited Release NV
☐ De Krans Cape Vintage 2013
☐ Groot Constantia Cape Ruby 2013

Hidden Gems

Cabernet Sauvignon
☐ Allesverloren 2013
☐ Breëland 2014
☐ Opstal 2013
☐ Simonsvlei Premier 2014

Durif/Petite Sirah
☐ Spotswood 2013

Grenache
☐ Four Paws 2014
☐ Piekenierskloof 2014

Merlot
☐ Cloof 2012
☐ Groote Post 2013
☐ Mount Rozier Beekeeper 2014

Mourvèdre
☐ Hawksmoor at Matjieskuil 2013

Pinotage
☐ Imbuko Du Plevaux 2013
☐ Onderkloof 2012
☐ Perdeberg Popular 2013
☐ Stanford Hills Jacksons 2014
☐ Vin du Cap Charmé 2014

Hidden Gems (continued)

Pinot Noir
- [ ] Lord's The Legend 2012
- [ ] Stellar Winery River's End 2014
- [ ] Virgin Earth 2013

Red Blends
- [ ] Ashton Cabernet Sauvignon-Merlot 2013
- [ ] Escapades Cabernet Sauvignon-Shiraz-Malbec 2014
- [ ] Jason's Hill Jason's Creek Classic Red 2012
- [ ] Stellar Running Duck Cabernet Sauvignon-Pinotage 2013
- [ ] Virgin Earth Shiraz-Viognier 2013

Shiraz
- [ ] Eagle's Cliff Wines-New Cape Wines Dwyka Hills 2014
- [ ] Garden Route 2013
- [ ] Kranskop 2012

Rosé
- [ ] Cape Dreams Pinotage 2014
- [ ] Fish Hoek Cinsaut 2015
- [ ] La Petite Ferme 2015

Chardonnay
- [ ] Eerste Hoop Wooded 2014
- [ ] Fröhlich Wooded 2014
- [ ] Linton Park 2014
- [ ] Slanghoek Private Selection 2015
- [ ] Wellington Bovlei Winemakers Selection 2014

Chenin Blanc
- [ ] Ashton 2015
- [ ] Ayama 2014
- [ ] Annex Kloof Xenna 2015
- [ ] Phizante Kraal 2015
- [ ] Teubes Malkopbaai 2014

Fernão Pires
- [ ] BLANKbottle Kortpad Kaaptoe

Riesling
- [ ] Bergsig Weisser Riesling 2012
- [ ] Highlands Road 2013
- [ ] Lothian 2014

Sauvignon Blanc
- [ ] Die Mas van Kakamas 2015
- [ ] Excelsior 2105
- [ ] Maison de Teijger Unwooded 2015
- [ ] Stellenbosch Vineyards Welmoed 2015

White Blends
- [ ] Allée Bleue Starlette Blanc 2015
- [ ] Boland One Creation White 2015
- [ ] Porcupine Ridge Viognier-Grenache Blanc 2014
- [ ] Quando Chenin Blanc-Viognier 2015

Dessert Wine, Unfortified
- [ ] Namaqua Noble Late Harvest 2014
- [ ] Roodezandt Late Harvest NV

Brandy
- [ ] Klipdrift Export

Buy Now, Drink Later

Cabernet Franc
- [ ] Edgebaston Camino Africana David Finlayson 2013
- [ ] Glen Carlou The Curator's Collection 2013
- [ ] Raka 2013
- [ ] Zorgvliet 2013

Cabernet Sauvignon
- [ ] Groenland Premium 2012
- [ ] Le Bonheur 2011
- [ ] Stark-Condé Three Pines 2013

Grenache
- [ ] Momento 2014

Merlot
- [ ] Lourensford 2013
- [ ] Mitre's Edge 2012

Pinotage
- [ ] Beyerskloof CWG Auction Reserve Traildust 2013

- [ ] Clos Malverne Reserve 2013
- [ ] Delheim Vera Cruz 2013
- [ ] Kanonkop Black Label 2013
- [ ] L'Avenir Single Block 2013
- [ ] Paardebosch 2014

Pinot Noir
- [ ] Catherine Marshall On Clay Soil 2013
- [ ] Litigo 2014
- [ ] Seven Springs 2013

Red Blends
- [ ] Akkerdraai Cabernet Sauvignon-Merlot 2013
- [ ] Anwilka 2012
- [ ] Boschkloof Epilogue 2013
- [ ] Diemersdal MM Louw Estate Red 2013
- [ ] Eikendal Classique 2013
- [ ] Glenelly Grand Vin de Glenelly 2010
- [ ] Keet First Verse 2012

Buy Now, Drink Later – Red Blends (continued)

- ☐ Lynx The Lynx 2012
- ☐ Olsen Cape Blend 2012
- ☐ Peter Falke Exclusive Blend 2013
- ☐ Stellenrust Timeless 2012
- ☐ Strydom CWG Auction Reserve Paradigm 2012
- ☐ Uitkyk Carlonet 2012
- ☐ Vergelegen GVB 2011

Shiraz/Syrah

- ☐ De Trafford Blueprint Syrah 2013
- ☐ Porseleinberg 2013
- ☐ Niel Joubert Shiraz 2013
- ☐ Thelema Shiraz 2012
- ☐ Van Loveren Christina Van Loveren Shiraz 2013
- ☐ Waverley Hills CW Reserve Shiraz 2012

Tinta Amarela

- ☐ Dagbreek 2014

Chardonnay

- ☐ Crystallum Clay Shales 2014
- ☐ Goudini Mirabilis Regis-Filia 2013

- ☐ Hamilton Russell 2014
- ☐ Nelson 2014
- ☐ Oldenburg 2014
- ☐ Restless River 2013

Chenin Blanc

- ☐ Bosman Optenhorst 2013
- ☐ Fledge & Co HoekSteen 2014
- ☐ Fram 2013
- ☐ Hogan 2014
- ☐ Patatsfontein Steen 2014

Sauvignon Blanc

- ☐ Strandveld Pofadderbos 2014

Semillon

- ☐ Escapades Grande Reserve 2015

White Blends

- ☐ Hughes Nativo White 2014

Port-Style

- ☐ Peter Bayly Cape Vintage 2010

About the Winery & Wines of the Year

In the course of tasting potentially 8,000 wines for this edition, those rated as 'outstanding', i.e. 4½ stars or 90-94 points on the 100-point scale, by individual judges were all entered into a second round of tasting. This was done blind (without sight of the label) by small panels, which included expert palates from outside Platter's team.

The wines regarded as superlative in a South African context were awarded the guide's highest rating, namely five stars (95-100 points). These standouts are listed above under the heading Five Stars. The highest-scoring five star wines were subjected to a further evaluation to determine the overall top scorers. The three wines – red, white and, for the first time this year, a dessert wine – which emerged from this stringent selection represent the pinnacle of SA winemaking and are recipients of the sought-after accolade, Wine of the Year.

The wines rated 94 points, which therefore did not make the five star selection but are extremely fine and collectible in their own right, are listed immediately below the Five Stars under the heading Highly Recommended.

Implicit in both the Five Star and Highly Recommended categories is the potential to improve with further bottle-maturation: 8-10 years, perhaps more, in the case of the reds and fortifieds, and around 4-6 years for the whites. (Proper storage is, of course, vital for sound maturation.) During the cycle of tasting, our team identified a number of high-quality bottlings, over and above the Five Stars and Highly Recommended wines, which show particular potential for cellaring. These ageworthy wines are listed under the heading Buy Now, Drink Later.

Also listed is a selection of wines which tasters feel are particularly worthy of note – interesting, attractive, unusual, unique, representative of an important trend etc. These Hidden Gems are also included in the A-Z directory and highlighted there with this icon: 🍷

Finally, there is the prestigious 'super award', Winery of the Year, recognising a winegrowing team who, in the opinion of the editor, are ambassadors par excellence for South African wine.

Further details about all releases listed in the Wines of the Year section will be found under the names of the relevant producers in the A-Z directory. The five star tasting is audited by Grant Thornton South Africa.

Tasters for this Edition

David Biggs

David discovered wine as an art student back in the 1960s and has been writing about it for more than 30 years. He was appointed wine columnist for the Cape Argus newspaper in 1979, and qualified officially as a wine judge in 2000. In 2001 he received a scroll of honour from the Cape Wine & Spirit Education Trust in recognition of his contribution to wine education in South Africa. David has been a judge in every Veritas competition since its inception, is a founder member of the Wine-of-the-Month tasting panel, and regularly judges at the Muscadel Championship and Terroir Wine Awards. In 2011 he was named a Living Legend of the wine industry. David has written several books on wine and cocktails, is a regular contributor to Good Taste magazine, and runs the wine website www.davidbiggsonline.com.

Winifred Bowman

A qualified physiotherapist and biomedical scientist, and holder of a PhD in Education, Winifred developed an interest in wine during her student days at Stellenbosch University and later through frequent travels to international winegrowing areas. She is a Cape Wine Master (and chair of the Institute of Cape Wine Masters), and judges wine regularly at local and international competitions. She also presents corporate and private wine tastings, teaches and writes about wine, brandy and food. Wine and brandy are Winnie's passions and she enjoys every moment talking about or tasting them.

Greg de Bruyn

Greg is an architect by profession, practicing in and around the Cape wine industry. He allowed wine to beguile him into leaving Johannesburg in 1999 to seek his future amongst the vines, first to establish and run a wine estate, and later as a specialist consultant in winery construction. He qualified as a wine judge in 1996 and a Cape Wine Master in 2000. Greg has sat on many of the major South African competitions and assessment panels, and has contributed to several publications and websites.

Joanne Gibson

Newly graduated and covering local politics for a community newspaper, Joanne was invited to the Gauteng launch of Springfield Estate. After hearing co-owner Abrie Bruwer wax lyrical about his soils, his vines, his family heritage, she was hooked on everything that goes into a good bottle of wine. She left Johannesburg for Cape Town, politics for wine, and received her Level 4 Diploma from the Wine & Spirit Education Trust in 2003 while working for Harpers Wine & Spirit in London. Named South African Wine Writer of the Year in 2009, and shortlisted in the 2010, 2012 and 2013 Louis Roederer International Wine Writers' Awards, the multitasking mother of two is a wine columnist, freelance contributor to numerous wine publications and, latterly, an associate editor of this guide.

Higgo Jacobs

Hailing from Calitzdorp, to some the port-wine capital of South Africa, Higgo graduated from the University of Stellenbosch with a law degree in 2002, but was constantly taking on wine roles with local vineyards, eventually spending nine years on either side of the cellar door: first making wine, then marketing and exporting it. Today, certified with the Court of Master Sommeliers (UK), he is co-founder of the South African Sommelier Association (SASA) and consults on a selection of hospitality wine programs, and to the wine industry at large. Higgo is a senior judge at the International Wine Challenge (IWC), and tastes for various local publications and competitions.

Tim James

With a home-base on his well-established blog, Grape.co.za, Tim, a Cape Wine Master, contributes freelance to various publications. He is one of few local wine journalists with an international reputation, and his wine writing has won him a number of awards. As to wine judging, he prefers a contextual, descriptive approach and doesn't participate in large-format competitions, but has been a taster (and associate editor) for this guide for many years. Tim's book, Wines of the new South Africa: Tradition and Revolution, was published in 2013.

Angela Lloyd

Writing, lecturing, broadcasting and making wine are some of Angela's undertakings during her more than 30 years' professional involvement with wine. Even so, it is still just one interest in her life though closely allied to another, cooking. When not tied to her laptop, Angela loves the outdoors: she grows vegetables, fruit and indigenous flowers in her and her husband's garden, while her daily walks with Syrah, their black Labrador, keep them both fit. Reading, cinema, theatre, music, rugby and cricket are other interests crammed into a busy life.

Cathy Marston

Cathy hails from Yorkshire, UK, and after completing her degree in English at Cambridge University, she joined Adnams Wine Merchants, passing all the Wine & Spirit Education Trust (WSET) exams, culminating in a diploma. She came to South Africa in 2001, and opened and ran The Nose Restaurant & Wine Bar, selling it after seven successful years. Cathy now concentrates on tasting, writing for local and international publications, and, increasingly, on wine education and edutainment events. She is an associate of the Institute of Wines & Spirits and was the first Approved Programme Provider in Africa for the Wine & Spirit Education Trust. Her first book, Love Your Wine, was published recently.

Fiona McDonald

Travel is said to broaden the mind, and Fiona, former editor of Wine magazine for eight years, has had her wine mind broadened by having been a long-serving jury president of a number of international wine competitions: Decanter World Wine Awards, International Wine Challenge, International Wine & Spirit Competition and Concours Mondial de Bruxelles. Initially trained as a news journalist, she got into wine by happy accident, helping to organise The Mercury Wine Week in between reportage and newsroom management as the night news editor on the Durban broadsheet. Currently freelancing, Fiona edits Cheers and Whisky magazines, and contributes to a range of publications and websites.

Ingrid Motteux

Enjoying wine with meals (the result of an Afro-Belgian childhood) led to Ingrid sitting her first wine exam at 23, unlocking a great love for the subject. During a decade spent setting up nuclear medicine departments in London and Hong Kong, she completed the UK WSET Diploma. Returning to South Africa, she explored various aspects of the local industry (working as a vineyard labourer, writer and lecturer) and attained the Cape WSET Wine Judge certification. An associate of the Institute of Wines & Spirits, Ingrid judges for the International Wine Challenge and runs Winewise, an independent wine consultancy servicing some of Africa's top safari lodges.

Gregory Mutambe

Encouraged to follow his father into accounting, Gregory instead found himself on a journey into wine and food, first as a winemaking assistant at Mukuyu, one of the handful of wineries in his home country, Zimbabwe, and later as a Cape Wine Academy student in Gauteng. Currently he is the Head Sommelier at Cape Town's 12 Apostles Hotel & Spa, superintending an award-winning winelist. Gregory, an epicure, has judged for the Standard Bank Top Ten Chenin Blanc Challenge, Master Chef South Africa, South African Airways, Nederburg Auction, Michelangelo and Best Value Wine selections, and twice been a finalist in the Bollinger Exceptional Wine Service Awards. He is enrolled in the Cape Wine Master and University of South Africa B. Comm. programmes, his aim being to become a wine economist.

Jörg Pfützner

German-born Jörg is an internationally trained and certified sommelier living in South Africa. Having worked at top restaurants in Hamburg and Cape Town, he started his own businesses: The Riesling Club, whose members have access to top European bottlings; and Fine Wine Events, which celebrates wine with specifically themed fine-wine and food tastings and festivals. Since completing his postgraduate diploma in Wine Business Management, Jörg continues to present and lecture locally and abroad, as well as manage a group of private cellars.

Christine Rudman

Christine's love affair with wine started when she joined the then Stellenbosch Farmers' Winery after a Johannesburg FMCG marketing career. Enrolling in the Cape Wine Academy, she achieved her Cape Wine Master qualification in 1986; left SFW to run the CWA for seven years; and has since been occupied with consultancy work, wine-judging, lecturing and writing. She has a wine column in Die Burger and Beeld newspapers, regularly contributes to Classic Wine and has published two editions of A Guide to the Winelands of the Cape. She travels widely, tastes on a variety of local and international panels and looks forward to working with wine for years to come.

Dave Swingler

A taster for this guide for two decades, Dave over the years has consulted to restaurants, game lodges and convention centres, taught wine courses and contributed to radio, print and other media. He is co-author of One Hundred Wines – An Insider's Guide to South African Wine, and drinks contributor to Posh Nosh. Dave is a long-standing member of the International Wine & Food Society, the South African consultant for its Annual Vintage Chart, and cellarmaster of the Cape Town branch. A psychiatrist by day, he's intrigued by language in general, and the lexicon of wine in particular.

Cathy van Zyl

Cathy started her wine journey on a bicycle: she asked her husband to ride South Africa's famed Argus Cycle Tour with her; he accepted if she attended a wine course with him. She has since notched up 17 more Cycle Tours and gone on to pass the Master of Wine examination. Cathy judges locally and internationally, is the current chair of the Institute of Masters of Wine's education committee, occasionally contributes to wine journals and websites around the world, but spends most of her wine-time as associate editor of this guide.

Meryl Weaver

The Cape winelands lured Meryl away from her legal career and, more than 20 years later, she remains firmly under their spell. She has conducted wine presentations abroad on SA wine on behalf of Wines of South Africa, lectures for the Cape Wine Academy, tastes and writes about wine, and judges for various wine competitions and magazines. Meryl qualified as a Cape Wine Master and has graduated with distinction from the Wine Judging Academy. She ensures, however, that the vinous learning curve continues by visiting wine-producing countries, combining some of her other passions, food and travel.

How to use this Guide

Note: The example text used here is illustrative and not complete or up to date. See A–Z for full details.

Producer's name

Our track-record-based rating system
See next page for an explanation

Listings of wines available during the currency of the book

Wine name, vintage, colour & style

Location: nearest major centre to winery, vineyard, head office

Map: See Maps section for winery's position

WO: Wine of Origin geographical unit, region, district or ward; wines described/rated bear the first-mentioned WO certification unless noted

Unless noted, red wines wooded; whites unoaked

Symbols
See next page for a complete list

Other attractions or activities available on the property

Bartinney Private Cellar

Perched high on the slopes of the Helshoogte Pas
owned by Michael and Rose Jordaan who are in
plantings interspersed with native fynbos on stee

★★★★ **Cabernet Sauvignon** Elegant & unde
fruit tempered by savoury Marmite hints, olive ta
lengthy finish. 12-18 months French oak, 50% n

★★★★☆ **Elevage** Poised & polished **10** oozes
Stellenbosch fruit shows minty notes on nose giv
balanced grippy tannins. Shades of dark chocolat

★★★★☆ **Chardonnay** Classically styled **13** co
citrus on nose before palate glides delicately into
ity & lengthy finish.

★★★★☆ **Sauvignon Blanc** Peaches & cream
green figs & quinces below. Good depth & length

Location/map: Stellenbosch ▪ WO: Banghoek/Stelle
10-4 ▪ Closed all pub hols ▪ Cellar tours by appt ▪ B
Stellenbosch) ▪ Owner(s) Rose & Michael Jordaan ▪
Ryno Maree (Oct 2010) ▪ 27ha/±17ha (cab, chard,
BWI champion ▪ Postnet Suite 231 Private Bag X50
bartinney.co.za ▪ S 33° 55' 34.66" E 018° 55' 56.79"

Barton Vineyards

Barton is a 200-ha working farm in the hills overl
offering a range of activities, farm produce and lu
stylish wines is still boutique in scale, critical accl
having to expand the cellar facilities to vinify othe

★★★★☆ **Winemakers Reserve** Maiden **11** n
elegance & balance than barrel sample. Understat
nuance. So tailored & sleek, belies its youthful inte

★★★★ **Shiraz-Cabernet Sauvignon** Youthfu
with garrigue scrub, pepper & a touch of cab's clea

Rouge (NEW) ⊘ ★★★★ 4-way blend **12**, shiraz c
ture, & merlot & malbec plump out fruit-filled inte

Blanc 13 ★★★☆ **Sauvignon Blanc 13** ★★★☆

Location: Bot River ▪ Map: Elgin, Walker Bay & Bot
ing, sales & cellar tours Mon-Fri 9–5 Sat 10–4 ▪ C
olive oil, marinated olives & proteas ▪ Barton Villa
winemaker(s)/viticulturist(s) PJ Geyer (Oct 2010)
raz, chenin, sauv, sem) ▪ 120t/20,000cs own label
River 7185 ▪ info@bartonvineyards.co.za ▪ www.b
2" ▪ F +27 (0)28-284-9776 ▪ **T +27 (0)28-284-**

Symbols
See next page for a complete list

🔆 ♿

tinney Private Cellars, a boutique wine estate
heir bio-diversity credentials with new
aced slopes.

Brief introduction/news update

1 (★★★★☆) improves on 10 with refined black
anilla & spice. Delightfully gritty texture & clean

All wines dry unless noted

istinction. Cab-led Bordeaux blend from
o plushy black fruit with herbal hints & nicely
thy finish.

Abbreviations
See next page for a list of abbreviations

orm of **12** showing oatmeal, cream & yellow
pineapples & tropical fruit, balancing oak/acid-

Taster/s initials

★★) preview moves on to flinty minerality with
concentrated appeal of **13**. — CM

Tastings, sales & cellar tour times (closed
Saturdays & Sundays but open public holidays
unless noted)

Est 2006 ▪ 1stB 2008 ▪ Tasting & sales Mon-Fri
Wine Bar Mon-Sat 11.30-9 (cnr Church & Bird Str,
ker(s) Ronell Wiid (consultant) ▪ Viticulturist(s)
18t/4,000cs own label 70% red 30% white ▪
abosch 7599 ▪ info@bartinney.co.za ▪ www.
(0)21-885-2852 ▪ **T +27 (0)21-885-1013**

Names of owner, winemaker, viticulturist &
consultant/s; year/month of appointment in
brackets

Production, in tons and/or 6-bottle cases (cs)
and red:white ratio

Postal & email address, website
(see www.wineonaplatter.com for social media
details)

T = Telephone number
F= Fax number

🔆 🏠 📷 ♿

he Bot River Valley, rich in biodiversity and
ommodation. Though the own portfolio of
sulting in French-trained winemaker PJ Geyer
ers' wines on contract.

d Bordeaux blend, now bottled, shows more
ed core of inky red fruit & violets with cedary
ll age with distinction.

nious **11** blend has a sappy texture, infused
ceousness. Supple structure enhanced by oak.
es though equal part cab adds pliable struc-
so tasted: **Shiraz Rosé 13 ★★★ Chenin**
⊘ **13 ★★★☆** — MW

Date established

Total hectares/hectares under vine (not necessarily in production); main varieties planted

WO: Walker Bay ▪ Est 2001 ▪ 1stB 2003 ▪ Tast-
aster Sun, Dec 25 & Jan 1 ▪ Lavender products,
er(s) Peter J Neill ▪ Cellarmaster(s)/
/30ha (cab, malbec, merlot, mourv, pinot, shi-
d 50% white 10% rosé ▪ IPW ▪ PO Box 100 Bot
eyards.co.za ▪ S 34° 15' 43.8" E 019° 10' 29.

GPS coordinates, based on Datum WGS 84

How to use this Guide

Our Track-Record-Based Rating System

General rating   ★★★★ **Caldera**
For 4-star or better wines, we give the 'track-record rating' over two or more vintages in the margin. Wines rated 4½ stars or more are set in red type

Vintage-specific rating   **06** (★★★☆)
Any differences from the general rating are noted in brackets beside the particular vintage

★★★★★	95–100 / 18–20 pts	Superlative. A South African classic
★★★★☆	90–94 / 17–17.5 pts	Outstanding
★★★★	86–89 / 16–16.5 pts	Excellent
★★★☆	83–85 / 15.5 pts	Very good/promising
★★★	80–82 / 15 pts	Characterful, appealing
★★☆	77–79 / 14.5 pts	Good everyday drinking
★★	73–76 / 14 pts	Pleasant drinking
★☆	70–72 / 13 pts	Casual quaffing
★	65–69 / 12 pts	Plain and simple
☆	60–64 / 11 pts	Very ordinary
No star	50–59 / 10 pts	Somewhat less than ordinary

Symbols

Winery symbols

- Ⓠ   Open for tasting (no fee unless noted)
- ⑪   Restaurant/refreshments
- ⌂   Accommodation
- ⊙   Other tourist attractions/amenities on the property
- ⊖   Bring your own (BYO) picnic
- Ⓐ   Child friendly
- Ⓔ   Wheelchair friendly (see page 622)
- Ⓝⓔⓦ   New winery

Wine symbols

- ⊘   Good value
- Ⓝⓔⓦ   New wine
- Ⓧ   Wine still selling, not retasted
- Ⓢ   Organic
- ◉   Biodynamic
- Ⓥ   Hidden gem

Abbreviations

% alc	Percentage alcohol by volume	NLH	Noble Late Harvest
1stB	First bottled vintage	NV	Non-vintage. Year of harvest not stated on label
BEE	Black Economic Empowerment		
BWI	Biodiversity & Wine Initiative/ WWF-SA Conservation Champion	RS	Residual sugar
		SAA	South African Airways (selected for First or Premium Class)
BYO	Bring your own (wine, picnic)		
Cs	Cases	SLH	Special Late Harvest
CWG	Cape Winemakers Guild	Veritas	SA National Bottled Wine Show
CWM	Cape Wine Master	WIETA	Wine & Agricultural Ethical Trade Initiative
Est	Date established		
g/l	Grams per litre	WO	Wine of Origin
IPW	Integrated Production of Wine		
IWC	International Wine Challenge		
IWSC	International Wine & Spirit Competition	cabernet/cab	cabernet sauvignon
		pinot	pinot noir
LBV	Late Bottled Vintage	chenin	chenin blanc
Malo	Malolactic fermentation	sauvignon/sauv	sauvignon blanc
MCC	Méthode cap classique	touriga	touriga nacional
MW	Master of Wine	tinta	tinta barocca

AA Badenhorst Family Wines 🔆 🏠 📷

Adi Badenhorst, part-owner (with cousin Hein) at this charming family farm and winery on the slopes of Swartland's Perdeberg, is one of the Cape's great characters, making some of the Cape's most characterful fine wines. Kalmoesfontein's cellar and vineyards were badly run down when Adi and his equally creative and energetic wife Cornelia arrived some ten years back, he having resigned as winemaker at the grand Rustenberg estate; but hard, thoughtful work has transformed it all. The cellar was stripped and re-established with cement and oak vessels, the old unirrigated bushvines tenderly brought back to high-quality, though ungenerous, production. Adi and his wines (made traditionally, with minimal intervention) play an important role in the ongoing vitality of the revolutionary Swartland.

AA Badenhorst range

★★★★☆ **Brak-Kuil Barbarossa** ⓝⓔⓦ From possibly the only SA planting (50 years ago, in Swartland's St Helena Bay ward) of this Italian red-wine grape, **14** deserves special notice. Spicy, with black fruit & earthy notes, fine-grained tannin, thrillingly bone-dry with moderate alcohol (13%).

★★★★★ **Ramnasgras Cinsault** ⓝⓔⓦ Animated **14** from farm's oldest cinsaut vines, bunch fermented in large old vats. Beautiful perfumes of rosepetal, red cherry & spice give way to harmonious mouthful of fruit supported by super-fine tannins, modest 12.3% alcohol; sleek & bone-dry. Underlines this cellar's oft-made point that concentration & power aren't needed to command attention.

★★★★☆ **Red** Two vintages tasted; both savoury, old-oak-matured blends shiraz, grenache, cinsault & tinta; effortless & timeless with mineral-tinged fruit, fine tannin structures. **14** more approachable than tighter & even better **13** (★★★★★); similarly complex Provençal herbs, black pepper & dark fruit detail. Will reward the patient.

★★★★☆ **CWG Auction Reserve Geel-Kapel Muscat de Frontignan** ⓝⓔⓦ Buckle up, you've not tasted as thrilling a skin-fermented white from SA as **13**. All about texture & form; super-fine & compact tannin from extended skin maceration, modest alcohol. A bone-dry beauty named for the Cape cobra: 'The wine may be dangerous if you don't have any "orange wine" antivenom!'

★★★★☆ **CWG Auction Reserve Graniet-Berg** ⓝⓔⓦ **13** co-fermented marsanne & 25% grenache blanc charms with quince, crushed stones & apple blossom notes, delivers flavours without overt heaviness; year in old oak lends breadth & support, not flavour.

★★★★ **Funky White Wine** ⓖ Latest release (only 1,000 375-ml bottles a year) of **NV** from 11 varieties, aged in solera. Nutty, salty & 'umami' savouriness, biting acidity & ultra-dry length. It's like fino sherry but without fortification or flor as in Spain. Enjoy young to preserve its thrilling freshness.

★★★★☆ **White** Vivid **14** an intricate (10-way) chenin-led marriage with impressive complexity on the nose & palate, the stonefruit & marmalade flavours heightened by well-judged acidity. Rich, but with same underlying minerality as subtler **12**, showier **11**. Co-fermented/aged in very old casks. No **13**.

Not tasted: **Kalmoesfontein Raaigras Grenache**, **Méthode Ancestrale**.

Secateurs range

★★★★ **Red Blend** ⊘ Generous & upbeat **13** co-fermented syrah/shiraz, grenache & cinsaut a departure from usual 8-way combo but still a most enjoyable, fruit-filled & spicy drink. Great value.

★★★★ **Chenin Blanc** ⊘ From old vines, **15** subtle aromas of nectarine, ginger & crushed stone; vigorous & precise flavours. Tasty & well priced; plentiful too, fortunately: 35,000 cases. **14** unreviewed.

Also tasted: **Rosé 15** ★★★☆ — JPf

Location: Malmesbury ▪ Map: Swartland ▪ WO: Swartland/Voor Paardeberg-Swartland/Swartland-Voor Paardeberg ▪ Est 2007 ▪ 1stB 2006 ▪ Tasting, sales & tours by appt ▪ Closed all pub hols ▪ Conferences ▪ Function venue for 130 people ▪ Conservation area ▪ Guest cottages ▪ Owner(s) Adi & Hein Badenhorst ▪ Winemaker(s) Adi Badenhorst (2006), with Jasper Wickens (2008) ▪ Viticulturist(s) Pierre Rossouw (Jan 1975) ▪ 60ha/23ha (cinsaut, grenache, shiraz, chard, chenin, rouss) ▪ 40,000cs own label 60% red 40% white ▪ PO Box 1177 Malmesbury 7299 ▪ adi@iafrica.com ▪ www.aabadenhorst.com ▪ S 33° 32' 38.01" E 018° 49' 7.42" ▪ F +27 (0)21-794-5196 ▪ **T +27 (0)82-373-5038**

Aaldering Vineyards & Wines

Since acquiring their estate in Stellenbosch's Devon Valley, Dutch businessman Fons Aaldering and wife Marianne have invested in a new cellar, luxury guest lodges and concerted local and international marketing (Africa, China, Europe). Season 2014/15 saw winemaker/viticulturist Guillaume Nell focus on soil analysis, moisture monitoring and crop reduction, auguring well for sustained quality.

★★★★ Pinotage Sweetly ripe **12** has wild bramble & mulberry fruit, full soft tannins; big 15% alcohol yet supple & better balanced than **11** (★★★☆).

★★★★ Shiraz Leafy edge slight detraction on **12** (★★★☆), but good ripe fruit shows through; big bodied & rustic, with hefty tannins & acidity reminiscent of beefy **11**.

★★★★ Pinotage Blanc Crisp & flavoursome blanc de noir, **14** has 12% sauvignon blanc adding zest to pinotage's overt fruitiness. Hints of both grape varieties in wild berries & steely edge.

★★★★ Sauvignon Blanc Subtle, balanced & polished **14** shows ripe gooseberry fruit on gentle but firm acidity. Layered herbaceous juiciness & focused finish in an unpretentious, restrained style.

Pinotage Rosé ★★★☆ Bubblegum & strawberries on part-oaked **14**, with tempered acidity & lime-mineral texture, pleasingly substantial dry flavours. Also tasted: **Lady M 14** ★★★ **Cabernet Sauvignon-Merlot 12** ★★★★ **Chardonnay 14** ★★★☆ — GdB

Location/map/WO: Stellenbosch ▪ Map grid reference: D4 ▪ Est 2004 ▪ 1stB 2007 ▪ Tasting & sales Mon-Thu 9-5 Fri 9-3 Sat (Nov-Apr) 9-3 ▪ Closed all pub hols ▪ Cellar tours by appt ▪ 3 luxury lodges (TGCSA 5 star) ▪ Owner(s) Marianne & Fons Aaldering ▪ Winemaker(s)/viticulturist(s) Guillaume Nell (Oct 2014) ▪ 20ha/19.7ha (cab, merlot, ptage, syrah, chard, sauv) ▪ ±120t/±18,300cs own label 70% red 30% white ▪ IPW ▪ PO Box 1068 Stellenbosch 7599 ▪ estate@aaldering.co.za ▪ www.aaldering.co.za ▪ S 33° 55' 9.81" E 018° 49' 8.14" ▪ **T +27 (0)21-865-2495**

Aan de Doorns Cellar

A cabernet sauvignon celebrating grower-owned Aan de Doorns' 60th anniversary joins the ±22,000 cases (and counting) of appealing, modestly priced wines available under the Worcester cellar's own label. The rest of the 32,000-ton production mostly goes to partner FirstCape, the hugely successful supplier of entry-level wines to UK supermarkets. Revamped labels and a new range are on the cards.

★★★★ Muscat d'Alexandrie Elegant fortified dessert; much appeal in its honey, floral & spice fragrance. **13** very delicate, fresh, with clean, uncloying finish.

Cabernet Sauvignon ★★☆ Medium-bodied **12** displays bright, crunchy blackcurrant fruit with toasty notes from 100% new French oak. Nicely rounded for current drinking. Also in 3L.

Doornroodt ★★ Fruity ruby cab, merlot partnership. **13** unpretentious with plenty bright red-berry flavours. **Chenin Blanc** ★★★ Generous fruity acids, moderate 12% alcohol on quaffable, dry **15**. Also in 3L pack. Also tasted: **Pinotage 13** ★★★ **Colombar Semi-Sweet 15** ★★ **Sauvignon Blanc 15** ★★★ **Red Muscadel 13** ★★★★ Not retasted: **Sparkling Demi Sec NV** ★★☆ **Cape Ruby 12** ★★★★ Discontinued: **Blanc de Noir**. — AL

Location/map/WO: Worcester ▪ Est 1954 ▪ Tasting & sales Mon–Fri 8–5 Sat 10-1 ▪ Closed all pub hols ▪ Tours during harvest by appt ▪ Owner(s) 58 members ▪ Cellarmaster(s) Johan Morkel (Nov 1993) ▪ Winemaker(s) Gert van Deventer (Sept 1997) & Ryno Booysen (Jan 2007) ▪ Viticulturist(s) Pierre Snyman ▪ 1,494ha (cab, ptage, chard, chenin, cbard) ▪ 32,887t/22,400cs own label ▪ PO Box 235 Worcester 6849 ▪ info@aandedoorns.co.za ▪ www.aandedoorns.co.za ▪ S 33° 41' 47.0" E 019° 29' 26.2" ▪ F +27 (0)23-347-4629 ▪ **T +27 (0)23-347-2301**

☐ **Abalone** see Whalehaven Wines
☐ **Abbotsdale** see Bryan MacRobert Wines
☐ **Abbotsville** see Org de Rac

Abbottshill ⓠ ⓐ

Cameron and Dianne Bain, boutique vintners on Swartland's Perdeberg, say they haven't crushed the past couple of harvests and at press time were out of stock but intended to rectify the situation by vinifying the 2016 vintage.

Location: Malmesbury ▪ Map: Swartland ▪ Est/1stB 2004 ▪ Tasting, sales & tours by appt ▪ BYO picnic ▪ Owner(s) Dynadeals One (Pty) Ltd ▪ Winemaker(s)/viticulturist(s) CA Bain ▪ 112ha/10ha (cab, mourv, shiraz) ▪ 1,250cs own label 100% red ▪ PO Box 433 Malmesbury 7299 ▪ cameron@empa.co.za ▪ S 33° 29' 26.4" E 018° 39' 25.3" ▪ **T +27 (0)82-492-0692**

Abingdon Wine Estate ⓠ ⑪ ⓞ

Ian and Jane Smorthwaite were pioneers of winemaking in the KwaZulu-Natal Midlands — the cooling altitude (1,150m) of their vineyards offsetting KZN humidity. They continue to innovate: their nebbiolo vines should be producing soon, and they're now proudly releasing the area's 'first certified estate sparkling wines'. Daughter Laurie is a wine-person too: one of only two accredited service providers in SA for the UK-based Wine & Spirit Education Trust, she has set up the KZN School of Wine on the estate.

Location: Lions River ▪ Map: KwaZulu-Natal ▪ Est 2004 ▪ 1stB 2007 ▪ Tasting room & restaurant open Sat/ Sun & pub hols 10-5 for personalised tastings & fresh country meals ▪ Weekday visits strictly by appt ▪ Weddings & corporate functions ▪ Owner(s) Ian & Jane Smorthwaite ▪ Winemaker(s)/viticulturist(s) Ian Smorthwaite ▪ 7ha/3ha (cab, shiraz, chard, sauv, viog) ▪ Lions River KZN Midlands ▪ jane@ abingdonestate.co.za, ian@abingdonestate.co.za ▪ www.abingdonestate.co.za ▪ S 29° 26' 36.71'' E 030° 09' 14.18'' ▪ F +27 (0)86-572-6877 ▪ **T +27 (0)33-234-4335/+27 (0)83-463-8503 (Jane)**

☐ **Abraham Perold Heritage Collection** *see* KWV

Accolade Wines South Africa

Owned by Champ Private Equity of Australia, Accolade Wines South Africa is part of the global drinks company Accolade Wines, whose portfolio includes some of the world's best-known wine labels. The SA business, based in Stellenbosch, is responsible for the global megabrand Kumala, Fish Hoek range of single varietals, and highly regarded Flagstone pinnacle wines, all separately listed.

Stellenbosch ▪ Owner(s) Champ Private Equity based in Australia ▪ Winemaker(s) Bruce Jack, Gerhard Swart, Ben Jordaan & Karen Bruwer ▪ 6.4m cs own label ▪ PO Box 769 Stellenbosch 7599 ▪ flagstone@ accolade-wines.com ▪ www.accolade-wines.com ▪ F +27 (0)21-852-5085 ▪ **T +27 (0)21-852-5052**

☐ **Adelberg** *see* Simonsig Estate
☐ **Ad Honorem** *see* Graham Beck Wines

Adoro Wines

Sibling of single malt Scotch producer Benriach, Adoro is where winemaker Ian Naudé and viticulturist Lucas de Kock indulge their passion for blending wines from many diverse terroirs. This edition also sees the launch of their superb Naudé Old Vines collection, featuring wines from vineyards planted up to 50 years ago. Ian and Lucas pay tribute to the 'dedicated winegrowers' who, amid the rush to follow market trends, 'maintained their commitment to our vinous heritage by not replanting their vineyards'.

Naudé Old Vines range ⓝⓔⓦ

★★★★☆ **Cinsault** Slightly earthy, rusty notes only enhance the appeal & encourage further taste consideration of silky smooth **14**, youthful yet poised, light bodied yet intensely redolent of cranberries, Morello cherries & wild strawberries, subtly spiced. 10% new oak.

★★★★☆ **Chenin Blanc** Fermented naturally with minimal handling (like all in range), **13** needs even more time to reach potential promised by lemon & oatmeal intensity, weighty viscosity balanced by fresh acidity. Calls for food & serious contemplation. 10% new oak.

★★★★☆ **Semillon** Remarkable **14** is crisp & fresh with less than 11% alcohol yet has firm backbone & sleek glossy texture from year new French oak, imparting only a pinch of savoury spice to layers of lime & green fig, with intriguing saline edge.

Adoro Wines range

★★★★☆ **Red Blend** (ℚ) **07**, revisited mid-2014, proves longevity of this multi-region blend. Shiraz (24%) adds meat, smoke & spice notes to blackcurrant backbone of cab & ripe plum softness of merlot, fruit still vibrant despite time in all-new oak & bottle age. Follows soft & accessible **06** (★★★★☆).

★★★★ **Sauvignon Blanc** (ℚ) **10** (★★★★) steely but not as penetrating as **09**, thanks to fleshy fruit & the softening effect of bottle maturation at the cellar.

★★★★☆ **Naudé White** (ℚ) On paper, **10** (★★★★) blend mostly chenin with semillon, sauvignon, is nothing out of the ordinary but, retasted mid-2014, lanolin-tinged savoury flavours of cucumber/pak choi are decidedly idiosyncratic. **09** was mostly semillon & sauvignon, dash chenin. Both styled for ageing.

★★★★☆ **Natural Sweet Mourvèdre** (⊘) Intentionally fromage-friendly & quite possibly unique; wooded **13** is sweet (56 grams sugar) but not at all cloying due to balancing acidity, with enough black cherry concentration & weight to take on an entire cheeseboard. No **11**, **12**. Swartland WO. — JG

Location: Stellenbosch ▪ WO: Western Cape/Swartland ▪ Est 2005 ▪ 1stB 2004 ▪ Closed to public ▪ Owner(s) Intra International ▪ Winemaker(s) Ian Naudé (May 2005) ▪ Viticulturist(s) Lucas de Kock (Aug 2005) ▪ 40% red 60% white ▪ PO Box 982 Stellenbosch 7599 ▪ info@adorowines.co.za ▪ www.adorowines.co.za ▪ **T +27 (0)83-630-3794**

☐ **Adua** *see* New Beginnings Wines

AD Wines   (ℚ) (NEW)

'Faint as a will 'o the wisp, crazy as a loon, sad as a gypsy serenading the moon.' The jazz classic Skylark is the theme song to this fulfilment (with the stellar Alheit Vineyards winecrafting team) of the dream of Cape Town advocate Adrian Dommisse of 'showcasing cinsault uncompromisingly, without any blending components and with minimal winemaking intervention'.

★★★★ **Skylark** One of the exciting new-wave cinsauts. **14** ex Darling grapes; minimum intervention, including whole-bunch ferment & old-oak maturation. Vast perfumed charm, fresh, clean & pure. A delight. — TJ, CvZ

Location: Cape Town ▪ WO: Darling ▪ Est 2013 ▪ 1stB 2014 ▪ Tasting by appt only ▪ Owner(s) Dommisse Holdings Pty Ltd, shareholder Adrian Dommisse ▪ Winemaker(s) Adrian Dommisse ▪ 2t/150cs own label 100% red ▪ PO Box 711 Hermanus 7200 ▪ adriandommisse@gmail.com ▪ www.adwines.co.za ▪ **T +27 (0)71-674-4316**

Aeternitas Wines   (ℚ)

No recent releases from Johan and Michelle Grimbeek, whose cellar is where their heart is — at home in Helderberg beach resort Strand. But that's understandable given their high-powered day jobs: he is winemaker for Kanu, she MD of the Cape Wine Academy Stellenbosch.

★★★★ **Syrah** (ℚ) Plush & utterly moreish, **08** heaped with sweet mulberry fruit, shows poise & finesse despite 15% alcohol. Wild ferment, like **07** (★★★★).

Not retasted: **Blanc 10** ★★★★ — DS

Location: Strand ▪ Map: Helderberg ▪ WO: Swartland ▪ Est 2005 ▪ 1stB 2007 ▪ Tasting by appt ▪ Closed all pub hols ▪ Owner(s) Johan & Michelle Grimbeek ▪ Cellarmaster(s)/winemaker(s) Johan Grimbeek (Jan 2002) ▪ Viticulturist(s) Various ▪ 4t/640cs own label 50% red 45% white 5% rosé + 8,000cs for clients ▪ 21 Livingstone Street, Strand 7140 ▪ aeternitaswines@telkomsa.net ▪ S 34° 6' 3.3" E 018° 49' 35.6" ▪ **T +27 (0)82-714-2095**

☐ **A Few Good Men** *see* Riebeek Cellars
☐ **African Dawn** *see* Rooiberg Winery
☐ **African Roots** *see* Seven Sisters
☐ **African Star** *see* Stellar Winery
☐ **African Terroir** *see* Jacques Germanier
☐ **African Tribe** *see* Baratok Wines

African Wines & Spirits

Wholesaling and marketing company owned by Edward Snell & Co, and responsible for entry-level label Craighall. An untasted Cab-Merlot, Sauvignon Blanc and Chardonnay-Sauvignon Blanc are available.

Cape Town ▪ Est 1999 ▪ Closed to public ▪ Owner(s) Edward Snell & Co ▪ Directors D Asherson, DV Hooper, IV Hooper, JM Pousson, B Coppen & A Kruger ▪ 40% red 60% white ▪ PO Box 318 Paarden Eiland ▪ iainh@esnell.co.za ▪ F +27 (0)21-510-4560/+27 (0)86-682-4922 ▪ **T +27 (0)21-506-2600**

☐ **Agaat** see Truter Family Wines
☐ **Ahrens Family** see The Ahrens Family

Akkerdal Wine Estate

Vine and soil gurus Eben Archer and Dawid Saayman assist Franschhoek owner, viticulturist and winemaker Pieter Hanekom in trialling unusual varieties alongside the classics. They introduced another three last year – 'something new for the market', which widely travelled Pieter, a keen tweeter, hopes to bottle for his 'wine angels'. Also look out for new releases of exceptional-years-only sauvignon and rosé.

Limited Releases

★★★★ Kallie's Dream ⓥ Shiraz-led blend, rest mourvèdre, grenache, carignan, viognier. Pure & very expressive **10** with red fruit permeated with fresh acidity & fine spicy tannins.

★★★★ TDT ⓥ **12** unusual blend of tempranillo, durif & tannat has intriguing dark perfumed fruit & supple tannins. Succulent, balanced but still youthful, with potential. Step up on **10** (★★★☆). No **11**.

Akkerdal range

★★★★ Shiraz ⓥ With dash mourvèdre, **12** mid-2013 still tight but dry tannins & oak (18 months) revealed underlying seriousness. Needed cellar time to reveal all its charms.

★★★★ Wild Boar ⓥ **09** conforms to no conventional template, with 5 different varieties including roobernet & tempranillo. Fruit driven but not facile, with fresh acidity, dry finish. No **07**, **08**.

Not retasted: **Merlot 12 ★★★☆ Passion Reserve 11 ★★★ Petit Noir 10 ★★★ SG Blush 13 ★★★☆** Not tasted: **Sauvignon Blanc**. — CE

Location/map/WO: Franschhoek ▪ Est 2000 ▪ 1stB 2001 ▪ Tasting & sales Mon-Fri 10-4 ▪ Fee R20pp ▪ Closed all pub hols ▪ Self-catering chalet ▪ Owner(s)/cellarmaster(s)/winemaker(s) Pieter Hanekom ▪ Viticulturist(s) Pieter Hanekom, advised by Eben Archer, Bennie Liebenberg & Dawid Saayman ▪ 18ha (barbera, cab f, carignan, durif, grenache, malbec, merlot, mourv, p verdot, roobernet, shiraz, tannat, tempranillo, chard, nouvelle, sauv, sem, viog) ▪ 6,000cs own label 95% red 4% white 1% rosé ▪ IPW, WIETA ▪ PO Box 36 La Motte 7691 ▪ wine@akkerdal.co.za ▪ www.akkerdal.co.za ▪ S 33° 52' 50.9" E 019° 3' 3.8" ▪ F +27 (0)21-876-3189 ▪ **T +27 (0)21-876-3481/+27 (0)82-442-1746**

Akkerdraai

After retiring as MD of global enterprise Media24, Akkerdraai owner Salie de Swardt turned his attention to the grapes on his Helderberg farm. With consultant Ronell Wiid, a Diners Club Winemaker of the Year, he's now launched the Bordeaux blend he promised last time, 'because my friends asked'.

★★★★ Cabernet Sauvignon-Merlot (NEW) ⓥ Merlot somewhat softens firm tannin structure from cab (85%) in commendably dry, savoury **13**. Bucks the trend in eschewing ingratiating vanilla sweetness & easy approachability. Needs (& will reward) 3+ years.

Not tasted: **Cabernet Sauvignon**. — CvZ

Location/map/WO: Stellenbosch ▪ Map grid reference: E8 ▪ Est 1956 ▪ 1stB 2007 ▪ Tasting Mon-Fri 9-5 Sat 9-12.30 ▪ Fee R25, waived on purchase ▪ Closed Easter Fri-Mon, Dec 25 & Jan 1 ▪ Walks/hikes ▪ Owner(s)/cellarmaster(s) Salie de Swardt ▪ Winemaker(s) Ronell Wiid (consultant), with Salie de Swardt (Jan 2013) ▪ Viticulturist(s) Ronell Wiid (consultant) ▪ 1.5ha (cab) ▪ 12t 100% red ▪ PO Box 22 Lynedoch 7603 ▪ saliedes@mweb.co.za ▪ S 33° 59' 53.52" E 018° 49' 50.94" ▪ F +27 (0)86-689-1841 ▪ **T +27 (0)21-881-3861/+27 (0)83-264-1463**

☐ **Alchemy** see Hartenberg Estate

Alexanderfontein

These wines are crafted for 'unpretentious pleasure' and 'enjoyment of the simpler aspects of life' by Ormonde Private Cellar in Darling.

Sauvignon Blanc ⊘ ⊛ ★★★☆ Darling in origin, darling by nature, **15** has a grassy nose leading to intense gooseberry, granadilla & lime flavours, dry with mouth-tingling acidity & a very long finish.

Merlot ★★★ As yet fruit-shy **14**, tasted soon after bottling, shows all the stewed plum succulence of its slightly smoky predecessor. **Chardonnay** ⊘ ★★★☆ Apart from peachy nose, lively unwooded **15** bursts with citrus zest, from lemony freshness on palate to dry grapefruit finish. Also tasted: **Cabernet Sauvignon 14** ★★★☆ **Shiraz 14** ★★★ **Chenin Blanc 15** ★★★ — JG

AlexKia Estate   ⓠ

Busier-than-ever retirees Franco and Carla Maestroni were en route to Malaysia when we caught up with them and got the happy news of a competition medal for their chardonnay. Wine combines with rosemary production at the Robertson farm, whose resident African Black Swifts feature on the labels.

Alexandra Cabernet Sauvignon ★★★☆ A rung above previous, **14** tank sample opens with dusty blackberries & dark chocolate, follows with cranberries & sour cherries, finishes pleasantly dry. **Chiara Chardonnay** ★★★ Unwooded **15** offers variety-true lemon-lime flavour plus hint of melon, brisk acidity leading to crisp, clean citrus conclusion. Also tasted: **Merlot Reserve 13** ★★★☆ — DB

Location/WO: Robertson ▪ Est 2004 ▪ 1stB 2006 ▪ Tasting by appt at La Verne Wine Boutique, Robertson ▪ Owner(s) Carla Maestroni ▪ Winemaker(s) André van Dyk (Rooiberg) ▪ ±90ha/7ha (cab, chard) ▪ ±70t/10,000cs own label 50% red 50% white + 8,000cs for clients ▪ PO Box 101 Robertson 6705 ▪ franco@alexkia.co.za ▪ www.alexkia.co.za ▪ **T +27 (0)82-575-9578/+27 (0)82-783-9825**

Alheit Vineyards   ⓠ

Cape wine doesn't get much closer to cult status than Chris and Suzaan Alheit's tiny offering. They won immediate acclaim, international and local, for their maiden vintage of Cartology, a first sign of how seriously they intend to express the Cape's heritage and terroirs through its old vines. The acclaim continues, as does their range to grow, as does their quest for special old vines – with Arrow Heart the latest of their single vineyard wines. But young vines are not excluded from their focus: 2015 saw the first harvest from a mixed block on Hemelrand, the Hemel-en-Aarde olive and grape farm where they rent a cellar, and they are also planting a high-altitude block at Ceres. Only white wines thus far. . .

★★★★★ **Magnetic North Mountain Makstok** Alheits' 2nd single-vineyard chenin, **14** (★★★★☆) off old, tiny-yield, ungrafted ('makstok'), dryland chenin from Olifants River. More austere in structure than Lazarus (drier, acidity more pronounced, less rich), even more relentlessly graceful, the fruit super-subtle, the stoniness stonier. Already profound, can only gain in complexity & depth for a decade, like debut **13**.

★★★★★ **Radio Lazarus 14** (★★★★☆) a brilliant follow-up to maiden **12** off resurrected old chenin vines on the Bottelary Hills. It has a graceful, delicately insistent richness & power, based on a complex harmony of ripe fruit (there's a core of sweet peach along with an earthy element) & fresh acidity. No **13**.

★★★★☆ **Arrow Heart Semillon** (ⁿᵉʷ) For the geeks. **14** from single Franschhoek vineyard. 75% red-skinned grapes, fermented separately on skins for a week – hence rich red-gold colour & tannic grip. Oxidative winemaking gives earthy, bruised apple note that scarcely detracts from purity & freshness.

★★★★☆ **Cartology** As usual, **14** from 4 old blocks of widely sourced chenin, one (11%) of semillon. The aromas of a hot, scrubby hillside, yet somehow cool. Mouthfilling richness with peachskin texture & mineral undertone. Piercing, lemony intensity; cruises to a long, clean finish. All these wines matured in old oak; hands-off winemaking. — TJ

Location: Hermanus ▪ Map: Elgin, Walker Bay & Bot River ▪ WO: Stellenbosch/Citrusdal Mountain/Western Cape/Franschhoek ▪ Est 2010 ▪ 1stB 2011 ▪ Tasting by appt only ▪ Owner(s)/winemaker(s) Chris & Suzaan Alheit ▪ Cellarmaster(s) Chris Alheit ▪ 27t/2,200cs own label 100% white ▪ PO Box 711 Hermanus 7200 ▪ chris@alheitvineyards.co.za ▪ www.alheitvineyards.co.za ▪ S 34° 20' 35.56" E 019° 18' 11.30" ▪ **T +27 (0)83-274-6860**

Alkmaar Boutique Vineyard (Ⓠ) (◎)

Bouwer and Janet Nell's boutique wine brand is inspired by the 1862 school building on their property and its founder, Marinus Stucki, from Alkmaar in the Netherlands. Another local hero, Abraham Izak Perold, Wellington-schooled viticulturist and father of pinotage, is the honoured 'Professor'.

The Old School range

★★★★ **Professor** Classy, elegant **12** pinotage a tribute to variety's creator, prof Perold. Tamed by judicious oak, vibrant ripe berry fruit, supple palate & focused finish. Rung above **11** (★★★☆).

Mistress ★★★★ Aromatic, almost medicinal **12** shiraz, mourvèdre, viognier is medium bodied & pleasant, juicy fruit offsetting rough tannins. Also tasted: **Master 12** ★★★ **Reunion 15** ★★★ — GdB

Location/WO: Wellington ▪ Map: Paarl & Wellington ▪ Map grid reference: G2 ▪ Est 2001 ▪ 1stB 2005 ▪ Tasting & sales Mon-Fri 10-4 Sat 10-2 ▪ Closed all religious pub hols ▪ Cellar tours by appt ▪ Walks (part of Wellington Wine Walk) ▪ Owner(s) Bouwer & Janet Nell ▪ Winemaker(s) Pieter-Niel Rossouw (Jan 2010, consultant), with Dawid Futhwa (Jan 2010) ▪ Viticulturist(s) Dawid Futhwa (Jan 2003) ▪ 9.9ha (cab, merlot, mourv, p verdot, ptage, shiraz, chard, viog) ▪ 50t/900cs own label 83% red 17% white + 12,000L bulk ▪ PO Box 1273 Blouvlei Road Wellington 7654 ▪ janet@alkmaarwines.co.za ▪ www.alkmaarwines.co.za ▪ S 33° 39' 37.98" E 019° 1' 55.14" ▪ **T +27 (0)21-873-0191**

Allée Bleue Wines (Ⓠ) (Ⓨ) (⌂) (◎) (Ⓢ) (♿)

Named after its bluegum-lined entrance, German-owned Allée Bleue has a diverse portfolio including accommodation, functions and an extensive cellardoor offering showcasing a 300-year heritage. Purchase of a neighbour Franschhoek farm last year brought more chardonnay and sauvignon into the cellar, necessitating additional tanks. Also installed just ahead of the early harvest were a press and cooling module. The delightful wines now have equally charming siblings named Blue Owl, listed separately.

Allée Bleue range

★★★★ **Pinotage** Plenty of charry oak on **13** (18 months, 60% new) but juicy, sweet black fruit handles it well, leading to a soft, dryish finish. Lovely example, excellent with food.

★★★★☆ **L'Amour Toujours** Continuing success of **10**, Bordeaux blend (mainly cab & cab franc with merlot & touch of petit verdot) **12** uses ripe WO Banghoek fruit to great effect. Rich yet elegant, handles both oak & alcohol (15%) with ease. **11** (★★★★) also tasted. Limited magnums made.

★★★★ **Chenin Blanc** ⊘ Balanced & assured **14** deftly uses gentle oak & lees-ageing to add richness to luscious lemon meringue & delicate floral notes. Tad more freshening acidity would equal perfection.

★★★★ **Sauvignon Blanc** Ripe, pungent **15** (★★★★) blazes with gooseberry intensity but lacks some of the finesse of **14**. Lots of tropical guavas & figs on just-dry wine. May settle & improve.

★★★★ **Isabeau** (⅛) Ripe tropical notes on **13** blend of chardonnay & semillon with dash of viognier. Toffee, toast & marmalade vie on palate before lengthy, though slightly hot finish. Walker Bay fruit.

★★★★ **Brut Méthode Cap Classique** Deliciously rich & savoury **12** delivers mouthfilling flavours of brioche, Marmite edged with lemon zest & cream. Good balancing acidity, excellent lengthy finish – a great fizz to partner food. Near-equal chardonnay & pinot noir ex Walker Bay. Improves on **11** (★★★★).

Also tasted: **Shiraz 13** ★★★★ **Cabernet Sauvignon–Merlot 13** ★★★ **Brut Rosé Méthode Cap Classique 13** ★★★★ Not retasted: **Cape Ruby 13** ★★

Starlette range

Shiraz Rosé ⊘ (🍷) ★★★★ Pretty-in-pink **15** delights with punnet-loads of strawberries & flowers. Lively acidity, fresh, just-dry finish. A summer sensation. **Blanc** ⊘ (🍷) ★★★★ Charming everyday quaffer **15** from sauvignon & chenin. Grassy, gooseberry nose, tropical fruit, just-dry finish.

Also tasted: **Pinotage 14** ★★★ Not retasted: **Rouge 13** ★★★ — CM

Location/map: Franschhoek ▪ WO: Franschhoek/Banghoek/Walker Bay/Coastal/Franschhoek-Walker Bay ▪ Est 1690 ▪ 1stB 2001 ▪ Tasting & sales Mon-Fri 9-5 Sat 10-5 Sun/pub hols 10-4 ▪ Tasting fee R25/4 wines ▪ Cellar tours by appt ▪ Bistro Allée Bleue ▪ Picnics (booking required) ▪ Jungle gym ▪ Tour groups by appt ▪ Gifts ▪ Farm produce ▪ Conferences ▪ Weddings ▪ Allée Bleue Kendall Cottage & Manor House ▪ Owner(s) DAUPHIN Entwicklungs-und Beteiligungs GMH (Germany) ▪ Winemaker(s) Van Zyl du Toit (Jul

2009), with Natalie Kühne (Jan 2012) ▪ Viticulturist(s) Douw Willemse (Sep 2008) ▪ 135ha/25ha (cab, merlot, ptage, pinot, shiraz, chard, chenin, sauv, sem, viog) ▪ 450t/35,000cs own label 34.5% red 55% white 5% rosé 5% MCC 0.5% fortified ▪ IPW ▪ PO Box 100 Groot Drakenstein 7680 ▪ info@ alleebleue.com ▪ www.alleebleue.co.za ▪ S 33° 51' 29.0" E 018° 59' 12.9" ▪ F +27 (0)21-874-1850 ▪ **T +27 (0)21-874-1021**

Allegria Vineyards   ⓠ ⌂

On Stellenbosch's scenic Polkadraai Hills, Jan and Annemarie Zevenbergen's shiraz grapes are husbanded and vinified by advisers Francois Hanekom and Louis Nel respectively. To taste the resulting wine, check into their luxury guest house or find it on a select winelist.

Shiraz ★★★☆ Pronounced mint & herbal notes on fresh **13**, moving on to cherries & chocolate with hints of smoke. Appetising & juicy. — CM

Location/map: Stellenbosch ▪ Map grid reference: B6 ▪ WO: Polkadraai Hills ▪ Est 2005 ▪ 1stB 2010 ▪ Tasting by appt ▪ Allegria Guest House ▪ Owner(s) Jan & Annemarie Zevenbergen ▪ Winemaker(s) Louis Nel (Nov 2009, consultant) ▪ Viticulturist(s) Francois Hanekom (Sep 2009, consultant) ▪ 2ha/0.5ha (shiraz) ▪ 4,200kg/500cs own label 100% red ▪ PO Box 24 Vlottenburg 7604 ▪ wine@allegria.co.za ▪ www.allegriavineyards.co.za ▪ S 33° 57' 29.79" E 018° 45' 31.63" ▪ F +27 (0)21-881-3210 ▪ **T +27 (0)21-881-3389**

Allesverloren   ⓠ ⓘⓘ ⌂ ⓐ ⓑ

The original vines serried on the slopes of Kasteelberg in Swartland produced their first crops around 1800, and while Allesverloren was planted mostly with wheat when 1st-generation Malan, Daniël Francois, bought the estate in 1872, it was the vineyard that fired his imagination. His sweet fortified evolved into today's Fine Old Vintage 'port', something of an SA institution and one of the first locally from traditional grapes. The vines remain Portugal influenced, producing trendy unfortified varietals and a 'Douro blend'. And they form a storied backdrop to the numerous activities at the cellardoor.

★★★★ **Touriga Nacional** ⊘ Maraschino cherries, tangerine nuance & subtle oak spicing tick all the boxes on fresh & poised **12**. Like **11** (★★★), characterful alternative to the usual red varietal suspects.

★★★★ **Três Vermelhos** ⓧ Older oak for the (unfortified) 'three reds' – souzão, tinta & touriga. Berry pudding, orange zest & black olive notes typical of these varieties, **12** lipsmackingly dry & characterful.

★★★★ **Red Muscadel** Delicious fortified **14** from single Kasteelberg vineyard. Opulent tones of cranberries, tealeaf, quince, orange & lime, heart-warming spirit gives tangy finale.

★★★★ **Fine Old Vintage** An enduring label, immediately accessible 'port' has typical notes of Xmas cake, nutmeg spice & tar, a fiery heart in a body of sweet fruit. **10** complex constellation of mostly tinta barocca, souzão, pontac plus malvasia rey, tintas roriz & francisca, touriga. Ready, with decade+ to go.

> **Cabernet Sauvignon** ⓥ ★★★★ Latest vintages step up. **13**'s generous dark fruit now masked by tarry oak, will integrate & unfold given year/2. **12** nudges next level, shows benefit of extra year in lovely cassis & graphite nuances, cab's firm tannin & freshening astringency. Both moderate 13.5% alcohol.

Tinta Rosé ⊘ ★★★ Sunset-hued dry **15** spice & pepper notes; a more serious expression, with satisfying length. Also tasted: **Shiraz 13** ★★★★ **Tinta Barocca 13** ★★★★ **1704 Red 14** ★★★ — CvZ

Location: Riebeek West ▪ Map/WO: Swartland ▪ Est 1704 ▪ Tasting & sales Mon-Fri 9–5 Sat 9–2 ▪ Fee R20pp ▪ Closed Easter Fri, Dec 25 & Jan 1 ▪ Cellar tours by appt ▪ Pleasant Pheasant Restaurant T +27 (0)22-461-2170 Tue 10.30-3 Wed-Sat 9-3 & 6-10 Sun 9-4 ▪ Facilities for children ▪ Conferences/functions T +27 (0)22-461-2253 ▪ Owner(s) Malan Boerdery Trust ▪ Cellarmaster(s) Danie Malan (Nov 1987) ▪ Winemaker(s) Danie Malan (Nov 1987), with Armand Lacomme (Aug 2012) ▪ 227ha/187ha (cab, shiraz & various port varieties) ▪ 100,000cs own label 100% red ▪ PO Box 23 Riebeek West 7306 ▪ info@allesverloren.co.za ▪ www.allesverloren.co.za ▪ S 33° 21' 32.5" E 018° 52' 24.1" ▪ F +27 (0)22-461-2444 ▪ **T +27 (0)22-461-2589**

☐ **Alluvia** see Brugman Wines
☐ **Alma Mater** see Lanzerac Wine Estate

☐ **Almara** *see* Southern Sky Wines

Almenkerk Wine Estate   ⓠ ⑪ ⊜ ⓐ

Vinified and offered for tasting at their showpiece cellar in Elgin, the Belgian/Dutch Van Almenkerk family's (untasted) portfolio includes Almenkerk Estate Syrah '12, Chardonnay '14 and Sauvignon Blanc '14; and Lace Vineyard Selection '12 (Bordeaux-Rhône red blend), Dry Rosé '15 and Sauvignon Blanc '14.

Location/WO: Elgin ▪ Map: Elgin, Walker Bay & Bot River ▪ Est 2004 ▪ 1stB 2009 ▪ Tasting, sales & cellar tours Wed-Sun 10-4 (Sep-May) & Tue-Sat 10-4 (May-Sep) ▪ Open pub hols except on Mon/Tue ▪ Meals/picnics by prior booking (min 20 pax), or BYO picnic ▪ Walks/hikes ▪ Conservation area ▪ Heliport ▪ Boule court ▪ Owner(s) Van Almenkerk family ▪ Cellarmaster(s) Joris van Almenkerk ▪ Winemaker(s) Joris van Almenkerk, with Danver van Wyk (Feb 2009) ▪ Viticulturist(s) Michael Keown (Jan 2014) ▪ 104.2ha/15ha (cabs s/f, malbec, merlot, mourv, p verdot, shiraz, chard, sauv, viog) ▪ 100t/5,000cs own label 65% red 30% white 5% rosé ▪ Brands for clients: De Mikke Patron, Pot Luck Club, Concierge Hotel DBN ▪ BWI, CVC member ▪ PO Box 1129 Grabouw 7160 ▪ info@almenkerk.co.za ▪ www.almenkerk.co.za ▪ S 34° 12' 55" E 019° 01' 57" ▪ **T +27 (0)21-848-9844**

☐ **Alta Casa** *see* Darling Cellars

Alte Neffen Wines

After a 35-year career (latterly at Solms-Delta), Hilko Hegewisch is 'doing his own thing' in Stellenbosch, with wine-partner and alte Neffe (literally 'old nephew') Helmut Peters driving sales in Germany. They call their Amarone-style vine-drying technique 'method kaperone' and, Hilko says, German wine drinkers, who know Italian wines, are fascinated. 'It's a good alternative to Amarone and much better value.'

Merlot Method Kaperone ⓝⓔⓦ ★★★ Fat & plush **13**, a raisiny mouthful with sweet plums & cherries. Just-off-dry sugar making it powerful & crowd pleasing at the same time. **Shiraz Method Kaperone** ★★★ Pronounced **13**, retasted shows lots of toasty oak, violets & smoked meats. From vine-dried grapes (like Merlot), the wine is rich & ripe with few grams sugar rounding out to a soft finish. — CM

Location/WO: Stellenbosch ▪ Est/1stB 2013 ▪ Closed to public ▪ Owner(s) Hilko Hegewisch & Helmut Peters ▪ Winemaker(s) Hilko Hegewisch ▪ 55t/1,000cs own label 100% red ▪ 22 Van Coppenhagen Street Rozendal Stellenbosch 7600 ▪ hilko@wineclick.co.za ▪ www.alteneffen.co.za ▪ F +27 (0)86-614-5993 ▪ **T +27 (0)21-887-9544/+27 (0)82-788-9505**

Alto Wine Estate   ⓠ ⓐ

Once part of a 17th-century Helderberg farm, Alto was established in the 1920s by the Malan family. Its location in Stellenbosch's 'Golden Triangle' reflects in the quality of its classically styled reds, but consistency comes from a rare continuity in cellarmasters. Witness the appointment last year of only the 5th winemaker in nearly a century: Bertho van der Westhuizen (ex Boschendal, Kleine Zalze), son of Schalk who retires after 15 years here, emulating a previous father-son handover from Piet to Hempies du Toit.

★★★★ **Cabernet Sauvignon** Svelte Stellenbosch cabernet; **12**'s blackcurrant fruit is balanced by savoury olive & tobacco notes in muscular, not ungenerous style. Satisfying now but will reward few years.

★★★★ **Shiraz** Similar smoke, leather & prune profile, but **12** improves on bolder, more robust **11** (★★★☆). Old fashioned, perhaps, but delightful.

★★★★ **Alto Rouge** A Cape institution, produced for more than half a century. 5-way blend led by cab franc & shiraz. Savoury **13** supple, smooth & flavourful. May not win trophies, but has myriad fans.
Not retasted: **Fine Old Vintage 08** ★★★★ Occasional release: **MPHS**. — DS

Location/map/WO: Stellenbosch ▪ Map grid reference: E8 ▪ Est 1693 ▪ 1stB 1921 ▪ Tasting & sales Mon-Fri 9—5 Sat/Sun 10—4 ▪ Fee R25 wine tasting/R10 FOV tasting ▪ Closed Good Fri & Dec 25 ▪ Pâté & wine pairing R50pp, advance booking required; FOV & chocolate pairing R45pp ▪ Hiking trail ▪ MTB track ▪ Owner(s) Lusan Premium Wines ▪ Cellarmaster(s)/winemaker(s) Bertho van der Westhuizen (May 2015) ▪ Viticulturist(s) Bertho van der Westhuizen & Danie van Zyl ▪ 191ha/83ha (cabs s/f, merlot, shiraz) ▪ 800t/100,000cs own label 100% red ▪ PO Box 104 Stellenbosch 7599 ▪ info@alto.co.za ▪ www.alto.co.za ▪ S 34° 0' 10.4" E 018° 50' 49.4" ▪ F +27 (0)21-881-3894 ▪ **T +27 (0)21-881-3884**

Altydgedacht Estate

The Parker family, represented by 5th-generation winegrower brothers Oliver and John, marches to the beat of its own drum, witness the rare-in-Cape barbera, varietal and blended, bone-dry gewürztraminer and other roads less travelled. Their estate, family farmed for over 160 years, is a homely haven amid Durbanville's suburban sprawl. Ongoing success and enduring appeal have warranted a new assistant winemaker and dedicated farm manager, plus extended eatery hours.

Parker Family Reserve range

★★★★ The Ollo Chardonnay, viognier, semillon & chenin in **14** medley named for longtime cellarmaster. Pungent aromas & a fleshy body brightened by crystalline acidity make for an alluring wine, worth seeking out. Oaked five months, 20% new.

Weisser Riesling ★★★☆ Intensely aromatic, pleasing **15** preview, with botrytis nuance adding dimension to variety's stony leanness. Also tasted: **Méthode Cap Classique Blanc de Blanc 13 ★★★★** Not retasted: **Pinot Noir 13 ★★★★** Not tasted: **Tintoretto**. Discontinued: **Semillon Noble Late Harvest**.

Altydgedacht Estate range

★★★★ Pinotage Sweet berries & vanilla toffee profile of tangy **14** suggest fun times, but fruit density & 30% new oak add gravitas. Needs year/2 for big tannins to meld, settle. Agreeable 13% alcohol.

★★★★ Sauvignon Blanc Sweaty, intense **15** in green/grassy style – & jolly good; unequivocal coolclimate example with underlying saline minerality.

Not retasted: **Barbera 13 ★★★☆ Gewürztraminer 14 ★★★☆** Occasional release: **Chardonnay**.

Ralph Parker range

Cabernet Sauvignon Limited Release ⑳ **★★★** Earthy **12** has blackcurrant whiff & firm tannins yet slips down easily. Not retasted: **Merlot Limited Release 12 ★★★★** Not tasted: **Shiraz**.

Tygerberg range

Cabernet Franc Blanc de Noir ★★☆ Cranberry twist to winter melon & red berry core of **15**, fresh & gently dry for chilled summer pleasure. **Chatelaine ★★★** Intensely scented **14** gewürztraminer, riesling & muscat; semi-sweet but enlivened by well-judged acidity. Perfect for spicy food. — DS

Location/WO: Durbanville ▪ Map: Durbanville, Philadelphia & Darling ▪ Est 1698 ▪ 1stB 1981 ▪ Tasting & sales Mon-Fri 9–5 Sat 9–4 Sun 11-3 ▪ Closed Easter weekend, Dec 25/26 & Jan 1 ▪ Cellar tours by appt ▪ B'fast & light lunches Mon-Sat 9-3.30 Sun 11-3 (T +27 (0)21-975-7815/eat@altydgedacht.co.za) ▪ Facilities for children ▪ Conferences ▪ Weddings/functions ▪ Conservation area ▪ Owner(s) Parker family ▪ Cellarmaster(s) Oliver Parker (1981) ▪ Winemaker(s) Etienne Louw (Jan 2006), with Marené de Beer (Jul 2014) ▪ Viticulturist(s) John Parker (1981), Gerrit Visser (Aug 2014, farm manager) ▪ 1,700ha/265ha (16 varieties, r/w) ▪ 1,300t total 360t/44,000cs own label 30% red 65% white 5% rosé ▪ PO Box 213 Durbanville 7551 ▪ info@altydgedacht.co.za ▪ www.altydgedacht.co.za ▪ S 33° 50' 46.6" E 018° 37' 26.4" ▪ F +27 (0)86-218-5637 ▪ **T +27 (0)21-976-1295**

Alvi's Drift Private Cellar

Founded in 1928 by Alvi van der Merwe, Alvi's Drift is now a fruitful partnership between his grandsons, medical doctor Alvi and lawyer/businessman Johan, who both inherited his love of winegrowing, with Linley Schultz, former chief winemaker at Distell. Although still off the beaten tourist track, it has grown from an insider's secret to a widely distributed brand specialising in pinotage, viognier and chenin blanc. Wines are made entirely from fruit grown on the farm, which is cultivated sustainably and uses organic compost also produced on the property.

AD range

★★★★ Drift Fusion ⊘ Secondary notes of smoke & leather as well as oak-derived spice & toasted nuts on velvety **11** (★★★★☆), more complex than suave **09** to whose cab, pinotage & shiraz blend is added 9% petit verdot, its richness balanced by fresh acidity. **10** sold out untasted.

★★★★ Albertus Viljoen Chenin Blanc Rich, creamy **13** (★★★★☆) barrel fermented (some naturally), worthy successor to maiden **12**, ripe cling peaches combining with zesty citrus, toasted nuts & vanilla in luscious mouthful, finishing refreshingly dry. Youthful **14**, also tasted, needs more time.

★★★★ **CVC Reserve** Chenin-led blend with lesser parts viognier & chardonnay, **13** has ripe white peaches & oak-derived vanilla while creamy **14** is more tropical. Label now reflects reserve status.

★★★★ **Thornlands Méthode Cap Classique** ⌖ Crisp & dry **NV** sparkling from 70% chardonnay & pinot has fine, persistent bead, with hints of lime & roasted walnut adding intrigue to green apple.

★★★★☆ **Muscat de Frontignan White** ⌖ Alluring fortified dessert, small-oak matured. Copper-hued **10** (★★★★★) 'dry' notes of tealeaf & cherry tobacco, 'moist' honey & fig jam, gingery caramel tail. Endless, unctuous mouthful! Easily trumps last **07**.

Not tasted: **Chardonnay**.

Signature range

★★★★ **Viognier** ⊘ A white for red-wine drinkers, **15** has a stonefruit & jasmine perfume, soft ripe peach & apricot flavours, a viscous texture balanced by acidic zing, & a lingering finish.

> **Chenin Blanc** ⊘ ⊛ ★★★★ Fresh & lively with nice viscosity, **15** bursts with pineapple & sweet citrus fruit, & a pithy finish. **Sauvignon Blanc** ⊘ ⊛ ★★★★ Aromatic **15** oozes granadilla & gooseberries before ending on a dry, ruby grapefruit note (& is that a savoury hint of asparagus?).

Pinotage ★★★ **14** is a strawberry/raspberry crush of a wine, light bodied but juicy with quite powdery tannins. **Pinotage Rosé** ⓝⓔⓦ ★★ Cheerful cherry-pink sipper, off-dry **15** smells like candyfloss & tastes like strawberries, would need serious chilling to be refreshing. Also tasted: **Cabernet Sauvignon 13** ★★★ **Merlot 14** ★★★ **Shiraz 13** ★★★ Not tasted: **Chardonnay-Viognier**.

Naughty Girl range

Sparkling Rosé ★★ At just 7.5% alcohol, the original 'Naughty Girl' **NV** sparkler is gently sweet with a pink candy blush & flirty cherry flavours. **Sparkling Sahara** ★★ The 'naughtiest' sister at 11.5% alcohol, also the driest, this **NV** fizz is fruity, foamy & fun. Also tasted: **Sparkling Nude NV** ★★ — JG

Location/map/WO: Worcester ▪ Est 1928 ▪ 1stB 2004 ▪ Tasting, sales & tours by appt ▪ Closed all pub hols ▪ Farm produce ▪ Owner(s) Bertie, Alvi & Johan van der Merwe ▪ Cellarmaster(s) Riaan Marais ▪ Winemaker(s) Riaan Marais, Alvi van der Merwe & Linley Schultz, with Anne van Heerden ▪ Viticulturist(s) Pierre Snyman (consultant) & Jan du Toit ▪ 6,000ha/420ha (ptage, shiraz, chard, chenin, muscat de F) ▪ ±7,500t/400,000cs own label ▪ IPW ▪ PO Box 126 Worcester 6850 ▪ info@alvisdrift.co.za ▪ www.alvisdrift.co.za ▪ S 33° 46' 25.8" E 019° 31' 53.7" ▪ F +27 (0)86-654-9425 ▪ **T +27 (0)23-340-4117**

☐ **Amandalia** *see* Rooiberg Winery

Amani Vineyards

New World-style wines are the norm here, as might be expected from a US-owned winery, the grapes off sustainably farmed vineyards on Stellenbosch's Polkadraai Hills skilfully vinified and available for tasting by appointment.

★★★★ **Merlot** ⌖ Powerful, alcoholic **11**, the ultra-ripe sweet fruit also giving plenty of flavour but less freshness, all supported by sensibly restrained oaking. With a lean muscularity allowing for ageing.

★★★★ **Cabernet Franc-Merlot** ⌖ Enticing **10** (★★★★), with drops cab & malbec, less classic than **09**. Fresh, spicy-leafy aromas; succulent flavours with modest savoury grip.

★★★★ **Forest Myers** ⌖ Amani's ripe charm on **11** from shiraz & mourvèdre, the blend giving some complexity. Typical fruit intensity too, quite soft though powerful; strong acid a bit awkward.

★★★★ **I Am 1** ⌖ Good-natured **11** cab-based Bordeaux blend with a drop of shiraz, offering spicy, sweet-fruited, bright charm in the most restrained & balanced of the reds. Ready, but could keep.

★★★★ **Chardonnay** ⌖ As was lively **11**, **12** (★★★★) naturally fermented & with only older barrels used for maturation. Easygoing balance of structure & fruit, gently rich, soft textured.

★★★★ **Kamili Chardonnay-Viognier** ⌖ **11** (★★★★) almost semi-sweet, unlike **10**, with easy charm. Structure from chardonnay & light oaking, with viognier's peachy richness, but no intensity.

Not retasted: **Cabernet Sauvignon 11** ★★★★ **Pinotage 11** ★★★ **Pendana Shiraz 11** ★★★ **Poppy Blush 12** ★★ **Sauvignon Blanc 12** ★★★ Occasional release: **Jordan Myers**. — TJ

Location/map: Stellenbosch ▪ Map grid reference: B6 ▪ WO: Stellenbosch/Upper Hemel-en-Aarde Valley/ Western Cape ▪ Tasting by appt only ▪ Owner(s) Lynde & Rusty Myers ▪ Winemaker(s) Chris van Reenen (Jan 2011) ▪ Viticulturist(s) Chris van Reenen (Jan 2011) & Chris Keet (2012-2015, consultant) ▪ 38ha/ 27.8ha (cabs s/f, merlot, mourv, shiraz, chard, sauv, viog) ▪ 235t 76% red 24% white ▪ EnviroWines ▪ PO Box 12422 Die Boord 7613 ▪ wine@amani.co.za ▪ www.amani.co.za ▪ S 33° 57' 54.3" E 018° 43' 59.5" ▪ F +27 (0)21-881-3931 ▪ **T +27 (0)21-881-3930**

☐ **Amatra** *see* Catherine Marshall Wines
☐ **Ama Ulibo** *see* Goedverwacht Wine Estate

Ambeloui Wine Cellar   ⓠ

Big changes to this 'little vineyard' ('ambeloui' in Cypriot) in Hout Bay, say the Christodoulou family, specialising in bottle-fermented bubblies since 1994. Their 20-year-old vines have been replanted to include third classic champagne variety pinot meunier. Reserved stocks plus fruit from a nearby vineyard will tide them (and us) over. Father-and-son team Nick and Alexis are also nurturing a potstill brandy.

★★★★☆ **Méthode Cap Classique Rosanne Rosé** ⓠ **NV** sparkler from chardonnay (52%) & pinot noir, base wine lightly oaked. Thrilling current release offers subtle red berry flavours, mellifluous texture & refreshing dry mousse. More yielding than sibling, both most satisfying.

★★★★☆ **Méthode Cap Classique** Urbane chardonnay-pinot noir (51/49) bubbly, 10% of base wine oaked; **13** 'Alexis' is aromatic, with a plush brioche character from long lees-ageing, like **12** 'Christo'. **11** 'Max' is tighter. Whatever the name (all family offspring), these are exquisitely focused, mouthwatering. — DS

Location: Hout Bay ▪ Map: Cape Peninsula ▪ WO: Western Cape ▪ Est 1994 ▪ 1stB 1998 ▪ Tasting by appt ▪ Owner(s) Nick & Ann Christodoulou ▪ Cellarmaster(s)/viticulturist(s) Nick Christodoulou (1994) ▪ Winemaker(s) Nick Christodoulou (1994), with Alexis Christodoulou (2009) ▪ 1ha/0.5ha (pinot, chard) ▪ 15t/3,000cs own label 100% MCC ▪ PO Box 26800 Hout Bay 7872 ▪ wine@ambeloui.co.za ▪ www.ambeloui.co.za ▪ S 34° 0' 49.5" E 018° 22' 55.4" ▪ F +27 (0)88-021-790-7386 ▪ **T +27 (0)21-790-7386/+27 (0)82-460-8399/+27 (0)82-880-1715**

Ameera   ⓠ

Relative newcomers Marc Machtelinckx and Kathleen Raemdonck are turning their Stellenbosch organically farmed wine and olive estate into something special, an Ameera ('Princess'). From nursing the vines back to health, to buying a neighbour property, to launching a first white bottling, their efforts and vision are bearing fruit. The wines, co-vinified by Marc, are now exported to Namibia and Belgium.

Ameera range

Cabernet Sauvignon ★★★★ Tobacco & dark plums, a salty liquorice savouriness in **13**, tasted prebottling. For drinking now & over the next 4 years. **Shiraz** ⓝⓔⓦ ★★★★ Mineral, scrub & cherries, there's lots going on in **13** preview, the supple tannins adding to the appeal. Also tasted: **Blanc de Noir 14** ★★ Not tasted: **Envie Sauvignon Blanc**.

Duel by Ameera range

Not tasted: **Cabernet Sauvignon-Shiraz**. — CR

Location/map/WO: Stellenbosch ▪ Map grid reference: D7 ▪ Est/1stB 2012 ▪ Tasting & sales Mon-Sat by appt ▪ Fee R30 ▪ Owner(s) Marc Machtelinckx & Kathleen Raemdonck ▪ Winemaker(s) Philip Costandius, Marius Roux (2012/23 vintages, both consultants) & Marc Machtelinckx ▪ 12.5ha/4.5ha (cab, shiraz) ▪ ±35t/1,000cs own label 80% red 20% rosé + 30,000L bulk ▪ PO Box 3949 Somerset West 7129 ▪ wine@ameera.co.za ▪ www.ameera.co.za ▪ S 33° 59' 42.62" E 018° 48' 40.08" ▪ F +27 (0)21-448-8611 ▪ **T +27 (0)21-881-3146**

☐ **Anchor Drift** *see* Viljoensdrift Fine Wines & Cruises
☐ **Ancient Earth** *see* Bellingham

Andersons Wines   ⓠ

Owner Ian Anderson planned to retire on his Plettenberg Bay property but now finds himself making an ever-improving young-vines boutique sauvignon with help from local guru Anton Smal. Not-good news from Ian about the next release, however: 'There will not be a '15 vintage due to a missed harvest.'

Leto Venus Sauvignon Blanc ★★★★ Named for the endemic Ghost Moth. Big improvement on previous, single-vineyard **14** has firm acidity, perky granadilla fruit, appealing lees texture. — GdB

Location/WO: Plettenberg Bay ▪ Map: Klein Karoo & Garden Route ▪ Est 2007 ▪ 1stB 2011 ▪ Tasting by appt ▪ Fee R5/wine ▪ Closed all pub hols ▪ Owner(s) Ian Anderson ▪ Winemaker(s) Anton Smal (Bramon Wines) ▪ Viticulturist(s) Ian Anderson, assisted by Anton Smal ▪ 22ha/2.5ha (sauv) ▪ 5.5t/600cs own label 100% white ▪ PO Box 2564 Plettenberg Bay 6600 ▪ ian@app.co.za ▪ S 33° 59' 17.7" E 023° 27' 15.1" ▪ **T +27 (0)83-453-3624**

Andreas Wines   ⓠ ⌂ ▣

After ten years' ownership, the Swedish Bokdal family have sold currently shiraz-only label Andreas to a group of UK winelovers and friends of David Croft, ex MD of Yorkshire Television and South Africa's Honorary Consul in that north English county. Team members new and old say they're looking forward to expanding the existing customer base and opening more local and export markets.

★★★★ Andreas Shiraz Opulent, round & soft as usual, **13** will reward fans of the warmer, rich side of shiraz. Stewed dark fruit, prunes & spice, slight developed characters suggest drinking it before **12**. — HJ

Location/WO: Wellington ▪ Map: Paarl & Wellington ▪ Map grid reference: G1 ▪ Est 2003 ▪ 1stB 2004 ▪ Tasting & sales by appt Mon-Fri 9—5 ▪ Closed all pub hols ▪ Cellar tours by appt ▪ Accommodation ▪ Weddings/functions ▪ Owner(s) David Croft ▪ Cellarmaster(s)/viticulturist(s) Howard Heughs & Eugenie Potter ▪ Winemaker(s) Howard Heughs & Ettienne Malan (consultant) ▪ 6ha/4.5ha (mourv, shiraz) ▪ 48t/ 3,168cs own label 100% red ▪ PO Box 892 Wellington 7654 ▪ andreas@ezinet.co.za ▪ www.andreas.co.za ▪ S 33° 37' 52.0" E 019° 2' 50.1" ▪ F +27 (0)86-664-5087 ▪ **T +27 (0)21-873-2286**

Andy Mitchell Wines   ⓠ

Undimmed by the sad passing of boutique winery co-founder, sailor and Cape Wine Master Andy Mitchell mid-2014, wife and daughter Vikki and Olivia Mitchell have established the planned half hectare of grenache, released one of three new wines, a rosé, the first from own grapes, and are designing a new cellar for Greyton home farm Heuningkloof.

★★★★ Elgin Pinot Noir Latest **13** (★★★) in light, fresh Elgin style; juicy cherry flavours dimmed by some stalky astringency, oak. **11** more elegant. No **12**.

Heuningkloof Shiraz Rosé (NEW) **★★★** Inviting strawberry hue/aromas on bone-dry **14**. Just under year on lees provides richer mouthfeel without spoiling fruit purity. **Swartland Chenin Blanc ★★★** Intriguing mix honey, oxidative notes with piquant freshness on **13**. Flavoursome but lean, enjoy over next year/2. No **12**. Not retasted: **Crooked Path Pinot Noir 12 ★★★☆ Crooked Path Shiraz 07 ★★★☆ Syrah-Grenache-Mourvèdre 12 ★★★ Méthode Cap Classique 11 ★★★☆** Not tasted: **Walker Bay Chenin Blanc**. Discontinued: **Breakfast Rock Syrah, Nerina Rosé**. — AL

Location: Greyton ▪ Map: Southern Cape ▪ WO: Elgin/Stellenbosch/Western Cape/Swartland/ Franschhoek-Paarl/Greyton ▪ Est/1stB 2003 ▪ Tasting, sales & cellar tours by appt ▪ Closed Easter Fri/Sun & Dec 25 ▪ Owner(s) Vikki Mitchell ▪ Winemaker(s) Olivia Mitchell (Jan 2008) ▪ 15t own label 42% red 21% white 13% rosé 24% MCC + 200cs for clients ▪ PO Box 543 Paarden Eiland 7420 ▪ olivia@ andymitchellwines.com ▪ www.andymitchellwines.com ▪ S 34° 2' 26.3" E 019° 37' 2.6" ▪ F +27 (0)86-611-2739 ▪ **T +27 (0)28-254-9045**

☐ **Angels Tears** *see* Grande Provence Heritage Wine Estate
☐ **Ankerman** *see* uniWines Vineyards

Annandale Wines   ⓘ 🍴 ♿

Owner, winemaker and viticulturist (and rugby legend) Hempies du Toit was a strong proponent of traditional winegrowing long before it became modish. His delightfully rustic estate on Annandale Road in the Helderberg is noteworthy, too, for extended barrelling and releasing vintages only when deemed ready, hence the venerable (but still spry) '05 Shiraz reviewed this edition.

★★★★ **Cabernet Sauvignon** ⓐ Serious-minded & classically styled. A melange of dark cherry & cassis on bold, spicy **04**, bottled after 7 years in barrel & showing similar fine form to previous.

★★★★ **Shiraz** Improving on **04**, **05** (★★★★☆) shows the vintage quality with savoury cured meat, dark creamy plums, fragrant fynbos & fine exotic spice. Vanilla oak rounds the seamless mouthful. Plenty of life ahead of this 11 year old!

★★★★ **Cavalier** ⓐ **04** Bordeaux-style blend with shiraz oozes spice & black fruit. Big & sturdy, yet balanced & smooth with lots of life after 7 years in barrel. More complex than **01** (★★★☆).

★★★★ **Nostalgia** ⓐ Tribute to old-style Cape reds & the founders of Alto Estate. From cab, shiraz & cinsaut – latter adding charming wild, raspberry notes in **NV**. From various years, mature but vibrant.

Not retasted: **Merlot 05** ★★★☆ **CVP 04** ★★★☆ — WB

Location/map/WO: Stellenbosch ▪ Map grid reference: E8 ▪ Est/1stB 1996 ▪ Tasting, sales & cellar tours Mon-Sat 9–5 ▪ Fee R25 ▪ Closed Easter Fri-Mon, Ascension Day & Dec 25 ▪ Farm produce ▪ BYO picnic ▪ Owner(s) Hempies du Toit ▪ Winemaker(s)/viticulturist(s) Hempies du Toit (1996) ▪ 72ha/45ha (cabs s/f, merlot, shiraz) ▪ 250t/10,000cs own label 100% red ▪ PO Box 12681 Stellenbosch 7613 ▪ info@annandale.co.za ▪ www.annandale.co.za ▪ S 33° 59' 49.2" E 018° 49' 50.9" ▪ F +27 (0)21-881-3562 ▪ **T +27 (0)21-881-3560**

Annex Kloof Wines   ⓘ 🍴 📷 ♿

Ten years ago Basson bothers Thys, Tobie and Hugo revived a legacy of winemaking dating from 1907, when patriarch Matthys first planted vineyards in the Perdeberg and made wine. His great-grandsons each own vineyards and these provide the fruit for the family label. Winemaker Hugo is mad about red wine and completely crazy about one variety in particular. Let the moniker 'Malbec King' be a clue.

Annex Kloof range

★★★★ **Malbec** Appetising **14** steps up on **13** (★★★☆) with fresh aromas of blackcurrants & cream, yielding to cherries & leather. Soft tannins & gentle oak round off a truly appealing wine.

★★★★ **Tulu** ⊘ Confident **14** shiraz-dominated Rhône blend is spicy & enticing. Hints of chocolate, coffee & liquorice, clean fruit, good length. Excellent value & oh-so-enjoyable. **13** sold out untasted.

Discontinued: **Shiraz**.

Xenna range

Shiraz ⊘ 🍷 ★★★☆ Fruit pastille nose of **14** spices things up with liquorice & cloves for yummy everyday sipper. **Chenin Blanc** ⊘ 🍷 ★★★☆ Fruity little number **15**, plenty of pungent guava & grapefruit notes offset by zippy acidity for delicious everyday drinking.

Discontinued: **Cabernet Sauvignon, Pinotage**. — CM

Location: Malmesbury ▪ Map/WO: Swartland ▪ Est/1stB 2006 ▪ AnnexKloof stall on N7: sales daily; tasting Fri 8-4.30 Sat 8-3 Sun 11.30-4.30 ▪ Farm: tasting, sales & cellar tours by appt only ▪ Closed Easter Fri-Mon, Ascension Day, Pentecost, Dec 16/25/26 & Jan 1 ▪ BYO picnic ▪ Walks/hikes ▪ Conservation area ▪ Owner(s) Hugo Basson, with brothers Thys & Tobie ▪ Winemaker(s) Hugo Basson (Jan 2006) ▪ 550ha (cab, grenache, malbec, merlot, mourv, ptage, shiraz, chard, chenin, sauv) ▪ 6,000t own label 95% red 5% white ▪ PO Box 772 Malmesbury 7299 ▪ hugo@annexkloofwines.co.za ▪ www.annexkloofwines.co.za ▪ S 33° 30' 39.1" E 018° 48' 22.5" (estate), S 33° 21' 5.69" E 018° 42' 36.87" (farmstall) ▪ F +27 (0)86-569-3957 ▪ **T +27 (0)22-487-3870 (cellar)/+27 (0)81-324-7888 (farmstall)**

Antebellum Winery   ⓘ

Under new vineyard manager and winemaker, MC Stander, this small producer on the slopes of the Riebeekberg is set to expand. New wines will join the current range – also in accordance with the precepts of the Swartland Independent Producers organisation (some other members of which make their wines in the Antebellum cellar), and more vineyards are being planted. A tasting venue, no doubt with splendid views across Riebeek-Kasteel and the Swartland, is also planned.

Chenin Blanc ⊕ ★★★☆ Attractive, subtly but fully fruited, lightly oaked **14**. 15% viognier adds note of ripe, sweet peach, even more apparent on the finish. A wine of great, easy charm. Just 12.1% alcohol.

Syrah ★★★☆ Naturally fermented (like all these), **14** preview has a smidgen of mourvèdre. Savoury-smoky aromas; bigger & heavier than previous, packed with sweet fruit & supported by soft, firm tannins. Also tasted: **Saffronne Rosé 15** ★★★ Not retasted: **Syrah-Cinsault-Mourvèdre 13** ★★★☆ — TJ

Location: Riebeek-Kasteel ▪ Map/WO: Swartland ▪ Est/1stB 2012 ▪ Tasting, sales & cellar tours by appt ▪ Owner(s) Herman & Mari Redelinghuys ▪ Winemaker(s)/viticulturist(s) MC Stander (Jan 2015) ▪ 17ha (ptage, shiraz, chenin) ▪ 2,400cs own label 55% red 45% white ▪ PO Box 148 Riebeek Kasteel 7307 ▪ herman@hermanredelinghuys.co.za, mcstander7@gmail.com ▪ www.antebellum.co.za ▪ S 33° 24' 19.8" E 018° 52' 15.0" ▪ F +27 (0)86-683-8132 ▪ **T +27 (0)79-280-0237**

AntHill Wines   Ⓨ

Barrel supplier Mark Howell's antennae are finely tuned to finding the odd special parcel of grapes to vinify for sale to faithful followers of this brand he owns with construction project manager Hylton Schwenk. See under Entre Nous for boutique parcels made 'with others'.

White Stone Sauvignon Blanc ⓦ ★★★☆ Aptly named **13** from Stellenbosch opens with stony minerality & dusty note, turning into greengage & stonefruit on bone-dry palate. Bright acidity freshens & counteracts the evident alcohol. Not retasted: **Cobbold Stone Red Blend 12** ★★★ Not tasted: **Long John Silver Pinot Noir**, **The Persian Shiraz**, **Davey Jones Locker**, **Pieces of 8**. — MW

Location: Somerset West ▪ WO: Philadelphia/Stellenbosch ▪ Est 1999 ▪ 1stB 2000 ▪ Tasting by appt ▪ Owner(s) Mark Howell & Hylton Schwenk ▪ Winemaker(s) Mark Howell (Feb 2000) ▪ 1,200cs own label 60% red 40% white ▪ 19 Immelmal Rd Somerset West 7130 ▪ www@telkomsa.net ▪ S 34° 4' 30.8" E 018° 52' 37.6" ▪ F +27 (0)86-668-4566 ▪ **T +27 (0)82-895-9008**

Anthonij Rupert Wyne   Ⓨ ⑪ ⓒ ⓑ

International businessman Johann Rupert's wine portfolio is vinified from own prime vineyards in Darling, Swartland, Elandskloof and Franschhoek, and marketed under the Anthonij Rupert flagship, L'Ormarins, Cape of Good Hope, Terra Del Capo and Protea labels, none reviewed this edition. The elegant brand home has twin cellardoors linked by specially built trams to the Franschhoek Motor Museum, which houses a remarkable collection of automobiles spanning more than 100 years.

Location/map: Franschhoek ▪ Est 1714 ▪ 1stB 1982 ▪ Two tasting rooms: Anthonij Rupert Mon-Sat 10–4.30; Terra del Capo Tue-Sun 10-4.30 ▪ Fee R15-R60 per flight ▪ Closed Good Fri & Dec 25 ▪ Antipasti Bar for light meals & refreshments ▪ Cheese, olive oil & honey ▪ Franschhoek Motor Museum T +27 (0)21-874-9002 Mon-Fri 10-4 Sat/Sun 10-3; admittance R60pp, seniors R50 & children (3-12 yrs) R30 ▪ Two specially built trams travel between the motor museum & tasting rooms ▪ Owner(s) Johann Rupert ▪ Winemaker(s) Dawie Botha (Jan 2005), Zanie Viljoen (Jan 2007), Vernon van Hoven (2012) & Mark van Buuren (2013) ▪ 4 farms: total ±1,100ha/±210ha (cabs s/f, carignan, cinsaut, grenache, marsanne, merlot, mourv, pinot, sangio, shiraz, chard, chenin, pinot grigio, rouss) ▪ ISO 14001:2009 ▪ PO Box 435 Franschhoek 7690 ▪ tasting@rupertwines.com ▪ www.rupertwines.com ▪ S 33° 53' 16.77 E 019° 0' 17.70" (Anthonij Rupert/Cape of Good Hope), S 33° 52' 47.36" E 019° 0' 10.91" (Terra Del Capo/Protea) ▪ F +27 (0)21-874-9111 ▪ **T +27 (0)21-874-9004/+27 (0)21-874-9041 (tasting)**

Anura Vineyards   Ⓨ ⑪ ⓒ ⓑ

Initially purchased to headquarter Tymen Bouma's optometry business, the frog-themed Paarl farm originally known as Sonop is now home to Forest Hill cheesery, Froggitt Foods, 12 Pigs Charcuterie, Wagon Trail microbrewery, The Trading Post deli and restaurant, and the Boumas' ever-expanding ranges of wines — all reached via a new entrance and road, with plans also in motion for a new tasting room, conference centre and residential development.

LB Series

★★★★ **Sangiovese** Fresh, bright **12** has smooth tannins & good splash of acidity to counter richness of spiced plums. Nicely balanced despite alcohol nudging 15%. **11** sold out untasted.

★★★★ **Shiraz** ⓥ Subtle, smooth & rounded, with floral scents & peppery spices, first-release **09** augurs well. Hints of Rhône with solid New World ripeness.

★★★★ **Cape Cuvée** Made to mature, intense yet elegant **13** has sumptuous blackberry fruit, with grippy tannins as well as brisk acidity to leave a tartly elegant impression. Pinotage (43%), merlot, cab franc & shiraz, some from Banhoek.

Discontinued: **La Traviata**.

Reserves & Limited Releases

★★★★ **Cabernet Sauvignon Reserve** Dark, brooding **12** has cassis & violets on nose leading to fresh blackberry & mulberry flavours with tobacco & clove, resulting in greater complexity than in **10** (★★★☆). **11** untasted.

★★★★ **Malbec Limited Release** Making a statement at ±15% alcohol, sweet-fruited **13** has remarkable balance & freshness for all its macerated black plums & melted dark chocolate. **11** & **12** not reviewed.

★★★★ **Merlot Reserve** Green apple tartness as well as plums on full-bodied **12** (★★★★), less plush than **10** despite ripeness suggested by 15% alcohol, very dry on finish. **11** not tasted.

★★★★ **Petit Verdot Limited Release** ⓥ Improving on **08** (★★★★), **09** has typical inky depth & spicy black fruit. Muscular but showing restraint. Reflects fine vintage, should soften with time in bottle.

★★★★ **Pinotage Reserve** Dense black berry fruit on velvety **12** with soft ripe tannins, freshness courtesy of balancing acidity & a pinch of herbs.

★★★★ **Syrah Limited Release** ⓥ Meaty butterscotch & white pepper dominate bold nose on **08**, but palate offers enticing scrub, delicate floral & sweet spicy notes over solid tannin backbone.

★★★★ **Chardonnay Limited Release** Only special barrels chosen for 'pinnacle' **14**, pear nose leading to tangy citrus intensity on palate, balanced by creaminess, flavours lingering after each sip.

★★★★ **Sauvignon Blanc Unfiltered Reserve** ⓥ **13**, with tiny new-oaked portion, mainly from Darling, where dryland bushvines yield intense gooseberry flavours with grapefruit finish.

★★★★ **Méthode Cap Classique Brut** Portion Robertson chardonnay combined with own plus 40% pinot noir helps outstanding **11** (★★★★★) sparkling rise to the occasion, more elegant, steely than **10**, with tart Granny Smith apple & cinnamon biscuit flavours enhanced by very fine & persistent mousse.

★★★★ **Cape Vintage Reserve** ⓥ Carefully crafted **10** port-style from Robertson tinta, 32 months in barrel. Fortified with aged brandy, shows traditional grippy spirit, restrained extraction.

Also tasted: **Chenin Blanc Limited Release 14** ★★★☆

Anura range

★★★★ **Arpeggio** ⓝⓔⓦ ⓥ Syrah/shiraz, mourvèdre & viognier notes rise & fall harmoniously in maiden **11**, in 'piano' rather than 'forte' style of fuller-bodied counterparts. Juicy, with sweet-tangy red fruit.

Rosé ★★☆ Now 100% shiraz, **14** is just-dry with red berry flavours, in particular cranberry adding tart freshness. **Chardonnay** ★★★☆ **14** represents great value, Golden Delicious apple from barrel-fermented own fruit combined with citrus freshness of tank-fermented component from Tradouw Highlands. Also tasted: **Merlot 13** ★★★ **Pinotage 13** ★★★★ **Legato 13** ★★★★ **Viognier Barrel Selection 14** ★★★★ Not retasted: **Pinotage-Syrah 13** ★★★ **Sauvignon Blanc 14** ★★★ **Cape Ruby Port NV** ★★★

Discontinued: **Frog Hill range**. — JG

Location: Paarl ▪ Map: Paarl & Wellington ▪ Map grid reference: C7 ▪ WO: Simonsberg-Paarl/Western Cape/Coastal/Paarl/Worcester ▪ Est 1990 ▪ 1stB 2001 ▪ Tasting, sales & cellar tours daily 9.30–5 ▪ Closed Good Fri, Dec 25 & Jan 1 ▪ Fee R45/cheese & wine, R25/wine only ▪ Trading Post Eatery & Deli open for b'fast & lunch Tue-Sun 9.30-4.30 ▪ Wagon Trail microbrewery ▪ Tour groups ▪ Farm produce ▪ Conferences ▪ Owner(s) Bouma family ▪ Cellarmaster(s) Tymen Bouma (1990) ▪ Winemaker(s) Johnnie Calitz &

Lance Bouma (Jan 2007) ▪ Viticulturist(s) Hannes Kloppers (Oct 1997) ▪ 240ha/120ha (cab, carignan, grenache, malbec, merlot, mourv, nebbiolo, p verdot, ptage, pinot, sangio, shiraz, tempranillo, chard, chenin, nouvelle, pinot gris, sauv, verdelho) ▪ 750t/60,000cs own label 80% red 17% white 2% rosé 1% fortified ▪ PO Box 244 Klapmuts 7625 ▪ info@anura.co.za, wine@anura.co.za ▪ www.anura.co.za ▪ S 33° 48' 41.4" E 018° 53' 19.8" ▪ F +27 (0)86-531-0057 ▪ **T +27 (0)21-875-5360**

Anwilka   ⓛ

Owned by the same group as Klein Constantia, including eminent Bordeaux men – and founders – Bruno Prats and Hubert de Boüard, this red-wine specialist in a quiet corner of Stellenbosch continues to reap the benefit of their long experience with growing and making fine wine. A holistic replanting programme, focused on sustainable farming such as practical and natural strategies to limit leafroll virus transmission, is well under way, while the 2015 harvest was the first test of its 'purpose-built for red wine production' facilities, including making the KC Red.

★★★★☆ **Anwilka** Elegant & composed red blend, **12** continues serious vein noted in **11** & **09** (**10** untasted); shiraz component upped to 87%, with cab (no petit verdot). Unforced & subtly oaked, with exotic & enticing cardamom overlay. More approachable than **11** but will reward up to decade cellaring.

★★★★ **Petit Frère** 'Little Brother' similar blend to grander sibling. **13** is wooded (30% new French) after unoaked **12**; similar savoury, graphite nuances but less settled, knit; needs further year/2. — CvZ

Location/WO: Stellenbosch ▪ Est 1997 ▪ 1stB 2005 ▪ Tasting & sales at Klein Constantia (see entry) ▪ Owner(s) Zdenek Bakala, Charles Harman, Bruno Prats & Hubert de Boüard ▪ MD Hans Aström ▪ Winemaker(s) Jean du Plessis (Aug 2008) ▪ Viticulturist(s) Piet Neethling, with Johan Wiese (consultant, both 1997) ▪ 48ha/±39ha (cab, merlot, p verdot, shiraz) ▪ 250t/±32,000cs own label 100% red ▪ PO Box 5298 Helderberg 7135 ▪ anwilka@mweb.co.za ▪ www.kleinconstantia.com ▪ F +27 (0)21-842-3983 ▪ **T +27 (0)21-842-3225**

Arendsig Handcrafted Wines   ⓛ ⓜ ⓢ ⓗ ⓒ

Arendsig co-owner and cellarmaster Lourens van der Westhuizen makes only single-vineyard wines in a boutique cellar on the Robertson family farm. The portfolio, untasted, includes Cabernet Sauvignon '13 Grenache '14, Shiraz '13, Chardonnay '15, Chenin Blanc '15, Sauvignon Blanc '15 and Viognier '14.

Location/map: Robertson ▪ Est/1stB 2004 ▪ Tasting & cellar tours by appt ▪ Tour groups ▪ Picnic baskets to be pre-booked, or BYO picnic ▪ Wedding/function venue ▪ Farmhouse (sleeps up to 10 people) ▪ Owner(s) Lourens & Frikkie van der Westhuizen ▪ Cellarmaster(s)/viticulturist(s) Lourens van der Westhuizen (2004) ▪ 95ha/12ha (cab, shiraz, chard, sauv, viog) ▪ 80t/3,000cs own label 50% red 50% white + 100t/3,000cs for clients ▪ Brands for clients: Esona, Mimosa, Star Hill ▪ PO Box 170 Robertson 6705 ▪ info@arendsig.co.za ▪ www.arendsig.co.za ▪ S 33° 55' 37.9" E 020° 0' 47.6" ▪ F +27 (0)86-535-0693/+27 (0)23-616-2090 ▪ **T +27 (0)84-200-2163/+27 (0)23-616-2835**

Arendskloof   ⓛ

These wines, mostly subtitled 'Voetspore', are the prestige bottlings of Christiaan Groenewald, owner/ winemaker at separately listed Eagle's Cliff Wines-New Cape Wines. Intended to complement good food, the Arendskloof labels are from single vineyards, 'made in a way to try and keep nature in the wines'.

★★★★ **Pinot Noir** Pioneer of variety in area. **15** more convincing than last-tasted **12** (★★★★). Delicate cherry fruit, supple tannins, genteel oak (10% new), moderate 13.5% offer immediate seamless drinkability as aperitif or lunchtime red. WO W Cape, as for all.

★★★★ **Pinotage** ⓛ **10** improves on flagging **08** with typical acetone & strawberry combo, easy sippability & interesting aloe lift. Ready now but will reward 3+ years cellaring. No **09**.

★★★★ **Tannat-Syrah** ⓛ Unusual & ambitious blend. **12** (★★★★☆) trumps last-tasted **09** (labelled 'Syrah-Tannat'). Spicy black plum & prune, firm but noble tannin (as expected from tannat).

★★★★ **Pinot Grigio** Well-crafted **15** has 'wet stone' minerality & smoky nuances, flavoursome & dry with a definite tug of tannin for mealtimes.

★★★★ **Sauvignon Blanc 15**'s (★★★) delicate blackcurrant notes overlain with almond aromas, enlivened by measured acidity. Unchallenging sipper, lacks texture & precision of **14**.

Cabernet Sauvignon (ⁿᵉʷ) ★★★★ Tobacco, cassis & faint leafy note on restrained & fresh **14**, showing well-managed oak (50% new). Could be broached now, kept ±5 years. **Coffee Pinotage** (ⁿᵉʷ) ★★★★ Mocha & sugared plum **15** has a pleasing lightness, is a well-made version of this trending style. For now & ±2 years. **Shiraz** (ⁿᵉʷ) ★★★☆ Exuding black cherry & black pepper, **13** is commendably dry but still tight, with lively acidity. Could show better in year/2. **Pinot Noir Rosé** (ⁿᵉʷ) ★★★ Palest onion skin hue, delicate strawberry & cream nuances; **15** nicely dry for charcuterie or solo enjoyment. Also tasted: **Chardonnay 14** ★★★☆ Not retasted: **Brut Rosé MCC 12** ★★★☆ — CvZ

☐ **Are We Having Fun Yet?** *see* Wine Village-Hermanus
☐ **Arniston Bay** *see* Stellenbosch Vineyards

Arra Vineyards   ⓠ

Quietly developed in the late 90s, this farm in Klapmuts changed hands in 2007, the Novak and Coventry family owners having fallen in love with the Cape during an earlier visit. Under their stewardship the cellardoor was opened and the portfolio expanded. The approach remains low key, the visitor venue open and welcoming, and Dee Wentzel, cellarmaster the past decade, in charge of the mostly red wines.

Reserve range

★★★★ **Cabernet Sauvignon** (ⓠ) Big & bold **09**, smooth textured but ultimately not unbalanced or overdone. Intense cassis, slight earthy note. No **08**.

★★★★ **Shiraz** (ⓠ) Rich, with layers of flavour – red & black fruit, a hint of vanilla, pepper & spice. **09** bright acidity, crunchy tannins. No **08**.

★★★★ **Viognier** (ⓠ) Evident oak spice on **11** (★★★☆) may since have melded with peachy, ginger fruit. Smooth & silky, fruitily dry finish. **09** more expressive; no **10**.

Not retasted: **Nobility 11** ★★★☆

Barrel Select range

★★★★ **Cabernet Sauvignon** (ⓠ) **08** (★★★☆) not as harmonious as **06**. Already quite evolved, with fruit yielding to a more savoury character. No **07**.

★★★★☆ **Shiraz** (ⓠ) Finesse & balance characterise **08**, with 3% mourvèdre. Layers of flavour including red berries & spice. Medium body, with fresh acidity & fine tannins.

★★★★☆ **Shiraz-Mourvèdre-Viognier** (ⓠ) Impresses with poise & complexity. Good concentration & fresh acidity on the palate. Start of some developed character lends further interest to early-drinking **08**.

Not retasted: **Mourvèdre 08** ★★★☆ Not tasted: **Pinotage**.

Arra Vineyards range

★★★★ **Cabernet Sauvignon-Petit Verdot-Merlot** (ⓠ) **10** over-delivers with plenty of dark fruit, attractive oak. Good concentration, firm but fine tannins. Should keep for a good few years.

Mourvèdre (ⓠ) ★★★★ Suitably exotic **10** with dark fruit & fynbos plus attractive hint of vanilla. Good concentration, smooth texture. **Shiraz-Cabernet Sauvignon** (ⓠ) ★★★ Unassuming **11** is medium bodied, with red & black fruit plus a little spice. Not retasted: **Merlot 10** ★★★ **Pinotage 10** ★★★☆ **Shiraz 10** ★★★☆ **Shiraz-Mourvèdre 10** ★★★ **Natural Sweet Viognier 12** ★★★ Not tasted: **Cabernet Sauvignon, Cape Blend, Blanc de Noir, Chenin Blanc, Viognier, Natural Sweet Red Blend.** — CE

Location/WO: Paarl ▪ Map: Paarl & Wellington ▪ Map grid reference: C8 ▪ Est 1998 ▪ 1stB 2001 ▪ Tasting & sales Fri-Sun 10-4.30 ▪ Owner(s) Arra Vineyards (Pty) Ltd ▪ Cellarmaster(s) Dee Wentzel (2006) ▪ Viticulturist(s) Willem Snyman (2014) ▪ 72ha/30ha (cab, merlot, mourv, ptage, ruby cab, shiraz, viog) ▪ 20,000cs ▪ PO Box 298 Klapmuts 7625 ▪ info@arrawines.com ▪ www.arrawines.com ▪ S 33° 49' 25.9" E 018° 51' 47.7" ▪ F +27 (0)21-875-5866 ▪ **T +27 (0)21-875-5363**

☐ **Artisan Collection** *see* Snow Mountain Wines

Arumdale Cool Climate Wines ⓠ

Mark Simpson traded apple and pear farming for this Elgin cool-climate boutique brand operating out of his wine shop in Grabouw town. Sales of these wines and siblings Robin Hood Legendary Wine Series (listed separately) continue to climb as fans succumb to their charm at shows and markets nationally.

Pink Shiraz ★★★ Bright cherry & plum succulence on **14** dry rosé, with the same modest alcohol (12%) as last. **Special LYC Sauvignon Blanc** ★★★ Creamy breadth & rounded stonefruit notes on **14**, atypical (but not unappealing) expression due to 4 months lees-ageing. Not retasted: **St Andrews 12** ★★★★ Not tasted: **Shiraz**. — FM

Location/WO: Elgin ▪ Map: Elgin, Walker Bay & Bot River ▪ Est 1962 ▪ 1stB 2003 ▪ Tasting & sales Mon-Fri 10-4 Sat 10-5 Sun 10-4 ▪ Fee R15/7 wines, waived on purchase of 2/more bottles ▪ Closed Easter Fri-Mon, Dec 25/26 & Jan 1 ▪ Owner(s) Mark Simpson ▪ Cellarmaster(s)/winemaker(s) Christo Versfeld (Villiersdorp Cellar) ▪ (cab, merlot, shiraz, sauv) ▪ PO Box 2 Elgin 7180 ▪ royalwine@arumdale.co.za ▪ www.arumdale.co.za, www.robinhoodlegendarywines.co.za ▪ S 34° 9' 14.51" E 019° 1' 48.22" ▪ F +27 (0)21-859-3430 ▪ **T +27 (0)21-859-3430**

Asara Wine Estate & Hotel ⓠ ⓜ ⌂ ⓞ ⓐ

The modern name of this historic Stellenbosch property – first granted in 1691 – alludes to the African gods Astar (earth), Asis (Sun) and Asase (sky). Under stewardship of estate manager Pete Gottgens since 2010, there have been major changes and improvements including a range of bedroom upgrades in 2015, new afternoon tea venue and lounge, fynbos gardens and, for brides, a spectacular 3,750 ice-berg roses – all contributing to a memorable, and awarded, winelands experience.

Speciality Collection

★★★★ **Bell Tower Estate Wine** ⓠ **11** first since **07**. Cab-headed Bordeaux quintet offers unshowy tobacco, dark berried notes & grip of firm ripe tannins. Satisfying; shows medium-term potential.

★★★★ **Avalon** From air-dried shiraz with 25% pinotage in **11** (★★★★); latter's stewed plum notes, nip concluding bitterness lend rustic note to local take on Italian Amarone style. Lacks concentration of **10**; notable kick of 15.5% alcohol in tail. Barrelled 3 years, 30% new. Also in magnum.

★★★★ **Carillon 13** Noble Late Harvest's sunny gold hue not quite matched in chenin's simple, lightly botrytised peachy fruit, spare flesh, nor as compared with pure, juicy **12** (★★★★★). Bright acidity, older oak ferment temper finishing sweetness. 500 ML.

Also tasted: **Nouveau 15** ★★ **White Cab 15** ★★ **Sundried Sauvignon Blanc 14** ★★★☆

Vineyard Collection

★★★★ **Cabernet Sauvignon 12** improves on **11** (★★★★☆) with elegant cedar-spiced cassis fragrance, the flavours equally fresh, focused & knit by fine, polished grip. Oaking, 20% new, 2 years, further refinement. Worth keeping 3-5 years.

Pinotage Rosé ★★★ Fresh, ripe raspberries, redcurrants on ruby pink **15**. Lingering fruity pleasure on bone-dry finish. **Chardonnay Lightly Wooded** ★★☆ Lemon & fresh honey nose on **13**. Juicy, with lightest of oak spicing, fruitily sweet tail. Also tasted: **Merlot 12** ★★★ **Petit Verdot 11** ★★★ **Shiraz 12** ★★★☆ **Cape Fusion 13** ★★★ **Chenin Blanc 14** ★★★ **Sauvignon Blanc 15** ★★★☆

Classic Collection

Merlot-Cabernet Sauvignon ★★☆ Smooth ripe mulberry fruit framed by gentle grip. No waiting necessary for **13**. Not retasted: **Rosé 14** ★★★ **Sauvignon Blanc 13** ★★☆ **Sauvignon Blanc-Chardonnay 14** ★★☆ Discontinued: **Shiraz**.

Cape Vinelands Collection ⓝⓔⓦ

Cabernet Sauvignon ★★ Pure yet simple juicy blackberry aromas, flavours lengthened by few grams of sugar; very gentle grip on previewed **14**. WO W Cape for all. **Merlot** ★★ Ex-tank, medium-bodied **14** shows spicy red plum freshness, gentle tannins. Portion oak influenced. **Merlot-Cabernet Sauvignon** ★★ **14** sweetish blend, including drop cinsaut to spice up juicy strawberry flavours. Rounded, ready. **Chardonnay Unwooded** ★★☆ Zesty ripe citrus appeal on **15** carries through on dry, clean finish. Great partner with grilled line fish. **Chenin Blanc** ★★ Chenin at its most modest on **15** gently fresh, dry quaffer. **Sauvignon Blanc** ★★ **15** brisk & dry with demure grassy flavours. **Sauvignon**

Blanc-Chardonnay ★★★ 15 marries sweet-fruited juiciness broadened by a creamy dab; clean & dry. Versatile with food or solo sipping — AL

Location/map: Stellenbosch ▪ Map grid reference: D6 ▪ WO: Stellenbosch/Western Cape ▪ Est/1stB 2001 ▪ Tasting Mon-Sat 10-6 Sun 10-4 ▪ Fee R30/3 wines, R50/5 wines ▪ Sales 10-5 ▪ Closed Dec 25 ▪ Tasting centre ▪ Cellar tours by appt ▪ Tour groups ▪ Five star hotel ▪ Raphael's restaurant ▪ Sansibar ▪ Deli ▪ Gift shop ▪ Function & banqueting facilities ▪ Conferences ▪ Weddings ▪ Vineyard walks ▪ Cookery school ▪ Cellarmaster(s) Francois Joubert (Sep 2009) ▪ Winemaker(s) Francois Joubert (Sep 2009) & Abé Beukes (consultant), with Dirk Tredoux (Jan 2015) ▪ Viticulturist(s) Allan Cockcroft (2013) ▪ 180ha/102ha (cab, merlot, p verdot, chard, sauv) ▪ 1,000t/90,000cs own label 70% red 30% white ▪ IPW ▪ PO Box 882 Stellenbosch 7599 ▪ info@asara.co.za ▪ www.asara.co.za ▪ S 33° 56' 35.00" E 018° 48' 31.00" ▪ F +27 (0)21-888-8001 ▪ **T +27 (0)21-888-8000**

Ashbourne   ⓠ

Farmed separately, the 113-hectare Ashbourne property on the eastern border of Hamilton Russell Vineyards is increasingly focused on organic cultivation. Owner Anthony Hamilton Russell notes the past year has been spent clearing alien vegetation and developing grazing camps for the organically farmed cattle. 'Their manure will go to the earthworm farm we've partnered with for earthworm tea, eventually supplying all our needs.' New in the cellar are two 500L Chinese antique stoneware 'wine jars', initially used to skin-ferment a low-alcohol semillon component for the Sandstone white, before doing duty for the whole-bunch syrah/shiraz destined for the Ashbourne red. Less unusual is a new ceramic 'egg', imported from Australia, which will be used to mature the Sandstone blend.

★★★★ **Ashbourne** Pinotage the major player among four Bordeaux varieties & shiraz in **10**; overall result homogeneous & classy. Already rounded, approachable, with plenty sweet ripe fruit & freshness. Can age few more years too.

★★★★☆ **Sandstone** Released at 5 years, unwooded blend gains in texture as well as flavour. **10** adds semillon (& greater density) to sauvignon (75%), chardonnay mix. Usual delicious qualities — vinosity, savouriness & vitality — feature in this food-friendly & still ageworthy individual.

Ashbourne Sauvignon Blanc-Chardonnay ★★★ Zesty sauvignon broadened by 20% creamy chardonnay, **15** shows richness, concentration of vintage with no loss of drinkability. Walker Bay WO. — AL

Location: Hermanus ▪ WO: Hemel-en-Aarde Valley/Walker Bay ▪ Est 1996 ▪ 1stB 2001 ▪ Tasting & sales at Hamilton Russell Vineyards ▪ Owner(s) Anthony Hamilton Russell ▪ Winemaker(s) Emul Ross (2014) ▪ Viticulturist(s) Johan Montgomery (2005) ▪ 113ha/24.35ha (cabs s/f, malbec, p verdot, ptage, shiraz, sauv, sem) ▪ 20t/2,000cs own label 50% red 50% white ▪ PO Box 158 Hermanus 7200 ▪ hrv@hermanus.co.za ▪ F +27 (0)28-312-1797 ▪ **T +27 (0)28-312-3595**

Ashton Kelder   ⓠ ⓞ ⓐ ⓖ

'Something for every vinotype' is what Ashton Kelder promises, and for good measure the 54-year-old grower-owned producer has added a spirit cooler to the portfolio, which covers everything from grape juice for kids to Reserve wines for sophisticates. Fans can taste the new arrival, made from red muscadel and packaged in a 340-ml bottle, at the recently enlarged tasting venue on the hill above Ashton town.

Reserve range
★★★★ **Roodewal** Switches from Bordeaux-shiraz in **11** (★★★★) to pinotage with cab & shiraz in improved **13**, showing serious intent in all-new French oaking. Savoury & vanilla nuances to the ripe berries, well-managed tannins & elegant cranberry conclusion.

★★★★ **Chardonnay Limited Release 14** reveals its 100% new-oak ferment in bold vanilla & toffee tones, but there's enough lemon curd, lime marmalade & sweet apricot fruit to balance the wood; finishes long & lemony. More structure & character than last-tasted **12** (★★★).

Ashton range

Cabernet Sauvignon-Merlot ⓥ ⓦ ★★★★ Same equal blend as previous but **13** goes up a notch with more generous red berry fruit, clean acid balance, soft tannins. Nice spicy farewell. **Chenin Blanc** ⓦ ★★★ Much-improved **15** has apple wafts & mouthfilling fruit salad flavours. Equally good solo or

> with food. Could even age a bit. **Satynwit** ⊘ ⊛ ★★★ Unwooded chenin, as previous, step-up **15** is charming, & shows some complexity in its array of ripe, full fruit flavours. Super seafood or poultry accompaniment. **Sauvignon Blanc** ⊘ ⊛ ★★★★ **15**'s bright green melon & guava flavours are served with controlled acidity along with clean citrus notes, a fruit salady finale.

Satynrooi ⊘ ★★★ Unoaked **14** mixes pinotage & ruby cab in a light & fruity pasta partner showing tobacco-tinged red berries & firm tannins. Also tasted: **Cabernet Sauvignon 14** ★★ **Pinotage 14** ★★ **Shiraz 13** ★★★ **Satynrosé 14** ★★ **Chardonnay Unwooded 14** ★★★ **Satynperlé 13** ★★ Not tasted: **Bonica Vin Doux, Red Muscadel.** — DB

Location: Ashton ▪ Map/WO: Robertson ▪ Est 1962 ▪ 1stB 1970 ▪ Tasting & sales Mon-Fri 8-5 Sat 10-4 ▪ Closed Good Fri & Dec 25/26 ▪ Cellar tours by appt ▪ Facilities for children ▪ Tour groups ▪ Farm produce ▪ Conferences & weddings ▪ Owner(s) 45 shareholders ▪ Cellarmaster(s) Sterik de Wet (Oct 2009) ▪ Winemaker(s) Simon Basson (Nov 2007) & Heinrich Coetzee (Sep 2013) ▪ Viticulturist(s) Hennie Visser (Vinpro) ▪ 1,280ha (cab, ptage, ruby cab, shiraz, chard, chenin, cbard, sauv) ▪ 21,614t/15m L total: 3% under own label 56% bulk & 41% grape juice concentrate ▪ Other export brands: Berryfields, Khoi Klaas, Mountain Stream ▪ ISO 22000, BWI, HACCP, IPW, WIETA ▪ PO Box 40 Ashton 6715 ▪ info@ ashtonkelder.co.za ▪ www.ashtonkelder.co.za ▪ S 33° 50' 12.1" E 020° 1' 48.3" ▪ F +27 (0)23-615-1284 ▪ **T +27 (0)23-615-1135**

Ataraxia Wines

Ataraxia is defined as a calmness or tranquil state of mind. Though a quarter century has passed since prime mover Kevin Grant graduated top-of-class from Elsenburg College, and gained seasoning in the US, Australia, New Zealand and France, and a long residency at Hamilton Russell in Hemel-en-Aarde before embarking on this venture, his energy and enthusiasm are undimmed. From a chapel-like 'wine lounge' modelled on vernacular Overberg architecture, built just over a decade ago on a promontory in Hemel-en-Aarde Ridge, Ataraxia's emphasis is on a sense of place. Ever meticulous in preparation – especially when it comes to the 14 soil types on the ±50 hectares – Kevin will not be drawn on precisely when his passion project, a long-gestated pinot noir, will join the critically acclaimed line-up.

★★★★☆ **Serenity** ⊗ Undisclosed blend, **11** (★★★★) not so serene as **10**. Very ripe, a few plummy notes but overall austere, densely tannic. May reach greater harmony with few years. Walker Bay grapes.

★★★★☆ **Chardonnay** Barrel ferment & 9 months oak (26% new) make for a toasty entry on youthful **14** (★★★★) otherwise showing similar taut, tangy, chiselled restraint to **13**, same full citrus profile. Hemel-en-Aarde Ridge WO.

★★★★ **Sauvignon Blanc** Overt lime zest held in check on juicy **15** from Elgin, with concentrated flinty finish. Impressive texture & length matches **14** from Walker Bay fruit. — FM

Location: Hermanus ▪ Map: Elgin, Walker Bay & Bot River ▪ WO: Western Cape/Hemel-en-Aarde Ridge ▪ Est 2004 ▪ 1stB 2005 ▪ Wine lounge: tasting & sales Mon-Fri 9-4 Sat 10-5 Sun in season only ▪ Fee R15pp for groups of 10 or more, refunded with individual purchase ▪ Closed Easter Fri/Sun, Dec 25 & Jan 1 ▪ Art exhibition ▪ Owner(s) Kevin Grant Wines (Pty) Ltd ▪ Cellarmaster(s)/winemaker(s) Kevin Grant (Sep 2004) ▪ Viticulturist(s) Kevin Grant (Sep 2004) & Rohan Breytenbach (Jun 2015) ▪ 47ha/12ha (pinot, chard) ▪ 83t/12,000cs own label 40% red 60% white ▪ PO Box 603 Hermanus 7200 ▪ info@ ataraxiawines.co.za ▪ www.ataraxiawines.co.za ▪ S 34° 20' 27.0" E 019° 18' 30.8" ▪ F +27 (0)28-212-1921 ▪ **T +27 (0)28-212-2007**

⊐ **Athena** *see* Long Mountain Wine Company

Auction Crossing Private Cellar

The 1938 cellar at this tiny Hex River Valley winery was refurbished (keeping the traditional open fermenters) and saw its first modern vintage in 2004. Grapes are sourced widely by winemaker Leon Dippenaar – Paarl and Durbanville in the case of the current releases.

Syrah ⓧ ★★★★ Spicy dark chocolate on **11** with peppercorns & black fruit. Coffee notes on palate sweep through to fresh, clean finish. **Viognier** ⓧ ★★★ Lightly oaked, flavourful **12** offers pleasantly fruity, spicy savouriness. Occasional release: **Syrah-Viognier**. — CM

Location: De Doorns ▪ Map: Worcester ▪ WO: Western Cape ▪ Est 2003 ▪ 1stB 2004 ▪ Tasting & sales Mon-Fri 9-5 Sat 9-2 ▪ Closed all pub hols ▪ Cellar tours by appt ▪ Bistro 'Inspirati' ▪ Facilities for children ▪ Tour groups by appt only ▪ Owner/s De Villiers Graaff, AJ Reyneke & Leon Dippenaar ▪ Cellarmaster(s)/winemaker(s)/viticulturist(s) Leon Dippenaar (Aug 2004) ▪ ±41ha/2ha (mourv, shiraz, viog) ▪ 10t/4,000cs own label 75% red 25% white ▪ The Pines PO Box 5 Hex River 6855 ▪ auctioncrossing@hexvalley.co.za ▪ www.auctioncrossing.co.za ▪ S 33° 29' 42.8" E 019° 34' 32.7" ▪ F +27 (0)23-357-9255 ▪ **T +27 (0)23-357-9655**

Audacia Wines ⓧ ⓧ ⓧ ⓧ ⓧ

This 'audacious' family-owned winery's passion for natural wines drove its collaboration with Stellenbosch University on patented cutting-edge technology, replacing oak with antioxidant-rich, low-tannin rooibos and honeybush wood, thereby obviating sulphites as a preservative. They continue to innovate, extending their range of no-sulphites-added reds with two similarly treated whites (from bought-in fruit) and working on low-alcohol/low-kilojoule wine, informatively back-labelled.

Audacia range

Merlot ★★★ **12** delivers pleasant sipping with ripe berry nose & palate, rounded tannins, some firmness from 33% new oak (mostly staves). **Shiraz** ★★★★ Mocha, dark chocolate & black pepper notes, **12** full bodied, savoury, with plump tannins; great to pair with game. Also tasted: **Cabernet Sauvignon 13** ★★★ Not retasted: **Rouge Noble NV** ★★★ **Jeté NV** ★★★ Discontinued: **Cabernet Franc**.

Rooibos Wooded No Sulphites Or Preservatives Added range

Cabernet Sauvignon ⓝⓔ ⓦ ★★★ Those who drink the tea will recognise the rooibos nuance on **14**, but also stewed fruit, hints of smoke & red berry; youthful & very appealing. **Shiraz** ⓝⓔ ⓦ ★★★ Dried buchu/rooibos notes, slight smokiness on **14**, plum & cherry hints, slides down effortlessly. Unusual wooding for these: rooibos & honeybush chips added in tank.

Not retasted: **Merlot 13** ★★★ — GM

Location/map/WO: Stellenbosch ▪ Map grid reference: E7 ▪ Est 1930 ▪ Tasting & sales Mon-Fri 9—4 Sat/Sun 11-4 ▪ Fee R20, waived on purchase ▪ Closed pub hols ▪ Root 44 market (food, arts, crafts, jewellery, kiddies area & bar) ▪ Owner(s) Strydom & Harris families ▪ Cellarmaster(s)/winemaker(s)/viticulturist(s) Michael van Niekerk (Aug 2009) ▪ 32ha/20ha (cabs s/f, malbec, merlot, p verdot, roobernet, shiraz) ▪ 120t/18,000cs own label 100% red ▪ IPW ▪ PO Box 12679 Die Boord 7613 ▪ info@audacia.co.za ▪ www.audacia.co.za ▪ S 33° 59' 45.7" E 018° 50' 2.9" ▪ F +27 (0)21-881-3137 ▪ **T +27 (0)21-881-3052**

Aufwaerts Co-operative ⓧ

Breedekloof family enterprise Aufwaerts produces mostly bulk wine but also bottles a limited-release hanepoot fortified dessert and a 5 year old brandy, Twee Eeue, named for the production process which straddled the 20th and 21st centuries. The distillery has been a national monument since the 1940s.

Location: Rawsonville ▪ Map: Breedekloof ▪ Tasting by appt ▪ Winemaker(s) Hennie de Villiers ▪ PO Box 51 Rawsonville 6845 ▪ hanepoot39@gmail.com ▪ S 33° 41' 42.4" E 019° 17' 33.7" ▪ F +27 (0)23-349-1202 ▪ **T +27 (0)23-349-1202**

Aurelia Wines ⓝⓔⓦ

Groote Post winemaker Lukas Wentzel's own specialist label debuts this edition with a champagne-method sparkling named for 18th-century matriarch Aurelia Stafforinus, wife of the first Wentzel to settle in the Cape. Made from Groote Post grapes, boutique-scale Aurelia is intended to 'recognise the uniqueness of Darling' and feed what Lukas describes as SA consumers' hunger for crafted bubblies.

Aurelia Méthode Cap Classique ★★★☆ Classic chardonnay/pinot combo in **13** bottle-fermented sparkler. Apple fresh, with racy bubbles & attractive brioche tones; bone-dry, slightly saline finish, savoury top notes. Stock up for summer sunsets. — WB, CvZ

Location/WO: Darling ▪ Est 2010 ▪ 1stB 2008 ▪ Closed to public ▪ Owner(s)/cellarmaster(s)/ winemaker(s) Lukas Wentzel ▪ 3t/600cs own label ▪ WIETA ▪ PO Box 102 Darling 7345 ▪ lukas@ grootepost.co.za ▪ **T +27 (0)22-492-2825/+27 (0)82-306-7373**

Autumn Harvest Crackling

Among SA's top sellers, these spritzy lower-alcohol wines are made by Distell. Also sold in larger bottles.

Crisp Perlé Rosé ⊗ **★★★** Crisp little pink **NV** party wine with a nice acid balance & the perkiness of tiny bubbles. Not retasted: **Crisp Perlé White NV ★★ Crisp Perlé Red NV ★** — DB

Avondale   Ⓥⓞⓐⓖ

Paarl wine estate Avondale is owned by the Grieve family, founders of a well-known SA health food and supplements range, so it's not surprising that son Johnathan, assuming management in 1999, converted the once conventionally farmed property into a model for sustainable winegrowing. Organic and biodynamic principles, backed by science, allow winemaker Corné Marais to follow an all-natural regimen in the underground gravity-flow cellar. Wines of great character are all certified organic, with names reflecting a holistic ethos further edified on their by-appointment Eco Wine Safari.

★★★★ Navitas ⊗ ⊙ Well-assembled, understated **08** is shiraz-led, rest mourvèdre, grenache. Medium bodied, with notes of red fruit & white pepper before a long, dry finish.

★★★★ Anima ⊙ Naturally barrel-fermented chenin; tangy quince & apricot with roasted walnut on broad-shouldered, rich **13**, commanding yet fresh & drying towards the slightly warm finish.

★★★★☆ Cyclus ⊙ Rich, perfumed 5-way white blend, native yeast fermented (20% new oak); chenin now equal with viognier & roussanne, dollops semillon & chardonnay. **13** (**★★★★**) as complex as **12** in its expression of the varieties, but lacks some of the class, intensity. Slight raisin note also a first.

★★★★ Armilla Blanc de Blancs ⊗ ⊙ Thrilling sparkling from chardonnay. **09** (**★★★★☆**) greater complexity than last-tasted **NV**, with apple, bruised pear & baked brioche character from part oaking, 2 years on lees as base wine, 3 in bottle. Fresh & tangy, superbly balanced. Delicious now, will develop.

Camissa ⊙ **★★★** Clever combination of muscat de Frontignan with more typical rosé varieties (mourvèdre, grenache), **14** offers spice & sweet floral perfumes, followed by surprisingly dry palate. Not retasted: **Samsara 09 ★★★★ La Luna 09 ★★★★** — HJ

Location/WO: Paarl ▪ Map: Paarl & Wellington ▪ Map grid reference: F6 ▪ Est 1996 ▪ 1stB 1999 ▪ Tasting & sales Mon-Sat by appt ▪ Fee R50pp ▪ Closed Easter Fri-Mon, Dec 25 & Jan 1 ▪ Cellar tours by appt only ▪ Eco Wine Safari Wed-Fri 10-4 by appt: R200pp incl MCC on arrival, tour & tasting in vyds, cellar tour ▪ Art exhibit ▪ Child friendly ▪ Owner(s) Grieve family/The Avondale Trust ▪ Winemaker(s) Corné Marais (Oct 2008), with Ivan September (Jan 2012) ▪ Viticulturist(s) Johnathan Grieve (Jul 1999) ▪ 300ha/70ha (cabs s/f, grenache, merlot, mourv, shiraz, chard, chenin, rouss, sem, viog) ▪ 500t/50,000cs own label 50% red 38% white 2% rosé 10% MCC ▪ EU Organic & USDA NOP organic ▪ PO Box 602 Paarl South 7624 ▪ wine@avondalewine.co.za ▪ www.avondalewine.co.za ▪ S 33° 45' 52.9" E 019° 0' 4.7" ▪ F +27 (0)21-863-1534 ▪ **T +27 (0)21-863-1976**

Avondrood Vineyards   Ⓥⓜⓐⓗⓞⓐ

The name of the Van Rensburgs' Breedekloof farm was inspired by its beautiful sunsets, perhaps best appreciated — glass of boutique vintner Albertus' handcrafted wines in hand — from the veranda of the mountainside guest cottage, one of several visitor and business amenities on or near the estate.

Location: Rawsonville ▪ Map: Breedekloof ▪ Est/1stB 2005 ▪ Tasting, sales & cellar tours Mon-Fri 8-12 & 1.30-5 Sat by appt (phone +27 (0)82-578-6841) ▪ Closed most pub hols ▪ Refreshments/food-and-wine tastings by appt or BYO picnic ▪ Conferences ▪ Walks/hikes ▪ Facilities for children ▪ Hewn-stone mountain cottage ▪ Owner(s) Albertus van Rensburg ▪ Winemaker(s) Albertus van Rensburg, with Johannes Damane ▪ Viticulturist(s) Pierre Snyman ▪ 80ha (cab, ptage, shiraz, chard, sauv, viog) ▪ 30t/4,200cs own label 40% red 60%

white ▪ PO Box 277 Worcester 6849 ▪ vineyards@avondrood.co.za ▪ www.avondrood.co.za ▪ S 33° 43' 32.9"
E 019° 20' 18.7" ▪ F +27 (0)86-210-5806 ▪ **T +27 (0)23-349-1858**

Avontuur Estate   ⓨ ⑪ ⓐ ⓖ

The scenic Avontuur property with its white-poled paddocks, verdant pastures and premium viticultural
terroir has been the source of equine thoroughbreds and characterful wines since the 1980s, when the
late Tony Taberer transplanted his champion racing stud from Zimbabwe to the Helderberg's sea-facing
slopes. Recently sons Michael and Philip carried out upgrades and expansions to the estate and its
cellardoor, continued educational and community development initiatives, and trimmed the wine portfolio to focus on the premium labels and ten-year-old brandy.

Avontuur Premiere range

★★★★ Dominion Royale Shiraz Reserve ⓧ **11** (★★★★) not as fleet of foot as **08** or standout **09**
(★★★★★). Stewy, meaty, with savoury black fruit. **10** not made.

Minelli Pinot Noir Reserve ★★★ Deep & savoury **11** has faint floral scents & spicy fruit, light &
uncomplicated. **Baccarat ★★★★** Wildflower, tea & blackcurrant notes mingle with vanilla oak &
cigarbox on **10** merlot-led Bordeaux blend. Supple tannins & structure, medium body. Also tasted:
Luna de Miel Chardonnay Reserve 14 ★★★ Sarabande Sauvignon Blanc Reserve 14 ★★★
Not retasted: **Above Royalty Liqueur Wine 09 ★★★☆**

Avontuur Estate range

Cabernet Sauvignon-Merlot ★★★ Medium-bodied **13** offers ripe dark berry fruit, subtle spice;
grippy tannins, but a juicy mouthful. **Pinot Noir-Chardonnay ★★☆** Palest blush on **15** rosé, fairly
neutral flavours, light & dry, portion oak aged. **Sauvignon Blanc ★★★ 15** herbaceous & crisp, with cut
grass nuance; vibrant, bright, with saline finish. Also tasted: **Cabernet Sauvignon 12 ★★ Cabernet
Franc 11 ★★★ Pinotage 13 ★★☆ Brut Cap Classique NV ★★★** Occasional release: **Above Royalty Noble Late Harvest**.

Brandy range

★★★★ 10 Year Private Collection 100% potstill from chenin. Sweet apricots, nuts, peardrop & cigar
smoke entice on the nose. Rich, with gorgeous depth of flavour; smooth, silky & very moreish. — WB

Location/WO: Stellenbosch ▪ Map: Helderberg ▪ Est 1850 ▪ 1stB 1990 ▪ Tasting & sales Mon-Fri 8.30–5 Sat/
Sun 9–4 ▪ Fee R30/5 wines ▪ Closed Good Fri, Dec 25 & Jan 1 ▪ Cellar tours by appt ▪ Tour groups ▪ Avontuur
Estate Restaurant ▪ Function venue ▪ Thoroughbred stud ▪ Owner(s) Taberer family ▪ Winemaker(s) /brandy
master(s) Jan van Rooyen (Jan 2011) ▪ Viticulturist(s) Pippa Mickleburgh (Sep 1999) ▪ 110ha/47ha (cabs s/f,
merlot, p verdot, ptage, pinot, shiraz, chard, sauv, viog) ▪ 405t/18,000cs own label 60% red 40% white ▪ PO
Box 1128 Somerset West 7129 ▪ info@avontuurestate.co.za ▪ www.avontuurestate.co.za ▪ S 34° 1' 33.2" E
018° 49' 23.8" ▪ F +27 (0)21-855-4600 ▪ **T +27 (0)21-855-3450**

Axe Hill   ⓨ

This Calitzdorp winery — founded by eminent winewriter the late Tony Mossop in the early 1990s — built
a reputation for Cape 'port' in inverse proportion to the modesty of its vineyard footprint. Its current
owners, since 2009, have expanded the range produced, with partner/cellarmaster Mike Neebe making
a number of table wines too, most notably from red Portuguese varieties (there should be a minimum of
70% of these in what proponents like him conceive of as a Calitzdorp Blend). Now, he says, 'white wines
have been produced for the first time after an upgrade of the cooling system'. Unsurprisingly, given this
growth, he also murmurs about a 'possible barrel cellar extension'.

★★★★ Shiraz ⓧ **13** (★★★) first since **10**. Ripely rich, with notes of smoked meat mingling with the
berry ones. Bold acidity a little unharmonious with the soft structure & sweet-fruited finish.

★★★★☆ Cape Vintage 12 is almost worryingly delicious for a young 'port', but there's the structure to
help it develop in bottle for a decade. Like **11** (★★★★★), led by touriga (here 60%), with souzão & tinta.
Rich & incipiently complex, the firm grip of tannin & spirit controlling the fruit, guiding it to a long, almost
dry finish.

Distinta ★★★☆ 13 from souzão & tinta, less ultra-ripe than previous, but still softly textured & rich. Lots of flavour – less firm tannin than Machado & not as complex, but perhaps more early charm. Also tasted: **Machado 13 ★★★☆ Cape White NV ★★★☆** Not retasted: **Cape Late Bottled Vintage 09 ★★★ Cape Ruby NV ★★★☆** Not tasted: **Dry Red**. — TJ

Location/WO: Calitzdorp ▪ Map: Klein Karoo & Garden Route ▪ Est 1993 ▪ 1stB 1997 ▪ Tasting, sales & cellar tours Mon-Sat by appt ▪ Owner(s) Axe Hill Winery (Pty) Ltd ▪ Cellarmaster(s)/winemaker(s) Mike Neebe (Oct 2007) ▪ Viticulturist(s) Johannes Mellet (Aug 2009, consultant) ▪ ±60ha/1.5ha (grenache, souzão, tinta barocca, tinta roriz, touriga nacional, viog) ▪ ±5t/±1,000cs own label 70% red 30% white ▪ Wesoewer Road Calitzdorp 6660 ▪ info@axehill.co.za ▪ www.axehill.co.za ▪ S 33° 30' 54.6" E 021° 41' 23.0" ▪ F +27 (0)11-447-3219 ▪ **T +27 (0)11-447-4366/+27 (0)44-213-3585**

Ayama Wines Ⓨ ⑪ ⊖ ⓐ ⑧

'Italian spirit and South African love' underpin the myriad developments at Voor Paardeberg's Slent farm, under custodianship of Attilio Dalpiaz, Michela Sfiligoi and partners from the old country since 2005. The buildings on the 330-year-old property are being transformed into a cellar, tasting area, olive oil facility, shop/deli and offices, 'and the happiness of watching old doors, windows, walls, poplar beams, bricks and rocks reviving to new life is huge'. Vermentino and petite sirah are among the exotics planted to help create 'a unique estate', and adored pinotage and chenin are earmarked for the first organic vineyard.

Leopard Spot range

★★★★ Red Ⓩ Shiraz, pinotage & mourvèdre the (unoaked) varieties in **13** (**★★★☆**) more modern than elegant & classic **10**. Flavoursome spicy dark berries, supple tannin. No **11**, **12**.

Not retasted: **White 13 ★★★☆**

Ayama range

Chenin Blanc ⑦ **★★★☆** Real interest & character on step-up **13**, starting to show tropical fruit richness offset by fresh zippy acidity. Also-tasted **14** continues in same vein – plenty of promise here.

Cabernet Sauvignon ★★★ Sweet, lively black fruit **13** with fresh, varietally correct flavours unhampered by wood (as are all these). **Merlot ★★★☆** Ripe, soft, berry compote **13** aims for commercial success & attains it in style. Also tasted: **Pinotage 13 ★★★ Shiraz 13 ★★★ Sauvignon Blanc 14 ★★★** Not retasted: **Chardonnay 13 ★★★**

Baboon Selection

Baboon's Back Shiraz ★★★☆ Kiss of old oak adds spice & charry notes to **13** whilst appetising aromas & flavours of cherries, leather & cloves keep interest going. Not retasted: **Baboon's Cuddle Pinotage 12 ★★★ Baboon's Swing Chenin Blanc 13 ★★★ Baboon's Cheek Viognier 12 ★★☆**

Slent range

Pinotage-Shiraz ⑦ **★★★** Cracking unoaked **14** cheers with plenty of juicy black fruit & fresh appeal. Uncomplicated but thoroughly enjoyable braai wine. WO W Cape, like Chenin-Sauvignon.

Chenin Blanc-Sauvignon Blanc ★★☆ Sweet tropical fruit nose on **14**, dryness of palate creates a surprise but overall, pleasant drink. Also tasted: **Cabernet Sauvignon-Merlot 13 ★★☆**

Méthode Cap Classiques

★★★★ Rosé Ⓩ Dry pink bubbles from pinot noir & 45% chardonnay, 2 years on lees (as for Brut). **11** (**★★★☆**) lovely, refreshing, but shade less panache than **10**.

★★★★ Blanc de Blancs Ⓩ **10** zesty sparkler from chardonnay improves on **08** (**★★★☆**). Poised & lingering, with modest 12% alcohol. **09** sold out untasted.

Not retasted: **Brut 10 ★★★★** — CM

Location: Paarl ▪ Map: Paarl & Wellington ▪ Map grid reference: B2 ▪ WO: Western Cape/Voor Paardeberg ▪ Est 2005 ▪ 1stB 2006 ▪ Tasting & sales open to public from Nov 2015 – see website for trading hours ▪ Meals/refreshments by appt; or BYO picnic ▪ Deli with fresh farm produce, olive oil, wines & much more ▪ Walks/hikes ▪ Child friendly ▪ Conservation area ▪ Owner(s) Slent Farms (Pty) Ltd (5 partners) ▪ Cellarmaster(s)/winemaker(s) Michela Sfiligoi (2005) ▪ Viticulturist(s) Attilio Dalpiaz (2005) ▪ 210ha/65ha (cab, carignan, grenache n/b, merlot, petite sirah, ptage, shiraz, chenin, sauv, vermentino, viog) ▪ 300t/40,000cs own label 40% red 58% white 2% rosé ▪ WIETA ▪ Suite 106 Private Bag X3041 Paarl 7620 ▪ info@slentfarms.com ▪ www.ayama.co.za ▪ S 33° 37' 22.5" E 018° 49' 19" ▪ F +27 (0)86-662-2765 ▪ **T +27 (0)21-869-8313**

☐ **Azania** *see* Jacques Germanier

Baarsma Wine Group

Stellenbosch-based Baarsma SA is a major exporter of South African wines, shipping wines to most of the major international markets. The group's Lyngrove brand is listed separately.

Stellenbosch ▪ Closed to public ▪ Owner(s) Baarsma Wine Group BV ▪ MD Chris Rabie ▪ Cellarmaster(s) Hannes Louw (since Jan 2005) ▪ PO Box 7275 Stellenbosch 7599 ▪ info@baarsma.co.za ▪ www.baarsma.co.za ▪ F +27 (0)21-880-0851 ▪ **T +27 (0)21-880-1221**

BABISA – Born & Bred in South Africa   ⓧ

Born & Bred in South Africa is a lifestyle brand whose various luxury product segments are being rolled out strategically. The Paarl-based wine division works with partner cellars to vinify and bottle wines to spec. CEO Paul Burger says a second blended red and 'a few whites' will follow in due course.

Lifestyle range
★★★★ Nicolas ⓧ Merlot-led Bordeaux blend from Paarl grapes is a leafy but bold & dense wine. **12** classically styled, with restrained fruit & serious tannin structure destined for a good future.

Not retasted: **Cabernet Sauvignon 12 ★★★☆**

Born & Bred in South Africa range
Not tasted: **Valerie Reserve**. — HJ

Location: Paarl ▪ WO: Western Cape ▪ Est 2008 ▪ 1stB 2007 ▪ Tasting by appt ▪ Tours to estates producing BABISA wines by prior arrangement ▪ Owner(s) BABISA Brand Innovation Holdings Ltd ▪ Cellarmaster(s)/winemaker(s)/viticulturist(s) Various ▪ 1,000cs own label 70% red 30% white ▪ PO Box 52185 Waterfront 8002 ▪ wines@babisa.com ▪ www.babisa.com ▪ F +27 (0)86-616-2794 ▪ **T +27 (0)71-232-8840**

☐ **Baboon Selection** *see* Ayama Wines

Babylon's Peak Private Cellar   ⓧ ⓧ ⓧ ⓧ ⓧ

The winery name, from the granite thumb on the Perdeberg locally known as Babylonstoren, signals that these wines are from some of the highest vineyards in the Swartland. The vines are part of a large farm, in the Basson family since 1919, previously supplying grapes to the big houses but also vinified for the own label since 2003. 5th-generation scion Christiaan has joined his father Stephan and oupa Kobus in the farming business. Aged 3, he's excused himself from preschool!

★★★★ SMG ⓧ Refined, characterful shiraz-based blend from mature vines. Swartland warmth in spicy, clean leather tones, richness & velvet grip of **10**.

★★★★ Chenin Blanc ⓧ **15** youthfully invigorating, with pure tropical, spicy concentration from dryland bushvines. Lees enriched for further texture; clean & fruitily long.

★★★★ Viognier-Roussanne 15 first since **11**. Individual 55/45 partnership harmonised in older oak. Elegant honeysuckle & spice fragrance reprised on agile yet richly textured palate. Should uphold area's excellent reputation for white blends once bottled.

Also tasted: **Shiraz-Carignan 14 ★★★☆** Not retasted: **Cabernet Sauvignon-Malbec 13 ★★★☆** Discontinued: **Syrah**. — AL

Location: Malmesbury ▪ Map/WO: Swartland ▪ Est/1stB 2003 ▪ Tasting & sales by appt only ▪ Pre-booked light refreshments for groups ▪ Conservation area ▪ Dams for fishing ▪ Self-catering cottage ▪ Owner(s) Stephan Basson ▪ Cellarmaster(s)/winemaker(s)/viticulturist(s) Stephan Basson (Jan 2003) ▪ 580ha/230ha (carignan, grenache, mourv, ptage, shiraz, chenin, rouss, viog) ▪ 20,000cs own label 65%

red 35% white + 500,000L bulk ▪ PO Box 161 Malmesbury 7299 ▪ info@babylonspeak.co.za ▪ S 33° 33' 40.8" E 018° 48' 38.6" ▪ F +27 (0)86-518-3773 ▪ **T +27 (0)21-300-1052**

Babylonstoren

Named after a nearby hill, Babylonstoren might be a showpiece estate but it also has a typical farm atmosphere with geese, chickens, turkeys and a donkey or two as a welcoming committee. Owners Koos Bekker, ex CEO of multinational media group Naspers, and wife Karen Roos, former editor of Elle Decoration, have gone to great lengths to retain the ambiance of a property established in 1692. The cellar is new, however, the story of the soils and wines innovatively depicted on its walls. Now using all home-grown fruit, bar for the rosé, winemaker Charl Coetzee and his team are crafting more interesting and balanced wines every vintage.

★★★★ **Shiraz 13** sees reduction in new wood (to 80%) & alcohol after oakier, bigger **12** (★★★★), better expressing variety's soft dark berries, savouriness. A tasty, supple mouthful with rounded tannins.

★★★★ **Nebukadnesar** ⓃⒺⓌ Flagship red from 5 Bordeaux grapes led by cab. **12** sumptuous, with ripe, sweet fruit still dwarfed by 100% new French oak. Enough fresh core, silky tannins for now & until ±2020.

★★★★ **Babel** Well-fruited & oaked Bordeaux quintet, cab-led with 22% shiraz augmenting flesh, savouriness, in **14**. Enough focus & mineral verve to allow for better harmony, interest over medium term. Improves on **13** (★★★★).

★★★★ **Chardonnay 13** full bodied & rich textured, luxurious feel expanded by notable lees influence, complementary oaking. Bone-dry, enlivening natural freshness ensures potential for further 2 or 3 years.

★★★★ **Chenin Blanc 15** (★★★☆) full of youthful vigour, crunchy red apple flavours. Tasty but less complex, rich than **14**.

★★★★ **Viognier 14** similar unshowy yet full-bodied style as **13** (★★★☆) but more concentrated. Oaked portion, lees enrichment increase complexity without losing focus on pure fresh apricot tones.

Also tasted: **Mourvèdre Rosé 15** ★★★ — AL

Location: Paarl ▪ Map: Franschhoek ▪ WO: Simonsberg-Paarl/Western Cape ▪ Est 1692 ▪ 1stB 2011 ▪ Tasting & sales daily 9-5 ▪ Tour groups by appt ▪ Farm shop ▪ Guided garden tours at 10 daily ▪ Hosted wine tasting, cellar tours daily 12-1 ▪ Babylonstoren Farm Hotel ▪ Bakery ▪ Babel Restaurant Wed-Sun 12-4; Garden Greenhouse for teas & light meals Mon-Sun 10-4 ▪ Garden Day Spa ▪ Winemaker(s) Charl Coetzee (Nov 2010), with Klaas Stoffberg (Sep 2013) ▪ Viticulturist(s) Hannes Aucamp (Jan 2010) ▪ 400ha/62ha (cabs s/f, malbec, merlot, mourv, p verdot, pinot, shiraz, chard, chenin, sem, viog) ▪ PO Box 167 Simondium 7670 ▪ cellar@babylonstoren.com ▪ www.babylonstoren.com ▪ S 33° 49' 26.73" E 018° 55' 39.08" ▪ F +27 (0)21-863-1727 ▪ **T +27 (0)21-863-1804**

Baccarat Wines

Nic and Ferda Barrow created this label when they couldn't find wines both stylish and easy-drinking enough for their boutique hotels. Having caught on in the Cape, Baccarat is moving into Gauteng, and a 'beautiful, floral' rosé is debuting along with winemaker Lisa Kruger.

Cabernet Sauvignon ★★★ Very pleasant everyday drinking **13** with black fruit & cream tweaked with a hint of mint. **Chenin Blanc** ★★★ Ripe, tropical **14** mixes sweet spicy notes with yellow fruit & shortish finish. Not retasted: **Chardonnay-Pinot Noir 13** ★★☆ — CM

Location: Stellenbosch ▪ WO: Western Cape ▪ Est/1stB 2013 ▪ Closed to public ▪ Owner(s) Nic & Ferda Barrow ▪ Winemaker(s) Lisa Kruger (2015) ▪ Viticulturist(s) Eben Archer ▪ 30% red 30% white 40% rosé ▪ chantal@barrowtrust.co.za, tharina@baccaratwines.co.za ▪ www.baccaratwines.co.za ▪ F +27 (0)44-279-1793 ▪ **T +27 (0)44-279-1791**

Backsberg Estate Cellars

The Back family this year celebrates a century of farming in the Simonsberg foothills, founder CL Back, grandfather of current co-owner Michael, having sold his butcher shop at Paarl station and bought a nearby farm at the instigation — the story goes — of a complete stranger. Winemaking commenced in the early 1920s. Sydney Back joined his father in 1936, and through talent, hard work and focus ultimately became the doyen of SA winemaking. Son Michael has handed the reins to the fourth generation, Simon and Jenny, while he concentrates on matters environmental – with such success, Drinks Business last year gave him its global Lifetime Achievement Award and the farm the Sustainability Award. Backberg's longtime stylistic goal of affordable wines with structure, finesse and drinkability continues in both the Backsberg and separately listed Tread Lightly ranges.

Flagship – Backsberg Family Reserve range

★★★★ Red Blend Classy, elegant **13** (★★★★★) switches to Bordeaux-style cab, malbec & merlot blend, takes step up on last-made **08** featuring cab & shiraz. Supple & lithe, full but restrained, packed with ripe black fruit, with delightfully endless liquorice tail. Coastal WO.

★★★★ White Blend Seriously conceived top label, **14** (★★★★★) blend of roussanne, sauvignon & chardonnay currently labours under a heavy oak mantle. Concentrated fruit core reveals itself with time, promising great things. Big, rich & silky, with endless finish. Last **09** also boldly flavoured.

Black Label range

★★★★ Pumphouse Shiraz Fine poise & weight on **12**, ripe cherry/plum fruit & appealing tobacco spices. Shows balanced elegance rather than power. 5% petite sirah/durif, all French oak.

★★★★ Klein Babylons Toren Stylish, focused cab, merlot & petit verdot blend. **13** has sweetly ripe berry fruit with appealing herbaceous undertones. Elegantly long finish with cassis & anise notes.

★★★★☆ Sonop Chardonnay ⓝⓔⓦ Very impressive newcomer to the all-black livery. **14** big & bold, solidly oaky (100% new barrels, 6 months) but beguilingly so. Skilled winemaking shows the complexity, mouthfilling flavour, silky texture & lingering finish.

★★★★ John Martin Reserve Sauvignon Blanc Since **85** debut, always oak fermented; named for estate's long-term manager – who hated wooded white wine! Latest releases more refined, as special. Rich & expressive, **14**'s ripe fruit prevails firmly over (French) oak. WO Coastal, like **13** (★★★★☆).

★★★★ Hillside Viognier 14 (★★★★) ramps up the oak to 100% new, which slightly overwhelms the peaches & violets, leaving hints of astringency & charred toastiness. Misses subtlety of **13**.

Not retasted: **Brut Méthode Cap Classique 10 ★★★★** Discontinued: **Beyond Borders Pinot Noir, Elbar**.

Premium range

★★★★ Cabernet Sauvignon ⊘ Bright & appealing fruit on **12** is bolstered by vibrant aromas & creamy tannins. Elegantly rounded shape, consistent finish. Middle range over-achiever. 10% malbec.

> **Chenin Blanc** ⓥ **★★★** Fresh & easy style with toned-down fruit. Pleasing heft & lime-mineral notes on **15**, over cling peaches. Pocket friendly.

Rosé ★★★ Simple, light & semi-sweet **NV** from grenache, shiraz, carignan & viognier. **Special Late Harvest ★★★★** Textbook gewürztraminer rosewater & litchi prettiness on **15**, full-sweet & packed with flavour. Also tasted: **Merlot 14 ★★★ Pinotage 14 ★★★ Shiraz 14 ★★★☆ Chardonnay 14 ★★★ Sauvignon Blanc 15 ★★★** Not retasted: **Dry Red NV ★★★**

Kosher range

Chardonnay ★★★ Pleasant but unremarkable **15**, unwooded, fresh & fruity. Not retasted: **Merlot 14 ★★★ Pinotage 14 ★★★ Brut Méthode Cap Classique 10 ★★★☆ Kiddush Sacramental Wine 12 ★★**

Fortified range

Cape Ruby ⊘ **★★★★** Port-style from cab franc & touriga, **NV** (**06**) on review was like drinking brandy-doused fruitcake: full bodied & rich. Not retasted: **Pinneau 10 ★★★☆**

Brandy range

★★★★ Sydney Back 1st Distillation ⊘ Dark amber on this 20 year old, rich texture, round & well matured, with marmalade, dark chocolate flavours. Loads of oaky vanilla & mature character, but a touch less fresh than the younger brandies. 100% potstill from chenin, as all.

★★★★ Sydney Back Finest Matured (10 Year Old) Inviting honey, dried apricot & marzipan aromas on the nose. Effortlessly elegant & light footed, with vanilla, toasty nuts, sweet tobacco & caramel.

★★★★ **Sydney Back Special Release (15 Year Old)** Complex nose of dried fruit & toasty nuts, hint of anise. Astounding intensity of apricot, peach & touch of sweet vanilla on the palate. Floral notes all the way & hint of orange peel. Retasted, as 10 Year Old. — WB, GdB, TJ

Location: Paarl ▪ Map: Franschhoek ▪ WO: Paarl/Western Cape/Coastal ▪ Est 1916 ▪ 1stB 1970 ▪ Tasting & sales Mon-Fri 9–5 Sat/Sun 10–4 ▪ Fee R15 ▪ Open 365 days a year ▪ Cellar tours by appt ▪ Self-guided tour of the cellar, brandy cellar, winery & historic corridors ▪ Backsberg Restaurant ▪ Facilities for children ▪ Tour groups ▪ Conferences ▪ Weddings & functions ▪ BYO picnic ▪ Hiking ▪ Mountain biking ▪ Bird watching ▪ Environmental talks ▪ Conservation area ▪ Sunday picnic concerts (summer) ▪ Owner(s) Michael Back & Simon Back ▪ Winemaker(s) Alicia Rechner (Jun 2012) ▪ Viticulturist(s) Clive Trent (Jul 1992) ▪ 130ha (cab, merlot, shiraz, chard) ▪ 900t/160,000cs own label 65% red 30% white 5% rosé ▪ PO Box 537 Suider-Paarl 7624 ▪ info@backsberg.co.za ▪ www.backsberg.co.za ▪ S 33° 49' 42.9" E 018° 54' 56.9" ▪ F +27 (0)21-875-5144 ▪ **T +27 (0)21-875-5141**

☐ **Badenhorst Family Wines** *see* AA Badenhorst Family Wines

Badsberg Wine Cellar

Breedekloof's grower-owned Badsberg is in the business of converting large tonnages into wine for partners in local brands and for export. But its wine team also makes time for small parcels under the own label, showing a particular penchant – and passion – for natural sweet wines and fortifieds.

★★★★ **Chardonnay Sur Lie** ⊘ Lightly oaked **14** punches above its price with complex lemon, fennel & floral bouquet, tangy acidity, engaging lime tail. Lipsmackingly delicious – buy loads! No **13**.

★★★★★ **Badslese** ⓟ Unwooded Natural Sweet dessert from chenin & muscat d'Alexandrie; only in best years (no **10**, **11**). With muscat portion upped to 30%, **12** (★★★★★) is pure indulgence: melting quince, melon & grape flavours, as scintillating & precise as **09**, our 2012 White Wine of the Year.

★★★★ **Noble Late Harvest** ⊘ Amber-hued **09** from unwooded chenin (80%) & hanepoot (20%) is at peak for ultimate enjoyment: sweet, rich apricots & roasted nuts, perfect for after dinner.

★★★★ **Red Muscadel** Consistent sweet fortified for year-round enjoyment: fireside in winter, on the rocks in summer. Tealeaf-nuanced **14** delivers signature raisin-sweet but balanced slipperiness.

★★★★ **Red Jerepigo** Classy fortified ruby cab **14** is another classic, packed with all things sweet, balanced by fiery fortification, ending long & seemingly dry.

Pinotage-Mocha Fusion ⊛ ★★★★ Chocolate, coffee & red berries jump out the glass of delightful, 'java-style' **14**. **Belladonna** ⊛ ★★★★ 2 vintages reviewed of blend shiraz & Bordeaux red grapes: **12** is cab-driven & sweet-fruited, with savoury herbal flavours; **13** is merlot-led, showing spicecake depth. Both well balanced, easy to sip.

Chenin Blanc ★★★ Easy-drinking **15** bright & appealing summer white with sunripe guava & melon flavours, thatchy complexity. Also tasted: **Merlot 13** ★★☆ **Perlé Moscato 15** ★★ **Sauvignon Blanc 15** ★★★ **Vin Doux 15** ★★★ Not retasted: **Special Late Harvest 13** ★★★ **Hanepoot Jerepigo 13** ★★★★ **Cape Vintage 09** ★★★ Occasional release: **Noble Late Harvest Limited Edition**. Discontinued: **Rosé**. — WB

Location: Rawsonville ▪ Map/WO: Breedekloof ▪ Est 1951 ▪ 1stB 1958 ▪ Tasting & sales Mon-Fri 9–5 Sat 10–1 ▪ Fee R20pp for groups of 10+ ▪ Closed all pub hols ▪ Cellar tours by appt ▪ BYO picnic ▪ Facilities for children ▪ Farm produce ▪ Conferences (40 pax) ▪ Conservation area ▪ Soetes & Soup (Jul) ▪ Owner(s) 26 members ▪ Cellarmaster(s) Willie Burger (1998) ▪ Winemaker(s) Henri Swiegers (2002) & Nicholas Husselman (2011), with Jaco Booysen (Jan 2007) ▪ Viticulturist(s) Nicholas Husselman (2011) ▪ ±1,500ha/±1,300ha (ptage, shiraz, chenin, cbard) ▪ ±30,000t ▪ 20% red 65% white 10% rosé 5% fortified ▪ ISO 22000:2009, IPW, WIETA ▪ PO Box 72 Rawsonville 6845 ▪ enquiries@badsberg.co.za ▪ www.badsberg.co.za ▪ S 33° 39' 40.1" E 019° 16' 9.2" ▪ F +27 (0)86-574-6091 ▪ **T +27 (0)23-344-3021**

☐ **Bag in Box Collection** *see* Jacques Germanier
☐ **Bain's Way** *see* Wellington Wines
☐ **Bakenskop** *see* Vinopoly Wines

☐ **Balance** *see* Overhex Wines International

Baleia Wines   ⑨ ⑥

Originally grain and sheep farmers, father and son Fanie and Jan-Hendrik Joubert planted vines near the holiday hamlet of Vermaaklikheid on the Cape's Garden Route and made the first wines in 2011. Their cellar and tasting venue are at Riversdale, where new winemaker Abraham de Klerk is making the first MCC bubbly to join the pinot noir, shiraz, tempranillo, oaked chardonnay and sauvignon blanc.

Location: Riversdale ▪ Map: Klein Karoo & Garden Route ▪ Est 2010 ▪ 1stB 2011 ▪ Tasting & sales Mon-Fri 9-5 Sat 10-1 ▪ Cellar tours by appt ▪ Olives & oil ▪ Owner(s) Fanie & Jan-Hendrik Joubert ▪ Winemaker(s) Abraham de Klerk ▪ 1,000ha/9.5ha (pinot, shiraz, tempranillo, chard, sauv) ▪ 80t/600cs own label 60% red 40% white ▪ PO Box 268 Riversdale 6670 ▪ info@baleiawines.com ▪ www.baleiawines.com ▪ S 34° 6' 36.89" E 021° 15' 18.48" ▪ F +27 (0)86-560-0367 ▪ **T +27 (0)87-234-8621**

☐ **Bales Choice** *see* Wade Bales Wine Society
☐ **Balthazar** *see* Roodezandt Wines
☐ **Bandana** *see* Klein Roosboom

Baratok Wines   ⑨ ⑥

Baratok owner Alex Boraine has moved his mostly export business from Paarl's main road to visitor-welcoming Hildenbrand Wine & Olive Estate outside Wellington, and launched an innovative venture, BuytheBarrel, which affords aspirant vintners the means to vinify, bottle, package and optionally market their very own wine brand. See the Make Your Own Wine section for details.

Location: Wellington ▪ Map: Paarl & Wellington ▪ Map grid reference: G2 ▪ Est 2012 ▪ Tasting by appt ▪ Delivery anywhere in South Africa ▪ Closed all pub hols ▪ Tour groups ▪ Olive oil ▪ Conferences ▪ Owner(s)/winemaker(s) Alex Boraine ▪ (cab, cinsaut, malbec, merlot, ptage, shiraz, chard, chenin, sauv, sem, viog) ▪ 27t/200,000L own label 60% red 40% white; 90,000L for clients + 480,000L bulk ▪ Brands for clients: African Tribe, Belle Vallee, Kipepeo, Terre de Papillon ▪ PO Box 668 Wellington 7654 ▪ alex@baratokwines.co.za ▪ S 33° 39' 33.3" E 019° 1' 46.3" ▪ **T +27 (0)84-582-6376**

☐ **Barber's Wood** *see* Celestina

Barista   ⑨

This is the brand introduced by leading SA wine distributor Vinimark upon spotting an emerging commercial appeal for pinotage exhibiting a marked mocha aroma and flavour. Burgeoning sales, including in the US, eventually paved the way for some cream to the coffee: a lightly wooded chardonnay.

> **Chardonnay** ⑦ ★★★ Lightly fruited **14**, 50/50 Elgin/Robertson fruit, has lemon freshness, creamy mouthfeel from part barrel ferment. Fun & easy.

Pinotage ★★★ Charry oak weighs heavily on **14**'s otherwise bright blueberry fruit. — WB

Location: Robertson ▪ WO: Western Cape ▪ Est/1stB 2009 ▪ Tasting at Val de Vie ▪ Owner(s) Vinimark ▪ Winemaker(s) Bertus Fourie ▪ 600t/60,000cs own label ▪ PO Box 6223 Paarl 7620 ▪ info@vinimark.co.za ▪ www.baristawine.co.za ▪ F +27 (0)21-886-4708 ▪ **T +27 (0)21-883-8043**

Barnardt Boyes Wines

Stellenbosch negociant business Barnardt Boyes Wines is part of a diverse group of companies, including luxury goods manufacturer Carrol Boyes Functional Art and citrus exporter FruitOne. More specifically, it is a collaboration between FruitOne MD John Boyes (Carrol's brother) and wine industry veteran Neels Barnardt, an old university friend. See also Carrol Boyes Collection.

Cabernet Sauvignon ⑭ ★★★ With just 60% oaked, expect loads of fruit. Cassis throughout **13**, the streamlined structure geared to early enjoyment. **Shiraz** ⑭ ★★★ Only 40% oaked to keep the wine fruit-fresh, **12** is smooth & curvaceous, oh so easy to drink. Also tasted: **Pinotage 12 ★★★ Premium Blend 12 ★★★** Not tasted: **Shiraz-Cabernet Sauvignon, Sauvignon Blanc.** — CR

Location: Stellenbosch ▪ WO: Western Cape ▪ Est 2012 ▪ 1stB 2009 ▪ Closed to public ▪ Owner(s) N Barnardt & J Boyes ▪ Winemaker(s) Hendrik Snyman (Jun 2013) ▪ 40,000cs own label 100% red ▪ Other export brands: Le Noe, Carrol Boyes Collection ▪ neels@barnardtboyes.com ▪ www.barnardtboyes.com ▪ F +27 (0)21-883-3491 ▪ **T +27 (0)21-883-3447**

☐ **Barney Barnato** *see* Douglas Wine Cellar
☐ **Barn Find** *see* Franki's Vineyards
☐ **Barony** *see* Rosendal Wines

Barrydale Winery & Distillery ⓠ

Working with Klein Karoo sibling Ladismith, both jointly owned by Southern Cape Vineyards and Elgin brandy distillery Oude Molen, Barrydale Winery & Distillery offers a small range of wines, with a few from Ladismith, selected each year on quality, at its cellardoor in Barrydale town. The internationally awarded brandies (most named for local 19th-century English-born wine and brandy tradesman Joseph Barry) form part a rebranding exercise still underway at the time of going to press.

Southern Cape Vineyards range
Ladismith Chenin Blanc ★★★ 15 bright & cheerful party wine with creamy apple pie flavours.
Barrydale Sauvignon Blanc ⑭ **★★★ 15** bursts with tropical fruit flavours, let down somewhat by bracing acidity. Not retasted: **Ladismith Ruby Cabernet 11 ★★ Barrydale Shiraz 13 ★★★ Ladismith Chardonnay 14 ★★☆ Barrydale Brut Rosé NV ★★★☆**

Brandy range
★★★★ Ladismith 8 Year Potstill Brandy ⑳ Clean aromas with abundant floral notes mixed with dried fruit. Lightish, elegant style, with muted fire, unobtrusive oak & a long dry finish.

Joseph Barry 10 Year Old ⑳ **★★★★** Dried fruit, floral wafts with cinnamon on well-matured, rich frame. More forceful, less fruity than Traditional bottling. Dry, lingering finish. **Joseph Barry Traditional** ⑳ **★★★★** 5-year-aged potstill, darker & more auburn of these. Hints of apple, pear, some citrus backed by toasty nut, vanilla & butterscotch. Balanced & smooth, oak hint on long finish. — WB, TJ

Location: Barrydale ▪ Map: Klein Karoo & Garden Route ▪ WO: Klein Karoo/Stellenbosch ▪ Est 1941 ▪ 1stB 1976 ▪ Tasting & sales Mon-Fri 9–5 Sat 9–1 ▪ Fee R25 for groups of 5+ ▪ Closed Easter Fri-Mon, Dec 25/ 26 & Jan 1 ▪ Owner(s) Southern Cape Vineyards (SCV) & Oude Molen Distillery ▪ Winemaker(s) / distiller Ferdi Smith ▪ ±110ha (cab, merlot, shiraz, chard, cbard, sauv) ▪ 28% red 72% white ▪ PO Box 59 Barrydale 6750 ▪ humanj@scv.co.za ▪ www.barrydalewines.co.za ▪ S 33° 54' 35.83" E 020° 42' 45.20" ▪ F +27 (0)28-572-1541 ▪ **T +27 (0)28-572-1012**

Barry Gould Family Wines ⓠ ⑪ ⌂ ◎ ⑧

Barry Gould's modestly named red blend is back in the guide after a short break, but the Elgin architect and boutique vigneron at press time had no white wine for review, and was moving production facilities so no cellar tours for the time being. No change, though, to his natural winemaking philosophy (basket pressing, spontaneous ferments, no filtration) or his 'hands-on, hands-in, hand-made' approach.

A Simple Red ★★★ Wild-yeast-fermented cab & merlot (50/50), **08** perfumed blackcurrant & soft vanilla; finishes tad warm (15% alcohol) but overall is appealing, simple in a good way. — WB

Location/WO: Elgin ▪ Map: Elgin, Walker Bay & Bot River ▪ Est 2003 ▪ 1stB 2004 ▪ Tasting & sales by appt ▪ Closed Good Fri, Dec 25 & Jan 1 ▪ Meals/functions by arrangement (up to 20 pax) ▪ Wildekrans Country House (B&B) + self-catering cottage ▪ Child-friendly ▪ Gifts ▪ Farm produce ▪ Conference venue (20 pax) ▪ 4-day fully guided slack-packing trail ▪ Owner(s) Barry Gould & Alison Green ▪ Cellarmaster(s) Barry Gould (2003) ▪ Winemaker(s) Barry Gould (2003), with family (2004) ▪ Viticulturist(s) Grapes bought in ▪ ±2t/200cs own label 100% red ▪ PO Box 7 Elgin 7180 ▪ gould.arc@wildekrans.co.za ▪ S 34° 12' 12.7" E 019° 8' 53.6" ▪ F +27 (0)21-848-9788 ▪ **T +27 (0)21-848-9788/+27 (0)82-901-4896**

Bartho Eksteen ⓠ ⑪ ◎ ⑧

After 29 years in the industry, mostly in cool-climate Walker Bay and latterly at Hermanuspietersfontein, Cape Winemakers Guild member Bartho Eksteen is now '100% focused' on this, the family wine brand,

and on nurturing ventures he's nobly initiated to support budding wine-makers (see Diners Club Bartho Eksteen Academy), —judges and —entrepreneurs. 18th-century Hemel-en-Aarde farm Attaquaskloof is the nexus, the old mill currently housing tastings (eats and sleeps in the planning). Wife Suné, Elsenburg wine graduate son Pieter Willem and daughter Shani, studying teaching, are fully involved.

★★★★☆ **Groepsdruk** (NEW) Bright black berry, exotic spice, fragrant lavender & compelling tannin structure announce stunning **13** blend warm/cool-climate blend shiraz, mourvèdre & grenache. Well-judged 21 months new French barrels. Radiates class, will continue to do so many years. WO W Cape.

★★★★ **Ouskool SMG** (NEW) Little brother of Groepsdruk, from Paarl shiraz, Hemel-en-Aarde mourvèdre & grenache. **13** delights with soft sweet black fruit, fragrant oriental spice & clever oaking (60% new).

★★★★ **Blom Rosé** (NEW) Palest salmon pink **15** from 4 Rhône varieties is dry & packs a flavour punch, with red summer berries, hints of vanilla spice (from brief oaking) & long savoury finish.

★★★★★ **CWG Auction Reserve Vloekskoot Sauvignon Blanc** Bunch-pressed, naturally older-oak-fermented **14** (★★★★) offers tangy citrus & granadilla with fresh thyme & salty mineral finish. Sharply focused, but misses the gravitas of exceptional **13**. Upper Hemel-en-Aarde fruit.

★★★★ **Meester Sauvignon Blanc** (NEW) Nettle & greenpepper flavours have instant appeal on **14** cool-climate expression of the variety. Small oaked portion (5%) adds to creamy mouthfeel & complexity.

★★★★ **Dom Méthode Cap Classique** (NEW) Sparkling from equal chardonnay & pinot noir, dash pinot meunier; **NV (11)** is round & fruity, with a creamy toastiness on the finish (though unoaked), soft persistent mousse. Perfect for smoked salmon canapés.

★★★★☆ **Soetmuis** (NEW) **15** Natural Sweet from old-vine Paarl chenin like a walk in a spring meadow. Delicate, sweet-scented, the perfumes turning mineral on complex palate with underlying creaminess to the rich rainbow of flavours. Minuscule 50-case production. — WB

Location: Hermanus ▪ Map: Elgin, Walker Bay & Bot River ▪ WO: Upper Hemel-en-Aarde Valley/Hemel-en-Aarde Valley/Western Cape/Paarl ▪ Est/1stB 2015 ▪ Tasting, sales & cellar tours Mon-Fri 10-5 Sat 10-2 ▪ Fee R20pp, on discretion of management ▪ Closed Easter Fri/Sun, Dec 25 & Jan 1 ▪ Facilities for children ▪ Gift shop ▪ Picnics available on request ▪ Conferences ▪ Functions & events ▪ Walks/hikes ▪ MTB route ▪ Historic buildings ▪ Owner(s) GROW Wynsentrum (Edms) Bpk, 1 shareholder ▪ Cellarmaster(s) Bartho Eksteen (Jan 2015) ▪ Winemaker(s) Pieter Willem Eksteen (Jan 2015, assistant) ▪ Viticulturist(s) various ▪ 5ha total ▪ 2,500cs own label 34% red 46% white 14% rosé 6% MCC ▪ IPW ▪ PO Box 1999 Hermanus 7200 ▪ wijnskool@hermanus.co.za ▪ www.wijnskool.co.za ▪ S 34° 23' 57.31" E 019° 13' 1.17" ▪ F +27 (0)86-554-0896 ▪ **T +27 (0)28-312-4612**

Bartinney Private Cellar   (Ⓠ) (🍴) (♿)

Michael and Rose Jordaan's boutique winery is perched high on the slopes of Stellenbosch's Helshoogte Pass, its steep, unterraced slopes dictating that everything must be done by hand. The small parcels of terroir-specific fruit are shepherded into the bottle with as little intervention as possible by winemaker Ronell Wiid, who also carefully selects top fruit from the surrounds for the Elevage blend. The other wines (WO Banghoek) are now all certified as 'estate' (Bartinney having been registered as a unit for the production of estate wine in late 2014) and this confirms 'the trust we put into our growing area'. Blessed with jaw-dropping views, the tasting venue now hosts Friday afternoon Wine & Tapas events.

Reserve range (NEW)

★★★★☆ **Cabernet Sauvignon** Selection of best cab barrels for this magnificent newcomer. **12** richer, denser crushed velvet feel than regular bottling, French oak (80% new) adding extra scented grandeur. Purity, freshness, overall harmony remain distinctive features. Many pleasures lie in store for the patient.

Bartinney range

★★★★☆ **Cabernet Sauvignon** Like all these reds, grand yet unostentatious & so well-proportioned it's tempting to drink them now but ageing will be richly rewarded. **12** pure, focused flavours of black berries, olives & subtle oak spice (50% new French) in creamy layers & lengthily refrained through dense, fine tannin. Also in magnum.

★★★★☆ **Elevage** Beautifully assembled Bordeaux quartet, **11** defined by cab's dark fruit tones, insistent though finely polished tannins. Spice, freshness, gently plush filling & savoury length complete this classy melange. Will offer pleasure, satisfaction for several years. Stellenbosch WO.

★★★★☆ **Chardonnay** A confident hand behind this layered, refined **14**. Flows seamlessly from its pickled lime freshness to more creamy, oatmeal breadth & prolonged savoury finish. Great balance, careful oaking; beneath its still youthful profile lies complexity worth waiting for. Magnum available.

★★★★☆ **Sauvignon Blanc** Previewed **15** reflects strength of vintage in its concentration & distinction. Full of sophistication, class, its riveting steely agility is paced by rich vinosity & bracing length. As promising at table as in the cellar. **14** (★★★★) shade less intense. — AL

Location/map: Stellenbosch ▪ Map grid reference: H5 ▪ WO: Banghoek/Stellenbosch ▪ Est 2006 ▪ 1stB 2008 ▪ Tasting & sales Mon-Fri 10-4 ▪ Wine & tapas Fri 12-7 ▪ Closed all pub hols ▪ Cellar tours by appt ▪ Bartinney Wine & Champagne Bar Mon-Sat 11.30-9 (T +27 (0)71-250-5814, cnr Bird & Church Str Stellenbosch) ▪ Owner(s) Rose & Michael Jordaan ▪ Winemaker(s) Ronell Wiid (consultant) ▪ Viticulturist(s) Ryno Maree (Oct 2010) ▪ 27ha/±17ha (cab, chard, sauv) ▪ 118t/4,000cs own label 70% red 30% white ▪ BWI champion ▪ Postnet Suite 231 Private Bag X5061 Stellenbosch 7599 ▪ info@bartinney.co.za ▪ www.bartinney.co.za ▪ S 33° 55' 34.66" E 018° 55' 56.79" ▪ F +27 (0)21-885-2852 ▪ **T +27 (0)21-885-1013**

Barton Vineyards

Winemaker PJ Geyer's boyhood fascination with fermentation started with mealies. He progressed to grapes, training and working locally and abroad (notably with Bordeaux's Moueix family). At Barton, he heads up the boutique winery where the Walker Bay breezes cool not only the 30 ha of vines but also the lavender, olive groves and guests in the recently extended luxury accommodation.

★★★★ **Merlot** Taut & structured **13**'s juicy red berry & chocolate flavours restrained in youth by brisk acidity & firm chalky tannins. Not as balanced as **12** (★★★★★), but deserves & will reward cellaring.

★★★★☆ **Winemakers Reserve** ⓥ Maiden **11** merlot-led Bordeaux blend, understated, refined core of inky red fruit & violets with cedar nuance. Tailored & sleek, will age with distinction.

★★★★ **Shiraz-Cabernet Sauvignon** ⓥ Youthful, harmonious **11** has a sappy texture, infused with garrigue scrub, pepper & touch of cab's clean herbaceousness. Supple structure enhanced by oak.

★★★★ **Sauvignon Blanc-Semillon** ⓥ **13**'s unwooded 61/39 blend raises the bar on **12** (★★★☆). Balanced, with refined fruit focus & minerality. An ageworthy, graceful table mate.

Pinot Noir Rosé (NEW) ★★★ Lovely balance on **14**. Dry styling, clean, savoury & crisp, perfect sunset aperitif – with the colour to match. **Chenin Blanc Reserve** (NEW) ★★★ Appealing stewed apple tone to **14**, older wood & extended lees-ageing add roundness & succulence; oak spice, though tad prominent mid-2015, should meld. **Chenin Blanc** ★★☆ **14** crunchy apple, zested with lime; tightly coiled fruit profile, leaner than previous; clean, racy flavours best with food. Also tasted: **Rouge 13** ★★★ **Sauvignon Blanc 14** ★★★ **Blanc 14** ★★☆ Not retasted: **Shiraz Rosé 13** ★★★ — MW

Location: Bot River ▪ Map: Elgin, Walker Bay & Bot River ▪ WO: Walker Bay ▪ Est 2001 ▪ 1stB 2003 ▪ Tasting, sales & cellar tours Mon-Fri 9–5 Sat 10–4 ▪ Closed Easter Fri & Mon, Dec 25 & Jan 1 ▪ Lavender products, olive oil & table olives ▪ Barton Villas ▪ Owner(s) Peter J Neill ▪ Cellarmaster(s)/winemaker(s)/viticulturist(s) PJ Geyer (Oct 2010) ▪ 200ha/30ha (cab, malbec, merlot, mourv, pinot, shiraz, chenin, sauv, sem) ▪ 120t/20,000cs own label 40% red 50% white 10% rosé ▪ IPW ▪ PO Box 100 Bot River 7185 ▪ info@bartonvineyards.co.za ▪ www.bartonvineyards.co.za ▪ S 34° 15' 43.8" E 019° 10' 29.2" ▪ F +27 (0)28-284-9776 ▪ **T +27 (0)28-284-9283**

☐ **Basco** see Blomendahl Vineyards

Bayede!

Previously sourcing from multiple producers, Bayede! has formed a joint venture with Robertson's Van Loveren to provide the wines for all its labels. Named for the traditional greeting reserved for the Zulu King, the bead-adorned wines are integral to what's believed to be one of Africa's first 'royal by appointment' brands. Its objectives are sustainable job creation and promotion of various industry sectors.

7 Icon Wines

★★★★ **Cabernet Sauvignon** ⓦ Stately **09** full bodied & elegant, with blackberry, cedar & mint complexity. Like generous **08**, should be ready now. Stellenbosch WO.

★★★★ **Merlot** ⓦ Choc/plum-toned **12** from Groenekloof step up on **11** (★★★★). No shrinking violet: mouthfilling & lipsmacking, smooth & polished, with fruit-sweet core, fine oak spicing.

★★★★ **Pinotage Reserve** ⓦ Hinting at blackcurrant & lavender, **10** previously noted as deserving more time to fully integrate. Stellenbosch WO.

★★★★ **Chardonnay** ⓦ Muted & light-footed **13** (★★★☆) from Robertson has similar lemon-cream tones as rounded & full-bodied **12**.

★★★★☆ **Chenin Blanc** ⓦ Ambitious **13** hedonistic glassful of peaches & limes, vanilla & butter. Emphatically dry & precise, as persistent as savoury **12**. Stellenbosch WO.

Not retasted: **Shiraz 11** ★★★ **Sauvignon Blanc 13** ★★★☆

King & Queen range

King Goodwill Shiraz ⓦ ★★★☆ **12** characterful & appealing, with supple tannins, savoury finish for solo sipping or mealtime enjoyment. Not retasted: **King Shaka Jubilee 12** ★★★ **Queen Thomo Chenin Blanc 13** ★★ Not tasted: **Queen Thomo Sauvignon Blanc**, **Queen Mantfombi Dry MCC Sparkling Rosé**.

Prince range

Red ★★★ Early-drinking **14** shiraz/cab combo (60/40) sparingly oaked, light textured for solo sipping. WO Robertson. **White** ★★★ Lively & flavoursome, gently pithy texture, **14** from 60% chenin & sauvignon appealing summer mouthful.

Shield range

The Prince Merlot ★★ Ready to drink **14**, soft & unchallenging, with choc finish. **The Prince Pinotage** ★★★ **14** standout in this range, more varietal character than other reds. Strawberry tones, bright & friendly sipper. Also tasted: **The Prince Sauvignon Blanc 14** ★★ Not retasted: **The Prince Cabernet Sauvignon 13** ★★★ Discontinued: **The Prince Cabernet Sauvignon-Shiraz-Merlot**, **The Prince Chenin Blanc**. — CvZ

Location: Paarl ▪ Map: Paarl & Wellington ▪ Map grid reference: E6 ▪ WO: Western Cape/Stellenbosch/Robertson/Groenekloof/Franschhoek ▪ Est 2009 ▪ Tasting & sales in showroom/office at 5 Stasie Street, Southern Paarl Mon-Fri or by appt ▪ Fee R30 ▪ Private VIP tastings at Villa Beanto Winelands Estate by appt only ▪ Closed all pub hols ▪ Tour groups by appt ▪ 60% red 30% white 10% rosé ▪ PO Box 7362 Northern Paarl 7623 ▪ anto@bayede.co.za ▪ www.bayede.co.za ▪ S 33° 45' 54.77" E 018° 57' 41.03" ▪ F +27 (0)21-863-4884 ▪ **T +27 (0)21-863-3406/+27 (0)83-650-3585**

☐ **Bayten** *see* Buitenverwachting
☐ **BC Wines** *see* Brandvlei Cellar
☐ **Beach House** *see* Douglas Green

Beau Belle   ⓦ ⓦ ⓦ ⓦ ⓦ

Former Gauteng property developer Tienie Lindeque and wife Estelle gladly share their Lynedoch farm's many facilities with those looking for a special winelands getaway. So too the fruits of their vineyard, expertly vinified off-site for the recently reconceptualised Beau Belle brand they want to see become synonymous with premium SA shirazes.

★★★★ **The Chapel Shiraz** ⓦ Cocoa & black pepper, dark hedgerow fruit core. Silky texture, polished tannins, **11**'s overall effect harmonious, well crafted to enjoy & cellar. Ends on a creamy espresso note.

Cooper Shiraz ⓦ ★★★★ Plums & brambleberries, deep & richly perfumed, an intriguing caraway seed note in the spicing — **13** very inviting. Succulent palate, vanilla flavoured & just enough grip for food, a bit of ageing. — WB, CR

Location/map/WO: Stellenbosch ▪ Map grid reference: C7 ▪ Est 2009 ▪ 1stB 2010 ▪ Tasting, sales & cellar tours by appt Mon-Fri 10-5 Sat 10-3 (first & last Sat of month) ▪ Closed Ash Wed, Easter Fri-Sun, Ascension day, Pentecost, Dec 25/26 & Jan 1 ▪ Meals/refreshments for groups of 10-50 by arrangement ▪ Olive oil ▪ BYO picnic ▪ MTB trail ▪ Weddings ▪ Chapel ▪ Special events/functions: contact Estelle at +27 (0)83-419-1761 ▪ Self-catering guest cottage (max 4 people) ▪ Owner(s) Lindeque Family Trust ▪ Directors Tienie & Estelle Lindeque ▪ Cellarmaster(s) Wilhelm van Rooyen (Jan 2014) ▪ Winemaker(s) Teddy Hall (Jan 2014) ▪ Viticulturist(s) Tienie Lindeque (Jan 2014), advised by Johan Pienaar (consultant) ▪ 36ha/23ha (shiraz) ▪ 220t/6,000cs own label 90% red 10% white + 40,000L bulk ▪ PO Box 156 Lynedoch Stellenbosch 7603 ▪ tienie@beaubelle.co.za ▪ www.beaubelle.co.za ▪ S 33° 59' 47.30" E 018° 46' 45.69" ▪ F +27 (0)86-670-6720 ▪ **T +27 (0)21-881-3808/+27 (0)83-522-0100**

Beau Constantia   (♀) (🍴) (📷)

Spectacular valley and mountain views match the viticultural potential on the Du Preez family farm high on the Constantiaberg. Classic French red varieties – cab franc and shiraz particularly promising – also flow into a limited-edition, seasonally available rosé (spring only!) Add select white wines, tapas and sushi, seven-days-a-week tastings, stylish split-level dining areas, and a small amphitheatre for concerts, and it's no wonder Beau Constantia is a go-to place for long lunches and special celebrations.

★★★★☆ Stella (NEW) Splendid limited-release shiraz/syrah; cool-origin perfume on delicate **12**, which announces itself as the cellar's new flagship. White pepper marries violets & berry pastille in a focused, perfectly poised, vivacious frame.

★★★★ Lucca Fair balance of capsicum with red & black fruit on **13** (★★★☆) from merlot & cab franc. Sweet, plush-fruited core, with freshness of **12** but not quite the complexity.

★★★★ Aidan Bordeaux/shiraz blend **13** (★★★★☆) dark fruited & brooding, with notable toasty oak & 32% petit verdot making an impression on the palate that is sweet & concentrated yet more burly than **12**, with gripping tannins.

★★★★ Cecily Viognier's charming varietal character on **14**, showing stonefruit & jasmine perfumes. Integrated oak in support, with slight buttered broad richness from barrel ageing (25% new).

Pierre (NEW) **★★★☆** 50% new oak manifests in coconut notes on youthful **14** blend sauvignon (75%) & semillon. Coaxing reveals greengage, cut flowers, granadilla & smoke. Quality fruit slightly subdued by wood mid-2015. Not tasted: **Pas de Nom Red**, **Pas de Nom White**. — HJ

Location/WO: Constantia ▪ Map: Cape Peninsula ▪ Est 2003 ▪ 1stB 2010 ▪ Tasting & sales Mon-Sun 10-4.30 ▪ Fee R55, waved according to purchase ▪ Closed Good Fri, Dec 25/26 & Jan 1 ▪ Wine bar, with sushi/tapas menu from Sushibox ▪ Amphitheatre for concerts & outdoor events ▪ Owner(s) Dormell Properties 139 (Pty) Ltd ▪ Winemaker(s) Justin van Wyk (Sep 2010) ▪ Viticulturist(s) Japie Bronn (Sep 2002, consultant) & Ewald Heyns (May 2015, farm manager) ▪ 22ha/±11ha (cabs s/f, malbec, merlot, p verdot, shiraz, sauv, sem, viog) ▪ 40t/4,000cs own label 80% red 20% white ▪ 1043 Constantia Main Road Constantia 7806 ▪ winesales@beauconstantia.com ▪ www.beauconstantia.com ▪ S 34° 0' 48.57" E 018° 24' 21.67" ▪ F +27 (0)21-794-0534 ▪ **T +27 (0)21-794-8632**

Beau Joubert Vineyards & Winery   (♀) (🍷) (🏠) (📷)

The name of this American-SA joint venture aptly combines the French word for 'beautiful' with the surname of the family that had sole ownership of the Polkadraai Hills estate for seven generations before welcoming in a group of families from Wisconsin, US, under entrepreneur Andrew Hilliard as MD.

Beau Joubert range

★★★★ Ambassador From 40% merlot for choc-plum intensity with 30% each cab & cab franc for blackcurrant backbone & leafy freshness, **11** a fine ambassador for Stellenbosch Bordeaux-style red.

Old Vine Chenin Blanc ★★★☆ 14 preview remarkably fresh & delicate considering six months in 100% new French oak, peach & spanspek softly enveloped by vanilla cream. **Fat Pig ★★★☆** Relatively light-bodied 'port' formerly made from pinotage, spicier **11** is 100% shiraz, adding allspice & savoury leather complexity to fruitcake sweetness. Calls for cheese. Also tasted: **Christmas Cabernet NV ★★★☆ Shiraz 11 ★★★ Sauvignon Blanc 15 ★★★** Not retasted: **Cabernet Sauvignon 10 ★★★☆** Not tasted: **Rosé**.

Oak Lane range

Chenin Blanc-Sauvignon Blanc ★★☆ Easy-drinking **15** has hints of greenpepper from 32% sauvignon, chenin's tropical contribution subdued apart from guava-like tone & crunch of starfruit. Not retasted: **Merlot-Cabernet Sauvignon 13 ★★☆ Shiraz-Cabernet Sauvignon 13 ★★★** — JG

Location/map/WO: Stellenbosch ▪ Map grid reference: B6 ▪ Est 1695 ▪ 1stB 2000 ▪ Tasting & sales Mon-Fri 8-5 Sat by appt ▪ Closed all pub hols ▪ Cellar tours by appt ▪ BYO picnic ▪ Walks/hikes ▪ Bird watching ▪ Self-catering guest cottage ▪ Owner(s) MD Andrew Hilliard ▪ Cellarmaster(s)/winemaker(s) Christian Kuun (Dec 2006) ▪ Viticulturist(s) Ian Engelbrecht (Nov 2010) ▪ 80ha/40ha (cabs s/f, merlot, pinot, shiraz, chenin, sauv) ▪ 280t/40,000cs own label 60% red 35% white 5% rosé + 10,000L for clients ▪ PO Box 1114 Stellenbosch 7599 ▪ info@beaujoubert.com ▪ www.beaujoubert.com ▪ S 33° 57' 11.6" E 018° 44' 25.5" ▪ F +27 (0)21-881-3377 ▪ **T +27 (0)21-881-3103**

Beaumont Wines   ⊘ ⊘ ⌂ ◎ ⊛

The best of the old combines with all that is new and creative at Bot River's family-run Compagnes Drift farm, home of Beaumont Wines. The hospitality and personal attention that draws scores of visitors here for picnics, fine art and jewellery, wine and entertainment remains as warm and welcoming. There is even more involvement by the younger guard, with plans to take the business forward in a dynamic way. Younger son Lucien Beaumont (ex Londolozi) will lead walks and trails on the farm's 350 ha of fynbos, while his wife Nadia takes up the marketing manager position. New and interesting wines by Lucien's brother Sebastian include a Loire-inspired demi-sec chenin and a Cape Blend celebrating friendship. Packaging has been revamped, drawing inspiration from the family crest, with a modern spin.

Beaumont range

★★★★ Pinotage Pinotage's fragrant plummy tones on **14** preview, complementary oak (16 months, 30% new) & dry, food-friendly tannins. Already elegant, potential to develop & step up on **13** (★★★☆).

★★★★☆ Ariane Bordeaux blend is cab-led in **13**, with cab franc, petit verdot & merlot (31/15/8). Classic cassis, leafy cedar tones, with refined structure & balance. Polished, with good length & potential to age elegantly. Magnums available. No **12**.

★★★★☆ R&B (NEW) Collaboration between brothers-in-wine Sebastian Beaumont & Marcus Riesie, celebrating 10 year friendship. **10** rich & spicy mix of mourvèdre, pinotage, shiraz & cab franc (34/30/30/6) in a fine-grained tannin framework. Already tempting, but will reward cellaring.

★★★★☆ Vitruvian ⊘ Intricate 6-way blend of mourvèdre, syrah/shiraz, pinotage, cab franc, petit verdot & malbec (38/25/19/8/8/2) in **12**, with lovely fruit intensity & melange of red berry, savoury & spicy flavours, sleek, well-tailored tannins. Larger formats made.

★★★★☆ Hope Marguerite Chenin Blanc Understated, restrained styling in **14** with lively tension; oak integration & less sugar (4.2 g/l) than **13** ensure long, clean apple & lime farewell. Proven pedigree from 41 & 37 year vines to deserve/reward cellaring. Also in 1.5 & 3L.

★★★★ Chenin Blanc 15 preview shows all the attributes of the variety well expressed in unoaked, polished style. Ample Golden Delicious apple, crisp & balanced for enjoyment now & over next few years.

★★★★ Chenin Blanc Demi-Sec (NEW) A fortuitous single (older) barrel from **13** botrytis-tinged grapes. Sweet (27 g/l sugar) glacé pineapple & lime flavours quiver with sweet-sour freshness & balance. Delicate, with racy intensity & lingering farewell. Only in 375ml and 1.5L.

★★★★ Goutte d'Or Noble Late Harvest-style chenin. Bottled **14** as decadently delicious as last year's preview. Unoaked (unusually for this wine) botrytis-tinged pineapple & honey; unctuous yet uncloying with delicate thread of tangy acidity & long almond nougat farewell.

★★★★ Cape Vintage 13 first since **09** of foot-crushed 'port' from equal tinta & pinotage. Rich dark chocolate & prune flavours in drier (82.6 g/l) style, with fine peppery tannins. Only 2 barrels made. 375 ml.

Syrah (NEW) **★★★★** Pre-bottled, tentatively rated **13** has spicy dark tones, supple dry tannins. Fruit tad subdued, brooding, oak (35% new) evident in youth, needs more time to develop. Also in 1.5, 3 & 5L.
Also tasted: **Mourvèdre 12 ★★★★** Not tasted: **Leo's Whole Bunch Chenin Blanc**. Discontinued:
Shiraz-Mourvèdre.

Raoul's range

Rosé ★★★ From old-vine tinta, bright & cheerful red fruits in tangy, fresh & dry summer styling. **15** great sunset sipper. Also tasted: **Constable House Shiraz-Cabernet Sauvignon 13 ★★★ Jackals River White 15 ★★★☆** Not tasted: **Red Blend**. — MW

Location/WO: Bot River ▪ Map: Elgin, Walker Bay & Bot River ▪ Est 1750 ▪ 1stB 1994 ▪ Tasting, sales & cellar tours Mon-Fri 9.30–4.30 Sat/Sun 10–3 ▪ Tasting fee R30pp ▪ Closed Easter Sun, Dec 25 & Jan 1 ▪ Light meals, platters & picnic baskets ▪ Farm produce ▪ Walking/hiking trails ▪ Conservation area ▪ 250-year old watermill ▪ Art/jewellery exhibits ▪ 2 historic self-catering guest cottages ▪ Owner(s) Beaumont family ▪ Cellarmaster(s)/winemaker(s) Sebastian Beaumont (Jun 2003) ▪ Viticulturist(s) Sebastian Beaumont (Jun 1999) ▪ 500ha/31ha (mourv, ptage, chenin) ▪ 150t/20,000cs own label 45% red 50% white 5% rosé ▪ BWI, IPW ▪ PO Box 3 Bot River 7185 ▪ info@beaumont.co.za ▪ www.beaumont.co.za ▪ S 34° 13' 27.2" E 019° 12' 24.9" ▪ F +27 (0)28-284-9733 ▪ **T +27 (0)28-284-9194**

Beeslaar Wines

This is the own label of Abrie Beeslaar (and wife Jeanne), winemaker with 18 years' experience, many of those at legendary Stellenbosch property Kanonkop. Their variety of choice is pinotage. Unsurprising, given Abrie's long-term personal affinity for, and professional affiliation with the variety. 'So young and poorly understood, there's much work to be done.'

★★★★☆ Pinotage As polished a pinotage as you'll find from man responsible for Kanonkop versions. Beeslaar's own is very different, **13** (**★★★★★**) tilting towards pinot noir's elegance, suppleness, replete with ripe & fresh cherry, raspberry flavours. Structured & oaked (18 months, 50% new French) for long ageing, as was maiden **12**. — AL

Location/WO: Stellenbosch ▪ Est 2011 ▪ 1stB 2012 ▪ Closed to public ▪ Owner(s) Abrie & Jeanne Beeslaar ▪ Cellarmaster(s)/winemaker(s) Abrie Beeslaar (Jul 2011) ▪ Viticulturist(s) Abrie Beeslaar ▪ 5t/750cs own label 100% red ▪ PO Box 93 Elsenburg 7607 ▪ info@beeslaar.co.za ▪ www.beeslaar.co.za ▪ F +27 (0)86-595-9424 ▪ **T +27 (0)83-663-3256/+27 (0)84-255-8686**

Bein Wine Cellar   ⓟ

Swiss émigrés and long-time winelovers Luca and Ingrid Bein traded the routine life of veterinarians for the vagaries of winegrowing after falling for the Cape winelands. Calling their small Polkadraai Hills property Pétrus Place, they planted Pomerol classic merlot and, with degrees in viticulture/oenology, apply knowledge and a technology-aided precision approach to produce diverse expressions of their favourite variety... and to cope with other challenges. They've countered SA's electricity crisis with a solar/battery array, expanding on their 'go-green' policy while ensuring a 'future that looks bright for us!'

★★★★ Little Merlot Return to form in **14** after **13** (**★★★★**). Fruit given focus by fresh acidity. Has a dab of cab & malbec (like flagship below, but no new oak). Achieves ripeness & refined balance.

★★★★☆ Merlot Flagship wine is a blend from vineyard parcels, rewarding precision viticulture. 60% new oak for **14**, with layers of dark berry flavours, lovely balance & intensity interwoven into elegant structure. Will age, though already tempting.

★★★★☆ Merlot Reserve ⓔ Only best vintages & 'best part of our vineyard'. **11** a classic. Elegant, intense, with lovely structure & length, deserves cellaring 6-8 years.

Also tasted: **Pink Merlot 15 ★★★** — MW

Location/map/WO: Stellenbosch ▪ Map grid reference: B6 ▪ Est 2002 ▪ 1stB 2004 ▪ Tasting, sales & cellar tours Mon-Sat by appt only ▪ Owner(s)/cellarmaster(s)/winemaker(s) Luca & Ingrid Bein ▪ Viticulturist(s) Luca Bein ▪ 3ha/2.2ha (merlot) ▪ 16t/2,400cs own label 80% red 20% rosé ▪ IPW ▪ PO Box 3408 Matieland 7602 ▪ lib@beinwine.com ▪ www.beinwine.com ▪ S 33° 57' 40.0" E 018° 44' 12.0" ▪ **T +27 (0)21-881-3025**

Belfield Wines   ⓟ ⌂

Small in stature but growing in following and reputation is this boutique winery in cool-climate Elgin. Its multiple attractions range from the diminutive red-only vineyards and ex-barn cellar — Mike Kreft's preserve – to the self-catering cottages and manicured gardens green-fingered wife Mel displays during annual Open Gardens weekends.

★★★★ Magnifica Cab named for Queen Protea, joined again by dabs cab franc & merlot in **13**. Juicy fruitcake & violet purity. Oak (28% new) is subtle & well knit. Serious, svelte & complex as **11**. No **12**.

★★★★ Aristata Keeping the standard, **12** is mostly cab with merlot & shiraz, also-tasted **13** merlot-based with cabs s & f. Ripe, restrained & elegant, with excellent concentration & depth.

Syrah ★★★☆ 13 mirrors **11** in lighter body. Succulent & lively black-fruit compote, good length. No **12**. — FM

Location/WO: Elgin ▪ Map: Elgin, Walker Bay & Bot River ▪ Est 2000 ▪ 1stB 2005 ▪ Tasting, sales & tours by appt ▪ Closed Dec 25 ▪ 3 self-catering cottages ▪ Owner(s) Mike & Mel Kreft ▪ Cellarmaster(s)/ winemaker(s)/viticulturist(s) Mike Kreft ▪ 5.5ha/2.5ha (cab, merlot, shiraz) ▪ 17t/2,000cs own label 100% red ▪ PO Box 191 Elgin 7180 ▪ mike@belfield.co.za ▪ www.belfield.co.za ▪ S 34° 10' 20.9" E 019° 1' 45.8" ▪ F +27 (0)86-613-3108 ▪ **T +27 (0)82-575-1849**

☐ **Bella Vino** see Nicholson Smith
☐ **Bellemore** see Bellevue Estate Stellenbosch
☐ **Belle Vallee** see Baratok Wines

Bellevue Estate Stellenbosch   ⓠ

'It's business as usual,' says winemaker Wilhelm Kritzinger of the Morkel family farm, noted for pioneering pinotage in the 1950s. Both pinotage and their other speciality, malbec, go to local retail giant Woolworths and the UK's Marks & Spencer, while recent bottlings of cinsaut and pinot noir for China are now also available from the estate in Stellenbosch's Bottelary Hills.

PK Morkel Collection

★★★★ Pinotage Opulent & concentrated **10**, revisited as a bottled wine, has plum & blackberry fruit, vanilla & spice appeal. Full bodied yet nimble, with ripe, mouthfilling tannins.

★★★★ Tumara Well-structured Bordeaux blend, mostly cab (50%), petit verdot (33%) with drops malbec, cab franc, merlot. **08** classic dark fruit, forest floor, earth & cedarwood. Like **07**, has sufficient grip for food & few years ageing.

Also tasted: **Petit Verdot 10 ★★★**

Morkel Collection

★★★★ Malbec 13 epitomises elegance & balance, marries vibrant cherry & plum fruit with dried herbs & spice for satisfying solo sipping or dinnertime pleasure.

Cinsaut (NEW) ⊘ **★★** Downy tannins & savoury tone on red-fruited **12** with mulberries & interesting hint of peat. **Pinot Noir** (NEW) **★★★** Among lightest in terms of both alcohol & oaking in this red-wine specialist's stable. **13** cherry & blackcurrant appeal, lovely dry & spicy tail. For now, year/2. Also tasted: **Shiraz 14 ★★★** Not retasted: **Pinotage 11 ★★★☆ Atticus Cape Blend 10 ★★★ Eselgraf Single Vineyard Chenin Blanc 13 ★★★★** Not tasted: **Sauvignon Blanc**. — GM

Location/map: Stellenbosch ▪ Map grid reference: C3 ▪ WO: Bottelary ▪ Est 1701 ▪ 1stB 1999 ▪ Tasting & sales Mon-Fri 10—4 Sat 11—4 ▪ Closed Good Fri, Dec 25 & Jan 1 ▪ Owner(s) Dirkie Morkel ▪ Winemaker(s) Wilhelm Kritzinger (Feb 2002) & Anneke Potgieter (Feb 2003) ▪ Viticulturist(s) Dirkie Morkel (Jan 1979) ▪ 291ha/151ha (cabs s/f, cinsaut, malbec, merlot, p verdot, ptage, pinot, shiraz, chenin, sauv) ▪ ±750t/±20,000cs own label 97% red 3% white; ±40,000cs for clients; balance in bulkwine & grapes ▪ Export brands: Bellemore, Bellemore Family Selection, Houdamond, Morkel, Tumara ▪ Labels for clients: Cap du Vin, Marks & Mapper, Provoyeur, Pure African, Sizanani, Woolworths ▪ BWI, IPW, WIETA ▪ PO Box 33 Koelenhof 7605 ▪ wilhelm@bellevue.co.za ▪ www.bellevue.co.za ▪ S 33° 52' 48.48" E 018° 45' 50.40" ▪ F +27 (0)21-865-2899 ▪ **T +27 (0)21-865-2055**

Bellingham   ⓠ ⓜ ⓞ ⓐ

Pioneering vintner Bernard Podlashuk, who revitalised the Bellingham estate and started the brand in the 1940s, no doubt would be delighted with the many awards recently bestowed on the top-tier wines that bear his name. Surely the founder would be just as pleased with the new brand home at the entrance to Franschhoek town, just a short distance from the farm founded by French Huguenots as 'Belle en Champ' ('Beautiful Fields'). It's a stylish, multifaceted space, which Bellingham shares with its sibling DGB brands, and an asset to Niël Groenewald, head winemaker and now also brand manager.

Bernard Series

★★★★ Bush Vine Pinotage Step-up **14** (★★★★☆) textbook pinotage: strawberry fruit, slight high-toned lift, refreshing acidity. Plus malleable tannins buffed by smart oaking (50% new). Even more so than bold **13**, excellent now & for many years.

★★★★ Basket Press Syrah Cassis & liquorice notes on **13** (★★★★★); glossy & polished, it glides incredibly tastily across the palate now but will improve & reward even more with few years ageing. As seamless, lingering as **12** but with greater gravitas.

★★★★ Organic Syrah ⊘ Previewed **12** has liquorice, eucalyptus nuances to its cassis & red berry bouquet, tarry oak notes cushioned by sweet fruit core. Shows more poise & presence than maiden **11** (★★★★), goes up a notch.

★★★★☆ Small Barrel SMV Pure & precise **13** Rhône blend repeats successful formula of improved **12** in its shiraz (80%), mourvèdre & viognier make-up, the perfectly judged 50% new oak giving subtle floral notes & spice. Enjoy now with a fine meal & cellar with confidence 5+ years.

★★★★ Old Vine Chenin Blanc **14** no wallflower: intensely flavoured with quince & white stonefruit, obvious oak (50% new) & crackling acidity. Delicious & impressive, though **13** (★★★★★) was finer.

★★★★☆ Whole Bunch Marsanne 🆕 Delicate & unusual camphor, sandalwood, pear & white peach complexity on aristocratic **14** from Voor Paardeberg grapes. Refined satiny & harmonious persistence. Inspired, supportive partial oaking: just 50% barrel fermented, only older wood. Brilliant debut!

★★★★☆ Whole Bunch Roussanne Rare-in-Cape white grape from Voor Paardeberg delivers restraint, persistence, ageability. Like **14**, **15** (★★★★★) impressive fruit purity & food-inviting grip from lees-ageing in stainless steel.

★★★★ Hand Picked Viognier Charming **15** polar opposite of full-bore **13** (★★★★): restraint & subtlety the hallmarks in floral & apricot fragrance, pithy grip & clean-cut finish; judicious older oak adds structure not flavour.

★★★★ Whole Bunch Grenache Blanc-Viognier No new oak for pure & confident **14** from Paarl grapes (vs **13**'s 60% new). Lively, dry & balanced, with 20% viognier contributing floral top notes.

Insignia Series

Mocha Java Merlot ★★☆ Barista's delight **14** exudes plummy java & choc aromas & tastes, for sweet, supple, slippery sipping. Also tasted: **Pinopasso Pinotage 14** ★★★ Not retasted: **Citrus Grove Chenin 14** ★★★

Ancient Earth range

Shiraz ★★★ **13**'s lighter styling for summer or winter enjoyment, preferably with 'Italian sausage & sun-dried tomato penne' say winemaking team. Also tasted: **Pinotage 14** ★★★ **Chardonnay 14** ★★☆ **Sauvignon Blanc 15** ★★★ Not retasted: **Cabernet Sauvignon 12** ★★★ **Merlot 13** ★★☆

Tree Series

Big Oak Red ★★☆ Not named for its wooding, which is minimal. Equal 40% portions shiraz & cab with malbec in fruity, easy **14**. For casual get-togethers. WO W Cape, as all these. Also tasted: **Berry Bush Rosé 15** ★★☆ **Pear Tree White 15** ★★ — CvZ

Location/map: Franschhoek ▪ WO: Coastal/Western Cape/Paarl ▪ Est 1693 ▪ 1stB 1947 ▪ Tasting & sales at Bellingham cellardoor, located at Franschhoek Cellar: Mon-Thu 10-6 Fri/Sat 10-9 Sun 10-5 ▪ Wine tasting, 6 wines with 6 cheeses, 6 wines with assorted chocolates ▪ Closed Easter Fri/Sun, Dec 25/26 & Jan 1 ▪ Alfresco style food & kiddies play area daily ▪ Farm produce ▪ Events venue (seat 300 pax) ▪ Owner(s) DGB (Pty) Ltd ▪ Winemaker(s) Niël Groenewald (Jul 2004), with Mario Damon (Jan 2002) ▪ Viticulturist(s) Stephan Joubert (2006) ▪ 4,000t/560,000cs own label 50% red 49% white 1% rosé ▪ ISO 9001:2000, HACCP, IPW, WIETA ▪ PO Box 52 Franschhoek 7690 ▪ bellingham@dgb.co.za ▪ www.bellinghamwines.com ▪ S 33° 54' 16.4" E 019° 6' 40.7" ▪ F +27 (0)21-876-4107 ▪ T +27 (0)21-876-2086

Bellpost ⓠ

When not upping the marketing ante to raise interest in their West Coast winery in Gauteng, owner Lollies Thiart and viticulturist son Nico are replacing vineyard blocks with clean material and planting unusual-in-SA varieties such as verdelho, durif and carmenère to assess their potential. Much to the delight of part-time winemaker (he's on the wine team at Namaqua nearby) and other son Koos.

Shiraz ★★★★ 11, unlike previous, is plush & friendly, with sweet cassis fruit, pliable tannins, smooth finish. **Chardonnay ★★★★** Lovely almond & hazelnut nuances, attractive lemon notes on just-bottled, unwooded **14**. Sauvignon-like grassy nuance is atypical but interesting. Also tasted: **Ruby Cabernet 11 ★★★★** Not retasted: **Merlot 13 ★★★ C'est la Vie 13 ★★★** — CvZ

Location: Vredendal ▪ Map/WO: Olifants River ▪ Est/1stB 2005 ▪ Tasting, sales & cellar tours by appt ▪ Owner(s) Lollies Thiart ▪ Winemaker(s) Koos Thiart (Jan 2005) ▪ Viticulturist(s) Nico Thiart (Jan 2005) ▪ 5ha/2ha (merlot, ruby cab, shiraz, chard, nouvelle, viog) ▪ 12t/1,800cs own label 80% red 20% white ▪ PO Box 39 Vredendal 8160 ▪ bellpost@starmail.co.za ▪ www.bellpost.co.za ▪ S 31° 36′ 24.1″ E 018° 25′ 0.6″ ▪ F +27 (0)27-213-2562 ▪ **T +27 (0)27-213-2562, +27 (0)82-619-2428**

☐ **Bell Tower** *see* Asara Wine Estate & Hotel

Bemind Wyne deur Ilse Schutte ⓠ ⓞ ⓝᴇᵂ

After 16 years at other wineries (latterly Lord's Wines), Ilse Schutte is relishing her long-dreamed-of role as an independent, vinifying hand-picked parcels. Her brand name, Beloved Wines, reflects her pleasure in sharing 'my love and passion for winemaking with loved ones'. She intends her small cellar and tasting venue in McGregor village to be more like a wine gallery, where visitors can experience 'the art of it all'. High-quality, timeless and elegant wines with a story are the Potchefstroom-raised vintner's goal.

Shiraz ★★★ Plums & white pepper but **14** is no pushover, the firm tannin backbone will ensure up to 5 years ageing. **Méthode Cap Classique Brut ★★★** Flavours come from the predominance of chardonnay (70%), with pinot noir, in **NV** zero-dosage sparkling. Winter melon, some citrus, dry & crisply refreshing. — CR, CvZ

Location/WO: McGregor ▪ Map: Robertson ▪ Est 2015 ▪ Tasting, sales & cellar tours Wed-Fri 9-5 Sat 10-4 ▪ Fee R20/4 wines, waived on purchase ▪ Closed Easter Fri-Sun, Pentecost, Dec 25/26 & Jan 1 ▪ Deli products ▪ Owner(s) Ilse Schutte ▪ Cellarmaster(s)/winemaker(s) Ilse Schutte (Jan 2015) ▪ 10-15t/ ±850cs own label 50% red 30% white 20% MCC ▪ IPW ▪ PO Box 446 McGregor 6708 ▪ ilse@bemindwyne.co.za ▪ www.bemindwyne.co.za ▪ S 33° 56′ 49″ E 019° 49′ 44″ ▪ F +27 (0)86-550-5999 ▪ **T +27 (0)83-380-1648**

Benguela Cove ⓠ ♿

Benguela Cove wine and residential estate is being rejuvenated by owners Penny Streeter OBE, health sector staffing entrepreneur, and husband Nick Rea. The vineyards overlooking Bot River lagoon and Sandown Bay benefit from the cool conditions, the wines from the skills of leading winecrafters. A strong international push complements local marketing through two new eponymous restaurants (in Somerset West and Sedgefield), planned onsite French/English contemporary eatery and new tasting centre.

Premium Selection
★★★★☆ Noble Late Harvest ⓝᴇᵂ **15** from sauvignon blanc. Subtle glacé pineapple, lime & kiwi aromas burst to life with wonderfully ripe & tangy flavours. Vivacious & beautifully balanced by vibrant acidity. Opulent smooth texture with delicious piquancy & length.

Merlot ⓝᴇᵂ **★★★★** Minty red fruit & a leafy nuance on **14**, dry & firm courtesy 18 months in 25% new oak. Still tight, needs further year/2 or decanting. **Pinot Noir** ⓝᴇᵂ **★★★** Appealing bouquet of berries & wild mushrooms, **14**'s palate yet to fully assimilate the oak (20% new), needs time's smoothing hand. **Chardonnay** ⓝᴇᵂ **★★★** Plenty of oak spice & butterscotch (20% new barrels) dominate **14**'s gentle lime & pear flavours, which may show more fruit in year/2. **Semillon-Sauvignon Blanc** ⓝᴇᵂ **★★★★** Previewed **15** 65/35 blend shows expected waxy lanolin & lemon flavours, mouthfilling breadth & balanced freshness. Focused flavours are classy, made for finest seafood. Also tasted: **Cabernet Sauvignon 14 ★★★★ Shiraz 14 ★★★★ Sauvignon Blanc 15 ★★★★** In abeyance: **Cabernet Franc.**

Matilda's Secret range (NEW)

Matilda's Secret ★★★★ 13 hearty, ripe & spicy blend of shiraz, grenache & viognier. Generous, friendly, with slight tannic grip for mealtimes or fun times. **14** (★★★) is shiraz & merlot, & somewhat sterner, tighter, with charry & herby tones needing time or a rich meal. **Sauvignon Blanc ★★★** Pre-bottling, **15** rounder, more approachable than premium bottling but shares the racy acidity & grapefruit farewell. Also tasted: **Rosé 15 ★★★** — MW

Location: Hermanus ▪ Map: Elgin, Walker Bay & Bot River ▪ WO: Walker Bay/Western Cape ▪ Est 2004 ▪ 1stB 2007 ▪ Tasting Mon-Sat 10-5 Sun/pub hols 10-4 ▪ Closed Dec 25 ▪ Fee R35pp ▪ Chocolate & wine pairing R85pp ▪ Sales Mon-Sat 10-5 ▪ Owner(s) Benguela Cove Investments (Pty) Ltd (Penny Streeter OBE) ▪ Winemaker(s) Kevin Grant, Niels Verburg, PJ Geyer & other artisan winemakers ▪ Viticulturist(s) Paul Wallace (2011, consultant) ▪ 206ha/66ha (cabs s/f, malbec, merlot, p verdot, pinot, shiraz, chard, sauv, sem, viog) ▪ 600t/4,400cs own label 50% red 50% white ▪ PO Box 327 Bellville 7535 ▪ info@benguelacove.co.za ▪ www.benguelacove.co.za ▪ S 34° 20' 45.0" E 019° 8' 15.7" ▪ **T +27 (0)83-645-6198/+27 (0)21-944-1041**

☐ **Ben Hur** see Blomendahl Vineyards
☐ **Berg en Dal** see Wine-of-the-Month Club

Bergheim (Q)

Enthused by food (and cooking), music and wine, general practitioner Edwin Jordaan micro-vinifies in rented cellar space on Paarl Mountain. 'Every bottle of wine wants to tell a story about terroir, cultivar and/or harvest,' Edwin says. 'My passion is seeing this happen with minimum interference.'

Bergheim range

★★★★ Mignon (Q) Older-oak-aged **13** (★★★★) is semillon & 35% sauvignon from Franschhoek; subtle fruit & pronounced acidity. Slightly less complex, weighty than **12**.

Not retasted: **Pinotage 12 ★★ Shiraz 12 ★★★**

Couple's Wine range

Not tasted: **Dry Red Ben**, **Dry White Celia**. — HJ

Location: Paarl ▪ Map: Paarl & Wellington ▪ Map grid reference: E6 ▪ WO: Paarl/Franschhoek ▪ Est/1stB 2000 ▪ Tasting by appt ▪ Owner(s) Edwin Jordaan ▪ Cellarmaster(s)/winemaker(s) Edwin Jordaan (Jan 2000) ▪ 4-6t/1,000cs own label 66% red 34% white ▪ PO Box 6020 Paarl 7622 ▪ drjordaan@gmail.com ▪ S 33° 45' 20.2" E 018° 57' 42.5" ▪ F +27 (0)21-862-7852 ▪ **T +27 (0)82-923-3115, +27 (0)21-863-1529**

☐ **Bergkelder** see Die Bergkelder Wine Centre

Bergsig Estate (Q) (¶) (◎) (⅄) (⅊)

This long-established Breedekloof family winegrowing and business concern has been bottling wine under its own label since the 1970s. Hence current cellarmaster De Wet Lategan, with brothers Louis and Plum are able to draw from decades-old vines for some of their premium wines, notably the recent Icarus White blend and outstanding new Chenin Blanc Reserve.

Limited Editions

★★★★ Cabernet Sauvignon Reserve Cassis, sandalwood, vanilla & cigarbox seamlessly integrated on balanced & elegant palate; medium body, with good flavour intensity & length on **12**. No **11**.

★★★★☆ Chenin Blanc Reserve (NEW) Blood orange, peach kernel, lemon tart, crushed rock & soy – an amazing spectrum in the bouquet of **14**, showing unusual density & concentration for a white wine, a clear structure, dry minerality & some oak tannins. A serious expression, suited to pair with the finest food.

Bergsig Estate range

★★★★ Icarus Red Unconventional combination of cab & touriga in equal parts on **12** (★★★★★), & to good effect. A step up from varietal range with more extraction & longer time in barrel – all new. Dark plums, spice & blackcurrants, good oak integration. Great balance as on **11**.

★★★★☆ **Icarus White 14** (★★★★) similar blend to **13** but less lipsmacking, more toasty, with new oak in driving seat. Mostly chardonnay & chenin, giving lemon & straw notes, plus subtle kerosene nuance from splash riesling. Drying tail from oak tannin clouds the fruit.

★★★★ **Cape Vintage** ⓥ Succulent, smooth & spicy 'port' from tinta. **04** similar to last-tasted **00**, generously flavoured but not sweet, sufficient fire to warm a winter night.

Weisser Riesling 🆕 ⓥ ★★★☆ Unquestionably riesling on nose, hint of kerosene development but also lots of steely dryness, green apple & stonefruit still on **12**. Light & crisp, welcome addition to the range – & the district. **Sauvignon Blanc** ⓥ ★★★☆ Attractive tropical fruit-punch aromas introduce fresh, harmonious, altogether delicious **15**, offering kiwi, guava & green fig. Also in magnum.

Chenin Blanc ★★★ Light, crunchy, mouthwateringly juicy summer sipper, **15** well poised & priced, as others in this range. Soft yellow fruit with savoury tail. **Gewürztraminer** ★★★ Well-crafted **15** shows sound balance & varietal integrity, few grams of sugar checked by bright acidity. Delicious curry partner. **Weisser Riesling Late Harvest** 🆕 ★★★☆ Ample terpene notes show more development than fresher, dry sibling; ample sweetness from late-harvested fruit, raisined sultanas, honey & lanolin on **13**. Also tasted: **Cabernet Sauvignon 12** ★★★ **Chardonnay 14** ★★★ **Cape LBV 06** ★★★☆ Not retasted: **Bulldozer Pinotage 13** ★★★ **Pinotage 11** ★★★☆ **Touriga Nacional 11** ★★★ **The Family Friend 11** ★★★ **Shiraz Rosé 12** ★★★ **Cape Ruby NV** ★★★☆ Not tasted: **Bouquet Light, Special Late Harvest.** Discontinued: **Sauvignon Blanc Brut.** — HJ

Location: Wolseley ▪ Map/WO: Breedekloof ▪ Est 1843 ▪ 1stB 1977 ▪ Tasting & sales Mon-Fri 8–5 Sat & pub hols 9–5 ▪ Fee R20 for groups of 10+ ▪ Closed Good Fri, Dec 25 & Jan 1 ▪ Cellar tours by appt ▪ Bergsig Bistro ▪ Organic food selection ▪ Facilities for children ▪ Farm produce ▪ Conferences ▪ Self-guided birdwatching route ▪ MTB route ▪ Conservation area, visits by appt ▪ Lategan family history & historical artefacts on display ▪ Soetes & Soup (Jul) ▪ Owner(s) Lategan family ▪ Cellarmaster(s) De Wet Lategan (Jan 1989) ▪ Winemaker(s) Chris du Toit (Jul 2003) ▪ Viticulturist(s) Louis & Plum Lategan (1991) ▪ ±400ha/253ha (cab, ptage, shiraz, touriga, chard, chenin, sauv) ▪ 3,200t/100,000cs own label 35% red 60% white 4% rosé 1% other + 140,000cs for clients ▪ Other export brands: White River, Bulldozer Pinotage ▪ Brand for clients: Woolworths ▪ BWI, BRC, IPW ▪ PO Box 15 Breërivier 6858 ▪ wine@bergsig.co.za ▪ www.bergsig.co.za ▪ S 33° 31' 7.78" E 019° 11' 37.14" ▪ F +27 (0)23-355-1658 ▪ **T +27 (0)23-355-1603**

Bergwater Winery
ⓥ 🍴 🥨 🏠 📷 ♿

Owned by brothers Stephan and Heimie Schoeman, Bergwater in Prince Albert Valley is the Groot Karoo's first and largest winery, with 63 ha of vineyards and a further ±1,400 ha of nature reserve. Wines are among several visitor attractions, including 4x4 and cycle trails, hiking, an airstrip and accommodation.

Reserve range

Cabernet Sauvignon ⓥ ★★★ **12** first since **09**. More harmony, dimension than standard label. Ripe dark fruit; firm backing that will benefit from short ageing. Not retasted: **Shiraz 09** ★★☆ **Royal Reserve 10** ★★ **Rosé 12** ★★ **Sauvignon Blanc 13** ★★☆ Not tasted: **Merlot.**

Bergwater range

Shiraz ⓥ ★★ Pleasant rustic style **12** has dark spice, hint oak & good freshness. **Rendezvous Red** ⓥ ★★ Shiraz, merlot & cab blend in no-frills, smooth **12**. Not retasted: **Cabernet Sauvignon 12** ★★ **Merlot 12** ★★ **Rendezvous White 13** ★☆ **Muscat d'Alexandrie 12** ★★ **Tinta Barocca 12** ★☆

Sparkling Wine range

Brut Sauvignon Blanc ⓥ ★★★ Frothy fun in **12** bubbly from sauvignon. Not retasted: **Sparkling Brut Rosé 12** ★★★ — AL

Location: Prince Albert ▪ Map: Klein Karoo & Garden Route ▪ WO: Prince Albert Valley/Western Cape ▪ Est 1999 ▪ 1stB 2003 ▪ Tasting & sales Mon-Thu 8–4.30 Fri 8-4 Sat/Sun 10-3 ▪ Fee R20 ▪ Cellar tours by appt ▪ Meals by prior arrangement ▪ BYO picnic ▪ Gifts ▪ Olives & olive oil ▪ Wedding/conference/function venue (up to 250 pax) ▪ 2 x self-catering guest houses ▪ Gravel airstrip for light aircraft (phone ahead) ▪ Hiking/mountain biking & 4x4 trail by arrangement ▪ Owner(s) Heimie & Stephan Schoeman ▪ Cellarmaster(s)/winemaker(s) Jacques Kruger (Jan 2013) ▪ 1,500ha/63ha (cab, merlot, shiraz, sauv) ▪ ±400-600t ▪ 80% red

15% white 5% rosé + bulk ▪ PO Box 40 Prince Albert 6930 ▪ wine@bergwater.co.za ▪ www.bergwater.com ▪ S 33° 16' 46.3" E 022° 13' 55.7" ▪ F +27 (0)86-541-7335 ▪ **T +27 (0)23-541-1703**

☐ **Bernard Series** *see* Bellingham
☐ **Berrio Wines** *see* The Berrio Wines
☐ **Berryfields** *see* Ashton Kelder

Beyerskloof Ⓣ Ⓜ ◎ ⑤

Since the maiden 1989 vintage, top Stellenbosch estate Beyerskloof has been indelibly associated with co-founder/owner Beyers Truter and with pinotage. He and winemaker son Anri fiercely champion the home-bred grape, and it remains the main focus here – though 2015 produced a maiden crop of shiraz, destined to join Cape Blends Synergy and if quality permits, Faith, the flagship. With the passing of winemaking duties from one generation to another, Anri sees the more accessible, fruit-driven pinotages attracting younger winedrinkers. But Beyers' revered hands aren't absent from the cellar: 'He does a lot of the 2am to 6am punch-down shifts,' says Anri, 'and is still involved in tasting throughout the winemaking process; it would be silly not to use one of South Africa's best red-wine palates and experience.'

★★★★☆ **CWG Auction Reserve Traildust Pinotage** (ℕ) Beyerskloof's CWG offering is, of course, pinotage. **13** classily swathed in 100% new French oak, its rich mocha tones presently dominating concentrated, fresh dark-cherry fruit. Very sleek, highly buffed tannins, only youthful edginess needs to settle.

★★★★☆ **Diesel Pinotage** Kingpin of winery's pinotages; treated like royalty, responds accordingly. **13** big (15% alcohol) but sleek, perfectly formed, with appealing freshness in its raspberry/red cherry fruit. Needs time for all-new French oak to meld; will reward patience.

★★★★ **Pinotage Reserve** Pinotage in smart, modern guise. Oak accessory (25% new) perfectly judged to complement fresh, ripe plummy fruit, plentiful juicy tannins on **13**. Good prospects.

★★★★ **Field Blend** Co-grown & -fermented cab-merlot, aged 5 years prior to release. **10** shade less appealing than standout **09** (★★★★★); pretty mint-laced cassis flavours shorter on flesh, concentration.

★★★★☆ **Faith** (②) Opulent & showy but **11** has better balance, harmony than **10**. All-new French oak well absorbed in ripe-fruited blend of pinotage & merlot (50/50), cab in usual holding role. Faith in ageability will be rewarded!

★★★★ **Synergy Cape Blend** Pinotage (42%) adds fruit notes to dominant cab, merlot influence in **13**. Balanced creamy/fresh contrast framed by firm, polished grip. Promises more savoury attraction with age.

Also tasted: **Pinotage 14** ★★★☆ Not retasted: **Cabernet Sauvignon-Merlot 12** ★★★ **Pinotage Dry Rosé 14** ★★★ **Chenin Blanc-Pinotage 14** ★★☆ **Lagare Cape Vintage 10** ★★★☆ — AL

Location/map: Stellenbosch ▪ Map grid reference: E3 ▪ WO: Stellenbosch/Western Cape/Coastal ▪ Est 1988 ▪ 1stB 1989 ▪ Tasting & sales Mon-Fri 9–4 Sat 9.30–4 ▪ Closed Easter Fri-Mon, Dec 25/26 & Jan 1 ▪ Cellar tours by appt ▪ Red Leaf Restaurant ▪ Farm produce ▪ Conferences (30 pax) ▪ Owner(s) Beyers Truter, Simon Halliday & Jan Morgan ▪ Cellarmaster(s) Beyers Truter (Jan 1988) ▪ Winemaker(s) Anri Truter (Jan 2004) & Travis Langley (Jan 2009), with Buddy Hendricks (Jan 2010) ▪ Viticulturist(s) Johan Pienaar (2000, consultant) ▪ 130ha/94ha (cab, merlot, ptage) ▪ 750t/240,000cs own label 96% red 2% white 2% rosé + 10,000cs for clients ▪ Brands for clients: Pick's Pick ▪ WIETA ▪ PO Box 107 Koelenhof 7605 ▪ reception@beyerskloof.co.za ▪ www.beyerskloof.co.za ▪ S 33° 53' 28.0" E 018° 49' 23.6" ▪ F +27 (0)21-865-2683 ▪ **T +27 (0)21-865-2135**

Bezalel-Dyasonsklip Wine Cellar Ⓣ Ⓜ ◎ Ⓐ

The Bezuidenhout family's estate in Upington offers a variety of attractions (hence its listing on the Northern Cape's Kokerboom Food & Wine Route) including tastings of father-and-son team Inus and Jan-Adriaan's new craft beer (and boutique wine, brandy and liqueur) in the upgraded visitor locale.

Bezalel Estate range (ℕ)

Shiraz ★★★ Translucent, unoaked **15** offers red berries & cherries, pleasant grape tannin grip; slips down easily courtesy smoothing sugar. **Colombard** ★★ Bone-dry **15** is nutty & earthy rather than guava-toned as expected. Chill well to up the refreshment. **Sauvignon Blanc** ★★☆ Water-white **15** hits the right varietal notes with grass & capsicum nuances, zesty acidity; appealing anytime sipper.

Brandy range (NEW)
Founder's Reserve XO Fine Potstill Brandy ★★★☆ Impressive packaging to back smooth ginger-caramel & khaki bush flavours on 10 year old potstill from eclectic mix of varieties: colombard, chardonnay, tinta barocca, cab, pinot noir & gewürztraminer. **VSOP Pure Alambic brandy ★★★** 5 year old sibling is rustic, with some cherry-chocolate notes, medicinal edge. Handsome packaging & from the same potstilled varieties as above. — WB, CvZ

Location: Upington ▪ Map: Northern Cape, Free State & North West ▪ WO: Northern Cape ▪ Est 1949 (farm)/1997 (cellar) ▪ 1stB 1998 ▪ Tasting, sales & cellar tours Mon-Fri 8.30–5.30 Sat 8–2 ▪ Fee R30-R75pp ▪ Large groups by appt ▪ Closed Easter Fri/Mon & Dec 25 ▪ Green Fig Café: breakfast, lunch & platters ▪ Venue for conferences & weddings (up to 280 pax) ▪ Owner(s) Bezuidenhout family ▪ Cellarmaster(s) Inus Bezuidenhout (1989) ▪ Winemaker(s)/viticulturist(s) Inus Bezuidenhout (1989), with Jan-Adriaan Bezuidenhout (2005) ▪ 60ha/44ha (cab, cornifesto, merlot, pinot, sangio, shiraz, touriga, chard, cbard, gewürz, merbein, sultana) ▪ ±1,000cs own label 100% red ▪ EuroGAP ▪ PO Dyasonsklip 8805 ▪ info@bezalel.co.za ▪ www.bezalel.co.za ▪ S 28° 36' 28.69" E 021° 6' 19.01" ▪ F +27 (0)54-491-1141 ▪ **T +27 (0)54-491-1325, +27 (0)83-310-4763**

☐ **Big Five** see Jacques Germanier
☐ **Big Flower** see Botanica Wines

Bilton Wines   (icons)

Biltons have farmed the Helderberg slopes since the late 1950s. Vegetables and fruit gave way to vines, overseen since 1996 by Mark Bilton, great-grandson of Sir Percy, the entrepreneur honoured in the flagship wine. The new generation is fully involved, in the person of Mark's son Simon, the general manager, who's introduced a new cellardoor tasting of the pirate-themed wines, Matt Black and Bonnie Anne.

Private Collection
★★★★ The Bilton (icon) 100% cab, **06** matured 3 years in '500% new oak' produced porty, inky, tannic leviathan, hopefully to emerge with grace.

★★★★☆ Sir Percy (icon) Cab leads in powerful **09 (★★★★)** Bordeaux-style blend with merlot & dab petit verdot. Not as spicy as **08** as mourvèdre omitted. Body & breadth from noticeable oak, all new. Discontinued: **Viognier**.

Cellar Selection
★★★★☆ Cabernet Sauvignon (icon) **08** structured & firm but beautifully smooth & rich overall. Light cocoa note adds complex nuance to palate.

★★★★ Shiraz (icon) Lovely concentration of **08** on par with **07**. Intense but seamlessly elegant, ripe blue/black berries & char hint from 80% new oak. Silky smooth texture, long rich tail.

Merlot ★★★☆ Green herbaceous notes on **08** give way to surprisingly ripe black fruit notes with some fennel & dark chocolate. Dryish tannins should soften nicely with food. Also in 1.5L, 5L & 12L.

Bilton range
Matt Black Red Blend ★★★☆ Thoroughly enjoyable **09** shiraz blend, revisited, continues to please with soft, juicy tannins rounded by cherry/smoke deliciousness. A cut above everyday quaffing. Also in 1.5L, 5L & 12L. Not retasted: **Bonnie Anne 14 ★★★** — CM

Location/map/WO: Stellenbosch ▪ Map grid reference: E8 ▪ Est 1694 ▪ 1stB 1998 ▪ Tasting & sales Mon-Sun 10–5 ▪ Fee R40/6 wines, R25 'pirate' tasting (2 wines), R55 dark Belgian chocolate & wine pairing (4 wines) ▪ Closed Good Fri, Dec 25/26 & Jan 1 ▪ Cellar tours Mon-Fri by appt ▪ Jungle gym & play area for children ▪ Vineyard walk ▪ Owner(s) Mark Bilton ▪ Winemaker(s) Ruan du Plessis ▪ Viticulturist(s) Ruan du Plessis (Dec 2004) ▪ 377ha/65ha (cab, merlot, mourv, p verdot, pinot, shiraz, chenin, sauv, viog) ▪ 100t/16,000cs own label 90% red 10% white ▪ IPW, WIETA ▪ PO Box 60 Lynedoch 7603 ▪ info@biltonwines.com ▪ www.biltonwines.com ▪ S 33° 59' 52.9" E 018° 50' 58.3" ▪ F +27 (0)21-881-3721 ▪ **T +27 (0)21-881-3714**

☐ **Birkenhead Estate & Brewery** see Walker Bay Vineyards
☐ **Bistro** see Zandvliet Wine Estate

Bizoe Wines ⓠ

Bizoe Wines encapsulates the personal relationship Somerset West-based Rikus Neethling has with wine. When not making his own pair (named after mother Henriëtta and wife Estalét) from bought-in grapes vinified in rented cellar space, he's sharing his knowledge of all things vinous with enthusiasts on his upscale wine tours and private tastings.

★★★★ **Estalét Syrah** Fascinating expression from Wolseley has improved with extra year, having integrated the acidity underpinning the pastille-like lavender, fynbos & liquorice flavours. **12** still youthful, stalky & somewhat sweet but a notch above lighter **11** (★★★☆).

★★★★☆ **Henriëtta 14** is the pick of recent vintages, achieving great complexity & flavour definition in a super-light frame. True finesse (12% alcohol) from dominant semillon, with 25% sauvignon (all from Franschhoek & Elgin, partly oaked). Delicately perfumed & fleshy. — HJ

Location: Somerset West ▪ WO: Western Cape ▪ Est/1stB 2008 ▪ Tasting & sales by appt or during tailor-made tours – booking essential ▪ Fee R1,500pp incl. transport & lunch ▪ Owner(s)/cellarmaster(s)/winemaker(s) Rikus Neethling ▪ Viticulturist(s) Org Viljoen ▪ 2,000cs ▪ Unit 189 Croydon Vineyard Estate Somerset West 7130 ▪ info@bizoe.co.za ▪ www.bizoe.co.za ▪ F +27 (0)86-653-8186 ▪ **T +27 (0)21-843-3307**

Blaauwklippen Vineyards ⓠ ⓡ ⊙ ⓐ ⓖ

17th-century Cape Dutch wine property Blaauwklippen has moved from traditional, family-owned homeliness to modern, multifaceted wine tourism over the past decade under German ownership. GM, winemaker and distiller Rolf Zeitvogel produces a carefully structured collection of single-varietal, vineyard-selected and blended wines. Premium brandies have joined the mix, as have spirits (see Gentleman Spirits entry). But tradition has not been discarded. Zinfandel, long a speciality, appears in several guises. The Blaauwklippen Blending Competition for wine enthusiasts is in its fourth decade. And the estate's continued branding based on its antique horse carriage collection is pure nostalgia.

Reserve Single Vineyard range

★★★★ **Shiraz** ⓠ Delightful, lithe **11** maintains standard of restrained **10**. Graphite edge to generous layered fruit. Textured, with focused, elegant aftertaste.

Not retasted: **Merlot 10** ★★★★ Not tasted: **Zinfandel**.

Blaauwklippen Vineyard Selection (BVS)

★★★★ **Cabriolet 12** improves on **11** (★★★☆) with array of ripe, savoury black fruit. Generously textured 3-way blend led by cab franc, dollops merlot & shiraz satisfies, ends on a dry, leafy note. Also in 1.5L.

★★★★ **Malbec Noble Late Harvest** ⓠ Chalky texture & cherry juice appeal to unusual **12** botrytised dessert that improves on **11** (★★★☆). Spicy, with cranberry tang. Sweet yet uncloying.

★★★★ **Viognier Noble Late Harvest** ⓠ Sun-dried pineapple & peach aromas on rich, honeyed **12** (★★★☆) dessert, light & tangy, dry-seeming finish. Last was scented **07**.

★★★★ **Zinfandel Noble Late Harvest** ⓠ Macerated raisin & spicy compote on less sweet **12**. Good harmony of fruit, sweetness & oak (50% new). Succulent, with long, 'dry' aftertaste.

Diva MCC ⓝⓔⓦ ★★★★ First zinfandel MCC bubbly in SA. Wild berry fruit, creaminess from extended lees-ageing, soft, smooth mousse delights on **NV** debut. Also tasted: **Zinfandel 11** ★★★★ **White Zinfandel 15** ★★★★ Not tasted: **Shiraz**.

Blaauwklippen Blending Competition (BBC)

Barouche ★★★ Blueberry & graphite spice on now-bottled **13**, 31st blending competition winner. Shiraz leads zinfandel, malbec & cab franc. Light, juicy & unfussy, like previous. Magnum only.

Blaauwklippen Cultivar Selection

Cabernet Sauvignon ★★★ **12** is rounded, with rich cassis fruit & toned body. Some depth, with rather dusty finish. Only partly oaked, as all these reds. **Chenin Blanc** ⊘ ★★★★ Improved **15** is tropical, tangy & crisp, with sunkissed ripe juicy orchard notes, lovely mouthfeel. WO W Cape, like next. **Sauvignon Blanc** ★★★ Riper, tropical-styled **15** offers pineapple & guava bounty balanced by flint & zest. Lively, clean acidity. Also tasted: **Malbec 12** ★★★ **Shiraz 13** ★★★ Not retasted: **Merlot 12** ★★★★ **Red NV** ★★☆ **Rosé 14** ★★★

Blaauwklippen Specialities

★★★★ Before & After Handsome packaging for aptly named **NV** from fortified zinfandel NLH (16% alcohol). A berry- & spice-saturated beauty, sweet & very moreish albeit not as luscious as previous.

★★★★☆ 10 Year Potstilled Brandy Light amber-gold glints entice, floral & tropical notes. Nutty, spicy oak supports the intense fruit flavours. Elegant balance & subtle texture, with all the mellow, mature notes given a lift on fresh finish. Retasted blend from colombard, sauvignon & chenin, like 8YO.

★★★★ 8 Year Potstilled Brandy Slightly younger sibling, with fresher flavours & greater depth, complexity, in new, finer blend. Smooth, fragrant, fresh citrus flavours on finish. 100% potstill.

Ons Sprankel (NEW) **★★★** Palest pink petillant rosé from undisclosed varieties. Off-dry **NV** with tiny frothy bubbles, low-alcohol party starter.

Terroir range (NEW)

Paradyskloof Cabernet Sauvignon ★★★ Playful & fun **13**, smooth, with supple tannin structure. Only partly oaked, as all the reds. **Paradyskloof Cabernet Franc ★★★** Soft & sweet fruited, with a leafy herbal edge in **13**, quite a brisk exit. Export only, as all these. **Paradyskloof Shiraz ★★★** Heady violet perfume, sweet & juicy, with cured meat notes on finish of easygoing **13**. **Padstal Cellarmaster's Blend ★★★ 13** is shiraz, zinfandel, malbec & petit verdot; succulent, with earthy notes, brisk, grippy finish. — WB

Location/map: Stellenbosch ▪ Map grid reference: E6 ▪ WO: Stellenbosch/Western Cape ▪ Est 1682 ▪ 1stB 1974 ▪ Tasting & sales Mon-Sat 10–6 (summer)/10-5 (winter) Sun/pub hols 10–5 ▪ Wine tasting; unique chocolate & wine experience ▪ Brandy tasting ▪ Closed Dec 25 & Jan 1 ▪ Food & wine pairing on request ▪ Wine blending on request ▪ Barrel station tasting (min 45 pax) ▪ Cellar tours 11-2 daily, booking advised ▪ Family market every Sun 10-3 (pony rides available) ▪ Bistro ▪ Deli ▪ Facilities for children ▪ Pony & tractor rides Mon-Sat by appt ▪ Gift shop ▪ Conferences ▪ Weddings/functions ▪ Walks/hikes & mountain biking ▪ Distillery: see Gentleman Spirits ▪ Owner(s) Blue Lion GmbH ▪ Winemaker(s) / brandy master(s) Rolf Zeitvogel (Sep 2003), with Albert Basson (Jul 2007) ▪ Viticulturist(s) Christo Hamman (Jan 2009) ▪ 160ha ▪ 500t/60,000cs wine & 650cs (x4-btl) brandy ▪ IPW ▪ PO Box 54 Stellenbosch 7599 ▪ marketing@blaauwklippen.com ▪ www.blaauwklippen.com ▪ S 33° 58' 23.3" E 018° 50' 51.0" ▪ F +27 (0)21-880-0136 ▪ **T +27 (0)21-880-0133**

Black Block Wines (NEW)

Derick Henstra and Peter Fehrsen have collaborated as architects for nearly 20 years, and as partners in Cape Town retailer Wine Concepts nearly as long, with a sustained and deep interest in wine – especially pinot noir. Hence this bottling in the 'bolder' style they favour. They make it at James McKenzie's cellar at Nabygelegen (with James as mentor), the grapes from a high-lying single block in Tulbagh.

★★★★ Pinot Noir Fruit-filled & rich, with sweet cherries & berries, refreshing acidity & fine tannins buffed by oak (20% new). **13** sleek & poised, drinks well now & has structure for some ageing. — TJ, CvZ

Location: Cape Town ▪ WO: Western Cape ▪ Est/1stB 2012 ▪ Closed to public ▪ Owner(s) Derick Henstra & Peter Fehrsen ▪ Winemaker(s) Derick Henstra & Peter Fehrsen, advised by James McKenzie (Nabygelegen) ▪ 100% red ▪ jacqui@blackblockwines.co.za ▪ www.blackblockwines.co.za ▪ **T +27 (0)21-421-6803**

☐ **Black Box** see Wineways Marketing

Black Elephant Vintners (Ⓛ)

Former Johannesburg investment business partners Kevin Swart ('black' in Afrikaans) and Raymond Ndlovu ('elephant' in Nguni) now collaborate with Franschhoek winemaker Jacques Wentzel on a collection of wines featuring unusual single-varietal bottlings. Quality comes from careful sourcing of mostly local fruit and traditional vinification, including use of older oak for the reds. Cellar space is rented at Bo La Motte, from where the wines sally forth (abroad too).

The Back Roads range

★★★★ Bakenshoek Grenache Noir (NEW) 30% bunch fermentation, older oaking allow variety's strawberry & sweet spice aromas to shine in delicious **14**. Sturdy – but oh so nicely dry & savoury – grape tannin & attractive Provençal herbs up the enjoyment.

★★★★ Matoppie Petite Sirah 'Durif' by another name, delectable by nature, **14** heady with blackberries, Asian spice & liquorice; generously fruited with a tannin structure for the brave – tackle with a steak or in ±3 years.

Not tasted: **Die Middagkrans Malbec**, **Die Perdeskoen Pinotage**.

Black Elephant Vintners range

★★★★ Amistad Pinotage (NEW) Cellarworthy **14** fruit-filled yet compact, dry & savoury with fine tannin frame, mulberry & savoury/nori complexity. Care taken with Stellenbosch & Wellington grapes: own yeasts (30% bunch pressed), 15 months in older oak.

★★★★☆ Chardonnay-Pinot Noir Brut MCC (NEW) Fresh & delicate **NV** sparkler has classic feel. Billowing brioche, red & yellow apple aroma, fine but gentle mousse from 27 months sur lie, lovely delineation of flavour. Mouthfilling, refreshing; one to seek out & enjoy now or cellar few years.

Two Dogs, a Peacock & a Horse Sauvignon Blanc ★★★★ Bright & breezy **15** with 5% oaked oldvine semillon has generous tropical fruit aromas & flavours given extra appeal by lipsmacking acidity, satisfying weight & length. Not retasted: **Amistad Syrah 12 ★★★☆ Nicolas Red 13 ★★★★ Timothy White 14 ★★★★** Not tasted: **Timothy White Viognier**. — JPf

Location/map: Franschhoek ▪ WO: Franschhoek/Western Cape ▪ Est 2013 ▪ 1stB 2012 ▪ Tasting, sales & cellar tours by appt ▪ Fee R25, waived on purchase ▪ Owner(s) Kevin Swart, Raymond Ndlovu & Jacques Wentzel ▪ Winemaker(s) Jacques Wentzel (Jan 2013) ▪ 80t/10,000cs own label 40% red 60% white ▪ IPW ▪ PO Box 686 Franschhoek 7690 ▪ sales@bevintners.co.za, jacques@bevintners.co.za, kevin@bevintners.co.za ▪ www.bevintners.co.za ▪ S 33° 54' 9.00 E 019° 7' 14.00" ▪ **T +27 (0)21-876-2903**

☐ **Black Forest** see Louis
☐ **Black Granite** see Darling Cellars
☐ **Black Label** see Backsberg Estate Cellars, Kanu Wines

Black Oystercatcher Wines (?) (♨) (⌂) (◎) (⚇) (♿)

The Black Oystercatcher home farm is on the windy Agulhas plain at Africa's southern tip, and the conservation-minded Human family have had to adapt to the often extreme climate, diverse and distinctive soil types, and location within the Nuwejaars Wetland Special Management Area. Their singular maritime terroir is reflected in a refreshed label design, and an ex-farm-only reserve range. Kajo Malek now assists co-owner/winemaker Dirk Human, and both are aided by a new quality-boosting cold room.

★★★★ Triton Second bottling of **13** has unheralded mocha notes creeping into otherwise delightful shiraz with splashes cab & cab franc. Cracked pepper, red cherry fruit, charming floral & fynbos accents.

★★★★ Blanc Fumé (②) Large-oak-fermented sauvignon, from special site within a top block. **10** intensely aromatic, vanilla/nut highlights, glorious rounded mouthfeel ex lees-ageing.

★★★★ Sauvignon Blanc 14 (★★★☆) a shade off **13**. Less intensity, roundness, but still elegantly formed. Lemony fruit with hints of wild scrub. Alcohol down to 12.5%.

★★★★☆ White Pearl Characterful semillon-sauvignon blend, **13** (★★★★) shows oxidative handling & leesy fatness, with striking wet-wool lanolin notes & herbaceous edge. Shade off previous **11**, but still appealing. **12** untasted.

Also tasted: **Rosé 14 ★★★☆** Not retasted: **Cabernet Sauvignon-Merlot 13 ★★★★** — GdB

Location/WO: Elim ▪ Map: Southern Cape ▪ Est 1998 ▪ 1stB 2003 ▪ Tasting, sales & cellar tours Mon-Fri 9-5 Sat/Sun 10-2.30 ▪ Sauvignon blanc vertical tasting by appt ▪ Closed Good Fri & Dec 24/25 ▪ Restaurant, function & wedding venue: kitchen open Tue-Sun 11-2.30, booking essential (venue@blackoystercatcher.co.za) ▪ Facilities for children ▪ Tour groups ▪ Conferences ▪ Conservation area ▪ Cycling route ▪ Annual Sauvignon Blanc & Oyster Festival (Dec); peak season programme; 1km braai for conservation on Heritage day ▪ Accommodation (stay@blackoystercatcher.co.za) ▪ Owner(s)/cellarmaster(s)/

viticulturist(s) Dirk Human ▪ Winemaker(s) Dirk Human, with Kajo Malek ▪ 1,550ha/18.5ha (cab, merlot, shiraz, sauv, sem) ▪ ±100t/±18,000cs own label 20% red 60% white 20% rosé ▪ BWI, IPW, WIETA ▪ PO Box 199 Bredasdorp 7280 ▪ wine@blackoystercatcher.co.za, orders@blackoystercatcher.co.za ▪ www.blackoystercatcher.co.za ▪ S 34° 37' 58.0" E 019° 49' 39.9" ▪ F +27 (0)86-666-7954 ▪ **T +27 (0)28-482-1618**

☐ **Black Pack** see Painted Wolf Wines

Black Pearl Vineyards ⒬ ⌂ ◉ ♿

Since joining her father Lance on Paarl mountainside farm Rhenosterkop in the mid-1990s, energetic American-born Mary-Lou Nash's nature-friendly approach has imbued not only her winemaking but other projects of interest to visitors: brewing craft beer, growing proteas, husbanding alpacas and Nguni cattle, and opening hiking trails through a tract of endangered renosterveld.

★★★★ **Mourvèdre** (NEW) Interesting combination of flavours (smoke, leather, cherry tobacco & meat) with softer, juicier tannins than expected. Whiffs of violets & grapefruit rind keep excitement going to slightly bitter finish. Promising **14** debut.

★★★★ **The Mischief Maker** ⊘ Like **12** (★★★★☆), **13** adds 15% mourvèdre to shiraz in a swirl of spice, smoke & black cherries. Integrated tannins, plenty of interest through to warmish finish.

★★★★ **Oro** ⊘ Forthright **14** (★★★★☆) steps up on **13** with black fruit, pepper, meatiness plus attractive leafy freshness. Concentrated, full-bodied & ripe blend of cab & shiraz (80/20) skilfully managed through to satisfying conclusion. Coastal WO.

★★★★ **Chenin Blanc** ⊘ Maintaining standards, **15** packs a delightful punch of fruit, given appetising edge by citrus acidity & leesy notes. Older Swartland vines. No **14**. — CM

Location: Paarl ▪ Map: Paarl & Wellington ▪ Map grid reference: D5 ▪ WO: Paarl/Coastal/Swartland ▪ Est 1998 ▪ 1stB 2001 ▪ Tasting, sales & tours just about anytime but phone ahead ▪ Closed Dec 25 ▪ Walks ▪ Lapa & camping facilities ▪ Self-catering cottage ▪ Conservation area ▪ Owner(s) Lance & Mary-Lou Nash ▪ Winemaker(s)/viticulturist(s) Mary-Lou Nash ▪ 240ha/7.2ha (cab, shiraz) ▪ ±5,000cs own label 90% red 10% white ▪ BWI, IPW ▪ PO Box 609 Suider-Paarl 7624 ▪ info@blackpearlwines.com ▪ www.blackpearlwines.com ▪ S 33° 44' 10.5" E 018° 53' 40.8" ▪ F +27 (0)86-617-8507 ▪ **T +27 (0)83-297-9796/+27 (0)83-395-6999**

☐ **Blacksmith** see The Blacksmith
☐ **Black Swan** see Hout Bay Vineyards
☐ **Black Tie** see Wineways Marketing

Blackwater Wine

Having spent eight years at award-winning Waterford, Francois Haasbroek was ready for '100% creative control' to build his own brand, sourcing grapes from under-appreciated blocks of the right varieties planted on the right sites. Among his latest discoveries are an exciting parcel of shiraz in Swartland and carignan in Darling, and he's been able to bring back a white blend after a break. Minimal intervention during winemaking — natural acidity, no additives, restrained use of oak — allows for natural expression of his finds — and time for managing a brand solo. He's particularly pleased to have sorted out distribution in Cape Town, securing listings in top restaurants and leading retailers.

★★★★ **Omerta** Drops variety from name, but partly bunch-fermented **14** (★★★★☆) is Cape carignan at its characterful best. Soulful, with wide array of aromas & flavours, vibrant acidity, endless savoury conclusion. Old oak. Ex Swartland, like **13**.

★★★★ **Cuvee Terra Lux Pinot Noir** 'For those who don't want sweet-fruited pinot' says Francois Haasbroek. Elegant **14** from 3 different Elgin sites. More generous than **13** (★★★★☆), shows red berry & earth tones, silky & attractively — & properly — dry.

★★★★ **Noir** Shiraz, 4% carignan from the Swartland, aged in neutral oak. Unlike **12** which was gentle with enough intensity for food, **13** in youth actually demands an accompaniment; the structure — grape tannin, elevated acidity & balanced 13% alcohol — is taut but thrilling, augurs well for future.

★★★★ **The Underdog Chenin Blanc** (❋) Unoaked **14** from Stellenbosch shows crisp apple, green melon & fresh herbs. Promising, fresh palate relatively lean mid-2014; should gain breadth & complexity with cellar-time it deserves.

★★★★ **Blanc** (NEW) Avante garde oak-fermented **14** from mostly old Swartland bushvine chenin, 15% semillon (ex 2013); former made in 'orange wine' style. White peach, dried herbs & dusty stone aromas give way to anticipated phenolic 'bite', smoothed on finish by the semillon.

Not retasted: **Cultellus Syrah 12** ★★★☆ Discontinued: **Prodigium Pinot Noir**. — JPf

Location: Stellenbosch ▪ WO: Swartland/Elgin/Stellenbosch/Western Cape ▪ Est/1stB 2010 ▪ Closed to public ▪ Owner(s) Blackwater Wines & Vines ▪ Cellarmaster(s)/winemaker(s)/viticulturist(s) Francois Haasbroek (Feb 2010) ▪ (carignan, cinsaut, pinot, shiraz, chenin) ▪ 15t/3,000cs own label 70% red 30% white ▪ 1 Trengrove Avenue Uniepark Stellenbosch 7600 ▪ info@blackwaterwine.com ▪ www.blackwaterwine.com ▪ **T +27 (0)82-329-8849**

Blake Family Wines

With almost 20 years as winemaker in Swartland, Andries Blake knows a thing or two about sourcing prime grapes there, and he and wife Marinda are using that vast knowledge for their boutique range. Blends are the focus for now but varietal bottlings are a possibility.

★★★★ **Amethyst** (❋) Shiraz-led red blend with pinotage, cab, 24 months new French barrels. Rich & deep **11** has black plum/prune ripeness, tobacco & cocoa notes. Amenable tannins, savoury but ripe.

Not retasted: **Tourmaline 13** ★★★★ — CR

Location: Malmesbury ▪ WO: Swartland ▪ Est 2013 ▪ 1stB 2011 ▪ Closed to public ▪ Sales via website ▪ Owner(s) Andries & Marinda Blake ▪ Cellarmaster(s)/winemaker(s) Andries Blake ▪ 5t/1,000cs own label 40% red 60% white ▪ PO Box 1121 Malmesbury 7299 ▪ info@blakefamilywines.com ▪ www.blakefamilywines.com ▪ **T +27 (0)82-922-6162**

BLANKbottle

Pieter Walser, since conceiving this project whose marketing focuses on internet and social media, has been doing just about everything: from sourcing grapes and making the wine to designing the sometimes quirky, always original and aesthetically compelling labels. Now the staff has trebled (to three!), but as production has grown too (with 26 varieties, from 47 vineyard parcels) there's little prospect of Pieter's 100-day harvest, centred on a cellar near Somerset West, involving driving less than his usual 13,000 kilometres. 'I sell stories,' he says, explaining the importance of his labels. But he also sells a lot of wine which has received much local and international praise.

★★★★ **Confessions of a White Glove Chaser** (NEW) From cab, **13** classic cassis & leafiness, opulent fruit intensity from Helderberg vines, old oak just a vessel. Poised & elegant, with long dry finish.

★★★★ **Professor Kukurowitz** Honours 50+ year old Wellington vineyard's founder. Wooded chenin **14** understated, rich & waxy, with subtle apple, lanolin & honey notes. Quietly intense, layered & long.

★★★★ **Epileptic Inspiration 14** semillon from Elgin, fermented in old oak (average 10 years, as for all these). Subtle & delicious greengage, lime & starfruit; so balanced & fresh, 14.5% alcohol unnoticeable.

★★★★ **DOK** Individual & complementary riesling, sauvignon, semillon blend (59/26/15) from Elgin. **14** pithy structure & crisp acidity, fresh herbaceous fruit cossetted by old oak.

★★★★ **Moment of Silence** Silky **14** (★★★☆) now chenin-led blend with chardonny. Demure & delicate, more subtly aromatic than **13**, which had some viognier. Still appealingly drinkable.

Familiemoord (❋) ★★★☆ Grenache, cinsaut, pinot noir blend in **14**. Scrubby red fruits, supple savoury drinkability & some underlying structure. As entertaining as the label & backstory, with a happy end. **Kortpad Kaaptoe** (❋) ★★★★ Unique (?) old-oaked fernão pires from Swartland, named for vineyard on 'shortcut' dirt road to Cape Town. **14** sweet tropical pineapple & rich oiliness balanced by lime flourish, more sprightly than previous. **Aasvoël** (NEW) (❋) ★★★★ Another rare thing: oak-aged verdelho. Rich & rounded but also fresh & satisfying mouthful of green fruits. **14** definitely prettier than its name ('Vulture')! From Stellenbosch.

Col. Mulscal Roos (NEW) ★★★☆ Fruit-forward styling for **13** shiraz, bold, ripe & spicy, perfumed red berries & floral tones. Still bit unsettled but promising lively drinkability over the next few years. **2nd Eulogy** (NEW) ★★★ Youthful, dark & a bit brooding **13** from Bot River tinta, dark fruit & liquorice nuance, firm chalky tannins seek robust fare. **Sigh of Relief** (NEW) ★★★★ Appealing Bordeaux red from Stellenbosch, **14** cab franc, cab, malbec with red berry perfume, mere hint of cab franc's piquancy; dry but pliable tannins, big 15% alcohol totally in balance. **Raw Hope** (NEW) ★★★★ Dense, dark & spicy **13**, unusual & seamless nebbiolo & carignan mix (75/25). Very appealing, not hugely complex but well crafted; surprisingly mild tannins for nebbiolo. **The Original Spaniard** (NEW) ★★★ Grenache, mourvèdre, carignan **13** from Swartland. Wild scrub & dark ripe berries, undemanding pliable tannins, clean dry farewell. Good with spicy tapas. **Another Bomb** (NEW) ★★☆ Amiable **14** sunset-hued semi-dry rosé from grenache, wooded. Plump & rounded, with warm afterglow ex 15% alcohol. Sip (slowly) with savoury canapés or cheeses. **Casting for Chris and Becoming Paul** (NEW) ★★★ Quirky but good expression of old-vine chenin, **14** ripe Golden Delicious apple, dried peach & straw; warm & rich with a red-wine feel, inviting food. WO Darling. Also tasted: **Im Hinterhofkabuff 14** ★★★★ **Nothing to Declare 14** ★★★☆ — MW

Location: Stellenbosch ▪ Map: Helderberg ▪ WO: Western Cape/Swartland/Elgin/Stellenbosch/Bot River/Darling/Wellington ▪ Est 2005 ▪ 1stB 2003 ▪ Tasting & sales Mon-Sat by appt ▪ Sales also via website ▪ Owner(s)/cellarmaster(s)/winemaker(s) Pieter H Walser ▪ Viticulturist(s) Various ▪ 5,000cs own label 50% red 50% white ▪ Lanrust Wine Estate, Winery Road, Somerset West 7129 ▪ pieter@blankbottle.co.za ▪ www.blankbottle.co.za ▪ S 34° 2' 41.1" E 018° 47' 16.0" ▪ F +27 (0)86-503-0974 ▪ **T +27 (0)21-842-2747/+27 (0)82-872-8658**

☐ **Bloem** see Noble Hill Wine Estate

Bloemendal Estate   (ⵏ) (ⵎ) (◎) (⅃)

More than 300 years old, and producing wine for almost a third of those, Durbanville's Bloemendal is undergoing a portfolio makeover under consultant Francois Haasbroek, working with wine man Boetman Langevelt, a decade at the estate this year, and more recent vine man/farm manager Lombard Loubser (like Francois, Waterford seasoned). 'Exciting new winemaking techniques' are being trialled, while vineyard rejuvenation continues and competition successes multiply.

Bloemendal Estate range

★★★★ **Tierberg Syrah** Plenty of potential in youthful **13**. Announced by heady white pepper, lily scents; currently palate tighter, less expressive, though all in balance to allow fruit to blossom with time. Also in 1.5L.

★★★★ **Chardonnay** Poised **14** combines weight & breadth with freshness. A whisper of toasty oak yet to integrate with the limy oatmeal flavours. An uncompromisingly dry finish also needs time to settle.

★★★★☆ **Suider Terras Sauvignon Blanc** Very low yield off windswept terraces, no wonder there's an almost tannic intensity to exceptional **14**. Now 100% oaked, 50% new, seamlessly absorbed in the lemongrass, blackcurrant features, & adding depth. One of best in difficult vintage.

★★★★☆ **Semillon 14** promises to be up with best of this variety. Smart oaking (used 500L French) enhances naturally silky texture & citrus peel, lemongrass concentration, though there is still a sense of tightness, linearity. All suggest lengthy lifespan.

★★★★☆ **Kanonberg** Classic cool-climate example of SA's fine sauvignon/semillon blends. **14** (★★★★★) youthful, well-matched & carefully oaked 65/35 mix. Great purity & intensity in the multi-layered lemongrass, fresh honey, tangerine flavours. Silky texture/bracing freshness will benefit from cellaring, like **13**.

★★★★ **Semillon Noble Late Harvest** (⊗) Barrel-fermented **13** dessert offers dark rye bread, apricot & integrated toasty oak. The nose slightly closed mid-2014, but shows good potential; round, soft & generous palate well balanced.

MCC Brut Nature (NEW) ★★★☆ From chardonnay & 35% Stellenbosch pinot noir. 2 years on lees impart brioche, bruised apple notes & pleasant richness to **12** bone-dry sparkling with brisk bubble.

Waterlily range

★★★★ **Shiraz 13** back on form after slightly bitter **12** (★★★☆). Enticingly fresh, with pure cool-climate spice, red fruits. Enough grip for development, pleasurable drinking over few years.

Merlot ★★★★ Perfectly ripe mouthful juicy plums on **13**. Older oak rounds off edges but finishes snappily clean, dry. Also tasted: **Shiraz Rosé 15** ★★★ **Sauvignon Blanc 15** ★★★★ Not retasted: **Cabernet Sauvignon 13** ★★★☆ **Malbec 13** ★★★☆ **Pinotage 13** ★★★☆ — AL

Location: Durbanville ▪ Map: Durbanville, Philadelphia & Darling ▪ WO: Durbanville/Coastal ▪ Est 1702 ▪ 1stB 1987 ▪ Tasting & sales Mon-Sat 10–5 Sun/pub hols 11–3 ▪ Bon Amis Bistro: weddings, evening functions & conferences ▪ Owner(s) Spirito Trade 82 (Pty) Ltd ▪ Winemaker(s) Boetman Langevelt (2006) & Francois Haasbroek (2012, consultant) ▪ Viticulturist(s) Lombard Loubser (2012) ▪ 135ha (cab, malbec, merlot, ptage, shiraz, chard, sauv, sem) ▪ PO Box 466 Durbanville 7551 ▪ info@bloemendalwines.co.za ▪ www.bloemendalwines.co.za ▪ S 33° 50' 22.1" E 018° 36' 1.4" ▪ **T +27 (0)21-975-9591**

Blomendahl Vineyards ⓠ

Blomendahl Vineyards is run by internationally experienced winemaker and negociant Franz Josef Blomendahl. Through an extensive network, Franz sources grapes across the winelands, including Elgin where he has a brand home open to the public by appointment. Wearing his other hat, he's setting up a Helderberg craft distillery to produce a local version of a traditional herb liqueur he makes in Germany.

Ben Hur range

Reserve ⒩ ★★★☆ From shiraz, **06** unusual lemon blossom fragance, dark berry & sour cherry flavours with tannic bite & dry finish for food. Not retasted: **Shiraz 07** ★★ **Quadrega 06** ★★★

Estate Collection

Basco Cabernet Sauvignon ⓥ ★★ Hints of cedar & sweet berries, **10** soft & fruity. **Basco Merlot** ⓥ ★★☆ **07** fruit sweetness held in firm tannic grip when last we tried. Should be ready now. Not retasted: **Môrewag Pinotage 06** ★★★ **Basco Chardonnay 10** ★★★☆ Not tasted: **Basco Pinotage, Blue Bay Shiraz, Môrewag Rosé, Basco Rosé, Bonny Bay Bushvine Chenin Blanc, Basco Sauvignon Blanc, Môrewag Cabernet Sauvignon, Môrewag Shiraz.**

Prime Bin range

Cabernet Sauvignon-Merlot ⓥ ★★★ Mix cab & merlot in black-fruited **06**, was dense & closely knit, should since have softened. Not tasted: **Lady in Red Rosé.**

Bonolo range

Not tasted: **Cabernet Sauvignon.** — DB

Location: Elgin ▪ Map: Elgin, Walker Bay & Bot River ▪ WO: Elgin/Simonsberg-Paarl/Western Cape ▪ Est 2003 ▪ 1stB 2006 ▪ Tasting by appt ▪ Owner(s) Blomendahl Trust ▪ Cellarmaster(s)/winemaker(s)/viticulturist(s) Franz Josef Blomendahl ▪ 126ha (cab, merlot, ptage, shiraz, chard, chenin) ▪ 480t/70,000cs own label 90% red 10% white ▪ PO Box 52019 Waterfront Cape Town 8002 ▪ franz@blomendahl.de ▪ www.blomendahl.de ▪ S 34° 13' 12.2" E 019° 2' 28.8" ▪ F +27 (0)21-859-1411 ▪ **T +27 (0)21-859-2937/+27 (0)72-692-6229**

Blouvlei Wyne ⓠ ⓖ

The easy-drinking wines in this range are made at Mont du Toit in Wellington, whose employees are shareholders in the business. Red wines from home-farm fruit are the focus; white grapes are brought in.

Blouvlei Selection ★★ Soft & fruity, with hints of vanilla on satisfying **12** from undisclosed varieties. New bottling tasted. Not tasted: **Sauvignon Blanc.** — WB

Location/WO: Wellington ▪ Map: Paarl & Wellington ▪ Map grid reference: G2 ▪ Est/1stB 2003 ▪ Tasting, sales & cellar tours Mon-Fri 9-4.30 Sat by appt ▪ Fee R15 ▪ Closed all pub hols ▪ Picnic area by arrangement ▪ Owner(s) BEE Company ▪ Winemaker(s) Abraham Cloete & Chris Roux ▪ Viticulturist(s) Ludwig Uys (Apr 2013) ▪ ±40ha/28ha (alicante bouschet, cabs s/f, merlot, mourv, p verdot, shiraz, tinta barocca) ▪ ±160t/10,000cs own label 70% red 30% white ▪ IPW ▪ PO Box 704 Wellington 7654 ▪ kelder@montdutoit.co.za ▪ www.montdutoit.co.za ▪ S 33° 39' 31.3" E 019° 2' 2.6" ▪ F +27 (0)21-864-2737 ▪ **T +27 (0)21-873-7745**

☐ **Blue Bay** *see* Blomendahl Vineyards

Blue Crane Vineyards

After buying the Blue Crane home farm near Tulbagh in 2009, Johannesburg mining businessman Fred Crabbia's investment in olive groves, indigenous vegetation and new vines is bearing fruit, with two attractive new wines emerging this edition from Zia Fox's cellar, undergoing refurbishment at press time. Merlot, a feature since debut in the guide a decade ago, has been discontinued and the vines uprooted.

SMV (NEW) ★★★☆ Promising debut **13** shiraz, mourvèdre & viognier, juicy & moreish, with blackcurrants & leather on the nose backed by spice & well-integrated tannins. Elegant & enjoyable. **Chenin Blanc** (NEW) ★★★ **14** carries decent amount of oak (60% new) well, integrating it with tropical fruit, marmalade & honey at finish. Also tasted: **Cabernet Sauvignon 13** ★★★☆ **Shiraz 13** ★★★ **Full Flight 13** ★★★☆ Not tasted: **Sauvignon Blanc**. Discontinued: **Merlot**. — CM

Location/WO: Tulbagh • Est 2001 • 1stB 2004 • Closed to public • Sales via website • Owner(s) Fred & Manuela Crabbia • Cellarmaster(s)/winemaker(s) Zia Fox • Viticulturist(s) Chris Fox • 138ha/9ha (cab, mourv, ptage, pinot, shiraz, chard, chenin, sauv, viog) • 4,000cs own label 75% red 25% white • BWI • PO Box 306 Tulbagh 6820 • info@bluecrane.co.za • www.bluecrane.co.za • F +27 (0)23-230-0825 • T +27 (0)23-230-0823

Blue Owl   (NEW)

The old Riversmeet Farm near Franschhoek, latterly incorporated into the Allée Bleue property, is the source of this new label, vinified at Allée Bleue by Van Zyl du Toit. The brand name alludes to the rich wildlife on sections of the property, in particular the barn-lodging owl that surprised the estate's staff with twin offspring, 'the cutest little creatures you can imagine'.

Merlot ⊘ ★★★☆ Lots of interest on **14**, plums & spice, whiffs of chocolate & iodine. Thoroughly enjoyable wine with a pleasing grippy finish. **Chardonnay** ⊘ ★★★☆ Fresh & zesty unwooded **15** makes confident debut, boasting lively lemon notes, hint of cream & well-managed acidity. Eminently drinkable. — CM

Location: Franschhoek • WO: Coastal • 1stB 2015 • Closed to public • Winemaker(s) Van Zyl du Toit • PO Box 100 Groot Drakenstein 7680 • info@alleebleue.com • www.alleebleue.com • F +27(0) 21-874-1850 • T +27(0) 21-874-1021

☐ **Bob's Your Uncle** *see* Boer & Brit

Boekenhoutskloof Winery   (♀) (♿)

The Franschhoek property was acquired in 1994 by a group of partners led by Tim Rands of wine company Vinimark. It has been much developed since — including conversion to organic — but the really spectacular development has been of Boekenhoutskloof qua brand: its production and reputation have both grown greatly, as have its holdings and interests elsewhere (including Porseleinberg, and The Wolftrap and Porcupine Ridge labels, listed separately). Marc Kent, partner, cellarmaster and inspiration since founding, is now 'morphing into a technical director', he says, with the 2015 advent of Gottfried Mocke (ex Chamonix) to lead the fine winemaking team and bring 'fresh thinking'. Marc seems almost as pleased with his fine new tasting room — tastings only by appointment, if you want to see why.

★★★★☆ **Cabernet Sauvignon** Gentle sheen of fynbos mingles with lavender & cassis/blackcurrant abundance on **13**. Elegant restraint but power in abundance, too, all-new French oak (25 months) lending structure & harmony; silky smooth & superbly long.

★★★★☆ **CWG Auction Reserve Syrah** (NEW) This from Swartland & Stellenbosch, same quality & ageworthiness as sibling. **13** is powerful yet cloaked with velvet; deep, dark, rich plum spice & cedar lightened by white pepper & violet lift. Tensile, sleek & muscular from 27 months in older oak.

★★★★☆ **Syrah** Violet whiffs seduce while the broad, dry & intense palate continues the affair. **13** expressive, nuanced, layered & integrated; dry, fine tannin grip. Swartland fruit joins Wellington, as in **12** (★★★★★). 25 months old oak. Natural ferment, 20% whole bunches. Also in 3L.

★★★★☆ **The Chocolate Block** Insatiable demand for this shiraz blend – 87,000+ cases of **14** (**13** 75,000!) with expressive inky cocoa notes coating deep black fruit; reined in but rounded & voluptuous with plush texture. 16 months oak for 90% of the blend, just 10% new. Also in 1.5 & 3L. WO W Cape.

★★★★☆ **Semillon** Textured, broad & well-defined **13** maintains form of previous. Similarly bunch-pressed with spontaneous ferment in barrel/concrete 'egg' & 12 months on lees. Tealeaf, preserved lemon & creamy biscuit notes; statuesque & long.

★★★★☆ **Noble Late Harvest** Typical botrytis peach/apricot & honey richness on **12** semillon. Gossamer light yet achingly beautiful, sweet & delicate, it finishes dry & clean. Harmoniously elegant with delightful marmalade tang. Oak (new, 30 months) is barely apparent. No **11**. — FM

Location/map: Franschhoek ▪ WO: Franschhoek/Coastal/Western Cape ▪ Est 1994 ▪ 1stB 1996 ▪ Tasting & sales by appt only ▪ Closed all pub hols ▪ Owner(s) Boekenhoutskloof Winery (Pty) Ltd ▪ Cellarmaster(s) Marc Kent (1994) ▪ Winemaker(s) Gottfried Mocke (2015), Jean Smit, Johan Nesenberend & Elsabé Engelbrecht, with Shaun Meyeridricks ▪ Viticulturist(s) Takkies Cloete ▪ 71ha/6.71ha (cabs s/f, merlot, sem) ▪ 60% red 39% white 1% rosé ▪ BDOCA, BRC, HACCP ▪ PO Box 433 Franschhoek 7690 ▪ info@boekenhoutskloof.co.za ▪ www.boekenhoutskloof.co.za ▪ S 33° 56' 33.0" E 019° 6' 28.0" ▪ F +27 (0)21-876-3793 ▪ **T +27 (0)21-876-3320**

Boer & Brit

The cleverly branded wine label of the direct descendants of two major Anglo-Boer War protagonists, 'Boer' Stefan Gerber and 'Brit' Alex Milner, has passed the 5-year milestone and, with Wellington Wines as production partner, 'things are looking rather sustainable'. A new project selecting individual sites around Wellington for vinification is in the works, and 'the most important, we are having fun'. Their Boer & Brit, Trans-Karoo, Suikerbossie Ek Wil Jou Hê and Bob's Your Uncle ranges untasted.

Location: Wellington ▪ Est 2010 ▪ 1stB 2008 ▪ Closed to public ▪ Owner(s) Stefan Gerber & Alexander Milner ▪ Winemaker(s) Stefan Gerber & Alex Milner (both Jul 2010) ▪ 30t own label 60% red 40% white ▪ Other export label: Bob's Your Uncle ▪ PO Box 4 Klapmuts 7625 ▪ alex@boerandbrit.com ▪ www.boerandbrit.com ▪ F +27 (0)86-531-7137 ▪ **T +27 (0)84-643-3600**

☐ **Boland Cellar** see Boland Kelder

Boland Kelder   ⓘ 🍴 📷

Now approaching its 70th anniversary, this substantial grower-owned Paarl winery (supplied by 57 farmers, with 1,900 ha of vines 'in five different climatic regions', they say, continues to show a dynamic will to develop, as well as to produce some ambitious wines. Testament to both is the new One Creation range, the one-off, unique wines blended from the best each season offers, and made in limited quantities by cellarmaster Johan Joubert and his team.

Reserve No. 1 range

★★★★ **Cabernet Sauvignon** ⊘ Solid oak aromas over sweet, juicy fruit on **13** preview. Dense & full, with gentle tannins carrying mulberry & liquorice core to good finish. Improves on last-tasted **11**.

★★★★ **Shiraz** ⊘ Pronounced black pepper nose on **12** gives way to sweet black fruit coupled with spicy Italian meats. Tannins quite dry & grippy, & will benefit from time or food but lots of potential.

★★★★ **Chenin Blanc** Lovely sunny tropical fruit on **14** is elevated by honeyed spices & lees fatness. Barely evident oak rounds off commendable effort. Natural ferment, as for most of these. WO Paarl.

★★★★ **Chenin Blanc Unwooded** (NEW) ⊘ Generously fruited **14**, bolstered by extended lees-ageing, offers eminently satisfying drinking. Broad, deep & rich on the palate, with lingering, focused finish.

Also tasted: **Merlot 12** ★★★★ **Pinotage 12** ★★★★ Note: range previously listed as 'Cellar Reserve'.

One Creation range (NEW)

★★★★ **Red Blend** Auspicious debut for previewed & tentatively rated **14** Cape Blend (pinotage – 50%, shiraz & grenache). Spicy fruit bomb with good underlying structure. Promising.

White Blend ⊕ ★★★☆ Lightly wooded chenin (52%), sauvignon & viognier, **15** barrel sample shows elements of all components in tasty & fresh composition. Good prospects once bottled.

Five Climates Single Varietal range

Chardonnay ★★★ Sweetly honeyed aromas, with satisfyingly ripe fruit on unwooded **15**, step up on previous. Also tasted: **Sauvignon Blanc 15** ★★★ — GdB

Location: Paarl • Map: Paarl & Wellington • Map grid reference: E4 • WO: Coastal/Paarl • Est/1stB 1947 • Tasting & sales Mon-Fri 9–5 Sat/pub hols 9–1 • Closed Easter Fri-Sun, Dec 25/26 & Jan 1 • Cellar tours by appt • Meals/refresments • Owner(s) 57 producing shareholders • Cellarmaster(s) Johan Joubert (2014) • Winemaker(s) Handré Barkhuizen (2009) & Bernard Smuts (2001), with Heidi Dietstein (2009), Carli Oosthuizen (2014) & Lodewyk Botha (2015) • Viticulturist(s) Jaco Engelbrecht (2012) • 1,900ha (cab, merlot, ptage, shiraz, chard, chenin, nouvelle, sauv, viog) • 21,881t/240,000cs own label 48% red 50% white 2% rosé + 330,300cs for clients • Other export brands: Lindenhof, Montestell • WIETA • PO Box 7007 Noorder-Paarl 7623 • info@bolandkelder.co.za • www.bolandkelder.co.za, www.bolandcellar.co.za, www.bolandwines.co.za • S 33° 48' 47.21" E 018° 48' 31.70" (farm), S 33° 41' 19.6" E 018° 57' 20.1" (deli) • F +27 (0)21-862-5379 • **T +27 (0)21-862-6190**

Bon Courage Estate   ⊕ 🍽 🛏 ♿

Three Bruwer generations have been behind the development of this fine Breede River-side property. Nearly a century's work started with Willie planting chenin and muscat in the 1920s. André established the label, earning kudos for sweet wines in the 1960s. The 1990s saw the advent of Jacques, adding to the range with particularly noteworthy shiraz and bottle-fermented bubblies. Vintage 2015's new assistant winemaker and elegant new livery were clearly well deserved.

Inkará range

★★★★ **Cabernet Sauvignon** More weight & extraction in these statement wines. 2 years all-new oak shows in waves of toasty richness on **13**, well absorbed by lush black berries & spice. Bold & crafted New World cab that's not for the faint-hearted.

★★★★ **Shiraz** Prominent coffee-mocha with rich bramble & concentrated black berries as **12**, but **13**'s (★★★☆) fluent, full-bodied, soft-textured palate is warmer, for fireside winter sipping.

Not retasted: **Pinot Noir 10** ★★★

Bon Courage Méthode Cap Classique range

★★★★☆ **Jacques Bruére Cuvée Rosé Brut** Part oaking, 48 months on lees & further 9 months under cork all point to serious intent with this prestige sparkling from 80% pinot noir & chardonnay. **09** (★★★★) shows more of its age in savoury farmyard nuance, with dried oregano & papaya. Not quite as pure & bright as **08** but equally complex & with a delicate, persistent mousse.

★★★★☆ **Cap Classique Jacques Bruére Brut Reserve** ⊕ Like all-chardonnay version, partly oaked, but extra ±36 months in bottle. Notes of sourdough & salted biscuits, mature palate of cured meats, baked limes & mushrooms on pinot/chardonnay **09** (★★★★) bone-dry sparkling. Misses the zingy freshness of **08** (★★★★☆) & **07**.

★★★★ **Cap Classique Jacques Bruére Brut Reserve Blanc de Blancs** ⊕ Excellent sparkling chardonnay, **09** smokiness from barrel fermented/lees aged component, green apple & lemon acidity.

Bon Courage range

★★★★ **Cabernet Sauvignon** ⊘ An honest wine, **13** has good varietal definition showing in earthy, herbal & capsicum notes with ample soft fruit & well-integrated oak in support. Better balanced & polished than **12** (★★★★).

★★★★☆ **Noble Late Harvest** ⊘ Botrytised riesling dessert back on form with fantail of sundried apple, honey, sultana & tangerine; **14** fully sweet & concentrated but with a beaming smile of acidity, which was missing on last **11** (★★★★). Praiseworthy low alcohol (9.9%). Should be in every connoisseur's cellar. 375 ml.

★★★★ **Red Muscadel** Musk candy, grenadine & jasmine on elegant **15** fortified, equal to White Muscadel's quality this vintage; already delicious but even better with time in cellar.

★★★★ White Muscadel Toffee apple, candied kiwifruit & pineapple, litchi & wild melon – it's happening on **15** fortified, as delightful & classy as previous with impressive balance given the full-sweet profile. Best put away for as long as possible.

Shiraz ★★★☆ 13 shows consistency with typical smoke, ripe primary fruit & charry oak. Serious weight & power at price point, a more grown-up vintage with sound structure. Also in magnum. **André's Fame Colombard ★★★** Light citrus & fresh blossoms on crisp **15**, substantial acidity to counter the few grains of sugar. Unsophisticated but pleasant quaffer. **The Gooseberry Bush Sauvignon Blanc ★★★** Was just 'Sauvignon Blanc'. Among drier whites in the range, **15** is crisp & zippy, with tropical fruit woven with dusty cut-grass notes. **Blush Vin Doux ★★** Unassuming **NV** carbonated rosé fizz from red muscadel, irresistibly sweet, nicely lifted by brisk bubbles. **Cape Vintage ★★★** Equal parts tinta, touriga & souzão, bringing slightly more complexity & classic quality to **14** 'port', with youthful spicy dark fruit & substantial tannins. Also tasted: **Pinotage 14 ★★☆ Hillside Red 13 ★★★ Chardonnay Prestige Cuvée 14 ★★★☆ Chardonnay Unwooded 15 ★★ Estate Blend 15 ★★★** Not retasted: **Gewürztraminer Dry 14 ★★☆ Gewürztraminer Special Late Harvest 14 ★★☆**

Like Father Like Son range

Chenin Blanc ★★★ Fresh, juicy & green-fruited **15** is softly dry, seamless & moreish. Also tasted: **Cabernet Sauvignon-Merlot 14 ★★ Pinotage Rosé 14 ★★** — HJ

Location/map/WO: Robertson ▪ Est 1927 ▪ 1stB 1983 ▪ Tasting & sales Mon-Fri 8–5 Sat 9–3 ▪ Fee R20pp for groups of 10+ ▪ Closed Good Fri, Dec 25 & Jan 1 ▪ Café Maude T +27 (0)23-626-6806 ▪ Facilities for children ▪ Olive oil ▪ Owner(s) André & Jacques Bruwer ▪ Winemaker(s) Jacques Bruwer, with Phillip Viljoen (Jan 2015) ▪ Viticulturist(s) André Bruwer ▪ 150ha (cab, pinot, shiraz, chard) ▪ 40% red 50% white 10% rosé ▪ Export brand: Three Rivers ▪ PO Box 589 Robertson 6705 ▪ wine@boncourage.co.za ▪ www.boncourage.co.za ▪ S 33° 50' 43.8" E 019° 57' 38.0" ▪ F +27 (0)23-626-3581 ▪ **T +27 (0)23-626-4178**

☐ **Bonne Esperance** see KWV

Bonnievale Wines   ⓘ ⓒ ⓐ ⓖ

Much of the focus at the grower-owned cellar outside Bonnievale village is on vineyard management, resulting in a portfolio with differing price:quality ratios but the single aim of being 'unpretentious' (the winery's slogan). Chief winemaker Marthinus Rademeyer and his team are delighted with vintage 2015 and, with food-and-wine pairing to spice up cellardoor visits, 'looking forward to an exciting year'.

Barrel Select range

★★★★ Shiraz ⓥ Maintains the standard in **13** smoky leather & dark cherry tones, juicy red berry flavours with finishing flick pepper. Tannin is soft, supportive & sufficient to reward keeping good few years. Also tasted: **Cabernet Sauvignon 13 ★★★☆**

Bonnievale range

Sauvignon Blanc ⓥ ⓣ **★★★☆** Definite step up in **15**, mouthfilling melange of grassy greenpepper & tropical fruit. Fresh & inviting summer fare.

Cabernet Sauvignon-Merlot ★★★ Succulent savoury berry flavours rounded in older oak, **14** ideal pizza or braai accompaniment. **Sauvignon Blanc Brut ★★** NV sparkler with grassy aroma, bouncy mousse & nice acid balance. Real party pleaser. **Natural Sweet Shiraz** ⓝⓔⓦ **★★** Something different, **NV** juxtaposes plum jam aroma with dusty hay nuance & 'sticky' raspberry flavours. For the adventurous sweet tooth. Also tasted: **Merlot 14 ★★☆ Shiraz 13 ★★ Cabernet Sauvignon-Shiraz 14 ★★★** Not retasted: **Chardonnay 14 ★★**

Riggton range

Red ★★ Tasted out of vintage sequence, unwooded **13** light-hued braai partner, soft & (as advertised on the front label) unpretentious. Also tasted: **White 15 ★★ Semi Sweet 14 ★★**

Perlé range

Dawn ★★ Low alcohol (9.5%) slightly sparkling **NV** chenin, fresh grapey flavour & sweet finish. Not retasted: **Dusk NV ★** — DB

Location/WO: Bonnievale ▪ Map: Robertson ▪ Est 1951 ▪ 1stB 1977 ▪ Tasting & sales Mon-Fri 9–5 Sat 10–1 ▪ Closed Easter Fri-Mon, Dec 25/26 & Jan 1 ▪ Cheese straws, biltong/droëwors & food and wine pairing ▪ Facilities for children ▪ Tour groups ▪ Conferences (12 pax) ▪ Christmas Market ▪ Owner(s) 110 members ▪ Winemaker(s) Marthinus Rademeyer (Dec 2009), Edwin Mathambo (Dec 2012) & Jean Aubrey (Jan 2014), with Izak de Vries (2015) ▪ Viticulturist(s) Sakkie Bosman (Nov 2006) ▪ 1,697ha (cab, grenache, malbec, merlot, mourv, ptage, shiraz, chard, chenin, cbard, sauv) ▪ 272,301t ▪ ISO 22 000, IPW, WIETA ▪ PO Box 206 Bonnievale 6730 ▪ info@bonnievalewines.co.za ▪ www.bonnievalewines.co.za ▪ S 33° 57' 27" E 020° 06' 06" ▪ F +27 (0)23-616-2332 ▪ **T +27 (0)23-616-2795**

☐ **Bonny Bay** see Blomendahl Vineyards
☐ **Bonolo** see Blomendahl Vineyards

Bon Terroir

Climate, soil and slopes were all just right for growing winegrapes. So thought the founders of this tiny Stellenbosch farm, who celebrated these conditions in its name. It all seemed propitious for red wine, so cabernet (sauvignon and a little franc) it was – crafted with the eminent Bruwer Raats.

★★★★ **Cabernet Sauvignon** ⊘ Attractive cassis & tomato cocktail notes on **11** (★★★☆), but fruit struggles to cope with firm tannin structure. Last, conducive-vintage **09** riper, more substantial. — JPf

Location/WO: Stellenbosch ▪ Est 2002 ▪ 1stB 2007 ▪ Closed to public ▪ Owner(s) Agri Marketing Exchange (Pty) Ltd, with shareholder Will-Mag Holdings Ltd ▪ Winemaker(s) Bruwer Raats (2007, consultant) ▪ 15.5ha/4ha (cabs s/f) ▪ 5t/600cs own label 100% red ▪ PO Box 12511 Die Boord 7613 ▪ willie@willmag.co.za ▪ www.bonterroir.co.za ▪ F +27 (0)86-622-8254 ▪ **T +27 (0)82-445-3440**

Bonview Wines

Negociant business Bonview was established in 2011 to produce wine and grape juice for export. Owner Teuns Keuzenkamp has long-term contracts with various Cape cellars, and targets mainly West Africa and China with 'quality wines that are affordable and attuned to the tastes of everyday wine consumers'.

Pegalle range
Cabernet Sauvignon ⊘ ★★★ **11**'s creamy oak-seamed plum character is quite serious yet very easy to drink. Not retasted: **Merlot 10** ★★ **Shiraz 11** ★★☆ — HJ, JP

Location: Stellenbosch ▪ WO: Western Cape/Stellenbosch ▪ Est 2011 ▪ 1stB 2012 ▪ Closed to public ▪ Owner(s) Teuns Keuzenkamp ▪ 5,700cs own label 95% red 5% white ▪ PO Box 1977 Somerset West 7129 ▪ bonview@telkomsa.net ▪ F +27 (0)86-224-9348 ▪ **T +27 (0)21-887-5812**

Boplaas Family Vineyards

No misnomer, this close-knit family enterprise has grower Carel Nel 'overseeing' two daughters, Margaux (winemaker) and Rozanne (marketer), on a Calitzdorp farm where grapes have been vinified since the mid-1800s. Originally distilled for brandy (by Carel's great-grandfather), the wines of the modern era have made Boplaas synonymous with world-class 'port'. Carel's skill in utilising the Klein Karoo's semi-arid, Douro-like growing conditions has been emulated by Margaux, with an MSc research paper on touriga nacional table wine and a leader of the local (and Portuguese) trend of using traditional 'port' varieties for table reds, hence the new touriga nacional and touriga francesa in the Family Reserve range.

Heritage Reserve range
★★★★★☆ **White Muscadel** Limited bottling in exceptional years to honour Nel family association with fortified muscadel since mid-1800s. From white muscadel, fragrant orange blossoms on **12** (★★★★★), honeyed & rich; delicious now but will reward lengthy cellaring, as with **11**.

Not retasted: **Red Muscadel 12** ★★★★☆

Family Reserve range
★★★★ **Touriga Francesa** (NEW) From Stellenbosch, scarce grape (4 ha in Cape!), **12** enchants with black fruit pastille flavours, hint of dark chocolate, rounded mouthfeel & fragrant mint finish.

★★★★☆ **Touriga Nacional** (NEW) The 'king of Portuguese grapes' sourced from Stellenbosch, Wellington & Calitzdorp for debut **12**, deliciously dry, with bright dark fruit mingling with exotic spice, firm tannins; deep & long. Will age well.

★★★★ **Gamka** Inky red blend of tourigas francesca & nacional, shiraz & tinta named for major Klein Karoo river. **13** seduces with scents & flavours of wild flower, allspice, plums & cured meats. Calitzdorp & Stellenbosch grapes.

★★★★ **Bobbejaanberg Sauvignon Blanc Reserve 15** from cool Upper Langkloof shows a bonanza of flavours — grapefruit, pineapple, green figs & pears. Freshening acidity already well integrated, supporting creamy lees complexity & lovely depth.

Not retasted: **Ring of Rocks 13** ★★★☆ **Pinot Noir Méthode Cap Classique 09** ★★★☆ Discontinued: **Cabernet Sauvignon**, **Shiraz**, **Cabernet Sauvignon-Shiraz**.

Boplaas range

★★★★☆ **CWG Auction Reserve Daniel's Legacy Cape Portuguese Red Blend** (NEW) **13** from best barrels of tourigas francesca & nacional, shiraz & tinta from Calitzdorp & Stellenbosch; honours Nel patriarch; array of dark fruit, sweet vanilla, licorice & cool leafy flavours. Harmonious, savoury, lipsmacking.

★★★★ **Cape Portuguese White Blend** (Ⓥ) Unusual & interesting **14** blend of 50% verdelho with chardonnay & sauvignon. Peachily fresh, with good balancing acidity & a rich mid-palate.

★★★★ **Straw Wine** (Ⓥ) From vine-dried viognier, unwooded, the **13** tropical fruit bomb is balanced by well-judged acidity & zippy finish.

★★★★☆ **CWG Auction Reserve Ouma Cloete Straw Wine** (NEW) Sun-ripe dry peach, fragrant fynbos & apricot blossom set the scene for a flavour explosion on **13**, from unoaked, air-dried, foot-crushed viognier. Sweet, exotic yet delicate with a dry-seeming, spicy exit.

★★★★ **Hanepoot Reserve** Fortified **14** dessert from 50+ year old vines planted by Danie Nel. 375 ml of liquid temptation, poised & a persistent, bright, orange marmalade finish.

★★★★ **Red Muscadel** (Ⓥ) **13** puts up a spirited attack which, with time, should mellow pleasingly. Raisins, Karoo dust & spicy flick; similar to zesty **12** (★★★☆) tank sample but showing greater weight.

★★★★☆ **Muscadel Reserve** Grapey, with an intense preserved ginger bite, **15** fortified dessert from white muscat de Frontignan is beautifully structured, with crisp acid, silky fruit & spicy sweetness (217 g/l sugar). A Klein Karoo classic in 375 ml.

★★★★☆ **Cape Vintage Reserve Port 12** (★★★★★) shows sleek muscularity in voluptuous mouthful of fruitcake, spicy plum pudding, nutmeg, clove & citrus, the concentrated fruit flavours well tamed by fiery alcohol. Will improve for 20+ years. Touriga, tinta & souzão, year oaked. WO W Cape, as was **11**.

★★★★☆ **Cape Tawny Port** (Ⓥ) NV from tinta, touriga, souzão. Nutty & spicy from long ageing in barrel, wonderfully balanced, shows mere hint of sweetness on the aftertaste.

★★★★ **Cape Vintage** Port-style fortified from touriga (80%), tinta & souzão. Pronounced pot-pourri notes on **13** combine with dark plums, chocolate & spice for a big mouthful. Grippy tannins suggest a good future. WO W Cape.

★★★★ **Cape Ruby** Delicious & well-balanced port-style NV offers delightful everyday drinking, with bright black & red berries, some raisin character & just-warming alcohol. Tinta (70%), touriga & souzão.

★★★★☆ **Cape Tawny Vintners Reserve Bin 1880** Adds '1880' to name. Concentrated nose on latest port-style NV with toffee apples, salted caramel, toasted hazelnuts & a touch of espresso; all layered with raisined fruit, wonderful oak/alcohol integration & unflagging finish. From tinta (85%) & touriga, cask-aged min 10 years. 375 ml.

★★★★★ **Cape Tawny Port** (Ⓥ) A tinta, touriga, souzão mix (90/8/2), **97** exceptionally classy. Rich & sleek, with superb spirit integration (±19%) from 12 years in old barrels.

★★★★ **Chocolate Cape Vintage 11** trumps 10 (★★★☆) port-style from tinta (70%) & touriga with creamy milk chocolate lushness, vivid dark fruit flavours leading to near-dry cocoa finish. WO W Cape.

★★★★☆ **Cape Tawny Reserve** (Ⓥ) Masterly **95** fortified from tinta (90%) & touriga 'made before Calitzdorp even became a WO district' says cellarmaster Carel Nel. 12 years in cask yield complex, intense medley of nuts, toffee, orange marmalade, lingering dry conclusion. 375 ml.

Tinta Barocca ★★★☆ **14** puts a smile on your face with loads of black/red fruit, vanilla sweetness & tarry finish. Bring on the peri-peri chicken! **Stoepsit Sauvignon Blanc** ★★★ **15**'s name celebrates 90th vintage of matriarch Roline Nel, who loves entertaining on her stoep (veranda) with this wine. Light bodied & fruity, radiates bonhomie. **Pinot Noir Brut Sparkling** ★★★ **15** dry bubbly displays true pretty-in-pink character, delicate red berries & lifting acidity to finish. Also tasted: **Pinotage 13** ★★★ **Shiraz 14** ★★★ **Tinta Chocolat 14** ★★★ **Touriga Nacional 14** ★★★ Not retasted: **Cabernet Sauvignon 12** ★★★ **Merlot 12** ★★☆ **Hanepoot 12** ★★★ **Red Muscadel Reserve 11** ★★★ **White Muscadel 13** ★★★ **Cape Pink NV** ★★★ **Cape White Port NV** ★★★ Not tasted: **Red Muscadel Vintners Reserve, Cape Tawny Show Reserve**.

Brandy range

★★★★★ **Potstill 20 Years Reserve** Ⓥ Gold coloured with hint of olive green on rim. Fruitcake, dried apricots, marzipan, sweet prune flavours, mingling with smooth vanilla. Super-complex, elegant & silky palate — both delicate & penetrating — leads to a gorgeous long finish. Just 500 bottles made.

★★★★☆ **Carel Nel 15 Years Reserve** Ⓥ Seductive, rich, with caramel, almonds & hint of smoke. Full bodied & mouthfilling, well integrated alcohol. Complex, strikes fine balance between rich fruit & oak. Less ethereal than 20YO, touch less drily refined.

★★★★☆ **Potstill 8 Years Reserve** Serious, effortlessly elegant 100% potstill (as is 20YO), revisited, shows caramel, sweet & smoky oak, fuller body with chocolate & dried fruit. Silky & complex, still youthful, with clean vanilla finish.

★★★★ **Carel Nel 5 Years Reserve** ⊘ New bottling improves with leafy fresh notes over dried apricot & pear. Fine depth of flavour, delicate & velvety, with a floral dry finish. 40% potstill, as is 15YO. All these from colombard, all unfiltered/fined.

Discontinued: **Potstill 10 Years**. — WB

Location: Calitzdorp ▪ Map: Klein Karoo & Garden Route ▪ WO: Calitzdorp/Western Cape/Stellenbosch/Upper Langkloof/Klein Karoo ▪ Est 1880 ▪ 1stB 1982 ▪ Tasting & sales Mon-Fri 8-5 Sat 9-3 Sun 10-2 ▪ Fee R35pp ▪ Closed Good Fri & Dec 25 ▪ Cellar tours by appt ▪ Facilities for children ▪ Gifts ▪ Farm produce ▪ Walks/hikes ▪ Conservation area ▪ Ring of Rocks ▪ Owner(s) Carel Nel ▪ Cellarmaster(s) Carel Nel (1982) ▪ Winemaker(s) Margaux Nel (Dec 2006) ▪ Viticulturist(s) Henry Kotze ▪ 2,300ha/70ha (cab, ptage, shiraz, tinta, touriga, chard, cbard, sauv) ▪ 55% red 45% white ▪ BWI, IPW ▪ PO Box 156 Calitzdorp 6660 ▪ info@boplaas.co.za ▪ www.boplaas.co.za ▪ S 33° 32' 8.0" E 021° 41' 1.9" (Boplaas), S 34° 4' 45.40" E 022° 8' 25.22" (Boplaas@Sea) ▪ F +27 (0)44-213-3750 ▪ **T +27 (0)44-213-3326**

☐ **Borg Family Wines** see Painted Wolf Wines
☐ **Born & Bred in South Africa** see BABISA — Born & Bred in South Africa

Boschendal Wines   Ⓥ ⑪ ⌂ ◎ Ⓐ ⑤

Established in 1685 by French Huguenot Jean Le Long, Boschendal was, in the 1980s, one of the first winefarms to gain an excellent reputation as a fine-dining destination. Purchased in 2012 by three South African entrepreneurs, the beautiful property at the foot of the Groot Drakenstein mountains has undergone a comprehensive upgrade. The Werf restaurant in the original cellar, with its new adjoining kitchen garden, under the care of well-known chef Christiaan Campbell; and the Olive Press, conference and wedding venues and luxury accommodation in the revamped labourers' cottages, are some of the renovations returning Boschendal to its glory days. 'All this can only benefit our wines,' confirms Jacques Roux, marketing director of DGB, owners of the wine portfolio. Along with the old favourites, the original blanc de noir and range of MCC sparklings, a new premium 10 Year Old brandy is set to be launched.

Cecil John Reserve range

★★★★☆ **Shiraz** Dark-hued, brooding flagship, **13** follows in authoritative style of **12** (★★★★☆); handsomely structured with firm, ripely dry tannins balanced by dense but unheavy texture & a freshness enlivening the waves of black pepper & dried herbs. Judicious oaking (10% new). WO W Cape.

Reserve Collection

★★★★ **Syrah** In less dense, fresher vein, **13** has pretty florals & herb attractions. Still austere & tight with bracing finish; some underlying substance should emerge, though lacks **12**'s (★★★★☆) generosity.

★★★★ **Grande Reserve** Latest **13** from undisclosed varieties, engages with soft black fruits & spice augmented by careful oaking; creamy texture, savoury concentration reined in by still insistent tannins. Worth waiting year/two, should improve for considerably longer. Stellenbosch WO.

★★★★ **Chardonnay** ⓐ **12** (★★★★☆) good lemon fruit intensity, well-judged wooding (third new) though not quite as persistent as **11** (★★★★★), which improved on **09**. **10** untasted.

★★★★ **Sauvignon Blanc 15** announced with focused steely attack. Lovely purity, clean lines, its 'sauvage' edginess balanced by breadth, weight & length of flavour. Has good few years' potential.

★★★★☆ **Grande Cuvée Méthode Cap Classique Brut** ⓐ Classy **09** chardonnay/pinot noir cele-brator has racy bubbles, baked apple & brioche notes, rich flavours buoyed by zesty acidity.

★★★★ **Jean Le Long Méthode Cap Classique** ⓐ Bone-dry & mineral sparkling from chardonnay. Oystershell & biscuit tones, **07** shows little of the creaminess expected from 5 years lees-ageing.

★★★★☆ **Méthode Cap Classique Brut** Drops 'Grande Cuvée' from name, remains **NV** but blend changes to chardonnay (51%) with pinot. Greater finesse, pure delicate citrus zest infused by pinprick creamy bubble & well-tuned dry finish. Worthy of any occasion. WO W Cape.

★★★★☆ **Vin d'Or 13** Noble Late Harvest from 100% riesling excites with gorgeous scented spice elab-orated by botrytis. Luscious flavours, cleansed by a riveting 10 g/l acid, culminate in explosive tangy tail. Just 10.5% alcohol adds to the any-time-of-day drinking pleasure.

Also tasted: **Méthode Cap Classique Brut Rosé NV** ★★★☆

Elgin Series

★★★★ **Pinot Noir 13** more youthfully revealing, characterful, than **12** (★★★★). Dark cherry, hint of undergrowth entice with incipient complexity. Lovely balance of flesh & region's typical freshness to the sweet fruit. Charms now; also 3 to 5 years' potential.

★★★★ **Chardonnay** Masterly expression of Elgin chardonnay, **13** (★★★★☆) combines delicacy with intensity in its nuanced citrus & toast features. Oak (45% new) enhances without imposing on freshness or effortless energy; satisfyingly long farewell. Last made was **11**.

★★★★☆ **Sauvignon Blanc** Cool-climate freshness, delicacy hallmarks of **14** (★★★★), the fruit purity just short of depth, length for higher rating. **12** long, vinous. No **13**.

1685 range

Merlot ★★★ Ripe, juicy plums on **14** backed by zippy freshness, lively grip. WO W Cape. **Shiraz-Cabernet Sauvignon** ★★★☆ Warmingly spicy berry mix; **13** full bodied, rich in flavour with firm but unharsh grip, just begging hearty winter fare. **Chardonnay-Pinot Noir** ★★★ Appealing cherry blos-som scents, flavours on pinky-beige **15** dry rosé. Medium bodied, with refreshing zesty conclusion. Also tasted: **Shiraz 13** ★★★ **S&M 14** ★★★ **Chardonnay 14** ★★★ **Sauvignon Blanc Grand Vin Blanc 15** ★★★☆

Boschendal Classics

Larone ★★★ **14** shiraz (70%) with mourvèdre, rounded in older oak offers hearty spicy, savoury fla-vours in firm but unharsh frame. WO W Cape. **Rachel's Chenin Blanc** ⓥ ★★★★ **15** steps up. Lots of ripe melon appeal, plump & sweetly juicy, finishing cleansing, balanced acidity. **Le Bouquet** ★★☆ Zippy, floral-scented **15** from a bouquet of varieties. Gently sweet & perfectly suited to al fresco dining. Also tasted: **Lanoy 14** ★★ **Blanc de Noir 15** ★★★ **Rose Garden Rosé 15** ★★☆ **Boschen Blanc 15** ★★★

Pavillion range

Pavillion Blanc ★★☆ Ripe fig tones daubed with muscat & fruit-lifting 7 grams sugar, juicy **15** from chenin, sauvignon & hanepoot. Also tasted: **Shiraz-Cabernet Sauvignon 14** ★★★ — AL

Location/map: Franschhoek ▪ WO: Coastal/Western Cape/Elgin/Stellenbosch ▪ Est 1685 ▪ 1stB 1975 ▪ Tasting & sales daily 11-5.30 (Oct-Mar) & 11-4.30 (Apr-Sep) ▪ Fee R35pp ▪ Chocolate & wine pairing R70pp, booking essential ▪ Closed Good Fri & Dec 25 ▪ Cellar tours daily 10.30, 11.30 & 3 ▪ Cheese plat-ters on request ▪ The Werf Restaurant ▪ Weddings & functions ▪ Facilities for children ▪ Tour groups ▪ Gifts ▪ Museum ▪ The Werf Cottages & Orchards Cottages (22 luxury cottages) ▪ Owner(s) DGB (Pty) Ltd ▪ Cellarmaster(s) JC Bekker (1986) ▪ Winemaker(s) Lizelle Gerber (whites, 2006) & Richard Duckitt (reds, 2015), with Lionel Leibrandt (1999) ▪ Viticulturist(s) Stephan Joubert (2006) ▪ 2,240ha/200ha (shiraz, sauv) ▪ 3,100t/500,000cs own label 32% red 43% white 14% rosé 11% sparkling ▪ WIETA ▪ Private Bag X03 Groot Drakenstein 7680 ▪ cellardoor@boschendal.co.za ▪ www.boschendalwines.com ▪ S 33° 52' 27.5" E 018° 58' 34.4" ▪ F +27 (0)21-874-1531 ▪ **T +27 (0)21-870-4200**

☐ **Boschenheuwel** *see* Wine-of-the-Month Club
☐ **Boschetto** *see* Stellekaya Winery

Boschheim   ②

Involved in international and local wine-consulting and -making, polymer scientist and boutique winery owner Andy Roediger vinifies for his own label whenever time allows. It's an ever-evolving range, the Stellenbosch-based Cape Wine Master having excellent grape contacts throughout the winelands.

Boschheim range

Mourvèdre ② ★★★☆ Perfumed **13** has bold & expressive pastille fruit intensity, firm savoury finish, good balance & oak integration. From Paarl vines. Not retasted: **Cabernet Sauvignon 09** ★★★☆
Pinot Noir 13 ★★★☆ **Elemental Shiraz 13** ★★★☆ **Ella Marie 11** ★★★☆

Muse range

Calliope ② ★★★☆ **11** almost equal portions cab & shiraz; has earthy elegance, delicate frame. Not retasted: **Cabernet Sauvignon 12** ★★★ — HJ

Location/map: Stellenbosch ▪ Map grid reference: E5 ▪ WO: Stellenbosch/Paarl/Western Cape ▪ 1stB 2003 ▪ Tasting & sales by appt ▪ Owner(s)/winemaker(s) Andy Roediger ▪ 1,800cs own label 85% red 15% white ▪ PO Box 3202 Matieland 7602 ▪ andy@roedigeragencies.co.za ▪ S 33° 55' 54.9" E 018° 50' 10.5" ▪ F +27 (0)21-886-4731 ▪ **T +27 (0)21-887-0010**

Boschkloof Wines   ② ⑪ ⊜

While offering a variety of wines, owner/cellarmaster Jacques Borman and winemaker son Reenen's true passion is shiraz, for which they are justifiably acclaimed. Their boutique Stellenbosch winery has released a single-block shiraz and future plans include more vineyard projects plus other Rhône varieties, some of which are already in barrel. 'Expect small batches of limited-release wines.' Their fans will be thrilled (and doubtless interested to read about Reenen's new Patatsfontein venture – see entry).

★★★★ **Cabernet Sauvignon** From 30+ year old vineyards. A cab template, **13** improves on **11** (★★★★☆) by offering cassis & cedar, a hint of mint chocolate, but the main attraction is the polished tannins, a hidden power. **12** sold out untasted.

★★★★☆ **Epilogue** ⑲ Flagship from a syrah/shiraz block in the Stellenbosch Hills. **13**'s 18 months French oak accounts for the cedar, spice array, & terroir for the Rhône-style character, wild berries, scrub, pepper. Succulent, streamlined, showcases the cellar's expertise with the grape.

★★★★☆ **Syrah** Combining Old World complexity with New World opulence, **13** has hedgerow berries, dark-toned spicing & black pepper, supported by a smoothly curvaceous body. Fine-grained tannins rein in any excess, provide for the future.

★★★★ **Conclusion** Cab-led 5-part Bordeaux-style blend, so expect structure, especially with 2 years French oak, 70% new. But it's the arresting fruit purity, vital & fleshy, that takes **13** (★★★★☆) to a higher level than **11**. Sleek, compact, with latent power, great length. **12** untasted.

Chardonnay ★★★ Portion unoaked to give freshness, fruit focus, rest 10 months in barrel, & **14** succeeds admirably. Citrus & melon, crisply elegant, a gentle savoury tail. Also tasted: **Merlot 12** ★★★★
Cabernet Sauvignon-Merlot 13 ★★★★ **Sauvignon Blanc 15** ★★★ — CR

Location/map: Stellenbosch ▪ Map grid reference: C6 ▪ WO: Stellenbosch/Western Cape ▪ Est/1stB 1996 ▪ Tasting, sales & cellar tours Mon-Fri 9-5 Sat 10-3 ▪ Fee R30 ▪ Closed Easter Fri-Sun, Dec 25 & Jan 1 ▪ Cheese & charcuterie platters ▪ BYO picnic ▪ Owner(s)/cellarmaster(s) Jacques Borman ▪ Winemaker(s) Reenen Borman (Jun 2010) ▪ Viticulturist(s) Jacques Borman, with Reenen Borman ▪ 30ha/19ha (cabs s/f, merlot, shiraz, chard) ▪ ±100-150t/6-8,000cs own label 90% red 10% white ▪ PO Box 1340 Stellenbosch 7599 ▪ boschkloof@adept.co.za, info@boschkloofwines.com ▪ www.boschkloofwines.com ▪ S 33° 57' 37.0" E 018° 46' 11.8" ▪ F +27 (0)21-881-3032 ▪ **T +27 (0)21-881-3293 (office)/+27 (0)21-881-3268 (cellar)**

Boschrivier Wines: NJT Boerdery

Paediatrician Theo de Villiers followed a dream, and expert advice, when converting inherited Overberg farmland, under wheat and onions in his great-grandfather's time, to vineyard in the 1990s. Initially supplying fruit to leading Walker Bay wineries, his vines and wines, supplemented by bought-in grapes, are co-tended by Mike Dobrovic (founder vintner of Mulderbosch, now widely consulting).

Shiraz ★★★ 13 sundried tomato, salami & paprika nuances, & very little of the rich fruit of **11** (★★★★). Warm, somewhat unfocused finish. **Sauvignon Blanc ★★★** Summer sipper **15** retains few grams of sugar to balance zippy acidity & clean, charming citrus character. WO Cape South Coast. Also tasted: **Cabernet Sauvignon 13 ★★☆** — HJ

Location: Stanford ▪ Map: Elgin, Walker Bay & Bot River ▪ WO: Overberg/Cape South Coast ▪ Est 1998 ▪ 1stB 2002 ▪ Tasting & sales Mon-Fri 8-5 Sat 9-5 ▪ Closed Dec 25 ▪ Restaurant ▪ BYO picnic ▪ Gift shop ▪ Farm produce ▪ Conferences (20 pax) ▪ Walking/hiking & 4x4 trails ▪ Self-catering farm house ▪ Owner(s)/viticulturist(s) Theodore de Villiers ▪ Winemaker(s) Mike Dobrovic ▪ 14ha (cab, shiraz) ▪ 7t/ha ±1,950cs own label 68.5% red 21% white 10.5% rosé ▪ Remhoogte Caledon p/a 70 Fairbairn Street Worcester 6850 ▪ drnjtdevilliers@mweb.co.za ▪ www.boschrivierwines.co.za ▪ S 34° 23′ 19.4″ E 019° 37′ 51.0″ ▪ F +27 (0)23-342-2215 ▪ **T +27 (0)23-347-3313/2 ext 3; +27 (0)76-736-0351**

Bosman Family Vineyards

Finishing first in the International Wine Challenge's Fairtrade Award and second in Drinks Business' Best Ethical Company of the Year were major validations for Wellington's Bosman family, whose concern for social and environmental sustainability is deep and enduring — 260 full-time staff have been sharehold-ers since 2008 (and the new name of the agri-business, Bosman Adama, recognises the forebear of many of the employee families). The Fairtrade wines (listed separately under De Bos Handpicked Vine-yards) and BFV bottlings are vinified by consultant winemaker Corlea Fourie, and include a de rigueur 'orange wine' and a rosé from all 47 varieties planted on the various home farms.

Unique Innovation range

★★★★ Adama Red ⑨ Rich & spicy shiraz-led sextet of Rhône varieties with dash zinfandel/primitivo in **13**. Generous in flavour but not overly dense or heavy; nicely rounded, dry finish. **11**, **12** untasted.

★★★★ Adama White Mostly chenin, with important input from chardonnay, grenache blanc & 4 oth-ers. **14** harmonious, understated, yet has nuance, energy & weight to benefit from cellaring. **13** not tasted.

Bosman Family Vineyards range

★★★★☆ Family Cuvée Erfenis 12 (★★★★) similar pinotage-led blend as **11**, not quite in same class. Presently bit earthy, sullen, with a bitter note. Hints of fresh sweet fruit may unfold in medium term. Discontinued: **30 Rosé**.

Fides range

★★★★ Fides Example of trendy 'orange wine' (skin fermented, 3 weeks) from equally fashionable gre-nache blanc, though **14** shows more orange (citrus) on nose than in colour. Good spicy impact but less weight than **13**. Savoury, firmly dry; best with food.

Special Vineyard Selection

★★★★ Cabernet Sauvignon Classic, elegant **08** improves on **07** (★★★★). Strong ruby hue, subtle maturing cassis, cigarbox features. Balanced freshness & well-integrated tannins. Holding well; good for further year/2.

★★★★ Pinotage 13 (★★★★) presently more oak dominated (100% new, some American) than **12**. Fresh, light texture & underlying pretty cherry, raspberry flavours may benefit from short-term ageing.

★★★★☆ Optenhorst Chenin Blanc From single vineyard planted in 1952, natural ferment in oak, 20% new. Each vintage tells its story, which in characterful **13** includes tiny portion botrytis, imparting tangy dryness & endless honeyed concentration. Soundly firm, fresh; maybe longer lived than **12**.

★★★★ Méthode Cap Classique Steen ⑳ **12** bubbly proves chenin blanc's versatility. Delicate yet full of vivacious sparkle & gentle creamy undertones. Nine months in older oak provides extra interest to this charmer.

Occasional release: **Dolce Primitivo**. — AL

Location: Wellington ▪ Map: Paarl & Wellington ▪ Map grid reference: G1 ▪ WO: Wellington/Western
Cape ▪ Est 1699 ▪ 1stB 2004 ▪ Tasting & cellar tours by appt ▪ Tasting fee R50pp, waived on purchase ▪
Sales Mon-Thu 8-5 Fri 8-4.30 Sat 10-3 ▪ Closed Sun, Easter Fri-Mon & Dec 25 ▪ Conservation area ▪
Bosman Release Celebration (Nov) ▪ Owner(s) Bosman family & Adama Workers Trust ▪ Cellarmaster(s)
Corlea Fourie (Nov 2006), with assistant winemaker Natasha Williams (Nov 2014) ▪ Viticulturist(s) Johan
Viljoen (Mar 2014) ▪ 300ha (47 varieties r/w) ▪ 3,000t/20,000cs own label 70% red 25% white 5% rosé
▪ Brands for clients: Sainsbury Supermarkets; The Cooperative ▪ BBBEE certificate (level 2), BWI, Fairtrade
▪ PO Box 9 Wellington 7654 ▪ taste@bosmanwines.com ▪ www.bosmanwines.com ▪ S 33° 37' 34.7"
E019° 01' 28.9" ▪ F +27 (0)21-873-2517 ▪ **T +27 (0)21-873-3170**

☐ **Bosman's Hill** see Saxenburg Wine Farm

Botanica Wines   ⓣ ⓜ ⓗ ⓒ

Ginny Povall made a huge leap of faith in 2008, exchanging her corporate consulting career in New York
for a run-down indigenous flower farm in Devon Valley, into which she sank her hopes and savings.
Here, emboldened by a few short winemaking courses, some harvests worked in local wineries and her
amazing resourcefulness, she has worked miracles. Young vines have sprung up on the steeply sloping
site (currently supplying the Big Flower range), the luxury guest house has been revived and her mainly
export markets are eagerly awaiting their next consignments. An arboretum, to serve as a novel tasting
room, is scheduled to become reality soon, and, fortune willing, a cellar of her own in the near future.

Mary Delany Collection

★★★★★ **Chenin Blanc** Seductive **14** as complex & enigmatic as previous. Grapefruit & citrus rind,
honeyed richness tempered by leesy minerality, spiced by careful partial oaking (none new). Silk textured
& generous, follows profoundly expressive **13** (★★★★★). Citrusdal Mountain grapes.

★★★★☆ **Chenin Blanc 'Untitled No 1'** ⓝ Tiny, exceptional batch of Citrusdal Mountain fruit
vinified separately, maiden **14** bursts with spicy baked apple fruit cosseted by plush lees-rich texture. Deliciously complex & individual interpretation of barrel-fermented, full-bodied chenin. 20% new oak.

Not tasted: **Pinot Noir**.

Big Flower range

★★★★ **Cabernet Sauvignon** Inky, opulent **14** (★★★★) perhaps over-extracted, lacks finesse of **13**.
Intense & chunky, with chalky tannins which may soften over time.

★★★★ **Arboretum** ⓝ Cab-led, 4-way Bordeaux-style blend is focused & concentrated, achieves
better balance than single-component siblings. **14** liquorice core with black fruit & ripe, soft tannins.

Cabernet Franc ⓝ ★★★★ Leafy, medicinal whiff on **14** follows to sweet-fruited, pencil lead-tinged
palate, with powdery tannins. Very tight; needs year/two to soften & meld. **Petit Verdot** ⓝ ★★★★
Joins fast-expanding number of varietal bottlings with **14**, even inkier than Cab, showing meaty, soupy
savouriness & dense tannins. Also tasted: **Merlot 14** ★★★★ **Rosé 15** ★★★★ — GdB

Location/map: Stellenbosch ▪ Map grid reference: D4 ▪ WO: Stellenbosch/Citrusdal Mountain/Western
Cape ▪ Est/1stB 2008 ▪ Tasting by appt ▪ Wine sales Mon-Fri 8-5 ▪ Farm produce ▪ Conferences ▪ Walks/
hikes ▪ Mountain biking trail ▪ Refreshments offered at Sugarbird Manor guest house ▪ Owner(s) Virginia
C Povall ▪ Winemaker(s) Virginia Povall (Jan 2008) ▪ Viticulturist(s) Francois Viljoen ▪ 21.6ha/5ha (cabs
s/f, merlot, p verdot, pinot) ▪ PO Box 12523 Die Boord 7613 ▪ ginny@botanicawines.com ▪
www.botanicawines.com ▪ S 33° 54' 18.5" E 018° 49' 25.4" ▪ **T +27 (0)76-340-8296**

Botha Wine Cellar   ⓣ ⓐ ⓒ ⓓ

Passers-by on the R43 between Worcester and Tulbagh would have seen the wrecker's ball demolish
two stores over the past year. A gleaming array of large-volume stainless steel tanks then arose at this
Breedekloof bulk wine specialist. The revamp didn't stop there: a reserve range was added to the bottled-wine line-up, website upgraded and new labels unveiled.

Reserve range ⓝ

Cabernet Sauvignon Reserve ★★★☆ **13** bold, juicy cassis notes cosseted by velvety texture & judicious tannic grip partly from 20 months oak age, 75% new. **Merlot Reserve** ★★★☆ Integration &

balance characterise **13**. Dark choc fruit nuances matched by wood spice & grip. Like cab, 75% new barrels but aged 18 months. **Barrel Fermented Chardonnay ★★★** Ripe peach & pineapple flavours face off against big oaky notes on **13**. **Bush Vine Barrel Fermented Chenin Blanc ★★★** Toasty wood (60% new French) masks stonefruit ripeness of **14**.

Dassie's Reserve range

Dassie's Rood ⊘ ⊛ **★★★** Cinsaut (50%) drives soft, cheery light-berried **13** blend with cab & ruby cab. Ideal braai companion also in 3L.

Also tasted: **Dassie's Blanc 15 ★★★** Not retasted: **Dassie's Rosé 13 ★★**

Botha range

★★★★ Hanepoot Jerepigo ⊘ Heady muscat honeysuckle ripeness & sweet ginger on **13** fortified dessert. Lovely balance & palate weight, light on its feet, with long tail.

Pinotage ★★★ 13 is supple, squishy & approachable, with ample ripe red fruit, spicy tail. **Chenin Blanc ★★★** Lively zip to green apricot tang on **15**, partly native yeast fermented. Clean, light & dry finish. **Sauvignon Blanc ★★★ 15** offers grapefruit zest on light-bodied palate. Summertime sipper. Also tasted: **Merlot 14 ★★★ Shiraz 13 ★★★** Not retasted: **Cabernet Sauvignon 09 ★★★ Chardonnay Brut NV ★★★ Cape Vintage Reserve 10 ★★★** Not tasted: **Light White, Red Jerepigo.** — FM

Location: Worcester ▪ Map/WO: Breedekloof ▪ Est 1949 ▪ 1stB 1974 ▪ Tasting & sales Mon-Fri 9–5 Sat 10–1 ▪ Closed Easter Fri-Sun, Dec 25/26 & Jan 1 ▪ Cellar tours by appt ▪ BYO picnic ▪ Conservation area ▪ Breedekloof Soetes & Soup festival ▪ Owner(s) Botha Wynkelder (Edms) Bpk ▪ Production manager Johan Linde (Nov 1996) ▪ Cellarmaster(s) Gerrit van Zyl (Nov 2007) ▪ Winemaker(s) Michiel Visser (Nov 1999) & Annamarie van Niekerk (Dec 2008), with Werner Swiegers (Aug 2013) ▪ Viticulturist(s) Jan-Carel Coetzee (Nov 2010) ▪ 1,969ha (cab, merlot, ptage, shiraz, chard, chenin, cbard) ▪ 38,199t/15,000cs own label 61% red 25% white 14% fortified ▪ ISO 22000:2009 ▪ BWI, IPW, WIETA ▪ PO Box 30 PK Botha 6857 ▪ admin@bothakelder.co.za ▪ www.bothakelder.co.za ▪ S 33° 34' 1.5" E 019° 15' 27.5" ▪ F +27 (0)23-355-1615 ▪ **T +27 (0)23-355-1740**

☐ **Bottega Family Wines** *see* Idiom Collection

Bottelary Winery ⓠ

A budget brand by Perdeberg Winery, from mostly dryland bushvines in the Coastal region.

Chenin Blanc ★★★ Back-to-form **15** is crisp & zippy, with a citrus grip. **Soft Smooth Red ★★ 13** soft & smooth, as per the label, with sweet berry flavours from mainly shiraz & cinsaut. Also tasted: **Rosé NV ★★ Semi-Sweet 14 ★★** Not retasted: **Merlot 13 ★★** — WB

Bouchard Finlayson

Vintage 2015 marked a quarter century of production for Bouchard Finlayson, named for viticulturist/cellarmaster Peter Finlayson and Burgundian Paul Bouchard, who started the Hemel-en-Aarde wine venture in 1989. Add another decade, and you have the time spent by Peter championing his beloved pinot noir since helping pioneer it here while at nearby Hamilton Russell. Citing the variety as ever the 'iconic challenge' (often equalled in excellence by their chardonnay), he finds 'obvious magic' in another, newer local speciality: the Piedmontese grape nebbiolo. Calling it a cornerstone component of the Hannibal red blend, he reports that new plantings have offered increased quantities since 2013. The vineyards, owned since 2000 by the Tollman family, are now planted to their arable maximum of 22 ha.

★★★★☆ Galpin Peak Pinot Noir Trademark sour cherry, dark fruit & spice stamp fabulous **13** (★★★★★), yards pacier than earthy **12** (★★★★), which shared a bright core with **11**. Latest vintage is svelte, with savoury components seamlessly spun into textured whole with echoing finish. A brilliant 'New World' rendition of the classic. Also in larger bottle formats, as for Hannibal.

★★★★☆ Tête de Cuvée Galpin Peak Pinot Noir Barrel selection with more new oak (87%) than sibling, the best of the best vintages. **12** gets extra year in bottle; bold, with nutty mushroom depth, yet retains supple polish of the variety at its best. No **11**.

★★★★☆ **Hannibal** Sangiovese-led 6-part marriage of Italian & French varieties, none Bordeaux. **13** back towards form of **11** (★★★★★) after über ripe **12** (★★★★); wild berries lie brooding in a fine tannin lattice, showing class, complexity & balance. Walker Bay vineyards.

★★★★☆ **Kaaimansgat Crocodile's Lair Chardonnay** One of Cape's revered chard sites, in Elandskloof, delivering powerful minerality & crystalline fruit purity; here well supported by judicious oak (just 70% wooded, 12% new). **14** fresh & elegant as usual, with trademark refinement. WO Overberg.

★★★★☆ **Kaaimansgat Limited Edition Chardonnay 14** bounces back to form after tiring **11** (★★★★). Rich & alluring, tighter than Elandskloof vineyard sibling above, will reward patience. Only 50% wooded, 100% new five months. Agreeable 12.4% alcohol. No **13** or **12**.

★★★★ **Missionvale Chardonnay** Butterscotch notes over iodine, soy & nut interest from home vineyard; **13** (★★★★★) advances the breeding with layered complexity, finely structured earthy core & dry tail. Eight months in oak (22% new) then 16 months in bottle. Impresses more than **12**.

★★★★ **Sauvignon Blanc** Cool-origin expression with lime & kiwi, crisp acidity & chalky dryness in **15**. Wonderful juxtaposition of generous flavour & lean weight, good for either solo sipping or with fine food.

★★★★ **Sauvignon Blanc Reserve** Block selection only in best years & 14% semillon distinguish **15** from sibling; gunflint & deep minerality accompany gooseberry tones in flinty finish. No **14** or **13**.

★★★★ **Blanc de Mer** Idiosyncratic, delicious mix riesling & viognier with splashes of chardonnay & chenin, unwooded. **14** loaded with juicy white peach & apricot, appley zing. WO Cape South Coast.

Also tasted: **Sans Barrique Chardonnay 14** ★★★★ — DS

Location: Hermanus ▪ Map: Elgin, Walker Bay & Bot River ▪ WO: Hemel-en-Aarde Valley/Overberg/Cape South Coast/Walker Bay ▪ Est 1989 ▪ 1stB 1991 ▪ Tasting, sales & cellar tours Mon-Fri 9–5 Sat 10–1 ▪ Fee R40pp for groups of 6+ ▪ Closed all pub hols ▪ Cheese & salami platters ▪ Gift shop ▪ BYO picnic ▪ Conservation area ▪ Nature walks by appt (guided & self-guided) ▪ Owner(s) The Tollman Family Trust ▪ Cellarmaster(s)/viticulturist(s) Peter Finlayson (1989) ▪ Winemaker(s) Peter Finlayson (1989), with Chris Albrecht (Nov 2010) ▪ 125ha/22ha (barbera, nebbiolo, pinot, sangio, chard, sauv) ▪ 280t/35,000cs own label 30% red 70% white ▪ BWI, IPW ▪ PO Box 303 Hermanus 7200 ▪ info@bouchardfinlayson.co.za ▪ www.bouchardfinlayson.co.za ▪ S 34° 22′ 54.0″ E 019° 14′ 30.9″ ▪ F +27 (0)28-312-2317 ▪ **T +27 (0)28-312-3515**

Boucheron Wines

Based in Gauteng, Boucheron has grown from a boutique-wine merchant founded by Fredy Pummer in 1996 to a full-fledged producer of close to 5,000 cases of own-label wines, including a white merlot, something rare in SA and made in a bone-dry, sushi-friendly style by cellarmaster Nicholas Ridley.

Location: Randburg/Kya Sand ▪ Est 1996 ▪ 1stB 2012 ▪ Closed to public ▪ Owner(s) Fredy Pummer ▪ Cellarmaster(s) Nicholas Ridley (Sep 2011) ▪ 4,932cs ▪ PO Box 870 Strathavon 2031 ▪ info@boucheron.co.za ▪ www.boucheron.co.za ▪ F +27 (0)11-708-3615 ▪ **T +27 (0)11-708-3444**

Boutinot South Africa   ⑨

The recently established local arm of a UK-based company of grape growers, winemakers, importers and agents worldwide uses rented cellar space to vinify small parcels of wine from grapes supplied by contracted growers (Boutinot has done business in SA for over 20 years). Manager/winemaker Marinda Kruger-Van Eck is seeking 'a suitable home' for a dedicated boutique cellar.

Mon Vieux range

★★★★ **Hell's Height Sauvignon Blanc** Crisp, ultra-fruity **14** is impressive, showy. Natural ferment & portion new oak impart richness, breadth to tropicality. Bold 14.5% alcohol adds to impression of sweetness. Stellenbosch fruit.

★★★★ **Acquifer Semillon** Delightfully rich & earthy **14** from Swartland grapes naturally fermented in small portion new oak, imparting perfect structure, breadth to pithy lemon & lime flavours.

Tea Leaf range 🆕

★★★★ **Chenin Blanc** Named for rooibos next to vines in high-altitude Piekenierskloof. Well-made **14** rich, crisp, abundantly fruity, with texture from half barrel-fermented portion & persistent mineral length.

Wandering Beeste range (NEW)
Syrah ★★★★ Effortlessly juicy, spicy, savoury **14** Swartlander has attractive simplicity & delightful personality. Year in older barrels astutely judged, leaving fresh fruit to shine.

Tiger Horse range
Shiraz-Mourvèdre-Viognier ⊘ ★★★ Was 'Shiraz-Mourvèdre'. Popular mocha appeal in easy-drinking, spicy **14**. Juicy, though nicely dry & savoury. Also tasted: **Chenin Blanc-Pinot Grigio 15** ★★★

Cape Heights range (NEW)
Chenin Blanc From Perdeberg vines, preview naturally fermented **15** too unsettled to rate.

Kindred range (NEW)
Cinsaut ★★★ Light-footed **13** from naturally fermented, lightly oaked Helderberg fruit, offers pure red fruit & fresh acidity. **Chenin Blanc** ★★★ Tropical pineapple **13** boldly flavoured & subtly oaked to ensure agreeable, uncomplicated enjoyment. Helderberg vines.

Percheron range (NEW)
Cinsaut ⊘ ★★★ Spicily sweet, light & supple **14** has plenty sweet red fruit flavours & serious edge to gently tannic tug. **Chenin Blanc-Viognier** ⊘ ★★★ Aromatic yellow peach on **15** preview ex Swartland, flavourful & fruity for everyday enjoyment.

Prime Cuts range (NEW)
Red ★★★ Spicily savoury **14** shiraz-led blend with pinotage, 2 others, easygoing, unpretentious drinking. **White** ★★★ Flavourful **15** preview ex Swartland chenin makes lively, crisply fresh summer sipper.

Windfall range (NEW)
Merlot ★★★★ Intriguing plum, cherry aromas in **13** from Elgin grapes, made in serious style with mostly new oak a little bold for delicate fruit. **Sauvignon Blanc** ★★★★ Earthy minerality in herbaceous preview **15** from lees-enriched Elgin fruit. Wild ferment adds interest. — IM

Location/map: Stellenbosch ▪ Map grid reference: H4 ▪ WO: Western Cape/Stellenbosch/Swartland/Elgin/Piekenierskloof ▪ Est/1stB 2011 ▪ Tasting, sales & cellar tours by appt ▪ Closed all pub hols ▪ Owner(s) Dennis Whitely & Michael Moriaty ▪ Cellarmaster(s)/winemaker(s) Marinda Kruger-Van Eck (May 2010) ▪ 80t/7,000cs own label 35% red 63% white 2% rosé + 7m L bulk ▪ Brands for clients: Cape Heights, Percheron, Tiger Horse ▪ marindak@boutinot.com ▪ www.boutinot.com ▪ S 33° 54' 41.7" E 018° 56' 32.0" ▪ F +27 (0)86-293-4577 ▪ **T +27 (0)82-357-2697**

☐ **Bovlei** *see* Wellington Wines
☐ **Bradgate** *see* Jordan Wine Estate
☐ **Brahms** *see* Domaine Brahms Wineries

Bramon Wines

Raised on a winefarm in inland Worcester, Peter Thorpe had an inborn passion for wine and working the land. With wife Caroline and children Bram and Manon (who gave their names to the venture), he pioneered vineyards near Plettenberg Bay on the Garden Route in the early 2000s. Today their boutique winery continues the initial focus on MCC sparkling, plus others, and there are 18 growers in the area.

Bramon range
★★★★☆ **Sauvignon Blanc MCC** ⓢ Bubbly with hallmark mineral complexity, seabreeze tang & effortless elegance. **10** (★★★★) showing honey, icing sugar, green apple complexity. Sweeter impression, less focus than **08**. **09** sold out untasted.

Not retasted: **Chardonnay MCC 12** ★★★★☆

The Crags range
★★★★ **Anton's Barrel** ⓢ Three Italians & a Frenchman (barbera, sangiovese, nebbiolo & cab) in savoury & bright **12**, interesting glassful from Fairview grapes, for now or few years.

★★★★ **Rosé** ⓢ Tank sample **14** intensely fruity, racy mix pinot noir (67%), shiraz. Emphatically dry but packed with flavour, lower 11% alcohol a bonus. For food & fans of a more serious style of pink.

★★★★ Sauvignon Blanc ⓦ Revisited **13** (★★★★★) shows cool-climate origin in 'wet pebble' minerality & green fig aromas, slight creaminess & tempered acidity courtesy year in bottle. Restrained & understated. Like **12**, needed time to unfurl its charms.

Not retasted: **Anton's Selection 13** ★★★★ — CvZ

Location: Plettenberg Bay ▪ Map: Klein Karoo & Garden Route ▪ WO: Plettenberg Bay/Coastal ▪ Est 2000 ▪ 1stB 2004 ▪ Tasting & sales daily 9-5.30 ▪ Fee R5/tasting glass, waived on wine purchase ▪ Closed Dec 25 ▪ Cellar tours by appt ▪ Restaurant ▪ Facilities for children ▪ Southern Crags Conservancy ▪ Owner(s) Private company ▪ Cellarmaster(s)/winemaker(s) Anton Smal (Feb 2010) ▪ Viticulturist(s) Peter Thorpe (2000) ▪ 10ha/6ha (chard, sauv) ▪ 50t/6,400cs own label 100% white ▪ PO Box 1606 Plettenberg Bay 6602 ▪ accounts@bramonwines.co.za ▪ www.bramonwines.co.za ▪ S 33° 57' 20.30" E 023° 28' 45.02" ▪ F +27 (0)86-589-6816 ▪ **T +27 (0)44-534-8007**

Brampton ⓦ ⓨ

Starting life in the Rustenberg cellars, and named for Brampton the champion Jersey bull, these upfront, fruit-driven 'lifestyle' wines are now made by Richard Duckitt (ex another DGB brand, Franschhoek Cellars), and can be tasted in Stellenbosch at the trendy brand home, Brampton Wine Studios, as well as a bespoke room in the Franschhoek Cellars tasting venue on Franschhoek town's main road.

Pinotage ★★★★ Improved **14** star in this year's line-up: engaging strawberry & mulberry fruit with a light tannin nudge for refreshing drinkability. **Rosé** ★★★★ Ex-tank, dry **15** a well-composed, satisfying picnic pink. From merlot, pinotage & shiraz, with sweet strawberry tone, appealing tug of tannin. **Sauvignon Blanc** ★★★ Fairly intense capsicum, green asparagus & grassy tones, **15** easy, flavourful summer white. WO W Cape. Also tasted: **Cabernet Sauvignon 13** ★★★ **Shiraz 13** ★★★ **OVR 13** ★★★★ **Unoaked Chardonnay 15** ★★★ — CvZ

Location/map: Stellenbosch ▪ Map grid reference: F5 ▪ WO: Coastal/Western Cape/Stellenbosch ▪ Est/ 1stB 1996 ▪ Tasting & sales Mon-Sat 10-6 ▪ Fee R25/3 wines R50/6 wines ▪ Closed Good Fri, Dec 25/26 & Jan 1 ▪ Light lunches & dinner 12-9; snacks & refreshments all day ▪ Owner(s) DGB (Pty) Ltd ▪ Winemaker(s) Richard Duckitt (May 2015) ▪ Viticulturist(s) Stephan Joubert (Nov 2006) ▪ 500t/80,000cs own label 40% red 55% white 5% rosé ▪ WIETA ▪ Private Bag X3 Groot Drakenstein 7680 ▪ brampton@ dgb.co.za ▪ www.brampton.co.za ▪ S 33° 56' 17.42" E 018° 51' 38.08" ▪ **T +27 (0)21-883-9097**

Brandvlei Cellar ⓦ ⓒ ⓖ

The grower-owned winery in the shadow of Jonaskop peak started out in 1955 on premises beside Brandvlei Dam and moved to the current location between Worcester and Villiersdorp 19 years later when the dam was enlarged. 'Quality wines that everyone can enjoy and afford' is the aim, and the small fraction of output that appears under the BC Wines label certainly hits that target.

BC Wines range

Ruby Cabernet-Merlot ⓦ ★★★ French/American oak infuses quaffable **14** with spicy mulled wine notes to back juicy red plums. Rounded & dry. **Chardonnay** ⓥ ⓦ ★★★ Oak influence sensitively judged on **15**. Provides lime/citrus zest, hint of creaminess to create all-round versatility. **Bacchanté** ⓦ ★★★ Happy mix chenin, colombard & soupçon spicy viognier. **15** off-dry but fruity rather than sweet. A charmer.

Also tasted: **Cabernet Sauvignon 14** ★★★ **Shiraz 14** ★★ **Chenin Blanc 15** ★★★ **Sauvignon Blanc 15** ★★ Not retasted: **Shiraz Rosé 13** ★★ **Hanepoot Jerepigo 13** ★★ — AL

Location/map/WO: Worcester ▪ Est 1955 ▪ Tasting & sales Mon-Thu 8–5 Fri 8–4.30 Sat 9-1 ▪ Closed all pub hols ▪ Cellar tours by appt only ▪ Conferences ▪ Owner(s) 19 members ▪ Cellarmaster(s) Jean le Roux (Aug 1995) ▪ Winemaker(s) Willie Biggs (Sep 2009) & Daneel Jacobs (Sep 2007) ▪ Viticulturist(s) Danie Conradie (Sep 2004) ▪ 1,630ha (cab, ptage, chard, chenin, cbard, sauv) ▪ 28,500t 20% red 80% white ▪ PO Box 595 Worcester 6849 ▪ sales@bcwines.co.za ▪ www.bcwines.co.za ▪ S 33° 48' 19.5" E 019° 28' 8.1" ▪ F +27 (0)23-340-4332 ▪ **T +27 (0)23-340-4215**

Breëland Winery ⊕ ⊕ ⊕ ⊕ ⊕

In conjunction with the renowned vine nursery team from Lelienfontein, Kosie and Lizelle Marais' Breëland estate is poised to become Breedekloof's first 'clone garden', a development which will 'provide a boost for wine quality in the area and make planting decisions easier for all local growers'.

Cabernet Sauvignon ⊕ ★★★ Early-drinking, wallet-friendly **14** fruit-filled & flavoursome, with harmonious oak.

Chenin Blanc Royal (NEW) ★★★☆ Fruit is the star of barrel-fermented **14**. White peaches, lemons & flowers, appealing viscosity & crisp finish. Also tasted: **Pinotage 14 ★★ Sauvignon Blanc 15 ★★★** Discontinued: **Chenin Blanc**. — CvZ

Location: Rawsonville ▪ Map: Breedekloof ▪ WO: Western Cape ▪ Est 1825 ▪ 1stB 2010 ▪ Tasting, sales & cellar tours Mon-Sat by appt ▪ Fee R10pp tour & tasting ▪ Closed Ash Wed, Easter Fri-Mon, Ascension day, Dec 25 & Jan 1 ▪ Pre-booked lunches (5 days prior notice) ▪ BYO picnic ▪ Walks/hikes ▪ MTB & 4x4 trails ▪ Conservation area ▪ Guest accommodation (mountain hut/farm house/camping) ▪ Owner(s) Kosie & Lizelle Marais ▪ Cellarmaster(s) Wickus Erasmus (Dec 2008) ▪ Winemaker(s) Wickus Erasmus (Dec 2008), with Jefry Fry (Jan 2009) ▪ Viticulturist(s) Wickus Erasmus, Kosie Marais ▪ 1,000ha/100ha (cab, cinsaut, ptage, shiraz, chenin, cbard, hanepoot, sauv, sem) ▪ 2,500t/500cs own label 20% red 80% white + 500cs for clients ▪ Brands for clients: Kaap Agri ▪ PO Box 26 Rawsonville 6845 ▪ wickus@breede.co.za ▪ www.buchukloof.co.za ▪ S 33° 39' 2.87" E 019° 13' 40.08" ▪ F +27 (0)86-562-6056 ▪ **T +27 (0)23-344-3129**

Brenaissance ⊕ ⊕ ⊕ ⊕ ⊕

Under owners Tom and Hayley Breytenbach, this Devon Valley property has undergone a (b)renaissance from an anonymous grape-growing farm into a wine and lifestyle destination (and Boran cattle stud). Fruit is vinified off-site by specialists in each variety or style. A new blanc de noir missed our deadline.

★★★★ **King of Clubs Cabernet Sauvignon** ⊕ Focused **09** shows complexity: mint, cedar, cassis, black olive, tobacco, cigarbox; ripe & supple tannins for youthful enjoyment or cellaring.

Queen of Hearts Merlot ⊕ ★★★ Plum & meat **10** juxtaposes ripe fruit & green leafy characters. Not retasted: **Jack of Diamonds Shiraz 09 ★★★☆ Full House Bordeaux Style Blend 10 ★★★** Not tasted: **Lord T Secret Blend, Ace of Spaces Blanc de Noir, Knight of White Chardonnay, Lady H Sauvignon Blanc**. — AL

Location/map/WO: Stellenbosch ▪ Map grid reference: D4 ▪ 1stB 2010 ▪ Tasting & sales Wed-Sun 11-5 ▪ Pizza & wine pairing ▪ Café Blanc de Noir restaurant ▪ Child friendly ▪ Conferences/functions ▪ Wedding venue & chapel ▪ Accommodation ▪ Boran cattle stud ▪ Owner(s) Tom & Hayley Breytenbach ▪ Winemaker(s) various ▪ 58.23ha/31.65ha (cabs s/f, malbec, merlot, p verdot, shiraz, chard) ▪ 5,058cs own label 70% red 30% white ▪ Suite 3, Private Bag X4, Die Boord, Stellenbosch 7613 ▪ info@brenaissance.co.za ▪ www.brenaissance.co.za ▪ S 33° 55' 4.31" E 018° 49' 7.82" ▪ **T +27 (0)21-200-2537**

☐ **Brendel Collection** *see* Le Manoir de Brendel

Brenthurst Winery

Having long made his boutique wines solo, Paarl-based advocate José Jordaan latterly assists winemaker Martin Fourie while vineyardist the past 25 years, Johan Wiese, oversees the Bordeaux vines.

Location: Paarl ▪ Est 1993 ▪ 1stB 1994 ▪ Open to public only by special appt ▪ Owner(s) José Jordaan ▪ Winemaker(s) Martin Fourie, assisted by José Jordaan ▪ Viticulturist(s) Johan Wiese (1991, consultant) ▪ 5ha (cabs s/f, merlot, p verdot) ▪ 15t ▪ PO Box 6091 Paarl 7622 ▪ martin@amatawines.co.za ▪ F +27 (0)21-424-5666 ▪ **T +27 (0)21-863-1154/1375, +27 (0)83-418-4110**

Bridge Wines ⊕

As the name of her business implies, Rosemary Mosia acts as a conduit to get wine to market, working with consultant viticulturists and winemakers to buy grapes and vinify wines which she sells into on- and off-consumption outlets including restaurants and liquor stores.

Chardonnay ⓦ ★★★★ Oak is a full partner in **13**, but in a good way: buttered toast, preserved citrus peel, crushed hazel nuts, melon. Finish is long & savoury, very food friendly. Partial barrel ferment. Not retasted: **Merlot Reserve 08** ★★ **Reserve Shiraz 10** ★★★ — CR, CvZ

Location: Cape Town ▪ WO: Wellington ▪ Est 2005 ▪ 1stB 2010 ▪ Tasting & sales Mon-Fri by appt ▪ Closed all pub hols ▪ Owner(s) Rosemary P Mosia ▪ Winemaker(s) Hennie Huskisson, with JG Auret (both consultants) ▪ Viticulturist(s) Vlok Hanekom ▪ 70% red 30% white ▪ 66 Loch Road, Rondebosch 7700 ▪ rmosia@yahoo.com, rmosia@thebridgewines.co.za ▪ www.thebridgewines.co.za ▪ F +27 (0)86-594-1501 ▪ **T +27 (0)21-686-2294**

☐ **Brink Family** *see* Pulpit Rock Winery
☐ **Broken Rock** *see* Riebeek Cellars
☐ **Broken Stone** *see* Slaley

Brothers Wines

After a successful corporate career, Capetonian Greg Castle in 2005 followed his passion and founded Brothers boutique winery, named for sons Dylan and Alex. Greg uses traditional methods to craft wines that are 'accessible and appealing to most folk who simply enjoy quality wine and quality of life'.

★★★★ **Legacy** Latest **13** Bordeaux-style quintet led by cab. Smartly composed: cab's tannins in command but plenty ripe fruit waiting emerge over next few years. Sense of classicism also shows in attractive cigarbox notes. No **12**.

Cabernet Sauvignon ⓃⒺⓌ ★★★★ **12** showing some meaty, savoury evolution in its sweet fruit. Fresh core & fine, ripe tannins well harmonised for current enjoyment & few more years. **Sauvignon Blanc** ★★★☆ **14** in riper, tropical mode but also nicely paced joie de vivre. Great accompaniment to 'noisy, lingering summer lunches'. Also tasted: **Chardonnay 14** ★★★☆ Not tasted: **Shiraz**. — AL

Location: Cape Town ▪ WO: Coastal ▪ Est/1stB 2005 ▪ Closed to public ▪ Owner(s) Greg Castle ▪ Cellarmaster(s)/winemaker(s) Greg Castle (2005) ▪ 10t/1,666cs own label 55% red 45% white ▪ PO Box 21681 Kloof Street Cape Town 8008 ▪ info@brotherswines.co.za ▪ www.brotherswines.com ▪ F +27 (0)86-528-6081 ▪ **T +27 (0)82-600-2555**

Brugman Wines

Previously listed in the guide as 'Alluvia', Brugman Wines continues as a family boutique brand distributing ('only by word of mouth') the wines named for matriarch Sandie and her daughters, Lisa and twins Ilse and Karla. Recent acquisition by the Brugman Group of Sure Global Travel & Global Events means the wines are available from their head office in Gauteng, as well as via email and the website. The intention is to craft an exclusive wine offering 'an über-sensory experience for the discerning palate'.

Princess range

★★★★ **Ilka Cabernet Sauvignon** ⓦ **11** ex barrel is a serious fellow. Layered blackcurrants & cedar, whiffs of scrub but firm tannins not integrated when tasted. Good potential, just needed time.

★★★★ **Ilka Sauvignon Blanc** ⓦ Ex-tank **13** (★★★★) shows apple & melon styling, ripe figs & an ample fresh-toned roundness. Less intense than last-tasted **10**.

Not tasted: **Lisa Vineyard Cabernet Franc**.

Queen range

★★★★☆ **Sandie Viognier Straw Wine** ⓦ Boldly styled in colour, alcohol & sweetness, yet **11** ex-barrel is sublime. Liquidised apricots, honey, quince preserve & barley sugar, but the palate surprises, sweetness with focus thanks to 18 months in barrel. 375 ml. WO Western Cape. — CR

Location: Stellenbosch ▪ WO: Banghoek/Western Cape ▪ Est 2002 ▪ 1stB 2005 ▪ Wines available via website or by email; also available from Sure Global Travel & Global Events head office in Gauteng T +27 (0)86-100-0748, wineshop@sureglobaltravel.co.za ▪ Owner(s) Brugman family ▪ PO Box 6365 Uniedal 7612 ▪ acquire@brugmanwine.com ▪ www.brugmanwine.com

Brunia Wines Ⓨ ⑪ ⓸

Willie and Annetia du Preez's brand is named for the silver-bloomed fynbos species Brunia laevis, and the wines are vinified from grapes on their Cold Mountain Vineyards property near Stanford under contract by specialist winemakers. The visitor venue is welcoming, with many and varied amenities on offer.

★★★★ **Pinot Noir** ⓔ Delicately spiced red cherries lead the way in harmonious **13** – bright & pure, showing lovely freshness throughout. Good balance, finesse & savoury finish.

★★★★ **Sauvignon Blanc** ⓔ Lime-scented **13** has fine mineral fruit core, smooth acidity, chalky finish & a steely dryness. Complex, made for fresh oysters. No **12**.

Not retasted: **Chardonnay 13** ★★★☆ **Semillon 13** ★★★★ Not tasted: **Shiraz**. — WB

Location: Stanford ▪ Map: Southern Cape ▪ WO: Walker Bay ▪ Est 2005 ▪ 1stB 2009 ▪ Tasting & sales by appt Tue-Sun 10-4 & daily during holidays ▪ Closed Dec 25/26 ▪ Light lunches, picnics & tractor rides ▪ Self-guided hiking trails ▪ Mountain biking ▪ Conservation area ▪ Owner(s) W P du Preez ▪ Winemaker(s) various ▪ Viti-culturist(s) Andrew Teubes (consultant) ▪ 417ha/17ha (pinot, shiraz, chard, sauv, sem) ▪ 75t/5,600cs own label 16% red 84% white ▪ PO Box 368 Stanford 7210 ▪ info@bruniawines.co.za ▪ www.bruniawines.co.za ▪ S 34° 28' 9.25" E 019° 39' 42.60" ▪ F +27 (0)86-669-6064 ▪ **T +27 (0)28-341-0432**

Bryan MacRobert Wines Ⓨ

Bryan MacRobert has gained a good deal of experience in making new-wave Swartland wines over the years, including a stint working in the cellar of Eben Sadie (Sadie Family). Bryan's own small operation has grown steadily, however, and in 2014 an old friend, Jean-Paul Stuyck, joined as business partner. The Swartland is still the focus, with many of the grapes they buy coming off vineyards that Bryan manages in the Malmesbury area.

Bryan MacRobert Wines range ⓝⓔⓦ

★★★★ **Field Blend 14** half syrah/shiraz, plus mourvèdre, cinsaut & carignan from Swartland & Darling grapes. Gorgeously perfumed, the full fruit fresh & unobscured by oak (2,500L foudres used). Restrained, balanced & dry, tightly knit, with fine texture. Firm dry tannins should soon harmonise. Also in 3L.

★★★★ **Steen** Characterful **14** a fine expression of chenin, leaning from fruitiness towards earthier, dried-herbal, dried peach spectrum, with a stony core. Good bite from acid & a hint of oak tannin.

Tobias range

★★★★ **Red (Shiraz-Cinsault-Mourvèdre)** Equal varietal partners on **14** (★★★★). Riper & sweeter than **13** – also 25% new oak now. More light-footed charm than depth, but nice tight structure, & richer than Abbotsdale version.

Not tasted: **White (Chenin Blanc)**.

Abbotsdale range

Red ★★★ Bright but mild red fruit character on fresh, easygoing, old-oaked **14** from shiraz with mourvèdre & cinsaut. Not tasted: **Rosé, Chenin Blanc**. — TJ

Location: Velddrif ▪ Map: Swartland ▪ WO: Swartland/Coastal ▪ Est/1stB 2010 ▪ Tasting by appt only ▪ Closed all pub hols ▪ Owner(s) Bryan MacRobert & Jean-Paul Stuyck ▪ Cellarmaster(s) Bryan MacRobert & Jean-Paul Stuyck (Jan 2015) ▪ Winemaker(s)/viticulturist(s) Bryan MacRobert (Jan 2010) ▪ (cinsaut, mourv, shiraz, chenin) ▪ 30t/1,500cs own label 45% red 45% white 10% rosé + 3,000cs for clients ▪ IPW ▪ bryan@bryanmacrobertwines.com, jp@bryanmacrobertwines.com ▪ S 33° 29' 12.64" E 018° 38' 50.53" ▪ **T +27 (0)71-223-3129/+27 (0)71-610-1284**

☐ **Buchu Berg** see Oude Compagnies Post Private Cellar

☐ **Buckleberry** see Louis

☐ **Buddy** see Overhex Wines International

Buffalo Creek Wines Ⓨ

Leroy and Mark Tolmay nobly ventured into wine with little knowledge or experience to benefit the staff on their McGregor farm – all profits are distributed among them. The father and son growers' aim is to produce easily drinkable wines at friendly prices. Current releases are: Merlot '14, Pinotage '14, Pinot Noir Rosé '15, Chardonnay '15 and Sauvignon Blanc '15. Dry Red temporarily sold out at press time.

Location: McGregor ▪ Map: Robertson ▪ Est/1stB 2005 ▪ Tasting, sales & cellar tours Mon-Fri 9-6 Sat 9-12.30 Sun by appt only ▪ Closed Easter Sun, Dec 25 & Jan 1 ▪ Owner(s) Leroy & Mark Tolmay ▪ Cellarmaster(s)/winemaker(s) Mark Tolmay (Jun 2005) ▪ 1,328ha/30ha (p verdot, ptage, pinot, merlot, chard, chenin, cbard, sauv) ▪ ±350-380t/500-600cs own label 65% red 25% white 10% rosé ▪ PO Box 124 McGregor 6708 ▪ info@buffalocreek.co.za ▪ S 34° 0' 2.97" E 019° 53' 11.94" ▪ F +27 (0)23-625-1727 ▪ **T +27 (0)23-625-1727**

Buitenverwachting   ⓠ ⓨ ⓞ ⓖ

Buitenverwachting was part of Simon van der Stel's original Constantia. The name dates to 1794 (though other names have also been used) and is the one under which it was revived, as an ambitious estate, by Richard and Christine Mueller in the early 1980s: a vital part of the rebirth of Constantia as a fine-wine area. Christine's son, Lars Maack, is part-owner and has for long untiringly run the show. Augmenting this valuable continuity is the long tenure of cellarmaster Hermann Kirschbaum – who's increasingly shared responsibility with Brad Paton, himself now celebrating a decade of winemaking here. Unshowy quality remains the watchword – although innovation and experimentation are never excluded. The farm name cedes prominence to the more easily pronounceable 'Bayten' on export labels.

★★★★ **Cabernet Sauvignon** Classic, youthful **13** needs time for tight tannins to soften. Nicely ripe & elegant, with a light herbal edge, not quite as convincing as outstanding **12** (★★★★☆), but lovely.

★★★★ **Merlot** Dry, savoury **11** dark plum fruit structured by well-integrated spicy oak in properly restrained, classic style which calls for food.

★★★★☆ **Pinot Noir Block 8** ⓝ **13** bound to be controversial, with richness & power not generally thought possible in Constantia reds, let alone pinot noir anywhere. Unashamedly bold & un-pinot like. Alcohol warms but fits snugly into supremely delicious, succulent & creamy conclusion.

★★★★☆ **Christine** Iconic SA Bordeaux-style blend & property's classic 'grand vin' in more accessible **11** vintage. Lush dense dark cherries & chocolate offered elegant restraint by sufficient balancing acidity & integrated, gentle tannic tug from all-new oak.

★★★★ **MPV** ⓝ Seductively perfumed **10** (unusual) blend in perfect harmony. Merlot's voluptuous plummy fruit lifted & rendered elegant by petit verdot's fresh acidity.

★★★★☆ **Chardonnay** Luxuriously creamy, complex **14** (★★★★★) offers scents of jasmine & classy oak. Seductively accessible, persistent peach & citrus flavours are rich & softly rounded, textured by lees & 10 months in barrel. **13** as graceful. Available in magnum.

★★★★ **Maximus** Confidently oaked, rich **13** (★★★★☆) in genteel mould. Late picking, lees-enrichment & lengthy 18 months in barrel contribute to breadth & intriguingly creamy texture, unusual in sauvignon blanc. Like last-tasted **11**, more subtle than imposing name suggests. **12** untasted.

★★★★☆ **Husseys Vlei Sauvignon Blanc** The most exhilarating of property's sauvignon trio, owes singularity to vineyard's soils & altitude. Intensely concentrated, perfumed **15** no exception, with vibrant layers pithy lime & passionfruit in precise balance with thrilling, savoury acidity. **14** untasted; **13** (★★★★★) exceptional.

★★★★☆ **Sauvignon Blanc** Invitingly succulent, fresh, sweet-fruited **15** (★★★★) as vibrant but perhaps not quite as complex as **13**; pleasurably soft & accessibly crisp. **14** sold out untasted.

★★★★☆ **3rd Time Lucky** Aromatic, spicy viognier, **14** (★★★★) soft & charming, with peach & apricot flavours in abundance. Not quite as fine as **13** but makes for deliciously flavourful earlier enjoyment.

★★★★☆ **1769** ⓥ Exceptional Noble Late Harvest from muscat de Frontignan. Unctuously sweet, marmalade-infused **13** is lighter-footed **12** (also tasted), both rendered delightfully dry at end by seamless acidity. Former's all-new oak superbly absorbed, latter saw older barrels.

Malbec ⓝ ★★★☆ Perhaps better in a blend, **12** has a slightly stalky aroma but attractively rich, ripe cherry & plum flavours. Firmly structured with warm finish despite moderate alcohol. Also tasted: **Blanc de Noir 15** ★★★ **Buiten Blanc 14** ★★★ Not retasted: **Meifort 10** ★★★☆ Not tasted: **Cabernet Franc, Méthode Cap Classique Brut.** — IM

Location: Constantia ▪ Map: Cape Peninsula ▪ WO: Constantia/Western Cape ▪ Est 1796 ▪ 1stB 1985 ▪ Tasting & sales Mon-Fri 9–5 Sat 10–5 ▪ Closed all pub hols ▪ Cellar tours by appt ▪ Buitenverwachting Restaurant ▪ Deli & coffee shop ▪ Picnic area ▪ Conferences ▪ Owner(s) Richard & Sieglinde (Christine) Mueller, Lars Maack ▪ Cellarmaster(s) Hermann Kirschbaum (Jan 1993) ▪ Winemaker(s) Brad Paton (Jan 2005) ▪ Viticulturist(s) Peter Reynolds (Jan 2001) ▪ 147ha/105ha (cabs s/f, merlot, chard, sauv) ▪ 800t/ 320,000cs own label 20% red 80% white ▪ PO Box 281 Constantia 7848 ▪ info@buitenverwachting.com ▪ www.buitenverwachting.com ▪ S 34° 2' 30.4" E 018° 25' 1.5" ▪ F +27 (0)21-794-1351 ▪ **T +27 (0)21-794-5190/1**

Burgershof

Fourth-generation Burgershof has successfully made the transition from traditional fortified desserts to modern, in-demand varietal and blended wines. These are mainly for Dutch supermarket chain Jumbo, but also available at local outlets La Verne Wine Boutique in Robertson and Ashton Wine Boutique.

Merlot ★★★ Revisited as bottled wine, unoaked **13** ripe cherries & plums throughout, softly juicy. WO W Cape. **Chardonnay** ★★★ 15's ripe citrus given light oaking, fresh & fruity styling. **Sauvignon Blanc** ★★★ 15 lime zest perfume broadening into melon flavours. Not retasted: **Cabernet Sauvignon-Shiraz 14** ★★★ Discontinued: **Pinotage**. — CR

Location: Robertson ▪ WO: Robertson/Western Cape ▪ Est 1864 ▪ 1stB 2000 ▪ Closed to public ▪ Sales at La Verne Wine Boutique & Ashton Wine Boutique ▪ Owner(s) HJ Reynecke ▪ Cellarmaster(s)/ winemaker(s)/viticulturist(s) Hennie Reynecke (Jan 1979) ▪ 68ha (cab, merlot, muscadel r/w, ptage, ruby cab, shiraz, chard, chenin, cbard, sauv) ▪ IPW, WIETA ▪ PO Box 72 Klaasvoogds River 6707 ▪ burgershof@barvallei.co.za ▪ www.burgershof.com ▪ F +27 (0)23-626-5433 ▪ **T +27 (0)23-626-5433**

☐ **Bush Camp** *see* Landskroon Wines
☐ **Bushman's Creek** *see* Wines of Cape Town

Bushmanspad Estate

At the foot of the Langeberg near Bonnievale, Menno Schaafsma's tranquil winery is well worth a detour, especially after recent tasting room refurbishments and creation of a shady al fresco area. In the restored centuries-old cellar next door, winemaker/viticulturist Arthur Basson oversaw an increase in production capacity, while on a viewsite high up the mountain slope, the guest cottages' decor was updated.

Bushmanspad range

★★★★ **The Menno** Ⓥ Shiraz-led mix, only in best years. Berry-rich **12** has a supple texture, its savoury seam adding complexity, flavour, definition, & promising a future. No **10**, **11**.

Rosé ★★ Fruit in abundance in merlot-led **15**, strawberries throughout, soft textured & easy. **Sauvignon Blanc** ⊘ ★★★★ Lemongrass & Rose's Lime Cordial, elegant **15** walks on the fresh side, some minerality creeping in at the end. Friendly 12.5% alcohol. Not retasted: **Cabernet Sauvignon 12** ★★★ **Cabernet Franc 12** ★★★ **Malbec 12** ★★★

Red Gold range

Blend ★★★ Cab, merlot with 4 others, **13**'s dark-toned richness is propped up by savoury, pliable tannins promising a good future. Already nicely accessible. Not retasted: **Shiraz 12** ★★★ — CR

Location: Bonnievale ▪ Map/WO: Robertson ▪ Est 2000 ▪ 1stB 2006 ▪ Tasting & sales Mon-Fri 8.30–5 ▪ Fee R20/6 wines ▪ BYO picnic ▪ Walks/hikes ▪ Self-catering cottages ▪ Owner(s) Menno Schaafsma ▪ Cellarmaster(s)/winemaker(s)/viticulturist(s) Arthur Basson (Feb 2011) ▪ 52ha (cabs s/f, malbec, merlot, mourv, shiraz, sauv) ▪ 400t own label 80% red 15% white 5% rosé ▪ PO Box 227 Bonnievale 6730 ▪ info@bushmanspad.co.za ▪ www.bushmanspad.co.za ▪ S 33° 53' 55.0" E 020° 11' 46.7" ▪ F +27 (0)86-268-3756 ▪ **T +27 (0)23-616-2961**

☐ **Butcher Shop & Grill** *see* The Butcher Shop & Grill

B Vintners Vine Exploration Co   ⓠ ⑭

B certainly covers the common 'Bruwer' bit in the names of the owners and vintners of this negociant business — Gavin Bruwer Slabbert and his cousin Bruwer Raats (of Raats Family Wines, where the wines are made). Together they seek out high-lying, cool-area vineyards, and vinify them in a way that reveals a sense of place — looking to tradition to help them 'follow a route to a future full of hope'.

★★★★ Liberté Pinotage Fragrant aromas of **14** from old vines most appealing, with more red than black fruit character. Only older oak used, to preserve purity & a rare delicacy in the world of pinotage.

★★★★ Strandwolf Chardonnay Lemony freshness, with floral & fynbos notes on subtly oaked **14**. Clean, pure & lifted; fine balancing acidity supports persistent finish, 12.5% alcohol helps downability.

★★★★☆ Harlem to Hope Fresh & very drinkable **14** from chenin & semillon with a dollop of muscat d'Alexandrie adding understated floral, grapey charm to the spice & lemon/peach notes. Older oak maturation gives breadth & a modicum of tannic grip. Dry, harmonious & rather elegant.

★★★★ De Alexandria 14's perfumed aromas show the unmistakable character of muscat, but in unusually subtle, refined guise. Not complex, but delightfully fresh, dry & light (11.5% alcohol).

Reservoir Road Pinot Noir ★★★☆ Dark-fruited **14** has unusual notes of black chocolate rather than more obvious fruit — though a sweet note comes amidst the dry tannins on an almost severe palate. Very tight — perhaps just time is needed to relax it & add pinot charm. — TJ, CvZ

Location/map/WO: Stellenbosch ▪ Map grid reference: B6 ▪ Est/1stB 2014 ▪ Tasting Mon-Fri by appt ▪ Fee R250 (2-10 pax) ▪ Closed all pub hols ▪ Owner(s)/cellarmaster(s) Bruwer Raats & Gavin Bruwer Slabbert ▪ own label 50% red 50% white ▪ PO Box 2068 Dennesig 7601 ▪ braats@mweb.co.za ▪ www.bvintners.com ▪ S 33° 58' 16.6" E 018° 44' 55.3" ▪ F +27 (0)86-647-8500 ▪ **T +27 (0)21-881-3078**

☐ **Cabrière** *see* Haute Cabrière
☐ **Café Culture** *see* KWV

Calais Wine Estate   ⓠ ⌂

Founded in 1692 by French Huguenot Jean Manje, who named the estate in Paarl's Daljosafat area after his home town, Calais' winemaking is on hold for now but some earlier releases in the Old-World-style Klein Valley flagship and New-World-fruity Calais ranges are available for tasting and sale.

Klein Valley range

St Katerina Barrel Fermented Viognier ⓥ **★★★** Attractive, peachy **13** has some richness & texture, sufficient acidity to refresh the creamy finish.

Calais range

Chardonnay ⓥ **★★** Unoaked **13** straightforward easy-drinker with tropical pineapple flavour. **Sauvignon Blanc** ⓥ **★★** Lightly tropical **13** for uncomplicated quaffing. Not tasted: **Merlot, Petit Verdot, Pinotage, Shiraz, Applause, Bel Canto, Cape Riesling, Chenin Blanc.** — IM

Location: Paarl ▪ Map: Paarl & Wellington ▪ Map grid reference: F4 ▪ WO: Wellington/Paarl ▪ Est/1stB 2000 ▪ Tasting by appt ▪ Sales daily 8-4 ▪ Guest accommodation ▪ Owner(s) Calais Wine Estate shareholders ▪ 23ha (cab, merlot, p verdot, ptage, ruby cab, shiraz, chard, chenin, sauv) ▪ 150t/3,000cs own label 70% red 30% white ▪ PO Box 9006 Klein Drakenstein 7628 ▪ info@calais.co.za ▪ www.calais.co.za ▪ S 33° 42' 32.1" E 019° 1' 24.6" ▪ **T +27 (0)21-868-3888**

☐ **Calico** *see* Osbloed Wines

Calitzdorp Cellar   ⓠ ⑪ ⊜ ⊚ ⊛

Forty years on from the maiden bottling (more than half under cellarmaster and winemaker Alwyn Burger), the welcoming grower-owned winery on the hill in Calitzdorp town continues to focus on fortified desserts (half hectares of touriga nacional and tinta barocca planted last year for their 'ports') and easy-drinking reds. Recent production tweaks include a filtration system to increase juice recovery.

★★★★ Hanepoot Fortified dessert **15** is back on track after last-tasted **12** (★★★★). Melon preserve, apricot & honey, rich & full-sweet (220 g/l sugar) but ending tangy. Very tasty.

★★★★ **White Muscadel** ⊘ Liquid sultanas with a freshening spicy, pineapple seam in fortified dessert **14** (★★★★☆). The beauty is that the richness, sweetness, is tempered by the other nuances, giving remarkable balance, appeal. Enjoy chilled. Even better than **12**. **13** untasted.

★★★★ **Golden Jerepigo** Sweetest of the cellar's fortified desserts, latest **NV** remains admirable & delicious. Honeyed raisins & sultanas throughout, full bodied & silky smooth. Serve over ice or with dessert.

Pinotage ⊛ ★★★ An individual take on pinotage, streamlined **14** has blueberries & cumin, other exotic spices, ends savoury.

Merlot ★★★ Juicy red berries, soft & smooth **14** is very easy to like & drink. **Chardonnay** ★★★ Lovely freshness in lightly oaked **14**, the melon & mango flavours adding to the appeal **Cape Ruby** ⊘ ★★★★ Rich & full bodied 'port', with smoky dark fruit & chocolate tones, **NV**'s fruitcake sweetness would ideally partner cheese & nuts, or just enjoy on its own after a meal. Also in 375 ml. Also tasted: **Cabernet Sauvignon 13** ★★★ **Shiraz 13** ★★ **Rosé NV** ★★ **Sauvignon Blanc 14** ★★★☆ Not retasted: **Touriga Nacional 13** ★★★ **Tinto 12** ★★★ Not tasted: **Limited Edition Muscat Delight**, **Hanepoot Muskadel Reserve**, **Red Muscadel**, **Cape Vintage**. — CR

Location/WO: Calitzdorp • Map: Klein Karoo & Garden Route • Est 1928 • 1stB 1976 • Tasting & sales Mon-Fri 9–5 Sat 9–1 • Closed Good Fri & Dec 25 • Cellar tours by appt • Tour groups • Farm produce • Picnics/meals by appt; or BYO picnic • Conferences • Succulent garden • Owner(s) 39 members • Cellarmaster(s) Alwyn Burger (1990) • Winemaker(s) Alwyn Burger (1990), with Abraham Pretorius • Viticulturist(s) Johannes Mellet (2005, consultant) • 286ha (13 varieties, r/w) • 5,000t/7,000ℓ own label 12% red 88% white • IPW • PO Box 193 Calitzdorp 6660 • manager@calitzdorpwine.co.za • www.calitzdorpwine.co.za • S 33° 32' 18.9" E 021° 41' 10.6" • F +27 (0)44-213-3328 • **T +27 (0)44-213-3301**

Camberley Wines   ⊛ ⊛ ⊛ ⊛ ⊛

Quantity surveyor John Nel celebrates two decades of specialising in reds on his small, immaculate property overlooking the scenic Banhoek Valley. What started as a hobby, hand-labelling 500-ml bottles of a Bordeaux blend in their dinky home cellar, has become expert production of a globally distributed range. Professional caterer wife Gaël treats visitors to gourmet breakfasts in the gracious garden setting, now also geared for cyclists (her husband is an avid sports lover).

Camberley Wines range

★★★★☆ **The 5th Element** ⊛ Pure, perfumed **11** has red & black fruit leaping from the glass. Heady alcohol (15%) noticeable but handled by the sweet, slightly jammy fruit. Plush & sumptuous, showing superb oak integration & intensity from 100% cabernet.

★★★★ **Cabernet Franc** ⊘ **10** has trademark alcoholic kick, but with attractive leafy blackcurrant, layers of tobacco & dark berry leading to plush, powerful end. Decanting or time needed.

★★★★ **Shiraz** Velvety **12** has property's boldness & power, with lush black fruit packed around a solid core of tannic grip. Pepper, dark-roast coffee & ash fan out the tail. Last tasted was ultra-ripe **10** (★★★★).

★★★★ **Cabernet Sauvignon-Merlot** ⊘ **10** in bold house style with ripeness in complex layers of dark & red fruit. Bright freshness on the nose & palate harmonises oak, acid & very big alcohol.

★★★★ **Philosophers' Stone** Rich, full, warming Bordeaux blend of cab (49%), cab franc & splash merlot. **11** (★★★) super-ripe, with dates & prunes combining with leather, sundried tomato & wet clay; to drink earlier than cab franc-led **10**.

Not retasted: **Pinotage 12** ★★★☆ Not tasted: **Sparkling Shiraz**, **Elixir Fortified Red**. Occasional release: **Cabernet Sauvignon Reserve**, **Elm Tree Merlot**, **Charisma**.

Prohibition range

Not tasted: **Red**, **White**. — HJ

Location/map/WO: Stellenbosch • Map grid reference: H4 • Est 1990 • 1stB 1996 • Tasting & sales Mon-Sat & pub hols 9–5 Sun 9-3 • Fee R40 max (depending on wine choice), waived on purchase • Closed Dec 25 & Jan 1 • Cellar tours by appt • Lunch/refreshments by appt; or BYO picnic • Cyclists breakfast • B&B guest cottage • Owner(s) John & Gaël Nel • Winemaker(s) John Nel • Viticulturist(s) Bennie Booysen • 7ha (cabs s/f, merlot, p verdot, ptage, shiraz, touriga) • ±35t/6,400cs own label 100% red • PO Box

6120 Uniedal 7612 ▪ john@camberley.co.za ▪ www.camberley.co.za ▪ S 33° 55' 8.9" E 018° 55' 58.3" ▪
F +27 (0)21-885-1822 ▪ **T +27 (0)21-885-1176**

Cameradi Wines

Casper Lategan is one of the less obtrusive winemakers in the Cape garagiste scene. But vinous stuff has
been happening in the cellar behind his Wellington house: more precisely a cabernet sauvignon and a
shiraz that are 'showing great' and that we look forward to tasting for the next edition.

Location: Wellington ▪ Est 1999 ▪ 1stB 2000 ▪ Closed to public ▪ Owner(s) Stelvest cc (Nic Swingler, Hendrik
du Preez & Casper Lategan) ▪ Winemaker(s) Casper Lategan (Jan 1999) ▪ 2t/260cs own label 100% red ▪ 48
Bain Str Wellington 7655 ▪ cas@lategans.co.za ▪ F +27 (0)21-873-4910 ▪ **T +27 (0)21-873-1225**

☐ **Camino Africana** *see* Edgebaston

Capaia Wine Estate

It's nearly two decades since Capaia was established on a Philadelphia hillside where only wheat had
grown before. It was a most ambitious effort by its German owners, with no expense spared in the vineyards or the winery, with one of the world's largest arrays of oak fermenters. Stephan von Neipperg, the
eminent owner of several fine wine domaines in France, has consulted here for some years, and now
joins Ingrid von Essen in a partnership, giving 'new momentum' to this estate.

★★★★ **Mariella's** ⓥ Graphite frames plush blue & black fruit of **11** cab, merlot, cab franc & petit
verdot with splash (8%) shiraz. Spicy oak adds body & length to lithe, rewarding & supple mouthful.

★★★★ **Merlot-Cabernet Sauvignon** ⓥ Intense & plush **10**, demure dark fruit & beautifully managed tannins, some spice, showy yet restrained. Firmer, better, than softly ripe **09** (★★★★).

★★★★ **ONE** ⓥ Flagship from petit verdot & cab with merlot, cab franc & 11% shiraz. Intense black
fruit with restrained herbal & tomato notes on **10** (★★★★), savoury, but chunkier, less fresh than **09**.

Sauvignon Blanc ★★★☆ **15** preview tangy, vibrant & typical lemon flint. Light yet succulent. — FM

Location/WO: Philadelphia ▪ Map: Durbanville, Philadelphia & Darling ▪ Est 1997 ▪ 1stB 2003 ▪ Tasting,
sales & cellar tours Mon-Fri 8-5; Sat/Sun tasting & sales at Mariella's ▪ Tour groups ▪ Mariella's restaurant
T +27 (0)21-972-1103/+27 (0)72-770-9695, mariellas@capaia.co.za ▪ Facilities for children ▪
Owner(s) Ingrid von Essen & Stephan von Neipperg ▪ Cellarmaster(s) Bernabé Strydom (Oct 2006),
assisted by Stephan von Neipperg ▪ Winemaker(s) Adriaan Burger (Oct 2010) ▪ Viticulturist(s) Schalk du
Toit (2009, consultant) ▪ 140ha/60ha (cabs s/f, merlot, p verdot, shiraz, sauv) ▪ 260t/26,000cs own label
85% red 15% white ▪ IPW ▪ PO Box 25 Philadelphia 7304 ▪ info@capaia.co.za ▪ www.capaia.co.za,
www.capaia.com ▪ S 33° 42' 45.9" E 018° 34' 6.9" F +27 (0)21-972-1894 ▪ **T +27 (0)21-972-1081**

☐ **Cap du Vin** *see* Bellevue Estate Stellenbosch
☐ **Cape Elephant** *see* Lutzville Cape Diamond Vineyards
☐ **Cape Auction** *see* Vinopoly Wines
☐ **Cape Avocet** *see* Rooiberg Winery
☐ **Cape Bay** *see* FirstCape Vineyards

Cape Chamonix Wine Farm

This part of the La Cotte farm in Franschhoek granted to Huguenot refugees in the late 17th century has
belonged for 25 years to German businessman Chris Hellinger, who re-established it as Chamonix. For
nearly the last 15 years, vineyards and cellar were creatively managed by Gottfried Mocke, who built and
established the estate's reputation as one of the leading producers in the Cape (it was this guide's Winery
of the Year in 2013). Gottfried moved to nearby Boekenhoutskloof in 2015, to be succeeded as cellarmaster by his assistant, Thinus Neethling. The vineyards, including new ones on promising sites, are
mostly unirrigated; they are on mountain slopes above Franschhoek town, and the coolness their altitude gives them is doubtless significant for the quality of fruit they deliver.

Reserve range

★★★★☆ **Pinot Noir** Impressive **14** has cherry, sultry spice & cured meat nuances, fine-grained tannins & an emphatic dry finish. Spontaneous ferment; more new oak (60% new, 14 months) than sibling. Deserves cellaring 5+ years.

★★★★☆ **Troika** Bordeaux red led by cab franc (40%) with cab in support, splashes petit verdot & malbec playing important spicing, structural roles. **13** fragrant & concentrated, with tightly coiled tannins. Like finely structured **12**, will reward the patient.

★★★★☆ **Chardonnay** From 29 year old elevated vineyard, authoritative **14** composed & restrained with oatmeal & citrus interplay, taut mineral core & integrated oak. Natural ferment mostly in oak (70% new), 20% in concrete 'egg'. For cellaring, like **13**.

★★★★☆ **White** Bordeaux blend ups the sauvignon to 75% (20% more than in **13**), drops the new oak to 40% (versus 50%) but retains its pedigree in **14**. Stately, with impressive purity of fruit, vibrancy & poise; lingering quince finish from semillon component.

Cape Chamonix range

★★★★☆ **Cabernet Franc** ⊘ Terrific **13** (★★★★★) shows greater poise & presence than impressive **12** debut; fresh red berry & blackcurrant fruit & bright acidity; full bodied, with graceful tannin support. Combo barriques & large vats; 15% new. Outstanding now, with long-haul potential.

★★★★ **Feldspar Pinot Noir** More obviously fruit-driven than Reserve & with less new oak (well-integrated 30%), **14** cherry & wet pebble aromas, elegant tannin frame, slightly earthy finish. As vibrant & youthfully tight as **13**.

★★★★☆ **Greywacke Pinotage** Despite no customary dash of pinot noir, **13** is the usual complex mix of early & late picked grapes (including desiccated portion) & bunch ferment/carbonic maceration. Sensitive oaking (25% new) gives free rein to the fruit, aids tannin integration, extends the savoury finish.

★★★★☆ **Chardonnay** Less new oak than Reserve (50%), also spontaneous fermentation in barrel. Attractive **14**'s yellow stonefruit, musk melon has almond nougat & walnut notes, palate invigorated by acidity. Delicious now, concentration & structure to improve few years.

★★★★ **Chardonnay Unoaked** Properly dry, like all these (mostly ±2 g/l sugar), **15** has 15% oaked portion, despite name. Feisty & packed with apple & lemon fruit, also a serious mineral seam.

★★★★ **Sauvignon Blanc** Fine spread of greengage, lime, kiwi & grass on flinty, smooth **15**, clean cut & long; 15% oaked portion, fruit intensity, crisp acid give structure for few years ageing.

> **Rouge** ⊛ ★★★★ Easygoing but elegant 4-way Bordeaux blend. **13**, with fine polished tannins, delivers melange blackcurrants, graphite. Chill lightly in summer.

In abeyance: **MCC Blanc de Blancs**. — GM

Location/map/WO: Franschhoek ▪ Est 1991 ▪ 1stB 1992 ▪ Tasting & sales Mon-Sun 8.30–5 ▪ Fee R60 ▪ Closed Dec 25 & Jan 1 ▪ Cellar tours by appt ▪ Restaurant T +27 (0)21-876-2393 ▪ Conservation area ▪ Marco Polo Lodge, Waterfall Lodge, Forest Suites & fully equipped self-catering cottages ▪ Owner(s) Chris Hellinger ▪ Cellarmaster(s)/winemaker(s)/viticulturist(s) Thinus Neethling (2015) ▪ 300ha/50ha (cabs s/f, malbec, merlot, p verdot, ptage, pinot, chard, chenin, sauv, sem) ▪ 220-250t/40,000cs own label 60% red 40% white ▪ IPW ▪ PO Box 28 Franschhoek 7690 ▪ marketing@chamonix.co.za ▪ www.chamonix.co.za ▪ S 33° 53' 60.0" E 019° 7' 34.0" ▪ F +27 (0)21-876-3237 ▪ **T +27 (0)21-876-8400**

Cape Classics   ⓘ

Proud times for Cape Classics as they celebrate 25 years of exporting SA wines, including these own labels, with particular focus on the US. New markets and opportunities for their consumer-friendly ranges are opening up internationally, while their unstinting support of a range of charities via the Indaba Educational Fund continues to uplift communities, making a real difference to the lives of many here at home.

Braai ⓝ ★★★ Sweet, meaty **13** has biltong & ripe fruit hints with plenty of smoky, toasty oak flavours. Mostly shiraz, with cab & grenache.

Indaba range

Mosaic ★★★ Ripe, fresh & easy-drinking **14** unwooded cab-led Bordeaux blend. Touch of banana confection at finish. **Chardonnay** ★★★ Very enjoyable, oak-brushed **14** with tropical fruits — guavas & mangoes — enlivened by just enough acidity to keep it fresh & interesting. Also tasted: **Merlot 14** ★★★ **Chenin Blanc 14** ★★★ **Sauvignon Blanc 14** ★★☆

Jam Jar range

Sweet Shiraz ★★ Gummy bears & fruit pastilles on **15**. People who like this sort of thing will find it the sort of thing they like. Lots do: 144,000 cases! Also tasted: **Sweet White 15** ★★ — CM

Location: Somerset West ▪ Map: Helderberg ▪ WO: Western Cape ▪ Est 1991 ▪ 1stB 1996 ▪ Tasting by appt only ▪ Owner(s) André Shearer ▪ Winemaker(s) Bruwer Raats (May 2010) ▪ 270,000cs own label 35% red 65% white ▪ PO Box 1695 Somerset West 7129 ▪ info@capeclassics.com ▪ www.capeclassics.com, www.indabawines.com, www.jamjarwines.com ▪ S 34° 4' 5.9" E 018° 53' 38.2" ▪ F +27 (0)21-847-2414 ▪ **T +27 (0)21-847-2400**

☐ **Cape Cult** *see* Darling Cellars
☐ **Cape Diversity** *see* Withington

Cape Dreams　　　　Ⓠ

Owner Bunty Khan's dream for her export-orientated venture is to gain international recognition as a marketer of top-quality wines at competitive prices 'while offering an enhanced palate experience'. With guarantee of style/supply, credible partners and customer service as first principles, she's clearly having considerable success, with wines shipped to 18 countries and counting.

Cape Dreams range

Pinotage Rosé ⊘ ⓥ ★★★★ Gentle strawberry notes & crisp liveliness make fresh & dry **14** a pleasing food accompaniment. **Colombar** ⊘ ⓥ ★★★ Even pre-bottling **15** is a merry sipper, with big guava wafts, tangy gooseberries & green apples to taste, fresh & frisky to the last drop.

Cabernet Sauvignon ★★☆ Tasty braai companion **14** preview has lingering dark berry & plum pudding flavours, perky dry finish. **Merlot** ★★★ Easy fireside sipper, **13** offers dark chocolate & dusty berries with a sour cherry twist to keep the flavours fresh, lively. **Selected Red** (NEW) ★★ **14** preview is an allsorts unwooded blend with pinotage. Bit unsettled mid-2015, with dusty hay & cranberry tones. **Natural Sweet Red** (NEW) ★★☆ Easy, un-sticky quaffing on offer in **13**, mix of mostly shiraz & cab, with tannin/acid balance giving a dryish impression. Also tasted: **Pinotage 13** ★★★ **Shiraz 13** ★★★ **Chardonnay** ⊘ **15** ★★★ **Chenin Blanc** ⊘ **15** ★★★ **Sauvignon Blanc 15** ★★

Reserve range

Pinotage ⊘ ★★★★ **11** plump strawberry fruit, creamy oak & banana notes, supple enough to uncork now or keep few years. Not retasted: **Cabernet Sauvignon 11** ★★★ **Shiraz 11** ★★★★ — DB

Location/map/WO: Robertson ▪ Est/1stB 2009 ▪ Tasting & cellar tours by appt ▪ Owner(s) Bunty Khan ▪ Cellarmaster(s) André van Dyk ▪ 600ha (cab, merlot, ptage, shiraz, chard, chenin, cbard, sauv) ▪ 60% red 40% white ▪ BEE, BWI, HACCP, ISO 9001 ▪ info@croftsales.co.za ▪ www.croftsales.co.za ▪ S 33° 46' 35.3" E 019° 45' 42.9" ▪ **T +27 (0)21-531-2016/+27 (0)83-792-7638/+27 (0)83-780-9428**

☐ **Cape Elements** *see* Nico van der Merwe Wines
☐ **Cape Haven** *see* Pulpit Rock Winery
☐ **Cape Heights** *see* Boutinot South Africa

Cape Hutton　　　　Ⓠ ◎

Located in scenic Blaauwklippen Valley on Stellenbosch's outskirts, the small winery belonging to maxillofacial surgeon Gerrit Wyma and wife Lesley takes its name from the dominant vineyard soil type. Attractions include a wedding/function venue and of course, wines, unready for review this edition.

Location/map: Stellenbosch ▪ Map grid reference: E7 ▪ Est 2003 ▪ 1stB 2004 ▪ Tasting, sales & cellar tours by appt 8-4.30 ▪ Weddings/functions ▪ Owner(s)/viticulturist(s) Gerrit & Lesley Wyma ▪ Winemaker(s)

Piet Smal (cab), Wynand Hamman (sauv) & Hilko Hegewisch (merlot) ▪ 2ha (merlot) ▪ PO Box 2200 Somerset West 7129 ▪ lesley@capehutton.com ▪ www.capehutton.com ▪ S 33° 58' 27.6" E 018° 51' 10.3" ▪ F +27 (0)21-880-0666 ▪ **T +27 (0)21-880-0527**

Capelands Estate

The small Somerset West estate of Johann Innerhofer and Laura Mauri boasts accommodation, a restaurant and, crucially, a walled vineyard supplying some of the grapes vinified at Lanrust Estate by Rocco de Villiers. No new wines tasted this year, but, says Johann, 'We do have 2014 and 2015 in barrel.'

★★★★ **Redstone** ⓥ With the **12** vintage moved to a second label, **13** drops the malbec & is straight cab from a small, mature Helderberg vineyard. More restrained in fruitiness than the Klein version, but still forthrightly ripe & generous; firmly structured & judiciously oaked.

★★★★ **Whitestone Chardonnay** ⓥ Interesting tropical, peachy ripeness on the aromas of **13**, while the finish shows citrus freshness. Crisp & flavoursome, with elegantly integrated acidity & modest oaking.

Not retasted: **Klein Redstone 12** ★★★★ — TJ

Location: Somerset West ▪ WO: Stellenbosch/Western Cape ▪ Est 2004 ▪ 1stB 2010 ▪ Tasting available at Capelands Restaurant during operating times only – see website for trading hours ▪ Guest house ▪ Owner(s) Capelands Resort Estate (Pty) Ltd ▪ Winemaker(s) Rocco de Villiers (Lanrust Estate) ▪ Viticulturist(s) Francois Hanekom (Feb 2009, consultant) ▪ 12.5ha/2.8ha (cab) ▪ 6t/1,333cs own label 100% red ▪ 3 Old Sir Lowry's Pass Road Somerset West 7130 ▪ restaurant@capelands.com ▪ www.capelands.com ▪ S 34° 6' 29.57" E 018° 53' 4.42" ▪ F +27 (0)86-299-3905 ▪ **T +27 (0)21-858-1477**

☐ **Capeman** *see* Darling Cellars

Capenheimer

South Africa's original perlé wine, launched in 1962. By Distell. Sold in 750ml & 1.5L bottles.

Capenheimer ⓥ ★★ Lightish, off-dry **NV** white with gentle sparkle, quite a fresh finish. — DB

Capensis

'From the Cape' is what the name means and what the chardonnay expresses – sourced as it is from widely spread vineyards winkled out by star viticulturist Rosa Kruger. But US influence is strong. Capensis is a joint project of two friends, Antony Beck, American-based director of Graham Beck Wines, and Barbara Banke, owner of substantial US company Jackson Family Wines. The wine is made at Graham Beck by Jackson's locally born and trained 'winemaster', Graham Weerts, who visits frequently.

★★★★ **Chardonnay** Barrel ferment/10 months ageing give vanilla & cinnamon, lemon lime refreshment. Streamlined, **14**'s lovely salty acidity brightens the experience, adds length. Rich without being overbearing. — CR, CvZ

WO: Western Cape ▪ 1stB 2013 ▪ Closed to public ▪ Owner(s) Jackson Beck (joint venture between Jackson Family Wines USA & Graham Beck Wines SA) ▪ Winemaker(s) Graham Weerts ▪ Viticulturist(s) Rosa Kruger (consultant) ▪ 45t/2,000cs own label 100% white ▪ info@capensiswines.com ▪ www.capensiswines.com ▪ **T +1 884-889-7365**

☐ **Cape of Good Hope** *see* Anthonij Rupert Wyne

Cape Point Vineyards

Founded 20 years ago by investment banker and developer Sybrand van der Spuy, Cape Point Vineyards was always out on a limb, breaking new viticultural ground, pushing the limits and challenging conventions. They single-handedly created a new sub-region in Noordhoek on the Cape Peninsula, producing unique and ageworthy cool-climate wines. The emphasis on top-end quality has been unwavering and the accolades have followed. Cellarmaster Duncan Savage has forged the estate's style and status almost from the start and his mark is indelibly printed on every bottling. The cellardoor is a centre of social activity, with its charming tasting/function venue hosting Sunday community markets, picnics and weddings, all in an idyllic lakeside setting high above the vineyards.

Cape Point Vineyards range

★★★★☆ **Chardonnay** Classically styled, generously fruited **14** maintains impressive standard. Barrel fermented & matured (14 months), but emphasis remains on fruit & texture, balance & suppleness. Cape Peninsula & Overberg vineyards.

★★★★☆ **Sauvignon Blanc Reserve** Industry benchmark, oak-matured **14** underscores pedigree. Profound expression of terroir & variety, unfurling multiple layers of spicy fruit & sumptuously rich lees with steely mineral notes. Finely crafted, deserving time & attention. **13** untasted.

★★★★ **Sauvignon Blanc 14** changes to 100% unwooded but retains all the appeal & class. Bright & vibrant yet satisfyingly plump (abetted by 3% semillon), with substance, texture & lingering finish.

★★★★ **Semillon** Returns to guide after a break with a limited release of barrel-matured **14**, showing great promise. Finely focused lanolin-beeswax with marzipan, bolstered by subtle brush of oak spice.

★★★★☆ **CWG Auction Reserve White** Selection from Sauvignon Reserve & Isliedh parcels, masterly **14** (★★★★★) stands above even these noble siblings & previous **13**. Intensely aromatic, but ripe, modulated & approachable, nuanced yet harmonious & integrated. Sophisticated pleasure.

★★★★☆ **Isliedh** Regal, understated stature of **14** sauvignon-semillon barrel-fermented classic demands respect. Intricately structured, weaving spices, beeswax & subtle floral notes into creamy, lees-rich platform. Still taut – needs cellar time.

Not tasted: **Cabernet Sauvignon**, **Noble Late Harvest**.

Splattered Toad range

Sauvignon Blanc ★★★ Pocket friendly & cheerful, **15** has crisp green-apple fruit, hint of pebbles. WO W Cape. Also tasted: **Syrah 14** ★★★ — GdB

Location: Noordhoek ▪ Map: Cape Peninsula ▪ WO: Cape Peninsula/Western Cape/Coastal ▪ Est 1996 ▪ 1stB 2000 ▪ Tasting & sales Mon-Sun 10-6 ▪ Fee R10-R60 ▪ Cheese/antipasti platters available during tasting hours ▪ Weddings & events ▪ Picnics & sundowners ▪ Facilities for children ▪ Weekly community market Thu evenings in summer ▪ Conservation area ▪ Owner(s) Sybrand van der Spuy ▪ Winemaker(s) Duncan Savage (Dec 2002), with Riandri Visser (Jul 2014) ▪ Viticulturist(s) Duncan Savage (Dec 2002), with Hendri Burger (Sep 2010) ▪ 22ha (chard, sauv, sem) ▪ 16,000cs own label 100% white; Splattered Toad, Stonehaven, The Point: ±50,000cs; ±3,000cs for clients ▪ Brands for clients: Woolworths ▪ BWI, IPW, Farming for the Future ▪ PO Box 100 Noordhoek 7985 ▪ info@cape-point.com ▪ www.capepointvineyards.co.za, www.splatteredtoad.co.za ▪ S 34° 5' 41.82" E 018° 22' 17.28" ▪ F +27 (0)21-789-0614 ▪ **T +27 (0)21-789-0900**

☐ **Cape Promise** *see* uniWines Vineyards

Cape Rock Wines   ⓠ ⌂

'Vergelegen' is a revered designation in SA wine, so it's appropriate that Olifants River Valley's top boutique winery should be based on an estate by that name. It follows the sale of Willie Brand's Oerwoud farm, where wine-making and -tasting were centered, and move to the riverside property where the vines are located. A new cellar and visitor centre have been constructed there, son and co-winemaker Gavin Brand says, and a soupçon of marsanne planted for the GRV blend.

★★★★☆ **SMV** Characterful flagship. Mainly shiraz, mourvèdre & viognier providing extra layers in **13**. Gently textured, with velvet tannins & just 13.5% alcohol (15% in **12**) but also full of flavour – spice, fynbos – freshness & enticing savoury persistence. Older French oak enhanced.

Not tasted: **Cabernet Sauvignon**, **Shiraz**, **SGMV**, **Capa Roca**, **Rosé**, **GRV**. — AL

Location: Vredendal ▪ Map/WO: Olifants River ▪ Est 2001 ▪ 1stB 2002 ▪ Tasting, sales & cellar tours by appt ▪ Closed Good Fri, Dec 25 & Jan 1 ▪ BYO picnic ▪ Owner(s) Willie Brand ▪ Cellarmaster(s) Willie Brand (Jan 2001) ▪ Winemaker(s) Willie Brand (Jan 2001) & Gavin Brand ▪ Viticulturist(s) Jeff Joubert (Jan 2001, consultant) ▪ 13ha/11ha (cab, carignan, grenache, mourv, shiraz, chenin, cbard, marsanne, rouss, viog) ▪ 40t/2,100cs own label 60% red 40% white ▪ PO Box 261 Vredendal 8160 ▪ caperockwines@gmail.com ▪ www.caperockwines.co.za ▪ S 31° 43' 3.12" E 018° 31' 26.37" ▪ F +27 (0)27-213-5567 ▪ **T +27 (0)27-213-2567**

☐ **Cape Soleil** *see* Jacques Germanier
☐ **Cape Sparrow** *see* TCB Wines
☐ **Cape Star** *see* Stellenview Premium Wines
☐ **Cape to Cairo** *see* Rogge Cloof
☐ **Cape to Cape** *see* Nordic Wines
☐ **Cape Tranquility** *see* Pulpit Rock Winery
☐ **Cape View** *see* Kaapzicht Wine Estate
☐ **Cape Vinelands** *see* Asara Wine Estate & Hotel
☐ **Cape West** *see* Namaqua Wines

Cape Wine Company   ⓠ ⓟ ⓝⓔⓦ

With help from Fairview's Charles Back, Erlank Erasmus founded Cape Wine Company in 2010 as a platform for practising his winecraft and sharing his creations with oenophiles worldwide. With HQ in Paarl, CWC is focused on product innovation and assisting brands get their wine from vine to shelf. In the wine below, Erlank salutes Dutch ancestor Pieter Erasmus, grantee in 1699 of a farm in today's Paarl district.

★★★★☆ **Erasmus Family** Impressive **14** from 3 Swartland sites; 50% carignan, with mourvèdre, grenache, shiraz; 20% new oak 14 months. There's aromatic scrub & fynbos, perfect tension between bountiful fruit & refreshing acidity, but what really impresses is the elegant & savoury persistence. — WB, CvZ

Location: Paarl = Map: Paarl & Wellington = Map grid reference: E5 = WO: Swartland = Est 2009 = 1stB 2014 = Tasting & sales Mon-Fri 8-6.30 Sat 8.30-3 = Fee R20 = Closed Good Fri, Dec 25 & Jan 1 = Restaurant Mon-Wed 8-6.30 Thu/Fri 8-9.30 Sat 8-3 = Tertia du Toit Gallery = Owner(s)/winemaker(s) Erlank Erasmus = 5,000cs own label 100% red = erlank@capewinecompany.co.za = S 33° 44' 36.9" E 018° 57' 46.1" = F +27 (0)86-515-9882 = **T +27 (0)21-872-9214**

☐ **Cappupinoccinotage** *see* Boland Kelder
☐ **Cap Vino** *see* Winkelshoek Wine Cellar

Carisbrooke Wines   ⓠ

The brand from lawyer-winegrower Willem Pretorius' Stellenboschkloof farm takes its name from the little train station of Carisbrooke, made famous by the Alan Paton masterpiece Cry, the Beloved Country.

Alan Paton Cabernet Sauvignon ★★★ Bold, brambly & serious **13** a shade harder than previous, with solid backbone & acidity inviting food or further bottle-ageing. — FM

Location/map/WO: Stellenbosch = Map grid reference: C6 = Est 1989 = 1stB 1996 = Tasting & sales Mon-Fri 10-2 = Closed all pub hols = Owner(s) Willem Pretorius = Cellarmaster(s)/winemaker(s) Kowie du Toit (1997), Willem Pretorius = Viticulturist(s) Kowie du Toit (1997) = 19ha/6ha (cab, sem) = 50t/800cs own label 100% red = PO Box 25 Vlottenburg 7604 = willem@carisbrooke.co.za = F +27 (0)21-881-3796/ +27 (0)86-518-8767 = **T +27 (0)21-881-3798**

☐ **Carmel Wines** *see* Wilde Haf Wines
☐ **Carnival** *see* Orange River Cellars
☐ **Carpe Diem** *see* Diemersfontein Wines

Carrol Boyes Collection

South African designer Carrol Boyes partners with her brother, farmer and financier John Boyes, in this range of limited-edition wines, featuring Carrol's bold and striking designs on the labels. See Barnardt Boyes Wines for contact details.

Shiraz ★★★ Dark plums & nutmeg, **13** has the structure to age but is already in perfect drinking mode, you won't want to wait. Franschhoek grapes. **Cape Blend** ★★★★ Pinotage in partnership with cab & merlot in succulent **13**, berry-rich & lavishly spiced from 80% new oak. Stellenbosch WO. — CR

Casa Mori   ⓠ ⌂ ◎

The Devon Valley 'House of Mori' provides a taste of Tuscany, from fresh produce (artichokes a speciality, olives in the offing, a 30-year-barrel-aged red wine vinegar being bottled) to a fresh batch of 2015 wines maturing in their recently upgraded cellar after a vintage hiatus. This includes a sangiovese rosé, promises new winemaker/GM John Kotze.

Location/map: Stellenbosch ▪ Map grid reference: D3 ▪ Est 1995 ▪ 1stB 2009 ▪ Tasting, sales & tours by appt ▪ Farm produce ▪ Conferences/functions ▪ Artichoke festival ▪ B&B facilities (3 rooms) ▪ Owner(s) Eugene Mori ▪ Winemaker(s)/viticulturist(s) John Kotze (2014) & Bruno Julian Mori (1997, consultant) ▪ 4.4ha/2.3ha (cab, malbec, sangio, shiraz, viog) ▪ 15t/2,000cs own label 97% red 1% white 2% rosé ▪ Other export label: Mori ▪ PO Box 71 Koelenhof 7605 ▪ casamoricucina@gmail.com ▪ www.casamori.co.za ▪ S 33° 53' 15.28" E 018° 48' 27.64" ▪ F +27 (0)21-865-2312 ▪ T +27 (0)21-865-2312/+27 (0)83-620-0016 (Eugene)/+27 (0)60-381-3381 (John)

Catch Of The Day

Catch of the Day's DeMorgenzon-seasoned winemaker, Warwick Denman, has become a shareholder in the Cape Town-based business and is helping transform it into 'an ecommerce platform for wine' – sourcing grapes and wines from reputable producers, and marketing small batches of interesting, good-value bottlings to young urbanites via mostly the web and social media, but also popup stores, tastings and more. A shiraz, chenin blanc and sauvignon blanc are planned, and pinotage and sparkling could feature in the strategy of 'bringing wine to the city'.

Location: Cape Town ▪ Closed to public ▪ Owner(s) Cunicsar Vintners cc ▪ Winemaker(s) Warwick Denman ▪ 8 Osborne Road Claremont 7708 ▪ warwickswines@gmail.com ▪ www.catchofthedaywines.com ▪ F +27 (0)86-624-4780 ▪ T +27 (0)84-993-8881

☐ **Cathedral Cellar** see KWV

Catherine Marshall Wines   ⓠ ⑪

Cathy Marshall now probably qualifies, though with undiminished vitality, as a veteran of Cape winemaking, notably of the pinot noir which has long been a central passion. Her small venture is now fully Elgin-oriented: it's where all her grapes are sourced, and vinified – the latter at Valley Green, where she also consults to Hannay Wines. Her experience leads only to further exploration, however, and she's working hard (including with geologists) to understand Elgin's varying soil profiles and how their idiosyncrasies translate into the aromatics, textures and structures of wine, of her beloved pinot in particular.

Catherine Marshall range

★★★★ Pinot Noir On sandstone soils. **13** signature forest floor, perfumed aromas. Fresh & balanced, more 'feminine' elegance than muscularity. Understated intensity, engaging now but ageworthy.

★★★★ Pinot Noir On Clay Soil Was 'Barrel Reserve'. On iron-rich clay soils. **13** hint of earthy savouriness, supple but firmer tannins, more 'masculine' styling, good intensity & balance. One for the cellar.

★★★★ Sauvignon Blanc Fresh herbaceous, stony minerality & a hint of passionfruit on **14**. Mid-palate weight from brush of oaked semillon & lees-ageing. Crisp & clean, with good food-pairing length.

Not retasted: **Myriad 08 ★★★** Not tasted: **Peter's Vision Merlot Reserve**.

Amatra range

★★★★ Merlot 14 ample rich & ripe dark berries & hint of mint. Full bodied, supple texture from some natural fermentation & old oak. Not as elegant & balanced as **13** (★★★★★). Needs time to harmonise.

★★★★ Chenin Blanc Jono's Wave From Elgin's only chenin block. Partly oaked **14** rich, well crafted, with layers of almond, apple flavours. Creamy succulence from lees-ageing but inherently fresh. Lovely length & intensity. Named for surfing son, who joined the business in 2013. — MW

Location/WO: Elgin ▪ Map: Elgin, Walker Bay & Bot River ▪ Est/1stB 1997 ▪ Tasting, sales & cellar tours by appt ▪ Closed Easter Fri-Sun, Dec 25 & Jan 1 ▪ Meals/refreshments by appt ▪ Owner(s) Cathy Marshall, Greg Mitchell, Jonathan Oxenham & Jeff Jolly ▪ Cellarmaster(s) Catherine Marshall (Oct 1996) ▪ Winemaker(s) Shawn Fortuin (Jan 2010) ▪ Viticulturist(s) Various ▪ 40-50t/8,000cs own label 60% red

37% white 3% fortified ▪ IPW ▪ PO Box 30913 Tokai 7966 ▪ cathy@cmwines.co.za ▪ www.cmwines.co.za
▪ S 34° 12' 12.07" E 019° 02' 35.10" ▪ F +27 (0)86-523-7479 ▪ **T +27 (0)83-258-1307**

Cavalli Wine & Stud Farm

The Smith family has transformed this property amid the rolling hills of the Helderberg into a showpiece destination estate. While the horse stud is the bedrock, and includes an equestrian centre, the area's history of winemaking is embraced. Alongside manicured paddocks lie recent virus-free, vermi-composted vineyards – the vines, made offsite, include bought-in grapes as vines mature to supply a home-grown range. All bear an equine theme, as do stylish dining, shopping and conferencing amenities.

Location: Stellenbosch ▪ Map: Helderberg ▪ Est/1stB 2008 ▪ Tasting & sales Wed-Sat 10-7 Sun 10-3 ▪ Closed Dec 26 & Jan 1 ▪ Equus Restaurant Wed-Sun bistro lunch & fine dining dinner ▪ Gift shop ▪ Conferences ▪ Banqueting facility (350 seater) ▪ Conservation area ▪ Art gallery ▪ Boutique ▪ Equestrian centre tours on Sat ▪ Owner(s) Smith family ▪ 80ha/28ha (cab, malbec, p verdot, shiraz, tempranillo, chard, chenin, verdelho, viog) ▪ 100t/6,500cs own label 45% red 40% white 15% rosé ▪ BWI, IPW, WIETA ▪ PO Box 102 Somerset West 7129 ▪ info@cavalliestate.com ▪ www.cavalliestate.com ▪ S 34° 0' 35.91" E 018° 48' 47.06" ▪ F +27 (0)86-766-6556 ▪ **T +27 (0)21-855-3218**

Cecilia Wines

A Wine of the Week plaudit from leading UK winewriter Jancis Robinson for a different producer's bottling from the same Citrusdal Mountain farm as her pinotage recently gave after-hours boutique vintner and Klawer Cellars winemaker Cerina van Niekerk further validation of the quality of the terroir. Strongly pro social responsbility, soft-spoken Cerina donates the proceeds from the wine to the local community.

★★★★☆ **Pinotage** Focused spicy plum on **14** preview, supple structure with intriguing perfumed nuance, clean intensity & balance despite highish alcohol. Natural winemaking & older oak allow Citrusdal Mountain fruit to shine.

In abeyance: **Shiraz-Mourvèdre**. — MW

Location: Klawer ▪ Map: Olifants River ▪ WO: Citrusdal Mountain ▪ Est 2010 ▪ 1stB 2007 ▪ Tasting by appt ▪ Owner(s) Cerina van Niekerk ▪ Cellarmaster(s)/winemaker(s) Cerina van Niekerk (2007) ▪ 2t/100cs own label 100% red ▪ PO Box 23 Trawal 8147 ▪ cecilia@mylan.co.za ▪ www.ceciliawines.co.za ▪ S 31° 51' 32.16" E 018° 36' 13.37" ▪ F +27 (0)86-617-0101 ▪ **T +27 (0)82-334-9422**

☐ **Cecil John** see Boschendal Wines

Cederberg Private Cellar

Fifth-generation David Nieuwoudt has taken the family's former fruit farm in the remote Cederberg Mountain range to heights undreamed of by his grandfather, who planted grapes here in 1973. Learning from the unique conditions, a landlocked site with an altitude of around 1,000 metres above sea level, among the highest in the Western Cape, David purchased a maritime site at Elim near Cape Agulhas in 2008. It now allows him to expresses cool climate on two fronts in his range, Cederberg and Ghost Corner, to wide critical acclaim. Deputies Alex Nel and Tammy Turck-Nel since 2011 have brought their own deft touches to a portfolio that now regularly features in the guide's gallery of five stars, this edition including a sparkling MCC, which speaks to the team's versatility.

Five Generations range

★★★★☆ **Cabernet Sauvignon** Barrel selection, all new French. Cassis & cigarbox, **13** has impressive richness, intensity, concentration. Stands for the family name (as next), must be worthy, & is. Mocha chocolate flavours & succulence make it accessible but the best still lies ahead.

★★★★☆ **Chenin Blanc** French barrel fermented/aged, third new, 14% viognier, **13** seduces with orange blossom, baked apple, the aromatic richness & flavour of roasted nuts. All resting on a seam of brisk acidity, which lifts, enlivens, lengthens, promising an illustrious future.

David Nieuwoudt Ghost Corner range

★★★★☆ **Pinot Noir** Elegant, delicate yet characterful, cherry/raspberry fruit gives a youthful vitality to well-crafted **14**, older oak well judged not to overwhelm. Some subtle earthy notes, touch of minerality make it even more interesting. Great purity, class. Elim fruit for this range.

★★★★☆ **Wild Ferment Sauvignon Blanc** Natural ferment, 9 months French oak, **14** has individual styling, quince & Bosc pear, hint of lemongrass, a ginger biscuit savoury seam. Delicious, has character & attitude, & despite the sleek elegance, is still tightly knit.

★★★★☆ **Sauvignon Blanc** Multi-dimensional **14** (★★★★★) doesn't settle on a particular style, is its own master, and trumps steely **13**. Green fig & summer meadow grasses, a wet pebble minerality, yet pithy grapefruit, a touch of lime in the flavours. Complex, involving, lots to admire.

★★★★☆ **Semillon** Carefully made to respect the fruit & terroir, but with partial oaking to add creamy breadth, elegant **13** is a cool-climate version of the variety. Nettles, a salty minerality, green fig & lime, it has signature finesse, refinement.

★★★★☆ **The Bowline** Referring to the 'king of knots' & how expertly sauvignon & semillon are tied together. Elegant, with intense capsicum, but as with all these, **14** has other layers, dusty minerality, green fig, oak's tantalising almond tone. Vital, with focused freshness.

Cederberg Private Cellar range

★★★★ **Cabernet Sauvignon** For earlier drinking than its big brother, but **13** still well-crafted, impressive, with cassis-laden curves. Fine-grained tannins a hidden strength, add exotic spice, savoury tones. Cederberg grapes for this range.

★★★★☆ **CWG Auction Reserve Teen die Hoog Shiraz** Serious, built for the long haul with all-new French oak, yet **13** respects the fruit. Deep, rich wild berries, lovely aromatics, violets, scrub, oak's dusty cocoa spicing. The structure is compact with good musculature for ageing, but already gorgeous for now.

★★★★ **Shiraz** A template for the variety: bramble berries, scrub & pepper, **13**'s plush fruit giving the sleek, compact structure an admirable succulence, masking the deep muscle tone.

★★★★ **Chenin Blanc** Mineral notes in the perfume continue into the flavours, sharing space with lemon zest. With an austerity, savouriness that could partner oysters, **15** (★★★★) less expressive than **14**.

★★★★ **Sauvignon Blanc** Litchi- & lime-flavoured **15**'s nervy tension bodes well for the future. This is freshness personified, admirable lime intensity on the extended length.

★★★★☆ **Blanc de Blancs Brut** MCC sparkling from chardonnay, third barrel-fermented. Freshness is paramount in masterly **10** (★★★★★), but it's the layers, nuances that captivate. Lemon zest, lemon cream biscuit notes from 52 months on the lees, pine nut richness from oak. Same extra-dry style as **09**.

> **Merlot-Shiraz** ⓥ ★★★★ Nice typicity in **13**, red berries, a herbaceous nuance, comes across as bright & fresh, harmonious. Gives smooth & juicy drinking pleasure. **Bukettraube** ⓥ ★★★☆ A gentle fruity intro, which doesn't prepare you for previewed **15**'s explosion of stonefruit flavours, tangy sweet, vibrant.

Also tasted: **Sustainable Rosé 15** ★★★ — CR

Location: Citrusdal ▪ Map: Olifants River ▪ WO: Cederberg/Elim ▪ Est 1973 ▪ 1stB 1977 ▪ Tasting Mon-Sat 9–12; 2–4.30 pub hols 9–11.30; 4-5.30 ▪ Fee R20 ▪ Closed Easter Fri/Sun, Dec 25 & Jan 1 ▪ Sales Mon-Sat 8-12.30; 2-5 Sun/pub hols 9-12; 4-6 ▪ BYO picnic ▪ Sanddrif Holiday Resort self-catering cottages; camping ▪ Walks/hikes ▪ Mountain biking ▪ Conservation area ▪ Rock climbing ▪ Sport climbing ▪ Observatory ▪ Owner(s) Nieuwoudt family ▪ Cellarmaster(s) David Nieuwoudt (Jan 1997) ▪ Winemaker(s) David Nieuwoudt (Jan 1997), with Alex Nel & Tammy Turck-Nel (Aug 2011) ▪ Viticulturist(s) Ernst Nieuwoudt (Jan 1960) ▪ 5,500ha/60ha (cab, shiraz, bukettraube, chenin, sauv) ▪ 600t/64,000cs own label 40% red 60% white ▪ PO Box 84 Clanwilliam 8135 ▪ info@cederbergwine.com ▪ www.cederbergwine.com ▪ S 32° 30' 12.8" E 019° 15' 27.7" ▪ F +27 (0)86-531-0491 ▪ **T +27 (0)27-482-2827**

Celestina

Her head might be occupied with running her multi-outlet wine retail business in Cape Town but Caroline Rillema's heart belongs to a handkerchief-sized vineyard parcel which she and partner Ray Kilian spend weekends tending at Baardskeerdersbos near Gansbaai. Black Oystercatcher winemaker Dirk Human shepherds the sauvignon and semillon into bottle.

★★★★ Sauvignon Blanc-Semillon 15 preview meets standard set by last-made **12**. Nettle, grapefruit & white pepper typical of this aromatic barrel-fermented blend (67/33). Taut & concentrated, with long mineral tail. — FM

Location: Gansbaai ▪ WO: Cape Agulhas ▪ Est 2004 ▪ 1stB 2009 ▪ Closed to public ▪ Owner(s) Caroline Rillema ▪ Winemaker(s) Dirk Human (Black Oystercatcher) ▪ Viticulturist(s) Caroline Rillema & Ray Kilian ▪ 3.4ha/1.85ha (sauv, sem) ▪ 6t/600cs own label 100% white ▪ c/o Caroline's Fine Wine Cellar, Shop 44 Matador Centre, 62 Strand Street, Cape Town 8001 ▪ carowine2@mweb.co.za ▪ www.carolineswine.com ▪ F +27 (0)21-419-8985 ▪ **T +27 (0)21-419-8984**

Cellar Cask

South Africa's first bag-in-box, launched in 1979, styled by Distell to meet rising demand for Natural Sweet wines with lower alcohol levels. Today in 750ml glass and 2L & 5L packs.

Select Johannisberger Rosé ★★ Sweet pink party wine from shiraz, ruby cab & merlot, **NV**. Strawberry flavours, easy, sippable. Also good with mild curry. **Select Johannisberger Red ★★** Casual picnic wine with clear ruby colour, scent of crushed mulberry, sweet & juicy taste. **NV**. Also tasted: **Select Johannisberger White NV ★★** — DB

☐ **Cellar Door** *see* Namaqua Wines
☐ **Cellar Foot** *see* Lammershoek Winery
☐ **Cellar Road** *see* Darling Cellars

Chabivin Champagne & MCC House

Chabivin is a boutique venture by local bubbly specialist Hendrik Snyman and the Charbaut family, producers of fine champagne near Epernay. Their Stellenbosch vineyard, cellar and visitor venue offers tastings of Charbaut and Chabivin sparklers and, if plans come together, an on-site restaurant.

Signature Series

★★★★ Brut Rosé Pink **12** from pinot noir, as with others in range 80% fermented in older oak. Three years on lees imparts some brioche complexity to delicate wild strawberry fruits. Creamy mousse, fruitily dry finish provide further elegance.

★★★★ Blanc de Blancs (NEW) Refined **12** from 100% chardonnay; soft whipped cream aromas, hint of nutty development gain further complexity from oaked portion. Tiny vivacious bead, sound but unharsh dry finish complete this quality bubbly.

Zero Dosage ★★★ Uncompromisingly dry **11**, mainly pinot noir with 25% chardonnay. Slight hightoned lift to its bruised apple notes; brisk but short-lived bubble. — AL

Location/map/WO: Stellenbosch ▪ Map grid reference: E7 ▪ Est 2008 ▪ Tasting & sales Tue-Fri 9-5 Sat/Sun 10-4; in winter by appt only ▪ Fee R30/3 MCC, R100/4 champagnes (NEW) ▪ Winemaker(s)/viticulturist(s) Hendrik Snyman ▪ 3ha/0.4ha (pinot, chard) ▪ ±8t/1,500cs own label 100% MCC ▪ PO Box 12456 Die Boord Stellenbosch 7613 ▪ info@chabivin.co.za ▪ www.chabivin.co.za ▪ S 33° 58' 24.27" E 018° 51' 8.17" ▪ F +27 (0)86-540-6237 ▪ **T +27 (0)21-880-1643**

☐ **Chameleon** *see* Jordan Wine Estate
☐ **Chamonix** *see* Cape Chamonix Wine Farm
☐ **Chapel** *see* Robertson Winery
☐ **Chapel Cellar** *see* Zanddrift Vineyards – Chapel Cellar
☐ **Charles Borro** *see* Govert Wines

Charles Fox Cap Classique Wines   ⓠ ⓐ

It's ten years since bubbly specialists Charles and Zelda Fox left Johannesburg for an old fruit farm in Elgin, and they celebrated by planting an extra 3 hectares of dry-farmed chardonnay and pinot noir for their small but expanding MCC house. The range gets a new flag bearer this edition, and there are plans to add a blanc de blancs by the end of next year to complete a quartet of fine, handcrafted sparklers.

★★★★☆ **Brut Rosé** ② Very fine-flavoured **11** sparkling from mainly pinot noir with chardonnay & pinot meunier. Flavours of raspberry Pavlova with subtle, balanced, savoury edge, freshening acidity & persistent, fine mousse. Enough depth of flavour to stand up to food.

★★★★☆ **Cipher** (NEW) Accomplished new flagship only in outstanding years. **11** near-equal pinot noir/ chardonnay, small portion oaked (as for Brut), 3+ years on lees have created a lively & exciting wine of Golden Delicious apple hue with ginger spice & creamy citrus length.

★★★★ **Vintage Brut** Change of style (from pinot noir-led to mostly chardonnay with pinots noir & meunier) in **12** (★★★★★) makes for slightly fresher wine than **11** with lively lemon & creamy orange peel notes. 28 months on lees add rich savoury character, lengthy finish to a classy wine. — CM

Location/WO: Elgin ▪ Map: Elgin, Walker Bay & Bot River ▪ Est 2007 ▪ 1stB 2010 ▪ Tasting, sales & cellar tours Mon-Fri 11-4 Sat/Sun 10-4 ▪ Fee applicable ▪ Closed Easter Sun, Dec 25/26 & Jan 1 ▪ Play area for children ▪ Owner(s) Charles & Zelda Fox ▪ Cellarmaster(s) Charles Fox (2010) ▪ Winemaker(s) Nicolas Follet (2010, consultant) ▪ Viticulturist(s) Kevin Watt (2008, consultant) ▪ 33.4ha/6.3ha (pinot noir/ meunier, chard) ▪ 4,000cs own label 100% MCC ▪ PO Box 105 Elgin 7180 ▪ charlesfoxmcc@gmail.com ▪ www.charlesfox.co.za ▪ S 34° 14' 14.38" E 019° 04' 41.99" ▪ F +27 (0)86-536-2924 ▪ **T +27 (0)21-300-1065/+27 (0)82-569-2965/+27 (0)82-471-3444**

☐ **Charmé** *see* Vin du Cap International

Chateau Libertas

The grandfather of SA's reds, available since 1932 and still a paragon of value and drinkability. By Distell.

Chateau Libertas ② ★★★ In usual consistent form, **13** plentiful well-sustained soft black berry fruit in a gentle rounded frame. Bordeaux varieties with shiraz & ruby cab. — AL

Chateau Naudé Wine Creation

Pretoria pharmacist Francois Naudé switched careers late in life, establishing himself in the early 90s as a winemaker (self-taught) on then fledgling Stellenbosch L'Avenir Estate. Armed with a sharp intellect, enquiring mind and ebullient personality, he became a champion at (and of) pinotage and barrel-treated chenin especially. Subsequent consultancies and service on various producer associations have been balanced with this eponymous boutique wine venture with son Francois jnr and daughter Melissa, producing select parcels of internationally acclaimed and distributed wines. A full-time mentoring role on one property has halted production (hopefully temporarily) of the Wingnut and Nuts About ranges. But the flagship Le Vin de François lives on, a special 27L bottle auctioned early 2015 in memory of Magda, beloved late wife, wine-partner and family matriarch.

Chateau Naudé range

★★★★☆ **Le Vin de François** 9 barrels from Paarl, Stellenbosch & Bot River for the 'best of the best' all-pinotage **13**. Lovely depth & intensity, with layers of dark chocolate, vanilla & sweet spice. Seamless, sappy & structured, will age with distinction though already balanced & stylish. Also in 1.5, 3, 5 & 9L.

Wingnut range

★★★★ **Cabernet Sauvignon** ② **10** a shade off stellar **09** (★★★★☆), but still shows classical elegance & restraint, underpinned by deft oaking.

★★★★ **Méthode Cap Classique Brut Rosé** ② Refined & flavoursome **10**, from chardonnay (70%) & pinotage, savoury freshness & fine creamy mousse. Perfect with ceviche or for any occasion.

Not retasted: **Pinotage 11** ★★★ **White Port 10** ★★☆ Not tasted: **Chardonnay**, **Chenin Blanc Barrel Fermented**.

Nuts About range

Chenin Blanc ② ★★★☆ Unshowy yet persuasive **11**, cool clean lines, complementary textural bounce, smooth yet long finish. Not retasted: **Shiraz 11** ★★★ — MW

Location: Stellenbosch ▪ WO: Stellenbosch/Wellington/Stellenbosch-Bot River-Paarl ▪ Est 2006 ▪ 1stB 2007 ▪ Closed to public ▪ Owner(s) Francois Naudé snr, Francois Naudé jnr & Melissa Naudé ▪ Cellarmaster(s) Francois Naudé (Jul 2007) ▪ 1,000cs own label 65% red 35% white ▪ 11 Weidenhof Street Stellenbosch 7600 ▪ naude@levindefrancois.co.za ▪ www.levindefrancois.com ▪ F +27 (0)86-651-3192 ▪ **T +27 (0)21-883-8469**

Chateau VO Extra Fine

This is one of the stalwarts among South Africa's quality modern-day blended brandies produced by Distell, though the brand has been around as such since 1921 and boasts a history dating back even further: it was originally sold wholesale by 19th-century liquor trading company Sedgwick's.

Chateau VO Extra Fine ⦵ ★★★ Decent, straightforward blended brandy designed for mixers. Not short of fruit & floral notes, rich enough, firm & smooth. — WB, TJ

Chennells Wines ⓠ

Blessed with top Helderberg terroir, Jeremy and Colleen Chennells converted just enough of their fruit estate's trees to vines to allow for personal care and involvement. Farming responsibly and holistically, their philosophy appears on each bottle: 'While we live, let us truly live.'

Viognier ⓦ ★★★★ Single-vineyard **14** is something different. Fermented in barrel, shows savoury oatmeal & peach pip flavours, variety's usual aromatics tamed. Lovely!

Not retasted: **Cabernet Sauvignon 10 ★★★★ Shiraz 10 ★★★ The Journey 12 ★★★ A Handful of Summers 13 ★★★** — CR

Location: Stellenbosch ▪ Map: Helderberg ▪ WO: Stellenbosch/Western Cape ▪ Est 2004 ▪ 1stB 2008 ▪ Tasting, sales & cellar tours Mon-Sun 9-5 by appt ▪ Closed all pub hols ▪ Owner(s) Jeremy & Colleen Chennells ▪ Cellarmaster(s)/winemaker(s) Jeremy Chennells & Chris Keet (Jul 2009, consultant) ▪ Viticulturist(s) Colleen Chennells & Chris Keet (Jul 2009, consultant) ▪ 5ha/3.2ha (cab, shiraz, viog) ▪ 26t/330cs own label 85% red 15% white ▪ Romond Vineyards, Klein Helderberg Road, Somerset West 7130 ▪ chennell@iafrica.com ▪ S 34° 1' 52.61" E 018° 49' 59.67" ▪ F +27 (0)21-683-6280 ▪ **T +27 (0)21-855-3905**

☐ **Chip Off The Old Block** see Ormonde Private Cellar
☐ **Chris Keet** see Keet Wines
☐ **Christina Van Loveren** see Van Loveren Family Vineyards
☐ **Christine-Marié** see Niel Joubert Estate
☐ **Cilliers Cellars** see Stellendrift – SHZ Cilliers/Kuün Wyne
☐ **Circle of Life** see Waterkloof
☐ **Circumstance** see Waterkloof

Cirrus Wines

A transcontinental venture between the owners of California's Silver Oaks Cellars, Ray Duncan and sons David and Tim, and Jean Engelbrecht of Rust en Vrede, aimed at 'capturing the very essence of shiraz influenced by both Stellenbosch and Napa'.

★★★★★ **Cirrus Syrah** Some changes in style but quality of **13** remains of the highest. Shy aromas open up to serene & structured mouthful of dark berries, spice, perfume & oak (now 100% French). Splash viognier adds elegance & grace to seriously beautiful wine. — CM

Location/WO: Stellenbosch ▪ Est/1stB 2003 ▪ Tasting & sales at Guardian Peak ▪ Owner(s) Jean Engelbrecht & Ray Duncan ▪ Cellarmaster(s) Coenie Snyman (Jun 2010) ▪ Winemaker(s) Roelof Lotriet (Sep 2014) ▪ Viticulturist(s) Dirkie Mouton (Jun 2010) ▪ 30t/3,626cs own label 100% red ▪ IPW ▪ PO Box 473 Stellenbosch 7599 ▪ info@cirruswines.com ▪ www.cirruswines.com ▪ F +27 (0)21-881-3388 ▪ **T +27 (0)21-881-3899**

☐ **Citrusdal Wines** see Piekenierskloof Wine Company

CK Wines

Bushveld-born Christian Kuun, seduced by wine while studying stock farming at Elsenburg, now immerses himself in winemaking as vintner for Beau Joubert as well as his own label. Inspired by his son's birth in 2009, CK reflects his love of red Bordeaux, fleshed out in 2015 with a limited-release sauvignon blanc, 'tickled with a little French oak', and a sparkling MCC, neither ready for tasting.

★★★★ **Sincera** ⓥ Appealing rich cocoa & oodles of succulent black fruit on pre-bottling debut **11**, 100% cab franc. Yielding & plush textured; harmonious oaking with long star anise & liquorice finish.

★★★★ **Integra** ⓥ Switches from varietal cab to 60/40 blend cab & cab franc in **10**, goes up notch on **09** (★★★★). Rich & ripe yet gently soft, heaps of cassis flavour, lovely mouthfeel & balance. — FM

Location/WO: Stellenbosch ▪ Est 2009 ▪ 1stB 2010 ▪ Closed to public ▪ Owner(s)/cellarmaster(s)/winemaker(s) Christian Kuun ▪ 1,000cs own label 70% red 15% white 15% MCC ▪ winemaker@ckwines.co.za, sales@ckwines.co.za ▪ F +27 (0)86-504-6209 ▪ **T +27 (0)82-615-8105**

Claime d'Or   ⓥ

Gold is referenced in the name of the boutique winery of husband and wife team Bernardo Rapoport and Magriet de Wet, sourcing from 10 ha of vines in the Goudmyn ('Gold Mine') area between Robertson and Bonnievale, and in the second range, Solidus, after a Roman empire gold coin.

Claime d'Or range

Chardonnay ★★★☆ Pleasing improvement on lightly oaked **14** with plenty of lemon curd, zesty fruit & creamy richness. Tad short but otherwise a very pleasant drop. **Sauvignon Blanc** ★★★ Green notes dominate on **14** with celery & mange tout yielding to a surprising richness on the palate (nearly 4 g/l sugar) & not unpleasant finish. Also tasted: **Cabernet Franc 12** ★★★☆ **Cabernet Sauvignon-Cabernet Franc 12** ★★★☆ Not retasted: **Pinot Noir 11** ★★★☆ **Shiraz 11** ★★★ Not tasted: **Cabernet Sauvignon Rosé**.

Solidus range

Cabernet Sauvignon ⓥ ★★★★ Supple **12** opens to bright blackberry fruit, lifted by cab's dusty/leafy notes. Elegant dinner companion now & for few years. Not retasted: **Unwooded Chardonnay 13** ★★★☆ — CM

Location: Robertson ▪ WO: Robertson/Western Cape ▪ Est/1stB 2008 ▪ Tasting & sales at Rietvallei Wine Estate ▪ Owner(s) Magriet de Wet & Bernardo Rapoport ▪ Cellarmaster(s)/winemaker(s) Kobus Burger (2002, Rietvallei) ▪ Viticulturist(s) Wilhelm Treurnicht (2007, Rietvallei) ▪ 10ha (cabs s/f, sauv) ▪ 30% red 60% white 10% rosé ▪ PO Box 2040 Parklands 2121 ▪ info@claimedorwines.co.za ▪ www.claimedorwines.co.za ▪ F +27 (0)86-691-7497/+27 (0)11-788-7346 ▪ **T +27 (0)11-447-8776**

Clairvaux Private Cellar   ⓥ ⊜ ⓖ

Winemaker and recently appointed manager Jaco van der Merwe is upbeat about the quality of the 2015 harvest at Robertson's Clairvaux Private Cellar. The family-owned business produces more than 3 million litres annually of mostly bulk wine for local and export markets, but also bottles a range of budget wines that can be ordered online or purchased from excellent local retailer, La Verne Wine Boutique.

Sandberg Purple ⓥ ★★ **13** pinotage, merlot & malbec combo, sturdy campfire companion. **Sauvignon Blanc** ★★★ Wallet-friendly, step-up **15** has immediate sauvignon appeal – grass, capsicum – plus white peach; packs a zesty, flavoursome punch. **Red Muscadel** ⓥ ★★★★ Fortified dessert to 'warm dem bones'. Jasmine-scented **12** reminiscent of sweet black tea; tangy lemon & well-integrated spirit cut the sweetness. Not retasted: **Cabernet Sauvignon 11** ★★★ **Shiraz 11** ★★ **Good Night Irene 14** ★★★ **Madonna's Kisses 14** ★★★★ **Cape Vintage 12** ★★★ — CvZ

Location/map/WO: Robertson ▪ Est/1stB 2000 ▪ Tasting & sales Mon-Fri 8-5 ▪ Closed all pub hols ▪ Cellar tours by appt ▪ BYO picnic ▪ Sales (at cellar price) also from La Verne Wine Boutique T +27 (0)23-626-4314 Mon-Fri 9-5.30 Sat 9-5 ▪ Owner(s) Wouter J de Wet snr & jnr ▪ Winemaker(s) / manager Jaco van der Merwe (Oct 2011) ▪ 200ha (cab, merlot, ptage, shiraz, chard, chenin, cbard, muscadel, sauv) ▪ 4,000t/3.2m L bulk ▪ PO Box 179 Robertson 6705 ▪ info@clairvauxcellar.co.za ▪ www.clairvauxcellar.co.za ▪ S 33° 48' 13.8" E 019° 52' 21.1" ▪ F +27 (0)23-626-1925 ▪ **T +27 (0)23-626-3842**

Clayton Wines

Swapping Scotland for South Africa and the security business for winemaking, Roger Clayton found kindred spirits among the Swartland Independent Producers. After a stint with DeanDavid, he's expanding his own portfolio under the Jolly Roger banner. Still working mainly with typical new-wave Swartland Rhône varieties, he's also exploring similarly on-trend Portuguese 'port' grapes after a vintage visit in 2014. A tinta barocca (not ready for tasting) may be released soon.

Jolly Roger range

★★★★ SMG (NEW) Swartland grapes, naturally fermented & lightly oaked, as for other red. **14** introduces 15% mourvèdre & equal shiraz, grenache, in a harmonious wine with an almost ethereal lightness.

★★★★☆ Chardonnay Ex Elgin, **14** (★★★☆) has light & lively stonefruit flavours with oatmeal/straw notes. Fresh & mouthwatering, but lacks the grip & intensity of **13** from Swartland bushvines.

Syrah-Grenache (NEW) **★★★☆** Equal blend has bright, red cherry & cranberry lightness typical of this producer. Could do with more substance, but **14** is delicate, pure & appetising. — HJ

Location: Riebeek-Kasteel ▪ WO: Swartland/Elgin ▪ Est/1stB 2013 ▪ Closed to public ▪ Wines available from Wine Kollective, Riebeek-Kasteel & Vino Pronto, Cape Town ▪ Owner(s) Roger & Natasha Clayton ▪ Winemaker(s) Roger Clayton (Jan 2013) ▪ 6t/400cs own label 50% red 50% white ▪ Postnet Suite 247, Private Bag X16, Constantia 7848 ▪ roger@unwined.co.za ▪ **T +27 (0)76-826-8500**

☐ **Clearsprings** *see* Trizanne Signature Wines

Clive Torr Wines ⓦ

A chance meeting with the late Robert Mondavi in Napa Valley inspired Clive Torr, then studying pomology to switch to winegrowing. Now a Cape Wine Master, wine educator and garagiste mentor, his eponymous venture involves handcrafted parcels in Elgin and the western slopes of the Cape Peninsula.

Clive Torr range

★★★★ Pinot Noir NW From warmer north-west slope in Elgin, riper, fuller cherry fruit bomb **14** is both fresh & confected, steps up on **13** (★★★☆) with touch sherbet & fresh grassy-green notes. Genuinely appealing, cries out for a savoury terrine.

Chardonnay (NEW) **★★★☆** Expressive **14** nose of sweet yellow plums & peaches with unusual banana hint, good acidity & depth. From Elgin. Also tasted: **Shiraz 13 ★★★ Viognier 14 ★★★** Not tasted: **Pinot Noir SE, Chenin Banc, Sauvignon Blanc**.

Scarborough Affair range

Shiraz ★★ Medicinal tones on retasted **13**, some sweet spice but herbal notes overwhelm. Not tasted: **Cabernet Sauvignon**. — CM

Location: Somerset West ▪ Map: Helderberg ▪ WO: Elgin/Cape Peninsula ▪ Tasting by appt ▪ Owner(s)/ winemaker(s) Clive Torr ▪ 26 Topaz Street Heldervue Somerset West 7130 ▪ clivetorrwines@mweb.co.za ▪ www.clivetorrwines.co.za ▪ S 34° 3' 19.09" E 018° 49' 1.51" ▪ F +27 (0)86-513-4034 ▪ **T +27 (0)82-557-0836**

Cloof Wine Estate ⓦ ⓦ ⓐ ⓐ ⓐ

There's more to this large former wheat farm near Darling than its annual Rocking the Daisies music festival, now in its tenth year (events and tasting room manager Ida van Tonder reports 'huge strides made in catering for special events'). Replanted to classic grape varieties in the late 1990s, under foreign ownership since 2003, and committed to conserving Darling's highly endangered veld types, Cloof keeps expanding its range – with local sales ramping up in response. International response to new-look labels, intending 'to reflect the uniqueness of what's inside the bottle' has been 'phenomenal'.

Premium range

★★★★ Cloof Shiraz ⓐ More sexy than its Signature stablemate, dense yet remarkably fresh **12** oozes ripe raspberry while hints of black pepper, smoked meat & sweet spice from year oak add intrigue.

★★★★ Cloof Lynchpin ⓐ **10** (★★★☆) first since **06**. Austere cab franc (70%) & merlot mix proffers brooding plum, with a tannic frame requiring decanting.

★★★★ **Syrah-Viognier** (NEW) A heady posy of blossoms on **13**'s nose from 5% viognier, along with white pepper & clove spice, leading to dark fruit & liquorice flavours, silky texture & dry, savoury finish.

★★★★ **Chenin Blanc** (NEW) Only 1,500 bottles of barrel-fermented **14** made by Jody Johannes as special old-bushvines project; heady honeysuckle & spicy cinnamon adding complexity to orange citrus & apricots, creaminess balanced by fresh acidity.

Merlot (🍷) ★★★★ Ripe plums on nose of **12**, sweet prunes, milk chocolate & fruitcake sweetness on palate balanced by mouthwatering prickle of acidity.

Not tasted: **Crucible Shiraz**.

Signature range

★★★★ **The Very Sexy Shiraz** Sweeter, softer, lighter than new Syrah-Viognier above, **13** (★★★★) is slightly less seductive than **12**, with cinnamon lifting berry fruit, white pepper to finish.

Cab Cult Cabernet Sauvignon (✓) (🍷) ★★★★ Many followers due to its sheer drinkability, juicy & moreish **13** has crushed ripe blackcurrant – even Ribena-like – intensity, soft & very approachable.

Also tasted: **The Dark Side Cabernet Sauvignon-Shiraz** (✓) 13 ★★★★ Not retasted: **Cloof Pinotage** 11 ★★★ **Inkspot Vin Noir** 11 ★★★ **The Very Vivacious Viognier** 14 ★★★★ Discontinued: **Summertime Sauvignon Blanc**.

Duckitt range

★★★★ **Cabernet Sauvignon-Merlot-Cabernet Franc** (✓) In leaner **13**, the wild berries & leafiness of 30% cab franc prevail, while the ripe cassis of cab is back in richer, more concentrated **14** preview (60% cab, 22% merlot, 18% cab franc).

Sauvignon Blanc (NEW) ★★★★ **15**'s pale appearance doesn't hint at aromatic burst of citrus to come, followed by intense tropical mouthful of granadilla & green melon, zesty dry acidity. Also tasted: **Chardonnay-Pinot Noir NV** ★★★★

Darling range

Rosy Darling (✓) ★★★ From pinotage, crisp dry **15** rosé has pink fruit intensity: guava, watermelon & ruby grapefruit. Not retasted: **Ruby Darling** 13 ★★★ **Daisy Darling Chardonnay Unwooded** 14 ★★★ **Happy Dragon Chenin** 13 ★★★ **Daisy Sweet Darling** 14 ★★★ **Daisy Darling** 14 ★★★

Bush Vine range

Rosé (NEW) ★★★ Crisp, dry **15** pink from pinotage, with – as it happens – pink tropical fruit notes. **Chenin Blanc** (NEW) (✓) ★★★★ **15**'s peach & honeysuckle promise doesn't quite deliver on palate, where creamy mouthfeel is balanced by lime zest with slight peach-pip bitterness on finish. — JG

Location/WO: Darling ▪ Map: Durbanville, Philadelphia & Darling ▪ Est/1stB 1998 ▪ Tasting & sales Mon-Sat 10–4 ▪ Closed Easter Fri/Sun, Dec 25 & Jan 1 ▪ Cellar tours by appt ▪ Meals/refreshments Tue-Sat 11-3 ▪ Farm produce ▪ Conservation area ▪ Game & eco drives by appt ▪ Child friendly ▪ Owner(s) Cloof Wine Estate (Pty) Ltd ▪ Winemaker(s) Christopher van Dieren (Jan 2002) & Jody Johannes (Jan 2012) ▪ Viticulturist(s) Peter Duckitt (May 2004) ▪ 1,300ha/135ha (cabs s/f, merlot, ptage, shiraz, chard, chenin, viog) ▪ 600t/100,000cs own label 88% red 12% white ▪ BWI champion ▪ PO Box 269 Darling 7345 ▪ info@cloof.co.za ▪ www.cloof.co.za ▪ S 33° 28' 58.1" E 018° 31' 23.4" ▪ F +27 (0)22-492-3261 ▪ **T +27 (0)22-492-2839**

Clos Malverne   (♀) (🍴) (📷) (♿)

Touted as Stellenbosch's smallest wine venture when boutique winefarming was rare in SA, Seymour and Sophia Pritchard's Devon Valley winery celebrates its 30th anniversary this year. It's maintained its personal touch and dedication to pinotage while growing in size and stature. Suzanne Coetzee is winemaker, viticulturist and manager, recently overseeing construction of a glass-walled barrel maturation space and addition of a 'cold' kitchen for an expanded al fresco dining area with verdant views.

★★★★ **Pinotage Reserve** Traditionally crafted, dark plum & wild heather scented **13**, savoury notes on firmly structured palate with good freshness & developing complexity. Will age well.

★★★★ **Auret** 2 vintages of flagship Cape Blend reviewed: **12** from cab, pinotage, dollops merlot & shiraz is smooth & elegant, with rich fruit flavours, fine tannins; all-new French oak; **13** (★★★★☆) similar profile but less complex, tannins need more time. No shiraz & 50% new oak.

★★★★ **Spirit of Malverne Limited Release** Step-up **12** (★★★★☆) Cape Blend pinotage (46%), cab & shiraz is lively & bright with concentrated black fruit flavours tempered by meaty savouriness & firm but supple tannins. 18 months in new French oak. Slightly more pinotage in **11**.

★★★★ **Ellie MCC** Unusual salmon pink sparkling from shiraz. Second disgorgement of **11** is very appealing, ripe red berry & soft spice nuances, fine bubbles & savoury ending.

Chardonnay ★★★☆ Bright, clove-spiced **14** from McGregor grapes, briefly oaked, delights with ripe fruit flavours & zesty lemon goodbye. **Sauvignon Blanc** ★★★☆ Only Devon Valley grapes for this label, showing juicy tropical fruit & green undertones in **14**. Friendly & succulent, lees-ageing providing smooth mouthfeel. Also tasted: **Merlot 13** ★★★★ **Cabernet Sauvignon-Merlot 13** ★★★☆ **Cabernet Sauvignon-Shiraz 13** ★★★ Not retasted: **Le Café Pinotage 12** ★★★★ **Sauvignon Blanc Brut Reserve NV** ★★★ Not tasted: **Auret Limited Release**. — WB

Location/map: Stellenbosch ▪ Map grid reference: D4 ▪ WO: Stellenbosch/Western Cape/Devon Valley ▪ Est/1stB 1986 ▪ Tasting & sales Mon-Sat 10—5 Sun 10-4.30 ▪ Fee R25/4 wines ▪ Closed Good Fri, Dec 25 & Jan 1 ▪ Cellar tours Mon-Fri ▪ The Restaurant @ Clos Malverne ▪ Tour groups ▪ Gifts ▪ Conferences ▪ Weddings/functions ▪ Walks/hikes ▪ Wellness Day Spa ▪ Owner(s) Seymour & Sophia Pritchard ▪ Cellarmaster(s)/viticulturist(s) Suzanne Coetzee (Oct 2010) ▪ Winemaker(s) Suzanne Coetzee (Oct 2010), with Mynardt Hitchcock (1999) ▪ 18ha (cab, ptage, sauv) ▪ ±200t/80,000cs own label 50% red 50% white ▪ PO Box 187 Stellenbosch 7599 ▪ info@closmalverne.co.za ▪ www.closmalverne.co.za, www.capeblend.co.za ▪ S 33° 54' 38.0" E 018° 48' 49.2" ▪ F +27 (0)21-865-2518 ▪ **T +27 (0)21-865-2022**

Clouds Wine Estate   Ⓟ ⑪ ⌂ ◎

That the international owners of this boutique luxury accommodation, conferencing and wedding venue atop Stellenbosch's Helshoogte Pass are serious about wine is clear. Having broadened their own tiny vineyard's varietal mix, they've commissioned star winemaker Donovan Rall (also vinifying for nearby Vuurberg and his own top-rated label) to extend the portfolio. Among the new line-up, a wooded chenin blanc and (untasted) shiraz, unsurprising given Donovan's long connection with the Swartland.

★★★★ **Pinot Noir** Elegant **14** (★★★★☆) adds evolved earthy, mushroom layers to more delicate **13**'s fresh berry vibrancy. Long & concentrated wine from Walker Bay fruit, 20% new barrels.

★★★★ **Chardonnay** ⓃⒺⓦ Lime & lees juxtaposition in delicious **14**; Ceres grapes, bunch pressed & naturally fermented in seasoned casks, yield vibrant acid tension amid oatmeal creaminess. Balanced, poised.

★★★★ **Chenin Blanc** ⓃⒺⓦ Classy **14** in oxidative style of new-wave Swartland, its grape origin, with underlying crystalline minerality that enlivens the broad flavours. Bunch pressed, wild yeasts, all old oak.

Also tasted: **Pink 14** ★★★☆ **Sauvignon Blanc 14** ★★★☆ — DS

Location/map: Stellenbosch ▪ Map grid reference: G5 ▪ WO: Western Cape/Stellenbosch/Swartland ▪ Est/1stB 1993 ▪ Tasting & sales Mon-Sat 10-5 ▪ Breakfast ▪ Hotel & self-catering villas ▪ Conferences ▪ Weddings & functions ▪ Owner(s) Paul Burema & Jolanda van Haperen ▪ Cellarmaster(s) Donovan Rall (Jan 2014, Vuurberg) ▪ Winemaker(s) Donovan Rall (Jan 2014, Vuurberg), with Paul Burema (Jan 2012) ▪ Viticulturist(s) Wynand Pienaar (Aug 2009, consultant) ▪ 4.5ha/2.7ha (cab, pinot, chard, sauv) ▪ 24t/2,500cs own label 40% red 60% white ▪ PO Box 540 Stellenbosch 7599 ▪ info@cloudsestate.co.za ▪ www.cloudsestate.co.za ▪ S 33° 55' 23.9" E 018° 55' 29.7" ▪ F +27 (0)21-885-2829 ▪ **T +27 (0)21-885-1819**

Clovelly Wines   Ⓟ

In between consulting for others, winemaker/viticulturist Jacques Fourie vinifies a small range under an own label. The wines (latest vintages not available for tasting) are mostly red and chiefly from fruit bought in from Stellenbosch (with chardonnay from Robertson), but they do include the grapes from a postage stamp cabernet vineyard on the family farm overlooking Devon Valley.

Location/map: Stellenbosch ▪ Map grid reference: D4 ▪ Est/1stB 2000 ▪ Tasting, sales & tours strictly by appt ▪ Owner(s) York Partnership t/a Clovelly Wines ▪ Winemaker(s)/viticulturist(s) Jacques Fourie ▪

4ha/3ha (cab) ▪ 90% red 10% white ▪ Postnet Suite 215 Private Bag X5061 Stellenbosch 7599 ▪ info@
clovellywines.com ▪ www.clovellywines.com ▪ S 33° 53' 54.1" E 018° 47' 52.3" ▪ F +27 (0)21-865-
2511 ▪ **T +27 (0)82-853-7190**

Cloverfield Private Cellar   ⓘ ♿

Family history has an honoured place – in the winery branding and name of the Shamrock Red – for the
much-loved Irish lass who bore Cloverfield patriarch Pietie Marais three sons and brought hope, love as
well as luck to the Robertson farm.

Shamrock Red ★★★ From mostly shiraz, latest lightly oaked **NV** (**14**) improves on previous; a touch
heavy & sweet, but this balanced by a decent grip of tannin & acid. **Shamrock Rosé** ⑲ **★★★** Rather
charming delicate raspberry character on tasty **15**; just off-dry but still crisp enough. **Chenin Blanc**
★★☆ 15 tank sample pleases more than previous, with thatchy, dried peach notes; well rounded with a
crisp bite. Also tasted: **Chardonnay Unwooded 15 ★★★** **Sauvignon Blanc 15 ★★★** Not retasted:
Chardonnay Wooded 14 ★★ — TJ

Location/map/WO: Robertson ▪ Est 1945 ▪ 1stB 2002 ▪ Tasting & sales Mon-Fri 9-5 ▪ Closed Easter Fri-Mon,
Dec 25 & Jan 1 ▪ Owner(s)/viticulturist(s) Pieter Marais ▪ Cellarmaster(s) Cobus Marais (2002) ▪
Winemaker(s) Cobus Marais (2002), with Gerald Smith (Jun 2009) ▪ ±200ha total (shiraz, chard, chenin,
sauv) ▪ 40% red 60% white ▪ PO Box 429 Robertson 6705 ▪ info@cloverfield.co.za ▪ www.cloverfield.co.za ▪
S 33° 49' 57.3" E 019° 55' 34.1" ▪ F +27 (0)23-626-3203 ▪ **T +27 (0)23-626-4118**

☐ **Cocoa Hill** *see* Dornier Wines

Cold Duck (5th Avenue)

Long-established sweet, low-alcohol carbonated sparkling rosé by Distell.

5th Avenue Cold Duck ⓥ **★★★** Scented pink party fizz, **NV**, simple but balanced, uncloying. — DB

☐ **Cold Mountain** *see* Brunia Wines
☐ **Collection** *see* Mooiplaas Estate & Private Nature Reserve

Collison's

Funky packaging in non-traditional (for brandy) blue and silver reflects brand owner Distell's intent to
appeal to a young, trendy, inclusively female market. But the name – recalling 19th-century Cape Colony distillers and traders, Englishmen John and Francis Collison – is a nod to SA's rich brandy heritage.

White Gold ⓥ **★★★☆** Near colourless (useful in cocktails). Light tropical fruity nose, hints of vanilla &
roasted nuts. Elegant, youthful; slightly sweet aftertaste. Blended; from chenin & colombard. — WB, TJ

Colmant Cap Classique & Champagne   ⓘ ♿

The Colmants – Jean-Philippe, wife Isabelle and five children – made a leap into the unknown when, in
2005, they swapped their masonry stone manufacturing business in Belgium for a 5-ha sub-division of the
original La Motte farm overlooking Franschhoek. They set about building their reputation on high-end MCC
sparkling wines with a remarkably consistent and consistent formula: own small blocks of classic varieties with
brought-in fruit, an all-NV range based on blending oak-matured base wine and reserve fractions, extended
lees maturation and late disgorgement. These techniques have been rewarded by an enviably reliable track
record and a string of awards. From the outset, they've also distributed a carefully selected range of champagnes. Their customer-friendly tasting room is a must for any lover of sparkling wine.

★★★★ Brut Rosé Latest **NV** follows form of previous (though now slightly drier). Appealing green
    apples, strawberries & quince laced with exotic spiciness. 70/30 pinot/chardonnay, 2 years bottle-aged.

★★★★☆ Brut Chardonnay Flagship of an exceptional range, **NV** offers intriguing spices & fruit pre-
    serves with a nutty, honeyed, delightfully lingering palate. Oak (20%) adds weight & breadth without
    intruding. Complex & elegant, exuding class. 45 months on lees.

★★★★☆ **Brut Reserve** Consistently impressive **NV** bubbly, near-equal pinot/chardonnay blend, achieves fine balance of creamy mousse, fresh acidity & richly layered fruit. Appealing citrus marmalade zest with nutty brioche. Elegant long finish. On lees 32 months.

★★★★ **Sec Reserve** Almost equal pinot & chardonnay, with 23 g/l sugar, produce a pleasantly creamy, fruity result. Refined & elegant **NV**, with distinct spiciness from 12% oak. On lees 32 months. — GdB

Location/map: Franschhoek ▪ WO: Western Cape ▪ Est 2005 ▪ 1stB 2006 ▪ Tasting & sales Mon-Fri 11-1; or by appt ▪ Fee R15 per ½ glass MCC ▪ Cellar tours on request ▪ Owner(s) Jean-Philippe Colmant ▪ Cellarmaster(s) Jean-Philippe Colmant ▪ Wine consultants Nicolas Follet & Pieter Ferreira ▪ Viticulturist(s) Paul Wallace (consultant) ▪ 5ha/3ha (pinot, chard) ▪ 7,400cs own label 100% MCC ▪ PO Box 602 Franschhoek 7690 ▪ info@colmant.co.za ▪ www.colmant.co.za ▪ S 33° 55' 22.4" E 019° 7' 37.3" ▪ F +27 (0)21-876-3732 ▪ **T +27 (0)21-876-4348/+27 (0)72-368-4942**

☐ **Commando** see Distell
☐ **Compagnies Wijn** see Oude Compagnies Post Private Cellar
☐ **Concierge** see Almenkerk Wine Estate
☐ **Concordia** see KWV
☐ **Condé** see Stark-Condé Wines
☐ **Confluence** see Douglas Wine Cellar

Conradie Family Vineyards   ⓠ ⓨ ⓐ ⓐ ⓞ ⓐ

Plenty of activity at this family-owned farm in Nuy Valley. The winemaking facility has doubled in size, with investment going into new equipment and tanks while on the people side, a dynamic new team has been formed for marketing and PR. All celebrated with the launch of the farm's first MCC bubbles.

Conradie Family Vineyards range
★★★★ **Friederich Conradÿ MCC Brut** ⓝⒺ Enjoyable **08** sparkling packs in plenty of yeasty creaminess with some ginger biscuit spice, hint of marshmallow & apple pie notes. 5 years on lees adds richness & texture. **09** follows in similar vein. From chardonnay.

Also tasted: **Sauvignon Blanc 15** ★★★★ Not retasted: **Cabernet Sauvignon-Pinotage 14** ★★☆ **Sweet Rosaline Perlé Rosé NV** ★★ **Rooi Muskadel 09** ★★☆

Single Vineyard Barrel Selection Reserve range
★★★★ **Pinotage** ⓖ Juxtaposition of sweet vanilla & choc with savoury bacon & spice in juicy **12**. Not retasted: **Cabernet Sauvignon 13** ★★★ Discontinued: **Shiraz**. — CM

Location/map: Worcester ▪ WO: Nuy/Western Cape ▪ Est/1stB 2004 ▪ Tasting, sales & cellar tours Mon-Fri 8.30–4.30 Sat 9-3 Sun 11-2; after-hours by appt ▪ Closed Good Fri, Ascension Day, Dec 25 & Jan 1 ▪ Nuy Vallei Restaurant & Guest House: meals daily 8-5, or by appt ▪ Facilities for children ▪ Tour groups ▪ Gift shop ▪ Farm produce ▪ BYO picnic ▪ Conferences ▪ Walks/hikes ▪ MTB & 4x4 trails ▪ Conservation area ▪ Annual Nuy Valley Feast (May) ▪ Owner(s) CP Conradie & Gareth Penny ▪ Cellarmaster(s) CP Conradie (Jan 2004) ▪ Winemaker(s) CP Conradie (Jan 2004), with Ronwan Griffiths (Sep 2009) ▪ Viticulturist(s) CP Conradie ▪ 4,500ha/83ha (cab, ptage, pontac, chenin, cbard, crouchen, muscadel w, pinot gris, sauv) ▪ 1,840t total 70t/5,400cs own label 50% red 25% white 25% rosé ▪ BWI ▪ PO Box 5298 Worcester 6851 ▪ wine@conradievineyards.co.za ▪ www.conradie-vineyards.co.za ▪ S 33° 39' 28.0" E 019° 37' 59.6" ▪ F +27 (0)86-509-4911 ▪ **T +27 (0)23-342-7025**

☐ **Conservation Coast** see Whalehaven Wines

Conspirare   ⓠ

Boutique vintner Henry Dowling hasn't vinified his blended red Conspirare in several years, but the '02 is still available from his Helderberg farm.

Location: Stellenbosch ▪ Map: Helderberg ▪ Est/1stB 2002 ▪ Tasting by appt ▪ Owner(s) HB Dowling/LRD Trust ▪ Winemaker(s) Henry Dowling ▪ 24ha (cabs s/f, merlot, shiraz, chenin) ▪ 250t/850cs own label 100% red ▪ PO Box 1210 Stellenbosch 7599 ▪ dowls@mweb.co.za ▪ S 34° 1' 18.4" E 018° 50' 54.6" ▪ F +27 (0)86-516-3086 ▪ **T +27 (0)21-855-0706**

☐ **Constantia de Tulbagh** *see* Montpellier

Constantia Glen   ⓛ ⑪

This prestigious wine farm in the Constantia heights was originally part of Simon van der Stel's vast Constantia estate. Forest and pasture gave way to vineyards only in 2000 when the Waibel family purchased the property and recognised its potential for Bordeaux grape varieties, red and white, thanks to the longer sunlight hours at this northern end of the valley. Busy with a replanting programme to increase blending opportunities, winemaker Justin van Wyk says his team is constantly working towards improving wine quality and furthering their 'biological' approach to viticulture. 'We have purchased a cover crop roller, which rolls the annual cover crop into a mulch, preventing the germination of weed seedlings in the work row, thus allowing us to minimise herbicide sprays.'

★★★★☆ **Constantia Glen Five** Powerful yet elegant **11** flagship blends all five Bordeaux red varieties (31% cab, 27% merlot, plus petit verdot, cab franc & malbec), hence the name. Clove & tobacco notes promise thrilling evolution of dense cassis & cherry core. 1.5 & 3L formats available.

★★★★☆ **Constantia Glen Three** Plush & velvety yet fresh **12** is about half merlot, equal cab & cab franc. With juicy blackcurrant, dark cherry & plum fruit, & fine tannin structure, this is an iron fist in a silk glove – already delicious, accessible, with a fine future. Also in magnum.

★★★★☆ **Sauvignon Blanc** Winning formula of (unwooded) 4% semillon added for palate weight works in creamy yet fresh, flinty **15**, typical elderflower perfume leading to intricate passionfruit & gooseberry, cling peach & kumquat flavours, with long, vibrant finish. **14** untasted.

★★★★ **Constantia Glen Two** Subtly but confidently rises above siblings in **14** (★★★★★) seamless Bordeaux-style white, richness of 30% barrel-aged semillon countering sauvignon's high acidity. Fruit flavours range from green melon to grapefruit but it's more about texture & minerality; should age even more gracefully than **13**. — JG

Location/WO: Constantia ▪ Map: Cape Peninsula ▪ Est 2000 ▪ 1stB 2005 ▪ Tasting & sales Mon-Sun 10-5 ▪ Tasting fees from R40-R80, waived according to purchase ▪ Closed Good Fri, Dec 25 & Jan 1 ▪ Cheese & charcuterie platters; various soups during winter ▪ Owner(s) Tumado Investments (Pty) Ltd ▪ Winemaker(s) Justin van Wyk (Dec 2011), with Megan van der Merwe (May 2015) ▪ Viticulturist(s) Etienne Southey (Sep 2012, farm manager) & Andrew Teubes (consultant) ▪ 60ha/28.5ha (cabs s/f, malbec, merlot, p verdot, sauv, sem) ▪ 160t/20,000cs own label 70% red 30% white ▪ PO Box 780 Constantia 7848 ▪ wine@constantiaglen.com ▪ www.constantiaglen.com ▪ S 34° 0' 39.6" E 018° 24' 30.6" ▪ F +27 (0)21-795-6101 ▪ **T +27 (0)21-795-6100**

Constantia Mist   ⓛ ⌂

After a break, property developer and between-times vintner John Schooling has a new vintage, vinified from his tiny Constantia vineyard by local wine man Gregory Louw. Only 250 (x 6) cases were made, so only a select few will get their hands on one of the Cape's more exclusive – and tasty – sauvignon blancs.

★★★★ **Sauvignon Blanc 14** first since **10**. Its cool-climate origin evident in the delicate yet resonating scents & purity. Bone-dry, with balanced savoury acid, it's best enjoyed in the flush of youth. — AL

Location/WO: Constantia ▪ Map: Cape Peninsula ▪ Est 2004 ▪ 1stB 2009 ▪ Tasting & sales by appt only ▪ Closed Good Fri & Dec 25 ▪ 4-star guest house (self-catering) ▪ Owner(s) Eagles Nest Property Investments (Pty) Ltd ▪ Cellarmaster(s) John Schooling (2009) ▪ Winemaker(s)/viticulturist(s) Gregory Louw (Silvermist Vineyards) ▪ 6.6ha/2.8ha (sauv) ▪ 5.4t/ha 250cs own label 100% white ▪ Postnet Suite 96, Private Bag X16, Constantia 7848 ▪ johns@stagprop.com ▪ www.constantiamist.co.za ▪ S 34° 1' 0.48" E 018° 24' 58.32" ▪ F +27 (0)21-794-4123 ▪ **T +27 (0)21-794-0904**

Constantia Uitsig   ⓛ ⑪ ⊚

Historically part of 17th-century Cape Governor Simon van der Stel's vast Constantia Valley landholding, this already vaunted wine producer seems set to take things up a notch under new owner Pieter Erasmus, CEO of SA retail giant Pepkor. Vines planted in the late 1980s are being systematically replaced by young Stellenbosch viticulture/oenology graduate Jacques du Plessis (ex Olifantsberg), who will eventually assume winemaking duties (vinification has been at neighbour Steenberg to date). Established luxury hospitality offerings (except for the revamped, renamed Open Door restaurant) have been closed. Renovated and new buildings (including a state-of-the-art winery) will follow 'green' principles, already evident in the restoration of the natural environment, reflected in delicate new 'bird' labels on wines available for tasting/sale in a charmingly rustic cottage.

★★★★ **Constantia Red** ⓦ Elegant, seamlessly integrated **12**, merlot-led blend with both cabs, flaunts abundant plum & red fruit, underpinned by well-structured tannins from mostly new barrels.

★★★★☆ **Chardonnay Reserve** Classy, confident **14** (★★★★) luxuriously oaked (half new), less thrilling than precise **13**, but still has creamy lees-enriched texture & peach-flavoured pithiness.

★★★★ **Sauvignon Blanc** Expressive preview **15** characterises young sauvignon in full flight. Light minerality underlies decent weight & richness in ultra-fresh, vibrant style.

★★★★★ **Semillon** Vibrant **14** has plenty of verve in more accessible, less remarkable vintage. Trademark earthiness underlies layers of deliciously sweet, creamily textured fruit wrapped around pithy core & structured oak, portion new. **13** (★★★★☆) flinty, austere.

★★★★★ **Natura Vista** Was 'Constantia White' in pretty new label design. Concentrated but less obviously imposing than usual, accessible **14** semillon, sauvignon blend has seamless fruit/acid/oak balance in freshly pithy, generously rich style & sustained flavourful finish.

★★★★ **Méthode Cap Classique** Expansive, confidently oaked & aged (3 years on lees) **12** all-chardonnay sparkling is generously bold & toasty. Ripe pear flavours persist, carried by gentle mousse.

★★★★ **Red Muscat d'Alexandrie** ⓦ Previewed **NV** dessert-style fortified shows overt grape aromas. Lacks wow-factor of previous, though moreish, sweet impression rendered dry by spicy tannins.

Also tasted: **Chardonnay Unwooded 15** ★★★ — IM

Location/WO: Constantia ▪ Map: Cape Peninsula ▪ Est 1980 ▪ 1stB 1988 ▪ Tasting Mon-Fri 10—6 Sat/Sun & pub hols 10—5 ▪ Fee R40 ▪ Closed Good Fri, Dec 25/26 & Jan 1 ▪ Wine Shop: deli items, gifts ▪ Hanepoot grapes sold annually ▪ Tour groups ▪ Open Door restaurant ▪ Chris Nixon cycling academy ▪ Owner(s) Constantia Uitsig Wine Estate (Pty) Limited ▪ Cellarmaster(s) JD Pretorius ▪ Winemaker(s) JD Pretorius & Jacques du Plessis ▪ Viticulturist(s) Jacques du Plessis (2015) ▪ 60ha/20ha (cabs s/f, merlot, chard, Muscat d'A, sauv, sem) ▪ 120t/20,000cs own label 10% red 90% white ▪ WIETA ▪ PO Box 32 Constantia 7848 ▪ jacques@uitsig.co.za ▪ www.uitsig.co.za ▪ S 34° 2' 51.9" E 018° 25' 27.5" ▪ F +27 (0)21-794-7605 ▪ **T +27 (0)21-794-6500**

☐ **Constitution Road** *see* Robertson Winery
☐ **Contours Collection** *see* Swartland Winery

Conviction

American David Brown and South African Clive Torr collaborate on this boutique label, vinified naturally at Romond on the Helderberg. The grapes are from a site in cool-climate Elgin known for ripening cab — ripe enough to translate into higher alcohol, in fact. 'It is what it is,' Clive shrugs.

Cabernet Sauvignon ★★★★ Convincing **14** shows usual soft styling: plush layers of very ripe fruit, pliable tannins for easy access; big 14.7% alcohol — down on **13** & **12**, actually — adds no heat, only smooth sweet nuance on finish. — CvZ

Location: Somerset West ▪ WO: Elgin ▪ Est/1stB 2009 ▪ Closed to public ▪ Winemaker(s) Clive Torr & David Brown, with Anne Howell ▪ 10ha ▪ 100cs ▪ 26 Topaz Street Heldervue 7130 ▪ clivetorr@bigfoot.com ▪ **T +27 (0)82-557-0826**

☐ **Cool Bay** *see* Boplaas Family Vineyards
☐ **Cooperative** *see* Bosman Family Vineyards
☐ **Coral Reef** *see* Wineways Marketing
☐ **Coral Tree** *see* FirstCape Vineyards

Corder Family Wines   ⓦ

Ian and Anette Corder report 'good inroads' into the US market with their Cool Climate Collection, now streamlined to comprise the four classics tasted below. The couple, he an advertising/marketing man, she a former wine tourism practitioner, are advised by seasoned viticulturist Kevin Watt, particularly au fait with Elgin's developing vineyard terrain.

Cool Climate Collection

★★★★ Chardonnay Sweet flourish of **14** not classic but will win many fans; warm baked custard viscosity offset by citrus tang. Lick (10%) of new oak; a satisfying drop.

★★★★ Sauvignon Blanc Most agreeable **14** combines herbaceous fresh-cut grass & riper peach/pear features in a textured body; loaded with flavour but ends a tad sweet.

Pinot Noir (NEW) **★★★** Delicate **13** gets much-needed heft from 15% shiraz, seasoned oak. **Syrah** (NEW) **★★★★** Seamless melange of spicy fruit, supple tannins & firming oak, **13** goes down very smoothly. Discontinued: **Special Reserve Shiraz**, **Corder Barrel Crafted Viognier**. — DS

Location/WO: Elgin ▪ Map: Elgin, Walker Bay & Bot River ▪ Est 2003 ▪ 1stB 2007 ▪ Tasting & sales Mon-Fri 9-2 Sat/Sun by appt ▪ Closed all pub hols ▪ Owner(s) Ian & Anette Corder ▪ Cellarmaster(s)/winemaker(s) Joris van Almenkerk (Mar 2010) ▪ Viticulturist(s) Kevin Watt (2004) ▪ 40ha/14ha (pinot, shiraz, chard, sauv) ▪ 90t ▪ own label 20% red 80% white ▪ PO Box 169 Elgin 7180 ▪ ian@corderwines.co.za ▪ www.corderwines.co.za ▪ S 34° 12' 8.10" E 019° 0' 47.46" ▪ F +27 (0)21-846-8460 ▪ **T +27 (0)21-846-8083**

☐ **Country Cellars** see Orange River Cellars
☐ **Couple's Wine** see Bergheim
☐ **Coutelier** see Domaine Coutelier

Cowlin Wines

A new company with a familiar name and owners, John and Lisa Cowlin, previously based on a farm in Simondium, sold in 2006. Lisa then moved abroad and on her return, father and daughter found their shared interest in wine as strong as ever, so they started a negociant business under the old name, selecting parcels delivering 'the best expression of the varieties'. A top-end varietal shiraz will replace the Jack's Jug shiraz-merlot selling out at press time, and a new red blend will be added in due course.

Rosé (NEW) **★★★** From shiraz & pinotage (60/40), **13** is a pretty pink with woody notes, dry & lightish; a savoury undertone gives food compatibility. **Sauvignon Blanc** (NEW) **★★★** 10% semillon adds a light lemon touch, rounds out sauvignon's acidity on lively grass- & asparagus-toned **14**. For drinking now, solo or with food. Discontinued: **Jack's Jug**. — WB, CvZ

Location: Cape Town ▪ WO: Stellenbosch ▪ Est/1stB 2014 ▪ Closed to public ▪ Owner(s) John & Lisa Cowlin ▪ Winemaker(s)/viticulturist(s) Hardy Laubscher (2014, consultant) ▪ PO Box 793 Noordhoek 7975 ▪ lisa@cowlinwines.com, john@cowlinwines.com ▪ www.cowlinwines.com ▪ **T +27 (0)72-973-9562**

☐ **Craighall** see African Wines & Spirits

Cranefields Wine   ⓠ

Focused on the export market (Hamburg-based merchant Siegfried Greve is co-owner), Cranefields wines (we await the next vintages to review) are named for South Africa's national bird, the Blue Crane, and sales of the brand help raise funds for birdlife conservation.

Location/map: Villiersdorp ▪ WO: Overberg ▪ Est/1st B 1995 ▪ Tasting by appt only ▪ Owner(s) SJ Greve & CJ Roux ▪ Winemaker(s) Christo Versfeld (Villiersdorp Cellar) & Riaan Wassüng (Jan 2005, Stellenbosch University Welgevallen Cellar) ▪ Viticulturist(s) Charl Roux (Feb 1998) ▪ 35ha (cab, merlot, shiraz) ▪ 220t/6,000cs own label 100% red ▪ PO Box 417 Villiersdorp 6846 ▪ cranefields@telkomsa.net ▪ www.cranefields.com ▪ S 34° 2' 45.99" E 019° 13' 59.64" ▪ F +27 (0)28-840-0440 ▪ **T +27 (0)28-840-2565**

Craven Wines   ⓠ

The 'natural', avant-garde winemaking approach taken by this young husband-and-wife pair (Australian Mick and local Jeanine) is not common in Stellenbosch, but expressing the vinous essence of that grand area though early picking of single-vineyard sites is what they focus on for their light, fresh and ebulliently drinkable wines. Their day jobs are also there: Jeanine makes wine for Dornier, Mick for Mulderbosch — which is also where their wines are made, in tiny quantities.

★★★★ Pinot Noir Faure Vineyard Adds origin to name from **14**. Better varietal expression than **13**. Less than 11% alcohol, but enough subtle intensity of flavour for sappy, sweet-fruited length. Finely balanced acidity, gentle tannin. Whole-bunch pressed & somehow redolent of naturalness.

★★★★ Syrah Faure Vineyard (NEW) Perfumed (spicy & floral) **14** is modest in the best possible sense. Remarkable sweet red-fruit flavour for just 11.4% alcohol. Finely structured, supple & hugely drinkable.

★★★★ Clairette Blanche (NEW) **14** half skin ferment, half just whole-bunch pressed to old oak. Slightly nutty, with clear oxidative notes; light & lean but with pervasive flavour — though not at all 'fruity'. Lipsmackingly drinkable. Natural yeast, unfined, unfiltered, like all these. Like above, 11% alcohol.

★★★★ Clairette Blanche Skin Fermented (NEW) Esoteric **14** fermented (like red wine) on its skins 10 days, then in old oak. More intense, austere, nutty version of Clairette, acid & tannin more obvious. Not unfresh.

Pinot Gris (NEW) **★★★☆** Skin contact (8 days) gives salmon colour to old-oaked **14**. Beautiful ethereal aromas but supple, crisply dry palate a touch insubstantial. No unripe hint at 11% alcohol. Tiny volume; export only. — TJ

Location/WO: Stellenbosch ▪ Est 2013 ▪ 1stB 2014 ▪ Tasting & sales by appt only ▪ Owner(s) Jeanine & Mick Craven ▪ Winemaker(s) Jeanine & Mick Craven (Jan 2013) ▪ 7t/700cs own label 60% red 40% white ▪ PO Box 972 Somerset Mall 7137 ▪ mick@cravenwines.com ▪ www.cravenwines.com ▪ **T +27 (0)72-701-2723**

Creation Wines   (symbols)

Co-owners Jean-Claude and Carolyn Martin infuse this Hemel-en-Aarde mountainside property with excitement and, yes, creativity. The couple are both from winemaking backgrounds: he Swiss-born and -trained, she from the Finlayson clan of leading local vintners. Converting pasture to vineyards amid indigenous vegetation, they bucked the trend with classic Bordeaux and Rhône varieties alongside the area's signature pinot noir and chardonnay. All are bearing exceptional fruit. New are a barrel selection, single-vineyard pinot noir and chardonnay under the Art of Creation label. A debut reserve merlot will soon be joined by grenache and, eventually, others. Superior sites for pinot and shiraz informed more plantings of both. Their new assistant winemaker is the third generation of one of Stellenbosch's venerable wine families. Cherry on the top: they're now officially a 'unit for the production of estate wine'.

Premium range

★★★★ Merlot 13 less wondrously aromatic than **12** but with same chalky texture & cocoa-rich flavours. Depth, concentration of flavour & body on well-judged oak platform (now 25% new).

★★★★ Reserve Merlot (NEW) **13** billows violets & fynbos; deeper, denser choc-mocha profile than standard label, sumptuous finish. Oaking, too, ramped up: 60% new, 18 months.

★★★★ Pinot Noir Most delicate of cellar's pinot noir trio. **14** hints of earth with primary cherry & berry features. Silky, layered on integrated oak base (25% new), long finish beautifully balanced.

★★★★☆ Reserve Pinot Noir Vineyard selection showing forest floor & loamy notes; lithe, supple, yet firmly structured, unfruity. Like **13** (★★★★★), **14** deeply textured, great flavour concentration & intensity in enduring finish. Polished oak, 45% new.

★★★★☆ The Art of Pinot Noir (NEW) Darkest, deepest, most textured of the three pinot labels. **13** gutsy, brooding & muscular, needing time to offer up all its charms. Best grapes, 30% bunch fermented to add freshness, 60% new oak one year. Beautiful composure, demands respect. 1,200 numbered bottles.

★★★★ Syrah Vibrant fruit melange — dark cherry, blueberry & plum — seamed with woodsmoke & spice. Structure is restrained, 14.5% alcohol well contained in supple & rewarding **13**.

★★★★ Merlot-Cabernet Sauvignon-Petit Verdot (symbol) **12** a tight, dense, tannic mouthful in youth, but concentration of flavour & body, as well as lengthy dry tail, bode well for few years in cellar.

★★★★☆ Syrah-Grenache Blackcurrant opulence contrasts with cocoa grip in spicy 80/20 blend. Chunky **13** (★★★★) is muscular, not as refined as **12**. Firm yet yielding oak (14 months oak, 25% new).

★★★★☆ Chardonnay New World juiciness in Old World style. **14** lavish but not blowsy, loaded with lemon curd & vanilla cream yet restrained; pure fruit perfectly framed by oak, just 25% new.

★★★★☆ **The Art of Chardonnay** (NEW) Serious fruit seriously oaked. Seriously priced too... Selected grapes bunch pressed, cask fermented/matured, 60% new. **13** packed with tropical flavours, full & weighty but ends fresh, dry. Not too subtle, quite a glassful. Just 600 numbered bottles made.

★★★★ **Viognier** Typical peach vivacity on fruity, unwooded **15**; apricot fullness cut by bouncy acid, dry chalky texture & mineral tang. Four months on fine lees, rich but not overblown.

Also tasted: **Sauvignon Blanc 15** ★★★★ **Sauvignon Blanc-Semillon 14** ★★★★ — DS

Location: Hermanus ▪ Map: Elgin, Walker Bay & Bot River ▪ WO: Walker Bay ▪ Est 2002 ▪ 1stB 2006 ▪ Tasting, sales & cellar tours daily 10-5 ▪ Closed Dec 25 & Jan 1 ▪ Lunch; wine & canapés; secret food & wine pairing; wine & chocolate pairing; tea pairing ▪ Kiddies' beverages & snack pairing, menu & designated play area ▪ Tour groups ▪ Wine accessories, books & souvenirs on sale ▪ Walking/hiking trails ▪ Predator-friendly farm ▪ Conservation area ▪ Art exhibition (paintings & sculptures) ▪ Events: blend your own bottle; barrel/true terroir tasting; vineyard safari on foot; regular musical performances & themed cultural events ▪ Owner(s) Jean-Claude & Carolyn Martin, Jonathan Drake ▪ Cellarmaster(s) Jean-Claude Martin (Jan 2006) ▪ Winemaker(s) Jean-Claude Martin (Jan 2006), with Michael Malan (Jul 2014) ▪ Viticulturist(s) Jean-Claude Martin & Peter Davison (consultant), advised by Johan Pienaar (all 2002) ▪ 35ha (cab, grenache, merlot, p verdot, pinot, shiraz, chard, sauv, sem, viog) ▪ 300t/50,000cs own label 65% red 35% white ▪ BWI, EnviroWines accredited, IPW ▪ PO Box 1772 Hermanus 7200 ▪ info@creationwines.com ▪ www.creationwines.com ▪ S 34° 19' 51.90" E 019° 19' 35.53" ▪ F +27 (0)28-212-1127 ▪ **T +27 (0)28-212-1107**

☐ **Creative Block** see Spier
☐ **Credo** see Stellenbosch Vineyards

Crios Bríde

The braided straw girdle belonging to the Celtic fertility goddess Brighid lends its name to this Stellenbosch boutique family winery, whose wines are made by Saltare's Carla Pauw.

★★★★ **Syrah-Carignan** (②) Powerful **07** concentrated molten dark fruit, good structure & ageability. **Chenin Blanc** (②) ★★★☆ Sumptuous & robust **07** ex Swartland vines. Not retasted: **Sauvignon Blanc 08** ★★★★ **Méthode Cap Classique 07** ★★★★ — MW

Location: Stellenbosch ▪ WO: Swartland/Darling ▪ Est/1stB 2007 ▪ Closed to public ▪ Owner(s) Yorke-Smith family ▪ Winemaker(s) Carla Pauw (Jan 2007, consultant) ▪ 2,500cs own label 15% red 25% white 60% MCC ▪ PO Box 2290 Dennesig Stellenbosch 7601 ▪ carlapauw@gmail.com ▪ F +27 (0)88-021-883-9568 ▪ **T +27 (0)21-883-9568**

Crows Nest (②) (🍽) (🍷) (📷) (🏠)

Marcel and Deidre de Reuck's winery on the western slopes of Paarl Mountain may be small, but the wines are big. Very big. To be expected from a vintner who spent eight years diving off Scotland's oil rigs, and believes 'wine should have a presence, shake you up a bit!'

Marcel de Reuck range
Syrah (②) ★★★★ **09** beefy, with 5 years in barrel & 15.5% alcohol. Integrated tannins, harmonious melange of dark berries, oak & savoury meaty flavours. Not tasted: **Cabernet Sauvignon**, **Cabernet Sauvignon-Merlot**, **Cabernet Sauvignon-Syrah**, **Chardonnay**.

Torres Claude range
Not tasted: **Crow's Nest**. — WB

Location: Paarl ▪ Map: Paarl & Wellington ▪ Map grid reference: D3 ▪ WO: Coastal ▪ Est/1stB 2002 ▪ Tasting, sales & cellar tours Mon-Fri 10–5 Sat/Sun & pub hols by appt ▪ Fee R25, waived on purchase ▪ Meals by appt; or BYO picnic ▪ Facilities for children ▪ Farm produce ▪ Weddings/functions ▪ Conservation area ▪ Owner(s) Marcel & Deidre de Reuck ▪ Winemaker(s) Marcel de Reuck ▪ 33.6ha/11.5ha (cab, shiraz) ▪ 60t/10,000cs own label 90% red 5% white 5% port ▪ PO Box 2571 Paarl 7620 ▪ dereuck@mweb.co.za ▪ www.dereuckwines.co.za ▪ S 33° 40' 33.0" E 018° 54' 25.4" ▪ F +27 (0)21-869-8714 ▪ **T +27 (0)21-869-8712**

Croydon Vineyard Residential Estate ⓠ ⓞ ⓐ ⓑ

The names of the wines made at this Helderberg residential estate reflect the character and story of the place. Portion 20 refers to the original farm, where the winery is, while the Title Deed range confirms that the house-owners are also co-owners of the vineyards and cellar. Some, in fact, get involved even before wines reach the bottle – including the occasional bit of grape-crushing by foot.

Title Deed range

★★★★ Cape Blend ⊘ Reworked blend in **13** omits pinotage, now equal cab/cab franc with 10% malbec. Pleasantly focused & substantial, showing black berries & currants with serious liquorice core.

Rosé ★★★ 15 dry shiraz has bright, steely raspberry fruit, light body, modest finish. Appealing pale rose colour. Also tasted: **Chenin Blanc 15 ★★**

Croydon range

Not tasted: **Covenant Pinotage, Portion 20.** — GdB

Location/WO: Stellenbosch ▪ Map: Helderberg ▪ Est/1stB 2004 ▪ Tasting & sales Mon-Fri 10-5 Sat 9-1 ▪ Closed all religious holidays ▪ Cellar tours by appt ▪ Facilities for children ▪ Tour groups ▪ Conferences ▪ Events ▪ Owner(s) Croydon Vineyard Estate ▪ Winemaker(s) Rikus Neethling (consultant), with Jannie Alexander ▪ Viticulturist(s) Nico Grobler (consultant) ▪ Vineyard manager(s) Ben van Zyl ▪ 8ha (cabs s/f, malbec, merlot, ptage, shiraz, chenin) ▪ 65t/4,000cs own label 95% red 5% white ▪ Unit 1 Croydon Vineyard Estate Somerset West 7130 ▪ admin@croydon-estate.co.za ▪ www.croydon-estate.co.za ▪ S 34° 2' 23.3" E 018° 45' 5.5" ▪ F +27 (0)21-843-3609 ▪ **T +27 (0)21-843-3610**

Crystallum

This small label is managed by the Finlayson brothers: architect Andrew and winemaker Peter-Allan. The latter came to wine via philosophy and economics after a happily failed attempt to escape his clan's enduring involvement in Cape wine. (Father Peter helped pioneer the Hemel-en-Aarde Valley as prime viticultural terroir from the late 1970s.) A working vintage in Burgundy partly inspired his focus on chardonnay and pinot noir, sourced from special sites throughout the valley and surrounding Overberg, and vinified naturally using wild yeasts and minimal sulphur. Crystallum is Latin for a crystal drinking cup, marking the label's birth in a straw-bale cellar at Crystal Kloof on Hemel-en-Aarde Ridge. Its new home is Gabriëlskloof, whose wines Peter-Allan now also oversees (having married the co-owner's daughter).

★★★★★ Bona Fide Pinot Noir Back-to-form **14** from a single Hemel-en-Aarde Valley vineyard is appealing, with gorgeous texture & complexity: earthy forest floor, sweet fruit & savoury finish. **13** (★★★★) less harmonious.

★★★★★ Cuvée Cinéma Pinot Noir Jaw-dropping perfumed grace on **14** from single Hemel-en-Aarde Ridge parcel. Displays a fine combination of richness & delicacy. Pure fruit & silky texture give early charm; structure bodes well for future enjoyment. Natural ferment, as all. **13** (★★★★★) also graceful.

★★★★★ Mabalel Pinot Noir From a high-lying young inland (Elandskloof) vineyard, **14** from all destemmed grapes. Concentrated & refined, marrying pure red berry fruit with spicy oak & long velvety exit. Well-judged oaking on all these pinots.

★★★★★ Peter Max Pinot Noir Dark cherry, bitter chocolate & allspice on the **14** perfumed nose. Intense & elegant, but without undue weight: fruit flavours are accented by a subtle smokiness & sexy spiciness that vibrate in the mouth. Includes high inland vineyard, some whole bunches.

★★★★★ Clay Shales Chardonnay Citrus, stone, wild flower & ripe pear – with toasty hint – on early complexity of **14** from high-altitude single vineyard. Rich & creamy palate, with succulent acidity carrying it to very long mineral finish. Vines just outside the Hemel-en-Aarde area, so WO Overberg.

★★★★★ The Agnes Chardonnay Blended from three vineyards in Hemel-en-Aarde & Overberg. **14** is full-flavoured, exuberant & precise. Silky mouthfeel with vibrant limy acid conclusion. Like Clay Shales, naturally fermented & sensitively oaked. — WB

Location: Bot River ▪ WO: Western Cape/Overberg/Hemel-en-Aarde Ridge/Hemel-en-Aarde Valley ▪ Fst 2006 ▪ 1stB 2007 ▪ Closed to public ▪ Owner(s) Crystallum Coastal Vineyards (Pty) Ltd ▪ Winemaker(s) Peter-Allan Finlayson (2006) ▪ 60t/7,000cs own label 60% red 40% white ▪ PO Box 857 Hermanus 7200 ▪ info@crystallumwines.com ▪ www.crystallumwines.com

☐ **Culemborg** *see* DGB
☐ **Culinaria Collection** *see* Leopard's Leap Family Vineyards
☐ **Curator's Collection** *see* Glen Carlou
☐ **Cutters Cove** *see* Robert Stanford Estate

Dâbar

Jannie Gutter's farm Vierfontein near Napier bears figs, flowers, blueberries and grapes – mainly sauvignon blanc and some chardonnay, shiraz and pinot noir. Farm manager Niel Schutte and new consultant viticulturist Conrad Schutte are focusing on quality enhancement using, among others, the rare-in-SA guyot (cane) pruning method. Another new presence is Rianie Strydom (Haskell Vineyards), bringing wide-ranging winemaking expertise to the team.

★★★★ **Pinot Noir** Forceful **14**'s (★★★★) intense hue, concentrated fruit & spice-tangerine attraction let down slightly by sappy oak finish. This also evident on pretty & delicate **13** but less so. Both much improve on maiden **11** (★★★).

Shiraz (NEW) ★★★★ Red fruits & black pepper on judiciously oaked (20% new) **13**. Commendable dryness, weight for food or solo sipping. **Cuveé Brut** (NEW) ★★★ MCC sparkling from chardonnay (60%) & pinot noir, among relatively few in SA with portion oaked base wine. This somewhat overwhelms the fruit on **11**, lends rustic styling. WO W Cape. Also tasted: **Sauvignon Blanc 15** ★★★ — WB, CvZ

Location: Napier ▪ WO: Napier/Western Cape ▪ 1stB 2010 ▪ Closed to public ▪ Owner(s) Jannie Gutter ▪ Winemaker(s) Rianie Strydom (Haskell Vineyards) ▪ Viticulturist(s) Conrad Schutte (consultant) ▪ 25ha (pinot, shiraz, chard, sauv) ▪ 50% red 50% white ▪ lukas@atwine.co.za ▪ **T +27 (0)83-306-9467/+27 (0)71-491-6183**

☐ **Da Capo Vineyards** *see* Idiom Collection

Dagbreek   (Ⓠ) (👜) (📷)

Out of 3rd-generation Breedekloof winegrower Peet Smith's small-scale portfolio always something new or different. This edition it's a maiden tinta amarela, aka trincadeira, locally rare Portuguese variety long associated with 'port' but also, as here, unfortified dry red. For his own new 'port', dedicated to his late father, Peet used a different Portuguese native, touriga nacional, the gold-standard grape for that style.

★★★★ **Tinta Amarela** (NEW) High-toned pot-pourri & red berry perfumes, supple tannins, lovely dryness & length; older-oak-matured **14** lipsmackingly fresh, well made.

Cape Vintage (NEW) ★★★★ Liquorice & Xmas pudding on 'port' from touriga, in striking 375 ml bottle. 19% spirit gives warmth but, overall, **13** is soft & smooth, best enjoyed relatively young. Also tasted: **Touriga Nacional 12** ★★★★ Not tasted: **Nebbiolo**, **Chenin Blanc Barrel Selection**. — CvZ

Location: Rawsonville ▪ Map/WO: Breedekloof ▪ Est/1stB 2009 ▪ Tasting, sales & cellar tours Mon-Sat by appt ▪ Closed all pub hols ▪ BYO picnic ▪ Walking/hiking trails ▪ Owner(s) Peet Smith ▪ Cellarmaster(s)/winemaker(s) Peet Smith (2009) ▪ Viticulturist(s) Leon Dippenaar (2009, consultant) ▪ 108ha/48ha under vine ▪ 7t/1,000cs own label 70% red 30% white ▪ WIETA ▪ PO Box 237 Rawsonville 6845 ▪ dagbreek@compnet.co.za ▪ www.dagbreek.co.za ▪ S 33° 39' 56.20" E 019° 18' 26.99" ▪ F +27 (0)86-529-2865 ▪ **T +27 (0)82-820-2256**

Dalla Cia Wine & Spirit Company   (Ⓠ) (🍴) (♿)

Giorgio Dalla Cia, celebrated Meerlust winemaker for 25 years and son of a famed Italian distiller, with scion George set up a distillery in Stellenbosch in 2004, exactly a decade after the production of 'grappa' (husk spirit) became legal in SA. In celebration, they've readied a limited, individually numbered and signed bottling of the original distillation. Also new, and innovative, is Dalla Cia Corretto, a snap-open, single-serving grappa sachet allowing Italophiles to quickly and conveniently 'correct' their espresso. Wine has been part of the DCW&SC portfolio from the outset, and it too leans towards the old country, no more so than in the Supertuscan-style flagship, Teano, honouring Italy's unification.

Dalla Cia Wine range

★★★★ Classico Cabernet Sauvignon 13 shows better concentration than **12** (★★★☆) but fruit remains distinctly, atypically plummy. Quality oak regime & careful handling show in supple, complex palate & finish. 10% petit verdot.

★★★★ Pinot Noir Intensely fragrant, seductively plush **13** (★★★★☆) a fine expression of this enigmatic grape. Opulent yet elegant, handling 18 months new oak with ease. Approachable now but, like last-tasted **11**, promises even better things with a few years cellaring. Also in magnum.

★★★★☆ Giorgio 12 (★★★★) Bordeaux-style blend, 60 % cab with merlot, petit verdot & cab franc is understated & elegant, but lacks the wow factor of **11** & standout **07** (★★★★★). Subtle fruit, spicy oak, may emerge in time. Magnum also available.

★★★★☆ Teano ⓐ Maiden release of flagship blend (third sangiovese, rest undisclosed French varieties), **11** shows brooding power & subtle spiciness in laudable 'Supertuscan' style. Attention-grabbing intensity, rich texture, lingering farewell. WO W Cape. Also in magnum, jéroboam.

★★★★ Chardonnay Ripe, rich & expressive **14** follows previous form with leesy texture, minimal wood. Appealingly fruity yet restrained, should improve with time in bottle.

Also tasted: **Sauvignon Blanc 15** ★★★★

Dalla Cia Husk Spirit range

★★★★★ 10 Year Old Celebration Cabernet Sauvignon-Merlot Limited release marks distillery's 10th anniversary. Last time a preview, now shows delicate hints of spicy plum, tobacco & tealeaves. Rich, with a velvet texture, delightfully mellow. Flavours of prune & hay add to complexity. Long-lasting sipper to be savoured. 500 ml, handsomely packaged.

★★★★ Cabernet Sauvignon-Merlot Premium Selection ⓐ Slight straw tinge to this more refined, less aggressive Premium (lightly oak-barrelled) version of the standard Husk Spirit from these varieties. Supple, gently unctuous palate, lingering finish.

★★★★ Pinot-Chardonnay ⓐ Fresh aromas of fruit & nuts; some delicacy, focus & refinement evident on a delightfully textured, smooth & balanced palate.

★★★★ Single Cultivar Organic Merlot ⓐ ⓒ High-toned note gives magnificent lift to red berry & floral aromas; sweet spice & some citrus buoy spirity finish (43% alcohol). Smooth & elegant.

Cabernet Sauvignon-Merlot ⓐ ★★★☆ Robust aromas & flavours – 'husky', quiet berry hint. Smooth enough, but with some rusticity. Not tasted: **Limited Edition Pinot Noir**. — WB, GdB, TJ

Location/map: Stellenbosch ▪ Map grid reference: E5 ▪ WO: Stellenbosch/Western Cape ▪ Est 2004 ▪ Tasting, sales & traditional Italian meals at Pane E Vino Food & Wine Bar, Mon-Fri 10-6 Sat 10-5 ▪ Owner(s) Giorgio & George Dalla Cia ▪ Winemaker(s) Giorgio Dalla Cia ▪ 18,000cs ▪ 7A Lower Dorp Street Bosman's Crossing Stellenbosch ▪ info@dallacia.com ▪ www.dallacia.com ▪ S 33° 56' 25.8" E018° 50' 50.1" ▪ F +27 (0)21-887-2621 ▪ **T +27 (0)21-888-4120**

Damarakloof

The vineyard on family farm Damarakloof near Paarl was once was a racetrack, deemed too gravelly for vines. Given the rise of SA old-vine chenin, owner Agnes de Vos feels 'it's appropriate to remember that ours was planted 63 years ago by my grandfather. He used mules and horses to plough the soil and dynamite sticks to blast out the rocks. We're returning to the old ways by composting with straw bales.'

Racetrack range

★★★★ Regale ⓐ When last tasted, **08** Bordeaux red returned to classic form after **06** (★★★☆). Fragrant, refreshingly demure & altogether delightful to drink. No **07**.

Chenin Blanc ★★★☆ Old-oak-fermented (part natural) **13**, rich stewed apple & spice zested with lime for satisfying if lively mouthful. Even better when acidity fully integrates in year/2. — MW

Location/WO: Paarl ▪ Map: Paarl & Wellington ▪ Map grid reference: A7 ▪ Est/1stB 2006 ▪ Function venue by appt ▪ Owner(s) Agnes de Vos ▪ Winemaker(s) Carla Pauw (Jan 2006) ▪ 19ha (cabs s/f, merlot, chenin) ▪ 10t/1,300cs own label 50% red 50% white ▪ PO Box 38 Elsenburg 7607 ▪ agnesdev@telkomsa.net ▪ S 33° 48' 41.79" E 018° 47' 21.19" ▪ F +27 (0)21-884-4304 ▪ **T +27 (0)21-884-4304**

☐ **Danie de Wet** *see* De Wetshof Estate

D'Aria Winery   ⓠ ⑪ 🏠 ◎ ⑧

'Cellarmaster Rudi von Waltsleben is both musician and winemaker,' says his assistant, Madri Dreyer, explaining the musical themes permeating D'Aria, formed in 1998 through the amalgamation of two historic Durbanville farms by a property investment and development company. 'Rudi's creative urge leads to D'Aria always trying something new and different.'

Reserve range

★★★★☆ **The Soprano Shiraz** Hits high notes with violets, star anise & piercing black berry & plum fruit; rich, powerful, with ripe tannins yet **13** also manages to be refreshing, bright & pure.

★★★★ **The Songbird Sauvignon Blanc 14**'s grass & greenpepper aromas harmonise deliciously with tropical flavours including granadilla & gooseberries, plump but on a steely frame, ending on zesty grapefruit note. Tiny portion oaked.

Not tasted: **The Following White Blend**.

Terra range

Cabernet Sauvignon-Merlot ★★★☆ Dollop of merlot (8%) adds to **13**'s sweet plum pudding richness but plays second fiddle to cab's structure & black fruit, coated in caramel dark chocolate from year in French oak. **Blush ★★★** A delicate pink from 52% merlot, picked early for freshness, rest sauvignon, picked later for tropical fruit, **15** is off-dry but fresh, with red cherry & peach flavours. Also tasted: **Merlot 13 ★★★ SV Shiraz 13 ★★★★ Sauvignon Blanc 15 ★★★★** Not tasted: **Lullaby Noble Late Harvest**.

Music range

Sauvignon Blanc ★★★☆ Redolent of elderflowers & clover, **15** is quite light & steely, for crisp everyday refreshment. WO W Cape. Also tasted: **Shiraz-Cabernet Sauvignon-Merlot 14 ★★★** Not retasted: **Pinotage-Shiraz 13 ★★☆**

Sparkling range ⓝⒺⓦ

> **Pop Song Sparkling Sauvignon Blanc** ⑦ **★★☆** Best name ever? Carbonated **15** sauvignon from Lutzville fizzes with fun as well as green apple & gooseberry flavours, moderate alcohol of 11.5% also worth celebrating.

Brandy range

The Piccolo 5 Year Potstill Brandy Ⓖ **★★★** Earthy ripe apricots, green herbal notes & a sherry cask edge. Uncomplicated, youthfully rough & fiery. 100% potstill from colombard. — WB, JG, TJ

Location: Durbanville ▪ Map: Durbanville, Philadelphia & Darling ▪ WO: Durbanville/Western Cape ▪ Est/1stB 2007 ▪ Tasting & sales Mon 12-6 Tue-Fri 10-6 (summer)/Mon 11-5 Tue-Fri 9-5 (winter) Sat 10-5 Sun 11-5 ▪ Fee R20 ▪ Closed Dec 25 & Jan 1 ▪ Cheese platters & gourmet burgers ▪ Play area for children ▪ Poplars Restaurant ▪ Conferences/functions ▪ Hiking & MTB trails ▪ 4-star guest cottages ▪ Owner(s) Barinor Holdings ▪ Brandy master Rudi von Waltsleben (2008) ▪ Winemaker(s) Rudi von Waltsleben (Nov 2007), with Madri Dreyer (2014) ▪ Viticulturist(s) Johan von Waltsleben (1998) ▪ 80ha/63ha (cab, merlot, shiraz, sauv) ▪ 400t/ 160,000cs own label 67% red 30% white 3% rosé + 400cs for clients & ±1,000btls x 500ml brandy ▪ M13 Racecourse Road Durbanville 7550 ▪ tasting@daria.co.za ▪ www.dariawinery.co.za ▪ S 33° 50' 28.6" E 018° 36' 36.2" ▪ F +27 (0)86-539-4519 ▪ **T +27 (0)21-801-6772**

Darling Cellars   ⓠ ⑪ ⑧ ⑤

Unirrigated bushvines (some 45 years old) are the overwhelming source of grapes for this large grower-owned cellar on the West Coast. Hardened against the dry conditions, they grow – nurtured by some 20 farmer-shareholders – on low hills inland from the Atlantic, many cooled by ocean breezes, and with a useful variousness of aspect. It's a combination of factors conducive to both fruit concentration and an elegant balance in the wine. The modern cellar is continually upgraded, and in 2015 received not only smart new machinery – and 'a splash of paint' – but also a new head winemaker, Pieter-Niel Rossouw.

Limited Releases

★★★★☆ **Sir Charles Henry Darling** Cabernet leads merlot, petit verdot, malbec & splash cab franc in ambitious flagship. **12** (★★★★) has dark berry fruit contained in cedary oak with a savoury tail but it's tight & tannic, without the resonance of **11** which also needed time to settle. 15 months cask, 70% new.

★★★★☆ **Lime Kilns** ⓐ A melange of opulent chenin, creamy chardonnay & spicy viognier melded in oak (five months). Unabashed **13** (★★★★) shade less poised than **11**. No **12**.

★★★★ **Blanc de Blancs Brut** ⓐ Vibrant **13** MCC sparkler from chardonnay has oystershell & lemon zest to cut plush brioche complexity; alluring finesse to bone-dry farewell. **12** untasted.

Discontinued: **Cellarmaster's Signature Selection No. 7**, **Cellarmaster's Signature Selection No.8**.

Premium range

★★★★☆ **Cabernet Sauvignon** ⓐ **10** has leafy tobacco top notes typical of cool region, supported by a core of cassis with poised ripe promise. Back on track after lesser previewed **09** (★★★★).

★★★★ **Shiraz** ⓐ **10** (★★★★) lacks the intensity & length of **09**. Lighter, with red fruits, bright spice & dry medium finish.

★★★★ **Sauvignon Blanc** Some steeliness & grassy grip contain the bouncy gooseberry fruit of **14**, give focus to the enduring flavour. With dash semillon, six months on lees.

★★★★ **Noble Late Harvest** ⊘ Back after a break, & with purpose! Cleanly defined botrytis aromas of **13** herald beautiful glossy summer fruit flavours, freshened by crisp acidity. From chenin, third wooded.

Also tasted: **Pinotage 12** ★★★ Not retasted: **Kroon 10** ★★★★ Discontinued: **Riesling**.

Reserve range

Arum Fields Chenin Blanc ★★★ Blossoms & ripe peach/pear features of **15** guarantee fruity quaffing & a soft landing. **Bush Vine Sauvignon Blanc** ★★★ Floral-toned **15** offers passionfruit interest & gentle acidity. Also tasted: **Quercus Gold Chardonnay 15** ★★★ Not retasted: **Terra Hutton Cabernet Sauvignon 13** ★★★ **Six Tonner Merlot 13** ★★★★ **Old Blocks Pinotage 13** ★★★ **Black Granite Shiraz 13** ★★★★ Discontinued: **Shiraz-Mourvèdre**.

Growers Signature Selection

Mariette ⓐ ★★★ Mostly chenin & viognier, **13** seductive aromas & flavours of tinned peaches; full, rounded, but dry. Discontinued: **The Chairman**, **Cinsaut-Cabernet Sauvignon**, **Chenin Blanc**.

Classic range

Merlot Rosé ★★ **15** blush charms with strawberry fruit, ends dry. **Chenin Blanc-Sauvignon Blanc** ⊘ ★★★ Chenin's bountiful tropical fruit salad flavours tethered by racy sauvignon in **15**. Also tasted: **Cabernet Sauvignon-Merlot** ⊘ **14** ★★☆

Chocoholic range

Pinotage ★★★ Generous, opulent, decadent – it's all in the name of popular off-dry **14**.

Sweet Darling

Rosé ★★ Vibrant pinepple notes in semi-sweet **NV** quaffer from bukettraube & ruby cab. **Red** ★ Fudge & cherry pop flavours on **NV** sweet sipper from merlot & 3 others. Also tasted: **White NV** ★★ — DS

Location/WO: Darling ▪ Map: Durbanville, Philadelphia & Darling ▪ Est 1948 ▪ 1stB 1996 ▪ Tasting & sales Mon-Fri 9–5 Sat 10–2 ▪ Closed Good Fri, Dec 25 & Jan 1 ▪ Cellar tours by appt ▪ Cheese platters ▪ Facilities for children ▪ Owner(s) 20 shareholders ▪ Winemaker(s) Pieter-Niel Rossouw (Sep 2014), with Carel Hugo (Jun 2009), Anthony Meduna (Oct 2011) & Maggie Venter (Jun 2014) ▪ 1,300ha (barbera, cab, carignan, cinsaut, grenache, malbec, merlot, mourv, ptage, shiraz, chard, chenin, riesling, sauv, sem) ▪ 7,500–8,500t/700,000cs own label 70% red 28% white 2% rosé ▪ Other export brands: Alta Casa, Black Granite, Cape Cult, Capeman, Cellar Road, Fountain Crossing, Mamrevale, Tabiso, Victoria Bay, Zantsi ▪ PO Box 114 Darling 7345 ▪ info@darlingcellars.co.za ▪ www.darlingcellars.co.za ▪ S 33° 26' 25.7" E 018° 31' 5.1" ▪ **T +27 (0)22-492-2276**

Darlington see Withington

Daschbosch see uniWines Vineyards

Dassie's Reserve see Botha Wine Cellar

David & Nadia Sadie

There's much that's new for David and Nadia Sadie — most importantly, 2nd son Malan. The star wine-growers have resigned their consultancies to join the ranks of the self-employed, and are based full-time in Swartland (David was raised there, though he's unrelated to its other famous Sadie). They've launched the first wines from the farm-focused Paardebosch project (see entry) with lawyer Des Kruger, and moved into the recently restored 220-year-old cellar on that property. Their 'David' venture sources more widely, from diverse blocks around Swartland. Nadia's the qualified viticulturist/soil scientist, David's the winemaker with experience at top-flight Saronsberg and Waterford, inspired by stints in the Rhône familiarising himself with Mediterranean varieties, and having helped resurrect Lemberg. Members of Swartland Independent Producers, the couple are in the front rank of the new generation making inspired wines from old vines, following a minimalist approach to achieve 'natural freshness and acidity'.

★★★★☆ **Grenache** Fashionable red grape, here sourced from 3 Swartland blocks (1 organically farmed), 50% bunch pressed, 11 months older oak. Like classy **13**, exceptional **14** (★★★★★) is wonderfully understated, with perfectly ripe grape tannins cradling delicate fruit.

★★★★☆ **Elpidios** Pace-setting Rhône blend, mostly shiraz (44%) & grenache (31%) with carignan, cinsaut & pinotage in **13** from 6 schist & granite sites. Savoury, with wild scrub notes & steely balance; superb now, will keep. Natural vinification — native yeasts, no additives, long lower sulphur, no fining/filtration, as for all. Also in 1.5 & 3L.

★★★★☆ **Chenin Blanc** Oxidatively styled **14** from Perdeberg vines (oldest planted 1960s). Ethereal apricot, white peach & pear aromas, flavours; like almond-toned **13**, emphatically dry, delicious, with hidden depths & sheathed power.

★★★★★ **Hoë-Steen Chenin Blanc** (NEW) Understated & regal **14** off 49 year old bushvines with unusually tall shoots, hence 'High Chenin'. Restrained pear & wet wool aromas, intense bruised apple flavours with seamless length, extraordinary purity & presence.

★★★★☆ **Skaliekop Chenin Blanc** (NEW) Attractive ferrous character on fresh hay & lemon-toned fruit, **14** the most forthcoming of the 3 new releases. Full palate lively & silky, harmonious, with delicate tangerine pith, saline conclusion. Youngest of the vineyards (1985), on shale ('skalie'); like maiden siblings, bunch pressed, minimal intervention, only older oak.

★★★★☆ **Perdekamp Semillon** (NEW) A single block of dryland bushvines planted 1960 on decomposed granite, named for adjacent paddock. Remarkable **14** slowly reveals its lemongrass charms & mineral underpin, bone-dry & steely with savoury persistence.

★★★★★ **Aristargos** Authoritative white blend evokes hidden ravines, rugged black scrub, terracotta & yellow soil thanks to 12 mostly dryland bushvine blocks, some 50+ years. Unlike **13**, **14** features substantial portion roussanne (with chenin, clairette blanche, viognier & semillon), touch livelier but no less seductive, thrilling. — CvZ

Location: Malmesbury ▪ Map/WO: Swartland ▪ Est/1stB 2010 ▪ Tasting by appt & subject to availability ▪ Owner(s)/winemaker(s)/viticulturist(s) David & Nadia Sadie ▪ (carignan, cinsaut, grenache, ptage, shiraz, chenin, clairette, rouss, sem, viog) ▪ 35t/3,700cs own label 50% red 50% white ▪ Swartland Independent Producers (2011) ▪ info@davidnadiasadie.co.za ▪ www.davidnadiasadie.co.za ▪ F +27 (0)86-512-4903 ▪ **T +27 (0)72-375-4336**

David Frost Wines

Champion golfer David Frost maintains his long association with wine, having financed his earliest golfing efforts picking grapes on his father's farm, with this own range of affordable, eminently drinkable wines. Exclusive to Pick n Pay stores nationwide, they can also be tasted at a venue on Main Road, Paarl.

Pinotage ★★★ Fresh, sappy & juicy **14** more modern style than last, with some choc/coffee hints, red cherries, tobacco in surprisingly elegant example. **Sauvignon Blanc** ★★★ Lashings of tinned grapefruit & green figs on fresh, crowd-pleasing **15**. Also tasted: **Cabernet Sauvignon 14** ★★☆ **Shiraz 14** ★★★ — CM

Location: Paarl ▪ Map: Paarl & Wellington ▪ Map grid reference: E5 ▪ WO: Western Cape ▪ Est 1994 ▪ Tasting & sales at Winefolk, 191 Main Rd Paarl Mon-Sat 8-6.30 ▪ Owner(s) David Frost ▪ Winemaker(s)

Erlank Erasmus ▪ 10,000cs 60% red 40% white ▪ PO Box 68 Main Road Paarl 7620 ▪ natalie@
winefolk.co.za ▪ www.frostwine.com ▪ S 33° 44' 36.9" E 018° 57' 46.1" ▪ T +27 (0)21-871-1850

☐ **David Nieuwoudt** *see* Cederberg Private Cellar

DeanDavid Wines

Founder of this small Swartland label, Dean Thompson ('David' is his dad), has had less time for the business in recent years, but wine partner Roger Clayton (see also Clayton Wines) stepped into the breach, searching out quality Swartland vineyards and making the wines at the Antebellum cellar.

★★★★ Two Mile Squared Syrah 12 (★★★★) more time in (older) oak than **11**. More serious intent, with extraction & weight compromising elegance. Savoury, dark fruited, meaty & bit puckering.

★★★★ One Mile Squared Chenin Blanc Still a limited release, **14** is now 100% barrel fermented (in older wood); richer than previous, mouthfeel a little slippery but retains its savouriness & composure.

Half Mile Squared Pinotage ⓐ ★★★☆ Youthful **13** exotic expression of pinotage, with blueberry & juniper in the perfume; palate more straightforwardly berry-driven but seriously easy to drink. — HJ

Location: Riebeek-Kasteel ▪ WO: Swartland ▪ Est/1stB 2003 ▪ Closed to public ▪ Wines available from Wine Kollective, Riebeek-Kasteel & Vino Pronto, Cape Town ▪ Owner(s) Dean Thompson, Roger Clayton, Peter Alexander & John Fulford ▪ Winemaker(s) Dean Thompson & Roger Clayton ▪ 5t/500cs own label 70% red 30% white ▪ Postnet Suite 247, Private Bag X16, Constantia 7848 ▪ roger@unwined.co.za, dean@unwined.co.za ▪ www.unwined.co.za ▪ T +27 (0)76-826-8500 (Roger)/+27 (0)71-233-8261 (Dean)

De Bos Handpicked Vineyards

These premium Fairtrade wines, available from leading restaurants and retailers nationwide, are sourced from farms in Upper Hemel-en-Aarde Valley, Wellington and Hermon owned and managed by Bosman Family Vineyards (see entry).

47 Varietal Rosé ⓝⒺⓦ ★★★ Melange of every variety in the Bosman vineholding. **14** Turkish delight & other exotic features, lightish body, bone-dry. **Sauvignon Blanc** ★★★☆ Cool-climate lemongrass & tangerine zest attractions in characterful **14**. Zippily dry, balanced lunchtime sipping. Also tasted: **Cabernet Sauvignon 13** ★★☆ **Merlot 14** ★★ **Chardonnay 14** ★★★ **Chenin Blanc 14** ★★★ Not tasted: **Pinot Noir**. — AL

De Breede Organic Vineyards

Boutique-scale Harteberstrivier estate just outside Worcester, its organic vines and 200-year-old cellar are the source of these characterful wines, now overseen and made by owner Debbie Alcock-Bousfield as a complement to her internationally awarded Gourmet Africa condiment range.

★★★★ Syrah ⓐ ⓢ Appealing freshness on bright-fruited **11** – a bit lighter, suppler, less extracted than the others, but still powerful & just as characterful.

1st XI Merlot ⓐ ⓢ ★★★☆ Violets, fruit pastilles & crème de cassis in abundance on **10**. Like Cab, touch jammy but more structure-giving tannins & finesse here; good juicy acidity, too. Enjoy soon. Not retasted: **Cabernet Sauvignon 12** ★★ **Little Red Rooster 13** ★★ **The Rooster 12** ★★★ **The Rooster Reserve 10** ★★★ — HJ

Location: Worcester ▪ Map/WO: Breedekloof ▪ Est 2006 ▪ 1stB 2009 ▪ Tasting by appt ▪ Owner(s)/viticulturist(s) Debbie Alcock-Bousfield ▪ Winemaker(s) Debbie Alcock-Bousfield & Isaac Mabeta (2009) ▪ 26ha/2.5ha (cabs s/f, malbec, merlot, p verdot) ▪ ±20t/2,000cs own label 99% red 1% rosé ▪ Certified organic by BCS ▪ PO Box 511 Worcester 6849 ▪ info@burchells.co.za ▪ www.gourmet-africa.com ▪ S 33° 37' 10.69" E 019° 22' 44.79" ▪ F +27 (0)86-684-7778 ▪ T +27 (0)23-342-5388

De Doorns Wynkelder (Koöp) Bpk

Taking convenience to a new level, there's an Engen service station at the same premises as De Doorns Wynkelder's tasting centre in De Doorns village, so you can fill up while you stock up. And, because the wine venue shares with the Tourism Centre, you can plan your Hex River Valley visit while sampling the range, which includes sweet and medium-dry 'sherry' (untasted this edition).

Location: De Doorns ▪ Map: Worcester ▪ Est 1968 ▪ Tasting & sales Mon–Fri 8–5 Sat 8–12 ▪ Cellar-master(s) Danie Koen ▪ Winemaker(s) Danie Koen, with Peter James Thomson ▪ PO Box 129 De Doorns 6875 ▪ ddwk@hexvallei.co.za ▪ www.dedoornscellar.co.za ▪ S 33° 29' 10.3" E 019° 39' 43.2" ▪ F +27 (0)86-579-1310 ▪ **T +27 (0)23-356-2100**

Definitum Wines

Aiming to introduce winelovers to the novel and exotic, Helderberg-based Fritz van der Merwe and De Wet Schreiber certainly tick the 'unusual' box with Benevolence, their current blend of SA, Bordeaux and Rhône varieties. Next is a Bordeaux red – with who knows what surprises in store...

Benevolence Cape Blend ★★☆ **13** mix of pinotage, malbec, shiraz, merlot & petit verdot improves on previous. Tasty if straightforward fruitcake flavours, with freshness & supple tannins to balance. Not tasted: **Petit Verdot**. — AL

Location: Strand ▪ WO: Stellenbosch ▪ Est/1stB 2009 ▪ Closed to public ▪ Owner(s) Fritz van der Merwe & De Wet Schreiber ▪ 520cs own label 100% red ▪ PO Box 917 Strand 7139 ▪ info@definitum.co.za ▪ www.definitum.co.za

De Grendel Wines   Ⓠ ⑪ ⓐ ⓑ

The Durbanville spread overlooking Table Mountain mourned third-generation owner Sir David Graaff beginning 2015. Following a family tradition of careers in farming and national politics, it was this grad-uate of Stellenbosch, Oxford and Grenoble who added wine and a modern winery to the farm's cattle and sheep stud. Under veteran winemaker Charles Hopkins, wines from high-lying and sea-facing sites have proved consistently excellent. Promising continuity is Sir David's eldest son De Villiers, also a Stellenbosch agriculture graduate and father of four. Supplying grapes for De Grendel while managing the family's Hex River fruit farms, he has overseen recently increasing production and is credited with tempting Michelin-starred restaurateur Jonathan Davies to manage De Grendel's classy restaurant.

★★★★ **Op Die Berg Pinot Noir** Sultry **13** (★★★★☆) broods in ruby robes mid-2015, dark cherry fruit & wisps of oak spice interweave in deep-pile texture brightened by acidity, which is crisp enough to con-tain 14.6% alcohol. 20% new oak; Ceres Plateau grapes, like **12**.

★★★★☆ **Shiraz** Whiffs of white pepper over densely concentrated blue berry fruit, **13** strongly built but supple, packed with accessible flavour; good line of acidity, wonderfully dry finish. 20% new oak, half American. 95% Paarl grapes, as for **12**.

★★★★ **Rubáiyát** Ambitious Bordeaux-style red blend a touch overdone in **12** (★★★★) but **13** better balanced; sappy tones of dominant petit verdot & 18 months 90% new oak add well-controlled muscular-ity. WO Coastal.

★★★★☆ **Sir David Graaff** (ⓝⓔⓦ) Honours the late founder. Shiraz (83%) & 4 Bordeaux varieties from low-yielding Firgrove vines handled for maximum extraction, lavished with new oak. Smoky leather tones, piquant spice & dense tannins cloak **13**'s fruit core for now, but promise of splendour over 10 years.

★★★★ **Op Die Berg Chardonnay** Stellar **14**'s (★★★★★) breathtaking poise & balance true to restrained house style, but intensity of flavour takes it to an even higher level than **13**. 40% of the fruit from Ceres vines unwooded for freshness; 8 months on lees. Ends dry, 13.5% alcohol in harmony.

★★★★☆ **Koetshuis Sauvignon Blanc** Complex & complete **15** is arresting: piercing green pea aro-mas with striking intensity of riverstone & gunflint give flavour without weight in the mouth; bone-dry, gently salty finish. 80% Darling fruit, none of sibling's semillon.

★★★★ **Sauvignon Blanc** Immensely appealing **15**, well-defined lime fruit with a nettle edge smoothed by 100 days on the lees; zippy acidity ensures fleshier 11% semillon portion remains in balance.

★★★★ **Viognier** Oak vanilla still evident on **15** preview but the rich, layered tropical fruit is cleaner, fresher (only 15% new oak) than on **14** (★★★★).

★★★★ **Méthode Cap Classique Brut** Dry **13** a classy bubble; elegant, understated assembly of 67% chardonnay & pinot noir, subtle biscuit character (14 months on lees), bright acidity & fine mousse.

Also tasted: **Merlot 13** ★★★☆ **Rosé 15** ★★★ **Sauvignon Blanc Noble Late Harvest 14** ★★★★ Not tasted: **Pinot Gris**. — DS

Location: Durbanville ▪ Map: Durbanville, Philadelphia & Darling ▪ WO: Durbanville/Coastal/Ceres Plateau ▪ Est 1720 ▪ 1stB 2004 ▪ Tasting & sales Mon-Sat 9–7 Sun 10–4 ▪ Closed Dec 25 ▪ Cellar tours by appt ▪ Conferences ▪ De Grendel Restaurant ▪ Owner(s) De Villiers Graaff ▪ Cellarmaster(s) Charles Hopkins (Oct 2005) ▪ Viticulturist(s) Kudzai Mwerenga (2009) ▪ 800ha/110ha (cabs s/f, merlot, mourv, p verdot, ptage, pinot noir/gris, shiraz, chard, sauv, sem, viog) ▪ 600t/35,000cs own label 35% red 50% white 15% rosé ▪ 112 Plattekloof Road Panorama 7505 ▪ info@degrendel.co.za ▪ www.degrendel.co.za ▪ S 33° 51' 2.5" E 018° 34' 18.4" ▪ **T +27 (0)21-558-6280**

☐ **De Haas** *see* Hazendal

☐ **Dekker's Valley** *see* Mellasat Vineyards

☐ **De Kleine Leeuwen** *see* Leeuwenberg

De Kleine Wijn Koöp

De Kleine Wijn Koöp is a Stellenbosch collective of creatives and wine experts specialising in small-scale, unusual bottlings with quirky names and packaging. After a brief sabbatical, the 'flip-flops and boardshorts' vintners are back with a trio of (untasted) releases: Dik Duidelijke Syrah '11 and tongue-twisting 'nerdy blends' Symourcinache '13 (shiraz/syrah, mourvèdre, grenache, cinsaut) and Chelomviorettellho '14 (chenin, palomino, viognier, clairette, verdelho), all from Swartland.

Location: Stellenbosch ▪ Est/1stB 2011 ▪ Closed to public ▪ Sales via email 9-5 ▪ Owner(s) Hendrik Stephanus Opperman Rabie, Etienne Dawid-Olivier Heyns, Johannes Diederick Pretorius, Rohan CY Etsebeth & Jan Georg Solms ▪ 800cs own label ▪ kantoor@dekleinewijnkoop.co.za ▪ www.dekleinewijnkoop.co.za

De Krans   ⊕ ⊕ ⊕ ⊚ ⊕ ⊕

Under Boets and Stroebel Nel, prime movers for the past three decades, De Krans has notched up a great many successes in competitions and professional tastings, not least the remarkable unbroken eleven-year run of five star ratings in this guide for its 'ports'. Louis van der Riet, who took the cellar reins in 2012, immediately hit the mark with a Diners Club Young Winemaker of the Year finalist bottling, Tinta Roriz '13. That the plaudit went to an unfortified wine, from a 'port' grape, highlights De Krans' continuing focus on not just refining the Portuguese varieties that are Calitzdorp's heritage and strength, but also re-imagining them for the new generation of winelovers. See also Garden Route and Le Sueur.

★★★★ **Tinta Barocca** ⊘ Unfortified **13** reprises the pleasantly dusty scents, sour cherry flavours noted in **12** (★★★★) but with more verve & intensity; the notably long, juicy finish ends crisply dry.

★★★★ **Touriga Nacional** ⊘ Keeping the standard & flavour profile, unfortified **14** opens with warm, dark savoury notes, then a cranberry tang kicks in for a crisp, fresh conclusion. Like **13**, very youthful, deserves time to show its best.

★★★★ **Tritonia** Potential-laden Calitzdorp Blend from touriga (66%), dollops tempranillo & tinta, unfortified. **13** chocolate & tobacco aromas, dark berry flavours still firmly gripped by tannins. Like **11**, needs & deserves time. No **12**.

★★★★☆ **Muscat De Frontignan** Was 'White Muscadel Jerepigo'. Barely bottled yet beguiling & delicious, fortified **15** is all honey & lemon on nose, silky smooth dried apricot & marmalade on palate, aromatic suggestions of Turkish delight & litchi. Perfect after-dinner drink. No **14**.

★★★★☆ **Cape Tawny Limited Release** Outstanding tawny port-style, 1,600 cases of gorgeousness from touriga, tintas amarela & barocca. Limpid pale amber invitation to latest **NV**, subtle & elegant aromas of leather & tobacco, plus gentle notes of dusty apricot & orange marmalade. The quietly amazing experience lingers on & on. WO W Cape.

★★★★☆ **Cape Vintage** ⊘ Always generous & juicy yet cellarworthy 'port'. **13**, previewed last time, since has knit & even better. Moreish Xmas pudding & brandy butter character with a fine balancing dusty sprinkle & active tannin underpin. From touriga (60%), tintas barocca & roriz, souzão.

★★★★★ **Cape Vintage Reserve** Phenomenal 11th maximum rating for this impressive, long-lived Cape port-style. **13** mostly touriga (60%) plus tintas barocca & roriz. Rich fruity elements (dark plums, cherries) & chocolate lifted by cinnamon spice. Endless, appealingly dusty finish. 19% alcohol perfectly synced, as always. Exceptional now & for decade-plus.

★★★★☆ **Original Espresso** ⊘ Xmas pudding in a glass, like previous, luscious fireside warmer takes the hedonism to a new level in latest **NV** bottling. Fortified touriga & tinta, plus 3 other 'port' grapes, it oozes raisins, dates & nuts — even brandy butter. Irresistible.

Zero Dosage Méthode Cap Classique ⓃⒺⓌ ⑦ ★★★☆ Highly unusual (unique?) bubbly from chardonnay, chenin & 'port' grape tinta barocca, all barrel-fermented. **13** warm fresh bread aromas, dried fig & apple flavours with a touch of black pepper in the persistent froth. Klein Karoo WO.

Tinta Roriz ★★★☆ Now bottled, unfortified **13** shows the warm nutty aroma previewed last time, plus a coriander nuance, the dark plum & cherry flavours buoyed by variety's tangy acidity. **Wild Ferment Unwooded Chardonnay** Was 'Chardonnay'. **15** pre-bottling sample shows good varietal tones of lemon & lime but mid-2015 too young to conclusively rate. **Moscato Perlé** ★★ **15** sweetish white muscadel, splash hanepoot, with a prickle of bubbles. Poolside fare with low 8.5% alcohol. Also tasted: **Basket Press Cabernet Sauvignon 15** ★★★ **Free-Run Unwooded Chenin Blanc 15** ★★☆ **Cape Ruby Premium NV** ★★★★ **Original Cape Pink** ⊘ NV ★★★ Not retasted: **Tinta Barocca Rosé 14** ★★★ — DB

Location: Calitzdorp ▪ Map: Klein Karoo & Garden Route ▪ WO: Calitzdorp/Western Cape/Klein Karoo ▪ Est 1964 ▪ 1stB 1977 ▪ Tasting & sales Mon-Fri 8–5 Sat 10–4 ▪ Tasting fee R25pp ▪ Closed Easter Fri/Sun & Dec 25 ▪ Pick your own apricots (last week Nov, 1st week Dec) & hanepoot grapes (±10 Feb–10 Mar) ▪ 'Braaivleis' by friends of Vygieshof Home for the Aged available on Wed & Sat during picking season ▪ Facilities for children school hols ▪ BYO picnic ▪ Walking trail ▪ Owner(s) De Krans Wines (MD Boets Nel & directors Stroebel Nel & René Oosthuizen) ▪ Winemaker(s) Louis van der Riet (Aug 2012) ▪ Viticulturist(s) Stroebel Nel (Jan 1988) ▪ 78ha/45ha (cab, tinta barocca/roriz, touriga nacional, chard, chenin & muscats) ▪ 500t/40—50,000cs own label 50% red 10% white 3% rosé 37% fortifieds ▪ IPW, BWI ▪ PO Box 28 Calitzdorp 6660 ▪ dekrans@mweb.co.za ▪ www.dekrans.co.za ▪ S 33° 32' 6.3" E 021° 41' 9.0" ▪ F +27 (0)44-213-3562 ▪ **T +27 (0)44-213-3314**

Delaire Graff Estate Ⓠ Ⓨ ⌂ ⊚ ⓖ

International diamantaire Laurence Graff's 'Jewel of the Cape Winelands', high on Stellenbosch's Helshoogte Pass, is a hedonist's dreamland: rolling gardens studded with eye-catching sculpture, super-luxurious hotel and spa, fine restaurants, a diamond room and exclusive boutiques, all rolled into a not-to-be-missed tourism destination. The award-winning DHK-designed winery boasts a spectacular art collection, newly expanded, and a warm welcome at all price points. The dynamism of the place is palpable, from the striving for ultimate quality in all things to the lofty plans for future development, the search for unique vineyard parcels and innovation in winemaking techniques. This edition sees the debut of an unusual chenin bubbly, inspired partly by winemaker Morné Vrey's 2011 visit to the Loire. The newcomer, Sunrise, aptly is named for a remarkable yellow sparkler cut and polished by Graff Diamonds.

Icon range

★★★★☆ **Cabernet Sauvignon Reserve** Massively proportioned, inky & dense, yet **13** shows delicate nuances & scented fragrance. 18 months in mostly new oak add subtle spice to perfectly modulated tannin texture & plush, ripe fruit.

★★★★★ **Laurence Graff Reserve** Pricey but worthy icon label, **12** comprises 5 best barrels of Cab Reserve with 4% splash of petit verdot. Class shows in purity of fruit & subtle detail, rather than raw power. Seductively plush with endless finish. **11** (★★★★★) included drop malbec.

★★★★☆ **Terrace Block Reserve** ⓃⒺⓌ Aristocratic barrel-fermented chardonnay, **14** is finely focused, big bodied & stately, with creamy citrus fruit, lees buttered toast & sweet marmalade finish. Stellar fruit quality & assured handling have produced a distinctly New World jewel from Banghoek single-vineyard.

★★★★☆ **White Reserve** Barrel selection of finest oak-fermented sauvignon & semillon, **13** maintains lofty standard. Fresh & approachable yet intricate & complex, promising even more in years to come. Stellenbosch & Franschhoek grapes.

★★★★ **Sunrise Brut Méthode Cap Classique** (NEW) Seriously conceived chenin-based **NV** sparkling with chardonnay & dash cab franc. Rich, yeasty sourdough with baked apple, offering substance & delicacy borne on creamy mousse.

Premium range

★★★★ **Merlot** Elegant, expressive **13** offers generously ripe berries & currants on firm but gentle tannins. Precise & pure, with mouthcoating texture & lingering finish.

★★★★★ **Botmaskop** High-flying 5-way Bordeaux blend maintains appeal in **13**. Aristocratic yet approachable, intricate yet focused, with beguiling black fruit & earthy, rich core. Refined & supple in youth, but promising great things in future years. Also in magnum.

★★★★ **Chardonnay Banghoek Reserve** Was 'Chardonnay'. **14**'s oak countered by opulent citrus fruit & honeyed buttery layers. Spicy, rich & ripe, with creamy texture, promising rewards for cellaring.

★★★★ **Chenin Blanc Swartland Reserve** Was just 'Chenin Blanc'. Assertively big & ripe, oak-spiced **14** from old bushvines has lees fatness with charming honey-melon fruit, all in subtle harmony.

★★★★☆ **Coastal Cuvée Sauvignon Blanc** Precise & complex **15** from Stellenbosch, Darling, Durbanville & Franschhoek shows subtle touches of oak & semillon, with softly plush lees texture. Youthful & sprightly (just-bottled when tasted) yet fine-tuned & focused, showing promise once settled.

★★★★ **Sauvignon Blanc** Edgy nettle & khaki bush notes on **14** (★★★★☆), previewed last edition. More settled now, but still a bit short of **13**'s intensity. WO W Cape.

★★★★ **Cape Vintage** Alluring black plum-pudding & tingling spirit bite on **13** 'port' from tinta & touriga. Opulently ripe fruit with tobacco & liquorice accents, showing youthful potential.

Not tasted: **Reserve Noble Late Harvest**.

Luxury range

Cabernet Franc Rosé ★★★☆ Understated but elegant **15** has well-mannered berry fruit, hints of rosepetal. Dry & totally refreshing. Also tasted: **Shiraz 14** ★★★★ Not retasted: **Old Bush Vine Chenin Blanc 14** ★★★☆ — GdB

Location/map: Stellenbosch ▪ Map grid reference: G5 ▪ WO: Stellenbosch/Banghoek/Coastal/Western Cape/Swartland ▪ Est 1983 ▪ 1stB 1984 ▪ Tasting & sales Mon-Sat 10-5 Sun 9.30-4 ▪ Fee R50/3 wines, R70/5 wines, R150/3 Reserve wines ▪ Cellar tours by appt (no tours during harvest) ▪ Gifts ▪ Farm produce ▪ Walks/hikes ▪ Art collection ▪ Delaire Graff & Indochine Restaurants ▪ 5-star Lodges & Spa ▪ Owner(s) Laurence Graff ▪ Winemaker(s) Morné Vrey (Jul 2009) ▪ Viticulturist(s) Kallie Fernhout (Jun 2010) ▪ 42ha/20ha (cabs s/f, malbec, merlot, p verdot, chard, sauv) ▪ 280t/34,000cs own label 40% red 55% white 5% rosé ▪ WIETA ▪ PO Box 3058 Stellenbosch 7602 ▪ info@delaire.co.za ▪ www.delaire.co.za ▪ S 33° 55′ 17.70″ E 018° 55′ 22.08″ ▪ **F** +27 (0)86-775-1720 ▪ **T +27 (0)21-885-8160**

Delavia Estate

Entrepreneur Merwe Viljoen's mountainside vines are in Stellenbosch's viticulturally prime 'Golden Triangle'. With advisers Rocco de Villiers (Custom Crush) and Francois Hanekom, he's aiming to produce small parcels of 'extremely high-quality wine, expressing the unique style of the Helderberg'.

Shiraz (NEW) ★★★ Smoked meat & spicy notes on modestly oaked, well-structured **14**; touch lighter in feel than Adagio but also with sweet suggestion, partly from big (15%) alcohol. **Adagio** ★★★☆ Like last-tasted **11**, heavily built **14** a 5-way Bordeaux blend led by cab & merlot. Ripe, big & plush, offering straightforward sweet berry fruit, with firm enough tannic underpinning. **Pinot Noir-Chardonnay** (NEW) ★★★ Delightful pale colour on easygoing, dry, gently berry-fruited **15** rosé, with unlingering, quaffable pleasantness. WO Coastal. — TJ

Location: Stellenbosch ▪ WO: Stellenbosch/Coastal ▪ Est 2009 ▪ 1stB 2010 ▪ Closed to public ▪ Owner(s) Merwe Viljoen ▪ Winemaker(s) Rocco de Villiers (Jan 2014, consultant) ▪ Viticulturist(s) Francois Hanekom (Jan 2013, consultant) ▪ 25ha/18.5ha (cabs s/f, merlot, shiraz, chard) ▪ 115t/225cs own label 100% red ▪ IPW ▪ PO Box 12275 Die Boord Stellenbosch 7613 ▪ rocco@capecrush.co.za, merwe@delavia.co.za ▪ **F** +27 (0)86-571-7688 ▪ **T +27 (0)82-821-4625**

Delheim Wines

'Deli's home' – Delheim – was founded by Hans and Deli Hoheisen back in 1949 on the historic Driesprongh farm on the slopes of the Simonsberg in Stellenbosch. Soon thereafter, young Spatz Sperling, Deli's nephew, arrived from Germany to help out (though all involved then had more enthusiasm and ambition than useful knowledge), and it was he and his family who over the years established Delheim as a significant producer and a popular destination for wine-loving tourists. The Vera Cruz estate, about three kilometres distant, was a later addition, and is now the source of some of Delheim's grandest wines. We see in this edition the positive impact made on all the wines by the arrival in 2012 of both winemaker Reg Holder and viticulturist Etienne Terblanche.

Estate range

★★★★☆ **Grand Reserve** Long-established flagship **13** from cab – last-made **08** had a little merlot (oaky **09** tasted by us, but declassified before release). Worth waiting. Subtly fragrant aromas of berries, spice & tobacco lead to darkly elegant, poised palate. Unshowy but convincing; deserves 5+ years.

★★★★ **Vera Cruz Pinotage 13** (★★★★★) less oaky than **12**, & a fine advert for the grape's more elegant possibilities. Fragrant aromas, excellent structure, the restrained tannins harmonising with fresh acid & deep sweet fruit. Lingering dry finish. Simonsberg–Stellenbosch WO, as for Edelspatz. Like other reds in range also in larger formats.

★★★★☆ **Vera Cruz Shiraz** Ripely generous, judiciously oaked **13** tempers power with sense of restraint. Plenty of fruit lurks among the grippy tannins, & so polished & refined that it's approachable now, though years off its best, when the balance will become more graceful & complexly harmonious.

★★★★ **Chardonnay Sur Lie** Naturally fermented, excellently oaked **14** less bold & more subtle than previous – nothing overt: fruit, oak, silky texture, firm structure all in balance.

★★★★★ **Edelspatz Noble Late Harvest 14** (★★★★☆) continues triumphant flow of quietly penetrating, delicately insistent, totally persuasive botrytis dessert from single vineyard riesling. 11.5% alcohol, no oak – ie, like **13** & previous in German rather than French style, but not greatly sweet or acidic. 375 ml.

Family range

★★★★ **Cabernet Sauvignon** Unpretentiously modest, very satisfying **13** both generous & restrained, still even a little tight. Well oaked – this giving some tobacco spice tempering the dark berry fruit.

★★★★ **Shiraz 13**'s forthcoming smoky-spicy-fruity aromas lead to approachably soft palate – but enough grip to support the slightly sweet fruit & help ensure some ageing potential.

★★★★ **Chenin Blanc** Combo of tank & barrel maturation on natural ferment **14**. Dried peach, thatchy notes; gently rounded, balanced & pleasant, with a touch of complexity & reasonable length.

Also tasted: **Merlot 13** ★★★ **Pinotage 13** ★★★★ Discontinued: **Unwooded Chardonnay**.

Heritage range

Gewürztraminer ★★★ Rosepetal & litchi fragrance on **14** well contained – doesn't gush forth. Offdry, one-dimensional & tasty. Also tasted: **Spatzendreck 14** ★★★☆

Lifestyle range

Sauvignon Blanc ★★★ Drops 'Heerenwijn' from name with **15**. Showily fruity & flavourful, well balanced, but unambitious. Rather brief in its offering, but a nice succulent bite. Stellenbosch & Darling grapes. Also tasted: **Cabernet Sauvignon-Shiraz 13** ★★★ **Pinotage Rosé 15** ★★★ — TJ

Location/map: Stellenbosch ▪ Map grid reference: F2 ▪ WO: Stellenbosch/Simonsberg–Stellenbosch/Coastal ▪ Est 1971 ▪ 1stB 1961 ▪ Tasting & sales daily 9-5 ▪ Cupcake & wine pairing, pre-booking essential ▪ Closed Easter Fri/Sun, Dec 25 & Jan 1 ▪ Cellar tours daily at 10.30 & 2.30 ▪ Delheim Restaurant ▪ Tour groups ▪ Gifts ▪ MTB trail ▪ Conferences ▪ Conservation area ▪ Events: see website for schedule ▪ Owner(s) Sperling family ▪ Cellarmaster(s) Reg Holder (Jan 2012) ▪ Winemaker(s) Altus Treurnicht ▪ Viticulturist(s) Etienne Terblanche (Aug 2012) ▪ 375ha/148ha (cab, ptage, shiraz, chard, chenin, riesling, sauv) ▪ 980t/120,000cs own label 50% red 30% white 20% rosé ▪ Brands for clients: Woolworths ▪ BWI champion, Level 2 BBEE, WIETA ▪ PO Box 210 Stellenbosch 7599 ▪ info@delheim.com ▪ www.delheim.com ▪ S 33° 52' 10.1" E 018° 53' 9.8" ▪ F +27 (0)21-888-4601 ▪ **T +27 (0)21-888-4600**

☐ **De Liefde** see Mountain Ridge Wines

De Meye Wines

This quiet Stellenbosch farm has long been in the Myburgh family; it's named after a river in Holland near where Myburghs lived before the first one arrived in the Cape in 1655. Current owners Jan and Philip (the latter is the MD) represent the fifth and sixth generations. It was only with the 1998 vintage, however, that some of the crop (previously all sold off to the merchant houses) was held back for an own label. Marcus Milner has been in the cellar from 2000, crafting rather elegant wines.

De Meye range

★★★★ **Cabernet Sauvignon** Pleasingly dry, savoury **12** (★★★★) lightly earthy, with decent, rugged grip balancing easy, elegant fruit flavours; tasty but not quite as convincing as **11**.

★★★★ **Trutina** Property's cabernet-led flagship with merlot, cab franc in **12**. Generously dense, fully ripe & rich fruit flavours coated by gently grippy tannins. Splash shiraz contributes to warm, spicy finish.

Shiraz ★★★☆ Dollop cab franc in smoky, earthy **13**. Nicely ripe & spicy but not jammy. **Chardonnay Unwooded** ★★★ Fresh **15**, uncomplicated peach & pear flavours; ideal as light lunchtime sipper. Also tasted: **Chenin Blanc 15** ★★★★ Not retasted: **Merlot 12** ★★★ **Shiraz Rosé 14** ★★★

Little River range

Cabernet Sauvignon ★★★ Dark-fruited, properly dry **13** in savoury lightly funky style. Not retasted: **Shiraz 13** ★★☆ — IM

Location/map/WO: Stellenbosch ▪ Map grid reference: E1 ▪ Est/1stB 1998 ▪ Tasting & sales Mon-Thu by appt Fri 12-5 Sat/Sun & pub hols 11-4 ▪ Fee R30/5 wines ▪ Closed Good Fri, Dec 25/26 & Jan 1 ▪ Cellar tours Mon-Fri by appt ▪ 'The Table at De Meye' open for lunch Sat-Sun, booking essential T +27 (0)72-696-0530, www.thetablerestaurant.co.za ▪ Farm produce ▪ Owner(s) Jan Myburgh Family Trust ▪ Winemaker(s) Marcus Milner (Sep 1999) & Lofty Ellis (consultant), with Aby Bodlani (Sep 2000) ▪ Viticulturist(s) Philip Myburgh & Johan Pienaar (Jan 2006, consultant) ▪ 100ha/65ha (cabs s/f, merlot, shiraz, chard, chenin) ▪ 300t/36,000cs own label 65% red 25% white 10% rosé ▪ IPW ▪ PO Box 20 Elsenburg 7607 ▪ info@demeye.co.za ▪ www.demeye.co.za ▪ S 33° 49' 0.7" E 018° 49' 48.8" ▪ F +27 (0)21-884-4154 ▪ **T +27 (0)21-884-4131**

☐ **De Mikke Patron** *see* Almenkerk Wine Estate

DeMorgenzon

After buying this under-performing property against Stellenboschkloof's slopes in 2003, business moguls and philanthropists Hylton and Wendy Appelbaum spared neither expense nor energy in realising its viticultural, aesthetic and natural biodiversity potential. Soil analyses and climatic data informed a vineyard overhaul; a new cellar arose from an Aussie design; and an on-site nursery supports large-scale re-introduction of indigenous vegetation in and around sustainably farmed vineyards. Similarly out-the-box thinker Carl van der Merwe, GM/cellarmaster since 2010, shares the ethos. Reds and whites perform equally under his baton, particularly in masterly blends. Shiraz and chenin (including a new Special Cuvée) are specialities; a pinot noir debuts this edition. And 15 ha of new chenin, chardonnay and roussanne will build the premium whites up to a crescendo.

Maestro range

★★★★ **Red** Ethereal, gorgeously perfumed **13** (★★★★☆) cab-led blend all 5 Bordeaux varieties. Classy, supple & restrained, needing time in glass to reveal spicy core & ample red fruit charm. Step up on **11** but don't expect a bold statement wine. No **12**.

★★★★★ **White** Masterly **14** (★★★★★) textured blend spicy roussanne & chardonnay, with grenache, chenin & viognier in supporting role. Fresh acidity focuses richness, while ferment in cement 'egg' & oak adds breadth. **13** voluptuously rounded.

Not tasted: **Red ('Rhône Blend').**

Reserve range

★★★★☆ **Syrah** ⊘ Convincing rendition of variety's Rhône origins in deep-hued, complex **12**. Vivid red fruit, white pepper in superb balance with supple oak (some new) & uplifting savoury acidity.

★★★★★ **Chardonnay** Complex, immensely inviting **14** (★★★★☆) touch less electrifying than stellar maiden **13** Platter White Wine of the Year. Two thirds new oak & time on lees judiciously executed to offer poised structure, generous richness & texture to layered elegant melange citrus & stonefruit.

★★★★☆ **Chenin Blanc** Seriously styled **14** from old bushvines, 10 months on lees prior to barrel selection. Real verve & personality, flaunting delicious layer upon complex layer of ripe apples, peaches & nuts. Richer, more generous style than new Special Cuvée bottling.

★★★★☆ **Special Cuvée Chenin Blanc** ⓃⒺⓌ Pristine & utterly austere **13** far steelier than Reserve, needing ample time to unfurl & reveal layered complexity lurking behind pithily textured lemon fruit, resolute acidity & earthy minerality. Wonderful tension imparts fascination to the markedly long finish.

DMZ range

★★★★ **Syrah** Ⓥ Vibrant fruit core & roasted spices in brightly youthful **12** interwoven with fine, supple tannins to produce authentic, boldly expressive syrah.

★★★★ **Chardonnay** Stylishly elegant, multi-regional **14** in harmonious, subtly oaked form with enough fresh yellow apple & stonefruit richness to satisfy. Flavourful sibling to Reserve.

★★★★ **Chenin Blanc** Pure-fruited, lightly oaked **15** has natural grace & charm. Most modest of property's trio of chenins offers unassertive clarity & greater depth, breadth than **13** (★★★☆). Delightful.

★★★★ **Sauvignon Blanc** Overt sauvignon character in ultra-crisp, characterful **14** (★★★☆) though also-tasted **15** more convincing, with zingy edge to lean, structured, minerally finish. Small portion oak adds texture, some breadth.

★★★★ **Concerto White** Textured viognier, roussanne led 5-way **14** blend from Stellenbosch fruit over-delivers, with full-flavoured yellow peaches & spice.

Pinot Noir ⓃⒺⓌ ★★★☆ Delightfully fresh, earthy **14**'s silky, textured, seamless charm has sufficient weight & interest to ensure agreeably savoury, flavourful sipping. WO W Cape, as all these unless noted. Also tasted: **Concerto Red 13** ★★★☆ Not retasted: **MCC Chenin Blanc NV** ★★★☆

Garden Vineyards range

Rosé Ⓥ ★★★ Floral, dry & fruity **14** from Rhône grapes has frank, unpretentious but genuinely tasty appeal, perfect lunch wine. — IM

Location/map: Stellenbosch ▪ Map grid reference: C5 ▪ WO: Stellenbosch/Western Cape ▪ Est 2003 ▪ 1stB 2005 ▪ Tasting & sales daily 10-5 ▪ Fee R30-R50 ▪ Closed Good Fri, Dec 25/26 & Jan 1 ▪ Cellar tours on request ▪ Conservation area ▪ Owner(s) Wendy & Hylton Appelbaum ▪ Cellarmaster(s) / GM Carl van der Merwe (Jul 2010) ▪ Winemaker(s) Carl van der Merwe (Jul 2010), with Hanneke Botha (Nov 2014) ▪ Viticulturist(s) Danie de Waal (Dec 2014) & Kevin Watt (consultant) ▪ 91ha/52ha (cab, grenache, merlot, mourv, shiraz, chard, chenin, rouss, sauv, viog) ▪ 252t/30,000cs own label 56% red 33% white 8% rosé 3% other ▪ BWI, IPW ▪ PO Box 1388 Stellenbosch 7599 ▪ info@demorgenzon.co.za ▪ www.demorgenzon.co.za ▪ S 33° 56' 22.99" E 018° 45' 0.17" ▪ F +27 (0)21-881-3773 ▪ **T +27 (0)21-881-3030**

☐ **Den** *see* Painted Wolf Wines
☐ **Denneboom** *see* Oude Denneboom
☐ **De Oude Opstal** *see* Stellendrift – SHZ Cilliers/Kuün Wyne

---

De Redley ⓆⓊ

A rare white merlot (untasted) is among the wines made to spec for this Stellenbosch-based boutique winery, under the direction of owners Nicholas Ridley and Fredy Pummer of Boucheron Wines.

Location: Stellenbosch ▪ Est/1stB 2012 ▪ Tasting available at select slowfood markets ▪ Owner(s) Nicholas Ridley & Fredy Pummer ▪ Cellarmaster(s) Nicholas Ridley (Sep 2011) ▪ Winemaker(s) Piet Bredell ▪ 7t/766cs own label 100% white ▪ info@deredley.co.za ▪ www.deredley.co.za ▪ F +27 (0)11-708-3615 ▪ **T +27 (0)11-708-3444**

Desert Rose Wines ⓦ

A 'fun sideline/garagiste project when we have time for it' is how busy nurseryman Alan van Niekerk and long-time Namaqua Wines supplier Herman Nel describe Desert Rose, the Vredendal boutique winery named for a Sting tune as well as the gypsum crystal 'roses' found on nearby surrounding plains.

Winemaker's Choice Cabernet Sauvignon ⓦ ★★★ Interesting salty nuance on blackcurrant-toned **11**, soft & vanilla-scented from 100% new American oak. **Shiraz** ⓦ ★★★ **09** dense & powerful, still tight when last tasted; structured to develop interestingly. Not retasted: **Cabernet Sauvignon 10** ★★☆
Winemaker's Choice Merlot 10 ★★☆ **Jada's Rose 09** ★★★★ **Nicola's Rose 10** ★★★☆ — DB, CvZ

Location: Vredendal ▪ Map: Olifants River ▪ WO: Western Cape ▪ Tasting by appt ▪ Owner(s) Alan van Niekerk & Herman Nel ▪ Winemaker(s) Herman Nel ▪ desertrose@nashuaisp.co.za ▪ S 31° 41' 33.1" E 018° 30' 5.9" ▪ F +27 (0)27-213-2858 ▪ **T +27 (0)82-809-2040/+27 (0)82-800-2270**

De Toren Private Cellar ⓦ

Business world émigrés Emil and Sonette den Dulk and their team combine smarts, competitiveness, perfectionism and love of wine to produce a trio of red blends, two at the upper end of SA wine's quality and price scales. Having bought their 'little piece of heaven' in the Polkadraai Hills outside Stellenbosch in 1991 as a country retreat, Emil and Sonette quickly learned of the sea-facing site's viticultural potential. After consulting experts and evaluating markets, they planted 13 different clones of the five classic Bordeaux red varieties in the diverse soils. 'Our objective is to develop and redefine the Bordeaux concept to be uniquely South African... achieving complex, balanced, expressive wines.' They credit attention to detail for success, most pleased in recent years by a US Wine Enthusiast Top New World Winery rating.

★★★★☆ **Fusion V** Cab-led (44%) 5-way Bordeaux blend, part natural ferment. **13** concentrated, with rich, fragrant fruit & well-managed ripe tannins. Mouthfilling & firmly structured, French & American oaking, year (half new), a well-judged support. Also in smaller & larger bottle formats.

★★★★ **La Jeunesse Délicate** Improved **NV** blend of unwooded rosé (48%) & oaked Bordeaux reds is light styled & intended for early enjoyment, lightly chilled, but also has a modicum of structure.

★★★★☆ **Z** Consistent, earlier-ready (but ageworthy) 5-way Bordeaux blend; merlot-led **13** shows intense berry flavours in harmony with oak & supple tannin structure. Lighter bodied than sibling, with delightful freshness & composure. Also in 1.5 & 3L. — WB

Location/map/WO: Stellenbosch ▪ Map grid reference: B6 ▪ Est 1994 ▪ 1stB 1999 ▪ Tasting, sales & cellar tours by appt ▪ Fee R180, waived on purchase ▪ Owner(s) Edenhall Trust ▪ Cellarmaster(s) Albie Koch (Oct 1998) ▪ Winemaker(s) Charles Williams (Dec 2008) ▪ Viticulturist(s) Juhan Hunlun (Nov 2013, assistant) ▪ 25ha/±21ha (cabs s/f, malbec, merlot, p verdot) ▪ 150t/11,000cs own label 100% red ▪ PO Box 48 Vlottenburg 7604 ▪ info@de-toren.com ▪ www.de-toren.com ▪ S 33° 57' 34.5" E 018° 45' 7.5" F +27 (0)21-881-3335 ▪ **T +27 (0)21-881-3119**

De Trafford Wines ⓦ

A practising architect making wine as a hobby before earning widespread acclaim and commercial success, David Trafford is one of SA's most thoughtful, creative winegrowers. In more than three decades on the secluded Stellenbosch family farm Mont Fleur, he has not deviated from the simple and the natural in his artisan cellar to express 'the magical' coaxed from the land. Vinifying grapes from selected vineyards (including next-door Keermont) to supplement Mont Fleur's meticulously sited 5 ha, he's honed charming rusticity to sophisticated power in internationally lauded reds and signature chenins. Now it's 'bit by bit' improvement and 'getting more organised in the cellar', the latter aided by the completed move of his path-breaking (separately listed) Sijnn wines to their new home in Malgas.

★★★★☆ **Cabernet Sauvignon** From 4 low-yield blocks 9-24 years old, liquorice-nuanced **12** a fine ambassador for the variety: classic dark fruit, iodine & graphite spicing, stately structure. 35% new oak (23 months) well integrated, will assist cellaring decade or more.

★★★★☆ **CWG Auction Reserve Cabernet Sauvignon** ⓝⓔⓦ Opulent **13** has rich fruitcake, blackcurrant & plum notes, cigarbox & wood spice complexity. Powerful, with underlying minerality; needs 5+ years even to begin showing its best. 50/50 best own block & neighbour Keermont. Also in magnum.

★★★★☆ **Cabernet Franc** From mountainside viewsite that 'screamed to be planted to cab franc'. Charming **12**, first off young vines, seductive tealeaf & cedarwood spice, bright red fruit & malleable tannins for early enjoyment, structure to improve few years. First since **08** from bought-in grapes.

★★★★ **Merlot** Excellent but not (yet) very expressive **11**; unlike early-approachable **10**, has athletic tannins that benefit from decanting now, will meld & reward good few years.

★★★★☆ **Blueprint Syrah** Despite vintage challenges, **13** approaches quality of **12** (★★★★★), our Red Wine of Year last edition. Ticks all fine syrah/shiraz boxes; lithe, precise & detailed, accessible early courtesy only old oak maturation. Grapes largely ex neighbour Keermont.

★★★★☆ **Syrah 393** Unfined/filtered, as all reds, **13** similar deep & broad vein as **12**, **11**; layered & refined, it has violet & pepper nuances, satisfying now but crafted to improve decade or more.

★★★★☆ **Syrah CSC** (NEW) Wind-reduced (by 50%) home shiraz crop supplemented in **13** with fruit from select Cape South Coast (Malgas, Upper Hemel-en-Aarde, Stanford) sites. Perfumed with mulberry & white pepper, concentrated & sleek, 14.7% alcohol unnoticeable.

★★★★☆ **Elevation 393** (Ⓧ) Merlot leads on **10** flagship blend named for home-vineyard altitude, cab & shiraz offer near-equal support. Light smoke & dried thyme nuance to blue/black fruit. Yielding & generous, rich, yet tautly muscular too, deserves time.

★★★★ **Chenin Blanc 14** (★★★★☆) wild yeast fermented in 15% new oak, a step up on **13**; ripe melon, yellow stonefruit & honey notes lifted by vibrant acidity, which also provides clean length & structure.

★★★★ **Straw Wine** 16th vintage of trailblazing air-dried chenin dessert; naturally-fermented, oak-aged **12** (★★★★★) in top form with appealing dried apricot, orange marmalade & honey notes, flinty hint; unashamedly sweet yet bright & uncloying. **11** (★★★★) more unctuous after ambrosial **10**. — GM

Location/map: Stellenbosch ▪ Map grid reference: G8 ▪ WO: Stellenbosch/Cape South Coast ▪ Est/1stB 1992 ▪ Tasting, sales & tours Fri & Sat 10–1, or by appt ▪ Fee R50, waived on purchase ▪ Closed all pub hols ▪ Owner(s) David & Rita Trafford ▪ Winemaker(s) David Trafford ▪ Viticulturist(s) Schalk du Toit (consultant) ▪ 200ha/5ha (cabs s/f, merlot, shiraz) ▪ 71t/7,000cs own label 70% red 30% white ▪ PO Box 495 Stellenbosch 7599 ▪ info@detrafford.co.za ▪ www.detrafford.co.za ▪ S 34° 0' 45.1" E 018° 53' 57.8" ▪ F +27 (0)86-542-3959 ▪ **T +27 (0)21-880-1611**

Deux Frères Wines   (Ⓧ) (⌂)

The two brothers in the boutique winery's name are Stellenbosch-based Stephan and Retief du Toit, who have moved vinification of their young-vine crop to nearby L'Avenir (where vine-and-wine man Stephan learnt his craft). He personally hosts by-appointment tastings at the home farm, and a barrel cellar will soon take shape there along with a block of cabernet franc.

★★★★ **Liberté** Alluring dark & perfumed berry fruit, with minty nuance, now starting to unfurl from dry chalky tannin structure of retasted **12** Bordeaux red. Still showing youthful restraint but will continue to develop & reward ageing. **11** (★★★★) still available (as 'Cabernet Sauvignon-Petit Verdot').

★★★★ **Fraternité 13**, like still-selling **12**, delicious smoky bacon & berry fruits clothing amenable tannins in fine 70/30 shiraz/mourvèdre blend. Supple, juicy now & for next few years.

Blanc de Noir ★★★ Step-up **15**, from mourvèdre, brisk & feisty bone-dry style. Tad more fruit than previous, quite juicy savoury flavours, but still needs food. — MW

Location/map/WO: Stellenbosch ▪ Map grid reference: E3 ▪ Est 2008 ▪ 1stB 2012 ▪ Tasting & sales by appt Mon-Fri 10-5 Sat 10-1 ▪ Closed Easter Fri-Mon, Dec 25 & Jan 1 ▪ BYO picnic ▪ Owner(s) M Wiehe, H Wiehe, S du Toit, R du Toit ▪ Cellarmaster(s)/viticulturist(s) Stephan du Toit (Jan 2008) ▪ 2.1ha (cab, malbec, mourv, p verdot, shiraz) ▪ 1,700cs own label 80% red 20% rosé ▪ PO Box 209 Koelenhof 7605 ▪ stephan@dfwines.co.za ▪ www.dfwines.co.za ▪ S 33° 52' 51.16" E 18° 50' 44.93" ▪ F +27 (0)86-621-2425 ▪ **T +27 (0)21-889-9865/+27 (0)82-371-4770**

De Villiers Wines

Cellarmaster on the eponymous Paarl family farm, Villiers de Villiers makes wine under an own label (with Reserve, Value and Heeren van Oranje Nassau ranges), and for export brands, under contract to buyers in a variety of markets including the Netherlands, Indian Ocean islands and China.

Location: Paarl ▪ Map: Paarl & Wellington ▪ Map grid reference: E6 ▪ Est/1stB 1688 ▪ Tasting & sales by appt ▪ Owner(s) De Villiers Family Trust ▪ Cellarmaster(s)/winemaker(s)/viticulturist(s) Villiers de Villiers (1980) ▪ 50,000cs own label 80% red 20% white ▪ Brands for clients: Huangtai Wines ▪ PO Box 659 Suider-Paarl 7624 ▪ vadev@mweb.co.za, info@devilllierswines.co.za ▪ www.devilllierswines.com ▪ S 33° 45' 43.3" E 018° 57' 40.8" ▪ F +27 (0)86-653-8988 ▪ **T +27 (0)21-863-2175**

Devonair

Owners of Devon Valley winery Devonair, Leon and Rina de Wit, in 2008 decided to replant their cabernet sauvignon boutique vineyard and, on advice, decided to stick with cab, establishing 3 different clones. Just 3,000 bottles of the first vintage from these young vines ('12), made by veteran wine man Ernst Gouws, will debut this year, after 4 years' maturation. 'We've learnt that a good cab needs time.'

The Cab ⓠ ★★★★ Medium-bodied 07 shows plush ripe blackberry fruit backed by a fine tannin structure & firm acid balance. Not tasted: **The Cab Family Reserve.** — WB

Location/map/WO: Stellenbosch ▪ Map grid reference: D3 ▪ Est 1994 ▪ 1stB 2000 ▪ Tasting & sales by appt ▪ Closed all pub hols ▪ 1 self-catering cottage ▪ Owner(s) Leon & Rina de Wit ▪ Winemaker(s) Ernst Gouws (Mar 2006) ▪ Viticulturist(s) Pierre de Wet (2012) ▪ 2.2ha (cab) ▪ 500cs own label 100% red ▪ PO Box 1274 Stellenbosch 7599 ▪ leon@devonair.co.za ▪ www.devonair.co.za ▪ S 33° 53' 44.45" E 018° 48' 27.46" ▪ F +27 (0)21-865-2327 ▪ **T +27 (0)21-865-2190**

Devon Hill

Geir Tellefsen's label from Devon Valley grapes is to be relaunched, he and team 'working around the clock' at press time 'to ensure the quality and consistency that Devon Hill consumers are accustomed to'.

Location: Stellenbosch ▪ Est 1994 ▪ 1stB 1996 ▪ Closed to public ▪ Owner(s) Geir Tellefsen ▪ Cellarmaster(s)/winemaker(s)/viticulturist(s) Therese de Beer (Jan 2011, consultant) ▪ 20,000cs own label 80% red 15% white 5% rosé ▪ geir@rosendalwinery.com ▪ F +27 (0)21-424-1571 ▪ **T +27 (0)21-424-4498**

Devon Rocks

No new wines from Jürgen and Brita Heinrich's small vineyard in Devon Valley, but their Pinotage '05 and '07, and Shiraz Rosé '09 are still available.

Location/map/WO: Stellenbosch ▪ Map grid reference: D3 ▪ Est 1998 ▪ 1stB 2003 ▪ Tasting, sales & tours by appt ▪ B&B accommodation ▪ Owner(s) Jürgen & Brita Heinrich ▪ Winemaker(s) Simon Smith (Louisvale) ▪ Viticulturist(s) Gawie du Bois & Paul Wallace (advisers) ▪ 4ha/3.5ha (ptage, shiraz) ▪ 4,400cs 57% red 18% white 25% rosé ▪ PO Box 12483 Die Boord 7613 ▪ info@devonrocks.co.za ▪ www.devonrocks.co.za ▪ S 33° 53' 9.9" E 018° 48' 30.1" ▪ F +27 (0)21-865-2621 ▪ **T +27 (0)21-865-2536**

Devonvale Golf & Wine Estate

Residents of tony Stellenbosch lifestyle estate Devonvale at harvest time invite family and friends to help pick the crop from vines fringing some of the fairways, for offsite vinification. In 2014, the first sauvignon was bottled. It proved so popular, volumes were doubled in 2015 — and flew off the shelves in weeks.

Provoyeur range

★★★★ **Cabernet Sauvignon** ⓠ 07 modern styling with rich cassis & mint. Sweet & spicy oak nuance integrated, giving sleek polished texture, ready to enjoy. **06** (★★★) was charry, chunkier.

Special Reserve Shiraz ⓠ ★★★★ 10 shows a supple structure, smooth, rich & elegant without being intense or complex; to drink now & for couple of years. Not retasted: **Shiraz 11** ★★ — MW

Location/map/WO: Stellenbosch ▪ Map grid reference: D3 ▪ Est 1997 ▪ 1stB 2004 ▪ Tasting by appt ▪ Fee R25pp ▪ Sales Mon-Sat 11–6 ▪ Chez Shiraz restaurant ▪ Tour groups ▪ Golf ▪ Pro shop ▪ Conferences ▪

Devonvale Golf Lodge ▪ Owner(s) Devonmust (Pty) Ltd ▪ Winemaker(s) Wilhelm Kritzinger (2004, Belle-vue Estate) & Riaan Wassüng (Stellenbosch University Welgevallen Cellar) ▪ Viticulturist(s) Southern Turf Management (2015) ▪ 117ha/1.7ha (shiraz, sauv) ▪ 14t/±2,000cs own label 85% red 15% white ▪ PO Box 77 Koelenhof 7605 ▪ info@devonvale.co.za ▪ www.devonvale.co.za ▪ S 33° 52' 59.6" E 018° 48' 15.0" ▪ F +27 (0)21-865-2601 ▪ **T +27 (0)21-865-2080**

DeWaal Wines

The De Waals of Uiterwyk in Stellenboschkloof celebrated three centuries on African soil in 2015. Now under custodianship of ninth-generation Pieter and winemaker brothers Chris (whites) and Daniël (reds), the farm's winegrowing is enmeshed with SA home-bred pinotage, looming large in their pre-dominantly red repertoire. The lofty Top of the Hill draws from bushvines in apparently SA's oldest block (65 years). From vines almost as ancient, the CT de Waal honours the forbear, the first, in the 1940s, to vinify the grape. Visitors to the recently updated tasting room view the venerable vines from the terrace.

DeWaal range

★★★★ **Cabernet Sauvignon** ⓥ Richly ripe **11** back on form after lesser **08** (★★★☆), offering suc-culent dark fruit & spice, underpinned by finely textured tannins from half new oak.

★★★★ **Merlot** ⓥ Some classic styling in well-structured **10**, less resolutely dry than last. Supple tan-nins support juicy black plum flavours to ensure harmonious conclusion.

★★★★ **CT de Waal Pinotage 13** elegant glassful with black cherry & floral bouquet, juicy intensity, silky finish; 60% new oak lends support, adds allspice complexity. Follows stellar **11** (★★★★☆). No **12**.

★★★★☆ **Top of the Hill Pinotage** Kingpin of estate's pinotage trio gets grand treatment: tiny yields from 60+ year old bushvines judiciously seasoned in all-new oak. Cassis & liquorice on **12** (★★★★) lead to compact, layered palate that hesitates to open & share its fruit. Less concentrated but more revealing, also-tasted **13** a beautiful medley of spicy red & black fruit, with greater freshness & better balance, more moderate alcohol (13% versus 14%).

★★★★ **Signal Rock** Cab-driven Bordeaux-style red with merlot, **09** (★★★★) has old-fashioned styl-ing: tealeaf, tomato & faint cassis; angular palate; dominant tannin. **08** was richer with more flesh.

Not retasted: **Pinotage 12 ★★★**

Young Vines range

Sauvignon Blanc ★★★ Tank sample **15** has vivid, energetic green grass & capsicum aromas & fla-vours, lots of zing. Also tasted: **Merlot 13 ★★★ Chenin Blanc 15 ★★★** Not retasted: **Shiraz 13 ★★★** — JPf

Location/map/WO: Stellenbosch ▪ Map grid reference: C5 ▪ Est 1682 ▪ 1stB 1972 ▪ Tasting & sales Mon-Sat & pub hols 10–4.30 ▪ Fee R30 ▪ Closed Sundays, Good Fri, Dec 25/26 & Jan 1 ▪ Meals/refreshments ▪ Art exhibitions ▪ Owner(s) Pieter de Waal ▪ Winemaker(s)/viticulturist(s) Chris de Waal & Daniël de Waal (whites/reds, consultants) ▪ 800t ▪ 50% red 50% white ▪ IPW ▪ PO Box 15 Vlottenburg 7604 ▪ admin@dewaal.co.za ▪ www.dewaal.co.za ▪ S 33° 56' 29.3" E 018° 45' 59.9" ▪ F +27 (0)86-648-0187 ▪ **T +27 (0)21-881-3711**

Dewaldt Heyns Family Wines

Celebrated Saronsberg winemaker and Cape Winemakers Guild member Dewaldt Heyns' own boutique-scale vinifications are about capturing 'the elegance and understated complexity that older vineyards offer'. The wines are intended as a tribute to Dewaldt's father and the Swartland, where he grew up.

Weathered Hands range

★★★★ **Shiraz** ⓥ Nodding to the Rhône, **09** is concentrated & flavoursome without being heavy, shows greater poise than very ripe but unshowy **08** (★★★★). Good fruit & tannin augur well for ageing.

★★★★ **Chenin Blanc** ⓥ From ±40 year old bushvines on weathered granite, **11** (★★★★☆) like pre-viously tasted **10** is elegant, perfumed, pure; the younger wine slightly richer, with bigger structure but similarly quickened by minerality.

Pinotage ⊛ ★★★★ **12** from old bushvines. Oak (55% new barrels) dominates the aromas, but ripe berry fruit emerges more on the palate. Juicy & well balanced, if not harmonious yet, with dry tannins & sweet-fruited finish. — TJ

Location: Tulbagh/Swartland ▪ WO: Swartland ▪ Est/1stB 2006 ▪ Tasting by appt at Saronsberg ▪ Owner(s) Dewaldt Heyns Family Wines ▪ Cellarmaster(s)/winemaker(s)/viticulturist(s) Dewaldt Heyns ▪ (ptage, shiraz, chenin) ▪ 15t/1,100cs own label 60% red 40% white ▪ dewaldt@dewaldtheyns.com ▪ **T +27 (0)82-441-4117**

De Wet Cellar   ⊗ ⊜ ⊛

As a stakeholder in FirstCape, Worcester's oldest winery is focused on supplying millions of litres to one of SA's great export successes. But a not insubstantial 30,000 cases of good-quality and -value wines are bottled under the owner-growers' own label, and conveniently available — in newly revamped packaging — from the cellardoor just off the main artery into the winelands.

★★★★ **Cravate** ⊛ Among first méthode cap classique sparklings from the region. 100% chardonnay, vibrant **10** raises bar on **09** (★★★★): lemon meringue taste, creamy mousse, clean citrus ending.

★★★★ **Red Muscadel** ⊘ Intense **15** fortified sweetie exudes honey & jasmine, fig jam & Turkish delight, lingering & warming conclusion. Also-tasted **14** (★★★★) similar attractions but shade less concentrated.

★★★★ **White Muscadel** ⊘ Charms & satisfies every time (without breaking the bank). **13** jerepiko has grapey aromas & flavours, honey & dried figs, a citrus lift on the finish. Delicious solo or with dessert.

★★★★ **Cape Ruby** ⊘ The team do this accessible, fruity style of 'port' so well. Their latest **NV** has rich & chewy prune & raisin flavours which linger long & cheerfully. Perfect way to end a good meal.

★★★★ **Cape Vintage** ⊛ **08** port-style is firm & luscious, with complex curry spice, Xmas cake & smoky aromas. From now-uprooted, ultra-rare-in-Cape pontac.

⌐ **Cabernet Sauvignon** ⊘ ⊛ ★★★ Add this to your list of must-buy good-value cabs — always on the ⌐ button. **14** plums & blackberries swaddled in vanilla (from 2nd-fill barrels), with fragrant black pepper ⌐ twist. **Chenin Blanc** ⊘ ⊛ ★★★★ Rung up from previous, **15** a mouthwatering basket of soft ripe ⌐ fruit (apple, apricot & peach), juicy to the end. ⌐

Chenin Blanc Wood Matured (NEW) ★★★ **14**'s older oak is merely a platform upon which crisp green-apple fruit performs, gooseberry-nuanced tangy acidity is perfect for seafood. Also tasted: **Shiraz 15** ★★★ **Pinotage Rosé** ⊘ **14** ★★★ **Sauvignon Blanc 15** ★★★ Not retasted: **Merlot-Cabernet Sauvignon 13** ★★★ **Chardonnay 13** ★★★★ **Petillant Fronté NV** ★★ **Hanepoot 13** ★★★★ — DB

Location/map/WO: Worcester ▪ Est 1946 ▪ 1stB 1964 ▪ Tasting & sales Mon-Fri 9–5 Sat 9–12 ▪ Closed all pub hols ▪ Cellar tours by appt ▪ BYO picnic ▪ Owner(s) 60 members ▪ Winemaker(s) Tertius Jonck (Sep 2007) & Phillip Vercuiel (Dec 2007) ▪ Viticulturist(s) Hennie Visser (Jul 2008, Vinpro) ▪ 1,000ha (cab, shiraz, chard, chenin, sauv) ▪ 15,500t/30,000cs own label 29% red 36% white 5% rosé 30% fortified + 10m L bulk ▪ ISO 22000, SGS ▪ PO Box 16 De Wet 6853 ▪ admin@dewetcellar.co.za ▪ www.dewetcellar.co.za ▪ S 33° 36' 24.2" E 019° 30' 36.5" ▪ F +27 (0)23-341-2762 ▪ **T +27 (0)23-341-2710**

De Wetshof Estate   ⊗ ⊚ ⊛

'To produce world-class chardonnays in a socially and ethically sustainable manner' has been the goal of industry heavyweight Danie de Wet and his marketing legend wife Lesca, and it's taken 'years of toil in vineyards and cellar' to reach the heights they have on their Robertson farm, five-time President's Export Achievement Award winner. A 1970s stint at Germany's Geisenheim inspired a lifetime of experimental work with plant material, clones and suitable sites. Among SA's pioneer explorers of chardonnay, Danie's seen sons Peter and Johann continue in similar vein, with additions of pinot noir, classic MCC sparklings and cabernet and merlot to an increasingly diversified, but meticulously researched portfolio.

De Wetshof Estate range

★★★★ **Naissance Cabernet Sauvignon** Classic & elegant **14**, lead pencil & blackcurrant whiffs, taut structure with overlay of smooth chocolate-wrapped berries, vanilla from year in 40% new French oak.

★★★★ **Thibault** ⓐ Impressive Bordeaux-style red, one of handful made over the years. **10** merlot (88%) & cab; elegant, with supple tannin structure. Age or decant now to appreciate fully.

★★★★ **Nature In Concert Pinot Noir** ⓐ **10**'s ebullient spice, earth & peppery cherry notes coupled with malleable tannins take it up a notch on choc-mocha **09** (★★★★). Enjoy solo or with food.

★★★★☆ **Bateleur Chardonnay** Flagship from 29 year old single-vineyard & named for majestic African eagle, **13** brims with citrus & vanilla (90% new oak), showing class, poise & complexity. Succulent, bright mouthfeel, harmony & unflagging finish – will reward the patient. Bigger bottle formats available.

★★★★ **Finesse Chardonnay** **14** from 4 different vineyards, punches above its weight with plenty of flavour, butterscotch richness from extended lees-ageing; crisp citrus acidity. Only 10% new barrels.

★★★★☆ **The Site Chardonnay** Fine new-barrel-fermented **14** from estate's oldest single Block 17B shows concentrated lemon zest freshness, apple blossom & pear flavours underpinned by creamy vanilla, hint of roasted nuts, silky mouthfeel. Ageworthy & a real gem.

★★★★ **Bon Vallon Chardonnay** ⓐ Going up a notch on **13** (★★★☆), unoaked **14** oozes tropical fruit, lime zest & granadilla, mouthfillingly rich from weekly lees stirring. Perfect for roast duck.

★★★★ **Riesling** Delightful **15** back to form after last-tasted **12** (★★★★) with perfumed nose of orange blossom, ripe apple & stonefruit. Off-dry, with bright, light-tripping fruit balanced by zesty acidity.

★★★★ **Sauvignon Blanc** ⓐ After **13** (★★★★), back-to-form **13** offers signature fresh lime fruit profile, depth & focus, with lemon blossom note, mouthfilling marzipan (from lees-ageing) & lemony finish.

★★★★ **Méthode Cap Classique Pinot Noir Brut** New disgorgement of sophisticated & dependable **08** sparkling owes its elegant brioche character to 60 months on fine lees, no dosage. Fine & stately.

★★★★☆ **Méthode Cap Classique Cuvée Brut** Champagne-method bubbly from chardonnay & pinot noir; lighter-footed **11** (★★★★) misses the mark of **08**, showing fine almond brioche notes, creamy mousse, balanced acidity & savoury conclusion.

★★★★☆ **Edeloes** ⓐ Exceptional botrytised riesling dessert wine, occasional release. **06** is voluptuous, complex & rich, with bright pineapple & apricot flavours complemented by pristine acid backbone for a clean lifted finish. Terrific length. 500 ml.

Also tasted: **Limestone Hill Chardonnay 15** ★★★☆

Danie de Wet range

★★★★ **Chardonnay Sur Lie** ⊘ Reliable unwooded, lees-aged label; **15** sparkles with ginger & lemon whiffs, silky mouthfeel & lush, rounded quality on long finish. Excellent value.

Also tasted: **Sauvignon Blanc 15** ★★★ Discontinued: **Cape Muscadel**.

Limelight range

Chardonnay ★★★ **15** unaoked is light bodied, balanced, easy & charming for early consumption. Not retasted: **Pinot Noir 12** ★★★ **Chardonnay-Pinot Noir 14** ★★★ — WB

Location/map/WO: Robertson ▪ Est 1949 ▪ 1stB 1972 ▪ Tasting & sales Mon-Fri 8.30–4.30 Sat 9.30–12.30 ▪ Closed Easter Fri/Sun/Mon, May 1, Dec 25/26 & Jan 1 ▪ Cellar tours by appt Mon-Fri 8.30–4.30 ▪ Conservation area ▪ Owner(s) Danie, Peter & Johann de Wet ▪ Cellarmaster(s) Danie de Wet (Jan 1973) ▪ Winemaker(s) Danie de Wet (Jan 1973), Mervyn Williams (2001) & Peter de Wet (2007) ▪ Viticulturist(s) Rudolf Kriel (2012), advised by Phil Freese & Francois Viljoen (both 1997) ▪ 600ha/180ha (cab, merlot, pinot, chard, riesling, sauv) ▪ 1,800t 85% red 90% white 1% rosé 1% MCC ▪ ISO 9001:2008, ISO 22000:2005, BBBEE Grade 2, BWI, CVC, Enviro Scientific, Integrity & Sustainability, IPW ▪ PO Box 31 Robertson 6705 ▪ info@dewetshof.com ▪ www.dewetshof.com ▪ S 33° 52' 38.0" E 020° 0' 35.1" ▪ F +27 (0)23-615-1915 ▪ **T +27 (0)23-615-1853**

☐ **De Wilde Haf** *see* Wilde Haf Wines
☐ **De Wit Family** *see* Signal Gun Wines

De Zoete Inval Estate   ⓛ

Respect for the heritage accumulated by five generations of Fraters over 130 years on their Paarl estate – originally granted in 1688 by the father of South African wine, Simon van der Stel – runs deep in John

Robert and wife Eulalia. They're building on that legacy by introducing Rhône-style wines, among others, suited to their soil, and naming them for family members.

★★★★ Oupa Bull Pinotage Reserve Fruit is masked by oak on **14** (★★★), less impressive than last-made **08** though the tail is appealingly succulent & spicy. Simonsberg–Stellenbosch WO.

Eulalia Shiraz (NEW) **★★★** Leathery blueberry ease to maiden **14**, given form by year on French/American oak staves. **Elizabeth Cabernet Sauvignon-Petit Verdot-Malbec** (NEW) **★★★** Bright, lively debut for **14** Bordeaux blend. Juicy, structured & approachable. **Connor SMG** (NEW) **★★★** Smoky red fruit & cedar notes on accessible **14** shiraz-led blend with mourvèdre & grenache. **Adrian Chardonnay-Viognier** (NEW) **★★★** 60/40 combo offers softly rounded yet light & zesty citrus notes on **15**. Discontinued: **Pinotage, Cabernet Sauvignon-Shiraz, Chardonnay, Chenin Blanc-Viognier-Semillon, Vintage Brut, Cape Vintage, Sweet Surrender Shiraz.** — FM

Location: Paarl ▪ Map: Paarl & Wellington ▪ Map grid reference: E6 ▪ WO: Paarl/Simonsberg–Stellenbosch ▪ Est 1878 ▪ 1stB 1976 ▪ Tastings & sales by appt ▪ Owner(s) DZI Agricultural Investments cc (John Robert & Eulalia Frater) ▪ Cellarmaster(s)/winemaker(s) John Robert Frater (1999) ▪ Viticulturist(s) Robert Frater ▪ 80ha/20ha (cab, grenache, malbec, mourv, p verdot, shiraz, chard) ▪ 200t/16,000cs own label 50% red 50% white ▪ Other export brands: Eskdale, Safari ▪ PO Box 591 Suider-Paarl 7624 ▪ info@dezoeteinval.co.za ▪ www.dezoeteinval.co.za ▪ S 33° 46' 35.9" E 018° 57' 50.9" ▪ F +27 (0)86-297-6981 ▪ **T +27 (0)21-863-1535/+27 (0)82-731-3898**

☐ **De Zuydpunt** *see* Group CDV

DGB

Well-established merchant house with strong portfolio of premium and own-brand wines, 'port' and 'sherry', including Bellingham, Beach House, Boschendal, Bernard Series, Brampton, Douglas Green, Franschhoek Cellar, Tall Horse, Legacy Johannisberger, Saints and Oude Kaap, some listed separately.

Wellington ▪ Est 1942 ▪ Closed to public ▪ Owner(s) DGB management, Brait Capital Partners ▪ Winemaker(s)/viticulturist(s) see Bellingham, Boschendal & Franschhoek Cellars ▪ PO Box 246 Wellington 7654 ▪ exports@dgb.co.za ▪ www.dgb.co.za ▪ F +27 (0)21-864-1287 ▪ **T +27 (0)21-864-5300**

☐ **D'Hero's** *see* Govert Wines
☐ **Diamond Collection** *see* Lutzville Cape Diamond Vineyards
☐ **Diamond Creek** *see* Wines of Cape Town
☐ **Dido** *see* Township Winery

Die Bergkelder Wine Centre (Ⓣ) (ⓞ) (ⓑ)

Literally 'Mountain Cellar', after the maturation facilities deep within Stellenbosch's Papegaaiberg, Die Bergkelder is the home of Fleur du Cap, listed separately. FdC wines can be tasted during a cellar tour and monthly salt pairing dinners, while other premium and super-premium wines in the Distell portfolio can be tasted and purchased at Die Bergkelder Wine Centre. The Vinotèque, now in its 32nd year, markets fine wines with the option of having purchases stored in perfect cellar conditions. T +27 (0)21-809-8281 ▪ info@vinoteque.co.za ▪ www.vinoteque.co.za.

Location/map: Stellenbosch ▪ Map grid reference: E5 ▪ All day tasting & sales Mon-Fri 8–5 Sat 9–2 ▪ Tour fee R45pp ▪ Open non-religious pub hols ▪ Tours Mon-Fri 10, 11, 2 & 3; Sat 10, 11 & 12; incl AV presentation; bookings: info@bergkelder.co.za ▪ T +27 (0)21-809-8025 ▪ Special group tours, private tastings by appt ▪ Owner(s) Distell ▪ PO Box 184 Stellenbosch 7599 ▪ info@bergkelder.co.za ▪ www.bergkelder.co.za ▪ S 33° 56' 8.8" E 018° 50' 54.7" ▪ F +27 (0)21-883-9533 ▪ **T +27 (0)21-809-8025**

☐ **Die Laan** *see* Stellenbosch University Welgevallen Cellar

Die Mas van Kakamas (Ⓣ) (ⓟ) (ⓐ) (ⓖ) (ⓞ) (ⓑ)

Vlok and Welna Hanekom, then teachers, started up 40 years ago with 1 ha of vines (and two donkeys). Today their estate on the Orange River near Kakamas covers almost 100 times that area, and the fruit is processed into table grapes, raisins, wine and spirit. Recent wine-grape plantings are now all in production, and a new fermentation cellar has been built for Danie van der Westhuizen's ever-improving range.

Die Mas range

Sauvignon Blanc (NEW) ⊕ ★★★ Interesting, attractive combination of tropical fruit & green underbrush in **15**, tangy, fresh & vibrant.

Petit Verdot (NEW) ★★★ **13** depth & plum/prune richness, a firm tannin structure that needs hearty food or a year/2 cellaring. **Chardonnay** (NEW) ★★☆ Lightish (12.5% alcohol), dry, citrus-seamed, just a touch of oak plus crisp freshness, **15** is very easy to like. Also tasted: **Merlot 11** ★★★ Not retasted: **Cabernet Sauvignon 12** ★★★ **Pinotage 14** ★★★☆ **Shiraz 11** ★★☆

Rooi Kalahari range

Droë Rooi Versnit ② ★★★ Coffee bean smoky nuance to cab, shiraz-led 3-way **NV** blend. Plush, velvety feel with ample plum & chocolate flavour. Not retasted: **Rooi Muskadel 11** ★★☆ **Rooi Jerepigo 12** ★★ **Cape Ruby 08** ★★★

Groen Kalahari range

Sauvignon Blanc ② ★★★ Lots of aromatic interest in **14**, grassy, wild herbal notes & lemon zest served up with the tang of pomelo. Not retasted: **Chardonnay 12** ★★☆

Goue Kalahari range

Hanepoot ② ★★★ **10** packed with sun-dried sultanas plus interesting pecan nut, almond nuance. Clean dry finish. Not retasted: **Wit Muskadel 10** ★★★ **Wit Jerepigo 08** ★★★

Brandy range

Die Kalahari Truffel ② ★★★★ 100% potstill from chenin delights with soft, genteel flavours of sun-dried fruit, hints of vanilla oak with dark chocolate & roasted almonds on the finish. **Vêr In Die Ou Kalahari** ② ★★★ Blended brandy from chenin is robust, fresh & vibrant, brims with ripeness & sweet fruit. Has fiery Kalahari sunsets deeply embedded in it. — WB, CR

Location: Kakamas ▪ Map: Northern Cape, Free State & North West ▪ WO: Northern Cape ▪ Est/1stB 2005 ▪ Tasting & sales Mon-Fri 8-5 Sat 8-1 ▪ Closed Easter Fri-Mon & Dec 25 ▪ 3-hr full farm tour on tractor-pulled wagon during tasting hours ▪ Meals/refreshments by appt; or BYO picnic ▪ Facilities for children ▪ Tour groups ▪ Gift shop ▪ Farm produce ▪ Conferences ▪ Walks/hikes ▪ Mountain biking trail ▪ Conservation area ▪ Camping facilities, 3 self-catering chalets & large lapa/bush pub ▪ Owner(s) Die Mas Boerdery (Pty) Ltd ▪ Cellarmaster(s)/winemaker(s)/viticulturist(s) Danie van der Westhuizen (May 2010) ▪ 1,400ha/80ha (cab, merlot, muscadel r/w, p verdot, pinot, ptage, sangio, shiraz, souzão, tinta, touriga, chard, chenin, cbard, sauv, viog) ▪ 350t/14,000cs own label 30% red 20% white 50% brandy ▪ PO Box 193 Kakamas 8870 ▪ winemaker@diemasvankakamas.co.za ▪ www.diemasvankakamas.co.za ▪ S 28° 45' 48.59" E 020° 38' 26.45" ▪ F +27 (0)86-531-9243 ▪ **T +27 (0)54-431-0245/+27 (0)82-931-5902**

Diemersdal Estate   ② (♨♨)

17th-century Durbanville farm Diemersdal has been in the hands of six generations of Louws, who effect change with sensitivity: the new tasting room/restaurant parking area does not intrude on historical Cape Dutch surrounds; the Estate label's family heraldry design was merely tweaked for greater appeal. Cellarmaster Thys Louw, with winemaker Mari Branders, are far more adventurous with their wines. They've pioneered signature Austrian white grüner veltliner locally, the successful result unsurprising given their deft touch with sauvignon blanc. Their speciality (though the reds are no slouches), sauvignon appears in several incarnations, adroitly slotted into the farm's four ranges and featured in the separately listed Sauvignon.com own brand and West Coast joint venture Sir Lambert.

MM Louw range

★★★★☆ **Estate Red** Most concentrated of the reds by some distance, **13** shows serious intent & bold conception yet retains a classy sense of place with lifted freshness & Bordeaux character (mostly cab). Already impressively accessible now but will reward cellaring for decades.

★★★★☆ **Sauvignon Blanc** More oxidative styling than the other sauvignons, & sees influence from oak (25% new French), giving woodsmoke nuance to **14**'s (★★★★) tangerine & marzipan fruit; intense but well-rounded & rich though it misses some of the freshness that balanced **13**'s opulence & power.

Reserve range

★★★★ **Grenache** ⊘ Fragrant & fresh cherry & red berry aromas. **13** vibrant, older oak not obscuring the fruit. Still tight, should start opening up around 2015. Previous was **11** (★★★☆).

★★★★ **Pinotage** Heady, ripe bramble & mulberry **14** introduces a palate that is deep & opulent, yet lively & focused. Charming sweet vanilla from 50% new oak. Clear step up from Estate version. Larger bottle formats available, as for Private Collection.

★★★★ **Private Collection** Blueberries, gunsmoke, spearmint & crème de cassis on harmonious 5-way Bordeaux red (cab-led). House's elegance with real refinement, unobstructed fruit purity on **13**. Lighter yet more generous & polished than **12** (★★★★).

★★★★☆ **8 Rows Sauvignon Blanc** Delicate, fresh, perfumed aromas introducing a typically lean & flinty palate, reveals layers of complexity with coaxing. **15** (★★★★) unwooded yet seriously mineral-structured, greener & more austere than **14**, lacking power & concentration.

★★★★☆ **Sauvignon Blanc** ⊘ **15** a compact sauvignon with real tension, serious enough to drink with fine food. Kiwi & passionfruit with slight herbal interest & an appealing savoury saline quality.

Also tasted: **Chardonnay 14 ★★★☆**

Diemersdal Estate range

★★★★ **Pinotage** Ripe, sweet dark fruit combines with smoke & black coffee in a typical pinotage. **14** (★★★☆) expresses good flavour intensity yet less finely crafted than **13**.

★★★★ **Grüner Veltliner** ⊘ Coming of age with real character. **14** (★★★★☆) from rare (here) Austrian variety has typical white pepper & spice, like **13**, with sweet lime, pear & celery. A wonderful food wine – aromatic, elegant, with lasting flavour.

★★★★ **Sauvignon Blanc** ⊘ Sound sense of place, showing typical Durbanville capsicum & nettle along with attractive fresh apple & peach notes on **15**. Clean, vibrant, balanced & fresh. Appetising finish.

Chardonnay Unwooded ⊕ ★★★☆ Good alternative to sauvignon blanc, with generous amounts of crunchy citrus fruit & white flowers. Clean, zippy & super-appetising **15**.

Also tasted: **Merlot 14 ★★★ Shiraz 14 ★★★★ Sauvignon Rosé 15 ★★★☆**

Matys range

Cabernet Sauvignon-Merlot ⊕ ★★★ Cherry, nutmeg, cinnamon & liquorice on wickedly delicious **14**, pocket-friendly cab-merlot that packs a big punch. WO W Cape for this range.

Also tasted: **Sauvignon Blanc 15 ★★★** — HJ

Location: Durbanville ▪ Map: Durbanville, Philadelphia & Darling ▪ WO: Durbanville/Western Cape ▪ Est 1698 ▪ 1stB 1976 ▪ Tasting & sales Mon-Sat/pub hols 9–5 Sun 10–3 ▪ Closed Good Fri, Dec 25 & Jan 1 ▪ Cellar tours by appt ▪ Diemersdal Farm Eatery ▪ Owner(s) Tienie Louw ▪ Winemaker(s) Thys Louw & Mari Branders ▪ Viticulturist(s) Div van Niekerk (1980) ▪ 210ha (cab, grenache, malbec, merlot, p verdot, ptage, shiraz, chard, grüner veltliner, sauv) ▪ 2,100t 50% red 50% white ▪ BWI, BRC, HACCIP ▪ PO Box 27 Durbanville 7551 ▪ info@diemersdal.co.za ▪ www.diemersdal.co.za ▪ S 33° 48' 6.3" E 018° 38' 25.1" ▪ T +27 (0)21-976-3361

Diemersfontein Wines   ⓛ ⑪ ⌂ ⊚

The bluegums had to go; they were threatening cottages. So David and Susan Sonnenberg turned the newly felled forest into an amphitheatre for summer opera evenings – something close to the hearts of these energetic patrons of the arts. Energy has typified everything achieved at this former Wellington fruit farm in the 16 years since the owners returned from the UK. There's now a restaurant and accommodation, an employee empowerment venture in Thokozani, vineyard walks and, of course, a winery which has had a bumper year, notching up medals from China to London to Stellenbosch. And, as ever-rising volumes attest, their much-emulated coffee-style pinotage remains a consumer favourite.

Carpe Diem Reserve range

★★★★ **Malbec** Vibrant cherry spice appeal on **14**. Soft & approachable yet structured from 14 months in 70% new oak. Balanced & long. **13** sold out untasted, no **12** made.

★★★★☆ **Pinotage 13** lives up to top billing of **12**. Gentle, soft & fresh with lively raspberry & cocoa appeal. Oak (16 months French & American) is apparent but matched by ripe fruit. Serious & long.

★★★★ **Chenin Blanc** Rich, ripe fruit-forward boldness on pear-toned **14** but with bright freshness & succulence to balance. Oaked third adds structure & length.

★★★★ **Viognier** Layered complexity with broad, leesy stonefruit on **14**. Honeyed & rich but showing restraint, freshness & elegance. Third oaked for just 7 months.

Diemersfontein range

★★★★ **Cabernet Sauvignon 14** improves on last-tasted **12** (★★★) in its focus, concentration, depth & length. Ripe, rounded fruitcake generosity balanced by elegant oak maturation (year, older French).

Pinotage ★★★☆ Frequently imitated, the original 'coffee' wine's **14** release keeps up the mocha note. Soft, easy-drinking & juicy, no wonder volumes now top 50,000 cases. **Summer's Lease** ★★★☆ **13** seductive Rhône-style red of shiraz, mourvèdre & dab viognier. Spicy plum succulence tempered by seasoned oak that adds dry grip & length. **For The Birds White** ★★★ **14** light fruity sipper from equal parts chenin & sauvignon with 10% viognier. Birdlife South Africa reaps the benefits of sales of this & red partner. Also tasted: **Shiraz 14** ★★★★ **Maiden's Prayer Red 13** ★★★ **Chenin Blanc 15** ★★★ **Maiden's Prayer White 14** ★★☆ Not tasted: **For The Birds Red**. — FM

Location/WO: Wellington ▪ Map: Paarl & Wellington ▪ Map grid reference: F2 ▪ Est 2000 ▪ 1stB 2001 ▪ Tasting & sales daily 10–5 ▪ Closed Dec 25 ▪ Cellar tours by appt ▪ Seasons Restaurant ▪ Tour groups ▪ Conferences ▪ Weddings ▪ Walks/hikes ▪ 3-star Diemersfontein Country House ▪ Owner(s) David & Susan Sonnenberg ▪ Winemaker(s) Francois Roode (Sep 2003), with Lauren Hulsman (Nov 2011) ▪ Viticulturist(s) Waldo Kellerman (Aug 2007) ▪ 180ha/60ha (cabs s/f, grenache, malbec, mourv, p verdot, ptage, roobernet, shiraz, chenin, viog) ▪ 600t/80,000cs own label 90% red 10% white ▪ BWI, HACCP ▪ PO Box 41 Wellington 7654 ▪ wine@diemersfontein.co.za ▪ www.diemersfontein.co.za ▪ S 33° 39' 41.1" E 019° 0' 31.1" ▪ F +27 (0)21-864-2095 ▪ **T +27 (0)21-864-5050**

☐ **Die Tweede Droom** *see* Groot Parys Estate

Dieu Donné Vineyards   ⓛ ⑪ ⓐ

This French-Mauritian-owned mountainside winery's awarded reds, whites and méthode cap classique sparkling are vinified by Stephan du Toit, a Cape Wine Master who this year celebrates two decades at the cellar's helm. Visitor-friendly attractions such as a restaurant and an on-site micro brewery make Dieu Donné a popular stop on the Franschhoek Wine Tram route.

Location/map: Franschhoek ▪ Est 1984 ▪ 1stB 1986 ▪ Tasting & sales Mon-Fri 9–5 Sat/Sun 10.30–5 ▪ Fee R20 ▪ Closed Dec 25 & Jan 1 ▪ Cellar tours Mon-Fri by appt ▪ Cheese platters ▪ Gifts ▪ Micro brewery ▪ Roca Restaurant ▪ Owner(s) Robert Maingard ▪ Cellarmaster(s)/winemaker(s) Stephan du Toit (May 1996) ▪ Viticulturist(s) Hennie du Toit (Apr 1988) ▪ 40ha (cab, merlot, shiraz, chard, sauv, viog) ▪ ±280t/ 33,000cs own label 60% red 32% white 3% rosé 5% MCC ▪ PO Box 94 Franschhoek 7690 ▪ info@ dieudonnevineyards.com ▪ www.dieudonnevineyards.com ▪ S 33° 53' 46.9" E 019° 7' 45.0" ▪ F +27 (0)21-876-2102 ▪ **T +27 (0)21-876-2493**

Diners Club Bartho Eksteen Academy   ⓛ ⓐ

Deciding it was time repay an industry that had supported him for more than two decades, accomplished wine man and Cape Winemakers Guild member Bartho Eksteen and wife Suné founded a winemaking academy at Bartho's Paarl alma mater, Boland Agricultural High School, with Diners Club support. The wines produced from the course are sold to help fund the initiative, and Bartho is especially proud that consistently high quality has helped debunk the notion that wines with 'school', 'college' or 'university' on the label are inferior 'because they appear to represent a young person's first attempt'. See also Bartho Eksteen entry, and note that Platter's Guide is a wholly owned subsidiary of Diner's Club SA.

Trees of Knowledge range

★★★★ **Wijnskool Shiraz** Inviting bright ruby glow, with brooding aromas of blackberry, mocha, violets & pepper. **13** lush, with terrific acid spine giving a lifted goodbye. Lovely cool-climate expression.

★★★★ **Wijnskool Sauvignon Blanc** Fragrant **14**, with piquant aromas of capsicum, grapefruit & fresh pineapple, is rich & expansive, with a generous texture & steely backbone.

Discontinued: **Diners Club Bartho Eksteen Academy range**. — WB

Location: Paarl/Hermanus ▪ Map: Paarl & Wellington ▪ Map grid reference: C3 ▪ WO: Cape South Coast ▪ Est/1stB 2011 ▪ Tasting, sales & cellar tours by appt ▪ Walks/hikes ▪ Nature reserve ▪ Owner(s) Bartho & Suné Eksteen ▪ Winemaker(s) Bartho Eksteen (Feb 2011), with Pieter Willem Eksteen (Jan 2012) & learners at Hoër Landbouskool Boland and other schools ▪ Viticulturist(s) Willie van der Linde (Hoër Landbouskool Boland); Pieter Carstens (De Bos Estate, Hermanus); Jadri Lötter (Vrede, Hermanus) — bought in grapes ▪ 9t/1,200cs own label 50% red 50% white ▪ PO Box 1999 Hermanus 7200 ▪ bartho@ hermanus.co.za, sune@hermanus.co.za ▪ www.wijnskool.co.za ▪ S 33° 39' 11.45" E 018° 52' 59.77" ▪ F +27 (0)86-554-0896 ▪ **T +27 (0)28-312-4612**

Dispore Kamma Boutique Winery

Following a self-imposed Rx, Philip Mostert and Hannes Coetzee have been on leave from their after-hours-only 'job' of vinifying and marketing a highly regarded shiraz. But fans will be delighted the Caledon-based medicos intend to don their garagiste boots and crush the 2016 harvest.

Location: Caledon ▪ Map: Elgin, Walker Bay & Bot River ▪ Est/1stB 2002 ▪ Tasting, sales & cellar tours by appt ▪ Owner(s) Philip Mostert & Hannes Coetzee ▪ Winemaker(s) Philip Mostert (Jan 2002), with Hannes Coetzee (Jun 2002) ▪ 150cs own label 100% red ▪ PO Box 272 Caledon 7230 ▪ disporekamma@ overnet.co.za ▪ S 34° 13' 40.2" E 019° 25' 10.5" ▪ F +27 (0)28-214-1077 ▪ **T +27 (0)28-212-1096**

Distell

Helmed by MD Richard Rushton, Distell is Africa's largest producer of wines, spirits, ciders and RTDs, and the SA leader with ±20% value share of the total local liquor market. From its Stellenbosch HQ, Distell produces some of South Africa's most successful and enduring brands. They include: 4th Street, Cold Duck (5th Avenue), Autumn Harvest Crackling, Capenheimer, Cellar Cask, Chateau Libertas, Drostdy-Hof, Fleur du Cap, Graça, Grand Mousseux, Grünberger, Ixia, Kellerprinz, Kupferberger Auslese, Monis, Obikwa, Oom Tas, Overmeer, Place in the Sun, Pongrácz, RED ESCape, Sedgwick's, Ship, Tassenberg, Taverna Rouge, Two Oceans, Virginia and Zonnebloem. Distell also owns the House of JC le Roux, a dedicated sparkling-wine cellar in Devon Valley. Then there are the stand-alone 'estate' labels: Nederburg, Plaisir de Merle and Lomond. Distell is also the co-owner, together with Lusan Holdings, of top Stellenbosch properties Alto, Le Bonheur, Neethlingshof, Stellenzicht/Hill & Dale, Uitkyk/Flat Roof Manor, and, with several local growers, of Durbanville Hills. Distell also has agreements with independent cellars Allesverloren, Jacobsdal and Theuniskraal to provide a range of services. Finally, there's the black empowerment venture on Papkuilsfontein farm near Darling, source of Earthbound wines. Brandy labels include Chateau VO, Collison's, Commando, Flight of the Fish Eagle, Klipdrift, Limosin, Mellow-Wood, Olof Bergh Solera, Oude Meester, Richelieu, Van Ryn and Viceroy. See Die Bergkelder for details about the Vinoteque Wine Bank, and separate entries for most of the above.

Stellenbosch ▪ PO Box 184 Stellenbosch 7599 ▪ info@distell.co.za ▪ www.distell.co.za ▪ **T +27 (0)21-809-7000**

☐ **Dixon's Peak** *see* Waverley Hills Organic Wines & Olives
☐ **Dolphin Bay** *see* Wines of Cape Town
☐ **Dolphin Sands** *see* Wines of Cape Town

Domaine Brahms Wineries

As executive mayor of 'city of excellence' Drakenstein (Paarl, Wellington, Hermon, Gouda and Saron), Domaine Brahms' prime mover Gesie van Deventer regrets she no longer has time to make wine but is delighted that 'young talented people, neighbours and friends extend my hand and assist with vineyards and wine'. That the results 'still win awards' suggests Gesie's 'angels' are as deft as they are enthusiastic!

★★★★ Shiraz ⓠ **10** improves on 08 (★★★☆) with lots of concentrated dark-berried fruit & hints of sweaty leather. Silky tannins, lower alcohol make for thoroughly enjoyable wine. **09** untasted.

★★★★ Chenin Blanc ⓠ Truly lovely **13**, first tasted since **06** (★★★★), floats softly & delicately into play with plenty of lively pineapples & cream touched by the gentlest of oak (15% new).

Quartet ⓠ ★★★☆ **12** merlot-dominated Bordeaux blend, brightly fruited, soft & enticing. Not retasted: **Cabernet Sauvignon 10** ★★★ **Sonato 11** ★★ **Unwooded Chenin Blanc 2014** ★★★ Not tasted: **Merlot, Pinotage**. — CM

Location/WO: Paarl ▪ Map: Paarl & Wellington ▪ Map grid reference: C3 ▪ Est 1998 ▪ 1stB 1999 ▪ Tasting & tours (vyd/cellar/wine) by appt ▪ Fee R5/wine ▪ Chapel & wedding/function venue ▪ Owner(s) Johan & Gesie van Deventer ▪ Winemaker(s)/viticulturist(s) Carmia Loubsher ▪ 12ha (cab, merlot, ptage, shiraz, chenin) ▪ 30,000L 90% red 10% white ▪ PO Box 2136 Windmeul 7630 ▪ brahms@iafrica.com ▪ www.domainebrahms.co.za ▪ S 33° 40' 27.28" E 18° 53' 29.24" ▪ F +27 (0)86-614-9445 ▪ **T +27 (0)21-869-8555**

Domaine Coutelier   ⓠ ⓐ

UK-born businessman Quint Cutler and French wife Floriane welcome German/SA winemaker Carsten Migliarina (of Migliarina Wines) as adviser to their Bordeaux-planted Domaine Coutelier, part of a 17th-century Devon Valley grape farm. They're adding two top-tier Coutelier and Reserve collections to their renamed Feast range, taking their first crop of SA rarity carmenère and finalising boutique cellar plans.

Festin range

★★★★ Chardonnay ⓠ **13** from Durbanville in showy style, with plenty of aroma & flavour (lemon, nut, oatmeal), supported by fairly discreet oak & a powerful acidity. Good long lemony finish.

Not retasted: **Cabernet Sauvignon 12** ★★★☆ Not tasted: **Merlot, Méthode Cap Classique**. — TJ

Location/map: Stellenbosch ▪ Map grid reference: D4 ▪ WO: Stellenbosch/Coastal ▪ Est/1stB 2012 ▪ Tasting, sales & cellar tours by appt ▪ Closed all pub hols ▪ Weddings/functions ▪ Owner(s) Quint Cutler ▪ Winemaker(s) Quint Cutler (March 2013) & Carsten Migliarina (Jan 2015, consultant) ▪ Viticulturist(s) Kevin Watt (May 2013, consultant) ▪ 4ha/3.5ha (cab, carmenère, merlot) ▪ ±21t/2,300cs own label 70% red 10% white 10% rosé 10% MCC ▪ 45 Blumberg Drive, Devon Vale, Stellenbosch 7600 ▪ quint.cutler@domainecoutelier.com ▪ www.domainecoutelier.com ▪ S 33° 54' 2.80" E 018° 47' 58.46" ▪ **T +27 (0)21-300-0649/+27 (0)79-498-0772**

Domaine des Dieux   ⓠ

These elevated Hemel-en-Aarde Ridge vineyards against mountain landmark Babylonstoren are to be extended with 'some interesting' cool-climate Italian varieties. Visitors can look forward to not only a wider selection (including fresh bottlings of their existing range) but also tastings on a new deck and a lawn terrace for picnics. Wines are vinified off-site by area, variety and style specialists.

★★★★ Syrah-Mourvèdre ⓠ **12** (★★★) tightly buttoned & lean, nothing like intense **11**. Piquant red fruit veined by really fresh acidity, may settle & bloom given time.

★★★★ Sauvignon Blanc ⓠ After flinty & herbaceous **11**, **12** (★★★) is tropical & lighter toned, tangy acidity underpinning a summer-styled easy-drinker with clean dry limy farewell.

★★★★ Rose of Sharon MCC Brut Rosé ⓠ Sweeter, more gregarious bubbles in **09** (★★★) than **08**, pale sunset orange with fresh berry/cherry tone, frothy & with no great depth.

★★★★ Claudia Brut MCC ⓠ **09** sparkling from undisclosed varieties. Lovely fresh apple, toasted nut & brioche flavours, mouthfilling, with creamy lees undertone. Shows refined balance, ready to enjoy.

Not retasted: **Josephine Pinot Noir 12** ★★★ **Chardonnay 11** ★★★☆ — MW

Location: Hermanus ▪ Map: Elgin, Walker Bay & Bot River ▪ WO: Hemel-en-Aarde Ridge/Walker Bay/Walker Bay-Elgin ▪ Est 2002 ▪ 1stB 2006 ▪ Tasting & sales at the vineyards Tue-Sun 11-4.30 ▪ Closed Easter Fri/Sun, Dec 25 & Jan 1 ▪ Owner(s) Domaine des Dieux (Pty) Ltd ▪ Winemaker(s) Kevin Grant, Niels Verburg & Gerhard Smith ▪ Vineyard manager Petrus Bothma ▪ Viticulturist(s) Johan Pienaar ▪ 28ha/20ha (pinot, shiraz & other red varieties, chard, sauv) ▪ 15,000cs own label 25% red 25% white 50% MCC ▪ PO Box 2082 Hermanus 7200 ▪ info@domainedesdieux.co.za ▪ www.domainedesdieux.co.za ▪ S 34° 19' 35.81" E 019° 19' 50.71" ▪ F +27 (0)87-230-6286 ▪ **T +27 (0)28-313-2126/+27 (0)83-536-5916**

☐ **Dombeya Wines** *see* Haskell Vineyards

Domein Doornkraal ⓛ ⓜ ⓐ ⓞ

Septuagenarian Swepie le Roux's long-time winemaking exploits in beautiful, arid Klein Karoo are supported by vineyardist Celia le Roux Mostert. Father and daughter welcome visitors to the family's off-the-beaten-track farm cottages, and offer convenience and local colour at their De Rust-area roadside shop, stocked with regional food, wine and spirit (muscadels, 'ports' and brandies of particular interest).

Domein Doornkraal range

★★★★☆ **Kaptein** Latest bottling of **NV** fortified old-vine muscadel is extraordinary. Two years in old French oak give tobacco & nut overlay to rich, beautifully balanced fruitcake flavours, with hints of dusty hay & raisins in the complex interplay. A delicious bargain.

Tickled Pink ★★☆ Pretty pink **NV** sparkler from muscadel with lively bubbles & strawberry sweetness. Perfect for a casual birthday toast. Montagu WO. **Kuierwyn** ★★☆ Natural Sweet from chenin, **15** clean acid balance, simple summer sipper which could also go well with curry. WO W Cape. **Majoor** ★★★ Subtle honey aroma from jerepiko-style hanepoot. Not-too-sweet **NV** could be a relaxing summer drink over crushed ice. WO W Cape. Also tasted: **Jerepigo NV** ★★★ **Luitenant NV** ★★★☆ **Pinta NV** ★★★☆ Not retasted: **Tanige Port 92** ★★★☆

Swepie Selection

Kannaland Rooi ★★ 'Kannaland' the local name for Klein Karoo. No-frills country red from merlot, pinotage & cab, unwooded **14** is earthy, with robust tannins & dry finish. Also tasted: **Kannaland Wit Chenin Blanc 14** ★★ **Kannaland Wit Sauvignon Blanc 14** ★★ — DB

Location: De Rust ▪ Map: Klein Karoo & Garden Route ▪ WO: Klein Karoo/Western Cape/Montagu ▪ Est 1880 ▪ 1stB 1973 ▪ Tasting & sales Mon-Fri 9-5 Sat 9-3 ▪ Closed Easter Fri/Sun & Dec 25 ▪ Light refreshments ▪ Farm produce ▪ Gifts ▪ Conference facility on farm ▪ Self-catering farm cottages & lodge ▪ Owner(s) Swepie, Piet & Celia le Roux ▪ Cellarmaster(s) Swepie le Roux (Apr 2011) ▪ Winemaker(s) Swepie le Roux ▪ Viticulturist(s) Celia le Roux Mostert ▪ 2,000ha/10ha (cab, merlot, muscadel, ptage, chard, chenin, cbard) ▪ 105t/4,000cs own label 15% red 15% white 70% fortified ▪ PO Box 14 De Rust 6650 ▪ wyn@doornkraal.co.za ▪ www.doornkraal.co.za ▪ S 33° 32' 43.5" E 022° 26' 42.6" ▪ F +27 (0)86-528-5633 ▪ **T +27 (0)44-251-6715**

☐ **Donatus** *see* Dornier Wines

Donkiesbaai ⓛ

Harvest 2015 was the fifth for Donkiesbaai Steen, original label in this terroir-specific range by Rust en Vrede owner Jean Engelbrecht, named for the West Coast resort (Donkin — 'Donkey' — Bay) where four generations of Engelbrechts have vacationed, glass of cold chenin in hand. Vintage 2015 was also the first with Roelof Lotriet, R&V's deputy winemaker, at the helm.

★★★★ **Pinot Noir** Plenty of earthy red & black fruit on **14** (★★★★☆), unobtrusively oaked (only older barrels) letting freshness & elegance sing forth. Improves on debut **13** with layers of flavour leading to very satisfying finish. Ceres fruit.

★★★★☆ **Steen** Majestic **14** effortlessly maintains standards, giving layer upon layer of fresh stonefruit, some tropical notes, creamy lees & just a hint of supportive oak (just 50% wooded, 10% new). Wonderful oatmeal texture from venerable Piekenierskloof vines.

★★★★☆ **Hooiwijn** Rich & unctuous **14** barrel-fermented chenin, dried on straw ('hooi') mats for a concentrated, lively mouthful of honey, dried apricots, butter & cream. Nicely balanced acidity offsets substantial sweetness for cheese or dessert. Ex Piekenierskloof, like **13** (★★★★). — CM

Location: Stellenbosch ▪ WO: Western Cape ▪ Est/1stB 2011 ▪ Tasting & sales at Guardian Peak ▪ Owner(s) Jean Engelbrecht ▪ Winemaker(s) Roelof Lotriet (Sep 2014) ▪ Viticulturist(s) Dirkie Mouton

(Jan 2011) ▪ 15t/1,200cs own label 50% red 50% white ▪ PO Box 473 Stellenbosch 7599 ▪ info@ donkiesbaai.com ▪ www.donkiesbaai.com ▪ F +27 (0)21-881-3000 ▪ **T +27 (0)21-881-3881**

☐ **Don Morris** *see* Govert Wines

Doolhof Wine Estate

Doolhof ('Labyrinth') was so named by early settlers in Wellington because of its seemingly confusing many hills and valleys. However, this topology allows for a multitude of vineyard aspects, reflected in the range diversity. Dating from 1707, the estate was bought by the Kerrison family in 2003 and transformed into a showpiece, which includes the luxe Grand Dédale Country House in the old manor.

Legends of the Labyrinth range

★★★★ **1712 Jacques Potier** Ⓥ Merlot-led, with 4 other Bordeaux varieties plus pinotage. **09** deeply rich, dark plums, vanilla, creamy coffee, the body smoothly juicy. Good grip from 2 years French barrels.

★★★★ **The Minotaur** Ⓥ Back on track after **08** (★★★☆), **09** has curves to spare. Spicy dark fruit &, thanks to pinotage, merlot, shiraz & malbec which comprise most of the blend, it is rich, power packed.

> **Dark Lady** Ⓥ ★★★★ Mainly pinotage, dab petit verdot in **13**. Mocha, cocoa-rich chocolate, indeed 'dark', but has succulent appeal, smooth tannins.

Not retasted: **Lady in Red 09** ★★★ **Theseus 09** ★★★★ **Lady in White 10** ★★★

Signatures of Doolhof range

★★★★ **Cabernet Franc** Vivid cherry/blackcurrant fruit throughout while single-vineyard **12**'s well-judged oaking gives a cedar seam & just enough firmness to promise a 5+ years future. No **10**, **11**.

★★★★ **Renaissance Cabernet Sauvignon-Merlot** Ⓥ After generous **06**, last-tasted **07** (★★★★) had blackcurrant & cigarbox, ripeness balanced by char from year in 40% new French oak.

★★★★ **Chardonnay Wooded** Only new oak for **10**, a rare older vintage release. Kumquat preserve, toasted hazelnuts, delicious mellow richness yet dry, a step up from **09** (★★★★). Worth a look.

Malbec ★★★☆ Black plums & fynbos, nice typicity on **12**, the herbal tone providing a counterpoint to usual fruit-driven styles. Drinks smoothly & well. Also tasted: **Cabernet Sauvignon 14** ★★★☆ **Pinotage 13** ★★★☆ **Chardonnay Unwooded 15** ★★★ **Sauvignon Blanc 15** ★★★☆ Not retasted: **Merlot 11** ★★★☆ **Petit Verdot 09** ★★★☆ **Shiraz 08** ★★★☆

Cape range

Crane Chenin Blanc ★★★ Passionfruit, hint of lime in tasty **15**, drier & lighter textured than also-tasted **14**, which has a fuller palate, melon flavours. WO Coastal. Also tasted: **Boar 13** ★★★ Not retasted: **Loerie Rosé 13** ★★ Discontinued: **Eagle**. — CR

Location: Wellington ▪ Map: Paarl & Wellington ▪ Map grid reference: H1 ▪ WO: Wellington/Western Cape/ Coastal ▪ Est 1995 ▪ 1stB 2003 ▪ Tasting & sales Mon-Sat 10–5 Sun 10-4 ▪ Fee R20/5 wines ▪ Closed Good Fri, Dec 25/26 & Jan 1 ▪ Cellar tours by appt ▪ Light lunches Tue-Sun 11-3; picnics by appt; wine & canapé pairings by pre-booking ▪ Conferences ▪ Walks/hikes ▪ Mountain biking & 4x4 trails ▪ 5-star Grand Dédale Country House ▪ Owner(s) Dennis Kerrison ▪ Cellarmaster(s)/viticulturist(s) Gielie Beukes (Aug 2014) ▪ Winemaker(s) Gielie Beukes (Aug 2014) & Rianie Strydom (consultant) ▪ 380ha/38ha (cabs s/f, malbec, merlot, p verdot, ptage, shiraz, chard, sauv) ▪ 300t/24,000cs own label 73% red 26% white 1% rosé ▪ BWI, IPW, WIETA ▪ PO Box 157 Wellington 7654 ▪ wine@doolhof.com ▪ www.doolhof.com ▪ S 33° 37' 35.6" E 019° 4' 58.7" ▪ F +27 (0)21-864-2321 ▪ **T +27 (0)21-873-6911**

Doran Vineyards

Irishman Edwin Doran bought Voor Paardeberg farm Far Horizons and the Horse Mountain brand that went with it in 2010. With old friend André Badenhorst, who had helped set up top Constantia wineries Buitenverwachting and Constantia Uitsig, he's revitalising the property. On the to-do list, after successful listings in the US and UK, is a blend from young chenin, roussanne and grenache blanc vines.

Doran Vineyards range

★★★★ **Shiraz** Impressive **13** ticks all the boxes: aromatic & flavoursome, structured, refreshing, lingering. Partial spontaneous ferment, year older oak. Should improve 3-5 years. **12** (★★★) a bit foursquare.

★★★★ **Chenin Blanc** ⊘ Older-barrel-fermented **13** (★★★★★) has more layers, goes up a notch: roasted almonds, honeysuckle & vanilla on nose; peach & pear on palate. Drinks easily with lovely acid-fruit tension, judicious oak support. Like **12**, understated but well crafted, rewarding. Swartland WO.

Rosie D Pinotage Rosé ★★ **14** is dry & unpretentious, with strawberry & cream appeal. Also tasted: **Pinotage 13** ★★★ **The Romy D 13** ★★☆

Horse Mountain range

Michele ★★ Merlot-dominated Bordeaux blend with cabs sauvignon & franc, **12** is light & crunchy for summer sunset sipping. Also tasted: **Chenin Blanc-Viognier 14** ★★★ Not retasted: **Pinotage 11** ★★★ **Shiraz 11** ★★☆ — CvZ

Location: Paarl ▪ Map: Paarl & Wellington ▪ Map grid reference: D1 ▪ WO: Voor Paardeberg/Swartland/ Western Cape ▪ Est 2010 ▪ 1stB 2012 ▪ Tasting Mon-Fri by appt Sat/Sun & pub hols 10-4 ▪ Closed Good Fri, Dec 25/26 & Jan 1 ▪ Owner(s) Edwin Doran & André Badenhorst ▪ Winemaker(s) Martin Lamprecht ▪ Viticulturist(s) Basson Potgieter ▪ 170ha/55ha (cabs s/f, merlot, ptage, shiraz, chenin, grenache blanc/ noir, rouss) ▪ 450t/30,000cs own label ▪ PO Box 2143 Windmeul 7630 ▪ andrebad@iafrica.com ▪ www.doranvineyards.co.za ▪ S 33° 34′ 56.12″ E018° 51′ 59.15″ ▪ F +27 (0)86-248-3160 ▪ **T +27 (0)61-024-4933**

☐ **Doreen** *see* Teddy Hall Wines

Dormershire Estate   ⓠ

Attorney Paul Frost maintains a small, 3-variety vineyard on the edge of Kuils River suburbia and wife Sunette makes the wine, both with consultants' help. Sunette honed her skills on reds – her first was an '02 shiraz accommodated on the couple's veranda (hence 'Stoep Shiraz') before a cellar was built.

Cabernet Sauvignon ⓠ ★★★★ As expected, juicier & earlier accessible than the Reserve, a savoury note makes **07** a good food match. **Shiraz** ⓠ ★★★ **07** toasted bread & spicy cherry flavours, ending dry. Ideal winter casserole red. Not retasted: **Reserve Cabernet Sauvignon 07** ★★★★ **Stoep Shiraz 07** ★★★ **Cabernet Sauvignon-Shiraz 07** ★★★★ **Sweet Red NV** ★★★★ Not tasted: **Rosé, Sauvignon Blanc**. — DB

Location: Kuils River ▪ Map/WO: Stellenbosch ▪ Map grid reference: A5 ▪ Est 1996 ▪ 1stB 2001 ▪ Tasting, sales & tours by appt only ▪ Closed all pub hols ▪ Owner(s) SPF Family Trust ▪ Winemaker(s) Sunette Frost & Kowie du Toit ▪ Viticulturist(s) Johan Pienaar (consultant) ▪ 8ha/6ha (cab, shiraz, sauv) ▪ ±50t/ 8,000cs own label 85% red 10% white 5% rosé ▪ PO Box 491 Bellville 7535 ▪ wine@dormershire.co.za ▪ www.dormershire.com ▪ S 33° 56′ 27.0″ E 018° 42′ 54.7″ ▪ F +27 (0)21-945-1174 ▪ **T +27 (0)21-801-4677/4991**

Dornier Wines   ⓠ 🍽 🏠 📷 🛏 ♿

Creativity is a recurring theme at the premium Stellenbosch Mountain wine estate owned by the Swiss family Dornier. Late founder and artist Christoph Dornier designed the flowing lines of the low-impact, modernist cellar and its reflecting pool for appreciation by visitors, including guests at Bodega Restaurant and the farm's luxury homestead. Inventiveness abounds in the cellar too. Recent experiments with barrel-fermented rosé, bunch-fermented pinotage and carbonic maceration of cab franc produced 'supremely rewarding results, changing our winemaking philosophy'. Imagination stretches to the vineyards, hence locally rare tempranillo and vine-desiccation for the Natural Sweet dessert wine.

Founders range

★★★★☆ **CMD** ⓠ Elegant flagship from malbec (80%), cab franc & petit verdot, 50% new oak in **12**. Spiced plums, cherry & fresh herbs; plushness reined in by firm, dry tannic finish. Will reward cellaring.

Donatus range

★★★★ **Red** Continues 4-way Bordeaux blend formula with cab in lead. Youthful **12** has large petit verdot (22%) component showing in brooding, concentrated dark fruit with solid oak support (30% new) evident in ground coffee & tobacco. For the long haul.

★★★★ **White** Elegant **14** still shy, closed, but with similar new-wave Dornier elegance compared to opulent **13** (★★★★☆). Mineral texture, fine balance & underlying freshness. Unusual blend chenin (76%) & semillon; some from Swartland & Bottelary.

Dornier range

★★★★☆ **Chenin Blanc Bush Vine** As previous, **14** all Swartland bushvine fruit, fermented in barrel, stainless steel & cement 'egg'. Finely woven, crunchy white peach & pear with floral interest. Real elegance & purity here — delicious improvement on **13** (★★★★). Modest alcohol a bonus.

★★★★ **Froschkönig Natural Sweet** From vine-desiccated chenin, **13** (★★★★☆) shows yet another facet of SA's 'king of white grapes'. 18 months in barrel add further complexity to the luscious sun-dried apricot, apple & honeysuckle flavours. Occasional release in 375 ml. Last tasted was **09**.

Syrah (NEW) ★★★ Lots of savoury spice, iron & game meat, **13** raised in older wood, as other reds in this range, with medium body & brisk acidity. **Tempranillo** ★★★ Rare varietal bottling, offering smoke & spice with clean ripe black fruit. Like previous, **13**'s tannins are chewy, with dry grip; best cellared or decanted. **Barrel Fermented Rosé** (NEW) ★★★★ Appealing onion skin colour, dry **15** is serious expression of rosé, from merlot, with candied red fruit, slight phenolic grip & fresh acidity. Also tasted: **Malbec 13** ★★★ **Merlot 13** ★★★ **Pinotage 13** ★★★★ **Semillon 14** ★★★★ Not retasted: **Cabernet Sauvignon-Merlot 12** ★★★★ Discontinued: **Cabernet Sauvignon**.

Cocoa Hill range

Red ★★★ Merlot & shiraz again dominant, crunchy **13** has bright fruit, herbal notes & savoury finish. WO W Cape. **Sauvignon Blanc** ★★★★ Tank sample **15** promises improved fleshiness & delicious tropical fruit. Nicely dry & appetising palate. Also tasted: **Rosé 15** ★★★ **Chenin Blanc 15** ★★★ — HJ

Location/map: Stellenbosch ▪ Map grid reference: F7 ▪ WO: Stellenbosch/Western Cape/Swartland ▪ Est 1995 ▪ 1stB 2002 ▪ Tasting & sales daily 10-5 ▪ Cellar tours by appt ▪ Dornier Bodega Restaurant: lunch daily 12-5 dinner (Oct-Apr) Thu-Sat ▪ Facilities for children ▪ Gift shop ▪ Conference venue ▪ Conservation area ▪ Homestead with 6 bedrooms & large entertainment areas ▪ Owner(s) Dornier family ▪ Winemaker(s) Jeanine Craven (Mar 2012) ▪ Viticulturist(s) Theunis Bell (Sep 2009) ▪ 180ha/55ha (cabs s/f, malbec, merlot, p verdot, ptage, shiraz, tempranillo, chenin, sauv, sem) ▪ 350t 65% red 28% white 7% rosé ▪ PO Box 7518 Stellenbosch 7599 ▪ info@dornier.co.za ▪ www.dornier.co.za ▪ S 33° 59' 31.00" E 018° 52' 19.00" ▪ F +27 (0)21-880-1499 ▪ **T +27 (0)21-880-0557**

Dorrance Wines   ⓟ 🍴

French barrel importer Christophe Durand (at home in the Cape since the mid 1990s — his wife Sabrina is of South African Indian origin) started his negociant winemaking in a tiny way, in rented facilities. Things have developed, and now grapes come from scattered vineyards to a winery in a heritage building in the heart of Cape Town. Vinification and maturation facilities in this unique cellar, with small wine shop and tasting room, are to be joined by 'a full-scale restaurant', says Christophe.

Dorrance range

★★★★☆ **Syrah Cuvée Ameena** Partly bunch-fermented **13** closed & unforgiving in youth, but has undeniable substance. Palate reflects Elgin's cool peppery red fruit, & a warmer, richer Swartland depth. Sensible oaking (2 years, 20% new), fine tannins for cellaring. No **12**. Also in magnum.

★★★★☆ **Chardonnay Cuvée Anaïs** Like **13**, standout **14** (★★★★★) from Franschhoek & Elgin fruit, naturally fermented. Rich, with integrated notes of 20% new oak. True to house style, offers restrained, classic fruit profile with good acidity to carry its full body. In magnums too.

★★★★☆ **Chenin Blanc Kama** From Swartland, **14** shows usual restraint but with fantastic depth & complexity. An enticing mix ripe fruit & minerals unfettered by new oak, it has a classic & invigorating feel.

Simply range

Rosé (NEW) ★★★ From cinsaut, **14** fresh & zesty, with nicely rounded palate, uncomplicated berry tones & smooth dry finish. Also tasted: **Rouge 14 ★★★☆ Blanc 14 ★★★** — JPf

Location: Cape Town ▪ Map: Cape Peninsula ▪ WO: Western Cape/Swartland ▪ Est/1stB 2000 ▪ Tastings & sales Mon-Fri 11-6 or by appt ▪ Wine shop ▪ Restaurant ▪ Owner(s) Christophe & Sabrina Durand ▪ Cellarmaster(s)/winemaker(s) Christophe Durand ▪ 11ha ▪ 30t/4,666cs own label ▪ 95 Hout Street Cape Town 8001 ▪ christophe@vinsdorrance.co.za ▪ www.vinsdorrance.co.za ▪ S 33° 55' 12.26" E 018° 25' 6.42" ▪ F +27 (0)86-588-2989 ▪ **T +27 (0)21-422-0659/ +27 (0)83-409-7071**

Douglas Green

'Good wine, at a good price, that people enjoy' was the philosophy of founder and negociant Douglas Green when he started trading from the Stukvat Bottlestore in Main Street, Paarl, in 1938. That remains the foundation of the enduring DGB-owned brand that bears his name, but the Paarl premises are no more. Instead, there's the chic, foodie- and children-friendly brand home it shares in Franschhoek with sibling labels including Bellingham and Franschhoek Cellar.

Vineyard Creations

Pinotage ★★★ Barista! Barista! Enticing coffee tones from oak staves, berry fruit on **14**, to enjoy young. **Shiraz ★★★** Spice & black pepper highlights on red-fruited **14**, with friendly tannins, touch oak; uncomplicated but convivial red. **Chenin Blanc ★★★** Nut & thatch aromas, mouthfilling **15** rounded & unchallenging for sipping at book club. Also tasted: **Cabernet Sauvignon 14 ★★★ Merlot 14 ★★ Chardonnay 15 ★★★ Sauvignon Blanc 15 ★★**

Diversity range

Merlot-Malbec ⊘ ★★★ Unwooded **14** generous melange of red berries, supple tannins don't need food. Also tasted: **Chenin Blanc-Sauvignon Blanc 15 ★★**

Douglas Green Signature Brands

Ribshack Red ★★ Dependable & friendly 60/40 pinotage & shiraz combo, **14** with usual few grams sugar for gulpability. Nice retro packaging. **St Augustine Cape Blend** ⊘ ★★★ Tweaked name for enduring label recognises pinotage component (45%) with shiraz & cab. Fruit-packed **14** offers smooth, succulent drinkability plus affinity with Sunday roast. **Beach House Rosé ★★** From pinotage, **15** faintly berried picnic basket staple with Turkish delight appeal, just-dry farewell. Also tasted: **Beach House Sauvignon Blanc 15 ★★★** Not retasted: **Cape Ruby Port NV ★★★★**

Sunkissed range

Natural Sweet Red (NEW) ★ Latest **NV** is light footed (8% alcohol) & light fruited. Drink soon. **Natural Sweet White ★★** Funky label for low-alcohol (8%) **NV**, litchi & Turkish delight tones with pineapple tang on the finish. From chenin & muscadel (60/40). Also tasted: **Natural Sweet Rosé NV ★☆**

Douglas Green Sherry-Styles

Dry Fino No. 1 ⓢ ★★★☆ Pale gold colour, very dry & aromatic, with green olive, savoury & salty nut flavours. Good balancing acidity, with a refreshing lift, spirity grip. Palomino & chenin from Worcester & Robertson, made in a solera, as all the Douglas Green sherry-style wines. **Full Cream No. 3** ⓢ ★★★☆ Smooth winter warmer: rich, with raisin, spiced nut & honey flavours, aromas; full bodied & mouthfilling, but not cloying. **Medium Cream No. 2** ⓢ ★★★☆ Pale amber delicately sweet, with layers of dried & candied fruit, nuts & spice. Smooth & silky, slips down easily, but has a refreshing orange zest finish. — CR, CvZ

Location: Wellington ▪ WO: Western Cape ▪ Est 1942 ▪ Closed to public ▪ Owner(s) DGB (Pty) Ltd ▪ Blending manager Dico du Toit (2012) ▪ Oenologist Jaco Potgieter (2000) ▪ Viticulturist(s) Stephan Joubert (2006) ▪ 50% red 49% white 1% rosé ▪ ISO 9001:2000, Fairtrade, HACCP, IPW, WIETA ▪ PO Box 246 Wellington 7654 ▪ douglasgreen@dgb.co.za ▪ www.douglasgreenwines.com ▪ F +27 (0)21-864-1287 ▪ **T +27 (0)21-864-5300**

Douglas Wine Cellar   ⓘ ⓐ ⓞ

Located in the Northern Cape town of Douglas, near the confluence of the Orange and Vaal Rivers, Douglas Cellar is owned by agribusiness GWK, as is sibling Landzicht, listed separately, whose wines are made here. There's a new tasting and conference centre, and a new assistant winemaker – so that, as viticulturist Hein Janse van Rensburg says, the cellar now has a Small Ian (Jooste) joining the Big Ian (Sieg). It sounds better in Afrikaans: Klein Ian, Groot Ian! The 'easily' accessible wine ranges include Confluence and Barney Barnato.

Location: Douglas ▪ Map: Northern Cape, Free State & North West ▪ Est 1968 ▪ 1stB 1977 ▪ Tasting & sales Mon-Fri 8–5 ▪ Closed all pub hols ▪ Cellar tours by appt ▪ BYO picnic ▪ Gifts ▪ Function/conference venue (up to 60 pax) ▪ Owner(s) GWK Ltd ▪ Cellarmaster(s) Ian Sieg ▪ Winemaker(s) Ian Sieg, with Ian Jooste ▪ Viticulturist(s) Hein Janse van Rensburg ▪ Douglas + Landzicht GWK: 350ha (cab, ruby cab, shiraz, chard, chenin, cbard, muscadels r/w) ▪ 40,000cs own label 20% red 40% white 5% rosé 35% fortified ▪ PO Box 47 Douglas 8730 ▪ wynkelder@gwk.co.za ▪ www.gwk.co.za ▪ S 29° 3' 57.0" E 023° 46' 7.8" ▪ F +27 (0)53-298-1845 ▪ **T +27 (0)53-298-8314/5**

☐ **Down to Earth** see Villiera Wines

Dragonridge   ⓘ ⓟ ⓐ ⓗ ⓞ ⓐ

The granite outcrops on Perdeberg saw rock climbing added to the activities at Fynbos Estate, eco-tourism getaway, wedding venue, nature reserve and home to Dragonridge wines. It's all natural and traditional for co-owner, vintner and Swartland Independent Producers member Johan Simons, from repurposing buildings to native ferments, basket pressing and eschewing fining/filtering on the wines.

★★★★ **Cabernet Savignon** ⓝ Bold blackcurrant, graphite & ink on unwooded **15**. Ripe, taut, dense, with dry fruit-tannin & lovely richness. Defined & rewarding. Decanting recommended.

Pinotage ⓝ ★★★☆ Vibrant fruit-forward **15**, vivacious, ripe, concentrated & generous with dry tail. Unoaked. Naturally made, as all these. **Chardonnay** ⓝ ★★★ Interplay of citrus tang with creamy lees notes on unwooded **15**. **Supernova** ⓝ ★★ Idiosyncratic **14** méthode ancestrale sparkler from chenin. Sourdough yeast, lees & oxidative caramel notes. Tangy to end. Also tasted: **Cosmos 15** ★★ **Capella 15** ★★★ Not retasted: **Sangiovese 13** ★★★★ **Jack's Red 13** ★★★ — FM

Location: Malmesbury ▪ Map/WO: Swartland ▪ Est 2004 ▪ 1stB 2006 ▪ Tasting, sales & cellar tours by appt ▪ Fee R30, waived on purchase ▪ Closed Good Fri, Dec 25/26 & Jan 1 ▪ Country meals by arrangement for groups of 8+ ▪ Facilities for children ▪ Farm produce ▪ BYO picnic ▪ Weddings/functions ▪ Conferences ▪ Walks/hikes ▪ MTB trail ▪ Simson-Simons Contract Nature Reserve ▪ Guest houses: 6-bedroom, 4-bedroom & 2 x 2-bedroom cottages ▪ De Perdestal Restaurant open for Sunday lunch (bookings only) ▪ Owner(s) Fynbos Estate (3 partners) ▪ Cellarmaster(s)/winemaker(s) Johan Simons (Jan 2004) ▪ Viticulturist(s) Johan Simons (Jun 1997) ▪ 320ha/13ha (cab, mourv, ptage, sangio, shiraz, chard, chenin, viog) ▪ 35t/1,400cs own label 50% red 25% white 10% rosé 5% Méthode Ancestrale ▪ Swartland Independent Producers ▪ P O Box 526 Malmesbury 7299 ▪ info@fynbosestate.co.za, info@dragonridge.co.za ▪ www.dragonridge.co.za ▪ S 33° 33' 28.9" E 018° 47' 5.6" ▪ F +27 (0)86-611-5125 ▪ **T +27 (0)22-487-1153**

☐ **Dragon's Back** see Kumala

Driehoek Wines   ⓐ ⓗ ⓞ ⓐ

The Du Toit family farm in the scenic Cederberg mountain conservancy area, long known as a hiking, camping and nature lover's destination, should be on the serious winelovers' radar too. Fifth-generation Charl du Toit's small, relatively young vineyard delivers excellent cool-climate quality and character, captured with help from award-winning neighbour David Nieuwoudt of Cederberg Private Cellar.

★★★★ **Mieke Pinot Noir** Adds 'Mieke' to name with improved **14** (★★★★★). Finesse & poise with subtle heather perfume, violet, wisp of vanilla & cranberry flavours on light-tripping palate. Smooth & fine textured; long savoury finish. Finer than **13** & maiden **12** (★★★★).

★★★★ **Shiraz** Classy, dark-fruited **13** (★★★★☆) trumps **12**, shows pristine berry, savoury spice & cedar flavours layered with sprinklings white pepper & lavender. Balanced oaking (60% new French/American, 15 months), with fresh finish.

★★★★ **Ludic Sauvignon Blanc** ⊘ Adds 'Ludic' to name. Pungent lemon zest, apple & quince scents underscored by herbal minerals & white flowers on stunning **15** (★★★★★). Bright & focused, with exceptional complexity, depth & clarity. Takes **14**'s excellent varietal expression up a level. — WB

Location: Citrusdal ▪ Map: Olifants River ▪ WO: Cederberg ▪ Est/1stB 2009 ▪ Sales Mon-Sat ▪ Closed Good Fri & Dec 25 ▪ Facilities for children ▪ Gift shop ▪ BYO picnic ▪ Walking/hiking & MTB trails ▪ Horse riding ▪ Bird watching ▪ Fishing ▪ Bushman paintings ▪ Conservation area ▪ Self-catering cottages & camping ▪ Beauty treatments ▪ Owner(s) Du Toit family ▪ Cellarmaster(s)/winemaker(s) David Nieuwoudt (Jan 2008, Cederberg) ▪ Viticulturist(s) Dawie Burger & Hennie Spamer (both Jun 2006), advised by David Nieuwoudt ▪ 375ha/5ha (pinot, shiraz, sauv) ▪ 3,500cs own label 40% red 60% white ▪ PO Box 89 Clanwilliam 8135 ▪ driehoekcederberg@gmail.com ▪ www.cederberg-accommodation.co.za ▪ S 32° 26' 34.40" E 019° 11' 24.32" ▪ F +27 (0)86-720-2474 ▪ **T +27 (0)27-482-2828**

☐ **Drift** *see* The Drift

Drostdy-Hof Wines ⓠ ⓐ ⓖ

Distell's well-established label salutes the old magistrate's court in Tulbagh, now a national monument, museum and elegant brand home. Value and a convenient range of pack sizes are attributes of the wines, doing particularly well in Scandinavia. 'Positive innovations' flowing from the tenure of new global marketing chief Tamsyn Parkins will be injected into the local market, promise the team.

Core range

Claret Select ★★ Fresh & fruity **NV** blend, smoothed by few grams sugar. Can take chilling. Also in various pack sizes, as most of the wines below. **Premier Grand Cru** ★★ Name associated with nothing grander than unfussy dry white; suits lightish, gentle fruity **NV** perfectly. **Stein Select** ★★ Fresh **NV** with gently sweet grapey flavours. **Late Harvest** ★★ Easy-drinking **NV**, gentle fruity sweetness & crisp, clean finish. Not retasted: **Cabernet Sauvignon 14** ★★★ **Merlot 14** ★★★ **Pinotage 14** ★★★ **Reserve Shiraz 12** ★★★☆ **Shiraz-Merlot 13** ★★☆ **Shiraz-Pinotage 14** ★★★ **Rosé 14** ★★ **Chardonnay 14** ★★★ **Chenin Blanc/Steen 14** ★★★ **Sauvignon Blanc 14** ★★ **Chardonnay-Viognier 13** ★★☆ **Adelpracht 14** ★★★☆

Light range

Extra Light ★ Briskly dry, plain **NV** white. Just 9% alcohol.

Natural Sweet range

Red ★★ Latest **NV** delicious smells, tastes of bowlful of fresh blackberries; juicily sweet but not cloying. Low alcohol (7.5%), as all this range. Also tasted: **Rosé NV** ★★ **White NV** ★★ — AL

Location/map: Tulbagh ▪ WO: Western Cape/Stellenbosch ▪ Est 1804 ▪ Tasting & sales Mon-Fri 9–5 Sat/pub hols 10–2 (last tasting 30min prior to closing) ▪ Tasting R20pp incl. museum visit ▪ Museum R10pp ▪ Closed Sun, Good Fri, Dec 25 & Jan 1 ▪ Private functions by arrangement ▪ Owner(s) Distell ▪ Cellarmaster(s) Wim Truter ▪ Winemaker(s) Pieter Badenhorst (reds) & Kirsten Basson (whites) ▪ Viticulturist(s) Annelie Viljoen ▪ PO Box 213 Tulbagh 6820 ▪ info@drostdywines.co.za ▪ www.drostdyhof.com ▪ S 33° 15' 23.3" E 019° 8' 57.5" ▪ F +27 (0)23-230-0211 ▪ **T +27 (0)23-230-0203**

Druk My Niet Wine Estate ⓠ ⓘ ⓐ ⓗ ⓐ

The Kirchner and Stein families' 17th-century estate in Paarl has been lovingly restored and refurbished, and now includes a boutique cellar and self-catering cottages. Close attention is also paid to the floral kingdom biosphere setting and, of course, the wines – top-end reds and chenin, some from old vines.

Flagship range

★★★★★ **Invictus** ⊘ Merlot-led **11** flagship blend (with cabs sauvignon & franc, splash malbec) in classic, plush Bordeaux style; seamless & understated, serious & balanced. A keeper.

★★★★☆ **T3** ⓦ Intriguing red fruit & leafy aromas on creative & one-of-a-kind **11** tempranillo (45%), tannat & tinta amarela blend. Fruit clarity shines in restrained, elegant style. WO Western Cape.

Not retasted: **T3 Reserve 13** ★★★ Not tasted: **C68 Chenin Blanc, C68 Puella**.

Druk My Niet Collection

★★★★ **Cabernet Sauvignon** ⓦ Boldly fruited **11** exhibits generous dark-toned flavours & firm yet elegant structure. Balanced vanilla oak adds complexity & velvet mouthfeel.

★★★★ **Cabernet Franc** ⓦ **11** (★★★☆) misses complexity of **10** (which showed dust, leaf, mint – you name it). Green, with quite hard tannin, herbal notes.

★★★★ **Malbec** ⓦ **11** offers loads of bright cranberry fruit, wild herbs & earthy tones. Good balance & supple structure with ageing potential. — WB

Location: Paarl ▪ Map: Paarl & Wellington ▪ Map grid reference: F4 ▪ WO: Paarl/Western Cape ▪ Est 2003 ▪ 1stB 2009 ▪ Tasting, sales & cellar tours by appt ▪ Fee R50pp ▪ Closed all pub hols ▪ Meals/refreshments on request ▪ BYO picnic ▪ Tour groups ▪ Walks/hikes ▪ Mountain biking trail ▪ Conservation area ▪ 3 self-catering cottages ▪ Owner(s) Georg & Dorothee Kirchner, Jens-Peter Stein ▪ Winemaker(s)/viticulturist(s) Lukas van Loggerenberg (Nov 2013) ▪ 24.5ha/9ha (cabs s/f, malbec, merlot, shiraz, tannat, tempranillo, tinta amarela, chenin, viog) ▪ 60t/3,500cs own label 80% red 20% white ▪ BWI, IPW ▪ PO Box 7383 Paarl 7620 ▪ georg.kirchner@dmnwines.co.za ▪ www.dmnwines.co.za ▪ S 33° 41' 23.26" E 019° 1' 40.23" ▪ **T +27 (0)21-868-2393**

☐ **Drunken Fowl** *see* Saxenburg Wine Farm

☐ **Duckitt** *see* Cloof Wine Estate

☐ **Duel** *see* Ameera

Dunstone Winery   ⓨ ⓨ ⌂ ⊚ ⓐ ⓑ

The Dunstone logo is a Weimaraner, featured throughout the property grounds and buildings, as well as on the front labels, and clearly a love of Lee and Abbi Wallis, owners since 2003 of this Wellington luxury country house, bistro and boutique winery. Another love is Shiraz, the name of said dog, and main focus of the wine activities here, current and future.

Dunstone range

★★★★ **Shiraz** Mixed spices, liquorice & black plums, no shortage of interest & attraction in **13**, savoury tannins well crafted. Mainly French oak, dab American, Hungarian. Drink now & for 5+ years.

Not tasted: **Merlot, Shiraz Rosé, Sauvignon Blanc**.

Stones in the Sun range

Not tasted: **Syrah**. — CR

Location/WO: Wellington ▪ Map: Paarl & Wellington ▪ Map grid reference: H1 ▪ Est/1stB 2006 ▪ Tasting, sales & cellar tours Wed-Sun 10-4, Mon-Tue by appt ▪ Fee R15pp, waived on purchase ▪ Closed Dec 25 & Jan 1 ▪ The Stone Kitchen ▪ Facilities for children ▪ Conferences ▪ Dunstone Country House luxury B&B guest house & self-catering cottage ▪ Owner(s) Abbi & Lee Wallis ▪ Winemaker(s) Lee Wallis & Robert Frith, with Neil Marais (Jun 2011) ▪ Viticulturist(s) Johan Viljoen (Icon Vines & Wines) ▪ 2ha/3.5ha (grenache, merlot, mourv, shiraz, viog) ▪ 20t/3,300cs own label 65% red 25% white 10% rosé ▪ PO Box 901 Wellington 7654 ▪ wine@dunstone.co.za ▪ www.dunstone.co.za ▪ S 33° 38' 5.3" E 019° 3' 36.8" ▪ F +27 (0)21-873-6770 ▪ **T +27 (0)21-873-6770**

☐ **Du Plevaux** *see* Imbuko Wines

Du Preez Estate   ⓨ ⊝ ⓑ

Breedekloof winegrowers since 1926, the Du Preez family have appointed Ferdinand Laubscher as head winemaker, noting: 'For one so young he brings a wealth of innovation which he personally sourced during his wine travels'. Ferdinand's brief is to marry innovation with best practice and 'age-old techniques' to express the estate's terroir. He will also oversee heavy investment in oak (justified by the character/quality of harvest 2015) and ongoing development of 'alternatives to artificial inputs'.

Du Preez Private Cellar range

Polla's Red ⊘ ★★★ Merlot leads four-way blend on approachable, unfussy **12**, notch up on previous. Also in magnum. WO W Cape. **Sauvignon Blanc** ⊘ ★★★ Flinty tropical hints on light & easy **15**. Also tasted: **Cabernet Sauvignon 13** ★★☆ Not tasted: **Merlot, Shiraz, Maranda Rosé Méthode Cap Classique, Hanepoot.** Discontinued: **Chardonnay.**

Rockfield range

Cabernet Sauvignon ⊘ ★★☆ Medium-bodied **NV** offers a graphite edge to cassis brightness. **Shiraz** ⊘ ★★☆ Softly ripe & spicy blue fruit on step-up **13**. Also tasted: **Merlot** ⊘ **NV** ★★★ **Sauvignon Blanc 14** ★★

Hendrik Lodewyk range

Méthode Cap Classique ★★☆ Uncomplicated tangy & crisp citrus marmalade notes on chardonnay-driven **NV** sparkler. Just 9 months on lees, unlike 48 of previous. Breedekloof WO. Also in magnum. Not tasted: **Petit Verdot.** — FM

Location: Rawsonville • Map: Breedekloof • WO: Western Cape/Breedekloof • Est 1916 • 1stB 1998 • Tasting & sales Mon-Fri 8–5 Sat 10–1 • Closed all pub hols • Cellar tours by appt, 2-day prior notice required • BYO picnic • Tour groups (max 20 pax) • Owner(s) Du Preez family • Cellarmaster(s)/winemaker(s) Ferdinand Laubscher (Oct 2014) • Viticulturist(s) Jean du Preez • 350ha (merlot, p verdot, ptage, shiraz, chard, chenin, cbard, nouvelle, sauv) • 5,000t • Other export brand: Martinique • IPW • PO Box 12 Route 101 Rawsonville 6845 • info@dupreezestate.co.za • www.dupreezestate.co.za • S 33° 41' 37.1" E 019° 16' 59.6" • F +27 (0)23-349-1923 • **T +27 (0)23-349-1995**

Durbanville Hills   ⓨ ⑪ ⓸ ⓧ ⓖ

In the late 1990s, some business-savvy Durbanville wine growers collaborated with industry giant Distell to build a cellar and vinify a shared label. Veteran cellarmaster Martin Moore's team shepherds wine from some 250 tanks (ranging from 6,000 to 100,000L capacity) and a couple of thousand barrels into nearly 2 million bottles. Though mainly exported, the three-tier range is available locally and includes sales from the hilltop edifice's tasting room and restaurant, with panoramic views of Table Mountain across Table Bay. New is the limited-edition Scouts range (not tasted), exclusive to wine club members. It features special bottlings of varieties like pinot gris and pinot noir, and blends including winery speciality sauvignon blanc, the passion of new white-wine maker Kobus Gerber.

Vineyard Selection

★★★★ **Biesjes Craal Sauvignon Blanc** A sauvignon for every palate here. This single vineyard version crackles with life; **15** more peppery, steely than siblings, with stony minerality & invigorating acidity.

Discontinued: **Luipaardsberg Merlot, Caapmans Cabernet Sauvignon-Merlot.**

Rhinofields range

★★★★ **Pinotage** ⑧ Full-bodied, ripe **12** is excellent in its opulence, though perhaps not quite as pure fruited as much-liked **11** (★★★★★).

★★★★ **Chardonnay** Peanut brittle nuttiness & spicy oak (cask-fermented) jostle with juicy tropical/pineapple fruit of **14**, the ample flavours refreshed (just) by acidity.

★★★★☆ **Noble Late Harvest** From sauvignon, as last, pale gold **14** (★★★★) inviting clean botrytis aromas, concentrated honeyed fruit, sweet low-alcohol tail missing the verve of scintillating **13**. 375 ml.

Also tasted: **Merlot 12** ★★★☆ **Shiraz 12** ★★★ **Sauvignon Blanc 15** ★★★☆

Durbanville Hills range

Pinotage ★★★ Cardamom & clove spice deftly balances ripe plum fruit of very gentle **13**. **Merlot Rosé** ★★★ Pretty in pink, **15** offers raspberries with a cranberry twist, ends nicely dry. **Sauvignon Blanc** ★★★ A trusted winelist stalwart; the cellar's 'all-purpose' bottling of the variety. Juicy **15** doesn't disappoint. Also tasted: **Cabernet Sauvignon 13** ★★★ **Merlot 13** ★★★ **Chardonnay 14** ★★★ Not retasted: **Shiraz 12** ★★★ — DS

Location/WO: Durbanville • Map: Durbanville, Philadelphia & Darling • Est 1998 • 1stB 1999 • Tasting & sales Mon-Fri 9-6 Sat 10–4 Sun 11–4 • Fee R50/8 wines incl crystal glass • Closed Dec 25 & Jan 1 • Chocolate/biltong and Rhinofields reserve food & wine pairing • Tasting room menu available daily •

Cellar tours Mon-Fri 11 & 3; 24 hour booking required ▪ Restaurant Tue-Sun 8.30-3; dinner 6-10 Wed-Sat (summer) & Fri (winter) ▪ Picnics (Oct-Apr) ▪ Facilities for children & cyclists ▪ Conferences ▪ Weddings/functions ▪ Owner(s) Distell, 9 farmers & workers trust ▪ Cellarmaster(s) Martin Moore (Nov 1998) ▪ Winemaker(s) Wilhelm Coetzee (reds, Sep 2008) & Kobus Gerber (whites, Jul 2015) ▪ Viticulturist(s) Henk van Graan (consultant) ▪ 770ha (merlot, sauv) ▪ 6,000t/300,000cs own label 40% red 58% white 2% rosé ▪ ISO 9000-1, ISO 14000-1, BWI, BRC, HACCP, IPW, WIETA ▪ PO Box 3276 Durbanville 7551 ▪ info@durbanvillehills.co.za ▪ www.durbanvillehills.co.za ▪ S 33° 49' 29.9" E 018° 33' 56.7" ▪ **T +27 (0)21-558-1300**

Dusty Heath Vineyard

Though based in the summer-rainfall Midlands of KwaZulu-Natal, Mark and Paula Haldane always fancied making wine. When some of their neighbours started doing it successfully, they thought why not? The resulting 'happy sexy wine' will be available for tasting onsite, and a functions venue open, once the Haldanes get the necessary licences. It's taking somewhat longer than expected but hopefully soon.

Cabernet Sauvignon ⓥ ★★★ Only 2nd fill barrels for **13**, naturally fermented, as all. Attractive blackcurrants, liquorice & scrub nose; light & dry, more gamay in character but very sippable. Not retasted: **Barrel No. 2 Red Blend 13** ★★ **Good Luck Blend 13** ★★★ — CR, CvZ

Location: Hilton ▪ WO: KwaZulu-Natal ▪ Est 2009 ▪ Closed to public ▪ Owner(s) Mark & Paula Haldane ▪ Cellarmaster(s)/viticulturist(s) Paula Haldane (Aug 2009) ▪ Winemaker(s) Paula Haldane (Aug 2009), with Maqua Madlala (Aug 2009) ▪ 20ha/2ha (cabs s/f, merlot, p verdot) ▪ 100% red ▪ dhvineyard@sai.co.za ▪ F +27 (0)86-542-8704 ▪ **T +27 (0)33-383-2001/+27 (0)82-901-4304**

Du'SwaRoo   ⓥ ⓘ

Former analytical chemist Tony Bailey, from Durban, and wife Nita, born in SWA (South West Africa/Namibia) moved to the Klein Karoo to grow olives and fruit. Making wine 'was supposed to be a hobby but the bug bit' and now their Calitzdorp boutique cellar has extra equipment (but remains the region's smallest), and Tony intends to produce small volumes of varieties sourced beyond the home farm.

Mistral ★★★ Appealing spice & berry nuances to dry rosé of **15** (uncertified) touriga, tinta & shiraz. Step up on previous. **Chinook** ⓝⓔⓦ ★★★ Appealing length & tropical fruit flavours on light, unwooded **15** (uncertified) from chenin. **Cape Vintage** ★★★★ Vibrant nutty spice & raisin notes on **11** port-style fortified, which retains 66/34 mix of touriga & tinta. Fiery core with good spirit integration. Also tasted: **Khamsin 12** ★★★ Not retasted: **Shiloh Winemakers Blend 13** ★★ **Sirocco Bin 3 NV** ★★★ Not tasted: **Shiraz**. — FM

Location/WO: Calitzdorp ▪ Map: Klein Karoo & Garden Route ▪ Est/1stB 2008 ▪ Tasting & sales by appt Mon-Fri 9-5 Sat 9-1 ▪ Closed all pub hols ▪ Wines also available at Withoek Cellar ▪ Farm produce ▪ Owner(s) Tony Bailey ▪ Cellarmaster(s)/winemaker(s)/viticulturist(s) Tony Bailey (2008) ▪ 0.6ha (shiraz, tinta, touriga); 1.5ha/20t hanepoot also grown but delivered to Calitzdorp Cellar ▪ 200cs own label 80% red 20% port ▪ PO Box 279 Calitzdorp 6660 ▪ duswaroo@telkomsa.net ▪ www.kleinkaroowines.co.za ▪ S 33° 30' 58.7" E 021° 41' 39.5" ▪ F +27 (0)44-213-3137 ▪ **T +27 (0)44-213-3137/+27 (0)83-378-8101**

Du Toitskloof Winery   ⓥ ⓜ ⓘ ⓔ

After exiting the Huguenot Tunnel and following the N1 north through dramatic mountain scenery into the suitably broad Breedekloof Valley, Du Toitskloof just off to the right is hard to miss. Even more so now that the cellar has been extended — once again. That's because this dynamic winery, established as a co-operative over half a century ago, knows what it takes to produce a broad range of consumer-friendly, pocket-pleasing wines year after year. Palate pleasing is Melissa's Food, now open at the cellardoor.

Quest range

★★★★☆ **Heroes Journey 1 Bordeaux Blend** ⓥ Cab-led (76%) **11** with equal merlot, petit verdot, is powerful, supple, complex & generous, with deeply scented aromas of cassis, tobacco & spicecake.

★★★★ **Heroes Journey 2 Rhône Blend** ⓥ Gorgeous blend of shiraz & 19% mourvèdre, **11** offers a melange of earthy, savoury, dark berry flavours & cherry preserve, mingling with firm but supple tannins.

Reserve Collection

Nebbiolo ⊘ ★★★★ Bright cherry vivacity on **13** echoes quality of last-made **10**. Typical spice & dry tannin but light & deliciously supple. Fairtrade certified, as all Du Toitskloof wines. Not retasted: **Dimension Red 12** ★★★ Discontinued: **Chardonnay-Viognier**.

Du Toitskloof range

Merlot ★★★ **14** ticks the boxes: light-bodied, succulent, spicy fruitcake flavour & ease of enjoyment. **Pinotage** ★★★ Ripe blueberry sweetness to juicy **13**, soft textured & approachable. **Chardonnay** ★★★ **15** continues the good form. Oak fermented portion (50%) frames juicy citrus well. Light & balanced with long, dry tail. **Sauvignon Blanc** ★★★ Old faithful, **15** maintains form of previous. Bright, sweet hints of granadilla & lemon add vibrancy to balanced palate. **Sparkling Brut** ★★☆ Crisp, zesty lemon zip of sauvignon-led **NV** sparkler retains appeal & form of previous. Unpretentious party starter. Also tasted: **Cabernet Sauvignon 13** ★★★ **Shiraz 11** ★★★ **Pinotage-Merlot-Ruby Cabernet 14** ★★☆ **Chenin Blanc 15** ★★☆ **Vin Doux Red Sparkling Wine NV** ★★★ Not retasted: **Cabernet Sauvignon-Shiraz 13** ★★★ **Beaukett 13** ★★☆

Tunnel range

Red ★★ Ideal **NV** cab for beginners: light, soft & unfussy with gentle berry fruit. **Moscato** ⊘ ★★☆ Floral appeal to balanced **NV** semi-sweet livened with 15% colombard. Uncloying yet clean to end. Also tasted: **Sweet Rosé NV** ★★ **White NV** ★☆ **Sweet Red NV** ★★

Dessert Wines

Hanepoot Jerepigo ★★★☆ Ambrosial honeyed seduction of balanced **14** fortified from muscat d'Alexandrie. Richly sweet but with a clean & dry finish. Drink now, say the team, or up to 50 years! Also tasted: **Red Muscadel 14** ★★★ Not retasted: **Cape Ruby 10** ★★★ Discontinued: **Noble Late Harvest**. — FM

Location: Rawsonville • Map: Breedekloof • WO: Western Cape • Est 1962 • Tasting & sales Mon-Fri 8–5 Sat 9–3.30 • Closed Good Fri, Dec 25 & Jan 1 • Cellar tours by appt • Melissa's Food Shop • Picnics in summer • Owner(s) 22 members • Cellarmaster(s) Shawn Thomson (Oct 1999) • Winemaker(s) Chris Geldenhuys (Mar 2005) & Willie Stofberg (Feb 2011), with Derrick Cupido (Jan 1993) & Jaco le Roux • Viticulturist(s) Leon Dippenaar (Jan 2005, consultant) • 900ha (cab, merlot, ptage, shiraz, chard, chenin, cbard, sauv) • 14,000t/±700,000cs own label 40% red 60% white • Fairtrade • PO Box 55 Rawsonville 6845 • info@dutoitskloof.co.za • www.dutoitskloof.com • S 33° 42' 9.2" E 019° 16' 8.9" • F +27 (0)23-349-1581 • **T +27 (0)23-349-1601**

DuVon Private Cellar ⓨ ⓐ ⓞ

When not growing grapes for bigger brands, Armand du Toit and his uncle, Alex von Klopmann, vinify small batches in the restored 1940s cellar on Little Italy farm in Robertson's De Goree district.

Location/map: Robertson • Est/1stB 2003 • Tasting, sales & cellar tours by appt • Conferences • Weddings • Guest house • Owner(s) Armand du Toit & Alex von Klopmann • Cellarmaster(s)/winemaker(s)/viticulturist(s) Armand du Toit • 29.5ha/27ha (cab, ruby cab, shiraz, chenin, cbard, sauv) • 400t/1,200cs own label 70% red 30% white • PO Box 348 Robertson 6705 • info@duvon.co.za • www.duvon.co.za • S 33° 48' 46.8" E 019° 47' 4.1" • F +27 (0)86-626-1490 • **T +27 (0)72-514-4204**

☐ **D'Vine** *see* Swartland Winery
☐ **Dwyka Hills** *see* Eagle's Cliff Wines-New Cape Wines
☐ **Dyasonsklip** *see* Bezalel-Dyasonsklip Wine Cellar

Eagle's Cliff Wines-New Cape Wines ⓨ ⓨ⓵ ⓞ ⓐ ⓰

These are the entry-level bottled wines of Christiaan Groenewald, who also successfully exports bulk wines to Europe. (His Diners Club Winemaker of the Year-lauded top label, Arendskloof/Voetspore, listed separately.) Last year's 700+ km Cape Epic cycle tour saw the 600 teams not only conquer Christiaan's vineyard sites in the mountains between Worcester and Villiersdorp, but also whoosh through his cellar!

Eagle's Cliff range

Shiraz-Pinotage ⊘ ★★★ Invariably vibrant & engaging blend. Another successful 80/20 marriage in **14**, with coffee, smoke & strawberry attractions. Well priced, too. **Shiraz Rosé** ⊘ ★★★

Flavoursome **15** ticks all the summer sunset boxes: dry, modest 12.5% alcohol, refreshing Granny Smith apple acidity. **Sauvignon Blanc ★★ 15** reined-in aromas & flavours, rounded acidity for uncomplicated & unchallenging enjoyment. Also tasted: **Pinotage** ⊘ **14 ★★★☆ Cabernet Sauvignon-Merlot** ⊘ **14 ★★★** Not tasted: **Chenin Blanc**.

Dwyka Hills range

Shiraz ⊘ ⊛ **★★★☆** Always punches above its weight, **14** no exception. Characterful olive tapenade nuances, balanced finish (even with 14.7% alcohol), unfettered by oak. Worth seeking out. WO W Cape.

Hoeksrivier range

Cabernet Sauvignon ⊘ **★★★** Wallet-friendly **11** has dusty berries & sweet vanilla. Not retasted: **Chenin Blanc 13 ★★★ Sauvignon Blanc 13 ★★** — CvZ

Location/map: Worcester • WO: Breede River Valley/Western Cape • Est 2000 • Tasting & sales Mon-Fri 8-3 • Closed all pub hols • Cheese & meat platters Mon-Fri 10-2 • Facilities for children • Tour groups • Owner(s)/winemaker(s) Christiaan Groenewald • 600ha/80ha • 40% red 60% white • PO Box 898 Worcester 6849 • christiaan@ncw.co.za • www.eaglescliff.co.za • S 33° 50' 25.4" E 019° 25' 7.4" • F +27 (0)86-236-4959 • **T +27 (0)23-340-4112**

Eagles' Nest   Ⓨ Ⓜ Ⓖ

Like a phoenix (or eagle) rising from the ashes, the Mylrea family's Constantia eyrie (which supports a local raptor research programme) overlooking False Bay was born of a potentially devastating fire in 2000. This decimated a pine forest leaving unstable, erosion-prone ground on the steep slopes. Following expert advice from, among others, viticulturist Kevin Watt and red-wine guru Martin Meinert, they developed terraced vineyards. The resultant specialist portfolio of distinctive, cool-climate wines has earned a tide of endorsements from winewriters, competitions and consumers around the world.

★★★★☆ Merlot 11 revels in care taken to create it, including multiply sourced barrels of various ages. While there's ample plum & complex spice attractions, fine-grained tannins, most impressive is savoury persistence in a country where fruit- & oak-sweet conclusions are norm.

★★★★★ Shiraz Well-deserved maximum rating for brilliant **12**, an unshowy but richly satisfying & complete wine. Echoes **11**'s (**★★★★★**) dark berry fruit spiced with black pepper & scrub, smooth polished lines & — the property's hallmark — resonating length. Composed & lithe, with a great future. French oak 16 months, half new. Also in magnum, as is Merlot.

★★★★☆ Viognier Restrained in SA context, **14** (**★★★★**) has none of **13**'s forthright peach & apricot notes, intriguing jasmine nuance. There is, however, texture & weight, savoury nuances for food. Barrel-fermentation, ageing (9 months, 10% new).

Little Eagle Rosé ⓃⒺⓌ **★★★★** Bollywood pink **15** successful example of the dry style, balanced, juicy & zesty for easy al fresco enjoyment. From merlot/shiraz, partial saignée. Also tasted: **The Little Eagle 13 ★★★** Not retasted: **Sauvignon Blanc 13 ★★★☆** — CvZ

Location: Constantia • Map: Cape Peninsula • WO: Constantia/Western Cape • Est 2001 • 1stB 2005 • Tasting & sales daily 10-4.30 • Fee R50pp, waived on purchase of R300+ • Closed Good Fri, Dec 25/26 & Jan 1 • Light meals • Owner(s) Mylrea family • Winemaker(s) Stuart Botha (2007), with consultant Martin Meinert (2001) • Viticulturist(s) Kobus Jordaan (2008), with consultant Kevin Watt (2001) • 38ha/12ha (merlot, shiraz, viog) • 90t/15,000cs own label 85% red 15% white • PO Box 535 Constantia 7848 • info@eaglesnestwines.com • www.eaglesnestwines.com • S 34° 0' 54.2" E 018° 24' 54.3" • F +27 (0)21-794-7113 • **T +27 (0)21-794-4095**

Eaglevlei Wine Estate   Ⓨ Ⓜ Ⓒ Ⓐ Ⓖ

Eaglevlei is a small family-owned Stellenbosch estate geared towards providing family/tourist-friendly attractions, the latest of which is weekend tastings in the newly upgraded cellar. The appointment of a tasting room manager and commencement of trade distribution in Cape Town and Johannesburg show their forward thinking, to introduce the unusually named wild bird range of wines to a wider market.

★★★★ **Kroonarend** ⓐ Now 100% merlot, previous **09** a shiraz blend. **12** (★★★☆) mixed berries, ripe & forthcoming, some tobacco flavours; still youthful, would reward cellaring few years.

★★★★ **Tiervoël** ⓐ Switches from Cape Blend to varietal pinotage in **12**. Complex & involving, cigarbox & cured meat shading to deep plummy fruit, the flavours savoury yet juicy. Intriguing scrub notes.

Red Affair ⓐ ★★★☆ Half pinotage with cab & merlot, **13** meaty, smoky, some mocha, the fruit showing on the palate, juicy & lively, finishing fresh. **Berghaan** ⓐ ★★★ Blanc de noir style **13**, cherries & cranberries, there's lovely fruit in the perfume & flavours, & a nice bite of acidity for freshness. **Breëkop** ⓐ ★★★ **12** unwooded chardonnay shows lively lime & granadilla notes, light footed but flavourful. Hemel-en-Aarde vines. Not retasted: **Roofarend 12** ★★★☆ **Dwerg Arend 14** ★★★ **Visarend 14** ★★ **Langkuif 13** ★★★★ **Lekkerbek Sweet Sparkling NV** ★★☆ — CR

Location/map: Stellenbosch ▪ Map grid reference: E1 ▪ WO: Stellenbosch/Swartland/Hemel-en-Aarde Valley/Western Cape ▪ Est/1stB 1997 ▪ Tasting & sales Tue-Sat 10–5 Sun 10-3 ▪ Fee R30, waived on purchase ▪ Eaglevlei Restaurant Tue-Thu 8-8 Fri/Sat 8-9 Sun 8-6 ▪ Facilities for children ▪ Tour groups ▪ Conferences ▪ Functions ▪ Owner(s) Rennert van Rensburg ▪ Cellarmaster(s)/winemaker(s)/viticulturist(s) Clarise Sciocatti-Langeveldt (Jan 2012) ▪ ±7ha (cab, merlot, ptage) ▪ 75t/14,000cs own label 70% red 25% white 5% rosé ▪ PO Box 969 Stellenbosch 7599 ▪ wine@eaglevlei.com, info@eaglevlei.com ▪ www.eaglevlei.com ▪ S 33° 49' 33.5" E 018° 48' 52.2" ▪ F +27 (0)21-884-4716 ▪ **T +27 (0)21-884-4713**

Earthbound   ⓠ

An apt name for wines certified organic and Fairtrade, a message boldly proclaimed on the colourful labels. Established in 1998, Earthbound is an empowerment joint venture between wine giant Distell, a consortium of taverners in Gauteng, and a local community trust. Home base is Papkuilsfontein farm in the cool Groenekloof ward near Darling, with grapes sourced from mostly unirrigated bushvines.

Pinotage ⓢ ★★★ Plums & liquorice, nice vanilla tones make **13** friendly & appealing, confirmed by the smooth, juicy texture. **Chenin Blanc** ⓢ ★★★ Zesty, with stonefruit & melon flavours, **15** has an attractive mineral note at the end. Nice food match. Also tasted: **Cabernet Sauvignon** ⓢ 13 ★★★ **Sauvignon Blanc** ⓢ 15 ★★★ Not retasted: **Pinot Noir 12** ★★☆ — CR

Location/WO: Darling ▪ Est 1998 ▪ 1stB 1999 ▪ Tasting by appt at Trinity Lodge, Darling ▪ Owner(s) Distell, Leopont 98 Properties, Maluti Groenekloof Community Trust & consortium of Gauteng-based black taverners ▪ Winemaker(s) Samuel Viljoen (Sep 2007) ▪ Viticulturist(s) Hannes van Rensburg (1998) ▪ 975ha/373.36ha (of which 172ha organically grown) ▪ 73% red 27% white ▪ BWI, Fairtrade, SGS, WIETA ▪ PO Box 184 Stellenbosch 7599 ▪ info@earthboundwines.co.za ▪ www.earthboundwines.co.za ▪ F +27 (0)21-882-9575 ▪ **T +27 (0)21-809-7000**

☐ **Eden Crest** see Lourensford Wine Estate
☐ **Edenhof** see Schalkenbosch Wines

Edgebaston   ⓠ

When David Finlayson purchased this Simonsberg farm outside Stellenbosch it was called Woodlands. He returned it to its original name of Edgebaston, also the area in England his mother, Jill, was born and raised in. After a year of increasing storage and cellar space, better vineyard management is the current focus, especially to achieve greater concentration in white wines. The search for old vineyards with super-premium potential is another focus, to meet increased demand for the Camino Africana range.

Camino Africana range

★★★★ **David Finlayson Cabernet Franc** ⓝⓔⓦ Third in Camino Africana range, bearing same evocative label, **13** cab franc sourced from variety's Helderberg heartland. Full bodied & rich, it's spiced by both fruit & oak (100% new, 300L). Firm & dry; cellar or drink now with veal or lamb dishes.

★★★★☆ **David Finlayson Pinot Noir Reserve** From same mature, experimental-clone vineyard as **12**, the fruit in **13** (★★★★) slighter, softer, leaving all-new French oak currently dominant. Harmony may be achieved in medium term but not **12**'s distinction.

★★★★☆ **David Finlayson Chenin Blanc Old Vine 14** more open, youthfully sumptuous than **13**, old-vine concentration remains from this 1947 Bottelary Hills vineyard. Elegant floral, pink apple features, currently shaded by new oak, have freshness & length for confidence in future integration.

Edgebaston range

★★★★ **Cabernet Sauvignon** Fragrant cab fruit introduces **13**, along with complementary if still evident new oak (60%) scents. Perhaps not as long or intense as **12**, the fruit is forward & silky, the grip forming but not overly aggressive. Includes drops of merlot & petit verdot.

★★★★☆ **David Finlayson 'GS' Cabernet Sauvignon 13** in characteristic bigger, more sumptuous style, with generous very ripe, dark cab fruit. Structured for lengthy ageing with dense, fine tannic grip. Named for legendary George Spies cabs from 1960s.

★★★★☆ **Reserve Cabernet Sauvignon** (NEW) David Finlayson has the knack of achieving balance with high alcohol: **12** hits 15% without obvious heat. Dark berry fruit & texture are very ripe & rich & easily soak up two years in 100% new oak, but the finish is dry with proper, ageworthy cab tannins.

★★★★ **Pinot Noir** (Ⓧ) Darker fruit spectrum provides touch more serious note in **13**; supple texture, freshness & gentle tannins ensure it remains in fruitier, approachable house style. WO W Cape.

★★★★ **Syrah 14**'s restrained aromas, silky smooth feel belies generous, richly spiced & lengthy flavours. Subtle oaking & rounded tannins allow for current enjoyment; peak maturity may be earlier than **13**'s.

★★★★ **The Pepper Pot** Previewed **14** (★★★) short on character of **13**. Shiraz with mourvèdre, tannat & grenache provide simple, very ripe flavours in easy-drinking style. Coastal WO.

★★★★☆ **Chardonnay 14** (★★★★) has many of **13**'s engaging features: creamy texture, freshness & restrained oaking, 25% new, but not grainy grip, an important textural feature, or core concentration. In lieu, clean citrusy bite & substance provide few years' potential.

Also tasted: **The Berry Box Red 13** ★★★☆ **Cast In Stone Sauvignon Blanc 15** ★★★☆ **The Berry Box White 15** ★★★ Not tasted: **DLDC Natural Sweet**. — AL

Location/map: Stellenbosch ▪ Map grid reference: F3 ▪ WO: Stellenbosch/Coastal/Western Cape ▪ Est/1stB 2004 ▪ Tasting by appt only ▪ Owner(s) David Finlayson ▪ Cellarmaster(s) David Finlayson (Jan 2004) ▪ Winemaker(s) David Finlayson (Jan 2004), with Franco Lourens (Jun 2013) ▪ 30ha/24ha (cab, shiraz, chard, sauv) ▪ 300t/60,000cs own label 60% red 40% white ▪ PO Box 2033 Dennesig 7601 ▪ david@edgebaston.co.za ▪ www.edgebaston.co.za ▪ S 33° 53' 33.82" E 018° 51' 17.61" ▪ F +27 (0)21-889-9572 ▪ **T +27 (0)21-889-9572/+27 (0)83-263-4353**

☐ **Edward Snell & Co** see Wellington VO

Eendevanger (NEW)

There's been just one vintage (2013) from the tiny 'Duck Catcher' label, and three naturally fermented (in neutral oak) wines – chenin blanc, pinot gris and riesling. But watch this space! says brand owner and winemaker Lucinda Heyns, jumping through legal and bureaucratic hoops associated with formalising a business entity. Namibia raised, Lucinda was introduced to wine by her father, originally from Stellenbosch where she graduated. After five years at Jordan, she landed dream jobs in California's Napa Valley with cult producers Screaming Eagle and Dalla Valle, and later in southern California working with cool-climate pinot noir and syrah/shiraz. 'My approach is to choose good vineyards in which I enjoy working, and then interfere as little as possible.'

Owner(s)/winemaker(s) Lucinda Heyns ▪ lucinda@eendevangerwines.com ▪ www.eendevangerwines.com ▪ **T +27 (0)84-370-4282**

Eenzaamheid (Ⓛ) (Ⓞ)

This 17th-century Paarl farm's 7th-generation growers nurture both the land and its people. Old dryland bushvines (chenin, cinsaut) and new plantings (grenache noir, malbec) supply quality fruit to leading brands. Meanwhile, son Janno Briers-Louw vinifies the boutique family label, assisted by Danny Arries, racking up qualifications courtesy of ongoing employee support programmes.

★★★★ **Cinsaut** 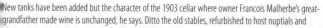 Fragrant red fruit – delicate raspberry, notably – & earthy element on delightful **14**, with purity unobscured by old oak. Light, fresh & elegantly structured by grape (not oak) tannin.

★★★★ **Pinotage 12** on the grape's more fragrant, elegant side – last-tasted **10** (★★★☆) was more chunky. Ripe, with big 14.5% alcohol well disguised in clean, dry package. Well-handled oak (10% new).

★★★★ **Cuvée** ⊘ Previously 'Cuvée 1693'. Last-tasted was **NV** (★★★☆), now vintaged. Remarkable value on warmly generous, plump-fruited, yet mouthwateringly fresh **13** blend of 5 varieties (shiraz the largest at 37%). Mostly old oak. Lovely now, but should grow a few years.

★★★★ **Chenin Blanc** Thatchy & floral **13** (★★★★★) matured in old oak, as was **12**. Light-footed & poised, well-padded with fruit giving a good length, with a fresh (though slightly coarse – perhaps just in youth) acidity. The evident unforced character is part of the pleasure. — TJ, CvZ

Location/WO: Paarl • Map: Paarl & Wellington • Map grid reference: B5 • Est 1693 • 1stB 2010 • Tasting by appt only • Conferences • Owner(s) Christo & Karina Briers-Louw • Winemaker(s) Janno Briers-Louw (Apr 2008) • Viticulturist(s) André Coetzee (Sep 2003) • 1,185ha/420ha (cab, cinsaut, ptage, shiraz, chenin) • 3,500t/2,500cs own label 75% red 25% white • PO Box 22 Klapmuts 7625 • wine@ eenzaamheid1.co.za • www.eenzaamheidwines.co.za • S 33° 44' 52.67" E 018° 50' 12.06" • F +27 (0)86-583-5741 • **T +27 (0)82-493-9930**

Eerste Hoop Wine Cellar ⓠ ⌂

Named for 17th century Cape governor Willem Adriaan van der Stel's hunting lodge, here in Theewaterskloof Valley, this boutique winery is co-owned by Belgian restaurateur Lode Lemahieu, who drives strong exports. 'Local sales are also in full throttle,' says winemaker/viticulturist Werner Barkhuizen, inviting visitors to stay at the new guest house.

Lodewijkx range
★★★★ **White Blend** Gaining in intensity, retasted chardonnay-led wooded **12**, with 36% chenin & 20% viognier, has peachy perfume, tangy orange & apricot flavours, creamy mouthfeel & lingering, leesy, savoury finish. Up a notch on **11** (★★★☆).

Eerste Hoop range
★★★★ **Cabernet Sauvignon** ⊘ **10** dense & rich, with black fruit, dark chocolate & liquorice. Oak (20% new) is well judged, making wine accessible now but worth keeping.

Wooded Chardonnay ⊛ ★★★☆ Aged in second-fill oak for 16 months, **14** is big & bold with toasted nut notes, zesty citrus bursting through to refresh.

Pinot Noir ⓝ ★★★ Fairly 'masculine' in style, **13** has deep, dark, ripe black cherry fruit as well as more savoury thyme, fennel, liquorice notes; aged in older barrels 20 months. Also tasted: **Blushing Bride Pinot Noir Rosé 14** ★★★ **Viognier 14** ★★★ Not retasted: **Shiraz 10** ★★★★

Witklip range
Shiraz ★★☆ Fruit-driven **13** has ripe, juicy plum fruit, six months on oak staves adding vanilla & baking spice to sweetish, easy-drinking appeal. Also tasted: **Chardonnay 14** ★★★ — JG

Location: Villiersdorp • Map: Elgin, Walker Bay & Bot River • WO: Western Cape • 1stB 2006 • Tasting, sales & cellar tours Mon-Sat by appt • Guest house • Owner(s) Belgium owners • Winemaker(s)/viticulturist(s) Werner Barkhuizen (May 2013) • 24.5ha/11ha (cab, grenache, mourv, pinot, shiraz, chard, chenin, viog) • 95t/14,000cs 55% red 42% white 3% rosé • Brands for clients: Oggendau, Skoon Vallei, Stilfontein • IPW • PO Box 89 Elgin 7180 • wine@eerstehoop.co.za • www.eerstehoop.co.za • S 34° 5' 23.7" E 019° 11' 50.7" • **T +27 (0)28-841-4190/+27 (0)82-754-4408**

☐ **Eighth Wonder Wines** *see* VinGlo Wines

Eikehof Wines ⓠ ⓟ ⌖

New tanks have been added but the character of the 1903 cellar where owner Francois Malherbe's great-grandfather made wine is unchanged, he says. Ditto the old stables, refurbished to host nuptials and other celebrations as part of the family's drive to share their passion for wine and the 'relaxed and intimate atmosphere' of their oak-shaded Franschhoek farm.

Cabernet Sauvignon ⊘ ★★★ **11** raises the bar with black fruit appeal, but firm oak still apparent. Not retasted: **Shiraz 12** ★★ Not tasted: **Merlot, Chardonnay, Sauvignon Blanc, Semillon-Chardonnay**. — FM

Location/map: Franschhoek ▪ WO: Franschhoek/Western Cape ▪ Est 1903 ▪ 1stB 1992 ▪ Tasting & sales Mon-Sun 10-5 (Sep-Apr) & 10-4 (May-Aug) ▪ Closed Good Fri, Dec 25 & Jan 1 ▪ Light lunch (Sep-Apr); cheese platters (daily) ▪ Weddings & functions ▪ Owner(s)/cellarmaster(s)/winemaker(s) Francois Malherbe ▪ 29ha/24ha (cab, merlot, pinot, shiraz, chard, sem) ▪ 28t/3,000cs own label 80% red 20% white ▪ PO Box 222 Franschhoek 7690 ▪ eikehof@mweb.co.za ▪ www.eikehof.com ▪ S 33° 52' 53.3" E 019° 3' 52.0" ▪ F +27 (0)21-876-2469 ▪ **T +27 (0)21-876-2469**

Eikendal Vineyards   ⊘ ⑪ ⌂ ◎ ⑧ ⑥

Chief winemaker/viticulturist Nico Grobler's notes about the tasting samples submitted for our review show an enormous focus, passion and attention to detail, traits amply reflected in his multi-awarded wines. He's been at the Swiss Saager family's winery on the Helderberg almost a decade, and he and more recent colleagues Christo Hanse and Willem van Kerwel are extending their varietal palette with grenache and mourvèdre vines, and specific clones of chardonnay (they also source around Stellenbosch, Elgin and Lutzville). New-shape red-wine tanks have been installed, freeing Nico to take 'as long as he likes' with his spontaneous ferments, and at the diverse and vibrant cellardoor there's a popular new eatery, with the team's Charisma blend a particularly tasty match with the Italian food.

Icon range

★★★★☆ **Classique** Refined blend mainly merlot, cab & polish of cab franc. **13** seamless & balanced, its gentle, sweet flesh braced by a rumble of tannin, fresh core. Both allow for current & future enjoyment.

★★★★☆ **Chardonnay 14** follows in footsteps of fine **13**. Still incredibly young but with characteristic delicacy, focus in its intricate, lacy weave citrus tones, gentle creaminess & elegant length. Structurally bit slighter than **13**, still shows good ageing potential. WO W Cape.

Reserve range

★★★★☆ **Cabernet Sauvignon** Immediate impression of class in finely crafted **13**. Elegant & fine-boned, the perfectly ripe flavours are fresh & lengthy, the texture silky behind dense tannin wall. Subtle oaking, 300L French, 40% new, enriches & adds to ageability.

★★★★ **Merlot** Compared with classic **12** (★★★★☆), **13** is tightly wound, tense & barricaded by dense, fine tannins. This closed phase looks to last for some time before glimpses of perfectly ripe, red fruits are fully revealed.

★★★★ **Pinotage 13** displays fruity charm with freshness, vivacity & engaging length. As drinkable as it is now, there's substance & form for further four or five years.

★★★★ **Charisma 13** unusual blend home-grown shiraz, petit verdot & splash sangiovese, older oak matured. Rich in flavour, lighter, vibrant in feel. Cranberry, sour cherry tang suggests great partner with tomato-based dishes.

★★★★ **Janina Unwooded Chardonnay** Extraordinarily expressive for unoaked chardonnay, **14** has wealth of pickled lime intensity, citrus zest but also substance from lengthy lees-ageing. Intriguing, worthy maturation prospects, more so than **13** (★★★★). WO W Cape.

★★★★ **Sauvignon Blanc** Part-oaked **14** (★★★★☆) ex Elgin & Lutzville, less about obvious fruit, more textural statement, with gentle varietal liveliness. Versatile food partner. **13** richer, lingering. — AL

Location: Stellenbosch ▪ Map: Helderberg ▪ WO: Stellenbosch/Western Cape ▪ Est 1981 ▪ 1stB 1984 ▪ Tasting & sales Mon-Sat 9.30-4.30 (Sep-May)/10-4 (Jun-Aug) Sun 10-4 ▪ Fee R20/4 wines ▪ Closed Good Fri, Dec 25/26 & Jan 1 ▪ Cellar tours Mon-Fri 10 & 2.30 ▪ Cucina di Giovanni @ Eikendal T +27 (0)21-855-5033 Tue-Sat lunch & dinner Sun lunch only ▪ Facilities for children ▪ Tour groups ▪ Conferences ▪ Walks/hikes ▪ MTB trail ▪ Flywaters fly fishing ▪ Cheetah Outreach ▪ Eikendal Lodge ▪ Owner(s) Substantia AG ▪ Winemaker(s)/viticulturist(s) Nico Grobler (2007), with Christo Hanse & Willem van Kervel (both 2012) ▪ 78ha/±50ha (cabs s/f, malbec, merlot, p verdot, chard) ▪ 250t/70-80,000cs own label 70% red 30% white ▪ IPW ▪ PO Box

2261 Stellenbosch 7601 ▪ info@eikendal.co.za ▪ www.eikendal.com ▪ S 34° 0' 46.7" E 018° 49' 24.5" ▪ F +27 (0)21-855-1027 ▪ **T +27 (0)21-855-1422**

☐ **Eksteens' Family Vineyards** *see* Stone Ridge Wines

Elana Wine ⚲

Effervescent media personality Elana Afrika-Bredenkamp will remember harvest 2015 mostly for the birth of her first child. As a vigneron, she likes to be hands-on, so didn't bottle a follow-up of her '12 shiraz, crafted with D'Aria's Rudi von Waltsleben, but it is still available from her website.

Shiraz ⚲ ★★★☆ Stylish **12** rich & slightly smoky, intensely vanilla-sweet. Plush & rounded, red wine for the dessert course. — WB, CR

Location/WO: Durbanville ▪ Est 2012 ▪ 1stB 2013 ▪ Tasting by appt only ▪ Cellarmaster(s)/viticulturist(s) Elana Afrika-Bredenkamp (2012) ▪ Winemaker(s) Elana Afrika-Bredenkamp (2012), with Rudi von Waltsleben (D'Aria, 2012) ▪ 6ha ▪ 7t/200cs own label 100% red ▪ M13 Racecourse Road Durbanville 7550 ▪ elana@elanaafrika.com ▪ www.elanaafrika.com ▪ F +27 (0)21-439-1480 ▪ **T +27 (0)83-593-6329**

☐ **Elandsberg** *see* Viljoensdrift Fine Wines & Cruises

Elemental Bob

Craig Sheard ('Farmer Bob' to his brother), after a decade working for someone else, now makes this project his very fulltime job ('I do it all!'), vinifying his bought-in grapes in rented space alongside the Alheits on the Hemel-en-Aarde Ridge. His devotion to interesting blends and 'natural' winemaking remains intense, but production and focus on brand identity are both increasing.

Location: Somerset West ▪ Est/1stB 2004 ▪ Closed to public ▪ Owner(s)/winemaker(s) Craig Sheard ▪ 1,200cs own label 40% red 60% white ▪ elementalbob@gmail.com ▪ www.elementalbob.co.za ▪ **T +27 (0)82-265-1071**

☐ **Elements** *see* Hartswater Wine Cellar

Elgin Heights ⚲ 📷

The shiraz, chardonnay, sauvignon blanc and MCC bubbly vinified by contracted winemakers from the Joubert family's Elgin farm, Smarag, missed our cut-off date but, when in stock, are available for tasting and sale by appointment at the Jouberts' Stellenbosch property, Rozendal.

Location/map: Stellenbosch ▪ Map grid reference: C6 ▪ WO: Elgin ▪ 1stB 2007 ▪ Tasting & sales by appt ▪ Conference facilities ▪ Owner(s) Ryk Joubert ▪ Winemaker(s) Andries Burger, Kobie Viljoen & Corné Marais (sauv/shiraz/MCC, consultants) ▪ Viticulturist(s) DD Joubert ▪ 111ha/70ha (cab, merlot, shiraz, chard, sauv, viog) ▪ PO Box 52 Vlottenburg 7604 ▪ mwddj@mweb.co.za ▪ www.elginheights.co.za ▪ S 33° 57' 2.60'' E 018° 45' 28.91" ▪ F +27 (0)86-648-1704 ▪ **T +27 (0)84-517-9300**

Elgin Ridge ⚲ 🍴 🛍 📷

Brian (in the cellar) and Marion (in the vineyards) Smith are now practising biodynamics on their former Elgin apple farm, long since certified organic. In fact it's recently doubled in size, giving more space to their large herd of Dexter cattle (useful for biodynamic preparation 500), and ploughing, trailer-pulling Percheron, Maddox. More pinot's been planted too. A maiden '11 rosé MCC bubbly is due this year.

★★★★ **282 Sauvignon Blanc** ⚲ **14**'s passionfruit, fig & lemon lead to lively mouthful balancing crunchy acidity & succulent fruit. Natural ferment, 9 months on lees & dash semillon for weight & texture.

282 Pinot Noir ⚲ ★★★☆ Rare certified-organic pinot noir; native-fermented **13** is earthy, with macerated berry flavours, sparingly oaked (only 20% new); slight glow from 14% alcohol. — JPf

Location/WO: Elgin ▪ Map: Elgin, Walker Bay & Bot River ▪ Est 2007 ▪ 1stB 2009 ▪ Tasting, sales & tours by appt Mon-Fri 10-4 Sat/Sun/pub hols by appt only ▪ Food & wine pairing during Elgin Open Gardens weekends 10-4 ▪ Farm produce ▪ BYO picnic ▪ Owner(s) Brian & Marion Smith ▪ Winemaker(s) Brian Smith ▪ Viticulturist(s) Kevin Watt (Apr 2007, consultant), with Marion Smith ▪ 20.2ha/5ha (pinot, chard, sauv, sem) ▪ 35t/3,000cs own label 20% red 80% white ▪ Organic certification ▪ PO Box 143 Elgin 7180 ▪ info@elginridge.com ▪ www.elginridge.com ▪ S 34° 12' 10.68" E 019° 0' 14.34" ▪ F +27 (0)21-846-8060 ▪ **T +27 (0)21-846-8060**

Elgin Vintners   ⓠ ⌂ ◉

Six Elgin Valley growers, versed in fruit but mostly new to winegrowing when entering the market over a decade ago, pooled their resources and corralled leading specialists in specific varieties and styles to vinify their grapes under a shared brand name. Encouraged by critical and commercial success, they've since partnered on a tasting venue with set hours (on member farm Elgin Orchards), country accommodation and a variety of outdoor activities and currently are collaborating on a new website.

★★★★☆ **Cabernet Sauvignon** ⊘ Elegant **09** raises the bar hugely on **08** (★★★). Classic dark fruit & leafy/herbaceous nuance, tightly bound in chalky dry tannin framework; fresh & elegant. Youthful, one for the cellar, with excellent potential.

★★★★ **Merlot 11** with a splash of malbec, trumps **10** (★★★☆). Refined & fresh, with subtle berry & leafy nuance. Clean dry tannins in supple support. Very young, has life & structure to reward cellaring.

★★★★☆ **Pinot Noir 12** now unfurling beautifully after 36 months in bottle, was very tight when sampled last year. Appealing earthy red berry flavours & piquantly fresh balance; 22% new oak well integrated. Will continue to improve for many years. Big leap ahead from savoury **11** (★★★★).

★★★★ **Syrah** Was 'Shiraz'. **10** (★★★) swaggeringly ripe (15.5 % alcohol) & dense, with viscous texture; oaking adds further spice. Demands robust fare. A style change from gentler & more balanced **09**.

★★★★ **Agama** ⓠ Savoury blend of cab, merlot & malbec (74/14/12) from 4 farms. **09** starting to reveal charm after 26 months in oak (25% new). Classically styled, with dense fruit core & supple tannins. Ageworthy, whereas **08** (★★★★) wasn't for keeping.

★★★★ **Chardonnay** ⓠ **12** less overt fruit richness than **11** (★★★★☆) & tad oaky mid-2014. Still has lovely core of tangy dried peach & lime. Shows cooler provenance & elegant styling, just needs time.

★★★★ **The Century** Very understated, food-friendly unwooded styling on **13** sauvignon/semillon (60/40) blend. Genteel beeswax & clean lemony tone; fresher than **12** (★★★☆), allow time to evolve into rating. Honours Elgin's centenarian Douglas Moodie.

Also tasted: **Sauvignon Blanc 15** ★★★☆ **Viognier 12** ★★★★ Not retasted: **Merlot Rosé 14** ★★★ — MW

Location/WO: Elgin ▪ Map: Elgin, Walker Bay & Bot River ▪ Est 2003 ▪ 1stB 2004 ▪ Tasting & sales Wed-Sun 10-4 ▪ Function facility ▪ MTB route ▪ Fynbos walks ▪ Fishing ▪ Birding ▪ Vineyard tours ▪ Homestead to rent for getaway weekends ▪ Owner(s) Derek Corder, Max Hahn, Alastair Moodie, James Rawbone-Viljoen, Rob Semple & Paul Wallace ▪ Cellarmaster(s)/winemaker(s) Various (Kevin Grant, Gavin Patterson, Nico Grobler, Martin Meinert, Niels Verburg, Joris van Almenkerk) ▪ Viticulturist(s) Paul Wallace ▪ ±75ha (cab, malbec, merlot, pinot, shiraz, chard, riesling, sauv, sem, viog) ▪ 750t/14,500cs own label ▪ BWI, IPW ▪ PO Box 121 Elgin 7180 ▪ info@elginvintners.co.za ▪ www.elginvintners.co.za ▪ S 34°10'52.18" E 019° 0'42.54" ▪ F +27 (0)86-646-3693 ▪ **T +27 (0)21-848-9587**

Elsenburg Agricultural Training Institute   ⓠ

Located on a 17th-century Stellenbosch winefarm, a government agricultural school since 1898 and seat of practical training for the Elsenburg Cellar Technology qualification as well as Stellenbosch University's Viticulture & Oenology degree, the Institute produces most of SA's modern-era winemakers and viticulturists. The wines and brandy listed below were made by final year students under guidance of resident winemaker Lorraine Geldenhuys.

Elsenburg range
★★★★ **Muscat d'Frontignan** ⓠ Bright, golden unfortified **13** oozing grape, orange marmalade & cinnamon aromas. Smooth, light-footed & bright, with deep intense flavour & vibrant citrus lift to end.

Cinsaut ⓠ ★★★☆ Unoaked **13** shows earthy black fruit on the nose, soft & easy flavours. Not retasted: **Sauvignon Blanc 13** ★★★☆ **Viognier 13** ★★★★ **Cape Vintage 11** ★★★★

Brandy range

★★★★☆ **Potstill 13 Years** (Ⓩ) From colombard, fragrant apricot, cashew & warm spice on the nose. Rich & smooth, with bright fruit flavours, hints of fresh apple & a long mellow taste in the mouth – harmonious, with great finesse. Attractive modern packaging. 500 ml. — WB

Location/map/WO: Stellenbosch ▪ Map grid reference: E2 ▪ Est 1976 ▪ Visits by appt ▪ Owner(s) Western Cape Government, Department of Agriculture ▪ Winemaker(s) Lorraine Geldenhuys (Jan 2013) ▪ 40ha (cinsaut, tinta barocca, cbard, muscadel, sauv, viog) ▪ 178t/1,363cs own label 65% red 35% white ▪ IPW ▪ Private Bag X1 Elsenburg, Muldersvlei 7607 ▪ lorraineg@elsenburg.com ▪ www.elsenburg.com ▪ S 33° 50' 40.87" E 018° 50' 12.28" ▪ F +27 (0)21-808-5484 ▪ **T +27 (0)21-808-5483**

☐ **Embrace** see Stellenrust
☐ **Emineo** see Rogge Cloof

Enfin Wines (Ⓠ) (NEW)

Susan van Aswegen, legal practitioner and member of the Garagiste Movement, doesn't actually say but we're guessing that the French name of her brand – 'Finally!' – alludes to a long-held dream to see her own wine in a bottle. Inspired by poodles Alice and Sebastian for the delightful front label, Elim for the cool-climate grapes and the ever more pervasive 'natural' winemaking movement to intervene as little as possible, she now has her sights set on a pinot noir, wooded sauvignon and MCC sparkling.

The Romanian Syrah ★★★☆ Molten plums, vanilla & coffee spice from Romanian oak, nuances of violets. **14** plush & velvety texture, full & round, best enjoyed young – no hardship! — CR, CvZ

Location: Cape Town ▪ WO: Elim ▪ Est/1stB 2014 ▪ Tasting by appt ▪ Owner(s)/winemaker(s) Susan van Aswegen ▪ 6t 90% red 10% white ▪ 28 Visvanger Road Melkbosstrand 7441 ▪ info@enfinwines.co.za ▪ www.enfinwines.co.za ▪ **T +27 (0)83-310-1679**

☐ **Engel** see Orange River Cellars
☐ **Enigma** see Zorgvliet Wines
☐ **Enon** see Zandvliet Wine Estate

Entre Nous (Ⓠ) (⌂)

'We're expecting a fabulous cabernet from the 2015 harvest; watch this space!' says Terry Winstanley, one of five friends who 'between us' (hence the brand name) make wine in Stellenbosch's Banhoek Valley from bought-in grapes. The three lawyers, quantity surveyor and wine barrel expert 'love the exciting mix of art, science and magic'.

Cabernet Sauvignon ★★☆ Tart sweet/sour plums & leafy tone to leaner **12**, feisty structure & dry tannins, better in a few years or with a meal. **Starboard** (NEW) ★★ Wittily named 'port', though **12** deviates from the template in both variety (shiraz) & style (overtly sweet & spicy, with still over-fiery spirit). Allow time to fully knit. Not retasted: **Chardonnay 12** ★★★★ Discontinued: **8:2:3**. — MW

Location/map: Stellenbosch ▪ Map grid reference: H5 ▪ WO: Stellenbosch/Western Cape ▪ Est/1stB 2000 ▪ Tasting, sales & cellar tours by appt ▪ BYO picnic ▪ Owner(s) Geoff Brooker, Mark Howell, Steve Kirk-Cohen, Andre Smalberger & Terry Winstanley ▪ Cellarmaster(s)/winemaker(s) Steve Kirk-Cohen, Andre Smalberger & Terry Winstanley (2000), Mark Howell & Geoff Brooker (2005) ▪ ±1,176cs own label 85% red 15% white ▪ c/o Terry Winstanley PO Box 695 Cape Town 8000 ▪ terry.winstanley@dlacdh.com ▪ S 33° 55' 25.96" E 018° 57' 03.12" ▪ F +27 (0)21-481-9516 ▪ **T +27 (0)21-481-6332**

Epicurean Wines

Just one, appropriately luxurious, wine is produced under this label, in the cellars of Rupert & Rothschild with input from the four socially and economically eminent winelovers behind the venture: Ron Gault, Mutle Mogase, Moss Ngoasheng and Mbhazima Shilowa. The name comes from Epicurus, the philosopher who understood pleasure as the measure of what is good.

★★★★ **Epicurean** ⓥ **10** (★★★★☆) expertly blends merlot with cab, cab franc & a dab petit verdot. Firmly built, but eschews power in favour of gently rich, bright-fruited elegance & suavity. Easily absorbs all-new oak. Modern, but not too fruity, with savoury vinosity. Will develop. **08** lighter; no **09**. — TJ

WO: Western Cape ▪ Est 2001 ▪ 1stB 2003 ▪ Closed to public ▪ Owner(s) Global Pact Trading 125 (Pty) Ltd ▪ Cellarmaster(s) Mutle Mogase, Mbhazima Shilowa, Moss Ngoasheng, Ron Gault (Nov 2002) ▪ Winemaker(s) Schalk Willem Joubert (consultant) ▪ 1,000cs own label 100% red ▪ WIETA ▪ PO Box 280 Parklands Johannesburg 2121 ▪ info@epicureanwine.co.za ▪ www.epicureanwine.co.za ▪ F +27 (0)11-530-9101 ▪ **T +27 (0)11-530-9100**

Equitania ⓥ 🍞 📷

Equitania in the Helderberg is the dream home of Esme Kruger de Beer, with a garden designed by a feng shui master. And a tiny vineyard, its crop vinified at Stellenbosch Hills since debut '08. Soon-to-be-bottled '12 is especially exciting, Esme says, as it's the first to be extra-long-aged (3 years) in oak.

★★★★ **Flag** ⓥ Classic Bordeaux-style aromas of berries & lead pencil on pleasingly restrained **12** (★★★★☆) preview. Like **10**, from cab, cab franc. Savoury & balanced; modestly oaked. No **11**.

Not tasted: **Fluke**. — TJ

Location/WO: Stellenbosch ▪ Map: Helderberg ▪ Est 2000 ▪ 1stB 2008 ▪ Tasting & sales by appt ▪ Fee R10 ▪ Closed all pub hols ▪ BYO picnic ▪ Walking/hiking trails ▪ Owner(s) Esme Kruger de Beer ▪ Winemaker(s) PG Slabbert (Stellenbosch Hills) ▪ Viticulturist(s) Gavin Dun (May 2007) ▪ 4.65ha/1.38ha (cabs s/f) ▪ 10.54t/12,000cs own label 100% red ▪ PO Box 5308 Helderberg 7135 ▪ esme14@mweb.co.za ▪ www.equitania.co.za ▪ S 34° 2' 26.15" E 018° 49' 5.51" ▪ F +27 (0)21-300-1092 ▪ **T +27 (0)21-300-1140/1**

☐ **Erasmus Wines** *see* Cape Wine Company

Ernie Els Wines ⓥ 🍴 📷 ♿

Golfing legend Ernie Els launched his venture into the wine world under the guidance of long-time friend Jean Engelbrecht (Rust en Vrede) in 1999, with his controversially priced Signature red Bordeaux-style blend. Soon after, parcels of vineyard assembled from various neighbouring farms were consolidated into the present showpiece estate. Local architects 2AD Space were commissioned to design the gracious, understated cellar on the northern Helderberg slopes, and Ernie Els Wines had a home. Initially aimed at the elite golfing export markets, newer ranges are bringing the brand back home and into more affordable price brackets. CWG member and cellarmaster from the outset, Louis Strydom, has maintained a strong emphasis on cabernet sauvignon and has begun a programme of clonal plantings to broaden his creative palette.

Ernie Els range

★★★★ **Cabernet Sauvignon** Well-focused, concentrated blackcurrant fruit on **13** albeit rather less nuanced than **12** (★★★★★). Showy, extroverted, but needs time to settle chalky tannins.

★★★★☆ **Proprietor's Cabernet Sauvignon** Powerhouse, massive **13** tightly concentrated, black hearted & robustly textured, but precise & focused, ticking all the boxes. Made for the long haul, should be more accessible after a few years' cellaring.

★★★★ **Proprietor's Syrah** Dense, intimidating, muscle-bound **13** still tightly woven & tough. Ripe black fruit glimpses through inky black mantle. May relent with several years in cellar.

★★★★☆ **Ernie Els Signature** Since its audacious launch in **00**, this flagship label has grabbed public attention, not least for its unprecedented (at the time) pricing. Beautifully crafted **12** 5-way Bordeaux blend maintains lofty standard, with power & subtlety in perfect balance.

★★★★★ **CWG Auction Reserve** Another lovingly crafted cab-shiraz-merlot blend, **13** is already plush & supple, with exuberant sweet berry fruit, belying massive density & muscular tannic undercarriage. Totally delicious, but showing nobility & class. Will reward cellaring.

★★★★ **Proprietor's Blend** Imposing 4-way Bordeaux blend plus shiraz, is inky black & dense, with aromatic liquorice & blackcurrant fruit. **13** (★★★★★) has power with subtlety, showing delicate rose-petal notes underlying robust, 'masculine' attitude. Up on **12**.

Also tasted: **Merlot 13 ★★★☆ Sauvignon Blanc 15 ★★★☆**

Big Easy range

★★★★ Red 6-way Rhône-style blend with cab, **14** is brawny & bold, packed with cherry/plum fruit, robust tannins & spicy herbaceousness. Appealing floral-scented notes, lengthy finish. Stellenbosch & Wellington grapes. Also in 3 & 5L.

Rosé ★★★ Dry, light, freshly fruity **15** from shiraz. Also tasted: **White 15 ★★★☆** — GdB

Location/map: Stellenbosch ▪ Map grid reference: F8 ▪ WO: Stellenbosch/Western Cape ▪ Est 1999 ▪ 1stB 2000 ▪ Tasting, sales & cellar tours Mon-Sat 9–5 ▪ Player's tasting R40/Major's tasting R60 (4 wines each) ▪ Closed Easter Fri/Sun, Dec 25 & Jan 1 ▪ Light lunches & cheese platters Tue-Sat ▪ Tour groups ▪ Gift shop ▪ Corporate events & functions ▪ Small conferences ▪ MTB trail ▪ Ernie Els' Trophy Room ▪ The Big Easy Restaurant at 95 Dorp Str ▪ Owner(s) Ernie Els ▪ Cellarmaster(s) Louis Strydom (Dec 1999) ▪ Winemaker(s) Louis Strydom (Dec 1999), with Danie van Tonder (2013) ▪ Viticulturist(s) Leander Koekemoer (2015) ▪ 72ha/45ha (cab, merlot, shiraz) ▪ 250t/18,000cs own label 90% red 10% white + 1,500cs for clients ▪ Brands for clients: SA Rugby ▪ PO Box 7595 Stellenbosch 7599 ▪ info@ernieelswines.com ▪ www.ernieelswines.com ▪ S 34° 0' 52.8" E 018° 50' 53.5" ▪ F +27 (0)21-881-3688 ▪ **T +27 (0)21-881-3588**

Ernst Gouws & Co Wines

Members of the Gouws family have been active in the Stellenbosch wine business for more than 150 years. Koelenhof-based Ernst and wife Gwenda are the current driving force, next-generation siblings Ezanne and Ernst jnr, both graduate winemakers from Stellenbosch University, 'slowly taking over'. A new bottle label, symbolising family cohesion in striking copper hues, is debuting to mark the transition.

★★★★☆ Nineteenfiftytwo Star of the line-up. Impressive body & complexity on **14** (**★★★★**), but not quite up to previous **11**. Sauvignon-semillon blend, partly barrel matured. Deftly handled oak lifts without dominating, lees-ageing adds fatness.

Shiraz ★★★★ Interestingly complex wild scrub/spicy nose on **13**, with full, almost chewy tannins & ripe black cherries. **Sauvignon Blanc ★★★** Pleasantly quaffable **15** showing juicy green apple flavours. Totally dry, but some fruit sweetness adds to the friendliness. Also tasted: **Chardonnay 14 ★★★★** Not retasted: **Merlot 12 ★★★★ Pinot Noir 12 ★★★ Pinotage 13 ★★★★** — GdB

Location/map: Stellenbosch ▪ Map grid reference: D1 ▪ WO: Stellenbosch/Coastal/Bot River ▪ Est/1stB 2003 ▪ Tasting & sales at Koelenhof Winery Mon-Thu 9-5 Fri 9-4 Sat 10-2 ▪ Fee R15pp ▪ Closed Easter Fri/Sun, Ascension day, Dec 25/26 & Jan 1 ▪ Facilities for children ▪ Owner(s) Ernst & Gwenda Gouws ▪ Cellarmaster(s) Ernst Gouws ▪ Winemaker(s) Ernst Gouws snr ▪ 60,000cs own label 40% red 60% white ▪ Other export brand: New Gate ▪ IPW ▪ PO Box 7450 Stellenbosch 7599 ▪ ernst@ernstgouws.co.za ▪ www.ernstgouws.co.za ▪ S 33° 50' 3.4" E 018° 47' 52.7" ▪ F +27 (0)21-865-2894 ▪ **T +27 (0)21-865-2895**

Esau Wines

Former chemical engineer Wim Hugo describes his Paarl venture as a 'micro-winery' – small but not garagiste (in fact, he plans to double production in the medium term). Focus is on red blends, with occasional varietals. A maiden '15 tempranillo mix is due in 2018, and the '13 vintage is being released late.

Holy Cow 🍷 **★★★★** Plush black berries & plums in **12** shiraz-led Cape Blend, ripe & full bodied. **Château Esau** 🍷 **★★★★ 12** big, dense but appealing Rhône blend hangs together well, with savoury-tinged flavours of black cherries & smoky meat. Not retasted: **Moerwetter 12 ★★★ Non Pareille 12 ★★★** Not tasted: **Cabernet Sauvignon Reserve, Grenache Reserve**. — GdB

Location/WO: Paarl ▪ Map: Paarl & Wellington ▪ Map grid reference: E6 ▪ Est/1stB 2010 ▪ Private tastings on request ▪ Owner(s) Wim Hugo ▪ Cellarmaster(s) Wim Hugo (2009) ▪ Winemaker(s) Wim Hugo & Jorrie Jordaan (both 2009) ▪ 3t/2,500L 100% red ▪ PO Box 3175 Paarl 7620 ▪ wim.hugo@gmail.com ▪ www.esau-wines.com ▪ S 33° 45' 20.2" E 018° 57' 42.5" ▪ **T +27 (0)79-875-4646**

Escapades Winery 🍷

The brainchild of three Greek friends, two leading winemakers, Evangelos Gerovassiliou and Vassilis Tsaktsarlis, and vintner Takis Soldatos, Sweden-based connoisseur and marketer, who built that country's top wine distribution company. Though they take turns to visit, the local operation is run by Kiwi winemaker Chris Kelly, who sources older and higher-altitude vineyards to get the desired result, concentration and complexity. Semillon is a particular focus, with a reserve wine released this edition. While the range grows and quality remains high, the wines are still mainly exported.

★★★★ **Pinotage** With house-style plush dark fruit, cocoa-rich chocolate spicing, **14** draws you in but is no pushover. Supple tannins already give drinking pleasure, with the latent power to age well.

★★★★ **Semillon** Elegant & refined, with well defined varietal character, **15**'s partial oaking a subtle enhancement. Shows lime cordial & beeswax, summer meadow grasses, fresh extended length.

★★★★ **Semillon Grande Reserve** (NEW) Differs from its sibling in 100% oaking, but **15** has similar elegance, flavour intensity & polish. Lime & greengage, almonds, its fynbos & flinty notes proclaiming cool growing conditions.

★★★★ **Semillon-Sauvignon Blanc** Oaked semillon portion adds gentle oat biscuit savouriness to **15**'s flinty, green fig character. Layered & interesting, has a touch of fynbos, is lifted by a grated lime zest tone. WO W Cape.

Cabernet Sauvignon-Shiraz-Malbec ⊕ ★★★☆ A seductive array of aromas, fresh prunes, café au lait, nutmeg, **14** is determined to impress, the silky, succulent structure another part of it. Also in magnum.

Also tasted: **Pinotage Rosé 15** ★★★ **Sauvignon Blanc 15** ★★★☆ — CR

Location/map: Stellenbosch ▪ Map grid reference: B4 ▪ WO: Coastal/Western Cape ▪ Est/1stB 2006 ▪ Tasting by appt ▪ Owner(s) Evangelos Gerovassiliou, Vassilis Tsaktsarlis & Takis Soldatos ▪ Cellarmaster(s) Vassilis Tsaktsarlis & Evangelos Gerovassiliou (both 2006) ▪ Winemaker(s) Chris Kelly (Oct 2010, consultant) ▪ (cab, malbec, ptage, shiraz, sauv, sem) ▪ 100t/10,000cs own label 40% red 50% white 10% rosé ▪ PO Box 99 Somerset Mall 7129 ▪ info@escapadewinery.com ▪ www.escapadewinery.com ▪ S 33° 54' 47.7" E 018° 44' 7.7" ▪ F +27 (0)86-585-6549 ▪ **T +27 (0)82-569-3371**

☐ **Eskdale** see De Zoete Inval Estate
☐ **Es La Vida** see Vinopoly Wines

Esona Boutique Wine   ⓠ 🍴

The Beattie family farm in Robertson offers visitors an intimate setting in a restored 90-year-old riverside cellar to enjoy limited-release, single-vineyard wines (currently sauvignon, blanc de noir, chardonnay and shiraz). Casual tastings are upstairs on a deck overlooking valley and mountains; pre-booked comparative vintage tastings paired with regional delights from Esona's deli are downstairs by candelight.

Location/map: Robertson ▪ Est 2002 ▪ 1stB 2010 ▪ Tasting & sales Mon-Fri 9-5 Sat 10-4 ▪ Closed Dec 25 & Jan 1 ▪ Std tasting; Taste-the-Difference tasting (2 vintages/3 cultivars); fruit preserve/chocolate/ music & wine pairing ±55 min, essential to book ▪ Taste-of-Africa meals (min 18 pax) by request ▪ Deli ▪ Owner(s) Rowan & Caryl Beattie ▪ Winemaker(s)/viticulturist(s) Lourens van der Westhuizen (Jan 2010, Arendsig) ▪ 17ha/9.83ha (pinot, shiraz, chard, chenin, cbard, sauv) ▪ ±250t/6,000cs own label 34% red 66% white ▪ PO Box 2619 Clareinch 7400 ▪ info@esona.co.za ▪ www.esona.co.za ▪ S 33° 54' 16.14" E 020° 0' 38.66" ▪ F +27 (0)21-787-3792 ▪ **T +27 (0)76-343-5833**

☐ **Essay** see MAN Family Wines
☐ **Eternal** see Kumala

Euphoria   ⓠ (NEW)

Chandré Petersen was a recipient of a Cape Winemakers Guild Protégé Programme award. She made her pinot noir from Ceres Plateau grapes while working at De Grendel in Durbanville under the mentorship of her guild colleagues. The wine was sold at charity dinners to raise funds for the programme.

★★★★☆ **Pinot Noir** Sleek **13** shows exceptional purity of fruit — cherries & raspberries melded with dark earth & judicious new oak (33%). Seamless & delicious now but with depth for cellaring. — WB, CvZ

WO: Ceres Plateau ▪ Est 2013 ▪ 1stB 2014 ▪ Tasting by appt ▪ Owner(s)/winemaker(s) Chandré Petersen ▪ 35cs own label 100% red ▪ chandrep25@gmail.com ▪ **T +27 (0)61-077-2512**

Excelsior Estate

(Y) (ΨΨ) (⌂) (⌂) (◎) (⊗)

This handsome property is owned by Freddie de Wet and son Peter, scions of a clan deeply rooted in the Robertson/Bonnievale area. Knowledge of the land has them utilise its lime-rich soils for quality wines and champion racehorses, celebrated on the labels of some of the premium bottlings. Affinity for people finds expression through support of a farm crèche, funding for a local school and a warm welcome for overnight guests and day visitors.

Excelsior Reserve range

★★★★ **Evanthuis Cabernet Sauvignon** Off farm's oldest vines, homage to champion Hackney horse imported in 1913. Fruitcake & cassis richness yet still streamlined, **13** already has palate appeal, plus good oak foundation for cellaring.

San Louis Shiraz ⊛ ★★★☆ Recognises never-say-die Guineas winner. Glossy fruit in **13**, the practice of using various barrels translates into cigarbox spicing, supple tannins. As sleek as its namesake.

Also tasted: **Gondolier Merlot 13** ★★★☆ Not retasted: **Agricola Sauvignon Blanc 12** ★★★☆

Excelsior Estate range

Sauvignon Blanc ⊛ ★★★ Passionfruit & litchi, **15** exuberantly fruity, sparks with youthful freshness.

Cabernet Sauvignon ★★★ Meaty plums & dried herbs, **13** shows nice layers & a succulent, curvaceous body for early enjoyment. **Merlot** ★★★ Loads of fruit in **14**, plush cherries & blackcurrants, making this a delicious drinking experience. Oak a hidden support. **Viognier** ★★★ Floral & peach notes in **15**, the touch of sweetness plumping the body. Nice freshness though, making it tasty & easy. Also tasted: **Paddock Shiraz 13** ★★★ **Purebred Red 14** ★★★ **Chardonnay 15** ★★★ Occasional release: **Caitlyn Rosé**. — CR

Location/map/WO: Robertson ▪ Est 1859 ▪ 1stB 1990 ▪ Tasting & sales Mon-Fri 10-4 Sat 10-3 ▪ Deli serving light lunches ▪ Picnics available on request, or BYO picnic ▪ Facilities for children ▪ Conferences ▪ 4-star Excelsior Manor Guest House ▪ Owner(s) Freddie de Wet ▪ Cellarmaster(s) Johan Stemmet (Aug 2003) ▪ Winemaker(s) Johan Stemmet (Aug 2003), with Kelly Gova (2005) ▪ Viticulturist(s) Freddie de Wet (1970) ▪ 320ha/220ha (cab, merlot, p verdot, shiraz, chard, sauv) ▪ 2,200t/320,000cs own label 75% red 25% white ▪ Other export brand: Stablemate ▪ BRC ▪ PO Box 17 Ashton 6715 ▪ info@excelsior.co.za ▪ www.excelsior.co.za ▪ S 33° 51' 15.1" E 020° 0' 25.6" ▪ F +27 (0)23-615-2019 ▪ **T +27 (0)23-615-1980**

Excelsior Vlakteplaas

(Y)

A bulk wine specialist based near De Rust in Klein Karoo, Danie Schoeman bottles only two wines – both fortified muscats – under his own label, and, interestingly, to date has opted to do so only in even years.

His Master's Choice range

Red Muscadel ⊘ ★★★★ Honey & blossoms on **12** raisin-sweet fortified charmer, just enough acid & tannic grip to prevent it being cloying. Not retasted: **White Muscadel 12** ★★★ — DB

Location: De Rust ▪ Map: Klein Karoo & Garden Route ▪ WO: Klein Karoo ▪ Est 1934 ▪ 1stB 1998 ▪ Tasting & sales by appt only ▪ Closed Easter Fri-Mon, Ascension Day, Dec 16/25/26 & Jan 1 ▪ Owner(s)/winemaker(s) Danie Schoeman ▪ 41ha (merlot, ptage, ruby cab, chenin, muscadel r/w) ▪ 490t/2,000cs own label 50% red 50% white ▪ PO Box 112 De Rust 6650 ▪ jjschoeman@telkomsa.net ▪ S 33° 29' 16.74" E 022° 35' 25.50" ▪ F +27 (0)44-241-2569 ▪ **T +27 (0)82-821-3556**

Fable Mountain Vineyards

(Y) (◎)

This isolated farm, straddling the Witzenberg Mountain slopes between Tulbagh and Wolseley, is part of Charles Banks' more populous and worldwide Terroir Selections portfolio. The biodynamically farmed property itself is well-populated, too: the winegrowing duo of Rebecca Tanner, Paul Nicholls and their family are joined by horses, chickens, pigs (destined for cured meat) and varied wildlife. The latest introductions, Nguni cattle, are being trained to plough the vineyards. 'It's nice to use indigenous animals,' Rebecca reasons; 'Nguni are tough as nails and require very little maintenance.' Also tough is a home-designed under-vine plough that copes with the rocky soils. The wines, including a new, serious rosé, continue to show the quality that comes from meticulous attention from vineyard to bottle.

★★★★★ **Syrah** Beguilingly scented, **13**'s (★★★★★) charms continue with its refined silky texture, freshness & fine ripe tannins. Despite overall sense of delicacy, there's great depth to the still primary spice, cured meat & bright red fruits; depth which deserves time to be revealed. Follows masterly **12**.

★★★★☆ **Night Sky** Subtle & refined, **13** offers layers of flavour – dark spice, florals & many more among its shiraz, grenache, mourvèdre components – in its fresh, precise form. Beautifully polished, it gives much pleasure now, especially decanted; yet a tightness suggests rewards of cellaring. Coastal WO.

★★★★ **Belle Flower** (NEW) Dry rosé from Swartland grenache, syrah & mourvèdre **14**, charms with its purity & vivacity. As in whole range, texture important element; here, weight, rounded firmness, from year on lees in concrete 'egg', lend extra dimension & enhance overall drinking pleasure.

★★★★☆ **Jackal Bird** **14** shows delicate vitality & purity, youthful harmony in the intricate weave of its chenin, grenache, roussanne, chardonnay & viognier make-up. Satiny texture, concluding pithy grip add dimension. Natural ferment in oak (15% new), concrete 'eggs'. WO W Cape. — AL

Location/map: Tulbagh ▪ WO: Tulbagh/Coastal/Western Cape/Swartland ▪ Est 1989 ▪ 1stB 2009 ▪ Tasting & cellar tours by appt only ▪ Conservation area ▪ Owner(s) Terroir Selections ▪ Winegrowers Rebecca Tanner & Paul Nicholls (both Jul 2009) ▪ 185ha/30ha (grenache, mourv, syrah, viog) ▪ PO Box 12817 Die Boord 7613 ▪ rebecca@fablewines.com ▪ www.fablewines.com ▪ S 33° 21' 7.9" E 019° 12' 46.1" ▪ **T +27 (0)78-315-3861/+27 (0)73-768-1600**

☐ **Fairhills** see Origin Wine
☐ **Fair Karoo** see Rogge Cloof
☐ **Fair Selection** see Nederburg Wines
☐ **Fairtrade Original** see uniWines Vineyards

Fairvalley Wines ⓥ

Fairvalley's slogan says it all: 'The hands that work the soil feed the soul.' One of SA's original employee empowerment ventures, wholly owned by 42 families at Fairview, Fairvalley ensures no compromise on standards in producing wines from Fairtrade-certified vineyards mostly in the Citrusdal area.

Sauvignon Blanc ⊘ ⓣ ★★★★ **15** preview drier than floral, peachy nose suggests; crisp & zesty, with lime & grapefruit intensity mellowing into sweeter citrus finish.

Pinotage ⊘ ★★★☆ Smooth **14** a deft step up on also-tasted raspberry bomb **13** (★★★), with dark cherry as well as hints of smoke, coffee & vanilla spice adding interest. Also tasted: **Cabernet Sauvignon 14** ★★★ **Chardonnay 14** ★★★ **Chenin Blanc 15** ★★★ — JG

Location: Paarl ▪ WO: Western Cape ▪ Est 1997 ▪ 1stB 1998 ▪ Tasting by appt only ▪ Fee R25 ▪ Closed Good Fri, Dec 25 & Jan 1 ▪ Sales at Fairview (see entry) ▪ Owner(s) Fairvalley Farmworkers Association ▪ Cellarmaster(s) Jaco Brand (2010) ▪ Winemaker(s) Jaco Brand, with Andries de Klerk (both 2010) ▪ 30,000cs own label 50% red 50% white ▪ Fairtrade ▪ PO Box 6219 Paarl 7620 ▪ wine@fairvalley.co.za ▪ www.fairvalley.co.za ▪ F +27 (0)21-863-2591 ▪ **T +27 (0)21-863-2450**

Fairview ⓥ ⓟ ⓒ ⓓ

This Paarl powerhouse was once rather inauspiciously known as Bloemkoolfontein ('Cauliflower Fountain') and the farm had a chequered past, forming part of eight insolvent estates – a habit current owner/vintner Charles Back says he is doing his best to break. Humour permeates everywhere at Fairview, whose labels now include separately listed Spice Route and Goats Do Roam and export-only, untasted Leeuwenjacht, previously Seidelberg. The old Seidelberg cellar has been incorporated into a new, extended Fairview cellar, where winemaker Adele Dunbar says the team is enjoying the extra equipment and tank space, not to mention having 'everything under one roof'. Colleague Anthony de Jager celebrates his 20th vintage here this year, which sees special wines reclassified under the Winemakers Selection.

Winemaker's Selections

★★★★ Caldera Wild strawberries galore on smooth, medium-bodied **13** (★★★★★), better balanced than **12**, now boasting slightly more grenache (48%) while shiraz & mourvèdre add pepper as well as lavender & heather nuances. Coastal WO.

★★★★ Extraño ⊘ Nudging higher rating, Rioja-like **12** blend of tempranillo with grenache & carignan tastes like choc-dipped, cinnamon-sprinkled berries, juicy & lively. Coastal WO.

★★★★☆ Homtini Formerly the name of Anthony de Jager's own shiraz, now a Supertuscan-style blend of sangiovese with cab, shiraz & merlot, **14**'s name ('Difficult Passage') does not refer to its drinkability: smooth, medium bodied, delicious. Coastal WO.

★★★★☆ Nurok White Blend Impressive **14**'s pear, peach & citrus flavours linger after each sip, viognier's heady perfume toned down as chenin resumes domination (43%) with roussanne adding savoury spice, grenache blanc bringing freshness & minerality.

★★★★ Méthode Cap Classique Brut Unusual MCC sparkling from jasmine-scented viognier (71%) with grenaches blanc & noir, **13** is like Appletiser for grown-ups, crisp & frothy, refreshingly dry.

★★★★☆ La Beryl Blanc Decadently golden rather than 'blanc', air-dried, unwooded **14** tones down rosepetal fragrance of muscat de Frontignan (15%) as chenin leads with tangy apricot & spiced candied oranges, unctuous sweetness balanced by fresh acidity.

Limited Releases

★★★★ Pegleg Carignan There's nothing off-kilter about deliciously rustic **12**, jammed with red berries & cherries, & nicely balanced with dusty tannins & lively acidity. **11** (★★★★) also from Swartland.

★★★★☆ Primo Pinotage **13** (★★★★) seems less powerful than **12**, nonetheless smooth & elegant with lavender, spice & smoke as well as red berry flavours, a slightly medicinal note on the finish.

★★★★☆ Cyril Back Dapper tribute to Charles Back's father, **13** so delicate considering its 26 months in new French oak, adding mere hints of dark chocolate & spice to black cherries, powerful in the ballet sense of powerful. Agter Paarl & Swartland grapes.

★★★★☆ Eenzaamheid Shiraz The first of three 'vineyard' shirazes, **13** from Paarl is all about texture, in this case rich & velvety, with cocoa-dusted blueberries & blackcurrants on nose, palate & finish, seamlessly integrated.

★★★★☆ Jakkalsfontein Shiraz Less weighty than its single vineyard siblings, medium-bodied **13** charms with lifted floral perfume notes, almost incense-like, as well as with fresh, lively mulberry fruit. A very pretty wine. WO Swartland.

★★★★☆ The Beacon Shiraz This Swartland vineyard is primarily about spice, **13** redolent of mixed spice as well as savoury coriander & black pepper, not to mention hints of leather, smoke & tobacco, all seasoning ripe black plum fruit.

★★★★ Oom Pagel Semillon From Darling bushvines, partly barrel fermented, **14** has citrus zest & pear intensity but mostly it's about rich texture, like creamy vanilla custard poured over spiced baked citrus. **13** sold out untasted. **12** was exceptional (★★★★★).

Fairview range

★★★★ Stellenbosch Cabernet Sauvignon Was 'Cabernet Sauvignon'. Poised **13** back on form after unfocused **12** (★★★★), dark plums & black berries, hint of cigarbox oak spice. Also in magnum.

★★★★ Barbera Piercing raspberry nose on **14**, red as well as dark berries coming to the fore on palate; smooth, with high natural acidity accentuating cinnamon spice. Coastal WO, as was **13** (★★★★☆).

★★★★ Mourvèdre Quite a savoury number, **14** characterised by black olive as well as black berry notes, smooth with leather & clove on the finish. Coastal WO.

★★★★☆ Petite Sirah ⊘ Nothing petite about inky **13**, again boldly impressing with luscious black cherries, liquorice & pinch of dried herbs, big & bold yet freshly balanced, with texture like velvet rubbed the wrong way that will soften over time.

★★★★ Pinotage Vibrantly youthful **14** shows more promise than **13** (★★★☆), floral fynbos aroma leading to mouthfuls of sweet dark plums, gritty but integrated tannins & pleasingly dry finish.

★★★★ Shiraz Lovely purity of red fruit on **13**, – redcurrants, raspberries, cranberries, ripe red plums on palate, rich & smooth, seamlessly integrated, with pinch of white pepper. Improves on **12** (★★★★☆).

★★★★ **Roussanne** Preview of **15** 'white Rhône grape' has subtly fragrant peach & mallow nose, more savoury than sweet on lees/oak-textured palate, fresh & crisp with ruby grapefruit finish. Fairview grapes. Rung up on maiden **14** (★★★☆).

★★★★ **Verdelho** (NEW) Textured & broad, (unwooded) **15** from Swartland makes impressive debut, with almost oily viscosity & intense pear & peach fruit, yet moderate 12% alcohol, ending clean, pithy, mineral.

★★★★ **Viognier** Pale pink-gold hue adds to jasmine-perfumed appeal of **15**, orange citrus & ground ginger spice combining with hints of vanilla from judicious oaking, quite viscous but elegant.

Tannat (circle) ★★★☆ Perfumed **13** is medium bodied & fresh despite quite rustic tannins, very plush dark berry/cherry fruit. Nudging higher rating.

Chardonnay ★★★☆ Evocative of lemon tart in all but sweetness, **14** is bone-dry but creamy with citrus freshness & vanilla spice. Coastal WO. **Darling Riesling** ★★★☆ Off-dry **15** (14.3 g/l residual sugar) calls for spicy Thai, its aromatic orange blossom nose & tartly sweet green apple & naartjie flavours balanced by mouthwatering acidity. **Viognier Special Late Harvest** ★★★ Sweet **15** has peach & litchi flavours, quite full bodied with balancing acidity, so not cloying. Also tasted: **Stellenbosch Merlot 13** ★★★☆ **Darling Chenin Blanc 15** ★★★★ **Darling Sauvignon Blanc 15** ★★★☆ **Sweet Red 14** ★★★ Occasional release: **La Beryl Rouge**.

La Capra range

Merlot ★★★ Liquorice finish to **14**, otherwise a chocolate-drizzled, plummy, soft fruitcake of a wine. From Stellenbosch & Paarl. **Chenin Blanc** ★★★ **15**'s pale green hue doesn't hint at the burst of citrus that comes with every sip, lively but nicely rounded. Coastal WO. **Pinot Grigio** ★★★ Tropical **15** has litchi & melon notes, quite a creamy mouthfeel considering that it's also light & fresh. WO Darling. Also tasted: **Cabernet Sauvignon 13** ★★★ **Malbec 14** ★★★☆ **Shiraz 14** ★★★ **Sauvignon Blanc 15** ★★★ Not retasted: **Pinotage 13** ★★★ Not tasted: **Sangiovese**, **Chardonnay**, **Viognier**. Discontinued: **Pinotage Rosé**. — JG

Location: Paarl ▪ Map: Paarl & Wellington ▪ Map grid reference: D6 ▪ WO: Paarl/Coastal/Darling/Swartland/Stellenbosch ▪ Est 1693 ▪ 1stB 1974 ▪ Tasting & sales Mon-Sun 9–5, last tasting 30min before closing ▪ R25/standard tasting, R60/master tasting ▪ Closed Good Fri, Dec 25 & Jan 1 ▪ The Goatshed Restaurant ▪ Tour groups by appt only ▪ Deli: artisanal cheeses & fresh farm breads ▪ Owner(s) Charles Back ▪ Winemaker(s) Anthony de Jager (Dec 1996), with Stephanie Betts (2010) & Adele Dunbar (2006) ▪ 500ha/300ha (cab, carignan, grenache, merlot, mourv, petite sirah, ptage, shiraz, tannat, tempranillo, chenin, sauv, viog) ▪ 2,100t/260cs own label 80% red 15% white 5% rosé ▪ ISO 9001:2001, BWI, BRC, Fairtrade, HACCP, IPW, WIETA ▪ PO Box 583 Suider-Paarl 7624 ▪ info@fairview.co.za ▪ www.fairview.co.za ▪ S 33° 46' 19.16" E 018° 55' 25.26" ▪ F +27 (0)21-863-2591 ▪ **T +27 (0)21-863-2450**

False Bay Vineyards　　　　　　　　　　　　　　　　　　　　　　　(Ω)

Intended for everyday enjoyment, False Bay and Peacock Wild Ferment are the more pocket-friendly offerings of Paul Boutinot's Helderberg-based Waterkloof winery. Apart from sourcing grapes more widely, winemaker Nadia Barnard fully adheres to Waterkloof's philosophy of uncompromised quality, with recent WIETA certification recognising that staff are also treated with respect.

Peacock Wild Ferment range

★★★★ **Chardonnay** (NEW) Beautifully balanced **14**, from Schapenberg, has apricot & nectarine aromas leading to fresh yet restrained citrus zestiness, offset by creamy mouthfeel & underlying minerality.

Sauvignon Blanc (circle) ★★★★ From cool pockets in the Helderberg, flinty **14** has squeeze of lime on stonefruit salad of flavours, intense with smooth texture & persistent finish.

Syrah ★★★★ Was 'Shiraz'. Fresh, vibrant **14** needs time but already bursts with red plum, berry & cherry fruit, a pinch of spice lifting this lighter-bodied red with moderate 13% alcohol even further. Also tasted: **Cabernet Sauvignon 13** ★★★☆ **Merlot 13** ★★★★ **Chenin Blanc 14** ★★★☆

False Bay range

Rosé ★★★ Pale pink, aromatic & dry **14** has red berry sweetness from old-vine Swartland cinsaut balanced by freshness & spice of mourvèdre from Elgin & Stellenbosch. Modest 12% alcohol. **Chenin Blanc ★★★** Fresher, drier & more focused than last year's fruit salad, **14** has lemony freshness & smooth minerality, stone- & star-fruit flavours. Also tasted: **Shiraz 13 ★★★ Chardonnay 14 ★★★☆ Sauvignon Blanc 15 ★★★** Not retasted: **Pinotage 13 ★★★☆** — JG

Location: Somerset West • WO: Stellenbosch/Western Cape/Coastal • Est/1stB 2000 • Tasting at Waterkloof • Owner(s) Paul Boutinot • Cellarmaster(s) Nadia Barnard (Jan 2013) • 160,000cs own label 30% red 65% white 5% rosé • IPW, WIETA • PO Box 2093 Somerset West 7129 • info@waterkloofwines.co.za • www.falsebayvineyards.co.za • F +27 (0)21-858-1293 • **T +27 (0)21-858-1292**

☐ **Fantail** *see* Morgenhof Wine Estate
☐ **Far & Near** *see* L'Avenir Vineyards
☐ **Farm Animals** *see* Osbloed Wines

Fat Bastard

What started out as an experimental chardonnay tasted in a dank cellar by two friends, UK wine brand creator Guy Anderson and French winemaker Thierry Boudinaud, and pronounced a 'fat bastard', has become a successful range on both sides of the Atlantic. In South Africa, it's made by Robertson Winery.

Cabernet Sauvignon ★★★★ Light, supple & fresh **13** has fruitcake appeal, well supported by 18 months new oak. **Merlot** (NEW) **★★★** Black fruit & brush of herbs on structured **13**. **Pinot Noir Rosé** (NEW) **★★★** Ripe berry juiciness & tang on dry **14**. Also tasted: **Pinotage 13 ★★★ Shiraz 13 ★★★ Chardonnay 14 ★★★ Sauvignon Blanc 15 ★★** Not retasted: **Pinot Noir 13 ★★★★** — FM

Feiteiras Vineyards   ⓠ

At the time of going to press, Feiteiras Vineyards, the small 'taste of Madeira' brought to Bot River by restaurateurs and liquor retailers Jose and Manuel de Andrade about a decade ago, had just been sold to Free State and Lesotho construction magnate Sandro Arcangeli. The first-generation Italian was still deciding on a new name for what will remain a wine producer with new wine tourism elements. Labels below available while stocks last.

Casa Merlot Rosé (ⓥ) **★★★** The unwooded edition of cellar's rosé duo; **12** coral hue, lovely dry redberry zing. **Verdelho** (ⓥ) **★★★★** Rare-in-Cape white grape, unwooded **13** tank sample picked early for freshness but doesn't sacrifice flavour — alluring lime, pineapple, honeysuckle, all in a fragrant, light, dry body. Not retasted: **Cabernet Sauvignon 11 ★★★★ Troca Tintas 13 ★★★★** Not tasted: **Vinho Forte Tinto, Vinho Forte Branco**. — CM

Location/WO: Bot River • Map: Elgin, Walker Bay & Bot River • Est 2003 • 1stB 2004 • Tasting & sales by appt • Owner(s) Sandro Arcangeli • 16.2ha/4.2ha (cab, merlot, mourv, shiraz, verdelho) • PO Box 234 Bot River 7185 • fabio@azraelwines.com • www.azraelwines.com • S 34° 14' 3.6" E 019° 12' 33.3" • **T +27 (0)82-412-7795**

Felicité

A sea of sickly sweet rosés encouraged the Newton Johnson family in the late 90s to introduce a 'classy' version, described in these pages as 'unashamedly dry rosé for grown-ups'. Now a standalone, extended label, Felicité — with Stettyn Cellar as winegrowing partner — still aims for drinkability with panache.

Rosé ★★★☆ Carnival pink & jammed with cranberries, **15** is bold & dry, for mealtimes. From shiraz & cinsaut, splash of sauvignon. **Chardonnay ★★★** **14** a glassful of crisp, vibrant citrus fruit unfettered by oak; direct & honest. WO W Cape for both. Not tasted: **Pinot Noir**. — DS

Fernskloof Wines   ⓠ 🍽 🏠 📷 🛏

Being certified organic, the small-batch wines made by Diederik le Grange dovetail nicely with the many nature/outdoor attractions on the family farm near Prince Albert in Groot Karoo. Handcrafting is the watchword: even the barrels are shaved and re-toasted on-site and, as might be expected, the mostly red wines are made naturally and traditionally, and bottled by hand.

Location: Prince Albert ▪ Map: Klein Karoo & Garden Route ▪ Est 2009 ▪ 1stB 2010 ▪ Tasting & sales Mon-Fri 9-5 Sat 10-5 Sun by appt 10-5 ▪ Closed Good Fri, Ascension Day & Dec 25 ▪ Facilities for children ▪ BYO picnic ▪ Walks/hikes ▪ 10km mountain running trail ▪ Conservation area ▪ Angeliersbosch guest house (up to 8 guests), no pets allowed ▪ Owner(s) Le Grange family ▪ Cellarmaster(s)/winemaker(s) Diederik le Grange (2010) ▪ Viticulturist(s) Diederik le Grange (2009) ▪ 1,026ha/7ha (cab, merlot, ptage, shiraz, chard) ▪ 40t/1,900cs own label 42% red 29% white 29% rosé ▪ BWI, Lacon Organic ▪ PO Box 41 Prince Albert 6930 ▪ info@fernskloof.co.za ▪ www.fernskloof.co.za ▪ S 33° 16' 23.77" E 022° 10' 55.60" ▪ **T +27 (0)23-541-1702**

☐ **Festin** see Domaine Coutelier
☐ **5th Avenue Cold Duck** see Cold Duck (5th Avenue)
☐ **51 Miles** see Winters Drift
☐ **56Hundred** see Nederburg Wines

Fijndraai Estate   ⌂ ◎

Expect interesting Mediterranean-style wines from owners Laurel van Coller and Veronique Kritzinger, made from a Stellenbosch vineyard once part of Welmoed by seasoned wine man Ken Forrester. Launching as the guide went to press was a shiraz, grenache, durif combo to partner the viognier-based white.

Location: Stellenbosch ▪ Est 2007 ▪ 1stB 2011 ▪ Sales via website ▪ Olive oil ▪ Walks/hikes ▪ Mountain biking trail ▪ Self-catering accommodation ▪ Equestrian centre ▪ Owner(s) Laurel van Coller & Veronique Kritzinger ▪ Winemaker(s) Ken Forrester (Jan 2010, consultant) ▪ Viticulturist(s) Pieter Rossouw (Feb 2011, consultant) ▪ 93ha/12ha (durif, grenache, sangio, shiraz, pinot grigio, rouss, viog) ▪ 134t/1,094cs own label 57% red 43% white ▪ WIETA ▪ PO Box 24 Lynedoch Stellenbosch 7603 ▪ info@fijndraai.com ▪ www.fijndraai.com ▪ **T +27 (0)82-817-6372**

☐ **Finch Mountain** see Rooiberg Winery
☐ **Firefly** see Stellar Winery

FirstCape Vineyards

Powerhouse export-only brand FirstCape was formed in 2002 as a joint venture between five Breede River Valley cellars and British marketer Brand Phoenix. Currently all bottling is done in the UK, and the wines available as: FirstCape (Five Cellars, Winemaker's Selection, Limited Release, Special Cuvée, Coral Tree, First Selection, Special Reserve); FirstCape Light (5.5% alcohol); FirstCape Sparkler; and FirstCape Rosé Sparkler. New markets in China (Five Cellars) and Canada (Cape Buy) are growing the footprint.

Location: Paarl ▪ Est 2002 ▪ Closed to public ▪ Owner(s) Aan de Doorns, Badsberg, De Wet, Goudini & Stettyn wineries ▪ Winemaker(s) David Smit ▪ WIETA ▪ PO Box 62 Simondium 7670 ▪ david@firstcape.com ▪ www.firstcape.com ▪ F +27 (0)21-874-8344 ▪ **T +27 (0)21-874-8340**

☐ **First Fruit** see Lourensford Wine Estate
☐ **First Selection** see FirstCape Vineyards
☐ **First Sighting** see Strandveld Wines

Fish Hoek Wines   ⓥ

This is the global mid-tier 'lifestyle' label made by the Accolade Wines SA team of Bruce Jack, Gerhard Swart and Karen Bruwer in the Flagstone cellar at Somerset West. 'One of those brands you look at and suddenly realise has doubled in volume, again!' As pleasing is Fairtrade accreditation, achieved in 2015.

Cinsaut Rosé (NEW) ⊘ 🍇 ★★★ **15** offers generous, genuinely fruity berry flavours. Perfectly delicious picnic wine.

Malbec (NEW) ⊘ ★★★ Savoury & dry but gorgeously fruity **14**, sweet wild berries & gentle tannic bite. **Merlot** ★★☆ Cheerful, succulent **14** all plum & chocolate. **Chenin Blanc** ★★★ Previewed **15** has oodles of fresh fruity flavour & zestiness for easy sipping. Also tasted: **Pinotage 14 ★★☆ Shiraz 14 ★★★ Sauvignon Blanc 15 ★★★** Discontinued: **Pinotage Rosé**. — IM

Location: Somerset West ▪ WO: Western Cape ▪ Tasting, sales & cellar tours at Flagstone Winery (see entry) ▪ Owner(s) Accolade Wines South Africa ▪ Winemaker(s) Karen Bruwer (Feb 2013), Gerhard Swart (Sep 2008) & Bruce Jack (1998) ▪ 50% red 50% white ▪ PO Box 769 Stellenbosch 7599 ▪ flagstone@accolade-wines.com ▪ F +27 (0)21-852-5085 ▪ **T +27 (0)21-852-5052**

- ☐ **Five Cellars** *see* FirstCape Vineyards
- ☐ **Five Climates** *see* Boland Kelder
- ☐ **Five Generations** *see* Cederberg Private Cellar
- ☐ **Five's Reserve** *see* Van Loveren Family Vineyards
- ☐ **Flagship** *see* Stellenbosch Vineyards

Flagstone Winery   ⓠ ⓗ

What started as SA-schooled, Aussie-trained vintner Bruce Jack's indoor/outdoor collection of winemaking paraphernalia in a Cape Town waterfront warehouse in the late 1990s has become a highly reputed winery in Somerset West, home of a brand now owned by multinational Accolade Wines. Remaining in charge of Flagstone (as well as Accolade's other SA-sourced brands Kumala and Fish Hoek), Bruce has stood fast on the quality, quirky individuality and 'yum' factor of Flagstone wines, despite steady increase in production and scope. Still the creative, philosophical lodestar, he credits 'team players' such as head winemaker Gerhard Swart for helping him 'tell the stories' of distinctive varieties and sites under each evocative label.

Time Manner Place range

★★★★☆ Pinotage Ambitious single-vineyard bottling in good years. Powerful, plush **13**'s dense ripe, spicy tannins underpin vibrantly fresh red fruit & alcohol's sweet impression. Genteel & polished, without losing character. From Breedekloof, like **12** (★★★★★).

Flagstone range

★★★★☆ Music Room Cabernet Sauvignon Softly ripe, warm & affable **13** (★★★★) seamless & well made if unexciting. Decent grip from 2 years in mostly American oak checks overtly sweet impression from both alcohol & fruit. Not as impressive as **12**.

★★★★ Writer's Block Pinotage Single Breedekloof vineyard **13** confidently smart & modern, offering abundant sweet red fruit & savoury spices, kept in check by polished tannins.

★★★★ Dark Horse Shiraz **12** as broodingly sombre as **11**, with punchy ripeness but lacking relative freshness & charm of also-tasted **13**, which is notably floral with compact dark fruit & roasted spices. Both vintages conclude sweetly warm.

★★★★ Dragon Tree Multi-regional cab, shiraz, pinotage blend, **13** (★★★☆) lively & sweet-fruited, perhaps not as convincing as **12**. Savoury spiciness makes tasty, appealing everyday drink.

★★★★ Treaty Tree Red ⓝⓔⓦ Ultra-juicy Bordeaux-shiraz blend, **13** not quite in same serious league as white counterpart, but seamlessly integrated with sufficient grip to frame richness.

★★★★☆ Free Run Sauvignon Blanc ⊘ Lively, herbaceous **14** not quite as thrillingly vibrant as also-tasted **13** & with touch less semillon. Cool-climate Elim & Elgin vines ensure intense aromas & appetisingly crisp layers of fruit, wound around tight mineral core. Expressive flavours have unfurled with 2 years in bottle.

★★★★ Word of Mouth Viognier ⓧ Expressive **13** shows ginger spice with orange stonefruit & citrus in elegant mouthful. Restrained oak (40% barrel-fermented) & well-managed alcohol give a fresh feel.

★★★★★ Treaty Tree Reserve White Blend ⊘ Distinctive semillon roundness & breadth to **14** (★★★★☆) partly barrel-fermented blend with (mostly) sauvignon from cool Elim vineyards. Layered herbs & stonefruit, though perhaps not as concentrated as stellar **13**.

Truth Tree Pinotage ⓝⓔⓦ ★★★ Vanilla spiciness mingles with sweetly jammy blackberry fruit of **14**. Also tasted: **Fiona Pinot Noir 13 ★★★★ Longitude 14 ★★☆ Noon Gun 15 ★★☆** Not retasted: **Last Word 09 ★★★☆**

Stumble Vineyards range

Malbec ★★★ Dollop pinotage in cheerful **14** from Swartland fruit, fresh acidity balances ripeness. **Verdelho ★★★** Focused **14** softened by touch sugar, lipsmacking crispness; some interest & appeal. Olifants River WO. Also tasted: **Merlot 14 ★★☆ Cape Blend 14 ★★ White Pinotage 14 ★★**

Poetry range

Cabernet Sauvignon ★★★ Tannins underpin generous dark fruit in pleasant, balanced **14**. Also tasted: **Merlot 14 ★★★ Sauvignon Blanc 14 ★★**

The Rustler range

Chenin Blanc ★★★ Splash viognier in appetising **14**, crisp green apples & lingering refreshing acidity. Also tasted: **Pinotage 14 ★★☆** Occasional release: **Sauvignon Blanc**.

Whispering Jack range

Chardonnay ★★★ Dash chenin in lightly oaked, mildly buttery & fresh **14**; balanced, straightforward. — IM

Location: Somerset West ▪ Map: Helderberg ▪ WO: Western Cape/Breedekloof/Swartland/Cape South Coast/ Elim/Overberg/Durbanville/Olifants River ▪ Est 1998 ▪ 1stB 1999 ▪ Tasting & sales Mon-Fri 10-4 Sat 10-3 ▪ Fee R20, waived on purchase ▪ Cheese & wine pairing, to be pre-booked ▪ Closed Sundays, Good Fri, Dec 25/ 26 & Jan 1 ▪ Cellar tours by appt ▪ Owner(s) Accolade Wines South Africa ▪ Winemaker(s) Gerhard Swart (Sep 2008) & Bruce Jack (1998), with Gerald Cakijana (Jan 2000) ▪ 70% red 30% white ▪ PO Box 769 Stellenbosch 7599 ▪ flagstone@accolade-wines.com ▪ www.flagstonewines.com ▪ S 34° 5' 26.38" E 018° 48' 30.04" ▪ F +27 (0)21-852-5085 ▪ **T +27 (0)21-852-5052**

Flat Roof Manor

This unpretentious range is made by Estelle Lourens at Uitkyk, which dates back to 1712 and boasts a two-storied Georgian homestead — one of only three left in the Cape. Its flat roof and quirky resident cat are the inspiration for the branding; the wines are under screwcap for easy access.

Malbec ⓝ **★★★** Previously blended away, now solo bottled; **14** has rustic charm, quite earthy with dark berry fruit & hint of mixed spice. **Pinot Grigio ★★★** Ever so slightly off-dry **15** has floral nose, with 14% sauvignon for green freshness & tangy citrus lift. Also tasted: **Merlot 14 ★★★** Not retasted: **Shiraz-Mourvèdre-Viognier 11 ★★★☆ Sauvignon Blanc Light 13 ★★** Discontinued: **Pinot Rosé Light**. — JG

Fledge & Co ⓠ

'Our nest of fledglings is sort of taking shape', says Leon Coetzee, who partners Margaux Nel in this small but dynamic 'terroirist' venture based at Calitzdorp, where Margaux is Boplaas winemaker. Stability seems unlikely, however, given more varieties proving irresistible, from different regions and off different soils — prompting 'a few more experiments' in the cellar. There's a solid core, however, expressed in a 'little mantra' Leon cites: 'Wine, it's made from grapes.'

Fledge & Co range

★★★★ KatVis Pinot Noir ⓝ **14** a unique blend of Elgin & Klein Karoo (BK5 clone) fruit; matured in old oak. Fresh & persistent, mixing fruity & savoury, subtle & succulent tannic grip. Fine balance.

★★★★☆ Red Blend ⓝ Delightful **12** blend of 'port' grapes souzão, touriga franca, touriga, from old Stellenbosch & Klein Karoo vines. Bright red & black fruit, with darker depths; intricate & complex, delicate & strong; supple, silky, finely balanced. Mostly, greatly drinkable.

★★★★☆ HoekSteen Unoaked old bushvine chenin ex Stellenbosch. **14** paler, more brilliant than Klipspringer; more gentle & perfectly balanced too. Lovely fragrant aromas (pear, dried peach, thatch); fine, clean, subtle intensity & long finish. Should develop well.

★★★★ Klipspringer Swartland Steen ⓝ **14**'s old bushvines yield (via natural ferment) typical Swartland breadth & depth — clean & fresh, with a touch of earthiness. Understated richness married to austerity, with a good bite.

★★★★ **Fumé Blanc** (NEW) Old-oaked **14** sauvignon from Upper Langkloof & Outeniqua vines. Characterful & a bit unusual, blending aromatic stoniness & sweet-fruited charm; elegant & refined, with modest alcohol.

★★★★ **Vagabond** 13 (★★★☆) all Klein Karoo viognier; old-oaked **14** has 40% Stellenbosch chenin. Also low-key, aromas more spicy-almond than fruity — viognier's peach on the finish. Fresh, light. Not tasted: **Hatchi**.

Experimental Barrels range
Not tasted: **Straw Wine**. — TJ

Location: Calitzdorp/Riebeek West ▪ WO: Western Cape/Stellenbosch/Elgin-Klein Karoo/Swartland/ Upper Langkloof-Outeniqua ▪ Est 2007 ▪ 1stB 2010 ▪ Tasting & sales by appt at Boplaas ▪ Closed all pub hols ▪ Owner(s) Margaux Nel & Leon Coetzee ▪ Winemaker(s) Margaux Nel & Leon Coetzee (both Jan 2007) ▪ Viticulturist(s) Margaux Nel (Jan 2007) ▪ 20t/2,000cs own label 40% red 60% white ▪ IPW ▪ winemaker@boplaas.co.za, leon.mrfoo@gmail.com ▪ www.thefledge.co.za ▪ **T +27 (0)82-828-8416/ +27 (0)72-385-6503**

Fleur du Cap   (Ⓠ)

Distell-owned Die Bergkelder ('Mountain Cellar') has been home to the prestige Fleur du Cap brand since its opening in 1968. Grapes, in significant volumes, are sourced from the far corners of the winelands, offering the wine team an enviable choice of components. Die Bergkelder Wine Centre centre in Stellenbosch (see entry), including the labyrinthine cellar burrowed into the Papegaaiberg hillside, includes among its visitor offerings unusual and fascinating wine-and-salt tastings (and pre-booked wine-and-salt pairing dinners). The Unfiltered Collection represents their no-holds-barred efforts to produce the best possible wines, but there are real stars in the Bergkelder Selection, too.

Unfiltered Collection

★★★★☆ **Cabernet Sauvignon** 2 vintages of consistently high-flying prestige label tasted: **12** has muscular but silky body, seriously deep black-fruit core & nervous herbaceous nuances. **13** follows form, if less integrated. Stellenbosch fruit spent 18 months in all-new French oak, like next.

★★★★ **Merlot** Big, intense & generous **12** shows class. Robust but smooth tannin structure with luscious black berry fruit, plum pudding & subtle rosepetal nuances. Stellenbosch vineyards.

★★★★ **Pinotage** (NEW) Serious & intense, but brimming with rich black fruit, **14** is youthful but shows promise. Dense, sweetly ripe mulberry & bramble on silky tannins. WO Coastal.

★★★★☆ **Chardonnay** Big, stately barrel-fermented **14** from Stellenbosch & Robertson vineyards, needs time to integrate. Fat & textural with buttery citrus highlights, following to lingering finish. Should blossom with a couple of years in bottle.

★★★★ **Chenin Blanc** (NEW) Overtly oaky **14** (though only partially barrel fermented), full bodied, ripe & flavoursome, still rather unknit but should settle & meld with time. Paarl, Darling grapes.

★★★★☆ **Sauvignon Blanc** Exuberantly youthful **15** preview already showing impressive form. Intense & concentrated yet bracingly crisp, offering a generous reflection of Darling origins. Deliciously intricate weave of granadilla, gooseberry & figs, cloaked in dusty mantle.

★★★★ **Semillon** Refined & classy, barrel-fermented **14** has zesty limes with spicy beeswax, reined-in oak & satisfyingly rich texture. From Gansbaai vineyards; WO W Cape.

Fleur du Cap Bergkelder Selection

★★★★★ **Laszlo** Stately merlot & cab blend, with 10% shiraz in **12**, flagship label pays tribute to Julius Laszlo, pioneer of barrel ageing in SA. Plush & decadently layered fruit with velvety tannins, muscular but precise, showing great potential. Stellenbosch grapes. Last tasted was **09** (★★★★★).

★★★★☆ **Noble Late Harvest** Perennial high-flyer, **14** unoaked botrytised chenin from Darling shows irresistible charm & complexity. Honeyed layers of dried apricot with glacé citrus, floral scents & exotic spices, bound by bracing acidity, all in sublime balance. 375 ml.

Cabernet Sauvignon ★★★☆ Good varietal character on **13**, perhaps missing nervous edginess, but offering solid tannins, ripe black fruit, spicy oak. **Natural Light Rosé** (NEW) ★★ Early harvested low-alcohol **15** from chenin, sauvignon & pinotage is tartly austere despite good few grams sugar.

. **Sauvignon Blanc** ★★★ Brisk & fresh **15** still showing fermentation character, but generously fruity & appealing. Darling, Elgin, Stellenbosch & Agulhas vineyards. Also tasted: **Merlot 13** ★★★ **Pinotage 13** ★★★☆ **Chardonnay 14** ★★★ **Chenin Blanc 15** ★★★ **Natural Light Chenin Blanc 15** ★★ Not retasted: **Shiraz 13** ★★★☆ — GdB

Location: Stellenbosch ▪ WO: Western Cape/Coastal/Stellenbosch/Darling ▪ Est 1968 ▪ 1stB 1969 ▪ Tasting, sales & tours at Die Bergkelder Wine Centre (see entry) ▪ Owner(s) Distell ▪ Cellarmaster(s) Andrea Freeborough (Aug 2005) ▪ Winemaker(s) Wim Truter (2014, reds) & Pieter Badenhorst (Dec 2006, whites), with Christoff de Wet (Sep 2010) & Elmarie Botes (2014) ▪ Viticulturist(s) Bennie Liebenberg (Apr 2001) ▪ ±17,000t/±290,000cs own label 47% red 53% white ▪ ISO 14001, ISO 9001, BRC, HACCP, IFS ▪ info@fleurducap.co.za, info@bergkelder.co.za ▪ www.fleurducap.co.za, www.bergkelder.co.za ▪ **T +27 (0)21-809-8025**

Flight of the Fish Eagle

'Perfect for first-time brandy drinkers,' says marketing manager Oupa Lehaha of one of Distell's most popular pure potstill brandies. Pitched particularly at young professionals and promoted through major ad and events campaigns, it's named after one of Africa's best-known raptors (for its evocative call).

★★★★ **Natural Brandy** ⓠ Pale gold colour belies intensity of the aroma (red berry fruit, orange, honey). Refined, with a long finish. Modern style; 100% potstill from chenin & colombard. — WB, TJ

☐ **Flippenice** *see* Tulbagh Winery
☐ **Flutterby** *see* Boland Kelder

Flying Cloud   ⓠ ⓝⓔⓦ

Long desirous to produce a creative, characterful and philosophical work, Cape Town advocate Donald Ackerman was inspired by Plato, Aquinas and many other great thinkers (and first-hand experience!) to choose wine as his medium. Undaunted by 'miserable failure' in 2013, he and the Strandveld Vineyards team overcame the troubled 2014 vintage to craft a wine (untasted by us) which has the energy, soul and authenticity Donald seeks.

Location: Cape Town ▪ Est 2013 ▪ 1stB 2014 ▪ Tasting by appt only ▪ Owner(s)/winemaker(s) Donald Ackerman ▪ 62cs own label 100% white ▪ 50 Keerom Street Cape Town 8001 ▪ flyingcloudwines@ icloud.com ▪ **T +27 (0)82-610-2422/+27 (0)21-422-2268**

Foothills Vineyards   ⓠ ⓟ ⓐ ⓞ

These wines originate on Klein Welmoed Wine & Olive Estate in the Helderberg foothills, where Glenn Hesse and Tim Featherby established a luxury guest house and boutique winery. Their pinot noir and chardonnay vines produced a first crop last year, but the owners aren't rushing to vinify the grapes, preferring to wait for the second or third vintage.

Syrah ⓥ ★★★★ Step-up **13** has garrigue scrub & lily notes, powdery tannins & fruit purity with commendable dry & savoury conclusion. Young shiraz vines showing potential.

Dry Rosé ★★★☆ Fruity but bone-dry mealtime companion **14** gets oomph from 6 months lees-ageing of its components, shiraz, viognier & dash semillon. Also tasted: **Sauvignon Blanc 14** ★★★ **The Partners 14** ★★★ — CvZ

Location/WO: Stellenbosch ▪ Map: Helderberg ▪ Est 2008 ▪ 1stB 2012 ▪ Tasting & sales by appt ▪ Fee R25 ▪ Meals/refreshments by appt ▪ Olive oil ▪ Conferences ▪ Luxury guest house (B&B) ▪ Owner(s) Glenn Hesse & Tim Featherby ▪ Winemaker(s) Bernard le Roux ▪ Viticulturist(s) Bennie Booysen ▪ 39ha/19ha (shiraz, sauv, sem, viog) ▪ 4,000cs own label 15% red 80% white 5% rosé ▪ IPW ▪ PO Box 647 Somerset Mall 7137 ▪ steve@foothillsvineyards.co.za ▪ www.kleinwelmoed.co.za, www.foothillsvineyards.co.za ▪ S 34° 0' 58.86" E 018° 47' 43.08" ▪ F +27 (0)21-842-2775 ▪ **T +27 (0)21-842-0045**

☐ **Foot of Africa** *see* Kleine Zalze Wines
☐ **Force Majeure** *see* Mother Rock Wines

☐ **Forresters** *see* Ken Forrester Wines
☐ **Fortress Hill** *see* Fort Simon Wine Estate

Fort Simon Wine Estate

This Bottelary Hills family farm's well-established portfolio of wines, internationally marketed, seems as rock-steady as its turreted fortress cellar and visitor centre, modelled on eccentric Duwisib Castle in Namibia. Built of stone gathered on the property by late founder and namesake Simon Uys, it's since been extended to include a functions venue and wedding chapel.

Platinum Collection

★★★★ **Viognier** ⓥ Vibrant & alive **12** (★★★) has ample nectarine & peach, with light nuttiness on dry finish, but shade less impressive than **09**.

★★★★ **Viognier Noble Late Harvest** Apricot pip, honey & sultanas jostle, with hint of toasty oak (though no new barrels used) on **11**. Moderate richness balanced to give an easy lightish feel. 375 ml.

Fort Simon Estate range

★★★★ **Shiraz** Darkly glowing **12** also has dark, fragrant fruitiness edged with spice. Nicely dry (though usefully rounded with a tiny bit of extra sugar). Approachable now, but firm structure more harmonious in a few years.

★★★★ **Chenin Blanc** Old-oak maturation lends roundness & silky texture to apricotty, pleasing but straightforward **14** (★★★★), with prominent acidity. Last tasted was **12**.

Rosé ★★★ Fresh & ripely tasty **14** from pinotage, merlot & shiraz. Easygoing, with a forceful acidity balancing the ripe strawberry fruit, making it dry enough for the particular. **Chardonnay** ★★★★ Toasty oak more dominant on the aromas of **14**, but better integrated on the palate, where succulent, zesty citrus comes forward to orchestrate a pleasing conclusion. Also tasted: **Cabernet Sauvignon 11** ★★★★ **Merlot 13** ★★★ **Sauvignon Blanc 15** ★★★★ Not retasted: **Pinotage 12** ★★★ **Barrel Select Merlot-Malbec 12** ★★★

Fortress Hill range

Shiraz ★★★ Welcoming gentle fragrance of fruit & spice on softly textured, judiciously oaked **13** – the most approachable & rewarding red in this range. **Sauvignon Blanc** ★★★ Easygoing & fresh **15** offers straightforward guava & tropical fruit character. Also tasted: **Merlot 14** ★★ **Merlot-Cabernet Sauvignon 14** ★★★

Michelle d'Or

Merlot-Cabernet Sauvignon ⓥ ★★★ Dried thyme & soft juicy berries on **12** 60/40 blend, good integration & length. WO W Cape, as all these. Not retasted: **Merlot** ★★★ **Shiraz** ★★★ **Sauvignon Blanc** ★★★ — TJ

Location/map: Stellenbosch ▪ Map grid reference: C4 ▪ WO: Stellenbosch/Western Cape ▪ Est 1997 ▪ 1stB 1998 ▪ Tasting & sales Mon-Fri 9.30–5 Sat 10–2 ▪ Fee R20/5wines ▪ Closed all pub hols ▪ Cellar tours by appt ▪ Venue for after-hours functions/weddings & conferences (120-140 guests) ▪ Wedding chapel ▪ Accommodation ▪ Owner(s) Renier, Petrus & Michéle Uys ▪ Winemaker(s) Stander Maass (Sep 2006) ▪ Viticulturist(s) Renier Uys ▪ 80ha (cabs s/f, malbec, merlot, p verdot, ptage, shiraz, chard, chenin, sauv, viog) ▪ 800t/80,000cs own label 70% red 25% white 5% rosé ▪ PO Box 43 Sanlamhof 7532 ▪ accounts@fortsimon.com ▪ www.fortsimon.co.za ▪ S 33° 55' 9.5" E 018° 45' 19.4" ▪ F +27 (0)21-903-8034 ▪ T +27 (0)21-906-0304

☐ **Foundation Stone** *see* Rickety Bridge Winery
☐ **Foundry** *see* The Foundry
☐ **Fountain Crossing** *see* Darling Cellars
☐ **Four Cousins** *see* Van Loveren Family Vineyards

4G Wines

Based near Stellenbosch, and sourcing from various carefully selected sites, 4G Wines is about building a South African 'first growth', says director Philipp Axt, adding this is not about flattering shareholders' or customers' egos. 'Our ambition is rather to create delicate, delicious and inimitable wine [by] combining European winemaking expertise, craftsmanship and innovative technologies with SA's outstanding natural assets and winemaking skills.' 4G's guiding spirit was Giorgio Dalla Cia, creator of iconic Meerlust Rubicon, and now French consultants Denis Dubourdieu and Valérie Lavigne are also on board.

Location: Stellenbosch ▪ Est 2009 ▪ 1stB 2010 ▪ Closed to public ▪ Owner(s) Private shareholders ▪ Winemaker(s) Mia Fischer, Giorgio Dalla Cia, Denis Dubourdieu & Valérie Lavigne ▪ 20t ▪ own label 100% red ▪ Other export brands: G, The Echo of G ▪ info@4g-wines.com ▪ www.4g-wines.com

Four Paws Wines ⓛ

Fans might sniff at the introduction of a canine label to the feline-themed portfolio this edition, but in fairness it is wittily named and the wine itself is rather pleasant. Certainly it's in line with brand owners and wine-industry professionals Rob Meihuizen, Gerda Willers and Anne Jakubiec's intention to offer 'variety and interest each vintage'. So sheath those claws and enjoy!

★★★★ **Pinotage** ⓥ Brambleberry notes on full-bodied **11** from Piekenierskloof, showing vanilla tone from year 30% new oak. Drinks easily & well but underlying seriousness invites cellaring ±5 years.

★★★★ **Picatso** Generous floral, tropical & grapey notes contrast nicely with delicate oaking (2nd fill) on **15** viognier & muscat d'Alexandrie dessert. Crackling acidity reins in the sweetness, adds to the enjoyment, vibrancy. 375 ml.

Grenache (NEW) ⓥ ★★★☆ **14** an elegant glassful, with fine-grained tannins, intense red & dark fruit bouquet spiced with cherry tobacco & nutmeg.

Vincent Van Dogh (NEW) ★★★★ Playful name, playful nature, **13** lively melange grenache, cinsaut & cab with pleasing savoury tone & deft oak touch (20% new). **Rosé** (NEW) ★★★ Food-friendly 3-way combo lightly oaked merlot, plus sauvignon, chenin. **15** dry, with pomegranate & spice nuances. Also tasted: **Sauvignon Blanc 15** ★★★ **Calico 15** ★★★ Not retasted: **Shiraz 12** ★★★ **Pablo 11** ★★★☆ **Chardonnay 11** ★★★☆ — GM

Location/map: Franschhoek ▪ WO: Western Cape/Piekenierskloof ▪ Est 2005 ▪ 1stB 2006 ▪ Tasting by appt at La Vigne, Robertsvlei Road, Franschhoek (contact Anne +27 (0)83-447-1376/Gerda +27 (0)82-375-0524) ▪ Owner(s) Rob Meihuizen, Gerda Willers & Anne Jakubiec ▪ Winemaker(s) Gerda Willers (2005) ▪ Viticulturist(s) Gerda Willers ▪ 60t/12,000cs own label 70% red 30% white ▪ PO Box 69 Simondium 7670 ▪ anne@southerntrade.co.za ▪ www.fourpawswines.com ▪ S 33° 53' 28.0" E 019° 5' 0.5" ▪ F +27 (0)21-874-2110 ▪ **T +27 (0)21-874-1033**

☐ **Four Secrets** see Stellenbosch Vineyards

4th Street

Low alcohol and on-the-go accessibility are features of these trendy Natural Sweet wines, some slightly sparkling and sold in colourful 'sixpacks' of 300 ml crown-capped bottles. By Distell.

Lightly Sparkled range

Natural Sweet Red ★★ Fizzy, sweet **NV** picnic wine with strawberry flavours & the brand's signature low alcohol (6.5%). 300 ml bottle, as for all these. Also tasted: **Natural Sweet Rosé NV** ★★ **Natural Sweet White NV** ★☆

4th Street range

Natural Sweet Rosé ★☆ Coral pink **NV** with raspberry lightness has a carefree, outdoorsy feel. 750 ml bottle, as all these. Also tasted: **Natural Sweet Red NV** ★☆ **Natural Sweet White NV** ★★ — DB

Foxwood Vineyards ⓛ ⓦ ⓐ ⓞ (NEW)

The partnership behind this label revives an older one. The great-grandfather of Matthew Krone (of the old winemaking family formerly at Twee Jonge Gezellen) and grandfather of Pieter de Vos had a business partnership dating to 1923. Pieter owns the luxury Johannesburg guest house Foxwood with Jan Groenewald, and the three now collaborate over wine. Winemaker Matt is currently renting cellar space and sourcing grapes from three Coastal areas.

★★★★ Chenin Blanc Opulent **12** boasts stonefruit, creamy vanilla & butterscotch from year in oak, a dab of plumping sweetness. Bound to be a hit. Widely sourced, like shiraz.

Shiraz ★★★☆ Prosciutto & red berry perfume draws you in to **11**'s smoothly juicy palate appeal, the dry finish the only indication of the underlying seriousness. — CR, CvZ

Location: Johannesburg ▪ WO: Coastal ▪ Est 2002 ▪ 1stB 2011 ▪ Tasting & sales at Foxwood House 13 5th Street Houghton Johannesburg Mon-Fri 10-5 Sat/Sun by appt 10-2 ▪ Restaurant: à la carte by appt 12-8 daily, Sunday buffet 12-3 ▪ Conferences (40 pax round table/100 pax cinema style) ▪ Cultural artifacts (1880-present) ▪ Owner(s) Pieter de Vos, Jan Groenewald & Matthew Krone ▪ Winemaker(s) Matthew Krone ▪ 50% red 50% white ▪ PO Box 1202 Houghton 2041 ▪ pieter@foxwood.co.za ▪ www.foxwoodvineyards.co.za, www.foxwood.co.za ▪ S 26° 9' 44.28" E 028° 3' 10.19" ▪ F +27 (0)11-486-2300 ▪ **T +27 (0)11-486-0935**

Fraai Uitzicht 1798

On Karl Uwe and Sandra Papesch's venerable Klaasvoogds mountainside farm, with luxury guest house and restaurant, a long-promised Châteauneuf-du-Pape style red is maturing. As a 'preview', Karl Uwe is releasing a solo bottling of blend component grenache. Besides Rhône grapes, his focus is on merlot.

Grenache ⓝ **★★★★** Lightly perfumed fruit aromas on **13** mingle with oaky notes. Very ripe fruit of no great intensity make for a soft & easy palate, though gently gripping. 15% alcohol not too intrusive.

Viognier ★★★ Toasty oak still dominates fruit on now-bottled **14** & adds rough finish to the supple palate, but some typical peach shines through. Not retasted: **Merlot 08 ★★★★ Syrah 13 ★★★** — TJ

Location/map: Robertson ▪ WO: Robertson/Western Cape/Klaasvoogds ▪ 1stB 2000 ▪ Tasting & sales daily 10-4 ▪ Closed Dec 24/25/31 & Jan 1 ▪ Restaurant ▪ 4-star guest house ▪ Owner(s) Karl Uwe Papesch ▪ Winemaker(s) Karl Uwe Papesch (2005) ▪ Viticulturist(s) Michael Marson ▪ 175ha/15ha (grenache, merlot, mourv, shiraz, viog) ▪ 3,000cs own label 95% red 5% white ▪ PO Box 97 Robertson 6705 ▪ info@fraaiuitzicht.com ▪ www.fraaiuitzicht.com ▪ S 33° 47' 43.0" E 020° 0' 18.2" ▪ F +27 (0)86-662-5265 ▪ **T +27 (0)23-626-6156**

Fram Wines ⓘ

While rising star boutique winegrower Thinus Krüger vinifies his range (named for a legendary19th-century Norwegian ship) in the Swartland, fruit is sourced from several areas, each selected for a specific variety in an endeavour to reflect both area and site. 'I'm looking for the difference each site makes. I'd never call the wine better or more special.' New in the cellar in 2015 included grenache gris, tinta barocca, carignan and 'a co-fermented Swartland cab-cinsaut, which looks really lekker'.

★★★★ Pinotage 13 more elegant, charming than **12** (**★★★★**). Light texture & natural fresh feel help highlight pure black cherry flavours. Oaking (older small barrels only) has polished pinotage's rougher edges. Citrusdal Mountain grapes.

★★★★★ Chenin Blanc Citrusdal Mountain grapes vinified to reflect origin. **14** (**★★★★★**) has haunting aromas of hay & dried pears, with a veil of earthiness from natural ferment in older oak. Great texture & intensity, plus positive bitter hint & contrasting delicacy of slow-fading flavour. As individual as **13**.

Also tasted: **Shiraz 14 ★★★★ Chardonnay 14 ★★★★** — AL

Location: Riebeek West ▪ WO: Citrusdal Mountain/Swartland/Robertson ▪ Est/1stB 2012 ▪ Tasting by appt only ▪ Owner(s)/viticulturist(s) Thinus Krüger ▪ Cellarmaster(s)/winemaker(s) Thinus Krüger (Dec 2012) ▪ 30t/2, 500cs own label 45% red 55% white ▪ PO Box 2272 Dennesig Stellenbosch 7601 ▪ thinus@framwines.co.za ▪ www.framwines.co.za ▪ **T +27 (0)72-545-4959**

Francois La Garde ⓘ

Running a specialist Stellenbosch mobile bottling and labelling company doesn't leave former oenology lecturer Piet Matthée much time to spend on his own champagne-method bubblies. But he manages to keep vinifying (at Zorgvliet) and disgorging enough to keep himself, fans and the spirit of the eponymous ancestor happy – even adding a new rosé this edition.

String of Pearls range
★★★★ **Brut Méthode Cap Classique** ② Marked dryness noted on **08** sparkling taken to new level in zero-dosage **09** (★★★), equal pinot noir & chardonnay. Alluring brioche & toasted nut aromas cut short by steely gunflint nuance on austere, food-demanding palate.

Rosé Méthode Cap Classique (NEW) ★★★☆ Delicious aperitif-perfect **09** similar specs to Brut MCC, pinot noir & chardonnay (50/50), but with a blush & balancing dab sugar. Delicate rosepetals & red fruit, long tangy finish. Not tasted: **Reinette Rosé Méthode Cap Classique**, **Blanc de Blancs Méthode Cap Classique**. — MW

Location/map: Stellenbosch ▪ Map grid reference: E5 ▪ WO: Franschhoek ▪ Est 2004 ▪ Tasting by appt ▪ Owner(s) PL Matthée ▪ Cellarmaster(s)/winemaker(s) Piet Matthée (Jan 2009) ▪ 15t/2,000cs own label 100% white ▪ PO Box 12366 Die Boord 7613 ▪ admin@technofill.co.za ▪ www.francois-lagarde.com ▪ F +27 (0)21-887-5274 ▪ **T +27 (0)21-887-3674**

☐ **Francois Le Vaillant** *see* Lutzville Cape Diamond Vineyards

---

Franki's Vineyards   ② ⊕ ⌂ ◎
Some of the grapes from this Swartland winery are sold off, some are vinified in the home cellar by Erica Joubert. She now has nephew Gerhard working with her, allowing two new wines to join the range. The idea is to 'use technology from the New World' with 'suitable elements from the Old World standards'.

Barn Find range
Mourvèdre Rosé (NEW) ★★★ **15** in modest, restrained style; light-feeling & dry, but no lack of fresh red fruit flavour. **Viognier** (NEW) ★★★☆ **15** tasted ex-barrel — only older oak used, but toasty notes still mingle with the subtle peach. Some voluptuousness, but not overdone, with balancing acidity & good texture. Also tasted: **Grenache 14** ★★★ **Joubert Red Blend 14** ★★★ — TJ

Location: Malmesbury ▪ Map: Swartland ▪ WO: Swartland/Western Cape ▪ Est 2004 ▪ 1stB 2007 ▪ Tasting, sales & cellar tours Mon-Fri 8-5 by appt ▪ Closed all pub hols ▪ BYO picnic ▪ Franki's Guest Lodge venue for small weddings & conferences ▪ Owner(s) Franco Afrique Technologies (Pty) Ltd ▪ Winemaker(s) Erica Joubert (Jan 2004), with Gerhard Joubert (2015) ▪ 700ha/22ha (grenache, mourv, viog) ▪ ±160t/450cs own label 98% red 2% white ▪ PO Box 972 Malmesbury 7299 ▪ erica.joubert@cropspec.co.za, jeanne@frankisvineyards.co.za ▪ www.frankisvineyards.co.za ▪ S 33° 20' 59.5" E 018° 32' 12.4" ▪ F +27 (0)86-660-3677 ▪ **T +27 (0)82-963-8045/+27 (0)82-888-3702**

Franschhoek Cellar   ② ⊕ ◎ ⑧ ⑤
Remodelling of the brand home has created a stylish tourist drawcard for not just Franschhoek Cellar but also DGB-owned siblings Brampton, Bellingham and Bernard Series. Al fresco dining, functions, children's play area and bespoke tasting lounges are housed in Franschhoek Cellar's original home on the town's main street, creating a link with other local landmarks featured in the wines' names.

Franschhoek Vineyards range
★★★★ **Shiraz** Flagship red is unpretentious, delicious & consistent. **13**'s red berries & white pepper are variety true & suffused with appetising vanilla; drinks well & should improve. Franschhoek WO, as next.
★★★★ **Semillon** Part natural ferment in 10% new oak for **14**. Ticks all the boxes for a cut-above summer white: lemon thyme & lanolin whiffs, toasty fruit flavours, refreshing acidity & moderate alcohol.

Village Walk range
Old Museum Merlot ★★★ Very sippable **14** with mocha nuance, hint of sweetness & brush of new oak well integrated. **Stone Bridge Pinotage** ★★★☆ Standout red in this range. Mostly old-oak-aged **14** has appealing strawberry fruit, fresh acidity & coffee finish; no rough edges. **Clubhouse Rosé** ★★☆ **15** preview raises the bar with a hint of complexity in the red & black berry flavours, food-friendly nudge of tannin, dry conclusion. **Statue de Femme Sauvignon Blanc** ★★★ Al fresco companion **15** can only be sauvignon: grass, capsicum & racy acidity — just what the fans expect. Also tasted: **The Churchyard Cabernet Sauvignon 14** ★★★ **Baker Station Shiraz 14** ★★★ **Our Town Hall Chardonnay 15** ★★★ **La Cotte Mill Chenin Blanc 15** ★★☆ — CvZ

Location/map: Franschhoek • WO: Western Cape/Franschhoek • Est 1945 • Tasting & sales Mon-Thu 10–6 Fri/Sat 10-9 Sun 10–5 • Wine pairing: 6 wines with 6 cheeses; 6 wines with assorted chocolates • Closed Easter Fri/Sun, Dec 25/26 & Jan 1 • Al fresco dining daily • Play area for children • Farm produce • Weddings • Conferences • Events venue (seat 300 pax) • Owner(s) DGB (Pty) Ltd • Winemaker(s) JD Rossouw • Viticulturist(s) Stephan Joubert (Nov 2006) • 300ha (cab, merlot, shiraz, chard, chenin, sauv, sem) • 30,000t 49% red 50% white 1% rosé • ISO 9001:2001, IPW • PO Box 52 Franschhoek 7690 • fhcellardoor@dgb.co.za • www.thefranschhoekcellar.co.za • S 33° 54' 16.4" E 019° 6' 40.7" • F +27 (0)21-876-4107 • **T +27 (0)21-876-2086**

☐ **Frans K Smit** *see* Spier

Freedom Hill Wines   Ⓠ 🍽 📷 🅰 ♿

Civil engineer Francois Klomp's Paarl hillside farm, established as a red-wine property in the late 90s, is now managed by industrial engineer daughter Chanine. Recent upgrades include a wedding and special events venue, landscaped gardens, seasonal picnics and platters, and novel wine pairings (try toffee and nuts). Current rebranding sees a gold sunbird take flight…

Freedom Hill range

Shiraz-Cabernet Sauvignon ★★★☆ Pleasantly substantial **12** shows plum pudding fruit, sweet spices, smooth tannins. 60/40 blend. **Chardonnay ★★★☆** First tasted since **10**, barrel-matured **14** has appealing lime & butter notes, well-restrained oak. Nicely balanced package. WO W Cape, like next. **Chenin Blanc ★★★** Cheerful, fruity **15** is light & refreshing, with demure 12% alcohol. Also tasted: **Pinotage 13 ★★★☆ Shiraz 12 ★★★ Sauvignon Blanc 15 ★★★★** Not tasted: **Cape Blend**.

Freedom Walk 1335/88 range

Not tasted: **Pinotage, Shiraz, Cape Blend**. — GdB

Location: Paarl • Map: Franschhoek • WO: Paarl/Western Cape • Est 1997 • 1stB 2000 • Tasting Mon-Fri 10-5 Sat 12-4 pub hols by appt • Closed Easter Fri/Sun & Dec 25 • Child friendly • Cheese & charcuterie platters, picnics available in season by appt • Wedding & function venue • Owner(s) Francois Klomp • Cellarmaster(s)/winemaker(s) Kowie du Toit (Feb 2007) • Viticulturist(s) Paul Wallace • 82ha/19ha (cab, ptage, shiraz) • ±70t/12,000cs own label 100% red • PO Box 6126 Paarl 7620 • info@freedomhill.co.za • www.freedomhill.co.za • S 33° 49' 48.33" E 019° 0' 35.90" • F +27 (0)86-244-9748 • **T +27 (0)21-867-0085**

☐ **Freedom Walk** *see* Freedom Hill Wines
☐ **Frid hem Gaard** *see* Migliarina Wines
☐ **Friesland** *see* Kaapzicht Wine Estate
☐ **Frisky Zebras** *see* United Nations of Wine
☐ **Frog Hill** *see* Anura Vineyards
☐ **Frogner** *see* Nordic Wines

Fröhlich Family Wines   Ⓠ NEW

Michael Fröhlich, owner of this boutique Bonnievale winery, had long supplied grapes to a local cellar but, he says, 'we realised that the true value of our passion could only be realised when we created our own wine'. The excitement of the first vintage vinified in their cellar, 2014, was marred by a 'disastrous bottling experience', but the character of 2015 was compensation. Quality wine that is unpretentious but typical of variety and terroir, is the totally laudable aim.

Wooded Chardonnay ⓦ **★★★** Citrus peel & pith, a gentle oatmeal biscuit overlay from oak, **14** is fresh, sleek & youthful. **Sauvignon Blanc** ⓦ **★★★** Delightfully light & fresh but in no way lacking personality or flavour, **15** has Rose's Lime Juice intensity, a tangy acidity that bodes well for some cellaring.

Rosé ★★★ 15 from merlot celebrates red berries in a fruity but dry charmer that has 'drink me' written all over it. **Chenin Blanc ★★★** Quince & fresh hay, **15** is fruity-fresh & softly rounded. **Viognier ★★★** Bursting with flowers & peaches, **15** showcases the aromatic side of the variety. — CR, CvZ

Location/WO: Bonnievale ▪ Map: Robertson ▪ Est 2013 ▪ 1stB 2014 ▪ Tasting by appt ▪ Owner(s) Michael
Ian Fröhlich ▪ Cellarmaster(s)/viticulturist(s) Salôme Buys-Vermeulen (Jun 2013) ▪ 63.35ha/21ha under
vine ▪ 200t 30% red 60% white 10% rosé ▪ GlobalGAP, WIETA ▪ fueltec@netactive.co.za ▪
www.frohlichfamilywines/facebook.co.za ▪ S 33° 58' 1.49" E 020° 8' 12.01" ▪ F +27 (0)23-616-2972 ▪
T +27 (0)23-616-2972

Fryer's Cove Vineyards   Ⓨ ⑪ ⓒ ⓖ

Unlocking the cool-climate maritime potential of vineyards on the near-deserted Atlantic shoreline near
desolate diamond divers' haunt Doring Bay led to this collaboration between West Coast grower Jan
'Ponk' van Zyl and Stellenbosch-based winemaker brother-in-law Wynand Hamman. An own small
vineyard and simple, sea-cooled cellar in a converted harbour building contribute to an expanding
range, requiring assistance from recent recruit Jacques Vos. The wines, tiny tasting room and rustic seafood eatery extending onto a wave-washed wooden jetty make for a special visitor experience.

★★★★ **Bamboes Bay Blanc Fumé** (NEW) From best grapes off older vines, **13** fermented over 3 months
(some whole berry) in small barrels, blended with previous vintages for complexity. Forthcoming vanilla-
laced tropical fruit; rich, with tangy acid lift & vibrancy.

★★★★ **Bamboes Bay Sauvignon Blanc 15** ex tank intense asparagus, nettle & gooseberry appeal,
tad hard finish. Also-tasted **14** brisk & engaging, with passionfruit, grass & lemon notes, herbal interest on
fine-tuned palate, pleasing weight from small oaked portion.

★★★★ **Doringbaai Sauvignon Blanc** Quirky label, serious wine. From Doring & Elands Bays,
Lutzville, seductive **15** greengage & nettle bouquet, tropical flavours, crunchy yet unaggressively acidic.

★★★★ **Noble Late Harvest** (NEW) Botrytis dessert **13**'s beautiful honeyed notes layered with orange &
dried mango; richness & sweetness effortlessly cleansed by acidity. From sauvignon blanc; 375 ml.

Shiraz (NEW) ★★★★ Earthy, peppery **14** shows good freshness & balance but lacks real concentration &
complexity. Also tasted: **Pinot Noir 14** ★★★★ **The Jetty Sauvignon Blanc 15** ★★★ — JPf

Location: Doring Bay ▪ Map: Olifants River ▪ WO: Western Cape/Bamboes Bay ▪ Est 1999 ▪ 1stB 2002 ▪
Tasting, sales & cellar tours Mon-Fri 8-5 Sat 10-5 ▪ Tasting fee, donations for public school ▪ Closed Sun
& Christian hols ▪ The Jetty restaurant open 10-4 (summer)/11-3 (winter), bookings on weekends &
pub hols ▪ West Coast walking trail ▪ Owner(s) Jan Ponk Trust, JH Laubscher Family Trust & Wynand
Hamman ▪ Cellarmaster(s) Wynand Hamman (Apr 1999) ▪ Winemaker(s) Jacques Vos (Dec 2014, assistant) ▪ Viticulturist(s) Jan van Zyl (Apr 1999), with Jacques Vos (Dec 2014) ▪ 6ha (pinot, sauv) ▪ 85t/
5,000cs own label 30% red 70% white ▪ PO Box 93 Vredendal 8160 ▪ admin@fryerscove.co.za, cellar@
fryerscove.co.za ▪ www.fryerscove.co.za ▪ S 31° 45' 53.1" E 018° 13' 55.8" ▪ F +27 (0)86-636-3295 ▪
T +27 (0)27-213-2312 (office)/+27 (0)27-215-1092 (tasting)

☐ **Future Eternal** *see* L'Avenir Vineyards

Gabriëlskloof   Ⓨ ⑪ ⓒ ⓐ ⓖ

This was a Bot River wheat and sheep farm until Bernhard Heyns and partners bought it in 2002 and
established a substantial, sustainably farmed wine estate (with olives important too). Soil analysis suggested planting Bordeaux and Rhône varieties, which remain the focus, joined by chenin blanc in 2015.
In another significant development, 2015 also saw the maiden harvest of cellarmaster (and son-in-law)
Peter-Allan Finlayson, of Crystallum fame, who inaugurated what looks set to be a new, hands-off wine
aesthetic, with spontaneous fermentation for most of the grapes.

Reserve range

★★★★ **Swartriver Shiraz** Fynbos, dried herb dryness on ripe **12**, with oak & sweetness rather less evident than on **11** (★★★★). Succulent, savoury & quite dense fruit; well supported by infrastructure of tannin & acid. Also in magnum.

★★★★ **Five Arches** Heavily oaked aromas on youthful **12** blend of 5 red Bordeaux varieties – a more
intense version of The Blend, with ripe berry fruit & firm, succulent tannins. Well balanced, on a largeish
scale. 1.5L available.

★★★★ **Magdalena 14** a 60:40 blend of well-oaked semillon & sauvignon working happily together. Gentle fragrance (fresh honey, flowers & wax there) leads to penetrating freshness in the context of broader flavours.

Also tasted: **Viognier 14** ★★★☆

Special Collection

★★★★ **Noble Late Harvest** ⓥ Unoaked **13** dessert from semillon with aromatic viognier (partly ex Elgin). Sweetly delicate, fresh & really charming — no great complexity or depth but poised & delightful.

Premium range

★★★★ **Sauvignon Blanc** Not too obvious, **15** an aromatic blend of riper (blackcurrant) & grassy elements. More interesting than **14** (★★★★). Fresh but unaggressive, carrying a core of fruit to a good finish.

Rosebud ★★★ Fruity, forward **15** from shiraz & viognier, drier & crisper than previous though also lightish alcohol (12.2%). Balanced, flavourful, with quite a tannic bite for a rosé. Also tasted: **Shiraz 12** ★★★★ **The Blend 12** ★★★☆ — TJ

Location: Bot River ▪ Map: Elgin, Walker Bay & Bot River ▪ WO: Bot River/Cape South Coast ▪ Est 2002 ▪ 1stB 2007 ▪ Tasting & sales Mon-Fri 9–5 Sat 11-3 ▪ Fee R15/4 wines or R30/8 wines, waived on purchase ▪ Closed Dec 24/25 ▪ Cellar tours by appt ▪ Restaurant ▪ Deli ▪ Child-friendly; dogs welcome ▪ Weddings (very limited availability) ▪ Annual market (Dec 11-12) ▪ Owner(s) Bernhard Heyns & shareholders Johan Heyns, Barry Anderson & Wally Clarke ▪ Cellarmaster(s) Peter-Allan Finlayson (Jul 2014) ▪ Winemaker(s) Christiaan van der Merwe (Jan 2011) ▪ Viticulturist(s) Barry Anderson (2001) ▪ 150ha/68ha (cabs s/f, malbec, merlot, mourv, p verdot, pinot, shiraz, sauv, sem, viog) ▪ BWI champion, IPW, WIETA ▪ PO Box 499 Kleinmond 7195 ▪ info@gabrielskloof.co.za ▪ www.gabrielskloof.co.za ▪ S 34° 14' 19.89" E 019° 14' 58.68" ▪ F +27 (0)28-284-9864 ▪ **T +27 (0)28-284-9865**

☐ **Game Reserve** see Graham Beck Wines

Gantouw Farm

Previously prime hunting ground for eland (gantouw), this mountainous Helderberg property is now farmed in an eco-friendly way by Linky and James Smith (founder of Wetherlys furniture and decor). In addition to olives and over 20 varieties of 'gourmet' garlic, they grow sauvignon and petit verdot without commercial fertilisers or pesticides. Vinification is by Yves Musfeld at nearby Onderkloof.

Sauvignon Blanc ⓥ ★★★ Gooseberries & passionfruit with a zinging fresh acidity that would be a good seafood match, **13** unmistakably sauvignon & for summer. — CR, CvZ

Location: Sir Lowry's Pass ▪ WO: Stellenbosch ▪ Est 2006 ▪ 1stB 2012 ▪ Closed to public ▪ Sales (wine, olives/olive oil, garlic) via website & social media ▪ Owner(s) James Alexander Smith ▪ Winemaker(s) Yves Musfeld (Jan 2012, Onderkloof) ▪ 25ha/3.3ha under vine ▪ 10t/1,600cs own label 100% white ▪ PO Box 2649 Somerset West 7129 ▪ james@gantouwfarm.co.za ▪ www.gantouwfarm.co.za ▪ F +27 (0)86-518-0518 ▪ **T +27 (0)83-794-6070**

☐ **Garajeest** see The Garajeest

Garden Route Wines   ⓥ ♿

De Krans' champion port-style maker Boets Nel revels in vinifying these unfortified wines from cool-grown vines in Waboomskraal Valley near George on the coastal Garden Route. The awarded Shiraz and Sauvignon Blanc are available at home base in Calitzdorp and Outeniqua Wine Emporium on the N12.

★★★★ **Sauvignon Blanc** ⊘ Ex tank, **15** wild fynbos & herbs, crisp green apple flavour, greenpepper & clean minerality on a firm acid base. Shows potential but needs short time to fully integrate.

> **Shiraz** ⊕ ★★★☆ Revealing its cool provenance, **13** is redolent of wind-blown sea foam & red berries; crisp cranberry flavours make it an ideal companion to roast pork or duck. — DB

Location: Calitzdorp ▪ Map: Klein Karoo & Garden Route ▪ WO: Outeniqua ▪ Est/1stB 2008 ▪ Tasting & sales at De Krans (see entry) ▪ Wines also available at Outeniqua Wine Emporium, Waboomskraal on N12 between George & Oudtshoorn ▪ Owner(s) Boets Nel ▪ Cellarmaster(s)/viticulturist(s) Boets Nel

(2008) ▪ 9ha (shiraz, chard, sauv) ▪ 80t/±3,000cs own label 50% red 50% white ▪ PO Box 28 Calitzdorp 6660 ▪ dekrans@mweb.co.za ▪ S 33° 32' 6.3" E 021° 41' 9.0" ▪ F +27 (0)44-213-3562/+27 (0)23-541-1702 ▪ **T +27 (0)44-213-3314/+27 (0)23-541-1702**

☐ **Garden Vineyards** *see* DeMorgenzon
☐ **Gecko Ridge** *see* Long Mountain Wine Company
☐ **Genade Water** *see* Nuweland Wynkelder

Genevieve Méthode Cap Classique   ⓥ

From promoting the wines of various Bot River producers, Melissa Nelsen took the next step: making her own, a champagne-method sparkling from the grapes of the area. Bearing her middle, suitably French name, the current 2010 follows her maiden 2008.

★★★★ **Genevieve** ⓥ **10** sparkling from chardonnay is fruit driven, as expected from blanc de blancs, the small oak-fermented portion almost invisible among crisp, bright appley bubbles. — MW

Location: Bot River ▪ WO: Overberg ▪ Est 2009 ▪ 1stB 2008 ▪ Tasting by appt ▪ Owner(s) Melissa Nelsen ▪ Viticulturist(s) Leon Engelke (2008) ▪ 16t/1,650cs own label 100% MCC ▪ PO Box 122 Elgin 7180 ▪ melissa@genevievemcc.co.za ▪ www.genevievemcc.co.za ▪ **T +27 (0)83-302-6562**

Gentleman Spirits   ⓥ

Globetrotting in search of the finest fruit, a suitable site and, um, kindred spirits to help him develop a portfolio of 'superlative distilled beverages', Hubertus Vallendar finally found all on Stellenbosch wine farm Blaauwklippen. Together with MD/winemaker Rolf Zeitvogel (already distilling potstill brandies) and Swiss partner Urs Gmuer, he's been producing grape husk spirits ('marc/grappa') and citrus eaux de vie since 2012, recently introducing gins. All are available from Blaauwklippen's special 'spirits room'.

Husk Spirit range

★★★★ **Malbec Noble Late Harvest** ⓥ Rich, elegant & oh-so-smooth, with honeysuckle & jasmine perfumes. Lively flow & silky texture, full flavours, integrated spirit – a party in your mouth!

★★★★ **Merlot** ⓥ Fresh, pure & enticing floral & spicy red berry nose; focused & fresh with soft, sweet berry flavours; concludes with a raspberry lift. 500 ml, as all.

★★★★ **Shiraz** ⓥ Colourless, as all these. Scented with notes of violet & lavender, black berries & exotic spice. Smooth, elegant, with a lovely depth & balance.

★★★★ **Zinfandel** ⓥ Wild flowers, dried herbs & warm spice introduce the silky palate & delicate fire. Clean, bright, with subtle nut & red berry perfume. Balanced, with spirit well integrated.

Zinfandel Noble Late Harvest ★★★★ Improved new bottling offers fragrant rose & violet perfume, on the palate honey & soft berries combine harmoniously for a satisfying sip.

Eau de Vie range

★★★★ **Lemon** ⓥ Upfront lemon blossom & rind jump out of the glass; zesty, creamy & fresh – fun with dessert or on the deck after lunch.

★★★★ **Orange** ⓥ Richly layered marmalade, orange rind & sweet-spiced orange flavours take over the palate. Depth, with elegance & a fresh, lifted finish. Delicious! — WB

Location/map/WO: Stellenbosch ▪ Map grid reference: E7 ▪ Est/1stB 2012 ▪ Tasting & sales at Blaauwklippen (see entry) ▪ Closed Dec 25 & Jan 1 ▪ Distillery tours by appt only ▪ Owner(s) Hubertus Vallendar, Urs Gmuer, Rolf Zeitvogel ▪ Brandy master(s) Hubertus Vallendar (Feb 2012) ▪ 1,000cs ▪ rz@ gentleman-spirits.com ▪ www.gentleman-spirits.co.za ▪ S 33° 58' 23.3" E 018° 50' 51.0" ▪ F +27 (0)21-880-0136 ▪ **T +27 (0)82-907-9787**

☐ **Ghost Corner** *see* Cederberg Private Cellar
☐ **Ghost Tree** *see* SylvanVale Vineyards
☐ **Giant Periwinkle** *see* The Giant Periwinkle
☐ **Giant's Peak** *see* Wine-of-the-Month Club

Gilga Wines

(medal) (house)

Cellarmaster Stefan Gerber (also of Boer & Brit) partners with John Rowan in this Stellenboschkloof boutique winery, whose untasted line-up includes varietal Syrah and blends Amurabi and Zagros. A spacious self-catering guest house on the property can be booked via the website.

Location/map: Stellenbosch ▪ Map grid reference: D5 ▪ Est/1stB 2002 ▪ Tasting & sales by appt ▪ Guest house ▪ Owner(s) John Rowan & Stefan Gerber ▪ Cellarmaster(s) Stefan Gerber (Jun 2010), with assistant winemaker Roelof du Toit (Jan 2014, consultant) ▪ Viticulturist(s) Stefan Gerber (Jun 2010) ▪ 4ha/3.5ha (grenache, mourv, shiraz, tempranillo) ▪ 10t/1,100cs own label 100% red ▪ PO Box 871 Stellenbosch 7599 ▪ info@gilga.co.za ▪ www.gilga.co.za ▪ S 33° 56' 46.1" E 018° 47' 20.6" ▪ F +27 (0)86-531-7137 ▪ **T +27 (0)84-515-6677**

☐ **Gilysipao** see Orange River Cellars
☐ **Girlfriends Wine** see Val du Charron
☐ **Glass Collection** see Glenelly Estate

Glen Carlou

(medal) (fork) (camera) (person) (wheelchair)

Since Donald Hess' Hess Family Estates bought out the Finlayson family, founders of this Paarl farm, it has become a destination venue. Apart from wine, there's the Hess Art Museum, a restaurant, tapas bar and speciality shop where wines from the other Hess estates may be purchased. The Curator's Collection, a range of limited-batch wines available from the winery only, was launched to celebrate Arco Laarman's 20 years in wine and five as Glen Carlou's cellarmaster. Celebrations were also in order for Glen Carlou Chardonnay, deemed by a US panel of ten sommeliers to be the joint-favourite to pair with oysters, when pitted against 30 international chardonnays and nine oyster species. What gave the SA wine the edge? 'It's the lime,' reckoned the participants.

Prestige range

★★★★☆ **Gravel Quarry Cabernet Sauvignon** Released as 5 year old, farm's top cab shows well-harmonised all-new French oak regime, still many years' potential. **10** powerful, stately, with impressively long sumptuous dark chocolate filling to its highly polished grip. A talking point wine, from best vineyards.

★★★★☆ **Quartz Stone Chardonnay** 14 (★★★★) reflects power associated with this single, old vineyard but lacks concentration, creamy layers of **13**. Carries 90% new oak well (balance concrete 'egg' ferment) on medium body, lightish, fresh flavours.

Also tasted: **The Welder 13** ★★★★

The Curator's Collection

★★★★ **Cabernet Franc** (NEW) Characterful debut, **13** displays clear leafy, spicy tones, fine-boned structure associated with variety. Good substance, freshness provides balance to allow for time needed to assimilate cedary oak (100% new).

★★★★ **Chenin Blanc** Unoaked **15** (★★★☆) very different from broader, wooded **13**, both ex Swartland. Delicate bruised apple purity takes a while to unfold from steely, taut frame. Reasonable length, gentle pithy nip suggests possible greater interest after year/2.

★★★★ **Viognier** (NEW) A breath of spring in **15**'s honeysuckle, apricot blossom fragrance. Uncluttered by oak, there's appealing fruit purity & freshness; also length & a sense of future complexity. Charming debut.

Not retasted: **Malbec 11** ★★★★ **Tannat 10** ★★★★ Not tasted: **Pinot Noir Reserve**.

Classic range

★★★★ **Cabernet Sauvignon** Ripe but well-proportioned **13** has sound dark-berry fruit concentration to balance determined tannin structure, 14% alcohol. Harmonised in all-older French oak.

★★★★ **Grand Classique** 12 bigger, sterner year, cab (50%) taking command of this Bordeaux quintet. There's fruit richness, layers of flavour & overall balance to warrant cellaring.

★★★★ **Petit Verdot-Tannat** (medal) Unusual but successful pairing. **11** rich in flavour & confidently built, though both its natural fresh feel & fine-grained tannins temper its full body.

★★★★ **Chardonnay** Bright fruited, New World style, carefully oaked for weight, breadth without dimming zesty pickled lime, juicy tropical flavours. **14** well balanced, supple & lingering.

★★★★ **Unwooded Chardonnay** 14 back on form after 13 (★★★★); richly textured with touch of pithy grip to focus ripe citrus, canned pineapple flavours. Concrete 'egg' ferment, 6 months lees-ageing.
Also tasted: **Merlot** 13 ★★★ **Pinot Noir** 13 ★★★★ **Sauvignon Blanc** 15 ★★★ Not retasted: **Syrah** 10 ★★★★ Discontinued: **Zinfandel**.

Limited Releases
Méthode Cap Classique ★★★ MCC from Robertson's Bon Courage, exclusive to Glen Carlou. Latest **10** chardonnay with 11% pinot; plain earthy lees features, brisk bubble.

Contemporary range
Tortoise Hill Red ★★ Sweet red fruits dimmed by determined grip on **13** cab, merlot partnership. WO W Cape. Also tasted: **Tortoise Hill White** 14 ★★ — AL

Location: Paarl • Map: Paarl & Wellington • Map grid reference: D7 • WO: Paarl/Swartland/Robertson/ Durbanville/Western Cape/Coastal • Est 1985 • 1stB 1988 • Tasting & sales Mon-Fri 8.30–5 Sat/Sun 10–4 • Fee R25-R50 • Closed Good Fri, Dec 25 & Jan 1 • Cellar tours by appt • Restaurant • Facilities for children • Tour groups • Gifts • Honey • Conferences • Conservation area • Hess Art Collection Museum • Owner(s) Hess Family Wine Estates Ltd (Switzerland) • Cellarmaster(s)/winemaker(s) Arco Laarman (Jan 2000) • Viticulturist(s) Marius Cloete (2000) • 145ha/68ha (cabs s/f, malbec, mourv, p verdot, pinot, shiraz, chard) • ±700t/ 100,000cs own label • PO Box 23 Klapmuts 7625 • welcome@glencarlou.co.za • www.glencarlou.co.za • S 33° 48' 44.85" E 018° 54' 12.88" • F +27 (0)86-215-8157 • **T +27 (0)21-875-5528**

Glenelly Estate   ⓦ ⓒ ♿

In her 90th year, May-Eliane de Lencquesaing shows no signs of slowing down. Repeated South African success in winning the Pichon Lalande Trophy at the International Wine & Spirit Competition was an initial attraction for her, then owner of that Bordeaux classed growth, to invest in the Cape. Thirteen years after development of what was an old fruit farm into vineyards and construction of a cellar, Glenelly on Stellenbosch's Simonsberg is undergoing further improvements with the building of a new home for Madame's noteworthy glass collection, renovations of the tasting room and space for a new food experience. It is anticipated these will be completed by mid-2016.

Lady May range
★★★★☆ **Lady May** ⓖ Classic cab, naturally fermented **11** still youthfully taut, with subtle lead pencil, dark fruit aromas; complementary oaking (100% new). Full bodied, but fine acid backbone & properly dry finish lend overall refinement. Includes a little petit verdot, merlot. Stellenbosch WO.

Grand Vin de Glenelly range
★★★★☆ **Red** Syrah/shiraz & cab, supported by merlot, petit verdot. **10** reflects sturdiness of vintage but also refinement associated with property. Look for syrah's resonating dark spice & savouriness, cab's ageworthy structure. Still youthful; potential to 2020 in 750ml, longer in magnum.

★★★★ **Chardonnay** House style expressive yet unshowy, as in **14**'s tropical purity, attractive creamy-fresh contrast & medium body. Natural ferment in 500L oak & lees-ageing provide extra nuance.

Glass Collection
★★★★ **Cabernet Sauvignon** Crunchily fresh blackberry flavours, tannic grip to balance & properly dry finish make **13** appetising mouthful. Subtle oaking, just 15% new, adds further appeal.

★★★★ **Merlot** A merlot to convince variety's naysayers. **13** reprises **12**'s focus & precision in its dark chocolate, plum layers, vibrant yet polished tannins. Savouriness is a bonus.

★★★★ **Syrah** Warming, rich & full of black pepper spice, **12** also shows a welcome freshness that makes it temptingly moreish. Year in oak, none new. More interesting than **11** (★★★☆).
Also tasted: **Chardonnay Unwooded** 14 ★★★☆ — AL

Location/map: Stellenbosch • Map grid reference: F4 • WO: Simonsberg–Stellenbosch/Stellenbosch • Est/1stB 2003 • Tasting & sales closed due to renovations, tasting available by appt • Closed Easter Fri/ Sun, Dec 25/26 & Jan 1 • Cellar tours by appt • Glass museum viewing by appt • Owner(s) May-Eliane de Lencquesaing • Cellarmaster(s) Luke O'Cuinneagain (Jan 2008) • Winemaker(s) Luke O'Cuinneagain (Jan 2008), with Jerome Likwa (Jan 2008) • Viticulturist(s) Heinrich Louw (2003) • 125ha/60ha (cabs s/ f, merlot, p verdot, shiraz, chard) • 500t/55,334cs own label 90% red 10% white • PO Box 1079

Stellenbosch 7599 ▪ wine@glenelly.co.za ▪ www.glenellyestate.com ▪ S 33° 55' 6.1" E 018° 52' 45.1" ▪
F +27 (0)21-809-6448 ▪ **T +27 (0)21-809-6440**

Glen Heatlie   Ⓨ

A Grenache-Shiraz '15 and Chenin Blanc '15, both unready for review, are the latest small-parcel
bottlings by after-hours vintner Joan-Marie Heatlie, based on the family farm near Worcester where her
Scottish great-grandfather distilled Heatlie's Prized Brandy in the 1880s.

Location: Worcester ▪ Est 2006 ▪ Tasting by appt only ▪ Owner(s) Orange Grove Trust ▪ Winemaker(s)
Joan-Marie Heatlie ▪ Viticulturist(s) Charlie Heatlie ▪ 3,100ha/45ha (cab, merlot, shiraz, chenin, chard,
cbard, sauv, sem) ▪ Orange Grove PO Box 18 De Wet 6853 ▪ joan@glenheatlie.co.za ▪ F +27 (0)23-341-
2708 ▪ **T +27 (0)82-364-4702**

Glenview Wines

Vintner and surfer Robin Marks continues to do steady online business, locally and abroad, by sourcing
wines from coastal vineyards for his own label (the brand name a reference to Glen Beach near Robin's
Camps Bay home). His selling point is easy-drinking, affordable quality.

Merlot ★★ Red-fruited 14, smooth & juicy, perfect pizza & pasta partner. **Sauvignon Blanc ★★★**
Tasty 15 has variety-true passionfruit & grassy notes, zippy acidity. WO W Cape. — GM

Location: Cape Town ▪ WO: Stellenbosch/Western Cape ▪ Est/1stB 1998 ▪ Closed to public ▪ Owner(s) Robin
Marks ▪ Winemaker(s) Danie Steytler jnr (consultant) ▪ 14,000cs own label 50% red 50% white ▪ PO Box
32234 Camps Bay 8040 ▪ bayexport@kingsley.co.za ▪ F +27 (0)21-511-2545 ▪ **T +27 (0)21-438-1080**

GlenWood   Ⓨ ⑪ ◎ ⑤

Secluded in Franschhoek's Robertsvlei, GlenWood was developed by former business consultant Alastair
Wood with hands-on involvement by locally born stalwart, cellarmaster/viticulturist DP Burger. Alien
vegetation was cleared to accommodate vines, and today sustainable farming practices accompany a
minimalist approach in the cellar, producing rare consistency of quality. New winemaker Zinaschke Steyn
takes the edge off, as does fine fare from the farm bistro enjoyed in restored natural surrounds.

Grand Duc range

★★★★☆ Syrah ⓍⓏ This range only in exceptional vintages; bunch pressing, wild yeast ferments &
100% new oak, 2 years. From Wellington fruit, 12 a beautifully crafted, balanced & complex wine showing concentrated plum, white pepper, blueberry aromas & flavours. Good for up to a decade.

★★★★☆ Chardonnay Bunch press, natural ferment, 2 years new oak, monthly bâtonnage, light filtration – that's a lot of... hands-off care in the making of 13 (★★★★★), which takes 12 up a notch with
opulent yellow peach & apricot fruit, vanilla, almond & chamomile complexity.

GlenWood range

★★★★ Merlot Chocolate-toned 13 delivers great fruit concentration, vivacity & purity plus blueberry &
cherry nuances; approachable tannin structure for now & few years keeping.

★★★★ Shiraz Perfumed 13's judicious oaking (30% new, 18 months) provides light spicing, elegant
mouthfeel for fine dining. There's also classic berry, rosemary complexity & a graceful finish.

★★★★☆ Chardonnay Vigneron's Selection Clever oaking (year 2nd fill) ensures wild-yeast-fermented 14's flamboyant fruit is unobscured. Full body, with refreshing acidity, stonefruit core, vanilla &
almond farewell. Like barrel-fermented 13, has a lot going on.

★★★★ Unwooded Chardonnay Worthy follow-on to ageworthy 13 (14 untasted), 15 5 months
lees-matured for extra mouthfeel & roundness; elegant, with mineral nuance for oysters.

Also tasted: **Sauvignon Blanc 15 ★★★** Not retasted: **Merlot-Shiraz 12 ★★★☆** Not tasted: **Semillon Vigneron's Selection**. — GM

Location/map: Franschhoek ▪ WO: Franschhoek/Coastal ▪ Est/1stB 2002 ▪ Tasting & sales Mon-Fri 11–4
Sat/Sun (Aug-May only) 11-3 ▪ Closed Easter Fri/Sun, Dec 25 & Jan 1 ▪ Tasting R50/cellar tour R150 ▪
Tours daily at 11; cellar tour with owner/winemaker available by prior arrangement, min 2 persons ▪ Bis-
tro@GlenWood open for lunch Thu-Tue ▪ Hikes ▪ Owner(s) Alastair G Wood ▪ Cellarmaster(s)/viticultur-

ist(s) DP Burger (Apr 1991) ▪ Winemaker(s) Zinaschke Steyn (Jan 2015) ▪ 49ha/30ha (merlot, shiraz, chard, sauv, sem) ▪ 150t/16,000cs own label 50% red 50% white ▪ BWI, IPW ▪ PO Box 204 Franschhoek 7690 ▪ info@glenwoodvineyards.co.za ▪ www.glenwoodvineyards.co.za ▪ S 33° 54' 56.7" E 019° 4' 57.0" ▪ F +27 (0)21-876-3338 ▪ **T +27 (0)21-876-2044**

Goats do Roam Wine Company   ⓐ

Born at Fairview in Paarl, this 'kid' is Charles Back of Fairview's fun range of highly drinkable, value-for-money, Fairtrade wines from mostly southern French varieties (hence the wordplay on Côtes du Rhône and Côte Rôtie) as well as Italian grapes sangiovese, barbera and nebbiolo (with cab) for The Goatfather.

★★★★ **Goat Roti** Merest smidgen of viognier (3%) adds fynbos perfume to dark plum, black berry, pepper & spice of silky **13**. Includes Stellenbosch grapes.

Goats do Roam Red ⊘ ★★★☆ Six Rhône varieties led by 60% shiraz are herded together in easy-drinking **14**, which tastes like cinnamon-sprinkled baked plums. WO W Cape. **Goats do Roam Rosé** ★★★☆ From its vibrant sunset blush to its strawberry & Morello cherry fruit, dry food-friendly **15** pink from five varieties (led by 37% shiraz) cries out for sundowner tapas. W Cape WO. Also tasted: **Goats in Villages Red 13** ★★★ **The Goatfather 13** ★★★☆ **Goats do Roam White 15** ★★★☆ — JG

Location: Paarl ▪ WO: Coastal/Western Cape ▪ Est/1stB 1998 ▪ Tasting & sales at Fairview ▪ Owner(s) Charles Back ▪ Winemaker(s) Anthony de Jager, with Stephanie Betts & Adele Dunbar ▪ PO Box 583 Suider-Paarl 7624 ▪ info@goatsdoroam.com ▪ www.fairview.co.za ▪ F +27 (0)21-863-2591 ▪ **T +27 (0)21-863-2450**

Goede Hoop Estate   ⓐ ⓐ ⓐ ⓐ

The vineyards of this well-established family estate climb the slopes of Stellenbosch's Bottelary Kloof, giving a wide range of conditions. Taking the grapes into the cellar (much of the wine is sold off in bulk) are consultant cellarmaster Albert Ahrens and, appointed in time for the fine 2015 vintage, Anton Bothma. The Heritage label is a joint venture between Albert and Goede Hoop's owner Pieter Bestbier — 3rd generation of his family here.

Heritage Wines

★★★★ **Estate Wine** ⓐ **11** blends merlot, pinotage, cab, shiraz, malbec & cinsaut to express the estate. More power than **10** (needs time), but some elegance, & depth of fruit too. Larger oak barrels.

★★★★ **Estate Straw Wine** ⓐ **10** from chenin; hugely sweet & concentrated, ripe fruit flavours.

Goede Hoop Estate range

Pinotage ★★★ Spicy **12** dry, savoury & well built, with firm acidity lending some elegance to warm finish. **Sauvignon Blanc** ★★★☆ Ultra-crisp, herbaceous **14**'s structured acidity lends some seriousness to Estate bottling. Also tasted: **Merlot 13** ★★★ **Shiraz 11** ★★★ Not retasted: **Cabernet Sauvignon 10** ★★★ **Chardonnay 13** ★★★ Not tasted: **Shiraz LBV Port**.

Domaine range

Sauvignon Blanc ★★★ Simple, tasty **15** accessible & flavoursome. Also tasted: **Chenin Blanc 14** ★★☆ Not retasted: **Merlot 13** ★★★ — IM

Location/map: Stellenbosch ▪ Map grid reference: C3 ▪ WO: Bottelary ▪ Est 1928 ▪ 1stB 1974 ▪ Tasting, sales & cellar tours Mon-Fri 9–4 Sat 10–1 ▪ Closed Easter Fri-Sun, Dec 24/25/26/31 & Jan 1 ▪ Pieter's private cellar: monthly 4-course gourmet meal with wine R325pp, booking essential (12 seats only) ▪ BYO picnic ▪ Mountain biking trail ▪ Owner(s) Pieter Bestbier ▪ Winemaker(s) Albert Ahrens (Jun 2009, consultant), with Anton Bothma (Oct 2014) ▪ 122ha/71ha (cab, cinsaut, malbec, merlot, ptage, shiraz, chard, chenin, sauv) ▪ ±600t/10,000cs own label 80% red 20% white & ±200,000L bulk ▪ PO Box 25 Kuils River 7579 ▪ goede@adept.co.za ▪ www.goedehoop.co.za ▪ S 33° 54' 32.0" E 018° 45' 14.0" ▪ F +27 (0)21-906-1553 ▪ **T +27 (0)81-283-1618**

Goedvertrouw Estate

For an authentic farm experience, head for Goedvertrouw near Bot River. Owner tannie Elreda Pillmann is a force of nature, making wine, fund-raising for Tommy Prins Foundation, featuring in Elgin Open Gardens Week and Bot River Spring Weekend, running a B&B, and cooking pre-booked 'boeremeals'.

Pinot Noir ② ★★ Earthy strawberry notes & hint of vanilla on light-hearted **09**. Not retasted: **Chardonnay 06 ★★★ Sauvignon Blanc 08 ★★★** Not tasted: **Cabernet Sauvignon**. — DS

Location: Bot River ▪ Map: Elgin, Walker Bay & Bot River ▪ WO: Overberg ▪ Est 1990 ▪ 1stB 1991 ▪ Tasting & sales by appt ▪ Home-cooked meals & accommodation by appt ▪ Play area for children ▪ Walks ▪ Farm produce ▪ Small conferences ▪ Conservation area ▪ Small art gallery ▪ Owner(s)/winemaker(s)/viticulturist(s) Elreda Pillmann ▪ 8ha (cab, pinot, chard, sauv) ▪ 70% red 30% white ▪ PO Box 37 Bot River 7185 ▪ goedvertrouw@breede.co.za ▪ S 34° 9' 56.7" E 019° 13' 24.1" ▪ F +27 (0)28-284-9769 ▪ **T +27 (0)28-284-9769**

Goedverwacht Wine Estate

To boost exports to existing European markets and reach into China and Africa, the Du Toits are investing heavily in their family estate near Bonnievale. They've acquired more land to plant mainly white varieties, improved cooling facilities in the cellar, achieved WIETA status and given their good-value range an appropriately upbeat and forward-looking name, Great Expectations.

Maxim range

★★★★ Cabernet Sauvignon ② Polished & modern. **11** similar leafy notes to elegant **10** (★★★★) but greater presence, complexity (chocolate, coffee, liquorice) from 100% new French oak.

Chardonnay ★★★★ Ripe clementine & smoke on smooth **14**, aged 8 months in 20% new oak; lovely lemony acidity & weight for food.

Great Expectations range

Shiraz ★★★★ Was 'An Acre of Stone Shiraz'. Step-up **13** has toasty oak (from well-managed staves), pepper & spiced red fruit. Balanced, with form-giving tannin, good dry finish. **Chardonnay ★★★** Papaya & nut nuances on fresh, lemon-toned **15**, unwooded, with enough palate weight for food. **Crane White Colombar ★★★ 15** lively passionfruit & guava, modest alcohol for sipping solo or with summer salads. **Sauvignon Blanc ★★★** Was 'The Good Earth Sauvignon Blanc'. **15** charms with nuances of wet pebbles & freshly mown lawn, rounded palate & soft end. Also tasted: **Crane Red Merlot 14 ★★★ Triangle 13 ★★★ Shiraz Rosé 15 ★★★ Sparkling Rosé Demi-Sec 15 ★★** — CvZ

Location: Bonnievale ▪ Map/WO: Robertson ▪ Est 1960's ▪ 1stB 1994 ▪ Tasting, sales & cellar tours Mon-Fri 8.30-4.30 Sat 10-1 ▪ Closed Easter Fri/Sun, Dec 25/26 & Jan 1 ▪ Mediterranean or quiche & salad platter; picnic basket for 2 (incl sparkling wine) — 2 days prior booking essential ▪ BYO picnic ▪ Tour groups ▪ Conservation area ▪ Owner(s) Jan du Toit & Sons (Pty) Ltd ▪ Winemaker(s) Henry Conradie (Aug 2005) ▪ Viticulturist(s) Jan du Toit, advised by Francois Viljoen ▪ 220ha/150ha (cabs s/f, merlot, p verdot, shiraz, chard, chenin, cbard, sauv) ▪ 2,700t/1.8m L 30% red 65% white 5% rosé ▪ Other export brands: Ama Ulibo, Kaapse Droom, Misty Kloof's, Mzanzi's, Soek die Geluk ▪ Brands for clients: Vinimark Trading ▪ BEE, BWI, IPW, WIETA ▪ PO Box 128 Bonnievale 6730 ▪ goedwachtestate@lando.co.za, winemaker@goedverwacht.co.za ▪ www.goedverwacht.co.za ▪ S 33° 55' 11.3" E 020° 0' 19.1" ▪ F +27 (0)23-616-2073 ▪ **T +27 (0)23-616-3430**

☐ **Gôiya** *see* Namaqua Wines
☐ **Goldcoast** *see* Val du Charron
☐ **Golden Chalice** *see* Southern Sky Wines
☐ **Golden Triangle** *see* Stellenzicht Vineyards
☐ **Goose Wines** *see* The Goose Wines

Goudini Wines

There've been big changes in the cellar at this grower-owned Breedekloof winery, including three new state-of-art, high-capacity bladder presses and more gravity-aided juice runoff, resulting in 'purer fruit and softer mouthfeel'. Winemaker/viticulturist Hendrik Myburgh says the top range, named for the long-lived desert plant Welwitchia mirabili, now has a dedicated barrel cellar with the latest technology.

Reserve range

★★★★ **Mirabilis Regis-Filia Chardonnay** ⊘ From Goudini grapes (previously Stellenbosch) **13** has less obvious oak (20% new), livelier fruit than **11** (★★★★); steps up with luxurious mouthfeel, good length, nutty-dry conclusion. No **12**.

★★★★☆ **Gevonden Hendrik de Wet Cape Hanepoot** ⓐ Marvellous fortified dessert wine from single-vineyard believed planted ca 1880. Unoaked **13** luxurious, smooth & very sweet but balanced by pinpoint acidity. Cellarworthy; 375 ml.

Mirabilis Regis-Filia Chenin Blanc ⓝⓔⓦ ★★★★ **14** wonderful lemon-lime intensity, 10% colombard for freshness & 50% new oak for breadth, vanilla appeal. Rich & big (though 14.5% alcohol not unbalanced or spiritous). A red-wine lover's white. Not retasted: **Mirabilis Primus-Capio 11** ★★★☆

Goudini range

Shiraz ★★☆ Smoky vanilla whiffs on improved lily & red plum **14**. Satisfying informal meal mate with bright acidity, supple grip from 14 months in older oak. **Unwooded Chardonnay** ⊘ ★★★★ **14** gets weight & richness from ripe yellow peach & tangerine fruit; similar big alcohol as previous but more balance, freshness. **Chenin Blanc** ★★★ Uncomplicated sipping delivered by characterful **15**, pretty floral & apricot bouquet, perky acidity & good length. **Brut Sparkling** ★★ Latest **NV** (**14**) from sauvignon has the usual 'wet pebble' nuance plus suggestion of blackcurrant. Light & frothy party fizz. Also tasted: **Merlot 14** ★★ **Ruby Cabernet-Merlot 14** ★★☆ **Sauvignon Blanc 15** ★★ Not retasted: **Cabernet Sauvignon 12** ★★☆ **Rosé 13** ★★ **Natural Sweet Red NV** ★★☆ **Natural Sweet NV** ★★ **Hanepoot 10** ★★★☆ Discontinued: **Pinotage**. — CvZ

Location: Rawsonville ▪ Map: Breedekloof ▪ WO: Goudini/Western Cape ▪ Est 1948 ▪ Tasting & sales Mon-Fri 9–5 Sat 9–2 ▪ Closed Good Fri, Dec 25/26 & Jan 1 ▪ Cellar tours by appt ▪ Bistro: light meals during tasting hours ▪ Fully licensed bar ▪ Conferences ▪ Owner(s) 40 members ▪ Cellarmaster(s) Hennie Hugo (Dec 1984) ▪ Winemaker(s) Hendrik Myburgh (Nov 2001), with Tinus le Roux (Jan 2010) & Marius Prins (Jul 2013) ▪ Viticulturist(s) Hendrik Myburgh (Nov 2001) ▪ 1,000ha (merlot, ruby cab, shiraz, chard, chenin, sauv) ▪ 22,000t/66,000cs own label 45% red 45% white 10% rosé ▪ PO Box 132 Rawsonville 6845 ▪ info@goudiniwine.co.za ▪ www.goudiniwine.co.za ▪ S 33° 41' 37.8" E 019° 19' 9.5" ▪ F +27 (0)23-349-1988 ▪ **T +27 (0)23-349-1090**

☐ **Goue Kalahari** *see* Die Mas van Kakamas
☐ **Gouverneurs** *see* Groot Constantia Estate

Govert Wines

The Stellenbosch-based Keuzenkamp family source export wines from around the Cape winelands for clients and their own labels Charles Borro, D'Heros, Don Morris, Loyal Brothers and Ruby Ridge.

Location: Stellenbosch ▪ Est 2002 ▪ 1stB 2007 ▪ Closed to public ▪ Owner(s) Teuns Keuzenkamp ▪ 180,000cs own label 80% red 5% white 15% rosé ▪ PO Box 1977 Somerset West 7129 ▪ info@govertwines.com ▪ www.govertwines.com ▪ F +27 (0)86-224-9348 ▪ **T +27 (0)21-887-5812**

Graça

Inspired by Portugal's vinho verde wines, these popular, modest-alcohol easy-drinkers are by Distell.

Rosé ⓐ ★★ Lots of flavour on sweetish **NV** from mostly white grapes. **Graça** ⓐ ★★ Fruity off-dry **NV** blend, tasty enough but pretty dilute. WO W Cape for both. — TJ

Graceland Vineyards   ⓠ

Small but ambitious, the McNaughton family estate in Stellenbosch's viticultural 'Golden Triangle' since inception almost 20 years ago has focused on handcrafted (by winemaker Susan) sumptuous reds, beautifully packaged. Taking the house style up a level — to 'really sumptuous' — is a planned select Cabernet Sauvignon '16 from young vines on some of the best soils, last in production in the 1960s.

★★★★ **Three Graces** ⓐ **12** reflects big, bold house style. Half cab provides firm structure, shiraz & merlot sweet, spicy plum flesh. Warming tail.

Colour Field ★★☆ **13** very ripe merlot with splashes cab, shiraz. Straightforward, chunky tannin conclusion. Not retasted: **Shiraz 12** ★★★ Not tasted: **Cabernet Sauvignon**, **Merlot**, **Strawberry Fields**. — AL

Location/map/WO: Stellenbosch ▪ Map grid reference: E7 ▪ Est/1stB 1998 ▪ Tasting & sales Mon-Fri by appt ▪ Fee R50 ▪ Closed all pub hols ▪ Owner(s) Paul & Susan McNaughton ▪ Cellarmaster(s)/winemaker(s)/viticulturist(s) Susan McNaughton (2001) ▪ 18ha/10ha (cab, merlot, shiraz) ▪ 55t/8,333cs own label 100% red ▪ Suite 144 Private Bag X4 Die Boord 7613 ▪ graceland@iafrica.com ▪ www.gracelandvineyards.com ▪ S 33° 59' 37.5" E 018° 50' 3.1" ▪ F +27 (0)86-556-4600 ▪ **T +27 (0)21-881-3121**

Graham Beck Wines ⓠ ⓰

Last year, this estimable winery on the Madeba wine and thoroughbred estate in Robertson, founded by late mining magnate Graham Beck, celebrated its silver jubilee. Along its 25-year journey, it's not only been a solid corporate citizen, investing in indigenous fauna and flora conservation and skills upliftment in the region, it's built an impressive range of wines. In particular, cellarmaster Pieter Ferreira and team have passionately pursued the perfect bubbly, their success evident in the respect paid their bottlings by judges, competitors and consumers worldwide. Plans on the drawing board to ensure another 25 years of excellence on the global stage include improved facilities and a heightened focus on R&D.

Ad Honorem range

★★★★☆ **Coffeestone Cabernet Sauvignon** ⓐ Regal Stellenbosch cab **12** quite reticent mid-2014, but decent grip & satisfying fruit intensity suggest it will evolve in similar manner to elegant **11**.

★★★★☆ **The Ridge Syrah** ⓐ Barrel selection from Robertson single-vineyard; spice & violet-perfumed **12** exudes confidence, is plush & polished, with better integrated tannins than **11** (★★★★).

★★★★ **The Joshua** Stellenbosch-sourced **12** co-fermented shiraz, 5% viognier seriously wooded (90% new oak, some American) & back on track. Unlike **11** (★★★★), has generous fruit & muscular structure for ±5 years improvement. Unforced but with bearing & precision.

★★★★★ **Ad Honorem** ⓐ Oak-spicy **09** (★★★★☆) grand vin is opulent & tarry, with impressive dark fruit, weight & length. More shiraz than noble **07** cab-shiraz blend (72:28).

★★★★ **Lonehill Chardonnay** Returns to the guide in best possible way! **14** (★★★★★), from home-grown fruit, is lithe & shapely, its well-judged oak (60% new) supporting the custard-seamed lemon fruit, harmonising with the palate weight & lees-buffed texture to deliver a hugely satisfying wine, with lots more to give. Different league to last-reviewed **10** (★★★☆) & **09**.

★★★★ **Bowed Head Chenin Blanc** Effusive vanilla, stonefruit & nuts on barrel fermented (40% new) from Agter Paarl dryland vines. **14** has immediate appeal plus concentration & balance for 3+ years ageing. No **13**, **12** similarly expansive.

★★★★☆ **Pheasants' Run Sauvignon Blanc** Just-bottled **15** already composed, expressive & as vivacious as **14**, showing similar complexity of cool khaki bush & blackcurrant along with fruit weight & grip on palate to balance Groenekloof's brisk acidity.

★★★★ **Rhona Muscadel** ⓐ Long since named for Rhona Beck, the late founder's wife, & Graham Beck Wines director Antony Beck's mother, who passed away in September 2015. Fragrant fortified dessert from Montagu, rounded in oak. **13** preview back on track after slightly spiritous **12** (★★★☆). Grapey, floral scents & satiny finish.

Méthode Cap Classique Sparkling range

★★★★ **Brut Rosé 10** from Stellenbosch & Walker Bay pinot noir (80%) & chardonnay demands attention with sanguine whiff on its patisserie aromas, weighty mid-palate ex 54 months lees-ageing in bottle.

★★★★ **Brut Rosé** Latest **NV** celebratory tipple from chardonnay (52%) & pinot; previous release was led by the black grape. Delicate strawberry attraction, fine bubbles & creamy mouthfeel courtesy 17 months lees-ageing.

★★★★☆ **Blanc de Blancs Brut** From Robertson chardonnay. Oaked portion adds breadth & depth to **10**. Lively lemon & brioche scents, endless creamy mouthful enlivened by oystershell minerality. 53 months lees contact; almost as profound as **09** (★★★★★) tasted last year.

★★★★ **Brut Zero** Understated **09** (★★★★☆) from Franschhoek chardonnay (78%) & pinot noir is ultra-dry but gains breadth from combo of 64 months lees-ageing, a wooded portion & a pinot noir component. Long & refined finish. Like **08**, there is plenty of future enjoyment in its still-unfurling depths.

★★★★☆ **Cuvée Clive** Flag bearer of the MCC sparklings. Latest disgorgement **09** (see April **15** date on the bottle) profoundly mineral, with elegant lemon persistence & freshness, creamy texture courtesy 69 months on lees. Chardonnay (80%, small portion barrel fermented) & pinot noir. No **08**.

Also tasted: **Brut NV** ★★★★ **Bliss Demi Sec NV** ★★★★

The Game Reserve range

★★★★ **Cabernet Sauvignon** Restrained **13** (★★★☆) has leafy note better managed in classy **12**; similar freshness & near-invisible oak support. From Firgrove, Stellenbosch, Groenekloof & Robertson. **Merlot** ★★★☆ Uncomplicated yet characterful & plummy **13** is medium bodied, fruity & easy. For everyday enjoyment. WO Coastal. **Shiraz** ★★★ Small portion American oak ups the sweet impression created by **13**'s ripe, smooth fruit overlaying it with creamy vanilla notes. Uncomplicated sipping guaranteed. Ex Stellenbosch fruit. **Chenin Blanc** ★★★ Preview **15** herbaceous & vibrant, immediate appeal enhanced by slight tannic tug. Lightly oaked. WO Coastal. Also tasted: **Pinotage 14** ★★★☆ **Chardonnay 14** ★★★ **Sauvignon Blanc 15** ★★★☆ Discontinued: **Viognier**.

Everyday Favourites

Railroad Red ★★★ **13** for the 'braai nation', with chewy tannins, succulent fruit – & no corkscrew required! Shiraz, cab & viognier seasoned with French/American oak (30% new). **Gorgeous** ★★☆ Cheeky pinot noir/chardonnay dry blush with front label to match the name. **15** moderate 11.5% alcohol. Also tasted: **Pinno 14** ★★☆ **Waterside Unoaked Chardonnay 15** ★★★ — CvZ

Location/map: Robertson ▪ WO: Western Cape/Coastal/Robertson/Stellenbosch/Paarl/Groenekloof/ Franschhoek ▪ Est 1983 ▪ 1stB 1991 ▪ Tasting & sales Mon-Fri 9–5 Sat/Sun 10–4 ▪ Tasting fees: classic is complimentary; deluxe R50, waived on purchase of R200+; MCC R75 ▪ Closed Good Fri & Dec 25 ▪ Owner(s) Graham Beck Enterprises ▪ Cellarmaster(s) Pieter Ferreira (Aug 1990) & Erika Obermeyer (Jan 2005) ▪ Winemaker(s) Pierre de Klerk (Oct 2010) ▪ Viticulturist(s) Dérick Hamman & Pieter Fouché ▪ 226ha (cabs s/f, grenache, merlot, p verdot, pinot, shiraz, chard, chenin, sauv); Robertson 150ha/ Stellenbosch 76ha ▪ 2,800t/540,000c own label ▪ ISO 14001, BWI champion, IPW, SABS 1841, WIETA ▪ PO Box 724 Robertson 6705 ▪ cellar@grahambeckwines.co.za, market@grahambeckwines.co.za ▪ www.grahambeckwines.com ▪ S 33° 48' 14.95" E 019° 48' 1.41" ▪ F +27 (0)23-626-5164/+27 (0)21-874-1712 (marketing) ▪ **T +27 (0)23-626-1214/+27 (0)21-874-1258 (marketing)**

☐ **Grand Beach Café** see Stellekaya Winery
☐ **Grand Duc** see GlenWood

Grande Provence Heritage Wine Estate   Ⓟ Ⓜ Ⓐ Ⓞ Ⓑ Ⓓ

It's owned by a Dutch-Belgian consortium, but this Franschhoek property's name goes back to its founding by a French Huguenot in 1694, though the handsome manor house is from the following century. Art, dining, accommodation, wedding and conference venues confirm that it's not just about wine here – but it is sufficiently intensely and interestingly so for cellarmaster Karl Lambour to have acquired two clay amphorae for vinifying some of his old-vine chenin.

Grande Provence range

★★★★ **The Grande Provence Red** Adds 'Red' to name. Flagship **12** (★★★★☆) blend from merlot & cab more restrained & regal than **11**; pure black fruit, sweet vanilla flavours with the 30 months in new French barrels well absorbed. Excellent balance & savoury, complex finish.

★★★★ **Chardonnay** Ⓐ **12** & **13** both tasted; they share classic aromas of vanilla, ripe melon & pear, with good fruit & oak influence on the balanced palate. Satisfying, lingering flavours.

★★★★ **The Grande Provence White** Ⓐ **13** blend of chenin blanc & viognier shows an intense but not very complex palate mirroring the aromas of pear skin, apricot blossom & vanilla-infused apple.

★★★★ **Chenin Blanc-Viognier 14** is 74% chenin. 31 year old vines give notes of clementine & peach on a clean, precise, concentrated palate. Joyful, balanced & long ending.

★★★★ **Grande Provence Brut** (NEW) Delightful MCC sparkling from 50/50 chardonnay & pinot noir. **09** soft, creamy mousse introduces delicate baked apple notes, waft of cinnamon, long spicy farewell.

Cabernet Sauvignon ★★★☆ **11** improves with succulent red fruit, dried herbs & touch of mocha.

Pinot Noir ★★★★ Ripe strawberry & earthy tones on **14**, fragrant fynbos & brush of dry tannins on the finish. Also tasted: **Sauvignon Blanc 15** ★★★ **Muscat d'Alexandrie 15** ★★☆ Not retasted: **Shiraz 10** ★★★★ **Rosé 14** ★★★

Vignerons Reserve 4 Barrel Selection

★★★★ **Chenin Blanc** (Ⓩ) Inviting aromas of green & tropical fruit. **13**'s dry palate shows vigour & an appealing complexity, but with a slightly warming finish.

★★★★ **Viognier** (Ⓩ) Varietal hallmark perfumes & flavours of white flowers & apricot, & the usual element of viscosity. **13** finish touch more unusual, with an interesting slightly saline note.

Not retasted: **Zinfandel 13** ★★★☆

Angels Tears range

Merlot-Cabernet Sauvignon ★★ Good everyday red, **14** fruity, easy, with smooth curves & food-inviting savouriness. Coastal WO. **Rosé** (✓) ★★★ Moreish off-dry **15** from merlot, cab, hanepoot, petit verdot, shiraz; lovely structure, easy-quaffing fun. WO W Cape. Also tasted: **Sauvignon Blanc 15** ★★ **Muscat d'Alexandrie-Chenin Blanc 15** ★★★ — WB

Location/map: Franschhoek ▪ WO: Franschhoek/Coastal/Western Cape/Wellington ▪ Est 1694 ▪ 1stB 2004 ▪ Tasting & sales Mon-Sun 10–6 (winter) & 10-7 (summer) ▪ Fee R40/4 wines, R50/7 wines, R100/food & wine pairing ▪ Group tastings in cathedral extension of art gallery (seat up to 80 pax) ▪ Cellar & gallery tours Mon-Fri 11 & 3 Sat/Sun by appt ▪ Wine blending sessions by appt ▪ Kiddies grape juice tastings ▪ Picnics ▪ The Restaurant at Grande Provence ▪ Tour groups ▪ Gift shop ▪ Conferences & weddings ▪ Art gallery ▪ Harvest festival ▪ The Owner's Cottage & La Provençale at Grande Provence ▪ Owner(s) Dutch & Belgium consortium ▪ Cellarmaster(s)/winemaker(s)/viticulturist(s) Karl Lambour (May 2012) ▪ 32ha/22ha (cab, merlot, chard, sauv) ▪ Grande Provence: 120t/10,000cs own label 60% red 40% white; Angels Tears: 600t/60,000cs own label 30% red 60% white 10% rosé ▪ PO Box 102 Franschhoek 7690 ▪ reservations@grandeprovence.co.za ▪ www.grandeprovence.co.za ▪ S 33° 53' 57.6'' E 19° 06' 10.5'' ▪ F +27 (0)21-876-8601 ▪ **T +27 (0)21-876-8600**

Grand Mousseux

Enduring (launched 1929) budget-priced sweet carbonated sparkling brand by Distell.

Vin Doux (Ⓩ) ★☆ Exuberant fizz **NV** that's launched a million brides, to be served well chilled. — DB

Grangehurst   (Ⓠ) (Ⓖ)

Jeremy Walker's winery – based in a cellar which used to be a squash court on the family's Helderberg smallholding – remains modest in size, though another Stellenbosch farm, bought with a partner in 2002, supplies cab for the cellar, these grapes supplemented by bought-in Helderberg fruit. This is one of the more serious-minded ranges in the Cape: 'still our handcrafted, traditional, unhurried classic red wines and our dry rosé'. Which doesn't preclude innovation: 2015 saw a new variety crushed – the rare local crossing called roobernet, from a neighbouring vineyard. 'Perhaps to be used in a blend a few years down the line...' Other interesting developments ahead involve both wine and visitor facilities – but (unlike some!) Jeremy prefers us to wait for completion before reporting them.

★★★★ **Cabernet Sauvignon Reserve** (Ⓩ) After charming **05**, classic **06** (★★★★★) showed bold ripe tannins, delicate blackcurrant fruit with extended finish. Tasted some years back.

★★★★ **Mourvèdre** (Ⓩ) With 14% shiraz, **08** is rich, fresh, spicy & dark fruited. Very 'masculine' wine – with burly 14.4% alcohol, but the palate is vibrant, with well-melded oak & lingering flavours.

★★★★☆ **Pinotage** Forest floor, juniper & venison notes on mature but lively & fresh **06**. Drinking well, with black fruit detail, fine tannin grip & attractive focus. Also-tasted **07** hedonistic & a bit more open with greater generosity, power & depth. Both include dash cab, have several years to go. Also in magnum.

★★★★ **Cabernet Sauvignon-Merlot** Though ripe, 07 (★★★★☆) seems cool, with subtlety ruling over obviousness. Classic aromas of cassis, wet earth & chocolate-laced cherries. Intriguing palate benefits from aeration. Like 06, youthful despite maturity. Also in magnum.

★★★★ **CWG Auction Reserve Akayla** ⓖ Listed without 'Akayla' suffix last time; 09 (★★★★☆) for 2015 Auction true to the classic, unhurried philosophy. Cab-led, with petit verdot & merlot, as was previous 07. Fruit concentration, but with restraint; needs 5+ years to open up & reach its full potential.

★★★★☆ **Grangehurst** ⓖ Flagship cab-led 07 (★★★★) blend with merlot, petit verdot, as was 06. House's restraint shows earthy dark fruit & hints of smoked redpepper; accessible, but vibrant acid & firm tannin give ageability.

★★★★☆ **CWG Auction Cape Reserve Blend** ⓖ Virile 09 for 2015 Auction from half cab, with pinotage, shiraz & dollop mourvèdre. Generous dark fruit with Asian spices & attractive toasty oak. Rich but with great definition & impeccable length. Despite 14.8% alcohol, there's a fine lift & freshness.

★★★★ **Nikela** Cape Blend 07 (★★★★★) opens slowly to reveal cassis & cherry fruit from near-equal parts cab & pinotage, mature forest floor & genteel spice ex 2 years older oak. Rich & complex, thanks to drops shiraz, merlot; like 06, fine dinner companion now, will reward cellaring ±5 years. Also in 1.5L.

★★★★☆ **Shiraz-Cabernet Sauvignon Reserve** ⓖ Complex cassis, redpepper, spice, leather & earthy notes on 05 (★★★★) after finer 03. Tasted some years back.

Also tasted: **Cape Rosé Blend 14** ★★★☆ — JPf

Location/WO: Stellenbosch ▪ Map: Helderberg ▪ Est/1stB 1992 ▪ Tasting & sales Mon-Fri 9–4 Sat/Sun 10-3 (plse phone to confirm) ▪ Fee for group tastings depends on wines being presented ▪ Closed Easter Fri-Mon, Dec 25/26 & Jan 1 ▪ Self-catering guest cottages ▪ Owner(s) Grangehurst Winery (Pty) Ltd ▪ Cellarmaster(s) Jeremy Walker (Jan 1992) ▪ Winemaker(s) Jeremy Walker (Jan 1992), with Gladys Brown (Jan 2002) ▪ ±13ha/6ha own (cab) + 8ha bought in grapes (merlot, p verdot, ptage, shiraz) ▪ 80t/10,000cs own label 90% red 10% rosé + 2,000cs for clients ▪ Brands for clients: Woolworths ▪ PO Box 206 Stellenbosch 7599 ▪ winery@grangehurst.co.za ▪ www.grangehurst.co.za ▪ S 34° 01' 02.9" E 018° 49' 50.5" ▪ F +27 (0)86-710-6070 ▪ **T +27 (0)21-855-3625**

☐ **Granny Smith** *see* Boland Kelder
☐ **Grape Grinder** *see* The Grape Grinder
☐ **Great Five** *see* Stellenview Premium Wines
☐ **Greendale** *see* Withington
☐ **Green Shebeen** *see* Org de Rac
☐ **Griffin** *see* Stettyn Cellar
☐ **Grimont** *see* Tulbagh Winery
☐ **Groblershoop** *see* Orange River Cellars
☐ **Groen Kalahari** *see* Die Mas van Kakamas

Groenland ⓠ ⓐ ⓒ ⓑ ⓔ

If consistent quality and ungreedy prices are what you're looking for, be sure to call at the Steenkamp family farm on Stellenbosch's Bottelary Road (or shop for their wines on the website, or now also on Pick n Pay Online)! You'll get good old-fashioned hospitality from the affable Kosie and his son, fellow winemaker Piet. They enjoy people and good humour, and, like their wines, shun pretension.

Premium range

★★★★ **Cabernet Sauvignon** 11 & 12 tasted. Both show opulently ripe blackcurrants, subtle herbaceous notes & reassuringly sturdy tannins. Intense & satisfying, with promising future.

★★★★ **Shiraz** Appealingly generous ripe cherry fruit on 12, with plump roundness & smooth tannins. Show the rewards of serious intent, 100% new oak. Also-tasted 11 (★★★★) a bit lighter, spicier.

★★★★ **Antoinette Marié** Intense dark fruit, fine structure impress on 12 blend of equal parts cab, merlot & shiraz. Also-tasted 13 follows form, with slight lift in youthful fruit. Taut tannins need time to soften. 11 sold out untasted.

Also tasted: **Merlot 13** ★★★☆

STEENBERG

www.steenbergfarm.com

Minutes from Cape Town, Miles from the World

Hotel reservations: +27 21 713 2222
email: reservations@steenberghotel.com

Catharina's Restaurant reservations: +27 21 713 7178
email: reservations@catharinasrestaurant.co.za

Bistro Sixteen82 reservations: +27 21 713 2211
email: reservations@bistro1682.co.za

We share the secrets of the south

Vineyard Ventures offers private, individually tailored tours and itineraries woven around your personal interests and preferences, based on our broad familiarity with this wonderful region and our extensive network of contacts.

Wine is our speciality, but we cover a fascinating variety of personal travel throughout Southern Africa. Our purpose is to go beyond the expected and make your dream holiday a reality.

With 20 years of experience,
we ensure a carefree and unforgettable adventure.

VINEYARD VENTURES

Tel: 021 434 8888 | Fax: 086 579 9430 | Cell: 082 920 2825
Email: vinven@iafrica.com | www.vineyardventures.co.za

SATSA
Southern Africa Tourism
Services Association
BONDED

WOOLWORTHS

THERE ARE
OVER **7000**
WINES IN
THIS BOOK.

YOU'LL FIND
THE **BEST**
OF THEM IN
ONE PLACE.

PRESENTS

iSommelier uses a revolutionary technology that filters the ambient air removing moisture, dust and pollutants. It seperates oxygen from nitrogen providing up to 90% of purified and concentrated oxygen. This advanced system enhances the flavors and aromas of the wine in just a few minutes and controls the air pressure ensuring a constant quality of the wine anywhere in the world.

Get the app!

Join the iFavine Network
Be part of the largest community ever known in the wine industry

WWW.IFAVINE.COM

z Last ed **05**
★★); showed p
tion in warm vi

ty Varying ble
, spice, cream
l, good tannin
ry vinosity in s

z-Viognier Co
leberries, ear
15% alc well

z-Merlot NEW
hoorland scrub,
constructed, gre

Chardonnay Meticulous
citrus intensity in 06's intro
boned burgundian savouriness.

★★ Viognier Ex-barrel 07 already
while oak works its magic on pal
food.

not Noir 🖴 **★★★★** Last tasted **05** (sam
nt, delicate redcurrant flavours; plenty o

ack Rock range

★★☆ Red Blend 🖴 S. Rhône-inspired
doesn't falter: violets, dried herbs,
mark lithe tannins welcome partic

★★ White Blend 🖴 Majority blend 4
06 almost overpowers with a pe
tangy, food-friendly, thanks to enli

num range

★★ Cabernet Sauvignon 🖴 Showing
same delectable cassis, dark choc
vintage, for drinking sooner. No ha

★★ Chenin Blanc 🖴 From old Hldrbe
gd chenin develops: citrus peel t
everything fresh, lively. Potential fo

e Winery of Good Hope range

henin Blanc ☺ 🖴 **★★★** Crammed wit
s quaffability personified.

ot Noir 🖴 **★★★★** Pvsly ex-barrel, 06 del
rs, hints of violets, captured in a fine-h
ntage ★★★★ Previewed last ed, striking
eenper spiced, with variety's trad

ODD BINS

Famous wine brands at a fraction of the price

Every now and then we source limited quantities of vintage releases from famous wine brands. Each of these wines is then judged by our panel of experts – including Jan Boland Coetzee, with the best of the batch each given a unique bin number under our own exclusive Odd Bins label. We then sell them to you at a fraction of the price and vow to keep the original label a closely guarded secret.

Taste one and the secret may reveal itself.

we bring the wine route to you
wine route

Checkers
better and better

Not for Sale to Persons Under the Age of 18.

ZORGVLIET
wines

Welcome to our haven...

Five kilometres outside Stellenbosch in the heart of the winelands you will find a place of serenity and ultimate beauty.

Zorgvliet Wine Estate nestled in the Banghoek Valley overlooking majestic mountains and vineyards. Today Zorgvliet boasts not only award winning wines but also a spectacular wedding venue, various function venues, a deli and picnic area. Zorgvliet wines features a picturesque Country Lodge with a private wine studio and outside pool area where guests can enjoy our magnificent views.

The unique contemporary Cape Dutch architecture blends in with the authentic restaurant dated 1692.

Experience the magical ambiance of a mountain braai, a picnic at the foot of the Simonsberg or you can enjoy wine tasting and barrel sampling in the modern wine cellar.

Zorgvliet Wine Estate is the ideal location for the wedding of your dreams. With exquisite views of the winelands that compliment the historic Cape Dutch architecture of the Estate, your wedding photos will be exquisite.

At dusk the valley becomes tranquil and filled with magic, the mountains are painted in the colours of our rainbow nation as the last rays of sunshine greet the valley good night. Share our haven and you will never be the same again as you will become a beholder of the spirit of the Banghoek Valley.

T: +27 (0)21 885 1399 | **E:** info@zorgvliet.com
www.zorgvlietwines.com

MUNDO VIDA
RESTAURANT

CERTIFICATE of EXCELLENCE
2015 Winner
tripadvisor

FINE WINES, EXCEPTIONAL CUISINE AND PANORAMIC OCEAN VISTAS

◀ 1ST FLOOR, UMDLOTI BEACH CENTRE,
1 SOUTH BEACH ROAD, UMDLOTI, KZN
EMAIL: info@mundovida.co.za

TEL: 031 568 2286
www.mundovida.co.za

Helena's
RESTAURANT

"The food was phenomenal and service above expectations."
- Reviewed on TripAdvisor, January 2015

"I recommend Helena's to anyone looking for a fantastic meal!"
- Reviewed on TripAdvisor, May 2015

"Very friendly service and excellent food. Hats off to the chef!"
- Reviewed on TripAdvisor, July 2015

Helena's Restaurant is housed in Coopmanhuijs Boutique Hotel & Spa,
which has consistently ranked #1 among all hotels in Stellenbosch.
We serve heritage food with finesse, often with subtle twists in the detail.

Tel: +27 (0)21 883-8207 l info@coopmanhuijs.co.za l www.coopmanhuijs.co.za
33 Church Street, Stellenbosch 7600, South Africa

J.

Joostenberg

Come rain or shine...
YOUR TABLE IS WAITING.

Joostenberg Bistro, Deli, Events, Wines & Butchery

Klein Joostenberg, R304, Muldersvlei, Stellenbosch
T 021 88 44 141 | **E** bistro@joostenberg.co.za
GPS 33 49'30.26" S   18 47'37.64" E
f /JoostenbergBistroEventsVenue   🐦 joostenberg_b
www.joostenberg.co.za | *Booking recommended for the bistro.*

DGB WINES INVEST ITS WINNINGS FROM INAUGURAL STANDARD BANK / CHENIN BLANC CHALLENGE 2014 IN MOBILE LIBRARY PROJECT

In April 2015, DGB Wines formally received its cheque of R20 000 as one of the winners in the inaugural **Standard Bank/Chenin Blanc Top 10 Challenge**, held in August 2014. As per the stipulations of the competition, the wine producers will invest the money in a project that will benefit its workforce – in this case, a R2.5 million mobile library that will serve nine farm schools in Du Toitskloof Valley.

In May 2015, DGB Wines and Du Toitskloof Cellars Winery launched a major education project – a R2.5 million mobile library/media centre that will, over a two-week cycle, service nine farm schools in the Franschoek region.

On 17 April, the project received another boost – the R20 000 prize money that DGB had won in the inaugural Standard Bank/Chenin Blanc Top Ten Challenge, hosted in 2014 by the Chenin Blanc Association of South Africa (CBA) and sponsored by Standard Bank for three years from 2014-2016. DGB's "rich and ripe *Bellingham the Old Orchard's 2013*" had been included in that list of South Africa's finest Chenin Blancs.

The prize money will go towards the library – simply known as the DGB/Du Toitskloof Mobile Library – per the stipulations of the Standard Bank/Chenin Blanc Top Ten Challenge. While most wine competitions reward the winemakers, the organisers decided that the prize money "must be used to reinforce the economic and social benefits in the workplace and to the workforce."

Which is what the mobile library will do, servicing nine farm schools in the Du Toitskloof Valley region where learners have little or no access to public libraries.

The R20 000 will be used to purchase a wide selection of books and electronic resources, explained Ree du Toit, Production Director at DGB. "We want the learners, as well as younger users and parents to make use of the library," said du Toit when the winemaker received its cheque from Willie du Plessis, Head of Business Banking: Western Cape at Standard Bank, at the Franschoek Cellars.

"The learners can not only take out books, but also use the computers for research and projects."

DGB had been involved in the establishment of the mobile library for some time, so it made sense to also direct the award towards the project, explained Niel Groenewald, Bellingham Chief Winemaker at DGB. The winemakers may not pocket the prize money, but the competition offers a different reward for them as it has created a platform where the many Chenin Blanc wines in the country can finally be rated.

"So it's not so much about the money as it is a review process that would determine which are the 10 best Chenin Blancs in the country, and which wines would be set as the benchmark," said Mr Groenewald.

"That's why we entered the competition, and why we – who see ourselves as a Chenin Blanc leader – are pleased with being among the top 10."

This ranking was one of the main objectives behind the Standard Bank/Chenin Blanc Top Ten Challenge, said Ina Smith, Manager of the CBA. "Chenin Blanc is now getting the recognition it deserves, and the top 10 is just a snapshot of the greatness that awaits the consumers."

Standard Bank chose to back the competition because of the value the wine industry adds to the country, both as an earner of foreign exchange and as a job creator, noted Mr du Plessis. "As a bank we want to invest in and support the wine industry to grow," he said. "In this case we looked at a particular cultivar, a cultivar that we believe will grow and offer consumers something different."

Great views, delicious food, exquisite wines

Situated on the slopes of Franschhoek Mountain, Haute Cabrière boasts arguably the best views over the valley. There is truly nothing better than relaxing with a glass of our Chardonnay Pinot Noir, or a bottle of Pierre Jourdan Cap Classique, paired with a delicious meal inspired by the seasonal produce grown on our farm.

Haute Cabrière Wines & Restaurant, Franschhoek Pass (R45), Franschhoek, 7690. +27 (0)21 876 8500 | cabriere.co.za

FOUNDED   ANNO 1694

HAUTE CABRIÈRE
THE HOME OF PIERRE JOURDAN

Full of Life

NGWENYA GLASS

The glass is always **greener**
on our side.

handmade • eco friendly • recycled • locally produced in Swaziland

P.O. Box 45, Motshane, Swaziland
www.ngwenyaglass.co.sz | ngwenya@ngwenyaglass.co.sz
T / F: +268 – 244 24053 | 244 24142 | 244 24151 | 244 24588
Fax from SA only: 086 5305 452
Watershed, V&A Waterfront, Cape Town | 021 418 0654

Legendary German engineering isn't just for cars.

The Liebherr WTB4212 – a versatile dual-temperature wine cooler which offers conditions similar to a wine cellar and is therefore ideal for the long term storage of both red and white wines.

Liebherr's silent operation and elegant design make it beautiful, and its ability to increase wine's flavour makes it powerful. See for yourself why Liebherr is the most advanced technology not on the road today.

Distributed in Southern Africa by
Liebherr-Africa (Pty) Limited
Vlakfontein Road, Fulcrum Industrial,
Springs, Gauteng
Tel: 011 365 2561/2/3
Fax: 086 674 9628
E-Mail: appliances.laf@liebherr.com

www. liebherr-appliances.co.za

Wine

Quality, Design and Innovation

RIO LARGO

OLIVE ESTATE

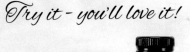

Try it – you'll love it!

GREAT QUALITY. GREAT TASTE.

Breede River Valley | Western Cape
+27 23 340 4776 | www.riolargo.co.za | info@riolargo.co.za

TERMS & CONDITIONS APPLY
DINERS CLUB IS A REGISTERED CREDIT PROVIDER (NCRCP983)

CLUBMILES

EXPAND YOUR HORIZONS

Not just a charge card, Diners Club
offers exclusive features such as
ClubMiles, which earns Miles that
you can redeem on any airline, any
seat, any time. You can also use them
to pay for accommodation, book
ocean cruises, shop online, and buy
vouchers from a growing list of select
partners. Apply for a Diners Club card
today and explore the world in ways
far less limited.

**JOIN THE CLUB AT
DINERSCLUB.CO.ZA**

VAN RYN'S DISTILLERY & BRANDY CELLAR

At Van Ryn's, visitors will experience an internationally award-winning range of brandies which are both luxurious and sumptuous. When you enter the chateau-style distillery, you encounter a quiet, tranquil and welcoming space. In the visitor centre you'll taste our world-renowned brandies. If you're in luck, you will see our 200 year old copper pot slowly distilling the Van Ryn's brandies of the future while part of our tour will allow you to see the coopers assemble the oak barrels in which Van Ryn's brandies are aged. Choose a pairing and experience the marrying of the aromas, tastes and textures of our brandies with locally-sourced foods and confections.

TASTING & SALES: Mon-Fri: (Oct-Apr) 09h00 - 18h00.
Mon-Fri: (May-Sept) 09h00 - 17h00,
Sat & Public Holidays: 09h00 - 16h00. Sun: (Oct-Apr only) 11h00 - 16h00.
Closed: Christmas Day, New Year's Day and Good Friday

DISTILLERY TOURS: Mon-Fri: 10h00, 11h30 & 15h00.
Sat & Pub Hols: 10h00, 11h30 & 13h00. No tours on Sundays

Tel: 021 881 3875 • Email: info@vanryns.co.za • Web: www.vanryn.co.za
Van Ryn Road, off R310, Vlottenburg -33.96535, 18.79590.
MAP REFERENCE: C2

Glassware delivered to your door

We offer a wide variety and supply to Public, Hotels, Restaurants & Wineries

Spiegelau

Luigi Bormioli

Paşabahçe

Rastal

Arcoroc

Libbey

Beer & Speciality

Decanters

distinctive brands

HOME OF PREMIUM BRANDS

021 854 4700 • www.dbrands.co.za
Buy on-line at **www.glassware-warehouse.co.za**

RUITERSVLEI

Good practice.
Good people. Good wine.

Ruitersvlei is located in the heritage Suider-Paarl valley in Southern Paarl. The Restaurant, Manor House, Guest Rooms and Old Cellar are all rich in historical significance and architectural value. The Old Cellar has been renovated as a venue for weddings, conferences and events. The stables are now Guest Rooms and the Manor House is in the process of being restored to its former glory. All this framed by mountains and vineyards that exude peace and tranquility so rarely found and seldom experienced.

Wine Tasting | Restaurant | Accommodation | Functions

Telephone: 021 863 0223/1517 | Email: info@ruitersvlei.co.za

www.ruitersvlei.co.za

A RESTAURANT WITH ROOMS

Restaurant Mosaic can be found in The Orient Private Hotel that is surrounded by the 280-hectare Francolin Conservancy. The Hotel offers ten stylish suites that you can retire to after dinner.

Chantel Dartnall is one of South Africa's highly regarded chefs and well known for her Botanical Cuisine where each plate is a visual and sensual delight. Mosaic's Sommelier Germain Lehodey, expertly matches hand-picked wines from around the world together with Chef Chantel to complement each individual dish. It is not surprising that both the Restaurant and Cellar at Mosaic has been awarded with a variety of international and local awards.

For enquiries please contact us on reservations@restaurantmosaic.com or visit our websites:
www.the-orient.net
www.restaurantmosaic.com
Tel: + 27 (0)12 371 2903/4/5

RESTAURANT MOSAIC

MOSAIC
AT THE ORIENT

www.jfhillebrand.com
11600 CUSTOMER RELATIONSHIPS
EFFICIENT AND COST-EFFECTIVE LOGISTICS OF
WINE·BEER AND SPIRITS
2185 PROFESSIONALS IN 83 COUNTRIES
54 OFFICES
THE FOREFRONT OF LOGISTICS & I.T. DEVELOPMENTS
6 CONTINENTS
FOUNDED IN 1844
600 000 TEU'S
100% BEVERAGE. 100% LOGISTICS.
JF Hillebrand South Africa
T +27 21 809 2000
capetown@hillebrandgroup.com
JFHillebrand
global beverage logistics

Classic range

Sauvignon Blanc ⊘ 🍷 ★★★☆ Typically dusty & racy, **15** has decent heft & finish, ripe gooseberries, softer acidity. Good value.

Antoinette Marié ★★★★ **11** shiraz, cab, merlot blend is appealing, fresh & spicy. Also-tasted **10** similar but riper plummy fruit. Also tasted: **Cabernet Sauvignon 09** ★★★☆ **Shiraz 11** ★★★

Landskap range

Chenin Blanc ★★★ **15** shows ripe stonefruit, softer acidity. Fresh & fruity style. Not retasted: **Shiraz-Merlot 12** ★★☆ — GdB

Location/map: Stellenbosch ▪ Map grid reference: B3 ▪ WO: Bottelary/Stellenbosch ▪ Est 1932 ▪ 1stB 1997 ▪ Tasting & sales Mon-Fri 10—4 Sat 10—1 ▪ Fee R15pp for groups of 6+, waived on purchase ▪ Closed Easter Fri/Sun & Dec 25 ▪ Cellar tours by appt ▪ Gift shop ▪ BYO picnic by appt ▪ Conference/function venue (20-60 pax) ▪ Kids parties ▪ Owner(s) Kosie Steenkamp ▪ Winemaker(s) Kosie Steenkamp (Feb 1975), with Piet Steenkamp (Jan 2001) ▪ Viticulturist(s) Piet Steenkamp (Jan 2001) ▪ 192ha/154ha (cab, merlot, ptage, shiraz, chard, chenin, sauv) ▪ 1,500t/±13,000cs own label 75% red 25% white ▪ BEE level 3, BWI, IPW ▪ PO Box 4 Kuils River 7579 ▪ steenkamp@groenland.co.za ▪ www.groenland.co.za ▪ S 33° 53' 48.9" E 018° 44' 5.3" ▪ F +27 (0)21-903-0250/+27 (0)86-571-4969 ▪ **T +27 (0)21-903-8203**

Groot Constantia Estate (🍷) (🍴) (📷) (🏠) (♿)

This is one of the most historically significant winefarms in the Cape, having been the home of Simon van der Stel, founding father of the wine industry. But it is also a hive of dynamic activity and creative modernity. 'There is still so much to do at Groot Constantia,' enthuses the estate's upbeat winemaker, Boela Gerber, who believes if one can't add value to a company, one should leave! His 15-year tenure here, together with that of CEO Jean Naudé and vineyard manager Floricius Beukes, combine to give the team 36 years of experience in the Constantia area, an invaluable asset — and they are still eager to learn. The viticultural expansion continues with each block managed with fine-tuned precision, to ensure optimum grape quality, and a resultant stellar line up of wines, natural, fortified, MCC sparkling and, on the distant horizon, a possible ultra-premium potstill brandy.

Gouverneurs range

★★★★☆ **Reserve Red** Merlot-led Bordeaux blend with cab franc, cab & petit verdot (44/32/21/3). **12** polished, with bright-fruited elegance, new oak (73%) effortlessly absorbed. Still youthful, but showing inherent balance & pedigree to age. **11** (★★★★) more subdued. Also in magnum.

★★★★☆ **Reserve White** Appealingly fresh, rich & waxy blend of semillon & sauvignon (75/25). Oak well judged, allows vibrant fruit to shine. Focused, with lovely sweet/sour tension & length. **13** classy food wine over next 3-5 years. **12** (★★★★) was a shade off.

Groot Constantia range

★★★★☆ **Cabernet Sauvignon 13** more restrained & tightly structured than stellar **12** (★★★★★). Latest still elegant & ageworthy but shows more of the leafy, herbaceous tones & less overt bright fruit intensity. Deserves cellar time to show true potential.

★★★★☆ **Merlot 13** still tightly buttoned, clearly classically styled. Refined but intense core of fruit, cedar & minty nuance in balanced but firm dry tannin structure. Elegant, polished & ageworthy — a sleeping beauty for the cellar.

★★★★ **Pinotage 13** (★★★★★) polished leather & red fruit flavours in modern, ripe & powerful styling. Quite showy & intense, oak well integrated. Bemedalled in youth, will be more handsome & urbane with maturity. Raises the bar on **12** which had a dash of shiraz.

★★★★☆ **Shiraz** Critically acclaimed **13** reverts to form after less focused **11** (★★★★). Layered intensity, white pepper, smoky bacon & sappy red fruits. Oak tannins (36% new, 13 months) still a tad imposing — just needs time to harmonise. **12** untasted. Also in magnum.

★★★★ **Constantia Rood 13** juicy 6-way blend with supple tannins, seamless & well crafted. Plenty of fruity charm now & over next 5 years. Classy step up on **11** (★★★). **12** untasted. Also in magnum.

★★★★☆ **Chardonnay** Focused lime & brioche tone to **14**. Finely tuned & understated, both fresh & creamy, oak the elegant understudy. Less overtly sumptuous than **13** but equally distinguished.

★★★★☆ **Grand Constance** Enchantingly perfumed Natural Sweet from red & white muscat de Frontignan, partly air-dried, skin fermented in older oak. **12** glacé pineapple & rich tropical fruits, sweet yet uncloying, balanced citrus freshness. Wonderful intensity at just 12% alcohol. **11** (★★★★) less refined.

★★★★☆ **Cape Ruby** Delicious **13** 'port' from touriga exudes ripe bramble berry fruit, rich & generous but balanced sugar (89 g/l), rounded tannins & integrated spirit. A quintessential Ruby!

Not retasted: **Blanc de Noir 14** ★★★ Not tasted: **Sauvignon Blanc, Semillon-Sauvignon Blanc, Méthode Cap Classique**. — MW

Location/WO: Constantia ▪ Map: Cape Peninsula ▪ Est 1685 ▪ 1stB 1688 ▪ Tasting & sales daily 9–6 ▪ Fee R45, R60 tasting & tour ▪ Closed Good Fri & Dec 25 ▪ Cellar tours 10-4 on the hour, every hour ▪ Simon's at Groot Constantia Restaurant; Jonkershuis Constantia Restaurant ▪ Facilities for children ▪ Tour groups ▪ Gifts ▪ Conferences ▪ Walks/hikes ▪ Conservation area ▪ Iziko Museum, manor house, historic buildings & orientation centre ▪ Owner(s) Groot Constantia Trust NPC RF ▪ Winemaker(s) Boela Gerber (Jan 2001), with Rudolph Steenkamp (Jan 2015) ▪ Vineyard manager Floricius Beukes ▪ Viticulturist(s) Andrew Teubes (2009) ▪ 170ha/±90ha (cab, merlot, ptage, pinot, shiraz, chard, muscat, sauv, sem) ▪ 483t/68,000cs ▪ Private Bag X1 Constantia 7848 ▪ enquiries@grootconstantia.co.za ▪ www.grootconstantia.co.za ▪ S 34° 1′ 37.44″ E 018° 25′ 27.39″ ▪ F +27 (0)21-794-1999 ▪ **T +27 (0)21-794-5128**

☐ **Grootdrink** see Orange River Cellars
☐ **Groot Eiland** see uniWines Vineyards

Groote Post Vineyards   🍷 🍴 📷 👤 ♿

The Pentz family transitioned with aplomb from dairy to wine on this large West Coast spread, 'the old man' Peter Pentz's success with the former emulated by son Nicholas' achievements with the latter. Supported by steadfast-since-the-start winemaker Lukas Wentzel and seasoned viticulturist Jannie de Clerk, they have utilised different aspects of their Darling hillsides for varieties that produce cool-climate class, including area specialities sauvignon blanc, shiraz and pinot noir (now also appearing as a rosé). The team's matching passion for nature, culture, cuisine and heritage conservation deserves a day trip.

Kapokberg range

★★★★ **Pinot Noir** 🖈 Raspberries, forest floor & slight floral perfume with spicy hint ex deft oaking (5% new); **13** smooth but noticeable tannins for food, cellaring few years.

★★★★ **Chardonnay** Smart oak detail (10 months, 15% new) lets the fruit shine through, adds complexity & creamy mouthfeel to citrus & pine needle-toned **14**.

★★★★☆ **Sauvignon Blanc** A selection of top blocks, now one of the most thrilling bottlings in the Cape. **14** doesn't disappoint: grapefruit, grass, gooseberry & lime complexity; bone-dry, with great length & depth, unexpected saline mineral nip in the finish.

Varietal range

★★★★☆ **Shiraz** Previewed & provisionally rated **14** (★★★★) opens with white pepper, liquorice, violets & cassis interwoven with meaty & plummy notes; finishes with strong, youthful tannins needing few years cellaring. **13** more graceful, sleek.

★★★★ **Unwooded Chardonnay 15**'s gentle melon, orange blossom & pear accented with minerals & lingering citrus farewell.

★★★★ **Riesling** Lightish 12.5% alcohol ideal for lunchtime sipping but **15** no pushover. Intense & flavoursome, with lime, florals & starfruit, racy acidity that lifts 17 g/l sugar to thrill the palate. Improves on **14** (★★★★) preview.

★★★★ **Sauvignon Blanc** Good ripe varietal expression marries with cool-climate freshness in **15**; gooseberry & passionfruit; racy acidity with a mineral edge. Tank sample **14** (★★★★) less vibrant.

Merlot 🍷 ★★★★ Smoky **13** with cherry, blue berry & clean farmyard whiff. Soft & juicy; for now.

Pinot Noir Rosé Limited Release (NEW) ★★★ Seductive **15**, delicate glassful of pomegranates, rosepetals & berries with dry tail, bright acidity. Only from Groote Post country market. Also tasted: **Chenin Blanc 15** ★★★☆

The Old Man's Blend range
★★★★ **The Old Man's Blend White** ⊘ Cut-above-everyday white. Unwooded, mostly sauvignon **15** with chenin, semillon for apple & citrus notes, breath & weight. **14** (★★★★) less piquant. Coastal WO. Also tasted: **The Old Man's Blend Red 14** ★★★

Méthode Cap Classique range
Brut Rosé ★★★ **NV** celebrator from chardonnay & pinot noir (20%). Dry, tangy, with berry & citrus notes, delicate bubbles. — GM

Location: Darling ▪ Map: Durbanville, Philadelphia & Darling ▪ WO: Darling/Coastal ▪ 1stB 1999 ▪ Tasting, sales & cellar tours Mon-Fri 9—5 Sat/Sun & pub hols 10—4 ▪ Fee R25 for groups of 10+ ▪ Closed Good Fri, Dec 25/26 & Jan 1 ▪ Hilda's Kitchen open for lunch Wed-Sun, booking essential ▪ Facilities for children ▪ Conferences ▪ Walks/hikes ▪ Farm drive to be pre-booked ▪ Conservation area & bird hide ▪ Groote Post country market last Sunday of the month Aug-Apr only ▪ Owner(s) Peter & Nicholas Pentz ▪ Winemaker(s) Lukas Wentzel (Nov 2000) ▪ Viticulturist(s) Jannie de Clerk (1999), advised by Johan Pienaar ▪ 3,000ha/100ha (cabs s/f, merlot, pinot, shiraz, chard, chenin, riesling, sauv, sem) ▪ 580t/ 64,000cs own label ▪ PO Box 103 Darling 7345 ▪ wine@grootepost.co.za ▪ www.grootepost.com ▪ S 33° 29' 0.5" E 018° 24' 35.0" ▪ F +27 (0)22-492-2693 ▪ **T +27 (0)22-492-2825**

Groot Parys Estate   ⓘ
The trio behind this Paarl winery — Dutch-born Peter Ras, Mariëtte Ras and Eric Verhaak — are passionate about chenin (hence the grape starring in most of their variously fermented, aged and blended wines), about sustainable winegrowing (note the 'organic' icons below) and about experimentation (witness the delightful new méthode ancestrale bubbly). Grootparys.blogspot.com (in Dutch) is the way to keep up with all the happenings.

Die Tweede Droom range
★★★★ **Chenin Blanc Dopkontak** ⊗ ⊘ Extended skin/lees-ageing & natural ferment give individual **13** a fino sherry nuttiness but there's also thatch & wet clay complexity. Bone-dry, pleasantly firm.

★★★★ **Chenin Blanc Vatgegis** ⊘ Subtle white peach & pear, toasted nuts & buttered brioche on old-oak-fermented **14**, with brisk acidity plumped by generous fruit. Should reward cellaring year/2.

★★★★ **Straw Wine** ⊗ ⊘ Characterful dessert from air-dried chenin. Previously noted as sold out, in fact still-available **12** similar to unctuous **11**, integrated all-new oak, endless orange marmalade farewell.

Wellustig Vatgegis Chardonnay (NEW) ⊘ ★★★ Only 47 cases of **14**, showing tangerine & orange notes, slight sawn wood character from 100% new oak, satisfying weight & dryness though unlingering. **Chenin Blanc Spontane Gisting** ⊘ ⊘ ★★★★ Spontaneously fermented **14** takes step up with attractive bruised apple character, estate's hallmark vivacious acidity. **Méthode Ancestrale** (NEW) ★★★★ Personality-packed **14** sparkling from mostly chenin has racy bubbles, buttered crumpet, Granny Smith apple attractions. Tad frothy but very individual & appealing. Enjoy well chilled. Also tasted: **Rosé Vatgegis** ⊘ ⊘ **14** ★★★ **Chardonnay Vatgegis** ⊘ **14** ★★☆ Not retasted: **Pinotage 14** ★★★ **Chenin Blanc Extra Matured 12** ★★★★ **Chenin Blanc Amfora Gegis 14** ★★★ **Chenin Blanc Sparkling 13** ★★★☆ In abeyance: **Chenin Blanc Wellustig Vatgegis**.

Special Projects
Pinotage-Chenin Blanc ⊗ ⊘ ★★★ Joint venture with Voor Paardeberg's Scali winery. Lovely light, cherry-scented red, the grapes co-fermented. **14** bone-dry, packed with flavour. Enjoy young. — CvZ

Location/WO: Paarl ▪ Map: Paarl & Wellington ▪ Map grid reference: E5 ▪ Est 1699 ▪ 1stB 1709 ▪ Tasting & sales by appt ▪ Owner(s) Eric Verhaak, Mariëtte Ras & Peter Ras ▪ Viticulturist(s) Gawie Kriel (consultant) ▪ 81ha/45ha (ptage, ruby cab, chard, chenin, cbard) ▪ 105t 90% white 10% rosé ▪ PO Box 82 Huguenot 7645 ▪ grootparys@wam.co.za ▪ www.grootparys.co.za ▪ S 33° 44' 48.0" E 018° 58' 41.6" ▪ **T +27 (0)76-567-8082**

Group CDV

Selling well over 1m cases, mainly to supermarkets in Europe, Group CDV (Cape Dutch Vignerons) is primarily a negociant though it also offers services to buyers of value-for-money South African wines. The ever-changing portfolio includes slightly higher-priced (over 5 euros) ranges like De Zuydpunt, and bottling for all labels is approached pragmatically: entry-level wines mostly done overseas, 'tricky' ones (eg sparkling, sweet and low-alcohol) in SA.

Vry Burger

Bourgeois Blanc ⓠ ★★★ Viognier's apricot & peach to fore on tank sample **13**, with chenin & grenache blanc. Full bodied, crisp & dry. Not retasted: **Bourgeois Rouge 13** ★★

Groupe LFE South Africa range

Grâce Blanche Natural Sweet ⓠ ★★ Delicate **13** balanced sweetness, low alcohol for all-day quaffing.

Klein Kasteelberg Private Bin range

Pinotage ⓠ ★★ Faint varietal banana, strawberry on lightly fruited, dry **12** sipper. Not retasted: **Merlot 12** ★★★ **Chardonnay 13** ★★ **Secco NV** ★★★

Klein Kasteelberg range

Pinotage ⓠ ★★ **12** doesn't shout the variety but is easy to drink. Not retasted: **Merlot 12** ★★ **Chardonnay 13** ★★

Nuwe Wynplaas range

Merlot ⓠ ★★★ Juicy fruit firmly gripped by tannins mid-2014, **12** for country fare. Not retasted: **Cabernet Sauvignon 12** ★★★ **Chardonnay 13** ★★

Klein Centennial range

Not tasted: **Pinotage, Shiraz Rosé, Chenin Blanc-Viognier**. — AL

Location: Somerset West ▪ WO: Swartland/Western Cape ▪ Est/1stB 2006 ▪ Closed to public ▪ Owner(s) Groupe LFE South Africa ▪ Cellarmaster(s) Nicky Versfeld (consultant) ▪ 1.2m cs own label 60% red 35% white 5% rosé ▪ Fairtrade ▪ PO Box 88 Somerset Mall 7137 ▪ rob@groupcdv.co.za ▪ www.groupcdv.co.za ▪ F +27 (0)21-851-3578 ▪ **T +27 (0)21-850-0160**

Grünberger

Introduced more than 60 years ago, the flattish, rounded 'bocksbeutel' flagon, first of its kind in South Africa, remains a feature of this lower-alcohol, mostly Natural Sweet range by Distell.

Spritziger ⓠ ★★★ Spritzy party wine from chenin/colombard, **14** semi-sweet, with grapey flavour.
Spritziger Rosé ⓠ ★★ Splash of ruby cab gives a blush to **14** gently sweet, slightly bubbly quaffer. Not retasted: **Rosenlese 14** ★★ **Freudenlese 14** ★★★ — DB

Grundheim Wines   ⓠ ♿

Stalwarts of Klein Karoo grape growing, winemaking and distilling, the Grundling family have launched their first red wine, a '14 Shiraz, and introduced a new label, Grundheim Craft Distillery, featuring apple and pear 'schnapps'. These join an array of fortifieds and spirits, including the traditional unmatured firewater half-jokingly named Withond ('Bull Terrier'): 'Once it bites, it doesn't let go'.

Fortified range

★★★★ **Rosyntjiewyn** ⓠ Jerepiko-style dessert, **11** (★★★) is 100% touriga & very sweet. Though checked by firm tannin, misses crispness & alcohol punch of previous **NV**, which included pinotage.
★★★★ **Late Bottled Vintage** ⓠ Commendable & complex port-style from touriga & tinta. **09** (★★★★), first since **05** (only touriga), is richly fruity & textured.
Not retasted: **Red Muscadel 12** ★★★ **White Muscadel 13** ★★ **Cape Ruby Port NV** ★★★ **White Port 10** ★★★ Not tasted: **Cape Vintage Port**.

Brandy range

Boegoe ⓠ ★★★ Blended 9 year old potstill with natural buchu, giving a minty, herbal character, dusty palate. For medicinal purposes or with a mixer for a refreshing drink. 375 ml. **Gemmer** ⊘

★★★☆ Blended 9 year old potstill, natural fresh ginger for a delightful balanced drink with spicy kick. Enjoy on its own or with ginger ale for a cocktail. **Kuipers** ⓨ ★★★ 5 year old blended brandy (43% alcohol) from colombard & chenin. Nuts, fynbos & dried apricot flavours; sweet, fragrant & spicy finish. **Potstill** ⓨ ★★★ 100% potstill from colombard & chenin. Firm & powerful, floral & dried fruit notes, hint of smoke & caramel. Leanish style, quite fiery for 9 year old. — WB, TJ, CR

Location: Oudtshoorn ▪ Map: Klein Karoo & Garden Route ▪ WO: Klein Karoo/Western Cape ▪ Est/1stB 1995 ▪ Tasting & sales Mon-Fri 9-5 Sat 9-1 ▪ Fee R20 for groups of 10+ ▪ Closed Easter Fri/Sun, Dec 25 & Jan 1 ▪ Owner(s) Danie Grundling ▪ Winemaker(s) Dys Grundling (1997) ▪ 25ha (cinsaut, muscadel r/w, ruby cab, tinta, touriga, cbard, hanepoot, palomino) ▪ 360t/10,000L own label 100% fortified ▪ PO Box 400 Oudtshoorn 6620 ▪ grundheim@absamail.co.za ▪ S 33° 37' 40.1" E 022° 3' 54.6" ▪ F +27 (0)86-616-6311 ▪ **T +27 (0)44-272-6927**

Guardian Peak Wines ⓨ ⑪ ⑤

Situated high on the Helderberg and commanding wonderful views of owner Jean Engelbrecht's other prestige property, Rust en Vrede, and surrounding vineyards, Guardian Peak is supplied by long-term contracted grape growers ensuring consistency and quality (note the 5 star gem below). Such stability also allows winemakers Philip van Staden and Pieter van der Merwe some freedom of expression, and specific parcels of fruit are finding their way into new wines slowly being added to the range – the rosé already proving a popular food-friendly option at the on-site restaurant.

★★★★ **Frontier** ⓨ 100% cab, showing lively blackcurrant & hint of fynbos on **13**. Chewy & dense but refined, with good depth & length. Spice from judicious use of 10% American oak adds interest.

★★★★☆ **Lapa Cabernet Sauvignon** Initially fairly muted **13** (★★★★★) opens to classic cab aromas & flavours of black berries, cedar & tar. Big, ripe & bold but not without grace; gritty tannins add texture, suggesting excitement to come. Well oaked, as was **12**. Stellenbosch WO.

★★★★ **Summit** Delightful yet concentrated mix of red fruits (plums, strawberries, raspberries) **13** given definition by firm, ripe tannins & powerful but integrated alcoholic punch. Syrah/shiraz (62%), mourvèdre & grenache, some from Breedekloof.

Rosé ⓝⓔⓦ ★★★ Pretty debut for dry **15** from cab promises strawberries & lots of summer fun. **Sauvignon Blanc** ★★★ **15** tank sample shy & floral, slim & slight with underlying promise of more to come. Also tasted: **Merlot 14** ★★★ **Shiraz 14** ★★★★ Discontinued: **Tannat-Malbec**. — CM

Location/map: Stellenbosch ▪ Map grid reference: E8 ▪ WO: Western Cape/Stellenbosch ▪ Est 1998 ▪ 1stB 2000 ▪ Tasting & sales Mon-Sun 9–5 ▪ Closed Easter Fri/Sun & Dec 25 ▪ Guardian Peak Winery & Grill ▪ Owner(s) Jean Engelbrecht ▪ Winemaker(s) Philip van Staden (Jan 2009), with Pieter van der Merwe (Jan 2013) ▪ Viticulturist(s) Dirkie Mouton (Jun 2010) ▪ 50,000cs own label 100% red ▪ Brands for clients: Pick's Pick ▪ IPW ▪ PO Box 473 Stellenbosch 7599 ▪ info@guardianpeak.com ▪ www.guardianpeak.com ▪ S 34° 0' 40.19" E 018° 50' 31.99" ▪ F +27 (0)21-881-3388 ▪ **T +27 (0)21-881-3899**

☐ **Guinea Fowl** see Saxenburg Wine Farm
☐ **Guru** see Hoopenburg Wines
☐ **Gwendolyn** see Saxenburg Wine Farm
☐ **Hagelsberg** see Middelvlei Estate
☐ **Halala Afrika** see Rudera Wines

Hamilton Russell Vineyards ⓨ ⑥

This pioneering winery, founded by the late Tim Hamilton Russell in the then viticulturally uncharted Hemel-en-Aarde Valley, last year celebrated its 40th anniversary. While dedication to Burgundy varieties chardonnay and pinot noir has been constant, there have been many changes. The move towards organic farming, including the use of earthworm tea in the vineyards, took a step further in 2015 with the harvesting of the first organic crop. This coincided with winemaker Emul Ross' first crush here, described as 'unusually early and brief' but showing promise. A new pinot noir fermentation cellar with a larger press and open fermenters, capable of holding the entire crop, helped. To cap the 40 year festivities, current owner Anthony Hamilton Russell was inducted as a Chevalier du Tastevin in Burgundy.

★★★★☆ **Pinot Noir** More interesting, typical pinot features on **14**: black cherries, hint undergrowth & spice but none of the mint on **13** (★★★★). Quite luscious, richly silky but well-contained by fresh thread acid, fine bracing tannins. Some magnums available.

★★★★☆ **Chardonnay 14** tribute to Hannes Storm's last vintage here. Thrilling, full of taut energy & incipient lime, oatmeal layers spread across its silky reach. Oaking, just 86% oaked, 26% new, 8.5 months provides subtle polish to maintain consistency in this ageworthy SA classic. — AL

Location: Hermanus ▪ Map: Elgin, Walker Bay & Bot River ▪ WO: Hemel-en-Aarde Valley ▪ Est 1975 ▪ 1stB 1981 ▪ Tasting & sales Mon-Fri 9–5 Sat 9–1 ▪ Closed Easter Fri/Mon, Dec 26 & Jan 1 ▪ Tours by appt ▪ Fynbos reserve & 2 wetlands ▪ Owner(s) Anthony Hamilton Russell ▪ Winemaker(s) Emul Ross (2014) ▪ Viticulturist(s) Johan Montgomery (2005) ▪ 170ha/52ha (pinot, chard) ▪ 18,704cs own label 50% red 50% white ▪ BWI Champion ▪ PO Box 158 Hermanus 7200 ▪ hrv@hermanus.co.za ▪ www.hamiltonrussellvineyards.com ▪ S 34° 23' 23.0" E 019° 14' 30.6" ▪ F +27 (0)28-312-1797 ▪ **T +27 (0)28-312-3595**

Hannay Wines

A rockstar team of winemakers (Cathy Marshall and Richard Kershaw) and viticulturist (Kevin Watt) join owner Malcolm Dicey at his boutique cellar in Elgin. Expansion work is now complete, creating room for many of the valley's top talents to custom-make their own wines. Meanwhile understanding of the unique vineyard sites available to the team improves apace.

★★★★☆ **Cabernet Franc** Excellent typicity on **13**, mixing subtle spice, black fruit & (ripe) signature leafiness to good effect. Improves over time, gentle oaking (no new) adds vanilla to lengthy & satisfying finish. Also in magnum. Different league to **11** (★★★). No **12**.

★★★★☆ **Chardonnay** (NEW) Delicious debut **14** combines buttered toast with pineapples & creamy citrus. Oak (1/3 new) needs time to integrate fully but fresh acidity (no malo) suggests wine should improve over next 3-5 years – certainly bears decanting before serving.

Not tasted: **Sauvignon Blanc**. — CM

Location/WO: Elgin ▪ Map: Elgin, Walker Bay & Bot River ▪ Est/1stB 2011 ▪ Tasting, sales & cellar tours by appt ▪ Fee R30 for groups of 10+ ▪ BYO picnic ▪ Light/buffet lunches by appt only ▪ Owner(s) Malcolm J Dicey ▪ Winemaker(s) Richard Kershaw & Catherine Marshall ▪ Viticulturist(s) Kevin Watt (2012, consultant) ▪ 72ha/13ha under vine ▪ 220t majority custom crush ▪ 50% red 50% white ▪ IPW, SIZA, WIETA ▪ PO Box 36 Elgin 7680 ▪ winemaker@hannaywines.co.za, info@valleygreen.co.za ▪ S 34° 12' 12.07" E 19° 02' 35.10" ▪ F +27 (0)86-718-2203 ▪ **T +27 (0)21-848-9770/+27 (0)71-676-9588**

Harrison Hope

US missionaries Ronnie and Janet Vehorn planted a small vineyard on a mountainous property in the Eastern Cape interior in the 1990s as a community skills development project. Self-taught winemaker Ronnie, recently with Vumile Makapela, ex Asara, has produced a few vintages (none reviewed).

Location: Queenstown ▪ Map: Eastern Cape ▪ Est 2000 ▪ 1stB 2009 ▪ Tasting & tours by appt ▪ Accommodation ▪ Owner(s) Ronnie & Janet Vehorn ▪ Cellarmaster(s)/viticulturist(s) Ronnie Vehorn ▪ Winemaker(s) Ronnie Vehorn, with Vumile Makapela (Aug 2014) ▪ 2ha (merlot, ptage, shiraz, chard, sauv) ▪ 2,000cs own label ▪ PO Box 1394 Queenstown 5320 ▪ rvehorn@gmail.com ▪ www.harrisonhope.com ▪ S 32° 10' 01.11" E 026° 50' 28.28" ▪ F +27 (0)40-842-9200 ▪ **T +27 (0)40-842-9444/+27 (0)82-808-5284**

Hartenberg Estate

The flagship wines are an homage to the people who shaped this renowned Bottelary Hills property over the years: the elegant chardonnay pays tribute to Eleanor Finlayson who farmed it in the 1950s; the Bordeaux blend and shiraz honour subsequent owner Ken Mackenzie ('Stork' being his WWII air force call sign). Helping shape the estate the past two decades is cellarmaster Carl Schultz, who drives the shiraz focus with multiple iterations including a CWG Auction bottling. His other passion is riesling, and visitors flock to the annual Riesling Rocks festival, a popular highlight along with the Shiraz & Charcuterie celebration. Enhancing the Hartenberg offering are the new Alchemy blends which in years to come will accommodate newly planted grenache.

Ultra Premium range

★★★★☆ **Gravel Hill Shiraz** Complexity & purity define **11** from gravelly terroir. Silky smooth & elegant but muscular, with rich black fruit, spice, ink & even cocoa nuances. Layered, refined; will age well.

Super Premium range

★★★★☆ **The Stork Shiraz** Offers ripe plum & blue fruit vibrancy & appeal. **12** gentle, rounded & juicy but with dry tannin squeeze. Identical oaking to Gravel Hill (19 months all-new French), difference is in the clay-rich soils. Layered, elegant & long.

★★★★☆ **The Mackenzie** Confident entry of blackcurrant on **12** Bordeaux trio led as always by cab with dabs merlot & petit verdot. Deep, dark & concentrated but with superb balance & lightly harmonious fruit & oak. Poised & polished with gentle regal presence. **11** (★★★★★) had dash malbec.

★★★★☆ **The Eleanor Chardonnay** Effortlessly elegant, understated **13** unfurls creamy clementine vibrancy on the palate. Sexy & refined, with perfect balance from 11 months in 60% new French oak. **12** sold out untasted.

CWG Auction Reserves

★★★★☆ **Merlot** (NEW) Cedar spice nuance underpins the refined blackcurrant & bramble notes of layered, expressive yet reserved **13**. Elegantly balanced oak mimics that of CWG Shiraz, 20 months all-new French. Fine dry tannin. Lingers on & on.

★★★★☆ **Shiraz** Svelte **13** is a ripe, pure, dark choc & black berry beauty, poised perfectly by understated oak (20 months new French). Iron fist & velvet glove, its leashed power & promise will reward careful cellaring. **12** untasted.

Premium range

★★★★ **Cabernet Sauvignon** Peppery edge to seductive black fruit notes of **12**. Textured, ripe & succulent, with a confidently assertive frame of oak from 17 months in 65% new French barrels.

★★★★ **Merlot** **12** retains form of **11** & **10** in bright, plush yet savoury black fruit palate with earthy notes. Defined, broad & deep. Small dabs cab, malbec & petit verdot.

★★★★ **Shiraz** Gentle violet & pepper sheen to plum fruit & spice on **12**. Restrained & elegant, with pliable, dry tannin from 17 months oak, half new.

★★★★ **Chardonnay** **13** returns to form after **12** (★★★★) with broad, creamy oatmeal & stonefruit ripeness. Vibrant citrus freshness balances oak (just 36% new French). Defined frame & focused length.

★★★★ **Riesling** Crisp, dry **14** (★★★★) displays a trace of honeyed lime zest from touch of botrytis. Taut & focused with lively green-apple succulence. A shade off **13**.

Cabernet Sauvignon-Shiraz ★★★★ Ripe, rounded **13** is savoury & broadly appealing but with nice concentration & balance. Also tasted: **Doorkeeper Shiraz** 13 ★★★★ **Sauvignon Blanc** 14 ★★★★ Not tasted: **Occasional Riesling**. Occasional release: **Riesling Noble Late Harvest**.

Alchemy range (NEW)

SMG (organic) ★★★ Spicy core of berry fruit is balanced by ripe succulence & light tannin squeeze on **13** syrah/shiraz, mourvèdre, grenache. **Syrah-Cabernet Sauvignon** (organic) ★★★★ Instantly engaging squishy black fruit on **13**, light easy-drinker with bright plum & pepper notes.

Merlot-Malbec-Cabernet Franc ★★★ Fruitcake generosity with dry spice highlights on **13** Bordeaux trio. Unfussy & supple with gentle grip. Coastal WO, like SMG. **Chenin Blanc-Semillon-Sauvignon Blanc** ★★★★ Lively fresh vibrance to perky stonefruit notes of **15**. Good body, breadth & length. — FM

Location/map: Stellenbosch ▪ Map grid reference: C4 ▪ WO: Stellenbosch/Coastal ▪ Est/1stB 1978 ▪ Tasting & sales Mon-Fri 9–5 Sat 9–4 Sun (Nov-Apr only) 10-4 ▪ Closed Good Fri, Dec 25 & Jan 1 ▪ Tasting fee refunded with purchase ▪ Cellar tours by appt ▪ Picnics & lunches 12-3.30 ▪ Light snacks, charcuterie and cheese platters served throughout the day ▪ Specialised food & wine pairings by appt only ▪ Facilities for children ▪ Walks/hikes ▪ Bird watching ▪ Bottelary Renosterveld Conservancy ▪ Function venue: outdoor & underground cellar ▪ Owner(s) Hartenberg Holdings ▪ Cellarmaster(s) Carl Schultz (Nov 1993) ▪ Winemaker(s) Patrick Ngamane (Jan 2001), with Oscar Robyn (Nov 2003) ▪ Viticulturist(s) Wilhelm Joubert (May 2006) ▪ 187ha/85ha (cab, merlot, shiraz, chard, riesling, sauv) ▪ 550t/60,000cs own label 80% red 20% white ▪ BWI, IPW ▪

PO Box 12756 Die Boord 7613 ▪ info@hartenbergestate.com ▪ www.hartenbergestate.com ▪ S 33° 53' 52.5"
E 018° 47' 30.4" ▪ F +27 (0)21-865-2153 ▪ **T +27 (0)21-865-2541**

Hartswater Wine Cellar   ⓦ

Deon Truter and his wine colleagues are part of the very large Orange River Cellars team, and their focus
is on easy-drinking, mostly sweet wines from vines in the Northern Cape's Hartswater irrigation region.

Elements range

Fire ⓦ ★★ Fully sweet **NV** rosé from ruby cab. **Rain** ⓦ ★★ Semi-sweet **NV** from colombard with
modest 10% alcohol. Not retasted: **Earth NV** ★★ **Wind NV** ★★ **Thunder NV** ★★

Overvaal range

White Jerepico ⓦ ★★ With fleshy raisin sweetness, **NV** fortified is from rare fernão pires. Not
retasted: **Red Jerepico NV** ★★★ — DB

Location: Hartswater ▪ Map: Northern Cape, Free State & North West ▪ WO: Northern Cape ▪ Tasting &
sales Mon-Fri 8.30-1, 2-5 ▪ Sales also from outlet in Hartswater; orders delivered to liquor stores in
Northern Cape (350-km radius), Free State & North West ▪ Cellar tours by appt ▪ Owner(s) Orange River
Wine Cellars ▪ Winemaker(s) Deon Truter ▪ 800t ▪ PO Box 2335 Hartswater 8570 ▪ deon@
wynkelder.co.za ▪ S 27° 55' 2.2" E 024° 49' 38.2" ▪ F +27 (0)53-474-0975 ▪ **T +27 (0)53-474-0700**

Haskell Vineyards   ⓦ ⓰ ⌂ ⓐ ⓹

Owned by international real estate magnate, American-born Preston Haskell IV, who clearly knew what
to look for in buying this prime 25-ha Stellenbosch property over a decade ago. Located in the sought-
after 'Golden Triangle' on the slopes of the Helderberg, it has a variety of soils, aspects and elevations,
particularly suited to shiraz and Bordeaux-style reds. Some supplementary fruit is bought, including for
wines requiring a specific terroir expression, like the Dombeya whites. Haskell is the premium label, with
the credentials to prove it (note the two 5 stars this edition), its wines polished and powerful, with great
ageing potential. The main focus is shiraz, two of the reds are this variety, and it features as a component
in the other reds. Dombeya, previously listed separately, is more commercially priced with a wider single-varietal range. All the wines are made at Haskell under the direction of Rianie Strydom.

Haskell range

★★★★☆ **Aeon Syrah** Dab of mourvèdre & 40% new oak (10% more than Pillars) gives deep & involving **12** a meaty tone, liquorice & savoury spice. Tannins also more evident but without detracting from the
enjoyment, a guarantee of a long life.

★★★★☆ **Pillars Syrah** Lots to admire in **12**, voluptuous dark-toned fruit, espresso nuances, a hint of
scrub, backed by a smoothly curvaceous body, fine tannins. Already accessible & pleasurable but deep
muscle tone promises a 10+ year future.

★★★★☆ **Haskell II** Mocha chocolate & spiced black plums in **11**, thanks to 60/40 shiraz/cab blend &
expert oaking, 18 months French, 30% new. Strikes the right balance between plush fruit & a tannin backbone which ensures a rewarding future.

★★★★☆ **Haskell IV** Cab dominant with merlot, a soupçon of petit verdot, shiraz, **10** (★★★★★)
demands to be taken seriously. Styled for the long haul, as was **09**, with all already in place, fruitcake
depth, tobacco notes on a savoury bed of fine-textured tannins.

★★★★☆ **Anvil Chardonnay** Beautifully crafted to give citrus-seamed **14** (★★★★★) an oak partnership that takes it to another level, though **12** was also fine. Sophisticated, elegant, poised & polished, with
a very long future. No **13**.

Dombeya range

★★★★ **Merlot** Expressive red berries yet **13**'s personality is more serious, geared to fine dining with its
firm but ripe tannins, savoury finish. Already drinking well, has a good future.

★★★★ **Boulder Road Shiraz** Straddling the Old World & New, **13** has Morello cherry depth &
piquancy, is sleekly curvaceous & polished with a hint of peppery wildness. Also-tasted **12** has meatier,
darker tones, with the same succulence & flair.

★★★★ **Fenix** Cab rules in Bordeaux-style **10**, with merlot, dab petit verdot. Dark toned, the liquorice, plush black plums verge on opulent, rescued by a seam of fine tannins for structure, a long future.

★★★★ **Chardonnay** Sleek & elegant **14** vibrates with citrus intensity, a far cry from oaky, gutsier versions. This is an aristocrat, already gorgeous, with a 4+ year future. WO Coastal.

Also tasted: **Sauvignon Blanc 15** ★★★☆ — CR

Location/map: Stellenbosch ▪ Map grid reference: E8 ▪ WO: Stellenbosch/Coastal/Western Cape ▪ Est 2002 ▪ 1stB 2008 ▪ Tasting & sales Tue-Fri 9–5 Sat/Sun 10-5 ▪ Fee R40 ▪ Closed Mon, Easter Fri-Mon & Dec 25 ▪ Cellar tours on special request only ▪ The Long Table Restaurant & Café Tue-Sun 9-5; dinner Fri (Sep-Mar) – booking essential ▪ Facilities for children ▪ Self-catering accommodation in The Residence and Cottage ▪ Owner(s) Preston Haskell ▪ Cellarmaster(s) Rianie Strydom (Jan 2005) ▪ Viticulturist(s) Aldert Nieuwoudt (Aug 2014) ▪ 25ha/13.5ha (cabs s/f, merlot, shiraz, chard) ▪ ±80t/3,600cs own label 80% red 20% white ▪ PO Box 12766 Die Boord 7613 ▪ info@haskellvineyards.com ▪ www.haskellvineyards.com ▪ S 34° 0' 13.9" E 018° 51' 38.4" ▪ F +27 (0)21-881-3986 ▪ **T +27 (0)21-881-3895**

Hathersage   ⓠ ⓞ

Presided over by handsome 1920s homestead Hathersage House (now a conference/wedding venue), expertly researched Bordeaux plantings and surrounding conservation land (once part of 17th-century Cape governor Willem Adriaan van der Stel's Vergelegen) hold out against Somerset West suburban creep. Increasingly exported wines are 'still passionately produced', says wine/admin officer Suzette Nel.

Merlot ★★★ Rich plummy fruitcake aromas on ex-barrel **13**. 15% petit verdot adds focus & freshness to otherwise big but well-balanced wine. **Bistro Red** ⓝⒺⓦ ★★ Robust, cab-franc led Bordeaux-style blend. Pre-bottling **13** sweet fruited, very dry, with gruff tannins. **Semillon** ★★★☆ **15**, tasted pre-release, first since **12**. Full bodied & rich textured, with expressive lemony wax features, hint oak vanilla. 10% sauvignon adds some zest, backbone. **Bistro White** ⓝⒺⓦ ★★☆ Full-flavoured, zesty sauvignon-semillon blend. Ex-tank **15** is dry, with hint alcohol glow in tail. Also tasted: **Cabernet Sauvignon 13** ★★ **Chardonnay 15** ★★ **Sauvignon Blanc 15** ★★★ Not tasted: **Mouille Grange**. Occasional release: **Special Edition Red Reserve**, **Special Edition White Reserve**. — AL

Location: Somerset West ▪ Map: Helderberg ▪ WO: Stellenbosch ▪ 1stB 2007 ▪ Tasting & sales by appt Mon-Fri 9-4 ▪ Closed all pub hols ▪ Tour groups ▪ Conference & wedding/function venue with catering (10-150 pax) ▪ Conservation area ▪ Owner(s) Stephan Holdings cc & Stephan Brothers (Pty) Ltd ▪ Winemaker(s) Michael Liedtke (Jan 2010, consultant) ▪ 40ha/12ha (cabs s/f, merlot, p verdot, shiraz, chard, sauv, sem) ▪ 52t/3,036cs own label 43% red 57% white ▪ PO Box 2517 Somerset West 7129 ▪ info@hathersage.co.za ▪ www.hathersage.co.za ▪ S 34° 4' 54.42" E 018° 51' 55.32" ▪ F +27 (0)21-851-8382 ▪ **T +27 (0)21-851-1644/+27 (0)21-851-5076**

Haute Cabrière   ⓠ ⓨ ⓖ

Celebrating his 60th birthday this year, charismatic founder Achim von Arnim still keeps a seasoned eye on operations alongside daughter-in-law and MD Christiane, but son Takuan is now fully in charge of winemaking at both the Pierre Jourdan bubbly cellar on Clos Cabrière estate and the still-wine facility on panoramic Franschhoek Pass, also home to the tasting room and ever-popular restaurant. New viticulturist and deputy cellarmaster Tim Hoek (ex Lithos) shares their fundamental winegrowing philosophy of 'sun, soil, vine, man' as they focus on chardonnay and pinot noir, the latter recently replanted.

Haute Cabrière range

★★★★ **Pinot Noir Reserve** Gets deserved 'Reserve' status in **12**, more serious than cheerful **11** (★★★☆). Fruits of the forest & earthy forest floor combine with elegantly integrated tannins & slightly savoury finish. Franschhoek WO. Also in magnum.

Unwooded Pinot Noir ⓥ ★★★ A 'red white wine' best served lightly chilled, **15** is bright ruby in colour with light tannins, sweet red berries & a hint of spice making it instantly approachable.

Also tasted: **Chardonnay-Pinot Noir 15** ★★★☆

Pierre Jourdan range

★★★★ **Ratafia** Latest honeyed yet citrusy **NV**, SA's only example of the 'other' drink from Champagne (a sweet fortified), reaches new heights with cheese. From chardonnay, available in new 375 ml bottle.

Brut ★★★ Reliable golden **NV** méthode cap classique sparkler from 60% chardonnay & 40% pinot noir has apple as well as citrus notes, with a buttery pastry richness. Also in 375 ml and 1.5L. Also tasted: **Tranquille NV** ★★★☆ **Cuvée Belle Rose NV** ★★★☆ — JG

Location/map: Franschhoek ▪ WO: Western Cape/Franschhoek ▪ Est 1982 ▪ 1stB 1984 ▪ Tasting & sales Mon-Fri 9–5 Sat/pub hols 10–4 Sun 11-4 ▪ Public cellar tour/tasting Mon-Fri at 11; cellarmaster's tour/tasting Sat at 11; private tasting/tour (pre-booked) ▪ Closed Good Fri, Dec 25/26 & Jan 1 ▪ Haute Cabrière Restaurant ▪ Tour groups by appt ▪ Owner(s) Clos Cabrière (Pty) Ltd ▪ Cellarmaster(s) Takuan von Arnim (2005), with Tim Hoek (Dec 2014) ▪ Viticulturist(s) Tim Hoek (Dec 2014) ▪ 30ha (pinot, chard) ▪ 40% red 60% white ▪ PO Box 245 Franschhoek 7690 ▪ marketing@cabriere.co.za ▪ www.cabriere.co.za ▪ S 33° 54' 51.8" E 019° 8' 8.2" ▪ F +27 (0)21-876-8501 ▪ **T +27 (0)21-876-8500**

Haut Espoir   ⓨ ⓐ ⓖ

The Armstrong family has been breathing new life into this hilltop Franschhoek farm for over a decade. Recently appointed winemaker Marozanne Bieldt works on reds to match the whites on quality, freeing up cellarmaster son Rob Armstrong to oversee biodynamic practices and liaise with Scherpenheuwel neighbours (including Boekenhoutskloof) on a nature conservancy.

★★★★ **Chardonnay** Quietly elegant, unassertive **11** (★★★☆), with hints of nuts & citrus. Good texture, though acid a little rough; moderate length. Like **10**, ready for drinking on release.

★★★★ **Semillon** Previewed natural-ferment **14** the first since **09**. Lemon & beeswax confirm variety, untrammelled by older oak used, which adds softness. Bone-dry & fresh; not intense, but characterful.

Gentle Giant ★★★☆ Most 'modern' & easily appealing of these reds, **10** Bordeaux blend with rare grape tannat is not gigantic but certainly friendly. Firm structure for red/black fruit. 5 years in old oak accounts for dryness on finish. Also tasted: **Cabernet Sauvignon 07** ★★★☆ **Shiraz 08** ★★★ Not retasted: **Cabernet Franc 08** ★★★ — TJ

Location/map: Franschhoek ▪ WO: Franschhoek/Stellenbosch ▪ Est 1999 ▪ 1stB 2004 ▪ Tastings, sales & cellar tours by appt ▪ Closed all pub hols ▪ Fynbos walks ▪ Conservation area ▪ Owner(s) Armstrong family ▪ Cellarmaster(s)/viticulturist(s) Rob Armstrong ▪ Winemaker(s) Rob Armstrong & Marozanne Bieldt ▪ ±23ha/12ha (cab, merlot, p verdot, shiraz) ▪ 70t/10,000cs own label 70% red 30% white ▪ BWI ▪ PO Box 681 Franschhoek 7690 ▪ wine@hautespoir.com ▪ www.hautespoir.com ▪ S 33° 56' 23.6" E 019° 6' 20.9" ▪ F +27 (0)21-876-4038 ▪ **T +27 (0)21-876-4000**

Havana Hills

Having undergone a transformation of wheatland to vineyard just ahead of the millennium, this West Coast farm with spectacular views across Table Bay to Table Mountain has now begun a process of revitalisation under a new owner. A fresh market-led approach aims to increase the visibility and presence of Havana Hills' wines in South Africa and the export market.

Kobus range

★★★★ **Chardonnay** Natural ferment **14** (★★★★) has citrus & nutty nose. Last-made **12** was lean, this is soft, creamy, with few grams sugar — no cloy thanks to zippy acid. Integrated new oak.

Also tasted: **Red 12** ★★★☆

Havana Hills range

★★★★ **Sauvignon Blanc** Citrus & tropical notes on **15** (★★★☆), less showy than Lime Road version. Light-feeling; green grip to the flavoursome soft-textured palate. Last-made **13** more dramatic & intense.

Shiraz ★★★☆ **11** has ripe, spicy fruit, well balanced, with supportive oaking (only 30% new, 18 months) for the lovely flavours. Comes across as more rich than sweet. Fairtrade certified, like many Havana wines. **Chardonnay-Pinot Noir** ★★★ Just 15% pinot noir on pale salmon-hued **14**. Forward aromas hinting at ripe strawberries. Flavourful, lightly fresh & neatly balanced rosé. Also tasted: **Merlot**

10 ★★★ **Chardonnay-Pinot Noir 14** ★★★ Not retasted: **Sangiovese 12** ★★★ **Cabernet Sauvignon-Barbera 09** ★★★☆ Not tasted: **Cabernet Sauvignon**. Discontinued: **Petit Verdot**.

Lime Road range

Shiraz-Mourvèdre-Viognier (NEW) ★★★ Rich & full-flavoured **13**, gently structured & well & unobtrusively oaked (like all these reds). Savoury element mingles nicely with the sweet dark fruit. WO W Cape. **Sauvignon Blanc** ⊘ ★★★ Exuberant **15** a leap forward. Limy accent adds interest to tropical fruit. Handles 8.4 g/l sugar well, finishes with green boiled-sweet note. Also tasted: **Cabernet Sauvignon-Merlot-Cabernet Franc 13** ★★★ **Cabernet Sauvignon Rosé** ⊘ **15** ★★★ Not tasted: **Shiraz**. — TJ

Location: Philadelphia ▪ WO: Philadelphia/Western Cape/Coastal ▪ Est 1999 ▪ 1stB 2000 ▪ Closed to public ▪ Owner(s) Xinxing Pang ▪ Winemaker(s) Piet Kleinhans (Sep 2008), Joseph Gertse (Jan 2000) & Mike Dobrovic (consultant) ▪ Viticulturist(s) Rudi Benn (Jan 2001) ▪ 260ha/60ha (barbera, cabs s/f, merlot, mourv, sangio, shiraz, sauv) ▪ 70,000cs own label 50% red 20% white 30% rosé ▪ Fairtrade, IPW, WIETA ▪ PO Box 451 Melkbosstrand 7437 ▪ sales@havanahills.co.za ▪ www.havanahills.co.za ▪ F +27 (0)21-972-1105 ▪ **T +27 (0)21-972-1110**

☐ **Hawk's Head** *see* Southern Sky Wines

Hawksmoor at Matjieskuil Ⓟ Ⓜ Ⓗ

These limited-release wines originate and generally are available only from venerable Paarl farm Matjieskuil, its restored Cape Dutch buildings with Table Mountain views run as Hawksmoor House luxury accommodation and wedding venue. Made off-site by various consultants, the wines appear under a new label depicting the manor house and resident German Shorthaired Pointer pair in the foreground.

Limited Releases

★★★★ **Algernon Stitch** Half each shiraz & mourvèdre in **12**, a lovely Morello cherry & liquorice richness with creamy mocha. Streamlined & polished, a bit of freshness giving lift, adding to the pleasure.

★★★★ **Saint Alfege's** Unwooded shiraz with 10% oaked mourvèdre in **12** (★★★★), yet spicing shows in the dark-toned fruit. Juicy, soft structure & appealing, but falls short of last-tasted **08**.

Mourvèdre (Ⓥ) ★★★★ Lots going on in **13**, opulent fruit, loads of savoury spice, scrub, even whiffs of campfire smoke, yet still offering lively, elegant drinkability. As does **12**, also tasted; darker toned, lovely cocoa, black pepper, similar smokiness. Both fewer than 200 cases, worth seeking out.

Cabernet Franc (NEW) ★★★★ Showing good typicity, **13** has blackberries, lead pencils, a faint herbal note & bright-fruited flavours. Should reveal even more over time. **Shiraz** ★★★ Plush dark fruit, elegant structure, **12** has an attractive liveliness, fresh finish. Also tasted: **Magdalen 15** ★★★ Not retasted: **Triginta Shiraz 11** ★★★★ **Cape Blend 09** ★★★★ **French Blend With A Cape Twist 09** ★★★★

Classic range

Serliana ★★★ From 30+ year old chenin. Earth & melon, some faint citrus notes, **15** is light & bone-dry. Also tasted: **Hawksmoor Pinotage 14** ★★★ — CR

Location/WO: Paarl ▪ Map: Paarl & Wellington ▪ Map grid reference: A7 ▪ Est 1692 ▪ 1stB 2005 ▪ Tasting by appt 10-4 daily ▪ Fee R35 ▪ Sales by appt daily ▪ Specialise in group tastings (10-20 pax), with option of lunch in the Cape Dutch manor house – prior arrangement essential ▪ Closed Easter Fri-Sun, Dec 25/31 & Jan 1 ▪ Luxury guest house ▪ Owner(s) Brameld Haigh ▪ Winemaker(s) various ▪ Viticulturist(s) Paul Wallace (2004) ▪ Farm manager Jan Lategan ▪ ±23ha (cab f, mourv, ptage, shiraz, chenin) ▪ ±130t/1,000cs own label 65% red 25% white 10% rosé ▪ PO Box 9 Elsenburg 7607 ▪ wines@hawksmoor.co.za ▪ www.hawksmoor.co.za ▪ S 33° 48' 47.4" E 018° 46' 14.1" ▪ F +27 (0)86-605-9008 ▪ **T +27 (0)21-884-4587**

Hazendal Ⓟ Ⓜ Ⓒ Ⓐ Ⓑ

Tourist-friendly Hazendal in Stellenbosch's Bottelary Hills dates from 1699, making it one of SA's oldest wine estates. Russian-born entrepreneur and current owner Mark Voloshin came to Cape Town for business, fell in love with the beauty of the winelands and bought Hazendal 21 years ago. After much careful restoration, the estate today has many attractions, not least a museum of Russian arts and culture.

Hazendal range

★★★★ Merlot ⓥ Satisfyingly full & intense, **09** ratchets up on **07** (★★★★) with savoury hints & black fruit on substantial tannins.

★★★★ Shiraz ⓥ Savoury core of red fruit, spicy dry tannins & bright acidity. Supple, juicy **08** (★★★★) shade off more structured **07**.

★★★★ Bushvine Chenin Blanc ⓥ Concentrated, rich & ripe stonefruit galore, with zesty freshness & leesy breadth. Long, creamy tail. **14** from 35 year old vines over-delivers, as did last-tasted **10** (★★★★).

★★★★☆ The Last Straw Harmony of acid (9 g/l) & sugar (198 g/l) balances **09** (★★★★) dessert from unbotrytised air-dried chenin, barrel aged. Slight loamy, bitter almond & praline nuance detract from honeyed appeal. Clean, dry finish. Follows delight of pure **08**.

Pinot Noir ⓝ **★★★** Easy & unfussy preview of **15** offers blueberry & cranberry succulence with light tannic grip from old oak. **Sauvignon Blanc ★★★** Light hearted & bright **14** has an unusually rounded palate due to maturation in barrel. Honeyed tail. Also tasted: **Shiraz-Cabernet Sauvignon 09 ★★★☆ White Nights Cap Classique NV ★★★★** Not retasted: **Wooded Chenin Blanc 09 ★★★★**

De Haas range

Red ★★★ Gentle succulence & lightness to fruity **14** unoaked Bordeaux-shiraz blend. Also tasted: **Rosé 14 ★★★ White 14 ★★★** — WB, FM

Location/map/WO: Stellenbosch ▪ Map grid reference: B3 ▪ Est 1699 ▪ 1stB 1950 ▪ Tasting, sales & Babushka farm stall 8-6 daily ▪ Tasting fee 25/5 wines ▪ Cellar tours Tue-Fri 11-3 ▪ Closed Jan 1 ▪ Hermitage Restaurant Tue-Sun 11–5 ▪ Picnics ▪ Conferences ▪ Functions ▪ Facilities for children ▪ Tour groups ▪ Gifts ▪ MTB trail ▪ Russian Arts & Culture Museum ▪ Owner(s) Dr Voloshin ▪ Winemaker(s) Wynand Pienaar ▪ 140ha/40ha (cab, merlot, pinot, shiraz, chenin, sauv) ▪ 50% red 50% white ▪ PO Box 111 Soneike 7583 ▪ info@hazendal.co.za ▪ www.hazendal.co.za ▪ S 33° 54' 2.7" E 018° 43' 9.1" ▪ F +27 (0)21-903-0057 ▪ **T +27 (0)21-903-5034/5**

- ☐ **HB Vineyards** *see* Hout Bay Vineyards
- ☐ **Head butt** *see* Rooiberg Winery
- ☐ **Heaven on Earth** *see* Stellar Winery
- ☐ **Heeren van Oranje Nassau** *see* De Villiers Wines
- ☐ **Heinrich Kulsen** *see* Kulsen Wines
- ☐ **Hendrik Lodewyk** *see* Du Preez Estate
- ☐ **Hercules Paragon** *see* Simonsvlei International
- ☐ **Heritage Heroes** *see* Nederburg Wines

Hermanuspietersfontein Wynkelder ⓠ ⓨ ⌂ ⓞ ⓖ

The winery with the 'proudly local' Afrikaans name (honouring the founder in 1855 of tourist-friendly coastal resort town Hermanus) is situated at the hub of the buzzing food, wine and shopping precinct at the entrance to Hemel-en-Aarde Valley. But the grapes mostly come from the Pretorius family co-owners' farm in the newer wine ward of Sunday's Glen further along Walker Bay. The focus of new cellarmaster Wilhelm Pienaar remains on sauvignon blanc and red blends (Bordeaux and Rhône), with a cabernet franc the only single-varietal red, aptly named Swartskaap, the 'Black Sheep' of the 'family'. Priding itself on operating sustainably both environmentally and socially, 'HPF' is a WWF-SA Conservation Champion and local community supporter through education charity Sondagskool 20/20.

Flagship Wines

★★★★☆ Die Arnoldus Cab-led Bordeaux quintet **11** shows serious intent along with purity & freshness: intense blackberry & juniper notes with a clean seam of redcurrant acidity. Ripe, refined, supple & complex with cedar, spice & smoky tobacco from oak seamlessly integrated. Also in magnum.

★★★★☆ Die Martha Full-bodied **12** Rhône-style blend of shiraz, mourvèdre, grenache, viognier shows elegance & presence, with spiced meat perfume, mocha, pepper & wild herb flavours. Supple texture, fresh & rich. A keeper. Walker Bay WO.

★★★★☆ **Die Bartho** Ⓠ Mix oak-fermented sauvignon (65%) & semillon, with splash nouvelle, all then a year in large oak. **12** more sombre toned than **11**. Bracing acid tension cloaks textural richness which time should expose.

Classic Wines

★★★★☆ **Swartskaap** 100% cab franc, **12** bright, vibrant with black & red berry fruit steeped in fragrant green herbs. Subtle oak spice adds to liquid silk texture. Superb expression of variety. A real gem!

★★★★ **Kleinboet** **12** younger brother of Arnoldus is no shrinking violet. Generous spicy berries & fruitcake, with good restraint, 50% new oak ageing. Lighter in build, but with personality. Walker Bay WO.

★★★★ **Sauvignon Blanc No 5** Ⓠ Distinctive oaked sauvignon. Improved **13** (★★★★☆) offers expressive tropical & fresh greenpepper aromas. Mouthfilling, with powdery texture, enhanced by regular lees stirring, hints of allspice on the lengthy goodbye, as in **12**.

★★★★ **Sauvignon Blanc No 7** Ⓠ Unoaked, intense & fresh, lees-enriched **14** lives up to expectation with bouncy tropical flavours, impressive concentration & focus, lemon zest twist to finish.

Bloos ★★★☆ Dry **15** rosé from Bordeaux red varieties is aromatic & fun. Touch of oak, lees-ageing complement plentiful berry fruit. Walker Bay WO. Also tasted: **Skoonma 13** ★★★★ **1855 Posmeester 14** ★★★ Discontinued: **Sauvignon Blanc No 3 Bergblokke, Sauvignon Blanc No 2.** — WB

Location: Hermanus ▪ Map: Elgin, Walker Bay & Bot River ▪ WO: Sunday's Glen/Walker Bay/Western Cape ▪ Est 2005 ▪ 1stB 2006 ▪ Tasting & sales Mon–Fri 9–5 Sat 9–4 Sun (15 Dec-15 Jan) 10.30-3 ▪ Closed Easter Fri/Sun, Dec 25/26 & Jan 1 ▪ Cellar tours on request ▪ Food & wine market Sat 9–1 ▪ Self-catering cottages ▪ Owner(s) The Pretorius Family Trust, Gerrie Heyneke ▪ Cellarmaster(s) Wilhelm Pienaar (Dec 2015) ▪ Winemaker(s) Kim McFarlane (Feb 2006) ▪ Viticulturist(s) Lochner Bester (Nov 2012) ▪ 320ha/ ±65ha (cabs s/f, grenache, malbec, merlot, mourv, p verdot, shiraz, nouvelle, sauv, sem, viog) ▪ 350t/ 25,000cs own label 50% red 40% white 10% rosé ▪ BWI champion ▪ Hemel en Aarde Village, Suite 47, Private Bag X15, Hermanus 7200 ▪ kelder@hpf1855.co.za ▪ www.hpf1855.co.za ▪ S 34° 24' 38.7" E 019° 11' 51.7" ▪ F +27 (0)28-316-1293 ▪ **T +27 (0)28-316-1875**

Hermit on the Hill Wines   Ⓠ

Having consolidated his new joint venture with longtime friend Krige Visser in Mount Abora Vineyards in the Swartland, boutique winemaker Pieter de Waal returns with a vengeance with his and wife Lohra's label. This fan of Arthurian legend continues his crusade against 'average': aptly named Coup d'Etat is from sought-after grapes from SA's oldest sauvignon block (circa 1965); among his ladies-in-waiting is an unusual grenache blanc/roussanne MCC sparkler.

★★★★ **Stellenbosch Syrah** Black fruits & pepper, olive tapenade on **13** at first; tightly wound, with terse tannin grip from 18 months in barrel. Like still-available **10**, needs time to unfold. No **11**, **12**.

★★★★ **The Second Crusade Chenin Blanc** (NEW) Youthful **14** competently marries 70% older-oaked fraction with unwooded portion to join ranks of interesting whites marching out of Swartland. Lovely dusty/mineral nuances to coiled fruit – decanting helps it unwind.

★★★★☆ **The Round Table Roussanne** ⊘ In contrast to full-bodied **13**, **15** from Voor Paardeberg is über fresh & zingy yet with an attractive slightly tactile element. Unwooded to fully express acacia, citrus marmalade & lemon fruit. Enjoy now & for ±3 years. No **14**.

★★★★☆ **Coup d'Etat** (NEW) **14** from SA's oldest sauvignon blanc vines, planted 1965 in Swartland. Ripe granadilla, orange & fresh apricot aromas. Though raised in old 500-litre oak no evidence of wood. Pure & intense with leesy complexity & invigorating acidity.

Knights in Tights Mourvèdre Luminoir ★★★★ Was 'Knights in Tights'. **15** from Swartland lives up to 'luminoire' moniker (for its rosé-like lightness) on nose but explodes with juicy flavour on palate. Light(ish) 12% alcohol too. Not tasted: **Aurora Grenache, Wellington Grenache, Aurora Syrah, Paarl Syrah, The Second Crusade, The Red Knight, Aurora Chardonnay, Aurora Blanc, The Infidel, The Souvenir Viognier, The White Knight, The Starry Knight.** — JPf

Location: Durbanville ▪ WO: Swartland/Stellenbosch/Voor Paardeberg/Paarl ▪ Est/1stB 2000 ▪ Tasting & sales by appt ▪ Owner(s)/cellarmaster(s) Pieter de Waal ▪ Winemaker(s) Pieter & Lohra de Waal ▪ bastardo, cinsaut, gamay, grenache n/b, malbec, mourv, shiraz, chard, chenin, rouss, sauv, viog ▪ 15t/

1,600cs own label 60% red 40% white ▪ PO Box 995 Bellville 7535 ▪ pieter@dw.co.za ▪ www.hermitonthehill.co.za ▪ F +27 (0)21-948-6666 ▪ **T +27 (0)83-357-3864**

Herold Wines   ⓦ ⓨ ⓐ ⓞ ⓩ ⓺

Undeterred by 'extreme' conditions on the steep, 450-600 m Cradock Peak slopes that helped launch the cool-climate Outeniqua wine ward in the late 1990s, Nico and Maureen Fourie are increasing sauvignon blanc and pinot noir, vinifying a maiden riesling and constructing a conference venue and mountain bike track through vineyards and indigenous fynbos.

★★★★ Pinot Noir Reserve (NEW) Density of colour signals seriousness of **13**, a rich, earthy example of the variety, with fulsome red berry features & a velvet texture. Nine months seasoned cask. Very satisfying.

Syrah (NEW) **★★★☆** Cool-climate elegance & white pepper character to svelte **13**; delicate but full of flavour. Modest 12.5% alcohol adds to light-on-the-tongue profile. Also tasted: **Red Men 13 ★★★ Sauvignon Blanc 14 ★★★☆** Not retasted: **Pinot Noir 'Screwcap' 13 ★★★★ Skaam Skaap 14 ★★★** Not tasted: **Cabernet Sauvignon, Merlot, Pinot Noir.** — DS

Location: George ▪ Map: Klein Karoo & Garden Route ▪ WO: Outeniqua ▪ Est 1999 ▪ 1stB 2003 ▪ Tasting, sales & cellar tours Mon-Sat 10-4 ▪ Fee R20, waived on purchase ▪ Closed Easter Sun, Dec 25 & Jan 1 ▪ Light refreshments/cheese platters during opening hours ▪ Picnic baskets/farm lunches with 2 days prior notice ▪ Facilities for children ▪ Tour groups ▪ Gifts ▪ Farm produce ▪ Conferences ▪ Walks/hikes ▪ Mountain biking ▪ Conservation area ▪ Self-catering cottages ▪ Owner(s) Nico & Maureen Fourie ▪ Winemaker(s)/viticulturist(s) Nico Fourie (Jul 2011) ▪ 324ha/6ha (cab, merlot, pinot, shiraz, chard, riesling, sauv) ▪ 35t/3,400cs own label 55% red 25% white 20% rosé ▪ PO Box 10 Herold 6615 ▪ info@heroldwines.co.za ▪ www.heroldwines.co.za ▪ S 33° 51' 49.4" E 022° 28' 9.9" ▪ F +27 (0)86-698-6607 ▪ **T +27 (0)72-833-8223**

Heron Ridge   ⓦ

New (2012) vintages from the Orpen family's small blocks of Helderberg cab and shiraz missed our deadline but part-owner Jane, mother of winemaker Harry, says they will become available during the year. Meanwhile the releases below are still selling and in fact should be at peak drinking age now.

Family Reserve range
Shiraz (ⓦ) **★★★☆ 06** is full bodied, slightly rough around the edges but not without charm. Red & black fruit, vanilla, hint of spice. Contains 13% cab.

Heron Ridge range
★★★★ Shiraz (ⓦ) **07** raised the bar on **06** (★★★☆), showed attractive rusticity & real liveliness, interest when last tasted. 30% oak well integrated.

Not tasted: **The Flight.** — CE

Location/WO: Stellenbosch ▪ Map: Helderberg ▪ Est 1997 ▪ 1stB 2001 ▪ Tasting, sales & cellar tours by appt ▪ Fee R20 ▪ Closed all pub hols ▪ Owner(s) Orpen family ▪ Cellarmaster(s)/winemaker(s) Harry Orpen (Jun 2014) ▪ Viticulturist(s) Paul Wallace (Sep 1999, consultant) ▪ 4.29ha/4ha (cab, shiraz) ▪ 20t/300cs own label 100% red ▪ PO Box 5181 Helderberg 7135 ▪ janeorps@gmail.com ▪ www.heronridge.co.za ▪ S 34° 2' 45.6" E 018° 47' 58.1" ▪ F +27 (0)86-613-6960 ▪ **T +27 (0)21-842-2501**

Het Vlock Casteel   ⓦ ⓨ ⓞ ⓺

The Vlok family, wine and table grape farmers near Riebeek-Kasteel since 1958, named their boutique brand after Cape Town's Castle of Good Hope. Vinified to spec by contractors, the wines are just one of a cornucopia of products and amenities on offer at their castle-like visitor venue, recently upgraded.

Merlot (ⓦ) **★★★** Rustic **10** with plum, farmyard tones, sweet & sour finish. Not retasted: **Cabernet Sauvignon 10 ★★ Shiraz 10 ★★★** Not tasted: **Sauvignon Blanc.** — AL

Location: Riebeek-Kasteel ▪ Map/WO: Swartland ▪ Est/1stB 2005 ▪ Tasting & sales Mon-Fri 9-5 Sat 9-2 ▪ Closed Good Fri & Dec 25 ▪ Tour groups ▪ Gift shop ▪ Farm produce: olives, olive oil, jams, chutneys etc – sampling available ▪ Conferences ▪ Café Merlot functions: by appt only ▪ Owner(s) Johan Louw Vlok ▪ Winemaker(s) Alecia Boshoff ▪ Viticulturist(s) Johan Vlok snr & Johan Vlok jnr ▪ 100ha (cab, merlot, ptage, shiraz, chard) ▪ 1,300t/14,000cs own label 100% red ▪ PO Box 8 Riebeek-Kasteel 7307 ▪ info@hetvlockcasteel.co.za ▪ www.hetvlockcasteel.co.za ▪ S 33° 23′ 22.74″ E 018° 53′ 40.75″ ▪ F +27 (0)86-720-6281 ▪ **T +27 (0)82-567-9132**

☐ **Hex River Crossing Private Cellar** *see* Auction Crossing Private Cellar

Hidden Valley Wines   ⓨ ⓜ ⓞ ⓑ

The ancient, decomposed granite soils on this estate high on the slopes of Stellenbosch's Helderberg will take change as it comes – and 2015 saw significant human development. The name alludes to the man who bought it in 1998 and developed its potential, Dave Hidden, but the farm has a new owner in Riaan Stassen, a former 'brilliant iconoclast' banker. In the cellar, Annalie van Dyk took in her first harvest, while 'Oom Grobbie' Grobbelaar retired from 17 years of managing the vines (there are 15 hectares of them, and 3 of olives), leaving Daniel Roux in charge.

★★★★☆ **Hidden Gems** Cab-based **13** (★★★★) with petit verdot, merlot. Modern, ripe style, like **12**, showy sweet fruit but not without finesse in its balance. Few years should resolve firm dry tannins.

★★★★ **Hidden Secret** Shiraz & tannat on **13**, as **12** (★★★★☆). Very ripe fruit gives perfumed, bright aromas (with spice from judicious oak), boiled sweet character. Firmly built; grippy tannins should resolve.

★★★★ **Sauvignon Blanc** Tropical, ripe notes on smartly structured & succulently textured **15**, its ingratiating light richness augmented by a few extra grams of sugar.

Viognier ⑲ ★★★☆ Modestly oaked **14** does show some spicy toastiness on nose & palate alongside restrained peach & apple. Not intense, but clean, balanced and dry. Also tasted: **Pinotage 14** ★★★☆ Discontinued: **Shipwreck Collection**. — TJ

Location/map/WO: Stellenbosch ▪ Map grid reference: F8 ▪ Est/1stB 1995 ▪ Tasting & sales: summer Mon-Thu 9-6 Fri 9-8 (sundowners on the deck) Sat/Sun 9-6; winter Mon-Fri 9-4 Sat/Sun 9-5 ▪ Fee R50pp ▪ Open pub hols, but closed Dec 25/26 & Jan 1 ▪ Cellar tours by appt ▪ Overture Restaurant ▪ Cheese/winter/chocolate platters ▪ Picnics, to be pre-booked ▪ Table olives & olive oil ▪ Tour groups by appt ▪ Conferences ▪ Weddings/functions ▪ Walks/hikes ▪ Conservation area ▪ Owner(s) Riaan Stassen ▪ Winemaker(s) Annalie van Dyk (Nov 2014) ▪ Viticulturist(s) Daniel Roux (Nov 2013) ▪ 28ha/15ha (cab, merlot, p verdot, shiraz, tannat, sauv, viog) & 4ha olives ▪ 130t/14,000cs own label 65% red 35% white ▪ BWI ▪ PO Box 12577 Die Boord 7613 ▪ info@hiddenvalleywines.com ▪ www.hiddenvalleywines.com ▪ S 34° 1′ 15.3″ E 018° 51′ 13.9″ ▪ F +27 (0)21-880-2645 ▪ **T +27 (0)21-880-2646**

Highberry Wines   ⓨ

Grapes for this new label, launched locally during the 2015/16 season with a sauvignon blanc and cabernet sauvignon (neither ready for review), are from vinegrower Andre Parker's farm Highberry on Helderberg's viticulturally vaunted Schapenberg Hill. The classic varieties are for the palette of winery co-owner and winemaker Werner Engelbrecht (ex Waterkloof). As third partner Jabulani Ntshangase (Thabani Wines) resides in New York, there's a strong focus on the US market.

Location: Sir Lowry's Pass ▪ Map: Helderberg ▪ 1stB 2014 ▪ Tasting by appt only ▪ Owner(s) Andre Parker, Werner Engelbrecht & Jabulani Ntshangase ▪ Winemaker(s) Werner Engelbrecht (Jan 2014) ▪ Viticulturist(s) Edward Etson (Jul 2003) ▪ 65ha/49ha (cabs s/f, malbec, merlot, p verdot, shiraz, chard, sauv, sem) ▪ 350t/2,000cs own label 50% red 50% white ▪ werner@highberry.co.za ▪ www.highberry.co.za ▪ **T +27 (0)21-852-3754**

High Constantia Wine Cellar   ⓨ ⓜ ⓒ

High Constantia once competed with its illustrious neighbour Groot Constantia for the favour of Europe's mid-19th century royal courts. Present owner David van Niekerk vinifies in a cellar 'reminiscent of High Constantia's original home for wine' and bottles under the High Constantia and Silverhurst labels.

Location: Constantia ▪ Map: Cape Peninsula ▪ Est 1693 ▪ 1stB 2000 ▪ Tasting, sales & cellar tours Mon-Fri 8–5 Sat 10-1 ▪ Fee R50 ▪ Closed Easter Sun, Dec 25 & Jan 1 ▪ BYO picnic ▪ Meals pre-arranged with private chef, Marc Wassung ▪ Owner(s) David van Niekerk ▪ Cellarmaster(s)/viticulturist(s) David van Niekerk (Jan 1999) ▪ Winemaker(s) David van Niekerk (Jan 1999) & Roger Arendse (Jan 2001) ▪ 14.5ha (cabs s/f, malbec, merlot, pinot, chard, sauv) ▪ 70t/11,000cs own label 52% red 15% white 3% rosé 30% MCC + 3,800cs for clients ▪ Brands for clients: Terra Madre ▪ Groot Constantia Rd Constantia 7800 ▪ david@highconstantia.co.za, info@highconstantia.co.za ▪ www.highconstantia.co.za ▪ S 34° 1' 31.3" E 018° 25' 36.1" ▪ F +27 (0)21-794-7999 ▪ **T +27 (0)21-794-7171/+27 (0)83-300-2064**

Highgate Wine Estate   ⓠ ⑪ ⓐ ⓐ

Among a handful of wineries bringing wine culture to KZN-Natal province, Rudi and Cindy Kassier's Highgate has a very charming home: Piggly Wiggly Village on the Midlands Meander. The former fresh produce growers took the opportunity to plant vines in 2005 as part of a trial, and have since bottled under the label Lions River as circumstances allow. Tasting and sales are by appointment; sales also at the excellent Meander Fine Wines outlet on the property.

Location: Howick ▪ Map: KwaZulu-Natal ▪ Est/1stB 2010 ▪ Tasting, sales & cellar tours by appt ▪ Closed Dec 25 ▪ Facilities for children ▪ Coffee shop (see www.pigglywiggly.co.za) ▪ Country shops catering for all ages ▪ Owner(s) Rudi & Cindy Kassier ▪ Winemaker(s)/viticulturist(s) Rudi Kassier ▪ 57ha/3.7ha (cab, merlot, ptage, shiraz, chard) ▪ 2.5t/840cs own label 50% red 50% white ▪ PO Box 1025 Howick 3290 ▪ rudi@pigglywiggly.co.za ▪ www.highgatewineestate.co.za ▪ S 29° 27' 29.92" E 030° 8' 8.66" ▪ F +27 (0)86-535-3187 ▪ **T +27 (0)82-895-1667/+27 (0)33-234-2911**

Highlands Road Estate   ⓠ ⑪ ⓐ ⓐ ⓑ

One of Port Elizabeth attorney Michael White's 'cellar rat' holidays led to a joint venture about a decade ago, converting an old Elgin fruit farm to vine. He's now sole owner, partnering since 2015 with winemaker Vanessa Simkiss on more au naturel wines. Chardonnay, riesling and some sweet wines expand the range, attracting attention along with bottle-aged sauvignon blanc.

★★★★ **Ruadh 13** sees tinta amarela (10%) join shiraz & mourvèdre in complex, spicy blend. Vibrant, juicy, with lovely dry grip from oak maturation, just 30% new. Improves on **11** (★★★).

★★★★ **Chardonnay** ⓃⒺⓌ Barrel ferment & 10 months on lees makes **14** rich, nuanced & complex, with acid contrast keeping it fresh & lively.

★★★★ **Sine Cera** Nettle & flint typicity of semillon (10% oaked) adds pungency to 50/50 mix with sauvignon on **14**, now bottled. Waxy richness to taut yet broad **13** shows influence of bottle age.

⸱ **Riesling** ⓃⒺⓌ ⓥ ★★★☆ Crisp crunchy vivacity & acid of **13** augurs well for ageability. Precise & typical. ⸱

Special Late Harvest ⓃⒺⓌ ★★★ Bright tangy sweetness of **14** from sauvignon blanc remains lively, clean & fresh. **Noble Late Harvest** ⓃⒺⓌ ★★★★ Creative tension of richness & limy acid zip on **14**, all sauvignon blanc. Balanced, clean dry finish. Also tasted: **Pinot Noir 12** ★★★★ **Rosé 13** ★★★ **Sauvignon Blanc 14** ★★★ Not tasted: **Slainte MCC Bubbly**. Discontinued: **Tinta Amarela**. — FM

Location/WO: Elgin ▪ Map: Elgin, Walker Bay & Bot River ▪ Est 2005 ▪ 1stB 2007 ▪ Tasting, sales & cellar tours Mon-Sun 10–4 ▪ Light lunches & picnics ▪ Facilities for children ▪ Fly fishing ▪ Boule court ▪ Owner(s) Michael White ▪ Winemaker(s) Vanessa Simkiss ▪ Viticulturist(s) Paul Wallace ▪ 28ha/10ha (pinot, shiraz, chard, sauv, sem) ▪ 30t/4,500cs own label 35% red 65% white ▪ PO Box 94 Elgin 7180 ▪ info@highlandsroadestate.co.za ▪ www.highlandsroadestate.co.za ▪ S 34° 14' 4.4" E 019° 4' 14.3" ▪ **T +27 (0)71-271-0161**

☐ **High Road** see The High Road

Hildenbrand Wine & Olive Estate   ⓠ ⑪ ⓐ ⓑ

Boutique vintner and international olive/olive oil judge Reni Hildenbrand is updating, expanding and re-introducing her extensive Wellington 'vegan- and vegetarian-friendly' wine range with assistance from consultant winemaker Alex Boraine (Baratok Wines). Among the additions (some not ready for tasting) are a barrel of 'orange' (skin-fermented) wine and two reds (one named Roikat joining other wines celebrating animal rescuer Reni's four-legged friends). New marketing initiatives include food-and-wine pairings and Alex's BuyTheBarrel venture (see under Make Your Own Wine).

Estate Single Vineyard range

★★★★ **Shiraz** Wild berry notes, bitter twist on bold, assertive **12** (★★★☆). Generous but unfocused fruit has un-knit leathery tannins & lingering hot alcohol (15%). Last-made **07** more restrained.

Cabernet Sauvignon Unwooded Pre-bottling sample **15** too unformed to rate. **Chardonnay ★★★** Was 'Chardonnay Unwooded', still is unoaked. **14** more precise, less funky than previous. Muted fruit, buttery-creamy lees, good length. **Chenin Blanc ★★★** Better balance on previewed **15**, with restrained fruit, measured acidity. Pleasant sipper. Also tasted: **Cabernet Sauvignon 12 ★★★ Shiraz Rosé 14 ★★** Not retasted: **Malbec 12 ★★★★ Chardonnay Barrique 13 ★★★ Semillon 13 ★★★ Sleepless Nights NLH Semillon 07 ★★★**

Estate Animal range

★★★★ **Wild Style Méthode Cap Classique** ⓥ Named for a racehorse, **12** sparkling from chardonnay & malbec spent 2 years on lees, giving a salty tang to the creamy citrus fruit. Balanced, fresh finish.

Roikat Shiraz (NEW) ★★ **14** malty cherry fruit laced with tangy acid, obvious tannins need time to settle & integrate. **The Duo Red Cuvée** (NEW) ★★★ Shiraz & cab blend with confected berries & ultra-soft, talcum-like tannins. **12** quirky but appealingly juicy. Not retasted: **Coconut & Angel 13 ★★★★ Emma & Asa 09 ★★★**

Hildenbrand Wines range (NEW)

Cape Riesling 15 tank sample too young to rate. — GdB

Location/WO: Wellington ▪ Map: Paarl & Wellington ▪ Map grid reference: G2 ▪ Est 1991 ▪ 1stB 1999 ▪ Tasting & sales Mon-Sat 10-4 Sun 9-12 by appt ▪ Wine tasting R50pp; olive & oil tasting R15pp ▪ Closed Easter Sat/Sun, Dec 24/25 & Jan 1 ▪ Food & wine evenings/lunch by appt ▪ Klein Rhebokskloof Country & Guest House ▪ Owner(s)/cellarmaster(s) Reni Hildenbrand ▪ Winemaker(s) Reni Hildenbrand, with Alex Boraine (consultant) ▪ ±4,500cs ▪ PO Box 270 Wellington 7654 ▪ info@wine-estate-hildenbrand.co.za ▪ www.wine-estate-hildenbrand.co.za ▪ S 33° 39' 33.3" E 019° 1' 46.3" ▪ **T +27 (0)82-656-6007**

Hill & Dale

Easy-drinking wines vinified from grapes off selected Stellenbosch vineyards at Stellenzicht (see that entry for tasting/sales information).

Cabernet Sauvignon-Shiraz ⊘ ⓣ ★★★☆ Consistent good-value performer is packed with juicy berry fruit & hint of spice. **13** well-crafted, elegant dry red. Also in magnum.

Pinotage ★★★ Banana, plum & creamy vanilla with hints of smoke in a plush package that's accessible & moreish. Previewed **14** for casual sipping or food pairing. **Dry Rosé Merlot ★★★** Luminous pink **15** is on form, delivers candied red fruit & creamy balance. **Sauvignon Blanc ★★★** Honest expression combining tropical fruit with grassy notes in youthful **15**, crisp & bone-dry, ready for summer. Also tasted: **Merlot 13 ★★☆ Shiraz 13 ★★☆ Chardonnay 14 ★★★ Pinot Grigio 15 ★★★** — HJ

Hillcrest Estate

⚲ ⓥ ⓒ

Durbanville's Hillcrest, part-owned by civil engineers Pete Inglis and Rick Haw, is seeing its geologically ancient soils increasingly utilised for quality vines, with chardonnay and pinot noir set to bring Burgundy to the hitherto pure Bordeaux/Loire mix. Newcomer Arno Smith is assuming responsibility for both winemaking (from original driving force, Graeme Read) and farm management (from co-owner Gerrie du Toit), and overseeing the opening of a craft brewery.

Metamorphic Collection

★★★★ **Quarry** Classically styled, plushly elegant **13** merlot ticks all the boxes: perfectly ripe & savoury, with beautifully layered plum fruit underpinned by spicy oak tannins.

★★★★☆ **Hornfels** Classy, polished **13** cab franc-led blend with cabernet, petit verdot & merlot, named for vineyard's shale soils. Mineral & herbal layers underlie generous, perfectly ripened berry fruit, framed by unobtrusive mostly new oak.

★★★★☆ **Atlantic Slopes** From ocean-facing slopes which yield distinctively earthy, pungently aromatic & exceptional sauvignon. Dash semillon in **15** fleshes out lean, steely mineral style which slowly unfurls to reveal complex citrus & passionfruit core.

Hillcrest Estate range

★★★★ **Cabernet Franc** Always the charmer of the trio of varietal reds. Serious but accessible **14** gorgeous perfume & seductively ripe fruit, kept in check by tannins from well-judged third new oak.

★★★★ **Malbec** Raspberry & sour cherry abound in **14** (★★★☆) but lack precise balance of **13**, as biting acidity briskly cleanses the palate.

> **Robbenzicht** ⊙ ★★★★ Succulent, savoury **14** merlot, cab blend over-delivers. Ample red fruit kept in check by integrated, spicy tannins. No dumbing down.

Also tasted: **Petit Verdot 14** ★★★★ Not tasted: **Cabernet Sauvignon Rosé, Sauvignon Blanc**. — IM

Location/WO: Durbanville ▪ Map: Durbanville, Philadelphia & Darling ▪ Est/1stB 2002 ▪ Tasting & sales daily 9–5 ▪ Fee R30 ▪ Closed Dec 25/26 & Jan 1 ▪ Cellar tours by appt ▪ Restaurant T +27 (0)21-975-2346 open daily for b'fast & lunch ▪ Wedding/function venue ▪ Farm produce ▪ MTB trail ▪ Conservation area ▪ Owner(s) PD Inglis, R Haw, G du Toit & E Menegablo ▪ Winemaker(s) Graeme Read (Jan 2003) & Arno Smith (Jan 2014) ▪ Viticulturist(s) G du Toit & Arno Smith ▪ 25ha (cabs s/f, malbec, merlot, p verdot, sauv) ▪ 60t/±6,000cs own label 45% red 55% white ▪ Private Bag X3 Durbanville 7551 ▪ cellardoor@hillcrestfarm.co.za ▪ www.hillcrestfarm.co.za ▪ S 33° 49' 38.2" E 018° 35' 25.9" ▪ F +27 (0)21-975-2195 ▪ **T +27 (0)21-970-5800**

Hillock Wines   ⊙ 🍴 🏠 📷

Andy Hillock, surgeon, aviator, grape grower and now solo winemaker (having worked with consultants previously) is stretching his wings on their Mymering Guest Farm outside Ladismith. He's released a first MCC bubbly (named after wife Penny) and has another on the lees for release in 2017.

Location: Ladismith ▪ Map: Klein Karoo & Garden Route ▪ Est 2010 ▪ 1stB 2011 ▪ Tasting, sales & cellar tours daily 10-5 ▪ Closed Dec 25 ▪ Light lunches & refreshments 10-5 daily ▪ Tour groups ▪ Gifts ▪ Farm produce ▪ Guided hikes & vineyard tours ▪ Mountain biking ▪ 4-star guest house (sleeps 20), Mymering Estate www.mymering.com ▪ Owner(s) Andy & Penny Hillock ▪ Winemaker(s) Andy Hillock ▪ Viticulturist(s) Riaan Steyn ▪ 400ha/50ha (shiraz, chard, chenin) ▪ 24t/3,600cs own label 50% red 50% white ▪ PO Box 278 Ladismith 6655 ▪ penny@mymering.com ▪ www.hillockwines.com ▪ S 33° 29' 55.24" E 021° 10' 18.65" ▪ F +27 (0)28-551-1313 ▪ **T +27 (0)28-551-1548**

☐ **Hill of Enon** *see* Zandvliet Wine Estate
☐ **Hills** *see* The Hills

Hilton Vineyards

Boutique vintner Richard Hilton, 'blessed with a second beautiful daughter' end 2014, has spent over a decade acquainting himself with special Helderberg and Elgin sites of his beloved shiraz and viognier. Greater understanding of the latter, he says, has resulted in two new versions. He's collaborated with Upland's organic grower/distiller Edmund Oettlé on a grappa-style viognier husk wine, and is planning an 'orange' viognier and a syrah/shiraz to be matured in French oak 'for a minimum of 36 months'.

★★★★ **Ironstone Syrah** Pure expression of the Helderberg site, unfettered by oak (only older wood, 21 months), **12** melds black berry fruit with whiffs of leather & a freshening salinity. Refined, satisfying drink.

★★★★☆ **The Dalmatian Syrah** Northern Rhône styling, with 5% co-fermented viognier, **12** creates thrilling toasted spice dimension to measured, elegant & enduring taste sensation. Helderberg grapes, barrel-aged an extended 28 months, 40% new oak.

★★★★ **Rose Quartz Viognier** (NEW) Ebullient older-oaked **14** has oodles of fruit personality, flavourful tropical richness, so much so it seems to end sweet despite being technically dry at 3 g/l residual sugar.

★★★★☆ **The Emperor Probus Viognier** (NEW) More courtly than sibling (both from Elgin), **14** finely & textured, with classy balance of tangy fruit & mineral features, refreshing acid, moderate 13.3% alcohol. 9 months in seasoned cask round edges; more vinous than simply fruity.

Discontinued: **Rockwater Fountain Viognier**. — DS

Location: Stellenbosch ▪ WO: Stellenbosch/Elgin ▪ Est 2003 ▪ Closed to public ▪ Owner(s) Richard Hilton ▪ Cellarmaster(s)/winemaker(s) Richard Hilton (2003) & Riaan Wassüng (2005) ▪ Viticulturist(s) Tjuks Roos & Richard Rose ▪ (shiraz, viog) ▪ 21t/2,600cs own label 35% red 65% white ▪ richard@ hiltonvineyards.co.za ▪ www.hiltonvineyards.co.za ▪ F +27 (0)86-618-4089 ▪ **T +27 (0)21-855-5244**

Hirst Wines ⓃⒺⓌ

Cape Town entrepreneur Luke Hirst is also the owner of trendy wine boutique Vino Pronto, so it's no surprise that he has an own label or that his Swartland-grown wines – vinified by young guns Johan Meyer and MC Stander – are aligned with the natural, 'less-is-more' winemaking movement. The Front Row (where rugby enthusiast Luke has spent some time) is mostly for the limited, more complex wines; bottlings 'for easy enjoyment' appear under the untasted River Horse label.

The Front Row range

★★★★ **Mourvèdre** Perfumed **14** characterful & interesting, if not entirely typical: has 4% syrah/shiraz, tastes as if it had cinsaut too! Succulent acidity energises intense fruit; balanced structure overall.

★★★★ **Chenin Blanc** Lightish, gentle & charming **14** surprisingly intense flavour for just 12% alcohol. Oxidative winemaking shows in bruised apple finish. Old oak & hands-off approach for both. — TJ, CvZ

Location: Cape Town ▪ WO: Swartland ▪ Est/1stB 2013 ▪ Closed to public ▪ Owner(s) Luke Hirst ▪ Winemaker(s) Johan Meyer & MC Stander (2013/2014, both consultants) ▪ Own label 50% red 50% white ▪ PO Box 12066 Hout Bay 7872 ▪ hirstluke1@gmail.com ▪ **T +27 (0)82-751-8169**

☐ **His Master's Choice** see Excelsior Vlakteplaas
☐ **Hoeksrivier** see Eagle's Cliff Wines-New Cape Wines

Hofstraat Kelder Ⓠ

The name of this small winery refers not to the Swartland vineyards it mostly draws on but a street in Malmesbury town. More bucolic-sounding is Myrtledene, the smallholding where Wim Smit, Jack de Clerq and Jerry Finley latterly make the wine – 'with passion', says Wim, who adds that 'family and friends make up the workforce'. Look out for the new Nebbiolo.

Renosterbos range

★★★★ **Barbera** Ⓠ **13** version of rare varietal bottling will please its fans more than **12** (★★★★). Cherries & slight balsamic whiffs, varietally correct high acidity that will easily stand up to rich food.

Nebbiolo ⓃⒺⓌ ★★★ Apart from lighter colour, **14** from Breedekloof doesn't shout the variety but offers plum & red berry compote in a warm body. **Shiraz** ★★★★ Elegant & pure **14** has heady fruit perfume with violets & aniseed, slight resin note combining with pepper & spice notes. Also tasted: **Cabernet Sauvignon 14** ★★★ **Merlot 14** ★★★ **Pinotage 14** ★★★★ Not retasted: **Chenin Blanc 13** ★★★ **Die Solder NV** ★★★★ **Cape Vintage 09** ★★☆ — HJ

Location: Malmesbury ▪ Map: Swartland ▪ WO: Swartland/Darling/Breedekloof ▪ Est 2002 ▪ 1stB 2003 ▪ Tasting, sales & tours by appt ▪ Owner(s)/cellarmaster(s)/winemaker(s) Wim Smit, Jack de Clercq & Jerry Finley ▪ 4t/505cs own label 100% red ▪ PO Box 1172 Malmesbury 7299 ▪ renosterbos@ cornergate.com ▪ S 33° 26' 56.1" E 018° 44' 1.8" ▪ F +27 (0)22-487-3202 ▪ **T +27 (0)83-270-2352**

Hogan Wines Ⓠ ⓃⒺⓌ

'After 7 years of working with various wineries in the Cape and overseas,' says Jocelyn Hogan Wilson, she has now teamed up with her parents, Dunstan and Trish Hogan in a small family concern. Jocelyn's new label eloquently expresses her commitment to a shift in emphasis in Cape winemaking, 'back to the farmers and the small-scale wine producers'. In rented space in Franschhoek, she vinifies grapes brought in from selected vineyards. A red wine was also made in 2015.

★★★★☆ **Chenin Blanc 14** from old Swartland bushvines – beautifully made, with no additives beyond some sulphur. Already complex aromas & flavours (floral, nutty, apple, pear, thatch), left pure by sensitive old-oak maturation. Fresh & bright, with a happily long-lingering finish. — TJ, CvZ

Location/map: Stellenbosch ▪ Map grid reference: H5 ▪ WO: Swartland ▪ Est 2013 ▪ 1stB 2014 ▪ Tasting by appt only ▪ Owner(s) Jocelyn Hogan Wilson ▪ Winemaker(s) Jocelyn Hogan Wilson (Nov 2013) ▪ 8t/ 690cs own label 40% red 60% white ▪ PO Box 2226 Dennesig 7601 ▪ jocelyn@mweb.co.za ▪ www.hoganwines.co.za ▪ S 33 55' 55.03'' E 018 57' 26.90'' ▪ **T +27 (0)21-885-1275**

Holden Manz Wine Estate   ⓠ 🍴 🏠 📷 ♿

Holden Manz's name dates back just half a decade to the purchase of the Franschhoek property by Gerard Holden and Migo Manz. Much revitalised, there is a luxury guest house, spa and restaurant, and a collection of contemporary African art in the town. Just in time for harvest 2015, Frenchman Thierry Haberer (fresh from working with eminent Bordeaux consultant Michel Rolland) arrived to take charge of the cellar.

Reserve range
★★★★☆ **Cabernet Franc 13** substantially ups the ante on maiden **12** (★★★★). Bold, brooding & powerful, with typical fynbos, cocoa & blackcurrant complexity. Refined, elegant, with dry, fine tannin. Oak – 50% new – well knit.

★★★★ **Syrah 13** retains form of **12**. Nuanced, multi-faceted palate with good harmony of oak & juicy black fruit. Bunch pressing & spontaneous ferment on 50% of the wine.

Avant Garde range
★★★★ **Big G** Merlot (40%) leads equal cab & cab franc in polished, succulent, deep, dark & enticing **12** blend. Lovely structured palate. As with **11**, long & rich. Alcohol (15%) easily assimilated.

Chardonnay ★★★☆ **14** ups the ante with Stellenbosch fruit offering tangy citrus, with light toasty overtones from barrel ferment, just 10% new oak. Not retasted: **Visionaire 12** ★★★☆ **Good Sport Cape Vintage 10** ★★★

Modern range
Rosé ★★★ Improved **15** is from shiraz, cab, cab franc & merlot. Bright, dry red-fruit succulence makes it ideal for poolside sipping. Also tasted: **Vernissage 14** ★★★☆

Contemporary range
★★★★ **Cabernet Sauvignon** Inky graphite depth to spicy cassis & cherry on **12** which improves on **11** (★★★). Fine dry tannin from integrated oak, just 18% new. Seamless long finish.

Also tasted: **Merlot 12** ★★★ **Shiraz 12** ★★★☆ — FM

Location/map: Franschhoek ▪ WO: Franschhoek/Western Cape ▪ Est 2010 ▪ 1stB 2005 ▪ Tasting, sales & cellar tours daily 10-5 ▪ Fee R30 ▪ Franschhoek Kitchen ▪ Spa ▪ Picnic area ▪ Holden Manz Country House ▪ Owner(s) Gerard Holden & Migo Manz ▪ Winemaker(s) Thierry Haberer (Dec 2014), with Annamarie Fourie (Apr 2015) ▪ Viticulturist(s) Tertius Oosthuizen (Sep 2010) ▪ 20ha/16ha (cabs s/f, merlot, shiraz) ▪ 110t/13,332cs own label 85% red 3.85% white 6.65% rosé 4.5% port ▪ IPW ▪ PO Box 620 Franschhoek 7690 ▪ info@holdenmanz.com ▪ www.holdenmanz.com ▪ S 33° 56' 6.3'' E 019° 7' 8.3'' ▪ F +27 (0)21-876-4624 ▪ **T +27 (0)21-876-2738**

Hoopenburg Wines   ⓠ 🍷 🏠 📷

At the Schmitz family's estate on the northern fringe of Stellenbosch, recently appointed cellarmaster Helanie Olivier's first wines are finding their way into bottle, their styling partly influenced by the weaker rand and the resultant need to use less new oak. Serendipitously, the more fruit-driven style works well in Hoopenburg's newer markets such as Zambia, Namibia and Zimbabwe, and in Asia, says GM Anton Beukes, who is delighted to be growing the business 'in very difficult times'.

Integer range
★★★★ **Cabernet Sauvignon** Farmyard entry on **12** (★★★) yields to black fruit & spice with astringent tannins asserting through to finish. Less appealing than **11**.

★★★★ **Syrah-Mourvèdre-Carignan** Interesting & enjoyable **12** mixes ±33% of each variety, showing spice, liquorice, leather & polish. Soft tannins, dry finish. 18 months in barrel, 40% new. Coastal WO.

★★★★ **Méthode Cap Classique Brut** ⊘ Honey & lemon curd on this fine **NV** dry sparkling from chardonnay. 15 months on lees add richness, & well-integrated bubbles dance through to a biscuity finish. Also tasted: **Chardonnay 14** ★★★☆ Discontinued: **Syrah**.

Hoopenburg Bush Vine range

Pinot Noir ★★★★ Tasty & juicy **12** from Elgin charms with cherries, tea, tobacco & spice. Soft structure, pleasant summer red. **Rosé** ★★ From merlot, **15** shows hints of coffee & strawberries with dry finish. **Chardonnay** ★★★ Fresh fruit salad on unwooded **14**, with nice depth of flavours (melons & lemons) & just enough fresh acidity to round off. **Sauvignon Blanc** ★★★ Pungent **15** shows attractive green fruit with typical lively acidity & freshness. Also tasted: **Cabernet Sauvignon** 13 ★★ **Merlot** 13 ★★☆ **Pinotage** 13 ★★★★ **Shiraz** 12 ★★ **Chenin Blanc** 15 ★★☆ Occasional release: **Shiraz-Cabernet Sauvignon**.

Guru range

Merlot ★★☆ Plenty of spice on **13**, finishes savoury & dry. Also tasted: **Sauvignon Blanc** 15 ★★ Not retasted: **Cabernet Sauvignon-Merlot** — CM

Location/map: Stellenbosch ▪ Map grid reference: E1 ▪ WO: Stellenbosch/Coastal/Elgin/Western Cape ▪ Est/1stB 1992 ▪ Tasting, sales & cellar tours Mon-Fri 8.30-4 ▪ Fee R20/6-8 wines ▪ Closed all pub hols ▪ BYO picnic ▪ Conferences ▪ Guest house T +27 (0)21-884-4534 ▪ Owner(s) Gregor Schmitz ▪ GM Anton Beukes (Aug 2009) ▪ Cellarmaster(s) Helanie Olivier ▪ Viticulturist(s) Gert Snyders ▪ 70ha/30ha (cab, merlot, shiraz, chard) ▪ 180t/40,000cs own label 80% red 18% white 2% MCC ▪ PO Box 1233 Stellenbosch 7599 ▪ info@hoopenburg.com ▪ www.hoopenburgwines.co.za ▪ S 33° 49' 33.4" E 018° 49' 9.3" ▪ **T +27 (0)21-884-4221**

☐ **Hope** see Almenkerk Wine Estate

Hornbill Garagiste Winery   Ⓟ Ⓜ Ⓐ Ⓞ

Architect John Dry seamlessly combines his love of wine, art and food at the Hermanus family home: wine is from vines around Walker Bay, handcrafted by John literally in the garage (a debut wooded chenin blanc missed our tasting deadline); art in the adjacent ceramics studio and art gallery; and food in the new Biga Bakery Café & Deli alongside.

Merlot Ⓝ ★★★ **12** a little gawky, with smoky edge to red fruit & dry tannin grip. Walker Bay WO. **Pinotage** ★★★★ Spicy plum compote succulence on **12**, less concentrated than predecessors. **Cape Blend** ★★★ Usual 50/50 pinotage & merlot on **12**, earthy tinge to bright berry notes. At 14.3%, alcohol is higher than previous. — FM

Location: Hermanus ▪ Map: Elgin, Walker Bay & Bot River ▪ WO: Western Cape/Walker Bay ▪ Est 2004 ▪ 1stB 2005 ▪ Tasting, sales & tours Mon-Fri 9-5 Sat 9-2 ▪ Closed Easter Fri/Sun, Dec 25 & Jan 1 ▪ Gifts ▪ Art gallery & ceramic studio ▪ Self-catering accommodation ▪ Biga artisan bakery & restaurant ▪ Owner(s) John Dry ▪ Winemaker(s) John Dry (2004) ▪ 6t/800cs own label 100% red ▪ PO Box 4 Hermanus 7200 ▪ hornbill@intekom.co.za ▪ www.hornbillhouse.co.za ▪ S 34° 24' 46.3" E 019° 11' 54.4" ▪ F +27 (0)28-316-3794 ▪ **T +27 (0)28-316-2696**

☐ **Horse Mountain** see Doran Vineyards
☐ **Horses of the Apocalypse** see Osbloed Wines
☐ **Houdamond** see Bellevue Estate Stellenbosch
☐ **House of GM & Ahrens** see The House of GM&AHRENS
☐ **House of JC le Roux** see The House of JC le Roux
☐ **House of Krone** see Twee Jonge Gezellen Estate-House of Krone

---

House of Mandela

The wines of this negociant business commemorate, say owners Makaziwe and Tukwini Mandela, 'the life and spirit of a great African soul, our father and grandfather, Rolihlahla Nelson Mandela'. At a charmingly playful level too: the brightly patterned labels of the easygoing (and Fairtrade-accredited) Thembu Collection allude to the bright dashiki shirts that Mandela favoured. The ranges have been created with the help of consultant (and former Fairview winemaker) Erlank Erasmus.

Royal Reserve range

★★★★☆ **Cabernet Sauvignon** ⓐ **12** first since **08**, now from Paarl & Stellenbosch grapes – with dollops of shiraz (adding floral notes to the aromas) & mourvèdre. Serious-minded wine; firmly, even powerfully structured; generous new oak – but all this in balance. Needs a few years to show its best.

★★★★ **Shiraz** ⓐ Big, burly **11**, like previous **07** from Paarl. Ripe, dark fruit flavours held in check by obvious oak, which should integrate in a few years. Finishes rather sweet, with some alcohol glow.

★★★★ **Chardonnay** ⓐ **13** (★★★☆) from Paarl follows **09** from Elgin. In lightish, elegant style, with balanced oaking, & a good vein of acidity enlivening the lemony, peachy flavours.

Vusani Series

Cabernet Sauvignon ⓐ ★★☆ Uncomplicated **11** firm yet comfortable with slight mint aroma. **Shiraz** ⓐ ★★☆ Fruit-flavoursome, plush & modestly oaked **12** has gently firm structure. Not retasted: **Merlot 11** ★★★ **Pinotage 13** ★★★

Thembu Collection

Cabernet Sauvignon ⓐ ★★☆ True varietal character on **13**. Like others in range, deftly styled with soft, ripe tannins & a little sweetness to add to the easy charm. **Sauvignon Blanc** ⓐ ★★☆ Some residual sugar adds to the easy, tropical-fruity pleasantness of **14**. Not retasted: **Merlot 13** ★★☆ **Pinotage 13** ★★☆ **Shiraz 13** ★★☆ **Chardonnay 13** ★★☆ **Chenin Blanc 13** ★☆

Méthode Cap Classique range

★★★★ **Brut** ⓐ Xhosa beads on the label, while fine gas beads enliven this chardonnay-based MCC (with pinot noir & a little pinotage). Crisply dry; fresh, balanced & flavourful. **NV**, ex Stellenbosch. — TJ

WO: Western Cape ▪ Est 2009 ▪ Closed to public ▪ Owner(s) Makaziwe Mandela & Tukwini Mandela ▪ Winemaker(s) Erlank Erasmus ▪ Viticulturist(s) Various ▪ 60% red 40% white ▪ info@ houseofmandela.com ▪ www.houseofmandela.com ▪ **T +27 (0)21-872-9214**

Hout Bay Vineyards   ⓐ ⓐ

Self-taught winegrowers Peter and Cathy Roeloffze, from the bottling and restaurant business respectively, have hand-hewn hearth, cellar and vineyard on their rocky Hout Bay mountainside property. Terraced slopes and poled vines (each supported by a single upright) produce a small, eclectic range, supplemented by bought-in grapes, with trial and error tempered by expert input.

Hout Bay Vineyards range

★★★★ **Petrus** ⓐ Roundly ripe, plush-textured shiraz-led blend. **11** appealing succulent fruit informed by well-judged oaking to finish sweet & spicy. WO W Cape.

★★★★ **Klasiek by Catherine** Lengthy lees-ageing (40 months) evident in bone-dry **11** (★★★) MCC sparkling's fine bead, hazelnut & bread aromas. Shows a bruised apple note, misses the elegance, vivacity of **10**. Chardonnay (56%) with pinots noir & meunier; also in magnum.

Sauvignon Blanc ★★★★ Forthcoming fig, gooseberry & nettle bouquet, zinging acidity, **14** juicy & lightish (12% alcohol). Also tasted: **Blush 14** ★★★ Not retasted: **Merlot 12** ★★★★ **Shiraz 12** ★★★★ Discontinued: **Cabernet Sauvignon**.

Black Swan range ⓝⓔⓦ

★★★★ **Cape Vintage** 'Port' from classic grapes ex Stellenbosch, **10** packed with dark chocolate, cassis & raisin flavours; rich, bold & oh so enjoyable now. Aged 5 years in 40 year old vats. — JPf

Location: Hout Bay ▪ Map: Cape Peninsula ▪ WO: Hout Bay/Western Cape/Stellenbosch ▪ Est 2001 ▪ 1stB 2004 ▪ Tasting, sales & cellar tours by appt ▪ Fee R40 ▪ Facilities for children ▪ Owner(s) Peter & Catharine Roeloffze ▪ Cellarmaster(s)/winemaker(s)/viticulturist(s) Peter & Catharine Roeloffze (both Jan 2004) ▪ 3.5ha/1.1ha (pinots meunier/noir, merlot, shiraz, chard, sauv, viog) ▪ 16t/2,500cs own label 40% red 20% white 20% rosé 20% MCC ▪ Other brand: HB Vineyards ▪ PO Box 26659 Hout Bay 7872 ▪ cathy@ 4mb.co.za ▪ www.houtbayvineyards.co.za ▪ S 34° 1' 31.0" E 018° 22' 31.0" ▪ F +27 (0)86-514-9861 ▪ **T +27 (0)83-790-3303**

☐ **Huangtai Wines** *see* De Villiers Wines

Hughes Family Wines ⓘ

Making and selling wine started in 2004 as a hobby for Argentina-born Billy Hughes and wife Penny, who sadly passed away since the last edition. 'She was initially a bit reluctant but eventually became the drive and soul of our family business,' Billy recalls. The vineyards in Swartland are grown using a 'trilogy approach': mineral soils, organic cultivation (certified since 2012) and, recently, biodynamic practices. An underground cellar built from old shipping containers was set to vinify the 2016 vintage.

Nativo range

★★★★ **Red Blend** ⓘ Rich in flavour yet light of foot, **11** is the essence of Swartland. Good potential. Mainly shiraz with equal parts mourvèdre, grenache, pinotage, tempranillo.

★★★★☆ **White Blend** ⓘ Sunny in appearance & aroma, **14** spring flowers & hay, lovely energy, concentration & harmony. Pleasingly understated despite 75% viognier in the blend (with chenin, grenache blanc & roussanne). Partial oaking allows fruit to shine. — AL

Location: Malmesbury ▪ Map/WO: Swartland ▪ Est 2000 ▪ 1stB 2004 ▪ Tasting by appt ▪ Owner(s)/cellarmaster(s) Billy Hughes ▪ Winemaker(s) Bryan MacRobert ▪ Viticulturist(s) Kevin Watt (Jul 2005, consultant) ▪ 52ha/27ha (grenache n/b, mourv, ptage, tempranillo, shiraz, chenin, rouss, viog) ▪ 180t total 25t/3,600cs own label 70% red 30% white ▪ Organic ▪ 6 Riverstone Road Tierboskloof Hout Bay 7806 ▪ billy@nativo.co.za ▪ www.nativo.co.za ▪ S 33° 20' 37.71" E 018° 43' 45.09" ▪ F +27 (0)86-549-1080 ▪ **T +27 (0)21-790-4824**

☐ **Hugh Masekela** *see* Veenwouden Private Cellar

Huguenot Wine Farmers

Privately owned wholesalers in Wellington, blending, marketing and distributing a range of liqueurs; spirits such as Huguenac Brandy and Buchu Brandy; wine brands including Huguenot (Cabernet, Smooth Red, Nagmaalwyn, Jeripico, Hanepoot) and Zellerhof 5L Vats (Smooth Red, Premier Grand Cru, Late Harvest); and Huguenot Fortified Sherry.

Wellington ▪ Closed to public ▪ Owner(s) JC Botha (Pty) Ltd ▪ Cellarmaster(s) Bill Matthee (1984) ▪ Trade enquiries Gert Brynard ▪ PO Box 275 Wellington 7654 ▪ gmbrynard@jcbotha.co.za ▪ F +27 (0)21-873-2075 ▪ **T +27 (0)21-864-1277**

Huis van Chevallerie ⓘ

The titular 'house' of Christa von La Chevallerie is family farm Nuwedam in Swartland, where the one-woman show welcomes visitors, but by appointment, please. 'I'm owner, winemaker, viticulturist and all the other titles that accompany the making of gorgeous sparkling wine!' She's released two more, including a rosé, harnessing signature SA varieties chenin and pinotage. Her experience(s) in German, French and Italian sparkling wine regions are shared with similarly impassioned local start-ups.

★★★★ **Filia 13** chenin MCC sparkling in bone-dry brut nature style. Most refined of the trio; oystershell, bruised apple & biscuity flavours at a pleasing 12% alcohol; will reward ageing. Zero dosage, as for Brut. Step up on **12** (★★★★☆).

★★★★ **Filia Brut** ⓝⓔⓦ MCC sparkler **13** only in magnum. Honeyed, toasted nut platform for chenin's vivacious fruit/acid character; mere granule sugar imparts rounder, richer feel than MCC sibling. Very engaging style, both creamy & fresh; ready to enjoy.

Circa ⓝⓔⓦ ★★★ NV bottle-fermented rosé sparkling (not MCC) from pinotage subtitled 'Rosecco', savoury & tangy, touch more sugar than the others ensures laid-back drinkability. — MW

Location: Malmesbury ▪ Map/WO: Swartland ▪ Est 2005 ▪ 1stB 2011 ▪ Tasting by appt only ▪ Closed most pub hols ▪ Owner(s) Chevallerie Family Trust ▪ Cellarmaster(s)/winemaker(s)/viticulturist(s) Christa von La Chevallerie ▪ 110ha/20ha (ptage, chenin) ▪ 100% sparkling wine ▪ PO Box 185 Malmesbury 7299 ▪ info@chevallerie.co.za ▪ www.chevallerie.co.za ▪ **T +27 (0)72-237-1166**

Hunneyball Wines   ⓠ ⌂ ◎

Swedish transplants and small-scale vignerons Jim Hunneyball and wife Marie have moved their grape sourcing and vinification to Stellenbosch, where local winemakers give much-welcomed encouragement and mentorship. The couple have also opened a guest house in the leafy heart of Stellenbosch town, and offer speciality guided wine tours to selected cellars in the area.

Hunneyball House (NEW) ★★★☆ Stellenbosch syrah/shiraz, grenache & mourvèdre fly the flag. **13** a dense, fruity assault but very smooth & deliciously accessible, carrying sweet berries in dry tail. Not retasted: **Cabernet Sauvignon 11** ★★★ — DS

Location/map: Stellenbosch ▪ Map grid reference: F5 ▪ WO: Western Cape/Stellenbosch ▪ Est 2012 ▪ 1stB 2011 ▪ Tasting by appt ▪ Guided wine/regional tours ▪ Hunneyball House 32 Herold Road Stellenbosch ▪ Winemaker(s) Jim & Marie Hunneyball ▪ 5t ▪ 100% red ▪ PO Box 795 Stellenbosch 7599 ▪ jim.hunneyball@gmail.com, marie@hunneyballhouse.com ▪ www.hunneyballhouse.com ▪ S 33° 56' 13.99" E 018° 51' 7.58" ▪ **T +27 (0)71-674-9379**

☐ **Hunterspeak** *see* Niel Joubert Estate
☐ **Hunting Family** *see* Slaley
☐ **Idelia** *see* Swartland Winery
☐ **Ideology** *see* Spier

Idiom Collection   ⓠ ⑪ ◎

The Bottega family celebrated a decade of winemaking in the Helderberg by opening a new visitor centre and restaurant at their mountain vineyards. The focus here remains on Italian varieties, and a regular festival offers visitors the chance to compare classic Italian wines with their local counterparts.

Idiom Collection

★★★★ **Nebbiolo** Savoury & tarry **11** starting to hit its straps with black fruit & perfume softening variety's tannins & high acidity. **12**, also tasted, more fruit forward, both suggesting they will reward patience.

★★★★ **Zinfandel** Back to form of **10**, **12** improves on powerful **11** (★★★★) with pronounced mint & herbs rounded by black cherries, chocolate & tobacco. For lovers of robust reds.

★★★★ **Cabernet Sauvignon-Merlot-Petit Verdot-Cabernet Franc** Showy **11** (★★★★) with plenty of sweet black fruit, though slightly unfocused & a bit thicker than **10**.

★★★★ **Cabernet Sauvignon-Pinotage-Merlot-Cabernet Franc-Petit Verdot** 30% pinotage with quartet of Bordeaux varieties make for meaty yet attractive **11**. Needs time & air but settles into savoury red fruit with upfront tannins & charry oak.

★★★★ **Viognier** An earthy entry to **13** before peaches & tealeaves break through onto rich & fat palate. Livened by good acidity & balanced by restrained alcohol, this is an enjoyable, if not most typical, viognier.
Also tasted: **Sangiovese 12** ★★★★ **Shiraz-Mourvèdre-Viognier 11** ★★★☆ Not retasted: **Sauvignon Blanc-Semillon 12** ★★★☆

900 Series

Barbera ★★★☆ Riper & softer than typical Italian counterpart, **11** settling into savoury stage with red berries & herbs. Also-tasted **12** needs time to balance out tannins & overripe fruit. Occasional release: **Cabernet Franc, Mourvèdre, Sangiovese**.

Heritage Series

> **Rosso** ⓥ ★★★☆ Order the pizza! **12** mainly sangiovese with 10% barbera, slightly stalky nose relaxes into chunky, juicy everyday glugger.

Bianco di Stellenbosch ★★★★ More character than expected from pinot grigio/gris, step-up **14** filled with pears & pear drops, hints of frangipane. Slightly hot finish, but better than most SA examples. Occasional release: **Super Rosso**. — CM

Location: Sir Lowry's Pass ▪ Map: Helderberg ▪ WO: Stellenbosch ▪ Est 1999/1stB 2003 ▪ Tasting & sales: new visitor centre opens in late 2015 — see website for opening hours ▪ Wine tasting; food & wine experience; deli & restaurant; fynbos perfumery & imported Vinotria.co.za Italian wine library ▪ Vineyard tours by appt ▪ 'Italia in Campagna' harvest festival (Feb/Mar) ▪ Owner(s) Bottega family ▪ Winemaker(s) Reino Thiart ▪ 35ha (barbera, cabs s/f, merlot, mourv, nebbiolo, p verdot, ptage, sangio, shiraz, zin, sauv, sem, viog) ▪ 85% red 15% white ▪ PO Box 3802 Somerset West 7129 ▪ wine@idiom.co.za ▪ www.idiom.co.za, www.bottegafamilywine.co.za ▪ S 34° 6' 17.25" E 018° 56' 26.11" ▪ F +27 (0)21-851-5891 (sales) ▪ **T +27 (0)21-858-1088 (vyds)/+27 (0)21-852-3590 (sales)**

iKapa Jazz Wines   (NEW)

'Enjoy your jazz with wine and thereby help keep the jazz legacy alive in South Africa' is the message that accompanies these wines, produced for iKapa Jazz Movement, a group of jazz lovers who encourage, nurture and develop talent through providing opportunities. iKapa, founder member of South African Jazz Appreciators (SAJA), based in Cape Town, also seeks to preserve jazz as an art form that enhances social interaction and self-discovery.

Cabernet Sauvignon-Pinotage ⊘ ★★★ Mainly cab, giving **14** blackcurrant flavours, with oak adding vanilla, while pinotage accounts for the juicy smoothness. Certified organic & Fairtrade, as all. **Rosé** ⊘ ★★ Lots of berries in **14**, from pinotage, dry, lightish & softly smooth. **Dry Sparkling** ⊘ ⊘ ★★★ Nice pear & apple styling in chenin-based **14**, crisply refreshing bubbly to serve to friends. **Semi Sweet Sparkling Rosé** ⊘ ★★ Semi-sweet fizz from pinotage, fun **14** has light-textured fruit pastille flavours. Also tasted: **Pinotage** ⊘ 14 ★★★ **Chenin Blanc** ⊘ 14 ★★★ — CR, CvZ

Location: Cape Town ▪ WO: Western Cape ▪ No 134 Fenyana Road Nyanga 7750 ▪ ntjana.timo@gmail.com, joesidambe@yahoo.com ▪ **T +27 (0)82-716-8256/+27 (0)84-994-0111**

☐ **iLike** see Tulbagh Winery
☐ **Imagine** see Southern Sky Wines

Imbuko Wines   (♀) (♔) (◎)

In only its second decade of operation, Wellington's Imbuko continues to grow and roll out a multifaceted marketing strategy featuring events, sponsorships, a wine club and more. All the while upliftment continues through the Releaf social initiative. Home farm fruit is supplemented with bought-in wine to supply the 120,000-case demand from 32 export markets.

Du Plevaux Private Collection

Pinotage ⊕ ★★★★ Open-tank ferment & brief ageing in large vats result in supple, juicy yet structured **13**, with dry raspberry spice tail. Wellington WO.

Shiraz ★★★ Nimble, spicy plum generosity with tannic core to balance, **13** ratchets quality on previous. Not retasted: **Sauvignon Blanc 14** ★★★★ **Chenin Blanc-Viognier 14** ★★★

Van Zijl range (NEW)

Shiraz-Mourvèdre ⊕ ★★★ Mourvèdre component is a mere splash (7%); **13** easy, cheerful red fruit & light grip.

Cabernet Sauvignon ★★★ Sweet cassis cheer on light **13** offers ample consumer appeal. **Pinotage** ★★★ Ripe, lithe & bright **13**, has bags of fruit with a gentle squeeze of tannin to balance. **Bushvine Chenin Blanc** ★★★ Tangy yet rich with pineapple, peach vibrancy on **15**. Gentle & light with some lees character adding interest. **Sauvignon Blanc** ★★★ Lemon sherbet & grass notes typical of variety, with fresh acidity on **15**. **Chardonnay-Viognier** ★★★ Chardonnay (93%) leads with citrus zip but viognier adds floral nuance to fleshy but focused **15**.

Imbuko range

Cabernet Sauvignon (♀) ★★ Ripe & foursquare **12**, a flavoursome red for country foods. Not retasted: **Chenin Blanc 14** ★★ **Sauvignon Blanc 14** ★★ Not tasted: **Iswithi Pinotage, Chardonnay.**

Pomüla range

Moscato Spumante ⓐ ★★★ Exuberant grapey flavours laced with minuscule bubbles, low-alcohol **NV** perlé from muscadel to be served well chilled. Not retasted: **Rosé 14 ★★**

Shortwood range

Red ⓐ ★★ Though sweet, **NV** on release not as friendly as expected. Not tasted: **White**. — FM

Location: Wellington ▪ Map: Paarl & Wellington ▪ Map grid reference: F4 ▪ WO: Western Cape/Wellington/Coastal ▪ Est/1stB 2004 ▪ Tasting Mon-Fri 9-4 Sat 9-1 ▪ Fee R20/5 wines ▪ Sales 8-5 ▪ Closed all pub hols; Dec 25-Jan 1 ▪ Cellar tours by appt only ▪ Food & wine pairing by appt ▪ Farm produce ▪ Owner(s) Imbuko Wines (Pty) Ltd ▪ Cellarmaster(s) Theunis van Zyl (2004) ▪ Viticulturist(s) Jan-Louw du Plessis ▪ 60ha (cab, cinsaut, merlot, ptage, shiraz, chenin, sauv, viog) ▪ 570t/120,000cs own label 60% red 40% white ▪ Other export brands: Makulu, Releaf Organic & Rebourne Fairtrade, Van Zijls Family Vintners, Kleine Kaap ▪ Fairtrade, IPW, ISO, Organic ▪ PO Box 810 Wellington 7654 ▪ wines@imbuko.co.za ▪ www.imbuko.co.za ▪ S 33° 40' 30.84" E 019° 01' 18.87" ▪ F +27 (0)21-873-7351 ▪ **T +27 (0)21-873-7350**

☐ **Imoya** see KWV Brandies
☐ **Indaba** see Cape Classics
☐ **Infiniti** see Stellenbosch Vineyards
☐ **Ingenuity** see Nederburg Wines
☐ **Inglewood** see Neil Ellis Wines
☐ **Inkará** see Bon Courage Estate
☐ **Insignia Series** see Bellingham
☐ **Integer** see Hoopenburg Wines

Intellego Wines

The name means 'understand', says owner-winemaker Jurgen Gouws; the scale featured on his original labels indicates the balance he seeks in his non-interventionist, 'natural' wines – though more recent labels have been decidedly more funky. Since leaving his position at Lammershoek in 2014, to concentrate on Intellego, Jurgen has been making his wines in rented space at Annex Kloof, on the lower slopes of the Paardeberg, in the Swartland from which he draws his (mostly organically farmed) grapes.

★★★★ **Chenin Blanc** ⓐ Melon, quince & lavender biscotti, **12** is wonderfully aromatic, different, the fruit & older oak combo well judged, allows both to shine. Round & ripe, finishes ultra-long. Could age 4+ years for those who can resist drinking it now. Takes perfumed **11** (★★★★) up a level.

★★★★☆ **Elementis Skin Contact** ⓐ From chenin, fermented 3 weeks on skins, 10 months old oak. Sauvignon-like dryness & acidity, lower alcohol (12.5%), but oh, **13**'s perfume & flavour! Peach & mango to start, evolving into a nutty, earthy, savoury beauty, svelte & pure. The name says it all.

Not retasted: **Kolbroek 12 ★★★☆ Syrah 13 ★★★★** — CR, CvZ

Location: Malmesbury ▪ WO: Swartland ▪ Est/1stB 2009 ▪ Closed to public ▪ Owner(s)/winemaker(s) Jurgen Gouws ▪ 1,000cs own label 40% red 60% white ▪ jurgen@intellegowines.co.za ▪ **T +27 (0)82-392-3258**

Iona Vineyards   ⓐ ⓒ

Andrew and Rozy Gunn's farm sits on an isolated Elgin plateau, which forced them to learn by trial and error rather than with help of neighbours. Today, thanks to greater vine age (the oldest block is 17 years) and an established winemaker (Werner Muller, with four vintages under his belt), they have a better understanding of their terroir. 'Respecting the limitations and unique potential of our farm is the thread that will endure in Iona wines,' say the Gunns, 'if we allow our sites to reflect our philosophy of maximum care and minimum intervention.' New nebbiolo vines are intended for the One Man Band blend.

Iona Vineyards range

★★★★ **Pinot Noir Limited Release** Elgin freshness & gentle tannins evident in **13**. Nicely composed, though sweet edge of oak (20% new) needs ±year to harmonise with luxurious dark cherry flavours.

★★★★ **One Man Band** Hearty (for elegant Elgin) shiraz-based blend, **10**'s meaty richness augmented with firm grip & energy from cabernet, merlot, petit verdot & mourvèdre partners.

★★★★☆ **Chardonnay 14** gorgeous follow up to elegant, complex **13** (★★★★★). Fruit youthfully expressive, riper lemon & lime juicy flavours, but not compromising its cool, clean lines & cushioning lees enrichment. Charming now, but plenty more pleasure in store.

★★★★☆ **Sauvignon Blanc** Now regularly includes portion oaked wine, drop semillon for added interest, accessibility. **14** shows cool-climate refinement in its unshowy tropical, citrus features, bouncy feel, both alleviate edginess of its current steely, bone-dry conclusion. Worth ageing few years.

Husk Spirit range

Corretto Ⓥ ★★★ From cab & merlot; light amber hue, playful label, fragrant black-fruit perfume; alcohol quite prominent – perhaps better to 'correct' your shot with an espresso. — WB, AL

Location/WO: Elgin ▪ Map: Elgin, Walker Bay & Bot River ▪ Est 1997 ▪ 1stB 2001 ▪ Tasting, sales & tours Mon-Fri 8–5 Sat by appt ▪ Closed all pub hols ▪ Walks/hikes ▪ Mountain biking ▪ Conservation area ▪ Owner(s) Andrew & Rozanne Gunn, Workers Trust ▪ Winemaker(s) Werner Muller (May 2011), with Thapelo Hlasa (Jun 1997) ▪ Vineyard manager Joseph Sebulawa ▪ 100ha/40ha (cab, merlot, mourv, p verdot, pinot, shiraz, chard, sauv) ▪ 250t/24,000cs own label 25% red 75% white ▪ BWI ▪ PO Box 527 Grabouw 7160 ▪ orders@iona.co.za ▪ www.iona.co.za ▪ S 34° 16' 42.2" E 019° 4' 58.2" ▪ F +27 (0)86-627-8960 ▪ **T +27 (0)28-284-9678**

☐ **Ithemba** *see* Stellar Winery
☐ **Iwayini** *see* Maiden Wine Cellars
☐ **Ixia** *see* Distell

Izak van der Vyver Wines

Living among Elgin's cool vineyards, general practitioner Izak van der Vyver couldn't resist having a go at producing his own wine. In the cellar of his friend Paul Cluver, he has vinified two rows of sauvignon from local farm Smarag since 2002.

★★★★ **Sauvignon Blanc** Cool climate shows in **14**'s fynbos, flint & figgy character, its flavours anchored by the acidity, intensifying the finish. **12, 13** untasted. — CR, CvZ

Location/WO: Elgin ▪ 1stB 2002 ▪ Closed to public ▪ Owner(s) Izak van der Vyver ▪ Cellarmaster(s) Andries Burger (Paul Cluver Wines) ▪ Winemaker(s) Izak van der Vyver (Jan 2002) ▪ 1.4t/±166cs own label ▪ PO Box 42 Grabouw 7160 ▪ drs@telkomsa.net ▪ F +27 (0)21-859-3607 ▪ **T +27 (0)21-859-2508**

☐ **Jabari** *see* Vin du Cap International

Jacaranda Wine & Guest Farm   Ⓠ ⓦ ⓗ

After years working in China, René and Birgit Reiser decamped to Wellington in 2009 and, watched over by Cape Eagle Owls, with great verve developed Jacaranda into a stylish guest farm with a boutique wine range, much expanded this edition. Their minute organically farmed vineyard is sadly now minus old cabernet and merlot but boosted by shiraz, mourvèdre and chardonnay.

Reserve Cabernet Sauvignon-Merlot ⓃⒺⓌ ★★★ Soft, rounded herb-brushed black fruit on **13** 51/49 blend. **SMV** ★★★ Plum spice of shiraz leads **13** Rhône blend with dashes mourvèdre & viognier, medium-bodied juicy sipper. **Sauvignon Blanc** ⓃⒺⓌ ★★ Lemony lightness to unfussy maiden **14**. **Méthode Cap Classique Brut Reserve** ⓃⒺⓌ ★★ **11** bubbly from chardonnay shows crisp apple tang on broad, yeasty yet light palate. Also tasted: **Old Vine Chenin Blanc** ⓃⒺⓌ **13** ★★ **Chenin Blanc 14** ★★ Not retasted: **Cuvée Rouge 11** ★★★ **Pinotage Rosé 12** ★★★ — FM

Location/WO: Wellington ▪ Map: Paarl & Wellington ▪ Map grid reference: F1 ▪ Est/1stB 2009 ▪ Tasting & sales Mon-Sat 10-5 ▪ Fee R30/6-8 wines (depending on availability), served with olives & bread ▪ Closed Easter Fri/Sun, Dec 25 & Jan 1 ▪ Mediterranean/cheese platters & picnic baskets by appt ▪ B&B: 2 cottage units, 1 family unit (4 pax) ▪ Owner(s) René & Birgit Reiser ▪ Cellarmaster(s)/viticulturist(s) René Reiser (Jun 2009) ▪ Winemaker(s) René Reiser (Jun 2009) & Jean-Paul Schmitt (2013) ▪ 3.5ha (mourv, shiraz, chard, chenin, viog) ▪ 9t/1,500cs own label 50% red 40% white 10% rosé ▪ PO Box 121 Wellington 7654 ▪ birgit@jacarandawines.co.za ▪ www.jacarandawines.co.za ▪ S 33° 36' 49.2" E 019° 0' 16.1" ▪ **T +27 (0)21-864-1235**

Jacobsdal ⓠ

'No change,' reports Cornelis Dumas, not unexpectedly considering this Stellenbosch winery's reputation for upholding tradition. Third (since 1966) and fourth generation (son Hannes) vinify two enduring reds from dryland bushvines in tried-and-true open concrete tanks using wild yeasts and little intervention.

Cabernet Sauvignon ★★★ Elegant **12** has cassis, liquorice & fennel hints; modest 20% new oak buffs the fruit, rounds the tannins for smooth & persistent flavour, farewell. **Pinotage ★★★** Sour cherry & blue berry notes with underlying dark choc, cinnamon; flavourful, well-made **12** invites hearty game dishes & casseroles. Also-available magnums extend the enjoyment. — GM

Location/map/WO: Stellenbosch ▪ Map grid reference: B6 ▪ Est 1916 ▪ 1stB 1974 ▪ Tasting on the farm by appt only ▪ Tasting & sales also at Die Bergkelder (see entry) ▪ Owner(s) Dumas Ondernemings (Pty) Ltd ▪ Cellarmaster(s) Cornelis Dumas ▪ Winemaker(s)/viticulturist(s) Cornelis Dumas, with Hannes Dumas ▪ 100ha (cab, ptage, chenin, sauv) ▪ 600t/26,000cs own label 100% red ▪ PO Box 11 Kuils River 7579 ▪ info@jacobsdal.co.za ▪ www.jacobsdal.co.za ▪ S 33° 58' 4.9" E 018° 43' 34.6" ▪ F +27 (0)21-881-3337 ▪ **T +27 (0)21-881-3336**

☐ **Jacoline Haasbroek Wines** *see* My Wyn

Jacques Germanier ⓠ ⓜ ⓐ ⓞ

An early pioneer of environmentally and socially sustainable farming in SA, Swiss-owned Jacques Germanier ('African Terroir' until recently) has redoubled its focus on organic and Fairtrade (along with its conventional wines). Accordingly, a collection of 'widely differentiated blends' is debuting in a custom, new-shape bottle, specially labelled and embossed with the winery logo. Previously by appointment, tastings at the scenic brand home, Sonop Farm near Paarl, are now available at set hours along with tourist and business facilities.

Organic range ⓝ

Sonop Cabernet Sauvignon-Merlot ⓥ **★★★ 14** preview 60/40 blend shows cassis, blue berry, cocoa & plum with chalky tannins. **Winds of Change Cabernet Sauvignon-Merlot-Shiraz** ⓥ **★★★☆** Dark berries, ripe red stonefruit, cigarbox & oriental spice on previewed **14**. Noticeable grape tannins are polished, given form by 9 months in new oak; augurs well for future. **Sonop Chardonnay-Sauvignon Blanc** ⓥ **★★★** Work-in-progress **15** gets its citrus tones, fresh lime conclusion from 60% chardonnay; gooseberry & melon tones, extra freshness from sauvignon. **Winds of Change Chardonnay-Sauvignon Blanc-Viognier** ⓥ **★★☆** Characterful 3-way combo ex-tank exudes freshness with green fig, asparagus, gooseberry & citrus in **15**; dry, crisp & balanced. — GM

Location: Paarl ▪ Map: Paarl & Wellington ▪ Map grid reference: C1 ▪ WO: Western Cape ▪ Est/1stB 1991 ▪ Tasting, sales & cellar tours Mon-Fri 9-5 Sat 10-2 ▪ Lunch available for larger groups on request – to book ahead ▪ Closed all pub hols ▪ Conferences ▪ Functions ▪ Conservation area ▪ Guest house ▪ Owner(s) Jacques Germanier ▪ Winemaker(s) Jaco Marais (Nov 2012) ▪ Viticulturist(s) Johan Barnard (Nov 2009) ▪ 75ha (cab, merlot, ptage, shiraz, chard, cbard, sauv, viog) ▪ 540t ▪ Brands for clients: Azania, Bag in Box Collection, Cape Soleil, Landela (organic), Milton Grove, Out of Africa, Sonop (organic), The Big 5, Tribal Skin, Tribal Spear, Tribal Sparkling, Winds of Change (organic) ▪ ISO 22000, BWI, Fairtrade, FOA, HACCP, IPW, Organic ▪ PO Box 2029 Windmeul Paarl 7630 ▪ admin@germanier.co.za ▪ www.germanier.co.za ▪ S 33° 37' 1.8" E 018° 50' 38.4" ▪ F +27 (0)21-869-8104 ▪ **T +27 (0)21-869-8103**

Jacques Smit Wines ⓠ ⓐ

Vine nurseryman Jacques Smit, who counts Calitzdorp 'port' champion Boets Nel among his longtime clients (and mentors when it comes to Jacques' artisan winemaking), provides an interesting stop on the Wellington Wine Walk, where visitors tarry for a tasting in wife Marina's shady garden.

Limited Releases

Cabernet Sauvignon ⓥ **★★★☆** Juicy & appealing **07** easygoing mealtime companion. Not retasted: **Shiraz 05 ★★★☆ Vine Valley 06 ★★★☆ Cape Ruby Roobernet Port 07 ★★★☆** — MW

Location/WO: Wellington ▪ Map: Paarl & Wellington ▪ Map grid reference: F2 ▪ Est/1stB 2003 ▪ Tasting, sales & tours by appt ▪ Closed Easter Fri/Sun/Mon, Ascension Day, Dec 25/26 & Jan 1 ▪ Facilities for chil-

dren ▪ Wellington Wine Walk ▪ Owner(s) Jacques & Marina Smit ▪ Cellarmaster(s)/winemaker(s)/viticul-
turist(s) Jacques Smit ▪ 60ha/32ha (cab, roobernet, shiraz, Cape riesling, chenin) ▪ 300t total 100% red ▪
Welvanpas PO Box 137 Wellington 7654 ▪ info@vines2wine.com ▪ www.vines2wine.com ▪ S 33° 39'
2.2" E 019° 1' 9.0" ▪ F +27 (0)21-873-2143 ▪ **T +27 (0)21-873-1265**

Jakkalsvlei Private Cellar (♀) (¶¶) (◎) (♨)

Primarily a bulk wine supplier, Jantjie Jonker has steadily increased own-brand volumes and now bottles 18,000 cases under the label of his farm near Herbertsdale, named for the many foxes and jackal in
nearby mountains. He's added a 250-seat restaurant and an MTB trail to the cellardoor attractions.

La Perlé Rosé ★★ Faint prickle on palate of **15** equal pinotage, red muscadel mix. Sweet, juicy & light
(only 10% alcohol). **Sauvignon Blanc ★★★** Taut lemon zest & flint typicity to **15**, good palate weight
& length. **Hanepoot ★★★★** Ambrosial barley sugar richness on **NV** fortified dessert. Very sweet but
not cloying thanks to focused dry-seeming finish. **Trop** (NEW) **★★★** Spell name backwards & you get
'Port', which **12** is, from tinta. Fiery, nutty, spicy, with harmony of ripe fruit & spirit though purists will
find it a little light. 375 ml. Also tasted: **Cabernet Sauvignon Reserve 13 ★★★ Mount Cuvée
Pinotage-Merlot 14 ★★☆ River Cuvée Chenin Blanc-Sauvignon Blanc 15 ★★★ Red
Muscadel NV ★★★** Not tasted: **Pinotage Coffee Edition.** — FM

Location: Herbertsdale ▪ Map: Klein Karoo & Garden Route ▪ WO: Western Cape ▪ Est 1987 ▪ 1stB 2008 ▪
Tasting & sales Mon-Fri 9.30-5 Sat 9.30-3 ▪ Closed Sun ▪ Cheese platters ▪ Deli ▪ Conferences ▪ Wed-
dings/functions (250 pax) ▪ Restaurant ▪ Facilities for children ▪ Walks/hikes ▪ MTB trail ▪ Jakkalsvlei
beer: Jackal Lager & Wolf Ale ▪ Seasonal food & wine pairings ▪ Pick your own hanepoot (Feb/Mar) ▪
Sundown festival (Apr) ▪ Owner(s)/cellarmaster(s)/viticulturist(s) JG Jonker ▪ 80ha/26ha (cab, merlot,
muscadel r, ptage, chenin, hanepoot, sauv) ▪ 350t/18,000cs own label 40% red 20% white 20% rosé
20% dessert + 150,000L bulk ▪ PO Box 79 Herbertsdale 6505 ▪ info@jakkalsvlei.co.za, catering@
jakkalsvlei.co.za, sales@jakkalsvlei.co.za ▪ www.jakkalsvlei.co.za ▪ S 33° 59' 15.31" E 021° 43' 9.33" ▪
F +27 (0)86-593-0123 ▪ **T +27 (0)28-735-2061**

Jakob's Vineyards (♀)

This parcel of cabernet, unusual for Hemel-en-Aarde, is the stuff of childhood dreams for former Johannesburg attorney André de Lange, and honours his father. Having previously put it towards a Bordeaux
blend, he and scientist wife Yvonne are focusing on a single-varietal expression, 'looking for simplicity
and striving for excellence', supported by Crystallum/Gabriëlskloof winemaker Peter-Allan Finlayson.

★★★★ Cabernet Sauvignon (♀) First since **06**, crafted **11** displays lively red berry aromas & earthy
tone, well-judged 30% new oak frames a very friendly, juicy palate. — JPf

Location: Hermanus ▪ Map: Elgin, Walker Bay & Bot River ▪ WO: Hemel-en-Aarde Ridge ▪ Est 2002 ▪ 1stB
2006 ▪ Tasting by appt ▪ Owner(s) André & Yvonne de Lange ▪ Winemaker(s) Peter-Allan Finlayson
(2010, consultant) ▪ Viticulturist(s) Johan Pienaar (Jun 2003, consultant) ▪ 5ha/1ha (cab) ▪ 5t/±500cs
own label 100% red ▪ PO Box 15885 Vlaeberg 8018 ▪ wine@jakobsvineyards.co.za ▪
www.jakobsvineyards.co.za ▪ F +27 (0)86-589-4619 ▪ **T +27 (0)82-371-5686**

☐ **Jam Jar** see Cape Classics
☐ **Jardin** see Jordan Wine Estate
☐ **Jason's Creek** see Jason's Hill Private Cellar

Jason's Hill Private Cellar (♀) (¶¶) (◎) (♨) (♿)

Ivy du Toit, supported by viticulturist husband Alister Oates, is a fifth-generation grape grower/supplier
in the Slanghoek Valley. She made a name as an award-winning, internationally experienced young
winemaker with her own red-led bottlings in a new cellar, named after an old farmhand and subsequently incorporated into a family-friendly visitors/functions venue.

Jason's Hill range

Cabernet Sauvignon ★★★ Smooth & sleek **13** has house's ripe-fruit styling but it's tempered with
balancing cab tannins for a more refreshing mouthful. Still bold & intense; better in a year/2. **Merlot**

★★★ Ultra-ripe prune & malty fruit, 14.5% alcohol deftly handled on **13**, which hangs together quite well despite the burly character. Also-tasted **11** similar 'no wallflower' personality, juicy steak companion. Also tasted: **Pinotage 13** ★★★ **Shiraz 12** ★★★

Jason's Creek range

Classic Red ⊕ ★★★ From petit verdot, merlot, cab franc, **12** aims for 'easy uncomplicated drinking' & succeeds admirably. House's ripeness evident but also a freshening herbal quality. — WB, CvZ

Location: Rawsonville ▪ Map/WO: Breedekloof ▪ Est/1stB 2001 ▪ Tasting & sales Mon-Fri 8–5 Sat 10-3 ▪ Closed Easter Fri-Sun, Dec 25 & Jan 1 ▪ Cellar tours by appt ▪ Bistro Mon-Sat 10–3 (also available for functions) ▪ Shop ▪ Facilities for children ▪ Spa ▪ Weddings/functions ▪ 6.5km hiking trail ▪ Owner(s) Du Toit family ▪ Cellarmaster(s) Ivy du Toit (Jan 2001) ▪ Viticulturist(s) Alister Oates (Jan 2004) ▪ 100ha ▪ 45% red 50% white 5% rosé ▪ PO Box 14 Rawsonville 6845 ▪ info@jasonshill.co.za ▪ www.jasonshill.co.za ▪ S 33° 39' 52.3" E 019° 13' 40.6" ▪ F +27 (0)86-523-6655 ▪ **T +27 (0)23-344-3256**

Jasper Raats Single Vineyard Wines   ⓠ

'Jasper Raats is smiling' says the winemaker behind these single-vineyard wines ('naturally' vinified and available at Longridge). His pinot noir, sourced from Elgin (where, he believes, there's just the right balance between high sunlight hours and relatively low temperatures), received 'rave reviews' abroad. And his sauvignon blanc from high-lying Helderberg farm Driefontein sold out early. He's therefore 'hugely excited' about the new Syrah in the portfolio, also from Driefontein.

★★★★ **Driefontein Syrah** ⓝ Blackberries, pepper & liquorice waft from the glass of forthcoming, polished **13**. Well built, 20 months older oak add svelte form & depth, light charcoal nuance on goodbye.

★★★★ **Cuvée Rika Pinot Noir** Sleek, modern **14** with bouquet of macerated strawberries & spiced cherries. Modest oaking (just 13% new), reined-in 13% alcohol perfect for fine dining. Benefits from decanting, should reward a few years cellaring. No **13**.

★★★★ **Driefontein Sauvignon Blanc** Older-barrel-fermented **14** is gooseberry & grass scented, shows finesse & elegance underpinned by minerals & appealing pithy texture. Achieves refreshment with moderate acidity & friendly 13% alcohol. — JPf

Location: Stellenbosch ▪ Map: Helderberg ▪ WO: Stellenbosch/Elgin ▪ Est 2010 ▪ 1stB 2011 ▪ Tasting & sales by appt only ▪ Closed Good Fri, Dec 25 & Jan 1 ▪ Owner(s) Vigneron Consulting Ltd ▪ Winemaker(s)/viticulturist(s) Jasper Raats (2010) ▪ 2ha (pinot, sauv) ▪ 13t/1,700cs own label 50% red 50% white ▪ jasper@longridge.co.za ▪ S 34° 0' 55.2" E 018° 49' 60.0" ▪ F +27 (0)21-855-4083 ▪ **T +27 (0)76-752-5270**

☐ **Jasper Wickens** see JC Wickens Wines
☐ **JC Kannemeyer** see Wolfkloof
☐ **JC le Roux** see The House of JC le Roux

JC Wickens Wines   ⓝ

Stellenbosch graduate Jasper Wickens' winemaking epiphany was the 2009 vintage at AA Badenhorst Family Wines. He'd worked crushes in Stellenbosch and Napa, but it took the Swartland to put his tertiary education into perspective. Here he fell in love with wine all over again, and with the old vines, the farm lifestyle, the traditional winemaking. Three stints in Spain and two in France have further broadened his outlook. Jasper's first own-wines were from the 2011 vintage, and he currently offers a '14 chenin and '14 red blend (mostly co-fermented cinsaut and grenache). He's thinking of renovating a cellar in the Perdeberg area, working with his own grapes and increasing his boutique production.

Est 2011 ▪ Owner(s)/winemaker(s) Jasper Wickens ▪ 500cs ▪ jcwickens@gmail.com ▪ **T +27 (0)72-461-4249**

☐ **JD Initial Series** see Jean Daneel Wines

Jean Daneel Wines

The accomplished Daneel family are proudly putting their signature on a gradually evolving range of bespoke wines reflecting increasing input from their Domaine Daneel vineyard near the rural Overberg town of Napier. It's where Jean, with wife René, the creative talents behind JD Wines' deli and decor treats, settled after more than three decades helping establish Buitenverwachting and Morgenhof as top SA wine properties. Winemaker Jean-Pierre has inherited his father's touch, with chenin being a particular focus. The variety features in a new Signature MCC sparkling, the maiden '15 slated for release next year. The Le Grand Jardin range and the Signature Red are on hold, the latter to be re-introduced alongside a new Directors Signature Red in a few years' time.

Signature Series

★★★★☆ **Chenin Blanc** Smartly oaked **14** from old bushvines perfect food wine, with fresh acid core & tightly wound apple & pear fruit. Lees-ageing provides lovely richness, texture to lively mouthwatering conclusion. WO W Cape. Also in magnum.

★★★★☆ **Sauvignon Blanc** Ultra-fresh, vibrantly herbaceous **14** offers complex, generous granadilla, fig fruit, underscored by steely, earthy minerality noted in debut **13**.

Not tasted: **Red**. Occasional release: **Directors Signature Red**, **Directors Signature Chenin Blanc**.

JD Initial Series

★★★★ **White** Splash chenin in **14** fleshes out sauvignon's austere steeliness. Lees enrichment ensures textural element to balanced fruit, acid combo. More harmonious than **13** (★★★☆).

Not tasted: **Red**.

Le Grand Jardin

In abeyance: **Red**, **Chenin Blanc**, **White**. — IM

Location: Napier ▪ Map: Southern Cape ▪ WO: Napier/Western Cape ▪ Est/1stB 1997 ▪ Tasting, sales & cellar tours by appt ▪ Closed Dec 25 & Jan 1 ▪ Restaurant & deli ▪ Owner(s) Jean & René Daneel ▪ Winemaker(s) Jean-Pierre Daneel ▪ 70t 40% red 60% white ▪ PO Box 200 Napier 7270 ▪ info@jdwines.co.za ▪ www.jdwines.co.za ▪ S 34° 28' 38.11" E 019° 54' 15.47" ▪ F +27 (0)28-423-3197 ▪ **T +27 (0)28-423-3724**

Jeu

This port-style wine by Nadia Barnard, cellarmaster at Waterkloof, is dedicated to her grandmother 'from whom I've learnt to love fortified wines'. Friend Margaux Nel, winemaker at port champion Boplaas, offered encouragement; Albert Bredell, member of another port-producing clan, provided the grapes.

Jeu ⓤ ★★★ Port-style from tinta, **10** delicious but not usual Ruby affability: chunky mouthful, lots of extracted flavours, very low sugar. Mid-2013 needed time to soften & unfurl. — WB, IM

Location/WO: Stellenbosch ▪ Est/1stB 2010 ▪ Closed to public ▪ Owner(s)/winemaker(s) Nadia Barnard ▪ jeuwines@gmail.com ▪ **T +27 (0)83-324-8466**

JH Meyer Signature Wines ⓤ

Johan 'Stompie' Meyer is a busy man. Apart from making wine for avant-garde Mount Abora he's radically expanding his own label — clearly a work in progress. Three serious pinot noirs expressing different terroirs might seem ambition enough, but there's also a project focusing on other varieties, and new plantings in the Outeniqua area. 'And also a few surprises from the 2016 vintage!'

JH Meyer Signature Wines range

★★★★ **Chardonnay** Floral notes & lemony acidity work well with light richness, some grip, & a touch of sweetness on **14**. Not fruity, but flavourful, with character & depth. Ex Elgin, like next.

Carbonic Pinot Noir ⓝⓔⓦ ★★★ An original idea: light, fresh Beaujolais-style pinot — whole-bunch carbonic ferment. Exuberant crushed strawberry dominates something earthier. Fairly quick-fading charm. **15** no new oak, as for all these.

Single Vineyards range

★★★★ Cradock Peak Pinot Noir (NEW) Strawberry fragrance on **14** ex Outeniqua; forest floor depth – most complex & interesting here. Impressive intensity for 12.8% alcohol, with firm tannins, though still light-feeling.

★★★★ Palmiet Pinot Noir Was just 'Pinot Noir'. **14** from Elgin has fresh raspberry perfume, which follows through to vibrant, pure-fruited palate. Gently but firmly built: light & juicy, with a tannic underpinning. These all 100% whole-bunch-pressed & 'naturally' made; only older oak barrels used.

Elands River Pinot Noir (NEW) **★★★☆** From Elandskloof. Characterful **14** less perfumed than others, despite 50% carbonic ferment; pleasant earthy note, but less fine fruit; fairly tannic, plus bright acidity. — TJ

Location: Riebeek-Kasteel ▪ WO: Elgin/Outeniqua/Elandskloof ▪ Est/1stB 2011 ▪ Private tastings on request ▪ Owner(s) Johan Meyer ▪ Cellarmaster(s)/winemaker(s)/viticulturist(s) Johan Meyer (2011) ▪ 18t total ▪ own label 80% red 20% white ▪ PO Box 396 Riebeek Kasteel 7307 ▪ jhmeyerwines@ gmail.com ▪ www.jhmeyerwines.co.za ▪ **T +27 (0)79-280-0237**

☐ **JJ Handmade Wines** *see* Stellenrust
☐ **John B** *see* Rietvallei Wine Estate
☐ **Jolly Roger** *see* Clayton Wines
☐ **Jonkheer** *see* Vinopoly Wines

Joostenberg Wines   ⓦ ⑪ ⌂ ◎ ⑧ ♿

There is always something creative happening on the old (1870s) Myburgh family farm between Paarl and Stellenbosch. It's either something bubbling or baking at the bustling Deli & Bistro, or experimental batches of wine, only a barrel or two, hence available mostly ex farm/deli (and not reviewed here). Released as the Small Batch Collection, there are a cab, touriga, roussanne and chenin/steen from one of the old organic blocks, labelled Kaalgat ('Naked') to convey the natural approach, here and throughout.

Premium range

★★★★ Klippe Kou Syrah (Ⓥ) Was just 'Syrah', name now alludes to rocky soils. **13** fresh & bright with peppery & dark chocolate flavours, well-judged older oak, silky texture & supple tannins. Will improve.

★★★★ Noble Late Harvest Name changed to indicate chenin partnered by viognier, semillon in **14** sweet dessert, older-oaked. Botrytis-tinged caramel, barley sugar & viognier's tangy peach. Different style to unctuous chenin-only **13**, equally delicious. Coastal WO.

Chenin Blanc (NEW) (Ⓥ) **★★★** Mostly about texture: richly woven, mouthfilling & creamy; **15** ripe apple & almond flavours, finishes a bit warm, could do with tad more freshness. **Die Agteros Chenin Blanc** (NEW) (Ⓥ) **★★★** From oldest chenin block, **14** lighter-bodied & -textured, fresher than younger sibling, genteel & harmonious. Also tasted: **Family Blend Red** (Ⓥ) **13 ★★★★** **Bakermat** (Ⓥ) **12 ★★★☆** **Fairhead** (Ⓥ) **13 ★★★** Discontinued: **Family Blend Rosé**, **Family Blend White**.

Little J range

In abeyance: **Shiraz**, **Chenin Blanc**. — MW

Location: Paarl ▪ Map: Paarl & Wellington ▪ Map grid reference: A7 ▪ WO: Paarl/Coastal ▪ Est/1stB 1999 ▪ Tasting & cellar tours by appt at the winery ▪ Sales daily 10–5 at the Deli on Klein Joostenberg Farm ▪ Closed Dec 25 & Jan 1 ▪ Joostenberg Bistro ▪ Facilities for children ▪ Tour groups ▪ Gifts ▪ Farm produce ▪ Honey shop ▪ Conferences ▪ Ludwigs rose nursery & Van den Berg garden centre ▪ Guest accommodation (3 double rooms), contact anette@joostenberg.co.za ▪ Owner(s) Philip & Tyrrel Myburgh ▪ Cellarmaster(s)/viticulturist(s) Tyrrel Myburgh (1999) ▪ Winemaker(s) Micu Narunsky (2014) ▪ 31ha (cab, merlot, mourv, shiraz, touriga nacional, chenin, rouss, viog) ▪ 120t/16,000cs own label 35% red 50% white 15% NLH ▪ PO Box 82 Elsenburg 7607 ▪ winery@joostenberg.co.za ▪ www.joostenberg.co.za ▪ S 33° 48' 47.21" E 018° 48' 31.70 (cellar), S 33° 49' 34.8" E 018° 47' 45.5" (deli) ▪ **T +27 (0)21-200-9903 (winery)/+27 (0)21-884-4141 (bistro/deli)**

Jordan Wine Estate   ⓦ ⑪ ⌂ ◎ ♿

Kathy and Gary Jordan's rise to the very pinnacle of Cape wine is underpinned by a remarkable work ethic and determination. Their entrepreneurial spirit has seen them expand and reinvent the estate, directly tackle export markets and embrace fine-dining and good living as integral parts of the great wine experience. They have partnered with chef George Jardin to establish an iconic winelands restaurant, launched the very impressive High Timber restaurant on the Thames in London, and now they've reinterpreted the boutique hotel with their luxury guest suites on the estate. This beautiful, impressive property, high above Stelleboschkloof, is an eloquent expression of what's possible with care, hard work and dedication. Watch out for a high-end barrel fermented chenin in the pipeline.

Jordan Estate range

★★★★☆ **Cabernet Sauvignon** Epitomises racy freshness of variety, with edgy herbaceous notes tempered by convincing black core. **12** more complex & nuanced than **11**, showing confident restraint. Should blossom with a few years in cellar.

★★★★ **Merlot** Previewed **13** shows familiar leafiness, underlain by sound, solid fruit base. Finely tuned, sweetly balanced & exuberantly youthful, showing promise once settled.

★★★★ **The Prospector Syrah** Delicious Rhône-style scrub & pepper on **13**. Subtle rather than bold, but bursting with ripe, spicy fruit & appealingly complex tobacco & savoury notes.

★★★★☆ **Cobblers Hill** Big bodied, dense & assertive Bordeaux-style blend, mostly cab/merlot **12** follows impressive form. Perfect balance of ripeness, fruit intensity & subtle spicing, with toned-down tannins, muscular litheness & resonating harmonious finish.

★★★★☆ **CWG Auction Reserve Sophia** Noble, statuesque **12** barrel selection from Cobblers Hill cuvée plus a reserve cab. Perennial high flyer is big & bold & distinctly New World but still beguilingly subtle. Shows promise for extended cellaring.

★★★★ **Chardonnay Barrel Fermented** Industry benchmark New World style, **14** (★★★★★) is a lesson in oak restraint, allowing full expression of sumptuous fruit, lees fatness & appealing beeswax scents. Fine balance of force & subtlety improves even on excellent **13**.

★★★★☆ **CWG Auction Reserve Chardonnay** Impressive special selection from Nine Yards vineyard. **14** shows family resemblance but spicier oak, even fuller body suggest long cellaring will reward. Bold, forthright yet refined.

★★★★☆ **Nine Yards Chardonnay** Rich, opulent citrus fruit on **14** is undaunted by solid whack of new oak. Larger-than-life flagship label still shows subtle balance, complex layers of spice & marmalade with fine texture & lingering finish.

★★★★ **Inspector Péringuey Chenin Blanc** Was 'Chenin Blanc Barrel Fermented'. Simply delicious **14** exudes appeal. Finely textured, lightly spiced by 50% oak-fermented fraction, showing ripe, wholesome stonefruit with a gentle acid grip.

★★★★ **The Real McCoy Riesling** Bracingly crisp, off-dry **15** one of the better local examples, showing variety's zest & spiciness with commendable focus. Youthful, but likely to develop in bottle. WO W Cape.

★★★★ **The Outlier Sauvignon Blanc** Partially (60%) barrel-fermented, sur-lie **14** is an entirely different creature to unoaked sibling. Soft, fat & understated but satisfying in an Old-Worldly way.

★★★★ **Sauvignon Blanc** Tank sample **15** still displaying ferment notes but already expressive & exuberantly generous. Ripe layers of summer fruit on a refreshingly crisp undercarriage.

> **Unoaked Chardonnay** ⊕ ★★★☆ Rich leesy texture on **14**, with overtly ripe citrus fruit. Very appealing, good length. Substance without attitude.

Not tasted: **Mellifera**.

Bradgate range

Chenin Blanc ★★★ Fruit emphasis on **14**, unoaked with 13% sauvignon. Bright & refreshing. Not tasted: **Syrah**, **Cabernet Sauvignon-Merlot**.

Chameleon range

> **Rosé** ⊕ ★★★☆ Appealing floral scents & ripe berries on **14** merlot-shiraz blend. Dry, refreshing, generous.

Also tasted: **Merlot No Added Sulphur 14** ★★★☆ Not tasted: **Cabernet Sauvignon-Merlot**, **Sauvignon Blanc-Chardonnay**. — GdB

Location/map: Stellenbosch ▪ Map grid reference: C5 ▪ WO: Stellenbosch/Western Cape ▪ Est 1982 ▪ 1stB 1993 ▪ Tasting & sales daily 9.30–4.30 ▪ Tasting fee R40pp, waived on purchase ▪ Cellar tours by appt Mon-Fri 9.30-4.30 ▪ Pre-booking required for: tasting & cellar tour R75pp; speciality tasting & cellar tours from R100pp; exclusive vineyard & cellar experience tours from R350pp ▪ Jordan Restaurant ▪ Jordan Bakery ▪ Conferences (50 pax) ▪ Walks/hikes ▪ Mountain biking ▪ Conservation area ▪ Visits to old prospector's mine shafts ▪ Fly fishing (catch & release) R100/adult & R50/child under 12, booking essential ▪ Jordan Luxury Suites ▪ Owner(s) Jordan family ▪ Cellarmaster(s) Gary & Kathy Jordan (1993) ▪ Winemaker(s) Sjaak Nelson (Jan 2002) ▪ Viticulturist(s) Gary Jordan (1983) ▪ 160ha/105ha (cab, merlot, syrah, chard, chenin, riesling, sauv) ▪ 850t/100,000cs own label 45% red 54% white 1% rosé ▪ Other export brand: Jardin ▪ Brands for clients: Pick's Pick, Woolworths ▪ BWI ▪ PO Box 12592 Die Boord Stellenbosch 7613 ▪ info@jordanwines.com ▪ www.jordanwines.com ▪ S 33° 56' 33.7" E 018° 44' 41.3" ▪ F +27 (0)21-881-3426 ▪ **T +27 (0)21-881-3441**

☐ **Joseph Barry** *see* Barrydale Winery & Distillery

Joubert-Tradauw Wingerde & Kelder Ⓟ ⑪ ⌂ ⊙ Ⓐ ⑆

Established by patriarch Schalk-Willem Joubert some 6 decades ago, the family farm in scenic Tradouw Valley has Karoo shale soils and cooling evening seabreezes rising up through Tradouw Pass – attributes which inform the two new wines: a pinot noir named for a fish species endemic to the local river, and cabernet franc (with Afrikaans spelling of 'Reserwe'). The already multifaceted visitor facilities are getting a private tasting venue and two extra garden areas.

★★★★ **Redfin Pinot Noir** (NEW) **13** shows distinctive spice with usual cherry, undergrowth nuances. A nip of bitterness only detraction to overall silky, fresh feel. Unfined/filtered.

★★★★ **Syrah** Ⓥ Revisited as bottled wine, smoky & savoury **11** (★★★★) has carefully crafted tannin structure to restrain opulent fruit, fine varietal black pepper & lily aromas. Follows **08** (no **09**, **10**).

★★★★ **Chardonnay Barrel Fermented** Bold, expressive **13**; creamy lees-enriched texture & full body balanced by lively acid. Well-judged oak enhances tasty oatmeal, nut, citrus flavours; good potential.

Reserwe Cabernet Franc (NEW) ★★★★ Quite exotic & ripely spiced **13**. Generous flavours with semblance of sweetness from alcohol, in fact bone-dry. Probably best over next 2/3 years. Also tasted: **R62 12 ★★★★** — AL

Location: Barrydale ▪ Map: Klein Karoo & Garden Route ▪ WO: Tradouw ▪ Est/1stB 1999 ▪ Tasting, sales & cellar tours Mon-Fri 9–5 Sat 10–2 ▪ Closed Easter Fri/Sun & Dec 25 ▪ R62 Deli Mon-Fri 9-3 Sat 10-1 breakfasts, lunches & Klein Karoo tapas ▪ Walks/hikes ▪ Mountain biking ▪ Conservation area ▪ Lentelus B&B (www.lentelus.co.za) ▪ Owner(s) Lentelus Family Trust ▪ Cellarmaster(s)/winemaker(s)/viticulturist(s) Meyer Joubert (1999) ▪ 1,100ha/30ha (cab, merlot, shiraz, chard) ▪ 5,000cs own label 70% red 30% white ▪ PO Box 15 Barrydale 6750 ▪ info@joubert-tradauw.co.za ▪ www.joubert-tradauw.com ▪ S 33° 55' 26.4" E 020° 35' 40.6" ▪ F +27 (0)86-555-3558 ▪ **T +27 (0)28-572-1619/+27 (0)82-815-3737/+27 (0)71-656-1230**

Journey's End Vineyards Ⓟ ⑪ ⌂ ⊙

These Gabb-family-owned Helderberg vineyards on windswept, sea-facing, stony Schapenberg Hill are benefiting from renewed focus on soil quality through sustainable farming practices ('happy soils, good wines'), while in the cellar Leon Esterhuizen – ten years in the driver's seat – is experimenting with carbonic maceration and looking to produce more single-vineyard wines.

Reserve range

★★★★ **Griffin Shiraz** Ⓥ **12** more elegant than powerful JE stablemate. Svelte, understated style shows perfumed red fruit & freshness with subtle oaking & structure. Good potential to develop.

★★★★☆ **Cape Doctor Cabernet Sauvignon-Merlot-Malbec-Cabernet Franc** Ⓥ **09** Bordeaux blend returns to form after all-cab **08** (★★★☆). Deftly oaked, showcases ample fruit. New World style with development potential for 4-6 years, but already tempting.

★★★★ **Destination Chardonnay** Sumptuous-styled **14** more opulent & oaked (70% new) than JE sibling; lime & toasty butterscotch flavours on a cream texture courtesy 80% malo. **13** untasted.

Journey's End range

★★★★ **Cabernet Sauvignon** Elegantly poised **09** returns to form in classic vintage, after lesser **08** (★★★★☆). Good core of cassis, mint & cedar in firm, supple structure with long, clean & dry finish.

★★★★ **Merlot** Restrained & reserved **12**, firm dry fruit & oak tannins. Definite potential to unfurl elegantly & allow fruit to shine with ageing. More inherent balance than **11** (★★★★).

★★★★ **Shiraz 11** dapper & juicy, with supple spicy oak support for layers of red fruit & pepper. Fresh & medium bodied; already entertaining with structure to reward ageing. No **10**.

★★★★ **Chardonnay** Livelier than opulent sibling, **14** only 20% malo & less new oak ensure freshness & focuses tangy fruit. Rich, balanced & flavoursome, though a shade off intensity of **13** (★★★★☆).

Cellar range

The Huntsman Shiraz-Mourvèdre ⊘ ★★★★ Attractive **13** 70/30 blend with loads of juicy red fruit & pepper, dry tannin & oak in harmony. Ready to enjoy now & over next few years. Also tasted: **The Pastor's Blend 13** ★★★ **Haystack Chardonnay 14** ★★★★ Not retasted: **Weather Station Sauvignon Blanc 14** ★★★★ — MW

Location: Sir Lowry's Pass ▪ Map: Helderberg ▪ WO: Stellenbosch ▪ Est 1995 ▪ 1stB 2001 ▪ Tasting only by appt Mon-Fri 9-5 ▪ Fee R50pp ▪ Closed Easter Fri-Mon, Dec 25 & Jan 1 ▪ Cheese platters & snacks by appt; or BYO picnic ▪ Conferences (20 pax) ▪ Walks/hikes ▪ Horse riding ▪ Mountain biking ▪ Conservation area ▪ Owner(s) Gabb family ▪ Cellarmaster(s)/winemaker(s) Leon Esterhuizen (Jun 2006) ▪ Viticulturist(s) Lodewyk Retief (Jun 2011) ▪ 50ha/30ha (cabs s/f, malbec, merlot, mourv, p verdot, shiraz, chard, sauv, sem, viog) ▪ 300t/30,000cs own label 60% red 40% white ▪ BWI, HACCP, IPW, WIETA ▪ PO Box 3040 Somerset West 7129 ▪ info@journeysend.co.za ▪ www.journeysend.co.za ▪ S 34° 6' 35.11" E 018° 54' 54.06" ▪ F +27 (0)86-540-1929 ▪ **T +27 (0)21-858-1929**

☐ **JP le Hanie Wines** *see* Vredevol Private Wine Cellar

Julien Schaal

Happiness is... making riesling in Alsace and chardonnay in SA. That's what Alsatian vintner Julien Schaal and new wife, Burgundy-born qualified winemaker Sophie Bollaert are doing. Having discovered SA in 2003, working at Newton Johnson in Hemel-en-Aarde as a cellarhand 'to learn English', he started bottling a local Syrah and Chardonnay from 2005, subsequently vinifying at Paul Cluver in Elgin. He's now specialising in chardonnay, specifically from cool-climate areas such as Elgin, Walker Bay, Villiersdorp and other high-lying Overberg sites. Joining his (now 'their') Mountain Vineyards and Evidence duo in 2016 are the single-vineyard Renaissance and Confluence.

★★★★☆ **Evidence Chardonnay** (NEW) Exquisite **13** has convincing, poised, regal richness. Complex, lees-infused oatmeal nuttiness mingles with citrus & stonefruit, structured by 14 months in barrels, third new. Elgin's coolness shines through in long, layered, steely conclusion.

★★★★☆ **Mountain Vineyards Chardonnay** Sheer purity & minerality in **14** from cool-climate (Elgin) fruit. Rapier-like acidity — no softening malolactic — underlies lime/citrus flavours; smart oaking (just 10% new) integrates seamlessly, lending complexity & dimension.

Discontinued: **Syrah**. — IM

Location/WO: Elgin ▪ Est 2004 ▪ 1stB 2005 ▪ Tasting by appt only ▪ Owner(s) Julien Schaal ▪ Winemaker(s) Julien Schaal & Sophie Bollaert ▪ 28t/4,000cs own label 100% white ▪ c/o PO Box 48 Grabouw 7160 ▪ julien@vins-schaal.com ▪ www.julienschaal.com ▪ **T +33 (0)6-10-89-72-14**

☐ **Juliet Méthode Cap Classique** *see* Tanja Beutler Wine Collection
☐ **Jumbo** *see* Burgershof

Juno Wine Company

Fronted by the Juno Bistro & Bakery in Paarl, this privately owned, internationally distributed brand now managed by winemaker Erlank Erasmus is named after the Roman goddess of marriage. Marketed as 'fun and funky', its richly colourful labels by artist Tertia du Toit celebrate working women and its Fairtrade accreditation contributes to empowering farm employees and their families.

Pinotage (NEW) ★★★ Charry, meaty **14** with sweet, soft tannins, enjoyable sipper. **Shiraz** ★★★ **14** fresh & juicy number with sweet fruit & warm leathery hints. **Sauvignon Blanc** ★★★ Very enjoyable **15** sappy, fresh mouthful of tinned grapefruits, green figs with tropical notes. Drier than previous & better for it. Also tasted: **Cabernet Sauvignon 13** ★★★ **Shiraz-Mourvèdre-Viognier 14** ★★☆ — CM

Location: Paarl ▪ Map: Paarl & Wellington ▪ Map grid reference: E5 ▪ WO: Western Cape ▪ Est 2004 ▪ Tasting & sales at 191 Main Rd Paarl Mon-Wed 8-6.30 Thu-Fri 8-9.30pm Sat 8–3 ▪ Open most pub hols ▪ Juno Bistro & Bakery ▪ Winemaker(s) Erlank Erasmus ▪ 60% red 40% white ▪ PO Box 68 Main Road Paarl 7622 ▪ winery@ junowines.com ▪ www.junowines.com ▪ S 33° 44' 36.9" E 018° 57' 46.1" ▪ **T +27 (0)21-872-0697**

☐ **Kaap Agri** *see* Breëland Winery
☐ **Kaapdal** *see* Robertson Wide River Export Company
☐ **Kaapse Droom** *see* Goedverwacht Wine Estate

Kaapse Familie Wingerde   (NEW)

The Cape families alluded to in the name of this new joint venture have been winegrowers for many generations: the De Waals in Paarl's Voor Paardeberg ward, marketing as Oude Denneboom, the Loubsers near Philadelphia (Kuypers Kraal) and the Le Rouxs on Paarl town's fringe (Vendôme). Besides the wines noted here, the KFW umbrella includes a Vendôme Sauvignon Blanc-Semillon '13, Kuypers Kraal Sauvignon Blanc '14 and Oude Denneboom Shiraz '13 and Chenin Blanc '15, listed separately.

Paarl Families Cabernet Sauvignon ★★★ Vibrant blackcurrants throughout **13**, dusted with sweet oak spice & drinking well. Not tasted: **Paarl Families Sauvignon Blanc.** — CR, CvZ

Location: Paarl-Philadelphia ▪ WO: Paarl ▪ vendome@icon.co.za ▪ www.kaapsefamiliewingerde.com ▪ **T +27 (0)21-863-3905**

Kaapzicht Wine Estate   (♀) (⌂) (◎)

Looking at the current range and what's planted, it's clear there are future plans in embryo, which is what this large family estate is about, providing for generations to come. Steytler-owned since 1946, brothers Danie and George are still involved, respectively, in the cellar and vineyards. Wives, German-speaking Yngvild and Mandy take care of export markets and look after guest venues and the entertainment. Danie jnr has been winemaker since 2009 while his wife Carin handles national sales. It is truly a family business. Only a third of the grapes are used, most harvested off unirrigated vineyards, the rest sold off. The main focus is red wines, with some noteworthy exceptions (1947 Chenin honours the date of its vineyard planting), and the wines have personality, reflecting the family's traditional values, with depth and power.

Steytler range

★★★★☆ **Pinotage** Always makes an impression. Small crop & 2 years new French oak, **12** is flavour-rich & concentrated. Prunes & black cherries, vanilla & nutmeg yet surprisingly elegant, polished, the supple tannins an equal partner, not intruding. No **11**.

★★★★☆ **Pentagon** Bold, serious version of 5-part Bordeaux-style blend; cab-led **12** shows intense cassis, expected structure. Beautifully crafted, tannins underpin wine's concentration & succulent depth, promise a long future. New oak, 2 years. No **11**.

★★★★☆ **Vision** Iconic Cape Blend, pinotage with cab & merlot, getting the best of all worlds. Cocoa-spiced plush plums & blueberries, & despite serious oaking, layered richness & complexity, **12** (★★★★★) has succulent, silky drinkability. Even finer than last-made **10**. Enjoy till 2025.

Kaapzicht range

★★★★ **Cabernet Sauvignon** Layers of interest in complex **12**, supporting its dark-fruited core, cocoa, hints of fynbos, tobacco, without putting a step wrong in the oaking. Harmonious, balanced, worth adding to the cellar. No **11**.

★★★★ **Merlot** (Ⓖ) Savoury & herbal, with earthy mulberry & tobacco aromas dominating **10** (★★★★☆), slighter than **08** but bulked-up by oak & dry tannin. No **09**.

★★★★☆ **Pinotage** (⊘) From bushvines. Intense blueberries & Morello cherries, an intriguing smoky nuance without making it darker, succulent fruit the hero in **12**. Perfectly judged oaking, a fine tannin structure for cellaring – but delicious already. No **11**.

★★★★ **Estate Red** Creative blend, shiraz & cab, dab petit verdot, pinotage. **11** deep pruney fruit loaded with savoury spice, succulent underpin to supple tannins. Delicious, improves on **10** (★★★☆).

★★★★★ **The 1947 Chenin Blanc** From SA's 2nd oldest chenin block. **14** bunch-pressed; ferment/ year in oak, 50% new. Striking, with layers of flavour, blanched almonds/pine nuts, kumquat preserve, all contained in svelte, polished body, ending savoury & long. Bottelary WO.

★★★★ **Kaleidoscope White** ⊘ Showcasing the art of unoaked blending, **15** has almost equal roussanne, verdelho, chenin & 3 others, so expect complexity, layers of flavours. A touch of sugar plumps the texture, gives a delicious sweet/sour effect.

> **Shiraz** ⊕ ★★★☆ Proudly New World, **12** boasts black plums, vanilla, creamy chocolate. A hedonist's delight, the ultra-smooth texture continues the seduction. **Chenin Blanc** ⊘ ⊕ ★★★☆ Lovely fresh fruit on **15**, lime & passionfruit, showing mouthwatering zesty intensity.

Pinot Noir (NEW) ★★★ Mocha perfume notes on dark fruited **13** prepare one for the savoury palate, this is food wine, with ageing potential. Also tasted: **Sauvignon Blanc 15** ★★★☆ Not retasted: **Bin-3 11** ★★★☆ **Kaleidoscope 13** ★★☆ **Ice 09** ★★☆ **Hanepoot Jerepigo 11** ★★★☆ **Cape Vintage 07** ★★★☆

Brandy & Husk Spirit range

★★★★ **15 Year Potstill** (NEW) As the brandy matured, it kept harmony & texture, gained in flavour complexity (the almond note particularly attractive), but perhaps lost some brightness, freshness.

Grape Husk Spirit (NEW) ⊘ ★★★★ Grappa-style from ripe aromatic varieties gewürztraminer & riesling, giving a gentle fragrant quality, the nuttiness touched with grape & raisin notes. Clean, fresh & persistent. 375ml. Discontinued: **10 Year Potstill**. — TJ, CR

Location/map: Stellenbosch ▪ Map grid reference: B4 ▪ WO: Stellenbosch/Wellington/Bottelary ▪ Est 1946 ▪ 1stB 1984 ▪ Tasting & sales Mon-Fri 9—4 Sat 9—12 ▪ Fee R20pp, waived on purchase ▪ Closed Easter Fri/Sun, Dec 24/25/26 & Jan 1 ▪ Cellar tours by appt ▪ Conference/function/wedding & braai venues ▪ Walks/hikes ▪ MTB trail ▪ Conservation area ▪ 2 self-catering cottages ▪ Owner(s) Steytdal Farm (Pty) Ltd/Steytler Family Trusts ▪ Cellarmaster(s) Danie Steytler snr (Jan 1979) ▪ Winemaker(s) Danie Steytler jnr (Feb 2009) ▪ Viticulturist(s) George Steytler (Jan 1984) & Schalk du Toit (Jun 2003) ▪ 190ha/162ha (cabs s/f, cinsaut, malbec, merlot, p verdot, ptage, shiraz, chard, chenin, hanepoot, rouss, sauv, sem, verdelho) ▪ 1,100t/60,000cs own label 70% red 30% white + 20,000cs for clients ▪ Other export brands: Cape View, Friesland, Vet Rooi Olifant ▪ PO Box 35 Koelenhof 7605 ▪ carin@kaapzicht.co.za ▪ www.kaapzicht.co.za ▪ S 33° 54' 47.7" E 018° 44' 7.7" ▪ F +27 (0)21-906-1622 ▪ **T +27 (0)21-906-1620/1**

☐ **Kadette** *see* Kanonkop Estate
☐ **Kakamas** *see* Orange River Cellars
☐ **Kalkveld** *see* Zandvliet Wine Estate
☐ **Kanah Winery** *see* Twelve Apostles Winery
☐ **Kango** *see* Mooiuitsig Wine Cellars

Kanonkop Estate

Widely regarded as a South African 'first growth', this legendary mostly red-wine estate is run as a very steady ship by owners and brothers Johann and Paul Krige. They are complemented by cellarmaster Abrie Beeslaar, only the third winemaker since bottling under Kanonkop's own label began in 1973. While the Bordeaux-style blend, Paul Sauer (named for the Krige's grandfather), is the anointed flagship, it is pinotage for which there's insatiable consumer demand. So popular is the Kadette range, currently showing double digit growth locally and overseas, an increase of 50% in production, oak maturation and warehousing facilities are being undertaken. Johann's view is that 'if you don't grow, you die! But it needs a dedicated team all sharing the same vision'.

Kanonkop Estate range

★★★★☆ **Cabernet Sauvignon 12** quintessential Kanonkop cabernet. Handsomely structured with fine-toned muscle, imposing tannic grip framing subtle walnut, dark fruit intrigue. Ageworthy classic from excellent vintage. 50% new oak. Also in larger formats.

★★★★☆ **Pinotage** Mid-tier of 3 pinotages in range, distinguished by its elegance, sophistication & purity. **13** wonderful harmony of ripe fruit, finely honed tannins & fresh core. Good now but plenty development in store, especially in larger formats.

★★★★★ **Pinotage Black Label 13** (★★★★★) celebrates vineyard's 60th anniversary in fine fashion. Serene in its concentration, with fine line of energy lifting ripe, dark fruits, viscosity. All in place, including new French oak, for lengthy ageing. As grand as **12**.

★★★★☆ **Paul Sauer** Cab-based flagship, with cab franc, merlot. **12** with usual richly vinous, muscular build; penetrating ripe fruit to balance concluding austerity. Beautifully composed, complemented by new oak, a long, fine future assured. Larger formats too.

Kadette range

★★★★ **Pinotage** Youngest member of Kanonkop's pinotage family huge success since first **12** (★★★★); **13** sold out untasted; tentatively rated **14** preview suggests continued strong demand. Grown-up yet approachable; generous dark berry flavours wrapped in rich, velvety feel; neat savoury conclusion.

Cape Blend ★★★ Pinotage plumminess leads fruit-forward **13**. Cab, merlot, cab franc add dimension to this easy-drinker, also in 1.5L. **Pinotage Dry Rosé** ★★★ Succulent mouthful of ripe red berries on fuller-bodied, food-friendly **15**. Well balanced, fruitily persistent. Stellenbosch WO, as all these. — AL

Location/map: Stellenbosch ▪ Map grid reference: F2 ▪ WO: Simonsberg–Stellenbosch/Stellenbosch ▪ Est 1910 ▪ 1stB 1973 ▪ Tasting & sales Mon-Fri 9—5 Sat 9—2 pub hols 10-4 ▪ Fee R30 ▪ Closed Good Fri, Dec 25 & Jan 1 ▪ Cheese platters in summer; traditional snoek barbecues by appt (min 15 people); or BYO picnic ▪ Conservation area ▪ Art gallery ▪ Owner(s) Johann & Paul Krige ▪ Cellarmaster(s) Abrie Beeslaar (Jan 2002) ▪ Winemaker(s) Alet de Wet (Dec 2014), with Jeremy Arries (2007) & Frikkie Elias (1992) ▪ Viticulturist(s) Koos du Toit (Jan 2004) ▪ 120ha/100ha (cabs s/f, merlot, ptage) ▪ 1,480t/220,000cs own label 98% red 2% rosé ▪ WIETA ▪ PO Box 19 Elsenburg 7607 ▪ wine@kanonkop.co.za ▪ www.kanonkop.co.za ▪ S 33° 51' 18.4" E 018° 51' 36.1" ▪ F +27 (0)21-884-4719 ▪ **T +27 (0)21-884-4656**

Kanu Wines ⓘ ♿

Named after a mythical African bird symbolising the promise of a bountiful harvest, the Kanu brand was hatched in the 1990s on Goedgeloof farm on Polkadraai Road as part of Hydro Holdings' Stellenbosch wine property portfolio which included Mulderbosch on the R304. Following various business and proprietary deals between 2010 and 2012, the two brands essentially swapped homes. Mulderbosch's former prime mover, Mike Dobrovic, is back as adviser, overhauling blocks he established in the late 1980s, replacing under-performing vines with 'interesting cultivars'. Meanwhile winemaker Johan Grimbeek introduces an ultra-premium white blend this year, melding fruit from old vines and unusual varieties.

Ultra Premium range ⓝ

★★★★ **'Maiden White Blend'** Previewed **NV** flag bearer mostly roussanne & grenache blanc, some viognier, naturally fermented in seasoned oak; profoundly aromatic, with scents of white flower & pear; rich dried apricot & peach pip allure adds to charm.

Premium range

★★★★ **Keystone** Clean-cut Bordeaux-style red with sappy choc-mint interest, **13** concentrated by bleeding off 35% juice, focused by 10 months in oak (35% new). **12** sold out before tasting. WO Coastal.

★★★★ **KCB Chenin Blanc** Bursting with ripe tropical melon flavours, **14**'s oak (French & Hungarian, 35% new) is well integrated with the sweet fruit. Grapes from Piekernierskloof.

★★★★ **Viognier 13** confirms uptick of **12**; like liquid confectionery; waves of apricot & marmalade jostle with oak in lusciously honeyed send-off. Not subtle, but delicious. 10 months seasoned cask.

★★★★ **Kia-Ora Noble Late Harvest** Botrytised chenin dessert; old gold **12** loaded with candied peel, piquant kumquat & almond hint, refined in all-new oak (17 months), balanced by vivacious acid. No **11**.

Shiraz ★★★ Soft berry compote character of **10** given form & focus by amenable tannins. WO W Cape. **GSM** ★★★☆ **11** grenache-led blend with shiraz & mourvèdre. Savoury red fruit shines through spicy oak (2 years, 65% new) in ripe package. WO W Cape. **Sauvignon Blanc** ★★☆ Grassy-green & crisp, pick-me-up **14** will kick-start a summer lunch. WO Coastal. Also tasted: **Cabernet Sauvignon 13**

★★★ **Merlot 14** ★★☆ **Chardonnay Barrel Fermented** ▪ 12 ★★★ **Chenin Blanc 14** ★★☆ Not tasted: **Rockwood**, **Giselle**. Discontinued: **Chardonnay-Pinot Noir**, **KCB Envy**.

Black Label range

Rifle Range Red ★★ 6-way **NV** blend ex Coastal vineyards hits the full-fruited spot; easy drinking without thinking. **Semi-Sweet Rosé** ★★ Grapey **NV** with pink tints, a modest, sweet drop. Also tasted: **Semi-Sweet White NV** ★★☆ **Natural Sweet Shiraz 13** ★ Not retasted: **Merlot Rosé NV** ★★ Not tasted: **Rifle Range White**. — DS

Location/map: Stellenbosch ▪ Map grid reference: E3 ▪ WO: Stellenbosch/Western Cape/Coastal/ Piekenierskloof ▪ Est/1stB 1998 ▪ Tasting & sales Mon-Fri 9.30–4.30 Sat 10-2 ▪ Fee R36pp ▪ Closed all pub hols ▪ Owner(s) Ben Truter Trust ▪ Cellarmaster(s)/winemaker(s) Johan Grimbeek (Jan 2002) ▪ Viticulturist(s) Mike Dobrovic (2014, consultant) ▪ 48ha/20ha (cab, merlot, chard, sauv) ▪ 200t/60,000cs own label 50% red 45% white 5% rosé ▪ BWI, WIETA ▪ PO Box 548 Stellenbosch 7599 ▪ info@kanu.co.za ▪ www.kanu.co.za ▪ S 33°53' 23.35" E 018°49' 8.44" ▪ F +27 (0)21-865-2351 ▪ **T +27 (0)21-865-2488**

☐ **Kap Hase** *see* Migliarina Wines

☐ **Karoo Classique** *see* Karusa Vineyards

Karusa Vineyards

For visitors exploring the rugged Klein Karoo along tourist route R62, Karusa in the Cango Valley near Oudtshoorn offers convenience on all fronts. Hospitable co-owner/cellarmaster Jacques Conradie produces small parcels of wine across a range of styles, from still and bubbly to dessert, 'port' and 'sherry'. A microbrewery caters for beer lovers, a tapas restaurant and deli for foodies and, at road's end in the foothills of the scenic Swartberg mountains, lie the world-renowned Cango Caves.

Location: Oudtshoorn ▪ Map: Klein Karoo & Garden Route ▪ Est/1stB 2004 ▪ Tasting & sales Mon-Fri 9.30–4 Sat 10–2.30 ▪ Closed Good Fri & Dec 25 ▪ Karoo Tapas Restaurant & Deli ▪ Microbrewery ▪ Conferences (30-40 pax) ▪ Owner(s) Karusa Partnership ▪ Cellarmaster(s) Jacques Conradie (2004) ▪ 8ha (grenache, mourv, muscadel r, ptage, shiraz, touriga nacional, chard, sauv, viog) ▪ 50-70t/5,000cs own label 30% red 50% white 5% rosé 15% other ▪ PO Box 1061 Oudtshoorn 6620 ▪ info@karusa.co.za ▪ www.karusa.co.za ▪ S 33°28' 36.0" E 022°14' 33.2" ▪ F +27 (0)86-600-3167 ▪ **T +27 (0)44-272-8717**

☐ **Kasteelberg** *see* Riebeek Cellars

Katbakkies Wine   ⓠ

Architect Andries van der Walt, inspired by a '63 Rustenberg cabernet, planted vines on both his Cederberg farm Katbakkies and Devon Valley property, collaborating with winemaking consultant Teddy Hall on a highly rated range, including attractive viogniers. Proceeds from a big wine order end 2015 was earmarked for a cellar refit, to date a 'shoestring' operation.

★★★★ **Cabernet Sauvignon** ⓠ **11** first tasted since '05. Classic style, built around its crunchy ripe fruit & form-giving grape tannins; well proportioned for current enjoyment & further few years.

★★★★ **Syrah Reserve** ⓠ Dense, complex **04**; firm structure, bold but balanced.

★★★★ **Chenin Blanc** ⓠ **10** more attractive savoury richness than sweetness, & delicious persistence. **09** (★★★☆) more obviously off-dry.

Not retasted: **Syrah 08** ★★★★ **Perpendiculum Viognier NV** ★★★ Not tasted: **Viognier**. — GdB

Location/map/WO: Stellenbosch ▪ Map grid reference: D5 ▪ Est/1stB 1999 ▪ Tasting & sales Mon-Sat by appt ▪ Closed all pub hols ▪ Owner(s) Andries van der Walt ▪ Cellarmaster(s) Andries van der Walt (1999) ▪ Winemaker(s) Teddy Hall (2002, consultant) & Andries van der Walt (1999) ▪ 29ha/10ha (cab, merlot, syrah) ▪ 1,000cs own label 40% red 60% white ▪ PO Box 305 Stellenbosch 7599 ▪ info@katbakkies.co.za ▪ www.katbakkies.co.za ▪ S 33°55' 37.4" E 018°49' 14.6" ▪ **T +27 (0)82-882-9022**

☐ **KC** *see* Klein Constantia Estate

Keermont Vineyards ⓠ

It's more than vines that grow on the Wraith family estate in the saddle between the Helderberg and Stellenbosch mountains. While plantings of marsanne and roussanne have increased the vineyard footprint to 29 ha, indigenous vegetation still beautifies much of the slopes. Growth in local and foreign markets has necessitated appointment of a bookkeeper and sales administrator but as Keermont is a team effort, you're just as likely to find them operating the corking machine or at the sorting table. Winemaker/viticulturist (and surfer) Alex Starey remains focused on fine-tuning great wines from great sites with minimum intervention in the cellar, including 'no removal of alcohol and very little new oak'.

Single Vineyard Series

★★★★☆ **Steepside Syrah** ⓩ Named after steep Helderberg vineyard site. Appealing & expressive lilies & red fruits introduce **12**. Savoury & well-fleshed mouthfeel with chewy tannins allow for current enjoyment but concentration & build for extended ageing. 20 months 2nd fill French oak, unfiltered.

★★★★☆ **Riverside Chenin Blanc 14** (★★★★★) reprises all that represented quality & character in **13**. Old vine concentration evident in its aromatic & flavour intensity: a fusion of dried peaches, orange zest & earthiness of natural ferment. Harmony is echoed in the pithy, energetic yet silky texture, wonderful persistence. Mix old/new wood; only 150 cases made.

Not tasted: **Topside Syrah**.

Annual Release range

★★★★ **Syrah** ⓩ Blend of single vineyards above plus 5% mourvèdre. Bigger, denser & lacking some of their exciting individuality. **12**'s dark spice, earthy tones subdued but has structure to age & evolve.

★★★★ **Keermont** ⓩ Flagship red; **12** refined Bordeaux quintet with dash syrah. Cab influential in ripe profile, flesh though merlot is main player. Fine, insinuating tannins suggest ageability.

★★★★ **Terrasse** Distinctive white blend named for terraced Stellenbosch Mountain home. Exuberant & harmonious **14** (★★★★★) chenin-led with chardonnay, sauvignon & sunny apricot tones from 5% viognier. Rich yet full of verve, trace of grip providing further dimension. Shines even brighter than **13**.

★★★★ **Fleurfontein** Sweet, vine-dried sauvignon blanc. **14** more honeyed, luscious than **12** (★★★★☆); peachy flavours lifted by clean thread of acid. Natural ferment in single barrel. **13** untasted.

Not retasted: **Companion 12** ★★★ — AL

Location/map/WO: Stellenbosch ▪ Map grid reference: F8 ▪ Est 2005 ▪ 1stB 2007 ▪ Tasting & sales Fri 10.30-1.30 or by appt ▪ Cellar tours by appt ▪ Owner(s) Wraith family ▪ Winemaker(s)/viticulturist(s) Alex Starey (Jan 2005) ▪ 156ha/29ha (cab, merlot, syrah, chenin) ▪ ±90t/3,000cs own label 65% red 33% white 2% sticky white ▪ BWI, IPW, IPW ▪ PO Box 713 Stellenbosch 7599 ▪ info@keermont.co.za ▪ www.keermont.co.za ▪ S 34° 0' 27.0" E 018° 53' 39.0" ▪ F +27 (0)21-880-0566 ▪ **T +27 (0)21-880-0397**

Keet Wines ⓠ

Chris Keet admits to being tempted to increase his range of wines, but contents himself with a focus which, he says, keeps him 'inspired to source the best grapes in Stellenbosch' and devote attention to detail for his one wine (volumes have grown substantially since the maiden 2009 vintage). As a consultant, Chris has also devoted attention to the wines and vineyards of numerous others, but this will mostly go following his appointment as winemaker to Quoin Rock.

★★★★★ **First Verse 12** 5-way Bordeaux-style blend shows a little toasty oak (just 15% new), & perhaps less fragrance than **11**, but still much charm & grace. Tannins well balanced against sweet fruit. A few years should harmonise, bring further complexity. — TJ

Location/WO: Stellenbosch ▪ Est 2008 ▪ 1stB 2010 ▪ Tasting by appt ▪ Owner(s) Christopher Keet ▪ Cellarmaster(s)/winemaker(s)/viticulturist(s) Christopher Keet (Oct 2008) ▪ 10t/1,500cs own label 100% red ▪ PO Box 5508 Helderberg 7135 ▪ chris@keetwines.co.za ▪ www.keetwines.co.za ▪ F +27 (0)86-544-3347 ▪ **T +27 (0)82-853-1707**

☐ **Keimoes** see Orange River Cellars
☐ **Keizer's Creek** see Roodezandt Wines

Kellerprinz

Budget-priced white for the sweet toothed, in 2L bottle, by Distell.

Late Harvest ⊘ ★★ Fresh, lively semi-sweet **NV** white with pear & peach flavours. — DB

☐ **Kelvin Grove** *see* Simonsvlei International

Ken Forrester Wines ⊘ ⊘ ⊘

In the mid-1990s Ken Forrester left the Johannesburg restaurant scene at the top of his game (Fedasa chairman) to restore derelict Stellenbosch farm Scholtzenhof to its original beauty and make some wine from its old chenin vines. Today the internationally acclaimed 'Chenin King' remains involved in the hospitality business as a partner in popular winelands restaurant 96 Winery Road but his main focus is championing SA wines around the world — not least his own range with its increased focus on Rhône-style reds — as well as welcoming visitors to the cellardoor's recently enlarged tasting area. 'In general our philosophy remains the same,' he says. 'To create a range of handcrafted, individually made wines that complement a wide variety of food styles and provide excellent value.'

Icon range

★★★★☆ **The Gypsy** Smooth, with barely perceptible tannins, grenache-led Rhône blend **12** is less lean than previous, softer, plumper, juicier, with lovely depth of dark red cherry, raspberry & blueberry fruit, hints of pepper & allspice (41% syrah/shiraz, 6% mourvèdre). WO W Cape.

★★★★☆ **The FMC** Mostly old-vine chenin harvested fully ripe. Smooth **13** is less OTT, more elegant than predecessor, repetitive harvesting (including some botrytis) & wild yeast barrel fermentation (in new oak) resulting in remarkable richness of texture & fruit/spice complexity, from apricot, peach & orange to vanilla, cinnamon & ginger.

★★★★☆ **'T' Noble Late Harvest** Barrel-fermented botrytised Stellenbosch chenin named for Mrs Forrester. Something so sweet shouldn't have so much finesse but in **12**, again, fresh acid & oak spice lift tropical lushness of honey-drizzled melon, pineapple & tangy apricot.

Occasional release: **FMC Première Sélection Moelleux**.

Cellar Exclusives range

★★★★☆ **Roussanne** Soft, almost velvety barrel-aged **13** has hedgerow flowers on the nose leading to peach & pear fruit, richly viscous texture, gentle balancing acidity, with lingering tangy impression somehow reminiscent of yoghurt-coated almonds.

Not tasted: **Sparklehorse**. Occasional release: **Three Halves**.

Ken Forrester range

★★★★ **Renegade** ⊘ **11** (★★★★★) even more focused than **10**, shiraz's blackcurrant & spice joined by juicy raspberry & red cherry of 26% grenache, with 14% mourvèdre adding grip as well as even more pepper & smoke. WO W Cape.

★★★★ **Old Vine Reserve Chenin Blanc** ⊘ From old Helderberg vines, exceptional **14** (★★★★★) is redolent of naartjies, apricots, cling peaches & fresh ginger, leesy & creamy like **13** but with relatively delicate vanilla oak spice due to less new wood (only 20%) & barrel time than FMC.

★★★★ **Sauvignon Blanc** Although **14** is crisp, dry & refreshing, it has a creamy texture similar to that of its chenin siblings, not to mention white peach & green apple flavours with a squeeze of lime. More delicious than previewed **13** (★★★★).

Merlot Reserve ⊘ ★★★★☆ Subtitled 'Pat's Garden', which must be lovely judging by soft, smooth **13** with ripe plum & black cherry fruit, hint of smoke, 15% cab franc bolstering structure.

Petit range

Pinotage ⊘ ⊘ ★★★★ Unwooded **14** bursts with succulent red berries, made in modern, fruit-forward style, as all these, where 'petit' also hints at 'small' difference made if all vineyard work is done by hand, providing job opportunities. **Rosé** ⊘ ★★★ Palest salmon pink **15** from grenache has heady rosepetal nose with red berry & cherry flavours; dry, refreshing & undoubtedly food friendly.

Cabernet Sauvignon (NEW) ★★★ Mostly for US market, **13** has very intense, ripe cassis nose so initially tastes drier than you expect, then sweetness reappears & persists on finish, as do powdery tannins. WO W Cape, as most of these. **Chardonnay** (NEW) ★★★ Also mainly for US market, **14** oozes pear & white peach ripeness, balanced somewhat by zesty lime acidity. **Chenin Blanc** ⊘ ★★★★ Sourced widely, unwooded **15** is a summery fruit salad of a wine, refreshing with pear, peach, melon, apple & even a hint of tangy grapefruit. Also tasted: **Cabernet Sauvignon-Merlot** ⊘ 13 ★★★☆ **Semi-Sweet** 15 ★★★ **Sauvignon Blanc** ⊘ 15 ★★★☆ — JG

Location: Stellenbosch ▪ Map: Helderberg ▪ WO: Stellenbosch/Western Cape ▪ Est/1stB 1994 ▪ Tasting & sales on home farm, cnr R44 & Winery Rd: Mon-Fri 9-5 Sat 9.30-3.30 ▪ Fee R60/6 wines, R100/entire range ▪ Closed Good Fri, Dec 25 & Jan 1 ▪ Sundays & after hours tasting available at 96 Winery Rd Restaurant ▪ Owner(s) Ken & Teresa Forrester ▪ Cellarmaster(s) Ken Forrester (1994) ▪ Winemaker(s) Ken Forrester (1994) & Martin Meinert ▪ Viticulturist(s) Pieter Rossouw (Oct 2009) ▪ (grenache, merlot, mourv, shiraz, chenin) ▪ 1,041t/148,000cs own label 35% red 65% white ▪ Other export brand: Workhorse (Marks & Spencer) ▪ Brands for clients: Woolworths ▪ ISO 9001:2000, BWI, HACCP, SEDEX, WIETA ▪ PO Box 1253 Stellenbosch 7599 ▪ info@kenforresterwines.com ▪ www.kenforresterwines.com ▪ S 34° 1' 31.06" E 018° 49' 05.92" ▪ F +27 (0)21-855-2373 ▪ **T +27 (0)21-855-2374**

☐ **Kevin Arnold** see Waterford Estate
☐ **Kevin King** see South Hill Vineyards
☐ **Khoi Klaas** see Ashton Kelder
☐ **Kindred** see Boutinot South Africa

Kingna Distillery ⓠ ⓞ

Besides wedding celebrants and conference delegates, Norbert Engel's farm at Montagu accommodates brandy lovers with his boutique distillery. Since 2007, brandy master Ruan Hunlun has been crafting colombard grapes into pure potstill: first a 5 Year Old and now an 8, probably followed by 10 and 12 as the 2,000L still and French/American oak barrels yield their riches over time.

★★★★ **Potstill Brandy 8 Year Old** (NEW) Karoo sunshine in a bottle! Gorgeous notes of violet & orange blossom leading to smooth enveloping candied fruit, entwined with gentle cinnamon spice & chocolate. **Potstill Brandy 5 Year Old** ⓧ ★★★ Smooth textured, light, 'feminine' & elegant, with fresh apricot, fynbos, clove & floral perfume; oak rather obvious. From colombard, like sibling. — WB, TJ

Location/WO: Montagu ▪ Map: Klein Karoo & Garden Route ▪ Est 2007 ▪ 1stB 2012 ▪ Tasting, sales & distillery tours Mon-Fri 10-5 Sat/Sun by appt ▪ Closed Easter Sat/Sun, Dec 25/26 & Jan 1 ▪ Tour groups ▪ Conferences ▪ Weddings/functions ▪ Owner(s) Norbert Engel ▪ Brandy master Ruan Hunlun (Jan 2005, consultant) ▪ 1,000ha/8ha (chenin, cbard) ▪ 140t/9,000L ▪ PO Box 395 Montagu 6720 ▪ ruan@kingna.co.za ▪ www.kingna.co.za ▪ S 33° 49' 45.87" E 20° 15' 39.10" ▪ F +27 (0)23-614-2721 ▪ **T +27 (0)23-614-2721**

☐ **Kipepeo** see Baratok Wines

Kirabo Private Cellar ⓠ ⓟ ⓐ ⓞ ⓑ

Breedekloof estate Watervalkloof, home of Kirabo (an African word meaning 'Gift from God'), has been farmed by six generations of the Le Roux family. Pieter and Karen le Roux sell off most of the grapes, but also vinify small parcels of red wine for regular, mostly private clients and visitors. The current releases are Merlot, Petit Verdot, Shiraz, Cupcake (merlot-shiraz) and No. 1ne (cab-shiraz).

Location: Rawsonville ▪ Map: Breedekloof ▪ Est 2002 ▪ 1stB 2003 ▪ Tasting, sales & cellar/vineyard tours Mon-Fri 8.30-5 Sat by appt ▪ Closed all pub hols ▪ Meals by appt only ▪ Facilities for children ▪ Tour groups ▪ Farm produce ▪ BYO picnic ▪ Walking/hiking/4x4 trails ▪ Weddings/functions ▪ Conservation area ▪ Owner(s) Pieter & Karen le Roux ▪ Cellarmaster(s) Pieter le Roux (2002) ▪ Winemaker(s) Pieter & Karen le Roux (2002) ▪ Viticulturist(s) Pieter le Roux ▪ 1,000t/10,000L total ▪ 10t own label 100% red ▪ IPW ▪ PO Box 96 Rawsonville 6845 ▪ info@kirabocellar.co.za ▪ www.kirabocellar.co.za ▪ S 33° 42' 36.68" E 019° 21' 27.55" ▪ F +27 (0)23-349-6764 ▪ **T +27 (0)23-349-6764**

Klawer Wine Cellars

(icons)

This large Olifants River producer's winemaking team, handling grapes off more than 2,000 ha of vines in two cellars (Klawer and Trawal), are itching to optimise special blocks and vineyards on their growers' farms. Impetus for the limited-edition, cellardoor-only range or separate brand being considered comes from recently appointed GM Andries Blake (dynamic former Swartland Winery cellarmaster with his own wine label), additional fermentation capacity, and marketing inroads into Russia and China.

★★★★ Hanepoot (icon) **09** fortified dessert shows intensity & freshness, well-handled sweetness, orange peel & apricot complexity. Cellar further for more delicious development. Rung above **08** (★★★★).

Cabernet Sauvignon (icon) **★★★** Best & most serious of the reds, **14** packs a lot of weight, offers value for money. Dark fruit & cedar, full & creamy. Will improve with short-term ageing. **Merlot ★★** Notably riper **14** has black plum & chocolate; typical tealeaf character still present on palate, providing dryness along with tannic finish. Best to decant or allow year or two. **Chardonnay ★★★** Less oak impression on **15**, with only 30% older wood, has lemon freshness & bone-dry grip. Leaner than previous, like other whites from this vintage. **Michelle Vin Doux Sparkling ★★☆** Complete jovial party package, from attractive blush appearance through lively fizz to dulcet finish. Low-alcohol **15** from red muscadel, touch sweeter than previous. **Red Muscadel ★★★★** Intensely sweet **14** appealing jasmine, orange syrup & red apple perfumes, touch more sugar than previous but still harmonious, with classy spirit warmth. Also tasted: **Pinotage 14 ★★☆ Shiraz 13 ★★ Chenin Blanc 15 ★★☆ Sauvignon Blanc 15 ★★** Not retasted: **Shiraz-Merlot 12 ★★☆ Viognier 13 ★★★★ African Ruby Rooibos NV ★★★★ White Muscadel 13 ★★★★ Travino Matador NV ★★** — HJ

Location: Klawer ▪ Map/WO: Olifants River ▪ Est 1956 ▪ Tasting & sales Mon-Fri 8–5 Sat 9–1 ▪ Facilities for children ▪ BYO picnic ▪ Conferences (office hours only) ▪ Owner(s) 92 members ▪ Manager Andries Blake ▪ Cellarmaster(s) Pieter van Aarde (Nov 2011) ▪ Winemaker(s) Roelof van Schalkwyk, Cerina van Niekerk, Christo Beukes, Bennie Avenant & Mariska de Bruyn ▪ 2,095ha (cab, merlot, ptage, ruby cab, shiraz, chard, chenin, cbard, hanepoot, muscadel, sauv, viog) ▪ 43,000t/60,000cs own label 40% red 40% white 5% rosé 15% other ▪ Other export brand: Travino ▪ ISO 22000:2009, Organic, DLG, IPW ▪ PO Box 8 Klawer 8145 ▪ klawerwyn@kingsley.co.za ▪ www.klawerwine.co.za ▪ S 31° 47' 34.9" E 018° 37' 36.1" ▪ F +27 (0)27-216-1561 ▪ **T +27 (0)27-216-1530**

☐ **Klein Centennial** *see* Group CDV

Klein Constantia Estate

(icons)

At Klein Constantia, one of SA's great wine estates, renovations and upgrades, including a bespoke maturation facility for the legendary Vin de Constance, are almost complete. This has given MD Hans Astrom, viticulturist Craig Harris and winemaker Matt Day and their teams — who favour a natural and holistic approach to winemaking — the opportunity to focus more on their own vineyards. Increasing attention is being paid to sauvignon blanc; six are reviewed below, each crafted with the intention of maximising site expression. The 2015 harvest was not only an early and fast one on 'KC', as it is affectionately known, the team fought night and day to protect their vineyards as an inferno devastated close to 5,000 hectares of national park and private land as well as dwellings.

Estate Wines

★★★★☆ Estate Red Blend 13 is 68% cab, with petit verdot & malbec. Firm, authoritative but not stern, with compact core of cassis fruit, attractive leafy nuance. Usual well-judged oaking: all new (vs 60% for **12**), 12 months (vs 16); both vintages (& previous) should reward long cellaring.

★★★★★ Perdeblokke Sauvignon Blanc Barrel selection of single-vineyard fruit ferment/9 months on gross lees. **13** (★★★★★) elegant expression of white blossoms, fresh hay & quince, with estate's salinity, savoury conclusion, impressive length & weight — not flavour — from old oak. Follows standout **12**.

★★★★ Sauvignon Blanc Block 381 (NEW) Natural ferment, minimal sulphur, year on gross lees in neutral barrel for single-vineyard with a sea view. Distinctive **14** almond, apricot kernel & bruised apple characters, plenty of extract, full mouthfeel & leesy farewell.

★★★★ **Metis Sauvignon Blanc** Joint venture with France's Domaine Pascal Jolivet, involving one of the highest blocks & 'natural, minimalistic and unconventional approach'. Step-up **14** (★★★★☆) has **13**'s peach purity & intensity, pleasing saline leanness & minerality, balanced rather than arresting acidity.

★★★★☆ **Organic Sauvignon Blanc** (NEW) ⊘ Engaging struck match tinge, faint grass & quince on (unwooded) **14**, 2nd vintage but new to the guide; more textural than aromatic, weightier than the estate bottling with gravelly pithiness, salty suggestion.

★★★★ **Sauvignon Blanc 14** subdued nose but vivacious palate of gooseberry, grass & house's signature quince. More focused than KC bottling, perhaps slightly less distinguished than estate siblings — but oh so well done, & with a delicacy of touch.

★★★★☆ **Brut Méthode Cap Classique** Like **11** sparkling, **12**'s (★★★★) appealing brioche tone hints at France but intense fruitiness is pure South Africa. Cask-aged chardonnay, 20 months on lees, packed with apple intensity, bracing acidity; tad less refined than previous.

★★★★☆ **Vin de Constance** Iconic, ageworthy dessert from unbotrytised muscat de Frontignan aged in French & Hungarian oak (some new). **11** (★★★★★) generous & satisfying with silky texture, sweetness lifted by racy acidity. 3 years oaked vs 4 for also-tasted **09** (★★★★), with similar candied orange, fynbos fragrance, vanilla fudge & glazed pineapple flavours. No **10**. Last tasted by us was **08**. Also in magnum.

Also tasted: **Riesling 14** ★★★★☆ Not retasted: **Chardonnay 13** ★★★★☆ Not tasted: **Sauvignon Blanc Block 382**.

KC range

Pinot Noir (NEW) ★★★ Lightish **14** easy-drinking styling with red cherries & toffee oak, bright acidity & juicy tail. WO W Cape. Also tasted: **Rosé 14** ★★★ **Sauvignon Blanc 14** ★★★★☆ Not retasted: **Cabernet Sauvignon-Merlot 12** ★★★★☆

Husk Spirit range

Spirit of Constance ⓧ ★★★ NV made from Vin de Constance husks, with powerfully grapey, floral scents. Soft, smooth, monolithic palate; lots of flavour but little finesse or delicacy. — WB, TJ, CvZ

Location: Constantia ▪ Map: Cape Peninsula ▪ WO: Constantia/Western Cape ▪ Est 1823 ▪ 1stB 1824 ▪ Tasting & sales Mon-Fri 9—5 Sat 10-5 (summer)/10—4.30 (winter) Sun 10-4 (summer only) ▪ Fee R30 ▪ Closed some pub hols ▪ Gift shop ▪ Estate honey for sale ▪ Collection of original Constantia bottles on display ▪ Owner(s) Zdenek Bakala, Charles Harman, Bruno Prats & Hubert de Boüard ▪ MD Hans Aström ▪ Winemaker(s) Matthew Day (2009) ▪ Brandy masters Matthew Day & Giorgio Dalla Cia (Dalla Cia) ▪ Viticulturist(s) Craig Harris (Oct 2013) ▪ 146ha/82ha (cabs s/f, malbec, merlot, p verdot, shiraz, chard, muscat de F, riesling, sauv, sem) ▪ 500t/80,000cs own label 30% red 70% white ▪ BWI champion ▪ PO Box 375 Constantia 7848 ▪ info@kleinconstantia.com ▪ www.kleinconstantia.com ▪ S 34° 2' 19.0" E 018° 24' 46.5" ▪ F +27 (0)21-794-2464 ▪ **T +27 (0)21-794-5188**

☐ **Kleindal** *see* Robertson Wide River Export Company

Klein DasBosch   ⓨ ⑪

Label vinified at Vriesenhof by Jan Coetzee for neighbour James 'Whitey' Basson, CEO of retailing empire Shoprite/Checkers. The wines can be tasted and purchased at Mont Marie Restaurant on Blaauwklippen Road, Stellenbosch. A selection also appears on a few other local restaurant lists and in Checkers stores.

Location/map: Stellenbosch ▪ Map grid reference: F7 ▪ Tasting & sales at Mont Marie Restaurant, Stellenbosch T +27 (0)21-880-0777 — phone ahead as tasting hours are subject to change ▪ Owner(s) James Wellwood Basson ▪ Viti/vini consultant Jan Coetzee (1997) ▪ Winemaker(s) Jan Coetzee (1994) ▪ ±25ha ▪ 90% red 10% white ▪ PO Box 12320 Stellenbosch 7613 ▪ annalette@kleindasbosch.com ▪ www.kleindasbosch.co.za ▪ www.montmarie.co.za ▪ S 33° 58' 56.0" E 018° 51' 44.5" ▪ F +27 (0)21-880-0999 ▪ **T +27 (0)21-880-0128/+27 (0)71-859-1773 (office)/+27 (0)21-880-0777 (tasting/sales)**

Klein Dauphine ⌂

The first cabernet was made in 2015, Diners Club Young Winemaker of the Year 2008 Ossie Sauermann reports, fleshing out the range of this Swiss-owned boutique Franschhoek Valley label. The 4-star guest cottage boasts spectacular mountain and valley vistas, making it a popular weekend getaway.

Location: Franschhoek ▪ Est 2001 ▪ 1stB 2003 ▪ Closed to public ▪ Fully equipped self-catering cottage (sleeps 2) ▪ Winemaker(s) Ossie Sauermann ▪ 2ha/0.5ha (cab, merlot) ▪ 3t 50% red 50% rosé ▪ PO Box 69 Simondium 7670 ▪ koch.willy@bluewin.ch ▪ www.kleindauphine.co.za ▪ **T +27 (0)21-876-2454**

Kleine Draken ⌘ 🍴 ♿

Still the sole kosher-only winery in SA, Kleine Draken aims to make 'good-quality, value-for-money Orthodox Union-certified wines under the supervision of the Cape Town Beth Din'. Replanting at home-farm Zandwijk on Paarl Mountain continues, winemaker Jean van Rooyen says, adding that his wines are vegan friendly as no animal products are used, and some are low alcohol.

Merlot ⓥ ★★ Inky simplicity to firm yet easy-drinking **13**. **Sauvignon Blanc** ★★ **15** clean & undemanding, with light fresh fruit. **Vin Doux** ⓥ ★★ Sweet watermelon notes on low-alcohol (8%) **NV** sparkler from sauvignon & riesling. **Natural Sweet Red** ⓥ ★★ Sweet herbal notes on **NV** merlot. Low-alcohol, like all the sweet desserts. Not retasted: **Cabernet Sauvignon 13** ★★★ **Kiddush NV** ★★ **Semi-Sweet Rosé NV** ★★ **Chardonnay 13** ★★ **Natural Sweet White NV** ★★ Not tasted: **Rosé**. Discontinued: **Dry Red**. — GdB

Location/WO: Paarl ▪ Map: Paarl & Wellington ▪ Map grid reference: D6 ▪ Est 1983 ▪ 1stB 1988 ▪ Tasting & sales Mon-Fri 8–4 ▪ Closed all pub hols & Jewish holy days ▪ Cellar tours by appt ▪ Pre-booked kosher picnics available ▪ Owner(s) Cape Gate (Pty) Ltd ▪ Winemaker(s) Jean van Rooyen (Dec 2007) ▪ Viticulturist(s) Frank Pietersen (1984) ▪ 12.5ha/8ha under vine ▪ 55t/20,000cs own label 50% red 47% white 3% rosé ▪ IPW, OU certified ▪ PO Box 2674 Paarl 7620 ▪ zandwijk@capegate.co.za ▪ www.kosherwines.co.za ▪ S 33° 46' 33.3" E 018° 56' 50.4" ▪ F +27 (0)21-863-1884 ▪ **T +27 (0)21-863-2368**

☐ **Kleine Parys** see Klein Parys Vineyards
☐ **Kleine Rust** see Stellenrust

Kleine Zalze Wines ⌘ 🍴 ⌂ 📷 ♿

With almost two decades at family-run Kleine Zalze, owner and MD Kobus Basson builds on a strong base of previous winemakers with the dynamic combination of Alastair Rimmer's international experience and RJ Botha's local perspective. Six well-defined ranges are made, from fruit off home vineyards or sourced elsewhere in Stellenbosch and beyond, and a slew of awards attests to the quality that can be achieved. With a core of premium-quality chenin, the Family Reserve '13 was the overall best white wine at Concours Mondial 2015, and Kleine Zalze was New World Producer of the Year at the international Sommelier Wine Awards 2015 in London. But it is about more than wine: Kleine Zalze is also a destination, with a residential estate, golf course, hotel, conference centre and acclaimed restaurant.

Family Reserve range

★★★★☆ **Cabernet Sauvignon** ⓥ Cherries & cassis stand proud in **10** despite 22 months new oak; there's lush ripeness further enhanced by grape sorting, 50% whole berry ferment. Coconut & tobacco attest to the oak influence but tannins are supple. Has a long future.

★★★★ **Pinotage** ⓥ Bold, alluring **09** a few years back had structure to contain — just — its 15+% alcohol.

★★★★ **Shiraz** ⓥ Flagship **10** (★★★★★) 22 months new French oak. Morello cherries, sweet spice & scrub perfume, hint of salty liquorice, a step up on **09**. Seductively flavoured, vanilla-brushed creamy dark fruit around a firm tannin backbone.

★★★★☆ **Chenin Blanc** Result of multi-vineyard blending, partial wood ferment, then year more in barrel, no fining, filtration. **14** has stonefruit & citrus, vibrates with youthful freshness, showcases the quality the variety can reach. Will age well.

★★★★☆ **Sauvignon Blanc** ⓩ Multifaceted **13** shows citrus, pear, green fig & sage, intensity deepens on the palate. Racy lemon/lime acidity, as on **12** (★★★★★) focuses the wine, giving length; so fresh & tightly held will age beautifully. WO W Cape.

Vineyard Selection

★★★★☆ **Cabernet Sauvignon** ⓥ **12** (★★★★★) boldly ripe, but its dark-fruited spicy richness & espresso tones don't prepare you for the savoury tannins. A serious wine with a long future, yet with tempering succulence for earlier enjoyment. **11** also opulently ripe.

★★★★ **Shiraz** Layered black cherries & spice, **12**'s opulence draws you in, holds your attention with the ripe, round & smooth texture. New World in style & proudly so.

★★★★ **Shiraz-Mourvèdre-Viognier** Dark tones, meat, hedgerow berries, a campfire smoke nuance, there's plenty of interest in **13**, the juicy smooth drinkability an added bonus.

★★★★ **Chardonnay Barrel Fermented** Boldly opulent, **14** is packed with flavour, yellow peach & mango. The oak influence, seen on the palate, anchors the flavours, & in combo with salty acidity, gives a long, savoury finish.

★★★★ **Chenin Blanc Barrel Fermented** ⓩ Quince & green melon, pure & focused, **14** has lovely rounded texture. Partial barrel ferment, plus oak maturation, as for also-tasted **13**. Stonefruit & pear, with oatmeal savoury tones, ending fruity-fresh & tangy.

Also tasted: **Pinot Noir 13** ★★★☆

Cellar Selection

Gamay Noir ⓣ ★★★ One of only a handful on the market. Unwooded to allow the fruit full expression, **15**'s blueberry/mulberry zesty vibrancy doesn't disappoint. Coastal WO.

Cabernet Sauvignon ★★★ Tasty easy-drinking version of the variety, **13** has supple tannins, blackcurrants, & just enough freshness for solo enjoyment. Coastal WO. **Chenin Blanc Bush Vines** ⓥ ★★★★ Template for well-priced, fruity style chenin, achieved through selective regional picking. **15** offers litchi & winter melon, zesty, nicely dry. Coastal WO. **Sauvignon Blanc** ★★★★ Softly fruity, fig & passionfruit, **15**'s pleasure is in the refreshing drinkability. A good food match. Also tasted: **Merlot 13** ★★★ **Pinotage 14** ★★★☆ **Gamay Noir Rosé 15** ★★★ **Chardonnay Unwooded 15** ★★★ Discontinued: **Cabernet Sauvignon-Merlot**.

Méthode Cap Classique Sparkling range

★★★★ **Brut Rosé** ⓝⓔⓦ ⓥ Same time on the lees as Brut (10 months) but here a pinot noir/chardonnay blend. **NV** goes on a charm offensive with its pale copper hue, red berry perfume & tangy fruity-freshness. Delicious.

★★★★ **Brut** ⓝⓔⓦ ⓥ Similar blend to Vintage Brut, chardonnay/pinot noir but less time on the lees, expect fresher flavours, more apple in **NV**. A class act: purity, perfect fruit/acid balance, good length.

★★★★ **Vintage Brut** ⓩ Dry bubbly that oozes flavour & personality. **09** chardonnay/pinot noir, partial barrel ferment, 3 years on the lees. Lemon zest/brioche notes, great length. Same blend but **10** is fresher, drier. Citrus & red berries melded into a biscuity, fine-beaded delight. Both Stellenbosch WO.

Zalze range

Chenin Blanc Reserve ⓣ ★★★☆ Partly barrel fermented then oak matured, enriching **13**'s melon & quince flavours. Kept youthful by the racy acidity, promising further cellaring confidence. Coastal WO.

Shiraz-Grenache-Viognier ★★★ Brambleberries & earthy notes in shiraz-dominant **14**, has succulence & good length. **Cabernet Sauvignon-Shiraz Rosé** ★★★ Ticks all the boxes for a summer wine, berry-flavoured **15** is dry, light textured & pinkly pretty. Coastal WO. Also tasted: **Shiraz-Mourvèdre-Viognier 14** ★★★ **Bush Vine Chenin Blanc 15** ★★★ Not retasted: **Malbec Reserve 13** ★★ **Pinotage 10** ★★☆ **Sangiovese 13** ★★★ **Sauvignon Blanc 14** ★★★

Foot of Africa range

Chenin Blanc ★★★ There's tropical fruit to spare in zesty, tangy **15**. Also tasted: **Shiraz-Viognier 14** ★★☆ — CR

Location/map: Stellenbosch ▪ Map grid reference: E6 ▪ WO: Western Cape/Coastal/Stellenbosch ▪ Est 1695 ▪ 1stB 1997 ▪ Tasting & sales Mon-Sat 9–6 Sun 11–6 ▪ Fee R25/5 wines ▪ Closed Good Fri, Dec 25 & Jan 1 ▪ Terroir Restaurant ▪ Kleine Zalze Lodge ▪ De Zalze Golf Course ▪ Conference/function venue ▪ Owner(s) Kobus Basson ▪ Cellarmaster(s) Alastair Rimmer (Sep 2014) ▪ Winemaker(s) RJ Botha (Dec 2012), with Zara Conradie (Feb 2008) ▪ Viticulturist(s) Henning Retief (May 2006) ▪ 90ha (cab, merlot, shiraz, chenin, sauv) & 200ha leased vyds ▪ 2,300t/400,000cs own label 40% red 50% white 10% rosé ▪ PO Box 12837 Die Boord 7613 ▪ quality@kleinezalze.co.za ▪ www.kleinezalze.co.za ▪ S 33° 58' 14.1" E 018° 50' 8.9" ▪ F +27 (0)21-880-0716 ▪ **T +27 (0)21-880-0717**

Klein Gustrouw Estate

Following renovation of the Cape Dutch homestead in Stellenbosch's Jonkershoek Valley and replanting of the vineyards by businessmen Jannie Mouton and Markus Jooste, joint owners since 2007, the focus here remains on a red blend (from blocks around the area) and a sauvignon blanc (ex own grapes) by second-generation Neil Ellis Wines winemaker Warren Ellis.

★★★★ **Reserve** Slow-starting **12** blend of cab, cab franc & shiraz unfolds to rich, spicy berry aromas with a dry, well structured, robust palate; fine tannins will benefit from further maturation. Also in 1.5L.

★★★★ **Sauvignon Blanc** Variety-true aromas of cape gooseberries & passionfruit emerge from **14**, delicious, juicy summer wine with good lift & mineral undertones on its longish palate. — JPf

Location: Stellenbosch ▪ WO: Jonkershoek Valley ▪ Est 1817 ▪ 1stB 1993 ▪ Closed to public ▪ Owner(s) Klein Gustrouw (Pty) Ltd ▪ Winemaker(s) Warren Ellis (2006) ▪ Viticulturist(s) Pieter Smit (consultant) ▪ ±23ha/±14ha under vine ▪ 70% red 30% white ▪ PO Box 6168 Uniedal 7612 ▪ info@ kleingustrouw.co.za ▪ F +27 (0)86-609-7229 ▪ **T +27 (0)21-882-8152/+27 (0)82-445-4074**

Kleinhoekkloof   ⓥ

The De Jongh family members this edition celebrate a decade of winemaking from their vineyards in the Langeberg's rocky mountain soils and cool, breezy climate. Initial vinifications were at Robertson Valley wineries but since 2011 Theunis de Jongh has made small parcels in their own cellar. The portfolio, aimed at niche markets, includes Merlot, Petit Verdot, Pinot Noir, Shiraz, Rosé and Sauvignon Blanc.

Location: Ashton ▪ Map: Robertson ▪ Est 2004 ▪ 1stB 2006 ▪ Phone ahead for opening hours ▪ Owner(s) Raudan Trust ▪ Cellarmaster(s)/winemaker(s) Theunis de Jongh (2011) ▪ Viticulturist(s) Loure van Zyl (Mar 2004, consultant) ▪ 114ha/11.8ha (merlot, p verdot, pinot, shiraz, sauv, viog) ▪ 110t/2,400cs own label 45% red 40% white 15% rosé ▪ Other export brand: Mountain Eye ▪ PO Box 95134 Waterkloof 0145 ▪ theunis@khk.co.za ▪ www.kleinhoekkloof.co.za ▪ S 33° 46' 51.87'' E 020° 03' 17.30'' ▪ F +27 (0)86-677-5399 ▪ **T +27 (0)23-615-2121**

☐ **Klein Kasteelberg** see Group CDV
☐ **Kleinood** see Tamboerskloof Wine – Kleinood Farm

Klein Optenhorst   ⓥ

Wellington owner-viticulturist Naas Ferreira says he spends a lot of time and effort keeping his nearly quarter-century-old, postcard-size pinot noir block in tip-top condition for MCC sparkling. His reward in 2015 was 'one of the most perfect crops we've ever harvested'. Made by specialist Pieter Ferreira, the rosé bubbles are snapped up during two annual open days in the family farm's gorgeous gardens.

★★★★ **Pinot Noir Méthode Cap Classique** ⓥ Soupçon Elgin fruit in **12** (★★★☆) sparkling. Friendly strawberries & cream aromas, crisp bright palate. moreish, but less fine than **11**. — HJ

Location: Wellington ▪ Map: Paarl & Wellington ▪ Map grid reference: H1 ▪ WO: Western Cape ▪ Est/1stB 2001 ▪ Tasting & sales by appt ▪ Owner(s) Naas Ferreira ▪ Cellarmaster(s)/winemaker(s) Pieter Ferreira (2009, consultant) ▪ Viticulturist(s) Naas Ferreira (2001) ▪ 0.25ha (pinot) ▪ ±1t from own vyds, additional fruit from Shannon Vineyards in Elgin ▪ 100% MCC ▪ PO Box 681 Wellington 7654 ▪ kleinoptenhorstwines@gmail.com ▪ www.kleinoptenhorst.com ▪ S 33° 37' 48.60'' E 019° 3' 19.54'' ▪ **T +27 (0)21-864-1210**

Klein Parys Vineyards

Owner and cellarmaster Kosie Möller's extensive wine business is based on the tranquil fringe of Paarl, at Klein Parys farm, one of the area's oldest (founded 1692). Like the wines and vines, the cellardoor is constantly rejuvenated and expanded, and now includes restaurant Mi Casa, featured on two new wine and lifestyle programmes on local TV channel KykNet.

Family Selection

★★★★ Jacob ⓥ Attractive **09** combo mainly pinotage, shiraz, cab franc & petit verdot.

Charl Sias ⓥ **★★★★** Full-bodied & ripe **10**, exotic méthode cap classique sparkling from chardonnay, nouvelle, viognier & sauvignon. Not retasted: **Beatrix 07 ★★★ Niclas 08 ★★☆**

Kleine Parys Selection

Shiraz ★★★★ Ripe, plummy **14** a big step up from previous. Appealing tobacco aromas, smoked meat & pepper. **Charmat Selection** ⓝⓔⓦ **★★★** First release of **NV** second-tier bubbly, unusually from chenin & semillon. Fresh, fruity & dry. Pleasant, easy-drinking. **Red Muscadel ★★★** Distinctive grapey vibrancy on **NV** fortified dessert, malty/medicinal hint, extreme sweetness offset by firm grip of spirit. Also tasted: **Cabernet Sauvignon 14 ★★★ Merlot 14 ★★★ Chenin Blanc 15 ★★★** Not retasted: **Pinotage 12 ★★★ Pinotage Coffee Style 11 ★★★ Chardonnay 13 ★★☆ Sauvignon Blanc 13 ★★☆ Méthode Cap Classique 09 ★★★** — GdB

Location: Paarl ▪ Map: Paarl & Wellington ▪ Map grid reference: E5 ▪ WO: Paarl/Western Cape ▪ Est 1692 ▪ 1stB 2002 ▪ Tasting, sales & cellar tours Mon-Fri 10-5 Sat 10-3 ▪ Fee R20/4 wines ▪ Closed Good Fri, Dec 25 & Jan 1 ▪ Facilities for children ▪ Conferences ▪ Weddings/functions ▪ Mi Casa Restaurant ▪ Owner(s) Kosie Möller ▪ Cellarmaster(s)/winemaker(s) Kosie Möller (2002) ▪ 56ha/45ha (cab, shiraz, chard, chenin) ▪ 1,800t/500,000cs own label 48% red 48% white 4% sparkling + 1m cs for clients ▪ Brands for clients: Millers Mile ▪ PO Box 1362 Suider-Paarl 7624 ▪ logistics@kparys.co.za ▪ www.kleinparysvineyards.co.za ▪ S 33° 45' 0.2" E 018° 58' 48.6" ▪ F +27 (0)21-872-8527 ▪ **T +27 (0)21-872-9848**

Klein Roosboom

Self-taught Karin de Villiers, wife of Durbanville Hills grower Jean, started this boutique winery in 2007 'to bottle my husband's passion for the vine'. Her own passion comes through in wines honouring family members, and in various pop-up events that regularly get her cellar 'moving and shaking'.

Klein Roosboom range

Nicol Merlot ★★★☆ Ever-improving tribute to older son, **13** has red berries & plums cloaked in slightly minty dark chocolate. **Marianna Roos Rosé** ⓝⓔⓦ **★★★** Winemaker's mother's memories live on in 'la vie en rose' **15** pink, from sauvignon & 25% merlot. Dry, with fresh berry flavours, calling for food at over 14.5% alcohol. Also tasted: **Jean Sauvignon Blanc 15 ★★★** Not retasted: **Johan Cabernet Sauvignon 12 ★★★☆ Janét Shiraz 13 ★★★ My Way 12 ★★★☆** Not tasted: **Marné Brut Méthode Cap Classique**.

Bandana range

Not tasted: **Blanc**. — JG

Location/WO: Durbanville ▪ Map: Durbanville, Philadelphia & Darling ▪ Est 1984 ▪ 1stB 2007 ▪ Tasting, sales & cellar tours Tue-Sun 10-4.30 ▪ Fee R25, waived on purchase (6 wines) ▪ Closed Good Fri, Dec 25/26 & Jan 1 ▪ Cheese & charcuterie platters ▪ Café Ruby T +27 (0)21-975-7965 open for breakfast & lunch ▪ Facilities for children ▪ Tour groups ▪ Season of Sauvignon festival (Oct) ▪ Owner(s) Jean de Villiers Trust ▪ Cellarmaster(s)/winemaker(s) Karin de Villiers (2007) ▪ Viticulturist(s) Jean de Villiers (1984) ▪ 260ha/130ha (cab, merlot, shiraz, chard, sauv) ▪ 3,000cs own label 40% red 60% white ▪ Postnet Suite #3 Private Bag X19 Durbanville 7551 ▪ info@kleinroosboom.co.za ▪ www.kleinroosboom.co.za ▪ S 33° 49' 6.24" E 018° 34' 25.86" ▪ F +27 (0)21-975-7417 ▪ **T +27 (0)82-784-5102**

☐ **Klein Simonsvlei** see Niel Joubert Estate
☐ **Klein Steenberg** see Steenberg Vineyards
☐ **Klein Tulbagh** see Tulbagh Winery
☐ **Klein Valley** see Calais Wine Estate

☐ **Klein Welmoed** *see* Foothills Vineyards

Klipdrift

One of SA's best-loved brands, nearing its 80th birthday and now not just the original Export blended brandy, but also a premium potstill (and the world's first brandy-based chocolate and coffee liqueur, Black Gold). Its iconic status – also as official spirit/brandy sponsor of SA's Springbok beloved rugby team – is celebrated by owner Distell at Klipdrift House on Robertson's main road, offering visitors boutique distillery tours, brandy-and-food pairings and long, lazy lunches.

★★★★☆ **Gold** ⓩ Seduces with complex aromas of dried apricot, raisin, orange peel & sweet spice. Finely textured, well rounded, much greater complexity than others. Vanilla & cinnamon come into greater focus just before long, fruit-filled finish. 100% potstill brandies of between 3 & 21 years age.

> **Export** ⊘ ⓥ ★★★★ The famous 'Klippies,' a standard blended brandy (30% potstill), but arguably the best of its type. Even more so with recent tweaks, which push it close to a higher rating. Remarkable quality at this price level. A pleasure to sniff those dried apricot, fynbos & toasty nut aromas, & so smooth & well balanced you could just about treat it as a liqueur brandy. From chenin & colombard, as all these.

Premium ⓩ ★★★★ Blend of 5-year-matured potstill with 70% unmatured spirit. Richer & fuller than Export, with greater maturity bringing sweet tobacco & spice from oak. Powerful, but not too harsh to sip neat. — WB, TJ

Location/map: Robertson ▪ Tasting Mon-Fri 9-5 Sat/pub hols 9.30-4 Sun (Oct-Apr) 10-3 ▪ Distillery tours Mon-Fri 10, 12 & 2.30 Sat/pub hols 10, 12 & 2 Sun (Oct-Apr) 11 & 1 – book ahead as opening & tour times may vary ▪ Brandy-and-food pairing ▪ Brandewyntuin restaurant ▪ Shop ▪ 4 Voortrekker Street Robertson 6705 ▪ info@klipdrift.co.za ▪ www.klipdrift.co.za ▪ S 33° 48' 40.86" E 019° 52' 55.63" ▪ **T +27 (0)23-626-3027**

☐ **Kloof Street** *see* Mullineux & Leeu Family Wines

Kloovenburg Wine & Olives

A shiraz, foot-crushed by winegrower Pieter du Toit's four children in 1997, resurrected winemaking on their Riebeek-Kasteel estate after a four-decade hiatus. It also birthed the Eight Feet label, now comprising a red and untasted white blend, for which more bushvine chenin, grenache blanc, roussanne and verdelho have been planted. Add wife Annalene's burgeoning olive business and little wonder an extra pair of hands, belonging to Jolandie Fouché, has joined the cellar.

★★★★ **Cabernet Sauvignon** Most classic of cellar's reds. Sleek **13** beautifully balanced cassis fruit & supple, yielding tannins. Lipsmacking in youth, rewards a few years' patience.

★★★★ **Shiraz** White pepper spicing to medium-weight, athletic **13**; well contained though ripe-fruit sweetness emerges in the finish. 15% bunch ferment adds freshness.

★★★★ **Eight Feet** Celebrates Du Toit juniors who crushed maiden modern vintage. Mostly shiraz, plus grenache, mourvèdre & carignan, **13** rich, velvety fruit, grainy tannins need bit more time to mesh.

★★★★ **Cape Vintage Shiraz** ⓩ Well-judged **08** port-style is welcomely lighter feeling, fruitcake & all but not dense, over-sweet or spirituous. 375 ml.

Merlot ★★★★ Medium-bodied **13** redolent of savoury smoked bacon, floral violet tones to subtle, elegant mouthful lifted by spice. **Sauvignon Blanc** ★★★★ Serious **15** has bracingly fresh frame for full fig flavour, intense grassy finish with persistence. **White From Red Brut** ★★★ Coppery pink **NV** carbonated dry sparkler from shiraz; quiet red-berry fruit lifted by busy bubble. Also tasted: **Barrel Fermented Chardonnay 15** ★★★☆ **Unwooded Chardonnay 15** ★★★ Not retasted: **Shiraz Rosé 14** ★★☆ Not tasted: **Naturally Fermented Chardonnay**. — DS

Location: Riebeek-Kasteel ▪ Map/WO: Swartland ▪ Est 1704 ▪ 1stB 1998 ▪ Tasting & sales Mon-Fri 9–4.30 Sat 9–2 Sun at Kloovenburg Pastorie Guest house 10.30-2 ▪ Fee R10 wine/olive tasting ▪ Closed Easter Fri-Mon, Dec 25/26 & Jan 1 ▪ Cellar tours during tasting hours ▪ Tour groups ▪ Gift shop ▪ Farm produce/olive products ▪ BYO picnic ▪ Walks/hikes ▪ Conservation area ▪ Christmas Market (Dec) ▪ Owner(s) Pieter du Toit ▪ Cellarmaster(s) Pieter du Toit (Jan 1998) ▪ Winemaker(s) Jolandie Fouché (Dec

2014) ▪ Viticulturist(s) Kobus van Graan (Jan 1998, consultant) ▪ 300ha/130ha (cab, merlot, shiraz, chard, chenin, grenache blanc, rouss, sauv, verdelho) ▪ 229t/24,000cs own label 55% red 40% white 4% rosé 1% sparkling ▪ PO Box 2 Riebeek-Kasteel 7307 ▪ info@kloovenburg.com ▪ www.kloovenburg.com ▪ S 33° 23' 36.3" E 018° 53' 27.5" ▪ F +27 (0)22-448-1035 ▪ **T +27 (0)22-448-1635**

☐ **Knor** *see* Knorhoek Wines

Knorhoek Wines   ⓨ ⓦ ⌂ ◎ ⓐ ⓖ

Taking its name from the far-off time when lions growled on these Simonsberg slopes, Knorhoek is a beautifully scenic estate farmed by two brothers, the fifth generation of Van Niekerks on this land. A popular venue for weddings, conferences and weekends away, with restaurant and recently upgraded guest house, Knorhoek's wines – made by scion Barry van Niekerk – more than match the country charm.

Pantére range

★★★★☆ **Cabernet Sauvignon** Inky **12** (★★★★) textured & delicious but a tad dry, grippier & less generously fruited than impressively crafted **11**.

★★★★ **Bordeaux Blend** ⓥ Bold fruitcake styling on **11**, like **09** a cab-led Bordeaux blend. Assured & rich, with layered, integrated fruit & oak, all-new French 2 years. Structured for the long haul. No **10**.

★★★★ **Chenin Blanc** ⓥ Heady honey notes vie with lively acid on confidently ripe **13**. Bright granadilla & peach supported by subtle oak. Similar to **12** (★★★★★) though not as opulent.

Knorhoek range

★★★★ **Cabernet Sauvignon** Boldly fruited yet succulent **12** (★★★★) shows good concentration & length. A shade off notable **10** (★★★★★) & **07**. **11**, **08**, **09** untasted.

★★★★ **Cabernet Franc** Poised & refined, with dark cocoa, earth & brush of fynbos, **13** is on par with **12**. Textured & silky smooth, with layers of flavour. 18 months older oak well knit.

Chenin Blanc ★★★ Honeyed overtone to fleshy **14**, with stonefruit juiciness. Also tasted: **Shiraz 13** ★★★ **Sauvignon Blanc 14** ★★★ Not retasted: **Merlot 12** ★★★★ **Pinotage 12** ★★★★ In abeyance: **Konfetti Rosé Sparkling**.

Two Cubs range

Rosé ★★★ Cranberry succulence & suggestion of sweetness ensure bags of appeal on **14** pink poolside sipper from shiraz & chenin. Stellenbosch WO. **Sauvignon Blanc** ★★★ Tangy citrus zest on lively **15**, uncomplicated & easy to drink. Also tasted: **Red Blend** ⓥ **14** ★★★ **Chenin Blanc 15** ★★★ Occasional release: **Pinotage**.

Knor range

Red Blend ⓥ ★★★ Shiraz leads in this **NV** blend which is likeable & cheery, albeit a touch chewy. **White Blend** ★★ Slight floral nuance to unfussy **14** blend, mainly chenin. Juicy & light. — FM

Location/map: Stellenbosch ▪ Map grid reference: F3 ▪ WO: Simonsberg–Stellenbosch/Stellenbosch ▪ Est 1827 ▪ 1stB 1997 ▪ Tasting, sales & cellar tours daily 10–5 ▪ Fee R20/5 wines ▪ Closed Dec 25 ▪ Towerbosch Restaurant Wed-Sun 11.30-3.30 (Sat/Sun booking essential T +27 (0)21-865-2958) ▪ Facilities for children ▪ Tour groups ▪ Gift shop ▪ Weddings/conferences ▪ Hiking trail ▪ Horse riding ▪ Conservation area ▪ 3-star guest house & self-catering cottages ▪ Owner(s) Hansie & James van Niekerk ▪ Cellarmaster(s)/winemaker(s) Barry van Niekerk (Jan 2014) ▪ Viticulturist(s) James van Niekerk (1977) ▪ ±80ha (cabs s/f, merlot, ptage, shiraz, chenin, sauv) ▪ 640t/20,000cs own label 51% red 42% white 4.65% rosé 2.35% sparkling & 184,500L bulk ▪ BWI ▪ PO Box 2 Koelenhof 7605 ▪ office@knorhoek.co.za, cellar@knorhoek.co.za, towerbosch@knorhoek.co.za ▪ www.knorhoek.co.za ▪ S 33° 52' 44.8" E 018° 52' 19.1" ▪ F +27 (0)21-865-2627 ▪ **T +27 (0)21-865-2114**

☐ **Kobus** *see* Havana Hills
☐ **Koelenbosch** *see* Koelenhof Winery

Koelenhof Winery

Recent record crops and growing overseas wine demand (led by China) have encouraged ongoing expansion of facilities at this Stellenbosch grower-owned winery. Now they've appointed a production manager, Erika van Zyl, whose position on the winemaking team has been filled by Elsa du Plessis, who debuts along with a shiraz-led blend in the good-value eponymous range.

Koelenbosch range

Pinotage ★★★ Piquant red berries, **12** bolstered by savoury tannins. Drink now & for 3+ years.
Sangiovese ★★ Nutmeg & cloves, Morello cherries, **14** offers light-textured drinkability. **Pinotage Rosé Méthode Cap Classique** ⊘ **★★★** Variety now recognised in name. Expressive raspberry perfume & flavours in ultra-dry **11** bubbly. Good aperitif or food partner. Also tasted: **Shiraz 12 ★★☆**
Sauvignon Blanc 15 ★★ Not retasted: **Merlot 11 ★★★ Nineteenfortyone 12 ★★★ Chenin Blanc Wooded 13 ★★☆**

Koelenhof range

Pinotage ⊘ **★★☆** Returns to the guide with vanilla-nuanced plums in **13**, finishing softly round & smooth. **Koelenberg** ⊘ **★★★** Shiraz-led 4-part blend, lightly oaked **12** offers spiced fruit appeal.
Koelenrouge (NEW) ⊘ **★★★ 12** lightly oaked semi-sweet charmer from shiraz, cab & merlot.
Koelnektar ★★ Rosepetal & litchi, there's delicate sweetness in **14** from gewürztraminer, low 10.5% alcohol. **Sauvignon Blanc Vin Sec** ⊘ **★★★** Passionfruit & litchi in semi-sweet **15**, livened by zesty bubbles. Also tasted: **Pinotage Rosé 14 ★★ Koelenhoffer 15 ★★ Pinotage Rosé Vin Sec 15 ★★**
Not retasted: **Hanepoot 13 ★★★ Pinorto 12 ★★★** — CR

Location/map/WO: Stellenbosch ▪ Map grid reference: D1 ▪ Est 1941 ▪ 1stB 1970's ▪ Tasting & sales Mon-Thu 9–5 Fri 9–4 Sat/pub hols 10–2 ▪ Closed Easter Fri/Sun, Ascension day & Dec 25 ▪ Facilities for children ▪ BYO picnic ▪ Conference/function venue ▪ Owner(s) 67 shareholders ▪ GM Andrew de Vries (2006) ▪ Winemaker(s) Martin Stevens (Nov 2003) & Wilhelm de Vries (2002), with Elsa du Plessis (Dec 2014) ▪ Viticulturist(s) Wilhelm de Vries (2010) ▪ 16,500t/22,000cs own label 45% red 45% white 8% rosé 2% fortified + 2,000cs for clients & 100,000L bulk ▪ Other export brand: Simonsbosch ▪ IPW ▪ PO Box 1 Koelenhof 7605 ▪ koelwyn@mweb.co.za ▪ www.koelenhof.co.za ▪ S 33° 50' 5.2" E 018° 47' 52.7" ▪ F +27 (0)21-865-2796 ▪ **T +27 (0)21-865-2020/1**

Koelfontein

Seven generations of Conradies have farmed fruit on this high-altitude, sometimes snow-dusted farm along the Gydo Pass near Ceres. Grapes for brandy distillation were replaced by shiraz and chardonnay in the 1990s, the cool-climate quality attracting top-notch winemaker Dewaldt Heyns from Tulbagh's Saronsberg (and Dewaldt Heyns Family Wines) as consultant.

★★★★ Shiraz ⊘ Two vintages tasted: plush **10** outclasses **11** (★★★★) with its violets, smoky plums, dark chocolate. Supple oak tannins give ageing backbone, savoury tones. A silky delight.

★★★★☆ Chardonnay Pineapple & citrus piquancy in **13**, its perfectly judged oaking showing as a toasted almond seam, yet another layer of complexity. Balances flavour richness with elegance, finishing on a zesty, vibrant note. — CR

Location/WO: Ceres ▪ Map: Tulbagh ▪ Est 1832 ▪ 1stB 2002 ▪ Tasting & sales Mon-Fri 9-4 Sat 10-1 ▪ Closed all pub hols ▪ Farm produce ▪ BYO picnic ▪ Walks/hikes ▪ Conservation area ▪ Die Kloof self-catering historic house (sleeps 6) ▪ Owner(s) Handri Conradie ▪ Winemaker(s) Dewaldt Heyns (2004) ▪ Viticulturist(s) Hennie van Noordwyk ▪ 950ha/±6ha (shiraz, chard) ▪ ±24t/2,400cs own label 50% red 50% white ▪ BWI ▪ PO Box 4 Prince Alfred's Hamlet 6840 ▪ wine@koelfontein.co.za ▪ www.koelfontein.co.za ▪ S 33° 15' 54.70" E 019° 19' 29.28" ▪ F +27 (0)23-313-3137 ▪ **T +27 (0)23-313-3304/3538**

Konkelberg

As a burgher in the early Stellenbosch settlement, the backstory goes, the way to circumvent the prohibition on trading outside the Dutch East India Company ambit was to rendezvous at Konkelberg, a 'connivance corner' where the Stellenbosch and Helderberg mountains intersect. It's just a short hop away from today's Longridge cellar, where Jasper Raats and team produce a white and red, a rosé in the works.

Blend 54 ★★★ Shiraz with 4 others, accounting for **13**'s dark-fruited, smoky character. Medium body, with enough tannin grip for a few years' ageing. **Sauvignon Blanc ★★★** Elegant, refined **14** strikes a balance between fruit, leafiness & minerality, nothing overt, a gentle mix of flavours. — CR, CvZ

Location/WO: Stellenbosch ▪ Est 2011 ▪ 1stB 2012 ▪ Tasting & sales by appt only ▪ Fee R20/3 wines ▪ Closed Good Fri, Dec 25 & Jan 1 ▪ Owner(s) Konkelberg Eiendoms Beperk ▪ Cellarmaster(s)/viticulturist(s) Jasper Raats (Jul 2011) ▪ 20ha/18ha (cab f, shiraz, chenin, sauv) ▪ 180t/25,000cs own label 48% red 48% white 4% rosé plus 1,000cs for clients ▪ PO Box 2023 Dennesig 7601 ▪ konkelberg@gmail.com ▪ www.konkelberg.co.za ▪ **T +27 (0)72-026-5044**

Koopmanskloof Wingerde

This early 19th-century Stellenbosch property on the viticulturally reputed Bottelary Hills comprises a sizable landholding of six farms, including one belonging to Koopmanskloof employees. A substantial 100-ha nature reserve, legacy of the late, redoubtable Stevie Smit, lies alongside vineyards currently being renewed by son Stephan, who's also expanding red-wine production facilities.

Koopmanskloof range

Cabernet Sauvignon ✓ **★★★★** Ready-to-enjoy **14**'s intense blueberry nose has hints of molasses & redcurrants. Generous, with polished tannins & satisfying weight; great with ostrich fillet. **Shiraz** ✓ **★★★★** Previewed **14**'s red fruit is spiced with clean leather, seamed with savoury; smooth tannins augur well for youthful enjoyment with or without food. **Pinotage Rosé ★★★** Chirpy **15** tank sample promises vivacious sunset sipping; dry, packed with berries, nicely spicy. **Sauvignon Blanc** ✓ **★★★** Variety-true **15** lightly textured but grabs attention with punchy cool grassy notes, riper tropical hints plus lime twist in the aftertaste. Also tasted: **Merlot 14 ★★★ Pinotage 13 ★★★ Chardonnay 15 ★★★ Chenin Blanc 15 ★★★** — GM

Location/WO: Stellenbosch ▪ Est 1801 ▪ 1stB 1970 ▪ Closed to public ▪ Private Nature Reserve ▪ Owner(s) Managed by Koopmanskloof Wingerde (Pty) Ltd ▪ Winemaker(s) Stephan Smit ▪ Viticulturist(s) Louwtjie Vlok ▪ 457ha (cab, carignan, merlot, ptage, roobernet, ruby cab, shiraz, chard, chenin, sauv, sem) ▪ ±3,700t/±2.5m L 50% red 50% white ▪ Other brands: Vredehoek, One World ▪ BWI, Fairtrade, IPW, WIETA ▪ PO Box 19 Koelenhof 7605 ▪ info@koopmanskloof.co.za ▪ www.koopmanskloof.co.za ▪ F +27 (0)86-560-7145 ▪ **T +27 (0)21-865-2355**

Kranskop Wines

This high-lying Langeberg Mountain vineyard is where Robertson-raised Newald Marais (30 years in corporate winemaking; consulting here before assuming sole ownership in 2010) has always wanted to be: hands in soil making wine to share as an experience. Set to make the experience even more pleasurable — and accessible to visitors with disabilities — are cellardoor upgrades in progress at press time.

★★★★ Viognier Noble Late Harvest Fruit to the fore in expressive **13**, molten apricot & pineapple, but the oak-effect caramel seam adds even more appeal. Richer, weightier than last-tasted **11** (**★★★★**).

Shiraz ⊛ **★★★** Has the expected spice & smokiness but **12**'s main attraction is the plush fruit, cherries & wild berries, allowed the spotlight by supporting oak. **Sauvignon Blanc** ⊛ **★★★★** Ideal food wine, citrus & green fig, **15**'s flavours bursting with vibrant health end on a mouthwatering limy acid note.

Tannat (NEW) **★★** Still quite closed, needing time, smoky, tarry **13** shows dark wild berries, the oak still in control of the flavours, though no hard edges. **12**, also reviewed, more accessible but predominantly savoury, should open further in 1-2 years. Also tasted: **Cabernet Sauvignon 12 ★★★ Merlot 11 ★★★ Pinot Noir 12 ★★★ Chardonnay 14 ★★★★ Viognier 14 ★★★★** — CR

Location/map: Robertson ▪ WO: Klaasvoogds ▪ Est 2001 ▪ 1stB 2003 ▪ Tasting, sales & tours Mon-Fri 10-4.30 Sat & pub hols 10-2 ▪ Closed Easter Sun & Dec 25 ▪ BYO picnic ▪ Owner(s)/viticulturist(s) Newald Marais ▪ Cellarmaster(s)/winemaker(s) Newald Marais (2008) ▪ 43ha/30ha (cab, merlot, pinot, shiraz, tannat, chard, sauv, viog) ▪ 240t/3,000cs own label 75% red 25% white ▪ BWI, IPW ▪ PO Box 49 Klaasvoogds 6707 ▪ newald@kranskopwines.co.za ▪ www.kranskopwines.co.za ▪ S 33° 47' 53.1" E 019° 59' 56.6" ▪ F +27 (0)23-626-3200 ▪ **T +27 (0)23-626-3200**

☐ **Krone** *see* Twee Jonge Gezellen Estate-House of Krone

Kronendal Boutique Winery

Insufficient water prompted Piet and Magdaleen Kroon to switch from growing fynbos (for an indigenous nursery) to vines on their boutique-scale property in Durbanville. Their founding philosophy of handcrafting and personal attention continues, and their desire is for the packaging of the Rhône blend (the Latin name translates as 'To Wonder At') to become more reflective of that artisanal approach.

★★★★ **Mirari 12** (★★★☆) similar shiraz-led blend as previous, some minty notes in its less concentrated flavours; brisk finish. **11** well rounded, balanced. Also available in 1.5L & 3L. — AL

Location/WO: Durbanville ▪ Map: Durbanville, Philadelphia & Darling ▪ Est 2003 ▪ 1stB 2006 ▪ Tasting, sales & cellar tours by appt ▪ Conference facilities ▪ Art ▪ Seasonal 'langtafel' lunches ▪ Owner(s) Pieter & Magdaleen Kroon ▪ Winemaker(s) Magdaleen Kroon ▪ 2ha/0.6ha (mourv, shiraz, tempranillo, viog) ▪ 4t/520cs own label 100% red ▪ PO Box 4433 Durbanville 7551 ▪ info@kronendalwine.co.za ▪ http://kronendal.belmet.co.za ▪ S 33°48' 30.78" E 018°36' 50.82" ▪ F +27 (0)86-603-1170 ▪ **T +27 (0)82-499-0198**

☐ **Kruger Family** *see* Stellenview Premium Wines

Kulsen Wines   ⓘ

Heinrich Kulsen is sold out of his first own-label wine, an impressive barrel-fermented chenin from 30-year-old Villiera bushvines, launched while on the three-year Cape Winemakers Guild Protégé Programme, offering promising young winemakers mentorships by CWG members. He hopes to continue focusing on old-vine whites, as well as Mediterranean reds.

Location: Stellenbosch ▪ Est/1stB 2013 ▪ Tasting by appt only ▪ Owner(s) Heinrich Kulsen ▪ Cellarmaster(s)/winemaker(s) Heinrich Kulsen (2013) ▪ kulsenwines@gmail.com ▪ www.kulsenwines.co.za ▪ **T +27 (0)73-234-6315**

Kumala   ⓘ

Owned by multinational Accolade Wines, Kumala has been a major SA export success story for over 15 years, with wines vinified from across the Western Cape going to some 40 countries (local tastings and sales at Accolade-owned Flagstone Winery). The Reserve range, featuring single-varietal regional wines (and innovative resin labels rendering the signature gold gecko on a black pebble in 3D) this edition welcomes a chardonnay and malbec.

Zenith range
Merlot-Cabernet Sauvignon-Shiraz ⊘ ★★★ Juicy off-dry **14** blend has dollop ruby cab & attractive savoury spiciness. Not retasted: **Rosé 14** ★★★ **Chenin Blanc-Chardonnay 14** ★★★

Reserve range

> **Swartland Malbec** 🆕 🍷 ★★★☆ Floral **14** flaunts ample personality in succulent, sweetly fruity mouthful. Fresh acidity & suitable tannic grip lend some elegance & structure.

Swartland Chardonnay 🆕 ★★★ Pleasingly fresh, lightly off-dry **14** in zesty tropical form, brushed with oak. Certified as WO W Cape. **Swartland Chenin Blanc** ★★★ Abundant melon, apple flavours in vibrantly fresh **14**, enhanced by touch complexity. Also tasted: **Swartland Shiraz 14** ★★★

Cape Collection
Merlot-Pinotage ⊘ ★★☆ Unassuming, off-dry & fruity **14** quaffer checked by decent grip.
Pinotage-Shiraz ★★ Sweet & smoky, mocha-toned **14** for early drinking. Also tasted: **Chardonnay-Semillon 14** ★

Core range
Shiraz-Mourvèdre ⊘ ★★☆ Lively, fresh & simply fruity **14** dry red with overly grippy finish. **Cabernet Sauvignon-Shiraz** ⊘ ★★☆ Nicely fresh, uncomplicated **14** has ample red fruit flavours. **Shiraz-Pinotage Rosé** 🆕 ★★ Off-dry **14** has some soft red fruit flavours & nicely dry finish. **Colombard-Chardonnay** ★★ Simple, light **14** isn't concentrated but shows agreeable freshness. **Sauvignon**

Blanc-Semillon ★★ Crisp appeal in light, dry, pleasantly straightforward **14**. Also tasted: **Cape Red NV** ★ **Rosé 14 ★☆ Cape White NV ★ Sauvignon Blanc-Colombard 14 ★☆ Medium Sweet White NV ★ Cape Medium Sweet Red NV ★** Not retasted: **Shiraz 12 ★★ Chardonnay 14 ★★★ Chenin Blanc-Chardonnay 14 ★★☆ Chenin Blanc-Viognier 13 ★★★** In abeyance: **Merlot-Ruby Cabernet**.

Winemakers Release

Ruby Cabernet-Merlot-Pinotage ⓧ **★★★** Tangy red fruit, hint of mint, dash of sweetness but fairly balanced **13**.

Dragon's Back

Dry Red ★ Mocha-tinged **NV**, fresh & easy ruby cab, cinsaut blend. **Medium Sweet White ★** Attractively crisp, sweet **NV** blend chenin, colombard. Also in magnum. Also tasted: **Medium Sweet Rosé NV ★★ Dry White NV ★ Medium Sweet Red NV ★**

Eternal range

Chenin Blanc-Chardonnay-Semillon ⓧ **★★★** Candy confection, fruity & ripe **14**, pleasant sipping. Not retasted: **Merlot-Cabernet Sauvignon-Shiraz 13 ★★★** — IM

Location: Somerset West ▪ WO: Western Cape/Swartland ▪ Tasting, sales & cellar tours at Flagstone Winery ▪ Owner(s) Accolade Wines South Africa ▪ Winemaker(s) Ben Jordaan (Jul 2002), Gerhard Swart (Sep 2008) & Bruce Jack (1998) ▪ 50% red 50% white ▪ PO Box 769 Stellenbosch 7599 ▪ flagstone@accolade-wines.com ▪ www.kumala.co.za ▪ F +27 (0)21-852-5085 ▪ **T +27 (0)21-852-5052**

Kupferberger Auslese

Liquid history, this 1952 Distell stalwart was among the first to benefit from cold and controlled fermentation of white wines.

Kupferberger Auslese ⓧ **★★** Last-tasted **NV** from widely sourced chenin is lightish, simple, but with better-balanced sweetness. — DB

Kuypers Kraal   ⓧ NEW

Consumers familiar with Fair Cape dairy products will have an instant connection with this new wine label, originating in Philadelphia north of Durbanville. The Loubser family has been farming in the area for 150 years, and the current generation, five brothers, also cultivate grapes. Previously vinifying for own and friends' consumption, they have now been persuaded by two other wine families, the De Waals (Oude Denneboom) and Le Rouxs (Vendôme) to go to market via the joint venture, Kaapse Familie Wingerde, listed separately. The debut Sauvignon Blanc will soon be joined by 'an excellent Pinotage'.

Sauvignon Blanc ★★★★ Lots going on, fennel, chopped herbs, gooseberries, **14**'s crisp dryness anchors the flavours. — CR, CvZ

Location: Philadelphia ▪ WO: Coastal ▪ Est 1991 ▪ 1stB 2014 ▪ Tasting & sales at Vendôme (see entry) ▪ Owner(s) Loubser brothers ▪ Cellarmaster(s) Altus le Roux (consultant) ▪ Winemaker(s) Bernard Smuts ▪ Viticulturist(s) Viljee Loubser ▪ 1,500ha/100ha (cab, ptage, sauv) ▪ 1,000t/400cs own label 100% white ▪ WIETA ▪ Malanshoogte Road Durbanville 7550 ▪ viljee@faircape.com ▪ www.faircape.com ▪ F +27 (0)21-972-1973 ▪ **T +27 (0)86-169-6455**

KWV   ⓧ ⓧ ⓧ ⓧ

Founded in 1918 as the Ko-operatiewe Wijnbouwers Vereniging van Zuid-Afrika, later accorded statutory control over the Cape wine industry, KWV has evolved into a producer of over 100 products represented in more than 100 markets globally, and a leader in the arena of black economic empowerment. Its long-standing international reputation for fine wines, fortifieds and brandies is matched by modern wine tourism initiatives, no more visibly than at stately La Concorde HQ in Paarl. See separate listings for KWV Brandies and Sherry-Style Wines. Note: KWV's wine ranges and brands (Abraham Perold Heritage Collection, Bonne Esperance, Café Culture, Cathedral Cellar, Classic Collection, Concordia, Laborie, Pearly Bay, Reserve Collection and Roodeberg) not tasted this edition.

Location: Paarl ▪ Map: Paarl & Wellington ▪ Map grid reference: E6 ▪ KWV Wine Emporium: Kohler Street, T +27 (0)21-807-3007/8 F +27 (0)21-807-3119, friederm@kwv.co.za, www.kwvwineemporium.co.za ▪ Tasting & sales Mon-Sat 9–4.30 Sun 11-4 ▪ Several food & wine pairings available ▪ Cellar tours: Eng Mon-Sat 10, 10.30 & 2.15; Ger 10.15; Sun Eng 11 ▪ Tour groups by appt ▪ Closed Good Fri, Dec 25 & Jan 1 ▪ KWV Sensorium: 57 Main Road, T +27 (0)21-807-3094, sensorium@kwv.co.za, www.kwvsensorium.co.za ▪ Tasting, sales & art museum Mon-Fri 9-4.30 Sat 9-2 ▪ Art & wine pairing ▪ Owner(s) KWV (Pty) Ltd ▪ Chief winemaker Johann Fourie ▪ Winemaker(s) Anneke du Plessis, Izelle van Blerk, Louwritz Louw, Kobus van der Merwe, Monique Fourie & Thornton Pillay ▪ Viticulturist(s) Marco Ventrella & De Wet Hugo ▪ PO Box 528 Suider-Paarl 7624 ▪ customer@kwv.co.za ▪ www.kwv.co.za ▪ S 33° 45' 46.87" E 018° 57' 59.92" (Emporium), S 33° 45' 43.26" E 018° 57' 44.06" (Sensorium) ▪ F +27 (0)21-807-3000 ▪ **T +27 (0)21-807-3911 (office)**

KWV Brandies

Their international reputation is as burnished as the massive copper pot and six-column stills that, together with several thousand barrels of maturing elixir, impress visitors to KWV's dedicated House of Brandy in Worcester. The 10, 12, 15 and 20 Year Old have each shone as the International Wine & Spirit Competition's World's Best Brandy, as have the Laborie Alambic and Imoya. Similar success at the International Spirits Challenge culminated in the trophy in 2015 for world's top brandy/cognac producer, a first for a non-cognac brand. Brandy master Pieter de Bod was particularly thrilled to preside over the release of two even more exceptional products: the evocatively packaged 30-year-old Nexus, among KWV's first brandies in the super-super-premium category, and XO Heritage Cognac, understood to be the first cognac produced under a South African-owned brand name.

★★★★★ **Nexus** (NEW) Superb packaging featuring individually crafted bottle & wooden casing sets the scene: fine floral notes, wafts of soft spice, dried pears & apple follow on to intense fruit on the palate. Elegant, regal & oh so smooth, with a dry lingering citrus bite on the finish. Astounding quality.

★★★★★ **20 Year Old** (✷) Exquisite aromas – sandalwood, apricot, scented flowers, hints spice & oxidative maturity. Rich & full, yet super-refined & delicate. A touch less forceful than 15YO, but more grace. Beautifully balanced, with supreme oak support. Long, mellow, mature notes carry to slightly sweet finish.

★★★★★ **15 Year Old Alambic** (✷) Attractive honey, soft spice & dried fruit with floral backing & some fine oak. Smooth, fine texture & good balance; great complexity from a range of citrus & rich fruitcake flavours. Mellow & mature, with everlasting finish.

★★★★★ **12 Year Old Barrel Select** (✷) Rich, robust with caramelised nuts, sun-dried peaches, pear drop on the nose. The palate is that & more. Layers of cashew nut flavours melt in the mouth, honey, dark chocolate & fine sprinkling of spice. A triumph.

★★★★★ **10 Year Old Vintage** (✓) Now 100% potstill & even more exquisite. Jewel bright & delicate, with fruity citrus aromas, dried apple, spice & dark chocolate on the palate. Rounded & full bodied, with a long mellow finish.

★★★★☆ **Laborie Alambic** Unique 5 year old potstill from chardonnay & pinotage. Revisited, is smoother with more depth (meriting higher rating), retaining its essential delicacy. Floral notes, hints of toasty almond & fresh apricot, seamlessly supported by gentle vanilla. Elegant 500 ml packaging

★★★★ **Imoya Fine Potstill** Modern, beautifully presented brandy, retasted this edition. Fresh fruity aromas & flavours; elegant, rich balance, subtle texture with nutty, spicy oak in support, lifted with a fresh spirity finish. 100% potstill of up to 20 years.

★★★★ **5 Year Old Superior** (✓) Notes of sweet caramel, fruit, nuts & vanilla. Excellent balance, clean & lightly fiery on sweet-tinged finish. Blended; could compete with pure potstills on their turf!

3 Year Old Finest Blend (✷) ★★★★ Less aggressive than many young blended brandies – sippable neat. Fruity nose with caramel, dark molasses, tealeaves. Sufficiently complex, balanced. — WB, TJ

KWV Sherry-Style Wines

Besides the Cape Tawny and Red Muscadel for which it has long been known, KWV's fortified range includes sherry-style wines – the pair below and an untasted Cape Pale Dry. All are from chenin blanc and colombard, aged a year in small barrels and a further 3-6 in solera.

★★★★ **Cape Medium Cream** Ⓞ Golden brown, with candied apricot, orange peel & caramelised nuts. Balanced, fresh yet savoury, gentle spirity warmth.

★★★★ **Cape Full Cream** Ⓞ Pale amber; stewed fruit, a delightful floral note; layered nuts & rich caramel, complex, elegant. Although sweet, uncloying finish is savoury, lifted by a spirity glow. — CR

Kyburg Wine Estate

Named for an historic village and castle in their native Switzerland, Fred and Rosmarie Ruest's Devon Valley estate this year marks a decade of mostly red-wine making from vineyards replanted soon after purchase in 1998. The anniversary coincides with the release of their first white, a chenin blanc from Coastal grapes, which missed our tasting deadline.

★★★★ **Shiraz** Ⓞ Spicy whiff livened up slightly jammy notes on **09** (★★★☆). Tasty, if more straightforward than still-available **08**.

33 Latitude ★★★☆ Cab-based **10** with merlot & shiraz a touch more graceful & together than the Cab, with good fruit depth along with savoury-succulent element. Also in magnum, like Select. **33 Latitude Select** (ⁿᵉʷ) ★★★★ Similar blend to straight version, but this **10** with all-new oak, which dominates aromas & flavours, & adds drying tannin. Might resolve in time, if fruit intensity is enough. Also tasted: **Cabernet Sauvignon 10** ★★★★ Not retasted: **Merlot 09** ★★★★ — TJ

Location/map: Stellenbosch ▪ Map grid reference: D4 ▪ WO: Devon Valley ▪ Est 1998 ▪ 1stB 2006 ▪ Tasting & sales by appt ▪ Self-catering guest house (exclusive use, rental min 2 weeks) ▪ Owner(s) Fred & Rosmarie Ruest ▪ Cellarmaster(s)/winemaker(s) Jacques Fourie (Jan 2006, consultant) & Chris Keet (2013-2015, consultant) ▪ Viticulturist(s) Frans Snyman (Jul 2006) & Chris Keet (2014-2015, consultant) ▪ 28ha/17ha (cab, merlot, shiraz) ▪ 150t/5,000cs own label 90% red 10% white ▪ PO Box 12799 Die Boord 7613 ▪ info@kyburgwine.com ▪ www.kyburgwine.com ▪ S 33° 54' 59.3" E 018° 49' 28.4" ▪ **T +27 (0)21-865-2876**

☐ **La Bonne Vigne** *see* Wonderfontein

Laborie Wine Farm Ⓞ ⑪ ⌂ ◉ ♿

KWV-owned showcase Laborie is an island of tranquility in bustling Paarl, with vineyards stretching up Paarl mountain, tastefully restored historic buildings and wide-ranging visitor offering. The wine portfolio is equally comprehensive and includes specialisations such as the unique Pineau de Laborie, sweet pinotage fortified with pinotage brandy. Low-alcohol range Lazy Days is a recent addition.

Location: Paarl ▪ Map: Paarl & Wellington ▪ Map grid reference: E6 ▪ Est 1691 ▪ Tasting & sales Sun-Thu 11-5 Fri & Sat 11-8 ▪ Fee R30/5 wines R35/farm tour & tasting ▪ Macaron & MCC R50 ▪ Charcuterie & wine R50 ▪ Chocolate & wine pairing R45 ▪ Olive & wine pairing R35 ▪ Closed all Christian pub hols ▪ Tours for large groups by appt ▪ Harvest Restaurant ▪ Tapas ▪ Carols by Candlelight ▪ Conferences ▪ Weddings/functions ▪ Laborie Guest House ▪ Owner(s) KWV (Pty) Ltd ▪ Winemaker(s) Johann Fourie & Kobus van der Merwe ▪ Brandy master Pieter de Bod (Nov 2011) ▪ Viticulturist(s) Marco Ventrella, with De Wet Hugo ▪ (p verdot, petite sirah, ptage, pinots noir/meunier, shiraz, chard, chenin, sauv) ▪ BWI, IPW, WIETA ▪ PO Box 528 Suider Paarl 7624 ▪ info@laboriewines.co.za ▪ www.laboriewines.co.za ▪ S 33° 45' 55.2" E 018° 57' 27.6" ▪ F +27 (0)21-863-1955 ▪ **T +27 (0)21-807-3390**

La Bri Estate Ⓞ ⑪ ◉

This Franschhoek estate is the name-bearing part of the first farm in the area allocated to refugee French Huguenots. Current innovation sees new plantings and new wines – including an MCC bubbly (untasted by us), and a Cellar Door range reflecting Irene Waller's experimentation. The latter will be available only at the estate – alongside a range of sensory experiences: adding to tastings of wine and chocolate and wine and biltong, the cellardoor now offers visitors the chance to sample wine with Turkish delight.

★★★★ **Cabernet Sauvignon Limited Release** Ⓞ Floral, cassis & earthy tones, with tightly wound palate; **12** firm, slightly grainy tannin should even out in time. Only in best years – last was **09** (★★★☆).

★★★★ **Merlot** Bright, immediately appealing **13**, with, at 35%, a little more new oak than **12** (★★★☆) & responding admirably. Supple, balanced & rather elegant, charming as La Bri's lovely labels.

★★★★ **Affinity** Cab (48%) & merlot lead **13** Bordeaux blend. More imposing than, say, Merlot, & more serious tannic structure. Neat, balanced; sweet fruit within elegance's bounds. Like Cab, also in magnum.

Chardonnay ★★★☆ **14** a winning combo of ripe fresh fruit & cleverly calculated oaking for a toasted nut hint. Ingratiatingly only just-dry, with lovely sweet pear notes. Also tasted: **Syrah 13** ★★★☆ Not retasted: **Viognier Limited Release 13** ★★★☆ — TJ

Location/map/WO: Franschhoek ▪ Est 1694 ▪ Tasting, sales & cellar tours Mon-Fri 10-5 Sat 10.30-4 ▪ Fee R35-R45pp, waived on purchase ▪ Closed Easter Fri/Mon, Dec 25/26 & Jan 1 ▪ Chocolate & wine pairing; biltong & wine experience; Turkish delight & wine pairing ▪ Cheese platters ▪ Bicycle friendly ▪ Old wine cellar open by appt ▪ Weddings & functions ▪ Part of Franschhoek tram route ▪ Owner(s) Robin Hamilton ▪ Winemaker(s) Irene Waller (Oct 2010), with Glen Isaacs (Jun 2009) ▪ Viticulturist(s) Gerard Olivier (Oct 2010) ▪ ±20ha/±15ha (cabs s/f, merlot, p verdot, shiraz, chard, viog) ▪ 100t/8,000cs own label 80% red 20% white ▪ PO Box 180 Franschhoek 7690 ▪ info@labri.co.za ▪ www.labri.co.za ▪ S 33° 55' 18.3" E 019° 7' 1.5" ▪ F +27 (0)86-275-9753 ▪ **T +27 (0)21-876-2593**

☐ **La Capra** see Fairview
☐ **La Cave** see Wellington Wines
☐ **Lace** see Almenkerk Wine Estate

La Chataigne $\textcircled{2}$ $\textcircled{a}$ $\textcircled{5}$

As a result of selling off part of 'The Chestnut' estate near Franschhoek, Richard Parkfelt and family are building new tasting and storage facilities, and curtailing the range as the sale included their cabernet, shiraz and chenin vineyards. They promise, however, that they'll retain the boutique styling of the brand, with handwritten labels and limited bottlings.

★★★★ **Semillon** Lively acidity, integrated oak, buttery conclusion on mainly older-oak-fermented **13**. Delivers the serious intent — plus lemongrass & lemon thyme attractions — missing from **12** (★★★☆).

Kastanje $\textcircled{\uparrow}$ ★★★☆ From low-yielding chenin with dash semillon, unoaked. **14** ticks all boxes with fresh acidity & pithy texture, long rounded conclusion. Begs for oysters.

Also tasted: **Marron 11** ★★★☆ **Rosé 14** ★★★ **Sauvignon Blanc 14** ★★★ — CvZ

Location/map/WO: Franschhoek ▪ Est 1972 ▪ 1stB 2003 ▪ Tasting & sales Mon-Sun 10-4 ▪ Closed all pub hols ▪ 3 guest cottages ▪ Owner(s) Parkfelt family ▪ Winemaker(s) Gerda Willers (2003, consultant) ▪ 17ha/10ha (merlot, ptage, sauv, sem) ▪ 120t/1,500cs own label 25% red 65% white 10% rosé ▪ PO Box 301 Franschhoek 7690 ▪ office@lachat.co.za ▪ www.lachat.co.za ▪ S 33° 52' 43.8" E 019° 3' 34.1" ▪ F +27 (0)86-545-1039 ▪ **T +27 (0)21-876-3220**

La Chaumiere Estate $\textcircled{2}$

Cape Town steelman Michael Pawlowski over the past several years has invested in stages in vineyard replanting, cellar expansion and portfolio development on his boutique Franschhoek riverside property. Separate vinification of pinot noir blocks and shiraz from young vineyards are now enlivening the wines, reports viticulturist/winemaker Wynand Pienaar, unveiling an unusual tannat blend.

★★★★ **Pinot Noir** Elegant & unshowy **14**, with delicate whiffs of elderberry, mulberry, cinnamon spice & cured meat. Smooth, with deft oaking (30% new) & well-judged acidity adding structure, length.

Winemakers Blend (NEW) ★★★☆ Rare-in-SA fusion of tannat & 4 Bordeaux reds; **13** juicy, flavour packed (mostly ripe red fruits & blue berries) with a liquorice nuance, tannat's tannins well under control. Also tasted: **Cabernet Sauvignon 13** ★★★ **Shiraz 13** ★★★☆ **Chardonnay 14** ★★★ Not retasted: **Méthode Cap Classique 10** ★★★ — GM

Location/map/WO: Franschhoek ▪ Est 2001 ▪ 1stB 2003 ▪ Tasting & cellar tours by appt ▪ Sales from local outlets ▪ Owner(s) Michael Pawlowski ▪ Winemaker(s)/viticulturist(s) Wynand Pienaar ▪ 5ha (cab, pinot, shiraz, chard) ▪ 24t/3,400cs own label ▪ Other export brand: You Raise Me Up ▪ PO Box 601 Franschhoek 7690 ▪ wynlpers@iafrica.com ▪ S 33° 54' 34.0" E 019° 6' 54.9" ▪ F +27 (0)21-876-2135 ▪ **T +27 (0)21-876-4830/31**

La Couronne Wines

(icons)

Franschhoek property developer Francois Smith, owner since 2011 of this French Huguenot-founded property, has appointed experienced Henk Swart as cellarmaster and, as the guide went to press, was phasing in a three-tier range and label revamp. The rejigged branding incorporates a hand-sketched sailing vessel, recalling 17th-century warship The Crown, to tie in with the farm's name.

★★★★ **Barrel Fermented Chardonnay** Wooded chardonnay returns to line-up with crafted **14**, alluring rich yet pure varietal fruit & balanced oak support (30% new); full & broad but with a bright core, juicy freshness & nutty tail.

★★★★★ **Muscadel** Reported 'discontinued' last time, fortified white muscat de Frontignan is back – & what a return! Latest luscious **NV** shows some age in colour & notes of sugared chestnuts, sultana, toffee apple & sweet pastry; intensely sweet, but the full-spectrum flavours still vivacious, inviting further cellaring if you can resist. Barrel-aged (2 years) Worcester grapes.

Malbec ★★★ Jammy fruit flavours on **13** but there's fair grip to the full-bodied palate. Best enjoyed early. Also tasted: **Shiraz 13** ★★★ **Portside Red 13** ★★ Not tasted: **Merlot, Pinotage, Merlot Rosé, Chardonnay Unwooded**. Discontinued: **Starboard White Sauvignon Blanc**. — HJ

Location/map: Franschhoek ▪ WO: Franschhoek/Western Cape ▪ Chocolate & wine tasting/sales Mon-Sun 11–4 ▪ Closed Christian religious hols ▪ Restaurant ▪ Wine tram ▪ Traditional braai & picnics to be booked in advance ▪ Facilities for children ▪ Tour groups ▪ Weddings ▪ Conferences ▪ Le Chais Villa (6 en-suite rooms) ▪ Winemaker(s) Henk Swart (May 2015) ▪ 21ha (cabs s/f, malbec, merlot, p verdot, ptage, shiraz, chard, sauv, viog) ▪ 160t/±25,000cs own label 60% red 40% white ▪ eldorette@lacouronnewines.co.za ▪ www.lacouronnewines.co.za ▪ S 33° 55' 8.9" E 019° 6' 40.9" ▪ **T +27 (0)21-876-3939/+27 (0)82-495-8579**

Ladera Artisan Wines

(icons)

Young Charles Ochse was delighted to start running the family fruit farm in Wolseley, as long as he could keep making wine; which he did, and does, finding grapes from all over for his after-hours artisan label (meaning 'Hillside'). Wide experience includes crushes here and abroad – including Mexico and Russia!

★★★★ **First Born Syrah** Out of step with restrained **11**, **12** (★★★) is the 'wild child' this year: very ripe (14.7% alcohol) with raisin nuance, racy acidity.

Not tasted: **Wild Child Chardonnay**. — JPf

Location: Wolseley ▪ Map: Breedekloof ▪ WO: Malmesbury ▪ Est/1stB 2009 ▪ Tasting, sales & cellar tours Mon-Sat by appt ▪ Picnics & longtable lunches in the fruit orchards by prior booking ▪ Owner(s) Charles Ochse ▪ Cellarmaster(s)/winemaker(s) Charles Ochse (2003) ▪ 6-8t/800cs own label 51% red 33% white 16% rosé ▪ PO Box 193 Wolseley 6830 ▪ info@ladera.co.za ▪ www.laderawines.co.za ▪ S 33° 28' 20.66" E 019° 11' 27.45" ▪ **T +27 (0)72-536-0055**

☐ **Ladismith Winery & Distillery** see Barrydale Winery & Distillery
☐ **Lady May** see Glenelly Estate
☐ **Lady Somerset** see Somerset Wines

La Ferme Derik

(icons)

The focus here is on export table grapes and macadamia nuts, but having studied winemaking part-time, family member Eurica Scholtz couldn't resist testing her skills on a small production (temporarily out of stock at press time), from old vines and bought-in grapes, to 'add to the package of what we offer'.

Location: Paarl ▪ Map: Paarl & Wellington ▪ Map grid reference: D3 ▪ WO: Paarl/Western Cape ▪ Est 1695 ▪ 1stB 1895 ▪ Tasting, sales & cellar tours by appt ▪ Function venue for 160 guests ▪ Owner(s) Hardus Otto ▪ Winemaker(s)/viticulturist(s) Eurica Scholtz ▪ 7ha (shiraz, grenache b/n, rouss, viog) + 45ha export table grapes & macadamia nuts ▪ 35t 10% red 90% white ▪ PO Box 2008 Windmeul 7630 ▪ functions@lafermederik.com ▪ www.lafermederik.com ▪ S 33° 40' 33.348" E 18° 55' 56.964" ▪ F +27 (0)21-869-8433 ▪ **T +27 (0)21-869-8380/+27 (0)82-953-0185**

Laibach Vineyards ⑨ ⌂

Since this German-family-owned estate in the prestigious Simonsberg-Stellenbosch ward achieved organic certification in 2012, there has been a steady proliferation of both actual ladybirds and the successful wines that bear their name (now accounting for most of the production). Doubtless the colourful mealy bug busters were quietly influential in the last grape harvest not only being the biggest yet but also showing some of the highest quality. About 5% of the vineyards are replanted each year, and cabernet is earmarked for the next round, based on the success of the stellar Widow's Block.

★★★★ **Widow's Block Cabernet Sauvignon** ⑨ Best-years-only tribute to former owner who advised planting cab (instead of shiraz). Single-vineyard **12** (★★★★★) follows **07** with fruit purity & intensity, fine tannins. Lovely polished texture, oak (50% new) in harmony. Will develop with distinction.

★★★★☆ **Claypot Merlot** ⑨ Meticulous fruit selection rewards with concentration, elegance & structure. **13**'s well-integrated oak (50% new) allows fragrant fruit to shine. Polished & youthful, many years of drinking pleasure ahead.

★★★★ **Merlot** Full-bodied **14**, featuring Ceres fruit, makes confident return to form after tighter **12** (★★★). Rich dark fruit & minty overlay, firm juicy, supple tannins; good intensity & length. **13** untasted.

★★★★☆ **Friedrich Laibach** ⑨ Integration & harmony the watchwords for this **11** Bordeaux red blend of cab & merlot with 1% cab franc. Light oak juxtaposed with dark concentration of ripe, juicy berries. Tobacco & cedar reminiscent of equally elegant **09**. No **10**.

★★★★ **The Ladybird Red** ⑨ A merlot & cab dominated blend with cab franc, petit verdot, malbec. **13** full flavoured, ripe & savoury; offers lively drinkability & enough structure for enjoyment over the next few years. Also in magnum.

★★★★ **Natural Sweet** ⑨ Delightfully light & tangy **14** from Bottelary chenin, delicate (7.5% alcohol) yet focused & really fresh. 'Designed to pair with duck pâte in top Belgian restaurants.' 375 ml.

Cabernet Sauvignon (NEW) ★★★★ Subtle **14**, a little dark & brooding mid-2015, firm fleshed & toned with underlying seriousness. Good varietal definition – just needs a bit more time to unfurl & reveal its charms. **The Ladybird Chenin Blanc** (NEW) ★★★ From 40 year old Bottelary bushvines, **15** waxy apple flavours, crisp yet plump & creamy too, the mid-palate richness balanced by acidity. Also tasted:
Laibach Seeger Pinot Noir 13 ★★★★ **Pinotage 14** ★★★★ **The Ladybird White** ⑨ **14** ★★★★
Discontinued: **Chenin Blanc**. — MW

Location/map: Stellenbosch ▪ Map grid reference: F1 ▪ WO: Simonsberg–Stellenbosch/Western Cape/ Stellenbosch/Ceres ▪ Est 1994 ▪ 1stB 1997 ▪ Tasting & sales Mon-Fri 10–5 Sat (Nov-Apr)/pub hols 10–1 ▪ Fee R10/4 wines ▪ Closed Easter Fri/Sun, Dec 25/26 & Jan 1 ▪ Cellar tours by appt ▪ Laibach Vineyards Lodge ▪ Owner(s) Petra Laibach-Kühner & Rudolf Kühner ▪ Cellarmaster(s)/winemaker(s) Francois van Zyl (Jan 2000) ▪ Viticulturist(s) / MD Michael Malherbe (Jun 1994) ▪ 50ha/37ha (cabs s/f, malbec, merlot, p verdot, ptage, chard, chenin, viog) ▪ 300t/48,000cs own label 70% red 30% white + 9,000cs for Woolworths ▪ BWI, Organic ▪ PO Box 7109 Stellenbosch 7599 ▪ info@laibachwines.com ▪ www.laibachwines.com ▪ S 33° 50' 43.3" E 018° 51' 44.2" ▪ F +27 (0)86-665-2839 ▪ **T +27 (0)21-884-4511**

La Kavayan

Long-time Stellenbosch friends and boutique vignerons Theo Beukes and Gabriël Kriel are aided in their quest for 'wines of timeless quality' by winemaker PG Slabbert. The brand name (meaning 'Jan's Cellar') recalls previous farm owner prof Jan Sadie.

Cabernet Sauvignon-Shiraz ★★★ 2 vintages reviewed: undemanding **10** (★★★) sweet fruit & dusty tannins; **12** more life & complexity with bright fruit, soft tannins & contrasting racy acidity, inviting food. Occasional release: **Cabernet Sauvignon**. — WB, FM

Location/WO: Stellenbosch ▪ Est 1999 ▪ 1stB 2001 ▪ Closed to public ▪ Owner(s) Theo Beukes ▪ Winemaker(s) PG Slabbert (2001, consultant) ▪ Viticulturist(s) Gabriël Kriel ▪ 2ha (cab) ▪ ±10,000L own label 100% red ▪ PO Box 321 Stellenbosch 7599 ▪ diana@lakavayan.co.za, theo@minpro.co.za ▪ F +27 (0)21-880-1122 ▪ **T +27 (0)83-601-9030/+27 (0)21-880-1646**

☐ **LAM** see Lammershoek Winery
☐ **Lambert's Bay's Finest** see Teubes Family Wines

Lammershoek Winery   ⓆⒾⒶ

Lammershoek on Swartland's Perdeberg is under new management, with new winemaker (Schalk Opperman) and viticulturist (Charl van Reenen) part of a fired-up team intent on 'taking Lammershoek to new heights'. Specifics were unavailable at press time, sales and marketing manager Zia van Rooyen du Toit saying only: 'We will in the near future release more information on what we have planned.'

Location: Malmesbury ▪ Map: Swartland ▪ Est 1999 ▪ 1stB 2000 ▪ Tasting, sales & cellar tours by appt ▪ Light lunch platters by appt or BYO picnic ▪ Owner(s) Lammershoek Farms & Winery (Pty) Ltd ▪ Winemaker(s) Schalk Opperman (Jan 2015) ▪ Viticulturist(s) Charl van Reenen (Jan 2015) ▪ 80ha (carignan, grenache, merlot, mourv, ptage, shiraz, tinta barocca, zin, chard, chenin, hárslevelü, rouss, sauv, viog) ▪ PO Box 597 Malmesbury 7299 ▪ info@lammershoek.co.za ▪ www.lammershoek.co.za ▪ S 33° 31' 30.2" E 018° 48' 21.1" ▪ F +27 (0)22-487-2702 ▪ **T +27 (0)22-482-2835**

La Motte   ⓆⒾⓄⒶⒶ

Purchased by the late Anton Rupert in 1970, this property dating from early 1695 is now owned and run by his daughter, Hanneli Rupert-Koegelenberg, with her husband, Hein Koegelenberg, as CEO. The couple believe stories play an important role in successful wine tourism: Pierneef à La Motte restaurant introduces visitors to traditional Cape winelands cuisine; the museum shares the history of Franschhoek Valley; and revered SA artist JH Pierneef's heritage collection is on permanent exhibition. Outdoor activities include a mountain hiking trail and themed walks. Cellarmaster Edmund Terblanche's elegant, classic wines are styled to be enjoyed with food and complement the quality of the wine tourism. His latest plans are to bottle the components of both the Syrah and Pierneef Syrah-Viognier in order to show the diversity and stylistic differences of each site.

Pierneef Collection

★★★★☆ **Syrah-Viognier** Was 'Shiraz-Viognier'. Cellar's much-awarded flagship & one of finest of genre. Viognier (10%) subtly, intriguingly perfumes shiraz spice, doesn't impose its own aroma. **13** elegant, silky with long, complex farewell.

★★★★ **Sauvignon Blanc** Dash semillon adds gravitas, breadth to cool, South Cape Coast-sourced **14**. Though quietly persuasive, the tangerine & honey flavours are led by creamy, viscous structure & lengthened by an urgent zesty tang. Great food style.

Discontinued: **Shiraz-Grenache**.

Classic Collection

★★★★ **Cabernet Sauvignon 13**'s classy aromas from perfectly ripe black berries spiced with cab franc & new oak. With a few years, the unintimidating austerity should yield to the elegant, sweet fruit.

★★★★☆ **Syrah** Brooding **13** is 100% shiraz, (previous brightened by inclusion other varieties). Sombre dark fruit tones in its tense texture; all in balance to allow for unfolding expression, suppleness with time.

★★★★ **Chardonnay 14** offers satisfaction in its bright pickled lime purity, medium body & carefully judged oak enrichment (just 25% new). Displays typical WO Franschhoek elegance, character.

★★★★ **Méthode Cap Classique 12** refined chardonnay, pinot noir blend (65/35), 15% of base wine oaked for creamy depth. Suave citrus, toasty features, pinprick bubble; bone-dry finish. Franschhoek WO.

★★★★☆ **Straw Wine** Striking red gold lights matched by no less arresting & generous honeysuckle & spice aromas. Sumptuous, succulent but oak (20% new) & taut acid trim sweeter edges. 375 ml of sheer hedonism! **NV** from viognier.

La Motte Collection

★★★★ **Millennium** ⊘ Merlot (57%) at its plush, grand best in **13**. Cab franc, malbec, petit verdot & cab provide freshness, layers of flavour. Some astringency needs rounding for usual approachability.

★★★★ **Sauvignon Blanc** ⊘ Regional diversity harnesses components for satisfying **15**. Notes of lemongrass, asparagus & tropical fruits, weight anchored by lees-ageing & clean, mineral tang. — AL

Location/map: Franschhoek ▪ WO: Western Cape/Franschhoek/Cape South Coast ▪ Est 1969 ▪ 1stB 1984 ▪ Tasting & sales Mon-Sat 9–5 ▪ Fee R50pp ▪ Booking essential for: group tastings 8-16 R60pp; themed tastings R200pp; food & wine pairing Fri 10 R130pp by appt only ▪ Closed Good Fri & Dec 25 ▪ Pierneef à La Motte ▪ Facilities for children ▪ Tour groups (max 16), booking essential ▪ Farm shop: lavender, vegetables, bread, gifts ▪ Booking essential for: hiking trail Mon-Sat 9-2 R50pp (duration 2-3hrs, not recommended for children under 10); guided hike Mon 9 R100pp; sustainable walk Tue 9-10 R50pp; historic walk Wed 10-11 R50pp; sculpture walk Thu 10-11 R50pp ▪ 35ha conservation area ▪ Museum Tue-Sun 9-5: Rupert family, history of La Motte, Cape Dutch architecture, life/art of JH Pierneef & other SA artists ▪ Monthly classical music concerts ▪ Owner(s) Hanneli Rupert-Koegelenberg ▪ CEO Hein Koegelenberg ▪ Cellarmaster(s) Edmund Terblanche (Dec 2000) ▪ Winemaker(s) Michael Langenhoven (Dec 2006) ▪ Viticulturist(s) Pietie le Roux (May 1986) ▪ 170ha/75ha (merlot, pinot, shiraz, chard, sauv, sem) ▪ 1,600t/ 200,000cs own label 38.2% red 61.5% white 0.3% sparkling + 30,000cs for clients ▪ Brands for clients: Woolworths ▪ ISO 14001:2004, BWI champion, HACCP, IPW, WIETA, EnviroWines, Farming for the Future ▪ PO Box 685 Franschhoek 7690 ▪ cellar@la-motte.co.za ▪ www.la-motte.com ▪ S 33° 52' 52.20" E 019° 4' 25.76" ▪ F +27 (0)21-876-3446 ▪ **T +27 (0)21-876-8000**

Landau du Val   ⓠ

When Jane and Basil Landau bought their historic Franschhoek farm, La Brie, in 1986, they didn't quite realise the significance of the unirrigated block of low-yielding bushvine semillon: planted in 1905, it is among the Cape's oldest vineyards. Other grapes from the farm are sold off – just the widely acclaimed semillon is vinified (by Wynand Grobler of Rickety Bridge) under the Landau du Val label.

★★★★ Semillon Private Selection From ultra-low-yielding centenarian vines. Effusive beeswax, lanolin & honey aromas & flavours, grapefruit-like pithy texture on **13**. Polished & refined, bone-dry & sympathetically oaked (25% new).

Occasional release: **Late Vintage Semillon Private Selection**. — JPf

Location/map/WO: Franschhoek ▪ Tasting by appt ▪ Sales at La Cotte Wine Sales, Franschhoek ▪ Owner(s) Basil & Jane Landau ▪ Winemaker(s) Wynand Grobler ▪ Viticulturist(s) Martin du Plessis & Pietie le Roux (consultant) ▪ 15ha under vine ▪ La Brie Robertsvlei Road Franschhoek 7690 ▪ basillandau@mweb.co.za ▪ S 33° 55' 34.3" E 019° 6' 34.1" ▪ F +27 (0)21-876-3369 ▪ **T +27 (0)82-410-1130**

☐ **Landela** see Jacques Germanier
☐ **Land of Hope** see The Winery of Good Hope

Land's End

As implied, the Land's End vines grow at the southern tip of Africa on the cool, windy Agulhas plain. The wines are made at Fairview.

★★★★ Syrah ⓥ Fynbos & a salty note complement bright dark berries on harmonious **12**, from vineyards 8 km from the ocean. Restrained fruit mingling with spicy oak. Will reward cellaring.

Sauvignon Blanc ★★★☆ 15 preview smacks of the sea with hints of fynbos scrub, still fairly fruit-shy but promises to open up into tropical fruit medley. — JG

☐ **Landskap** see Groenland

Landskroon Wines   ⓠ ⓐ ⓐ ⓐ ⓐ

This family estate in Paarl, home to winegrowing since the 17th century, in 1974 bottled the maiden wine under the label Landskroon, after Landskrona, home of the original Swedish owner, Jan Holsmit. A cinsaut was the first release, and that red grape – sometimes spelt 'cinsault' and newly fashionable here – remains a fixture on the Landskroon price list, solo and blended. Perhaps the 'cinsaut revolution' happening all around will inspire resolutely unflashy cellarmaster and co-owner Paul de Villiers to surprise us with a rockstar version of the estate's heritage variety in coming vintages...

Paul de Villiers range

★★★★ Cabernet Sauvignon Impressive **13** in similar vein to polished **12** with savoury oak detail, refined tannins & fresh acidity for cellaring good few years. Try matching with charcuterie platters.

★★★★ Merlot Very good expression of this unforgiving variety. Candyfloss-toned **13** intense plum & cassis fruit, as confident as **12**, with latter's perfect tension between richness, acidity & tannic grip.

★★★★ **Shiraz** ⓔ Step-up **12** effusive vanilla bouquet, plush fruit centre, peppery conclusion: a hedonistic glassful. More concentrated than **11** (★★★☆), should reward even more with time.

★★★★ **Reserve** ⓔ Flagship blend shiraz & merlot plus dollops cab & touriga. **11** has cedar oak welcome, leading to bright fruited, medium body with balanced tannins. Needs a year or so to settle.

> **Chenin Blanc Barrel Fermented** ⓝⒺⓦ ⓥ ★★★★ Rich & appealing **14**, vanilla highlights to lemon-apricot tones. Enough interest & substance now for solo or (sea)food, or cellar few years.

Landskroon range

★★★★ **Cape Vintage** ⓔ Much-awarded port-style, **11** from tintas barocca & amarela, souzão & touriga; balanced sweetness, approachable grip & exotic orange rind, potpourri wafts.

Cabernet Sauvignon ★★★ **13** upfront cassis & tobacco, firm tannins & verve. What more do you want from an everyday cab? **Merlot** ★★★ **13** packed with wild berries & plums, smooth & friendly for easy enjoyment. **Cinsaut-Shiraz** ★★★ Spicy **13** very gluggable with friendly bitter-chocolate tannic hug. **Chardonnay** ★★★ Lifted floral notes on unoaked **15**'s bright lemon nose, some nutty complexity & perky tail. **Sauvignon Blanc** ★★★ Fennel/liquorice accents on grassy **15**, enlivened by ruby grapefruit acidity & flavours. WO W Cape. **Paul Hugo White** ★★★ **15** stars deftly handled viognier (80%) & chenin, unchallenging yet flavoursome. Stock up for summertime. Also tasted: **Pinotage 13** ★★ **Shiraz 13** ★★★☆ **Cabernet Franc-Merlot 13** ★★★ **Blanc de Noir Pinotage Off-Dry 15** ★★ **Chenin Blanc Dry 15** ★★★ **Chenin Blanc Off-Dry 15** ★★★ Not retasted: **Cinsaut 12** ★★ **Bush Camp Our Daily Red 09** ★★★ **Paul Hugo Red 12** ★★ **Bush Camp Blanc de Noir 11** ★★ Not tasted: **Bush Camp The Sundowner**. — CvZ

Location: Paarl ▪ Map: Paarl & Wellington ▪ Map grid reference: D6 ▪ WO: Paarl/Western Cape ▪ Est 1874 ▪ 1stB 1974 ▪ Tasting & sales Mon-Fri 8.30–5 Sat (Oct-May) 9.30-1 ▪ Closed Sun, Easter weekend, Dec 25 & Jan 1 ▪ Fee R10/5 wines, waived on purchase of 6btls ▪ Cellar tours by appt Mon-Fri 9-4 ▪ BYO picnic ▪ Play area for children ▪ Permanent display of Stone Age artefacts ▪ Self-catering cottage ▪ Owner(s) Paul & Hugo de Villiers Family Trusts ▪ Cellarmaster(s) Paul de Villiers (Jan 1980) ▪ Winemaker(s) Michiel du Toit (Nov 2014) ▪ Viticulturist(s) Hugo de Villiers jnr (1995) ▪ 330ha/190ha (cab, cinsaut, merlot, ptage, shiraz, souzão, tinta amarela, tinta barocca, touriga nacional, chenin, chard, sauv, viog) ▪ 78% red 14% white 8% port ▪ IPW ▪ PO Box 519 Suider-Paarl 7624 ▪ huguette@landskroonwines.com ▪ www.landskroonwines.com ▪ S 33° 45' 38.34" E 018° 54' 58.38" ▪ F +27 (0)21-863-2810 ▪ **T +27 (0)21-863-1039**

Landzicht GWK Wines   ⓔ

Vineyards are not common in the Free State, but that's where the Landzicht wines originate, around Jacobsdal. The grapes are vinified, however, across the provincial border at Douglas Wine Cellar in the Northern Cape – also owned by agribusiness GWK. New-look labels are being being phased in, inspired by the Northern Cape side of things.

Cabernet Sauvignon Reserve ★★★ Nutty blackberry aroma on this wooded version, **12** cranberry & sour cherry notes, firmer tannins which could see it age a while. **Merlot Reserve** ⓝⒺⓦ ★★ Red berries & milk chocolate flavours on oaked **13**, firm tannins & long dry finish. Try with pizza. **Blanc de Blanc** ★★☆ Lightweight, uncomplicated **15**, fruity, with green apple & peach flavours. **Rosenblümchen** ★★ Natural Sweet rosé offering rosepetals, Turkish delight & low alcohol (8%). **NV** party fun to be served chilled. **Red Muscadel** ★★★ Now vintage dated (**15**), well-made fortified glows pale amber, radiates flowers, honey & sweet grapiness. Try over crushed ice for tasty summer drinking. Also tasted: **Cabernet Sauvignon 14** ★★☆ **Merlot 14** ★★ **Chenin Blanc 15** ★ **Blümchen NV** ★★ **White Muscadel 14** ★★★ Not tasted: **Nagmaalwyn, Hanepoot, Red Jerepigo, Ruby Port, Oak Matured**. — DB

Location: Jacobsdal ▪ Map: Northern Cape, Free State & North West ▪ WO: Northern Cape/Douglas ▪ Est 1976 ▪ 1stB ca 1980 ▪ Tasting & sales Mon-Fri 8-5 ▪ Closed all pub hols ▪ Owner(s) GWK Ltd ▪ Winemaker(s) Ian Sieg, with Ian Jooste ▪ Viticulturist(s) Hein Janse van Rensburg ▪ Production: see under Douglas Wine Cellar ▪ PO Box 94 Jacobsdal 8710 ▪ landzicht@gwk.co.za ▪ www.gwk.co.za ▪ S 29° 8' 35.5" E 024° 46' 42.8" ▪ F +27 (0)53-591-0145 ▪ **T +27 (0)53-591-0164**

☐ **Langeberg Wineries** *see* Wonderfontein
☐ **Langtafel** *see* Mooiplaas Estate & Private Nature Reserve

Langverwacht Wynkelder

Two significant anniversaries this edition: crushing of the first grapes 60 years ago, when the Bonnievale winery was Boesmansrivier Winecellar (founded 1954); and the arrival of Johan Gerber, incumbent cellarmaster and 30-year veteran. Today's Langverwacht is owned by a relatively small group of growers and produces mostly bulk wine. Shiraz, chardonnay and colombard are specialities under the 8,000-case own label, available from the cellar and a few local wine shops.

Location: Bonnievale ▪ Map: Robertson ▪ Est 1954 ▪ Tasting, sales & tours Mon-Fri 8-5 ▪ Closed all pub hols ▪ Owner(s) 25 members ▪ Cellarmaster(s) Johan Gerber (Dec 1986) ▪ Winemaker(s) Theunis Botha (Dec 2005) ▪ Viticulturist(s) Hennie Visser (Jul 2008) ▪ 640ha (cab, ruby cab, shiraz, chenin, chard, cbard, sauv) ▪ 13,500t/8,000cs own label 64% red 36% white ▪ IPW ▪ PO Box 87 Bonnievale 6730 ▪ info@langverwachtwines.co.za ▪ www.langverwachtwines.co.za ▪ S 33° 57' 32.8" E 020° 1' 35.3" ▪ F +27 (0)23-616-3059 ▪ **T +27 (0)23-616-2815**

Lanner Hill

The Lanner Hill brand is a partnership between seasoned winemaker and Cape Winemakers Guild member, Nicky Versfeld, and the Tullie family. It is also the name of the family farm, open for visits by appointment in Darling's cool Groenekloof hills that have become synonymous with top sauvignons.

★★★★ **Sauvignon Blanc** ⓐ Like **11** preview, **13** flies the Darling flag, ticking all the variety's boxes. Lovely fruit purity & racy acidity end with a clean-cut flinty farewell. **12** sold out untasted.

Not retasted: **Merlot 11** ★★★★ — MW

Location/WO: Darling ▪ Map: Durbanville, Philadelphia & Darling ▪ Est 1999 ▪ 1stB 2002 ▪ Tasting by appt ▪ Sales Mon-Fri 9-3 via email/phone; from farm by appt only ▪ Owner(s) David & Nicola Tullie ▪ Winemaker(s) Nicky Versfeld (2002) ▪ Viticulturist(s) David Tullie ▪ 91ha/51ha (cab, merlot, p verdot, shiraz, sauv, sem, viog) ▪ 450-500t/1,000cs own label ▪ PO Box 220 Darling 7345 ▪ tulliefamilyvineyards@gmail.com ▪ S 33° 23' 36.54" E 018° 22' 10.22" ▪ F +27 (0)22-492-3664 ▪ **T +27 (0)22-492-3662/+27 (0)82-882-2260/ +27 (0)21-863-4925 (Anton du Toit, marketing & sales)**

Lanzerac Wine Estate

Situated at the entrance to Stellenbosch's beautiful Jonkershoek Valley, venerable Lanzerac (including 5-star hotel, spa, restaurants and winery) epitomises style and grace. Mrs English, who in 1914 bought and renamed the estate after her friend, General Lanzerac, is reputed to have bottled their first wines from 21 varieties. The current team, including winemaker Wynand Lategan, is more focused in their viti-cultural choices, aiming to restore Lanzerac to its full glory. Mrs E would be proud of their Heritage range, honouring her legacy and that of the Cape's pioneer commercial pinotage. The vineyard replanting project is now complete, as are the elegant tasting, function and deli refurbishments.

Heritage range

★★★★ **Pionier Pinotage** Named for world's first commercial pinotage release in 1961. **12** & **13** tasted. Quintessential pinotage profile: some high-toned sweet strawberry, smoky fruit & liquorice. **12** (WO Stellenbosch) quite dense, with good grip & balance; **13** more austere, structured & savoury. Both a shade off **11** (★★★★☆), needing cellar time to harmonise.

★★★★ **Le Général** Cab-led Cape Blend with 7-13% pinotage; **13** classic leafy cassis aromas & firm, chalky tannins; shows youthful restraint though with more depth than leaner **12** (WO Stellenbosch, also tasted), which is very tight. Both fresh & built for the long haul, with some merlot in their make-up, absent in finer **11** (★★★★☆).

★★★★☆ **Mrs English** Two releases from Jonkershoek chardonnay, both with splash pinot blanc & in more elegant, understated style than assertive **12**, same persistent finish. **14** fresher than **13** (★★★★), with toasted nut & caramel overlay; supple, succulent, with lovely fruit purity. **13** shows earthy evolution, some pear & bruised apple. Sleek & ready to savour.

Premium range

★★★★ **Cabernet Sauvignon** Leafy walnut & cassis entry on **13** unfurls to show a more powerful, riper personality (14.9% alcohol) tempered by acidity & chalky tannins from 18 months oak (30% new). Still integrating, needs more time.

★★★★ **Merlot** Appealing blue berry fruit with perfumed nuance on **13**, sappy dry tannins; riper than previous, with a juicy core & lively fresh balance; oak well integrated. Will reward ageing.

★★★★ **Pinotage** Dark, dense cherry/plum fruit from 3 Stellenbosch blocks. **13** (★★★) ripeness tempered by acidity & muscular tannins. Tad disjointed in youth, with warm farewell. More robust than **12**.

★★★★ **Chardonnay** Preview of **14**, with 13.7 % pinot blanc, quite toasty (80% barrel fermented, 20% new) mid-2015, succulent & enduring pear & lime flavours will shine with decanting & some ageing.

Blanc de Blancs Brut (NEW) ★★★★ Engagingly flavoursome **NV** (**13**) bubbly from chardonnay, with hazelnuts, citrus peel & bright fruitiness. Surprisingly creamy & expressive for 18 months on lees. WO Stellenbosch. Also tasted: **Sauvignon Blanc 15** ★★★

Alma Mater range

Chenin Blanc (符) ★★★ **15** bursts with chenin's bright fruit; crisp & crunchy, this balanced charmer exudes drinkability. WO Stellenbosch, as all these.

Also tasted: **Shiraz 13** ★★★ **Rosé 15** ★★★ — MW

Location/map: Stellenbosch ▪ Map grid reference: G5 ▪ WO: Jonkershoek Valley/Stellenbosch ▪ Est 1692 ▪ 1stB 1957 ▪ Tasting & sales daily 9–5 ▪ Cellar tours at 11 & 3 ▪ Closed Dec 25 ▪ Deli platters; wine & chocolate tasting; picnic baskets ▪ 5-star Lanzerac Hotel, Spa & Restaurants ▪ Conferences ▪ Weddings/functions ▪ Owner(s) Lanzerac Estate Investments ▪ Cellarmaster(s) Wynand Lategan (Jan 2005) ▪ Viticulturist(s) Danie Malherbe (2008) ▪ 150ha/46ha (cab, merlot, ptage, chard) ▪ 500t/24-26,000cs own label 55% red 30% white 15% rosé ▪ BWI ▪ PO Box 6233 Uniedal 7612 ▪ winesales@lanzerac.co.za ▪ www.lanzeracwines.co.za ▪ S 33° 56' 14.7" E 018° 53' 35.5" ▪ F +27 (0)21-887-6998 ▪ **T +27 (0)21-886-5641**

La Petite Ferme Winery   (♀) (♍) (⌂) (◎)

Behind the scenes at the Dendy Young family's ever-popular restaurant, guest house and boutique winery, Frans Malies' hard work in the vineyards has paid off, earning him the coveted Franschhoek Farm Worker of the Year title. The Dendy Youngs say their winning secret is patience ('no short cuts!').

La Petite Ferme range

★★★★ **Cabernet Sauvignon** (♀) Silky **13**, dense blackcurrant & dark chocolate-dipped cherry fruit, lifted by slightly herbaceous freshness & savoury hint of green olive.

★★★★ **Merlot** Despite all the richness — plums, choc-mocha, Christmas pudding spices from 15 months in French & American oak, 25% new — **14** is fresh & slips down easily.

★★★★ **Shiraz** At just 13% alcohol & with restrained red fruit, **14** is no New World blockbuster. More complex than **13** (★★★★) with hints of white pepper & smoked meat, any fruit sweetness countered by fresh acidity, slight tannic grip.

★★★★ **The Verdict** Bordeaux-style flagship from 80% cab franc with equal cab & merlot. Bursting with black berries & plums, **13**'s intensity is from vine-dried grapes. Rich but silkily so.

★★★★ **Barrel Fermented Chardonnay** True to form, **14** is redolent of citrus from its orange blossom nose to its marmalade-on-toast finish, with lime zest & lemon cream texture in between.

★★★★ **Batonnage Sauvignon Blanc Reserve** Latest **NV** subtle smoke/flint note to gooseberry & lime, creamy texture from lees stirring, tangy conclusion.

★★★★ **Viognier** Nothing over the top about **15**; less ripe/tropical than **14**, it's crisp & dry with restrained peach & pineapple notes, ginger-spiced nuts courtesy 15% older oak portion.

Also tasted: **Baboon Rock Unwooded Chardonnay Wild Yeast Fermented 15** ★★★☆ **Sauvignon Blanc 15** ★★★☆

Maison range

Rosé ★★★ Crisp & dry **15**, made from merlot, calls for Mediterranean tapas spread, very food friendly with its refreshing acidity, cranberry & red plum flavours, moderate 12% alcohol.

Also tasted: **Rouge** ⊘ **14** ★★★☆ Discontinued: **Blanc**. — JG

Location/map: Franschhoek ▪ WO: Franschhoek/Western Cape ▪ Est 1972 ▪ 1stB 1996 ▪ Tasting daily at 11 by appt ▪ Fee R50pp, tasting complimentary if lunch is booked ▪ Sales daily 8.30-5 ▪ Cellar tours from 11-12.30 ▪ Restaurant ▪ Guest suites ▪ Tour groups ▪ Gift shop ▪ Weddings ▪ Owner(s) Dendy Young family ▪ Cellarmaster(s)/winemaker(s) Mark Dendy Young (1996) ▪ Viticulturist(s) John Dendy Young ▪ Farm manager Frans Malies ▪ 16ha/14ha (cabs s/f, merlot, shiraz, chard, sauv, viog) ▪ 60-70t/12,000cs own label 40% red 50% white 10% rosé ▪ PO Box 55 Franschhoek 7690 ▪ jomark@mweb.co.za ▪ www.lapetiteferme.co.za ▪ S 33° 55' 6.43" E 019° 8' 10.32" ▪ F +27 (0)86-720-6284 ▪ **T +27 (0)21-876-3016**

La Petite Provence Wine Company   ⓘ

Essentially a wine club, with wines made mainly for Franschhoek's La Petite Provence Residential Estate owners from on-site cabernet and merlot vines, this small business also exports some of its production to, among others, Europe (from where many residents hail) via satellite 'clubs', agents and distributors.

Cabernet Sauvignon ★★★ With dashes merlot & cab franc, **12**'s supple dry tannins frame gentle cassis flavours & spice; accessible, unshowy, honest cab expression unfettered by oak (as all these). **Mélange** ★★★ Merlot, cab & cab franc are the **12** mélange. Lithe & balanced, with subtle fruit in a modest but appealing blend with good table manners. Also tasted: **Merlot 12** ★★ — MW

Location/WO: Franschhoek ▪ Est 2001 ▪ 1stB 2005 ▪ Tasting & sales Mon-Sat by appt ▪ Owner(s) La Petite Provence Wine Trust ▪ Winemaker(s) Johan van Rensburg (2003, La Provence) ▪ 3.5ha (cab, merlot) ▪ 30t/ 900cs own label 100% red ▪ 2 Cabernet Drive, La Petite Provence, Franschhoek 7690 ▪ info@ lapetiteprovence.co.za ▪ www.lapetiteprovence.co.za ▪ **T +27 (0)21-876-4178/+27 (0)21-876-4554**

La Petite Vigne   ⓘ

Perhaps more visible through his partnership in Black Elephant Vinters, Kevin Swart and family continue to produce soupçons of their all-cabernet Daniel Collection Amazing Grace – more like a soupçonette in harvest 2013, with just 300 bottles made. A (tiny) new cab block is set to come on-stream at their Franschhoek holding this year, and they're looking to release a little later to allow more time in bottle.

Location/map: Franschhoek ▪ 1stB 2012 ▪ Tasting & tours by appt only ▪ Owner(s) Kema Consulting (Kevin & Mandie Swart) ▪ Cellarmaster(s) Kevin Swart (Jan 2012) ▪ Winemaker(s) Kevin Swart (Jan 2012), with Gary Swart & Jospeh Ratabana (both Jan 2012) ▪ Viticulturist(s) Jacques Wentzel (Jan 2012, consultant) ▪ 3.3ha/2.5ha (cab) ▪ 3t/450cs own label 100% red ▪ PO Box 686 Franschhoek 7690 ▪ kevin@lapetitevigne.co.za ▪ S 33° 54' 9.00 E 019° 7' 14.00" ▪ **T +27 (0)21-876-2903**

La Residence   🍽 🏠 📷 ⒩ᴇᴡ

The grapes for these wines are grown on the Franschhoek property where Liz and Phil Biden's luxury hotel is located (with some suites almost among the vineyards), and the intention, of course, is to 'provide guests and interested persons with good quality wine'. The experienced and eminent DP Burger of nearby GlenWood is entrusted with the vinification.

Nicole Charlotte ★★ 100% cabernet, **13** tobacco & mint notes to cassis fruit, generous sweet vanilla from 80% new oak. Needs year/2 for tannins to soften, mesh with succulent fruit. Also in 375ml & 1.5L, as next. **Alexandra Frances** ★★★ Cinnamon & vanilla spicing to red plums on easygoing **13** from shiraz; early drinkability ensured by fresh acidity, supple tannins. **Rosemary Jane** ★★★ Rosé from cabernet, prettily packaged **14** palest onion skin hue, strawberries & cream flavours, delicate & dry. Perfect for al fresco dining. Also in 375ml. — TJ, CvZ

Location/WO: Franschhoek ▪ Est 2007 ▪ 1stB 2010 ▪ Closed to public ▪ Restaurant, reservation required ▪ Hotel ▪ Gift shop ▪ Owner(s) Liz & Phil Biden ▪ Winemaker(s) DP Burger (Jan 2010, consultant) ▪ Viticulturist(s) Pietie le Roux (Jan 2007, consultant) ▪ 30ha/4.9ha (cab, shiraz) ▪ 1,072cs own label 60% red

40% rosé ▪ Suite 44 Private Bag X19 Franschhoek 7690 ▪ info@laresidence.co.za ▪ www.laresidence.co.za
▪ **T +27 (0)21-876-4100**

Lateganskop Winery

The Lategan family have been vinegrowing in the Wolseley area for more than 100 years. Oupa Willie, who reached a remarkable 102, built a cellar in 1969, founding a legacy that continues today. Most of the wine is sold in bulk but a small portion bottled under the own labels. The new Zahir White forms part of the Breedekloof Chenin Blanc Initiative, aimed at terroir expression, especially of old vineyards.

The Zahir range
White (NEW) ★★★☆ 100% chenin from 21 year old bushvines, **14** barrel fermented/matured, giving hay, melon character, savoury finish. Not retasted: **Red 12** ★★★☆

Lateganskop range
Livia's Laughter Méthode Cap Classique ★★★☆ Bubbly named after only daughter among eleven 6th-generation Lategan siblings. Oaked **12**, from chardonnay, has ginger biscuit tones, delicious tangy acidity. Not retasted: **102 NV** ★★★☆

Twins range
Sauvignon Blanc ★★★☆ Softly fruity **15** offers apple & pear flavours, zippy freshness. Discontinued: **Pinotage**. Range previously known as 'Twin's Peak'. — CR

Location: Wolseley ▪ Map: Breedekloof ▪ WO: Breedekloof/Western Cape ▪ Est 1969 ▪ 1stB 2004 ▪ Tasting & sales Mon-Fri 8–12 & 1–5 ▪ Closed Easter Fri-Mon, Dec 25/26 & Jan 1 ▪ Cellar tours by appt ▪ Owner(s) 5 members ▪ Cellarmaster(s) Heinrich Lategan (Oct 2008) ▪ Winemaker(s) Heinrich Lategan, with Kéan Oosthuizen (May 2011) ▪ 238ha (cab, ptage, chard, chenin, sauv, sem) ▪ 2,900t/600cs own label 30% red 70% white & ±2m L bulk ▪ PO Box 44 Breërivier 6858 ▪ lateganskop@breede.co.za ▪ www.lateganskop.co.za ▪ S 33° 30' 57.27" E 019° 11' 13.65" ▪ F +27 (0)86-637-6603 ▪ **T +27 (0)23-355-1719**

La Terre La Mer

Co-founder, businessman and philanthropist Mark Wiehahn has new partners in this boutique winery on East London's Nahoon River: helicopter pilot Nicholas Cooke and multi-interest businessman Alwyn Krull. The trio are united by their passion for wine and, quips Mark, the challenge of being 1,000 km from the winelands. No wine was made in 2015; the 2016 crush will be vinified in a new cellar.

Location: East London ▪ Map: Eastern Cape ▪ Est/1stB 2008 ▪ Tasting, sales & cellar tours strictly by appt only ▪ Owner(s)/winemaker(s) Mark Wiehahn, Nicholas Cooke & Alwyn Krull ▪ Viticulturist(s) Grapes ex Mountain View/Lammershoek, Swartland ▪ 2.5t shiraz ▪ 30 Plymouth Drive, Nahoon Mouth, East London 5241 ▪ mw-assoc@mweb.co.za ▪ **T +27 (0)83-701-3148**

Lathithá Wines

Meaning 'sunrise', Lathithá is an empowerment venture headed by Sheila Hlanjwa, inspired by a wine marketing course at Stellenbosch University to get local communities similarly enthused. Sheila's new vintages, made at Hoopenburg, missed our tasting deadline.

Location: Cape Town ▪ Tasting by appt only ▪ Wine Boutique, Shop 17a, New Langa Junction Center, Cape Town ▪ Owner(s) Sheila Hlanjwa ▪ Winemaker(s) Helanie Olivier (Hoopenburg) ▪ 100ha (cabs s/f, malbec, merlot, shiraz, zin, viog) ▪ Washington Shopping Centre Langa 7455 ▪ sheila@lathithawines.co.za ▪ www.lathithawines.co.za ▪ **T +27 (0)73-393-5676**

L'Avenir Vineyards

L'Avenir, in the Simonsberg hills outside Stellenbosch, has always had a distinctly French tone. Past French-origin owners Mark Wiehe and Michel Laroche, and the current AdVini company, have all added to the quality and legacy of the estate. 'Proudly South African' (as well as French), they focused on pinotage and chenin blanc and the varieties rewarded the attention, bringing the farm's its early acclaim. The opening of their handsome new Pinotage Lounge, dedicated to tastings of the grape, is both an underscore of their ongoing commitment and a celebration of the character and versatility of pinotage (look for it in the blend of the new Brut sparkling). Visitors can savour the magic at, what else?, the Pinotage Deck, a special outdoors tasting platform at the highest point on the farm.

Single Block range

★★★★☆ **Pinotage** From farm's 21 year old single-vineyard. **13** silky, smooth but firm tannins, with layers of dark, scented fruits & integrated oak. Intense & complex, shining example of this variety. Already shows beautiful balance, but will age with distinction.

★★★★ **Chenin Blanc** Baked apple & spice, floral nuance from acacia barrels. **14** 100% wood fermented/aged but in harmony with fruit, bright acidity. Tad closed & understated mid-2015, deserves some time to unfurl. Also in magnum.

Provenance range

★★★★ **Cabernet Sauvignon 13** (★★★☆) in lighter more herbaceous style despite 14% alcohol. Dry tannins, piquant freshness, but less structure & depth than **12**.

★★★★ **Pinotage** Ample berry fruit & some savoury tobacco notes clothing fine amenable tannins, **13** supple balance with some underlying seriousness that doesn't detract from juicy drinkability. Also in 1.5L.

★★★★ **Chenin Blanc** ② Unoaked, easy-drinking styling for **13** (★★★★), dry, ample apple & honey flavours; initially bright & flavoursome but fades quite quickly. White peach & beeswax-toned **14**, also tasted, steelier, with good concentration & length, satisfying weight & freshness.

Also tasted: **Stellenbosch Classic 13** ★★★★ Not retasted: **Merlot 13** ★★★☆

Future Eternal range

★★★★ **MCC Brut** (NEW) Fresh, balanced & versatile dry sparkling from chardonnay, pinotage, pinot noir, pinot meunier (35/30/25/10). **12** clean shortbread & apple flavours with a creamy texture from 36 months on the lees.

Also tasted: **Brut Rosé Méthode Cap Classique 13** ★★★★ Discontinued: **Blanc de Blancs**.

Far & Near range

Chenin Blanc ★★★★ Spiced apple & quince on **14**, complemented by oak (20%, older). Creamy, with vivacious limy twist, delightful on its own or with a meal. **Sauvignon Blanc** ★★★ Ripe, tropical **15** with a touch of grassiness; dry, balanced fruit & freshness for easy enjoyment. Also tasted: **Rosé de Pinotage 15** ★★★ Not retasted: **Pinotage-Merlot 13** ★★★ Not tasted: **Pinotage**. — MW

Location/map: Stellenbosch ▪ Map grid reference: E3 ▪ WO: Stellenbosch/Coastal ▪ Est/1stB 1992 ▪ Tasting & sales Mon-Fri 9–5 Sat 10–4 ▪ Fee based on tasting option selected ▪ Closed Easter Fri/Sun, Dec 25 & Jan 1 ▪ Cellar tours by appt ▪ Child friendly ▪ Function venue ▪ Luxury 4-star Country Lodge ▪ Owner(s) AdVini ▪ Winemaker(s) Dirk Coetzee (Aug 2009), with Mattheus Thabo (Jan 2007) & Francois Conradie (Jan 2014) ▪ Viticulturist(s) Leigh Diedericks, with Johan Pienaar ▪ 64.9ha/27.26ha (cabs s/f, merlot, ptage, chenin, sauv) ▪ 250t/41,000cs own label 44% red 38% white 18% rosé ▪ IPW ▪ PO Box 7267 Stellenbosch 7599 ▪ info@lavenir.co.za ▪ www.lavenirestate.co.za ▪ S 33° 53' 7.78" E 018° 50' 37.12" ▪ F +27 (0)21-889-5258 ▪ **T +27 (0)21-889-5001**

La Vierge Private Cellar

Vintage 2015 elicited superlatives from the team at these Hemel-en-Aarde dryland vineyards, planted on virgin soils (hence 'La Vierge'). 'Excellent, with great-quality grapes; look out for some outstanding future single-block wines.' No doubt these will include more seductive pinot noirs, to the delight of winemaker Gerhard Smith, a self-confessed pinotphile, settling in after eight crushes in New Zealand.

La Vierge Collection

★★★★ **La Vierge Noir** Top of the range pinot noir, fruit from coolest vineyard lavished with new oak (20%) & longer bottle maturation in **13**; complex mushroom & farmyard features, savoury & streamlined.

★★★★ **Original Sin** Steely capsicum leads out **15** sauvignon, but softer acidity balances, spotlights slatey mineral core. Focused, intriguingly salty, perfect for seafood. Dash wooded semillon adds to gravitas.

Last Temptation ⊘ ★★★ Sampled from tank, bone-dry **15** riesling has stonefruit flavours & tingling core of acidity. Excellent as an aperitif; versatile at table.

Anthelia ★★★☆ Round, rich shiraz, oozes fleshy mulberries, **13** is deliciously drinkable – but note 15% alcohol. **Jezebelle ★★★☆** Sleekly built chardonnay; **14**'s lime & white peach features crackle with fresh acidity, partial oaking (20% new) fills out the balanced palate. Also tasted: **The Affair 14 ★★★☆ Nymphomane 13 ★★★☆** Not retasted: **Seduction Pinot Noir 13 ★★★☆** Not tasted: **Satyricon**. — DS

Location: Hermanus ▪ Map: Elgin, Walker Bay & Bot River ▪ WO: Hemel-en-Aarde Ridge/Cape South Coast ▪ Est 1997 ▪ 1stB 2006 ▪ Tasting & sales Mon-Sun 10–5 ▪ Closed Good Fri & Dec 25 ▪ Cellar tours by appt ▪ La Vierge Restaurant & Champagne Verandah ▪ Tour groups by appt ▪ Owner(s) La Vierge Wines (Pty) Ltd & Viking Pony Properties 355 (Pty) Ltd ▪ Winemaker(s) Gerhard Smith (Nov 2012), with Alexander Grier (Nov 2013) ▪ Viticulturist(s) Petrus Bothma (2008) ▪ 44ha (pinot, sangio, shiraz, chard, riesling, sauv, sem) ▪ 160t 60% red 40% white ▪ PO Box 1580 Hermanus 7200 ▪ info@lavierge.co.za ▪ www.lavierge.co.za ▪ S 34° 22' 22.3" E 019° 14' 29.4" ▪ F +27 (0)28-312-1388 ▪ **T +27 (0)28-313-0130**

Lazanou Organic Vineyards

The organic ethos at this tiny family estate near Wellington goes way beyond the vineyards, encompassing home-grown food and harmony with nature at all levels. Their popular Open Day allows visitors to partake of their bounty in al fresco splendour, and there's attractive new guest accommodation in the converted cowshed. Their first MCC bubbly is due next year.

★★★★ Syrah-Mourvèdre Reserve More flamboyant, ripe & spicy than sibling. 27 months new oak (25% American) impart distinct clove & smoky bacon, espresso nuance. Supple tannins, polished, but oak needs time to harmonise on **13**.

★★★★ Chenin Blanc-Chardonnay-Viognier **14** & **15** tasted. Similar seamless, aromatic blends with genteel but insistent scented peach & fresh ginger nuance, especially on **15**. Both beautifully fresh & balanced, but **15** fractionally brighter & tangier, with slightly lower alcohol (12.5%) & more acidity.

Viognier **15** too young to rate fairly. Also tasted: **Syrah** **13 ★★★★ Syrah-Mourvèdre** **13 ★★★★ Chenin Blanc** **05 ★★★☆** Not tasted: **Chardonnay**. — MW

Location/WO: Wellington ▪ Map: Paarl & Wellington ▪ Map grid reference: F1 ▪ Est 2002 ▪ 1stB 2006 ▪ Tasting & sales by appt ▪ Open days with wine & food pairing – booking required ▪ Tour groups ▪ Farm produce ▪ Cowshed Cottage ▪ Owner(s) Josef Lazarus & Candice Stephanou ▪ Winemaker(s) Rolanie Lotz (Jan 2011, consultant) ▪ Viticulturist(s) Johan Wiese (Jan 2006, consultant) ▪ 8.48ha/5.54ha (mourv, shiraz, chard, chenin, viog) ▪ 50t/6,000cs own label 50% red 50% white ▪ Organic certification by Ecocert ▪ PO Box 834 Wellington 7654 ▪ wine@lazanou.co.za ▪ www.lazanou.co.za ▪ S 33° 35' 59.58" E 018° 59' 36.12" ▪ F +27 (0)86-670-9213 ▪ **T +27 (0)83-265-6341**

☐ **Lazy Days** *see* Laborie Wine Farm
☐ **Le Bistro** *see* Zandvliet Wine Estate

Le Bonheur Wine Estate

If it ain't broke, don't fix it, the saying goes and brand Le Bonheur certainly requires no tinkering. It's stronger than ever, with the same classic and elegant styling associated with stalwart Sakkie Kotzé over his 20+ year tenure continuing under the younger guard at the gracious estate near Stellenbosch.

★★★★☆ Cabernet Sauvignon Cab shows its authoritative tannic stamp on **11** vintage. Firmly structured, but not ungenerous, with classic cassis, prune & cedar flavours. Enhanced by 18 months French oak, powerful but streamlined, will reward cellaring.

★★★★ Prima Consistently classy blend of merlot, cab franc, cab, 58/28/14 in **10** (★★★★★) which raises the bar on **09**. Still so fresh, with rich berry fruit & cool, leafy nuance. More new oak (65%) well integrated, finely tailored tannins. Ageworthy, but already tempting.

Sauvignon Blanc ★★★☆ Gentle passionfruit & herbaceous flavours with clean balanced acidity & some mid-palate leesy breadth. **15** tangy grapefruit twist favours food. Stellenbosch WO. Also tasted: **Chardonnay 15 ★★★★** Occasional release: **Tricorne, Single Vineyard Sauvignon Blanc**. — MW

Location/map: Stellenbosch ▪ Map grid reference: F1 ▪ WO: Simonsberg–Stellenbosch/Stellenbosch ▪ Est 1790s ▪ 1stB 1972 ▪ Tasting & sales Mon-Fri 9–5 Sat/Sun 10–4 ▪ Fee R25/5 wines ▪ Closed Good Fri & Dec 25

▪ Cheese platters ▪ Picnics ▪ Conferences ▪ Outdoor film evenings, every last Friday of the summer months — booking essential ▪ Owner(s) Lusan Premium Wines ▪ Winemaker(s) Lauren Behrens (Oct 2013) ▪ Viticulturist(s) Rudi Buys & Jaco van der Berg (both Oct 2013) ▪ 163ha/75ha (cab, merlot, chard, sauv) ▪ 600t/60,000cs own label 30% red 70% white ▪ PO Box 104 Stellenbosch 7599 ▪ info@lebonheur.co.za ▪ www.lebonheur.co.za ▪ S 33° 50' 1.0" E 018° 52' 21.4" ▪ F +27 (0)21-875-5624 ▪ **T +27 (0)21-875-5478**

☐ **Leeumasker** *see* Maske Wines

Leeuwenberg ⓠ

Wine trader Tanja Kastien-Hilka's belief that gaps exist for SA wine in Germany led her to mobilise her local contacts and export 1,000 cases of her own brand, Drie Kleine Leeuwen (after sons Yannick, Ben and Raphael), in 2010. Today there are 3 ranges, volumes top 6,000 cases, markets across Europe are served and the new Leeuwenberg Wine Bar in Wiesbaden serves Tanja's and other premium SA wines.

Flagship range

★★★★ **Two Barrels Shiraz** Unmistakably New World in styling, **12** (★★★☆) has forthcoming plush dark cherries, heaps of vanilla spicing, a creamy texture. Very easy to like but lacks the class of **11**.

Barrel Selection Merlot ⓃⒺⓌ ★★★☆ Pre-bottled **12** ticks all the boxes, piquant red berries, dark chocolate, a herb nuance, nicely smooth texture, dry finish. Already accessible, can be cellared for a few years. Bot River WO, like Shiraz. **Red** ⓃⒺⓌ ★★★☆ Cabs sauvignon & franc, with shiraz, dab of petit verdot, 15 months in new French oak, give **13** structure, cedar & white pepper notes but at core is enough dark-toned fruit to handle the firm tannins. Not yet at peak but promises well. Also in magnum.

Cellar Selection

Petit Verdot ⓃⒺⓌ ★★★☆ Fruitcake, scrub, white pepper, deep & dark **13** has an attractive smoky, savoury palate. Still in its youthful prime, should open up more with cellaring; give it time — nudges the next level. **Directors Reserve White** ⓃⒺⓌ ★★★ Chenin with 8% oaked viognier, **14** parades peach pip & quince perfume, becomes more mineral on the palate, a slight almond savouriness. Subdued, but a great food wine. Bot River WO. Also in magnum. Also tasted: **Cellar Blend 13** ★★★☆ Not tasted: **Directors Reserve Red**. Discontinued: **Shiraz-Cabernet Sauvignon, Chardonnay-Pinot Noir**.

Drie Kleine Leeuwen range

Sauvignon Blanc ⓃⒺⓌ ★★★☆ Guava & passionfruit, youthfully fresh **15** has an appealing vibrancy, zesty length. Also tasted: **Merlot 13** ★★★ Not tasted: **Pinotage Rosé**. Discontinued: **Chardonnay Unwooded**. — CR

WO: Philadelphia/Bot River ▪ Est/1stB 2010 ▪ Tasting only in Wiesbaden, Germany Mon-Fri 11-7 Sat 10-6 ▪ Closed all pub hols ▪ Owner(s) Tanja Kastien-Hilka ▪ Winemaker(s) Frank Kastien & Kobie Viljoen ▪ 6,000cs own label 60% red 40% white ▪ PO Box 422 Franschhoek 7690 ▪ sales@leeuwenbergwines.com ▪ www.leeuwenbergwines.com ▪ **T +49 (0)611-308-6778**

☐ **Leeuwenjacht** *see* Fairview

Leeuwenkuil Family Vineyards

Willie and Emma Dreyer are among the Cape's most substantial vineyard owners, with large holdings in Swartland and Voor Paardeberg — some of whose grapes find their way into bottles bearing highly important names. The last five years or so have seen them also appearing under the Dreyers' own label (named for their home farm) to growing acclaim. Fashionable-chic cinsaut and rare-in-the-Cape marsanne now join the line-up of grapes — room for expansion is essentially unlimited, so watch this space.

Heritage series

★★★★ **Syrah** Was 'Premium Shiraz'. Remarkable **13** (★★★★★) without stalky touch of **12**. Full, spicy generosity speaks even more of dry stones & warm scrubby hillsides than of intense dark fruit. Powerful but exquisite, succulent tannins guard the fruit to emerge in years to come. Lingers for ages.

★★★★ **Chenin** ⓧ Was 'Premium Chenin'. Stonefruit, thatch; hints of smoke & earth on **13**. More enigmatic, subtle & silky than standard (unwooded) version. Tight & restrained, needs time to blossom. Like Shiraz, natural ferment.

Cinsault ⓝ ★★★½ Subtle perfume on riper-styled **14** of sweet red fruit with savoury underpinning. Tasty combo elegance & rusticity, with modest tannic grip; but lacks concentration to help it to a long, satisfying finish. Repays decanting in youth. **Marsanne** ⓝ ★★★★ **14** a welcome addition of this unusual variety (with 10% roussanne). Characterful, with stone, floral, dried grass notes. Subtle & supple rather than concentrated, with a modest finish. Good lemony acid. WO Voor Paardeberg

Leeuwenkuil range

★★★★ **Family Reserve White** ⊘ Ex-tank, fresh, flavourful, interesting **14** is 50% chenin with 6 others! Repeats success of **13**, with citrus & stonefruit; richness enlivened by succulent acid. Great value. WO Coastal.

Shiraz ⓦ ★★★ Easygoing, expressive **14** preview with ripe sweet fruit plus some fynbos notes. Taut enough smooth tannin to ground the full-flavoured exuberance. **Chenin Blanc** ⊘ ⓦ ★★★ Fresh notes of thatch & dried peach on flavoursome **15**. Deftly balanced & rather delicious, if not persistent.

Also tasted: **Cinsaut Rosé** ⊘ **15** ★★★ Not retasted: **Family Reserve Red 12** ★★★★ — TJ

Location: Swartland ▪ WO: Swartland/Coastal/Voor Paardeberg ▪ Est 2008 ▪ 1stB 2011 ▪ Closed to public ▪ Owner(s) Willie & Emma Dreyer ▪ Cellarmaster(s) Pieter Carstens (Aug 2008) ▪ Winemaker(s) Gustav Fouche & Johan Gerber (both Dec 2012), Corrien Geleijnse & Bernard Allison (both Jan 2012), Madré van der Walt (Sep 2013), with Jehan de Jongh (Aug 2008) ▪ Viticulturist(s) Koos van der Merwe (Dec 2008) & Claude Uren (Jan 2012) ▪ 4,550ha ▪ 36,500t/27m L 70% red 30% white ▪ Fairtrade, WIETA ▪ PO Box 249 Koelenhof 7605 ▪ kobus@leeuwenkuilfv.co.za ▪ F +27 (0)21-865-2780 ▪ **T +27 (0)21-865-2455**

Le Fût   ⓠ ⓐ

Trevor and Joan Ernstzen indulged their love of wine just over a decade ago by buying and restoring an old Paarl wine farm. They combine running a special functions venue with tending vines. Most of the crop is sold, except for just enough for a fût or two of their own wine.

Shiraz Reserve ⓧ ★★★ Development shows on interesting **07**. Not heavy (though big 15% alcohol) though shy on fruit, with more savoury, smoky & earthy notes to follow. — JP

Location/WO: Paarl ▪ Map: Paarl & Wellington ▪ Map grid reference: F5 ▪ Est 2004 ▪ 1stB 2005 ▪ Tasting by appt ▪ Conference/function/wedding venue ▪ Owner(s) Trevor & Joan Ernstzen ▪ Winemaker(s) Trevor Ernstzen (Nov 2004) ▪ Viticulturist(s) Joan Ernstzen (Nov 2004) ▪ ±17ha/9ha (shiraz, chenin, cbard, riesling) ▪ 80t/600cs own label 100% red ▪ PO Box 156 Paarl 7622 ▪ wine@lefut.co.za ▪ www.lefut.co.za ▪ S 33° 44' 34.38" E 019° 0' 39.90" ▪ F +27 (0)86-675-5114 ▪ **T +27 (0)83-561-1555**

☐ **Legacy Johannisberger** *see* DGB
☐ **Legends of the Labyrinth** *see* Doolhof Wine Estate

Le Grand Chasseur Wine Estate   ⓠ ⓖ

'The great hunter' – the splendid African Fish Eagle that frequents this stretch of the Breede River gives its name to the own label of this large Robertson property, where five generations of De Wets have farmed. It's been some years, however, since we have tasted any new releases.

Location/map: Robertson ▪ Est 1881 ▪ 1stB 1999 ▪ Tasting by appt ▪ Closed all pub hols ▪ Owner(s) Albertus de Wet ▪ Cellarmaster(s)/winemaker(s) Carel Botha (Jan 2011) ▪ Viticulturist(s) Francois Viljoen (Jan 1998, consultant) ▪ ±1,300ha/300ha (cab, merlot, ptage, ruby cab, shiraz, chard, chenin, cbard, muscadel w, nouvelle, sauv) ▪ ±4,500t ▪ IPW ▪ PO Box 439 Robertson 6705 ▪ cellar@lgc.co.za, sales@lgc.co.za ▪ www.lgc.co.za ▪ S 33° 48' 26.8" E 019° 52' 40.1" ▪ F +27 (0)23-626-1048 ▪ **T +27 (0)23-626-1048**

☐ **Le Grand Jardin** *see* Jean Daneel Wines
☐ **Leipoldt 1880** *see* Wineways Marketing

Leipzig Winery

Francois and Lida Smit's Leipzig farm in scenic Nuy Valley near Worcester has gained red-wine barrel- and bottle-maturation cellars since last edition, plus an as yet untasted Bordeaux red blend and wood-fermented chenin blanc, from old Durbanville vines. The many cellardoor attractions now include Saturday morning cheese and charcuterie platters 'to pair with the fabulous wines'.

Master Blend ★★★ Mostly cab & pinotage, with rounding merlot & dollop malbec. Though young, **14** is already open, with gentle tannin structure & good fruit lifted by unoaked merlot portion. WO W Cape, like White. **Viognier ★★** Unpretentious **14**, peach & floral notes, moderate & gentle varietal character. WO Nuy. **White Leipzig ★★★** Flagship white is a 4-way blend of mainly chardonnay & viognier, mostly older-oaked. Like debut **13**, **14** is appealingly unforced, with moderately intense peach, apple & slight nutty tones. Also tasted: **Chardonnay 14 ★★☆ Chenin Blanc 14 ★★ Sauvignon Blanc 15 ★★★** Not retasted: **Cabernet Sauvignon 13 ★★★ Pinotage 13 ★★★ Shiraz 13 ★★** — JPf

Location/map: Worcester ▪ WO: Stellenbosch/Western Cape/Nuy ▪ Est/1stB 2013 ▪ Tasting, sales & cellar tours Tue-Sat 10-3; or by appt ▪ Closed Ash Wednesday, Easter Mon, Dec 25 & Jan 1 ▪ Cheese & charcuterie platters Sat 11.30-2 ▪ Facilities for children ▪ Tour groups ▪ Conferences ▪ Weddings/functions ▪ Walks/hikes ▪ MTB trail ▪ Guided tours by appt: historic buildings & art ▪ Leipzig Country House ▪ Owner(s) Francois & Lida Smit ▪ Cellarmaster(s)/winemaker(s) Mark Carmichael Green (Feb 2013, consultant) ▪ 10ha/4.5ha (sauv) ▪ 26t/2,917cs own label 49% red 51% white ▪ PO Box 5104 Worcester 6849 ▪ winery@leipzigcountryhouse.co.za ▪ www.leipzigcountryhouse.co.za ▪ S33° 38' 29.90" E 019° 38' 9.44" ▪ F +27 (0)86-295-5116 ▪ **T +27 (0)23-347-8422**

Le Lude Méthode Cap Classique

In 2009, Nic and Ferda Barrow, who own a portfolio of hotels and country houses, decided to build a specialist méthode cap classique cellar in Franschhoek. They proudly claim to be the first Cape cellar to ferment and mature a proportion of their MCC under cork – as opposed to crown cap – which 'gives a unique dimension to the wine'. The maiden Brut and Brut Rosé were released after we went to press. An exciting project is a newly planted test vineyard in cool, high Sutherland.

Location/map: Franschhoek ▪ Est 2009 ▪ 1stB 2012 ▪ Tasting, sales & cellar tours Mon-Fri 10-5 Sat & pub hols 10-4 Sun 11-4 ▪ Restaurant ▪ Guest house ▪ Owner(s) Nic & Ferda Barrow ▪ Winemaker(s) Paul Gerber (May 2010) ▪ Viticulturist(s) Eben Archer (2011/12, consultant) & Alain Deloire (2011/12, consultant/research) ▪ 6.2ha/3.4ha (pinot noir/meunier, chard) ▪ 100t/55,000 btls own label 100% MCC ▪ PO Box 578 Franschhoek 7609 ▪ info@lelude.co.za ▪ www.lelude.co.za ▪ F +27 (0)44-279-1793 ▪ **T +27 (0)87-754-9926**

Le Manoir de Brendel

Consultant winemakers are employed by Christian and Maren Brendel, German proprietors of this exclusive Franschhoek guest house and winelands function venue, to vinify house wines from the small riverside vineyard. The sauvignon blanc returns to the guide this edition after a lengthy absence.

Brendel Collection
Sauvignon Blanc ★★★ Quiet tropical ripeness on **15** offset by invigorating freshness. Not retasted: **Cabernet Sauvignon 07 ★★★ Merlot 06 ★★★ Pinotage 08 ★★☆ Shiraz 06 ★★★**

Le Manoir de Brendel Collection
Shiraz ⦵ ★★★ 05's stewed fruit showing bottle-age nutty character, drink soon. — AL

Location/map/WO: Franschhoek ▪ Est/1stB 2003 ▪ Tasting daily 12-4 ▪ Fee R40pp, waived on purchase ▪ Sales daily 7.30-4.30 ▪ Closed Good Fri, Dec 25/26 & Jan 1; also closed when booked for weddings/conferences ▪ Facilities for children ▪ Gift shop ▪ Conferences: day package (60 pax)/overnight package incl 9 rooms ▪ Walks ▪ Weddings (up to 60 pax) with chapel & wooden terrace on the river ▪ 5-star guest house (9 suites) ▪ Owner(s) Christian & Maren Brendel ▪ Winemaker(s) Cerina de Jongh & Gerda Willers ▪ Viticulturist(s) Paul Wallace (consultant) ▪ 30ha/±23ha (cab, merlot, ptage, shiraz, chard, chenin, sauv, sem) ▪ ±150t ▪ PO Box 117 La Motte Franschhoek 7691 ▪ lmb@brendel.co.za ▪ www.le-manoir-de-brendel.com ▪ S 33° 52' 52.8" E 019° 3' 42.2" ▪ F +27 (0)21-876-4524 ▪ **T +27 (0)21-876-4525**

Lemberg Wine Estate   Ⓥ Ⓨ 🥪 🏠 📷 ♿

Winemaker Niël Russouw is packing his bags – for France's Languedoc, to gain experience with grenache noir that will guide his decisions when the vines planted in 2012 come into full production this year. Also coming online is a new hárslevelü vineyard which went into the ground at the same time. This was a variety nurtured by winegrowing pioneer Janey Muller when she established the Tulbagh winery in 1978. Current owner Henk du Bruyn is determined to maintain the tradition.

Yellow Label range

★★★★ **Spencer** From pinotage. New-oak portion distinguishes this from sibling. Succulent, vanilla & cardamom scented **13** (★★★★☆) restrained, like sophisticated **12**. Marries well-managed tannins, seamless drinkability with presence & authority.

★★★★ **Nelson** (NEW) Glorious red fruit & spice on **13**, syrah/shiraz with drop carignan. Subtle meaty highlights, tealeaf tannin, refreshing acidity assist 50% new oak give form to full-fruited core.

★★★★ **Hárslevelü** Rare-in-SA white grape, long associated with Hungarian sweet white, here made dry & oxidatively. Waxy **14** silk texture on a full body, white peach freshness. Worth seeking out.

★★★★☆ **Lady** Innovative mix of oxidatively made (in older wood) viognier (52%), semillon (21%) dashes hárslevelü, sauvignon. Nutty & sleek **14** with seemingly boundless dried peach & pear flavours, liquorice tail. As succulent & refined as **13**. WO W Cape.

★★★★☆ **Surin** Ⓥ Standout dessert from vine-dried sauvignon, older oak fermented. **12** (★★★★) barrel sample's decadent richness well refreshed by lively acidity, though touch more unctuous than **11**.

Not retasted: **Pinot Noir 13** ★★★

White Label range

★★★★ **Sauvignon Blanc** Pre-bottling, **15** (★★★★☆) bone-dry with khaki bush & spice nuances, subtle cassis & grass. Charming but not as persistent as **14**. Rating provisional.

Pinotage ★★★ Characterful early-drinking **14** mixes berries with slight leathery note, sweet-sour palate. No new oak, as for all these reds; whole-berry ferment. WO W Cape. Also tasted: **Cape Blend 14** ★★★★ **Syrah Blanc de Noir 14** ★★★ Not retasted: **Syrah 13** ★★★ — CvZ

Location/map: Tulbagh ▪ WO: Tulbagh/Western Cape ▪ Est 1978 ▪ Tasting, sales & cellar tours Mon-Fri 9-5 Sat/Sun 10–3 ▪ Fee R25, waived on purchase ▪ Closed Dec 25 ▪ Meals, cheese platters & picnics by appt – book prior to visit ▪ BYO picnic ▪ Table olives & olive oil ▪ Function venue (40-60 pax) ▪ Self-catering guest cottage (sleeps 4) ▪ Fly fishing (equipment available) ▪ Sunset rowboat trips by prior arrangement ▪ Owner(s) Henk du Bruyn ▪ Winemaker(s) Niël Russouw (Jan 2014) ▪ Viticulturist(s) Niël Russouw (Jan 2014) & consultants ▪ 21ha/9ha (grenache, ptage, pinot, shiraz, hárslevelü, sauv, viog) ▪ 100t/11,000cs own label 60% red 30% white 9% rosé 1% vine dried sauv ▪ IPW, Envirowines (2012) ▪ PO Box 221 Tulbagh 6820 ▪ suzette@lemberg.co.za ▪ www.lemberg.co.za ▪ S 33° 18' 8.27" E 019° 6' 23.06" ▪ F +27 (0)21-300-1131 ▪ **T +27 (0)21-300-1130**

☐ **Le Noe** *see* Barnardt Boyes Wines

Leopard Frog Vineyards

Canadian-born vigneron David John Bate uses this Fairtrade and WIETA-accredited label as a showcase for interesting, sometimes unique vinifications. While several featured in earlier editions, including a blend that reunites cab and its parents, cab franc and sauvignon blanc, are still available, new (untasted) craftings include a white blend of 13 varieties from Stellenbosch, a méthode cap classique bubbly from pinotage and a pinot noir aged an extraordinary 5 years in new oak. See also United Nations of Wine.

Location: Stellenbosch ▪ Closed to public ▪ Owner(s) Dogwood Trust ▪ Cellarmaster(s)/winemaker(s) David John Bate (Jun 2005) ▪ 300cs own label 60% red 40% white ▪ Fairtrade, WIETA ▪ 8 Royal Ascot Lane Sandown Sandton 2196 ▪ info@leopard-frog.com ▪ www.leopard-frog.com ▪ F +27 (0)11-883-0426 ▪ **T +27 (0)11-884-3304**

Leopard's Leap Family Vineyards Ⓨ 🍴 📷 Ⓐ

Originally focused on the UK market, Leopard's Leap since 2000 has grown into a global label reaching more than 40 countries. At the chic brand home in Franschhoek, owners Hein Koegelenberg and Hanneli Rupert-Koegelenberg encourage visitors to experience the way wine and food enhance one another with, among others, a new tutored pairing of six wines from the Culinaria Collection with food partners created by resident chef Pieter de Jager. Social and environmental concern is expressed through support for, among others, the Cape Leopard Trust and Open Book Literary Festival.

Culinaria Collection

★★★★ **Grand Vin** Classy cigarbox notes & cab franc's leafy spice introduce **13** Bordeaux-style quintet. Elegance, freshness & purity also impress. The fine, ripe tannins will benefit from further year or two.

★★★★ **Shiraz-Grenache** Ⓥ Well-conceived & satisfying **12**, light, fresh texture, fine peppery zest. Careful oaking (15% new) enriches, rounds & fills out the savoury persistence.

★★★★ **Chenin Blanc** Was 'Chenin Blanc-Grenache Blanc'. Creamy, honeyed **14** step up from **13** (★★★). Flavours enhanced by old, large oak fermentation, 10% grenache blanc. Rich but not heavy, invigoratingly clean conclusion.

Méthode Cap Classique ★★★☆ Latest **NV** sparkling fresher, more citrus-toned & lively in its bright bubble than previous. 55% chardonnay with pinots noir & meunier. Also tasted: **Pinot Noir-Chardonnay 14** ★★★ **Muscat de Frontignan 14** ★★★

Family Collection

Shiraz-Mourvèdre-Viognier ★★★☆ **12** light on fruit & deep texture expected from this blend. Short, rather gravelly finish.

Classic range

Cabernet Sauvignon ★★☆ Easygoing, straightforward cassis flavours in **13** framed by gentle tannic grip. **Shiraz** ★★☆ Generous spicy aromas, some from oak, on **13**; tangy tannins softened by few grams sugar. **Chardonnay-Pinot Noir** (NEW) ★★ Dusty pink **15** rosé, gentle raspberry fruit, just-dry. **Chenin Blanc** ★★★ **15** in fresh & fruity style; tropical tones well sustained on dry finish. Also tasted: **Merlot 13** ★★ **Cabernet Sauvignon-Merlot 13** ★★ **Chardonnay 15** ★★ **Sauvignon Blanc 15** ★★

Lookout range

Pinotage Rosé ★★ Pink marshmallow & raspberry sherbet, as advertised on back label of **15**. Also fresh fruity acidity for uncomplicated dryish drinking pleasure. Also tasted: **Cabernet Sauvignon-Shiraz-Cinsaut 14** ★ **Chenin Blanc-Chardonnay 15** ★★ **Semi Sweet 15** ★★ — AL

Location/map: Franschhoek • WO: Western Cape • Est 2000 • Tasting & sales Tue-Sat 9-5 Sun 11-5 • Standard tasting fee R25/5 wines; Culinaria tasting R40/6 wines (incl one food taster paired with one of the Culinaria wines) • Culinaria food & wine pairing R120pp Fri 12-1.30 only, booking essential • Hands-on cooking classes • Shop: lifestyle gifts, wine accessories, tableware, linen ware, kitchen utensils & equipment, food literature • Rotisserie lunches Wed-Sun 11.30-3 • Child friendly • Owner(s) Hanneli Rupert-Koegelenberg & Hein Koegelenberg • Cellarmaster(s) Eugene van Zyl (Nov 2002) • 600,000cs own label 60% red 39% white 1% rosé • PO Box 1 La Motte 7691 • info@leopardsleap.co.za • www.leopardsleap.co.za • S 33° 53' 08.7" E 019° 04' 49.1" • F +27 (0)21-876-4156 • **T +27 (0)21-876-8002**

☐ **Leopard Spot** see Ayama Wines
☐ **Le Piquet** see Org de Rac

Le Pommier Wines Ⓨ 🍴 🏠 📷 Ⓐ

Like many other properties at the top of Stellenbosch's Helshoogte this was originally an apple farm, hence the name. Today it boasts a country-style vineyard lodge and restaurant, petting zoo and other treats for children, and wedding and conference facilities. The wine range is made by nearby Zorgvliet.

Jonathan's Malbec ★★★☆ Named after a bull that once decimated the grape harvest, whose photo takes pride of place on **13**'s label! This is a big wine, with scrub, blackberries, some cocoa & a nice savoury tannin grip. **Red Blend** (NEW) ★★★ Merlot-dominant 4-part Bordeaux blend, ripe **12** has expressive dark fruit, vanilla spicing adding to the richness, the firm tannins showing its serious side.

Olivia ⓃⒺⓌ ★★★☆ Semillon/sauvignon gives **14** its minerality, wet pebble flintiness, the 9 months in barrel adding a biscuit tone. Finishes clean, fresh & long. Also tasted: **Rosé 14** ★★★ **Sauvignon Blanc 14** ★★★★ Occasional release: **Cabernet Sauvignon Reserve**. Discontinued: **Chenin Blanc, Five-Three-Five, Natural Sweet Sauvignon Blanc.** — CR, CvZ

Location/map: Stellenbosch ▪ Map grid reference: H4 ▪ WO: Banghoek ▪ Est/1stB 2003 ▪ Wine tasting Mon-Sun 9-5 ▪ Facilities for children ▪ Petting zoo ▪ Picnics ▪ Le Pommier Restaurant ▪ Accommodation ▪ Owner(s) Melanie van Schalkwyk ▪ Winemaker(s) Bernard le Roux (Zorgvliet) ▪ Viticulturist(s) Hannes Jansen van Vuuren ▪ 16ha/4.8ha (malbec, sauv) ▪ 4,000cs own label 45% red 55% white ▪ PO Box 1595 Stellenbosch 7599 ▪ gm@lepommier.co.za ▪ www.lepommier.co.za ▪ S 33° 55' 8.58" E 018° 55' 43.14" ▪ F +27 (0)21-885-1274 ▪ **T +27 (0)21-885-1269**

Le Riche Wines   Ⓠ

Specialisation is key, as Etienne le Riche has so ably proved. His label born after moving from Rustenberg in the mid-1990s to a rented property and buying in grapes, he made cabernet sauvignon his main focus. In the process he has earned the reputation as one of SA's top red-wine producers, always with cabernet, long lived and fine, at core. Essentially a family business, with son Christo taking charge of winemaking in 2010, and daughter Yvonne involved in sales, marketing and anywhere else required (and awarded Cape Wine Master in 2015), Etienne's role as cellarmaster is to keep the vision on track. Now with a dedicated smallholding home and cellar in the Helderberg, grapes for the Le Riche range continue to be sourced from around Stellenbosch.

★★★★ **Cabernet Sauvignon** Classic blackcurrant & cedar, just a nuance of scrub in **13**, a template for cab. Succulent & silky yet a proven track record, the polished tannins promising more ageing potential.

★★★★☆ **Cabernet Sauvignon Reserve** Following on **11** (★★★★★) with plush fruit, impressive complexity, **12** showcases the Le Riche skill with cab. Smoothly curvaceous with polished tannins, the wine extends beyond fruit to fennel, cigarbox, an array of spices. Take your time here.

★★★★☆ **CWG Auction Reserve Etienne Le Riche Cabernet Sauvignon** Has the same stream-lined structure as Reserve Cab but different perfume, flavours. **12** brambleberries, cocoa, dried herbs, more Old World than New in the supple tannins, elegance, yet enough deep muscle tone for ageing.

★★★★ **Richesse** Bordeaux-style blend made for earlier drinking, but at the cellar's high standard. **13** cab & merlot, with 3 others, a cassis-laden polished delight, all elements in harmony.

Not tasted: **Chardonnay**. — CR

Location/WO: Stellenbosch ▪ Map: Helderberg ▪ Est 1996 ▪ 1stB 1997 ▪ Tasting, sales & cellar tours Mon-Fri 8.30-4.30 Sat by appt ▪ Closed all pub hols ▪ Owner(s) Etienne le Riche ▪ Cellarmaster(s) Etienne le Riche (Jan 1997) ▪ Winemaker(s) Christo le Riche (Jan 2010), with Mark Daniels (Sep 2000) ▪ 70t/9,000cs own label 90% red 10% white ▪ PO Box 5274 Helderberg 7135 ▪ wine@leriche.co.za ▪ www.leriche.co.za ▪ S 34° 0'52.87" E 018° 48' 9.06" ▪ F +27 (0)21-842-3472 ▪ **T +27 (0)21-842-3472**

☐ **Les Coteaux** *see* Mont du Toit Kelder
☐ **Les Fleurs** *see* Southern Sky Wines

Le Sueur Wines   Ⓠ ⓃⒺⓌ

Calitzdorp-based Louis Le Sueur van der Riet's output won't exceed 3-5 barrels, and even that might not be bottled in any given year, but his micro-label has a larger goal: 'To change people's perceptions of the Klein Karoo and get them excited' by experimenting with new and interesting techniques, and old and forgotten local varieties. De Krans cellar chief by day, Louis points to parallels with the climate of Swartland and says this creates the potential to make chenin blanc, among others, of similar quality.

★★★★ **Natural Barrel Fermented Chenin Blanc** Calitzdorp grapes, naturally vinified in well-sea-soned oak, for just 125 cases of distinctive **14**. Nut & thatch, slight 'brandy cask' character. Smooth & creamy, with fruit-sweet finish. — WB, CvZ

Location/WO: Calitzdorp ▪ Est 1987 ▪ 1stB 2014 ▪ Tasting & sales at De Krans ▪ Owner(s)/cellarmaster(s)/winemaker(s)/viticulturist(s) Louis van der Riet ▪ 2t/130cs own label 40% red 60% white ▪ PO Box 28

Calitzdorp 6660 ▪ lesueurwines@gmail.com ▪ www.dekrans.co.za ▪ F +27 (0)44-213-3562 ▪ **T +27 (0)44-213-3314**

☐ **L'Huguenot** *see* Leopard's Leap Family Vineyards

Libby's Pride Wines   ⓠ

'Never think your dream is beyond your reach' is Elizabeth Petersen's motto. With star sign Leo, which she associates with strength and pride, she's intent on developing Libby's Pride into South Africa's most successful black-woman-owned wine business.

Cabernet Sauvignon ★★☆ Unwooded **14** retains tone of **13** in its sweet, bright & easy black-fruit cheer. **Merlot ★★☆** Ripe berry simplicity & appeal to unoaked **14**, easy-drinking & slightly sweet. Not retasted: **Shiraz 13 ★★ Signature Red 13 ★★ Chardonnay 14 ★☆ Sauvignon Blanc 14 ★★☆** — FM

Location: Wellington ▪ WO: Western Cape ▪ Tasting & sales by appt at Linton Park ▪ Owner(s) Elizabeth Petersen ▪ Winemaker(s) JG Auret (2007, Linton Park) ▪ Viticulturist(s) Rudolf Jansen van Vuuren (2012, Linton Park) & Johan Viljoen (consultant) ▪ 720t/10,000cs own label 75% red 25% white ▪ info@libbyspridewines.com ▪ www.libbyspridewines.com ▪ F +27 (0)86-215-1811 ▪ **T +27 (0)82-745-5550**

☐ **Liberator** *see* The Liberator
☐ **Liberty** *see* Piekenierskloof Wine Company

Lieben Wines   ⓠ

While still advising The Goose Wines, Alwyn Liebenberg is devoting more of his energies to his own labels: established Quinta do Sul, with port-styles from Calitzdorp family vines; and Lieben, from selected pockets of pinot noir and, now chardonnay, beautifully packaged with origami-themed labels.

Lieben Wines range
★★★★ Pinot Noir Red cherry, raspberry aromas & flavours, grape tannin nip on **13** (★★★★). Natural ferment, 10% new oak; from widely sourced fruit versus **12**'s Walker Bay origins.

Chardonnay ⒩ **★★★☆ 14** from 7 clones (some 30 years old) around Stellenbosch, natural ferment/ ageing in 40% new French barrels. Smoky, with faint citrus tones, nutty oak flavours & grip on finish.

Quinta do Sul range
★★★★ Cape Vintage ⓠ Traditional 'port' grapes plus shiraz, tannat. Very ripe & fruit-sweet **09** is plump & pliable, more Ruby in style, with less spirit attack & tannic grip than a typical Vintage. Not tasted: **The Library**. — CvZ

Location: Calitzdorp/Hermanus ▪ Map: Klein Karoo & Garden Route ▪ WO: Western Cape/Klein Karoo/ Stellenbosch ▪ Est 2005 ▪ 1stB 2008 ▪ Visits by appt ▪ Owner(s) Alwyn Liebenberg ▪ Cellarmaster(s)/ winemaker(s) Alwyn Liebenberg (Jun 2005) ▪ 10ha/2.5ha (shiraz, souzão, tannat, tinta amarela/ barocca/roriz, touriga) ▪ 5t/580cs own label ▪ 54 Siffie Crescent Vermont 7201 ▪ alwyn@ liebenwines.co.za ▪ www.quintadosul.co.za ▪ **T +27 (0)82-610-2279**

Lievland Estate   ⓠ ⓜ ⌂ ♿

Shiraz has long been the forte of early 18th-century Stellenbosch estate Lievland, and it continues to feature varietally and in the amicable Lievlander blend. The sauvignon, a consistent performer, is especially good this year and would perfectly complement the summer picnic fare available by arrangement.

Lievlander ★★★ Accessible, mocha-laced **14** made for easy, fruity drinking. Nicely dry & savoury Bordeaux/shiraz blend. **Sauvignon Blanc ★★★☆** Expressive, vibrant **15** shows typical herbaceous character in crisply mineral tastiness. Not retasted: **Merlot 11 ★★★ Shiraz 11 ★★★** — IM

Location/map/WO: Stellenbosch ▪ Map grid reference: F1 ▪ Est/1stB 1982 ▪ Tasting, sales & cellar tours by appt T +27 (0)71-325-5382 ▪ Closed Dec 25 ▪ Summer picnic baskets by arrangement ▪ B&B accommodation ▪ Owner(s) Susan Colley ▪ Winemaker(s) Kowie du Toit (2004) ▪ Viticulturist(s) Conrad Schutte (2010, Vinpro) ▪ 50ha (cab, merlot, shiraz) ▪ 250t/10,000cs own label 95% red 5% white ▪ PO Box 66

Klapmuts 7625 ▪ lievland@icon.co.za ▪ www.lievland.co.za ▪ S 33° 50′ 29.5″ E 018° 52′ 34.8″ ▪ F +27 (0)86-628-1917 ▪ **T +27 (0)21-875-5226**

☐ **Like Father Like Son** *see* Bon Courage Estate

L'illa

The Robertson farm has been in the family of Nadia Cilliers for 6 generations, and this Noble Late Harvest is made by Nadia and her husband in the Hemel-en-Aarde cellar of the Newton Johnson clan into which she married. They're taking advice from 'the best brains' in the business to 'breathe new life' into the chenin blanc vineyard, which turns 40 this year. No '13, and '14 missed our deadline.

Location: Hermanus ▪ Est/1stB 2006 ▪ Tasting & sales at Newton Johnson Vineyards ▪ Owner(s)/winemaker(s) Gordon & Nadia Newton Johnson ▪ Viticulturist(s) AA Cilliers (Jan 1973) ▪ (chenin) ▪ 220cs own label 100% white ▪ PO Box 225 Hermanus 7200 ▪ gordon@newtonjohnson.com, nadia@newtonjohnson.com ▪ www.newtonjohnson.com ▪ F +27 (0)86-638-9673 ▪ **T +27 (0)28-312-3862**

☐ **Limelight** *see* De Wetshof Estate
☐ **Lime Road** *see* Havana Hills
☐ **Limestone Rocks** *see* Springfontein Wine Estate

Limosin

A blended brandy in Distell's extensive stable, Limosin owes its name to maturation (for three years) in barrels made of oak from France's Limousin forests. This adds the colour and flavour characteristics specifically sought for Limosin, part of the SA brandy scene for decades.

Limosin Extra Fine ⓥ ★★★ Uncomplex blended brandy, best for cocktails or with mixer. Caramel obvious on fruity nose. Rather sweet, with a dark, dense, spirity finish. — WB, TJ

☐ **Lindenhof** *see* Boland Kelder

Lingen ⓥ

Planned to yield a single-vineyard blended red, the Krige family's vines in Stellenbosch's Jonkershoek Valley are just 200 m from the Oude Nektar/Stark-Condé farm where the wine is made. Yet soil differences mean the Lingen is softer, fynbos scented, compared with its neighbour's. Helping cellarmaster José Conde shepherd the fascinating terroir nuances into bottle is acclaimed 'vine whisperer' Kevin Watt.

★★★★ **Lingen** Cab with shiraz, petit verdot & petite sirah from tiny interplanted block. **13** perhaps not as elegant or long lived as **12**, but rich, warm, supple & with delicious dark chocolate flavours. — MW

Location: Stellenbosch ▪ WO: Jonkershoek Valley ▪ Est 2003 ▪ 1stB 2008 ▪ Tasting & sales at Stark-Condé Wines ▪ Owner(s) JD Krige Family Trust ▪ Cellarmaster(s) José Conde (Jan 2003) ▪ Winemaker(s) José Conde (Jan 2003), with Elizma van Wyngaard (2012) ▪ Viticulturist(s) Andrew Klinck, with Kevin Watt ▪ 7ha/2ha (cab, p verdot, shiraz) ▪ 14t/508cs own label 100% red ▪ PO Box 389 Stellenbosch 7599 ▪ info@stark-conde.co.za ▪ www.stark-conde.co.za ▪ F +27 (0)21-887-4340 ▪ **T +27 (0)21-861-7700/+27 (0)21-887-3665**

Linton Park Wines ⓥ 🍴 ⊙

Owned by UK multinational Camellia, whose diverse interests include agriculture in southern Africa, Linton Park celebrates its local heritage through the Louis Fourie 1699 label, honouring Louis Fleurij, original owner of Wellington home farm Slangrivier. Dominated by single varieties, the ranges (including separately listed Rhino of Linton Park) may feature more blends when new vines come on-stream.

Reserve range

★★★★ **Cabernet Sauvignon** ⓥ Dark, charry brooding quality to **10** (★★★★). Extracted & firm, with sombre oak spice notes. Last-tasted **08** more expressive & brighter.

★★★★ **Merlot** Earthy chocolate tones with graphite & tar on **11**. Firm dry tannin on a somewhat lean body indicative of 2 years French/American oak, third new for 1st year then all older cask.

★★★★ **Shiraz** Harvest-boosted **09** (★★★★), svelte composition of spice aromas, mulberry fruit & lissome tannins. 2 years in wood; first 33% new, second all seasoned. Outclasses **08** (★★★☆) & **07**.

Linton Park range

De Slange Rivier ⊙ ★★★☆ Merlot/shiraz **11** a wine to take home to mother: cheerful berry features, cool minty refreshment & most agreeable tannins make for a great drink. **Chardonnay** ⊙ ★★★★ Cracking value **14** in broad, rich & creamy style of previous. Fruit is ripe & oak is obvious but complementary (50% new, year).

Shiraz ★★★★ Vibrant black cherry/berry spice to ripe **11**, with savoury olive tones, & dry tannin twist from year oaking, 33% new. Also tasted: **Cabernet Sauvignon 13** ★★★★ **Café Cabernet 14** ★★☆ **Merlot 13** ★★★☆ **Sauvignon Blanc 14** ★★★

Louis Fourie 1699 range

Chardonnay ★★★ Attractive tension between tangy grapefruit juiciness & creamy vanilla nuttiness of oak on medium-bodied **14**. Not retasted: **Cabernet Sauvignon 13** ★★★ Occasional release: **Merlot**, **Shiraz**, **Chenin Blanc**, **Sauvignon Blanc**. — DS

Location/WO: Wellington ▪ Map: Paarl & Wellington ▪ Map grid reference: G1 ▪ Est 1995 ▪ 1stB 1998 ▪ Tasting, sales & cellar tours every last Thu-Sat of the month 9-4, other days by appt only ▪ Closed all pub hols ▪ Meals/refreshments by appt ▪ 4x4 & MTB trails ▪ Annual harvest festival Mar/Apr ▪ Owner(s) Camellia PLC UK ▪ Winemaker(s) JG Auret (2007) ▪ Viticulturist(s) Rudolf Jansen van Vuuren (2012) & Johan Viljoen (consultant) ▪ 210ha/84ha (cab, merlot, pinot, shiraz, chard, sauv, viog) ▪ 720t/120,000cs own label 50% red 40% white 10% rosé ▪ Fairtrade ▪ PO Box 1234 Wellington 7654 ▪ sales@ lintonparkwines.co.za, info@lintonparkwines.co.za ▪ www.lintonparkwines.co.za ▪ S 33° 36' 40.1" E 019° 2' 15.0" ▪ F +27 (0)21-873-0851 ▪ **T +27 (0)21-873-1625**

☐ **Lion Creek** *see* Napier Winery
☐ **Lion Ridge** *see* Valley Vineyards Wine Company
☐ **Lion's Drift** *see* Silkbush Mountain Vineyards
☐ **Lion's Pride** *see* Stellenrust
☐ **Lions River Vineyards** *see* Highgate Wine Estate
☐ **Liquor City** *see* Orange River Cellars
☐ **Lisha Nelson Signature Wines** *see* Nelson Family Vineyards

Lismore Estate Vineyards ⓘ ⊙ ⓘ

Celebrating its tenth vintage this year, Lismore was established on the lower slopes of the Riviersonderend Mountains by Californian expatriate and aspirant winegrower Samantha O'Keefe. It's beneficially cool here, genuinely cold in winter, but with summer rain adding to the challenges. This is one of the Cape's more remote estates, its vineyards among a handful in the Greyton ward. Current releases of Shiraz, Chardonnay, Barrel Fermented Sauvignon Blanc and Viognier untasted.

Location: Greyton ▪ Map: Southern Cape ▪ Est 2003 ▪ 1stB 2006 ▪ Tasting & sales by appt ▪ Facilities for children ▪ Tour groups ▪ Walking/hiking & mountain biking trails ▪ Owner(s)/winemaker(s) Samantha O'Keefe ▪ 232ha/12ha (shiraz, chard, sauv, viog) ▪ 45t/6,000cs own label 20% red 80% white ▪ PO Box 76 Greyton 7233 ▪ wine@lismore.co.za ▪ www.lismore.co.za ▪ S 34° 4' 25.23" E 019° 41' 16.83" ▪ **T +27 (0)82-343-7913**

☐ **Literature Wine** *see* Nordic Wines

Lithos Wines ⓘ

Venture capitalist and vintner Sean Emery, with a wine and vine consultant, has taken charge of the Helderberg boutique winery he owns with wife Lorraine. No wines available for review this edition.

Location: Sir Lowry's Pass ▪ Map: Helderberg ▪ Est/1stB 2012 ▪ Tasting, sales & cellar tours Mon-Fri 8-5 by appt Sat/Sun by appt ▪ Fee R50, waived on purchase ▪ Closed all pub hols ▪ Owner(s) Sean & Lorraine Emery ▪ Cellarmaster(s) Sean Emery, with consultant ▪ 16ha/2ha (ptage, syrah) ▪ 20t/2,600cs own label

90% red 10% blanc de noir ▪ Postal Suite 346 Private Bag X15 Somerset West 7129 ▪ winemaker@lithos.co.za ▪ www.lithos.co.za ▪ S 34° 6' 12.66" E 018° 55' 15.28" ▪ F +27 (0)860-552-5521 ▪ **T +27 (0)21-858-1851**

Litigo Wines

As the name suggests, a legal practitioner is behind this boutique brand. 'Being a trademark lawyer must unfortunately remain my day job,' says Eben van Wyk, who handcrafts (deftly, let the record show) tiny quantities of pinot noir — only 3 barrels of '14 — alongside Peter-Allan Finlayson of Crystallum, with 'as little as possible winemaking interference'.

★★★★☆ **Pinot Noir** Dark cherry, bitter chocolate & allspice seduce on the **14** perfumed nose. Intense & elegant without undue weight: the fruit flavours are accented by a subtle smokiness & sexy spicing that vibrate in the mouth. Pure delight! Some whole bunches in natural ferment. — WB

Location: Cape Town ▪ WO: Hemel-en-Aarde Valley-Hemel-en-Aarde Ridge-Elandskloof ▪ Est 2011 ▪ 1stB 2012 ▪ Closed to public ▪ Owner(s) Eben van Wyk ▪ Winemaker(s) Eben van Wyk & Peter-Allan Finlayson (both 2011) ▪ 1.5t/160cs own label 100% red ▪ Postnet Suite 134, Private Bag X1005, Claremont 7735 ▪ info@litigowines.com ▪ www.litigowines.com ▪ F +27 (0)21-683-5952 ▪ **T +27 (0)82-803-4503**

☐ **Little Brown Job** see Cranefields Wine
☐ **Little J** see Joostenberg Wines
☐ **Little River** see De Meye Wines
☐ **Live-A-Little** see Stellar Winery
☐ **Living Rock** see Withington
☐ **Lodewijkx** see Eerste Hoop Wine Cellar
☐ **Logo** see Onderkloof

L'Olivier Wine & Olive Estate

Though mainly known as a tourist destination, with luxury accommodation and many amenities in a scenic Stellenboschkloof setting, family-owned L'Olivier does have 22 ha hectares under vine, from which boutique quantities are vinified off-site for the own label.

Cabernet Sauvignon ⓥ ★★★ Time has softened the tannins, melded them with the dark plum fruit to give pleasurable enjoyment right now: **08** at perfect drinking age. Meaty tones, some liquorice are part of the appeal. Not retasted: **Chardonnay 13** ★★☆ **Sauvignon Blanc 13** ★★★ — CR, CvZ

Location/map: Stellenbosch ▪ Map grid reference: D5 ▪ WO: Western Cape ▪ Tasting & sales by appt only ▪ Fee R50 ▪ Accommodation in manor house/villa (sleeps 8) & two cottages (sleeps 6) ▪ Owner(s) Theuns Kuhn ▪ Viticulturist(s) Hendrik Pieterse ▪ 22ha (cab, chard, sauv) ▪ ±120t/2,914cs own label 30% red 70% white ▪ Stellenboschkloof Road Stellenbosch 7600 ▪ info@lolivierestate.com ▪ www.lolivierestate.com ▪ S 33° 55' 37" E 018° 46' 54" ▪ F +27 (0)86-519-0615 ▪ **T +27 (0)21-881-3218**

Lomond

Uilenkraal River Valley near shark diving hotspot Gansbaai is the source of these wines, whose floral names reflect a sustainable farming ethos. Named for a local mountain peak and now in its second decade, the joint venture between Lomond Properties, Stellenbosch drinks giant Distell and a staff trust deserves recognition for helping pioneer cool-climate appellation Cape Agulhas, having developed 120 ha of vines on virgin land with the mantra 'Natural wines to reflect a unique site' firmly in mind.

★★★★☆ **Cat's Tail Syrah** ⓥ **12** lovely follow-up to **11**. Enjoys real cool-climate scented purity, lightness of touch & freshness despite 15% alcohol. There's toothsome savouriness in the swish, plush texture & minerality in the prolonged tail.

★★★★ **Conebush Syrah** Characterful resonating spice on **13** single-vineyard bottling diminished by present disjointed thick texture, gravelly acid. Time may bind to an extent but lacks inherent freshness of **11**. **12** untasted.

★★★★ **Syrah** ⊘ Very ripe, with some alcoholic heat subduing dark chocolate, spice notes on **12**. Careful extraction, oaking enhance smoothness, current drinkability.

★★★★ **SMV** ⊘ Commendably realised, approachable Rhône-style blend. **13** mainly shiraz, padded by 12% mourvèdre; full of life, energy & floral, spice fragrance (thanks to understated 6% viognier).

★★★★ **Pincushion Sauvignon Blanc** ⊘ **13** (★★★★) riper vintage gives more voluptuous feel to tropical fruit; maintains fresh backbone, though little hot on finish. **12** vibrant & poised.

★★★★ **Sugarbush Sauvignon Blanc** ⊘ Most enjoyable, distinctive of these **13** sauvignons. Heady quince, ripe lime scents & juicy flavours which linger deliciously long.

★★★★ **Snowbush** ⊘ Unoaked sauvignon, nouvelle balanced by oaked semillon, viognier, in **13**. Good weight, zestily clean conclusion — if a bit light on fruit intensity compared to **12** (★★★★☆).

★★★★ **SSV White Blend** ⊘ **14** 80% unoaked sauvignon with oaked semillon & 4% viognier. Typical cool-climate white peach, lemongrass & honey ensemble carried lengthily by lovely freshness.

Also tasted: **Merlot 12** ★★ **Sauvignon Blanc 15** ★★★★ Not retasted: **Pinot Noir 13** ★★★★ — AL

Location: Gansbaai ▪ Map: Southern Cape ▪ WO: Cape Agulhas ▪ Est 1999 ▪ 1stB 2005 ▪ Tasting & sales at Farm 215 Mon-Sun 9-4 by appt ▪ Closed all pub hols ▪ Guest accommodation, restaurant, conferences, hiking trail, conservation area (www.farm215.co.za) ▪ Owner(s) Lomond Properties, Distell & workers trust ▪ Cellarmaster(s)/winemaker(s) Kobus Gerber (2004) ▪ Viticulturist(s) Wayne Gabb (1999) ▪ 1,100ha/120ha (merlot, syrah, nouvelle, sauv) ▪ 750t 40% red 60% white ▪ ISO 9002, BWI ▪ PO Box 184 Stellenbosch 7599 ▪ lomond@capelegends.co.za ▪ www.lomond.co.za ▪ S 34° 34' 12" E 019° 26' 24.00" ▪ F +27 (0)21-882-9575 ▪ **T +27 (0)21-809-8381**

Londinium Wines

The maiden vintage ('10) of Somerset West-based Alan Bent's colourfully named shiraz received the nod from some serious UK palates. It's now nearly sold out and follow-ups '11 and '12 were snapped up ex barrel. Fans will be pleased a chenin and rosé are in the pipeline.

The Dog's Bollocks Shiraz ⊘ ★★★ From Stellenbosch vines, **10** is high toned, with rum-&-raisin notes & curry leaf spicing, intense sweet-sour twist. For early drinking. — CvZ

Location: Somerset West ▪ WO: Stellenbosch ▪ Closed to public ▪ Owner(s) Alan & Christine Bent ▪ Cellarmaster(s) Alan Bent ▪ Winemaker(s) John Kotze ▪ 200cs own label 100% red ▪ PO Box 3747 Somerset West 7129 ▪ wineandwhales@telkomsa.net ▪ **T +27 (0)21-852-6545**

Longbarn Winery

Given that it 'adds greatly to final flavour', natural yeast fermentation is now a fixture at David and Sue Power's serene property in Wellington's Agter Groenberg. Here winemaking takes place as advertised — in the Georgian-era barn, refurbished and equipped to suit the Powers' tiny output and hands-on style.

Sauvignon Blanc ★★★★ Now bottled, spontaneously fermented **14** shows lifted gooseberry & musk melon fruit, clean-cut acidity with enough balance for mealtimes or fun-in-the-sun times. Occasional release: **Pinot Noir**. — GM

Location/WO: Wellington ▪ Map: Tulbagh ▪ Est/1stB 2006 ▪ Cellar tours by appt ▪ Owner(s) David & Sue Power ▪ Winemaker(s) David Power (Feb 2006) ▪ Viticulturist(s) David Power (Sep 2003) ▪ 69ha/4ha (pinot, sauv) ▪ 7t/280cs own label 100% white ▪ PO Box 1295 Wellington 7654 ▪ david@longbarn.co.za ▪ www.longbarn.co.za ▪ S 33° 34' 13.6" E 019° 3' 53.6" ▪ F +27 (0)86-611-1534 ▪ **T +27 (0)21-873-6396**

☐ **Longmarket** *see* Woolworths

Long Mountain Wine Company

International drinks company Pernod Ricard continues to invest in their SA wine operation, promoting their Long Mountain and Gecko Ridge brands within sub-Saharan Africa and beyond. The key market locally remains Ghana, following the opening of offices there last year, while overseas Sweden and Ireland are proving equally successful for these popular brands.

Long Mountain range

Ruby Cabernet ★★ Juicy & appealing **14** unwooded tank sample shows forthright red fruit with sweet meaty notes on the side. A perky pal for pizza or pasta. **Chenin Blanc** ★★ Pre-bottling, **15** pleasant pineapple aromas & fresh fruit salad flavours. **Sauvignon Blanc** ★★ Correct & pleasant **15** with touch of sugar for easy-drinking accessibility. Also tasted: **Cabernet Sauvignon** 14 ★★ **Merlot** 14 ★★ **Pinotage** 14 ★★ **Chardonnay** 15 ★★ Not retasted: **Shiraz Reserve** 13 ★ **Rosé** 13 ★ Discontinued: **Pinotage Reserve**.

Gecko Ridge range

Chardonnay ★★ Fresh yellow fruits on lightly oaked **15**, simple & uncomplicated. WO W Cape, as all the Geckos. **Chenin Blanc** ★★ Fruity **15** shows tropical fruit notes (banana & pineapple) in everyday sipper. Also tasted: **Cabernet Sauvignon** 14 ★★ **Pinotage** 14 ★★

Athena range

Not retasted: **Sparkling Rosé NV** ★★ — CM

Location: Cape Town ▪ WO: Breede River Valley/Western Cape ▪ Est/1stB 1994 ▪ Closed to public ▪ Owner(s) Pernod Ricard ▪ Cellarmaster(s)/winemaker(s) Morne van Rooyen (Jan 2013) ▪ 50,000cs own label 55% red 40% white 5% rosé ▪ 2nd Floor, The Square, Cape Quarters, 27 Somerset Road, Cape Town 8005 ▪ morne.vanrooyen@pernod-ricard.com ▪ www.longmountain.co.za ▪ F +27 (0)86-775-3777 ▪ **T +27 (0)21-405-8800**

Longridge Wine Estate

Ⓛ Ⓜ Ⓒ Ⓖ

Home to a corporate wine brand before being acquired in the mid-2000s by Dutch national Aldo van der Laan, Longridge on the Helderberg flanks celebrated a 'big year' in 2015, taking in the first officially certified organic harvest, and relaunching the single-vineyard chardonnay Clos du Ciel, made from what cellarmaster Jasper Raats calls 'a true SA grand cru site' planted by former owner John Platter (this guide's founder). Jasper and colleague Hendrien de Munck also unveiled a new ultra-premium wine, Ou Steen, a Vouvray-inspired chenin blanc from Stellenbosch vines more than 30 years old.

Ultra Premium range

★★★★☆ **Ekliptika** Stylish Bordeaux blend of best batches cab franc, merlot & cab, naturally fermented. **13**'s well-judged oak supports a ripe yet fresh palate which impresses with fine silky tannins; aromas of red & black fruit, espresso & hints of toast draw you in.

★★★★☆ **Clos du Ciel** (NEW) With intensity & focus, aromas pour out of **13** chardonnay — honeysuckle, vanilla, ripe apples & hazelnut; tight palate has classic feel, with balanced oaking (100% new), moderate alcohol & upbeat acidity making an ideal food partner. Also in magnum.

★★★★☆ **Ou Steen Enkel Wingerd Chenin Blanc** (NEW) Single-vineyard chenin is honeyed & rich in **13**, distinctly off-dry but with lipsmacking acidity & restrained oaking, offering a range of flavours from minerals to stonefruit & citrus. In magnum too.

★★★★ **Edelgoud** Forthcoming orange & lemon marmalade, hints of spiced plums, honey, granadilla — **12** unwooded botrytised dessert is a trove of scents & tastes. Effortless, with sense of weightlessness on the palate. From sauvignon versus **11**'s verdelho.

Premium range

★★★★ **Pinotage** Embracing elegance over power, **13** very well balanced with ripe tannins lending support & grip; lightly spiced dark berries & meaty/savoury notes make a sophisticated departure from banana-toned **12**.

★★★★ **Shiraz** Ⓐ Crushed velvet feel highlights concentrated flavours on well-structured, long **08**. Smart oak polish, rather than dryness of **07** (★★★★). WO W Cape.

★★★★☆ **Chardonnay** Complex & fresh **13** shows aromas of orange peel, green almonds & hint of butterscotch. Well-judged oaking supports relatively full palate offering wide spectrum of classic chardonnay flavours. Also-tasted **14** (★★★★) similar but with a little less concentration & evolution.

★★★★ **Chenin Blanc** Confident **14** is complex & flavourful with white peach & quince notes, judicious vanilla oak detail & support. Very good, as is also-tasted **13**, little less vibrant but more concentrated.

Also tasted: **Cabernet Sauvignon** 13 ★★★☆ **Merlot** 13 ★★★☆

Méthode Cap Classique range

★★★★☆ **Brut Vintage Reserve** ⓐ In best years only. Finely textured & elegant **09** sparkling from chardonnay & pinot noir leaps forward from **08** (★★★★). Aromas of pear, brioche & ripe apple, the palate both dry & generous. 60 months on lees, giving beautifully persistent, fine mousse.

Also tasted: **Brut Rosé NV** ★★★☆ **Brut Blanc de Blancs NV** ★★★☆

Lifestyle range

Rouge ⓥ ★★★☆ Dry & tasty **13** 5-way blend is mostly shiraz, offers black pepper & dark fruit succulence wrapped in amenable tannins. Also tasted: **Emily** ⓝ **15** ★★★ **Blanc** ⓥ **14** ★★★ — JPf

Location: Stellenbosch • Map: Helderberg • WO: Stellenbosch/Western Cape • Est 1841 • 1stB 1992 • Tasting & sales Mon-Sat 10-5 (last tasting at 4.30) • Closed Good Fri, Dec 25 & Jan 1 • Cellar tours by appt • Longridge Restaurant T +27 (0)21-855-4082, restaurant@longridge.co.za • Private dining room available • Tour groups • Gift shop • MTB trail • Owner(s) Van der Laan family • Cellarmaster(s)/viticulturist(s) Jasper Raats • Winemaker(s) Jasper Raats, with Hendrien de Munck • 38ha (cab, merlot, pinot, chard, chenin) • 255t/30,000cs own label 45% red 45% white 5% MCC • PO Box 2023 Dennesig 7601 • info@longridge.co.za • www.longridge.co.za • S 34° 0' 55.2" E 018° 49' 60.0" • F +27 (0)21-855-4083 • T +27 (0)21-855-2005

☐ **Lookout** *see* Leopard's Leap Family Vineyards
☐ **Lord Somerset** *see* Somerset Wines

Lord's Wines   ⓠ ⓟ ⓐ

Once part of the Oosthuizen family's fruit, vegetable and export protea farm, these 13 ha were planted when viticulturist scion Jacie persuaded friends to join him in a wine venture. He chose well: at 500 m in the mountains above McGregor, the site is among Robertson's highest and coolest — perfect for aromatic whites like nouvelle and for pinot noir, now also available in an untasted fun-and-funky Craft bottling.

★★★★ **Chardonnay Barrel Fermented** With personality, presence, **14** improves on **13** (★★★☆) & boldly shows its wares: orange peel & hazelnuts underpinned by zinging acidity, a long flavourful tail.

Pinot Noir The Legend ⓐ ★★★ Was 'Pinot Noir'. Piquant cherries, red berries throughout **12** give a liveliness, brightness that's good enough for solo enjoyment, without food.

Méthode Cap Classique Brut ★★★★ White peach & bruised apple in latest **NV** chardonnay (60%), pinot noir dry bubbly. Elegant & lightish (12% alcohol) but no shortage of flavour. Also tasted: **Pinot Noir Rosé 15** ★★ **Sauvignon Blanc 15** ★★★ Not retasted: **Shiraz 11** ★★★ Not tasted: **Nectar Natural Sweet**. — CR

Location/WO: McGregor • Map: Robertson • Est 2005 • 1stB 2006 • Tasting, sales & cellar tours Mon-Fri 9-4 Sat 10-3 Sun/pub hols by appt • Saturday platters & wine • Farm produce • Owner(s) Jacie Oosthuizen • Cellarmaster(s)/winemaker(s) Jacie Oosthuizen (2006) • Viticulturist(s) Jacie Oosthuizen (Jan 2003) • 33ha/13ha (pinot, shiraz, chard, nouvelle, sauv) • 90t/13,200cs own label 50% red 45% white 5% rosé • PO Box 165 McGregor 6708 • lordswinery@breede.co.za, sales@lordswinery.com • www.lordswinery.com • S 33° 59' 20.98" E 019° 44' 28.39" • T +27 (0)23-625-1265

☐ **L'Ormarins** *see* Anthonij Rupert Wyne
☐ **Lorna Hughes** *see* Stonehill

Lorraine Private Cellar   ⓠ ⓟ ⓐ ⓐ

Cellarmaster Johan de Wet is deeply attached to this land, where his family has been growing wine for five generations. Small wonder: the farm is situated in a fertile valley with clear rivers, diverse soils, late sunrises and long afternoon shadows cast by the Du Toitskloof Mountains — perfect conditions for vines.

Cape Harmony ⓐ ★★★★ Aptly named, ripe-berried melange of cab, merlot & pinotage, **12** supple, supportive tannins & well-judged oak. Ready to enjoy. Not retasted: **Love Of My Life Pinotage Rosé 13** ★★★ **Chardonnay 12** ★★ **Sauvignon Blanc 13** ★★ Not tasted: **Shiraz, Viognier**. — MW

Location: Rawsonville ▪ Map: Breedekloof ▪ WO: Goudini/Western Cape ▪ Est 1996 ▪ 1stB 2002 ▪ Tasting, sales & cellar tours by appt ▪ Closed all pub hols ▪ Outdoor wine tasting & picnic by appt; or BYO picnic ▪ Tour groups ▪ Walks/hikes ▪ MTB trails ▪ Conservation area ▪ Owner(s) Lorraine Trust (Johan & Lori Ann de Wet) ▪ Cellarmaster(s)/winemaker(s) Johan de Wet (Jan 2002) ▪ Viticulturist(s) Leon Dippenaar (2003, consultant) ▪ ±417ha/155ha (cab f, merlot, p verdot, ptage, ruby cab, shiraz, chard, chenin, nouvelle, sauv, viog) ▪ 2,000t total 50t/±8,400cs own label 45% red 50% white 5% rosé ▪ Fairtrade ▪ PO Box 2 Rawsonville 6845 ▪ info@lorraine.co.za ▪ www.lorraine.co.za ▪ S 33° 42' 43.14" E 019° 15' 40.83" ▪ F +27 (0)86-664-2279 ▪ **T +27 (0)23-349-1224**

☐ **Lorry** see Corder Family Wines

Lothian Vineyards   ⓥ ⌂ ⊚

The Wilson brothers, third-generation grape growers after Scottish grandmother and mother Isobel, continue to transform their former protea farm on the banks of Elgin's Palmiet River, with more chardonnay grafted over from sauvignon to keep up with the demand. A recent visit to Burgundy certainly will have provided further inspiration.

Vineyard Selections
★★★★ Pinot Noir Perfumed **13** (★★★) lovely berry compote character with smooth texture & modest acidity; riper fruit & more evident oak (30% new) than **12**, misses some of its fresh elegance. Might gain more harmony with time.

Riesling ⓥ **★★★★** Refreshing aperitif style, delicate star/kiwi fruits & pine needles; light, dry & tangy with piquant lemon twist on improved **14**.

Isobel Mourvèdre Rosé ⓝⓔⓦ **★★★** Sunset pink **15**, savoury cranberry tone, pleasantly crisp sipper with clean dry farewell. Also tasted: **Chardonnay 13 ★★★** — MW

Location/WO: Elgin ▪ Map: Elgin, Walker Bay & Bot River ▪ Est 2004 ▪ 1stB 2010 ▪ Tasting by appt ▪ Honey ▪ Conferences ▪ Weddings/functions ▪ Conservation area ▪ Luxury guest house (8 double en-suite rooms) ▪ Owner(s) Wilson family ▪ Winemaker(s) Stefan Gerber (2010) ▪ Viticulturist(s) Kevin Watt (Mar 2009) ▪ 46ha/13ha (mourv, pinot, chard, riesling, sauv, viog) ▪ 60t 25% red 75% white ▪ IPW ▪ 68 Reservoir Rd Somerset West 7130 ▪ info@lothianvineyards.com ▪ www.lothianvineyards.com ▪ S 34° 11' 31.49" E 018° 58' 57.78" ▪ **T +27 (0)21-859-9901/+27 (0)82-565-7869**

Louiesenhof Wines   ⓥ ⓨ ⌂ ⊚ ⓐ ⓖ

Stephan Smit, the prime mover here, learnt eco-values in his early studies in Germany, inspiring a 'bio-organic wine' way back in 1991. Respect for the environment persists, as evidenced by Louiesenhof's support for the Bottelary Hills Conservancy and by striving to make wines 'in harmony with nature'.

Louiesenhof range
Free Run Pinotage ⓝⓔⓦ **★★★★** With fragrant mulberry & whiffs of coffee, **14** is balanced & juicy, ends on house's savoury note. **Perroquet Pinot Duo Pétillant Rosé** ⓝⓔⓦ **★★★** The 'pinot duo' are pinotage & pinot grigio/gris, made off-dry in rosepetal pink **14**, showing savoury notes & cured meat finish. **Sauvignon Blanc ★★★ 14** is barely there, with racy lemon acidity & a salty edge. Not retasted: **Pinotage 10 ★★★ Premier Collection Shiraz 11 ★★★★ Premier Collection Cabernet Sauvignon-Cabernet Franc 11 ★★★ Cape Blend 10 ★★★ Chardonnay Sur-Lie 11 ★★★**

Dessert Wine range
Roobernet Cape Ruby ⓥ **★★★** Youthful **10** fortified has spicy, medicinal notes. Pleasantly dry, dusty, with typical sweetness. Not retasted: **Sweet Red NV ★★ Perroquet Cape Tawny NV ★★★★**

Brandy range
3 Year Old Blended Brandy ⓥ **★★★** 100% potstill, from colombard (like next). Fresh & fruity, a touch sweet, with little oak influence. Ideal for mixing or cocktails. **Marbonne 16 Year Brandy** ⓥ **★★★** Less fresh than younger one, with earthy, oaky notes along with fruit & spice. Fairly rich & smooth, if not harmonious. — WB

Location/map/WO: Stellenbosch ▪ Map grid reference: E4 ▪ Est 1991 ▪ 1stB 1995 ▪ Tasting & sales Mon-Fri 9–5 Sat/Sun 10-5 ▪ Fee R30-R40pp ▪ Closed Good Fri, Ascension day & Dec 25 ▪ Bistro open daily 10-3, group bookings advised ▪ Play area for children ▪ Tour groups ▪ Gift shop ▪ Farm produce ▪ Conferences (20 pax) ▪ Conservation area ▪ Hiking & MTB trails ▪ Antique brandy kettle on display ▪ B&B guest house ▪ Owner(s) WS Smit Watergang Trust ▪ Cellarmaster(s) WS Smit ▪ Brandy master(s) Stefan Smit & Jos le Roux (both 1991) ▪ Winemaker(s) Jos le Roux ▪ Viticulturist(s) Stefan Smit (1991) ▪ 135ha (cabs s/f, merlot, ptage, shiraz, chard, chenin, pinot grigio, sauv) ▪ 900–1,000t/675,000L ▪ BWI, IPW, WIETA ▪ Koelenhof Road (R304) Stellenbosch 7601 ▪ info@louiesenhof.co.za ▪ www.louiesenhof.co.za ▪ S 33° 53' 34.7" E 018° 49' 35.3" ▪ F +27 (0)21-865-2613 ▪ **T +27 (0)21-865-2632 (office)/+27 (0)21-889-5550 (cellar)**

Louis

Winemaker Louis Nel had experience in some fine local cellars before deciding to concentrate on his own range. He shows a quirky sense of humour with the naming of the latest addition to his eclectic collection (eclectic? 'just like the winemaker', says this member of the Cape Winemakers Guild). The Titanic Cab is, he says, 'a big wine that goes down easily', like the ship. And it doesn't like ice . . . . Grapes for this and other wines are widely sourced, and made in rented space: a 'light' model he calls it, giving him great flexibility.

Louis range

★★★★ **Cabernet Sauvignon** ② The ripe, lush aspects of impressively tasty **09** are checked by melting tannins, savoury acid & resolute dryness. Like **08** (★★★★☆), will benefit from few years.

★★★★ **Sauvignon Blanc** ② Tropical fruit mingles with grass, lemongrass & citrus on partly oaked **14** from Darling. Intense, it's more refined than Buckleberry but also powerful, with forthright crisp acidity.

Discontinued: **Cabernet Sauvignon-Merlot**.

Black Forest range

Shiraz-Merlot ② ★★★★ Stylish, rather clever **13**, 90/10 blend, has choc & cherry – just like the gateau it's named for. Very soft, ripe & easy, though with some deft savoury underpin.

Buckleberry range

Cold Fermented Sauvignon Blanc ★★★ In established exuberantly fruity style, friendly **15**'s ripe but green-tinged tropicality does have a tight firm core. From Stellenbosch grapes.

Titanic range

Cabernet Sauvignon ★★★ Ripe cab's typical dark berry aromas & flavours complemented by some tobacco & spice on firm-tannined, dry but sweet-fruited **13**. Ex Stellenbosch. — TJ

Location: Stellenbosch ▪ WO: Western Cape/Stellenbosch/Darling ▪ Est/1stB 2007 ▪ Closed to public ▪ Owner(s) Louis Nel ▪ Cellarmaster(s)/winemaker(s) Louis Nel (Jan 2007) ▪ 15t/3,000cs own label 50% red 50% white ▪ 9 Forest Street Stellenbosch 7600 ▪ louis@louiswines.com ▪ www.louiswines.com ▪ **T +27 (0)82-775-8726**

☐ **Louis Fourie 1699** *see* Linton Park Wines

Louisvale Wines

Specialising in chardonnay since inception in 1989, Devon Valley's Louisvale Wines is replanting its oldest blocks at a rate of some 2 ha per annum, according to viticulturist-winemaker Simon Smith, himself a kingpin here for almost two decades. The house's signature grape features in two of the three new bottlings; the third is sourced off-farm. Planning for a new tasting venue is underway.

Louisvale range

Chardonnay ★★★★ Supple **14** has deepest colour of these chardonnays, hinting at more oak (50% new), as does light toasty, smoky element alongside the fruit. Rather more intense than others too. **Méthode Cap Classique Rosé Brut** (NEW) ★★ Bubbles disappear fast, but pinot adds quiet berry lift to chardonnay base on **NV. Méthode Cap Classique Brut** (NEW) ★★ Fresh, clean & dry **NV** from chardonnay, with brief simple flavour, but the bubbles are even briefer once the initial foam is over. Also tasted: **Dominique 14** ★★★★ **Chardonnay-Pinot Noir 15** ★★★ **Chavant 14** ★★★ **Chardonnay Unwooded 15** ★★☆

Stone Road range

Merlot ★★★ Soft & tasty, pleasantly unassuming **14**, neatly balanced, with just a little tug of tannin. **Sauvignon Blanc** ★★★ Full-flavoured, tropical **15** has easy, soft texture – the acidity just a trifle harsh on the finish, but pretty enjoyable all round. Also tasted: **Shiraz** (NEW) 13 ★★★ Not tasted: **Cabernet Sauvignon**. — TJ

Location/map: Stellenbosch ▪ Map grid reference: D4 ▪ WO: Stellenbosch/Coastal ▪ Est/1stB 1989 ▪ Tasting, sales & cellar tours Mon-Fri 10-5 ▪ Fee R20 ▪ Closed all pub hols ▪ BYO picnic ▪ Owner(s) Louisvale Wines (Pty) Ltd ▪ Directors Altmann Allers, Hendrik Kluever, Johann Kirsten & Zane Meyer ▪ Winemaker(s)/viticulturist(s) Simon Smith (Jul 1997) ▪ 34ha/23ha (cab, merlot, chard) ▪ 220t/16,000cs own label 50% red 50% white ▪ PO Box 542 Stellenbosch 7599 ▪ winery@louisvale.com ▪ www.louisvale.com ▪ S 33° 54' 32.3" E 018° 48' 24.3" ▪ F +27 (0)21-865-2633 ▪ **T +27 (0)21-865-2422**

Lourensford Wine Estate   (♀) (¶¶) (◎) (♿)

Years of viticultural experimentation are now being rewarded with fruit concentration and elegance on businessman Christo Wiese's vast, multifaceted estate, set in a mountain amphitheatre on the outskirts of Somerset West. 'On a cool property, you keep on learning,' quips CEO Koos Jordaan, gratified that their plan is also coming together in the cellar, one of SA's largest and most technologically advanced. There is a general upgrade planned of all the tourist facilities to complement the existing mini-village of craft-orientated ventures, purveying everything fine from coffee, pastries, chocolate and cheese to art and jewellery. There is also a restaurant and function venue, not to mention a host of outdoor events and activities on offer, the major portion of the property being dedicated to conservation.

Limited Releases

★★★★☆ **Merlot** Richer, riper fruit & better balance than Lourensford bottling. **13** firm, chalky oak tannins (mostly new oak) streamline the dense core. Serious & confident, just needs time or decanting.

★★★★☆ **Reserve Red Blend** (♀) Barrel selection of estate's best cab & merlot, 65/35 proportion in **11**. Sleek & muscular, dense kernel of dark fruit sheathed in dry, fine tannins (partly from 100% new French, 2 years). Youthful but polished, with pedigree to age. No **10**.

★★★★☆ **Chardonnay** Appealing lime & toasted nuts underscored by creamy butterscotch on **14**. Elegant balance & fruit intensity render 14.5% alcohol unobtrusive. Less new oak than previous, natural fermentation & lees-ageing impart succulence & freshness, to raise the bar on **13** (★★★★).

★★★★ **Viognier** Oak-fermented **13** (★★★★★) captures the essence of viognier even more than **12**. Enchanting perfume & spice, transformed into a vivacious beauty by bright & balancing acidity, not often achieved with this variety. Succulent, rich but focused & fresh.

★★★★☆ **White Blend** Drops 'Reserve'. Understated, refined & complex **12** from sauvignon with 13% chardonnay & a drop of oaked viognier. Ripe peach, delicate white flower & herbaceous tones, beautifully balanced, with clean limy thread & long farewell.

★★★★☆ **Semillon Noble Late Harvest** (♀) An unctuously rich elixir, oak-fermented **12** is dessert on its own! Cornucopia of sweet caramel, pineapple, wild fynbos honey & toasted nut flavours, yet still vibrant, balanced & tangy. No **10**, **11**.

Lourensford range

★★★★ **Méthode Cap Classique Rosé** (♀) Tangy & vivacious **11** pink sparkling from pinot noir (92%) with splash chardonnay. Freshness focuses bright & savoury red fruit. Rich, creamy tone from partial oaking & 33 months on the lees.

★★★★☆ **Méthode Cap Classique** Sea spray & green apple on **10** (★★★★) chardonnay & pinot (88/ 12) sparkling. Clean, refined, but somewhat aloof after 50 months on lees – needs time to settle & become more expressive. Less rich & creamy than **09**, still a classy food partner.

Cabernet Sauvignon ★★★ **13** remarkably supple & balanced already, clean leafy & dark fruits, dry pliable tannin structure, suave & velvety texture. **Shiraz** ★★★★ Lively, juicy drinkability & supple structure with a touch of spice from 13% new oak. Savoury/plummy **13** ready to enjoy now & over next few years. **Sauvignon Blanc** ★★★★ Racy, flinty **14**, with brush of oak & lees ageing plumping mid-palate. Light bodied but not simple, elegantly clean & balanced, ready for the table. Also tasted: **Merlot 13** ★★★ **Shiraz-Mourvèdre-Viognier 13** ★★★★ Not retasted: **Chardonnay 13** ★★★★

River Garden range

Rosé ★★★ 15 flavoursome sunset sipper from merlot, mourvèdre, shiraz & touch durif. Balanced & lively, with clean savoury/cherry tones & pleasing dry finish. **Chardonnay** ⊘ **★★★☆** Unoaked chardonnay with panache, **15** pleasing drinkability, smooth texture, fresh & lemony with the gentlest hint of viognier's aroma (1%). Also tasted: **Shiraz-Cabernet Sauvignon 13 ★★★ Sauvignon Blanc 15 ★★★** Not retasted: **Cabernet Sauvignon-Merlot 13 ★★★**

First Fruit range (NEW)

Pinot Noir Rosé ★★ Grapes unused for bubbly give **15** just-picked freshness, bright & tangy cherry flavours. Crisp & light (9.9% alcohol), perfect for picnics/al fresco occasions. — MW

Location: Somerset West ▪ Map: Helderberg ▪ WO: Stellenbosch/Western Cape ▪ Est 1999 ▪ 1stB 2003 ▪ Tasting, sales & cellar tours daily 9-5 ▪ Fee R30-R60 ▪ Closed Good Fri & Dec 25 ▪ Millhouse Kitchen ▪ Tour groups ▪ Art gallery ▪ Harvest Market ▪ Coffee Roastery ▪ Cheesery ▪ Function hall ▪ Conservation area ▪ Owner(s) Christo Wiese ▪ Winemaker(s) Hannes Nel (Nov 2002), with Timothy Witbooi (May 2005) ▪ Viticulturist(s) Piet Uys ▪ 4,000ha/135ha (cab, merlot, pinot, shiraz, chard, sauv, viog) ▪ 1,200t/240,000cs own label 40% red 58% white 2% rosé ▪ Brands for clients: Eden Crest (Checkers) ▪ BRC, BWI champion, HACCP, WIETA ▪ PO Box 16 Somerset West 7129 ▪ info@lourensford.co.za ▪ www.lourensford.com ▪ S 34° 4' 3.7" E 018° 53' 44.2" ▪ F + 27 (0)21-847-0910 ▪ **T +27 (0)21-847-2300**

Lovane Boutique Wine Estate   ⓠ ⑪ ⌂ ▣

After some hand-holding by the previous owners, winemaker and co-proprietor Hennie Visser vinified the 2015 harvest solo, and better half Theresa praises the result as 'exceptional', with yields up by about 1T/ha. The past year also witnessed extensions and renovations, and a restaurant opening on the Stellenbosch estate, home to a luxury guest house, conference venue and that pocket of vines.

★★★★☆ Isikhati ⓠ **09 (★★★★)** cab-led blend, with telling input from petit verdot & cab franc; developed leafy features, tannins softened. 42 months cask. Less sprightly & refreshing than **07**. No **08**. **Cabernet Sauvignon (NEW) ★★★☆** Burly **10** has dollops of cab franc & petit verdot. Forward characters of sombre sweet fruit, oak spice & tobacco; ripe juicy tannins, & less power than 15% alcohol suggests. Approachable now, but no hurry. **Unfiltered Blanc de Noir ★★★** Peachy-pale **14**, its cab fruit giving ripe berry notes & also a light tannic grip. Pleasingly balanced & bone-dry. **Cape Vintage (NEW) ★★★** Very tasty **12** 'port' from cab, with notes of fruitcake & honey; lightly structured for this style & ready now. Not retasted: **Cabernet Sauvignon Berries Only 09 ★★★☆ Cabernet Sauvignon Umgidi 07 ★★★** In abeyance: **Cabernet Sauvignon Iziko, Cabernet Sauvignon Tamkulu, Cabernet Sauvignon Umbhidi Wholeberry, Cabernet Franc Iliwa, Petit Verdot Umama, Summer Mist, Méthode Cap Classique, Sweet 77**. — TJ

Location/map/WO: Stellenbosch ▪ Map grid reference: D6 ▪ Est 2003 ▪ 1stB 2006 ▪ Tasting, sales & cellar tours Mon-Sun 10-5 ▪ Tasting fee R20, waived on purchase ▪ Closed all pub hols ▪ La Forchetta Restaurant ▪ Conferences ▪ Lovane Guest House ▪ Owner(s) Hennie & Theresa Visser ▪ Winemaker(s)/viticulturist(s) Hennie Visser ▪ 3.6ha/2.5ha (cabs s/f, p verdot) ▪ PO Box 91 Vlottenburg 7604 ▪ info@lovane.co.za ▪ www.lovane.co.za ▪ S 33° 57' 09.74" E 018° 48' 02.38" ▪ F +27 (0)21-881-3546 ▪ **T +27 (0)21-881-3827**

Lowerland   ⓠ (NEW)

Hennie Coetzee, fifth generation of Coetzees in this Northern Cape area traditionally devoted to sheep farming, had a dream 'of red wine and red meat'. So he planted vines on this large mixed farm in 2000; for many years, small quantities of grapes were sent far south for stylistic experimentation with the help of many seasoned winemakers. Now the aim is to challenge the image of this area as a wine producer. Son Bertie took over the farm's wine affairs in 2013, with an increasingly natural approach and a determination to express his terroir. The wines are made in Paarl.

Tolbos Tannat ★★★☆ Dusty dark berries, a lot of ripeness, verging on plum jam, **13**'s palate quite juicy with soft tannins, easy accessibility. Lightly structured, the oak not much in evidence. **Witgat Viognier ★★★** Gentle stonefruit & melon, the oaking giving biscuit flavours, **13** is the Northern Cape's take on viognier, zesty with appealing drinkability. — CR, CvZ

Location: Prieska ▪ Map: Northern Cape, Free State & North West ▪ WO: Northern Cape ▪ Est 2000 ▪ 1stB 2006 ▪ Tasting & cellar tours by appt ▪ Owner(s) Hennie Coetzee family trust ▪ Winemaker(s) Johnnie Calitz (Anura) ▪ Viticulturist(s) Hennie Coetzee, Bertie Coetzee (May 2013) ▪ 12,000ha/14ha (cab, merlot, mourv, p verdot, shiraz, tannat, chard, cbard, viog) ▪ 150t/300cs own label 80% red 20% white ▪ PO Box 292 Lowerland Prieska 8940 ▪ bioboer1@gmail.com ▪ www.instagram.com/bioboertie ▪ S 29° 29' 15.28" E 023° 0' 28.41" ▪ F +27 (0)86-677-0848 ▪ **T +27 (0)83-349-9559**

☐ **Loyal Brothers** *see* Govert Wines
☐ **Luca & Ingrid Bein** *see* Bein Wine Cellar

Luddite Wines   (?) (¶¶) (◎) (⅚)

'Totally naked' is Niels Verburg's way of emphasising that nothing at all was added to the '14 chenin during vinifcation, but the burly winemaker's colourful phrase well describes the resolutely traditional, zero-additive, machinery- and mechanisation-eschewing approach that's been fundamental to the Luddite way since its inception 16 years ago (long before 'nudity' became fashion). Said chenin vintage is also noteworthy for being the first to include a portion of grapes grown on the Bot River home farm by viticulturist wife Penny. Aside from a warm welcome, scenic surrounds and seriously fine wine, reasons to visit now also include pre-booked food-and-wine pairings.

★★★★☆ **Shiraz** Inky ruby **11** is complex, layered & powerful. Focused velvety sweet/savoury fruit & vanilla oak seduce the senses while big alcohol (15%) is well hidden. 25% new oak. Also available in magnum, 3, 5 & 9L. Made to last.

★★★★☆ **Saboteur 12** (★★★★★) a highpoint for this bold & big blend shiraz, cab, mourvèdre. Textured mouthful of bright, succulent, rounded black fruit, fynbos & dried herbs. Firm oak backbone yet silky, fine tannins & spicy cured meat lift on long finish. From 5 Bot River blocks, like **10**. **11** untasted.

★★★★ **Chenin Blanc** Orchard fruit & creamy citrus zest on broad **14**, from mostly 40-60 year old vines, naturally fermented in older oak with no additions. Balanced & complex, made for food (& in youth benefits from decanting). Overberg WO. — WB

Location: Bot River ▪ Map: Elgin, Walker Bay & Bot River ▪ WO: Walker Bay/Western Cape/Overberg ▪ Est/1stB 2000 ▪ Tasting, sales & cellar tours by appt ▪ Food & wine pairing by appt ▪ Closed Dec 25 & Jan 1 ▪ Farm produce ▪ Walks/hikes ▪ Conservation area ▪ Owner(s) Niels Verburg (2000) ▪ Viticulturist(s) Penny Verburg (2000) ▪ 17ha/5.8ha (cab, mourv, shiraz, chenin) ▪ 30t/3,500cs own label 100% red + 4,000cs for clients ▪ Brands for clients: Elgin Vintners, Oneiric, Ridgelands, Wilde Haf ▪ PO Box 656 Bot River 7185 ▪ info@luddite.co.za, niels@luddite.co.za ▪ www.luddite.co.za ▪ S 34° 12' 50.5" E 019° 12' 24.1" ▪ F +27 (0)28-284-9045 ▪ **T +27 (0)28-284-9308/+27 (0)83-444-3537**

LuKa Wine Estate   (?)

A pioneer of small-scale winegrowing in Plettenberg Bay, this family winery is now in the hands of Mark and Anneke Barnard, who are expanding the vineyards (previously just sauvignon blanc) to include pinot noir and chardonnay for an MCC bubbly. No cellar yet — the wines are still made at nearby Bramon.

Sauvignon Blanc ★★★ Cool maritime climate evident in delicate **14**. Faint elderflower bouquet, slight salty tang & rounded finish; perfect for oysters. — CvZ

Location/WO: Plettenberg Bay ▪ Map: Klein Karoo & Garden Route ▪ Est 2008 ▪ 1stB 2011 ▪ Tasting by appt ▪ Owner(s) Mark & Anneke Barnard ▪ Cellarmaster(s)/winemaker(s) Anton Smal (Bramon Wines) ▪ Viticulturist(s) Mark Barnard ▪ ±7ha/1.5ha (sauv) ▪ 8t/1,122cs own label 100% white ▪ PO Box 92 Knysna 6570 ▪ info@lukawines.co.za ▪ www.lukawines.co.za ▪ S 34° 2' 28.14" E 023° 15' 57.56" ▪ F +27 (0)44-533-6782 ▪ **T +27 (0)83-767-6218/+27 (0)82-498-7112**

☐ **Lula** *see* Rudera Wines

Lusan Premium Wines

Umbrella organisation for Alto, Le Bonheur, Neethlingshof, Stellenzicht (and its value brand Hill & Dale) and Uitkyk (including Flat Roof Manor). See separate entries.

Stellenbosch ▪ Closed to public ▪ imstrydom@distell.co.za ▪ F +27 (0)21-883-8941 ▪ **T +27 (0)21-883-8988**

☐ **Luscious Hippos** see United Nations of Wine

Lutzville Cape Diamond Vineyards   ⓛ ⑪ ⓐ ⓖ

One of SA's largest wineries, Lutzville Cape Diamond Vineyards on the West Coast produces both bulk and bottled wine, and cellarmaster Gideon Theron and team say they approach both categories with equal seriousness. The bottled wines benefit from only free-run juice being used. Harvest 2015 showed 'remarkable' quality, and was vinified with new technology to enhance flavour extraction and mouthfeel.

Francois Le Vaillant range

★★★★☆ **Noble Late Harvest** ⓐ Worthy addition to botrytis dessert category. From chenin, hedonistic **12** distinctive dried apricot & citrus peel flavour, lovely freshening acidity.

Not retasted: **Pinotage** 12 ★★★☆

Diamond Collection

★★★★ **Cabernet Sauvignon** ⓥ Fuller, more focused **13** is rounder & sleeker than **12** (★★★☆). Appealing & convincing blackcurrant with hints of spicy liquorice, suggesting better fruit ripeness.

★★★★ **Oaked Chenin Blanc** ⓩ Finely integrated oak bolsters solid, ripe fruit on **13**, with mineral emphasis & silky texture. From cooler Koekenaap & warmer Lutzville blocks.

★★★★ **White Muscadel** First since **10**, **14** is sumptuously honeyed, delightfully spicy & intensely sweet. Typical grapey fruit with zest & preserves, nice spirit grip.

Sauvignon Blanc ★★★★ Pungent khaki bush aromas, satisfying intensity & complexity on **14**. Koekenaap-sourced fruit. Lipsmacking acidity, creamy lees texture. Also tasted: **Shiraz 13** ★★★★ **Ebenaezer 13** ★★★★ Not tasted: **Chardonnay, Semillon**.

Lutzville range

Chenin Blanc ★★ Fresh & crisp **15** is pleasant but shows little concentration. Hint of litchi & pear.
Sauvignon Blanc ★★★ Appealing gooseberry & granadilla fruit over dusty pebble, hay, on refreshing **15**. Also tasted: **Cabernet Sauvignon 14** ★★ **Merlot 14** ★★ **Pinotage 14** ★★ **Shiraz 14** ★★★ **Chardonnay 15** ★★★ Not retasted: **Shiraz Rosé 14** ★★★ Discontinued: **Viognier**. — GdB

Location: Lutzville ▪ Map: Olifants River ▪ WO: Lutzville Valley ▪ Est 1961 ▪ 1stB 1980 ▪ Tasting, sales & cellar tours Mon-Fri 9-5 Sat 9-2 ▪ Closed Sun, Easter Sat, Dec 25 & Jan 1 ▪ Coffee shop & restaurant Mon-Fri 9-4 Sat 10-1 ▪ Function/conference venue ▪ Owner(s) Lutzville Wingerde Beperk ▪ Cellarmaster(s) Gideon Theron (Nov 2005) ▪ Winemaker(s) Jaco van Niekerk (Sep 2009), Brenda Thiart (Nov 2011) & Andries Eygelaar (Jan 2014) ▪ Viticulturist(s) Gideon Engelbrecht (Sep 2009) ▪ 2,100ha (cab, merlot, ptage, pinot, ruby cab, shiraz, chard, chenin, cbard, nouvelle, sauv, sem, viog) ▪ ±48,000t/400,000cs own label 11% red 89% white ▪ BRC, IPW, WIETA ▪ PO Box 50 Lutzville 8165 ▪ info@lutzvillevineyards.com ▪ www.lutzvillevineyards.com ▪ S 31° 33' 35.9" E 018° 21' 0.2" ▪ F +27 (0)27-217-1435 ▪ **T +27 (0)27-217-1516**

Lyngrove   ⓛ ⑪ ⓐ ⓐ

In prime Helderberg terroir between Somerset West and Stellenbosch, Lyngrove's vistas of False Bay and Table Mountain are among the attractions prized by guests at the 5-star country house and conference centre. In the vineyard chenin and pinotage are particular focuses, the former soon to appear in an old-vines bottling; the latter's footprint currently being extended. Also imminent are pinot noir MCC bubbles.

Platinum range

★★★★ **Pinotage 13** dense, plummy, perfumed core of fruit still enveloped in firm juicy tannins. 30% new oak imparts a sweetish vanilla dimension. Sleek & rich, serious styling that will reward ageing.

★★★★ **Shiraz** Earthy, leathery tone on **12** with some sweet vanilla spicing from more new oak (40%) than last. Ripe (14.8 % alcohol) & muscular, with well-tailored tannins. Deserves cellaring.

Not tasted: **Latitude**.

Reserve range

Chardonnay ★★★☆ Showing serious intent, part barrel-fermented **14** mouthfilling & rich butterscotch & vanilla cream flavours, freshened by a limy thread. Also tasted: **Shiraz-Pinotage 13** ★★★★

Lyngrove Collection

Pinotage ★★★ Only oaked red here; **14** high-toned strawberries & plums, bright & lively with smooth tannins, ready to enjoy solo or with spicy cuisine. **Chenin Blanc** ★★★ Loads of ripe Golden Delicious apple on **15** crowd pleaser, crunchy & crisp, light but vividly fruited. Also tasted: **Cabernet Sauvignon 13** ★★★★ **Merlot 14** ★★★★ **Shiraz 14** ★★★ **Sauvignon Blanc 15** ★★★

Lyngrove range (NEW)

Brut ★★★ NV sparkler from chenin, with green apple aroma, sherbetty bubbles & unsubtle texture perhaps better with canapés than solo. WO W Cape. — MW

Location: Stellenbosch ▪ Map: Helderberg ▪ WO: Stellenbosch/Western Cape ▪ Est/1stB 2000 ▪ Tasting & sales Mon-Fri by appt Sat/Sun 9-3 breakfast & wine tasting ▪ Guest house ▪ Conferences (12 pax) ▪ Winemaker(s) Hannes Louw & Danielle le Roux (Jun 2006) ▪ Viticulturist(s) André van den Berg ▪ 76ha (cab, merlot, p verdot, ptage, shiraz, chard, chenin, sauv) ▪ 100,000cs own label 70% red 20% white 10% rosé ▪ WIETA ▪ PO Box 7275 Stellenbosch 7599 ▪ wine@lyngrove.co.za ▪ www.lyngrove.co.za ▪ S 34° 1' 8.7" E 018° 48' 10.2" ▪ F +27 (0)21-880-0851 ▪ **T +27 (0)21-880-1221**

Lynx Wines $\bigcirc$

Spanish-born engineer-turned-grower Dieter Sellmeyer started making wine solely for family consumption. Now the Franschhoek boutique winery offers a range so wide 'it often surprises visitors', which hasn't dissuaded Dieter and daughters from adding more! 'I've always loved a good pinot noir,' he says, undeterred by a climate regarded as not cool enough. Golden Lynx celebrates recent motion-activated camera sightings of their long-elusive resident namesake (and an array of wild compadres).

Premium range

★★★★ **Cabernet Sauvignon 13** good, honest varietal expression, as was **12** (★★★★). Fruity cassis notes well supported by cedar & mint, a chocolate-like suppleness to the medium-bodied palate.

★★★★☆ **The Lynx** Complete change for flagship red: now 100% cab franc compared to Rhône blend **11** (★★★★) & better for it. **12** big step up, too, from lower-priced Cab Franc sibling, with leaf spice adding interest to deep fruit, polished tannins & bright acidity.

★★★★ **Shiraz** Good & typical spice, dark berries & dark chocolate, **13** is plush fruited & well balanced, with integrated oak & fine tannins.

★★★★ **Xanache 13** continues as pleasant 4-way Bordeaux blend, combining mint & garrigue scrub notes with plummy fruit that is accessible now & will reward further cellaring.

Pinot Noir (NEW) ★★★★ Strawberry, tealeaf & forest floor unhindered by overt oak (all older barrels). Commendable first stab **14** is honest & elegant if a little lean. **Golden Lynx** (NEW) ★★★ **15** Natural Sweet from viognier has no signs of botrytis complexity; simply sweet, with bruised orange notes & a tangy finish. 375 ml. Also tasted: **Cabernet Franc 13** ★★★ **Grenache 13** ★★☆ **SMV 13** ★★★☆ **Viognier 14** ★★★★ Not tasted: **Sweet Lynx**.

Classic range

Vino Tinto ★★★☆ **13** good partner for the white in this drinkable value range. Shiraz now the driving force, marrying Bordeaux varieties in balanced, crunchy red. **Vino Blanco** ★★★☆ 21% roussanne introduced to unwooded blend in **15**, aromatic party starter. Crisp & juicy, with pineapple & floral notes, savoury ending. Coastal WO. Also tasted: **Blanc de Noir 15** ★★★ **Viognier Tardio NV** ★★★ — HJ

Location/map: Franschhoek ▪ WO: Franschhoek/Coastal ▪ Est/1stB 2002 ▪ Tasting, sales & cellar tours Mon-Fri 10–5 Sat 10-3 Sun & pub hols by appt ▪ Fee R30 (tasting & tour) ▪ Owner(s) Vista Hermosa (Pty) Ltd ▪ Cellarmaster(s) Dieter Sellmeyer (Jan 2002) ▪ Winemaker(s) Helgard van Schalkwyk (Nov 2010) ▪ Viticulturist(s) Kevin Watt ▪ 26ha/11ha (cabs s/f, grenache, merlot, pinot, shiraz, viog) ▪ 90t/7,000cs own label 50% red 15% white 35% rosé ▪ IPW ▪ PO Box 566 Franschhoek 7690 ▪ winemaker@lynxwines.co.za ▪ www.lynxwines.co.za ▪ S 33° 51' 46.1" E 019° 2' 14.6" ▪ F +27 (0)21-867-0397 ▪ **T +27 (0)21-867-0406**

☐ **Maankloof** *see* Mountain River Wines

Maastricht Estate

Having realised the long-held dream of an own wine label with the name of their 18th-century Durbanville farm, Wheaty Louw and his family have started by-appointment on-site tastings. Vinification is still at nearby Diemersdal, where Wheaty's son works alongside his cousin and namesake, Thys.

★★★★ **Shiraz** ⓠ Soft **13** (★★★☆) shows slightly confected ripe red fruit & some spice, with moderately firm palate. More of an easy-drinker than the intense & soulful **12**.

★★★★ **Sauvignon Blanc** Delicious **15** offers capsicum whiffs &, like **14** (★★★★), a hint of Granny Smith apple on refreshing, bone-dry finish.

Not retasted: **Cabernet Sauvignon 13** ★★★ **Pinot Noir 13** ★★★ **Pinotage 13** ★★★☆ — DS

Location: Durbanville ▪ Map: Durbanville, Philadelphia & Darling ▪ WO: Durbanville/Western Cape ▪ Est 1702 ▪ 1stB 2009 ▪ Tasting by appt only, for groups of 4–8 people — contact Annelize Louw T +27 (0)82-570-3399 to arrange ▪ Owner(s) Wheaty Louw ▪ Cellarmaster(s) Thys Louw jnr (Jan 2009) ▪ Viticulturist(s) Wheaty Louw (1986) & Thys Louw jnr ▪ 105ha (cab, ptage, pinot, shiraz, sauv) ▪ ±1,100t/3,000cs own label 40% red 60% white ▪ wine@maastricht.co.za ▪ S 33° 50' 22.86" E 018° 35' 26.79" ▪ F +27 (0)86-521-9062 ▪ **T +27 (0)21-976-1995**

☐ **Maestro** *see* DeMorgenzon

Maiden Wine Cellars ⓠ

Part-time wine-tour operator Danie Hattingh's small negociant house was founded in the mid-1990s with America and Europe as focuses, gradually expanding to Asia. His Private Reserve red blend is in steady demand in the US and Malaysia, the latter also the prime outlet for his newer label, Iwayini.

Location: Gordon's Bay ▪ Est 1995 ▪ 1stB 1999 ▪ Tasting/tours by appt; also tailor-made wine tours (max 6 people) ▪ Owner(s) Danie Hattingh ▪ 3,700cs own label 100% red ▪ PO Box 185 Gordon's Bay 7151 ▪ mwines@mweb.co.za ▪ www.maidenwines.co.za ▪ F +27 (0)86-688-1177 ▪ **T +27 (0)82-554-9395**

Main Street Winery ⓠ

Artisan vintner Marais de Villiers' small-scale venture in a shared cellar on Paarl's major thoroughfare has become increasingly part-time as he's so busy with his day job of providing equipment and advice to wine production start-ups, hence no Main Street wines for tasting.

Location: Paarl ▪ Est/1stB 1999 ▪ Tasting & tours by appt ▪ Owner(s)/winemaker(s) Marais de Villiers ▪ 200cs own label 100% red ▪ PO Box 2709 Paarl 7620 ▪ mainstreet@mweb.co.za ▪ F +27 (0)21-872-3006 ▪ **T +27 (0)21-872-3006**

Maison ⓠ ⓘ ◎

Interior/homeware gurus Chris Weylandt and Kim Smith's chic Franschhoek estate's name aptly translates as 'Home'. Their stylish wines are the focus of a marketing drive, including a local guest house incentive programme, appearance at Johannesburg's Winter Fair and new website. Ongoing are invitations to loyal customers to Friday Fondue and other 'decadent evenings' à la maison.

★★★★ **Shiraz** ⓠ **12** still very youthful, unsettled. Slightly richer than **11**, with sweeter red berry fruit (1% raisined viognier co-fermented), but careful extraction, oaking allow for overall harmony.

★★★★ **Chardonnay 14** displays elegance, distinction of Franschhoek chardonnays. Ripe lemony lees-rich aromas, succulent flavours are characterful yet unshowy, & well set off by sensitive oaking (30% new). A fresh thread focuses & deliciously prolongs the attractions.

★★★★ **Single Vineyard Chenin Blanc Reserve** Ex same vineyard as unoaked version, totally different. Food-friendly **14** fuller, richer but with steely core, less obvious fruit. Toasty oak, 20% new French, complements, needs time to integrate.

★★★★ **Single Vineyard Chenin Blanc** Unoaked **14** scintillatingly pure, taut, also flourishes honeyed ripe fruit. Lees-ageing provides weight, breadth not at expense of cool, clean lines, tingling length. Interesting potential.

★★★★ **Straw Wine** A mouthful of juicy white peaches in **13** (★★★★). Very smooth & not overly cloying but lacks intensity of **12**. From air-dried, barrel-fermented chenin.

Méthode Cap Classique ★★★ Creamy, nutty evolution on **10** refreshed by brisk bubble. Bone-dry but not harsh. 100% chardonnay, old oak fermented, 4 years on lees. Also tasted: **Viognier 14** ★★★ Not tasted: **Blanc de Noir**. Discontinued: **Cape Ruby**. — AL

Location/map/WO: Franschhoek ▪ Est 2005 ▪ 1stB 2008 ▪ Tasting & sales Tue-Sun 10-5 ▪ The Kitchen @ Maison (fusion bistro, lunch 12-5) ▪ Deli (charcuterie, pâtés, preserves & more) ▪ Weddings & functions ▪ Owner(s) Chris Weylandt & Kim Smith ▪ Winemaker(s)/viticulturist(s) Antwan Bondesio ▪ 11ha/4.5ha (shiraz, chard, chenin, viog) ▪ 50% red 50% white ▪ PO Box 587 Franschhoek 7690 ▪ reservations@ maisonestate.co.za ▪ www.maisonestate.co.za ▪ S 33° 53' 09.7" E 019° 4' 39.80" ▪ F +27 (0)21-876-2116 ▪ **T +27 (0)21-876-2116**

Maison de Teijger ⓠ

Durbanville anaesthetist and small-batch vintner Charl van Teijlingen, wife Danél and children Matthew and Elda-Marie since 2004 have vinified classic red wines in their De Tyger Street home's double-garage for marketing off-site through group tastings such as wine clubs. Their focus is moving to three varieties – malbec, petit verdot and the 'white savage' – but the route to market remains the same.

Sauvignon Blanc range ⓝ

Sauvignon Blanc Unwooded ⓖ ★★★ Grapefruit & blackcurrant **15** a zippier version of oaked sibling, no less attractive. Worth seeking out at the price.

Sauvignon Blanc Wooded ★★★ Small oaked portion adds palate weight, cleverly tones down the acidity on attractive **14**, scented with peas, grass & typical Durbanville dust. Could improve over year/2.

Malbec range

Malbec Reserve ⓝ ★★☆ Smooth, fruity **11**, plums & meaty nuances, slips down easily but disappears quickly. 21 months oaked. Range previously listed as 'Durbanville'.

Pinot Noir range

Elgin ⓖ ★★★☆ Lifted red cherry on **11** from clone D115. Bright, food-craving acidity refreshes.
Walker Bay ⓖ ★★★★ Part of 6-bottle tasting pack from 4 farms. **11** has a tart bite to end but is most balanced of the range. PN 777B clone. Not retasted: **Durbanville Black Foil 11** ★★★★ **Durbanville Gold Foil 11** ★★★☆ **Durbanville Gold Screwcap 11** ★★★ **Paarl 11** ★★☆

Petit Verdot range

Petit Verdot ⓖ ★★★ Brooding fruit, tart & rich, following to bold tarry palate with good acid cleanout. **11** fine varietal exposition. — CvZ

Location: Durbanville ▪ Map: Durbanville, Philadelphia & Darling ▪ WO: Durbanville/Elgin/Bottelary ▪ Est/1stB 2004 ▪ Tasting by appt only ▪ Owner(s) Charl van Teijlingen ▪ Cellarmaster(s) Charl van Teijlingen (2004) ▪ Winemaker(s) Charl van Teijlingen, with Danél van Teijlingen (both 2004) ▪ 5-9t/±300cs own label 80% red 20% white ▪ PO Box 2703 Durbanville 7551 ▪ charlvt@kingsley.co.za ▪ S 33° 49' 02.20" E 018° 39'01.56" ▪ F +27 (0)21-975-0806 ▪ **T +27 (0)21-975-0806/+27 (0)83-456-9410**

Major's Hill Estate ⓠ ⓗ ⓑ

Wine and brandy lovers will be equally at home on Dewald Louw's farm. Named Klipdrift, it's the birthplace of the famous namesake brandy, fondly known as 'Klippies', whose brand home is in Robertson town a few minutes away (see separate Klipdrift entry). The brandy's originator and sometime farm owner, Major Kosie Marais, in turn gives his name to the wine range, currently including Cabernet Sauvignon '13, Merlot '11-'13, Pinotage '11-'13, Shiraz '11-'13, Chardonnay '15 and Sauvignon Blanc '15.

Location/map: Robertson ▪ 1stB 2002 ▪ Tasting & sales Mon-Fri 9.30-1; 2-5 Sat 10-4 ▪ Closed Easter Fri, Dec 25/26 ▪ Cellar tours by appt ▪ Facilities for children ▪ Major's Rest Guest House ▪ Owner(s)

Dewald Louw ▪ Cellarmaster(s) Alkie van der Merwe ▪ Winemaker(s) Alkie van der Merwe (Jan 2003) ▪ Viticulturist(s) Acker Hattingh ▪ 52ha (cab, merlot, ptage, shiraz, chard, sauv) ▪ 15,000cs own label 60% red 40% white + 15,000cs for customers + 100,000L bulk ▪ PO Box 561 Robertson 6705 ▪ info@ majorshill.co.za ▪ www.majorshill.co.za ▪ S 33° 49' 45.2" E 019° 53' 10.7" ▪ F +27 (0)23-626-6096 ▪ **T +27 (0)23-626-6093**

☐ **Makulu** see Imbuko Wines
☐ **Malan de Versailles** see Versailles

Malanot Wines   Ⓟ Ⓖ

From a grape-growing family in the Perdeberg area, predictably Marius Malan gravitated to wine, though perhaps the intensity was unexpected: he's a producer, online bulk wine seller, consultant and Cape Wine Master! Always on the lookout to improve the wines and increase his export sales, ranges have been realigned (the wine names remaining evocative). There are now two Family Reserve wines, with a third, pinotage, to follow. A small-scale cellar has been established at Summerhill near Stellenbosch.

Family Reserve range

★★★★ **Triton Syrah** Was 'Family Reserve'. Ripe black plum & cherry richness with layered complexity, **13** offers scrub, white pepper, liquorice spicing. Still an infant, oak has given a sturdy foundation for cellaring. No **12**, **11**. Paarl WO.

★★★★☆ **Chardonnay** ⓃⒺⓌ Pure & focused, **14** was made as naturally as possible: wild yeast, barrel ferment/aged, no adjustments, unfined. Taut elegance, lime-infused flavours, gentle almond tones, it vibrates with health.

Malanot range

> **Bush Pig** ⊘ Ⓣ ★★★★ Lightly oaked, expressive **14** chenin blanc is generously fruity, white peach & tropical tones, has a tasty, silky elegance.

Also tasted: **Vino Café Pinotage** ⊘ **13** ★★★☆ Not tasted: **Cherry Blossom**, **Flower Pot**. — CR

Location/map: Stellenbosch ▪ Map grid reference: E3 ▪ WO: Stellenbosch/Western Cape/Paarl ▪ Est/1stB 2006 ▪ Tasting & sales by appt ▪ Cellar tours by appt & during harvest only ▪ Owner(s) Malanot Wine Projects cc ▪ Cellarmaster(s)/winemaker(s)/viticulturist(s) Marius Malan (Jan 2006) ▪ 500t/40,000cs own label 80% red 20% white + 2,000cs for clients ▪ PO Box 592 Strand 7139 ▪ info@malanot.com ▪ www.malanotwines.co.za ▪ S 33° 52' 57.71" E 018° 50' 49.39" ▪ **T +27 (0)72-124-7462**

☐ **Malkopbaai** see Teubes Family Wines
☐ **Mamrevale** see Darling Cellars

MAN Family Wines   Ⓟ

A partnership among three friends, José Conde of Stark-Condé and brothers Tyrrel and Philip Myburgh of Joostenberg, the name MAN derives from the initials of their respective wives, Marie, Anette and Nicky. Described by a customer as 'everyday drinking wines for the wine geek', the grapes are sourced mainly from Agter Paarl, which also serves as inspiration for some of the evocative names. The repackaged, site-specific Tormentosa line-up, named for the Portuguese 'Cabo Tormentosa' (Cape of Storms), includes some old-vine and bushvine wines, a particular area of interest for the partners.

Tormentoso range

★★★★ **Reserve Red** ⓃⒺⓌ Shiraz/mourvèdre, with grenache, cinsaut. Complex **13** offers cocoa-rich chocolate, leather, a berry mix, backed by polished tannins & a fresh lift, making this a drinking pleasure.

> **Old Vine Chenin Blanc** Ⓣ ★★★★ Bushvine vineyard planted 1977. Old vines plus 10% American oak gives **14** palate weight, fruit intensity. Nice typicity, good ageing potential. Paarl WO.

Mourvèdre ★★★☆ Perfume of brambleberries & scrub, mix of savoury spices including turmeric, all reflected back in **13**'s smoothly textured flavours. Paarl WO, as for Reserve. Not retasted: **Cabernet**

Sauvignon 13 ★★★☆ **Old Vine Cinsaut 13** ★★★☆ **Bush Vine Pinotage 13** ★★★☆ **Touriga Nacional 13** ★★★☆ **Syrah-Mourvèdre 13** ★★★

Essay range
Chenin Blanc-Viognier ⊘ ★★★ Dash viognier's floral tones dominate the perfume but chenin's fresh & fruity flavours anchor **14**, give it drinkability. Not retasted: **Syrah 13** ★★★☆

MAN Family Wines range
Skaapveld Shiraz ★★★ Textbook smoky dark fruit, liquorice tones, smooth-textured **14** goes down oh so easy. **Méthode Cap Classique Brut** (NEW) ★★★ From chardonnay, **NV** has Granny Smith apple lively zestiness, its racy acidity the perfect palate-cleansing aperitif. Also tasted: **Ou Kalant Cabernet Sauvignon 14** ★★★ **Jan Fiskaal Merlot 14** ★★★ Not tasted: **Bosstok Pinotage**, **Padstal Chardonnay**, **Free-Run Steen Chenin Blanc**, **Warrelwind Sauvignon Blanc**. — CR

Location: Stellenbosch/Paarl ▪ WO: Coastal/Paarl/Western Cape/Stellenbosch ▪ Est 2001 ▪ Tasting & sales by appt ▪ Owner(s) MAN Vintners (Pty) Ltd ▪ Cellarmaster(s) Tyrrel Myburgh (2001) ▪ Winemaker(s) Francois Bezuidenhout (Jul 2011) ▪ 250,000cs own label 60% red 40% white ▪ PO Box 389 Stellenbosch 7599 ▪ info@manwines.com ▪ www.manwines.com ▪ F +27 (0)21-887-4340 ▪ **T +27 (0)21-861-7759**

Manley Private Cellar   ⊘ (¶) ⌂ ⌂

Plans to plant more pinotage 'to meet demand' have materialised at this destination Tulbagh property with its now 8-ha vineyard, accommodation and varied special events facilities. Demand remains overseas driven and a new range for export only is envisaged. Meanwhile local growth is 'slow, but loyal', says winemaker/viticulturist Stefan Hartmann, whose creations were not available for review this year.

Location/map: Tulbagh ▪ Est/1stB 2002 ▪ Tasting & sales Wed-Fri 10–4 Sat 10-3 ▪ Fee R25, waived on purchase ▪ Cellar tours by appt ▪ Closed Good Fri & Dec 25 ▪ Luxury B&B ▪ Restaurant ▪ Wedding & conference facilities ▪ Chapel ▪ Walks ▪ Owner(s) Manley Wine Lodge (Pty) Ltd ▪ Winemaker(s)/viticulturist(s) Stefan Hartmann ▪ 38ha/8ha (cab, merlot, ptage, shiraz) ▪ PO Box 318 Tulbagh 6820 ▪ stefan@manleywinelodge.co.za ▪ www.manleywinelodge.co.za ▪ S 33° 16' 15.8" E 019° 8' 43.8" ▪ F +27 (0)23-230-0057 ▪ **T +27 (0)23-230-0582**

☐ **Manor House** see Nederburg Wines
☐ **Marais Family** see Wonderfontein
☐ **Marcel de Reuck** see Crows Nest

Marianne Wine Estate   ⊘ (¶) ⌂ ⌂ (⅙)

After over a decade on the Simonsberg, Bordeaux's Dauriac family continues to tweak its portfolio, with a shiraz and red blend under the Selena label joining the Marianne and Natana ranges. Ongoing development of visitor facilities includes meat and cheese platters, a 'make your own wine' experience and re-conceptualised eatery Floreal Brasserie.

Marianne range
★★★★ **Cabernet Sauvignon** ⊘ Dramatic **09** has plenty of fruit weight & power but also balance thanks to fresh acidity, firm tannins.
★★★★ **Merlot** Cedar aromas entwine with savoury notes in lovely, soft, ripe **12**; supple tannins afford early enjoyability after 20 months in cask, 40% new.
★★★★ **Floreal 12** blend of cabernet with merlot & syrah/shiraz indulged 19 months in barrel, 80% new; an alluring, complex & assimilated melange. Delicious now, it will also repay cellar time.
Sauvignon Blanc ★★★★ Liberal oaking (70% of **14**, 50% new) imparts a developed creamy lees character & sweet finish. Also tasted: **Pinotage 12** ★★★☆ **Shiraz 12** ★★★☆ Not retasted: **Rosé 14** ★★★ Occasional release: **Desirade**.

Natana range
Cuvée Rouge ⊘ ★★★ Plummy dry red with unobtrusive tannins for easy drinking. **13** from pinotage & shiraz. WO W Cape. Not retasted: **Syrah 13** ★★★

Selena range (NEW)

Syrah ★★★ Unusual maturation one year in hermetically sealed steel tank with monthly nano-oxygenation. **12** is both tight & steely. This & next WO W Cape. **Cuvée Rouge ★★★ 13** syrah/shiraz with pinotage & merlot; easy, plummy without tannic hindrance. Pinotage & cab drive dusty, earthy-toned **12** (**★★**). Both part-aged in old cask. — DS

Location/map: Stellenbosch ▪ Map grid reference: G1 ▪ WO: Simonsberg-Paarl/Western Cape ▪ Est/1stB 2004 ▪ Tasting, sales & cellar tours Mon-Sun 11–7 (summer)/11-6 (winter) ▪ Fee R50/5 wines, waived on purchase ▪ Wine & biltong pairing; meat & cheese platters ▪ Picnics ▪ Floreal Brasserie ▪ Panoramic tasting deck ▪ Gift shop ▪ 1hr 'grape to wine' tour ▪ 4-star accommodation ▪ Owner(s) Dauriac family ▪ Winemaker(s) Francois Haasbroek (Dec 2012, consultant) ▪ Viticulturist(s) Andri Hanekom (Jan 2015) ▪ 36ha/±20ha (cab, merlot, ptage, shiraz, sauv) ▪ 100t/16,000cs own label 90% red 5% white 5% rosé ▪ PO Box 7300 Stellenbosch 7599 ▪ info@mariannewinefarm.co.za ▪ www.mariannewines.com ▪ S 33° 49' 57.6" E 018° 53' 37.4" ▪ **T +27 (0)21-875-5040**

☐ **Marimba** *see* Southern Sky Wines

Marklew Family Wines   (Ⓠ) (◎)

Prime Simonsberg family estate De Goede Sukses was a grape producer for 30 years before siblings Bill and Haidee Marklew renovated the old cellar in the early 2000s and began making boutique wine from part of the crop. Cellar chief Duan Brits is now advised by Australian Richard Rowe, and there's much excitement about the China market, and a reserve shiraz and rosé MCC sparkling due soon.

★★★★ Capensis Best-barrel cab, merlot & cab franc blend. Attractively earthy **13**, cassis & herb scents, fruit-layered palate & lively finish. Slightly more new oak than others.

★★★★ Chardonnay Atypical green mango nuance to part-oaked **13**'s red apple & matchstick bouquet, unusual yet attractive cucumber twist in tail; balanced glassful, with integrated modest wooding.

Cape Flora Pinotage ★★★★ Dark fruit bouquet & the promised fynbos nuance, **12** interesting earth & iron notes; medium bodied & firm but accessible, should hold few years. Also tasted: **Cabernet Sauvignon 13 ★★★★ Merlot 12 ★★★ Sauvignon Blanc 15 ★★★** — JPf

Location/map: Stellenbosch ▪ Map grid reference: F1 ▪ WO: Simonsberg–Stellenbosch ▪ Est 1970 ▪ 1stB 2003 ▪ Tasting, sales & tours by appt ▪ Tour groups (max 20) ▪ Private/business functions for small groups ▪ Walks ▪ Mountain biking ▪ Conservation area ▪ Owner(s) Marklew family (Edward Dudley, Edward William, Lyn & Haidee) ▪ Winemaker(s) Duan Brits (2003-2007; Sep 2012), advised by Richard Rowe (Jan 2015) ▪ Viticulturist(s) Billy Marklew (Jun 2001), with Duan Brits (Sep 2012) ▪ 58ha/45ha (cabs s/f, merlot, ptage, shiraz, chard, sauv) ▪ ±300t/5,000cs own label 80% red 20% white ▪ BWI, IPW ▪ PO Box 17 Elsenburg 7607 ▪ wine@marklew.co.za ▪ www.marklew.co.za ▪ S 33° 50' 35.7" E 018° 51' 50.3" ▪ F +27 (0)21-884-4412 ▪ **T +27 (0)21-884-4412**

☐ **Martinique** *see* Du Preez Estate
☐ **Marvelous** *see* Yardstick Wines

Mary Le Bow Trust

The grapes come from an Ashton farm owned by the Frater family, vinified by Bruce Jack of Flagstone fame – the late James Frater and Bruce having been good friends. James' mother Angela has distant ancestors buried in the crypt of London's St Mary le Bow Church, giving rise to the name.

★★★★ Mary le Bow (Ⓖ) Powerful **11** (**★★★★**) roughly equal cab & shiraz, 23% petit verdot. Misses finesse of **09** & seems to be tending to an ever more imposing style. No **10**. — CE

Location: Somerset West ▪ WO: Western Cape ▪ 1stB 2005 ▪ Wine sales Mon-Fri 8.30-4 ▪ Owner(s) Frater family ▪ Winemaker(s) Bruce Jack ▪ 516cs own label 100% red ▪ PO Box 3636 Somerset West 7129 ▪ info@thedrift.co.za ▪ F +27 (0)86-563-9533 ▪ **T +27 (0)86-150-2025**

Maske Wines   ⓦ 🖐

No new vintages ready for review, but Wellington exporters Erich and Janine Maske say a strapping young cabernet, which winemaking consultant Kobie Viljoen has dubbed 'a "meneer" of a wine', will debut this year. Meanwhile the cab-shiraz blend, named for a visit to a tattoo parlour, is still available.

Maske range

Tattoo ⓦ ★★★ **11** shiraz & cab combo very ripe & fruit-sweet, easy to drink. WO W Cape. Not tasted: **Cabernet Sauvignon**, **Merlot**, **Chenin Blanc**.

Leeumasker range

Not tasted: **Cape Blend**. — CvZ

Location: Wellington ▪ Map: Paarl & Wellington ▪ Map grid reference: G2 ▪ WO: Western Cape ▪ Est/1stB 2000 ▪ Tasting & sales Mon-Sun by appt ▪ Closed Ash Wed, Easter Fri/Sun & Dec 25 ▪ BYO picnic ▪ Owner(s) Erich & Janine Maske ▪ Winemaker(s)/viticulturist(s) Outsourced ▪ 7ha/5ha (cab, merlot, chenin) ▪ 80% red 20% white, blends outsourced ▪ Klein Waterval PO Box 206 Wellington 7654 ▪ laureat@iafrica.com ▪ www.maskewines.co.za ▪ S 33° 40' 4.2" E 019° 2' 37.3" ▪ F +27 (0)21-873-3408 ▪ **T +27 (0)21-873-3407**

☐ **Mason's Hill** *see* Mason's Winery

Mason's Winery   ⓦ 🍴

Calling sulphur-intolerant winelovers! Derek Clift, who tends small parcels of vines on his stonemason family's Paarl Mountain farm (and quarry) for vinifying in shared cellar space in town, is a fellow sufferer so uses minimal amounts. Shiraz is a speciality that, with occasional other releases (none ready for review), can be found at local steakhouse Hussar's Grill.

Location: Paarl ▪ Map: Paarl & Wellington ▪ Map grid reference: E6 ▪ Est/1stB 2001 ▪ Tasting & sales by appt at Hussar Grill Paarl, adjacent to cellar ▪ Owner(s) JA Clift (Pty) Ltd – Clift family ▪ Cellarmaster(s)/winemaker(s)/viticulturist(s) Derek Clift (2001) ▪ 47ha/4ha (shiraz) ▪ 30t/2,000cs own label 100% red ▪ Main Street Suider-Paarl 7646 ▪ masons@cliftgranite.co.za ▪ www.cliftgranite.co.za ▪ S 33° 45' 20.5" E 018° 57' 42.6" ▪ F +27 (0)21-863-1601 ▪ **T +27 (0)83-228-7855**

☐ **Maties** *see* Stellenbosch University Welgevallen Cellar
☐ **Matilda's Secret** *see* Benguela Cove
☐ **Matys** *see* Diemersdal Estate

Matzikama Organic Cellar   ⓦ

Organic red-wine grapes from Klaas Coetzee's Olifants River vines, established in 1994 and originally contributing to his own brand, latterly have gone to nearby Stellar Winery. Consequently Klaas, Stellar's production chief, has resorted to buying in organic grapes for his latest bottlings!

The Tidal Phase Pinot Noir ⓦ ⓥ ★★★★ Lovely fruit purity in **14**, succulent berries, oak in gentle support, pinor noir at its essence. Very small production. WO Koekenaap. Not retasted: **The Moon Phase Shiraz 14** ★★★ — CR, CvZ

Location: Vredendal ▪ Map: Olifants River ▪ WO: Koekenaap/Swartland ▪ Est/1stB 2001 ▪ Tasting by appt ▪ Owner(s)/winemaker(s)/viticulturist(s) Klaas Coetzee ▪ 12ha/2.5ha (cab, shiraz, tannat) ▪ 24t 100% red ▪ PO Box 387 Vredendal 8160 ▪ klaas@matzikamawyn.co.za ▪ www.matzikamawyn.co.za ▪ S 31° 36' 34.37" E 018° 44' 11.32" ▪ **T +27 (0)82-801-3737**

McGregor Wines   ⓦ 🖐 🛒

The unpretentious wines of this grower-owned winery are made just down the road from pastoral McGregor village, known for homely hostelries, excellent eateries, village markets, mountain walks and annual Ride2Nowhere mountain bike stage race, named for the cul de sac leading out of town.

Winemaker's Reserve range

★★★★ **Cabernet Sauvignon 12** improves on last-tasted **08** (★★★★) with classy oak spice aromas laced with dense blackcurrant fruit. Solid tannins carry to long, precise finish.

McGregor range

Pinotage ★★★ Appealingly juicy & fruity, **13** shows well now. **Colombard ★★★** Pleasantly fruity, fresh **15**, with zesty acid. **Sauvignon Blanc ★★** Tangy acidity on **15**, straightforward, with greenish fruit. **White Muscadel ★★★** Honey & butterscotch aromas, **11** fortified midwinter comforter is overtly sweet, with modest acidity. WO W Cape. Also tasted: **Cabernet Sauvignon-Merlot 13 ★★★ Chenin Blanc 15 ★★ Red Muscadel 14 ★★★** Not retasted: **Shiraz 11 ★ Chardonnay 14 ★★★ Cape Ruby 10 ★** Discontinued: **Ruby Cabernet, Pinotage Rosé**. — GdB

Location: McGregor ▪ Map: Robertson ▪ WO: McGregor/Western Cape/Robertson ▪ Est 1948 ▪ 1stB 1978 ▪ Tasting & sales Mon-Fri 8–5 Sat 9-1 ▪ Closed Good Fri, Dec 25/26 & Jan 1 ▪ Cellar tours by appt ▪ BYO picnic ▪ Owner(s) 27 members ▪ Winemaker(s) Elmo du Plessis, with Jean-Prieur du Plessis ▪ 14,000t 22% red 78% white ▪ IPW, WIETA ▪ PO Box 519 McGregor 6708 ▪ info@mcgregorwinery.co.za ▪ www.mcgregorwinery.co.za ▪ S 33° 56' 5.4" E 019° 50' 56.3" ▪ F +27 (0)23-625-1829 ▪ **T +27 (0)23-625-1741/1109**

☐ **Meander** *see* uniWines Vineyards

Meerendal Wine Estate ⓘ 🍴 🏠 📷 🛏 ♿

The dates 1702 and 1969 (founding and first bottled vintage) speak of heritage and tradition but Durbanville's Meerendal recently has seen much stylish revitalisation. And it continues unabated, in line with their slogan 'Home of Food & Wine'. The boutique hotel has been extended, and a cellar barrel room converted into a function venue. Cycling, already a focus via hosting the globally televised Absa Cape Epic Tour grand finale, gets a fillip with Tuesday mountain bike night rides. Talking tradition, one of the estate's stalwart grapes, merlot, features in two of the trio of wines debuting this edition.

Prestige range

★★★★ Heritage Block Pinotage ⓥ Accomplished version from 1955-planted bushvines. Elegant **10** (★★★★★) pays homage to Old World restraint with fairly moderate alcohol & proper dryness, while offering vibrant strawberry fruit. No **08**, **09**. Flavours on **07** were muted by firm tannins.

Merlot Prestige (NEW) **★★★★** Hints of sweet berry jam, leafy spices & savoury meat. **13** medium bodied, easy drinking, appealing without real gravitas. **Heritage Reserve** (NEW) **★★★★** Cape Blend of pinotage, merlot, pinot noir, shiraz has poise & balance, with generous red fruit; **12** an elegant & mild-mannered wine rather than the 'wow' implied in the ambitious pricing. Not retasted: **Merlot Reserve 07 ★★★★ Bin159 Shiraz 07 ★★★★** Not tasted: **Liza, Bin 242 Sauvignon Blanc, Blanc de Blancs Méthode Cap Classique**. Discontinued: **Natural Sweet**.

Standard range

★★★★ Cabernet Sauvignon Convincingly full & dense **12**, last tasted as a barrel sample, has rounded out & blossomed. Ripe blackcurrant fruit on solid but smooth tannins. Improves on last-tasted **10** (★★★).

★★★★ Pinotage Since last year's preview, **12** (★★★★) has acquired typical varietal high-toned perfumes, crushed bramble fruit. Solid & ripe, with youthfully firm tannins. **11** was soft & pliable.

★★★★ Méthode Cap Classique (NEW) Maiden release of **11** dry bubbly from chardonnay/pinot noir shows commendable brioche roundness from extended lees-ageing (42 months), with baked apple fruit. Elegantly balanced, with creamy mousse. WO W Cape.

Chardonnay Unwooded ★★★★ Buttery lemon, hint of sugar make for pleasantly plump **14**, generously full & fruity. Also tasted: **Merlot 12 ★★★★ Pinotage Rosé 15 ★★★ Sauvignon Blanc 15 ★★★★** Not retasted: **Pinot Noir 11 ★★★★ Shiraz 10 ★★★★** Discontinued: **Chardonnay Wooded**. — GdB

Location: Durbanville ▪ Map: Durbanville, Philadelphia & Darling ▪ WO: Durbanville/Western Cape ▪ Est 1702 ▪ 1stB 1969 ▪ Tasting & sales Mon-Sun 9-6 ▪ Closed Good Fri, Dec 25 & Jan 1 ▪ Cellar tours by appt ▪ Crown Restaurant & Wine Bar at Meerendal T +27 (0)21-975-0383, Mon-Sun 7am-10pm ▪ Facilities for children ▪ Tour groups ▪ Farmers market once a month ▪ Weddings/functions ▪ Walking/running trials ▪ Mountain biking ▪ Renosterveld conservation area ▪ The Meerendal Boutique Hotel ▪ Owner(s) Privately owned ▪ Cellarmaster(s)/winemaker(s) Liza Goodwin (Sep 2006) ▪ Viticulturist(s) Victor Rossouw (Feb 2007) ▪ 220ha/50ha (merlot, ptage, pinot, shiraz, chard, sauv) ▪ 500t/50,000cs own label 75% red 20% white 5% rosé ▪ IPW ▪

Private Bag X1702 Durbanville 7551 ▪ info@meerendal.co.za ▪ www.meerendal.co.za ▪ S 33° 47' 55.8" E
018° 37' 26.2" ▪ F +27 (0)21-975-1657 ▪ **T +27 (0)21-975-1655**

☐ **Meerhof** *see* Antebellum Winery
☐ **Meerkat** *see* Welbedacht Wine Estate

Meerlust Estate   ⓠ

The long and continuing history of this fine family estate in Stellenbosch has little parallel in the Cape,
certainly in conjunction with a tradition of fine winemaking. The lovely old manor house is lived in now
by Hannes Myburgh, descendant of the Johannes Myburgh who bought the property in 1757 and developed the land and the charming complex of buildings. There's also valuable continuity (on a shorter
scale!) in cellar and vineyard: Chris Williams has made Meerlust wine, in a brilliant blend of elegant classicism and riper, fruitier modernism, since 2004 (much longer, if one takes into account his time as assistant), while Roelie Joubert has been chief tender of the vines since 2001. Importantly, as underlined by
their recent Fairtrade accreditation, Hannes Myburgh ensures there's also genuine, pervading concern for
the whole Meerlust community's wellbeing.

★★★★☆ **Cabernet Sauvignon** Seamless integration: all building blocks of elegant & restrained **12** –
glossy blackcurrant fruit, lithe tannins, judicious oaking (65% new), invigorating acid & balanced 13.5%
alcohol – are placed, melded & polished. Also in magnum.

★★★★☆ **Merlot** Tall, dark & handsome in refined house style, **13** redolent of violets, roasted game bird
& piquant spice. 9% aromatic cab franc, splash petit verdot & deft 60% new oak focus the mineral core.

★★★★☆ **Pinot Noir** Of delicate mien, crafted from 27 year old vines, takes time in glass to reveal its
silken charm. **13** (★★★★) red-fruited, with savoury acidity in its seamless whole; stalkier than **12** & not
quite as profound.

★★★★☆ **Rubicon** Superlative **10** (★★★★★) follows sensational **09**, maintains classicism of this flagship cab-dominated (65%) Bordeaux blend. Plush, the dark fruit absorbs & integrates the oak influence
(60% new, 21 months) within complex, dense structure. For the long haul.

★★★★ **Chardonnay** Shift from earlier broad, oxidative style to more lightly fruited expression complete
with **14**; no loss of subtlety, breeding or class. Silk textured, for earlier enjoyment. Year in barrel, 55% new.
Occasional release: **Red**. — DS

Location/map/WO: Stellenbosch ▪ Map grid reference: B8 ▪ Est 1693 ▪ 1stB 1975 ▪ Tasting & sales Mon-
Fri 9–5 Sat 10–2 ▪ Fee R30 ▪ Closed all pub hols ▪ Cellar tours by appt ▪ Owner(s) Hannes Myburgh ▪
Cellarmaster(s) Chris Williams (Jan 2004) ▪ Viticulturist(s) Roelie Joubert (2001) ▪ 400ha/106ha (cabs s/
f, merlot, p verdot, pinot, chard) ▪ 500t/50,000cs own label 90% red 10% white ▪ Fairtrade ▪ PO Box
7121 Stellenbosch 7599 ▪ info@meerlust.co.za ▪ www.meerlust.co.za ▪ S 34° 1' 1.7" E 018° 45' 24.7" ▪
F +27 (0)21-843-3274 ▪ **T +27 (0)21-843-3587**

Meinert Wines   ⓠ

It takes a lot of courage to turn your back on a major corporate appointment as Anglo American-owned
Vergelegen's winemaker, overseeing the vineyard plantings and French-designed underground cellar
construction, but that's exactly what Martin Meinert did to follow his own dream of 'a small private
vineyard and winery'. It's situated in Stellenbosch's Devon Valley, and he's just finished his 20th vintage
there 'which is surprising since it feels we've just begun'. In this time he married, giving rise to the La
Barry wines, in honour of wine-and-food-loving wife Leigh Ann (née Barry). He regards cabernet as his
best variety, and unexpectedly but of necessity is replanting the 1989 vineyard to maintain quality.

Meinert Wines range

★★★★ **Cabernet Sauvignon** Deep, rich & complex **12** shows plums & prunes, tobacco, some fennel &
dried herbs, & while the cellaring potential is not in question, it already drinks well; smooth & streamlined.
Also in magnum.

★★★★☆ **Synchronicity** Cab-led flagship with Bordeaux varieties plus pinotage, natural ferment, 36
months in barrel, 80% new. And it shows in **11**, plush & silky, plums/cherries seasoned with spice &
liquorice, & deep muscle tone for long life. Also in 1.5L.

★★★★ **La Barry Sauvignon Blanc** Created for Martin Meinert's wife (née Barry) as wedding gift, this suits her taste. Lemongrass, hint of fennel, lovely leafy tones in **15**, palate showing intense passionfruit. Includes dash oaked semillon. Also-tasted **14**, 100% sauvignon, more mineral finish, perfect for food.

★★★★☆ **Semillon Straw Wine** Vine-dried grapes off the farm's only white-wine vineyard; oak fermented. Apricot & tangerine, full-sweet but not cloying, **14** rescued by acidity, leaving the flavours tangy, deliciously easy to drink. Intense & memorable. Also 375 ml.

Also tasted: **Printer's Ink Pinotage 13** ★★★☆ Not retasted: **Merlot 11** ★★★☆ **La Barry Red 11** ★★★

Family Collection

★★★★ **Pinot Noir** Ⓥ Elgin-sourced **12** seductively perfumed, raspberries & cedar, crystallised violets. Despite 18 months oak, retains variety's signature succulence, elegance. Savoury enough to love food.

┌───
The Italian Job Ⓥ ★★★☆ A different take on blanc de noir: from merlot, pale copper coloured, bunch pressed, year in French barrels. Expressive red berries in **14**, bone-dry, ending slightly savoury. An ideal food wine. **The German Job Riesling** (NEW) Ⓥ ★★★★ From Elgin, hence the intensity, **14**'s floral & pineapple intro leads to a svelte body with a dab of sugar, but the racy acidity makes it taste dry. Delicious.
└───

Not retasted: **Riesling 13** ★★★ In abeyance: **Chardonnay**. — CR

Location/map: Stellenbosch ▪ Map grid reference: D4 ▪ WO: Devon Valley/Elgin ▪ Est 1987 ▪ 1stB 1997 ▪ Tasting Mon-Sat strictly by appt only ▪ Closed all pub hols ▪ Owner(s) Martin Meinert ▪ Cellarmaster(s)/winemaker(s) Martin Meinert (Nov 1997) ▪ Viticulturist(s) Henk Marconi (Jan 1991) ▪ 16ha/12ha (cabs s/f, merlot, p verdot, ptage, sem) ▪ 90t/8,000cs own label 67% red 33% white ▪ PO Box 7221 Stellenbosch 7599 ▪ info@meinertwines.com ▪ www.meinertwines.com ▪ S 33° 54' 1.8" E 018° 48' 50.2" ▪ F +27 (0)86-662-7728 ▪ **T +27 (0)21-865-2363**

☐ **Melck's** see Muratie Wine Estate

Melkboomsdrift Wines   Ⓟ ⑪ ⌂ ◎

Hilsa van den Heever, boutique vintner and owner of Melkboomsdrift Guest Lodge & Conference Venue on the Olifants River near Lutzville, skipped the past few seasons of her all-red range but holds stock of some older vintages and at press time had plans to vinify the 2016 harvest.

Location: Lutzville ▪ Map: Olifants River ▪ Tasting & sales Mon-Fri 9-5 ▪ Melkboomsdrift Lodge serving farm breakfasts, dinner/picnic baskets on request; also self-catering ▪ Conference venue (20 max) ▪ Owner(s)/cellarmaster(s)/winemaker(s) Hilsa van den Heever ▪ Viticulturist(s) Jeff Joubert ▪ (cab, merlot, ptage, shiraz) ▪ PO Box 1124 Vredendal 8160 ▪ info@melkboomsdrift.co.za ▪ www.melkboomsdrift.co.za ▪ S 31° 36' 15.24" E 018° 24' 19.86" ▪ F +27 (0)27-217-2535 ▪ **T +27 (0)27-217-2624**

Mellasat Vineyards   Ⓟ ⑪ ◎ ⑤

Norfolk grain farmer turned winegrower Stephen Richardson is planning a vertical tasting to celebrate the 10th edition of his blanc de noir-style white pinotage, a quarter of which goes to — any guesses? — the US, home of white merlot. His range, unfettered by convention, is matched by wife Janet's creative food offerings on their Paarl farm, towered over by the spires of the Du Toitskloof Mountains.

Premium Exclusives

★★★★ **Tempranillo-Cabernet Sauvignon** Rich & earthy **12** packed with ripe fruit flavour, wafts of fynbos & warm spice; delightfully artisanal & well structured, built to last a few years. Old oak.

★★★★ **Viognier** Barrel-fermented in Romanian oak, **14** oozes peach blossom & apricot with clove & vanilla perfume. Mouthfilling & firm, a hint of bitterness limits the finish. 10 months in cask, 38% new.

Mellasat Premium range

★★★★ **'Sigma' White Pinotage** Blanc de noir vinified in Romanian oak, **14** confirms the uptick of **13**. Heady tropical features add interest to vinous depth & spicy complexity. 7% new wood.

Also tasted: **Chardonnay 13** ★★★☆ **Tuin Wyn 11** ★★★ Not tasted: **'M'**.

Dekker's Valley range

Revelation ★★★ Cab, shiraz, pinotage blend. Now bottled, **11** is vividly fruity, with supple tannins for uncomplicated sipping (probably in winter, given 15% alcohol). **Seraphic ★★★ 14** chardonnay-led unoaked blend tasted pre-bottling as 'White Blend' last edition, now shows bright citrus, floral notes & firm acidity. Also tasted: **Shiraz 13 ★★☆ Shiraz Rosé 14 ★★☆** Discontinued: **Chenin Blanc**. — DS

Location/WO: Paarl ▪ Map: Paarl & Wellington ▪ Map grid reference: G5 ▪ Est 1996 ▪ 1stB 1999 ▪ Tasting & sales Mon-Sat 9.30-5.30 Sun/pub hols 10-4 ▪ Closed Good Fri, Dec 25 & Jan 1 ▪ Cellar tours by appt ▪ Light lunches for groups/tours or private dinner functions by appt; picnics in summer & cheese platters in winter; pop-up seasonal restaurant & other food-based events ▪ Tour groups ▪ Conferences ▪ Paarl Ommiberg Festival ▪ Owner(s) Stephen Richardson ▪ Cellarmaster(s) Stephen Richardson (Jan 1999) ▪ Winemaker(s) Faizel Samuels (Jan 2014) ▪ Viticulturist(s) Poena Malherbe (Sep 1996) ▪ 13ha/8ha (cab, ptage, shiraz, tempranillo, chard, chenin, viog) ▪ 50t/3,500cs own label 40% red 50% white 10% rosé ▪ IPW ▪ PO Box 7169 Paarl 7623 ▪ mellasat@mweb.co.za ▪ www.mellasat.com ▪ S 33° 44' 30.0" E 019° 2' 31.0" ▪ F +27 (0)21-862-4525 ▪ **T +27 (0)21-862-4525**

☐ **Mellow-Wood** *see* Distell

☐ **Mentors** *see* KWV

☐ **Mercia Collection** *see* Mooiplaas Estate & Private Nature Reserve

Merwida Winery

Owned by cousins Schalk and Pierre van der Merwe, the Merwida cellar takes in grapes from several Breedekloof properties owned by the family, here for over 170 years. Their growing portfolio of own-label bottlings will please those looking for good-value, lower-alcohol wines. Their new status as WWF-SA Conservation Champions will please those looking to protect the environment.

★★★★ Barbera ⊘ A quality expression of the Italian variety, **14** has new-oak-derived coffee notes over classy perfumed red fruit & roasted herbs. Crisp acidity & muscular flavours more than a match for food. Also in magnum. **13** sold out untasted.

★★★★ Sauvignon Blanc ⊘ Round & rich courtesy 3 months on lees, generous tropical notes flesh out the zippy kiwi & green apple profile of **15**, with a broad finish.

Pinotage Rosé ★★☆ With strawberries-&-cream aroma & soft, barely dry candyfloss flavour, **15** is an absolute charmer. **Chenin Blanc** (NEW) **★★★☆** Oak-fermented/aged **15** preview full & flavoursome, ripe melons & creamy oatmeal buoyed by acid zip. **Pinot Grigio** (NEW) **★★☆** Tank sample **15** clean & fresh, slately interest in mineral food styling. Also tasted: **Cabernet Sauvignon 13 ★★★ Pinotage 13 ★★★ Chardonnay 15 ★★★☆ Cuvée Brut NV ★★ White Muscadel 15 ★★★☆** — DS

Location: Rawsonville ▪ Map/WO: Breedekloof ▪ Est 1963 ▪ 1stB 1975 ▪ Tasting & sales Mon-Fri 8-12.30 & 1.30–5 Sat 9–1 ▪ Closed Easter Fri-Mon, Dec 25-Jan 1 ▪ Merwida Country Lodge T +27 (0)23-349-1435 ▪ Owner(s) Schalk & Pierre van der Merwe ▪ Cellarmaster(s)/viticulturist(s) Magnus Kriel ▪ Winemaker(s) Magnus Kriel (Dec 2000), with Sarel van Staden (Aug 1982) & Lieza van der Merwe (Jan 2015) ▪ 700ha (cab, merlot, shiraz, chard, chenin, sauv, sem, viog) ▪ 15,000t/10,000cs own label 40% red 60% white ▪ ISO 22000, BWI champion, Fairtrade, IPW, WIETA ▪ PO Box 254 Rawsonville 6845 ▪ wines@merwida.com ▪ www.merwida.com ▪ S 33° 41' 24.9" E 019° 20' 31.1" ▪ F +27 (0)23-349-1953/+27 (0)86-557-5686 ▪ **T +27 (0)23-349-1144**

☐ **Metamorphic** *see* Hillcrest Estate

Metzer Wines

After 4 years (and 2 kids) in Switzerland, working for that country's biggest importer of SA wines, boutique vintner Wade Metzer and family are 'returning to the motherland' in time for the 2016 crush. Having helped build a large portfolio of SA brands, Wade notes that in Europe the excitement around SA as a category is palpable. 'There's work to be done to develop a regional footprint on many of our products, but the future is oh so bright!!' His own focus will remain on shiraz and shiraz-based blends.

★★★★☆ **Syrah 12** (★★★☆), first since **09**, has splash grenache adding to spice & red fruit perfume; palate is darker, brooding, & bound up in some rather dry tannins. Time or decanting needed to reveal the underlying fruit. Minimalist winemaking (natural ferment, no fining/filtration etc) for all these.

★★★★ **The Kitchen Sink Syrah** ⓥ **10** (★★★★) showed big, ripe fruity aromas & some sweet flavours on firm base, but a little more awkward & oaky than maiden **05**, with drying tannins.

The Kitchen Sink Red Blend (NEW) ★★★ As name implies, **13** is a varietal hodgepodge (but mostly syrah/shiraz), widely sourced & food styled, with tomato cocktail aromas, firm chalky tannins & understated red-fruit flavours. Discontinued: **Vitamin B Syrah**, **Vitamin B Blanc**. — MW

Location: Somerset West ▪ WO: Western Cape/Stellenbosch ▪ Est/1stB 2004 ▪ Tasting by appt ▪ Owner(s)/winemaker(s) Wade Metzer & Barry Holfeld ▪ 16t/2,400cs 100% red ▪ info@metzerwines.com ▪ www.metzerwines.com, www.kitchensinkwine.com ▪ **T +27 (0)72-279-7645**

M'hudi Wines

Founders of the first SA wine estate owned and managed by a black family, the Rangakas describe the story of M'hudi as 'a relentless pursuit of one's aspirations'. With a presence in several countries, distribution deal with Bidvest FoodService and recent SAA listings, their leap into wine – with no prior knowledge – is a validation of matriarch Malmsey Rangaka's dictum: life's more exciting if you take risks.

Platinum range

★★★★ **Cabernet Sauvignon** ⓥ Well-made **11** generous rendition of cab: lithely textured tannins support lush blackcurrant fruit, delivering great value & a properly dry finish.

★★★★ **Pinotage** ⓥ Vibrant, plush harmonious **11** made to charm with juicy, succulent red fruit & hint mocha for unpretentious enjoyment.

★★★★ **Shiraz** ⓥ Generously flavoured, balanced **11**, plush, dense, dark fruit & ripe tannins exerting perfectly integrated savoury grip. Temptingly moreish.

M'hudi Wines range

Pinotage ⓥ ★★★★ Quite exotic spice, raspberry perfume, bright & fresh flavours on **12**. Year oak, 30% new, lends attractive extra dimension. Good now & for few years. Stellenbosch WO.

Say Lovey range

Pinotage ⓥ ★★★ **12** in modern, juicy-fruity, dry style for immediate enjoyment. **Shiraz** ⓥ ★★★ Well-rounded & ready **12**, full of dark berries & spice. Hearty winter warmer. **Sauvignon Blanc** ⓥ ★★★ Gentle tropical tones on **13**. Fresh, dry but unharsh for easy sipping. Not retasted: **Cabernet Sauvignon 12** ★★ **Medley 12** ★★★ **Chenin Blanc 13** ★★★ — AL

Location: Stellenbosch ▪ WO: Paarl/Stellenbosch ▪ Est 2005 ▪ Closed to public ▪ Conferences (up to 70 pax) ▪ Owner(s) Rangaka family ▪ Winemaker(s) outsourced ▪ 70,000cs own label 80% red 10% white 10% rosé & sparkling ▪ WIETA ▪ PO Box 30 Koelenhof 7605 ▪ malmsey@mhudi.com ▪ www.mhudi.com ▪ **T +27 (0)78-750-4494/+27 (0)73-833-2815**

☐ **Mia** see Nordic Wines
☐ **Michelle d'Or** see Fort Simon Wine Estate

Micu Narunsky Wines

Israeli-born jazz musician and winemaker Micu Narunsky's day job at Joostenberg leaves little time for his own boutique brand, but he did fit in some bottling and labelling for a release around press time. The plan is to continue production this year and possibly add a rosé to the portfolio.

★★★★ **lemanjá** Rustic & raisined nose on **11** (★★★) leads to savoury core, less together than **10**. From touriga (83%) with tinta barocca.

La Complicité ★★★★ Complete style change from last-tasted **11** (★★★★) for quirky but interesting **13**. Now a blend, mostly colombard with muscadel & gewürztraminer, deliberate oxidisation adds savoury, nutty notes while hefty alcohol reinforces sherry-like appeal. Fresh acidity, great finish, recommended with tangy hard cheese. Stellenbosch WO. Not retasted: **Olodum 10** ★★★★ — CM

Location: Somerset West ▪ WO: Coastal/Swartland/Stellenbosch ▪ Est 2005 ▪ 1stB 2006 ▪ Tasting by appt ▪ Owner(s)/cellarmaster(s)/viticulturist(s) Micu Narunsky ▪ Winemaker(s) Micu Narunsky, advised by Francois Naudé ▪ 4.8t/450cs own label 85% red 15% white ▪ PO Box 427 Somerset Mall 7137 ▪ micunarunsky@gmail.com ▪ www.micunarunsky.com ▪ T +27 (0)73-600-3031/+27 (0)21-855-2520

Middelvlei Estate   ⓛ ⑪ ⌂ ◉ ⑧ ⑤

Two Momberg brothers bought Middelvlei in Stellenbosch's Devon Valley in 1919, and it remains in the family, run by another pair of brothers, Tinnie and Ben. Aside from Tinnie's wine, many family amenities await visitors including a lunchtime barbecue restaurant (with marshmallows for kids to braai).

★★★★ **Free Run Pinotage** ⓛ Mocha-laced, fresh & harmonious **13** (★★★★) has appetising acidity to offset sweet red fruit flavours; not quite as complex as **12**.

★★★★ **Shiraz** ⓛ Spicy, savoury **13** (★★★★) harmonious, smooth textured. Less depth than **10** but nicely integrated & pleasurable. **11**, **12** sold out untasted.

★★★★ **Momberg 12** was cab, pinotage with dash shiraz. **13** has shiraz in lead, with pinotage, merlot, mourvèdre. Pleasant, somewhat solid, balanced; good fruit; firm but smooth tannins need a few years.

Also tasted: **Pinotage-Merlot 14** ★★★ **Chardonnay Unoaked 15** ★★★ Not retasted: **Cabernet Sauvignon 13** ★★★ — TJ

Location/map: Stellenbosch ▪ Map grid reference: E4 ▪ WO: Devon Valley/Western Cape/Stellenbosch ▪ Est 1941 ▪ 1stB 1973 ▪ Tasting & sales daily 10–4.30 ▪ Fee R15pp ▪ Closed Good Fri, Dec 25 & Jan 1 ▪ Cellar tours by appt ▪ Traditional lunchtime braai 7 days a week; evenings by prior arrangement for groups of 15+ ▪ Facilities for children ▪ Conferences ▪ Walking/hiking & MTB trails ▪ Cottage (2 pax) ▪ Owner(s) Momberg family ▪ Cellarmaster(s)/winemaker(s)/viticulturist(s) Tinnie Momberg (Feb 1992) ▪ 160ha/110ha (cab, merlot, ptage, shiraz, chard, sauv) ▪ 650t/60,000cs own label 95% red 5% white ▪ Other export brands: Hagelsberg, Red Falcon ▪ IPW, WIETA ▪ PO Box 66 Stellenbosch 7599 ▪ info@middelvlei.co.za ▪ www.middelvlei.co.za ▪ S 33° 55' 41.2" E 018° 49' 55.9" ▪ F +27 (0)21-883-9546 ▪ T +27 (0)21-883-2565

Midgard   (NEW)

New to the guide but already into its fourth vintage, this big-hearted private venture supports the Elkana Hostel at the Alta du Toit Aftercare Centre in Cape Town's northern suburbs, where intellectually disabled adults from all Western Cape communities live and work. Grapes contributed by Durbanville growers are vinified by Nomada Wines' Riaan Oosthuizen and the profits from sales are donated to the hostel. The Viking ancestry of one of the benefactors is the inspiration for the brand name.

Sauvignon Blanc ★★★ Walleting-pleasing **15** punches above price point, worth seeking out. Fresh & appealing, with grass & fig tones, zesty & food friendly throughout. — WB, CvZ

Location/WO: Durbanville ▪ Est/1stB 2012 ▪ Closed to public ▪ Winemaker(s) Riaan Oosthuizen (Nomada Wines) ▪ 2-3t/±300cs own label 100% white ▪ PO Box 2703 Durbanville 7551 ▪ charlvt@kingsley.co.za ▪ T +27 (0)83-456-9410

Migliarina Wines   ⓛ

Stellenbosch boutique vintner Carsten Migliarina always knew he wanted to make wine; his first was as a teenager using table grapes. The journey since has included wine courses, contract cellar work and stints as a sommelier locally and abroad. He exports, and never stops looking for new wines to make – this edition a grenache from Wellington which, like his other new vintages, missed our tasting deadline.

★★★★ **Shiraz** ⓛ Ripe flavours, definite oak presence & some richness on **12** from Stellenbosch, yet with some sure-footed elegance. It all adds up to an attractive fruity-savoury proposition.

★★★★ **Chardonnay** ⓛ Quietly elegant, properly dry, harmonious **13** with notes of nut, citrus & oatmeal, the oaking unobtrusively supportive.

★★★★ **Chenin Blanc** ⓛ Bright, fresh floral & tropical tones with green edge on very lightly oaked **13** – a good advertisement for Elgin chenin. A fine, even challenging, acidity balances the succulence.

Not tasted: **Grenache.** — TJ

Location: Stellenbosch ▪ WO: Elgin/Stellenbosch/Wellington ▪ Est 2001 ▪ 1stB 2002 ▪ Tasting by appt only ▪ Owner(s)/winemaker(s) Carsten Migliarina ▪ 2,600cs own label 45% red 55% white + 350cs for clients ▪ Brands for clients: Kap Hase, Fridhem Gaard ▪ PO Box 673 Stellenbosch 7599 ▪ carsten@ migliarina.co.za ▪ www.migliarina.co.za ▪ **T +27 (0)72-233-4138**

☐ **Miko** *see* Mont Rochelle Hotel & Vineyard

Miles Mossop Wines

One of South Africa's star winemakers, Miles Mossop's own labels – named for his three children – as well as those he makes at Tokara reflect an ability to consistently deliver wines of great polish, integrity and distinctiveness. The more recent Introduction series comprises varietal wines from older blocks, generally in poorer soils and unirrigated. 'Made with the same philosophy as the other wines', they're intended to be fruit-forward, earlier drinking and more affordable. But clearly they're not dumbed down.

Miles Mossop range

★★★★☆ **Max** Youthful **12** (★★★★★) blend half cabernet, equal merlot, petit verdot shows fine breeding in pure, expressive red fruit, structured by tight tannins from almost 2 years in barrel. Classic, polished & elegant; deserves time in bottle, like **11**.

★★★★★ **Saskia** Exquisitely appealing **13** (★★★★★) oaked blend chenin, viognier, clairette, verdelho (as was **12**); effortlessly flaunts clean, richly textured layers of peach & apricot fruit, wrapped around tightly focused acid core. Judicious oaking adds final well-placed touch as persistent flavours unfurl throughout long, confident finish. Coastal WO.

★★★★☆ **Kika** Gorgeous **14** (★★★★★) a perfectly poised, seamless, botrytis dessert from chenin, oak matured. Zippy acidity cleanses unctuously sweet dried fruit flavours & adds measured grapefruit marmalade twist. Even more superb than **13**.

The Introduction range

★★★★☆ **Chenin Blanc** Delightful charm in **13** (★★★★) more accessible, less serious than **12**. Brush new French oak adds lightly spicy dimension to full, rich peach, apple flavours.

Red (Ⓝ) ★★★☆ Vibrant, charmingly spicy **13** delivers abundant fruitiness in merlot blend with malbec & cabernet. Glossy coating of tannins makes for pleasurable sipping. Not tasted: **Viognier**. — IM

Location: Stellenbosch ▪ WO: Stellenbosch/Coastal ▪ Est/1stB 2004 ▪ Closed to public ▪ Owner(s)/ winemaker(s)/viticulturist(s) Miles Mossop ▪ 15t/2,750cs own label 36% red 55% white 9% NLH ▪ PO Box 7339 Stellenbosch 7599 ▪ miles@milesmossopwines.com ▪ www.milesmossopwines.com ▪ F +27 (0)21-808-5911 ▪ **T +27 (0)82-413-4335**

☐ **Milkwood** *see* The Grape Grinder
☐ **Millberg** *see* Tulbagh Winery
☐ **Millbrook** *see* Valley Vineyards Wine Company
☐ **Millers Mile** *see* Klein Parys Vineyards
☐ **Stone** *see* Stettyn Cellar
☐ **Millstream** *see* DGB
☐ **Milton Grove** *see* Jacques Germanier

Mimosa Boutique Wines

Ⓨ Ⓜ Ⓗ Ⓒ Ⓐ

At Montagu's Mimosa Lodge the freshest seasonal ingredients are deliciously prepared by Swiss-born chef patron Bernhard Hess, who also handcrafts wines with a consultant winemaker to complement the menu. Much excitement at press time, as the cellar was getting its own tasting area and restaurant serving breakfast and lunch.

Reserve range

★★★★ **Alambic 5 Year Old Potstill** Dark amber, with complex nose of dried pears, candied lemon peel, roasted nuts. Long, satisfying flavours, showing fine, smooth intensity & touch of caramel on finish.

Reserve (Ⓥ) ★★★☆ Bordeaux blend **12**, led by cab (62%) marriage of intense sweet fruit & oak. Very fresh, racy acidity needs time to harmonise. WO W Cape.

Mimosa range

★★★★ Shiraz ⊘ Hedonistic, fragrant aromas of lavender, dried herbs & warm spice set the pace on **12**. Harmonious & flavoursome, with balance & poise. Drinks well & will reward ageing. WO W Cape.

★★★★ Chardonnay Barrel-fermented **14** more complex than **13** (★★★☆), fragrant ripe apple aromas, rich & creamy lemon curd & vanilla flavours & enduring citrus finish.

★★★★ Natural Sweet ⓃⒺⓌ Deliciously mouthfilling barrel-fermented **13** riesling oozes ripe nectarine, lemon blossom perfume to the deep but uncloying flavour, terrific acid balance to the dry finish. 500 ml.

Sauvignon Blanc ★★★☆ 14 ripe tropical fruit flavours, creamy mouthfeel from lees-ageing & perky lemon zest goodbye. Also in 500 ml. Also tasted: **Cabernet Sauvignon 13 ★★★☆** — WB

Location: Montagu ▪ Map: Klein Karoo & Garden Route ▪ WO: Robertson/Western Cape ▪ Est 2004 ▪ 1stB 2003 ▪ Tasting & sales daily 9-5 ▪ Tour groups ▪ Conservation area ▪ 4-star Mimosa Lodge: 23 rooms, conference centre, pool, boule pitch, wine cellar, tasting room & Ma Cuisine restaurant ▪ Owner(s) Bernhard Hess ▪ Cellarmaster(s)/winemaker(s)/viticulturist(s) Lourens van der Westhuizen (consultant) ▪ 5ha/3ha (cab, shiraz, chard, sauv) ▪ 20t/2,480cs own label 70% red 30% white ▪ PO Box 323 Montagu 6720 ▪ bernhard@mimosa.co.za ▪ www.mimosawines.co.za ▪ S 33° 47' 27.59" E 020° 6' 44.55" ▪ F +27 (0)86-535-0720 ▪ **T +27 (0)23-614-2351**

Miravel ⊕ ⑪ ⌂

Maarten and Janine van Beuningen's boutique-scale winemaking is both an end in itself and a showcase for their Helderberg grapes, some sold off to top names. A rebranding and repositioning exercise for their label in 2012 is paying off, Maarten says, and demand is now such that red wines are made every year.

★★★★ Ella Family Reserve Cabernet Sauvignon 12 (★★★☆) with some petit verdot, warmer & more approachable than **10**. Ripe berry & polished leather tone, for earlier enjoyment. No **11** made, as for all the reds.

★★★★ 1952 Family Blend 12 supple & succulent cab, merlot, petit verdot steps up on **10** (★★★☆) with oak well meshed with ample fruit; most balanced of the reds, with clean dry tannins. Ready.

Sauvignon Blanc ★★★ Returns to steely mode with really tangy acidity, grassy flavour & firm grip courtesy some lees-ageing. Sprightly **14** best with food. Also tasted: **Merlot 12 ★★★☆ Pinotage 12 ★★★ Nigma 13 ★★★☆** Occasional release: **Cabernet Sauvignon**. — MW

Location/WO: Stellenbosch ▪ Map: Helderberg ▪ Est 2002 ▪ 1stB 2005 ▪ Tasting & sales Mon-Sat & pub hols by appt ▪ Closed Ash Wed, Easter Fri-Mon, Ascension Day, Pentecost, Dec 25/26 & Jan 1 ▪ Meals & cheese platters by prior arrangement ▪ Self-catering Fynbos Cottage ▪ Owner(s) Maarten van Beuningen ▪ Winemaker(s) Gerda Willers (whites) & André Liebenberg (reds, 2012) ▪ Viticulturist(s) Francois Hanekom (Apr 2007) & Paul Wallace (Jun 2004, consultant) ▪ 39ha/27ha (cab, merlot, p verdot, ptage, chenin, sauv) ▪ 200t/815cs own label 60% red 40% white ▪ PO Box 5144 Helderberg 7135 ▪ maarten@miravel.co.za ▪ www.miravel.co.za ▪ S 34° 1' 58.7" E 018° 46' 46.9" ▪ F +27 (0)21-842-3154 ▪ **T +27 (0)21-842-3154**

☐ **Mischief Maker** see Valley Vineyards Wine Company
☐ **Miss Molly** see Môreson
☐ **Misty Kloof's** see Goedverwacht Wine Estate

Misty Mountains Estate ⊕ ⑪ ⌾

Returning to the guide after a break is the estate established by businessmen Louwrens le Roux and André van Vuuren on virgin land in the Klein River hills near Stanford, also home to a natural spring. The maiden wine, a sauvignon blanc, was vinified off-site but a cellar was soon built and the wine range extended (unusually, the public can sample the line-up from barrel by appointment). New since last time is winemaker Neil Patterson, whose eponymous own brand debuts separately this edition.

Shiraz ★★★ Intriguing floral notes on **10** add interest to dark-toned flavours, liquorice, black pepper & leather. Accessible now, can still age. **AnaMae Sauvignon Blanc ★★★** Was 'Sauvignon Blanc Reserve'. Nice cool-climate terroir reflection in **15**, elegant (13% alcohol), wet pebble minerality, with a refreshing hint of lime. **Sauvignon Blanc ★★★** A limy freshness throughout **15** matches the light-textured appeal, ends on a mineral note. — CR, CvZ

Location: Stanford ▪ Map: Elgin, Walker Bay & Bot River ▪ WO: Walker Bay ▪ Est 2004 ▪ 1stB 2008 ▪ Tasting & sales Mon-Fri 10-5 Sat 10-2 ▪ Closed Good Fri & Dec 25 ▪ Barrel tasting on request ▪ Cellar tours by appt ▪ Cheese platters ▪ Conferences (±60 pax) ▪ Owner(s) Misty Mountains Estates (directors LL le Roux & A van Vuuren) ▪ Winemaker(s) Neil Patterson ▪ Vineyard manager(s) Robert Davis ▪ 46ha/16ha (mourv, shiraz, sauv, sem) ▪ PO Box 1874 Hermanus 7200 ▪ info@mistymountains.co.za ▪ www.mistymountains.co.za ▪ S 34° 25' 04" E 019° 25' 35" ▪ **T +27 (0)82-973-5943**

Mitre's Edge   ⓨ ⓐ ⓞ

Winemaker Lola Nicholls and mechanical engineer-turned-winegrower husband Bernard in late 2015 delighted in presenting their long-planned Bordeaux-style blend. Named Sholto (Gaelic for 'sower'), it honours Lola's father Martin Sholto Hunting, whose 'passion for farming' during three decades on this Klapmuts property left a legacy they've built on since 1999, developing vineyards, wines (including two impressive new single-variety reds), olive groves and guest accommodation.

Flagship range

★★★★☆ **Cabernet Sauvignon** Rich & poised, with authoritative intensity, **12**'s oak effortlessly absorbed into dense cassis fruit. Supremely balanced, svelte tannin structure already tempts but worth cellaring 4-8 years. Confident step up from last-made **08** (★★★☆).

★★★★☆ **Cabernet Franc** ⓝⓔⓦ Adds green walnut piquancy to scented berry flavours in **12**; quite understated & the most subtle in this range. Refined balanced & elegant with lovely freshness & length. Ready now & over next 3-5 years.

★★★★☆ **Merlot** Minted blueberries, floral & leafy tones in a cool, finely woven tannin structure. **12**'s deft oaking provides subtle support, allows lovely fruit purity to shine. Still an infant, with good future. Great advance since last **08** (★★★).

★★★★ **Petit Verdot** ⓝⓔⓦ Handsome **12**, intense ripe flavours & length; perfumed berries, inky notes on bed of surprisingly pliable tannins for this variety. Ripe, modern styling, with fruit to carry 15% alcohol.

★★★★☆ **Sholto** ⓝⓔⓦ Classic cassis & leafy cedar notes on **12** Bordeaux blend (cab, merlot, cab franc, malbec, petit verdot 39/26/17/9/9). Structured & elegant, subtle fruit profile. Lengthy oaking, as for Cab, 20% new. Already harmonious, greater rewards with ageing.

Mitre's Edge range

Shiraz ★★★☆ Confident return to form with **12**, offers lively but smooth spiced-plum drinkability with some underlying seriousness & structure. Not retasted: **Cabernet Sauvignon 11** ★★★☆ **Rosé 14** ★★ **Viognier 14** ★★★☆

ME Range

Classic Red ⓥ ★★☆ Crunchy red fruit & leafy tannins in cab-led **NV**, billed as 'braai aperitif'. — MW

Location: Paarl ▪ Map: Paarl & Wellington ▪ Map grid reference: C8 ▪ WO: Simonsberg-Paarl ▪ Est 1999 ▪ 1stB 2004 ▪ Tasting & sales by appt Mon-Fri 9-5 Sat 9-1 ▪ Cellar tours by appt ▪ Guest house B&B ▪ Olive oil ▪ Owner(s) Bernard & Lola Nicholls ▪ Winemaker(s) Lola Nicholls (2004), with Bernard Nicholls ▪ Viticulturist(s) Danie Kritzinger (consultant) ▪ Vineyard manager Bertus de Clerk ▪ 28ha/18ha (cabs s/f, malbec, merlot, p verdot, shiraz, chenin, viog) ▪ 28t/3,072cs own label 80% red 9% white 1% rosé ▪ PO Box 12290 Die Boord 7613 ▪ info@mitres-edge.co.za ▪ www.mitres-edge.co.za ▪ S 33° 49' 47.3" E 018° 52' 34.4" ▪ F +27 (0)21-875-5965 ▪ **T +27 (0)21-875-5960**

☐ **MM Louw** *see* Diemersdal Estate

MolenVliet Oosthuizen Family Vineyards   ⓨ ⓐ ⓞ

Former SA rugby hero Ockie Oosthuizen and wife Susan's MolenVliet lifestyle venue in Banhoek Valley offers luxury accommodation, weddings and conferences – and this collection of Bordeaux-inclined red wines, made by Bernard le Roux at nearby Zorgvliet.

Private Collection

★★★★ **Cabernet Sauvignon** Liquorice, black cherries & cherry tobacco oak – beguiling fragrances on **13** (★★★☆), given form by cab's tannins, taut but not drying. First vintage tasted since **07**.

Merlot (NEW) ★★★ **13** ripe plum & malty tones, stemmy tannins that lift the palate; flavours are unlingering but would work well with winter stews & tomato pastas. **Duet** (NEW) ★★★ **13** marries 60% cab, merlot in milk chocolate- & berry-infused mouthful, good food partner now & for the next year/2. **Quartet** (NEW) ★★★★ Cab, merlot with 7% each petit verdot, cab franc in **13** successful, if somewhat stern, nod to Bordeaux. Not retasted: **Proprietors Selection 05** ★★★ — CvZ

Location/map/WO: Stellenbosch ▪ Map grid reference: H4 ▪ Est/1stB 2005 ▪ Tasting & sales by appt ▪ Fee R80 ▪ Wedding/conference venue ▪ Self-catering accommodation/B&B ▪ Owner(s) Ockie & Susan Oosthuizen ▪ Winemaker(s) Bernard le Roux ▪ 14ha/8ha (cab, merlot, shiraz) ▪ 13t/±2,500cs own label 100% red ▪ PO Box 6288 Uniedal 7612 ▪ info@molenvliet.co.za ▪ www.molenvliet.co.za ▪ S 33° 54' 52.9" E 018° 56' 30.6" ▪ F +27 (0)21-885-1684 ▪ **T +27 (0)21-885-1597**

Momento Wines   ⊘

Marelise Niemann's small range was born with a Swartland grenache five years ago, made in the Beaumont cellar, where she was winemaker. She left there at the end of 2014 to 'focus and grow' her own project, and made her next vintage as part of a little group of like-minded, exciting young winemakers renting cellar space at Gabriëlskloof in Bot River. Her approach is determinedly hands-off, wanting to respect and express the grape and the place where it grew: 'Less is more.' Much more, in this case.

★★★★ **Grenache 14** (★★★★★) expresses sweet Swartland fruit with accents of earth & stone. Clean, fresh, intricate, lightly muscular – even a touch severe in its youth (it deserves time for greater harmony & complexity; decant now). From same old-vines as last-made **11**. Also in larger bottle formats.

★★★★ **Tinta Barocca** ⊘ **13** another exercise in 'hands-off' winemaking to give elegant, fresh & pure delight. Well structured, with a good but unaggressive grip. Delightful, but serious. Should keep.

★★★★☆ **Chenin Blanc-Verdelho 14** blend from Bot River & Darling grapes, the 15% verdelho adding something greenly herbal & floral to chenin dried peach aromas & palate. Still tight mid-2015, subtle, silky & fresh. Long, fascinating finish to enjoy with pleasure & regret as it slowly fades. Will develop. — TJ

Location: Bot River ▪ WO: Swartland/Bot River/Western Cape ▪ 1stB 2012 ▪ Private tastings on request ▪ Owner(s)/winemaker(s) Marelise Niemann ▪ 6t/630cs own label 36% red 64% white ▪ marelise@ momentowines.co.za ▪ www.momentowines.co.za ▪ **T +27 (0)82-968-8588**

☐ **Moments Collection** see Teddy Hall Wines

Monis Wines

This fortifieds-only cellar is based in Paarl, but draws fruit from areas renowned for each style: muscadel from Breede River, Portuguese varieties for the port-styles from Calitzdorp and Paarl, and chenin for the sherry-styles from Stellenbosch. The fortifying brandy spirit is from parent group Distell's own distilleries.

Monis Wines

★★★★☆ **Wood Matured Muscadel** ⊘ 500 ml of irresistible dried orange zest, spice, muscat complexity. **04**'s rich, silky sweetness disciplined by 5 years older oak, tangy acid. Breede River fruit.

★★★★ **Tawny Port** ⊘ Gorgeous **96** ex Paarlberg tinta & cinsaut still selling.

Vintage Port ⊘ ★★★★ From Calitzdorp grapes. Dried fruit, leather & touriga's fragrance enhance **06**, with its warming spirity tail. Slightly more concentration would lead to higher rating.

Monis Sherry-Styles

★★★★ **Full Cream** Richest, sweetest of range, starting with amber colour, followed by an assault of perfumes, flavours: toffee, vanilla, roasted nuts, honey cake, a savoury note at end giving definition. **Medium Cream** ★★★★ Candied fruit & butterscotch, a powerful nutty seam throughout. Notable freshness despite the sweetness makes it a pleasure to drink. Serve with soups or as an aperitif on cold days. **Pale Dry** ★★★☆ From chenin, matured under flor for 3 years, then transferred to solera for a further 3 years. Salt & tealeaf first impression, then pear & nut flavours, adding richness to the savoury taste. Enjoy chilled. — CR

Location: Paarl ▪ WO: Stellenbosch/Breede River Valley/Calitzdorp ▪ Est 1906 ▪ Closed to public ▪ Owner(s) Distell ▪ Cellarmaster(s)/winemaker(s) Dirkie Christowitz (Aug 1979) ▪ 52,000cs 100% fortified ▪ PO Box 266 Paarl 7620 ▪ dchristowitz@distell.co.za ▪ www.moniswines.co.za ▪ F +27 (0)21-872-2790 ▪ **T +27 (0)21-860-1601**

☐ **Mon Rêve** *see* Simonshoogte

Mons Ruber Wine Estate

The Meyer brothers' traditional Karoo cellar was among the first to re-apply for a distilling licence in the 1990s after prohibition on private production, resurrecting a rare wood-fired copper potstill for a pair of brandies. Also available in the tasting room, a 19th-century toll house once graced by at least one poet (CJ Langenhoven) and one princess (later Queen Elizabeth II), are dessert wines Elegantia and Regalis.

Fortified range

Regalis ⊘ ★★★ Uncertified **NV** (**07**) jeripiko from white muscadel with sunshiny fruit, gentle muscat spice; packed with sweetness. Not retasted: **Elegantia 10** ★★☆

Brandy range

★★★★ **Estate Potstill Brandy** ⊘ Muscat d'Alexandrie origin shows subtly on bright, grapey, floral fragrance. Easy, smooth & balanced, with effective oak maturation. Old-style label gives **03** vintage.

Buchu Brandy ⊘ ★★★ A quirky, light yellow medicinal brandy, infused (very noticeably) with round-leaf buchu plant. Fiery finish. From cinsaut. — WB, TJ, JP

Location: De Rust ▪ Map: Klein Karoo & Garden Route ▪ Est ca 1850 ▪ 1stB 1985 wine/1995 brandy ▪ Tasting & sales Mon-Fri 9–5 Sat 9–1 ▪ Closed all pub hols ▪ Farm produce ▪ Hiking trail in proclaimed conservation area ▪ BYO picnic ▪ Owner(s) Radé & Erhard Meyer ▪ Brandy master Radé Meyer (1990) ▪ Winemaker(s) Radé Meyer ▪ Viticulturist(s) Radé Meyer (1990) ▪ ±1,800ha/38ha (cab, cinsaut, muscadel r/w, chard, chenin, hanepoot, palomino) ▪ ±500t/20,000cs own label 50% red 50% white & ±178cs brandy ▪ PO Box 1585 Oudtshoorn 6620 ▪ monsruber@gmail.com ▪ S 33° 32' 1.0" E 022° 28' 38.9" ▪ F +27 (0)86-566-6550 ▪ **T +27 (0)44-251-6550**

Montagu Wine Cellar

Tourist-friendly Montagu's 'home' cellar's slogan is 'Be part of the legend', and by 'legend' they can mean only one thing: their famously sweet and decadent fortified muscadels. The white version regrettably was unready for tasting this edition but the red, complete with legendary buy-it-by-the-bootload price tag, was showing at its cockle-warming best.

★★★★ **Red Muscadel** Bright copper-hued, grapey & rich **14** fortified dessert is better balanced than last **12** (★★★☆), its luscious spicy boiled sweet flavours cleansed by a fine alcohol zing. Also in 250 ml.

Cabernet Sauvignon ★★☆ Fruitcake aromas & ripe juicy plums give unoaked **14** smooth-drinking appeal. Also tasted: **Merlot-Ruby Cabernet 14** ★★ **Chenin Blanc 15** ★★ Not retasted: **Colombar 14** ★★ Not tasted: **White Muscadel**. Discontinued: **Late Harvest**. — WB

Location/WO: Montagu ▪ Map: Klein Karoo & Garden Route ▪ Est 1941 ▪ 1stB 1975 ▪ Tasting & sales Mon-Fri 8–5 ▪ Closed all pub hols ▪ Farm produce ▪ Owner(s) 54 members ▪ Executive manager Jacques Jordaan (2013) ▪ Winemaker(s) Hermias Vollgraaff (Aug 2013), with Jean Slabber (Dec 2014) ▪ Viticulturist(s) Johannes Mellet (2005, consultant) ▪ 620ha (11 varieties r/w) ▪ 16,000t/11,000cs own label 12% red 82% white 6% muscadel ▪ IPW ▪ PO Box 29 Montagu 6720 ▪ sales@montaguwines.co.za ▪ www.montaguwines.co.za ▪ S 33° 46' 37.3" E 020° 7' 58.4" ▪ F +27 (0)23-614-1793 ▪ **T +27 (0)23-614-1125**

Mont Destin

It's unclear if there's shiraz in the al fresco red-wine bath at this boutique cellar between Paarl and Stellenbosch (noted for its Luis Barragan architecture), but chances are good, given its pervading presence in the wines (and the 'grappa' made from the skins of flagship Destiny Shiraz). The owners are Ernest and Samantha Bürgin, the latter celebrating two decades of winemaking. The tasting room is now open during the week — a visit includes a personal tour of the cellar.

Mont Destin range

★★★★☆ **Destiny Shiraz** Barrel selection made ahead of blending others in line-up, only released when ready. **11** a tour de force flaunting very ripe dark fruit, 15% alcohol. Big & bold, it has sufficient concentration, tannin for balance & longevity. Finely crafted, 33% new oak well melded. Also in 1.5L.

★★★★ **Passioné** Shiraz (39%) with mourvèdre, cinsaut, grenache in **11**. Attractive macerated cherries, blackberries & allspice; plump & flavoursome palate lifted by tannin grip, supported by 30% new oak.

Also tasted: **11 Barrels 14** ★★★

Husk Spirit range

★★★★ **Spirit of Destiny** ⓠ From shiraz husks, this hand-labelled spirit is smooth, gentle & flavoursome. Bright, with hint of smoke, perfect for late evening with an espresso. — WB, JPf

Location/map: Stellenbosch ▪ Map grid reference: G1 ▪ WO: Paarl/Stellenbosch/Simonsberg-Paarl ▪ Est/ 1stB 1998 ▪ Tasting, sales & cellar tours Mon-Fri 9-4 Sat by appt ▪ Closed all pub hols ▪ Open air red wine bath ▪ Rustic self-catering accommodation in thatched rondawel ▪ Owner(s) Ernest & Samantha Bürgin ▪ Winemaker(s) Samantha Bürgin (May 1996) ▪ Viticulturist(s) Bertus de Clerk (2006, consultant) ▪ 10ha/ 7ha (cab, cinsaut, grenache, mourv, shiraz, viog) ▪ 15t/2,000cs own label 100% red ▪ IPW ▪ PO Box 1237 Stellenbosch 7599 ▪ info@montdestin.co.za ▪ www.montdestin.co.za ▪ S 33° 49' 58.9" E 018° 53' 27.8" ▪ F +27 (0)21-875-5870 ▪ **T +27 (0)83-288-4985**

Mont du Toit Kelder

Du Toits have been winefarming in the Cape since 1691, and for the past 20 years Johannesburg advocate Stephan du Toit's love for classic red wine has been expressed by continuing the tradition at the foot of Wellington's Hawequa Mountain (silhouetted on his labels). Said labels are set to become more visible in the Western Cape market, Stephan says, having enjoyed great success in Gauteng.

Mont du Toit Kelder range

★★★★ **Le Sommet** Bold & powerful **08** (★★★★★) from cab, petit verdot & alicante bouschet ups the ante on **06**. Vibrant dark berries & fynbos, with firm, balanced tannins. Savoury, deliciously dry; for a special occasion. Year in barrel. WO Paarl. No **07**.

★★★★☆ **Mont du Toit** ⓠ Flagship red in **08** regains form of **06** with 'secret blend' from Wellington fruit, after austere **07** (★★★★). Harmonious, moreish, with a velvety palate of ripe dark berries, supple tannins & firm structure from 2 years oak maturation.

Not tasted: **Hawequas**.

Les Coteaux range

★★★★ **Cabernet Sauvignon 13** (★★★☆) big & dry, with dark fruit flavours & bold tannins from 16-18 months in oak. Lacks the depth of **11**. **12** sold out untasted.

★★★★ **Cabernet Franc** ⓠ **12** offers gentle sweet red fruit in harmony with fragrant leafy herbs. A little lighter & juicier than the others, though as serious-minded; modest & sensitive oaking.

★★★★ **Sélection** ⊘ Elegant & unusual **12** Bordeaux/tinta barocca blend shows bright fruit, tobacco & dried herb notes. Appealing savoury notes on long finish. **11** sold out untasted.

Also tasted: **Merlot 13** ★★★ Not retasted: **Shiraz 11** ★★★☆ — WB

Location: Wellington ▪ Map: Paarl & Wellington ▪ Map grid reference: G2 ▪ WO: Wellington/Paarl ▪ Est 1996 ▪ 1stB 1998 ▪ Tasting, sales & cellar tours Mon-Fri 9-4.30 Sat by appt ▪ Fee R15/R35 ▪ Closed all pub hols ▪ Hiking trails ▪ BYO picnic, picnic area by arrangement ▪ Guest cottages ▪ Owner(s) Stephan du Toit ▪ Cellarmaster(s) Bernd Philippi & Loftie Ellis (1997, consultants) ▪ Winemaker(s) Chris Roux (2012), with Abraham Cloete (Jan 2005) ▪ ±40ha/±28ha (alicante bouschet, cabs s/f, merlot, mourv, p verdot, shiraz, tinta barocca) ▪ ±165t/±16,000cs own label 100% red & ±2,000cs for clients ▪ IPW ▪ PO Box 704 Wellington 7654 ▪ kelder@montdutoit.co.za, marketing@montdutoit.co.za ▪ www.montdutoit.co.za ▪ S 33° 39' 27.72" E 019° 1' 45.81" ▪ F +27 (0)21-864-2737 ▪ **T +27 (0)21-873-7745**

☐ **Montebello** see Wine-of-the-Month Club

Monterosso Estate ⓠ

Brothers Orneglio and Francesco De Franchi run the Stellenbosch grape and olive estate they grew up on, after Italian-born father Socrate bought it in 1977, naming it after his Liguria home town. Small parcels, vinified in the estate cellar, are increasingly targeted at Gauteng, in line with a new marketing strategy.

Sangiovese Socrate ⊘ ★★★☆ Only older barrels on **14**, but shows some dry spicy oak, along with dark cherry fruit. Juicy, with firm tannins & savoury power. **Sauvignon Blanc** ★★★ Easygoing but crisply fresh & tropical-toned **14** with boiled sweet element; dry enough, though. Also tasted: **Cabernet Sauvignon-Merlot** ⊘ **14** ★★★★ **Chenin Blanc Old Bush Vine 14** ★★☆ — TJ

Location/map/WO: Stellenbosch ▪ Map grid reference: E4 ▪ Est/1stB 2000 ▪ Tasting, sales & cellar tours by appt only ▪ Owner(s) Francesco & Orneglio De Franchi ▪ Cellarmaster(s)/winemaker(s) Orneglio De Franchi (Jan 2000) ▪ Viticulturist(s) Francesco De Franchi & Orneglio De Franchi (both Jan 2000) ▪ 83ha/60ha (cab, merlot, ptage, sangio, shiraz, chard, chenin, riesling, sauv, sem) ▪ 540t/760cs own label 60% red 40% white ▪ PO Box 5 Stellenbosch 7599 ▪ defranchivin@mweb.co.za, monterosso@mweb.co.za ▪ www.monterosso.co.za ▪ S 33° 54' 6.8" E 018° 50' 10.4" ▪ F +27 (0)21-889-7081/+27 (0)21-889-5021 ▪ **T +27 (0)21-889-7081/+27 (0)21-889-5021**

☐ **Montestell** see Boland Kelder
☐ **Montino** see Riebeek Cellars

Montpellier ⓠ 🍴 🏠 ◎ ⓐ

Lots new on Johannesburg advocate Lucas van Tonder's very old arm (three centuries in 2014). New-clone pinot noir for future MCC bubbles, and a restaurant serving 'boerekos with a twist' plus additional self-catering accommodation opening soon, reports winemaker Ettienne Malan (himself a new recruit).

Location/map: Tulbagh ▪ Est 1714 ▪ Tasting, sales & tours Mon-Fri 9–5 Sat/Sun & pub hols 10-3 ▪ Pre-booked cheese platters & light meals available during tasting hours ▪ Tour groups: gazebo with pizza oven to be pre-booked ▪ Deli ▪ Olives ▪ Walking/hiking trails ▪ Renosterbos conservation area ▪ Guest house/B&B/self-catering ▪ Weddings: Dome & Cathedral venues ▪ Events ▪ Owner(s) Lucas J van Tonder ▪ Winemaker(s) Ettienne Malan (Aug 2015) ▪ 482ha/60ha (cab, merlot, p verdot, pinot, shiraz, chard, chenin, gewürz, viog) ▪ 300t/4,400cs own label 48% red 27% white 25% MCC + 150,000L bulk ▪ PO Box 79 Tulbagh 6820 ▪ marica@montpellier.co.za ▪ www.montpellier.co.za ▪ S 33° 16' 30.4" E 019° 6' 40.0" ▪ F +27 (0)23-230-1574 ▪ **T +27 (0)23-230-0656**

Mont Rochelle Hotel & Vineyard ⓠ 🍴 🏠 ◎

Part of Sir Richard Branson's dynamic Virgin Limited Edition portfolio, the winery at this luxury boutique hotel overlooking Franschhoek is being equally vigorous in redeveloping the cellar and vineyard. Infrastructure upgrades, including a new barrel room with managed humidity 'to control the "angels share"', are being followed by new equipment to make the process 'more conducive to quality wine production'. And vine gurus VinPro are helping raise fruit quality 'exponentially', possibly leading to some replanting.

Mont Rochelle range

★★★★ **Syrah** With dark chocolate, spice & white pepper, **08** is more complex than **07** (★★★☆), shows some power but graceful tannins, too, from 2 years older oak & bottle ageing.

Chardonnay ⓦ ★★★☆ Had 'Barrel Fermented' prefix. Attractive **14** yellow stonefruit & honey whiffs, creamy texture from lees-ageing & harmonious oak nuance. Dash viognier adds floral charm.

Artemis Red ⊘ ★★★★ Was just 'Artemis'. **09** cab-led with 6% each petit verdot, shiraz, mourvèdre. Commendable balance, with cigarbox, menthol & forest floor notes to pique the interest. **Artemis White** ⓝⓔⓦ ⊘ ★★★★ Appealing & fairly complex blend of part-oaked chardonnay, semillon & viognier, **14** with aromatic green apple, citrus & peach-vanilla to enjoy poolside this summer & the next few. Also tasted: **Cabernet Sauvignon 08** ★★★★ **Sauvignon Blanc 14** ★★★ Not retasted: **Merlot 07** Discontinued: **Rosé, Unwooded Chardonnay.**

Miko Premier range

Not tasted: **Cabernet Sauvignon, Chardonnay Sur Lie.** — GM

Location/map/WO: Franschhoek ▪ Est 1994 ▪ 1stB 1996 ▪ Tasting & sales 10–7 daily ▪ Fee available on request ▪ Wine tasting closed Dec 25 ▪ Cellar tours Mon, Wed, Fri at 11 (pre-booking required) ▪ Miko Restaurant & The Country Kitchen ▪ Mont Rochelle Hotel & Vineyard ▪ Picnics ▪ Walking/hiking trails ▪ Educational wine tastings – booking essential ▪ Owner(s) Virgin Limited Edition ▪ Cellarmaster(s)/winemaker(s)/viticulturist(s) Dustin Osborne ▪ 33ha/12.5ha (cab, merlot, shiraz, chard, sauv, sem) ▪ 90–120t/12,000cs own label 60% red 40% white ▪ PO Box 448 Franschhoek 7690 ▪ wine@montrochelle.virgin.com ▪ www.montrochelle.virgin.com ▪ S 33° 54' 52.1" E 019° 6' 21.9" ▪ F +27 (0)21-876-3788 ▪ **T +27 (0)21-876-2770**

☐ **Mon Vieux** *see* Boutinot South Africa
☐ **Mooiberg** *see* Zidela Wines

Mooi Bly Winery   ⓘ 🍴 🏠 📷

Originally from Belgium, the Wouters family settled in Paarl and gained not only a son-in-law but a winemaker in Erik Schouteden, who was instrumental in planting tannat. One of the rarer varieties in the winelands, it and malbec set Mooi Bly apart. There have been some winemaking changes and some 'extra experiments', the team divulge, and they look forward to reveal the results here next time.

Selection range

★★★★ **Malbec** Punchy & forthright **10** shows no-holds-barred malbec floral aromas & spice over concentrated black fruit, backed with tarry integrated tannins. Accomplished & enjoyable.

★★★★ **Tannat** Lovely example of this rare-in-SA French grape, **10** ripe mouthful of black cherries with perfume & aromatic spice – cinnamon & clove. Grape's big tannins well integrated & balanced by concentrated fruit. Improves on **09** (★★★☆).

Cultivar range

Not tasted: **Cabernet Sauvignon, Shiraz, Chardonnay, Chenin Blanc.** — CM

Location/WO: Paarl ▪ Map: Paarl & Wellington ▪ Map grid reference: F4 ▪ Est/1stB 2005 ▪ Tasting, sales & cellar tours by appt ▪ Fee R50pp ▪ Closed Dec 25 & Jan 1 ▪ BYO picnic ▪ Walks ▪ 6 self-catering cottages ▪ Owner(s) Wouters family ▪ Cellarmaster(s)/winemaker(s) Erik Schouteden (Jan 2005) ▪ Viticulturist(s) Erik Schouteden (Feb 2001) ▪ 32ha/18ha (cab, malbec, shiraz, tannat, chard, chenin) ▪ 70t/6,000cs own label 50% red 50% white ▪ PO Box 801 Huguenot 7645 ▪ wine@mooibly.com ▪ www.mooibly.com ▪ S 33° 41' 7.0" E 019° 1' 21.9" ▪ F +27 (0)21-868-2808 ▪ **T +27 (0)21-868-2808**

Mooiplaas Estate & Private Nature Reserve   ⓘ 🍴 🏠 📷 ⓐ

At Stellenbosch family estate Mooiplaas, it all begins at the convivial langtafel ('long dining table') which is why the elegant, gabled manor house is regularly opened for luncheons and dinners. Visitors arrive as guests but leave as members of the Roos clan. 'Wonderful things happen when strangers sit around a table, break bread and drink wine,' says regular host, co-owner and cellarmaster Dirk Roos.

Mercia Collection

★★★★ **Tabakland Cabernet Reserve** ⓥ Best cab barrels only for this prestige label. **10** is intense & ripe, showing well-tuned black fruit with just enough vitality & freshness for a good future.

★★★★ **Watershed Syrah** ⓥ Robust but aristocratic **12**, with classy scrub & peppery aromas showing through; toasted coffee notes hopefully will integrate with time. No **10**, **11**.

★★★★ **Rosalind** Top-range Bordeaux-style blend from cab, cab franc & merlot. 3 vintages tasted: **09** dark & serious with luscious fruit; **10** more restrained, highlighting nervous cab tones; **11** lighter, leafier, showing tarry blackcurrant fruit.

★★★★ **Houmoed Bushvine Chenin Blanc** ⓥ Seriously conceived, wooded **13** shows complex spicy fruit. Bone-dry & robust, oak needs to integrate further. Returns to form after lesser **12** (★★★☆).

★★★★ **Duel Méthode Cap Classique** ⓥ Rich, creamy & very satisfying sparkling from pinot noir & chardonnay, 36 months on lees. Latest **NV** more classic: baked apples mingle with warm brioche aromas.

Classic range

★★★★ **Cabernet Sauvignon** 2 vintages tasted: 08 (★★★☆) has tangy acidity with sour cherry fruit, sturdy tannin structure. 09 more focused, showing a robust tarry core, refined black fruit, earthy aromas.

★★★★ **Chenin Blanc Bush Vine** Super-ripe fruit with marmalade undertones, 14 follows form. Oxidative, leesy & full bodied, with creamy texture, gentle acidity & sweet tropical sunshine finish.

Not retasted: **Pinotage** 13 ★★★☆ **Sauvignon Blanc** 13 ★★★★

Langtafel range

White ⊘ ★★★ Sauvignon, semillon & chenin blend, 14 is perky & refreshing, fruity & light. Also tasted: **Red** 14 ★★ **Rosé** 14 ★★ — GdB

Location/map: Stellenbosch ▪ Map grid reference: B4 ▪ WO: Stellenbosch/Coastal ▪ Est 1806 ▪ 1stB 1995 ▪ Tasting & sales Tue-Fri 9—4.30 Sat 10—4 Sun 10.30-3.30 ▪ Fee R25/5 wines, waived on purchase ▪ Closed Mon, Easter weekend, Dec 25/26 & Jan 1/2 ▪ Gourmet picnic hampers & cheese platters, booking essential ▪ Langtafel (32 seater) luncheons or dinners every ±8-10 weeks in the manor house (a National Monument), enquire for dates ▪ Taste Experience presented by Dirk Roos in the 'voorkamer' (10-18 guests), booking essential ▪ Guest accommodation ▪ Walks/hikes ▪ Mountain biking ▪ Horse riding, riding lessons & trail rides ▪ Child friendly ▪ 60ha private nature reserve ▪ Owner(s) Mooiplaas Trust ▪ Cellarmaster(s) Louis Roos (1983) ▪ Winemaker(s) Louis Roos (1983), with Dirk Roos ▪ Viticulturist(s) Tielman Roos (1981) ▪ 250ha/100ha (cabs s/f, p verdot, ptage, pinot, chard, chenin, sauv) ▪ 750t/ 50,000cs own label 57% red 41% white 2% rosé ▪ Other export brand: The Collection ▪ BWI, IPW ▪ PO Box 104 Koelenhof 7605 ▪ info@mooiplaas.co.za, wine@mooiplaas.co.za ▪ www.mooiplaas.co.za ▪ S 33° 55' 16.3" E 018° 44' 21.4" ▪ F +27 (0)86-604-4312 ▪ **T +27 (0)21-200-7493**

Mooiuitsig Wine Cellars ⌂

Mooiuitsig, the Jonker family's drinks enterprise, has a substantial portfolio (including mostly sweet wine, 3 and 5 Year Old brandy, and Pale Dry, Medium Dry, Medium Cream and Old Brown 'sherry'), an own distribution network and even retail outlets. Accommodation is offered near their Bonnievale HQ.

Location: Bonnievale ▪ Est 1947 ▪ Closed to public ▪ Stay-overs at De Rust Lodge info@ outdoorarena.co.za; T +27 (0)23-616-2444 ▪ Owner(s) Jonker family ▪ Winemaker(s) Nico van der Westhuizen, with Lazarus Kholomba ▪ Viticulturist(s) Casper Matthee ▪ 150ha total ▪ 2,900t ▪ PO Box 15 Bonnievale 6730 ▪ info@mooiuitsig.co.za ▪ www.mooiuitsig.co.za ▪ F +27 (0)23-616-2675 ▪ **T +27 (0)23-616-2143**

☐ **Mooiuitzicht** *see* Mooiuitsig Wine Cellars
☐ **Moonlight Organics** *see* Stellar Winery

Môreson ⚗ 🍴 📷

Over two decades since the maiden solo harvest in 1994, the 'Morning Sun' is still rising for the Friedman family. Their Franschhoek farm's wine offering is increasingly chardonnay-centric: 'We now boast 11 different clones of our favourite variety, from which we produce six different wines/MCCs,' says GM Nikki Friedman. Their hospitality offering also continues to expand, most recently with the addition of a wedding/function venue. 'We've repurposed our orchid nursery and transformed it into a fantastic space for an occasion. We have also completed the installation of a solar plant. Reducing our impact on the environment remains an important theme here.'

Môreson range

★★★★ **Cabernet Franc** 12 (★★★★☆) takes 11's spearmint freshness to new heights, as minty dark chocolate combines with raspberry & early plum fruit; lithely powerful; lingering spicy finish.

★★★★☆ **Pinotage** No longer with 10% cinsaut, 13 has greater purity of dark black berry fruit than 12, piercingly evident on nose, softening on palate with stewed plums & mocha; lingering finish. Coastal WO.

★★★★ **Mata Mata** ⊘ First vintage exclusively from Franschhoek grapes (40% merlot, 28% each cab & cab franc, malbec), 12 (★★★★★) has lovely black-fruit purity supported by soft tannins & fresh acidity. Even more balanced & elegant than 11, also tasted for the 2015 edition.

★★★★☆ **Mercator Premium Chardonnay** ⓦ Think pineapples & nectarines with a few squeezes of lime, elegant **13** is ripe & juicy but dry, rich & creamy but restrained, with fermentation (40% wild) in French oak (50% new) adding toasted almond & spice complexity.

★★★★ **Knoputibak** ⓦ Conceived to showcase Franschhoek's regional identity, **13** (★★★★☆) is more refined than **12**, with 25% semillon (from 50 year old dryland bushvines) adding smooth beeswax texture to chardonnay's creamy lemon intensity.

★★★★ **Solitaire Blanc de Blancs Méthode Cap Classique** Made from free-run (chardonnay) juice only (the press fraction going into Miss Molly bubbly), 18 months on lees, improved latest **NV** has lime & lemon freshness with crumbly biscuit notes, a bit like lemon creams without the sugar.

★★★★ **The Fudge** From vine-dessicated chardonnay, delicious **13** dessert also spent year in oak, adding vanilla & baking spice complexity to buttery, fudgy, tropical fruits & golden sultanas.

Also tasted: **Sauvignon Blanc 14** ★★★★ **Pink Brut Rosé NV** ★★★★ Not retasted: **Dr Reason Why 13** ★★★★ Not tasted: **Magia**.

Miss Molly range

Not tasted: **In My Bed Cabernet Sauvignon-Merlot, Kitchen Thief Sauvignon Blanc, Hoity Toity Chenin Blanc-Viognier, Petit Rosé, Méthode Cap Classique**. — JG

Location/map: Franschhoek • WO: Franschhoek/Coastal • Est 1983 • 1stB 1994 • Tasting, sales & cellar tours daily 9.30–5 • Fee R40 • Closed Dec 25 • Bread & Wine Restaurant daily 12-3 & Miss Molly Charcuterie Bar (for lighter meals) daily 11-3 • Charcuterie produced by Neil Jewell • Breadmaking • Exotic Plant Company • Wedding/function venue • Owner(s) Richard Friedman • Winemaker(s) Clayton Reabow (May 2007) • Viti-culturist(s) James McNaught Davis • 35ha/±18ha (chard, chenin) • ±120t 30% red 45% white 25% MCC • EuroGAP, IPW • PO Box 114 Franschhoek 7690 • sales@moreson.co.za • www.moreson.co.za • S 33° 53' 11.9" E 019° 3' 30.6" • F +27 (0)21-876-2348 • **T +27 (0)21-876-3055**

☐ **Môrewag** see Blomendahl Vineyards

Morgenhof Wine Estate   ⓦ ⓦ ⓐ ⓐ ⓐ ⓐ

Schalk Pienaar has taken charge of the vineyards, and as befits a property under French ownership since 1993 (Anne Cointreau is from the famous French cognac and liqueurs family), the vines chosen to augment current plantings are the classics: cabernet and chardonnay. Diverse aspects and soils (samples of the latter on display at the cellardoor) on Stellenbosch's Simonsberg allow for careful matching of variety to site, and for Andries de Klerk to create still, sparkling and fortified wines to match different style and price points. Extolling the estate's many virtues is new marketing/sales chief Anita Streicher Nel.

Morgenhof Estate range

★★★★ **Cabernet Sauvignon** ⊘ Fresh enjoyment in accessible **12**'s abundant, expressive black-currant fruitiness. Couple years in barrel structure & impart nicely savoury tannic grip.

★★★★ **Merlot** Leafy, herbaceous edge to elegant red-fruited **11** (★★★★), slightly less concentrated than **10**.

★★★★ **Merlot-Cabernet Franc** Expressive, perfumed **11** seriously styled blend significant step up from **10** (★★★☆). Oak spice (from 2 years in barrel) underpins convincing black & red fruit flavours, imparts supple structure & complexity.

★★★★ **The Morgenhof Estate** ⓦ Flagship red from 5 Bordeaux grapes. **06** noticeable acidity but better knit when revisited mid-2013. Delicious aromas persist, tannin supports the fruit.

★★★★ **Brut Reserve** Full, persistent mousse carries red pear flavours of bone-dry **10** chardonnay, pinot noir MCC sparkling. Couple of years on lees imparts freshness & complexity to lean, focused style.

Also tasted: **Chardonnay 14** ★★★★ **Chenin Blanc 14** ★★★★ Not retasted: **Sauvignon Blanc 14** ★★★★ Not tasted: **Cape LBV**. Occasional release: **Noble Late Harvest**.

Fantail range

Pinotage Rosé ★★☆ **14** softened by fruity sweetness. Fresh & light, perfect for picnics. Stellenbosch WO, as most of these. Also tasted: **Pinotage 13** ★★★ Not retasted: **Cabernet Franc-Cabernet Sauvignon 11** ★★★ **Sauvignon Blanc-Chenin Blanc 13** ★★☆ — IM

Location/map: Stellenbosch ▪ Map grid reference: F3 ▪ WO: Simonsberg–Stellenbosch/Stellenbosch ▪ Est 1692 ▪ 1stB 1984 ▪ Tasting & sales Mon-Fri 9–5.30 (Nov-Apr) & 9-4.30 (May-Oct); Sat/Sun 10–5 (Nov-Apr) & 10-3 (May-Oct) ▪ Fee R35pp ▪ Closed Good Fri, Dec 25 & Jan 1 ▪ Cellar tours/viewing of underground barrel cellar on request ▪ Cheese platters ▪ Morgenhof Restaurant ▪ Facilities for children ▪ Conferences ▪ Weddings/functions ▪ Heli-pad ▪ Conservation area ▪ Morgenhof Manor House ▪ Owner(s) Anne Cointreau ▪ Winemaker(s) Andries de Klerk (Jan 2012) ▪ Viticulturist(s) Schalk Pienaar (Dec 2014) ▪ 212ha/78ha (cabs s/f, malbec, merlot, chenin, chard) ▪ 410t/70,000cs own label 60% red 38% white 2% rosé ▪ BWI, IPW ▪ PO Box 365 Stellenbosch 7599 ▪ info@morgenhof.com ▪ www.morgenhof.com ▪ S 33° 53' 38.5" E 018° 51' 39.2" ▪ **T +27 (0)21-889-2000**

Morgenster Estate

This fine estate on the slopes of Stellenbosch's Schapenberg was once (briefly) part of the original Vergelegen. After 1708 this section was bought by a refugee Huguenot, who built the splendid manor house — on its gable the 'morning star' in a scallop which provides the logo of the modern estate of Italian businessman Giulio Bertrand, who acquired the property in 1992. His origins provide the obvious background for the Italian varieties grown here, as well as the estate's famous olive oil. A Frenchman, though, Pierre Lurton of prestigious Cheval Blanc in Bordeaux, has been significant in providing support. Giulio's ever-ambitious investment continues, with a host of innovations, from flood alleviation works to 'new and refined farming practices', to a new restaurant. An octogenarian, the signore's energy in developing his estate remains remarkable.

Morgenster Estate range

★★★★☆ **Lourens River Valley** Deep cocoa & blackcurrant notes on estate's other Bordeaux blend. Cab franc leads the way on **12** with merlot & dab (5%) cab in support. Sexy, succulent & plush yet elegant, supple & generous. Gentle tannic squeeze on long tail.

★★★★☆ **Morgenster** Focused & effortlessly elegant, taut & refined **12** sees merlot up to 72% from 59% on **11**. Cab & petit verdot season & support the seamless blend, as does 60% new French oak. Rounded, svelte, layered & deeply complex. Years of life ahead.

★★★★ **White** Precise, focused **14** (★★★★☆) sees semillon toned down from 49% on **13**, sauvignon hiked to 58%. Concentrated, taut & long with subtle interplay of oak (40% new) & bright, vivacious lemony fruit.

Italian Collection

★★★★ **Nabucco** Nebbiolo reigns supreme in **13** paean to Italian opera, like others here. Deep & dark yet seductive, with firm core, juicy life & dry, fine tannin on long tail.

★★★★ **Tosca** Cab & merlot scaled down while sangiovese rises to 69% in **13**. Light, supple & sylphlike, it's rewarding & full of typical cherry spice. A step up on **12** (★★★☆).

Also tasted: **Caruso 15** ★★★☆

NU Series 1

★★★★ **Merlot** ⟨Ø⟩ Medium bodied & accessible, **13** (★★★★☆) still has notable tannin grip to balance ripe cherry/cocoa succulence. Harmonious, as was slightly more impressive **12**.

Cabernet Franc ⟨NEW⟩ ★★★★ **14** preview shows earthy cocoa & fynbos depth with spice & texture. Tannic grip noticeable but it's still young. Also tasted: **Sangiovese 15** ★★★★ **Sauvignon Blanc 15** ★★★ Not retasted: **Cabernet Sauvignon 13** ★★★★☆ — FM

Location: Somerset West ▪ Map: Helderberg ▪ WO: Stellenbosch ▪ Est 1993 ▪ 1stB 1998 ▪ Tasting & sales Mon-Sun 10–5 ▪ Tasting fee R40 wine/R35 olive oil & olive products ▪ Closed Good Fri & Dec 25 ▪ Restaurant 95@ morgenster ▪ Owner(s) Giulio Bertrand ▪ Cellarmaster(s) Henry Kotzé (Oct 2009) ▪ Winemaker(s) Henry Kotzé (Oct 2009), with consultant Pierre Lurton (Nov 1997, Château Cheval Blanc) ▪ Viticulturist(s) Corius Visser (Apr 2014) ▪ 200ha/40ha (cabs s/f, merlot, nebbiolo, p verdot, sangio, sauv, sem) ▪ 90% red 5% white 5% rosé ▪ BWI, IPW, SIZA ▪ PO Box 1616 Somerset West 7129 ▪ info@morgenster.co.za ▪ www.morgenster.co.za ▪ S 34° 51' 2.9" E 018° 53' 7.8" ▪ F +27 (0)21-852-1141 ▪ **T +27 (0)21-852-1738**

☐ **Mori Wines** see Casa Mori

☐ **Morkel** see Bellevue Estate Stellenbosch

Mostertsdrift Noble Wines

Emergency modifications to the old cooling unit (the new one having been vandalised) by co-owner André Mostert allowed his sister and winemaker Anna-Mareè Uys to vinify a small quantity of rosé and chardonnay in 2015. The 'rescue' wines – along with the backstory, some earlier vintages and a warm welcome – are available from the family's cellardoor in Stellenbosch.

Merlot Rosé ★★★ Softly sweet **15** offers abundant berry flavours for easy, cheerful enjoyment. **Chardonnay** ★★ Part-oaked **15** is tropical toned, made to drink soon. Not retasted: **Cabernet Sauvignon 07** ★★★ **AnéRouge 07** ★★★ **Cape Blend 08** ★★★ Not tasted: **White Muscadel**. — IM

Location/map/WO: Stellenbosch ▪ Map grid reference: E4 ▪ Est/1stB 2001 ▪ Tasting, sales & cellar tours by appt ▪ Fee R10pp for groups ▪ Meals for groups by prior arrangement ▪ Facilities for children ▪ Conference venue ▪ Owner(s) André Mostert & Anna-Mareè Uys (Mostert) ▪ Cellarmaster(s)/winemaker(s) Anna-Mareè Uys (Jan 2001) ▪ Viticulturist(s) Nico Mostert (Jan 2001) ▪ 13ha/±8ha (cab, merlot, pinot, chard, hanepoot) ▪ ±80-100t/3,986cs own label 70% red 10% white 20% rosé + 15,000L bulk ▪ PO Box 2061 Dennesig Stellenbosch 7601 ▪ winemaker@mostertsdrift.co.za ▪ www.mostertsdrift.co.za ▪ S 33° 53' 31.7" E 018° 50' 17.6" ▪ F +27 (0)86-516-1730 ▪ **T +27 (0)73-194-9221**

Mother Rock Wines   (NEW)

Johan Meyer, winemaker for Mount Abora and his own JH Meyer Signature Wines, now has a third 'gig' as co-owner with UK importer Ben Henshaw of this recently launched venture. Bottling under the label Force Majeure, the pair seek to make honest, natural wines with character and a sense of place, and dream of the day when the SA market learns to appreciate 'terroir'. There's a chenin blanc, cinsaut rosé and red blend available, and a second label Witch in the pipeline.

Location: Riebeek-Kasteel ▪ Est/1stB 2014 ▪ Owner(s) Johan Meyer & Ben Henshaw ▪ Winemaker(s) Johan Meyer ▪ 35t/6,000cs own label ▪ PO Box 396 Riebeek Kasteel 7307 ▪ motherrockwines@gmail.com ▪ www.motherrockwines.com ▪ **T +27 (0)79-280-0237**

Mount Abora Vineyards   (♀)

Pieter de Waal and Krige Visser (both would admit to being a touch eccentric and wholly wine-passionate) took full ownership of this Swartland label after something of a shake-up. It continues to polish its local and international reputation in the avant-garde of the Cape's move to more refreshing, unmanipulated and 'authentic' wines. They're made by Johan Meyer in the Antebellum winery near Riebeek-Kasteel, fully embracing the precepts and ideals of the Swartland Independent Producers. The name comes from the imaginary landmark in Coleridge's poem 'Kubla Khan', whose 'Abyssinian maid' is also behind the name of the red blend.

★★★★☆ **Saffraan** ⊘ A great advert for cinsaut as a quality grape. **14** already enticing, with red fruit & more (floral, perhaps), though stressing minerality rather than fruit. Fresh, bright & light (12% alcohol) but subtly tannic & not without power or ability to develop many years. From old bushvines.

★★★★☆ **The Abyssinian** Lightly oaked, naturally made **13** from syrah/shiraz (57%) with mourvèdre & cinsaut, has Saffraan's red brightness but in darker, more sombre, & slightly bolder context. More difficult to understand, but worth it. Decant in youth; rather leave a good few years!

★★★★ **Koggelbos** **13** from old dryland bushvine chenin. Pale, rich gold; oxidative broadness, succulent & interesting. Whole-bunch ferment & 9 months in old oak. Just off level of fresher **12** (★★★★★). — TJ

Location: Riebeek-Kasteel ▪ WO: Swartland ▪ Est/1stB 2012 ▪ Tasting & sales at The Wine Kollective in Riebeek-Kasteel ▪ Owner(s) Vinotage (Pty) Ltd ▪ Winemaker(s) Johan Meyer ▪ 2,150cs own label 60% red 40% white ▪ PO Box 396 Riebeek Kasteel 7307 ▪ wine@abora.co.za ▪ www.abora.co.za ▪ **T +27 (0)82-413-6719/+27 (0)79-280-0237/+27 (0)83-357-3864**

Mountain Oaks Organic Winery ⓠ ⓞ

It was the wish to farm organically that led the Stevens family to the Slanghoek Valley, where the project was eased by conducive conditions. Today the farm is certified organic, and estate produce is available along with pre-booked tours and talks on organic farming.

★★★★ **Pinotage** ⓐ ⓥ After juicy **10, 11** (★★★★) preview had ripe raspberry scent & delicious flavours, but perhaps not the depth for its ambitious structure. Drying tannin might resolve in time.

Eikenbosch Red ⓐ ⓥ ★★★ Lively, pleasant **10** cab/cab franc blend balances ripe flavours with more spicy, savoury character. Firmly structured. Not retasted: **Le Jardin Rouge 11** ★★ Not tasted: **Le Jardin Rosé, Chardonnay Reserve, Eikenbosch White, Le Jardin**. — TJ

Location: Rawsonville ▪ Map: Breedekloof ▪ WO: Slanghoek ▪ Est/1stB 2003 ▪ Tasting, sales & cellar tours by appt ▪ Farm tours & talks on organic farming by appt ▪ Farm produce ▪ Owner(s) Stevens family ▪ 200ha/16ha (cabs s/f, ptage, shiraz, chard, chenin) ▪ 20-30t own label 70% red 20% white 10% rosé ▪ SGS organic certification ▪ PO Box 68 Rawsonville 6845 ▪ eikenbosch@iafrica.com ▪ S 33° 38' 16.1" E 019° 13' 36.0" ▪ F +27 (0)86-613-6687 ▪ **T +27 (0)23-344-3107**

Mountain Ridge Wines ⓠ 🤝 ⓞ ⓰

Wine, made under the baton of recent transplant (from Knorhoek in Stellenbosch) Arno Albertyn, a wedding and function venue, and monthly farmer's market with fresh produce, art and music are all among the attractions of the Mountain Ridge cellardoor. It's somewhat off the beaten path in Wolseley, but with an address that translates as 'Love Street' and a bubbly named Smooch, can you resist?

Romansrivier range

Cabernet Sauvignon Reserve ★★★★ Retasted **11** showing more harmoniously, with the plentiful dark berries in alliance with oak's tobacco & spice, leading to good dry finish. Big & impressive. Also tasted: **Shiraz Reserve 11** ★★★★

Mountain Ridge range

★★★★ **Shiraz** ⓐ Likeable, friendly, old-oaked **11** (★★★) without the ambitions of big, dramatic **10**. Ripe, spicy & flavourful, but rather edgy; finishes on a sweet note.

Merlot (ⓝⓔⓦ) ★★ Pleasant choc-mint notes on **13** become a bit greener on the palate. Big, grippy & slightly sweet. Also tasted: **Cabernet Sauvignon 12** ★★★ **Sauvignon Blanc 15** ★★

De Liefde range

Aanstap Rooies Dry Red ★★ Cheerful red fruit on burly but juicy, nearly dry cab-merlot **NV** (**14**) unwooded blend. **Smooch Vonkelwyn** ★★ Briefly foaming, briefly flavoursome off-dry pink bubbly. **NV**. Not retasted: **The Long & Wine'ing Road Dry White 14** ★★★ — TJ

Location: Wolseley ▪ Map: Breedekloof ▪ WO: Western Cape ▪ Est 1949 ▪ 1stB 1976 ▪ Tasting & sales Mon-Fri 8–5 ▪ Closed all pub hols ▪ BYO picnic ▪ Ramkiekie Farmer's Market ▪ Wedding & function venue (140-160 pax) ▪ Owner(s) 20 members ▪ Cellarmaster(s) / GM Arno Albertyn (Jan 2014) ▪ Winemaker(s) Christo Stemmet (Jan 2010) ▪ Viticulturist(s) Pierre Snyman (consultant) ▪ 400ha (cab, shiraz, chenin, cbard) ▪ 9,000t/8,000cs own label 48% red 37% white 15% rosé ▪ IPW ▪ PO Box 108 Wolseley 6830 ▪ sales@mountainridge.co.za ▪ www.mountainridge.co.za ▪ S 33° 28' 26.04" E 019° 12' 10.44" ▪ F +27 (0)23-231-1102 ▪ **T +27 (0)23-231-1070**

Mountain River Wines

Run from one of historic Paarl Main Street's elegantly restored homes, De Villiers Brits' negociant business, founded in the early 1990s when newly democratic SA's wine exports took off, has carved a place for both its bulk and bottled wines in markets as diverse as the UK, India, China and Russia.

Mountain River range

★★★★ **Pinotage** ⓐ **09** (★★★★), successor to ageworthy **06**, high-toned raspberry fruit, vanilla fudge nose, black fruit pastille core & coconut tail from 20% American oak.
Not retasted: **Chardonnay 12** ★★★

Maankloof range

Sauvignon Blanc ⊘ ★★★☆ Appealing grapefruit & flinty tone to step-up **15**. Crisp & tangy fruit, lovely clean-cut balanced freshness. Ideal for summer picnics. Not retasted: **Cabernet Sauvignon 13** ★★ **Pinotage 13** ★★ **Shiraz 13** ★★ Not tasted: **Chenin Blanc**.

Zaràfa range

Pinotage Tank sample too unformed to rate. **Shiraz** ⊘ ★★★ **14** preview plenty of sweet spice & redcurrants in ripe, fruit-forward unwooded style. Very friendly tannins for laid-back easy drinking. **Rosé** ⊘ ★★☆ Pre-bottled sample **15** from mixed cultivars, with scented rosepetal nuance, fresh dry flavours & modest alcohol. Appealing sunset sipper. Also tasted: **Sauvignon Blanc** ⊘ **15** ★★★☆ Not retasted: **Cabernet Sauvignon 13** ★★

Ukuzala range

Not tasted: **Dry Red**, **Dry White**. — MW

Location: Paarl ▪ WO: Western Cape ▪ Est 1993 ▪ 1stB 1998 ▪ Closed to public ▪ Owner(s) De Villiers Brits ▪ Cellarmaster(s) De Villiers Brits, with consultants ▪ 1.2ha (shiraz) ▪ 60,000cs own label 60% red 40% white ▪ 146 Main Road Paarl 7646 ▪ dev@mountainriverwines.co.za, mattie@mountainriverwines.co.za ▪ www.mountainriverwines.co.za ▪ F +27 (0)21-872-3255 ▪ **T +27 (0)21-872-3245/6/7/8**

☐ **Mountain Shadows** see Wineways Marketing
☐ **Mountain Stream** see Ashton Kelder

Mount Babylon Vineyards   ⓠ

Pioneers in Hemel-en-Aarde Ridge, Mount Babylon Vineyards' Johan and Yolanda Holtzhausen are planting more pinot noir as part of an increasing focus on MCC bubbly (their unusual shiraz-based Pioneer Brut Reserve '12 unready for tasting). With neighbour Creation Wines, they're launching a new sparkling named Elation, and turning their tasting venue into a champagne lounge opening early 2016.

Location: Hermanus ▪ Map: Elgin, Walker Bay & Bot River ▪ Est 2002 ▪ 1stB 2007 ▪ Tasting, sales & cellar tours by appt ▪ Cheese platters ▪ Owner(s) Johan Holtzhausen ▪ Winemaker(s) Jean-Claude Martin (2008, consultant) & Johan Holtzhausen ▪ Viticulturist(s) Johan Pienaar (2002, consultant) ▪ 65ha/7ha (pinot, shiraz, viog) ▪ ±38t/±400cs own label 90% red 10% white ▪ PO Box 7370 Stellenbosch 7599 ▪ info@mountbabylon.co.za ▪ www.mountbabylon.co.za ▪ S 34° 19' 44.0"   E 019° 19' 34.3" ▪ F +27 (0)21-855-2768 ▪ **T +27 (0)21-855-2768/+27 (0)84-511-8180**

Mount Pleasant Vineyards

Former London banker, now active music patron in arty Darling, Alfred Legner also tends a small, walled vineyard in this West Coast village. Made for the Legner family by Wim Smit at Malmesbury's Hofstraat Kelder, the shiraz is from the clos, the chenin from a local vineyard.

Darling Pascale's Shiraz ★★★☆ Elegant **13** sports a vibrant label & clearly shows cool origin in white pepper, bitter cherry & savoury, earthy notes. Tightly wound still, decant or cellar year/2. Not retasted: **Darling Pascale's Chenin Blanc 13** ★★★☆ — HJ

Location/WO: Darling ▪ Est 2009 ▪ 1stB 2011 ▪ Closed to public ▪ Owner(s) Legner family ▪ Winemaker(s) Wim Smit (Dec 2010, Hofstraat) ▪ Viticulturist(s) Alfred Legner (Jun 2006) ▪ 0.2ha/0.1ha (shiraz) ▪ 2t/ha 66cs own label 100% red ▪ 11 High Street Darling 7345 ▪ info@darlingmusic.org ▪ **T +27 (0)72-015-1653**

Mount Rozier Estate

Adopting the name of the Helderberg farm acquired in 2012 by the Gabb family, this supermarket-based brand of nearby Journey's End Vineyards (also Gabb owned) focuses on 'delivering a good, quaffable drop for under R50 a bottle' from selectively sourced bought-in wine. The vineyards on the prime Schapenberg Hill site contribute to premium Journey's End bottlings.

Beekeeper Merlot ⊘ ⓦ ★★★☆ Perfectly ripened, charming **14** over-delivers: bright red berry, plum fruit tucked in by softly spicy tannins. **Peacock Chardonnay** ⓦ ★★★ Exuberant, tasty, lightly oaked **13** has honeyed aromas, lipsmacking flavours of ripe apples & yellow peaches. **Flower Garden Sauvignon Blanc** ⊘ 🍷 ★★★☆ Full-flavoured tropical freshness belies unexpressive nose in **14**. Delightful, balanced summer sipper.

Also tasted: **Myrtle Grove Cabernet Sauvignon 14** ★★★ **Tobacco Street Shiraz 14** ★★★ — IM

Location: Sir Lowry's Pass ▪ Map: Helderberg ▪ WO: Stellenbosch ▪ Est/1stB 2011 ▪ Wine sales Mon-Fri ▪ Owner(s) Gabb family ▪ Winemaker(s) Leon Esterhuizen ▪ Viticulturist(s) Lodewyk Retief ▪ (cab, merlot, shiraz, chard, sauv) ▪ HACCP, IPW, WIETA ▪ PO Box 3040 Somerset West 7129 ▪ wines@mountrozier.co.za ▪ www.mountrozier.co.za ▪ S 34° 6' 21.22" E 018° 54' 35.80" ▪ F +27 (0)86-540-1929 ▪ **T +27 (0)21-858-1929**

☐ **Mount Sutherland Continental** see Super Single Vineyards

Mount Vernon Estate

Originally from Durban, KwaZulu-Natal, the Hooper family some years ago settled on the Simonsberg foothills near Paarl for a lifestyle change. Their small-scale label debuted in our 2005 guide, and has since featured red and white varieties and blends under the Mount Vernon and Three Peaks ranges. Two new Rhino Tears blends provide financial support to anti-poaching projects in SA's national parks.

Location: Paarl ▪ Est 1996 ▪ 1stB 2005 ▪ Closed to public ▪ Owner(s) David & Debbie Hooper ▪ Cellarmaster(s) Debbie Hooper (Jan 2003) ▪ Winemaker(s) Brendan Butler (Jan 2015) ▪ Viticulturist(s) Philip du Toit (Jun 1997) ▪ 160ha/57.5ha (cab, malbec, merlot, p verdot, ptage, shiraz, chard) ▪ 210-225t/5,300cs own label 80% red 15% white 5% rosé ▪ PO Box 348 Klapmuts 7625 ▪ john@mountvernon.co.za ▪ www.mountvernon.co.za ▪ F +27 (0)86-618-9821 ▪ **T +27 (0)21-875-5073**

Moya Meaker

(NEW)

This young brand honours the mother of Genevieve Curl, SA-born wife of Canadian businessman and wine aficionado David Curl, also owner of French châteaux Gaby and Moya. After many years away, Genevieve in 2010 persuaded David to buy land locally, and the Curls and their young family now divide their time between Bordeaux and Elgin. The vines on Moya Meaker, pinot noir and syrah/shiraz, represent two other great French wine regions. Production is overseen by Gaby's oenologist, Damien Landouar, who aims for 'concentration, elegance and persistence' as well as 'pleasure and conviviality'.

★★★★ **Syrah** Cocoa-dusted dark fruit, scrub & savoury notes, **13**'s succulence belies the serious tannins promising a 5 year future. **12** (★★★☆) an intriguing mix of meat extract & sour cherries, now at peak drinking age. — CR, CvZ

Location/WO: Elgin ▪ Est 2010 ▪ 1stB 2012 ▪ Closed to public ▪ Owner(s) David Curl ▪ Winemaker(s) Damien Landouar (2010) ▪ 4.5ha (pinot, syrah) ▪ 28-30t own label 100% red ▪ Habibi Farm, Valley Road, Elgin 7180 ▪ tom.davey@chateau-dugaby.com ▪ www.chateau-gaby.com ▪ **T +27 (0)21-844-0977**

Mulderbosch Vineyards

 🍷 ◎ ♿

Progress at this dynamic Stellenbosch winery has included WIETA accreditation for the rosé. 'Achieved in concert with our dedicated base of grape gowers,' winemaker Adam Mason notes. 'It also reflects our ethos as an organisation to social responsibility.' The varietal focus of owner Charles Banks of Terroir Capital, as well as Adam and co-winemaker Mick Craven is chenin blanc, with the three single-vineyard wines offering 'incredible insight into not only chenin but the sites and each unfolding vintage'. Adam mentions Block A as a standout in 2015, a year which 'saw a new level of fruit intensity and freshness attributable to the incredible conditions'. The team is happy that with the gradual recovery of the home farm's wetlands, bird species such as the African Snipe, Spoonbill and Yellow Billed Duck have returned.

Mulderbosch Vineyards range

★★★★☆ **Faithful Hound** ⊘ Consistently outstanding Bordeaux red, **13** (★★★★★) led by cab, cab franc, fleshed out by merlot, malbec, petit verdot. Too good not to enjoy now with its generous & forthcoming sweet, ripe black/red berries, creamy base & gentle tannin. Enough substance for the medium term, like **11**.

★★★★ **Chardonnay** Attractive part-oaked **14** similar ready satisfaction as **13** but concentration, structure to mature. Mixes pickled lime & leesy richness with precision, purity & lingering freshness. Stellenbosch WO.

★★★★☆ **Chardonnay Barrel Fermented** ⓐ Elegant & complex, **12** shows seamless integration between mineral, limy fruit & oak (50% new, 18 months). Expansive mouthfeel, good length though still tight core of flavour. Will reward cellaring. No **11**.

★★★★ **Chenin Blanc Steen op Hout** **14** follows in footsteps of moreish **13** with ripe yellow peach enticement & hint honey. Usual 10% oaked portion broadens, adds bounce to juicy flavours.

★★★★ **Faithful Hound White** **14**'s higher percentage semillon than **13** (72% vs 57%) evident in more waxy, savoury features, smooth viscous feel. Sauvignon plays subtle refreshing role. Food-friendly style, judiciously oaked; possibly ready sooner than **13**. Tasted just after bottling, needs time to settle.

★★★★ **Sauvignon Blanc Noble Late Harvest** Vintage conditions encouraged botrytis in **14**, pungently evident here along with peaches & apricots. Oak, both new/used, increases opulence to already luscious fruit but concludes clean, not overly sweet.

Cabernet Sauvignon Rosé ⓥ ★★★ Perennial winner, especially in the US. Zestily fresh **15** provides mouthful of juicy strawberries & cream, lingering fruity tail. WO Coastal.

Also tasted: **Sauvignon Blanc 14 ★★★☆**

1000 Miles range

★★★★☆ **1000 Miles Sauvignon Blanc** ⓐ **13** shows more youthful restraint than **12** (★★★★★); distinctive lime zest, blackcurrant intensity yet to unfold. Sleek & taut rather than zesty, with cool resonance in its endless fantail persistence. 14 months in 500L French oak seamlessly absorbed. Lovely prospects.

Single Vineyards range

★★★★☆ **Block A** Floral **14** (★★★★) prettiest of trio but unlike **13** doesn't appear to have quite the same backbone. Few grams of sugar, evident in tail, may harmonise, mellow over medium term.

★★★★ **Block S2** This Stellenbosch single-vineyard chenin trio vinified identically (& sold as a pack) to reveal individual identity. Natural ferment/ageing 11 months in older French barrels. Cinnamon-spiced baked apples on **14** (★★★★☆), rich yet full of energy & potential. More expressive than **13**.

★★★★☆ **Block W** **14** most steely & taut of trio. Delicate (just 13% alcohol) yet great intensity of bruised apple flavour; tangily mouthwatering conclusion. All well reined in; really does suggest a stayer. — AL

Location/map: Stellenbosch ▪ Map grid reference: C6 ▪ WO: Western Cape/Stellenbosch/Coastal ▪ Est 1989 ▪ 1stB 1991 ▪ Tasting & sales Tue-Sun & pub hols 10-6 ▪ Fee R50-R70 ▪ Closed Mon, Easter Fri-Mon, Dec 25 & Jan 1 ▪ Pizzas & cheese boards, gourmet burgers, cappuccinos, artisanal beer, juice ▪ Olive oil ▪ Bocce ball courts (Italian boule) ▪ Conservation area ▪ Owner(s) Terroir Capital ▪ Winemaker(s) Adam Mason (Dec 2011), with Mick Craven (Jan 2013) ▪ Viticulturist(s) Adam Mason (Jun 2013) ▪ 80ha/45.2ha (cabs s/f, merlot, p verdot, shiraz, chard, chenin, sauv, viog) ▪ BWI, IPW, WIETA ▪ PO Box 12817 Die Boord Stellenbosch 7613 ▪ info@mulderbosch.co.za ▪ www.mulderbosch.co.za ▪ S 33° 56' 56.00" E 018° 45' 57.00" ▪ F +27 (0)21-881-3514 ▪ **T +27 (0)21-881-8140**

Mullineux & Leeu Family Wines   ⓠ

Chris and Andrea Mullineux in 2014 surprised no one when they won this guide's coveted Winery of the Year accolade. Diverted (thankfully) into wine from intended careers in respectively bean counting and spacefaring, the couple founded their Swartland winery in 2007. Through talent, passion and a lot of hard work they accumulated a cult following and enviable international acclaim for their boutique-scale, naturally handcrafted wines. The SA- and California-born Mullineux recently forged a partnership with Indian businessman Analjit Singh, and together with deputy Tremayne Smith and vine adviser Rosa Kruger are taking the business to the next level. This edition they're also taking their achievements in the guide to a new high, with an extraordinary haul of five maximum 5 stars (this from a yet more stringent selection process) plus the Red Wine of the Year accolade and the newest of our prestige awards, Dessert

Wine of the Year. There surely can be no more deserving recipients of this year's ultimate distinction, and so for the second time in as many years, we're delighted to name Mullineux & Leeu our Winery of the Year 2016. For a profile of our worthy winners, see under Winery & Wines of the Year.

Mullineux Terroir Specific range

★★★★☆ **Iron Syrah** This edition's preeminent red wine is from an organically farmed parcel outside Malmesbury, on iron soil, with corresponding ferrous/savoury nuance; **13** (★★★★★) deeper hued & firmer structured than Schist stablemate but with similar white pepper perfume. Complex, muscular but sleek, & more integrated & balanced than **12**, it richly deserves the title of Red Wine of the Year 2016.

★★★★☆ **Schist Syrah** From 2 best schist-based Kasteelberg shiraz/syrah blocks, **13** reveals alluring white pepper & perfumed nuance, supremely balanced & fresh; fruit purity, almost delicate, but with refined intensity & length. This & sibling identically vinified to highlight effect of terroir. Already tempting. These reds also in magnums.

★★★★★ **Granite Chenin Blanc** ⓃⒺⓌ Stellar **14** on Perdeberg granite soils, delivers understated elegance, lovely fruit purity with a long racy farewell. Apple, almond, even some ripe pear, all quite subtle. Very refined, with lowest alcohol & sugar, & highest acidity of the 3 chenins; balanced, smooth & lively.

★★★★☆ **Quartz Chenin** The best quartz-rich Kasteelberg (single) block in **14** shows similar flavour profile, brightness & smooth texture to **13**. A classy expression of chenin in a style in between the rounder, richer tone of Schist & refined focus & acidity of Granite.

★★★★☆ **Schist Chenin Blanc** From 2 Kasteelberg schist-grown vineyards, **14** noticeably ripe with quickening mineral vein & citrus freshness. Streamlined, with real mouthfilling presence & intensity. All 3 chenins naturally fermented/year in old oak, this the most expressive & richest in youth.

Occasional release: **Granite Syrah**.

Mullineux range

★★★★☆ **Syrah** A blend of the three soil types distinguished in the terroir-specific range, **13** clean pepper overlay to subtle spiced fruit profile. Fine, integrated tannin management ensures silky smooth texture, seamless & supple with inherent freshness. In magnums too.

★★★★☆ **CWG Auction Reserve The Gris Semillon** From 50 year old 'gris' (red-skinned) semillon, **14** (★★★★★) though touch riper than **13** still marvellously understated with subtle honeycomb, lanolin, greengage tones; similar minerality & racy freshness; modest 12.5% alcohol, effortless balance & charm. All in a master-crafted old-oak frame. Engaging now, will develop beautifully.

★★★★☆ **White Blend** A Cape standard bearer for this genre, from old vines. Chenin-led **14** (★★★★★), with clairette, viognier & splash semillon gris, similar baked apple & almond flavours & waxy texture to **13**, but more immediately opulent & appealing. Natural ferment in barrel & foudre, with further oak maturation (20% new).

★★★★★ **Olerasay Straw Wine** ⓃⒺⓌ Chenin blanc from vintages 2008-2014, fractionally blended solera-style (hence 'pig Latin' name!). **NV** richly woven, with layered glacé pineapple, caramel, citrus peel & toasted hazelnuts; vast 260 g/l sugar is uncloying, with lovely freshness, piquancy & length at just 11% alcohol. A Bacchanalian masterpiece, deserved recipient of the inaugural Dessert Wine of the Year award.

★★★★★ **Straw Wine** ⓧ Star amongst the Cape's vin de paille-style dessert wines. Naturally older-barrel-fermented **13** decadently sweet (269 g/l sugar) & viscous, threaded with chenin's pervasive & piquant freshness. Lingering nougat, honey & dried fruit flavours drawn to long & tangy conclusion.

Kloof Street range

★★★★ **Swartland Rouge 14** (★★★☆) blends syrah/shiraz, grenache, carignan, mourvèdre, tinta & cinsaut (86/5/4/2/2/1) in a rounded, dark-fruited melange, not as sappy & fresh as **13**, but smooth & ready to savour.

Not tasted: **Old Vines Chenin Blanc**. — MW

Location: Riebeek-Kasteel/Franschhoek ▪ Map: Swartland/Franschhoek ▪ WO: Swartland ▪ Est 2007 ▪ 1stB 2008 ▪ Tasting, sales & tours by appt: Swartland Fri only, Franschhoek Mon-Thu ▪ Owner(s) Mullineux & Leeu Family Wines (Pty) Ltd ▪ Cellarmaster(s) Chris & Andrea Mullineux (May 2007) ▪ Winemaker(s) Andrea Mullineux (May 2007), with Tremayne Smith ▪ Viticulturist(s) Chris Mullineux (May 2007), with Rosa Kruger ▪ 28ha (carignan, cinsaut, mourv, shiraz, chenin, clairette, viog) ▪ 160t/

16,000cs own label 58% red 40% white 2% dessert ▪ PO Box 369 Riebeek-Kasteel 7307 ▪ info@
mlfwines.com ▪ www.mlfwines.com ▪ S 33° 22' 34.13" E 018°50' 23.74" (Riebeek-Kasteel) S 33° 54'
33.43" E 019° 6' 14.85" (Franschhoek) ▪ F +27 (0)86-720-1541 ▪ **T +27 (0)76-974-6679**

Muratie Wine Estate   (Ⓠ) (ⓎⅠ) (ⓐ) (ⓒ)

The Melck family estate is steeped in history and tradition, from its gnarled oaks and cobwebbed tasting
room to its wine labels commemorating important historical figures. Important contemporary figures
include viticulturist Conrad Schutte, exceptionally knowledgeable about the Simonsberg ward, and
winemaker Hattingh de Villiers, whose maiden harvest in 2015 was 'exciting but smooth' thanks to
some expert advice and modern technology including a state-of-the-art destemmer and a new cooling
unit in the barrel cellar. 'This has upset the angels as their "share" has diminished somewhat,' jokes
Hattingh, adding: 'It is still our philosophy that the wine must speak for itself.'

Premium range

★★★★ **Martin Melck Cabernet Sauvignon** As previous, **12**'s styling is bold, hedonistic. Wild mint,
dark cherry & mocha bouquet followed by rich & succulent fruit in a powdery tannin frame.

★★★★ **George Paul Canitz Pinot Noir** ⓥ Ripeness shows in **12**'s cherry, plummy fruit without
compromising the structure. Remains sleek, streamlined, finishing savoury-dry. Drink now & for 5+ years.

★★★★☆ **Ronnie Melck Shiraz** Honours family patriarch & industry luminary who loved shiraz. Customary meatiness, power in **12**, with white pepper, pot-pourri & vanilla spicing courtesy French/American
oak regime. Like **11**, succulent, smooth textured, structured for the long-haul.

★★★★☆ **Ansela van de Caab** ⓥ Cab-led Bordeaux blend generously oaked because **11**'s fruit richness accepts it. Opulent dark plums, berries, a savoury almost peppery seam of spice, yet enough succulence to give current drinking pleasure. Very good ageing potential.

★★★★ **Isabella Chardonnay** Vibrant & flavoursome **14**, with structure & nutty nuances from 9
months in oak. Less bold & emphatic than **12**, as attractive. **13** untasted. Stellenbosch WO.

★★★★☆ **Isabella Chardonnay Reserve** (NEW) Natural ferment in barrel, finished in stainless steel,
unfiltered & unfined – lots of care taken for **14** debut. Fruitier than sibling, more complex, too, with enticing apricot, kumquat & roasted pine nut characters. Good now, should reward cellaring few years.

★★★★ **Laurens Campher** **14** chenin-led 5-way combo, 40% fermented/aged in new oak. Effusively
perfumed with pineapple, yellow stonefruit & coconut, multi-layered & open palate. Fine blend but not as
savoury or long as **13** (★★★★☆). Stellenbosch WO.

★★★★ **Lady Alice Méthode Cap Classique** Attractive onion skin hue, profusion of racy bubbles, **12**
has red fruit aromas, weight & richness from 90% pinot noir, brioche from 22 months on lees, & citrus hints
from soupçon chardonnay. Creamier, less racy than **11**.

> **Alberta Annemarie Merlot** ⓥ ★★★☆ 'Fine steak or salty mature cheddar' suggest the team to
> accompanying olive tapanade & dried rosemary scented **12**. Full bodied & rounded, would suit solo sip-
> ping, too. Stellenbosch WO.

Fortified Wines

★★★★☆ **Amber Forever** ⓥ Fortified dessert from muscat d'Alexandrie. Wonderful floral & fruit styling in **13**, richly sweet & distinctive, irresistible. WO W Cape.

★★★★ **Ben Prins Cape Vintage** Perfumed **11** 'port' from undisclosed Portuguese varieties effortlessly
balances its immense tannin frame with alcohol & sweetness. **10** (★★★★☆) more opulent.

★★★★ **Cape Ruby** ⓥ Deep rich fruitcake & brandy, this port-style **NV**'s perfume is seductive & the
flavours don't disappoint either, finish with enlivening alcohol grip.

Melck's range

Melcks Pinot Noir Rosé (NEW) ★★ Appealing everyday sipping from delicate, rosepetally **15** with
lipsmacking dry finish. WO W Cape. Also tasted: **Blended Red 13** ★★★ **Sauvignon Blanc 15** ★★★
Occasional release: **Cabernet Franc Rosé**. — GM

Location/map: Stellenbosch ▪ Map grid reference: F2 ▪ WO: Simonsberg–Stellenbosch/Stellenbosch/
Western Cape ▪ Est 1685 ▪ 1stB ca 1920 ▪ Tasting & sales daily 10–5 ▪ Fee R30/5 wines R50/chocolate

pairing experience ▪ Closed Good Fri, Dec 25 & Jan 1 ▪ Cellar tours by appt ▪ Farm Kitchen Wed-Sun 12-3 ▪ Cheese platters ▪ Function venue ▪ Art gallery/exhibition ▪ Guest cottage ▪ Harvest festival ▪ Live music ▪ MTB trail ▪ Owner(s) Melck Family Trust ▪ Winemaker(s) Hattingh de Villiers (Jul 2014) ▪ Viticulturist(s) Conrad Schutte ▪ 110ha/42ha (cab, merlot, p verdot, pinot, shiraz, chard, chenin, hanepoot, port, verdelho) ▪ 300t/80,000cs own label 60% red 18% white 2% rosé 20% other ▪ BWI, IPW ▪ PO Box 133 Koelenhof 7605 ▪ info@muratie.co.za ▪ www.muratie.co.za ▪ S 33° 52' 14.8" E 018° 52' 35.1" ▪ F +27 (0)21-865-2790 ▪ **T +27 (0)21-865-2330/2336**

☐ **Muse** *see* Boschheim

Mvemve Raats Ⓠ

Accolades and international honours continue to fall the way of this collaboration of two good friends. Mzokhona Mvemve (the Cape's first qualified black oenologist) and Bruwer Raats (of Raats Family Wines) source the grapes for their 'blend of stars' from carefully selected Stellenbosch vineyards and each variety is vinified separately, at the Raats cellar, before the all-important blending begins.

★★★★☆ **MR de Compostella** A Cape benchmark, **13** (★★★★★) powerful yet elegant cab franc-led 5-way Bordeaux blend, like **12**. Aromas richly mix cassis, dark chocolate & undergrowth, echoing on a palate that's muscular but focused & athletic, ready now & toned (33% new oak) to go the distance. — JPf

Location/map/WO: Stellenbosch ▪ Map grid reference: B6 ▪ Est/1stB 2004 ▪ Tasting & sales by appt ▪ Closed all pub hols ▪ Owner(s) Bruwer Raats & Mzokhona Mvemve ▪ Cellarmaster(s)/viticulturist(s) Bruwer Raats & Mzokhona Mvemve (both Jan 2004) ▪ Winemaker(s) Bruwer Raats & Mzokhona Mvemve (both Jan 2004), with Gavin Bruwer Slabbert (Feb 2010) ▪ (cabs s/f, malbec, merlot, p verdot) ▪ 10t/900cs own label 100% red ▪ PO Box 2068 Dennesig Stellenbosch 7601 ▪ braats@mweb.co.za ▪ www.raats.co.za ▪ S 33° 58' 16.6" E 018° 44' 55.3" ▪ F +27 (0)86-647-8500 ▪ **T +27 (0)21-881-3078**

MVH Signature Wines Ⓠ

Matthew van Heerden, Diners Club Young Winemaker of the Year and the seasoned hands behind this boutique label, fully subscribes to the new-wave ethos of 'showcasing exceptional vineyard sites' and 'natural wines and winemaking'. Judging from the review below, it's little wonder the Webersburg winemaker's first own release sold out immediately. Next is his other specialisation, pinot noir.

★★★★★ **Chardonnay** Ⓝ A symphony of nuts, citrus & stonefruit, sinuous & polished despite the flavour boldness. Wonderful purity in **14**, laser precision, impossible not to be impressed. Delicious, but save some for ageing — it has a rewarding future. Stellenbosch & Elgin grapes, naturally vinified. — CR, CvZ

Location: Stellenbosch ▪ WO: Western Cape ▪ Est/1stB 2013 ▪ Tasting & sales at Webersburg ▪ Owner(s) Matthew van Heerden ▪ Winemaker(s)/viticulturist(s) Matthew van Heerden (Jan 2013) ▪ 5t/400cs own label 50% red 50% white ▪ IPW ▪ PO Box 3428 Somerset West 7129 ▪ mvhwines@gmail.com ▪ F +27 (0)21-881-3217 ▪ **T +27 (0)21-881-3636/+27 (0)82-520-9338**

☐ **My Best Friend** *see* Zandvliet Wine Estate

My Wyn Ⓠ Ⓨ ⓒ

Jacoline Haasbroek's first three barrels were for home consumption — and thus literally 'my wyn' (my wine) — but latterly parcels of the ebullient boutique vintner's 15 bottlings (the latest a red blend, Les Grandes Horizontales) are available from local eateries, overseas retail outlets (such as Jacoline's German importer's wine shop, named My Wyn in her honour), and her tiny Franschhoek mountainside cellar.

Location/map: Franschhoek ▪ Est/1stB 2001 ▪ Tasting, sales & cellar tours Mon-Fri 10-1 Oct-Apr; after hours, weekends & pub hols by appt or as indicated on the gate ▪ Fee R50pp, waived on purchase ▪ Sunset MCC tastings on koppie (15min walk, weather permitting) by appt only ▪ Cheese platters by prior booking ▪ Owner(s) Jacoline Haasbroek ▪ Winemaker(s) Jacoline Haasbroek (2001) ▪ 1,250cs own label 40% red 20% white 20% port 20% MCC ▪ IPW ▪ PO Box 112 Franschhoek 7690 ▪ tastewine@ telkomsa.net ▪ www.mywynfranschhoek.co.za ▪ S 33° 53' 29.3" E 019° 8' 3.6" ▪ F +27 (0)86-608-0233 ▪ **T +27 (0)21-876-2518/+27 (0)83-302-5556**

☐ **Mzanzi's** *see* Goedverwacht Wine Estate

Nabygelegen Private Cellar (ⓠ) (ⓐ) (ⓞ)

Success with the two labels produced on this traditional, visitor-friendly Wellington winefarm, resurrected in recent years by owner James McKenzie, has warranted a 'large-scale restructuring'. The eponymous brand from mostly home-farm grapes now stands apart (and is listed separately) from the Snow Mountain artisan wines, grown in 'interesting high-altitude vineyards'.

★★★★ **Merlot** Dusty **14** (★★★☆) has staying power, firm structure & good support from oak, but lacks the opulence of **12**. **13** sold out untasted.

★★★★☆ **1712** (ⓠ) Majestic **11**, first tasted since '07, merlot-dominated Bordeaux blend starts mint-choc-chip before unfolding into dark berries & cherries, hints of polish & leather. Smooth, silky tannins & back to mint for finish. Very satisfying – cries out for roast lamb!

★★★★ **Scaramanga Red** Cab, merlot & malbec with 20% tempranillo shows consistent serious form, **14** having the warmth of the vintage & perhaps peaking earlier. Wild spice & coconut combining with ripe dark fruit & slight herbaceous tones. Coastal WO.

★★★★ **Scaramanga White** (ⓠ) Fabulous Cape white blend **14** comes charging out the blocks with lots of fresh & dried apricots, resinous texture, light perfume & spice. Mainly chenin with chardonnay & 10% verdelho, wooded, 30% new American. WO W Cape.

Cabernet Sauvignon (ⓝⓔⓦ) ★★★ **14** still unsettled & tight mid-2015, coaxing reveals cranberry & prune in a medium frame that shows some elegance but not (yet) the balance of others in range. Also tasted: **Chenin Blanc 15** ★★★★ **Sauvignon Blanc 15** ★★★ **Lady Anna 15** ★★★ — HJ

Location: Wellington ▪ Map: Paarl & Wellington ▪ Map grid reference: H1 ▪ WO: Wellington/Coastal/Western Cape ▪ Est 2001 ▪ 1stB 2002 ▪ Tasting, sales & cellar tours Mon-Fri 10-5 Sat 10-1 ▪ Closed all pub hols ▪ Tour groups ▪ Conferences/functions ▪ Small weddings ▪ Walks/hikes ▪ Mountain biking trail ▪ Self-catering luxury accommodation ▪ Owner(s) Avalon Vineyards (Pty) Ltd ▪ Cellarmaster(s) James McKenzie (Jan 2002) ▪ Viticulturist(s) Johan Wiese (May 2001, consultant) ▪ 35ha/17ha (cab, merlot, p verdot, tempranillo, chenin, sauv) ▪ 180t/24,000cs own label 50% red 50% white ▪ PO Box 302 Wellington 7654 ▪ marketing@nabygelegen.co.za ▪ www.nabygelegen.co.za ▪ S 33° 37' 54.7" E 019° 3' 51.2" ▪ **T +27 (0)21-873-7534**

☐ **Naledi** *see* Savanha

Namaqua Wines (ⓠ) (ⓨ) (ⓞ) (ⓐ)

One of SA's largest wine brands, Namaqua (evoking SA's rugged West Coast countryside colloquially called Namaqualand) is produced in two cellars supplied by some 200 growers around Vredendal and Spruitdrift. Investment is ongoing, recently upgraded fermentation facilities allowing production chief Len Knoetze and his team to cover all bases, from the popular 5L bag-in-box to parcels of premium wines. Joining the Spencer Bay Winemakers Reserve range, to date featuring classic reds, is a Cape West Limited Release label with two whites. These and most other Olifants River Valley wines are offered at their recently revamped Die Keldery tourism centre and restaurant.

Spencer Bay Winemakers Reserve range

★★★★ **Cabernet Sauvignon** (ⓠ) **11** (★★★) more savoury, lacks generosity of **08** & **09**. Firm oak tannins (18 months new) & brisk acidity restrain fruit in youth. Needs time or food. **10** sold out untasted.

★★★★ **Pinotage** (ⓠ) After modern, mulberry-centred **10**, **11** (★★★) shows retro stewed fruit & banana; leaner & savoury styling with over-generous acidity.

★★★★ **The Blend** (ⓠ) Cassis & firm tannins dictate the styling of the **11** cab-led 5-way Bordeaux blend. Core of dark fruit still tightly coiled though less masked by oak than other reds.

Not retasted: **Pinot Noir 12** ★★★ **Shiraz 11** ★★★★

Cape West Limited Releases (ⓝⓔⓦ)

Chardonnay ★★★★ Youthful **15** barrel sample shows ample ripe pear & creamy oatmeal, with complementary part-oaking (20% new). Riper, rounder style but a clean thread of lime acidity freshens, ensures food compatibility. WO W Cape, like next. **Sauvignon Blanc** ★★★☆ Pre-bottling, **15** flinty asparagus notes & zesty acidity; oaked fraction & some lees-ageing add flesh to pleasing structure. Lovely balance & freshness, long food-pairing farewell.

Namaqua range

> **Noble Late Harvest** ⊛ ★★★ Unusual but pleasant **14** botrytis dessert from pinotage, unwooded. Moderately sweet with a delightful savoury undertone, giving a strawberries in balsamic vinegar effect. Low alcohol, balanced, would work well with soft cheeses or fresh fruit desserts. 375 ml.

Chenin Blanc ⊘ ★★★ Floral & some tropical flavours, very crisp & crunchy **15**, plumper, fruitier than previous. Happy summer sipper. **Sauvignon Blanc** ⊘ ★★★ Vibrant **15** steps up with intense herb, passionfruit & flint tones, feisty & fresh, with plenty of fruit intensity for versatile food matching. WO W Cape. **Red Muscadel** ★★★★ Rich & warming **14** fortified, tasted from barrel, is rose scented, sweet yet uncloying. Robust raisin flavours would make a great fireside partner. **Hanepoot Jerepigo** ★★★ Delicate acacia aromas on previewed **13** fortified, intensely sweet & decadent. Part-oaking creates a rounder, mellower profile, to sip contemplatively in winter. Not retasted: **Beach Braai NV** ★★ **Cabernet Sauvignon** 12 ★★☆ **Merlot** 12 ★★☆ **Pinotage** 11 ★★☆ **Shiraz** 12 ★★ **Chenin Blanc-Sauvignon Blanc** 14 ★★★ **Sauvignon Blanc-Semillon** 14 ★★★ **Guinevere Méthode Cap Classique** 07 ★★★☆ **White Muscadel** 12 ★★★★ **Cape Ruby NV** ★★

Cellar Door range

Pinotage ⊘ ★★★ **12** loads of banana, spicy plummy fruit & mocha nuance, dry cinnamon-dusted tannins. Bright, pleasant everyday red. Not retasted: **Pinotage-Malbec** 11 ★★☆

Gôiya range

Sauvignon Blanc-Chardonnay ⊘ ★★☆ Enduring entry-level brand; first tasted since **07**, **14** 50/50 will appeal widely: creamy, rounded & plumped by touch sugar, has drinkability in its DNA. — MW

Location: Vredendal ▪ Map: Olifants River ▪ WO: Olifants River/Western Cape ▪ Est/1stB 2002 ▪ Tasting & sales Mon-Fri 8–5 Sat 9–3 ▪ Closed Easter Fri-Mon, Ascension day & Dec 25/26 ▪ Cellar tours Mon-Fri 10 & 3, book ahead ▪ Die Keldery Restaurant T +27 (0)27-213-3699/8 Mon-Fri 8-5 & dinner Thu-Fri 7-10 Sat 9-3 Sun buffet 11-3 booking required ▪ Facilities for children ▪ Conferences ▪ Owner(s) 200 members ▪ Production manager Len Knoetze ▪ Winemaker(s) Driaan van der Merwe, Dewald Huisamen, Roelf Retief, Koos Thiart, Johan Weideman & Reinier van Greunen ▪ Viticulturist(s) Stoney Steenkamp, Dirk de Bruyn & Marina Cornellisen ▪ 4,990ha ▪ 113,692t/9.3m cs 20% red 80% white ▪ PO Box 75 Vredendal 8160 ▪ info@namaquawines.com ▪ www.namaquawines.com ▪ S 31° 42' 34.9" E 018° 30' 15.6" ▪ F +27 (0)27-213-3476 ▪ **T +27 (0)27-213-1080**

Napier Winery   ⊘ ⊛ ◎ ♿

Family-owned Napier Winery in the Groenberg foothills takes its name from Sir George Napier, governor of the Cape Colony, who in 1840 oversaw the naming of the nearby town after the Duke of Wellington, vanquisher of Napoleon. Sir George also gives his name to the fine, traditionally made potstill brandy.

Napier range

★★★★ **Cabernet Sauvignon** Charred, tarry notes meld surprisingly well with dense blackcurrant fruit on single-vineyard **13**. Full-bodied, ripe & wholesome, with satisfying finish. Oak may settle with time.

★★★★☆ **Red Medallion** Seriously conceived cab-led 5-way Bordeaux blend has stature & character. **11** (★★★★) subtlety & nuance rather than power, but noble oak & ripe fruit lend charm. Tad off **10**.

★★★★ **St Catherine** Wooded, single-vineyard chardonnay, **13** still oak-spice heavy but showing succulently ripe marmalade-tinged fruit with beeswax tones. Elegantly balanced yet rich, lingering.

Not retasted: **Greenstone** 12 ★★★☆

Lion Creek range

Cabernet Sauvignon ★★★ Dark, full plum pudding fruit with atypical spiciness on **13**. Quirky but pleasant. Also tasted: **Cabernet Sauvignon-Shiraz** 13 ★★★ **Chenin Blanc-Sauvignon Blanc** 14 ★★★

Brandy range

★★★★ **Sir George Potstill Brandy** Ⓢ From 100% chenin, vibrant gold potstill, matured 5 years. Fresh apple, caramel on nose mingle with dried peach & pear on palate. Well structured, with sweet tobacco edge & lemon drops on finish. Smooth & elegant; appropriately packaged. — WB, GdB

Location: Wellington ▪ Map: Paarl & Wellington ▪ Map grid reference: G2 ▪ WO: Wellington/Western Cape ▪ Est 1989 ▪ Tasting, sales & cellar tours Mon-Fri 8–5 Sat 10–3 ▪ Fee R20 ▪ Closed Easter Fri-Mon, Dec 25/26 & Jan 1 ▪ Tapas platters, pre-booked ▪ Conferences ▪ Owner(s) Michael & Catherine Loubser ▪ Cellarmaster(s)/winemaker(s)/viticulturist(s) Leon Bester (Apr 2000) ▪ 135ha/±89ha under vine ▪ 70% red 30% white ▪ Other export brand: Sir George ▪ PO Box 638 Wellington 7654 ▪ info@ napierwinery.co.za ▪ www.napierwinery.co.za ▪ S 33° 38' 37.0" E 019° 2' 24.8" ▪ F +27 (0)21-864-2728 ▪ **T +27 (0)21-873-7829**

☐ **Natana** see Marianne Wine Estate
☐ **Nativo** see Hughes Family Wines

Natte Valleij Wines   Ⓨ ⌂ ◎ ♿

On the 300th anniversary of their cellar, fairly unchanged over the centuries, Stellenbosch brothers Alexander (the 'Brit' in Boer & Brit) and Marcus Milner (also De Meye winemaker) 'with some excitement and trepidation' installed a brand-new cooling unit just ahead of last year's early season. Further excitement arrived in the shape of not one but two French harvest interns and, in time for Easter, a concrete 'egg'. Plus 'some fantastic reviews internationally'. The line-up includes Natte Valleij Cinsaut, P.O.W. (red blend) and Dry Hanepoot; and The Blend (red) under the Swallow label, none tasted.

Location/map: Stellenbosch ▪ Map grid reference: F1 ▪ Est 1715 ▪ Tasting, sales & cellar tours Mon-Sat by appt ▪ Closed all pub hols ▪ Facilities for children ▪ Conference/indaba venue ▪ Art gallery & art classes ▪ Artifacts & various paintings ▪ Natte Valleij B&B/self-catering cottages ▪ Owner(s) Milner family ▪ Winemaker(s) Alexander Milner (2005), with Marcus Milner (2010) ▪ 28ha total ▪ 30t/2,000cs own label 90% red 10% white ▪ PO Box 4 Klapmuts 7625 ▪ wine@nattevalleij.co.za ▪ www.nattevalleij.co.za ▪ S 33° 50' 3.6" E 018° 52' 43.2" ▪ **T +27 (0)21-875-5171**

☐ **Natural Star** see Stellar Winery

Naughton's Flight

Francis Naughton worked for many years for SFW (precursor of Distell) following his 'flight' from his native Ireland (he retains plenty of the accent and a bit of the blarney). With him from the start has been consultant Ronell Wiid in the cellar, making boutique-scale wines.

Shiraz Ⓢ ★★★★ Nicely maturing **08** in the customary style, stressing the leathery, savoury side rather than the fruity – but there's a good touch of red berry succulence on the lean but balanced, structured palate. Not retasted: **Tribua 09** ★★★★ **Délice 09** ★★★ Not tasted: **Viognier**. — TJ

Location: Constantia ▪ WO: Stellenbosch/Coastal ▪ 1stB 2003 ▪ Closed to public ▪ Owner(s) Francis Naughton ▪ Winemaker(s) Ronell Wiid (consultant) ▪ (carignan, mourv, shiraz, viog) ▪ ±20,000 btls ▪ 25 Willow Rd Constantia 7806 ▪ naughts@mweb.co.za ▪ F +27 (0)21-794-3928 ▪ **T +27 (0)21-794-3928**

☐ **Naughty Girl** see Alvi's Drift Private Cellar

Nederburg Wines   Ⓨ 🍴 ◎ ♿

From late 18th-century Cape Dutch winefarmer Philippus Wolvaart's home – his manor house an iconic SA winelands image – to modern-day corporate big brand, Paarl-based Nederburg, its widespread growers and long-serving cellarmasters have adeptly balanced tradition and innovation, popular tastes with connoisseurs' choices. As of 2016, well-versed Andrea Freeborough leads the youthful, dynamic team. But 15-vintage veteran Razvan Macici will still influence as multi-brand-owning Distell's chief winemaker. Expanding on its historic German and traditional French styles, Nederburg's recent focus on Mediterranean wines has seen a Spanish red blend join the flagship Ingenuity range, and experimentation with grenache blanc, roussanne, albariño, verdelho and viura. Botrytis-prone grasa de cotnari from Razvan's birthplace Romania promises a new slant to Nederburg's signature Noble Late Harvest desserts. Overall, exciting times for an old favourite . . .

II Centuries range

★★★★☆ **Cabernet Sauvignon** Premium-priced flagship. Understated but regal **11** from Groenekloof. Intense but not heavy ripe berry flavours, smart oaking (30 months) & tannin frame, lively persistence. Fine successor to **10** (★★★★★) from Paarl.

★★★★☆ **Sauvignon Blanc** (NEW) A blast of fresh green herbs, sea salt & tang of grapefruit announce **14**, worthy addition to this super-premium range. 10% oaking provides depth & complexity. Only 226 cases produced from Darling vines.

Ingenuity range

★★★★☆ **Red Italian Blend** ② Sangiovese & barbera, & a dollop nebbiolo, **11** does not disappoint. Great aromatic complexity with rich berries, chocolate, nuts & spices on the palate, taut, polished tannins, lingering finish. **12** similar quality & vibrant personality, just younger.

★★★★☆ **Red Spanish Blend** ② Vivacious local take on tempranillo (85%) & graciano, **12** richly textured red summer berries, supple fine-grained tannins, great freshness to finish. Paarl grapes, combo French & American oak, new, 15 months.

★★★★☆ **White Blend** Splendid 8-part sauvignon-led blend which includes aromatic varieties, some oaking. Floral **14** offers layers of intense fruit, spice & vibrant freshness, depth & impeccable balance. Will age gracefully.

Manor House range

★★★★ **Shiraz** ② Bright scrub & hedgerow fruit mingle with cinnamon & clove spice in **12**, supported by a peppery texture, velvet end. Also-tasted **13** is fresh, perfumed & in the same vein, with vivid fruit flavours, fluid texture. Both from Philadelphia, great promise.

Not tasted: **Cabernet Sauvignon**. Discontinued: **Fairtrade Shiraz-Mourvèdre**.

Heritage Heroes range

★★★★ **The Brew Master** Saluting Nederburg founder Johann Graue, improved **13** (★★★★★) merlot-led 4-way Bordeaux blend has captivating blackcurrant perfume, ripeness & spicecake, with firm tannin grip & texture. Last made was cellarworthy **11**.

★★★★☆ **The Motorcycle Marvel** Characterful Rhône-style blend from carignan, grenache, shiraz & dollop mourvèdre. **13** shows concentrated earthy hedgerow fruit, black pepper & lavender. Spice & compelling tannins round off this flavour explosion. No **12**.

★★★★☆ **The Anchorman** Four different fermentation techniques on **14** capture chenin's character admirably. Remarkable textural interplay between focused & pure crunchy apple flavours, creamy vanilla & ground almond; restrained & harmonious. Get some!

★★★★ **The Beautiful Lady** Semi-sweet gewürztraminer **14** from Stellenbosch allures with typical rosepetal fragrance & pristine acid structure to balance the ripe fruit for a lipsmacking dry-seeming finish. Back to form after **13** (★★★★).

★★★★☆ **The Young Airhawk** Inspired, ageworthy older-barrel-fermented sauvignon; outstanding **14** (★★★★★) has many layers of citrus & stonefruit flavour, hugely appealing creamy texture. Shows greater clarity & focus than equally complex **13**.

Private Bin range for Nederburg Auction

★★★★☆ **Cabernet Sauvignon Private Bin R163** Brooding **11** from Paarl, plump & packed with blackberry & chocolate, defined by fine ripe tannins (French & American oak for 18 months). Plush & silky, with an endless conclusion.

★★★★☆ **Merlot Private Bin R181** **12**'s deep core of marinated berry fruit, concentrated layers of integrated vanilla oak, supple tannins are tinged with crushed fresh herbs. Harmonious & elegant – a joy to drink. No **11**.

★★★★ **Pinot Noir** Opaque ruby, foot-crushed & handcrafted **13** exudes classic pinot smells & tastes: ripe strawberry, cherry, savoury mushroom. Delicate & elegant with an appealing zesty acid.

★★★★☆ **Shiraz Private Bin R121** Powerful **12** from Paarl a serious expression of the variety. Mouthfilling, layered with exotic coriander spice & charcuterie from 18 months in combo French, Hungarian & American oak; rich conclusion. Will reward the patient.

★★★★☆ **Sauvignon Blanc Private Bin D234 14** (★★★) shows a nose of perfumed citrus & basil; brisk, bright mineral acidity, with breadth from regular lees stirring. Misses the depth of **13**.

★★★★☆ **Edelkeur** Revered Noble Late Harvest from unoaked chenin; noted for fruit intensity & complexity, light-footed nature. **14** doesn't disappoint with exuberant melon & apricot flavours, fynbos honey nuances. Extremely long, lifted & focused thanks to a piercing mineral acidity. Low alcohol; 375 ml.

Not tasted: **Grenache Private Bin**. Discontinued: **Sauvignon Blanc Private Bin D215, Semillon Private Bin D266, Viognier Private Bin D212, Sauvignon Blanc-Chardonnay Private Bin D253, Sauvignon Blanc-Semillon Private Bin D252, Gewürztraminer Special Late Harvest Private Bin S354**.

Fair Selection

Sauvignon Blanc ★★★ From Groenekloof, **15** green plum & apple blossom perfumes, tasty mealtime companion with well-weighted dry fruit flavours. Not tasted: **Cabernet Sauvignon**.

Winemaster's Reserve range

★★★★ **Edelrood (Cabernet Sauvignon-Merlot)** Ever-dependable & well-priced Bordeaux-style red; latest **13** brims with ripe berry perfume, perfectly oaked; again punches above its weight.

★★★★★ **Noble Late Harvest** ⊘ Only botrytis dessert from Nederburg freely available, as respected as its scarcer siblings. Unwooded **14** mostly chenin & 10% muscat de Frontignan from Paarl. Richly aromatic & flavoursome: crème brûlée, gingered apricot & honey on a seam of steely/tangy acidity. Fabulous value, as was **13** (★★★★☆).

> **Malbec** (NEW) ⓦ ★★★☆ Pure aromas of blackberry, liquorice & dark chocolate, **14** sturdy but upbeat on finish. WO Coastal. **Baronne (Cabernet Sauvignon-Shiraz)** ⓦ ★★★☆ Cab-shiraz blend a longtime friend of many casual drinkers (& serious ones too). Velvety berry-spiced **14** epitomises drinkability, offers great value. **Chardonnay** ⓦ ★★★★ Citrus-scented, lightly oaked **14** is soft & creamy but finishes with a tangy flourish, ticking all the drinkability boxes. **Pinot Grigio** ⓦ ★★★★ Off-dry summer fun in a bottle! Honeysuckle-perfumed **15** packed with fresh apple flavour, lovely brisk finish.

Riesling ★★★ Appealing dryish **15** is perfumed with rosepetals, delicately fruity with a crisp tail. WO Coastal. Also tasted: **Cabernet Sauvignon 13** ★★★☆ **Cabernet Sauvignon Rosé 15** ★★★ **Sauvignon Blanc 15** ★★★ Not tasted: **Merlot, Special Late Harvest**.

56Hundred range

> **Cabernet Sauvignon** ⓦ ★★★ Dark berries in **14** are soft, fleshy & supple, framed by easy tannins for cheerful enjoyment. Lightly oaked as all reds here. **Merlot** (NEW) ⓦ ★★★ Sun-ripe plums, genteel tannins on **14**, juicy yet savoury mouthful for al fresco enjoyment. **Pinot Noir** (NEW) ⓦ ★★★ With touches grenache & carignan, **14** fragrant dusty strawberries & a friendly grip in the goodbye. **Pinotage** (NEW) ⓦ ★★★ Super-smooth anytime sipper, **14** entices with generous bright plum fruit laced with chocolate. **Shiraz** (NEW) ⓦ ★★★ Hints of spice on succulent dark hedgerow fruit, gentle tannin bite in **14**.

Pinot Grigio (NEW) ★★★ Water-white **15** perfumed & satisfying summer refresher to serve chilled. **Sauvignon Blanc** (NEW) ★★★ Bright & breezy tropical fruit followed by lipsmacking zingy finish on **15**. Also tasted: **Chenin Blanc 15** ★★☆

Foundation Collection

> **Cabernet Sauvignon** ⓦ ★★★ Smoky French-oak-spiced **14**'s plush black fruit offers just-picked freshness, smooth & approachable now. **Duet (Shiraz-Pinotage)** ⓦ ★★★ Accessible, unassuming & just-dry **14** is shiraz-led (60%) but packed with pinotage's fresh juicy flavours & texture. Like Pinotage, genteel seasoning from brief French/American oaking. **Chardonnay** ⓦ ★★★ French/American combo in **15** lends hint vanilla, buttered toast to lemon curd & jasmine tones; lovely fresh conclusion for seafood or solo sipping. **Stein** ⓦ ★★★ Semi-sweet **15** chenin a luscious & fresh mouthful from the peach

orchard; suits spicy Cape Malay dishes. **Chardonnay-Viognier** ⊛ ★★★ With peach melba flavours & brush of spice, **15** has moderate alcohol & subtle depth from older oak ferment/ageing. **Première Cuvée Brut** ⊛ ★★★ Dependable **NV** dry sparkling from chenin, sauvignon & chardonnay is citrus- & apple-toned, with myriad racy bubbles, zesty tail to get the party started. WO Coastal.

Lyric (Sauvignon Blanc-Chenin Blanc-Chardonnay) ★★★ Perennial sunset-sipping favourite. **15** mostly sauvignon, with herbal notes & dryish tropical flavours, finishes with a tangy lime twist. Also tasted: **Merlot 14** ★★★ **Pinotage 14** ★★★ **Rosé 15** ★★☆ **Chenin Blanc 15** ★★★ **Sauvignon Blanc 15** ★★★ Not tasted: **Shiraz**, **Shiraz-Viognier**, **Cabernet Sauvignon-Shiraz**. Discontinued: **Sauvignon Blanc-Chardonnay**. — WB

Location: Paarl ▪ Map: Paarl & Wellington ▪ Map grid reference: F5 ▪ WO: Western Cape/Paarl/Coastal/Groenekloof/Stellenbosch/Philadelphia/Darling ▪ Est 1791 ▪ 1stB ca 1940 ▪ Tasting & sales Mon-Fri 8–5 Sat 10–2 (May-Sep)/10–4 (Oct-Apr) Sun 11–4 (Oct-Apr) ▪ Various tasting fees, waived on purchase of R100+ ▪ Closed Good Fri, Dec 25 & Jan 1 ▪ Cellar tours Mon-Fri 10.30 & 3 Sat 11 Sun 11 (Oct-Apr) ▪ Large groups/foreign language tours by appt only ▪ Visitors' centre: wine tasting, cheese & wine pairing ▪ Historic Manor House (national monument) featuring The Red Table restaurant, open Tue-Sun T +27 (0)21-877-5155 ▪ Tour groups ▪ Gifts ▪ Conferences ▪ Museum ▪ Conservation area ▪ Owner(s) Distell ▪ Cellarmaster(s) Andrea Freeborough (Jul 2015) ▪ Winemaker(s) Samuel Viljoen (reds, 2014) & Natasha Williams (whites, 2013), with Heinrich Kulsen (whites) ▪ Viticulturist(s) Unathi Mantshongo & Henk van Graan ▪ 1,100ha (cab, carignan, grenache, malbec, merlot, p verdot, ptage, shiraz, tannat, tempranillo, chard, riesling, sauv, sem) ▪ 18,000t/2.8m cs own label ▪ ISO 0001:2008, ISO 14001:2004, BWI, HACCP, IPW, BRC, SGS organic ▪ Private Bag X3006 Paarl 7620 ▪ nedwines@distell.co.za ▪ www.nederburg.co.za ▪ S 33° 43' 15.4" E 019° 0' 9.4" ▪ F +27 (0)21-862-4887 ▪ **T +27 (0)21-862-3104**

Neethlingshof Estate ⊛ ⊛ ⊛ ⊛ ⊛

Owned by Lusan Premium Wines, Distell's joint venture with German financier Hans Schreiber, Neethlingshof dates back to 1705, its history shaped by many colourful characters after whom one of the Short Story Collection wines is named. Other names reflect farming initiatives that have seen the estate attain WWF-SA Conservation Champion status. Winetasting options include the Flash Food, Slow Wine pairing: bite-sized portions of 'fast food with a twist' matched with De Wet Viljoen's wines.

Short Story Collection
★★★★ **Owl Post Pinotage** Estate-grown (as are all), single-vineyard **13** packs a punch of dark chocolate-dipped cherry & banana flavours with vanilla & cinnamon oak spice. Deftly balanced at 14.5% alcohol. Also in 3L, like Caracal.

★★★★☆ **Caracal** Sleek & muscular **13** has violets & pencil shavings on the nose, hinting at the complexity that should increasingly complement cab's youthful blackcurrant fruit; juicy, ripe plum notes of 20% merlot; & fresh lift of 12% cab franc. Also magnums.

★★★★ **Six Flowers** Blooming far earlier than floral **13**, wooded **15** has citrus zest & creaminess from chardonnay while viognier, gewürztraminer & riesling add perfume & spice to the fresh fruitiness of chenin & sauvignon. **14** sold out untasted.

Not tasted: **Maria**.

Neethlingshof range
★★★★ **Chenin Blanc** ⊘ Delicious **15** has citrus acidity to balance ripe tropical fruit flavours as well as guavas-and-custard texture; fresh dry finish. Takes **14** (★★★★) to next level.

★★★★ **Gewürztraminer** ⊘ Off-dry **15** has everything you'd hope for in a partner for spicy food: aromatic honeysuckle nose, litchi fruit & hints of Turkish delight, zesty acidity & ginger to finish.

★★★★ **Sauvignon Blanc Single Vineyard 15** nudges higher rating with intensity of stone- & tropical-fruit, quite full bodied with underlying flintiness, vibrant freshness & long finish. **14** untasted.

Shiraz ⊛ ★★★☆ Soft & accessible **12** is plush, with macerated mulberries, dense fruit made all the more delicious by hints of smoke, pepper & underlying liquorice.

Merlot ★★★☆ **13** is a gently spiced plum pudding of a wine, soft & juicy, no trace of green, just a hint of coffee at the end. **Pinotage** ★★★★ Whiff of vanilla-spiced banana bread on **14**, medium bodied with juicy plum fruit, hints of coffee & dark (hot?) chocolate to complement that banana bread... Also tasted: **Cabernet Sauvignon** 12 ★★★★ **Malbec** 13 ★★★★ **Cabernet Sauvignon-Merlot** 13 ★★★★ **Chardonnay Unwooded** 15 ★★★ **Sauvignon Blanc** 15 ★★★☆ — JG

Location/map/WO: Stellenbosch ▪ Map grid reference: D5 ▪ Est 1692 ▪ 1stB 1880 ▪ Tasting & sales Mon-Fri 9–5 Sat/Sun 10-4 ▪ Fee R35pp ▪ Closed Good Fri & Dec 25 ▪ Cellar tours by appt ▪ 'Flash Food & Slow Wine' pairing R65pp — booking recommended for 6+ ▪ Jungle gym ▪ Tour groups ▪ Conferences ▪ Conservation area ▪ Annual music concert in conjunction with Die Woordfees (Mar); Wednesday night live music during summer months ▪ Lord Neethling Restaurant & Palm Terrace ▪ Owner(s) Lusan Premium Wines ▪ Cellarmaster(s) De Wet Viljoen (Jun 2003) ▪ Winemaker(s) Jacobus van Zyl ▪ Viticulturist(s) Hannes van Zyl & Nico Nortje ▪ 273ha/95ha (cabs s/f, malbec, merlot, p verdot, ptage, shiraz, chard, chenin, gewürz, riesling, sauv, viog) ▪ 1,400t/100,000cs own label 55% red 45% white ▪ BWI champion, WIETA ▪ PO Box 104 Stellenbosch 7599 ▪ info@neethlingshof.co.za ▪ www.neethlingshof.co.za ▪ S 33° 56' 28.2" E 018° 48' 6.7" ▪ F +27 (0)21-883-8941 ▪ **T +27 (0)21-883-8988**

Neil Ellis Wines   (Ⓟ) (Ⓨ) (Ⓖ)

What started as a solo venture grew into a family business, and has become an even stronger and more quintessential one in recent years, as the highly esteemed Neil Ellis hands over the hard work to the next generation — though himself remaining fully involved. Warren is the winemaker, while Charl is responsible for commercial activities and Margot for brand management. Neil was the Cape's first real negociant, seeking out interesting parcels around the winelands to sell under his own name: Neil Ellis Vineyard Selection was launched exactly 30 years ago, and the top wines are still sourced from Jonkershoek, Elgin, Groenekloof and Piekenierskloof. Unlike 30 years ago, the whole concern now has a single home, in handsome premises on Helshoogte Pass, just outside Stellenbosch town.

Vineyard Selections

★★★★☆ **Cabernet Sauvignon** Masterly **12** has ripe berry aromas & lingering flavours tempered, restrained & made more complex by superbly handled all-new oak maturation. Properly dry, but grandly reserved rather than austere. Deserves time, as it has a long, fine future. Jonkershoek Valley fruit.

★★★★ **Cinsaut Noir** (Ⓝ) **12** in fuller, bigger, riper style than much modern Cape cinsaut. Some new oak doesn't upset the sweet fruit charm. Approachable now, but firm structure & balance allow for some ageing. Groenekloof WO.

★★★★☆ **Grenache** (Ⓟ) Fragrant & expressive **11** from low-yield old Piekenierskloof vines. Composed yet intense, shows real presence. Lovely fruit purity & silky & seamless structure. To savour over 5+ years.

★★★★ **Rodanos** **11**'s 6-way blend led by 69% shiraz, 18% grenache. **10** (★★★★) showed more oak than fruit, but this is well balanced. Sweet red fruit, savoury note; firm but easy structure. WO W Cape.

★★★★ **Amica** Previously had semillon, but **14** all from Groenekloof sauvignon. New oak well contained & supportive, adds spice to tame the aromatics, as well as some firmness of grip. Dry, restrained & elegant. Not tasted: **Pinotage**. Discontinued: **Syrah**.

Premium range

★★★★ **Cabernet Sauvignon** (Ⓟ) Fresh, darkly bright fruit on **12**, supported by clever oaking. Balanced, firm, savoury, juicy — not demanding, but serious enough; good now, should develop.

★★★★ **Cabernet Sauvignon-Merlot** With some cab franc too in **13**, as usual. Also as usual, offers early drinkability while keeping serious. Sweet fruit, succulent firm structure, altogether satisfying. Stellenbosch WO.

★★★★ **Elgin Chardonnay** (Ⓝ) Clean-scented & fresh, **14**'s pear & citrus supported by unobtrusive oak. Generous & balanced with good acidity. Tight (but satisfying) in youth; should develop a few years.

★★★★☆ **Groenekloof Sauvignon Blanc** (✓) Some green, freshly acidic character on **15** (★★★★★), but mixing happily with citrus & tropical (passionfruit) notes. The palate very well composed, both lipsmacking & almost sumptuous. **14** had similar flinty & herbaceous character.

Aenigma Red ★★★☆ Cab with shiraz & a little cinsaut adding brightness in **13**. Pleasingly fruity & easy but with sufficient grip. Stellenbosch WO. **Aenigma White** ★★★☆ Very different from previous blend, **14** neatly melds chardonnay citric broadness with aromatic sauvignon blanc; lemony freshness cuts richness very neatly. Balanced & pleasing, if not long or intense. WO W Cape. Also tasted: **Shiraz 13** ★★★★ Not tasted: **Pinotage**. Discontinued: **Stellenbosch Chardonnay**. — TJ

Location/map: Stellenbosch ▪ Map grid reference: G5 ▪ WO: Groenekloof/Stellenbosch/Western Cape/Jonkershoek Valley/Piekenierskloof/Elgin ▪ Est 1986 ▪ 1stB 1984 ▪ Tasting & sales Mon-Fri 9.30-4.30 Sat/pub hols 10—5 ▪ Fee R25 premium range/R45 vineyard selection range ▪ Closed Good Fri, Dec 25/26 & Jan 1 ▪ Antipasto platters ▪ Tour groups ▪ Owner(s) Neil Ellis Wines (Pty) Ltd ▪ Winemaker(s)/viticulturist(s) Warren Ellis (2006) ▪ 100,000cs own label 50% red 50% white ▪ Brands for clients: Woolworths ▪ WIETA ▪ PO Box 917 Stellenbosch 7599 ▪ info@neilellis.com ▪ www.neilellis.com ▪ S 33° 55' 34.92" E 018° 53' 32.46" ▪ F +27 (0)21-887-0647 ▪ **T +27 (0)21-887-0649**

Neil Patterson Wines   ⓘ (NEW)

Neil Patterson was Anthonij Rupert cellarmaster for 10 years before following his dream to launch his own label. He now has, he says, the Cape's 'first full range of wines with no added sulphites'. The biggest challenge, he adds, is educating consumers about such wines, given that 'they are so used to the chemical influence that sulphite makes on aroma and palate'. A Family Reserve label missed our deadline.

Neil Patterson range

★★★★ **Chenin Blanc** A nod to 'orange' wine, oxidative styling successfully done. Oak-aged **13** has abundant cinnamon/nutmeg-dusted apple pie aromas & tastes; nutty, salty nuances reminiscent of a Spanish palo cortado sherry.

Sauvignon Blanc ★★★ Guaranteed to spark debate at the dinner table; **14** shifts the paradigm of sauvignon from grass & wet pebble to fennel & earth; round & almost oily.

Signature range

Cabernet Sauvignon ★★☆ Umami, soy & dense cassis characters on chewy & tad stewed **12**. Malo in older barrel, 2 years ageing. Natural ferment, no chemical additions, as both ranges. — CR, CvZ

Location/map: Stellenbosch ▪ Map grid reference: E5 ▪ WO: Franschhoek ▪ 1stB 2009 ▪ Tasting, sales & cellar tours by appt only ▪ Owner(s) Neil & Robyn Patterson ▪ Cellarmaster(s)/winemaker(s) Neil Patterson (May 2012) ▪ 30t/4,500cs own label 65% red 35% white ▪ 6 Santhagen Road, Devon Valley, Stellenbosch 7600 ▪ admin@pattersonwine.com ▪ www.pattersonwine.com ▪ S 33° 56' 31.63" E 018° 49' 45.46" ▪ F +27 (0)21-887-2376 ▪ **T +27 (0)21-887-2377**

Nelson Family Vineyards   ⓘ ⌂ ◎ ⓐ ⓑ

The Nelson family's peaceful Paarl property plays host to many a perfect wedding as well providing the venue for a wide variety of other events. Wine production enters its third decade this year, having commenced in 1995. In charge of the cellar today is founder and patriarch Alan Nelson's daughter Lisha.

Lisha Nelson Signature Wines

★★★★☆ **Cabernet Franc** ⓖ Pungent varietal aromas on **10** before generous mouthful of intense fruit. Mid-2013's still-taut tannins & new French oak since may have settled.

★★★★ **Dad's Blend** ⓖ Cab franc-dominated **09** Bordeaux blend with tomato nuance giving way to blackcurrants, capsicum, hint of coffee.

Nelson Estate range

★★★★ **Shiraz** Sleek, creamy vanilla oak (20% American) on plush **09**. Still youthful but oh so settled & seamless, with classic red berry & pepper nuances. Step up on tannic **08** (★★★★).

★★★★ **Chardonnay** Simple (but elegant) packaging belies complexity of **14**. Prominent oak (100% new French) enlivened by lemon acidity, nutty overlay. Mouthfilling richness offset by bright fruit core. Better balanced than last-tasted **11** (★★★☆).

Rosé ⓥ ★★★ **15** from 4 black grapes commendably dry & savoury, with subtle grip for food. Worth seeking out.

Noble Late Harvest (NEW) ★★★☆ From semillon, aged in new French oak, **14** lovely dried apricot & pear notes, persistent flavours, though unctuous sweetness not entirely refreshed by delicate peachy acidity. Best served well chilled. Also tasted: **Cabernet Sauvignon-Merlot 09** ★★★☆ **Sauvignon Blanc 15** ★★★

Nelson's Creek range
Chenin Blanc ★★★ Cheerful **15** thatch & spice, some dustiness. Soft flavours for effortless drinkability. Also tasted: **Shiraz 12** ★★★ **Pinotage Rosé 15** ★★★ — CvZ

Location: Paarl ▪ Map: Paarl & Wellington ▪ Map grid reference: D3 ▪ WO: Paarl/Western Cape ▪ Tasting, sales & cellar tours by appt only ▪ Closed all pub hols ▪ Facilities for children ▪ Tour groups ▪ Conferences ▪ Weddings ▪ Walks/hikes ▪ MTB trails ▪ Guest accommodation ▪ Owner(s) Alan Nelson ▪ Cellarmaster(s) Lisha Nelson (Nov 2007) ▪ Winemaker(s) Lisha Nelson (Nov 2007), with Solly Hendriks (Apr 2011) ▪ Viticulturist(s) Petrus de Villiers ▪ 142ha/46ha (cabs s/f, merlot, p verdot, ptage, shiraz, chard, chenin, sauv, sem) ▪ 210t/9,340cs own label 30% red 60% white 10% rosé ▪ IPW ▪ PO Box 2009 Windmeul 7630 ▪ lisha@nelsonscreek.co.za ▪ www.nelsonscreek.co.za ▪ S 33° 39′ 31.2″ E 018° 56′ 17.3″ ▪ F +27 (0)21-869-8424 ▪ **T +27 (0)21-869-8453**

☐ **Nelson's Creek** *see* Nelson Family Vineyards

New Beginnings Wines (Ⓠ)
This long-established label, owned by vineyard staff, is flying to new heights and destinations under the wing of mentors and wine exporters FMS Food & Beverages. After the launch of Skipper's Collection in Japan in 2014, orders for other private labels have been received from Bolivia, Demark, Kenya and the US, and CEO Anton Blignault is confident on building on these successes in the year ahead.

Family Collection
★★★★ **Cabernet Sauvignon** ⊘ Supple & sexy **13** improves on last-made **10** (★★★) with ample ripe cassis fruit, good concentration & structure, light tannin grip.

Merlot (NEW) ⊘ ★★★☆ Unoaked **13** offers squishy blueberry appeal in spades. Medium body, with cocoa finish. **Chardonnay** ★★★ Attractive white peach tone, **15**'s brief oaking adds weight, breadth; fresh, with lipsmacking acidity. Piekenierskloof grapes. Not retasted: **Pinotage 12** ★★★ **Chenin Blanc 13** ★★★ Not tasted: **Shiraz, Pinotage Rosé, Shiraz Rosé**.

Skipper's Collection
Classic Dry Red (Ⓠ) ★★★ Light-bodied **10** from Darling has blueberry tang & succulence on defined frame. Not tasted: **Classic Dry White**. — FM, CvZ

Location: Cape Town ▪ Map: Cape Peninsula ▪ WO: Voor Paardeberg/Darling/Western Cape/Paarl ▪ Est 1996 ▪ 1stB 1999 ▪ Tasting by appt only ▪ Owner(s) Klein Begin Farming Association ▪ Brand manager FMS Food & Beverages SA cc ▪ 13ha/10ha (cab, ptage, shiraz, chard, chenin) ▪ 20,000cs own label 70% red 25% white 5% rosé ▪ Unit 6, Tafelberg Hof, Upper Wandel Street, Gardens, Cape Town 8001 ▪ info@fms-wine-marketing.co.za ▪ www.fms-wine-marketing.co.za ▪ S 33° 55′ 58.08″ E 018° 24′ 47.16″ ▪ F +27 (0)21-413-0825 ▪ **T +27 (0)21-426-5037**

☐ **New Cape Wines** *see* Eagle's Cliff Wines-New Cape Wines
☐ **New Gate** *see* Ernst Gouws & Co Wines

Newstead Lund Family Vineyards (Ⓠ) (Ⓨ) (◎)
Ex-international polo player Doug Lund and wife Sue were among the Plettenberg Bay wine district pioneers with their New Zealand-inspired vine portfolio of sauvignon, chardonnay and pinot noir, planted in 2006. The wines are made by local go-to vini man Anton Smal, and available from — among others — the cellardoor, now extended to accommodate increasingly popular 'farm to fork' lunches.

Sauvignon Blanc ★★★☆ Melon, kiwi & guava fragrance reflects the cool origin. Light-bodied **14** shows more fruit, less saline character than previous, possible sign of maturing vines. **Méthode Cap Classique Rosé** (NEW) ★★★☆ Bone-dry **13** bubbly mostly pinot noir (with 17% chardonnay) helps entrench MCC in this exciting appellation (& comes dressed for the occasion in elegant blush attire).

More savoury, less deliciously fruity than Brut, but similar balance & craftsmanship. Not retasted: **Chardonnay 13** ★★★ Not tasted: **Méthode Cap Classique Brut**. — HJ

Location/WO: Plettenberg Bay ▪ Map: Klein Karoo & Garden Route ▪ Est 2008 ▪ 1stB 2012 ▪ Tasting & sales Tue-Sat 10-4 ▪ Closed Dec 25 ▪ Cellar tours by appt only ▪ Farm to fork lunches, booking required ▪ Tour groups ▪ Gift shop ▪ Farm produce ▪ Walks ▪ Mountain biking/guided cycle tours ▪ Owner(s) Doug & Sue Lund ▪ Cellarmaster(s)/winemaker(s) Anton Smal (Jan 2011, consultant) ▪ Viticulturist(s) Doug Lund & Gift Lwazi ▪ 11ha/5ha (pinot, chard, sauv) ▪ 24t/4,500cs own label white & MCC ▪ PO Box 225 The Crags 6602 ▪ info@newsteadwines.com ▪ www.newsteadwines.com ▪ S 33° 57' 7.24" E 023° 28' 18.66" ▪ T +27 (0)44-534-8331 (office)/+27 (0)84-586-1600/+27 (0)83-616-0010

Newton Johnson Vineyards   ⓘ ⑪ ⑤

This Hemel-en-Aarde farm houses three Newton Johnson families: Dave Johnson and Felicity (née Newton) who founded the estate in the mid-1990s; and two sons with their families – Bevan (marketing manager) and Gordon (winemaker with wife Nadia). The estate's ever-growing reputation never precludes innovation – with new wines, for example: most recently, developing the Cape's first albariño is making great progress. Gordon's Cape Winemakers Guild membership will be, they say, 'an exciting avenue for us to release some ideas, as 2015 allowed us to prepare for and pinpoint some exceptional cuvées'. Assiduous, meticulous and creative work in cellar and vineyard doesn't cease: 'Keeping the vineyard honest in the wine is essential for us, and knowing when to step in or let go in the winemaking.'

Family Vineyards range

★★★★★ **Pinot Noir** Uniquely remarkable record of five star ratings – it's never failed. Low yields in **14** meant all the fruit from farm's top three sites combined here, with no single vineyard bottlings. As always, a triumph of subtle insistence; pure fruit integrated with succulent acidity, understated tannins & sensitive oaking in an elegant composition. Its power belies its demure demeanour.

★★★★☆ **Granum** Cellar as adept with Rhône varieties on weathered iron-rich granite as it is with Burgundian grapes from clay-rich earth. Shiraz with 23% mourvèdre, year in barrel, 20% new; fine **13** expresses violets & forest floor fruit twirled with ethereal spice in deft, elegant ensemble.

★★★★★ **Chardonnay** Exquisitely textured with a chalky minerality, **14** interleaves crisp citrus fruit & wood spice (22% new barriques) with a stern acidity. Poised & elegant, it will reward ageing. **13** (★★★★★) was also pretty thrilling.

Newton Johnson range

★★★★ **Walker Bay Pinot Noir** The anima of its Family Vineyards peer, off younger vines & flatter slopes but loaded with cherry & red-berry personality. **13** bright & attractive. 14% new cask 11 months.

★★★★ **Full Stop Rock** Suave shiraz with grenache & mourvèdre named for jagged landscape of origin. **12** redolent of violets with an earthy profile, retains dry elegance. Mostly seasoned oak. WO Walker Bay.

★★★★ **Southend Chardonnay** Full & broad, brash even, a praise singer for more regal Family Vineyards offering. **14** butterscotch & crème brûlée braced by tingling acidity. From a single block, 17% new oak, 11 months.

★★★★ **Sauvignon Blanc** Grassy edginess of emphatic **15** smoothed by smidgen wooded semillon; myriad flavour components in precise balance. Sunday's Glen & home grapes melded with Elgin fruit.

★★★★☆ **Resonance** Echoing the maritime character of the place, **14**'s (★★★★★) powerful 20% semillon adds reverberating depth of flavour to the crackling freshness of sauvignon, all in harmonious balance. Great length of flavour promises more in bottle with time. WO Walker Bay; while **13** was Cape S Coast.

Not tasted: **Block 6 Pinot Noir, Mrs. M Pinot Noir, Windansea Pinot Noir**. — DS

Location: Hermanus ▪ Map: Elgin, Walker Bay & Bot River ▪ WO: Upper Hemel-en-Aarde Valley/Walker Bay/Cape South Coast ▪ Est 1996 ▪ 1stB 1997 ▪ Tasting & sales Mon-Fri 9–4 Sat 10–2 ▪ Closed all pub hols ▪ 'Restaurant @ Newton Johnson': lunch 12-3 Wed-Sun (Apr-Nov)/Tue-Sun (Dec-Mar) & dinner Fri-Sat 6-9 ▪ Owner(s) Newton Johnson family ▪ Cellarmaster(s) Gordon Newton Johnson (Jan 2001) ▪ Winemaker(s) Gordon Newton Johnson (Jan 2001) & Nadia Newton Johnson (Aug 2006) ▪ Viticulturist(s) Dean Leppan (Sep 2010) ▪ 140ha/18ha (grenache, mourv, pinot, shiraz, albariño, chard, sauv) ▪

240t/20,000cs own label 50% red 50% white ▪ PO Box 225 Hermanus 7200 ▪ wine@
newtonjohnson.com ▪ www.newtonjohnson.com ▪ S 34° 22' 9.7" E 019° 15' 33.3" ▪ F +27 (0)86-638-
9673 ▪ **T +27 (0)28-312-3862**

☐ **New World Collection** *see* Zidela Wines

Nicholson Smith

Recently established Nicholson Smith is a joint venture between Nabygelegen owner/winemaker James
McKenzie and his Gauteng/Mpumalanga agent Jason Neal. Bolstered by wine show successes, most of
the new releases answer 'the growing trend to sweet wines' with the fillip of low alcohol.

Pandora's Box range

Bell Pepper Cabernet Sauvignon (NEW) ★★ NV shows sweet dark berry fruit, with a dusting of spice,
slips down easily. **The Black Bird Merlot** ★★ Sweet plum fruit on juicy **NV**, balanced everyday red.
Also tasted: **The Persian Connection Shiraz NV ★★★ Lock 1855 Merlot-Cabernet Sauvignon
NV ★★★ The Gooseberry Sauvignon Blanc NV ★★**

Bella Vino range

Perky Pink (NEW) ★★ As implied, **NV** rosé is pink & perky, with soft, squishy red-berry flavours, floral
perfume & low alcohol. **Seductively Sweet White** (NEW) ★★ Low-alcohol (8.5%) **NV** sweet sipper,
serve well chilled on a hot summer's day. **Sassy Sweet Red** (NEW) ★★ Smooth, spicy red plum fruit,
sweet & easy **NV**, with low alcohol. Also tasted: **Sultry Red NV ★★ Sublime White NV ★★** — WB

Location: Johannesburg ▪ WO: Western Cape ▪ Est 1997 ▪ 1stB 2012 ▪ Closed to public ▪ Owner(s) Jason
Neal ▪ Winemaker(s)/viticulturist(s) James McKenzie (2012) ▪ 40,000cs own label 70% red 20% white
10% other ▪ PO Box 1659 Jukskei Park 2153 ▪ jason@nicholsonsmith.co.za ▪ www.nicholsonsmith.co.za
▪ F +27 (0)11-496-2952 ▪ **T +27 (0)11-496-2947**

Nick & Forti's Wines   ⓠ

Started just over ten years ago as a celebration of 'life, friendship and superb wine', the venture between
restaurateur Fortunato 'Forti' Mazzone and Saronsberg winery owner Nick van Huyssteen continues to
flourish. The range, made by Dewaldt Heyns at Saronsberg, is available at the winery and Forti's Pretoria
restaurant, Ritrovo, his stores and the selected outlets and restaurants he supplies.

Shiraz ★★★★ Charming, very approachable **13**, ripe & sweet fruited, with berry, spice & gentle tannin
buffed by light oaking. **Epicentre** ★★★★ Perky red fruit & spice vibrancy to **13** Bordeaux quintet.
Designed with food in mind, it is textured, ripe & ready to enjoy. Discontinued: **Viognier**. — FM

Location: Tulbagh/Pretoria ▪ WO: Coastal ▪ Est/1stB 2004 ▪ Tasting at Saronsberg Cellar ▪ Owner(s)
Fortunato Mazzone & Saronsberg ▪ Winemaker(s) Dewaldt Heyns (2004) ▪ 4,000cs own label 85% red
15% white ▪ Box 25032 Monument Park Pretoria 0105 ▪ ritrovo@mweb.co.za ▪ www.saronsberg.com ▪
F +27 (0)12-460-5173 ▪ **T +27 (0)12-460-4367**

Nico van der Merwe Wines   ⓠ

Nico van der Merwe, longtime cellarmaster at Saxenburg, has produced his own premium wines since
1999, and the past few years have seen his ambition of owning his own cellar slowly come together. The
tiny Mas Nicolas spread on Stellenbosch's Polkadraai Hills is not only up and running but 'running ideally,' after the installation recently of three red-wine fermenters and a new press. A half hectare of sauvignon is next. Nico's winemaking philosophy remains traditional, hands-on — and averse to screwcaps.

Flagship range

★★★★☆ **Mas Nicolas Cape** Cabernet & shiraz (55/45) fly the flag here, **13** (★★★★★) ever elegant
with understated layers of intense black fruit & plum; savoury coriander-spiced meat & mocha oak tones
add to great depth. Half new wood 14 months. Even more special than last-made **09**.

Nicolas van der Merwe range

★★★★☆ Syrah Last-made **07** was big & muscular. Fast forward to **13**, which is polished, buffed & refined. Beautiful mulberry fruits interplay with powdery tannin in lissome structure; lovely to drink. All-new French oak, 14.5% alcohol in check.

★★★★☆ Red Cab-led Bordeaux-style **13** (★★★★) redolent of cassis, herbs & spice but less voluptuous than merlot-led **09**, which radiated pure red berry & graphite in elegant balance. No **10 – 12**.

★★★★ White Sauvignon (76%, ex Robertson) & oak-fermented Darling semillon team up in fine-grained **15**, vibrant with a tingling minerality. Worth keeping. Follows exceptional **13** (★★★★☆). No **14**.

★★★★ Méthode Cap Classique Brut Latest **NV** (**09**) sparkler is 72/28 chardonnay & pinot noir (previous was 100% chard), with bakery aromas & real gravitas from five years on lees. WO W Cape.

Five to Nine Sauvignon Blanc ⑭ **★★★** Grapes harvested between 5 & 9 am; reductive style of **15** produces steely tension, somewhat cushioned by few grams sugar in tail.

Robert Alexander range

★★★★ Shiraz ⑫ Savoury **13** shows complexity in ripe black fruit, fynbos, dried herbs, cured meat, along with richness & depth; good balance & length. Super value too – stock up! No **10 – 12**.

Merlot ★★★ Medium-bodied **14** with rich berry fruit is balanced & satisfying.

Cape Elements range

Cape Elements ⑫ **★★★☆** Shiraz, cinsaut & grenache in **11**. Fresh, juicy & bright, with dark berry & spice flavours, great depth. Delightful all-year appeal. WO W Cape. — DS

Location/map: Stellenbosch ▪ Map grid reference: B6 ▪ WO: Stellenbosch/Western Cape ▪ Est/1stB 1999 ▪ Tasting & sales by appt only ▪ Owner(s) Nico & Petra van der Merwe ▪ Cellarmaster(s)/winemaker(s) Nico van der Merwe ▪ 50t/4,000cs own label 80% red 20% white ▪ PO Box 12200 Stellenbosch 7613 ▪ nvdmwines@vodamail.co.za ▪ S 33° 57' 48.2" E 018° 43' 51.8" ▪ F +27 (0)21-881-3063 ▪ **T +27 (0)21-881-3063**

Nico Vermeulen Wines   ⑨

Nico Vermeulen's more than three decades' winegrowing experience inform this small family label (the sauvignon-semillon blend still a work in progress at press time) as well as the wines of Ruitersvlei, where he consults and both portfolios are available for tasting.

★★★★ The Right Red ⊘ ... is shiraz, as usual, though **13** is quietly elegant where last-made **10** was bold, tannic. Understated leather & cinnamon on nose, choc-laced red berries on palate. For fine dining.

★★★★ The Right Two Reds ⊘ Sophisticated merlot/cab **13** with food-friendly savoury-tangy undertone to gutsy cranberry fruit; different league to last-tasted **05** (★★★).

The Right White ★★★☆ Fresh, cheerful **15** from sauvignon, unusual but appetising fruit profile of pineapple, peach & green apple in a crisp, dry body. Not tasted: **The Right Two Whites**. — DB

Location: Paarl ▪ WO: Coastal/Western Cape ▪ Est/1stB 2003 ▪ Tasting by appt at Ruitersvlei Wines ▪ Owner(s)/viticulturist(s) Nico Vermeulen ▪ Winemaker(s) Nico Vermeulen, with Judy & Izelle Vermeulen ▪ 3,000cs own label & 240,000L bulk export ▪ 3 Pieter Hugo Str Courtrai Suider-Paarl 7646 ▪ nicovermeulen@webmail.co.za ▪ F +27 (0)21-863-2048 ▪ **T +27 (0)21-863-2048/+27 (0)82-553-2024**

Niel Joubert Estate   ⑨

It's nearly 120 years since Piet Joubert bought the Klein Simonsvlei farm in Paarl that is now the Joubert family's wine estate – with Niel jnr in the cellar and Daan among the vines. But just 20 years since they first held back some grapes off their extensive vineyards for an own label. Now there's a new white blend, and a malbec on the way.

Christine-Marié range

★★★★ Cabernet Sauvignon ⑫ Refined, elegant flagship, **09** has poise, balance & structure, with enticing blackcurrant fruit. Step up from last-tasted **06** (★★★★).

★★★★ Shiraz ⑫ **08** shows development, but retains concentration & ripeness. Exotic tobacco aromas & silky tannins, well-judged oak add to appeal.

★★★★ **Méthode Cap Classique** ⊗ Opulent & attractive **09** dry bubbly from chardonnay, harbours powerful yeasty influence. Rich, creamy & persistently dry. Improves on **08** (★★★☆).

Not retasted: **Merlot 06** ★★★☆ **Chardonnay 08** ★★★☆ **First Kiss Fortified Chenin Blanc 09** ★★★☆ Discontinued: **Viognier**.

Niel Joubert Estate range

★★★★ **Shiraz** ⊘ Generous with varietal tones (smoke, some meatiness, dusty plums), **13**'s long, pepper-tinged fruity flavours & finish are excellent now, have a good future. More serious than **12** (★★★☆).

Merlot ★★★☆ Step-up, lightly wooded **13** a most attractive, balanced glassful of chocolate, soft dark berry fruit & silky tannins. **Rosé** ★★★ From pinotage, as usual, salmon pink **15** is soft but crisp, with ripe berry flavours, finishes bone-dry for tasty lunchtime quaffing. **Sauvignon Blanc** ⊘ ★★★☆ Elegant partner for seafood, **15**'s acidity is soft, flavours are clean & varietal gooseberry & crushed herb tones linger long. **Herr Leicht** (NEW) ★★☆ Light & easy to drink, **14**'s blend sauvignon blanc, splashes nouvelle & chenin offers an appealing spread of greener (grass & bellpepper) tones & plumper tropical fruits. Also tasted: **Cabernet Sauvignon 13** ★★★ **Pinotage 13** ★★★☆ **Chardonnay 14** ★★☆ **Chenin Blanc 15** ★★★ — DB

Location: Paarl ▪ Map: Paarl & Wellington ▪ Map grid reference: C8 ▪ WO: Western Cape/Paarl ▪ Est 1898 ▪ 1stB 1996 ▪ Tasting & sales Mon-Fri 9-4 by appt ▪ Closed all pub hols ▪ Owner(s) Joubert family ▪ Cellarmaster(s) Ernst Leicht ▪ Winemaker(s) Ernst Leicht, with Niel Joubert jnr (May 2011) ▪ Viticulturist(s) Daan Joubert ▪ 1,000ha/300ha (cab, merlot, ptage, shiraz, chard, chenin, sauv) ▪ 1,953t/±160,000cs own label 49% red 50% white 1% rosé ▪ Other export brand: Hunterspeak ▪ GlobalGAP, IPW ▪ PO Box 17 Klapmuts 7625 ▪ wine@nieljoubert.co.za ▪ www.nieljoubert.co.za ▪ S 33° 49' 54.7" E 018° 54' 3.2" ▪ F +27 (0)86-599-0725 ▪ **T +27 (0)21-875-5936**

☐ **Niels Verburg** see Luddite Wines

Nietgegund

Stellenbosch lawyer Jan Dreyer's tiny vineyard in Blaauwklippen Valley, surrounded by red-wine royalty, enjoys the attentions of two top advisers, Francois Hanekom (vineyard) and Ronell Wiid (cellar), and the hope is to release the new vintage of the fine red blend, conveniently QR-coded, sometime this year.

★★★★ **Pro Amico** ⊗ Merlot spiced by 10% shiraz; serious intent evident in firm structure & judicious oaking (30% new). **10** preview since should have settled into its provisional rating. — WB

Location/WO: Stellenbosch ▪ Est 2004 ▪ 1stB 2008 ▪ Closed to public ▪ Owner(s) Nietgegund Boerdery (Edms) Bpk ▪ Winemaker(s) Ronell Wiid (Jan 2013, consultant) ▪ Viticulturist(s) Francois Hanekom (Sep 2006, consultant) ▪ 3.4ha/1ha (cab, merlot, shiraz) ▪ 4t/100cs own label 100% red ▪ IPW ▪ PO Box 12684 Die Boord 7613 ▪ jan@dreyer.za.net ▪ **T +27 (0)21-880-0738**

Nietvoorbij Wine Cellar ⊗

Charmingly set on an avenue of oaks, Nietvoorbij Cellar is owned by the Agricultural Research Council. During harvest many hundreds of tiny experimental batches are vinified here for clients by winemaker and Elsenburg graduate Craig Paulsen. Knowledge gained is used to develop a range of good quality (often good value) wines for Nietvoorbij's commercial label, new vintages of which unready for review.

Location/map: Stellenbosch ▪ Map grid reference: F4 ▪ Est 1963 ▪ 1stB 1992 ▪ Tasting & sales Mon-Fri 9–4 ▪Closed Sat/Sun & all pub hols ▪ Owner(s) Agricultural Research Council ▪ Winemaker(s) Craig Paulsen ▪ Viticulturist(s) Guillaume Kotze ▪ 32ha (cabs s/f, malbec, merlot, ptage, shiraz, chard, sauv, viog) ▪ 75t/6,000cs own label 56% red 40% white 4% port ▪ Private Bag X5026 Stellenbosch 7599 ▪ cellar@arc.agric.za, winesales@arc.agric.za ▪ www.arc.agric.za ▪ S 33° 54' 43.5" E 018° 51' 48.9" ▪ **T +27 (0)21-809-3091/3084/3140**

Nieuwedrift Vineyards ⊗ 🍴 🛍 ◎ ⓐ

Johan Mostert's Piketberg vineyards are dwarfed by his wheatfields — this is the Swartland, after all — and he vinifies only some of his harvest. But, for his friendly wines, his winemaking fits many of the precepts of the local avant-garde, using older oak barrels and (for the blanc de noir and chenin) sponta-neous fermentation.

Shiraz ★★★ Easygoing **13** preview shows ripe but light sweet fruit, tempered by smoky tobacco notes.
Blanc de Noir ★★★ Fresh fruity fragrance on **15** from shiraz, tasted ex tank. Lots of flavour, neatly bal-anced, good dry finish. Also tasted: **Chenin Blanc 15 ★★★** Not retasted: **Méthode Cap Classique 12 ★★★** — TJ

Location: Piketberg ▪ Map/WO: Swartland ▪ Est/1stB 2002 ▪ Tasting, sales & cellar tours Mon-Fri 9–1 & 2–6 Sat 9–2 ▪ Closed Easter Fri/Sun, Dec 25/26 & Jan 1 ▪ Meals on request; or BYO picnic ▪ Facilities for children ▪ Tour groups ▪ Conferences ▪ Owner(s)/viticulturist(s) Johan Mostert ▪ Cellarmaster(s) Johan Mostert (Jan 2002) ▪ 151ha/20ha (shiraz, chard, chenin, cbard) ▪ 410t total 10t/1,316cs own label 28% red 40% white 16% rosé 16% MCC ▪ PO Box 492 Piketberg 7320 ▪ nieuwedrift@patat.za.net ▪ S 32° 58' 28.1" E 018° 45' 10.6" ▪ F +27 (0)88-022-913-1966 ▪ **T +27 (0)22-913-1966/+27 (0)82-824-8104**

19th Wines

Veteran vintner Ernst Gouws and winemaker son Ernst jnr (Ernst Gouws & Co Wines) researched the per-fect wine to enjoy at the '19th hole' by asking golfers themselves. The resulting wine portfolio (untasted) now has national distribution, and is exported to two countries (a third is in prospect).

Location: Stellenbosch ▪ Est 2012 ▪ 1stB 2013 ▪ Closed to public ▪ Owner(s) Ernst Gouws jnr & Leon de Wit ▪ Winemaker(s) Ernst Gouws snr & Ernst Gouws jnr ▪ 3,000cs own label 50% red 50% white ▪ PO Box 580 Stellenbosch 7599 ▪ ernst@the19th.co.za ▪ www.the19th.co.za ▪ F +27 (0)86-768-6376 ▪ **T +27 (0)21-865-2895**

Nitida Cellars

This was a run-down Durbanville sheep farm before engineer Bernhard Veller and wife Peta purchased it as their home, then set about transforming it into a prime family-oriented wine and lifestyle destination. From outdoor activities to conservation and social responsibility projects, Bernhard's guiding hand is everywhere — especially in making wines that 'we love to drink', of which only the best are bottled. A member of the prestigious Cape Winemakers Guild since 2005, Bernhard has been joined in the cellar by Daniel Keulder (ex Groot Constantia), whose experience in making craft beer is giving him new ideas...

★★★★ Cabernet Sauvignon 13's cassis nose explodes into plush mouthful underpinned by firm but ripe tannins; elegant, with promise of cigarbox & leather complexity to come.

★★★★ Pinot Noir (ⓃⒺⓌ) So pretty, from its light colour & floral nose to red cherry/berry flavours, **13** also has a serious side: earthy mushroom notes & firm tannic structure. A very elegant debut.

★★★★ Shiraz Whiff of fynbos as well as white pepper & clove on glossy **13**, layered with blackcurrants & wild berries; a fresh, elegant expression compared with big & bold **12** (★★★★).

★★★★☆ Calligraphy 13 greets with a bouquet of violets & a box of dark chocolates, courtesy of plummy merlot (58%) while cab franc (21%) brings raspberries & a whiff of verdant forest freshness to the black fruit & structure of cab (17%) & dash petit verdot.

★★★★ Riesling 15 has a lavender & lightly ginger-spiced nose leading to lime, even lime cordial, con-centration in the mouth, which waters due to vibrant acidity that cuts through 7.6 g/l sugar to finish on a dry, grapefruity, flinty note. Follows exceptional **14** (★★★★★).

★★★★ Sauvignon Blanc Less typically 'green' due to very warm ripening conditions, **15** has luscious white peach & sweet melon fruit enlivened by lemongrass & fresh acidity, rounded out by 5% semillon.

★★★★ Semillon Creamy **14** has 5% sauvignon to boost acidity, balancing 50% barrel-fermented semillon's rich texture & flavours reminiscent of baked apricot crumble with vanilla & cinnamon spice.

★★★★★ Coronata Integration Smooth, silky **14** combines barrel-fermented semillon (60%) for creamy texture & baking spice with tank-fermented sauvignon for fruit purity, this vintage less 'green' than **13** (★★★★☆) — more 'golden' (yellow apples & cling peaches), with tangy apricot finish.

★★★★☆ Wild Child (ⓃⒺⓌ) 90% sauvignon blanc plus semillon, **15**'s wild streak comes from natural fer-ment in French oak, 45% new, adding creamy texture, hint of smoke, pinch of white pepper to fresh lime, Granny Smith, white peach fruit — beautiful balance already with more complexity to come.

★★★★ **The Matriarch** Fresher than **13** (★★★☆), **14** MCC sparkling has delicate citrus fruit as well as biscuity richness, fast & frothy bubbles melting in mouth to enhance lingering impression of creaminess. Not retasted: **Matriarch in Red 12** ★★★ Not tasted: **Chardonnay**, **Club Select Sauvignon Blanc**. Occasional release: **Modjadji Semillon Noble Late Harvest**. — JG

Location/WO: Durbanville ▪ Map: Durbanville, Philadelphia & Darling ▪ Est/1stB 1995 ▪ Tasting & sales Mon-Fri 9–5 Sat 11–4 Sun 11-3 ▪ Fee R20/4 wines R50/range ▪ Closed Good Fri, Dec 25/26 & Jan 1 ▪ Cassia Restaurant T +27 (0)21-976-0640; conference & function venue at Cassia (200 pax) ▪ Tables at Nitida T +27 (0)21-975-9357, www.tablesatnitida.co.za ▪ Facilities for children ▪ Mountain biking, part of Hillcrest/Majik forest trail (www.tygerbergmtb.co.za) ▪ Conservation area ▪ Annual festivals: Season of Sauvignon (Oct); Feast of the Grape (Mar); Cellarbake (Mar); Soup, Sip & Bread (Jun) ▪ Owner(s) Bernhard & Peta Veller ▪ Cellarmaster(s) Bernhard Veller ▪ Winemaker(s)/viticulturist(s) Daniel Keulder (Jan 2015) ▪ 35ha/16ha (cabs s/f, p verdot, riesling, sauv, sem) ▪ 220t/18,000cs own label 30% red 70% white + 3,000cs for clients ▪ Brands for clients: Woolworths, Checkers ▪ PO Box 1423 Durbanville 7551 ▪ info@nitida.co.za ▪ www.nitida.co.za ▪ S 33° 50' 3.8" E 018° 35' 37.0" ▪ F +27 (0)21-976-5631 ▪ **T +27 (0)21-976-1467**

Noble Hill Wine Estate

'Having made estate wine in Simonsberg-Paarl since 2009, we now do so exclusively,' says winemaker Kristopher Tillery. 'We feel that Noble Hill's estate focus allows us to follow our soils and climate, and make terroir-driven wines that stand apart from consumer-driven styles.' Rodney Zimba, viticulturist the past 15 years, is establishing more mourvèdre for the burgeoning rosé, and replanting the 20-year-old merlot. The family owners' US roots are celebrated in the restaurant's Baja- and California-style cooking.

Noble Hill range

★★★★ **Cabernet Sauvignon 11** (★★★☆) light on fruit, flesh after riper **10**. More green walnut than blackberry flavours & grainy, brusque tail. Best drink sooner rather than later.

★★★★ **Merlot 12** is silky & fresh, the flavoursome black plum & bitter chocolate fruits slipping down smoothly & lingering. French oak, 30% new, enriches, increases ageing potential.

★★★★ **Syrah 12** more serious, interesting than **10** (★★★★). Good depth of dark spice, smoked meat & ripe berries nicely supported by rounded tannins & a little supple flesh. Includes splashes mourvèdre, viognier. **11** sold out untasted.

★★★★ **Estate Blend** Sternly structured **12** cab-based with merlot, petit verdot & cab franc providing some useful freshness & flesh. Should gain more flavour interest over next 3-5 years. Also in magnum.

Mourvèdre Rosé ★★★ Fresh, cinnamon-spiced **15**. Easygoing sipper with decent fruity length. Also tasted: **Chardonnay 14** ★★★ **Sauvignon Blanc 15** ★★ **Viognier 14** ★★★

Bloem range

Syrah-Mourvèdre ★★★ Out-to-please **14** juicy mouthful soft dark berries & spice. Rounded & ready. Paarl WO. Also tasted: **Chenin Blanc-Viognier 14** ★★ — AL

Location: Paarl ▪ Map: Franschhoek ▪ WO: Simonsberg-Paarl/Paarl ▪ Est/1stB 2001 ▪ Tasting & sales daily 10–5 ▪ Fee R30, waived on purchase ▪ Cellar tours by appt only ▪ Food & wine pairing option ▪ Hitachino Nest Japanese craft beer available at winery ▪ cosecha Restaurant ▪ Picnic baskets ▪ Facilities for children ▪ Farm-produced extra virgin olive oil ▪ Conservation area ▪ Owner(s) Noble Hill Trust ▪ Winemaker(s) Kristopher Tillery ▪ Viticulturist(s) Rodney Zimba (2001) & Johan Viljoen (consultant) ▪ 50ha/30ha (cabs s/f, merlot, mourv, p verdot, shiraz, chard, sauv, viog) ▪ PO Box 111 Simondium 7670 ▪ info@ noblehill.com ▪ www.noblehill.com ▪ S 33° 49' 38.0" E 018° 56' 12.1" ▪ **T +27 (0)21-874-3844**

☐ **Noble Nomad** see Rosendal Wines

Noble Savage

These fun wines from Bartinney Private Cellar, branded as a 'sexy blend of mischief', are best enjoyed at Bartinney Wine & Champagne Bar in Stellenbosch town centre (they're not available from the farm). Business manager Lisa van der Berg has this update: 'Two new mischief makers are joining the line-up: one a flaming redhead, the other with a bubbly personality. Visit the wine bar to meet them.'

★★★★ **Sauvignon Blanc** ⊘ Pre-bottling sample **15** full of energy, drive, accompanied by delicious tropical fruity acids & bounce. Expressive but not showy. Different league to **14** (★★☆) & **13** (★★★).

Cabernet Sauvignon-Merlot ⊗ ★★★★ Supple mouthful of ripe soft berries on quietly persuasive **12**. Fresh, properly dry & rounded in older oak for current enjoyment.

Cabernet Sauvignon Rosé ★★★ Tourmaline pink **15** fresh yet smooth, with generous wild strawberry fruit extended by few grams sugar. — AL

Location/map: Stellenbosch ▪ Map grid reference: F5 ▪ WO: Stellenbosch/Western Cape ▪ Est 2006 ▪ 1stB 2008 ▪ Tasting & sales at Bartinney Wine & Champagne Bar Mon-Sat 11.30-9 (T +27 (0)71-250-5814, 8 Bird Str Stellenbosch) ▪ Owner(s) Rose & Michael Jordaan ▪ Winemaker(s) Ronell Wiid (2012, consultant) ▪ 13,000cs own label 50% red 50% white ▪ Postnet Suite 231 Private Bag X5061 Stellenbosch 7599 ▪ info@bartinney.co.za ▪ www.noblesavage.co.za, www.bartinney.co.za ▪ S 33° 56' 18.36" E 018° 51' 36.81" ▪ F +27 (0)21-885-2852 ▪ **T +27 (0)21-885-1013**

Nomada Wines   ⓠ

No longer nomadic but advising a plethora of small wine producers, Riaan Oosthuizen finds time to make wine with wife Gina in the boutique cellar (with tasting venue) on Durbanville's Morgenster farm.

Rustica Sauvignon Blanc (NEW) ⊗ ★★★★ Lime, passionfruit, some fresh sage, **15** is packed with fruit freshness, lipsmackingly zesty, lively.

Cabernet Franc (NEW) ★★★ Appealing **13** has subtle herbaceous whiffs, brambleberries, a beef extract note, sleek polished structure. In abeyance: **Georgina**, **Sauvignon Blanc**, **Rustica**. — CR, CvZ

Location/WO: Durbanville ▪ Map: Durbanville, Philadelphia & Darling ▪ Est/1stB 2007 ▪ Tasting by appt only ▪ Owner(s) Riaan & Gina Oosthuizen ▪ Winemaker(s)/viticulturist(s) Riaan Oosthuizen (2007) ▪ 66ha/7ha (cabs s/f, merlot, chenin, sauv) ▪ 55t total 10t/2,000cs own label 40% red 60% white + 6,000cs for clients ▪ Brands for clients: Klein Roosboom Wines, Red White Pink Wines, Schaap Wines (Netherlands), Signal Gun Wines ▪ PO Box 5145 Tygervalley 7536 ▪ nomadawines@gmail.com ▪ S 33° 50' 15.70" E 018° 36' 23.88" ▪ **T +27 (0)83-280-7690**

Nordic Wines

Negociant Peter Tillman sources wines for export under various labels, mainly to Scandinavia courtesy of business partner Norwegian Wiggo Andersen. Having moved HQ from Malmesbury to Robertson, Nordic also sells Robertson Valley wines to customers in the areas covered by his courier service between Robertson, Plettenberg Bay and Cape Town.

Location: Robertson ▪ Est 2007 ▪ 1stB 2010 ▪ Closed to public ▪ Wine orders Mon-Fri 9-5 from export offices: Nordic Wines, Robertson ▪ Owner(s) Wiggo Andersen & Peter Tillman ▪ Winemaker(s)/viticulturist(s) consulting ▪ Other export brands: Cape to Cape, Frogner, Literature Wine, Mia, Selma, Wedgewood ▪ PO Box 896 Robertson 6705 ▪ info@nordicwines.co.za, peter@nordicwines.co.za, alison@nordicwines.co.za ▪ www.nordicwines.co.za ▪ F +27 (0)23-626-1031 ▪ **T +27 (0)23-626-1413/+27 (0)83-283-5354**

Nova Zonnestraal Estate   ⓠ (NEW)

Part of the original Alphen estate, dating back to the 1700s, Constantia's Nova Zonnestraal has been in Lynn Marais Rowand's family for 80 years and noted for olives, indigenous trees and horses. Vine-wise, focus has shifted from table grapes to sauvignon blanc – 'the terroir is ideal, and it's never too hot or too cold'. The wine is made on a boutique scale at Steenberg by consultant Roger Burton; long-term plans include leveraging Lynn's hospitality contacts to list it in top UK hotels and restaurants.

★★★★ **Constantia Royale Sauvignon Blanc** Lovely fruit expression in elegant **15**, lemongrass & litchi, with underlying mineral notes which strengthen in the flavours. — CR, CvZ

Location/WO: Constantia ▪ Map: Cape Peninsula ▪ Est 1997 ▪ 1stB 2015 ▪ Tasting by appt only ▪ Closed all pub hols ▪ Owner(s) Lynn Marais Rowand ▪ Cellarmaster(s) JD Pretorius (Dec 2014, consultant) ▪ Winemaker(s) Roger Burton (Oct 2013, consultant) ▪ Viticulturist(s) Joseph van Wyk Contractors (Nov

2013) ▪ 16ha/7ha (sauv) ▪ 15t/2,220cs own label 100% white ▪ Suite 193, Private Bag X16, Constantia 7848 ▪ wine@constantiaroyale.co.za ▪ www.constantiaroyale.co.za ▪ S 34° 0' 18.00" E 018° 26' 60.00" ▪ F +27 (0)21-794-4642 ▪ **T +27 (0)21-794-4841**

☐ **NU Series 1** *see* Morgenster Estate
☐ **Nuts About** *see* Chateau Naudé Wine Creation
☐ **Nuwehoop** *see* uniWines Vineyards

Nuweland Wynkelder

There's always something interesting from this winery because owner/winemaker Juan Louw can't resist small parcels from neighbouring or nearby farms when he spots something unusual or old. Hence often having only limited volumes of particular wines, which do not necessarily repeat – and are always given idiosyncratic names. He's in the right area, Malmesbury, with access to Swartland, Darling, Philadelphia and Durbanville, all with tempting vineyard pocket treasures. Finding particular success with his individually styled sweet wines, he says these will be an increasing focus in the future.

Genade Water range

★★★★☆ **Rosyntjiewyn** 'Straw Wine' renamed, 50% sauvignon, with chenin, bukettraube, hanepoot, 15 months barrel aged, as all these sweet wines. Barley sugar & dried apricots in now-bottled **NV**, a ginger biscuit savoury seam. Very sweet but a tangy acidity perks up the flavours. 375 ml.

★★★★ **Goue Jeripigo** Was 'Hanepoot', air-dried grapes, fortified & oaked. Now bottled, improved **NV** shows candied fruit, barley sugar, a mouthfilling syrupy richness best served chilled. 375 ml.

★★★★ **Rooi Jeripigo** Was 'Muskadel'. Oaked fortified blend red & white muscat de Frontignan from Goudini. Now-bottled **NV** has hedonistic raisin sweetness, full bodied, unctuous, like drinking dessert.

Not retasted: **Juan II 13** ★★★ **Wilna 12** ★★★☆ Not tasted: **Haasbek Tinta Barocca**.

Louw range

Mariëtha Merlot ⊘ ★★★ Named after winemaker's mother. **13** pulpy red berries with a thread of freshness adding appeal, tannins in balance, promising longevity. Not retasted: **Granietmyn Shiraz 13** ★★★ **Koffieklip Chenin Blanc 14** ★★★ **Gesuierde Sauvignon Blanc 14** ★★★ Not tasted: **Rooipad Cabernet Sauvignon**, **Makstok Pinotage**, **Olmo Ruby Cabernet**. — CR

Location: Malmesbury ▪ Map: Durbanville, Philadelphia & Darling ▪ WO: Swartland/Malmesbury/Coastal ▪ Est 2007 ▪ 1stB 2008 ▪ Vygevallei farmstall & Nuweland wine house (R27): Tasting & sales Mon-Sat 10-6 Sun 10-4 ▪ Closed Dec 25 & Jan 1 ▪ Cellar tours by appt only ▪ Restaurant ▪ Facilities for children ▪ Tour groups ▪ Gifts ▪ Art ▪ Farm produce ▪ Conferences ▪ Owner(s) Juan Louw ▪ Winemaker(s)/viticulturist(s) Juan Louw (Jan 2007) ▪ 300ha/96ha (cab, merlot, ptage, tinta barocca, chenin, sauv) ▪ 560t/1,500cs own label 45% red 35% white 20% dessert ▪ PO Box 283 Malmesbury 7299 ▪ vygevallei@ nuweland.za.net ▪ www.nuweland.za.net ▪ S 33° 24' 03.87" E 018° 16' 41.73" ▪ **T +27 (0)78-111-7913**

☐ **Nuwe Wynplaas** *see* Group CDV

Nuy Wine Cellar

The many fans of Nuy Valley's grower-owned winery will notice a major reorganisation and extension of the wine portfolio this edition, with new bottlings, fresh names for established line-ups and revamped packaging. To match, there's a new tasting venue and bistro at the cellardoor, where their consistently fine fortifieds continue to charm and delight palates as well as pockets.

Mastery range

★★★★ **Cabernet Sauvignon** Was 'Barrel Selection'. **13** dark blackberry notes with savoury tobacco; complex berry flavours & still-assertive tannin, auguring well for the future.

★★★★ **Pinotage** New bottling of **13**, longer aged in only older oak. (Last edition's was 'Barrel Selection'.) Earthy forest floor aromas, plums & banana suggestion, subtle wood hints. Lively cranberry flavour, tangy finish. **10** (★★★) was leaner. **11**, **12** sold out untasted.

★★★★ **Shiraz** Was 'Barrel Selection Syrah'. **13** smoky, savoury dark berries & cranberries; fairly rich flavours checked by firm tannins & a grippy finish needing few years to soften. Patience should be rewarded.

Chardonnay (NEW) (🍷) ★★★★ Understated oaking yields vanilla & biscuit overlay to soft lemon & pineapple palate in really attractive **14**.

Legacy range

★★★★ **Argilla** (NEW) Shiraz, pinotage blend in **13**, with appealing tobacco & savoury nuances to the black cherry & mulberry flavours, juicy finish.

★★★★☆ **50 Vintages** (Ⓠ) Listed as 'Red Muscadel Limited Release' last edition. 1,500 bottles of this fortified & barrel-matured **NV** nectar released to mark Nuy's 50th anniversary. Rich & refined, with subtle tannic grip. Do try to cellar some.

Not tasted: **Colcareo**, **Méthode Cap Classique**.

Inspiration range

★★★★ **Red Muscadel** Personality-packed fortified **14** (★★★★☆) warmly welcomes you with raisins, sultanas, orange rind, persimmon, raspberry & warm honey – all this offered with delicacy, panache. Sheer delight to end a perfect meal, as was **13** & previous.

★★★★☆ **White Muscadel** Underlining this team's mastery of fortified muscadel, **14** yet another deliciously light-footed glass of liquid sunshine. Jasmine-perfumed raisins & citrus, lemon marmalade flavour, honeyed finish goes on & on. Like **13** (★★★★★), will develop beautifully.

Sparkling Wine Off-Dry (🍷) ★★★ Was 'Sauvignon Blanc Sparkling Vin Sec'. Foamy **15** is sweetish but sauvignon's clean, crisp acidity makes it lively, fun to drink, as do the green apple flavours.

Muscat Sparkling Wine (NEW) ★★☆ Coral pink **15** with persistent bubbles, pleasant semi-sweet raspberry & marmalade tone, everyday patio pleaser. Also tasted: **Chenin Blanc 15** ★★☆ **Sauvignon Blanc 15** ★★☆ Not retasted: **Chardonnay 13** ★★★★ **Chant de Nuit NV** ★☆ Not tasted: **Cabernet Sauvignon**, **Koffiepit Pinotage**, **Shiraz**, **Colombar Semi-Sweet**.

3L Slim Pack range

Rouge de Nuy ★★☆ **NV** three-way blend pinotage, cab & merlot with easily sippable chocolates & berries, perfect for braais & parties. Not tasted: **Blanc de Blanc**. — DB

Location/map: Worcester ▪ WO: Nuy ▪ Est 1963 ▪ Tasting & sales Mon-Fri 9–4.30 Sat 9–3 ▪ Closed Good Fri, Dec 25/26 & Jan 1 ▪ Bistro & farmstall ▪ Owner(s) 19 members ▪ Cellarmaster(s) Christo Pienaar (Sep 2003) ▪ Winemaker(s) Charl Myburgh (Dec 2012) ▪ Viticulturist(s) Pierre Snyman (Vinpro) ▪ 770ha (cab, merlot, muscadel, ptage, shiraz, chard, chenin, cbard, nouvelle, sauv) ▪ 16,600t/10,000cs own label ▪ PO Box 5225 Worcester 6849 ▪ wines@nuywinery.co.za ▪ www.nuywinery.co.za ▪ S 33° 39' 8.7" E 019° 38' 30.9" ▪ F +27 (0)86-520-1782 ▪ **T +27 (0)23-347-0272**

☐ **Oak Lane** see Beau Joubert Vineyards & Winery

Oak Valley Wines

(🍷) (🍴) (🏠) (📷) (♿)

Oak Valley is a large family-run estate whose rich history is integrally woven into the character and destiny of Elgin Valley. The talented younger guard have taken over, with son Christopher Rawbone-Viljoen as marketing manager of a dynamic farming enterprise that includes everything from free-range meat, cut flowers, fruit to wine and a range of tourist attractions. New winemaker Quentin Gobregts was lured back from Margret River, Australia, after the sad passing of Pieter Visser in 2014. There are delicious new wines: a riesling grafted over from viognier, a semillon and (untasted) single-variety cabernet franc. The rebranded sauvignon, Fountain of Youth, refers to both the fresh spring discovered by the founder, Sir Antonie Viljoen in 1898, and the wine's longevity and brightness.

★★★★ **Pinot Noir** Alluring perfumed berries, white pepper & mushroom aromas & flavours, **13** firm oak tannin support (30% new, 9 months). Lively & fresh, just needs time to harmonise & shine.

★★★★ **Shiraz 14** (★★★★) quite feisty & fresh in youth, spicy oak & cherry flavours in a tussle. Light impression with supple tannins, but shade off the balance & integration of last-tasted **11**.

★★★★ **The Oak Valley Blend** Bordeaux red is cab & merlot led in **09** (★★★★★), with cab franc, petit verdot. Intensely fruited core, dark scented berries & fresh cedar, oak the integrated understudy in a fine-grained, supple tannin structure. Streamlined & so well groomed it disguises inherent power. An ageworthy leap up in quality on **08** (★★★☆) & **07**.

★★★★☆ **Chardonnay** Subtle citrus, minerals & hint of butterscotch, **14** is understated with fine fruit/acid balance & oak integration. From 2 vineyards at different elevations. Fresher (only 10% malo as opposed to 80%), more elegant & refined than **13** (★★★★).

★★★★★ **Stone & Steel Riesling** (NEW) ✓ Exhilaratingly fresh & racy debut for **15**. Exudes white flower, pineapple & nectarine; quivers with freshness & sweet/sour fruit, acid tension; great fruit purity, intensity & length, all at just 11.12% alcohol. A piquant delight!

★★★★☆ **Fountain of Youth Sauvignon Blanc** ✓ Was just 'Sauvignon Blanc'. **14** clean-cut grapefruit, passionfruit flavours tightly knit with some minerality, tempered by lees-aged creaminess & splash oaked semillon. Already balanced but aptly named, plenty of fresh vibrancy for development. Step up on **12** (★★★★). No **13**.

★★★★ **Semillon** (NEW) Subtle lanolin aromas on **13** blossom into honeycomb, white peach & hint of citrus; rich waxy texture courtesy natural ferment & lees-ageing; balanced, with ample freshness & length, lovely varietal expression & poise.

★★★★★ **Mountain Reserve White Blend** Exceptional sauvignon-led duo with oaked semillon. **11** toasted hazelnut, dried peach & some minerality enriched by creamy lees, but overall impression is tangy & lively. Youthful, with good development potential. — MW

Location/WO: Elgin ▪ Map: Elgin, Walker Bay & Bot River ▪ Est 1898 ▪ 1stB 2003 ▪ Tasting & sales Mon-Fri 9–5 Sat/Sun 10-4 ▪ Closed Easter Mon, Dec 25/26 & Jan 1 ▪ The Pool Room Restaurant ▪ Deli: artisanal breads, homegrown free-range meats & charcuterie ▪ Self-catering 1-bedroom cottage ▪ Walks/hikes ▪ MTB trail ▪ Conservation area ▪ Owner(s) AG Rawbone-Viljoen Trust ▪ Winemaker(s) Quentin Gobregts (Sep 2014) ▪ Viticulturist(s) Quentin Gobregts (Sep 2014), assisted by Kevin Watt ▪ 30ha (cabs s/f, merlot, pinot, shiraz, chard, riesling, sauv, sem) ▪ ±100t/±15,000cs own label 45% red 55% white ▪ BWI champion, GlobalGAP, IPW, WIETA ▪ PO Box 30 Elgin 7180 ▪ wines@oak-valley.co.za ▪ www.oakvalley.co.za ▪ S 34° 9' 24.4" E 019° 2' 55.5" ▪ F +27 (0)21-859-3405 ▪ **T +27 (0)21-859-4110**

Obikwa

Following her appointment as global marketing manager for this entry-level Distell label, available in over 40 countries, Thandi Ntuli is looking to inject some 'positive innovations' from the booming Asia-Pacific market into the SA arena.

Pinotage (🍷) ★★★ Wild brambly black berries on well-structured **14**, ripe, with choc-dipped banana sweetness. **Pinotage Rosé** ★★☆ **15** may be a bright pink berry-licious quaffer but its zippy acidity & dry finish also make it a versatile food match. **Pinot Grigio** (🍷) ★★ With appealing lemon blossom nose, pineapple & apricot flavours, **14** seems drier than previous vintage, slight pétillance adding to impression of freshness. Not retasted: **Cabernet Sauvignon 14** ★★★ **Merlot 14** ★★ **Shiraz 14** ★★ **Chardonnay 14** ★★★ **Chenin Blanc 14** ★★★ **Sauvignon Blanc 14** ★★☆ **Cuvée Brut 14** ★★☆ Not tasted: **Moscato**. — JG

Oldenburg Vineyards   (🍷) (🍴) (🏠) (♿)

This farm in Stellenbosch's spectacular Banhoek Valley had been much neglected before Adrian Vanderspuy returned to his roots, after many years abroad, to buy it and set about its rejuvenation. Vineyards first, of course, but the old homestead has also been fully renovated, as a 'short-stay luxury villa'. Widely experienced Philip Costandius arrived to take charge of vineyards and cellar in 2014 and is now identifying prime sites or patches of vines, planning on handling their fruit separately. Meanwhile awards for the wines multiply.

★★★★☆ **Cabernet Sauvignon** Underlines serious cab player status with **12**, following on from brilliant **11** (★★★★★) with similar concentration & intensity, fine-woven tannins & fruit purity – but without the extraordinary finesse we noted last time. Perhaps more of a sleeper vintage, requiring patience.

★★★★ **Cabernet Sauvignon Barrel Selection** ⓥ Restrained & perfumed **09**, with delicacy rather than intensity the hallmark of this selection. House-style big alcohol (15%) & all-new oak well managed.

★★★★ **Cabernet Franc** Impressive structure from relatively young vines – promising. **12** shows typical crushed leaf & eucalyptus spice combined with redcurrants & plum; fine & polished tannins.

★★★★ **Merlot** ⓥ Fruity **11** followed by herbaceous **12** (★★★★), bouquet garni, crushed leaf, sugared plum nuances, with hints capsicum, cedar. There's good acidity, with dry tannins, but needs year/2.

★★★★☆ **Syrah** Ever-improving label. Bold spice, black fruit & pepper are undeniably syrah/shiraz. 'Masculine' & dense, **12** is starting to integrate the tannins & oak, revealing some perfume with coaxing, but needs a few more years. Also in magnum. **11** (★★★★) was über-ripe, jammy.

★★★★ **Chardonnay** Sound oak integration (50% new wood) & elegant dryness on **14**. Citrus & peach supported by interesting wet clay, sandalwood & underbrush nuances. Ready to enjoy but will cellar well.

★★★★ **Chenin Blanc** A serious, full-bodied expression of the grape, partial barrel ferment (50% new) provides weight & toasty notes with tangy apricot & jasmine. **14** worthy of focused food pairing – not for casual sipping. Step up on **13** (★★★★).

Also tasted: **Rhodium Red Blend 12** ★★★★ — HJ

Location/map/WO: Stellenbosch ▪ Map grid reference: H5 ▪ Est 1960s ▪ 1stB 2007 ▪ Tasting & sales Mon-Fri 10-4.30 Sat & pub hols 10-4 (Oct-May)/by appt (Jun-Sep) ▪ Fee R30 ▪ Closed Good Fri, Dec 25/26 & Jan 1 ▪ Refreshments for sale: cheese platters, biltong, etc. ▪ Luxury accommodation in The Homestead (exclusive use, sleeps up to 12 in 6 bedrooms) ▪ Owner(s) Adrian Vanderspuy ▪ Winemaker(s)/viticulturist(s) Philip Costandius ▪ 50ha/30ha (cabs s/f, merlot, shiraz, chard, chenin) ▪ 227t/8,000cs own label 57% red 43% white ▪ PO Box 2246 Dennesig 7601 ▪ cellardoor@oldenburgvineyards.com ▪ www.oldenburgvineyards.com ▪ S 33° 55' 7.61" E 018° 56' 8.75" ▪ F +27 (0)21-885-2665 ▪ **T +27 (0)21-885-1618**

☐ **Old Harbour** *see* Whalehaven Wines
☐ **Old Man's Blend** *see* Groote Post Vineyards
☐ **Old School** *see* Alkmaar Boutique Vineyard

Old Vines Cellars

'It was lonely,' recalls Irina von Holdt, back in 1995 when she put a seriously conceived chenin blanc in an attention-grabbing royal blue bottle and jump-started the variety's renaissance in SA. Now, the Cape Wine Master and co-owner with daughter Françoise Botha, says she's loving the energy of young winemakers embracing chenin and proud that so many consumers are following suit. Future Old Vines winegrowers are in training, Fran's eldest interested in the cellar workings and his brother far more interested in the tractor hauling the grapes.

Old Vines range

★★★★ **Barrel Reserve Chenin Blanc** Last a preview, **13** has accentuated oxidative style & big oak, with honeysuckle scent & buttery tones. Generous body, muted white stonefruit. From Bottelary vineyards.

★★★★ **Chenin Blanc** ⓥ Ageworthy unwooded version. Hints of white nuts & earthiness on **14**. Extended lees-ageing brings creamy texture & complex layering of somewhat understated fruit. Possibly a tad down on last-tasted **12** (★★★★★). Stellenbosch WO.

In abeyance: **Baron von Holdt**, **Vintage Brut**.

Springvalley range

Shiraz-Merlot ⓥ ★★★★ 2nd bottling of **13**, tasted from tank, shows black fruit pastilles, more serious tarry notes with liquorice spiciness. Smoother & better integrated. **Sauvignon Blanc** ★★★ Wild herbaceous aromas on unsettled **15**, provisionally rated tank sample. Plenty of body & substance from

Helderberg fruit. Also tasted: **Chenin Blanc-Sauvignon Blanc 15 ★★★** Not tasted: **Merlot**. Occasional release: **Pinotage**. — GdB

Location: Cape Town ▪ WO: Coastal/Stellenbosch ▪ Est/1stB 1995 ▪ Closed to public ▪ Owner(s) Irina von Holdt & Françoise Botha ▪ Winemaker(s) Irina von Holdt ▪ 20,000cs own label 40% red 60% white + 8,000cs for clients ▪ 50 Liesbeek Rd Rosebank 7700 ▪ info@oldvines.co.za ▪ www.oldvines.co.za ▪ F +27 (0)21-685-6446 ▪ **T +27 (0)21-685-6428**

Olifantsberg Family Vineyards ⓘ

It was love at first sight for Elizma Visser, so the move here (from Waverley Hills Organic) as winemaker/viticulturist has her delighted and enthused about growing and developing the Leeuwerik family farm, and being involved 'from vine to bottle'. A unique site on Breedekloof's Brandwacht Mountain, some rarer varieties, a traditional hands-on approach and the drive to create 'wines of very high quality' make Elizma 'genuinely excited about what Olifantsberg is going to produce in the future'.

★★★★ Syrah 12 mirrors **11 (★★★★)** in meaty, leathery tones, pepper spiciness, but fruit is elevated a notch. Charming plum pudding & black cherries, with velvet tannin grip. 10% cab.

★★★★ Silhouette (new) Rhône-style **13** from shiraz/syrah (±10% ex Swartland) & 3 others. Luscious, fragrant red fruit; juicy & satisfyingly layered (if just a tad brief, precluding higher rating), firm tannins.

★★★★ Blanc de Noir Pretty salmon-pink shiraz, **14** is dry but fattened by lees-ageing, appealing lean fruitiness. Substantial, elegant & refined. Fermented in large oak, aged in tanks.

★★★★ Chenin Blanc (new) Promising debut, **14** widely sourced & naturally fermented. Big & dense, lashings of tropical fruit elegantly brushed with oak. Long, lithe & seductively plush, focused finish.

★★★★☆ Blanc Revamped blend in **14** leads with roussanne & grenache blanc, splash chardonnay. Less oxidative than previous, but stunningly dense & rich. Large older oak doesn't intrude but expresses the delicately complex fruit & silky texture. Unlike **13**, only Breedekloof grapes.

Not retasted: **Pinotage 13 ★★★★☆** Occasional release: **Chardonnay**. Discontinued: **Cabernet Sauvignon**. — GdB

Location: Worcester ▪ Map: Breedekloof ▪ WO: Breedekloof/Western Cape ▪ Est 2003 ▪ 1stB 2005 ▪ Tasting & sales Mon-Fri by appt ▪ Owner(s) Paul J Leeuwerik ▪ Winemaker(s)/viticulturist(s) Elizma Visser (Jun 2015) ▪ 95ha/18ha (carignan, grenache n/b, mourv, ptage, shiraz, chard, chenin, rouss) ▪ 100t/±13,000cs own label 50% red 50% white ▪ PO Box 942 Worcester 6849 ▪ winemaker@olifantsbergwines.com ▪ www.olifantsbergwines.com ▪ S 33° 35' 42.76" E 019° 21' 42.39" ▪ **T +27 (0)79-376-1466**

Olof Bergh Solera

A rarity in the local brandy arena, Distell's Olof Bergh is matured in a dedicated cellar at Goudini in the Breede River Valley using a solera, where different batches are racked down tiers of barrels for a final product with a greater percentage of cask-aged distillate than the usual blended brandy.

Olof Bergh Solera ⓐ **★★★** Blended brandy, sippable but best for cocktails & mixers. Straightforward, with nice fruity fragrance to sniff & some caramel & oak vanilla coming through. — WB, TJ

☐ **OloPam** see New Beginnings Wines

Olsen Wines ⓘ ⓘ

A decades-old partiality for pinotage persuaded American physicist Greg Olsen (the third civilian in space, in 2005) to buy this Klein Drakenstein property (co-owned with daughters Kimberly and Krista). Extensive research is guiding their new plantings of the variety plus five others – but only half a hectare of each so the boutique cellar is not stretched.

Cabernet Sauvignon (new) ★★★ Opaque, plush & blackcurrant-toned, **12**'s fruit-sweet, oak-sweet palate refreshed & extended by commendably firm tannins. This & other reds combo French/American oak (2 years, 10% new). **Merlot (new) ★★★** Like Shiraz, **12** has crème de cassis nuance, enlivened by bright acidity & supple tannins. **Cape Blend (new) ★★★★** Black plum, raspberry & dates on appealing **12** mix pinotage (43%) & dollops shiraz, cab & merlot. Sleek tannins, less obvious oak vanilla than others; a more balanced package. Also tasted: **Pinotage 12 ★★★☆ Shiraz 12 ★★★★** Not retasted: **Chenin Blanc 14 ★★★☆** Not tasted: **Chardonnay**. — CvZ

Location/WO: Paarl ▪ Map: Paarl & Wellington ▪ Map grid reference: G5 ▪ Est/1stB 2002 ▪ Tasting by appt only ▪ Fee R50pp depending on sales ▪ Farm-style jams & olive oil ▪ Owner(s) Greg Olsen & daughters ▪ Cellarmaster(s)/viticulturist(s) Armand Botha (2000) ▪ Winemaker(s) Armand Botha (2007) & Loftie Ellis (consultant) ▪ 15ha ▪ 1,500cs own label 80% red 20% white ▪ EuroGAP ▪ PO Box 9052 Huguenot 7645 ▪ olsenwines@mweb.co.za ▪ www.olsenprivatevineyards.co.za ▪ S 33° 44' 4.7" E 019° 3' 5.0" ▪ F +27 (0)21-862-2589 ▪ **T +27 (0)21-862-3653**

Onderkloof $\textcircled{Q}$ $\textcircled{a}$ $\textcircled{o}$

Having returned to his parents' prime Schapenberg property near Somerset West in 2012, armed with a BSc from Geisenheim University, Swiss-born Yves Musfeld is asserting his authority on winemaking, vineyard revitalisation (higher yields indicating that 'the vines appreciate our efforts') and introducing South Africans to wines that were previously mostly destined for export.

Onderkloof range

Pinotage 🍷 **★★★☆** From dryland bushvines, full-bodied **12** has intense red berry/cherry fruitiness with intriguing hints of spice, coffee, liquorice & even smoky bacon coming through.

Shiraz ★★★☆ Brimming with dark, ripe blackberries & blueberries, **12** is smooth with well-integrated oak spice, a pinch of white pepper & whiffs of leather adding interest. Not retasted: **Sir Lowry 11 ★★★ Chenin Blanc 12 ★★★ Sauvignon Blanc 13 ★★★ Floreal Blanc de Blanc 13 ★★★** Not tasted: **Cabernet Sauvignon, Cabernet Franc, Bottleneck Rosé, Chardonnay**.

Logo range 🆕

Cabernet Franc ★★★ Fresh is the operative word for **13** debut, medium bodied with mulberry fruit as well as mildly herbal mulberry leaf notes. — JG

Location: Somerset West ▪ Map: Helderberg ▪ WO: Stellenbosch/Western Cape ▪ Est 1998 ▪ 1stB 1999 ▪ Tasting, sales & cellar tours by appt ▪ Conservation area ▪ Self-catering cottages ▪ Owner(s) Beat Musfeld ▪ Winemaker(s) Yves Musfeld (Jan 2012) ▪ Viticulturist(s) Botha Marais (Aug 2012) ▪ 64ha/17ha (cabs s/f, ptage, shiraz, chard, chenin, muscat d'A, sauv) ▪ 100t ▪ PO Box 90 Sir Lowry's Pass 7133 ▪ info@onderkloof.com ▪ www.onderkloof.com ▪ S 34° 6' 37.9" E 018° 53' 49.2" ▪ **T +27 (0)21-858-1538**

☐ **Ondine** see Ormonde Private Cellar
☐ **One Creation** see Boland Kelder

Oneiric Wines $\textcircled{Q}$ $\textcircled{a}$ $\textcircled{o}$

Oneiric, 'of or pertaining to dreams', describes Matt and Jennifer Pascall and family's aspiration to bottle wines from their Elgin property on the border of the Kogelberg Biosphere under an own brand. Middle child Shan is the MD and prime mover, bringing boundless enthusiasm and a fresh perspective to the young brand. Vinification is by contracted specialists and, for visitors, the cellardoor offers a gift shop with arts and crafts, scenic walks and other allures.

Location: Elgin ▪ Map: Elgin, Walker Bay & Bot River ▪ Est 2007 ▪ 1stB 2009 ▪ Tasting & sales by appt only ▪ BYO picnic ▪ Gift shop ▪ Walks/hikes ▪ Conservation area ▪ Owner(s) Pascall family ▪ Winemaker(s) Niels Verburg ▪ Viticulturist(s) Paul Wallace (Aug 2007, consultant) ▪ 64ha/8ha (cab, merlot, syrah, chard, sauv) ▪ ±90t/5,000cs own label 65% red 35% white ▪ shan@oneiric.co.za ▪ www.oneiric.co.za ▪ S 34° 14' 31.0" E 019° 03' 05.8" ▪ **T +27 (0)71-481-9560**

☐ **One World** see Koopmanskloof Wingerde

Oom Tas

Distell big-volume white depicts winefarmer 'Uncle Tas' beaming from retro label. In 1, 2 & 5L bottles.

Oom Tas 🍷 **★** Amber hue implies sweetness but latest **NV** is bone-dry, dilute. — MW

Opstal Estate   🍷 🍴 📷 🛏 ♿

Dynamic 7th-generation Attie Louw has introduced two more wines to the Slanghoek family estate's Heritage range: a Carl Everson red blend (honouring his great-grandfather) and a semillon under the new Barber label (named for his grandfather). The Barber is all about single-varietal, limited-release, experimental wines, with recently planted carignan and roussanne promising more possibilities. Themed food-and-wine evenings bring winegrowers and guests together to focus on the region's strengths.

Heritage range

★★★★☆ **Carl Everson Cape Blend** 🆕 From equal shiraz, pinotage & cab, **13**'s bright fruit is the focus, the oak (some new) providing an ample frame; harmonious, mouthfilling & balanced.

★★★★☆ **Carl Everson Chenin Blanc** Opstal's calling card, from 35 year old home vineyard, naturally vinified. Serious **14** displays complex layers of tropical & green fruit, baked cinnamon custard – packed with flavour, the dry end belying the rich palate. Only older oak.

★★★★☆ **The Barber Semillon** 🆕 **13** from 18 year old vines shows spicy sun-dried peaches & pears, creamy mouthfeel lifted by dashes of lemon zest; satisfying and carefully coiffured; will age beautifully.

Opstal Estate range

★★★★ **Hanepoot** Great typicity of raisin, spice & fragrant, floral lift, following to sun-drenched viscosity. **14** fortified dessert has wonderful cleansing acidity to balance the sweet richness.

Cabernet Sauvignon 🍷 ★★★★ Taut, structured **13** has fresh lift to bright cherry aroma; red-fruited flavours, with light juicy appeal & dry firm end. **Sauvignon Blanc** 🍷 ★★★ White fruit & blossoms welcome you on **15**, delightful creamy mouthfeel from extended lees-ageing, fresh acid adds a bright end.

Syrah-Viognier Blush ★★★☆ Barely blushing, fragrant strawberry & musk on co-fermented, step-up **15** rosé. Lovely intensity of juicy flavours, tangy dry finish. Also in magnum. Also tasted: **The Mill Iron 15** ★★★ **Sauvignon Blanc Sparkling Sec 15** ★★☆ **Chardonnay Barrel Dessert 13** ★★★☆

Sixpence range

Sauvignon Blanc-Semillon 🍷 ★★★ **15** friendly & fun, hay & dry grassy foil to tropical zest of sauvignon.

Also tasted: **Cabernet Sauvignon-Merlot 14** ★★★ — WB

Location: Rawsonville ▪ Map: Breedekloof ▪ WO: Slanghoek/Breedekloof ▪ Est 1847 ▪ 1stB 1978 ▪ Tasting, sales & cellar tours Mon-Fri 9–5 Sat 11–3 Sun by appt ▪ Closed Easter Fri-Mon, Dec 25/26 & Jan 1 ▪ Cheese platters ▪ Restaurant Wed-Sun 9–5 ▪ Facilities for children ▪ Tour groups ▪ Gift shop ▪ Farm produce ▪ Conferences ▪ Conservation area ▪ MTB trail ▪ Quarterly music/theatre shows with dinner ▪ Quarterly farmers market ▪ Owner(s) Stanley Louw ▪ Winemaker(s) Attie Louw (Sep 2010) ▪ Viticulturist(s) Gerhard Theron (Jan 2002) ▪ 419ha/101ha (cab, ptage, shiraz, chard, chenin, muscat d'A, sauv, sem, viog) ▪ 1,500t/15,000cs own label 20% red 55% white 20% rosé 5% dessert ▪ BWI, IPW, WIETA ▪ PO Box 27 Rawsonville 6845 ▪ wine@opstal.co.za ▪ www.opstal.co.za ▪ S 33° 38' 19.8" E 019° 13' 40.8" ▪ F +27 (0)23-344-3002 ▪ **T +27 (0)23-344-3001**

Orangerie Wines   🍷

As well as supplying grapes to others from this large, venerable Perdeberg farm, young Pieter Euvrard has made some wines in his tiny cellar with a minimal-intervention approach. There have been plantings on the farm of scarcer varieties, and more will follow – and more wines soon, we hope.

Location: Malmesbury ▪ Map: Swartland ▪ Est 1707 ▪ 1stB 2009 ▪ Tasting, sales & cellar tours by appt only ▪ Paardeberg Conservation Area ▪ Owner(s)/viticulturist(s) Loffie & Pieter Euvrard ▪ Winemaker(s) Pieter Euvrard (2009) ▪ 200ha/70ha (cab, malbec, merlot, mourv, ptage, shiraz, chard, chenin, rouss, sauv, verdelho, viog) ▪ 15t/600cs own label 60% red 40% white ▪ PO Box 92 Malmesbury 7299 ▪ orangeriewines@yahoo.com ▪ www.orangeriewines.co.za ▪ S 33° 32' 20.8" E 018° 49' 55.6" ▪ F +27 (0)22-487-3046 ▪ **T +27 (0)22-482-2169**

Orange River Cellars Ⓨ ♿

'What better way to celebrate 50 years of winemaking excellence than with an exceptional 2015 harvest?' Senior winemaker Rianco van Rooyen speaks for an enthusiastic, extensive team of vini- and viti-culturists at five cellars in the Northern Cape towns of Groblershoop, Grootdrink, Kakamas, Keimoes and and nerve centre Upington. Grapes come from some 850 grower-shareholders whose 4,200 ha of vines line SA's mighty Orange River, cutting east through this vast, arid landscape to the Atlantic Ocean. Extreme weather conditions – witness 10-degree temperatures causing bud-destroying frosts in 2014 – do not deter ongoing vineyard renewal, upping quality (a shiraz joins the reserve range) and boosting exports. Encouraging visitors to this starkly beautiful part of the winelands is a new tasting centre opening in Upington this year.

Reserve range

★★★★ Straw Wine Sunshiny ripe tropical fruit in a bottle! **14** air-dried, older-barrel-fermented chenin seduces with intense fruit flavours & terrific balancing acid. Clean & bright. 375 ml.

Lyra Shiraz Reserve Ⓝ **★★★☆** Savoury & spicy maiden **13** combines 50/50 unoaked & oaked components for harmonious dark-berry & dusty tannin offering. Also tasted: **Lyra Vega 12 ★★★☆** Not retasted: **Chenin Blanc de Barrique 13 ★★★**

Orange River Cellars range

★★★★ Soet Hanepoot Sun-dried peaches suffuse bold, richly sweet **NV** fortified dessert. Hits the spot with excellent balance of sugar & alcohol, finishes whistle clean. Very moreish & super value.

★★★★ Red Muscadel Floral & winter melon scents, & brilliant tawny hue seduce on grapey **13** jerepiko-style dessert. Richly sweet but not cloying, great length & complexity. Stock up!

★★★★ White Muscadel Ⓧ Broad, rich barley sugar, sun-dried pineapple & muscat typicity to **13** (**★★★★★**) fortified, which improves on lighter **12** (**★★★★☆**) & seamless **11**. Elegant, long & beautifully balanced, its dry finish is focused by flavours that linger long.

Cabernet Sauvignon ★★★ Soft & fruity **13** with a brush of oak for easy appeal. **Pinotage ★★★** Mocha & chewy fruit pastilles on **14**, lightly oaked. Pleasing & very sippable. **Shiraz ★★★** Spicy, welcoming mouthful of dark berries & plums on **13**. Dashes petit verdot & tannat add a savoury touch to the enjoyment. **Chardonnay ★★★ 14** is bright, with orange blossom perfume, succulent, creamy mouthfeel from lees stirring. Some oaked chenin adds interest. **Colombard** Ⓧ **★★★** Uncomplicated, friendly (11.8%) **15** is a joy, with vibrant guava & apple flavours, spicy farewell. **Rosé Natural Sweet ★★★** Up-a-notch **15** blends morio muscat & pinotage in delightful & juicy rosé. Wafts of Turkish delight & rosepetals. Low alcohol (9.7%) **White Jerepigo ★★★☆** Succulent apricots & dried pears on fortified **NV** from chenin. Sweet, deep & rich, with a lingering spicy marmalade goodbye. Also tasted: **Ruby Cabernet** Ⓧ **14 ★★★ Chenin Blanc 15 ★★★ Sauvignon Blanc 15 ★★★ Nouveau Natural Sweet 15 ★★ Red Jerepigo NV ★★★☆ Cape Ruby 13 ★★★** Not retasted: **Sparkling Rosé 14 ★★★☆ Sparkling Brut 14 ★★★ Sparkling Doux 14 ★★★** — WB

Location: Upington ▪ Map: Northern Cape, Free State & North West ▪ WO: Northern Cape ▪ Est 1965 ▪ 1stB 1968 ▪ Tasting & sales Mon-Fri 8–4.30 Sat 8.30–12 ▪ Fee R10/5 wines ▪ Closed all pub hols ▪ Cellar tours Mon-Fri 9, 11 & 3 (Jan-Mar) ▪ Owner(s) ±850 shareholders ▪ Cellarmaster(s) Gert Visser ▪ Cellar managers Bolla Louw (Kakamas), Johan Dippenaar (Keimoes), Johan Esterhuizen (Upington), Jim de Kock (Grootdrink), Riaan Liebenberg (Groblershoop), with winemakers (in same cellar order) George Kruger/Marko Pentz/Stephan Steenkamp; Rianco van Rooyen/Mariken Jordaan; Jopie Faul/Philan Gumede/Renier Baard; Rudi de Wet; Mynhardt van der Merwe ▪ Viticulturist(s) Henning Burger (viticultural services manager), with (in same cellar order) Ockert Vermeulen, Chris Kalp, Francois Ozrovech, Dirk Sutherland ▪ 4,200ha (ptage, ruby cab, shiraz, chard, chenin, cbard, muscat varieties) ▪ 123,000t/20m L own label 10% red 50% white 20% rosé 20% other + 30m L for clients/bulk ▪ Other export labels: Engel, Gilysipao, Star Tree ▪ Ranges for customers: Country Cellars & Carnival (Spar); Seasons Collection (Liquor City) ▪ FSSC 22 000, IPW ▪ PO Box 544 Upington 8800 ▪ info@orangeriverwines.com ▪ www.orangeriverwines.com ▪ S 28° 26' 33.0" E 021° 12' 30.6" ▪ F +27 (0)54-332-4408 ▪ **T +27 (0)54-337-8800**

☐ **Oranjerivier Wynkelders** *see* Orange River Cellars

Org de Rac

⠀(Q)(M)(△)(◎)(⬤)

A sense of dynamism and growth at Swartland organic producer Org de Rac, its cellarmaster Frank Meaker reporting rising volumes in Sweden (including 3L bag-in-boxes), new markets in Belgium and Germany, and a listing with Whole Foods in the UK. New varieties in production mean new blends, certified organic by recently appointed Control Union. A holistic approach aimed at achieving yet more consumer-friendly wines and realising the full potential of each variety is a major focus moving forward.

Reserve range

★★★★ Cabernet Sauvignon (Ⓩ) (✿) Classy blackcurrant & damson fruit with iodine, tobacco & earth notes on **13** show promise of improvement with time in bottle. Generous body & length. No **12**.

★★★★ Shiraz (Ⓩ) (✿) Smoky, spicy & plump, **13** is youthful but has bright future. Honest, ripe fruit & chalky tannins need time to integrate, but the right components are in place.

Reserve Chardonnay (NEW) (✿) ★★★★ **14**'s fruit peeping out from a heavy oak mantle mid-2015, but behind all the wood spice is a promisingly full, ripe body which hopefully will emerge over time. Not retasted: **Merlot 13 ★★★**

Org de Rac range

★★★★ La Verne Méthode Cap Classique (✿) Well-structured, elegant **12** follows form of debut **11**. Crisply acidic, dry chardonnay blanc de blancs with baked apples & shortbread on energetic mousse. **La Trio Rouge** (✿) ★★★★ Youthfully reticent **14** preview, blend of shiraz, grenache & mourvèdre shows bright red-cherry fruit & aromatic herbs. Oak still evident, but plenty of promise. **Unwooded Chardonnay** (✿) ★★★ Light, fresh & perky **15** offers enjoyable everyday drinking. **La Trio Blanche** (NEW) (✿) ★★★ Chenin, roussanne & verdelho blend, unwooded, light & fruity **15** preview is cheerful if brief. **The Old Pumphouse Cape Ruby Port** (NEW) (✿) ★★★ Somewhat old-school styling for **NV** 'port' from cab & shiraz, plummy/grapey fruit flavours with heady spirit overlay needing time to knit. Also tasted: **Cabernet Sauvignon** (✿) 14 ★★★ **Shiraz** (✿) 14 ★★★ **Merlot-Mourvèdre Rosé** (✿) 15 ★★★ **Lightly Wooded Chardonnay** (✿) 15 ★★★ Not retasted: **Merlot 13 ★★★ Shiraz-Cabernet Sauvignon-Merlot 14 ★★☆**

Le Piquet range

Cabernet Sauvignon-Merlot (Ⓩ) (✿) ★★★ Convincing cassis fruitiness on lighter body of **13** tank sample. Sweet vanilla spice, soft tannins, ripe & accessible. Not retasted: **Cabernet Sauvignon-Merlot-Shiraz Reserve 13 ★★★☆**

Green Shebeen range

The Blend (Ⓩ) (✿) ★★☆ **NV** amiable cab/merlot packed with juicy fruit & easy tannins.

Husk Spirit range

★★★★ Le Genio (Ⓩ) (✿) Husk spirit from **14** merlot nicely done. Nutty, with floral violet & lavender scents; elegant, creamy, some roasted nut, sweet berry fruit complexity. Smooth & long. — WB, GdB

Location: Piketberg ▪ Map/WO: Swartland ▪ Est 2001 ▪ 1stB 2005 ▪ Tasting, sales & tours Mon-Fri 9–5 Sat 9–1 ▪ Closed Good Fri, Dec 25 & Jan 1 ▪ Meals/refreshments/cheese platters by prior arrangement, contact cindy@orgderac.co.za; or BYO picnic ▪ Tour groups ▪ Weddings/functions (120 pax) ▪ Conferences ▪ Walks/hikes ▪ Mountain biking ▪ Conservation area ▪ Game viewing ▪ Owner(s) Nico Bacon ▪ Cellarmaster/GM Frank Meaker (Jul 2013) ▪ Winemaker(s) Jurgen Siebritz (Sep 2014) ▪ Viticulturist(s) Henry Bredenkamp ▪ 59ha (cab, grenache, merlot, mourv, shiraz, chard, chenin, rouss, verdelho) ▪ 650t/ 62,500cs own label 85% red 10% white 5% rosé ▪ Other export brand: Abbotsville ▪ Control Union (Organic) ▪ PO Box 268 Piketberg 7320 ▪ wine@orgderac.co.za ▪ www.orgderac.co.za ▪ S 32° 57' 44.3" E 018° 44' 57.4" ▪ F +27 (0)21-913-3923 ▪ **T +27 (0)22-913-2397/3924**

Origin Wine

⠀(Q)

Headquartered near Stellenbosch, Origin's 10 million case production caters to diverse local and international markets, and includes Fairhills, among the leading Fairtrade wine brands globally.

Location/map: Stellenbosch ▪ Map grid reference: D3 ▪ Est/1stB 2002 ▪ Tasting strictly by appt ▪ Owner(s) Bernard Fontannaz ▪ Cellarmaster(s) Ferdi Coetzee (2013) ▪ Wine sourcing manager Hermias Hugo (2011) ▪ Winemaker(s) Seugnét Rossouw (2007), with Terence Capes & LizeMari Geldenhuys ▪

10m cs ▪ 50% red 40% white 10% rosé ▪ BRC, DLG, Fairtrade, HACCP, IFS, WIETA ▪ PO Box 7177 Stellenbosch 7599 ▪ info@originwine.co.za ▪ www.originwine.co.za ▪ S 33° 52' 39.07" E 018° 48' 35.50" ▪ T +27 (0)861-ORIGIN/+27 (0)21-865-8100

Ormonde Private Cellar

Nico Basson bought this Darling farm in 1970 to start what became a highly acclaimed dairy stud. He also planted vines, long before the area known for quality wine. Today his family produces a flagship range, Ormonde, made from the best grapes; Ondine, official wine of the South African Ballet Theatre; separately listed Alexanderfontein, crafted for 'unpretentious pleasure'; and Chip Off The Old Block, single-vineyard wines made in celebration of Basson generations to come.

Ormonde Premium Blends

★★★★☆ **Vernon Basson** ⓥ After lighter **07** (★★★★), velvety **08** marks return to a richer style, with concentrated cassis of cab lifted by leafy freshness of cab franc to ensure elegance, while lengthy bottle-maturation has added notes of meaty, leathery complexity.

Not retasted: **Theodore Eksteen 08** ★★★★

Ormonde Barrel Selected range

★★★★ **Shiraz** A welcome return (first since **09**), plush **13** has black fruit layered with dark chocolate, liquorice & black pepper, brooding intensity lifted by fresh acidity.

★★★★ **Chardonnay** Deft oaking (only 50% wooded, 25% new) gives creamy oatmeal softness & hint of vanilla to nectarine & lime zest freshness of elegant **13**. Not made in **12**.

★★★★ **Sauvignon Blanc** Returns in **15**, after 2-year absence, redolent of green fig/pepper, with tropical gooseberry & granadilla flavours, wet-stone-sleek with fresh, lingering lemongrass finish. Coastal WO.

Also tasted: **Cabernet Sauvignon 11** ★★★★ Not tasted: **Pinot Noir**.

Single-Vineyard Chip Off The Old Block range

Sauvignon Blanc ⓥ ★★★★ **15** is crisp & dry, fresh & aromatic, its grassy greenpepper nose leading to sweet-sour Granny Smith intensity with underlying flinty minerality. Coastal WO.

Cabernet Sauvignon ★★★★ Juicy **13** has ripe black berry fruit, soft tannins & vibrant acidity, finishing slightly warm with a hint of liquorice. Also tasted: **Merlot 13** ★★★ **Shiraz 13** ★★★

Ondine Specialities

★★★★ **Cabernet Franc** ⓥ Fresher than last-made **10**, almost silky with smooth tannins, **13** has tobacco leaf nose & hints of dark chocolate but mostly abounds with raspberry & red cherry fruit.

★★★★ **Sauvignon Blanc** Lemongrass & stonefruits on **14**, ripe pineapple too, with delicious balance between soft mouthfeel & zingy acidity, refreshing but by no means lightweight. Step up on **13** (★★★☆).

Also tasted: **Chardonnay 14** ★★★★ **Semillon 14** ★★★★ Not retasted: **Merlot 11** ★★★★ Not tasted: **Malbec, Pinot Noir, Chenin Blanc**. — JG

Location: Darling ▪ Map: Durbanville, Philadelphia & Darling ▪ WO: Darling/Coastal ▪ 1stB 1999 ▪ Tasting & sales Mon-Fri 9–4 Sat/pub hols 9–3 ▪ Closed Good Fri, Dec 25/26 & Jan 1 ▪ Chocolate & wine tasting by appt R50pp – tasting fee applies to Ormonde range only ▪ Facilities for children ▪ Walks ▪ Owner(s) Basson family ▪ Winemaker(s) Hennie Huskisson ▪ Viticulturist(s) Theo Basson ▪ ±300ha (cabs s/f, merlot, mourv, p verdot, pinot, shiraz, chard, chenin, sauv, sem) ▪ 1,000t/70,000cs own label 40% red 60% white ▪ BWI ▪ PO Box 201 Darling 7345 ▪ info@ormonde.co.za ▪ www.ormonde.co.za ▪ S 33° 22' 20.2" E 018° 21' 23.6" ▪ F +27 (0)22-492-3470 ▪ T +27 (0)22-492-3540

Osbloed Wines

Somerset West-based Bertus van Niekerk's varied career includes a clerical one, hence some biblical wine names. With a boutique wine business ably assisted by oenology student son Hendrik, he sources grapes widely for the ranges. And he's having fun, as his wine names attest.

Icon range
★★★★ **Wonderbare Raadsman** ⓠ 13 (★★★☆) a cornucopia of bright red berry fruits, succulent & delicious. Light, gentle & yielding but with structure & length. Lighter than introductory **12**, blend of pinotage & parents cinsaut & pinot noir.

Calico range
Ebony ⓠ ★★★ Fynbos note to **13** from cab franc, with deep, black & blue berry palate. Cocoa nuance adds interest. Good structure, definition & length. Not retasted: **Auburn 13** ★★☆

Farm Animals range
★★★★ **Osbloed** ⓠ Textured five-way Bordeaux/shiraz blend from Philadelphia grapes. **12** ups game on **10** (★★★★). Serious & brooding, dark fynbos-tinged tobacco & hedgerow fruit.
Not tasted: **Hanekam, Blommetjie**.

Horses of the Apocalypse range
★★★★ **Black Horse Cabernet Sauvignon** ⓠ Pure typicity to nose & palate of **13**, which improves on **12** (★★★★). Balanced, poised & yet fresh. Yielding but defined structure, good length.

Pale Horse Riesling ⓠ ★★★ Apple & pear blossom delicacy of **13** mimics previous; broad & long. Not retasted: **Red Horse Cinsaut Noir 13** ★★★★ **White Horse Chardonnay 13** ★★☆ — FM

Location: Somerset West ▪ Map: Helderberg ▪ WO: Coastal/Durbanville/Stellenbosch/Elgin ▪ Est 2009 ▪ 1stB 2010 ▪ Tasting, sales & cellar tours daily — please call ahead ▪ Tasting fee R20, waived on purchase ▪ Owner(s) Bertus van Niekerk ▪ Cellarmaster(s) Bertus van Niekerk (Jan 2010) ▪ Winemaker(s) Bertus van Niekerk (Jan 2010), with Hendrik van Niekerk (2011) ▪ 600cs own label 75% red 25% white ▪ 33 Eagle Crescent Somerset West 7130 ▪ bertus@osbloed.com ▪ www.osbloed.com ▪ S 34° 5' 26.22" E 018° 51' 55.87" ▪ **T +27 (0)83-400-2999**

Oude Compagnies Post Private Cellar   ⓠ ⓞ
Advocate and vintner Jerry Swanepoel and family celebrate their farm's history as a 17th-century Dutch East India Company (VOC) outpost and mid-19th century wine producer with modern-era Rhône-style reds (and an envisaged '16 grenache-shiraz MCC bubbly). From Tulbagh mountainside, fynbos-ringed vines, vinified in an old stone cellar, they're unique in being officially sanctioned to bear the VOC logo.

Compagnies Wijn range
The Buchu Trail ⓠ ★★★ Fruit-forward shiraz-mourvèdre blend. **13** good savoury substance; like all reds, burly tannins need cutting with rich meat dishes. **The Homestead** ⓠ ★★★☆ Evocative cinnamon & mulled wine scents on **13** shiraz, grenache, mourvèdre blend. Rich but not overly heavy; lively acid & rounded tannins add satisfying drinkability. **Ruby Blanc** ⓠ ★★ More ruby than blanc, **14** rosé has billowing pinotage fruit, full body & dryish tail. Not retasted: **Cabernet Sauvignon 11** ★★ **Shiraz 11** ★★ Not tasted: **Grenache, Merlot, Mourvèdre, Pinotage, Pinotage Grand Reserve, Caap Ensemble, Buchu Berg, Cabernet Sauvignon-Merlot, Mourvèdre-Merlot.** — AL

Location/map/WO: Tulbagh ▪ Est 1996 ▪ 1stB 2003 ▪ Tasting, sales & cellar tours by appt ▪ Walking trail (flower season Sep-Oct) ▪ Hiking trail 1-2 days (sleepover on Obiqua mountain in own tent) ▪ Mountain bike (difficult) & 15km off-road motorbike trails ▪ Owner(s) Jerry Swanepoel Family Trust ▪ Cellarmaster(s) Jerry Swanepoel ▪ Winemaker(s) Jerry Swanepoel, with Ervin Koen (Jul 2011) ▪ Viticulturist(s) Marius Robert (consultant) ▪ 235ha/18ha (cab, grenache, merlot, mourv, ptage, shiraz) ▪ 70t/10,000cs own label 90% red 10% rosé + 20,000L bulk ▪ Other export brand: Buchu Berg ▪ PO Box 11 Tulbagh 6820 ▪ swanepoel@intekom.co.za ▪ S 33° 14' 56.9" E 019° 6' 49.1" ▪ F +27 (0)23-230-0840 ▪ **T +27 (0)23-230-0840**

Oude Denneboom   ⓠ ⓐ ⓞ
The De Waal family offer visitors to their Voor Paardeberg property a trio of delights: wine, wildlife and wide open spaces. Farming here for 140 years, their deep roots in Cape wine have sparked collaboration with equally established vintners, the Le Rouxs of Vendôme in Paarl and Loubsers of Kuypers Kraal in Philadelphia, to market their individual labels under the banner Kaapse Familie Wingerde (see listings).

Chenin Blanc ★★★☆ Was 'Grysbok Chenin Blanc'. Mouthwateringly fresh, overtly guava-toned **15** shows satisfying concentrated tropical fruit flavours. Also tasted: **Shiraz 13** ★★★☆ In abeyance: **Eland**, **Steenbok**. — IM

Location/WO: Paarl ▪ Map: Paarl & Wellington ▪ Map grid reference: C2 ▪ 1stB 2003 ▪ Tasting by appt; also available at Vendôme ▪ 4-star self-catering cottages ▪ Private game reserve ▪ Owner(s) De Waal family ▪ GM Willem de Waal ▪ Viticulturist(s) Willem de Waal ▪ 199ha/±62ha (cab, mourv, ptage, shiraz, chenin, nouvelle, viog) ▪ 600t/1,000s own label 60% red 40% white ▪ WIETA ▪ PO Box 2087 Windmeul 7630 ▪ info@oudedenneboom.co.za ▪ www.kaapsefamiliewingerde.com ▪ S 33° 37' 47.28" E 018° 51' 55.08" ▪ F +27 (0)86-552-2695 ▪ **T +27 (0)21-869-8072**

☐ **Oude Kaap** *see* DGB

Oude Meester

Venerable Oude Meester brandy was launched exactly 70 years ago, heralding the arrival of Distillers Corp (now Distell) as one of SA's leading producer-wholesalers. The four current bottlings showcase the array of styles a master distiller achieves through blending and barrel maturing over different timespans.

★★★★★ **Souverein** ⓢ A fairly recent label & amongst the elite of the Cape's older potstill brandies – minimum 18 years in oak. Lightish amber colour to yellow rim. Thrilling floral & spice notes, more delicate than Reserve, even more complex. Not a roughness or jagged edge. Serene, silken, very long.

★★★★☆ **Demant** ⓢ Fine value offered with this 3-10 year matured potstill brandy, introduced in 2006 to celebrate Distell's diamond jubilee. Stressing a fresh, lighter elegance rather than full richness, like all in this range. Satisfying blend of maturing floral notes along with fruitier youthful ones.

★★★★☆ **Reserve 12 Year Old** ⓢ Molten gold colour. Aromas suggest some development – nutty & spicy along with fruit & honeysuckle. Fuller, richer than Demant, as elegant & dry, with restrained oak backing. Complex, lingering, mellow finish.

VSOB ⓢ ★★★☆ Standard blended brandy, first step of a ladder of quality in this range. Good fruity nose & palate, some dry oak & sweet forcefulness. Great for mixing, but possible to sip solo. — WB, TJ

Oude Molen Distillery

The name Oude Molen harks back to the Stellenbosch 'home' of early 20th-century French-born distiller René Santhagens, who inspired local distillers to adopt the strict cognaçais methods of brandy-making, based on double distillation in copper potstills. But the distillery itself has been based in its classy, visitor-friendly forest setting in Elgin for several years. Having in 2013 linked up with Southern Cape Vineyards, owner of Barrydale and Ladismith winery/distilleries, Oude Molen is streamlining their internationally award-winning ranges and adopting the new industry-wide style of labelling designed to provide a uniform, more accurate and consumer-friendly indication of the style of brandy in the bottle (as elucidated in the Brandy Styles section of this guide). Fresh bottlings, boasting stylish new liveries, were being prepared at the time of going to press.

★★★★☆ **René Single Cask** ⓢ All potstill, minimum 6 year maturation. Label shows cask & bottle numbers (about 600 bottles in each). More refined than Solera; a little less showy on the nose, but loads of fruit & flowers, with hints of prune & caramel. Rich, but some real finesse, & a long, soft finish.

★★★★ **100 Reserve** ⓢ Potstill component of this blended brandy oak-matured 5 years before blending. Dried fruit notes & touch of creamy vanilla for smooth sipping, even without a mixer (43% alcohol).

★★★★ **VOV Rare Vintage Selection** ⓢ 14 years matured pure potstill. Lightish colour, medium rich; more oak & sweetness than others in range. Lovely aromas & flavours: fruit, flowers, nuts, vanilla.

Solera Grand Reserve ⓢ ★★★☆ 100% potstill matured for consistency in solera. Nutty sherry notes, some jasmine fragrance as part of a pleasing complexity. Smooth & subtly persistent. — WB, TJ

Location: Elgin ▪ Map: Elgin, Walker Bay & Bot River ▪ Distillery tours & tasting Mon-Fri 11-4 (booking advisable) Sat by appt only (for groups of 10 and more) ▪ Fee R50pp (incl tour & tasting) ▪ Brandy sales Mon-Fri 9-5 ▪ Closed Sun & all pub hols ▪ Tour groups ▪ Gift shop ▪ Conferences ▪ 4x4 trail ▪ MTB trail ▪ Brandy master(s) Kobus Gelderblom (Jun 2013, consultant) ▪ PO Box 494 Grabouw 7160 ▪ info@

oudemolen.co.za ▪ www.oudemolen.co.za ▪ S 34° 8' 27.77" E 019° 1' 15.64" ▪ F +27 (0)21-859-3192 ▪
T +27 (0)21-859-2517

☐ **Oude Rust** see Mooiuitsig Wine Cellars
☐ **Out of Africa** see Jacques Germanier

Overgaauw Wine Estate   ⓦ 🍴 ♿

There have been van Veldens — and the winery they built — at this Stellenboschkloof farm for well over
100 years. Four have held the title of winemaker, with young David succeeding most recently to his
father Braam (who still plays a role here), and it was a fine idea to include photographs of the quartet on
the wines' back labels. Much of historical import has happened here: Overgaauw was among the local
pioneers of Bordeaux-style red blends, chardonnay, and Portuguese 'port' varieties. Its merlot was the
first varietal bottling of the grape, and the sylvaner is now surely a unique contribution to Cape wine.

Overgaauw Estate range

★★★★ **Cabernet Sauvignon** ⓦ Unlike previous, serious-minded **12** not at all burly, though also fragrant. Savoury & vinous, with sweet fruit & dry tannins in quietly refined whole. Needs a few years.

★★★★ **Merlot** Dark cherries & choc on confident & convincing **13**. Medium bodied, elegant & fresh,
with dry but succulent-savoury tannic structure. Customary restrained & thoughtful oaking.

★★★★☆ **Tria Corda** ⓦ **12** blends cab, merlot & touch cab franc, as did bold **11** (★★★★), but this,
though fully ripe, returns to more graceful, restrained classicism of **09**. Subtle dry tannins in balance with
sweet ripe fruit & savoury vinosity. Already delicious, can only gain with a good few years.

★★★★ **Cape Vintage** ⓦ The oldest current port-style release in the winelands? Mature **94**, from six-
tet port varieties, as pleasant & moderate as usual in its levels of sweetness, richness, power & grip.

Sylvaner ★★★☆ Gentle fruity, floral fragrance on this unique-in-SA **15**. Easy to enjoy, but dry & quite
elegant, with a serious flinty structure. 'Amazing ageing potential' suggests the winemaker. Also tasted:
Touriga Nacional 14 ★★★☆ **Chardonnay 14** ★★★★ **Sauvignon Blanc 15** ★★★

Shepherd's Cottage range

Cabernet Sauvignon-Merlot ⓦ ★★★☆ Easygoing **13** touch ingratiatingly sweet (though firmly
built) for those who like an element of austerity; dead right for others. — TJ

Location/map/WO: Stellenbosch ▪ Map grid reference: D5 ▪ Est 1905 ▪ 1stB 1970 ▪ Tasting & sales Mon-Fri
9–4 Sat 10–2 ▪ Fee R20pp for groups of 6+ ▪ Closed Easter Fri-Mon, Dec 25/26 & Jan 1 ▪ Restaurant open for
lunch Fri-Sun from 12.30 (Sep-May only) T +27 (0)83-651-4003, booking essential ▪ Owner(s) Braam &
David van Velden ▪ Winemaker(s) David van Velden (Jan 2003) ▪ Viticulturist(s) David van Velden; Vinpro ▪
100ha/60ha (cabs s/f, merlot, touriga, chard, sauv, sylvaner) ▪ 60% red 40% white ▪ Other export brand:
Sandrivier ▪ HACCP, IPW ▪ PO Box 3 Vlottenburg 7604 ▪ info@overgaauw.co.za, restaurant@overgaauw.co.za ▪
www.overgaauw.co.za ▪ S 33° 56' 52.1" E 018° 47' 33.4" ▪ **T +27 (0)21-881-3815**

Overhex Wines International   ⓦ 🍴 ⓞ ⓐ ♿

The playful Balance logo of an elephant perched on a stool isn't only for fun; it also sums up the mantra
of this globally operating, Worcester-based wine business: balance in all things, from ethical trading and
staff empowerment to wines that seriously over-deliver on price (especially since top ranker Jean
Daneel's appointment as advisory winemaker). A warm welcome awaits at Balance Bistro, where executive chairman Gerhard van der Wath particularly recommends the three-course Sunday lunch.

Survivor range 🆕

★★★★ **Pinotage** Aged in new French oak, full-bodied preview **14** has dark chocolate, liquorice, spice
& chewy tannins in addition to abundant mulberry fruit, balanced despite alcohol over 14.5%.

★★★★ **Merlot-Cabernet Sauvignon** Previewed **14** has soft ripe plums & fruitcake spice from 60%
merlot, while 15 months in French oak has added vanilla sweetness to cab's blackcurrant core, slightly
warm finish (14.5% alcohol).

★★★★☆ **Chenin Blanc** ⊘ Standout in ambitious new range from Swartland fruit, **15** has appealing
floral nose with tangy sweet-sour apricot exploding on palate, creaminess balanced by sherbity acid, pinch
of turmeric to finish.

★★★★ **Sauvignon Blanc** Far more serious than its crisp & fruity Balance counterpart, Swartland-sourced **15** preview has tropical gooseberry, granadilla & zesty grapefruit notes against creamy backdrop from 40% wooded component.

Balance Winemaker's Selection

Cabernet Sauvignon ⊘ ★★★☆ Medium-bodied **14** delivers on richness promised by nose of sweet black berry fruit, soft & supple after initial prickle dissipates. **Chenin Blanc** ⊘ ★★★☆ There's a pleasant underlying creaminess to summery, floral **15**, dry with fresh acidity cutting through ripe cling peach & nectarine flavours. Also tasted: **Pinot Grigio 15** ★★★ Not retasted: **Pinot Noir 14** ★★★ **Sauvignon Blanc 14** ★★★ Not tasted: **Merlot, Pinotage, Shiraz, Chardonnay**.

Balance Best Blends

Cabernet Sauvignon-Merlot ⊘ ★★★ Easy-drinking **14** has ripe black fruit flavours & soft tannins, fantastic burger wine with a mere hint of pencil-shaving oak spice. **Shiraz Rosé** ⊘ ★★★ Ever so slightly off-dry **15** has bright red berry flavours & a pinch of cinnamon to add interest. Also tasted: **Semi-Sweet Muscat 14** ★★ **Sauvignon Blanc-Semillon** ⊘ **15** ★★★☆ Not tasted: **Pinotage-Shiraz, Chardonnay-Pinot Noir, Chenin Blanc-Colombar**. Discontinued: **Shiraz-Merlot**.

Balance Buddy range

Sweet Rosé ⊘ ★★★ NV party pink has 15% chenin added to pinotage, candyfloss nose, sweet but not cloying thanks to nice acidity. Not retasted: **Sweet White NV** ★★ **Sweet Red NV** ★★

Balance Sparklings

Sweet Temptation Sparkling ⊘ ★★ Fun **NV** rosé fizz from pinotage almost cooldrink-like with its sweet strawberry & glacé cherry flavours. Not retasted: **Boldly Brut Sparkling NV** ★★ **Lusciously Fruity Sparkling NV** ★★ — JG

Location/map: Worcester ▪ WO: Western Cape ▪ Est/1stB 2006 ▪ Tasting & sales Mon-Thu 8–5 Fri 8-4 Sat/Sun 9-4 ▪ Closed Easter Fri-Tue & Dec 22-Jan 6 ▪ Cellar tours by appt ▪ Balance Bistro Wed-Sun 10-4 ▪ Facilities for children ▪ Tour groups ▪ Conferences ▪ Weddings & functions ▪ Owner(s) G van der Wath ▪ GM Gert van Wyk ▪ Winemaker(s) Willie Malan (2002) & Ben Snyman (Dec 2010), with Dirk Rust (Jan 2012) ▪ Viticulturist(s) Dirk Bosman ▪ 10,500t ▪ 34% red 64% white 2% rosé ▪ ISO 22000, Fairtrade, WIETA ▪ PO Box 139 Worcester 6849 ▪ marketing@overhex.com ▪ www.overhex.com ▪ S 33° 39′ 28.6″ E 019° 30′ 55.8″ ▪ F +27 (0)23-347-1057 ▪ **T +27 (0)23-347-5012**

Overmeer Cellars

Enduring no-frills range (since 1996) by Distell, with modest alcohol levels. Variously in 3L and 5L packs.

Red ★★ NV pizza/pasta wine with medium body, soft, slightly herby berry fruit. **Late Harvest** ★★ Fresh, lightish tropical **NV** with balanced sweetness, clean finish. Also tasted: **Sweet Rosé NV** ★★ **Grand Cru NV** ★★ **Stein NV** ★★ — WB

☐ **Over the Mountain** *see* Seven Springs Vineyards
☐ **Overvaal** *see* Hartswater Wine Cellar

Owl & Vine

This negociant-style concern, in the business of creating cleverly packaged brands, has already been around a year or two. Simon Wibberley and David Cope (a hipster himself, who's learnt a thing or two about what young wine-drinkers want from running his wine bar, Publik, in Cape Town) work with different winemakers, renting cellar space in Stellenbosch. They aim at unpretentious drinkability, 'for people who are after a good, consistent wine without worrying about regional or varietal snobbery'.

Alphabetical Vin Ordinaire ★★★★ Dominated by cab & shiraz, **12** blend mixes pure fruit & fynbos aromas. Refreshing, clean-cut & stimulating, with a serious dry tannic structure. From Swartland & Stellenbosch grapes. **Dirty Julie Dry White** ★★★ 'A good white wine with bad intentions' say the producers about this characterful **14** from rather rare verdelho. Light floral charm, succulent & dry, without much in the way of intensity or length. — TJ, CvZ

Location: Cape Town ▪ WO: Stellenbosch/Western Cape ▪ Est 2010 ▪ 1stB 2008 ▪ Closed to public ▪
Owner(s) David Cope & Simon Wibberley ▪ 6,300ccs own label 87% red 13% white ▪ hello@
owlandvine.com ▪ www.alphabetical.co.za, www.owlandvine.com

Paardebosch Wines   ⓠ

Big changes at this historic Perdeberg farm, with top rankers David and Nadia Sadie joining lawyer Des
Kruger as partners in a project to make wines off the home vineyards (some very old) within the guidelines of the Swartland Independent Producers. 'We believe in a pure, fresh and natural style where site
and soil are at work,' they affirm. The venerable cellar was thoroughly overhauled in time for the 2015
harvest – the Sadies' own-label wines (see David & Nadia Sadie) are also now made here.

★★★★ **Pinotage** Gorgeously scented **14** (★★★★☆) even more exciting than last-made **12**. Ripe but
   light-feeling (12.5% alcohol), almost delicate but firmly structured, with fine dry tannins – a combo rare
   in pinotage. Matured in old oak, preserving fresh purity of the fruit. Deliciously serious – & vice versa.

★★★★ **Rosé 15** from 6 red varieties, 60% in old barrels for 5 months. Like **14** (★★★★), though a touch
   more profound, fresh & gently fruited with an earthy element, round & textured. For serious winelovers.

★★★★ **Chenin Blanc** Quietly elegant, lightly oaked **14** (now bottled) has fresh fynbos notes, with ripe
   subtle fruit, all in balance with understated structural force & mineral vitality. — TJ

Location: Malmesbury ▪ Map/WO: Swartland ▪ Est/1stB 2014 ▪ Tasting by appt & subject to availability ▪
Owner(s) David & Nadia Sadie, Des Kruger ▪ Winemaker(s)/viticulturist(s) David & Nadia Sadie (2014) ▪
45ha/16ha (malbec, ptage, chenin, sem) ▪ 25t/2,500cs own label 45% red 55% white ▪ Swartland Independent Producers ▪ info@davidnadiasadie.co.za, deskruger21@gmail.com ▪ www.davidnadiasadie.co.za ▪ S
33° 32' 41.41" E 018° 49' 36.14" ▪ **T +27 (0)72-375-4336/+27 (0)82-565-4218**

PaardenKloof   ⓠ

PaardenKloof, the first wholly black-owned wine estate in the Overberg, resides in a valley on the northern face of Babylonstoren Mountain, which separates Bot River from Hemel-en-Aarde. Most of the 1,430
ha, fynbos-rich property is conserved but ±23 ha of vineyard were established from 2004 and the first
vintage pressed in 2008. Only ±40% of the harvest is vinified by contracted winemakers for the boutique label, the balance sold to other premium brands. An on-site tasting venue is in the planning.

PaardenKloof Private Collection

★★★★☆ **Die Fynboshuis Cabernet Sauvignon** Debuted as 'Renosterveld', since renamed. Bright &
   concentrated red berry fruit, exotic dried flower aromas & flavours on **10**, with outstanding structure &
   dimension: elegant, lush & sumptuous with persistence.

Peter Clarke Collection

★★★★ **The Long Road Shiraz** Aromatic plum, fynbos & white pepper aromas on **10**. Perfectly judged
   oak provides framework for lush, bright fruit, rounded mouthfeel & restraint.

★★★★ **Bend In The Road Sauvignon Blanc** Cool-climate expression, **14** with lime & grapefruit on
   nose; bright & focused flavours, refreshing orchard & fynbos notes with piquant conclusion.

Not retasted: **Gaiety Sauvignon Blanc 2011** ★★★ — WB

Location/WO: Bot River ▪ Map: Elgin, Walker Bay & Bot River ▪ Est 2003 ▪ 1stB 2007 ▪ Tasting & tours by
appt ▪ Sales Mon-Fri 9-5 ▪ Winemaker(s) Kobie Viljoen, Niels Verburg, Christo Versfeld & Adam Mason ▪
Viticulturist(s) Kevin Watt (Dec 2006) ▪ 23.6ha (cab, pinot, shiraz, sauv) ▪ BWI, IPW, WIETA ▪ PO Box 381
Bot River 7185 ▪ info@paardenkloof.co.za ▪ www.paardenkloof.co.za ▪ S 34° 17' 44.1" E 019° 14' 5.4" ▪
F +27 (0)28-284-9419 ▪ **T +27 (0)28-284-9824**

Packwood Wines   ⓠ ⑪ ⌂ ⓐ

Packwood, on the periphery of Knysna Forest, is a country estate owned by Peter and Vicky Gent (originally from England), complete with luxury accommodation, dairy herd and small vineyard, grapes from
which Vicky herself vinifies with advice from estimable Teddy Hall (Teddy Hall Wines).

★★★★ **Sauvignon Blanc** 15 preview shows more of tangy verve & freshness of **12** than **13** (★★★). Tight & flinty, with racy grapefruit flavours. Fine intensity & cool-picked purity & length. Good food wine. **14** untasted.

Pinot Noir ⊘ ★★★ Pleasantly savoury **13**, earthy & meaty notes, some stewed red fruit & broad structure. **Pinot Noir Rosé** (NEW) **15** pre-bottling sample too unformed to rate conclusively. Not tasted: **Gent Méthode Cap Classique**. — MW

Location/WO: Plettenberg Bay ▪ Map: Klein Karoo & Garden Route ▪ Est 2006 ▪ 1stB 2009 ▪ Tasting & sales Mon-Fri 11-3 Sat/Sun & pub hols by prior arrangement ▪ Cheese & wine lunch – book ahead ▪ Small tour groups by appt ▪ Farm produce ▪ Hikes ▪ Mountain biking trail ▪ 4-star country house & self-catering cottages ▪ Owner(s) Peter & Vicky Gent ▪ Winemaker(s) Vicky Gent, advised by Teddy Hall (consultant) ▪ Viticulturist(s) Vicky Gent (Jan 2006) ▪ 380ha/3.5ha (pinot, chard, sauv) ▪ 5t/10,000cs own label 30% red 70% white ▪ PO Box 622 Knysna 6570 ▪ vicky@packwood.co.za ▪ www.packwood.co.za ▪ S 34° 0' 18.77" E 023° 13' 43.33" ▪ **T +27 (0)44-532-7614**

☐ **Paddagang** see Tulbagh Winery

Painted Wolf Wines   ⊘

This close-knit 'pack' is as peripatetic as its beloved endangered African Wild Dog (aka Painted Wolf). Its members (worldwide stakeholders contributing equity or skills) are led by winemaker Jeremy Borg and photographer wife Emma. Jeremy's team sources grapes widely for vinifying in various cellars. Emma visits 'the more challenging' markets (Japan, Russia, Hong Kong, China), uses long-standing tourism connections to woo Africa, and leaves the UK, SA and Canada to Jeremy. Their conservation commitment goes beyond building their always interesting brand: they donate to and fund-raise for SA's Endangered Wildlife Trust, UK's Tusk and Canada's Pacific Wild.

Black Pack range

★★★★ **Stellenbosch Pinotage** ⊘ Lovely nose, showing fresh banana loaf, brooding fruit; seriously oaked **11** has better balance & composure of fruit & oak than **10** (★★★☆).

★★★★ **Pictus IV** Flagship blend of Swartland shiraz, grenache & mourvèdre. **12** combines power & charm in succulent, rich-fruited & polished style. Similar to **11**, which was 'Pictus III'.

★★★★ **Roussanne** Naturally fermented in 50% new French oak, **14** shows shy peach, dried apricot & lovely composure; floral but also nutty & creamy, following to distinct wet stone pithiness. WO Paarl.

Not retasted: **Chenin Blanc 12** ★★★☆ Not tasted: **Merlot**, **Shiraz**.

Pack range

★★★★ **Lycaon Grenache** ⊘ ⊙ **13** from Swartland, with dollop shiraz, is smooth, fragrant & earthy. Succulent & understated, shows a silky tannin structure & savoury finish.

★★★★ **Guillermo Pinotage** Super varietal expression from Swartland, **13** preview has a fresh red-berry intensity laced with coconut & vanilla; packed with flavour yet focused through to the spicy end.

★★★★ **Penny Viognier** Ex Swartland, organically grown, wild-yeast-fermented **14** now bottled shows exuberant fruit, creamy peach melba with supportive vanilla oak & textured mouthfeel.

Not retasted: **Rosalind Pinotage Rosé 14** ★★★

Peloton range (NEW)

★★★★ **Blanc** Viognier & chenin blend with roussanne, chardonnay & marsanne hits the mark in **14** with intense orchard fruit tones, creamy mouthfeel from some oaking. Balanced & focused.

Rouge ★★★☆ Succulent & fruity blend of shiraz, pinotage, mourvèdre & grenache; pre-bottling, **13** has the yum factor with rich, smooth & satisfying structure, lovely blueberry top note.

Cape 'Hunting' Blends

Madach ⊘ ★★★☆ Plums & ripe berry allure on **12** from mix pinotage, grenache, cinsaut. Savoury & juicy, showing toasty oak; dry finish. Not tasted: **Lekanyane**.

The Den Comfort Wines

Shiraz (NEW) ★★★ Coffee, dried herb & spice attractions on ex-tank **14** from Paarl. Touch of grenache adds to juicy, fruity enjoyment. **Chenin Blanc** ★★★☆ **15** has honeysuckle, ripe apples & spice, supported by good balancing acid, gentle oaking (10%) & dollop chardonnay adding some grip, complexity. Swartland WO. Also tasted: **Cabernet Sauvignon 14 ★★★ Pinotage 14 ★★★ Rosé 15 ★★★ Sauvignon Blanc 15 ★★★** — WB

Location: Paarl ▪ Map: Paarl & Wellington ▪ Map grid reference: E6 ▪ WO: Coastal/Paarl/Swartland/Stellenbosch ▪ Est/1stB 2007 ▪ Tasting & sales by appt Mon-Fri 10-5 ▪ Fee R50 ▪ Closed Easter Fri-Mon, Dec 25 & Jan 1 ▪ Owner(s) Jeremy & Emma Borg, & 16 'pack members' ▪ Cellarmaster(s) Madre van der Walt ▪ Winemaker(s) Jeremy Borg ▪ 20ha (grenache, mourv, ptage, shiraz, viog) ▪ 30t/18,000cs own label 75% red 20% white 5% rosé ▪ Other export brand: Pedals ▪ PO Box 1489 Suider Paarl 7624 ▪ sales@paintedwolfwines.com ▪ www.paintedwolfwines.com ▪ S 33° 46' 14.8" E 018° 57' 14.6" ▪ **T +27 (0)21-863-2492**

☐ **Palesa Fairtrade** *see* uniWines Vineyards
☐ **Pandora's Box** *see* Nicholson Smith
☐ **Pantére** *see* Knorhoek Wines
☐ **Papillon** *see* Van Loveren Family Vineyards

Paradisum

This is the rather exotic by-blow of Peter-Allan Finlayson, whose grapes for his Crystallum label mostly originate in the Hemel-en-Aarde: Paradisum was conceived as a Swartland project, but home-turf fruit creeps in. The approach is non-interventionist and exploratory, with techniques like whole-bunch fermentation. The wine is now made at Gabriëlskloof, where Peter-Allan is winemaker.

★★★★ Paradisum 12 (★★★★★) drops the mourvèdre that was in **11**, adds 30% cinsaut to 40% shiraz (both ex Swartland) & Hemel-en-Aarde grenache. The result is both delicious & elegant: dry, restrained, not obviously fruity, but with lovely sweet red-fruit overtones. Firm grip; will repay keeping. — TJ

☐ **Paradyskloof** *see* Vriesenhof Vineyards
☐ **Parker Family** *see* Altydgedacht Estate

Paserene

'Wine is a massively complex, sophisticated, living thing,' says Vilafonté winemaker Martin Smith. His own-brand name derives from the Passeriformes order of birds, including the swallow depicted on his award-winning labels (reflecting his decade as flying winemaker between SA and California). See the bird alight on a girl's finger on his upcoming third wine, Union…

★★★★☆ Marathon 13 undisclosed field blend has improved in bottle. Has similar mulberry & plum fruit, lingering berry finish rounding out fine-grained tannins from 16 months in barrel (30% new) as last edition's tank sample, with extra violet & jasmine complexity.

★★★★ Chardonnay Now bottled, **13** from Elgin vines is amalgamated & enticing: roasted pine nuts & almond, chamomile & stonefruit attractions; clean-cut acidity & citrus farewell. Natural ferment/matured 16 months in old oak. — GM

Location: Stellenbosch ▪ WO: Western Cape/Elgin ▪ Est/1stB 2013 ▪ Closed to public ▪ Owner(s)/viticulturist(s) Martin Smith ▪ Cellarmaster(s)/winemaker(s) Martin Smith (Jan 2013) ▪ 6t/560cs own label 60% red 40% white ▪ info@greatscottcreative.com ▪ **T +27 (0)71-379-2674**

Passages Wine

American couple Ron Gault and Charlayne Hunter-Gault (eminent banker and journalist) are fortunate enough to now divide their time between presidentially fragranced Martha's Vineyard on the US East Coast and sun-kissed Florida, but the passion for their SA-sourced wine brand (established to support democratic SA, made by Ernst & Co) is undimmed, and in fact is spreading to the US West Coast.

Merlot ★★★ Distinctly menthol-edged blackcurrant fruit, juicy & sappy, leaner body on **12**, with dash of malbec. **Cabernet Sauvignon-Merlot ★★★★** Just a splash (8%) of merlot in **12**, which is opulently fruity, soft textured & juicy. Not retasted: **Pinotage 13 ★★★★ Chardonnay 13 ★★★** — GdB

Location: Stellenbosch ▪ WO: Stellenbosch/Wellington/Coastal ▪ 1stB 2006 ▪ Closed to public ▪ Owner(s) Ronald T Gault & Charlayne Hunter-Gault ▪ Cellarmaster(s)/winemaker(s) Ernst Gouws (2007, consultant) ▪ (cab, merlot, ptage, chard) ▪ ±10,000cs own label 70% red 30% white ▪ gaultronald@gmail.com ▪ www.passageswine.com

Patatsfontein

In a salvage operation that's welcomely replaying across the winelands, Boschkloof's youngblood winemaker Reenen Borman is partnering with Montagu growers Fritz Schoon and Henk Kotze to give an old and special vineyard, previously anonimised at the local co-op, 'a chance to stand on its own feet and show what it can deliver'. Chenin/steen is the (superb) opener, Reenen noting the variety is no longer associated with quality wine from the area 'but we're changing that'. Prepare for more exhilaration as other seniors get to show their 'massive potential to become some of SA's best'.

★★★★☆ **Steen** 14 single-vineyard chenin from Montagu has Old World styling, faint stonefruit, lemongrass & green olive notes, & very dry; earthy & mineral, moderate alcohol, perfect balance. Nothing overt, has quiet assurance. More a 'sense of being' than a wine. — CR, CvZ

Location/WO: Montagu ▪ 1stB 2014 ▪ Closed to public ▪ Owner(s) Fritz Schoon, Reenen Borman & Henk Kotze ▪ Winemaker(s) Reenen Borman ▪ 220cs own label

☐ **Pater** *see* Van Loveren Family Vineyards

Paul Cluver Estate Wines   ⓠ ⑪ ⓒ ⓖ

Cluver family farm De Rust, dating from 1896, lies in the Kogelberg Biosphere in cool-climate Elgin. Visionary Paul Cluver snr pioneered commercial winefarming here in the late 1980s and became a leader in environmental and social sustainability. The younger generation, who subscribe to the same principles, took over in 2003 (4 of the 5 siblings are involved here) and continue to build the reputation of the thriving and diverse business. Boundlessly energetic and savvy Paul jnr and his equally switched-on brother-in-law, winemaker Andries Burger, almost literally leave no stone unturned to produce ever-finer and terroir-expressive wines. They're now starting to pick at 10 pm so the grapes are 'ready by 6 am' and cool enough to obviate mash chilling. Above, on the cellar roof, a new solar array is obviating much of the conventional-power need.

CWG Auction Reserves

★★★★☆ **Pinot Noir** Grapes selected from the highest vineyard, aged 11 months in 25% new oak. Red cherry fruit, coriander-spiced cured meat & earthy flavours enthral on **13**. Complex structure, silky, terrific lift to finish. 90 cases produced.

★★★★☆ **The Wagon Trail Chardonnay** Bunch-pressed grapes, naturally fermented in 33% new oak for **14**. Steely aromas of lemon peel, apple blossom & nutmeg lead to richness, gaining complexity in the mouth; dense, with loads of energy from 27 year old vines.

Paul Cluver Estate Wines range

★★★★ **Pinot Noir** 4 clones, some natural fermentation in **14**; perfumed floral & lush strawberry notes, silkier tannins than any pinot in this stable. Soft & ripe, with a moderate concentration & juicy finish.

★★★★ **Seven Flags Pinot Noir** Only the best barrels of Burgundian clone 113 for flagship label; improved **13**'s (★★★★★) delicately spiced black cherries light-trip on the tongue, the well-judged oaking (20% new) provides a supportive framework. Seamless, refined & elegant. Only 600 cases. **12** more restrained.

★★★★☆ **Chardonnay** Wild-fermented, barrel-selected **14** shows steely aromas & flavours of lime, apple blossom, wet stone & clove — no edges, no excess weight, just fruit intensity & elegant restraint. Refined, balanced & textured — worth cellaring.

★★★★★ **Seven Flags Chardonnay** Winemaker's true expression of terroir, both barrel & site selected. Buttered almond cake, clementine & lemon blossom fragrance on natural ferment **14**, 25% in new oak. Great depth, volume of fruit & oak flavours, yet delicate & understated. Only 360 cases.

★★★★☆ **Gewürztraminer** ⊘ Off-dry styled but beautifully balanced **14**. Spicy ginger wraps around rosepetal, honeydew melon & Turkish delight. Breadth & depth, with lemon drop precision on the finish. Classy fusion food partner.

★★★★ **Close Encounter Riesling 14** sweeter (34.2 g/l) than sibling but superbly balanced, tasting drier courtesy of racy acidity. Delicate bouquet of sweetness & freshness in featherlight (±9% alcohol) delivery.

★★★★ **Dry Encounter Riesling 14**'s ±8 g/l sugar offset by tangy lime, fynbos & mineral underpin; part large-oak fermented. Taut & intense, with zesty balance & lingering farewell.

★★★★☆ **Riesling Noble Late Harvest** Slimline elegant packaging & appealingly low 10.5% alcohol for this exceptional botrytis dessert wine, partly wooded, packed with fragrant & intense dried apricot, lime & honey flavours on dazzling **14**.

Also tasted: **Village Pinot Noir 14** ★★★★☆ Not tasted: **Sauvignon Blanc**. — WB

Location/WO: Elgin ▪ Map: Elgin, Walker Bay & Bot River ▪ Est 1896 ▪ 1stB 1997 ▪ Tasting & sales Mon-Fri 9–5 Sat/Sun (summer) 9–3 & Sat/Sun (winter) 10-2; tasting centre closed Sundays for period of 6 weeks in winter (Jul-mid Aug), phone ahead to confirm ▪ Fee R50 for groups, limited to 10 pax per group ▪ Closed Easter weekend, Dec 25/26 & Jan 1 ▪ Conservation area (part of Kogelberg Biosphere UNESCO heritage site) ▪ MTB track & bike park open to public, fee payable ▪ Open air amphitheatre hosting concerts Nov-Mar ▪ Fresh Restaurant T +27 (0)71-563-6020 | niki@freshatpaulcluver.co.za, booking essential ▪ Owner(s) Cluver family ▪ Cellarmaster(s) Andries Burger (Nov 1996) ▪ Winemaker(s) Andries Burger (Nov 1996), with Drew Harty (Oct 2013) ▪ Viticulturist(s) Rudi Zandberg (Dec 2013) & Kevin Watt (Mar 2005, consultant) ▪ 80ha (pinot, chard, gewürz, riesling, sauv) ▪ 20% red 80% white ▪ Brands for clients: Woolworths, ScruCap ▪ BWI champion ▪ PO Box 48 Grabouw 7160 ▪ info@cluver.com ▪ www.cluver.com ▪ S 34° 10' 6.2" E 019° 5' 8.1" ▪ F +27 (0)21-844-0150 ▪ **T +27 (0)21-844-0605**

☐ **Paul de Villiers** *see* Landskroon Wines
☐ **Paulina's Reserve** *see* Rickety Bridge Winery
☐ **Paul René** *see* Wonderfontein

Paul Roos Farming   ⓠ (NEW)

Educator and revered head of the top Stellenbosch school that bears his name, the late Paul Roos was born on the farm currently owned by his relative, Tjuks Roos. With brother Johan, Tjuks for many years has championed the education of staff and particularly their children, and this new label, vinified and mentored by Gus Dale, affords winelovers the opportunity to support the worthy creche-to-varsity cause through purchases of the blends below via web/email and an on-site tasting and education venue.

★★★★ **Die Filantroop** Naturally barrel-fermented shiraz (dollops cab, merlot, pinotage), **14** offers violet-scented blue berries; harmonious & layered, ripe fruit balanced by powdery tannins.

★★★★ **Die Skoolhoof** 'Nail biting' 51 day natural ferment for **14** chenin, chardonnay (20%); white stonefruit & florals, ripe & rich yet tantalisingly dry, mere 20% new oak a deft touch. — WB, FM

Location/WO: Stellenbosch ▪ Map: Helderberg ▪ Est 2008 ▪ 1stB 2014 ▪ Tasting, sales & cellar tours by appt ▪ Owner(s) Tjuks & Johan Roos, Paul Roos Farming Trust ▪ Winemaker(s) Augustus Dale (Jun 2012), with Ricardo Adams (1998) ▪ Viticulturist(s) Pete Adams (1974), with Jan Julius ▪ 24ha/18ha (cab, merlot, ptage, shiraz, chard, chenin) ▪ 6t/±700cs own label 50% red 50% white ▪ IPW, GlobalGAP, WIETA ▪ PO Box 397 Stellenbosch 7599 ▪ info@paulrooswine.com ▪ www.paulrooswine.com ▪ S 34° 0' 57.5" E 018° 49' 2.6" ▪ F +27 (0)86-645-6706 ▪ **T +27 (0)21-855-3628**

Paul Wallace Wines   ⓠ

'Witnessing every moment of the changing seasons' is one of the perks of finally settling on their Elgin farm, say leading viticultural adviser Paul Wallace and wife Nicky, aka 'Nix', the dynamo behind the family brand. Son Mark and Elsenburg classmate Vanessa Simkiss, winemaker at nearby Highlands Road, are the hands behind the sweet addition to the range. Also new is a red blend, sold only from the tasting room, where a convivial atmosphere, rugby on the TV and soup on the stove in winter are also offered.

★★★★ **Black Dog Malbec** Big boy in the range, named for Jake the Labrador-Rottweiler cross. **12** returns to full power with concentrated black fruit & spice. Good acid lift to muscular structure. **11** skipped.

★★★★ **Crackerjack** (NEW) Late-released **09** blend of cab, merlot & malbec, 26 months in French barriques. Mature & soft but far from old, showing (new) leather, cedar, bouquet garni & bellpepper nuances. Obvious cool origin.

★★★★☆ **The Nix Noble Late Harvest** (NEW) Favourable **14** vintage conditions allowed this excellent older-oak-matured botrytis dessert, honouring the lady of the house. Intensely rich & varied flavours — apricot, pineapple, honeycomb & jasmine — but vibrant, showing sauvignon blanc's suitability for the style.

Also tasted: **Brave Heart Pinot Noir 14** ★★★★ **Little Flirt Sauvignon Blanc 14** ★★★ — HJ

Location/WO: Elgin ▪ Map: Elgin, Walker Bay & Bot River ▪ Est/1stB 2004 ▪ Tasting facility open Saturdays, other days by appt or when open sign is displayed ▪ Chocolate & wine pairing ▪ Owner(s)/viticulturist(s) Paul Wallace ▪ Winemaker(s) Paul Wallace, advised by various other winemakers ▪ 25ha/10.5ha (malbec, pinot, sauv) ▪ 90t/1,000cs own label 60% red 40% white ▪ BWI, IPW ▪ PO Box 141 Elgin 7180 ▪ wallovale@mweb.co.za ▪ www.wallovale.co.za ▪ S 34° 12' 58.67" E 019° 03' 32.18 ▪ F +27 (0)86-646-3694 ▪ **T +27 (0)21-848-9744/+27 (0)83-255-1884/+27 (0)82-572-1406**

☐ **Pavillion** see Boschendal Wines
☐ **Peacock Wild Ferment** see False Bay Vineyards

Pearl Mountain   (🍷) (🍴) (📷)

Previously listed as Retief Wines, Pearl Mountain's brand home in the heights above Paarl is a happening place, with the recently opened Mediterranean-style Blacksmith's Kitchen restaurant and tasting venue abuzz with visitors, a wedding/function venue under construction and 3 ha of vines being redeveloped. Consultant wine man Robert Frater has been busy too, creating a charming new wooded chardonnay.

Retief range

★★★★ **Wagon Trail Shiraz** Revisited **12** now much more integrated & shapely, rich fruit flavours ably supported by firm controlled tannins. Shows better than last-tasted **05** (★★★).

★★★★ **Avis Chardonnay** (NEW) Previewed **14** marked but attractive toast/toffee wood influence, butteriness, nicely underpinned by crisp lemon curd flavour & hint of tropical fruit in the lingering finale.

Not retasted: **Three Oaks Cabernet Sauvignon 12** ★★★ **Above The Mist Merlot 12** ★★★

Stubborn Man range

Not tasted: **Chardonnay Unwooded**. — DB

Location/WO: Paarl ▪ Map: Paarl & Wellington ▪ Map grid reference: E4 ▪ Est 1747 ▪ 1stB 2004 ▪ Tasting & sales Tue-Sat 11.30-5 Sun 11.30-4 ▪ Closed Mondays, Dec 25 & Jan 1 ▪ Blacksmith's Kitchen Tue-Sat 11.30-9.30 Sun 11.30-4 ▪ Weddings & functions ▪ Owner(s) Pearl Mountain Wines (Pty) Ltd ▪ Winemaker(s) Robert Frater (2004, De Zoete Inval) ▪ Viticulturist(s) Graham Retief ▪ 11.8ha (cab, merlot, shiraz, chard, chenin, sauv) ▪ 92t/13,300cs own label 75% red 25% white ▪ PO Box 709 Northern Paarl 7623 ▪ info@pearlmountain.co.za ▪ www.pearlmountain.co.za ▪ S 33° 41' 44.4" E 018° 57' 11.1" ▪ F 021-872-9983 ▪ **T 021-872-9507/+27 (0)21-870-1550 restaurant & tasting**

☐ **Pearly Bay** see KWV
☐ **Pecan Stream** see Waterford Estate
☐ **Pedals** see Painted Wolf Wines
☐ **Pegalle** see Bonview Wines
☐ **Pella** see Super Single Vineyards
☐ **Peloton** see Painted Wolf Wines
☐ **Percheron** see Boutinot South Africa

Perdeberg Winery   (🍷) (🍴) (🛍) (📷)

If the oft-repeated phrase 'quality wine in made is the vineyard' is true, the 33 owner-growers of Perdeberg Winery believe they have an inherent advantage. With well over 2,000 ha in various demarcated areas, they have many different sites from which to vinify. The vines are 75% unirrigated, 50% bushvine and average yields a modest 7.8 t/ha – quality potentiators that increasingly are realised – and recognised by influencers around the world. The brand persona, with the striped 'horses' in the name of the winery and its mountain backdrop, remains unpretentious and friendly to the environment, people and purses. See also Waka Waka, Bottelary Winery, Saam and Perdeberg Winery The Vineyard Collection.

Dryland Collection

★★★★ **Cabernet Sauvignon** ⓐ Substantial, expressive **12** shows class after promising **11** debut. Dense & dark, with plush, supple fruit core & solid tannin backbone. Good value, too.

★★★★ **Pinotage** ⓐ Stylish expression of variety, **12** emphasises vibrant red fruit while reining in wilder tendencies. Elegant & plush, like **11**.

★★★★ **Shiraz** ⓐ Rhône-like pepper & scrub spicing on big, opulent & fruity **12**. Hefty tannin & appealing sinuous minerality should integrate & soften with time. Confirms class of **11**.

★★★★ **Joseph's Legacy** Shiraz-led **13** blend with cab, petit verdot & mourvèdre is elegant & fragrant, showing dark fruit coiled around supple tannins. Will age 5-6 years.

★★★★ **Barrel Fermented Chenin Blanc** 2 vintages reviewed: **13** (★★★★★), revisited, has benefitted from extra year; seamless integration of fruit & judicious part-oaking for an intense core of pure apple, pear & mineral notes with great persistence. A class act. **14** is similar but sweeter & not as complex.

★★★★ **Chenin Blanc** Bright stone/tropical fruit on unoaked **14**. Creamy & rich from lees-stirring, with delicious pink grapefruit lift to finish.

> **Sauvignon Blanc** ⓦ ★★★☆ Upfront green peppers, fynbos & tropical fruit fragrance announce improved **14**. Good expression of variety with a lime twist finish. WO Coastal.

Not retasted: **Pinot Noir-Chardonnay 14** ★★★☆ Not tasted: **Chardonnay-Viognier**.

Speciality range

★★★★ **Méthode Cap Classique Pinot Noir Rosé** Second disgorgement of **12** crisply dry traditional-method sparkling offers delicate strawberry cheesecake flavours, fine mousse & yeasty finish. Harmonious & delicious. Coastal WO.

★★★★ **Méthode Cap Classique Chenin Brut** New dégorgement of **12** presents crunchy apple fruit over shortbread & brioche, delivered on a fine, lingering creamy mousse. Underscores chenin's versatility.

★★★★☆ **Weisser Riesling** ⓐ Impressive Natural Sweet shows this noble variety to benefit. Piercing acid scythes through layers of honeyed raisin essence. **11** vinified in seasoned barrels.

Rex Equus range

Occasional release: **Red Blend**.

Popular range

> **Pinotage** ⊘ ⓦ ★★★☆ Ripe plums delight on **13**, juicy, with hints of spice. Be adventurous & try with grilled sardines.

Shiraz ⊘ ★★★☆ Mulberries & savoury notes on **13**, welcoming & moreish, with dry fynbos finish.
Chardonnay ⓝ ★★★ Mouthfilling **14** is light & bright with orchard fruit flavours & zesty goodbye.
Chenin Blanc ★★★ Tropical fruit flavours on bright **15** party wine. Will not disappoint its many fans.
Sparkling Rosé ★★★ Candyfloss pink **15** is fun, low in alcohol & offers not-too-sweet apple & berry flavours. Also tasted: **Cabernet Sauvignon 13** ★★★ **Merlot 13** ★★★ **Cabernet Sauvignon-Merlot 13** ★★★ **Sauvignon Blanc 15** ★★★ Not tasted: **Sparkling Chenin Blanc, Soft Smooth Red**.
In abeyance: **Rosé**. — WB

Location: Paarl ▪ Map: Paarl & Wellington ▪ Map grid reference: B3 ▪ WO: Paarl/Coastal ▪ Est 1941 ▪ 1stB 1942 ▪ Tasting & sales Mon-Fri 8—5 Sat 9.30—2 ▪ Closed Easter Fri-Mon, Dec 25/26 & Jan 1 ▪ Cellar tours Mon-Fri by appt ▪ Meals, pre-booked week in advance, for groups of 10+ ▪ BYO picnic ▪ Annual October festival ▪ Owner(s) 33 shareholders ▪ Cellarmaster(s) Albertus Louw (Oct 2008) ▪ Winemaker(s) Riaan Möller (Dec 2006) & Dylan Dowell-Ellis (Sep 2014) ▪ Viticulturist(s) Heinie Nel (Jul 2013) ▪ 6,000ha/2,564ha (cab, cinsaut, merlot, ptage, shiraz, chard, chenin, sauv) ▪ 18,000t/300,000cs own label 63% red 37% white ▪ BWI, HACCP, IPW, WIETA ▪ PO Box 214 Paarl 7620 ▪ info@perdeberg.co.za ▪ www.perdeberg.co.za ▪ S 33° 39' 30.00" E 018° 49' 37.00" ▪ F +27 (0)21-869-8245 ▪ **T +27 (0)21-869-8244**

Perdeberg Winery The Vineyard Collection

Perdeberg Winery's vineyard footprint covers well over 2,000 hectares around Paarl, Malmesbury, Durbanville and Stellenbosch, and from this trove of vines, the team says, 'small parcels with unique identities and of high quality' are selected to bottle for this debut label.

Pinotage ★★★ Sweet plum fruit on balanced, easy **13**; freshness from unoaked component. **Shiraz** ★★★ Spicy dark berry flavours on uncomplicated **13**, grip from robust tannins, savoury ending. **Chenin Blanc** ★★★ Bright summer orchard fruits abound on **14**, deliciously dry, with a zippy finish. — WB

Location/WO: Paarl ▪ Tasting & sales at Perdeberg Winery ▪ Owner(s) 33 shareholders ▪ Cellarmaster(s) Albertus Louw (Oct 2008) ▪ Winemaker(s) Riaan Möller (Dec 2006) & Dylan Dowell-Ellis (Sep 2014) ▪ Viticulturist(s) Heinie Nel (Jul 2013) ▪ PO Box 214 Paarl 7620 ▪ info@perdeberg.co.za ▪ www.perdeberg.co.za ▪ F +27 (0)21-869-8245 ▪ **T +27 (0)21-869-8244**

☐ **Pernod Ricard** *see* Long Mountain Wine Company

Peter Bayly Wines ⓟ

'Living free range' in Calitzdorp's secluded Groenfontein Valley, Peter and Yvonne Bayly handcraft Portuguese varieties planted in ancient shale soils. Demand for the more recent unfortified blend, Peter Bayly III (Three), is such that they're contemplating One and Two, while continuing with their first love, 'port'.

★★★★ **Cape Vintage** Attractive port-style **10** from touriga (44%) with tinta & souzão. Bright raisin, choc & orange peel giving way to concentrated fruit, leather & spicy warmth. Will benefit from few years keeping. Also in 375 ml.

III ★★★ Cloud of dark berries & some chocolate on **13** give way to more meaty, savoury notes on blend of three (unfortified) Portuguese varieties. Bit thicker & less fun than **12**. Not retasted: **Cape Late Bottled Vintage 08** ★★★ **Cape White NV** ★★★ Not tasted: **Cape Pink**. — CM

Location/WO: Calitzdorp ▪ Map: Klein Karoo & Garden Route ▪ Est 2002 ▪ 1stB 2004 ▪ Tasting, sales & tours by appt ▪ Owner(s) Peter Bayly Wines (Pty) Ltd ▪ Winemaker(s)/viticulturist(s) Peter Bayly ▪ 6.6ha/1.2ha (tinta, touriga, souzão) ▪ ±8t/±1,320cs own label ▪ PO Box 187 Calitzdorp 6660 ▪ info@baylys.co.za ▪ www.peterbayly.co.za ▪ S 33° 27' 16.70" E 021° 45' 34.86" ▪ F +27 (0)86-513-2727 ▪ **T +27 (0)44-213-3702**

☐ **Peter Clarke Collection** *see* PaardenKloof

Peter Falke Wines ⓟ 🍴

The winery owned by German entrepreneur Franz-Peter Falke is in Stellenbosch's mostly red-wine 'Golden Triangle' and, fittingly, the focus is on styles of own cabernet and shiraz/syrah, with other grapes sourced in Elgin and Paarl, among others — all vinified by the very able Louis Nel (Louis Wines). The stylish cellardoor, with plush outdoor lounge, was designed by Franz-Peter's French partner, Danièle Görtz.

Signature range
★★★★ **Syrah 13** full bodied but with easy flow in its still primary floral, spicy fragrance, supple texture & rounded grip. Complementary oaking completes promising picture. Step up on **12** (★★★★).

★★★★ **Exclusive Blend** Cab leads in **13** Bordeaux-style three-way blend. Very ripe, sumptuous though with sense of freshness in its sweet fruit, & well contained by a firm structure. Promising future.

PF range
Ruby Blend ★★★☆ Rich, savoury cab/shiraz partnership. **13** has flavour intensity, firm dry finish to complement hearty game dishes. WO W Cape. **Blanc de Noir** ★★★ Appetising **15** from cab. Delicate, fresh, & has few grams sugar to balance, lengthen generous black berry fruit Also tasted: **Pinot Noir 14** ★★★ Not retasted: **Cabernet Sauvignon 13** ★★★★ **Sauvignon Blanc 14** ★★★ — AL

Location/map: Stellenbosch ▪ Map grid reference: E8 ▪ WO: Stellenbosch/Western Cape ▪ 1stB 2003 ▪ Tasting & sales Tue-Sun 11-7 ▪ Fee R45 ▪ Closed Good Fri, Dec 25/26 & Jan 1 ▪ Cheese platters & refreshments ▪ Owner(s) Franz-Peter Falke ▪ Winemaker(s) Louis Nel (2013, consultant) ▪ Viticulturist(s) / GM Werner Schrenk (Jan 2009) ▪ 24ha/±5ha (cab, shiraz) ▪ 100t/12,000cs own label 65% red 25% white 10% rosé ▪ PO

Box 12605 Stellenbosch 7613 ▪ marketing@peterfalkewines.co.za ▪ www.peterfalkewines.com ▪ S 34° 0' 2.1" E 018° 50' 19.3" ▪ F +27 (0)21-881-3667 ▪ **T +27 (0)21-881-3677**

☐ **Petit** *see* Ken Forrester Wines

Pfeifer's Boutique Wines   ⓠ

Co-owner and winegrower Pascal Pfeifer advises that vintages 2005 to 2007, the last Caelum Syrah made, are still available from his family's Helderberg farm.

Location: Stellenbosch ▪ Map: Helderberg ▪ Est 2000 ▪ 1stB 2003 ▪ Tasting & sales by appt ▪ Closed Easter Fri/Sun, Dec 25 & Jan 1 ▪ Owner(s) Pascal & Maya Pfeifer ▪ Winemaker(s)/viticulturist(s) Pascal Pfeifer (Jun 2006) ▪ 1.675ha/1.4ha (shiraz) ▪ 14-16t/±150cs own label 100% red ▪ IPW member ▪ PO Box 5238 Helderberg 7135 ▪ enquiries@pfeifersvineyard.co.za ▪ www.pfeifersvineyard.co.za ▪ S 34° 01' 10.98" E 018° 47' 17.06" ▪ F +27 (0)86-616-8850 ▪ **T +27 (0)21-842-3396**

☐ **Philip Jonker** *see* Weltevrede Estate

Phizante Kraal   ⓠ 🍴 ◎

Durbanville's Brink family has been involved in winegrowing for 4 generations. André and Ronelle Brink held back some grapes (most are sold off) to launch their brand in 2005 – fulfilling a 'lifelong dream' of a range produced (at Diemersdal) 'in an environmentally sensitive and ethically responsible manner'.

Flagship range 🆕
Anna De Koning ★★★☆ Handsomely packaged own single-vineyard chenin substitutes freshness for rich weight in **14** barrel-fermented limited release. Bruised melon, stewed quince & hint of soy on a very soft body, best enjoyed soon.

Phizante Kraal range
★★★★ Sauvignon Blanc ⊘ Slight alcohol warmth on otherwise fully ripe & boldly aromatic **15**, offering a fantail of tropical fruit & typical cool crunchiness, though palate perhaps less crafted than **14**.

Chenin Blanc 🍃 **★★★★** Stonefruit & melon introduce a tangy palate that's clean & balanced, with lipsmacking finish. **15** great-value unwooded chenin.

Also tasted: **Cabernet Sauvignon 13 ★★★ Shiraz 13 ★★★☆** — HJ

Location/WO: Durbanville ▪ Map: Durbanville, Philadelphia & Darling ▪ 1stB 2005 ▪ Tasting & sales Tue-Fri 9-4 Sat 10-2.30 ▪ Fee R20 ▪ Restaurant Tue-Fri b'fast 8-11 lunch 12-2.30 Sat brunch 10-2.30 ▪ Closed Easter weekend, Dec 25 to early Jan ▪ Sauvignon Blanc Festival; Sip, Soup & Bread Festival ▪ Owner(s) André & Ronelle Brink ▪ Winemaker(s) Thys Louw (Jan 2005, Diemersdal) ▪ Viticulturist(s) André Brink ▪ 50ha (cab, shiraz, chenin, sauv) ▪ 5,100cs own label ▪ PO Box 8 Durbanville 7551 ▪ wines@ phizantekraal.co.za ▪ www.phizantekraal.co.za ▪ S 33° 47' 46.73" E 018° 40' 12.96" ▪ F +27 (0)21-975-3589 ▪ **T +27 (0)21-825-0060**

PicardiRebel

The PicardiRebel nationwide drinks chain offers wine shoppers a number of affordable options under house brand/occasional label The Naked Truth.

Est 1994 ▪ PO Box 1868 Cape Town 8000 ▪ F +27 (0)21-469-3434 ▪ **T +27 (0)21-469-3301**

Pick n Pay

A wide range of producers' own brands appear on the shelves of this national supermarket chain, along with an own portfolio mostly sourced from Robertson Winery, Swartland Winery and Orange River Cellars. Managed by Pick n Pay Corporate Brands' Neil Cooke, the selection includes boxed and bottled single varieties and blends, some carbonated sparklings and increasingly popular low-alcohol options.

Enquiries Neil Cooke ▪ Pick n Pay Corporate Brands PO Box 1960 Bedfordview 2008 ▪ ncooke@pnp.co.za ▪ www.picknpay.co.za ▪ F +27 (0)86-616-5949 ▪ **T +27 (0)11-856-7000**

☐ **Pick's Pick** *see* The Butcher Shop & Grill
☐ **Piekeniers** *see* Tierhoek

Piekenierskloof Wine Company

Reasoning that they grow grapes, not minneolas, and many of their wines are from upland wine ward Piekenierskloof, the largely anonymous source of some pretty smart SA labels, 'Citrusdal Wines' are rebranding and making a step change. New roussanne and chardonnay blocks are taking shape, young grenache and tempranillo coming on-stream and a Piekenierskloof Fairtrade farm, Oudam, joining the stable to enhance their sustainability credentials. Barrel ageing, and wines from old bushvines and single vineyards – in Piekenierskloof, of course – are increasing focuses.

Bergendal range (NEW)
Grenache Noir ★★★☆ Fragrant red berries, some scrub, even lavender, pre-bottled **14** knows how to turn on the charm. Lovely to drink, plush, supple, harmonious. **Chenin Blanc** ★★★ American/French oak lends previewed **15** a nuttiness that works well with the melon/thatch flavours. Will open even further over year/2.

Piekenierskloof range (NEW)

> **Grenache Noir** ⟲ ★★★☆ Showing lovely typicity, dark-fruited **14** preview has scrub & violet nuances, white pepper from French/American barrels & a lively, juicy structure.

Chenin Blanc ★★★ Ex-tank **15** has crunchy apple freshness, a gently curvaceous body from touch of sugar. Swartland WO. **White Blend** ★★★ Mainly chenin, with grenache blanc & chardonnay, working well together in **15** pre-bottling sample. Stonefruit & melon, ending on a flinty food-compatible note. Not tasted: **GMT**.

Six Hats Fairtrade range
Cabernet Sauvignon ★★★ Cassis & chocolate, smooth & juicy **14** is very easy to like. WO W Cape.
Rosé ★★ From pinotage, **15** sampled from tank is more mineral than fruity, an ideal food companion.
Chenin Blanc ★★★ Ex-tank, sleek **15** has apple & pear freshness, friendly 12.5% alcohol & offers nice mouthfeel, satisfying drinkability. Swartland grapes. Also tasted: **Pinotage 14** ★★★ **Shiraz 14** ★★☆ **Chardonnay 15** ★★☆ **Sauvignon Blanc 15** ★★★ — CR, CvZ

Location: Citrusdal • WO: Piekenierskloof/Swartland/Western Cape • Est/1stB 2007 • Closed to public • Owner(s) Charles Back, Mike Paul & other grape farm owners • Cellarmaster(s) Jaco Brand (Nov 2009) • Winemaker(s) Welma Visser (Nov 2013) & Andries de Klerk (Nov 2009) • Viticulturist(s) Charl du Plessis (Nov 2009) • 550ha (cab, cinsaut, grenache n/b, merlot, mourv, ptage, ruby cab, shiraz, tannat, chard, chenin, hanepoot, pinot grigio, sauv, viog) • 9,000t/50,000cs own label 45% red 50% white 5% rosé + 200,000cs for clients • Brands for clients: Co-op, Fairtrade Original, Liberty, M&S, Sainsbury's • Fairtrade, HACCP, IPW, WIETA • PO Box 41 Citrusdal 7340 • info@citrusdalwines.co.za • www.piekenierskloofwines.co.za • F +27 (0)22-921-3937 • **T +27 (0)22-921-2233**

☐ **Pierneef Collection** *see* La Motte
☐ **Pierre Jourdan** *see* Haute Cabrière
☐ **Pillar & Post** *see* Stellenrust
☐ **PK Morkel** *see* Bellevue Estate Stellenbosch

Place in the Sun

Deon Boshoff, appointed cellarmaster of Distell's Adam Tas production facility at the tender age of 32, is the son of farm employees and learned his trade on a bursary open to the community. So it's appropriate that this Fairtrade-accredited brand for which he now vinifies aspires to 'actively contribute to South Africa's social transformation' by channelling a portion of sales to a farm employees' trust.

Merlot ★★★ Interesting spice, farmyard & red berry features in **14**, easy, appetising. **Sauvignon Blanc** ★★★ Green-toned **15** is flinty, limy & appley; a refreshing dry package. Also tasted: **Shiraz 14** ★★★ Not retasted: **Cabernet Sauvignon 13** ★★★ **Chardonnay 13** ★★★ — DS

Location/WO: Stellenbosch ▪ Est/1stB 2010 ▪ Closed to public ▪ Owner(s) Distell ▪ Cellarmaster(s)/ winemaker(s) Deon Boshoff (2010) ▪ Viticulturist(s) Annelie Viljoen (2010) ▪ 1,000t ▪ ISO 9001 & ISO 14001 (pending), Fairtrade, IPW ▪ PO Box 184 Stellenbosch 7599 ▪ dboshoff@distell.co.za ▪ www.placeinthesun.co.za ▪ **T +27 (0)21-809-7000**

Plaisir de Merle   ⓘ 🍴 🏠 📷 👤 ♿

Simonsberg foothills estate Plaisir de Merle has been in the stable of Distell (then Stellenbosch Farmers' Winery) since 1964, with winemaker Niel Bester in charge of the cellar since the first branded (and much-lauded) '93 vintage. Grapes from the vast vineyards, which include some unusual varieties, also feed other members of the Distell family. The manor house, a fine example of Cape Dutch architecture, makes an elegant pre-booked function, conference and wedding venue.

★★★★ **Malbec** 🆕 Just 350 cases from a single 13 year old vineyard. Vibrant **11** intense red berry flavours in a body that's attractively lithe & even leanish despite 14.6% alcohol.

★★★★ **Grand Plaisir** 70% cab-based Bordeaux quintet plus 10% shiraz in sensational **09** (★★★★☆), bramble fruit laced with spice tucked into fine powdery tannins; great concentration of flavour & velvet texture a rung up on maturing **08**. All-new wood. WO Simonsberg-Paarl.

★★★★ **Chardonnay 14** is generous, opulent yet retains varietal definition & balance; pickled lime, oatmeal tones, lees-enriched texture & mineral lift on finish. 9 months in oak, half new. WO W Cape.

★★★★ **Sauvignon Blanc** Pungent **15**'s tropical/fig fullness balanced by a flinty note, 14% alcohol absorbed in penetrating length of flavour. Includes Darling grapes, 2 months on lees, bone-dry.

Petit Plaisir ★★★☆ 50% shiraz- & cabernet-led 5-way blend (with dash viognier), 'petit' only in name: **13** brims with primary sweet berry fruit, ready for enjoyment. WO W Cape. **Grand Brut Méthode Cap Classique** ★★★☆ Appealing **12** bubbly from chardonnay (70%) & Stellenbosch-grown pinot noir, 2 years on lees; loads of green apple flavour, persistent & refreshing. Also tasted: **Cabernet Sauvignon 12** ★★★★ **Merlot 13** ★★★★ **Shiraz 11** ★★★☆ — DS

Location: Paarl ▪ Map: Franschhoek ▪ WO: Paarl/Western Cape/Simonsberg-Paarl ▪ Est/1stB 1993 ▪ Tasting, sales & cellar tours Mon-Fri 9–5 & 9-6 (Nov-Apr) Sat 10-4 (all year) Sun 10–2 (Nov–Apr) ▪ Tasting fee R50 ▪ Closed Good Fri, Dec 25 & Jan 1 ▪ Cheese platters available during trading hours R90 ▪ Children welcome ▪ Gifts ▪ Manor House (sleeps 8) can be booked for functions, conferences & weddings ▪ Owner(s) Distell ▪ Cellarmaster(s) Niel Bester (1993) ▪ Viticulturist(s) Drikus Heyns & Freddie le Roux ▪ 974ha/400ha (cabs s/f, malbec, merlot, p verdot, pinot, shiraz, chard, sauv) ▪ 800t/80,000cs own label 80% red 20% white ▪ ISO 9001:2008, ISO 14001:2004, BRC, BWI, SGS, WIETA ▪ PO Box 121 Simondium 7670 ▪ info@plaisirdemerle.co.za ▪ www.plaisirdemerle.co.za ▪ S 33° 51' 0.0" E 018° 56' 36.2" ▪ F +27 (0)21-874-1689 ▪ **T +27 (0)21-874-1071**

Plettenvale Wines   ⓘ 🍴 🏠

Boutique winegrower Gloria Strack van Schyndel, inspired on a 2007 Tuscan 'walking and cooking tour', is making great strides on her small property near coastal resort town Plettenberg Bay. She's become 'totally self-sufficient' in key aspects of producing her MCC bubbly, now exported to the UK; planting more pinot noir; and opening an eatery offering food-and-wine pairings.

Dry Rosé ★★★ Appealingly bright hued, **14** from pinot noir & chardonnay has MCC sparkling's acidity & lean grip without the bubbles. Really zingy, with musk & strawberry nuances. **Brut Rosé Méthode Cap Classique** ★★★☆ Light salmon-coloured appetiser from pinot noir & chardonny, **13** steps up in freshness with lively bubbles, firm acidity, pinot-driven red fruit. Also hints of house-style salinity with savoury extras. Not retasted: **Chardonnay 13** ★★★ — HJ

Location/WO: Plettenberg Bay ▪ Map: Klein Karoo & Garden Route ▪ Est 2008 ▪ 1stB 2011 ▪ Tasting & sales by appt ▪ Restaurant ▪ Self-catering cottages ▪ Owner(s) Gloria Strack van Schyndel ▪ Winemaker(s) Anton Smal (consultant) ▪ Viticulturist(s) Paul Wallace (Nov 2007, consultant) ▪ 5.3ha/ 2.3ha (pinot, shiraz, chard) ▪ PO Box 2103 Plettenberg Bay 6600 ▪ info@plettenvalewines.co.za ▪ www.plettenvalewines.co.za ▪ S 34° 04' 53.9" E 023° 19' 41.4" ▪ F +27 (0)44-533-9146 ▪ **T +27 (0)44-533-9146/+27 (0)82-322-0765**

☐ **Poetry** *see* Flagstone Winery
☐ **Poker Hill** *see* Somerbosch Wines
☐ **Polkadraai** *see* Stellenbosch Hills Wines
☐ **Polo Club** *see* Val de Vie Wines
☐ **Pomüla** *see* Imbuko Wines

Pongrácz

Specialist méthode cap classique bubbly brand named after Desiderius Pongrácz, Dachshund-loving aristocrat who fled the Hungarian uprising, settled in Stellenbosch in 1958 and went on to become chief viticultural adviser to Distillers Corporation, Distell's precursor.

★★★★ **Desiderius** ⓥ 2nd disgorgement of **08** (★★★★☆) sparkling follows previous impressive form: 70% chardonnay with pinot noir offer delightful brioche & lemon shortbread. Silky mousse carries to lengthy roasted nut finish. First since **03**. WO W Cape, as all.

★★★★ **Pongrácz Brut** Restrained but appealing pinot noir/chardonnay (55/45) sparkler, **NV** showing apple pie & shortbread with hints of strawberry. Creamy, persistent mousse, subtle lemon biscuit finish.

Pongrácz Brut Rosé ★★★ **NV** pink bubbly from pinot noir & chardonnay (55/45) with tangy strawberry juice character, slight sweetish edge. Attractive if not complex or nuanced. — GdB

Porcupine Ridge

Boekenhoutskloof's original 'value range' continues to expand in terms of range (and reputation) as well as volume, with a new lightly oaked chardonnay and a chenin blanc — the latter from the Swartland, like the Rhône-inspired wines. Grapes are vinified in the Boekenhoutskloof-owned Helderberg Winery cellar.

★★★★ **Syrah** ⓥ Brooding dark hues on **14** (★★★★☆), palate shows tad less intensity than **13**'s but it's succulent, rich & rewarding, with good body.

> **Viognier-Grenache Blanc** ⓟ ★★★★ Bold peach ripeness on broad, honeyed **14**. Lovely structure with good depth & intensity from partial oak & lees-ageing.

Chardonnay (NEW) ★★★ Effortless ease to light, creamy citrus appeal of **14**. Oak (80% for six months) contributes to good body & length. WO W Cape. **Chenin Blanc** (NEW) ★★★ Broad, rich yet gentle **14**, rounded, ripe pineapple & stonefruit flavour with long tail. Also tasted: **Cabernet Sauvignon** ⓥ **14** ★★★☆ **Merlot** ⓥ **14** ★★★★ **Sauvignon Blanc 15** ★★★ Not tasted: **Syrah-Viognier**. — FM

Porseleinberg

This Swartland farm had only a few shiraz vineyards when Boekenhoutskloof acquired it in 2009 and Callie Louw inaugurated a major planting programme based on organic (partially biodynamic) principles — chickens and Nguni cattle playing their part too. The parental Franschhoek winery takes most of the grapes (which already play a part in the famous Boekenhoutskloof Syrah, among others), but Callie is crafting his one wine from the oldest vines here, in accord with the 'natural' approach of the Swartland Independent Producers. The result is one of SA's most distinctive, and most sought-after, syrahs.

★★★★☆ **Porseleinberg** ⓥ **13** was 60% in foudres, 40% in concrete 'egg', after whole-bunch natural ferment, while **12** (★★★★★) was unoaked. Lovely perfume (smoke, spice, floral) leads to supple, subtly intense palate, its fine muscular austerity matched by fruit depth; needs/deserves many years to harmonise. — TJ

Location: Malmesbury ▪ WO: Swartland ▪ Est 2009 ▪ 1stB 2011 ▪ Closed to public ▪ Owner(s) Boekenhoutskloof Winery Pty Ltd ▪ Winemaker(s)/viticulturist(s) Callie Louw (Jun 2009) ▪ 85ha/30ha (shiraz) ▪ 6t/600cs own label 100% red ▪ Organic EU Control Union ▪ PO Box 433 Franschhoek 7690 ▪ callie@porseleinberg.com ▪ www.porseleinberg.com ▪ F +27 (0)86-566-9332 ▪ **T +27 (0)79-884-2309**

☐ **Porter Mill Station** *see* Tulbagh Winery
☐ **Postcard Series** *see* Stark-Condé Wines

Post House Vineyards   ⓘ 🍽 🏠 ♿

Having set up home in an old post office building next to the Helderberg village of Raithby, boutique vintner Nick Gebers naturally chose a philatelic theme for his wines. From the appropriately inky Penny Black to the Chinese-inspired Golden Monkey, each carries a historical explanation and a yarn to entertain you while you sip. Soon there will be more for you to sip, as Nick is extending the cellar.

★★★★ **Bulls Eye Cabernet Sauvignon** With 12% dash petit verdot in **13**, another blockbuster with 15% alcohol, huge fruit density, solid tannins. But there's a refreshing savoury character, too.

★★★★ **Missing Virgin** Sturdy Cape Blend pinotage (70%) & petit verdot, **13** has stewed berry, oriental spice & gamey notes; solidly built with firm tannins, resolute 15.5% alcohol.

★★★★ **Penny Black** Powerful **13** more successful shiraz, Bordeaux, chenin blend than almost too dense **12**. There's big & chewy tannins plus a welcome berry & spice lift, 15% alcohol deftly handled.

★★★★ **Stamp Of Chenin** **14**'s ripe pineapple, peach & citrus interwoven with vanilla & honey from French, American oak ferment (spontaneous), ageing. Full bodied, rich yet impressively dry & persistent.

★★★★☆ **Treskilling Yellow** ⓥ Now bottled, **12** Noble Late Harvest chenin delivers on promise, improves on **10** (★★★★). Spicy mulled honey, dried apricots & orange zest in a rich, rounded body with delicate but effective acidity. 19 months small oak. No **09**, **11**.

Also tasted: **Black Mail Merlot 12 ★★★☆ Merry Widow Shiraz 13 ★★★☆ Blueish White 14 ★★★** Not retasted: **Blueish Black 13 ★★★☆** Not tasted: **Golden Monkey**. — GM

Location/WO: Stellenbosch ▪ Map: Helderberg ▪ Est/1stB 1997 ▪ Tasting, sales & cellar tours Mon-Fri 9-5 Sat by appt ▪ Fee R30 ▪ Closed all pub hols ▪ BYO picnic ▪ Guest house ▪ Owner(s) Nicholas Gebers ▪ Cellarmaster(s) Nick Gebers ▪ Winemaker(s) Nick Gebers, with Riana Theart ▪ 70ha/39ha (cab, merlot, p verdot, ptage, shiraz, chenin, sauv) ▪ 200t/16,000cs own label 65% red 35% white ▪ PO Box 5635 Helderberg 7135 ▪ info@posthousewines.co.za ▪ www.posthousewines.co.za ▪ S 34° 1' 8.1" E 018° 48' 41.6" ▪ F +27 (0)21-842-2409 ▪ **T +27 (0)21-842-2409**

☐ **Post Tree** see Valley Vineyards Wine Company
☐ **Pot Luck Club** see Almenkerk Wine Estate
☐ **Prime Cuts** see Boutinot South Africa
☐ **Private Collection** see Saxenburg Wine Farm
☐ **Prohibition** see Camberley Wines
☐ **Protea** see Anthonij Rupert Wyne
☐ **Provenance** see L'Avenir Vineyards, Saronsberg
☐ **Provoyeur** see Devonvale Golf & Wine Estate

Pulpit Rock Winery   ⓘ 🍽 🏠 📷 ♿

Lying on the foothills of the Swartland's Kasteelberg, Pulpit Rock takes its name from a distinctive craggy outcrop on that mountain. The Brink family have grown grapes here for over half a century, but made their own wine first in 2004. Their style is fruit driven, something they believe is dictated by the soil and climate, whose diversity also gives a unique character.

Reserve range

★★★★ **Pinotage** ⓥ Youthful **12** (★★★★★) has a real sense of place: pure, unshowy perfume; big but beautifully proportioned, oak (80% new) just needs time to integrate. Follows sturdy **10**.

★★★★ **Chardonnay 13** better balanced than **12** (★★★), still needs a while for oak (40% new French) to fully integrate with hazelnut, spicy, tangy citrus mix. Medium bodied, fruitily dry.

Chenin Blanc (NEW) ★★☆ Ripe, honeyed chenin challenged by 100% new French oak in **14**. Alcohol glow alleviated by few grams sugar. Also tasted: **Cabernet Sauvignon 13 ★★★ Shiraz 13 ★★** Not retasted: **Petit Verdot 12 ★★★☆ Louisa 12 ★★★☆**

Brink Family range

Merlot ★★★ 13 pleasantly fleshed with sound plummy fruits. Firm finish allows for further year/2.
Shiraz ★★★ Full-bodied, hearty **13**, with rich spicy flavours, backbone for few years. **Pinotage Rosé**

★★ Coral pink **15**. Fresh, ripe strawberry flavours lifted by few grams sugar. Also tasted: **Pinotage 14** ★★★ **Chenin Blanc 15** ★★ Not retasted: **Cabernet Sauvignon 13** ★★★ **Chardonnay 14** ★★☆

Swartland Stories
Chenin Blanc-Viognier ★★ **15** chenin with floral lift from 15% viognier. Bracingly fresh. Not retasted: **Shiraz-Pinotage-Grenache 13** ★★ — AL

Location: Riebeek West ▪ Map/WO: Swartland ▪ Est 2003 ▪ 1stB 2004 ▪ Tasting & sales Mon-Fri 9–5 Sat 10–2 ▪ Closed Easter Fri-Sun, Dec 25/26 & Jan 1 ▪ Cellar tours by appt ▪ BYO picnic ▪ Walks/hikes ▪ MTB trail ▪ Annual olive festival (May) ▪ Self-catering accommodation ▪ Owner(s) Brink family ▪ Winemaker(s) Riaan van der Spuy (Dec 2011) ▪ Viticulturist(s) Marco Roux (Dec 2008, consultant) ▪ 600ha/450ha (cab, grenache, merlot, mourv, p verdot, ptage, shiraz, chard, chenin) ▪ 650t/30,000cs own label 70% red 29% white 1% rosé + 200,000L bulk ▪ Other export brands: Cape Haven, Cape Tranquility ▪ PO Box 1 Riebeek West 7306 ▪ info@pulpitrock.co.za ▪ www.pulpitrock.co.za ▪ S 33° 20' 47.4" E 018° 51' 14.1" ▪ F +27 (0)22-461-2028 ▪ **T +27 (0)22-461-2025**

☐ **Pure African** *see* Bellevue Estate Stellenbosch

Quando Vineyards & Winery ⓠ

Bruwer brothers Fanus and Martin responded to friends asking 'when, when, when' they were creating their own brand by naming it after the 1960s bossa nova pop song. The small cast, treading the global stage, recently received a 'stylish' label makeover, sauvignon blanc's 2015 star turn warranted a Natural Sweet, and their mourvèdre rosé remains a hit.

Chenin Blanc-Viognier ⓦ ★★★☆ Old-vine chenin ferments two weeks before 29% viognier joins the tank, lees-ageing adds breadth to **15**; oatmeal richness cut by tropical fruit zing. Also in 500 ml.

Mourvèdre Rosé ⓥ ★★★ Salmon glints & cranberry twist on dry & zesty **15** crowd pleaser. Also tasted: **Sauvignon Blanc 15** ★★★☆ **Natural Sweet Sauvignon Blanc 15** ★★★ Not retasted: **Pinot Noir 12** ★★★ — DS

Location: Bonnievale ▪ Map/WO: Robertson ▪ Est/1stB 2001 ▪ Tasting & sales by appt ▪ Closed all pub hols ▪ Owner(s) F M Bruwer cc ▪ Cellarmaster(s)/winemaker(s) Fanus Bruwer (Jan 1991) ▪ Viticulturist(s) Martin Bruwer (Jan 1991) ▪ 190ha/80ha (mourv, chenin, sauv) ▪ 6,000cs own label 10% red 90% white ▪ PO Box 82 Bonnievale 6730 ▪ info@quando.co.za ▪ www.quando.co.za ▪ S 33° 56' 9.6" E 020° 1' 28.8" ▪ F +27 (0)23-616-2752 ▪ **T +27 (0)23-616-2752**

☐ **Quay 5** *see* Two Oceans
☐ **Quest** *see* Du Toitskloof Winery
☐ **Quinta do Sul** *see* Lieben Wines

Quoin Rock Winery ⓠ

Something extraordinary is afoot when one of the Cape's most celebrated consultants drops almost everything to focus on one venture – the rebirth of already highly regarded Quoin Rock. Chris Keet believes this to be one of 'the' Cape projects, initiated by recent Ukranian owners, the Gayduk family. Iconic wines are the goal, and sweeping re/developments are in progress in both the Simonsberg and Elim/Agulhas vineyards, and back home in the Stellenbosch cellar, where sustainability and holistic treatment of resources are special focuses. Debut under refreshed branding is due next year.

Location/map: Stellenbosch ▪ Map grid reference: F3 ▪ Est 1998 ▪ 1stB 2001 ▪ Tasting by appt ▪ Closed Easter Fri/Sun, Dec 25/26 & Jan 1 ▪ Owner(s) Quoin Rock Wines (Pty) Ltd ▪ Cellarmaster(s) Chris Keet ▪ Winemaker(s) Jacques Maree (Jan 2015, assistant) ▪ Viticulturist(s) Nico Walters (Sep 2012) ▪ 193ha/15ha (cabs s/f, merlot, mourv, shiraz, sauv, viog) ▪ 200t/22,000cs own label 55% red 35% white 7% MCC 3% dessert ▪ PO Box 1193 Stellenbosch 7599 ▪ info@quoinrock.co.za ▪ www.quoinrock.com ▪ S 33° 52' 42.5" E 018° 52' 2.3" ▪ **T +27 (0)21-888-4740**

Raats Family Wines

Bruwer Raats might well thrive in Touraine on the Loire, given his fascination with its great varieties, chenin blanc and cabernet franc. But his specialisation works well enough in the Cape, where he carefully sources his grapes from contracted vineyards dotted around Stellenbosch and vinifies them at his place on the Polkadraai Hills. Bruwer is a big man, and it's almost paradoxical that his wines tend to be so delicate and refined. He does, incidentally, extend his range to other varieties in his winemaking collaborations with old friend Mzokhona Mvemve and cousin Gavin Bruwer Slabbert – listed separately under Mvemve Raats and B Vintners, respectively.

★★★★☆ **Cabernet Franc** Vibrant **13**, with subtle aromas of berry, spice & undergrowth, needs time in the glass to unfold & reveal its potential. Balanced & elegant, it has beautiful ripe tannins, an energising freshness & unobtrusive oaking (25% new). Worthy successor to seamless & intense **12**.

★★★★ **Dolomite Cabernet Franc** Fruit-driven **14** almost unruly, with boundless berry & spicy tealeaf notes, lively acidity & firm but fine tannin. Similar joie de vivre to **12**, will please for good few years.

★★★★ **Red Jasper** Smart & accomplished **12** (★★★★☆) radiates ripeness (blackberries & currants), well reined in by chewy tannins & enlivened by balancing acidity. Cab franc-led Bordeaux blend as is shyer, also-tasted **13**, both styled for serious contemplation, deserving good food & friends.

★★★★☆ **Old Vine Chenin Blanc 14** opens up (with a little patience) to multi-layered aromas of apple, ginger, dried flowers & a hint of custard. The full palate has balanced intensity, with a kaleidoscope of evolving flavours; the long finish has a pebbly, mineral feel. Lightly oaked. In magnums too.

★★★★ **Original Chenin Blanc** Like bouncy **13**, unwooded **14** cut above your everyday tipple. Sophisticated melange quince, naartjie, pear & green peaches; steely mineral persistence. — JPf

Location/map/WO: Stellenbosch ▪ Map grid reference: B6 ▪ Est/1stB 2000 ▪ Tasting & sales by appt only ▪ Closed all pub hols ▪ Owner(s) Bruwer Raats ▪ Cellarmaster(s) Bruwer Raats (Jan 2000) ▪ Winemaker(s) Gavin Bruwer Slabbert (Feb 2010) ▪ Viticulturist(s) Bruwer Raats (Jan 2000) & Gavin Bruwer Slabbert (Feb 2010) ▪ 30ha (cab f, chenin) ▪ 150t/20,000cs own label 40% red 60% white ▪ PO Box 2068 Dennesig Stellenbosch 7601 ▪ braats@mweb.co.za ▪ www.raats.co.za ▪ S 33° 58' 16.6" E 018° 44' 55.3" ▪ F +27 (0)86-647-8500 ▪ **T +27 (0)21-881-3078**

☐ **Racetrack** *see* Damarakloof
☐ **Radford Dale** *see* The Winery of Good Hope

Rainbow's End Wine Estate

Civil engineer Jacques Malan invested in a steep-sloped Banhoek fruit farm in the 1970s. As the area gained recognition as prime viticultural terroir, he and sons Anton and Francois, suitably qualified and similarly inspired, planted vines from 2000. Converting existing buildings, vinifying traditionally, farming sustainably, they've created their pot of gold: an internationally marketed portfolio of reds and rosé.

Reserve range

★★★★☆ **Family Reserve** Drops 'Bordeaux Blend' from name, but polished, small-volume flagship **12** remains a merlot-led blend with both cabs & petit verdot. Compact, rich dark fruit has smokily spiced charcuterie edge to pique interest. Pleasingly dry finish supported by seamlessly integrated oak tannins.

Estate range

★★★★ **Cabernet Sauvignon** Tightly structured, wonderfully expressive **13** delivers convincing blackcurrant, dark plum flavours. Plenty charm & complexity in seamless, stylish rendition of this variety.

★★★★ **Cabernet Franc** Seriously styled **13** (★★★☆) lacks some of the charm & freshness of **12**. Ripe, meaty finish rendered savoury by nicely structured tannins.

★★★★☆ **Cabernet Franc Limited Release** Single-vineyard bottling. Gorgeously perfumed **13** charming, polished & bold. Dense, concentrated fruit core with mint chocolate richness & confident finish, underpinned by fine-grained tannins.

★★★★ **Merlot** Elegant **14**'s integrated tannins are woven into nicely ripe red plum, mint choc flavours & ensure firm, dry conclusion. **13** sold out untasted.

★★★★ **Shiraz** 13 fruit bomb delivers abundant flavour — berries, roasted spices — wrapped in silky tannins which ensure lovely savoury grip.

Also tasted: **Mystical Corner** 14 ★★★☆ **Rosé** 14 ★★★ — IM

Location/map: Stellenbosch ▪ Map grid reference: H5 ▪ WO: Banghoek ▪ Est 1978 ▪ 1stB 2002 ▪ Tasting, sales & tours by appt ▪ Fee R25, waived on purchase of 4+ btls ▪ Closed Dec 25 & Jan 1 ▪ Sales also via website, delivery free of charge ▪ Conservation area ▪ Owner(s) Malan family ▪ Cellarmaster(s) Anton Malan (Nov 2000) ▪ Winemaker(s) Anton Malan (Nov 2000) & Francois Malan (Jan 2005) ▪ Viticulturist(s) Francois Malan (Jan 2005) ▪ 52ha/21.6ha (cabs s/f, malbec, merlot, p verdot, shiraz) ▪ 120t/ 8,200cs own label 90% red 10% rosé ▪ IPW, WIETA ▪ PO Box 2253 Dennesig 7601 ▪ info@ rainbowsend.co.za ▪ www.rainbowsend.co.za ▪ S 33° 56′ 25.8″ E 018° 56′ 42.6″ ▪ F +27 (0)21-885-1722 ▪ T +27 (0)21-885-1719/+27 (0)83-411-0170/+27 (0)82-404-1085

Raka

Piet Dreyer's ebullience was somewhat tempered the past year by emergency open-heart surgery shortly before harvest. To spare the patriarch and owner any concern, all on the Stanford farm, family and staff alike, rallied round and worked extra hard, handling the early crush with aplomb. So much so, Jorika Dreyer chuckles, her father seemed somewhat taken aback that things could run so smoothly without him. 'But at least he knows he doesn't have to worry unnecessarily.' And doubtless the former squid fisherman was consoled and buoyed by becoming a grandfather — three times over! Unable to meet sustained demand for a full-fledged eatery, the Dreyers have created a small deli stocked with local produce 'so customers will at least have something to nibble on while tasting'.

★★★★ **Cabernet Sauvignon** ⊘ Austere, unyielding & nervous, 13 (★★★★★) is quintessential cab, with classic forest floor earthiness, liquorice spices & deep, dark fruit core. Demands & rewards close attention with subtle herbaceous nuances, velvety tannins, lingering finish. Step up from last-made 10.

★★★★☆ **Cabernet Franc** ⊘ Strikingly bold 13 grabs attention with intense blackcurrants, herbaceous hints & delicate floral notes. Finely poised despite hefty body, offering velvet-gloved power & subtle layering. Remarkable value.

★★★★ **Barrel Select Merlot** Best 30 barrels (of 180) for this label. Up a notch on 12 (★★★★), heavyweight 13 shows black plum & cherry fruit over robust tannins. Convincing fruit core follows to satisfying finish. Toasty, charred oak undertones should settle.

★★★★ **Mourvèdre** ⊛ Meaty, fragrant coriander spice allures on 11. Firmly structured & made for food, the sweet-savoury marriage is harmonious & moreish. A lifting sour cherry finish delights.

★★★★ **Petit Verdot** Meaty-savoury with bold blackcurrant fruit & subtle rosepetal scent, 13 is dense, dark & forceful. Youthfully gangly structure, but should settle & mature gracefully. No 11, 12.

★★★★☆ **Biography Shiraz** ⊘ Immensely satisfying flagship label, 12 gushes with ripe, rich plum pudding fruit, laced with sweet spices & peppery scrub aromas. Silky smooth texture, savoury meaty undertones & finely modulated acidity.

★★★★☆ **Five Maidens** ⊛ Knockout 11 5-way cab-led Bordeaux-style commemorates 10 years of the Dreyer family in wine. Elegant intensity, without excess weight. Great vibrancy & persistence.

★★★★ **Quinary** 5-way Bordeaux-style red, cab-led. 2 vintages tasted: 11 is focused & integrated, with noble black fruit, supple tannins. 12 shows bold blackcurrants & mulberries on tarry backbone with aromatic herbs. Both finely formed & elegant. Various larger bottle formats available.

★★★★ **Figurehead Cape Blend** 6-way blend 13 successfully harnesses 30% pinotage with Bordeaux quintet. Full bodied, with wild berry lift, spicy & satisfying, drinking well now.

Sangiovese ★★★☆ Juicy-fruity & earthy, 13 shows food-friendly rustic appeal. Stewed prunes & tomato cordial echo Italian provenance. **Sauvignon Blanc** ★★★☆ Dusty pebbles, bubblegum aromas on just-bottled 15. Appealingly lean & focused palate, good weight, intensely fruity. Also tasted: **Malbec** 13 ★★★ **Pinotage** 13 ★★★☆ **Spliced** 13 ★★★ **Chenin Blanc** 14 ★★★ Not retasted: **Rosé Dry** 14 ★★★ — GdB

Location: Stanford ▪ Map: Elgin, Walker Bay & Bot River ▪ WO: Klein River/Western Cape/Cape South Coast/Coastal ▪ Est/1stB 2002 ▪ Tasting & sales Mon-Fri 9—5 Sat 10—2.30 ▪ Tasting fee: 4 wines on daily tasting list free, other wines R10/wine ▪ Closed Sun, Good Fri & Dec 25 ▪ Cellar tours & large groups by appt ▪ BYO picnic ▪ Conservation area ▪ Owner(s) Piet Dreyer ▪ Winemaker(s) Josef Dreyer (Jan 2007) ▪ Viticulturist(s) Pieter Dreyer (Jan 2007) ▪ 760ha/62ha (5 Bdx, mourv, ptage, sangio, shiraz, sauv, viog) ▪ 350t/30,000cs own label 75% red 17% white 8% rosé ▪ BWI, IPW ▪ PO Box 124 Caledon 7230 ▪ info@rakawine.co.za ▪ www.rakawine.co.za ▪ S 34° 23' 56.1" E 019° 37' 26.7" ▪ F +27 (0)86-606-5462 ▪ **T +27 (0)28-341-0676**

Rall Wines ⓠ

A prominent if peripatetic figure among the newer generation of dynamic winemakers driving the revolutionary reputation of the Swartland, Donovan Rall has put down roots there, leasing part of the barrel cellar at Annex Kloof for his acclaimed own label. All Swartland fermentations will be done there, grapes from other areas vinified in Stellenbosch's Vuurberg cellar where his day job keeps him busy. His winemaking studies completed in 2005, Donovan travelled to gain work experience before tackling his maiden bottling in 2008. 'Now I can grow!' albeit in a small way, with minute (600-bottle) volumes of old-vine cinsaut and grenache blanc set to join the list in future.

★★★★☆ **Red** Deliberate focus on Swartland's delicacy, with understated sangfroid in balanced, classy **13**; whole bunches (50%) in ferment add minty freshness & natural tannin to frame pretty red & black berry fruit, with dash white pepper. 88% shiraz, rest grenache; only seasoned oak.

★★★★☆ **White** Super, silky, naturally fermented blend chenin, verdelho, chardonnay & viognier from Swartland & Stellenbosch. **14** has mineral texture & depth, with astounding balance, surreal length of flavour. Supportive older oak & seamless acid spine underlie poise in a salty-tang finish. — DS

Location: Swartland ▪ WO: Swartland/Coastal ▪ Est/1stB 2008 ▪ Tasting, sales & cellar tours by appt ▪ Owner(s)/winemaker(s)/viticulturist(s) Donovan Rall ▪ 20t/1,000cs own label 50% red 50% white ▪ info@rallwines.co.za ▪ www.rallwines.co.za ▪ **T +27 (0)72-182-7571**

☐ **Ralph Parker** see Altydgedacht Estate

Rannoch Farm

Proud of their Scottish heritage, owners Rory and Ricky Antrobus named their Helderberg farm after Loch Rannoch in Scotland. 'The island in our lake and the surrounding scenery are reminiscent of the highlands,' explains viticulturist Rory, who nurtures a single hectare of cabernet. 'Avondale in Paarl has been making our wine successfully for the past five years and this partnership should continue.'

★★★★ **Cabernet Sauvignon** Unshowy, handsome **11** (no **10**) gives typical berries, moderate depth of fruit & tobacco expressing all-new but not excessive oak. Few years will aid serious tannic structure. — TJ

Location/WO: Stellenbosch ▪ Est 1999 ▪ 1stB 2003 ▪ Closed to public ▪ Owner(s) Rory & Ricky Antrobus ▪ Winemaker(s) Corné Marais, with Ivan September (both Jan 2010, Avondale) ▪ Viticulturist(s) Rory Antrobus (Mar 1999) ▪ 8ha/1ha (cab) ▪ 6t/500cs own label 100% white ▪ PO Box 5667 Helderberg 7135 ▪ rory@gmint.co.za ▪ **T +27 (0)21-842-3601**

☐ **Raoul's** see Beaumont Wines

Rare Earth Vineyards ⓠ ⌂ ⊚

No new vintages of the funkily named/packaged SAV sauvignon blanc or Champu MCC bubbly, but no shortage of news from John 'Chick' Legh's polo, accommodation and wine estate in Plettenberg Bay's sylvan The Crags. Opening as the guide went to print was a 'spectacular' new function and wedding venue 'set among vineyards, paddocks, pastures and forests... with stunning views'. Sounds irresistible.

Location: Plettenberg Bay ▪ Map: Klein Karoo & Garden Route ▪ Est 2009 ▪ 1stB 2012 ▪ Tasting Tue-Sun 9-4 ▪ Chocolate & wine pairing ▪ Weddings & events ▪ Guest house (Rare Earth Retreats www.rareearthretreats.co.za) ▪ Owner(s) John Legh ▪ Cellarmaster(s)/winemaker(s) Anton Smal (2012, consultant) ▪ Viticulturist(s) Llyod Kasimbi ▪ 163ha/3.99ha (pinot, chard, sauv) ▪ PO Box 295 The Crags 6602 ▪ vineyards@rareearth.co.za ▪ S 33° 55' 58.32" E 023° 26' 21.40" ▪ F +27 (0)44-534-8387 ▪ **T +27 (0)44-534-8387/+27 (0)76-582-0122**

☐ **Ready Steady** *see* Southern Sky Wines
☐ **Rebourne Fairtrade** *see* Imbuko Wines
☐ **Rebus** *see* Romond Vineyards
☐ **Red Chair** *see* Rooiberg Winery

RED ESCape

Made by Stellenzicht, RED ESCape is positioned as an antidote to the demands of 24 x 7 connectedness.

Red Blend ★☆ Unashamedly sweet & bold **13**, with inklings of milk chocolate & spice. — AL

☐ **Red Falcon** *see* Middelvlei Estate
☐ **Red Gold** *see* Bushmanspad Estate
☐ **Red Tape** *see* Tanja Beutler Wine Collection
☐ **Red White Pink** *see* Nomada Wines

Reiersvlei   ⓠ

Just under a decade ago, Russell Inggs and wife Elize transplanted themselves from Johannesburg to the higher slopes of the Swartberg in the Groot Karoo and realised a long desire to make their own wine. After 'enjoyment of life' saw bottling dates postponed last edition, there are several new wines and vintages this time. Longer term, Russell wonders what the 'prevailing drought will do for quality'.

Pinotage Reserve (NEW) ★★☆ Lengthy 40 months in French oak, 15% new, has smoothed but not dimmed bright cranberry, raspberry tones on **11**. Concludes with bitter nip. **Tinta Barocca** (NEW) ★★★ Fortified & aged 6 months in 100% new French oak, **14** smells of fresh earth & spice with clean flavours & not overly sweet. A tasty nightcap. **Alchemy** (NEW) ★★☆ NV fortified blend petit verdot, touriga & tinta barocca. Oak (73% new) lends sweet, rather disjointed note to dryish, lean frame. Also tasted: **Pinotage 11** ★★ **Tinta Barocca 11** ★★ **Cape Blend 12** ★ **Red Muscadel 14** ★★★★ Not retasted: **Shiraz 11** ★★ **Cape Vintage Port 10** ★★ Not tasted: **Touriga Nacional**, **Sauvignon Blanc**. — AL

Location: Prince Albert ▪ Map: Klein Karoo & Garden Route ▪ WO: Prince Albert Valley ▪ Est 1999 ▪ 1stB 2010 ▪ Tasting, sales & cellar tours: Jun1-Oct 31 by appt only; Nov 1-May 31 Mon-Fri 10-3 or by arrangement ▪ Closed Sat/Sun, Easter Fri-Mon, Dec 25/26 & Jan 1 ▪ Owner(s) Reiersvlei Investments CC (Russell & Elize Inggs) ▪ Cellarmaster(s)/winemaker(s)/viticulturist(s) Russell Inggs (Sep 2007) ▪ 113ha/9ha (cab, p verdot, ptage, red muscadel, shiraz, tinta, touriga, sauv) ▪ 70t/3,600cs own label 90% red 10% white ▪ PO Box 33 Prince Albert 6930 ▪ reier@pawireless.co.za ▪ S 33° 16' 50" E 022° 14' 38" ▪ F +27 (0)23-541-1983 ▪ **T +27 (0)23-541-1983/1556**

☐ **Releaf Organic** *see* Imbuko Wines

Remhoogte Wine Estate

The farm on the Simonsberg slopes in Stellenbosch was run down when Murray and Juliet Boustred bought it in 1994. Now it's a thriving family estate with their two sons firmly in place: Chris in cellar and vineyards, Rob driving sales and marketing. Winemaking has become more non-interventionist, and as part of the aim to reflect the estate's terroir there's a return to 'looking at blends as the way forward', signalled by the revival of the Estate Blend which from 2013 will include all four red varieties grown.

Reserve range

★★★★☆ **Sir Thomas Cullinan** Ambitions announced with first sip of plush **12** flagship. Based on Chris Boustred's favourite, merlot, with 25% cab, it has power & refinement. Richness of dark fruits leavened by freshness & fine tannins. Ferment/aged in oak, 40% new. Should develop well.

★★★★☆ **Honeybunch Chenin Blanc** Aptly named barrelled chenin, harvested from morning side only of single old vineyard. **14** (★★★★) has lifted honey fragrance, flavours with touch more botrytis character but little short on **13**'s concentration, length.

Estate range

★★★★ **Aspect Merlot** From special high-lying vineyard with south-west aspect, hence name. **13** (★★★★★) echoes positives of **12**: fragrant, perfectly ripe fruit, freshness & just hints of flesh, depths to emerge from tight frame. Should blossom into classy beauty.

★★★★ **Bushvine Pinotage 13**, just under 15% alcohol, shows big can be beautiful. It's all freshness with lingering bright raspberry, cherry fruits & silky feel. Polished tannins add focus, form, for medium-term ageing.

★★★★ **Estate Blend 12** first since **07** (★★★★), now a fine shiraz/cab mix. As with other reds, freshness & gentle approach to extraction, oaking, mask high alcohol. Shiraz's dark berry, savoury tones, supple flesh to fore, cab (ferment in 7,000L oak) structurally important. Promising future.

Discontinued: **Terroir Cabernet Sauvignon**, **Valentino Syrah**.

Lifestyle range

★★★★ **Chenin Blanc** ⊘ Quality & price always smileworthy qualities in this partially oaked chenin. **14** has ripe, spicy scents & plenty of juicy bounce. Wild ferment & ageing on lees add extra intrigue.

Not retasted: **Soaring Eagle 12** ★★★★ — AL

Location/map: Stellenbosch ▪ Map grid reference: E3 ▪ WO: Simonsberg–Stellenbosch ▪ Est 1812 ▪ 1stB 1995 ▪ Tasting & sales Mon-Fri 9–5 Sat 10-4 ▪ Closed Easter Fri-Sun, Dec 25/26 & Jan 1 ▪ Cellar tours by appt ▪ Picnic baskets, booking required ▪ Pizzas, cheese platters, craft beer ▪ Functions ▪ Walks/hikes ▪ Game ▪ Guest cottage ▪ Owner(s) Murray Boustred Trust ▪ Cellarmaster(s) Chris Boustred (Jan 2011) ▪ Winemaker(s)/viticulturist(s) Chris Boustred (Jan 2007) ▪ 55ha/25ha (cab, merlot, ptage, shiraz, chenin) ▪ 130t/10,000cs own label 80% red 20% white ▪ BWI, IPW ▪ PO Box 2032 Dennesig 7601 ▪ info@ remhoogte.co.za ▪ www.remhoogte.co.za ▪ S 33° 53' 4.2" E 018° 51' 4.6" ▪ F +27 (0)21-889-6907 ▪ **T +27 (0)21-889-5005**

Re'Mogo Wines ⓘ ♿

Founded in 2004 by black entrepreneurs to establish business interests in wine, among other sectors, Re'Mogo (Setswana for 'standing together', illustrated on the label by giraffes with necks intertwined) is fronted by Thamsanqa Hombana. Based in Khayamandi, Stellenbosch, and Gugulethu, Cape Town, the brand currently sources wines from Olifants River.

Pinotage ⊘ ★★★ Ripe **14** has vanilla-tinged prunes & black plums, coming across almost sweet on the palate though wine is dry. Good tannin grip. Certified organic & Fairtrade, as all. **Rosé** (NEW) ⊘ ★★ From pinotage, giving a berry character to **14**, finishing softly dry & fruity. **Chenin Blanc** (NEW) ⊘ ★★☆ Vibrant, with zesty freshness that gets the taste buds going, **14** offers passionfruit, crunchy apple. **Semi Sweet Sparkling Rosé** (NEW) ⊘ ★★ Fruity & fun bubbly from pinotage, **14**'s fruit pastille & semi-sweet flavours are ideal party fare. Also tasted: **Cabernet Sauvignon-Pinotage** ⊘ **14** ★★☆ **Chardonnay** ⊘ **14** ★★★ **Dry Sparkling** ⊘ ⊘ **14** ★★★ — CR, CvZ

Location/map: Stellenbosch ▪ Map grid reference: E4 ▪ WO: Western Cape ▪ Est 2004, Trust est 2011 ▪ Tasting & sales Mon-Fri & pub hols 9-3 Sat 9-12 by appt only ▪ Owner(s) Simatule Trust t/a Remogo Holdings ▪ Winemaker(s) Klaas Coetzee (Stellar Winery) ▪ 50% red 50% white ▪ George Blake Street Stellenbosch 7599 / NY147 No. 7 Gugulethu 7750 ▪ remogo.holdings@gmail.com ▪ www.remogo.co.za ▪ S 33° 55' 9.47" E 018° 51' 7.90" ▪ F +27 (0)86-610-7047 ▪ **T +27 (0)82-638-6774**

☐ **Renosterbos** see Hofstraat Kelder

Restless River ⓘ ♨ ⊖

Anne and Craig Wessels' shed is now a cellar at their boutique set-up in the Hemel-en-Aarde, while they feel (a decade on) that they better understand their vines and cool sites, and their resolutely non-interventionist winemaking approach. 'We're happy to finally be doing everything so naturally, all under one roof.' Happy too at their maiden pinot noir crop. The only problem is the pleasant one that increased recognition (including new exports) means that their tiny volumes last year sold out in 3 months.

★★★★☆ **Cabernet Sauvignon** Characterful, rather unusual **12** (★★★★) first offers dried herbal fragrance, already hinting at complexity. The herbal quality becomes a touch greener on palate, but good length points to some intensity of fruit. Fine tannin structure. Integrated oaking, like **11**.

★★★★☆ **Chardonnay** Again, but maybe more so, **13** combines understated oak, tight intensity & power with generous citrus fruit & stony element. Poised & balanced; fine line of natural acidity. Probably the best yet of this impressively developing wine. — TJ

Location: Hermanus • Map: Elgin, Walker Bay & Bot River • WO: Upper Hemel-en-Aarde Valley • Est 1999 • 1stB 2005 • Tasting, sales & tours daily by appt • Closed all pub hols • Charcuterie, cheese platters & refreshments — booking essential • BYO picnic • Owner(s) Craig & Anne Wessels • Winemaker(s) Craig Wessels (Jan 2005) • Viticulturist(s) Kevin Watt (2012) • 20ha/7ha (cab, pinot, chard) • 10t/1,000cs own label 50% red 50% white • PO Box 1739 Hermanus 7200 • anne@restlessriver.com • www.restlessriver.com • S 34° 21' 26.11" E 19° 16' 32.80" • **T +27 (0)28-313-2881/+27 (0)82-650-3544**

☐ **Retief Wines** *see* Pearl Mountain
☐ **Reuben's** *see* The Goose Wines
☐ **Revelation** *see* Osbloed Wines

Reverie   ⓠ

Jacques de Klerk (also winemaker at The Winery of Good Hope) has a continuing programme of 'meticulous pruning and soil management' to hopefully preserve and rejuvenate the fine old block of Swartland chenin blanc (planted 1978) from which he makes the single wine for his boutique label. Exports have got under way, the family is growing (a second child) — all is well.

★★★★☆ **Chenin Blanc** Some will find **14** too delicate, airy, & light (at a mere 12% alcohol, flirting with peril!); others will revel in the subtlety & lingering purity of the nuances. Oxidative handling in old oak adds a hint of bruised apple as well as breadth — but the stony, saline quality is from the old Swartland vineyard. — TJ

Location: Stellenbosch • WO: Swartland • Est 2011 • 1stB 2012 • Tasting & sales by appt • Closed all pub hols • Owner(s) Jacques de Klerk • Cellarmaster(s)/viticulturist(s) Jacques de Klerk (Nov 2011) • Winemaker(s) Jacques de Klerk (Nov 2011), with Amelie de Klerk (Nov 2011) • 125cs own label 100% white • 5 Birkenhead Road Somerset West 7130 • reveriechenin@gmail.com • **T +27 (0)82-783-7647**

☐ **Rex Equus** *see* Perdeberg Winery

Reyneke Wines   ⓠ ⓞ ♿

Co-owner and viticulturist Johan Reyneke is delighted his neighbours continue to see the benefit of the organic approach; the Stellenbosch family farm Uitzicht has gone beyond that and is registered as biodynamic, a rare distinction in the Cape. 'We're converting another neighbour's vineyards to organic, bringing the count to four. More and more are knocking on the door to join our organic study group.' An Environmental Philosophy post-grad with Twitter handle @ZAVineHugger, Johan's passionate concern for the vines and well-being of the land is matched in the cellar by the brilliance of Rudiger Gretschel, chief guru at wine company Vinimark (which has an interest in the Reyneke brand). As one of the Cape's top wineries, its success continues to grow internationally and locally: the Vinehugger brand has been launched onto Woolworths retail shelves with positive results.

Biodynamic range

★★★★ **Pinotage** Ⓥ ⓞ Usual perfumed complexity on **12**. Forthcoming sweet fruit, its purity unchallenged by maturation in large older casks; big tannins; good dry finish. Few years will benefit.

★★★★☆ **Reserve Red** ⓞ **13** is straight syrah/shiraz, which it announces with authority & elegance in a flourish of deep & heady dark spice. More savoury than the Syrah, its rich vinosity is contained by fresh, form-giving tannins. Intense & unbelievably sustained finish.

★★★★☆ **Syrah** ⊘ ⓞ One of SA's great-value shirazes. **13** (★★★★★) richly scented with dark spice, herbs & ripe berries; similar sweet-fruited enticements lengthily reprised in its generous succulence, dry conclusion. Older oak simply rounds, fruit remains the focus. **12** was also very fine.

★★★★ **Cornerstone** ⓖ Plenty of spice & fleshy charm in cab franc-based **13**; merlot, cab add nuance & structure to warrant ageing. Light feel, a modest hint of new oak (20%) & ripe, dry tannins.

★★★★☆ **Chenin Blanc** ⓖ Power in **14**, as in all these wines, derives from concentration rather than alcohol (just 12.9%). Fruit purity (red apple, peach), lees- & subtle oak-enrichment combine in a masterly expression of chenin, sure to gain further intrigue over the years, which its structure & intensity will allow.

★★★★☆ **Reserve White** ⓖ **14** beautifully textured, both silky & with sense of firmness from portion 4 months on skins & natural ferment in mostly new oak. Structural elegance complements blackcurrant features reflecting lighter sauvignon blanc vintage. **13** (★★★★★) more concentrated.

★★★★ **Sauvignon Blanc** ⓖ Well balanced, with oaking (30%) attuned to difficult sauvignon vintage, **14** has some characteristic silkiness, weight & liveliness, but generally slighter than **13** (★★★★☆).

Organic range

Shiraz-Cabernet Sauvignon ⓥ ★★★ Increased cab (49%) lends more serious & grippy edge to **14**. Lacks immediate charm of also-tasted **13** (23% cab) with its supple, spicy approachability, well-tempered tannin. Coastal WO. Also tasted: **Sauvignon Blanc-Semillon** ⓥ **15** ★★★ — AL

Location/map: Stellenbosch ▪ Map grid reference: B6 ▪ WO: Stellenbosch/Coastal/Western Cape ▪ Est 1863 ▪ 1stB 1998 ▪ Tasting, vineyard walk & cellar tours by appt only ▪ Sales Mon-Fri 10-4 ▪ Paintings by Mila Posthumus on display ▪ Owner(s) Reyneke Wines (Pty) Ltd ▪ Cellarmaster(s) Rudiger Gretschel ▪ Winemaker(s) Rudiger Gretschel, with Jessica Garlick (Jan 2014) ▪ Viticulturist(s) Johan Reyneke ▪ 40ha/ 32ha (cabs s/f, merlot, ptage, shiraz, chenin, sauv) ▪ 270t/30,000cs own label 70% red 30% white + 2,000cs for clients ▪ CERES (organic), Demeter (biodynamic), IPW, WIETA ▪ PO Box 61 Vlottenburg 7604 ▪ wine@reynekewines.co.za ▪ www.reynekewines.co.za ▪ S 33° 57′ 27.7″ E 018° 45′ 7.0″ ▪ F +27 (0)21-881-3285 ▪ **T +27 (0)21-881-3517/3451**

Rhebokskloof Wine Estate   ⓟ ⓜ ⓞ ⓐ ⓖ

The centuries-old Paarl estate owned by Siebrits and Albie Laker of civils group ASLA is leaving no stone unturned in pursuit of the goal of becoming a top 10 producer. Under eminent 'wine manager'/mentor Francois Naudé, range updates continue the main focus on shiraz, Rhône blends, chardonnay and chenin blanc. Nikey van Zyl has come on board as viticulturist/farm manager (Karin Louw returning to the cellar to assist Rolanie Lotz), and is overseeing the last of the major replantings. Rhebokskloof is on the official list of producers of 'estate wine', and most of the blocks are registered as single-vineyards.

Flagship range

★★★★☆ **The Rhebok** Emphatic luxury statement. **13** Cape Blend of shiraz, pinotage (40%), splash mourvèdre lavished 2 years all-new French oak. Thrilling integration of buffed plum/mulberry fruit, fine-grained tannins & bold 14.5% alcohol; big in all ways.

Mountain Vineyards Reserves

★★★★ **Black Marble Hill Syrah** ⓥ Serious (21 months new oak) shiraz — best portion of best vineyard. Suave, smoky **12** concentrated yet not weighty; savoury tang adds freshness.

★★★★ **Sandstone Grove Chardonnay** Oak vanilla & oatmeal dominate **14** mid-2015 but underlying lemon & lime fruit likely to open with year or two in bottle & bring harmony. 30% new cask, 11 months. Not retasted: **Design Shiraz 12** ★★★☆

Vineyard Selections

Shiraz ★★★☆ Full, ripe mulberry opulence of **12** laced with white pepper, friendly 10% American wood adds vanilla gloss. **Chardonnay** ★★★★ Fresh oak (20% new) envelopes **14** mid-2015, but generous if still-tight citrus tones suggest wine will unfold over year/2 & become a classy food partner. WO Coastal. Also tasted: **Pinotage 13** ★★★★ **The MGS 12** ★★★★ Not retasted: **Viognier 13** ★★★★

Cellar Selections

Flat Rock Red ⓝⓔⓦ ★★★ **13** pinotage/shiraz blend in chunky, rustic mode; barbecue wine. Some Darling fruit. **Sauvignon Blanc** ★★★ Green apple & grass of **15** a pleasant pick me up from Stellenbosch grapes. **Hillside White** ⓝⓔⓦ ★★ Chenin, chardonnay & viognier give peach & pineapple tastiness to **14**, unencumbered by oak. Some Stellenbosch grapes. Also tasted: **Cabernet Sauvignon-Shiraz 13** ★★★★ **Bosstok Chenin Blanc 15** ★★★

Sparkling Wines

★★★★ **Méthode Cap Classique** ⓢ New livery for dry bubbly from chardonnay reflects serious **08**. 5 years on lees give richness cleaned by pinpoint mousse. Lifts bar on **07** (★★★☆).

Not retasted: **Rosé Sparkling 14** ★★★ — DS

Location: Paarl ▪ Map: Paarl & Wellington ▪ Map grid reference: D3 ▪ WO: Paarl/Coastal/Stellenbosch ▪ 1stB 1975 ▪ Tasting & sales Mon-Fri 9-5 Sat/Sun 10-3 ▪ Fee R20/5 wines ▪ Cellar tours by appt ▪ Rhebokskloof Restaurant open daily for b'fast & lunch; dinner Fri & by appt ▪ Facilities for children ▪ Tour groups ▪ Gifts ▪ Weddings, functions & conferences ▪ Mountain bike & hiking trails ▪ Live concerts ▪ Owner(s) Siebrits & Albie Laker, ASLA Group ▪ Winemaker(s) Rolanie Lotz (Jan 2007), with Karin Louw (2007) ▪ Viticulturist(s) Nikey van Zyl (Nov 2014) ▪ 180ha/38ha (cab, carignan, durif, grenache n/b, mourv, p verdot, ptage, shiraz, chard, chenin, marsanne, rouss, viog) ▪ 250t/30,000cs own label 75% red 20% white 5% rosé + 3,000cs for buyers own brands ▪ CVC member ▪ PO Box 2637 Paarl 7620 ▪ info@ rhebokskloof.co.za ▪ www.rhebokskloof.co.za ▪ S 33° 41' 6platters___new.1" E 018° 55' 56.6" ▪ F +27 (0)21-869-8386 ▪ **T +27 (0)21-869-8386**

☐ **Rhinofields** *see* Durbanville Hills
☐ **Rhino of Linton Park** *see* The Rhino of Linton Park
☐ **Rhino Tears** *see* Mount Vernon Estate

Richard Kershaw Wines ⓠ

Owner-winemaker Richard Kershaw also has a prestigious Master of Wine diploma tucked under his arm. He established his boutique winery in Elgin to create clonally selected wine grown in its cooler climate, focusing on the two varieties he believes best suited to the area. Richard's next project is 'terroir-specific clone-identified wines'. No doubt they will also receive the acclaim he's becoming accustomed to, locally and abroad — with 11 export markets, 'most interestingly Beaune', in the heart of Burgundy.

Kershaw Clonal Selections

★★★★★ **Elgin Syrah** Allspice & white pepper frame focused iodine-tinged dark berry fruit. Exceptional **13** (★★★★★) quieter in youth than **12** debut, but savoury notes & tempered tannins on song to complement richer dishes & amplify the 'umami' tone of both food & wine. Half new casks, 17 months.

★★★★★ **Elgin Chardonnay** A masterpiece in understatement; precise, classy... & delicious. Maximal taste from minimal intervention: no pumps used, no additions. **14** (★★★★★) scintillates; refined, but rich, complex & earthy, with a taut minerality & ethereal oak. A keeper, like **13**. — DS

Location/WO: Elgin ▪ Map: Elgin, Walker Bay & Bot River ▪ Est/1stB 2012 ▪ Tasting by appt ▪ Owner(s) Richard Kershaw ▪ Cellarmaster(s) Richard Kershaw (2012) ▪ 25t/±2,700cs own label 45% red 55% white ▪ PO Box 77 Grabouw 7160 ▪ info@richardkershawwines.co.za ▪ www.richardkershawwines.co.za ▪ S 34° 12' 12.07" E 19° 02' 35.10" ▪ F +27 (0)86-637-6202 ▪ **T +27 (0)21-200-2589**

☐ **Richard's** *see* Richard Kershaw Wines

Richelieu

This South African brand is French in name, and straddles SA and France in character as demonstrated by the two brandies featured below. A third, Richelieu XO Cognac Fine Champagne is produced in Cognac (entitling it to be labelled 'cognac'), courtesy of a French company founded in 1962 by the late Anton Rupert of Distillers Corporation (now Distell, which owns the brand).

★★★★ **10 Year Vintage Brandy** Fine example of rare category of SA brandy, with well-matured spirit & potstill (30% minimum) components. Slightly altered blend shows lovely silkiness with the elegant dry richness, the fruit not too fruity, floral notes sidling into the complexity. Nudges higher rating.

Richelieu International ⓢ ★★★ Tweaked & improved blended brandy shows some nice complexity of aroma but the spiritous, slightly heavy body still calls for a mixer to dilute the force. — WB

Rickety Bridge Winery

This venerable Franschhoek property, part of the original La Provence farm granted to the first French Huguenots, has a winemaking history dating back to the 18th century. Its first owner, the widow Paulina de Villiers, lends her name to the super-premium range; current British owner, Duncan Spence, has transformed the property. The wine team under Wynand Grobler has steadily ratcheted up the bar, and the hospitality staff have created varied, family-welcoming cellardoor attractions, including most recently a range of wine ice-creams, made from the Foundation Stone wines and various fruits.

Icon Wines

★★★★☆ **The Bridge** Flagship from cab, seriously oaked (100% new, 25 months). Like **09**, **12** restrained & subtle, with firm structure & controlled power; shows wonderful integration of cool fruit & fine wood tannin. No **12**, **11**.

★★★★☆ **Road to Santiago** ⓝⓔⓦ From 110 year old Franschhoek semillon, **14** comes with ambitious price tag, but then only 900 bottles made – & do they sing! Exotic mandarin overlay to initially oaky vanilla, cinnamon & nutmeg characters, but then it all slows down, evens out, finishes regally & thrillingly dry.

Paulina's Reserve range

★★★★ **Cabernet Sauvignon** Quiet **12** (★★★★), sappy with slight herbaceous lift to dark fruit; more like iron-fisted **10** than fruit-filled **13**.

★★★★ **Semillon** Lanolin & wax nuances to **12**'s fennel tone, smooth entry & creamy finish with unobtrusive oak. None of the oxidative styling of **11** or oak sweetness of **10** (★★★★☆). Fermented/aged 13 months 25% new French barriques.

Not tasted: **Chenin Blanc**, **Sauvignon Blanc**.

Foundation Stone range

★★★★ **White** Like compelling **13**, **14** worth seeking out. Complex blend led by chenin, 15% each ugni blanc/trebbiano, roussanne & grenache blanc, drop viognier. White peach, apricot, nutty richness. Barrel fermented/aged before blending. WO W Cape.

Also tasted: **Rosé 15** ★★★ Not retasted: **Red 13** ★★★☆

Rickety Bridge range

★★★★ **Merlot** Serious & successful **13** has attractive sanguine, ferrous notes; as compact & intense as dark-fruited **12**, with 20% new oak adding form not flavour.

★★★★ **Shiraz** ⓥ **12** smoky & tarry; ripe, plush & long with bright acidity, tannic grip refreshes. Like savoury **11**, needs year/2 to meld. WO W Cape.

★★★★ **Chardonnay 14** reflects care taken (natural ferment in 15% new barriques, remainder in large old oak). Intensely flavoured, with smooth persistence, better wood integration than buttery **13** (★★★★).

★★★★ **Méthode Cap Classique Brut Rosé** Pretty antique lace hue, tiny dancing bubbles belie serious nature of latest **NV**. Pinot noir takes the lead (53%) to contribute the weight & berry fruit, chardonnay the lively conclusion. Also adding breadth & complexity is 30% barrel fermented portion.

Sauvignon Blanc ★★★ Vivacious **15** boasts forthcoming capsicum & grass, zesty tail. Perfect spring libation. WO W Cape. **Noble Late Chenin Blanc** ⓝⓔⓦ ★★★★ Old-oak-fermented **14** shows marzipan, thatch & lemon complexity, lively acidity to cleanse the palate. Savoury nuance for those who prefer less treacly desserts. Also tasted: **Pinotage 14** ★★★ **Chenin Blanc 15** ★★★ Not tasted: **Méthode Cap Classique Blanc de Blancs**. Discontinued: **Natural Sweet Chenin Blanc**. — WB, CvZ

Location/map: Franschhoek ▪ WO: Franschhoek/Western Cape/Swartland ▪ Est 1990 ▪ Tasting, sales & cellar tours Mon-Sat 9–7 (Dec-Mar) 9-5 (Apr-Nov) Sun 10-5 ▪ Closed Dec 25 & Jan 1 ▪ Fee R30, waived on purchase ▪ Paulina's at Rickety Bridge ▪ Facilities for children ▪ Gift shop ▪ Conferences ▪ Weddings ▪ Rickety Bridge Manor House ▪ Owner(s) Duncan Spence ▪ Cellarmaster(s)/winemaker(s) Wynand Grobler (Nov 2007) ▪ 91ha/39ha (cab, merlot, shiraz, chard, chenin, sauv, sem) ▪ 195t/28,000cs own label 45% red 45% white 10% rosé ▪ PO Box 455 Franschhoek 7690 ▪ info@ricketybridge.com ▪ www.ricketybridge.com ▪ S 33° 53' 58.5" E 019° 5' 27.6" ▪ F +27 (0)21-876-3486 ▪ **T +27 (0)21-876-2129**

Rico Suter Private Cellar ⓠ ⓐ

This large family property in Breedekloof has reverted to being a red-wine-only producer (unless a drop of viognier blended with shiraz counts), including a cinsaut – the grape currently a favourite of many local sommeliers. Rico Suter, with input from son Carlo, vinifies them, other son Bruno cares for the vines.

★★★★ **Cabernet Sauvignon-Syrah** ⓠ **12** (★★★☆) shows touch of cab's herbaceousness & slightly astringent tannins, last edition needed year/two to settle. Shade off still-selling **06**.

Cinsaut ⓠ ★★★☆ Engaging, characterful **12**, perfumed red fruit with mocha overtone, bone-dry & very quaffable. Not retasted: **Cabernet Sauvignon 05 ★★★ Petit Verdot 04 ★★★☆ Pinotage 12 ★★★☆ Syrah-Viognier 12 ★★★☆** — MW

Location: Worcester ▪ Map/WO: Breedekloof ▪ Est/1stB 2004 ▪ Tasting & sales by appt ▪ Guest house (bookings: erika@ricosuterwines.com) ▪ Owner(s) Suter Family Trust ▪ Winemaker(s) Rico & Carlo Suter ▪ Viticulturist(s) Bruno Suter (2004) ▪ 750ha/45ha (cab, cinsaut, p verdot, ptage, shiraz, sauv, viog) ▪ 8-15t/ha ▪ PO Box 38 Breerivier 6858 ▪ rico@ricosuterwines.com ▪ S 33° 31' 39.00" E 019° 15' 13.00" ▪ F +27 (0)86-642-6591 ▪ **T +27 (0)23-355-1822**

Ridgeback ⓠ ⓟ ⓐ ⓒ ⓒ ⓒ

The founders of this mountainside winery transplanted themselves to Paarl from Zimbabwe. Hence the signature Rhodesian Ridgeback, a southern African hunting dog combining tenacity with a gentleness of spirit. Toit Wessels, who started here as a student viticulturist 16 years ago, is now winemaker and GM. Last season he oversaw new chenin and cab plantings, and the launch of a bubbly (unready for review).

★★★★ **Cabernet Sauvignon 13** classic cab dark fruit & cedar in fresh balance. Sappy fruit core supported by lithe tannins & integrated oak (48% new). Already tempting but definitely ageworthy.

★★★★ **Cabernet Franc** Cab franc's signature walnut piquancy & dark perfumed fruit supported by ripe, balanced tannin & oak structure. **13** supple & juicy, with a long spicy farewell. Elegant & ageable.

★★★★ **Shiraz** Rich, dark & spicy but balanced, with well-crafted oak. **13** fresh & succulent, a serious undertone that will grace the table & improve in the cellar. Dapper step up on **11** (★★★★). **12** untasted.

★★★★ **Journey** ⓠ Well-crafted merlot-led Bordeaux blend in **13**. Flavoursome dark berry fruit clothes fine amenable tannins. Vibrant & juicy, dry finish. Enjoy now & over the next few years.

★★★★ **His Master's Choice** Shiraz-led **12** (★★★★☆) with mourvèdre & grenache (82/13/12), raises the bar on **11**. Savoury & streamlined, with new oak (75%) well integrated into generous dark fruit, liquorice & sprinkling of white pepper. A puppy, needing time to grow into its paws.

★★★★ **Chenin Blanc** Rich & aromatic **14** from bushvines. Spicy pineapple & peach flavours enhanced by oak fermentation/maturation & a dab of Natural Sweet viognier. Appealingly bright & drinkable.

★★★★ **Viognier 14** clean & tangy interpretation of this aromatic variety. Mixed-origin oak ferment/ ageing adds succulent & spicy flair, but fruit still the star. Not as flamboyant as **13** (★★★★☆) but balanced & vivacious solo or with spicy fare.

★★★★ **Natural Sweet Viognier 15** continues in piquantly fresh style. Lively, light (10.5% alcohol) & racy dessert wine that exudes pineapple & lime.

Also tasted: **Merlot 13 ★★★ Sauvignon Blanc 15 ★★★** Not retasted: **SGMV 13 ★★★** — MW

Location/WO: Paarl ▪ Map: Paarl & Wellington ▪ Map grid reference: D3 ▪ Est 1997 ▪ 1stB 2001 ▪ Tasting & sales Mon-Sat 10-5 (summer)/10-4 (winter) Sun 10-4 ▪ Fee R25/5 wines, R50/10 wines ▪ Closed Good Fri, Dec 25 & Jan 1 ▪ Cellar tours by appt ▪ The Deck Restaurant Tue-Sun 9.30-3.30 ▪ 4-star/5-room Ridgeback Guest House ▪ Hiking trails ▪ Children's play area ▪ Owner(s) Kilimanjaro Investments ▪ Cellarmaster(s)/ winemaker(s) Toit Wessels (Jan 2007) ▪ Viticulturist(s) Toit Wessels (Mar 2000) ▪ 65ha/35ha (cabs s/f, grenache, merlot, mourv, p verdot, shiraz, sauv, viog) ▪ 300t/30,000cs own label 60% red 35% white 5% sweet ▪ BWI, WIETA ▪ PO Box 2076 Windmeul Paarl 7630 ▪ tasting@ridgeback.co.za ▪ www.ridgebackwines.co.za ▪ S 33° 40' 24.9" E 018° 54' 53.5" ▪ F +27 (0)21-869-8146 ▪ **T +27 (0)21-869-8068**

☐ **Ridgelands** see Luddite Wines

Riebeek Cellars

Whilst prestigious neighbours in the Swartland grab attention with their small quantities of handcrafted wine, Riebeek Cellars continues to offer not only plentiful everyday bottlings but also more ambitious ranges which allow the winemaking team to flex their vinous muscles and try new ideas. All can be tasted in the wine boutique in Riebeek-Kasteel town centre, handily open every day of the week.

Kasteelberg range

★★★★ **Shiraz** Spice, sweet black fruit, alcohol & oak all combine to much better effect in **13** than **12** (★★★★). Still big & powerful but multiple layers of flavour should come right given time.

Viognier ★★★★ Pretty & perfumed **13** starts with flowers, giving way to charry spice & stonefruit. All-new French oak doesn't quite tame hefty alcohol, but overall, a pleasant drink. Not retasted: **Méthode Cap Classique NV** ★★★ **Soet Steen NV** ★★★☆ Not tasted: **Chenin Blanc**.

A Few Good Men range

Chardonnay ★★★★ Happy improvement for **14** with attractive buttery/creamy notes on pineapples & stonefruit. Slightly warm at finish but overall a fairly well-balanced drop. Also tasted: **Cabernet Sauvignon 13** ★★★ **Shiraz 13** ★★★☆ Not retasted: **Merlot 10** ★★★ **Pinotage 11** ★★★

Riebeek Cellars Collection

Chardonnay (ⓥ) ★★★ Drier than previous & all the better for it, unwooded **14** is fresh & citrussy with some creaminess, zippy acidity & good length. Great fun to drink.

Cabernet Sauvignon ★★★ Good varietal character on **14**, ripe black fruit, savoury/Marmite tang. Like all these, has few grams of sugar to add to the obvious, easy charm. **Cabernet Sauvignon-Merlot** ★★★ Fresh & juicy **14**, partly oaked, with soft tannins & sweet ripe fruit for everyday easy drinking. **Pinotage Rosé** ★★★ Palest of pale pinks, slightly confected flavours of pomegranates & watermelons on just-dry **15**. Also tasted: **Pinotage 13** ★★★ **Shiraz 14** ★★★ **Chenin Blanc 15** ★★ Not retasted: **Merlot 13** ★★★ **Shiraz-Cinsaut 13** ★★★ **Sauvignon Blanc 14** ★★ **Pieter Cruythoff Brut NV** ★★★ **Cape Ruby Port NV** ★★★

Montino range

Petillant Light (ⓐ) ★★ Semi-sweet, grapey **NV** perlé white. Low alcohol, as all these. Not retasted: **Petillant Natural Sweet Rosé NV** ★ **Petillant Natural Sweet Red-Rosso NV** ★ — CM

Location: Riebeek-Kasteel ▪ Map/WO: Swartland ▪ Est 1941 ▪ Tasting & sales Mon-Fri 9-5 Sat 9-4 Sun 10.30-4 (wine boutique) ▪ Closed Good Fri, Dec 25 & Jan 1 ▪ Cellar tours by appt ▪ BYO picnic ▪ Owner(s) ±40 shareholders ▪ Cellarmaster(s) Zakkie Bester (Dec 1999) ▪ Winemaker(s) Eric Saayman & Alecia Boshoff (Jan 1997/Dec 2004), with Wouter Loubser (Jan 2015) ▪ Viticulturist(s) Tharien Hansen (Jul 2013) ▪ 1,200ha (cab, carignan, merlot, mourv, ptage, shiraz, tinta amarela, chard, chenin, sauv, viog) ▪ 17,000t/300,000cs own label 50% red 40% white 10% rosé & ±80,000cs for clients ▪ Brands for clients: Broken Rock, Rocheburg, Royal, Steenbok ▪ BWI, Fairtrade ▪ PO Box 13 Riebeek Kasteel 7307 ▪ info@riebeekcellars.co.za ▪ www.riebeekcellars.co.za ▪ S 33° 22' 58.0" E 018° 54' 54.5" ▪ F +27 (0)22-448-1281 ▪ **T +27 (0)22-448-1213**

Rietvallei Wine Estate

Family-owned Rietvallei is one of the oldest wine estates in Robertson, growing, vinifying and marketing under the Rietvallei Estate, Stonedale and John B labels.

Location/map: Robertson ▪ Est 1864 ▪ 1stB 1975 ▪ Tasting & sales Mon-Fri 8.30–5 Sat 10–2 ▪ R25pp for groups of 15+ ▪ Closed Easter Fri/Sun, Dec 25 & Jan 1 ▪ Cellar tours by appt ▪ Cheese platters, book ahead for groups of 6+ ▪ Farm produce ▪ Conservation area ▪ Owner(s) Kobus Burger ▪ Cellarmaster(s)/winemaker(s) Kobus Burger (2003) ▪ Viticulturist(s) Wilhelm Treurnicht ▪ 215ha/130ha (cab, red muscadel, shiraz, chard, sauv) ▪ 2,500t/110,000cs own label 40% red 50% white 5% rosé 5% fortified + 950,000L bulk ▪ PO Box 386 Robertson 6705 ▪ info@rietvallei.co.za ▪ www.rietvallei.co.za ▪ S 33° 49' 25.7" E 019° 58' 39.4" ▪ F +27 (0)23-626-4514 ▪ **T +27 (0)23-626-3596**

☐ **Riggton** see Bonnievale Wines

Rijk's ⓠ ⌂ ◎ ♿

Abandoning Cape Town for life in the country exactly 20 years ago, Rijk's owner and viticulturist Neville Dorrington chose unfashionable Tulbagh, where he bought a large plot of virgin land. Though advised to plant fruit, he established vines instead. Today he and long-time winemaker Pierre Wahl specialise in chenin, pinotage and shiraz, and their stellar track record is a fitting reward for Neville's prescience and pioneering spirit. As is the recent expansion of the pinotage plantings, which will necessitate cellar extensions within the next four years.

Reserve range

★★★★★ Pinotage Selection of 10 best barrels, perfumed **11** with both power & finesse. Bright red berries, brooding oak spice & hints of coffee; cordial-like intensity amplified by marked alcohol, yet the whole is integrated, precise & focused. **10** (★★★★☆) spoke of warm vintage.

★★★★ Shiraz Higher percentage new oak (50%) on the Reserve bottling well knit, **11** shows more savoury elegance than **10**, fine tannins on plush palate, but lacks concentration of others in this range.

★★★★ Chenin Blanc ⓥ **09** will reward fans of fully ripe, barrel-fermented chenins with brush of sweetness. Youthful yet drinks well already, though shade off fine expression of **08** (★★★★☆).

Private Cellar range

★★★★ Pinotage Ripe & silky **11** shows serious intent & concentration. Varietal rustic notes combine with youngberry jam & hints of tar. Less powerful than Reserve, more elegant than Touch of Oak.

★★★★★ Shiraz Pure & concentrated black berries with slight stalky interest, **10** is well crafted, a commanding presence, but remains moreishly fresh & savoury. Young & powerful fruit effortlessly assimilates serious oaking (40% new) & high alcohol. **09** sold out untasted.

★★★★ Chenin Blanc Super-lively **12** (★★★★★) hits its stride with best oak integration yet & wonderful youthful freshness encapsulating opulent fruit & charming sweetness (7.5 g/l sugar vs 1.8 g/l for **11**).

★★★★★ Méthode Cap Classique Brut (NEW) Decent lees-ageing period (2 years) & bottle-ageing of final product make for rich & complex **12**, showing deliciously pure fruit, crisp acidity & a tangy, savoury finish. 100% chardonnay.

Touch of Oak range

★★★★ Pinotage ⓥ **12** (★★★☆) varietally true banana, spiced mulberries & smoke; surprisingly bold, concentrated & serious for this range. Some Swartland fruit. **11** more satisfying though less typical.

★★★★★ Chenin Blanc ⊘ Ripe & fleshy peach & pear on **13**, wonderfully pure with only 30% wooded component, very nicely integrated. Excellent poise & harmony – a consistent benchmark for rich but lightly wooded fruity chenin. Coastal WO.

Also tasted: Shiraz 12 ★★★★ — HJ

Location/map: Tulbagh ▪ WO: Tulbagh/Coastal ▪ Est 1996 ▪ 1stB 2000 ▪ Tasting & sales Mon-Fri 10–4 Sat 10–2 ▪ Fee R10/wine, waived on purchase ▪ Closed Easter Fri-Mon, Dec 25 & Jan 1 ▪ Cellar tours by appt ▪ Rijk's Guest House ▪ Conferences ▪ Owner(s)/viticulturist(s) Neville Dorrington ▪ Winemaker(s) Pierre Wahl (Jan 2002) ▪ 135ha/36ha (carignan, grenache noir, mourv, ptage, shiraz, tinta amarela, chard, chenin, viog) ▪ 210t/24,000cs own label 75% red 25% white ▪ IPW ▪ PO Box 400 Tulbagh 6820 ▪ wine@rijks.co.za ▪ www.rijkswine.com ▪ S 33° 16' 1.5" E 019° 8' 42.0" ▪ F +27 (0)23-230-1650 ▪ **T +27 (0)23-230-1622**

Rivendell ⓠ ⑪ ◎ Ⓐ

Heimo and Maria Thalhammer's small Bot River vineyard is planted with just two varieties, sauvignon blanc and shiraz, vinified off-site by local consultant winemakers for enjoyment on-site in their bistro and tasting room, as well as by guests using their function venues.

★★★★ Shiraz ⓥ Violets & perfume intro to **13** (★★★☆), which just misses fine texture of **12** but still pleases with meaty flavours, mixed with black plums & spice.

★★★★ Sauvignon Blanc ⓥ **14** lots of gooseberries & guavas on nose before lashings of tinned grapefruit, threaded with bracing acidity; dies away for soft finish. Tad less impressive than **13** (★★★★☆).

Not retasted: Rosé 14 ★★★☆ — CM

Location: Bot River ▪ Map: Elgin, Walker Bay & Bot River ▪ WO: Bot River/Walker Bay ▪ Est 2008 ▪ 1stB 2011 ▪ Tasting & sales daily 9-5 ▪ Cheese platters ▪ Restaurant open for b'fast, lunch & dinner; cater for functions of various sizes ▪ Picnics in summer, to be pre-booked ▪ Facilities for children ▪ Tour groups ▪ Venue for weddings & seminars with fully equipped kitchen (94 pax inside) ▪ Walks/hikes ▪ Owner(s) Whales & Castle Investments (Pty) Ltd, with shareholders Heimo & Maria Thalhammer ▪ Winemaker(s) Kobie Viljoen (Mar 2010, consultant) & PJ Geyer (Feb 2013, Barton) ▪ Viticulturist(s) Schalk du Toit (Mar 2008, consultant) ▪ ±8ha/±4ha (shiraz, sauv) ▪ 32t/1,000cs own label 33% red 67% white ▪ PO Box 570 Onrusrivier 7201 ▪ office@rivendell-estate.co.za ▪ www.rivendell-estate.co.za ▪ S 34° 18' 5.22" E 019° 8' 32.23" ▪ F +27 (0)28-284-9597 ▪ **T +27 (0)28-284-9185/9597**

☐ **River Garden** see Lourensford Wine Estate

RiverGold Private Cellar   Ⓨ ⊖ ⊚ (NEW)

It was the striking colour of the reflected sunset on the Breede River which prompted the name of Boyce Naidoo's estate near Bonnievale. Envisioning an 'unforgettable experience' arising from a 'combination of fine wine, accommodation and a venue with stimulating architecture', Boyce has engaged the 40+ years' experience of viticulturist Herman Jonker and talents of winemaker and neighbour Lourens van der Westhuizen to craft a boutique range, untasted this edition.

Location: Bonnievale ▪ Map: Robertson ▪ Est/1stB 2010 ▪ Tasting by appt ▪ Closed Sun, Dec 25 & Jan 1 ▪ BYO picnic ▪ Conference facilities ▪ Owner(s) Boyce Naidoo ▪ Cellarmaster(s)/winemaker(s) Lourens van der Westhuizen (2009, consultant) ▪ Viticulturist(s) Herman Jonker (2011) ▪ 30ha/8ha (cab, merlot, shiraz, chenin, sauv) ▪ 25t/2,500cs own label 50% red 50% white ▪ WIETA ▪ PO Box 1065 Robertson 6705 ▪ graeme@ rivergold.co.za ▪ S 33° 55' 42.63" E 020° 0' 46.61" ▪ F +27 (0)23-616-2181 ▪ **T +27 (0)23-616-2218**

☐ **River Grandeur** see Viljoensdrift Fine Wines & Cruises
☐ **River Horse** see Hirst Wines
☐ **Riverscape** see Viljoensdrift Fine Wines & Cruises
☐ **River's End** see Stellar Winery
☐ **Robert Alexander** see Nico van der Merwe Wines

Robertson Wide River Export Company

Joint venture between Robertson Winery and Vinimark, handling all the cellar's exports under labels such as Robertson Winery, Kaapdal, Kleindal, Silversands and Veldt. See Vinimark for contact details.

Robertson Winery   Ⓨ ⊚ ⓰

2015 was a bumper year in terms of both production (record 38,200 tons) and quality, say the winemaking team at this dynamic grower-owned winery, established in an old chapel in 1941. Since the first own-label bottling in 1984, there has been constant refinement of the multifaceted offering. So much so that the flagship range, featuring unique top-quality parcels from member farmers, has outgrown its cellar in Robertson town centre and is now vinified at the newly purchased ex-KWV Vinova facility. Whether it's bag-in-box, bottle, sweet, sparkling or dry, Robertson Winery has it covered.

Constitution Road range

★★★★☆ **Shiraz 12 (★★★★)** a sophisticated, ripe & richly fruited mouthful but a tad lighter, less intense, than **11**. Succulent dark spicy elements on a poised, long palate.

★★★★ **Chardonnay** (NEW) Confident, nuanced debut of structured **13**. Creamy richness is countered by zippy citrus highlights. Refined & long. Oak is all French, all new.

Vineyard Selection range

★★★★ **Prospect Hill Cabernet Sauvignon 13** matches tone of **12** in its depth, density & gentle tannic grip from just 30% new French oak. Fruit is the hero with cassis succulence & light fynbos brush.

★★★★ **Wolfkloof Shiraz** (Ⓩ) From cool Langeberg slope, **12** continues powerful modern style, just 40% new oak makes for greater harmony, acidity adds tangy freshness.

★★★★ **Kings River Chardonnay** ⓦ Single block on Kings River farm, **13** repeats last-tasted **11**'s rating. Curvaceous but well structured; fresh yet elegant & long.

★★★★ **Retreat Sauvignon Blanc** Lemon sherbet tartness typifies **14** (★★★), simpler & less concentrated than **13**.

Also tasted: **Phanto Ridge Pinotage 13** ★★★☆

Winery range

Cabernet Sauvignon ★★★ Light silky texture to juicy blackcurrant generosity of **14**. Supple & easy. Oak, as with most reds in range, is from staves. **Pinot Noir** ★★★ Steady as she goes for light yet firm **14**. Abundant forest floor verve & smoky sheen too (though unwooded). **Pinotage** ★★ Bright & breezy raspberry cheer on easy **14**. **Cabernet Sauvignon-Shiraz** ★★★ Cabernet has a 2% edge over shiraz in medium-bodied **14**. Juicy, with some density & light tannic grip. **Pinot Grigio** ★★ Simple lemon sherbet crispness to **15**. **Lightly Sparkling Sauvignon Blanc** ⓝⓔⓦ ★★☆ Prickle of tiny bubbles adds interest to light, zippy, lemongrass & flint flavour of maiden **15**. **Gewürztraminer Special Late Harvest** ★★★ Sweetly heady rose-scented **15** is charming & light bodied. The tail tastes dry & clean courtesy of focused balance of fruit & acid. **White Muscadel** ★★★ Clean, sweet muscat seduction on well-balanced & -defined **12**. Also tasted: **Merlot 14** ★★★ **Ruby Cabernet** ⊘ **14** ★★★ **Shiraz 14** ★★☆ **Chardonnay 15** ★★★ **Chenin Blanc 15** ★★★ **Sauvignon Blanc 15** ★★★☆ Not retasted: **Viognier 14** ★★★ **Beaukett 14** ★★★ **Méthode Cap Classique 07** ★★★ **Cape Ruby 08** ★★★ Not tasted: **Red Muscadel**.

Chapel range

Cabernet Sauvignon-Merlot ⊘ ★★☆ Light oaking (4 months on staves) adds extra dimension to bright berry charm of **14**, which improves on previous. Includes splashes ruby cab, shiraz. Also in 500 ml & 1.5L, like next two. **Chenin Blanc-Colombar** ★★ Vivid peach & nectarine life to light-bodied **14** quaffer. **Sweet Red** ⓝⓔⓦ ★★ Fynbos edge to plummy black fruit on low-alcohol **NV** sweetie. Clean dry finish. Also tasted: **Extra Light NV** ★★ **Semi-Sweet NV** ★★ **Natural Sweet Rosé NV** ★★

Natural Sweet range

Rosé ★★ Tangy **NV** low-alcohol pink with bright, sweet succulence. Unfussy summertime sipper. Also tasted: **Red NV** ★★ **White NV** ★☆

Light Cultivar range

Extra Light Merlot ★★ Fruity blackberry tang & light backbone to easy low-alcohol (10%) **14**. **Pinotage Rosé** ★★ Low-alcohol (9%) **15**, with simple & easy red-berry succulence. Also tasted: **Light Chenin Blanc 15** ★★ **Extra Light Sauvignon Blanc 15** ★☆

Sparkling Wines

Sweet Red ★★ Foamy spicy plum zip on sweet **NV** fizz. Light 7.5% alcohol, like most in range. **Brut** ★★ Lively lemon crispness & bright bubble on **NV** sparkler. Alcohol 12%. Also tasted: **Sweet Rosé NV** ★★ **Sweet White NV** ★★

One-Litre Combibloc range

Merlot ⊘ ★★★ **14** keeps up standard of ripe fruitcake bounty of **13**. Soft textured with light oak frame. **Chardonnay** ⊘ ★★★ Gentle citrus appeal to **15**. Fresh & light with nice body. **Selected Stein** ★★ Light floral nuance to low-alcohol (10.5%) **NV** white. Dry finish. Also in 500 ml, like next. **Fruity Late Harvest** ★★ Gently sweet, juicy peach tones to low-alcohol (10.5%) **NV** white. **Smooth Sweet Red** ★★ Cheery berry freshness & light sweetness on unwooded **NV**. Also tasted: **Cabernet Sauvignon** ⊘ **14** ★★★ **Smooth Dry Red NV** ★★ **Sauvignon Blanc 15** ★★★☆ **Crisp Extra Light NV** ★☆ **Crisp Dry White NV** ★★ **Natural Sweet Rosé NV** ★★ **Natural Sweet White NV** ★☆

Two-Litre Certified Cultivar Slimline range

Ruby Cabernet ★★★ Fynbos edge to gentle black fruit on revisited **14**. Light & friendly. **Chenin Blanc** ★★★ Unfussy, zippy & zesty green apricot ease to **15**. Also tasted: **Cabernet Sauvignon 14** ★★★ **Merlot 14** ★★★ **Shiraz 14** ★★★ **Chardonnay 15** ★★★ **Sauvignon Blanc 15** ★★★☆

Three-Litre Cultivar Slimline range

Shiraz ★★☆ Squishy plum ease & approachability to light-bodied unfussy **14**. **Extra Light Sauvignon Blanc ★☆** Pithy grapefruit airiness to **15**. Just 10% alcohol. **Natural Sweet White ★☆** Grapey tang & freshness to sweetly simple **NV** low-alcohol white. Also tasted: **Cabernet Sauvignon 14 ★★★ Merlot 14 ★★★ Chardonnay 15 ★★★ Sauvignon Blanc 15 ★★☆**

Three-Litre Blended range

Smooth Dry Red ★★ Light-bodied red fruit vibrancy & ease to smooth, unfussy **NV**. **Crisp Dry White ★★** Interplay of guava & lemon zest on tangy **NV** white. **Refreshing Extra Light ★☆** Shy grassy notes on tangy low-alcohol (9.5%) **NV** white. **Johannisberger Semi-Sweet White ★☆** Honeyed tail balances zippy lemon entry of refreshing **NV**. Also tasted: **Natural Sweet Red (Slimline Packed) NV ★★ Natural Sweet Rosé (Slimline Packed) NV ★☆ Johannisberger Semi-Sweet Red NV ★☆**

Brandy range

★★★★ William Robertson 7 Year Potstill ⓝ Smooth & refined, with more ripe fruit complexity (built around apricot) than the two blended versions — this 100% potstill — though recognisably family in stressing the less obviously fruity components. Lower 38% alcohol gives more elegance.

William Robertson 5 Year ⓝ ⊘ **★★★** Prunes, dried peach & nuts, & a hint of mustiness on this blended brandy, designed for mixing, but neither very heavy nor very fiery. Like other 5 year version, with 40% potstill component. **5 Year ★★★** Rather fresher aromas of prunes & dried peach on this version of 5 year matured blended brandy, though also a trifle idiosyncratic. Fairly smooth & not too fiery, with a dry conclusion. These brandies all from colombard & distilled at Oude Molen. — TJ, FM

Location/map/WO: Robertson ▪ Est 1941 ▪ 1stB 1987 ▪ Tasting & sales Mon-Fri 9—5.30 Sat/pub hols 9-3 Sun 9—1 ▪ Closed Good Fri, Dec 25 & Jan 1 ▪ Cellar tours by appt ▪ Conferences ▪ Small wine museum ▪ Owner(s) 43 members ▪ Cellarmaster(s) Bowen Botha (Jan 1982) ▪ Winemaker(s) Francois Weich (Sep 1997), Jacques Roux (Jan 2001), Thys Loubser & Olivia Poonah (both Jan 2012) ▪ Viticulturist(s) Briaan Stipp (May 2005) ▪ 2,200ha (cab, shiraz, chard, chenin, sauv) ▪ 38,200t ▪ ISO 22000, WIETA ▪ PO Box 556 Robertson 6705 ▪ info@robertsonwine.co.za ▪ www.robertsonwinery.co.za ▪ S 33° 48' 36.8" E 019° 52' 51.4" ▪ F +27 (0)23-626-6807/+27 (0)23-626-4788 (sales) ▪ **T +27 (0)23-626-7080/+27 (0)23-626-8817 (sales)**

Robert Stanford Estate   ⓠ ⓟ ⓞ ⓐ

Established in 1855, this hillside property once owned by the entrepreneur Sir Robert Stanford is one of Walker Bay's oldest, and home to winegrowing since the 1890s. But heritage is not standing in the way of vineyard fine-tuning 'to optimise the maritime climate', director Jan Malan says, adding that a sweet wine is joining the range, the on-site distillery has additional products and a new festival is on the cards.

Sir Robert Stanford Estate range

★★★★ Shiraz ⓧ Potentially boisterous blackberry fruit of **10** cajoled into order by layers of warm spice; lovely composure & unwavering length of flavour swaddle 14.9% alcohol.

★★★★ The Hansom 13 cab with cab franc & merlot first since **10**. Clean, ripe, full berry fruit. Unshowy, restrained, despite some sweetness (offset by big acidity). Modestly oaked; firm, quiet tannins.

★★★★ Sauvignon Blanc Some sweet softness evident on undemanding but suave **14** (**★★★☆**), along with good, balanced flavours. Less persistent than last-tasted **12**.

Pinot Noir ⓝ **★★★☆** Bright, fresh red cherry notes on lightly oaked **13**. Notable acidity rather than tannin provides structure; flavours pleasing rather than intense. **Amber** ⓝ **★★★** Provisionally rated pre-bottling sample of **14** dessert from hanepoot is grapey-sweet but well balanced with acid for clean, almost dry-finishing effect. Also tasted: **Rosé 14 ★★★** Occasional release: **Chenin Blanc**.

Cutters Cove range

Shiraz-Viognier ★★☆ Quietly perfumed aromas on **14**. Lightly oaked, soft, ripe & unassuming — well calculated for easy pleasure. WO W Cape. Also tasted: **Chenin Blanc 14 ★★★** — TJ

Location: Stanford ▪ Map: Elgin, Walker Bay & Bot River ▪ WO: Walker Bay/Western Cape ▪ Est 1855 ▪ 1stB 2008 ▪ Tasting & sales Fri-Mon 10-3.30 ▪ Closed Good Fri, Dec 25 & Jan 1 ▪ Madre's Kitchen Thu-Mon 8-4 ▪ Facilities for children ▪ Gift shop ▪ Farm produce ▪ Conservation area ▪ Distillery ▪ Tractor tours/vineyard walks by appt ▪ Owner(s) Robert Stanford Vineyards (Pty) Ltd ▪ Winemaker(s) RJ Botha (Kleine

Zalze) ▪ Viticulturist(s) Jan Malan (Jan 2003) ▪ 176ha/60ha (pinot, shiraz, chenin, sauv) ▪ 320t/2,500cs
own label 40% red 30% white 15% rosé 15% MCC ▪ BWI champion ▪ wines@robertstanfordestate.co.za
▪ www.robertstanfordestate.co.za ▪ S 34° 25' 49.41" E 019° 27' 49.98" ▪ F +27 (0)86-655-6944 ▪
T +27 (0)28-341-0647

Robin Hood Legendary Wine Series

Mark Simpson, owner of this fun, food-styled quartet (and separately listed, upmarket Arumdale Cool
Climate Wines), intends the Robin Hood 'fourpack' as an accompaniment to the whole meal, beginning
with Maid Marian (hors d'oeuvres) and finishing with Friar Tuck (dessert, cheese, even curry/masala).

Robin Hood ★★★ Though it has few grams sugar, **NV** cab/shiraz is driest of all. Light, pleasant black &
blue berry fruit. Elgin grapes, as all. **Little John** ★★★ Tropical pineapple & lemon waft on off-dry **NV**
sauvignon blanc. Light & gentle. Also tasted: **Maid Marian NV** ★★ **Friar Tuck NV** ★★ — FM

☐ **Rocheburg** *see* Riebeek Cellars
☐ **Rockfield** *see* Du Preez Estate

Rogge Cloof   ⓘ ⑪ ⌂ ⌖ ⍟

Wine pioneer (and new mother) Bi-Anne du Toit, only the second vinegrower in the emerging Sutherland-Karoo district, has joined forces with her neighbours from across the road in an 'umbrella' boutique
venture featuring her fledgling Snowfield brand, the longer-established Emineo and Cape to Cairo
labels, and brand-new Fair Karoo, Salpeterkop and Sneeukop. The wines are made on-site and in partner
cellars around the Western Cape, and increasingly will showcase the operation's own high-altitude vineyards near Sutherland, officially SA's coldest town and home to the SA Astronomical Observatory (hence
the highly unusual inclusion of stargazing in Rogge Cloof's list of visitor amenities).

Emineo range
★★★★ **Liber II JLS** ⓘ Poised **07** cab (65%) with merlot & pinotage. When last tasted, minty choco-
late aromas, lively cassis underpinned by acidity & tannin.
★★★★ **Liber III RG** ⓘ **07** big, ebullient shiraz with splash mourvèdre ex Durbanville & Swartland.
Seriously styled, with polished oak when tasted some time ago.
Not retasted: **Liber I OCG 06** ★★★☆

Cape to Cairo range
Syrah ⓘ ★★★ Accessible **07**'s ripe fruit wrapped in sweet oak, pleasing lingering savouriness when
tasted some years ago. Breede River Valley WO. — KM, CvZ

Location: Sutherland ▪ WO: Durbanville/Breede River Valley/Coastal ▪ Est 1756 ▪ 1stB 2006 ▪ Tasting,
sales & cellar tours by appt ▪ Meals & picnics available ▪ Facilities for children ▪ Tour groups ▪ Gift shop ▪
Farm produce ▪ Walks/hikes ▪ Conservation area ▪ 4x4 trail ▪ MTB trail ▪ Museum ▪ Guest house ▪ Nature
reserve ▪ Stargazing ▪ Cellarmaster(s)/winemaker(s)/viticulturist(s) Bi-Anne du Toit ▪ 2,500ha total ▪
(mourv, shiraz, viog) ▪ 95% red 4% white 1% fortified ▪ Other export brands: Cape to Cairo, Emineo, Fair
Karoo, Salpeterkop, Sneeukop, Snowfield ▪ Off the R354, Roggeveld Karoo, Sutherland 6920 ▪ info@
roggecloof.com ▪ www.roggecloof.com ▪ S 32° 28' 44.3" E 020° 39' 12.3" ▪ **T +27 (0)23-004-0673**

Romond Vineyards   ⓘ ⌂ ⌖

As promised last edition, Romond Vineyards have new wines, including a varietal cabernet franc which
'hopefully will confirm Helderberg's West Peak as the prime terroir for this grape', notes André
Liebenberg, advertising commercials director and boutique vintner with wife Rhona. The couple's welcoming cellardoor, with said peak a majestic backdrop, is the venue for unsurprisingly popular group
tastings. 'We spare no effort to make them memorable.'

Rebus range
★★★★ **Fanfaronne** ⓘ Fragrant **09** (★★★★★) best yet; complex, classic cab franc leads Bordeaux
blend with cab, merlot. Savoury fruit balances firmly structured tannins. Step up from **07**; no **08**.
Cabernet Franc ★★★☆ **10** shows maturity in its colour. Herbal aromas turn to more herbaceous
character of full-fruited but not intense palate. Strong, dry grip. Note 15.4% alcohol. **Merlot**

★★★★ Big, ripe **12** shows dark fruit, with hints of tobacco & chocolate. Both softly textured & drily lean; powerful & grippy. **Cape Cuvée** (NEW) ★★★★ From pinotage (68%) plus cab & merlot, **11** declares itself with deep, enticing aromas. Though also very ripe, a touch lighter & fresher than the other reds tasted this year, though nearly 3 years in barrel makes for some dry, oaky dustiness. Not retasted: **Pinotage 09** ★★★★ **Impromptu 10** ★★★☆ — TJ

Location/WO: Stellenbosch ▪ Map: Helderberg ▪ Est 1993 ▪ 1stB 2003 ▪ Tasting, sales & tours by appt Mon-Sat 10-5.30 Sun 11-5.30 ▪ Fee R40, waived on purchase ▪ Closed Easter Fri-Sun, Dec 25/26 & Jan 1 ▪ Olive oil ▪ The Vintner's Loft self-catering apartment ▪ Owner(s) André & Rhona Liebenberg ▪ Winemaker(s) André Liebenberg ▪ Viticulturist(s) Francois Hanekom (May 2007) ▪ 11.5ha/9.5ha (cabs s/f, merlot, ptage) ▪ PO Box 5634 Helderberg 7135 ▪ info@romond.co.za ▪ www.romond.co.za ▪ S 34° 1' 52.61" E 018° 49' 59.67" ▪ F +27 (0)21-855-0428 ▪ **T +27 (0)21-855-4566**

☐ **Roodeberg** *see* KWV

Roodezandt Wines   (wine)(age)(wheelchair)

Under stalwart cellarmaster Christie Steytler (36 vintages here), grower-owned Roodezandt remains a producer of mostly bulk wine — well over 20 million litres — for brand owners in SA and abroad. But Christie and team also invite visitors to the Robertson cellardoor to taste and buy the own bottlings.

Roodezandt range

Late Harvest (NEW) ⊘ ⊛ ★★★ Mostly chenin, but splash white muscadel is noticeable on light, grapey **NV**. Skilfully crafted, bright acidity makes for easy & moreish semi-sweet.

Cabernet Sauvignon ★★★ Perfumed red fruit & spice with herbal interest on **13**. Juicy & sweet fruited; cheerful, well-balanced expression of the variety. **Sauvignon Blanc** ★★★ Tentatively rated **15** tank sample is very young but already shows pungent peach & citrus blossom aromas, clean & zippy flavours in fine balance. Also tasted: **Syrah 13** ★★★ **Chenin Blanc 15** ★★★ Not retasted: **Red Muscadel 12** ★★★ Discontinued: **Special Late Harvest**.

Balthazar range

★★★★ **Chardonnay Brut Méthode Cap Classique** (age) Elegant top-label sparkling. **09** shows appealing marzipan notes, toned yet generous body, nutty conclusion.

Keizer's Creek range

The Red (age) ★★ Unwooded plush-fruited **NV** blend offers light, uncomplicated party fun. Near-equal pinotage, cab & merlot. — HJ

Location/map/WO: Robertson ▪ Est 1953 ▪ Tasting & sales Mon-Fri 9-5 ▪ Cellar tours by appt Mon-Fri 8-12 & 2-5 ▪ Closed all pub hols ▪ Sales (at cellar price) also from La Verne Wine Boutique Mon-Fri 9-5.30 Sat 9-5 ▪ Facilities for children ▪ Owner(s) 60 members ▪ Cellarmaster(s) Christie Steytler (May 1980) ▪ Winemaker(s) Jean du Plessis (2012), with Tiaan Blom (Oct 2005) ▪ Viticulturist(s) Jaco Lategan (Dec 2006) ▪ 1,800ha (cab, merlot, ptage, ruby cab, shiraz, chard, chenin, cbard, muscadel w, sauv) ▪ 30,000t/23m L bulk ▪ BSCI, HACCP, IPW, WIETA ▪ PO Box 164 Robertson 6705 ▪ info@roodezandt.co.za ▪ www.roodezandt.co.za ▪ S 33° 48' 33.2" E 019° 52' 47.3" ▪ F +27 (0)23-626-5074 ▪ **T +27 (0)23-626-1160**

Rooiberg Winery   (wine)(food)(camera)(age)(wheelchair)

Formerly a co-operative, Robertson's progressive grower-owned private company Rooiberg is driven by three Ps: profit, people and planet, CEO Johan du Preez says. To this end comes concerted expansion in China, the US, Africa and Russia (among more than 20 international markets receiving their bulk and bottled wine). Contract crushing is done for others (including black economic empowerment companies), and sustainable winegrowing includes some organic production and conservation of over half its combined landholding.

Reserve range

★★★★ **Pinotage** 100% new oak for these well-crafted reds. **14** smoky bacon aroma, sour cherry & cranberry flavour bolstered by firm tannins & hint of savoury saltiness. Should mature well.

★★★★ **Shiraz** Smoky savoury aromas & full, ripe berry flavours, **14** with the usual assertive tannic bite boding well for ageing. Pair now with rich roasts or stews.

★★★★ **Chardonnay** Vanilla wafts usher in big, mouthfilling lemon-lime flavours on **14**, butter toffee hints from all-new oak on long citrus finish.

Also tasted: **Cabernet Sauvignon 14** ★★★☆ Not retasted: **Cape Blend 13** ★★★☆ Discontinued: **Merlot**.

Rooiberg range

★★★★ **Red Muscadel** We noted **13** fortified dessert as 'perfect for fireside sipping, or over ice for a summer pleaser'. **14** (★★★★☆) is more serious, deserving of contemplation. Vast honeyed raisin richness (264 g/l sugar) thrillingly balanced by acidity to fine, lively finish.

Cabernet Sauvignon-Merlot (Roodewyn) ★★★ Interesting dusty hay aroma, **14** crisp red berry flavours which linger attractively. Includes 10% petit verdot. **Pinotage Rosé** ★★ **15** tank sample is crisp, softly dry & refreshing, a pretty party sipper. **Chardonnay** ★★★ Unwooded **15** is fresh & clean, with green apple crispness & touch of lemon. Made for seafood. **Cape White Colombar** ★★★ Sprightly **15** is a step up. Green herbs & guava, crisp pineapple flavour, touch of sweetness on the finish. **Sauvignon Blanc** ★★ **15** appealingly combines grassy green leaves & tropical fruit salad tones with understated acidity. **Brut Sparkling** ★★ Fresh green apple tones & lively mousse, **NV** is a crisp & dry breakfast bubbly. **Blanc Natural Sweet** ★★★ From white muscadel, **15** tank sample has tangy acidity which gives a drier feel than expected from 45 g/l sugar. Finishes crisp & refreshing. **Cape Vintage** ★★★★ Port-style **13** from pinotage is rich & Christmasy, with notes of butter toffee, nuts & raisins, spirity mouthfeel. Will mature well. Also tasted: **Cabernet Sauvignon 13** ★★★ **Merlot 14** ★★ **Pinotage 14** ★★★ **Shiraz 14** ★★★★ **Mountain Red 14** ★★ **Chenin Blanc 15** ★★★ **Flamingo Sparkling NV** ★★ **Red Natural Sweet 14** ★★ **Rosé Natural Sweet 15** ★★ Not retasted: **Vin Doux Sparkling NV** ★★

Red Chair range

Bean There Pinotage ★★☆ With nutty aroma & cranberry crispness, **14** is good solo or with pizza/pasta. Also tasted: **De Lite Sauvignon Blanc 15** ★★ — DB

Location/map/WO: Robertson ▪ Est 1964 ▪ 1stB 1974 ▪ Tasting & sales Mon-Fri 9–5.30 Sat 9–4 ▪ Fee R10pp for tour groups ▪ Closed Good Fri, Dec 25 & Jan 1 ▪ Bodega de Vinho restaurant & bakery Mon-Fri 8–5.30 Sat 9–4 ▪ Facilities for children ▪ Tour groups ▪ Gift shop ▪ Rooiberg Conservancy ▪ Owner(s) 30 members ▪ Cellarmaster(s) André van Dyk (Oct 2002) ▪ Winemaker(s) André Scriven (Jan 2008), with Pieter Rossouw (Jan 2013) ▪ Viticulturist(s) Hennie Visser (2007, Vinpro consultant) ▪ 667ha (cab, merlot, ptage, ruby cab, shiraz, chard, chenin, cbard, sauv) ▪ 13,000t/100,000cs own label 35% red 65% white ▪ Other export brands: African Dawn, Amandalia, Cape Avocet, Finch Mountain, Tembana Valley, Zebra Collection ▪ Brands for clients: AlexKia, Cape Dreams, Headbutt, Woolworths ▪ ISO 9001:2000, BWI, HACCP, IPW, LACON Organic ▪ PO Box 358 Robertson 6705 ▪ info@rooiberg.co.za ▪ www.rooiberg.co.za ▪ S 33° 46' 35.3" E 019° 45' 42.9" ▪ F +27 (0)23-626-3295 ▪ **T +27 (0)23-626-1663**

☐ **Rooi Kalahari** *see* Die Mas van Kakamas

Rookiewino.com

Colleen Norkie decided, after ten years in the wine industry (she handles social media for Warwick Estate), to make a barrel of her own wine. The experiment, she says, 'turned into a life lesson and an amazing journey of discovery'. Under the mentorship of 'winemaking guru' Nic van Aarde she learnt that making wine is not only a science but also 'a fine art that requires focus, patience and determination'.

Cabernet Sauvignon ★★★★ Only 280 bottles of wild ferment, unfiltered **13** older-oaked. Fruit-sweet & supple, drinks easily, ends tad warm. — WB, CvZ

Location: Stellenbosch ▪ WO: Simonsberg–Stellenbosch ▪ Est/1stB 2013 ▪ Closed to public ▪ Owner(s) Colleen & Angus Norkie ▪ Winemaker(s) Colleen Norkie & Nic van Aarde ▪ 45cs own label ▪ rookie@rookiewino.com, guru@rookiewino.com ▪ www.rookiewino.com

Rosendal Wines

A new management team at this direct-to-customer wine business brings in a wealth of talent from outside the industry, focused on increasing the customer base both in Africa and overseas. New brand 'Noble Nomad', with wacky names and off-the-wall stories, is finding much favour with their fans.

Reserve range

★★★★ **Hilltop Shiraz** From Stellenbosch fruit, **12** structured for the long haul, with firm tannin giving form to dense & fruit-filled core.

★★★★ **Red Rock** (NEW) Merlot-led Bordeaux blend **11** shows fine structure & tannins wrapped around ripely elegant black fruit. Hints of smoke & coffee from 2 years in oak, 1/3 new. From Durbanville fruit.

★★★★ **Black Spice** (NEW) **12** Rhône blend shiraz & grenache make for elegant mouthful of black plummy fruit. Well named, with most of the spice coming from fruit (no new wood), ending with lick vanilla in tail.

★★★★ **Serenity Chardonnay** Poised **13**, judicious marriage spicy new oak (50%), creamy texture (9 months sur lie) & ebullient lemon & lime. Bright & easy yet complex solo sipper.

★★★★ **Cape Ruby** (NEW) From Calitzdorp, with all the class & concentration you'd expect. 3 classic 'port' grapes in **NV**, full bodied & ripe, typical whiffs of chocolate, orange peel, cloves & raisins. Nicely integrated alcohol, long finish.

Hilltop Merlot (NEW) ★★★★ Smoke & char somewhat mask sweet, ripe berry fruit on **12**. Lovely vanilla finish, though. May well improve. Not retasted: **Black Eagle 08** ★★★★ Not tasted: **Classic Cuvée**.

Rosendal range

★★★★ **Sauvignon Blanc** Delightful **14** delivers classic sauvignon aromas of green fig before peppers, asparagus, grass & limes, edged with creamy texture from some skin contact & lees-ageing.

★★★★ **HVIT** (NEW) Excellent **14** blend of chenin, grenache blanc & roussanne. This is summer in a glass — flowers, blossoms, peach stones & ginger spice. Fresh & lively, a great partner for aromatic food.

Also tasted: **Merlot 13** ★★★ Not retasted: **Chenin Blanc 13** ★★★ Not tasted: **Syrah**.

Noble Nomad range (NEW)

He Stole My Horse Shiraz-Cabernet Sauvignon ★★★ Easy-drinker **14**, spicy & charry notes slightly overwhelm juicy fruit. **He Slept Under the Stars Sauvignon Blanc** ★★★ Another candidate for maddest name ever! Delightful easy-drinking **14** with a dollop of sugar making for a fresh, tropical fruit bomb.

Barony range

August Cabernet Sauvignon ★★★ Cassis & graphite notes, austere, grippy mouthfeel — **11** is classic cab but beginning to tire, enjoy soon. Not tasted: **Bønne Pinotage**, **Heidi Shiraz**, **Cecile Sauvignon Blanc**. — CM

Location/map: Robertson ▪ WO: Western Cape/Calitzdorp ▪ 1stB 2003 ▪ Tasting, sales & cellar tours Mon-Sat 8-5 Sun 9-1 ▪ Fee only charged for groups of 10+ ▪ Wine & Lindt chocolate tastings ▪ Restaurant & guest house ▪ Spa & wellness centre ▪ Conferences ▪ Owner(s) Du Toit Britz, Mike Harvey & Geir Tellefsen ▪ Cellarmaster(s)/winemaker(s) Therese de Beer (Jan 2012) ▪ 18ha ▪ 80% red 15% white 5% rosé ▪ PO Box 3 Suite 128 Roggebaai 8012 ▪ info@rosendalwinery.com ▪ www.rosendalwines.com ▪ S 33° 48' 7.8" E 019° 59' 19.0" ▪ F +27 (0)21-424-1570 ▪ **T +27 (0)21-424-4498 (sales)/+27 (0)23-626-1570 (farm)**

Ross Gower Wines

The memory of one of the top winemakers of his time lives on in the name of this small Elgin property and the irrepressible spirit of wife Sally. Before his passing in 2010, free-thinking Ross, Sally and two sons Robert and James had rooted a small vineyard, built a rammed-earth cellar and established a wine portfolio. Subsequently continued with a consultant's help, the range currently comprises just two MCC bubblies pending decisions on future developments.

Pinot Noir Méthode Cap Classique Brut ★★★ Fruity champagne-method sparkling **08**, dapper & appealing aperitif or food partner. **Chardonnay Méthode Cap Classique** ★★★★ Bottle-fermented **11** bubbly offers fresh, creamy quaffability for any occasion. — HJ

Location/WO: Elgin ▪ Map: Elgin, Walker Bay & Bot River ▪ Est 2003 ▪ 1stB 2004 ▪ Tasting & sales by appt ▪ Glen Stuart self-catering cottages ▪ Conservation area ▪ Owner(s) Gower family ▪ Winemaker(s) James Gower ▪ 83ha/±7ha (shiraz, sauv) ▪ 20,000cs own label 5% red 10% white 85% MCC ▪ PO Box 161 Elgin 7180 ▪ info@rossgowerwines.co.za ▪ www.rossgowerwines.co.za ▪ S 34° 14' 17.7" E 019° 7' 3.7" ▪ F +27 (0)86-611-2179 ▪ **T +27 (0)21-844-0197**

☐ **Rowlands** *see* Southern Sky Wines
☐ **Royal** *see* Riebeek Cellars
☐ **Ruby Ridge** *see* Govert Wines

Rudera Wines

Owner Riana Hall, based in Jonkershoek Valley in Stellenbosch, reminds us that she's celebrating Rudera's 'sweet sixteenth' – the first bottling was the millennium year. Initial offerings were of famously successful chenin, but the classically oriented range spread rapidly. The home cellar makes winetasting an elaborate and sensorially adventurous affair, with a number of pairing options available. Few new bottlings reported on this year: Riana wants to hold back the wines till they are a little more ready.

★★★★☆ **Cabernet Sauvignon** Though ripe-fruited & powerful, savoury **12** from a mix of Stellenbosch & Paarl grapes is nicely balanced between youthful exuberance & disciplined constraint, built on firm foundations of concentration & structure. The dry finish is crucial.

★★★★☆ **Platinum Cabernet Sauvignon** Usually more substantial in all ways than the Cab. No **10** made, but subtly perfumed **11** fits the part: in modern but restrained style, the fruit focused, with a lilting sweetness of fruit & long finish. Youthful – evident oak should harmonise in a few years. Ex Stellenbosch.

★★★★ **Syrah** Fragrant floral notes lift red/black fruit on good, serious **12**. Supportive oaking. Ripe & rather big – 14.5% alcohol glows on the finish. Like **11** (★★★★☆) will benefit from some time in bottle.

★★★★ **De Tradisie Chenin Blanc** Richness & breadth on **11**, with notes of ripe apple, earth & smoky melon. Touch drier than Robusto, with balancing acid core. Like next, natural ferment; oaked (10% new). WO Stellenbosch.

★★★★☆ **Robusto Chenin Blanc** Sweet-fruited, rich & full-bodied but effectively dry **12**, despite some residual sugar which adds to the wine's harmony, with the richness balanced by a light intensity, even an element of austerity. Lingering finish testimony to the quality of the ripe grapes. Stellenbosch WO.

★★★★☆ **Noble Late Harvest** Oak-matured **10** dessert from chenin with smatterings chardonnay, viognier & sauvignon. Excellently balanced, with right hint of honeyed botrytis adding complexity to luscious ripe peach & tart apricot.

Not retasted: **Platinum Chenin Blanc 09** ★★★☆ — TJ

Location/map: Stellenbosch ▪ Map grid reference: G6 ▪ WO: Western Cape/Stellenbosch/Elgin ▪ Est 1999 ▪ 1stB 2000 ▪ Tasting by appt only ▪ Fee R50pp/5 wines, waived on purchase ▪ Specialised tastings (min 4/max 16 pax): food & wine pairing R280pp; chocolate & wine pairing R180pp; sensorial tasting R100pp ▪ Owner(s) Riana Hall ▪ Cellarmaster(s) Chris Keet (2011-2015, consultant) ▪ 15ha/10ha (cab, shiraz, chenin) ▪ ±120t/15,000cs own label 50% red 50% white ▪ IPW ▪ PO Box 589 Stellenbosch 7599 ▪ riana@rudera.co.za ▪ www.rudera.co.za ▪ S 33° 56' 26.5" E 018° 54' 14.3" ▪ **T +27 (0)21-882-8214**

☐ **Rudi Schultz Wines** *see* Schultz Family Wines
☐ **Ruins** *see* Bon Cap Organic Winery

Ruitersvlei Wines

'Lots of exciting changes' promised last edition are happening under a new team led by Helena d'Oliveira, whose 'simple ethos' – good food, good wine and good people – is evident in the fresh, seasonal meals and picnics offered by the Mountainside Restaurant, accommodation in renovated cottages, functions in the rustic old cellar, walking and planned quad biking trails, and varied water activities, with yet more attractions envisaged. And the 'good wine'? It's by widely seasoned Nico Vermeulen.

Shiraz Reserve (NEW) ★★★ From Sir Lowry's Pass vines, **08** is smooth & integrated, with plum & prune notes, less typical tangerine nuance. Has held up well but best enjoyed soon. **Rosé** (NEW) ★★★ Sauvignon (52%) & pinotage in harmony in **15** preview. Berry-fresh, some leafy features, brisk & lipsmackingly dry with enough grip for food. **Chenin Blanc** ★★★ Appealing nut & thatch nuances, some honeyed bottle age on still-vivacious **14**; bone-dry & brisk, satisfying. Also tasted: **Sauvignon Blanc 14** ★★★ Not tasted: **Cabernet Sauvignon, Merlot, Pinotage, Shiraz.** In abeyance: **Private Collection.** — CvZ

Location: Paarl ▪ Map: Paarl & Wellington ▪ Map grid reference: D6 ▪ WO: Paarl/Coastal ▪ Tasting & sales Mon-Sun 9-5; in season (from mid Sep) tastings continue till 10pm at restaurant ▪ Mountainside Restaurant (mountainside@ruitersvlei.co.za) open daily for breakfast & lunch; refreshments & picnic baskets ▪ Weddings & conferences ▪ 11 guest rooms ▪ Various water activities on the dam, incl. fishing & boating ▪ Owner(s) Ruitersvlei Holdings (Pty) Ltd ▪ Winemaker(s) Nico Vermeulen ▪ 120ha ▪ PO Box 532 Suider-Paarl 7624 ▪ marketing@ruitersvlei.co.za ▪ www.ruitersvlei.co.za ▪ S 33° 45' 10.8" E 018° 54' 28.0" ▪ F +27 (0)21-863-1443 ▪ **T +27 (0)21-863-1517**

☐ **Runner Duck** *see* Vergenoegd Wine Estate
☐ **Running Duck** *see* Stellar Winery

Rupert & Rothschild Vignerons   (꘠) (꘡꘡) (◎) (꘢)

The internationally acclaimed wines from this glossy venture between the Rupert family and Baron Benjamin de Rothschild were not available for review, but the current releases are '12 Baron Edmond (Bordeaux red blend), '13 Classique (red blend) and '14 Baroness Nadine (wooded chardonnay).

Location: Paarl ▪ Map: Franschhoek ▪ Est 1997 ▪ 1stB 1998 ▪ Tasting & sales Mon-Fri 10-4.30 Sat 10-4 ▪ Closed all religious holidays, Dec 26 & Jan 1 ▪ Champagne, wine & food tasting ▪ Chef's luncheon menu ▪ Owner(s) Rupert family & Baron Benjamin de Rothschild ▪ Winemaker(s) Yvonne Lester (Sep 2001) & Clive Radloff (Jun 1997) ▪ 90ha (cabs s/f, merlot, p verdot) ▪ 1,200t/170,000cs own label 95% red 5% white ▪ ISO 14001, HACCP, IPW ▪ PO Box 412 Franschhoek Valley 7690 ▪ info@rupert-rothschildvignerons.com ▪ www.rupert-rothschildvignerons.com ▪ S 33° 50' 14.5" E 018° 56' 51.1" ▪ F +27 (0)21-874-1802 ▪ **T +27 (0)21-874-1648**

☐ **Rupert Wines** *see* Anthonij Rupert Wyne

Russo Family Vintners   (꘠)

One of the Cape's first winemakers, Pierre Rousseau, who arrived in 1688, inspired Henk and Terèsa Rossouw to make wine on their Durbanville smallholding and, nearly 10 years on, the whole family is involved. Further inspiration, if needed, doubtless will come from their joining the rejuvenated Garagiste Movement of SA, which provides support to small-batch vignerons (see section Make Your Own Wine).

★★★★ **Bordeaux Blend** Was 'Russo'. Mature dinner companion **08** showing forest floor bottle-age & balance. Knit & rounded; satisfying fruitiness, dry finish & modest alcohol. Mostly cab franc, cab & merlot. **Cabernet Franc** ★★★★ Limited stock of **08** available ex cellardoor. Still fresh, with crisp cranberry fruit & some leafiness. Harmonious, ready to drink. Seasoned with mix French & Hungarian oak, as are all these. **Symphony** (NEW) ★★★★ **09** cab-led Bordeaux blend less youthful than siblings, no less interesting. Graphite & meaty tones followed by true cab austerity on the palate. Enjoy soon. — WB, CvZ

Location/WO: Durbanville ▪ Map: Durbanville, Philadelphia & Darling ▪ Est 2004 ▪ 1stB 2007 ▪ Tasting, sales & tours by appt only ▪ Closed all pub hols ▪ Owner(s) Henk & Terèsa Rossouw ▪ Winemaker(s) Terèsa Rossouw (2007) ▪ 6.5ha/4ha (cabs s/f, malbec, merlot, p verdot) ▪ 35t/800cs own label 100% red ▪ PO Box 4402 Tyger Valley 7536 ▪ teresa@russowines.co.za ▪ www.russowines.co.za ▪ S 33° 48' 37.9" E 018° 37' 04.3" ▪ F +27 (0)21-979-1996 ▪ **T +27 (0)21-979-1960**

Rustenberg Wines   (꘠) (◎) (꘢)

This, one of the great names in Cape wine, is a family estate and winery on a grand scale (and of great natural and architectural beauty). The family is the Barlows: the historic property was acquired by industrialist Peter Barlow in the 1940s (he reunited Schoongezicht and Rustenberg, split in 1810); Simon

Barlow is the fully involved current owner, and his son Murray took over as cellarmaster in 2011. Wine has been made here continuously, it seems, since the late nineteenth century – a continuity rare in the Cape. The rich heritage is, of course, a responsibility as well as a privilege, and the family were understandably chuffed at Rustenberg being named the 2015 Trophy Wine Show's 'Most successful producer', with trophies for site-specific wines Peter Barlow and Five Soldiers.

Flagship range

★★★★☆ **Buzzard Kloof Syrah** From one of the coolest sites on Rustenberg, planted with French clones. Perfumed & modern **12** good few notches up from Stellenbosch sibling, with higher concentration & extraction, ample fruit & pepper. Decanting recommended in youth.

★★★★ **John X Merriman** Perfumed, leafy **12** (★★★★☆) is typical Rustenberg Bordeaux expression, marrying red & black fruit with pencil lead & herbal notes. 5-way blend, mostly cab & merlot; much more balanced & characterful than **11** (★★★☆) & **10**.

★★★★ **Stellenbosch Chardonnay** Premium white grape of the estate & with good reason. Generous fresh lime with salted butter richness, savoury soy & chalk complexity on **14**. 100% malo with full lees & oak ageing – will delight fans of full bore chard. Stellenbosch WO.

Site Specific range

★★★★☆ **Peter Barlow** Opaque, still-youthful purple-black hue; layered & sumptuous **09** combines power & finesse, shows class & ageability of both the vintage & 100% Simonsberg cab. Raised in 64% new French oak, 24 months, has all hallmarks of a classic; keep for as long as you can resist.

★★★★☆ **Five Soldiers** Named for the stone pines guarding the renowned chardonnay block. All elements of Stellenbosch version with more power & body; **12** (★★★★) not as refined as **11**; 70% new oak gives buttered brioche & fresh rye overtones; bottle-age starting to show, ready to drink.

Regional range

★★★★ **Stellenbosch Cabernet Sauvignon** (NEW) Cellarworthy **13** shows elegance & structure typical of top Stellenbosch cab. Cedar, peppermint, coriander & liquorice combine with harmony & flair.

★★★★ **Merlot** One of the bolder, more structured merlots from Stellenbosch, **13** stages welcome return (no **11**, **12**) with cocoa dusting to blackcurrant fruit, very fine drying tannin. Even better after 2-5 years.

★★★★ **RM Nicholson** Popular WO Stellenbosch blend, **13** shiraz dominant, with merlot & cab; combines ripe juicy fruit with spice & dusty notes. Ready to drink but will live long under its screwcap.

★★★★☆ **Straw Wine** Opulent richness on **12** (★★★★) from air-dried chenin & crouchen blanc; raisin & honey notes in a concentrated, syrupy palate missing some of the fresh acidity of **11**. Coastal WO.

Stellenbosch Rosé (NEW) ★★★ Two vintages tasted, both from petit verdot, softly dry, ready for summer sipping; **14** (★★★) musk & sugared plum notes; **15** lighter coloured, slightly fresher, equally crowd pleasing. Also tasted: **Stellenbosch Shiraz 13** ★★★★ **Stellenbosch Roussanne 14** ★★★☆ **Stellenbosch Sauvignon Blanc 15** ★★★☆ — HJ

Location/map: Stellenbosch ▪ Map grid reference: G4 ▪ WO: Simonsberg–Stellenbosch/Stellenbosch/Coastal ▪ Est 1682 ▪ 1stB 1892 ▪ Tasting & sales Mon-Fri 9–4.30 Sat 10–4 Sun 10-3 ▪ Closed Good Fri, Dec 25 & Jan 1 ▪ Garden ▪ Filming ▪ Owner(s) Simon Barlow ▪ Cellarmaster(s) Murray Barlow (Nov 2011) ▪ Winemaker(s) Randolph Christians (Nov 1995), with Gareth le Grange (2003) & Craig Christians (Jun 2012) ▪ Viticulturist(s) Simon Barlow (Aug 1987), with Tessa Moffat (Nov 2013) ▪ 880ha/±110ha (cabs s/f, grenache n/b, malbec, merlot, p verdot, shiraz, chard, rouss, sauv, sem) ▪ ±1,200t/120,000cs own label 51% red 47% white 2% other ▪ BWI, IPW ▪ PO Box 33 Stellenbosch 7599 ▪ wine@rustenberg.co.za ▪ www.rustenberg.co.za ▪ S 33° 53' 44.8" E 018° 53' 33.6" ▪ **T +27 (0)21-809-1200**

Rust en Vrede Estate

This may be one of SA's oldest (and most prestigious) estates but that doesn't mean it remains unchanged. Owner Jean Engelbrecht has engaged in several recent developments including remodelling and expanding the tasting venue and cellar facilities, as well as building a brand-new barrel hall to house future vintages of the estate's fine reds. Nothing stands still in the vineyards either, with a rolling replanting programme ensuring quality fruit going forward. The award-winning restaurant continues to deserve its top ten accolades, and for more casual diners a winemakers lunch option is now available, to be enjoyed with a glass of red on the cellardoor terrace or inside by the warmth of the fire.

Estate Vineyards range

★★★★☆ **Cabernet Sauvignon** Effortlessly maintaining standard of excellent **12**, **13** has classic cab aromas of blackcurrants, cedar perfume & vanilla spice. Handles 100% new oak with panache, concentrated mid-palate & lengthy finish indicating a wine for the long term.

★★★★☆ **Single Vineyard Cabernet Sauvignon** **12** showing all cab's finest traits in powerful expression of individual terroir. Black fruit, enlivened by hints of violets with savoury undertones, delightfully gritty texture & spicy vanilla finish. 75% new oak. Return to form after oakier **11** (★★★★).

★★★★ **Merlot** Warm plumcake aromas persist on **14**, enlivened by some dark chocolate hints & spicy notes. Upfront tannins should mesh in time, delicious savoury notes suggest meaty food matches.

★★★★☆ **Single Vineyard Syrah** Already approachable **13** mixes pungent aromas of smoked meats, coriander & perfume with ripe black plums & cherries. Enough concentration to handle both 15% alcohol & 75% new oak with aplomb in harmonious, elegant mouthful.

★★★★☆ **Syrah** Plenty to admire already about **13**, shy but definitely feels as if more to come, continuing standard of **12**. Dense black fruit with whiffs of coffee, smoke, violets & spice, edged with toasty oak & grippy tannins only needing time to become very fine.

★★★★☆ **1694 Classification** Uniting the single-vineyard syrah & cab in flagship wine, **12** exudes power, polish, concentration & class. Ripe dark berries & chocolate, whiffs of cigarbox & spice all backed by seamlessly integrated 100% new oak, keeping interest alive until lengthy tail.

★★★★☆ **Estate** Cab-led **12** continues to prove a perfect partner for syrah/shiraz & touch of merlot. Soft, ripe berried fruit with splashes of fragrant tealeaves overlays fine-knit tannins, fresh acidity & appetising texture. 100% new wood, 15% American. Various bottle formats available up to 27L. — CM

Location/map/WO: Stellenbosch ▪ Map grid reference: E8 ▪ Est 1694 ▪ 1stB 1979 ▪ Tasting, sales & cellar tours Mon-Sat 9–5 ▪ Fee R40/4 wines & R70/6 wines, waived on purchase ▪ Closed Easter Fri/Sun, Dec 25 & Jan 1 ▪ Winemaker's lunch ▪ Rust en Vrede Restaurant ▪ Gift shop ▪ Owner(s) Jean Engelbrecht ▪ Cellarmaster(s) Coenie Snyman (Dec 2006) ▪ Winemaker(s) Coenie Snyman (Dec 2006), with Roelof Lotriet (Nov 2011) ▪ Viticulturist(s) Dirkie Mouton (Jun 2010) ▪ 50ha/45ha (cab, merlot, shiraz) ▪ ±300t/40,000cs own label 100% red ▪ IPW ▪ PO Box 473 Stellenbosch 7599 ▪ info@rustenvrede.com ▪ www.rustenvrede.com ▪ S 33° 59' 54.0" E 018° 51' 22.5" ▪ F +27 (0)21-881-3000 ▪ **T +27 (0)21-881-3881**

☐ **Rusthof** *see* Mooiuitsig Wine Cellars
☐ **Ruyter's Bin** *see* Stellenrust

Saam Mountain Vineyards   ⓘ

These wines are sourced from specific blocks on farms owned by 3rd-generation family growers in Paarl and other Coastal areas, and vinified by the team at Perdeberg Winery, where tastings/sales are offered.

Saam Mountain Premium Selection

★★★★ **Middelburg Chenin Blanc** Fragrant citrus blossom & vanilla entice on part-oaked **13**. Ripe stonefruit, lemon curd on the palate – rich & intense flavours follow through to unflagging finish

Heldersig Shiraz-Viognier ★★★ Bright, spicy berry fruit on **13**; easy & crowd pleasing. Not retasted: **Shiraz-Mourvèdre-Petit Verdot 12** ★★★★ Not tasted: **Koopmanskraal Shiraz.**

Saam Mountain Cellar Selection

Sauvignon Blanc ★★☆ Not much intensity to **14**'s tropical & greenpepper flavours; for early drinking. Not tasted: **Cabernet Sauvignon**, **Pinotage**, **Shiraz**, **Chenin Blanc**. — WB

Location: Paarl ▪ WO: Paarl/Coastal ▪ Tasting & sales at Perdeberg Winery ▪ Owner(s) 33 shareholders ▪ Cellarmaster(s) Albertus Louw (Oct 2008) ▪ Winemaker(s) Riaan Möller (Dec 2006) & Dylan Dowell-Ellis (Sep 2014) ▪ Viticulturist(s) Heinie Nel (Jul 2013) ▪ PO Box 214 Paarl 7620 ▪ info@perdeberg.co.za ▪ www.perdeberg.co.za ▪ F +27 (0)21-869-8245 ▪ **T +27 (0)21-869-8244**

☐ **Sabi Sabi** *see* Stellenrust

Sadie Family Wines ⓘ

Eben Sadie's Swartland winery has twice been the guide's Winery of the Year (2010, 2015) – a fraction of the recognition this charismatic and hard-working winemaker has received internationally and locally. His new-millennium debut, Columella, was made while he was still working for Spice Route. By the time it was joined by Palladius, he had an old shed on the Paardeberg, since grown into a substantial winery, where his two siblings are also part of the team. 2009 brought the Old Vine Series, with grapes from previously virtually ignored, old vineyards. The grapes (as for the Signature Series blends) are vinified with minimal intervention, to best express variety and site. All are snapped up by private buyers and retailers even before their official release. Eben has now closed down his parallel project, Sequillo, in order to concentrate fully on the Sadie Family wines.

Signature Series

★★★★★ **Columella** Widely noted as one of SA's top reds. Light, subtle **13** focuses more on elegance & purity than power, with lowest alcohol yet & expressive, fresh red berry fruits. Fine textured, supple blend Swartland shiraz with mourvèdre & grenache, year each in cask & foudre.

★★★★★ **Palladius** Like **12**, transcendent, rich & complex **13** (★★★★★) 8-way chenin-led blend fermented in concrete 'eggs' & clay pots; time on lees weaves textures & generous flavours into harmonious, elemental core. Immense interest & charm; accessible, but for the long haul. These in larger formats too.

Old Vine Series

★★★★★ **Pofadder** Wild berries & spice in **14** from old Riebeek-Kasteel cinsaut vineyard, plus something intriguingly darker, deeper & rather less silky than **13** (★★★★★). Succulence balanced by fresh acidity, fine grape tannins & ample breadth fashioned by time in old foudres.

★★★★★ **Soldaat** Translucent, delicate & utterly expressive **14** Piekenierskloof grenache. Non-interventionist winemaking allows ethereal pure ripe cherries, cinnamon spice to shine brightly through in hauntingly pale depth & power. Fresh, appetising acidity & silky lightness; long, minerally finish.

★★★★★ **Treinspoor** **14** Swartland tinta barocca feels like Soldaat's no-frills, overalled brother. Lively, with dry, grippy tannin, generous (but still masked) raspberry fruit & spritzy, appetising acidity. Eben Sadie's own 'red of the vintage', needs time to settle down & reveal its inner self.

★★★★★ **Mev. Kirsten** Most intense, ripe & fleshy of the chenin-based trio, though still incredibly agile, this is definitive Stellenbosch chenin from vines over a century old. Profound **14**'s sweet, ripe fruit fleshes out fine acid backbone throughout in astonishingly fresh & engaging completeness. Quite magical.

★★★★★ **Skurfberg** Exceptionally vibrant, delicately scented **14** Olifants River dryland chenin flaunts supremely rich, delicious citrus-edged ripe fruit, focused by precise, textured acidity & minerality. Profound young wine possesses great clarity & deep complexity, with a lot more to offer with time in bottle.

★★★★★ **Kokerboom** Semillon blanc (no gris this vintage) in tight, austere **14** from Skurfberg vines, basket pressed & raised in foudres. Linear & focused, with rapier-like acidity & stony, mineral elegance (has lowest alcohol yet), demanding plenty time in bottle to reveal well-concealed fruit.

★★★★★ **'T Voetpad** Field blend from one of the Cape's oldest vineyards. Chenin, semillon co-fermented in foudre with palomino, splash muscat in **14** (★★★★★) to produce generous, expressive & remarkably textured wine; complex flavours honed by precise acidity & attractive pithiness. Rich, like **13**.

★★★★★ **Skerpioen** Equal chenin, palomino in taut **14** blend brings back bracing sting in tail – missing in **13** (★★★★★), from vines grown in unique chalky West Coast soils (WO Swartland). Perfect fruit, acid balance & lower alcohol ensures impressive harmony in pithily structured, lively & profound wine. — IM

Location: Malmesbury ▪ Map: Swartland ▪ WO: Swartland/Olifants River/Piekenierskloof/Stellenbosch ▪ Est 1999 ▪ 1stB 2000 ▪ 5 public tastings annually – bookings essential, contact sales@ thesadiefamily.com ▪ Owner(s) The Sadie Family (Pty) Ltd ▪ Winemaker(s)/viticulturist(s) Eben Sadie (1999) ▪ 25ha (cinsaut, grenache n/b, mourv, syrah, tinta barocca, chenin, clairette, palomino, rouss, sem, verdelho, viog) ▪ 60t/8,000cs own label 50% red 50% white ▪ PO Box 1019 Malmesbury 7299 ▪ office@thesadiefamily.com ▪ www.thesadiefamily.com ▪ S 33° 31' 31.0" E 018° 48' 18.1" ▪ F +27 (0)86-692-2852 ▪ **T +27 (0)76-151-7131**

☐ **Safari** *see* De Zoete Inval Estate
☐ **Sainsbury** *see* Bosman Family Vineyards

St Francis Point Vineyards   ⓠ

The vineyards planted by Ian and Jean Fynn in 2009 on the coastal dunes a kilometre from the sea, at St Francis Bay in the Eastern Cape, are maturing well. Their olive trees too are prospering, and the preserved tract of indigenous bush is 'a delight for many'. 'We no longer run a full time restaurant,' adds Jean, 'but the space makes an ideal venue for weddings and functions.'

Sauvignon Blanc (NEW) ★★☆ **15** forthcoming grassy notes, light 11.5% alcohol & balanced acidity for satisfying solo sipping. — TJ, CvZ

Location/WO: St Francis Bay • Map: Eastern Cape • Est 2009 • Tasting by appt • Owner(s) Jean Fynn • Winemaker(s) Ian Fynn & Albertus van Rensburg • Viticulturist(s) Ian Fynn (2009) • 3.5ha (chard, sauv, sem) • PO Box 355 St Francis Bay 6312 • jfynn@intekom.co.za • S 34° 11' 6.61" E 024° 50' 34.05" •
T +27 (0)42-294-0548/+27 (0)82-491-3373

☐ **Saints** see DGB
☐ **Salpeterkop** see Rogge Cloof

Saltare   ⓠ

The tasting venue opened last year across the road from the Stellenbosch cellar is proving successful for Christoff and Carla Pauw's boutique brand, with frequent small groups of visitors enjoying personal tastings and events by winemaker Carla. Wine-wise, focus continues on sourcing from organic or eco-sensitively farmed vineyards. 'It's great to smell the fynbos as you walk among the vineyard rows,' says Carla.

★★★★ **Syrah** Ripe blackberries & blueberries on step-up **12** (★★★★☆) improves on **11** with fynbos notes, touch of spice, delicate oak & supportive tannins. Layers of flavour show complexity at lengthy finish. From Swartland fruit including tiny tweak of carignan.

★★★★ **Specialis** Ⓥ Perfumed **08** blend merlot & cab plus a little cab franc. Juicy ripe fruit firmly underpinned by fresh, brisk acidity. WO Paarl. Previous was lavish **06** (★★★★).

★★★★ **Chenin Blanc** Ⓥ Richly textured **12** from Swartland naturally fermented in older barrels, freshened by extended lees-ageing. Not quite as concentrated & focused as **11** (★★★★★).

★★★★ **Old Vines Chenin Blanc** Rich & satisfying **13** impresses with savoury lanolin notes offset by subtle honeyed wood. Ripe yellow stonefruit with steely core, wonderful texture from natural ferment.

★★★★ **Méthode Cap Classique Brut Rosé** Pale onion skin hue on **NV** sparkling belies depth of flavour from 2 years on lees. Plenty of creamy yeastiness backing up pinot noir's fresh cranberry & currant while acidity light-trips to fine finish. Zero dosage, as all these. Somerset West vines.

★★★★☆ **Méthode Cap Classique Brut Blanc de Blancs** Rich & intense **NV** spent 4 years on lees, with 15% oaking of Robertson chardonnay. Savoury notes with creamy lemon curd & ginger biscuits. Wonderfully integrated, fine persistent bubbles, excellent intensity on tantalisingly dry finish leaves you wanting more.

★★★★ **Méthode Cap Classique Brut Nature** Lots of salty biscuit notes on improving **NV** sparkler give way to nuts, cream, white peach & some marzipan. Brisk acidity & fine persistent mousse culminate in bone-dry finish. Part-oaked Robertson & Somerset West fruit.

★★★★☆ **Méthode Cap Classique Brut Reserve** Now equal chardonnay & pinot noir, & 'only' 3 years on lees – enough time to develop rich creamy notes on the ripe, spicy yellow fruit; **NV** bone-dry & thrillingly tingly, lengthy finish. Will improve. Robertson & Somerset West grapes, portion oaked. Also in magnum. — CM

Location/map: Stellenbosch • Map grid reference: F5 • WO: Swartland/Western Cape/Paarl/Robertson • 1stB 2005 • Tasting & cellar tour by appt • Tasting & sales also every Sat at Stellenbosch Slow Food Market, Oude Libertas • Owner(s) Christoff & Carla Pauw • Cellarmaster(s)/winemaker(s) Carla Pauw (2005) • 19t/2,200cs own label 15% red 15% white 70% MCC • 30 Die Laan Stellenbosch 7600 • info@saltare.co.za • www.saltare.co.za • S 33° 56' 15.85" E 018° 52' 7.69" • F +27 (0)88-021-883-9568 •
T +27 (0)21-883-9568

☐ **Sandrivier** see Overgaauw Wine Estate
☐ **Sandveld** see Tierhoek

Santa Cecilia   Ⓨ � ⌂ ◎

Witty non-conformist Anton Espost makes a little wine in a cellar in Swartland's Riebeek-Kasteel, where minimal intervention is the word ('perhaps out of laziness'). His Santa Cecilia bottlings celebrate chenin and include an Oppie Dop (skin-contact) version; the 'anarchist' range Tres Estrellas (currently El Presidente and El Pervertido) has labels printed in Spanish and Russian to recognise the role of those languages 'in making the world a more interesting place'.

Location: Riebeek-Kasteel ▪ Map: Swartland ▪ Est/1stB 2008 ▪ Tasting facility in The Wine Kollective: Mon-Sat 10-5 Sun 10-3 ▪ Closed Good Fri, Dec 25 & Jan 1 ▪ Gifts ▪ Farm produce ▪ Adjacent Bar Bar Black Sheep Restaurant ▪ Overnight facility 'The Santa Cecilia Boudoir' ▪ Owner(s)/winemaker(s) Anton Espost ▪ 2,000cs own label 30% red 70% white ▪ PO Box 61 Riebeek-Kasteel 7307 ▪ espost@telkomsa.net ▪ S 33° 23' 1.48" E 018° 53' 46.54" ▪ **T +27 (0)22-448-1008/+27 (0)76-012-9204**

Sarah's Creek

In Malherbe family hands since 1888, DCM Boerdery's wine brand is named for the stream on the Robertson home farm where, generations ago, a young daughter was habitually enchanted by dragonflies and birds. Cabernet Sauvignon '13, Merlot '14 and Sauvignon Blanc '15 are current releases.

Location: Robertson ▪ Closed to public ▪ Owner(s) Dirk C Malherbe ▪ Winemaker(s) Marga Malherbe ▪ 20ha (cab, merlot, sauv) ▪ PO Box 6531 Welgemoed 7538 ▪ info@sarahscreek.co.za ▪ www.sarahscreek.co.za ▪ **T +27 (0)76-838-6507**

Saronsberg   Ⓨ ⓪ ⌂ ◎

When Pretoria businessman Nick van Huyssteen came south to buy two Tulbagh farms in 2002 he named the new estate after the mountain rising above it (its lower slopes hosting one farm while the other stretches down the valley). A serious fire hastened vineyard replanting to feed the fine new cellar and art-filled tasting room. From the start, with Dewaldt Heyns the chief wine-person, Saronsberg has played a vital role in establishing Tulbagh as good red-wine country, especially for Rhône varieties, while its own reputation has soared. Now, says Dewaldt, 'rather than trying new gimmicks to stay in the news, our focus is to consolidate and build on Saronsberg's success, pushing the boundaries of quality and building on our track record of consistency.'

Saronsberg range

★★★★☆ **Shiraz** As usual **13** manages to include a graceful note in its balanced, handsome robustness. Sweet ripe fruit firmly cushioned on supportive tannic structure & oaking (90%) that is not intrusive. This internationally & locally much awarded wine has a track record of ageability.

★★★★☆ **Seismic** Many years since **08** tasted. **09** (★★★★) cab-based blend maturing well; full-throttle aromas promise the big, sweet, showy (slightly unfresh) flavours then delivered. WO Coastal.

★★★★☆ **Full Circle** Aromas offer both plummy & cherry-red fruit on shiraz-led **13** blend with grenache, mourvèdre, viognier, as usual the most complex & refined in this range, remarkably fresh given big 14.5% alcohol, all-new oak & few grams sugar. Generous & open, succulent & savoury. A touch less sweet in effect (though a little more sugar) & more tannic than the Shiraz.

★★★★ **Viognier** Ⓥ Peachy, floral **13** (★★★★) perhaps less exuberant than **12**. Flavourful, but heavy texture, obvious oak & a few grams of residual sugar lessen freshness. (Tasted as unfinished sample.)

★★★★ **Brut Méthode Cap Classique** Flavourful (fruity rather than steely) but fresh & drily elegant **11** from chardonnay shows benefit of 3 years on lees, but further bottle age will add to its harmony.

★★★★ **Six Point Three Straw Wine** Ⓥ Name reflects the 6.3 (Richter scale) magnitude of the 1969 Tulbagh earthquake. **07** from air-dried sauvignon, naturally fermented & nearly 3 years in new oak (well integrated). Intriguing, gorgeous & sweet; not intense, but balanced & fresh.

Also tasted: Grenache 12 ★★★★☆ Sauvignon Blanc 15 ★★★

Provenance range

★★★★ **Rooi** Ⓥ **12** (★★★★) from all five Bordeaux red grapes, as was **11**. Fruity & ripe, overtly friendly but with firm enough tannic grip. Rather simple, with sweetish finish. WO Coastal.

Shiraz ★★★☆ 13 less impressive than ambitious **12** (★★★★☆). Has ripe berry & spice aromas & generally a sweet-fruited charm abetted by 3.7 g/l of sugar. Unobtrusively oaked, with gentle tannins – altogether very approachable now. WO Coastal. Also tasted: **Shiraz Rosé 15 ★★** Not retasted: **Earth in Motion 14 ★★★** — TJ

Location/map: Tulbagh ▪ WO: Tulbagh/Coastal/Western Cape ▪ Est 2002 ▪ 1stB 2004 ▪ Tasting & sales Mon-Fri 8–5 Sat 10–2 ▪ Fee R50pp ▪ Closed Easter Fri/Sun, Ascension day, Dec 25 & Jan 1 ▪ Cellar tours by appt ▪ Olive oil ▪ BYO picnic ▪ Artworks & sculptures on display ▪ Christmas in Winter Tulbagh festival (Jun) ▪ Self-catering guest cottages ▪ Owner(s) Saronsberg Cellar (Pty) Ltd ▪ Cellarmaster(s) Dewaldt Heyns (2003) ▪ Winemaker(s) Dewaldt Heyns (2003), with Helienne van Zyl (2015) ▪ Viticulturist(s) Dewaldt Heyns (2003) & Chris Immelman (2012) ▪ 550ha/50ha (shiraz) ▪ 500t own label 70% red 30% white ▪ BWI, WIETA ▪ PO Box 361 Tulbagh 6820 ▪ info@saronsberg.com ▪ www.saronsberg.com ▪ S 33° 14' 48.2" E 019° 7' 2.0" ▪ F +27 (0)23-230-0709 ▪ **T +27 (0)81-267-2751/+27 (0)23-004-0435**

☐ **SA Rugby** see Ernie Els Wines

Sauvignon.com

With its pixellated vine leaf logo and active social media presence, Sauvignon.com is the brainchild of Diemersdal's internet-savvy cellarmaster, Thys Louw.

Cabernet Sauvignon ⊘ **★★★☆** Fruity, sparingly wooded cab has bitter cherry & sour fig with gentle herbal interest on **14**. Lightish body, with easy-drinking appeal. **Sauvignon Blanc ★★★** Typical, if generic **15**. Crisp & grassy, with lime notes, dry finish. — HJ

Location: Durbanville ▪ WO: Western Cape ▪ Est/1stB 2010 ▪ Closed to public ▪ Owner(s) Thys & Tienie Louw ▪ Winemaker(s) Thys Louw & Mari Branders (both Jan 2010) ▪ Viticulturist(s) Div van Niekerk (Jan 2010) ▪ 40% red 60% white ▪ PO Box 27 Durbanville 7551 ▪ info@sauvignon.com ▪ www.sauvignon.com ▪ F +27 (0)21-979-1802 ▪ **T +27 (0)82-442-1317**

Savage Wines

'Savage by name but not by nature' epitomises Duncan Savage's approach. The Cape Point Vineyards winemaker's personal range of fragrantly nuanced wines celebrates the rebirth of out-of-favour varieties (and some timeless classics) from far-flung vineyards. Duncan jokes about drinking a bit more witblits firewater than he's used to in his search for unique parcels, which he and his father farm to their unique formula. Exciting things are happening with cinsaut, grenache and chenin, the emphasis firmly on elegance. The range has expanded from the original Red and White, with more plans in the pipeline.

★★★★☆ Syrah ⓃⒺⓌ Blockbuster showpiece **14**, boldest of the newcomers, has great character & presence. Aromatically scented, with exotic spices & tobacco, ripe & supple black berries & soft, velvety texture. Drink now & many years hence. Cape Peninsula WO. Future vintages will be 'The Girl Next Door'.

★★★★☆ Red Subtlety & depth outshine raw power in beautifully poised, graceful blend of syrah/shiraz, cinsaut, grenache & touriga from across the Cape. **13** exudes class. Sweetly floral & aromatic, with silky texture & layered complexity.

★★★★★ CWG Auction Reserve Follow the Line ⓃⒺⓌ Equal parts cinsaut, grenache & syrah/shiraz from Darling & Piekenierskloof, **13** is deeper, fuller than its namesake but retains heady perfume & varietal focus. Stunning complexity & layering, showing great cellaring potential. Older 500L barrels, 14 months.

★★★★☆ Follow the Line ⓃⒺⓌ Delicately delicious cinsaut, grenache & syrah/shiraz blend from Darling & Piekenierskloof, **14** offers ethereal floral scents with sweetly spiced berry juice. Full & ripe, with silky texture, showing beauty in subtlety.

★★★★☆ White Barrel-fermented sauvignon (75%) & semillon from Villiersdorp area, **14** is seriously conceived & impressive. Heavy oak spice needs time to settle, but underlying fullness & subtle fruit will prevail. Beautifully poised, with creamy texture. Only wine here with new wood, 25%. — GdB

Location: Cape Town ▪ WO: Western Cape/Cape Peninsula ▪ Est 2006 ▪ 1stB 2011 ▪ Closed to public ▪ Owner(s) Duncan Savage ▪ Winemaker(s)/viticulturist(s) Duncan Savage (Jan 2006) ▪ 20t/2,000cs own label 60% red 40% white ▪ info@savagewines.com ▪ **T +27 (0)21-785-4019**

Savanha

This Spier-owned, mainly exported premium wine brand 'celebrates the vibrant energy of the South African sun, in a fun, relaxed and social way'.

Naledi range

★★★★ **Cabernet Sauvignon** ⓠ Naledi is Sotho for 'star' & **12** shines brightly: attractively compact berry fruit woven with firm tannins, dry & tangy, & in need of a few years to soften.

Not tasted: **Chardonnay**. — DS

Saxenburg Wine Farm   ⓠ ⓟ ⌂ ⓞ

The Swiss Bührer family's highly regarded estate in Stellenbosch's Polkadraai area has been producing standout wines under cellarmaster Nico van der Merwe since its rebirth in 2000. The estate has an enviable reputation for classical styling, consistent quality and well-defined product ranges. Shiraz has long been a speciality, and this edition there's a new Drunken Fowl bottling emblazoned with a suitably light-hearted version of Saxenburg's guinea fowl emblem. Fiona Bührer, daughter of owners Adrian and Birgit, who helped launch the 'baby shiraz' in Cape Town, says the farm team 'love to share our experience and passion', and they've extended the tasting hours 'so you may enjoy a glass or two with us after work'.

Saxenburg Limited Release

★★★★☆ **Shiraz Select** Standard bearer of cellar & its shiraz trio – **11** has the requisite gravitas. Aromatic white pepper a backdrop for ripe, coffee/choc-toned mulberry fruit master-crafted into stunning package. A blockbuster, but beautifully balanced. All-new oak, 50/50 French & American. No **10**.

Private Collection

★★★★ **Cabernet Sauvignon** Classy, restrained **12**'s fruits of the forest & dark mocha tones combine with firm oak (30% new) in mouthwatering finish. Also in magnum, as for all the reds.

★★★★ **Merlot** Understated **12** offers layers of silky mulberry fruit, warm spice & dark chocolate within a firm frame, showing lovely balance. Third new French oak.

★★★★☆ **Shiraz** Bold wild berry fruit flavours leavened with delicate lavender, lifted by pepper spice & liquorice in seamless **13**. Good ageing potential, like **11**. **12** sold out untasted.

★★★★☆ **Chardonnay** ⓠ Opulent yet elegant barrel-fermented **13** maintains the pattern. Offers many intense layers of dense, buttery citrus, crushed stone, vanilla & flowers; bold precise oaking (year French, only 10% new). A keeper.

★★★★ **Sauvignon Blanc** Consistent & dependable label. Now-bottled **14** shows concentrated grapefruit & lime flavours, & a good whiff of sea air; refreshing minerality on the dry finish.

★★★★ **Méthode Cap Classique** ⓠ NV (**10**) bubbly from chardonnay is dry, vibrant, with fine mousse & creamy texture from 36 months lees-ageing.

Also tasted: **Pinotage 13** ★★★★ Occasional release: **Le Phantom Brut Cap Classique**.

Drunken Fowl range ⓝ

Shiraz ★★★ Playful label for newest of cellar's shiraz trio. Dollops of lissom spicy fruit on just-dry **13**.

Guinea Fowl range

Red ★★★ Merlot, cab & shiraz blend. **13** previewed last edition remains smooth & fruity, a delicious everyday tipple. Also tasted: **White 14** ★★★ Occasional release: **Rosé**.

Concept range

Grand Vin Blanc ⓠ ★★★ Fun & fruity entry-level **NV** from sauvignon & chenin, bursts with ripe fruit & zesty acidity. Not retasted: **Grand Vin Rouge NV** ★★ — DS

Location: Kuils River ▪ Map/WO: Stellenbosch ▪ Map grid reference: A5 ▪ Est 1693 ▪ 1stB 1990 ▪ Tasting & sales Mon-Fri 10–6 Sat/Sun 10–5 ▪ Fee R20/R35 ▪ Closed Good Fri, Dec 25 & Jan 1 ▪ Cheese platters ▪ Wedding/function venue ▪ Gifts ▪ Conservation area ▪ Game park ▪ Saxenburg guest cottages ▪ Owner(s) Adrian & Birgit Bührer ▪ Cellarmaster(s) Nico van der Merwe (Nov 1990) ▪ Winemaker(s) Nico van der Merwe (Nov 1990), with Edwin Grace (Jan 2005) ▪ Viticulturist(s) Donovan Diedericks (Apr 2008) ▪ 195ha/85ha (cabs s/f, malbec, merlot, ptage, shiraz, chard, chenin, sauv, viog) ▪ 650t/100,000cs own label 78% red 20% white 2%

rosé ▪ Other export brands: Bosman's Hill, Gwendolyn ▪ PO Box 171 Kuils River 7580 ▪ info@saxenburg.co.za ▪ www.saxenburg.co.za ▪ S 33° 56' 47.9" E 018° 43' 9.4" ▪ **T +27 (0)21-903-6113**

☐ **Say Lovey** see M'hudi Wines

Scali ⓆⓀ

Willie de Waal is the fifth generation on gracious, certified organic Schoone Oord estate in Voor Paardeberg, home of Scali wines (unavailable for review). The farming tradition is likely to continue, with five children between the ages of four and fifteen, who deeply enrich Willie and wife Tania's lives. Recently the couple explored the Gaillac area of France to learn more about the méthode rurale style of single-ferment vinification, it being used by Willie and Tania for their chenin-based sparkling, Ancestor.

Location: Paarl ▪ Map: Paarl & Wellington ▪ Map grid reference: C1 ▪ Est/1stB 1999 ▪ Tasting, sales & cellar tours Mon-Sat by appt ▪ Closed all pub hols ▪ Self-catering cottage ▪ Owner(s) Willie & Tania de Waal ▪ Cellarmaster(s)/winemaker(s) Willie & Tania de Waal (Aug 1999) ▪ Viticulturist(s) Willie de Waal (Feb 1991) ▪ 270ha/70ha (cab, merlot, ptage, shiraz, chard, chenin, rouss, sauv, viog) ▪ 45t/6,000cs own label 67% red 33% white ▪ CERES (vyds, wines certified organic) ▪ PO Box 7143 Paarl 7620 ▪ info@scali.co.za ▪ www.scali.co.za ▪ S 33° 36' 70.6" E 018° 51' 49.5" ▪ F +27 (0)86-617-5040 ▪ **T +27 (0)21-869-8340**

☐ **Schalk Burger & Sons** see Welbedacht Wine Estate

Schalkenbosch Wines ⓆⓀⓄ

The luxury guest lodgings, for whose benefit the Schalkenbosch wine brand was mostly founded, are now complemented by new tasting and function venues. Also recent, though long seasoned and highly reputed (Overgaauw, Lourensford), is consultant winemaker Chris Joubert. And freshly cleansed of aliens are a further 20 hectares of mountain slopes, burnishing the Tulbagh estate's eco-credentials.

Schalkenbosch range

★★★★ **Cumulus** Ⓠ After impressive deep berry flavours on **10**, similar dark fruit from Bordeaux quintet less intense on **11** (★★★★). Densely layered tannins may benefit from ageing.

★★★★ **Stratus** Ⓠ Shiraz-led flagship, **11** (★★★★) less characterful than **10**. Red berries boosted by few grams sugar, but oak still dominant mid-2014. May gain greater harmony with time.

Méthode Cap Classique ★★ **11** first since **07**, 85/15 chardonnay & pinotage, bright lemon/lime flavours & toasty undertone. Good pick-me-up style: 10% alcohol & perky bubble. Not tasted: **Viognier**.

Edenhof range

Nighthawk 409 ★★★★ Mourvèdre leads satisfying **13** partnered by shiraz, viognier & grenache; smooth, dense but unheavy with well-paced spice, dark berry, meaty features & savoury length. **Rosé** ★★★ Eye-catching tourmaline pink **15** from cab franc, shiraz & merlot. Tasty & lingering wild red berry flavours too; refreshing, dry summer sipping. **Chardonnay** ★★★ **15** spiced with just one French oak barrel, lifts soft lemon, creamy tones; briskly dry. Also tasted: **Cabernet Sauvignon 13** ★★ **Pinotage 13** ★★★★ **Cabernet Sauvignon-Merlot 13** ★★ **Sauvignon Blanc 15** ★★ Not retasted: **Shiraz 13** ★★ Discontinued: **Merlot, Blanc de Blancs**. — AL

Location/map: Tulbagh ▪ WO: Tulbagh/Coastal ▪ Est 1792 ▪ 1stB 2002 ▪ Tasting, sales & tours by appt ▪ Closed all pub hols ▪ Tour groups ▪ Weddings/functions ▪ Walking/hiking & MTB trails ▪ Conservation area ▪ Self-catering cottages ▪ Owner(s) Platinum Mile Investments ▪ Winemaker(s) Chris Joubert (consultant) ▪ Viticulturist(s) Johan Wiese & Andrew Teubes ▪ 1,800ha/37ha (cab, shiraz) ▪ 140t/20,000cs own label 80% red 18% white 2% rosé ▪ BWI champion ▪ PO Box 95 Tulbagh 6820 ▪ info@schalkenbosch.co.za ▪ www.schalkenbosch.co.za ▪ S 33° 18' 49.7" E 019° 11' 59.9" ▪ F +27 (0)86-519-2605/+27 (0)86-654-8209 ▪ **T +27 (0)23-230-0654/1488**

Schenkfontein Kelders

A sibling to separately listed Winkelshoek, and previously a supplier of bulk wine to one of the majors, family-owned Schenkfontein stepped into the packaged wine arena in 2014 with three wines from own

1692
Spier

Taste three hundred years of heritage.
Ethical farming, the health of the soil and the people who work it.
Artistic endeavour and absolute care in the crafting of our wines.
This is what matters to us.

ESTABLISHED IN 1692

WINE. FARM-TO-TABLE RESTAURANT. PICNICS. HOTEL. CONFERENCING.
021 809 1100 | www.spier.co.za

f www.facebook.com/spierwinefarm @SpierWineFarm #spiermemories

THE ART OF FINE WINE

Exclusive auction wines purchased especially for you.

Over the years, we have been adding to our established collection of fine wines by purchasing annually from the country's only two specialist wine auctions –the Nedbank Cape Winemakers Guild Auction and the Nederburg Auction.

So, next time you visit one of our participating restaurants, ask to see the wine list and experience artistry of the Cape's finest.

f /tsogosun 🐦 @tsogosun

(ʊ) TSOGO SUN

KLEINE ZALZE
STELLENBOSCH
ANNO. 1695

A unique Cape Winelands experience

AWARD WINNING WINES | TERROIR RESTAURANT | KLEINE ZALZE LODGE

Wine Business Report 2014: The number one South African "On-Premise" wine brand in the UK

2015 Concours Mondial De Bruxelles, Best White Wine: Family Reserve Chenin Blanc 2013

UK 2015 Sommelier Wine Awards: New World Producer of the Year

☎ +27 (0)21 880 0717   🌐 www.kleinezalze.co.za

NOTHING ADDED EXCEPT NATURE ITSELF

AT OAKHURST WE ARE DEDICATED TO ENSURING PREMIUM QUALITY AND PURE ENJOYMENT. RIGHT FROM OUR TREES TO YOUR TABLE.

Discover more at **www.oakhurstolives.co.za**.
To contact us email **info@oakhurstolives.co.za** or call **+27 83 269 6999**.

 facebook.com/oakhurstolives @OakhurstOlives

CITY SIGHTSEEING OFFICIAL TOUR

Hop-On Hop-Off

CitySightseeing South Africa

The BEST way to see Cape Town & Joburg!

All Day - Every Day!

- **Cape Town**: Easy access to Table Mountain, Kirstenbosch, Townships, Beaches and Constantia Wine Farms
- **Johannesburg**: Easy access to Carlton Centre, Gold Reef City, Braamfontein, Maboneng and Soweto
- Open-Top, double-decker, circular bus tours of two of Africa's most vibrant cities!

PURPLE Wine Tour to Constantia, Cape Town

BUY ONLINE & SAVE
www.citysightseeing.co.za

0861 733 287

FOR BOOKINGS

+27 (0) 21 880 9500
info@phstellenbosch.com
proteahotels.com/stellenbosch

PROTEA HOTEL
STELLENBOSCH

LOCATED IN THE HEART OF THE WINELANDS.

FEEL AT HOME WITH NATURE AND WINE

Protea Hotel Stellenbosch is a historical little gem that offers GUESTS access to some of the best wine farms in South Africa. The hotel offers GUESTS a complimentary scheduled shuttle service to and from the Stellenbosch town and a variety of vouchers to different wine farms nearby. GUESTS can also enjoy comfortable and spacious accommodation and delicious meals from Die Wingerd restaurant while overlooking breathtaking views of the surrounding wine farms.

Terms and Conditions apply.

REAL VALUE

SolarWorld

REAL VALUE

THE FIRST CHOICE FOR SOUTH AFRICA'S AGRICULTURAL INDUSTRY

1975 · SOLARWORLD · 2015
40 YEARS
REAL VALUE

Rooibos Ltd (1 MW)

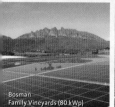

Bosman Family Vineyards (80 kWp)

Ceres Fruit Growers (1 MW)

Stellenpak (420 kWp)

WITH MORE THAN 40 YEARS OF TECHNOLOGY EXPERIENCE, SOLARWORLD OFFERS

» Highest quality solar modules made in Germany

» Linear 30 year performance guarantee

» More than a 30 year presence in Africa

» Established African distributor and installer network

↗ **WWW.SOLARWORLD.CO.ZA**

SolarWorld Africa (Pty) Ltd.
Lower Long Street · Cape Town
Email: contact@solarworld.co.za · Tel: (021) 421 8001

WINE, DINÉ
AND DELIGHT

LUCE AT HYDE PARK
SOUTHERN SUN
HYDE PARK SANDTON
T: +27 (0)11 341-8080

LEVEL FOUR
54 ON BATH
T: +27 (0)11 344-8400

SAN RESTAURANT
SANDTON SUN
T: +27 (0)11 780-5000

For breathtaking views of Johannesburg, look no further than Tsogo Sun.

For the finest take on traditional and trendy local dining, Tsogo Sun restaurants will delight you. Choose to be charmed at **Luce** where authentic Italian cuisine and the freshness of expertly prepared sushi is seamlessly brought together. Opt for a variety of classic dishes with a contemporary twist at **Level Four**. Or indulge at the **San** restaurant which places great emphasis on cosmopolitan dishes that are prepared using the freshest seasonal produce.

For more information on these or any of our other great restaurants log onto **tsogosun.com**

f /tsogosun 🐦 @tsogosun

◯ TSOGO SUN

Body & Solgar

Raw instead of refined. Stairs instead of elevator.

Whole grain instead of processed.

Doing the best for your body can really be good for your soul.

But even if you live well, you still may not be getting all the vitamins and minerals you need. At Solgar, we get it. After all, we've focused on wellness for over 65 years. That's all we do. And when it comes to supplements, we practically invented them.

Today, we still craft our vitamins and minerals in small batches to help ensure consistency and purity. And we always strive to make as many products as possible natural, vegetarian, plus dairy and gluten free. Focusing on wellness never gets old. Neither does feeling good throughout your life. So have a great journey. Solgar is with you all the way.

 SOLGAR® Live Vibrantly. Since 1947

SOLGAR | It's Your Choice.

SOLGAR *Vitamins* | **INNOVATION AND QUALITY** *Since 1947*

Available from Independent Health Stores and Healthcare Practitioners
For more information e-mail infosa@solgar.com | www.solgar.co.za | Tel 011 462 1652

CAREFULLY MANUFACTURED in the USA BY SOLGAR LABORATORIES

WINE VILLAGE

HERMANUS

VOTED ONE OF *South Africa's Best* **WINE SHOPS**

Open 7 days a week

Mon-Fri: 09:00 - 18:00
Sat: 09:00 - 17:00
Sun: 10:00 - 15:00

TEL: +27 (0) 28 316 3988
Hemel-en-Aarde Village
Hermanus, South Africa

wine@hermanus.co.za
www.winevillage.co.za

GPS Coordinates: S34°24'40.7" E019°12'1.9"

FOR THE **LARGEST SELECTION** OF FINE **SOUTH AFRICAN WINES**

The Neethlingshof **Short Story** Collection

DE WET VILJOEN, CELLARMASTER AT NEETHLINGSHOF, CONTINUES TO CREATE WINES WHICH PAY TRIBUTE TO THE SKILLS AND DETERMINATION OF ITS FOUNDER, MARIA MARAIS. HER DEEP LOVE OF THE LAND IS CELEBRATED AND CLEARLY EVIDENT IN THE RESTORATION OF THE FARM AND ESTATE TO ITS ORIGINAL NATURAL SPLENDOR BEAUTIFULLY CAPTURED BY THE **SHORT STORY COLLECTION**. THESE WINES ARE A CELEBRATION OF OUR COMMITMENT TO SUSTAINABILITY AND AN ABIDING EXPRESSION OF OUR DEEP LOVE OF THE LAND.

NEETHLINGSHOF
FROM THE HOUSE MARIA BUILT

NEETHLINGSHOF.CO.ZA

Not for Sale to Persons Under the Age of 18.

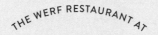

THE WERF RESTAURANT AT

BOSCHENDAL

*Innovative country cuisine guided
by the rhythms of the seasons*

WINE TASTING & SALES | VINEYARD & CELLAR TOURS | PICNICS
RESTAURANTS | FARMSHOP & DELI | ACCOMMODATION

BOSCHENDAL FARM ESTATE
Pniel Road R310, Groot Drakenstein, Franschhoek, Cape Winelands
www.boschendal.co.za   reservations@boschendal.co.za   021 870 4274
GPS Co-Ords 33°52.650'S 18°58.364'E

EAT
LOVE
WINE

Serving the finest steaks
complimented by an impressive
wine selection with international
appeal. The Meat Co is a 'must
visit' destination.

**The Meat Co Melrose Arch,
Johannesburg**

Monday – Sunday
12PM – 10:30PM

+27 11 684 1787 / 8

**The Meat Co Montecasino,
Johannesburg**

Sunday – Thursday
11AM – 10:30PM

Friday – Saturday
11AM – 11:30PM

+27 11 511 0235

www.themeatco.com

TheMeatCo

 The Meat Company South Africa

signature

RESTAURANT

CELEBRATING LIFE

SANDTON
Tel 087 940 3880 / 011 884 8888
sandton@signaturerestaurant.co.za

BROOKLYN
Tel 012 941 1277
brooklyn@signaturerestaurant.co.za

Pick n Pay

OUR SOUTH AFRICAN
WINES
ARE MORE THAN FINE.

South Africa has always
produced some of the finest
wines in the world. Now many
of those local wines have found
a home in Pick n Pay, alongside
a wide range of international
best sellers.

For inspirational wine choices,
visit www.picknpay.co.za/wine
or call our Customer Care Line
0800 11 22 88.
Toll-free landline.
Cellphone rates apply.

EAT GOOD

FEEL GREAT

The Grill Jichana is a modern and stylish Grill House that offers from prime beef cuts and Karoo lamb to free-range chicken, fish and vegetarian dishes.

THE GRILL JICHANA – GROUND FLOOR AT THE ELANGENI TOWER.

Southern Sun Elangeni & Maharani
63 Snell Parade, Durban 4001
t: 27 31 362 1300 I e: garika.ramdarie@tsogosun.com

THE
GRILL
JICHANA

Riedel recognises that the bouquet, taste, balance and finish of a wine is affected by the shape of the glass from which it is drunk. Over forty years ago Claus Riedel began his pioneering work to create stemware that would match and complement different wines and spirits.

"The Finest glasses for both technical and hedonistic purposes are those made by Riedel. The effect of these glasses on fine wine is profound.

I cannot emphasize enough what a difference they make."

Robert M Parker Jr - The Wine Advocate.

RIEDEL
THE WINE GLASS COMPANY

GRAPE ❖ VARIETAL SPECIFIC®

For more information & stockists in other areas please contact our Johannesburg Showroom: Pilrig, 1 Rockridge Road, Parktown | Tel: +27 11 482 9178 | e-mail: riedel@reciprocal.co.za

www.reciprocal.co.za

EXPERIENCE A
Journey of the senses

Bordeaux, Vineyards & Chateaux
Bordeaux to Bordeaux | 8 days

For lovers of food and wine, this Uniworld Boutique River Cruise show-cases the best that Bordeaux has to offer. You'll sail three stunning rivers on one amazing journey, all aboard your elegant floating hotel. Savour the unique heritage of southwest France, from delightful Pauillac, the gateway to the storied Médoc wine route, to elegant Bordeaux. With Uniworld's **true all-inclusive** river cruising experience, you´ll discover the *douceur de vivre* this region is known.

Wine & Culinary Highlights Include:

• *Taste regional delights, including duck confit, caviar d'Aquitaine, and oysters.* • *Visit the cellars of Premier Grand Cru in Saint-Émilion and savour the world's most highly rated wines.* • *Exclusive artisanal wine-pairing lunch at Château de Cazeneuve.* • *Discover the beautiful Médoc vineyards on a bicycle ride with wine tasting*

UNIW❦RLD.
BOUTIQUE RIVER CRUISE COLLECTION®

Call us on **(011) 280 8440** or visit **uniworldcruises.co.za**

 UniworldRiverCruises   @UniworldSA   #exploreuniworld

NGWENYA GLASS

The glass is always **greener**
on our side.

handmade • eco friendly • recycled • locally produced in Swaziland

P.O. Box 45, Motshane, Swaziland
www.ngwenyaglass.co.sz | ngwenya@ngwenyaglass.co.sz
T / F: +268 – 244 24053 | 244 24142 | 244 24151 | 244 24588
Fax from SA only: 086 5305 452
Watershed, V&A Waterfront, Cape Town | 021 418 0654

Zevenwacht

ANNO 1800

Indulge your senses
on breathtaking Zevenwacht

- Exquisite Award Winning Wines.
- Children welcome and catered for.
- Mouthwatering cuisine at our a la carte restaurant in the historic Manor House.
- Delicious picnic baskets to order and enjoy in a paradisical setting on tree shaded lawns.
- Luxurious accommodation in our 4 star Country Inn, with Vineyard Cottages or self-catering Chalet also available.
- Impressive function and conference facilities available.

Treat yourself to a delightful sensory experience. Whether you come for the day or spend a night, we'll exceed your expectations.

tel: +27 (21) 900 5700 | info@zevenwacht.co.za | www.zevenwacht.co.za
Langverwacht Road, Kuils River, South Africa
On the Stellenbosch Wine Route

and partner grapes in the Piketberg-Citrusdal area (the chardonnay missed our deadline last time). Winemaker/viticulturist Hendrik Hanekom has since shepherded several new labels into bottle.

Cabernet Sauvignon (NEW) ★★ Modest sweet berry aromas on 5-month-oaked **15** with an easygoing tannic grip. **Shiraz** ★★★ Pick of the red bunch: very ripe dark plummy fruit on **15**, soft but firm tannin. Flavours don't linger. Reds all unwooded or lightly oaked. **Chenin Blanc** ★★★ A little thatch, a soupçon of dried peach on pleasant, very easy & light **15**. Also tasted: **Merlot** (NEW) **15** ★★ **Pinotage** (NEW) **15** ★★ **Dry Rosé** (NEW) **15** ★★ **Chardonnay** (NEW) **15** ★ **Colombar** (NEW) **15** ★ **Sauvignon Blanc** (NEW) **15** ★★ — TJ

Location: Piketberg ▪ WO: Swartland ▪ Est 2000 ▪ 1stB 2014 ▪ Closed to public ▪ Cellarmaster(s)/ winemaker(s)/viticulturist(s) Hendrik Hanekom (Nov 2010) ▪ 500ha/51ha (ptage, shiraz, chenin) ▪ 500t/150,000L own label 30% red 70% white ▪ PO Box 2 Eendekuil 7335 ▪ hendrik@winkelshoek.co.za ▪ www.winkelshoek.co.za ▪ F +27 (0)22-942-1488 ▪ **T +27 (0)22-942-1484**

Schultz Family Wines   ⓠ

'Not much change within my small setup,' says Rudi Schultz ruefully. The 'setup' is what he calls his 'attempt to make hand-crafted ultra-premium wines at sensible prices'. His illustrious job as Thelema winemaker is what holds things up. But his '13 Cabernet Sauvignon is putting in some bottle maturation time and will be featured next year, he promises. And he's proud of the consistency of his '13 Syrah being the 12th consecutive vintage to get 90+ points in Wine Spectator.

★★★★ **Syrah** Restrained **13** from Bottelary needs time in the glass to reveal its black fruit, leather & Asian spice nuances; firm tannins are balanced by measured fruit concentration & intensity making it more accessible in youth than **12**, but sufficient structure for 5+ years improvement.

Occasional release: **Reserve Syrah**. — JPf

Location/WO: Stellenbosch ▪ Est 2002 ▪ Tasting by appt ▪ Closed all pub hols ▪ Owner(s) Rudi Schultz ▪ Cellarmaster(s)/winemaker(s) Rudi Schultz (Jan 2002) ▪ Viticulturist(s) Dirkie Morkel ▪ 12t/1,000cs own label 100% red ▪ 8 Fraser Road Somerset West 7130 ▪ rudi@thelema.co.za ▪ F +27 (0)21-885-1800 ▪ **T +27 (0)82-928-1841**

Scrucap Wines

'LUX* Resorts & Hotels in the Indian Ocean, China and the Middle East offer a lighter, brighter alternative to traditional five-star holidays,' says consultant Kent Scheermeyer. 'This philosophy extends to Scrucap, a refreshingly modern selection of wines from elite Cape producers.'

★★★★ **Reserve Cabernet Sauvignon** (NEW) Solid ripe fruit & long finish hint at future complexity, but **11** somewhat dominated in youth by oak & drying tannin. From The Winery of Good Hope.

★★★★ **Pinot Noir** Elegantly crafted with lovely silky texture, from De Grendel. Fresh balance, layers of polished red fruit but **14** (★★★★) not as alluring or complex as **13**.

★★★★ **Reserve Syrah** (NEW) The Winery of Good Hope's naturally fermented **13** shows delicate floral/ fynbos notes, fresh acidity, gentle tannins & lightest oak touch highlighting dark plum & berry fruit.

★★★★ **Swartland Blend 12** is 8-way combo from AA Badenhorst, large older oak only. Fruit-filled, slightly meaty, grape tannin bite & modest 12.5% alcohol make it a pleasure to drink.

★★★★ **Chardonnay 14** from Paul Cluver is rich & ripe with fragrant baked apple & roasted nut flavours. Smooth, balanced, lovely interplay between oaky & fresh lemon on palate.

★★★★ **Riesling** (ⓠ) **13** by riesling star Paul Cluver, subtle perfumed lime & kiwifruit in tangy balance with creamy undertone from semi-sweet styling. Beautifully light, fresh & delicious.

★★★★ **Sauvignon Blanc** (ⓠ) Feisty & flavoursome **13** by Paul Cluver raises the bar on **12** (★★★★). Cream texture threaded with racy passionfruit flavours, vivacious balance, long tangy farewell.

★★★★ **Popcap Brut MCC** Bubbly from chardonnay. **NV**'s citrus zing tempered by year on lees, breadth from 12% oak-aged reserve wine & splash pinot noir. A super aperitif from Steenberg.

Sauvignon Blanc ★★★☆ **15** by De Grendel proffers fresh, floral aromas & serves up a tropical fruit feast nicely controlled by zippy acidity. **Popcap Rosé MCC** (NEW) ★★★★ Candyfloss pink **NV** sparkling suggests a party. It is! A zesty mousse & lively dry finish call for fun in the sun. Chardonnay & pinot noir

9 months on lees. From Steenberg. Also tasted: **Merlot 13** ★★★☆ **Shiraz 13** ★★★☆ **Three Valleys Blend 13** ★★★☆ **Rosé 15** ★★☆ **Chenin Blanc 14** ★★★☆ — WB, GdB, JG, JPf, DS

WO: Western Cape/Elgin/Stellenbosch/Coastal/Swartland ▪ Est 2011 ▪ Closed to public ▪ Cellarmaster(s) Andries Burger (Paul Cluver), JD Pretorius (Steenberg), Charles Hopkins (De Grendel), Edouard Labeye (The Winery of Good Hope), Sjaak Nelson (Jordan), Adi Badenhorst (AA Badenhorst) & Schalk Opperman (Lammershoek) ▪ 20,000cs own label 40% red 40% white 10% rosé 10% MCC ▪ ksconsult@mweb.co.za ▪ www.luxresorts.com ▪ **T +27 (0)83-484-8781**

Seal Breeze Wines

No mid-life crisis for Joan Wiggins, rather mid-life joy after buying back the family's diamond-rich West Coast winegrape farm just over a decade ago and immersing herself in winemaking. Self-taught, she shares skills (and lust for life) with Journey of Hope breast cancer survivors during harvest and spoils buyers of her magnums with a sparkler in each bottle.

Shiraz ⓦ ★★★★ Star of the range. Pre-bottling, **13** rich & ripe red fruit with white pepper, cardamom & clove dusting. Supple, silky; succulent, very long, spicy farewell. Different league to previous, as all these reds. **Sauvignon Blanc** ⓦ ★★★ Previewed **14** cool & fresh expression of the variety, balanced, with immediate 'drink me' appeal & clean greengage/starfruit flavours. Not retasted: **Cabernet Sauvignon 13** ★★★ **Merlot 13** ★★★☆ — MW

Location: Lutzville ▪ Map: Olifants River ▪ WO: Lutzville Valley ▪ Est 2004 ▪ 1stB 2005 ▪ Tasting, sales & cellar tours Mon-Fri 9–4 Sat 9–12 ▪ Closed Easter Fri-Mon, Ascension Day, Dec 25 & Jan 1 ▪ Meals/refreshments by prior arrangement ▪ Facilities for children ▪ Tour groups ▪ BYO picnic ▪ Owner(s)/viticulturist(s) Joan Wiggins ▪ Cellarmaster(s) Joan Wiggins (Feb 2004) ▪ Winemaker(s) Joan Wiggins (Feb 2004), with Toy Brand (Feb 2006) ▪ ±92ha/±70ha (cab, merlot, shiraz, chenin, cbard, hanepoot, sauv) ▪ 1,200t/1,560cs own label ▪ PO Box 33 Lutzville 8165 ▪ jwiggins@kingsley.co.za ▪ www.sealbreezewine.co.za ▪ S 31° 34' 50.1" E 018° 19' 9.8" ▪ F +27 (0)27-217-1458 ▪ **T +27 (0)84-505-1991**

☐ **Season's Collection** *see* Orange River Cellars
☐ **Secateurs** *see* AA Badenhorst Family Wines
☐ **Secret Cellar** *see* Ultra Liquors

Sedgwick's Old Brown

Venerable Distell brand, blend of jerepiko and dry 'sherry', in 200ml, 375ml, 750ml, 1L and 2L.

Sedgwick's Old Brown ⊘ ⑨ ★★★ Fortified winter warmer since 1916. **NV**'s deep amber hue prepares you for the richness to come: candied fruit, honey & raisins, a lovely sherry-style sweetness. — CR

☐ **Selena** *see* Marianne Wine Estate
☐ **Selma** *see* Nordic Wines
☐ **Semara** *see* Wine-of-the-Month Club
☐ **Sentinel** *see* Wine-of-the-Month Club
☐ **Sequillo Cellars** *see* Sadie Family Wines
☐ **Seriously Cool** *see* Waterkloof
☐ **7even** *see* Zevenwacht

Seven Sisters

Seven indeed, from the West Coast village of Paternoster, and by their wines shall you know their names. Sister Vivian (Kleynhans) took the lead in launching the range for their company, African Roots, nearly a decade back. The Stellenbosch cellar is more recent, a restaurant set to open there at press time.

Carol Cabernet Sauvignon ★★☆ Unwooded **14**, juicy quince & strawberry fruit, soft texture. **June Merlot** ★★ **14**, unoaked, shows stewed fruit, easy tannins. **Vivian Sauvignon Blanc** ★★☆ **14** from Breede River vines, fresh & light, tiny hint of sweetness. Also tasted: **Dawn Pinotage-Shiraz 14** ★★★☆ Not retasted: **Odelia Bukettraube 13** ★★ **Yolanda Moscato 12** ★★ **Twena Sweet Rosé 14** ★★★ — GdB

Location/map: Stellenbosch ▪ Map grid reference: D7 ▪ WO: Western Cape/Swartland ▪ Tasting & sales at Seven Sisters Farm, Welmoed Rd, off Annandale Rd, Lynedoch, Stellenbosch – phone ahead ▪ Owner(s) African Roots Wine ▪ Winemaker(s) Vivian Kleynhans ▪ PO Box 4560 Tygervalley 7536 ▪ vivian@africanrootswines.com ▪ www.sevensisters.co.za ▪ S 33° 59' 23.41" E 018° 46' 34.35" ▪ F +27 (0)86-514-5569 ▪ **T +27 (0)71-049-4109/+27 (0)83-624-0391**

Seven Springs Vineyards

Britons Tim and Vaughan Pearson's farm, pioneer of a future Shaw's Mountain demarcation between Hermanus and Caledon, delivers increasingly impressive results in the guide and internationally. While their wine approach is hands-off (and vinification by Riana van der Merwe is off-site, pending a long-dreamed-of cellar mooted for 2017), their social media presence is distinctly and warmly fingers-on.

★★★★ **Pinot Noir** Subtle oak nuances on **13** give way to voluptuous cherry, raspberry fruit. Light & elegant, with downy tannins, sufficient form for now & 3-5 years.

★★★★ **Chardonnay** ⓥ **12** improves on **11** (★★★★) in its refinement & restraint. Subtly supportive oak (older barrels only, year); malo eschewed, therefore vibrantly fresh & seamlessly long.

★★★★ **Sauvignon Blanc** Raises the bar on rounded & full **12** (★★★★). **13** citrus, greengage & wet pebble complexity, gooseberry & lime persistence, pinpoint acid balance.

Not retasted: **Syrah 12** ★★★☆ **Unoaked Chardonnay 13** ★★★☆ — GM

Location: Hermanus ▪ WO: Overberg ▪ Est 2007 ▪ 1stB 2010 ▪ Closed to public ▪ Owner(s) Tim & Vaughan Pearson ▪ Winemaker(s) Riana van der Merwe (Nov 2009) ▪ Viticulturist(s) Peter Davison (Jul 2007, consultant) ▪ 12ha/±8ha (pinot, syrah, chard, sauv) ▪ ±67t/10,000cs own label 60% red 40% white ▪ Other export brand: Over the Mountain ▪ Private Bag X15 Suite 162 Hermanus 7200 ▪ tim@7springs.co.za ▪ www.7springs.co.za ▪ F +27 (0)86-571-0623 ▪ **T +27 (0)28-316-4994 (office)/ +27 (0)82-487-7572 (winemaker)**

Shannon Vineyards   ⓥ ♿

Situated in Elgin and owned by James and Stuart Downes, Shannon first built an enviable reputation on the quality of the grapes supplied to several elite winemakers. Then, in 2009, the brothers' own label, vinified in Hemel-en-Aarde by Gordon and Nadia Newton Johnson, debuted. Shannon wines have since enjoyed a 'second' reputation as among SA's finest, and most expressive of their cool, meticulously nurtured and very beautiful origin. Ever careful not to dilute their brand nor the quality of the fruit they grow, the Downes have planted a new pinot noir vineyard on 'probably the best-suited soils to date'.

★★★★☆ **Mount Bullet Merlot** A Cape benchmark. **12** similar noble bearing & athletic build, suave fruit to **11**. Incredibly complete, with persistent savoury conclusion, structure for decade-plus cellaring.

★★★★☆ **Rockview Ridge Pinot Noir** Iron fist in velvet glove **13**, pretty cherry & vanilla aromas followed by powerful palate of tightly wound acidity, assertive tannins, dense fruit core. For the long haul.

★★★★☆ **Sanctuary Peak Sauvignon Blanc** Portion (11%) new-oak-fermented semillon adds lanolin & vanilla nuances to **14**'s white peach & citrus fruit, gives weight & texture to its lean minerality. Elegant & complete, unreliant on acidity for presence or persistence. Even better with few years age.

★★★★ **Semillon** Barrel fermented (50% new) **14** (★★★★★) has a smoky edge to its lemon-toned fruit, perfectly poised acidity & very good length. Deserves year/2 to show at best, like debut **12**. **13** untasted.

★★★★☆ **Macushla Pinot Noir Noble Late Harvest** ⓥ 'My Darling' deliciously idiosyncratic dessert, naturally fermented in older oak. **12** (★★★★), first tasted since **09**, so easy to drink now, next year... or in 10. — CvZ

Location/WO: Elgin ▪ Map: Elgin, Walker Bay & Bot River ▪ Est 2000 ▪ 1stB 2003 ▪ Tasting & sales by appt ▪ Owner(s) Stuart & James Downes ▪ Winemaker(s) Gordon Newton Johnson & Nadia Newton Johnson ▪ Viticulturist(s) Kevin Watt (consultant) ▪ 75ha/15.5ha (merlot, pinot, sauv, sem) ▪ 100t/10,000cs own label 66% red 34% white ▪ BWI, Global GAP, IPW, Tesco's Natures Choice ▪ PO Box 20 Elgin 7180 ▪ james@shannonwines.com ▪ www.shannonwines.com ▪ S 34° 11' 3.9" E 018° 59' 3.6" ▪ F +27 (0)21-859-5389 ▪ **T +27 (0)21-859-2491**

☐ **Shepherd's Cottage** *see* Overgaauw Wine Estate

Ship

Another piece of Distell-owned South African wine patrimony, launched in 1929.

Ship ⓐ ★★ Raisiny jerepiko-style fireside comforter. **NV.** — DB

Shoprite Checkers

SA supermarket chain Shoprite Checkers boasts an actively marketed in-store 'wine route' offering top selections from 80+ local labels (including Nederburg Auction) and some 50 international producers. Its own Odd Bins range, selected by an expert panel, remains a top seller.

Enquiries: Stephanus Eksteen ▪ 160,000cs own label 50% red 40% white 10% rosé ▪ PO Box 215 Brackenfell 7561 ▪ seksteen@shoprite.co.za ▪ www.shoprite.co.za ▪ F +27 (0)21-980-4421 ▪ **T +27 (0)21-980-4000**

☐ **Short Story** *see* Neethlingshof Estate
☐ **Short Street** *see* Valley Vineyards Wine Company
☐ **Shortwood** *see* Imbuko Wines
☐ **Signal Cannon** *see* Vondeling

Signal Gun Wines   ⓐ ⓐ ⓐ

The range launched in 2006 by MJ de Wit as a hobby, with grapes off the old Hooggelegen family farm in Durbanville, soon developed into project Ke-Monate ('That's Nice!'), with tasting room, restaurant, more wines and, now, two craft beers named Ystervark and Bontebok after indigenous porcupine and antelope species. Coming soon are chenin blanc vines.

De Wit Family Reserves

★★★★ **Sea Smoke Sauvignon Blanc** Named for frequent ocean mists & fogs blanketing this, area's highest vineyard (455 m). **14** in finer form than **13** (★★★☆), intense gooseberry on nose, tropical fruit flavours with salty tang, full citrus finish.

Not retasted: **WRM Shiraz 10** ★★★☆ **B Loved Méthode Cap Classique 12** ★★★☆

Signal Gun range

Merlot ★★★☆ Attractive warm Christmas cake aromas on **13**, leading to balanced palate with firm structure, savoury finish. **Chardonnay** ★★★☆ Unoaked **15** is all tropical fruit & ripe apples, a hint of lemon, smooth & creamy. A delight! Also tasted: **Rosé 14** ★★★☆ **Sauvignon Blanc 14** ★★★☆ Not retasted: **Shiraz 11** ★★★☆

Tin Hill range

Sauvignon Blanc ⊘ ★★★☆ Green-toned **14** goes up a notch with greenpepper & fresh herbs, lees-ageing gives complexity, lipsmacking tangy exit. **Muy-Scatty** ★★★ Charming name for light just-dry blend muscat d'Alexandrie & sauvignon; **14** soft & fruity, with fragrant floral perfume. Also tasted: **Pinotage 14** ★★★ **Merlot-Cabernet Sauvignon 14** ★★★ — WB

Location/WO: Durbanville ▪ Map: Durbanville, Philadelphia & Darling ▪ Est/1stB 2006 ▪ Tasting & sales Tue-Sat 9.30-5 Sun 9.30-4 ▪ Fee R20 ▪ Closed Good Fri, Dec 25 & Jan 1 ▪ Ke-Monate Restaurant ▪ Conferences ▪ Conservation area ▪ Owner(s) WRM de Wit ▪ Cellarmaster(s)/winemaker(s) Riaan Oosthuizen (2011), MJ de Wit (Jan 2006) ▪ Viticulturist(s) Walter Smith ▪ 210ha/95ha (cab, merlot, ptage, shiraz, chard, sauv) ▪ 19t/2,000cs own label 50% red 50% white ▪ PO Box 364 Durbanville 7551 ▪ wine@ signalgun.com ▪ www.signalgun.com ▪ S 33° 49' 13.26" E 018° 36' 40.32" ▪ F +27 (0)86-611-8747 ▪ **T +27 (0)21-976-7343**

Signal Hill Wines   ⓐ ⓐ

Named after a peak above Cape Town, Signal Hill is situated in the city centre and latterly has had a remarkable and unique focus on tiny bottlings off metropolitan vineyards. The 'flagship' block, a few rows in residential Oranjezicht named Clos d'Oranje, is now biodynamically cultivated, reports

Jean-Vincent Ridon, debonair French founder of the winery and originator of the 'city vines' concept. Less good news for fans of the splendid shiraz from those apparently ungrafted vines (the '06 earned 5 stars in this guide) is that there is no new release – 'not to our level of expectation'. Cushioning the blow is a new pair of old-vine bottlings, wider sourced (as are several recent releases) but equally beguiling.

Single Barrel range

★★★★ **Malbec** Loaded with personality & bursting with juicy fruit, **14** is vibrant but not over the top; a supple frame supports classy Durbanville fruit to persistent finish. Only very old oak, only 285 bottles!

★★★★ **Pinot Noir** ⓓ **10** lighter style than **08** standard bottling, also from Stellenbosch fruit, with more appetising acidity & cranberry flavours imparting an elegant cool-climate feel.

★★★★ **1771 Heritage Vine** ⓓ One 240-year-old city centre chenin vine bore 20 bottles of this intriguing **11** curiosity: full of flavour, with a sweet impression despite low alcohol & sugar.

★★★★☆ **Pineau de Ludovic** ⓓ Contemplative **NV** aperitif; chenin-colombard blend spent a decade in barrel. 200 g/l sugar & 16% alcohol on complex & delicious fortified wine. Stellenbosch/Paarl fruit.

Discontinued: **Kalk Bay Blanc de Noir**.

Signal Hill range

★★★★ **Old Bush Vines Cinsault** ⓃⒺⓦ **12** mimics the texture of pinot noir; subtle dusty, earthy berry fruit on a refined, well-weighted palate seasoned 2 years in old cask; genteel 12.3% alcohol. Ex Durbanville, Darling.

★★★★ **Grenache Noir** Pioneer varietal bottling in SA. **14** a wine of contrasts: very pale but not short of power, sweetly fruited yet bone-dry, light on its feet but with an appealing earthiness. Durbanville vines.

★★★★☆ **Camps Bay Vineyard** ⓓ **10** (★★★★), from mourvèdre, just 250 bottles off coastal suburban vines. Fine **09** was maiden harvest.

★★★★☆ **Clos d'Oranje** ⓓ From tiny apparently ungrafted shiraz vineyard in Oranjezicht, Cape Town. Both **08** & **09** spicily vibrant, authentic & convincing, with ripe red fruit & integrated tannins.

★★★★ **Grenache Blanc** ⓓ **08** subtle scents, silky, & savoury mineral core. From Piekenierskloof.

★★★★☆ **Old Vines Semillon** ⓃⒺⓦ Tulbagh grapes oak-fermented/aged on lees 3 years (half new wood), further year sur lie in tank. Fascinating **11** vibrantly crisp & fresh, beautifully textured, the 15% alcohol secreted away in a fine structure.

★★★★ **Méthode Cap Classique Pinot Noir** ⓓ **06** sparkling disgorged on demand. Lovely mature aromas. Bone-dry, unsulphured.

★★★★ **Crème de Tête Muscat d'Alexandrie NLH** ⓓ Last tasted was hedonistic **03**.

★★★★★ **Eszencia** ⓓ Magnificent **NV** (**02**), probably a one-off, sweet & rich, nervy acidity.

★★★★☆ **Vin de l'Empereur Solera** ⓓ Unctuous **NV** from solera of Constantia muscat d'Alexandrie.

Not tasted: **Olympia Cabernet Franc**, **Straw Wine**. — DS

Location: Cape Town ▪ Map: Cape Peninsula ▪ WO: Coastal/Durbanville/Stellenbosch/Piekenierskloof/Constantia/Western Cape ▪ 1stB 1997 ▪ Tasting, sales & cellar tours Mon-Fri 11-6 Sat 11-3 in season ▪ Closed all pub hols ▪ Charcuterie & tapas during open hours ▪ Owner(s) Signal Hill Wines cc ▪ Cellarmaster(s) Jean-Vincent Ridon ▪ Winemaker(s)/viticulturist(s) Laurence Buthelezi ▪ 1ha ▪ Heritage Square, 100 Shortmarket Street, Cape Town 8001 ▪ info@winery.co.za ▪ www.winery.co.za ▪ S 33° 55' 15.06" E 018° 25' 5.54" ▪ F +27 (0)21-422-5238 ▪ **T +27 (0)21-424-5820**

☐ **Signatures of Doolhof** *see* Doolhof Wine Estate

Sijnn ⓠ 🍴

Sibling to top-rated De Trafford and a star in own right, this winery sits in scenic isolation atop a stony promontory above the river Breede ('Sijnn' in Khoisan; rhymes with 'Seine') near Malgas, 15 km from the ocean. Much to celebrate here in 2015, notably the maiden harvest for the new cellar and winemaker Charla Haasbroek. A BSc graduate, Charla has worked at Kanonkop, Tokara and in California. She describes the harvest as delivering 'a smaller crop but with beautiful colour and intensity'. There were a few teething issues and 'the dreaded power outages', says co-winemaker/-owner David Trafford, who visits (from Stellenbosch) around three times a month. Winelovers visit in their numbers on weekends, treating the long dirt road as 'a bit of an adventure'. More adventures will come with new plantings like assyrtiko, garnacha/grenache peluda and petit manseng, all farmed and vinified as naturally as possible.

★★★★ **Cabernet Sauvignon** 12 best to date. Beautiful, cool violets & fresh black berry scents; abundance of pure, fresh flavours in gently fleshed body, all invigorated by tiny, vibrant tannins. More elegant & satisfying than 11 (★★★★).

★★★★☆ **Syrah** 13 continues variations on cool-climate theme; all different, special. Lovely vibrant, spicy attack, even a sense of ruggedness within its elegant frame. It concludes with a similar spicy flourish. The flesh is there, just needing time for wine to settle into itself.

★★★★☆ **Touriga Nacional** Builds on individuality with each vintage. 13, in David Trafford's estimation, best yet, has similar violets, earthy spice as previous but with more depth, concentration & incredible length. Flesh & frame are seamlessly integrated, balanced, allowing for current enjoyment or cellaring with confidence.

★★★★ **Sijnn** Syrah/shiraz clearly lead singer in 11 with its dark spice, choc tones & padded feel. Partners touriga, mourvèdre, trincadeira & cab add freshness & bright tangy nuance. A tasty, balanced mouthful. Also in 375 ml & 1.5L.

★★★★ **CWG Auction Reserve !uri** (NEW) Translates as 'White'; components as for regular bottling, but viognier in the lead. 14 also bolder style, more about texture, structure, mere apricot hint in tail; some oaky notes yet to integrate. May gain more interest with year/2. Natural ferment oak, half new. Unfiltered.

★★★★☆ **White** With quiet presence & intrigue, 14 blends 82% chenin, with viognier & roussanne. Haunting honeysuckle & summer blossoms fragrance are echoed in the smooth, creamy texture & lengthened by gentle mineral thread. Natural ferment in oak, 15% new. Unfiltered. Also in 375 ml, 1.5L & 3L.

Also tasted: **Low Profile 13** ★★★☆ **Saignée 13** ★★★★ — AL

Location/WO: Malgas ▪ Map: Southern Cape ▪ Est 2003 ▪ 1stB 2007 ▪ Tasting at Sijnn Sat 10-3, or by appt ▪ Vintners platters ▪ Closed all pub hols ▪ Sales only at De Trafford (see entry) ▪ Owner(s) David & Rita Trafford, Simon Farr, Quentin Hurt ▪ Winemaker(s) David Trafford & Charla Haasbroek (Dec 2014) ▪ Viticulturist(s) Schalk du Toit (2002, consultant) ▪ 125ha/16ha (cab, mourv, shiraz, touriga nacional, trincadeira, chenin, rouss, viog) ▪ 60t/5,400cs own label 73% red 20% white 7% rosé ▪ PO Box 495 Stellenbosch 7599 ▪ info@sijnn.co.za ▪ www.sijnn.co.za ▪ S 34° 19' 0.27" E 020° 36' 41.37" ▪ F +27 (0)86-542-3959 ▪ **T +27 (0)21-880-1398**

Silkbush Mountain Vineyards　　　　　　　　　　　　　　　🏠

Established and reputed as a supplier of top-quality grapes to some of SA's majors, this California-owned spread below Breedekloof's Sybasberg (Silkbush Mountain) exports its own brand to the US and is forming a presence at home. Range expansions promised earlier have materialised – rather tastily.

Easy Red (NEW) ★★ Easy by name & nature, unoaked 13 supple melange mainly merlot & pinotage, 3 others, approachable with enough grip for food. **Summer White** (NEW) ★★ Chenin, chardonnay lead the fruity 5-way outdoorsy sipper, 14 lively unwooded citrus & tropical mouthful. Also tasted: **Pinotage 12** ★★★☆ **Viognier 14** ★★★ Not retasted: **Shiraz 10** ★★★ — GM

Location: Wolseley ▪ WO: Breedekloof ▪ Est 2000 ▪ 1stB 2007 ▪ Closed to public ▪ Kingsbury Cottage (self-catering), www.silkbush.net/kingsbury ▪ Owner(s) Silkbush Holdings LP ▪ Winemaker(s) Bennie Wannenburg (2007, consultant) ▪ Viticulturist(s) Anton Roos (2000) ▪ 143ha/87ha (cabs s/f, malbec, merlot, mourv, p verdot, ptage, shiraz, sauv, sem, viog) ▪ 1,200t/10,000cs own label 100% red ▪ Other export brand: Lion's Drift ▪ PO Box 91 Breërivier 6858 ▪ anton@silkbush.net ▪ www.silkbush.net ▪ F +27 (0)86-520-3261 ▪ **T +27 (0)83-629-1735**

☐ **Silverhurst** see High Constantia Wine Cellar

Silvermist Vineyards　　　　　　　　　　　　　　　　🍷 🍴 🏠 📷

The panoramic views across False Bay alone are worth the visit, but this boutique-size, organically certified estate offers so much more: luxury accommodation, fine-dining at the acclaimed La Colombe restaurant, winetasting at the Green Vine Eatery, picnics and hiking. On the upper slopes of Constantiaberg, there's something for thrill-seekers too – among the longest zip-line experiences in southern Africa.

★★★★☆ **Single Vineyard Sauvignon Blanc** Ⓥ ♡ **14**, a classy step up on **13** (★★★☆), from low-yielding vines; lovely intensity in piquant balance with fine mineral thread, vivacious yet focused.

Sauvignon Blanc Ⓥ ★★★★ Mostly cool & herbaceous tones but also hints of ripe tropical fruit, **14** really tangy mouthful especially given modest alcohol; racy freshness favours food. Not tasted: **Cabernet Sauvignon**, **Rocket Dog Red**. — MW

Location/WO: Constantia ▪ Map: Cape Peninsula ▪ Est 1984 ▪ 1stB 2010 ▪ Tasting & sales Mon-Sun 10-4.30 ▪ The Green Vine Eatery open daily 8-5.30 for breakfast, lunch, wine tasting & all day foods ▪ La Colombe Restaurant, www.lacolombe.co.za or reservations@lacolombe.co.za ▪ Silvermist Mountain Lodge ▪ Conferences ▪ Weddings/functions ▪ Picnics ▪ Walks/hikes ▪ Conservation area ▪ Cape Town Ziplining ▪ Owner(s) Constantia Ridge Estates (Pty) Ltd ▪ Cellarmaster(s)/winemaker(s)/viticulturist(s) Gregory Brink Louw (Jan 2005) ▪ 22ha/6ha (cab, shiraz, sauv) ▪ 5.2t/580cs own label 30% red 70% white ▪ CERES organic ▪ PO Box 608 Constantia 7848 ▪ silvermistvineyards@gmail.com ▪ www.silvermistvineyards.co.za ▪ S 34° 0' 51.93" E 018° 24' 5.13" ▪ F +27 (0)21-794-7602 ▪ **T +27 (0)21-794-7601**

☐ **Silver Myn** see Zorgvliet Wines
☐ **Silversands** see Robertson Wide River Export Company

Silverthorn Wines

This bubbly-only house in Robertson was founded by Karen and John Loubser (he the MD and sometime winemaker of Steenberg, in far-off Constantia). Later investment meant they were able to create a full portfolio of sparklings of their own. Volumes continue to grow, along with the acclaim: a notable triumph was at the 2014 Six Nations Wine Challenge, when Green Man '11 was voted best sparkling wine, best white wine, and joint best wine of the show. John's first Silverthorn wine on the Cape Winemakers Guild Auction was named for the family's beloved Rottweiler.

★★★★ **The Genie NV** MCC sparkling rosé from shiraz is serious fun. Subtle raspberry & spice entice, fine mousse from 17 months on lees leads to unashamedly frivolous, fruity yet crisp & dry finish.

★★★★☆ **CWG Auction Reserve Big Dog** ⓝ Complex **10** MCC sparkler from chardonnay & pinot noir billows candied apples, brioche & nuts; fine, gentle celebratory mousse; relatively full body from partial oaking & long (53 months) on lees, extended by wonderful vivacity. WO W Cape.

★★★★☆ **Jewel Box** Chardonnay-led **11** MCC with 40% pinot noir gets 'masculine' nuance ex 60% oaked portion; fine mousse, endless finish from 42 months on lees. Complex, creamy & rich with vanilla, pear & brioche, lifted by characteristic saline nuance. WO W Cape.

★★★★☆ **The Green Man** One of SA's benchmark blanc de blancs. Sophisticated & elegant **12** is understated yet commands attention with impressive definition, focus & obvious care taken. 100% chardonnay, 29 months on lees, 10% oaked portion. — JPf

Location: Robertson ▪ WO: Robertson/Western Cape ▪ Est 1998 ▪ 1stB 2004 ▪ Closed to public ▪ Owner(s) Silverthorn Wines (Pty) Ltd ▪ Cellarmaster(s)/winemaker(s)/viticulturist(s) John Loubser (1998) ▪ 10.5ha/4ha (cab, shiraz, chard) ▪ 50t/4,100cs own label 66% white 34% rosé ▪ IPW ▪ PO Box 381 Robertson 6705 ▪ john@silverthornwines.co.za, karen@silverthornwines.co.za ▪ www.silverthornwines.co.za ▪ **T +27 (0)21-788-1706**

☐ **Simelia** see Woestkloof Estate
☐ **Simonay** see Simonsvlei International
☐ **Simonsbosch** see Koelenhof Winery

Simonshoogte ⓥ ⓐ

Owner since December 2014, entrepreneur Alex Kerrod has wasted no time placing his stamp on what was Mon Rêve Estate in the Simonsberg foothills, notably aligning the farm name, Simonshoogte, with the wine branding, and building a 200-ton cellar, fitted with stoneware open fermenters along with more conventional equipment. Watch for a single-block merlot, a cab and a cab-merlot blend, and a wine bar in the working cellar, 'giving a real winemaking experience'.

Location: Paarl ▪ Map: Paarl & Wellington ▪ Map grid reference: D7 ▪ Est 2009 ▪ 1stB 2011 ▪ Tasting, sales & cellar tours by appt ▪ Fee R20pp, waived on purchase ▪ Closed Easter Fri/Sun, May 1, Dec 25 & Jan 1 ▪ Facilities for children ▪ Owner(s) Rapitrade 652 (Pty) Ltd ▪ Winemaker(s) Marius Malan (Jan 2012) ▪ Viticulturist(s) Stian Mooiplats ▪ 12ha/±6ha (cab, merlot, shiraz, muscat d'A) ▪ 8,000L own label 94% red 6% white + 12,000L for clients ▪ PO Box 116 Franschhoek 7690 ▪ alexk@icon.co.za ▪ S 33° 49' 4.98" E 018° 54' 47.21" ▪ **T +27 (0)82-659-7649**

Simonsig Estate　　　　　　　　　　　　　　Ⓥ ⑪ ⓐ ⓐ ⓖ

Family is important at this large and successful Stellenbosch estate with lovely vistas of Simonsberg Mountain (hence the name 'View of Simonsberg'). Run by the sons of trailblazer Frans Malan (whose many firsts include SA's first bottle-fermented sparkling, with a new photo exhibit in the disgorging cellar honouring the milestone), Johan is cellarmaster while CEO/viticulturist Francois' son has joined the business on the marketing side. Taking the family connection even further a prestige cabernet, The Garland, launches this edition from grapes off a vineyard on the Simonsberg slopes belonging to maternal relatives. Unsurprisingly, the Malans are meticulous about caring for their staff and the environment, as their accreditation with a variety of standards organisations, listed in the contact details below, attests.

Malan Family Selection

★★★★☆ **The Garland** (NEW) Single cabernet vineyard on Simonsberg belonging to Malan relatives. Serious, 26 months new French oak, long bottle maturation, **08** has impressive depth & structure. Black cherries & cassis, some fynbos notes, savoury spice, still in the early stage of development.

★★★★☆ **Redhill Pinotage** Single-vineyard & always impressive, **12** shows the fruit intensity & silky structure the variety can achieve with the right provenance. Blackberry, maraschino cherries, an array of spices, including vanilla, fine-grained tannins, it's a sultry temptress.

★★★★★ **Merindol Syrah** Showing house-style opulent ripeness reflecting the single-vineyard terroir, **13** has loads of flavour, dark fruit, tapenade, mocha chocolate, on a supple bed of tannin, the flavours succulent, concentrated.

★★★★☆ **Tiara** Standout cabernet-led 5-way Bordeaux blend, always beautifully made, **12** also delivers. An iron fist in a velvet glove, intense cassis throughout, coating the tannins, smoothly curvaceous. Still in its youthful prime, a long future ahead.

★★★★ **Frans Malan Cape Blend** Ⓥ **11** has lower 64% pinotage with cab & dash of merlot. Oak vanilla spices up generous bramble & blackcurrant fruit, supported by ripe, soft tannins.

★★★★ **Aurum Chardonnay** Ⓥ Prime vintage **09** (★★★☆) swamped by potent oak, buttery/yeasty lees notes mid-2013. Weighty, rich & ripe, may emerge in time, like last-tasted **07**.

★★★★ **Chenin Avec Chêne** Name means 'with oak' which **14** displays stylishly, a cedar, marzipan savoury richness in partnership with vivid tropical fruit. Better balance than **13** (★★★☆), the acidity adding zest & length.

CWG Auction Reserves

★★★★☆ **Heirloom Shiraz** Complex, layered **13** combines ripe, voluptuous fruit with careful crafting (new French oak 36 months), giving the winelover an involving experience. Morello cherries, dried herbs, scrub, the oak showing as white pepper, campfire smoke. Irresistible.

Cultivar Selection

★★★★ **Roussanne** Limited release (267 cases), **14** offers a different take on wooded whites. Opulent & full bodied, with orange blossom, fynbos honey & candied melon notes, savoury & dry.

> **Chenin Blanc** ⊘ ⓟ ★★★☆ Nice stonefruit & tropical flavours on curvaceous **15**, brightened by vibrant limy acidity, giving freshness & length. Great value.

Labyrinth Cabernet Sauvignon ★★★☆ Already accessible but **12** was made for the longer haul (21 months French/American oak). Intense cassis, attractive savoury shading, backed by firm but ripe tannin. **The SMV** ★★★☆ Previewed **14**, the acronym representing shiraz (77%), mourvèdre, dash viognier. Dark but not brooding, mocha & black plums, pepper, the structure supple, satisfying. **Chardonnay** ★★★☆ Oak ferment/ageing, accounting for the roasted nut overlay in **14**, but there's a good citrus core & freshness to balance it. Also tasted: **Pinotage 13** ★★★ **Cabernet Sauvignon-Shiraz 14** ★★★ **Gewürztraminer 15** ★★★☆ **Sunbird Sauvignon Blanc 15** ★★★★ Not retasted: **Mr Borio's Shiraz 12** ★★★☆

Adelberg range

Sauvignon Blanc ⊘ ⊛ ★★★☆ Ripe but 'green' styling in **15**, fennel & lemongrass, perfect Asian food fare, with zesty gooseberry notes at the end. Small portion semillon. Great value.

Also tasted: **Cabernet Sauvignon-Merlot 13** ★★★ **Sensation Sweet Red 14** ★★☆

Méthode Cap Classique Sparkling range

★★★★ **Kaapse Vonkel Brut Rosé** Pale blush MCC bubbly from mainly pinot noir with pinotage, dash pinot meunier, **14** offers red berry aromas, gains green apple steeliness on the palate. Elegant, dry, with extended fresh length.

★★★★☆ **Cuvée Royale** Prestige blanc de blancs MCC sparkling from partially oaked chardonnay, **11** spent 44 months on its lees, giving a creamy texture, the flavours remaining citrus-fresh, youthful. Sleekly elegant, pure & focused, a class act.

★★★★ **Kaapse Vonkel Brut** First SA MCC keeps up its quality standard. Classic pinot noir/chardonnay blend, **13** exudes freshness, the apple tart tones laced with lemon, wakening the taste buds.

Dessert Wines

★★★★ **Vin de Liza** ⊗ Noble Late Harvest from sauvignon & semillon. After simpler **09** (★★★☆), **10** satisfies with silky, gently unctuous charm.

★★★★ **Cape Vintage Reserve** ⊗ First recorded since **94** (LBV), all-shiraz port-style **09** is liquid Christmas pudding, complete with brandy! Dense, spicy & rich, made for cold winter nights.

Not retasted: **Straw Wine 11** ★★★☆

Exclusive range ⊛

Gees Van Die Wingerd Husk Spirit Gewürztraminer ★★★☆ Lovely aromatic, grapey, floral fragrance carries though to the palate. A touch unharmoniously fiery on the finish, though, hinting at a slightly bitter coarseness. A promising first 'spirit of the vineyard'. — TJ, CR

Location/map: Stellenbosch ▪ Map grid reference: E2 ▪ WO: Stellenbosch/Coastal/Western Cape ▪ Est 1953 ▪ 1stB 1968 ▪ Tasting Mon-Fri 8.30–4.30 Sat 8.30–3.30 Sun 10-2.30 (Nov-Apr) & 11-2.30 (May-Oct) ▪ Sales Mon-Fri 8.30–5 Sat 8.30–4 Sun 10-3 (Nov-Apr) & 11-3 (May-Oct) ▪ Fee R30pp (incl glass) ▪ MCC tour & tasting; MCC & cake pairing, book ahead ▪ Closed Good Fri, Dec 25 & Jan 1 ▪ Cellar tours daily at 11 (booking advised) ▪ Cuvée restaurant ▪ Facilities for children ▪ Tour groups ▪ Gifts ▪ Farm produce ▪ Conferences ▪ 4x4 Landrover experience ▪ Labyrinth vineyard ▪ Owner(s) Malan Family Trusts ▪ Cellarmaster(s) Johan Malan (1981) ▪ Winemaker(s) Debbie Thompson (Nov 1999) & Hannes Meyer (Jul 2009), with Charl Schoeman (Dec 2012) ▪ Viticulturist(s) Francois Malan (Jan 1981) & Tommie Corbett (Nov 2008), with Conrad Schutte (Vinpro) ▪ 210ha (cab, merlot, ptage, pinot, shiraz, chard, chenin, sauv) ▪ 2,700t/340,000cs own label 27% red 43% white 30% MCC ▪ BWI, HACCP 2009, IPW, SANAS, WIETA ▪ PO Box 6 Koelenhof 7605 ▪ wine@simonsig.co.za ▪ www.simonsig.co.za ▪ S 33° 52' 12.1" E 018° 49' 31.7" ▪ F +27 (0)21-888-4909/4916 ▪ **T +27 (0)21-888-4900 (farm)/+27 (0)21-888-4932 (Cuvée)/+27 (0)21-888-4915 (tasting)**

Simonsvlei International ⊙ ⊛ ⊚ ⊗ ⊗

Constituted in the aftermath of World War II to grow quality wines on a larger and sustainable scale, Simonsvlei took its name from the father of the South African wine industry, Simon van der Stel, and this Paarl area's vlei (wetlands) landscape. Co-founder Sonny le Roux in 1945 expressed a vision of 'quality wines at affordable prices' and that's still the mantra today. A 'rainbow' offering aims to please everyone, from grandpa and grandma with their sweet tooth to junior jungle-gymming outside the cellardoor while dad and mom taste the charming easy-drinkers.

Hercules Paragon range

★★★★ **SMCV** ⊗ Shiraz, mourvèdre, cinsaut & viognier **12** blend is a delight, with soft & supple tannins, packed with perfumed berry, savoury & earthy flavours. Invites spicy grilled meat dishes.

Cabernet Sauvignon ★★★☆ **12** first since **09**. Deep in colour & rich dark berry fruit; Oak, 20% new French, & cab tannins well integrated for current drinking. Will go for further 2-4 years. Also tasted: **Shiraz 13** ★★★ Not retasted: **Sauvignon Blanc 14** ★★★★

New Generation range

Toffee Chunk Syrah ★★★ More fruit — spice, berries — in **13** than Pinotage; caramel & vanilla too. Big & chewy with chunky tannins. Also tasted: **Ja-Mocha Pinotage 13** ★★☆

Premier range

Cabernet Sauvignon ⑦ ★★★ **14** bright, crunchy blackcurrant fruits fleshed out by subtle oaking (20% new French 8 months, as rest of reds in this range). Nicely balanced structure. A steal at the price.

Merlot (NEW) ★★ **13** austere, grippy with quiet funky, plummy notes. **Shiraz Rosé** (NEW) ⊘ ★★★ Eye-catching sunset pink **15**; spicy wild strawberry features, zesty freshness equally noteworthy. Perfect al fresco sipping. **Zenzela Pinotage Rosé** (NEW) ★★ Pretty pink blush, tangy red fruit dimmed by **15**'s concluding bitterness. Also tasted: **Pinotage 14** ★★★ **Shiraz 14** ★★★ **Chenin Blanc** ⊘ **15** ★★★ **Sauvignon Blanc** (NEW) **15** ★★ **Humbro Red Jerepiko NV** ★★★ Not retasted: **Cabernet Sauvignon-Merlot 13** ★★★ **Chardonnay 13** ★★★

Lifestyle range

Merlot ⊘ ★★☆ Easy-drinking **14** pleases with sweet plum compote features, tangy tail. This, rest of range, unoaked. **Simonsrood** ⊘ ★★☆ Smooth **NV** shiraz/cab blend; few grams fruit-lifting sugar enhance drinkability. **Extra Light Natural Sweet Rosé** (NEW) ★★ Pearly pink **NV** with gentle summer berry flavours, clean, not over-sweet finish. Just 8% alcohol. Also tasted: **Cabernet Sauvignon 14** ★★☆ **Pinotage 14** ★★ **Shiraz** ⊘ **14** ★★☆ **Chenin Blanc 15** ★★★ **Sauvignon Blanc 15** ★★ **Simonsblanc NV** ★★

Simonay range

Dry Red ★★ Fresh juicy berry flavours on zesty & versatile **NV**. 5L bag-in-box, as all in this range. Also tasted: **Dry white NV** ★★ **Natural Sweet Rosé NV** ★ — AL

Location: Paarl ▪ Map: Paarl & Wellington ▪ Map grid reference: D7 ▪ WO: Western Cape ▪ Est/1stB 1945 ▪ Tasting & sales Mon-Fri 8—5 Sat 8.30—4.30 Sun (Sep-Apr) 11—3 ▪ Fee R20pp ▪ Cellar tours by prior arrangement ▪ Closed Good Fri, Dec 25 & Jan 1 ▪ Eat@Simonsvlei upmarket family restaurant serving slow cooked country fare, cellar priced wine ▪ Kids play area ▪ Conference & function venue (100 pax) ▪ Conservation area ▪ Owner(s) 65 shareholders ▪ Winemaker(s) Ryan Puttick (Nov 2010), with Mari Kotze (Jan 2012) ▪ Viticulturist(s) Ryan Puttick (Nov 2010) & Francois van Zyl ▪ 1,158ha (shiraz, chenin) ▪ 7,400t ▪ 55% red 45% white ▪ Brands for clients: Kelvin Grove, Ocean Basket, Woolworths ▪ BWI, Fairtrade, HACCP, IPW, WIETA ▪ PO Box 584 Suider-Paarl 7624 ▪ steven@simonsvlei.co.za ▪ www.simonsvlei.com ▪ S 33° 47' 24.9" E 018° 55' 49.1" ▪ F +27 (0)21-863-1240 ▪ **T +27 (0)21-863-3040**

☐ **Simplicity** *see* Weltevrede Estate
☐ **Simply** *see* Dorrance Wines
☐ **Since 1922** *see* Villiersdorp Cellar
☐ **Sir George** *see* Napier Winery
☐ **Sirkel** *see* Scali

Sir Lambert Wines

Named after 19th century seafarer Sir Robert Lambert, this is a joint venture between Diemersdal cellar chief Thys Louw and partners. Hand harvested (exclusively by locals, as part of the winery's support for the Lamberts Bay community), the grapes are from a 10-ha block just 3 km from the cold Atlantic ocean.

★★★★ **Sauvignon Blanc** Figs, guavas & fleshy yellow fruit over crushed stone, the **15** palate has weight without sweetness, texture & length. Bone-dry but moreish, perfect for West Coast seafood feasts. Discontinued: **The Admiral's Shiraz**. — HJ

Location/WO: Lamberts Bay ▪ Map: Olifants River ▪ Est 2004 ▪ 1stB 2007 ▪ Tasting by appt in Lamberts Bay or Mon-Sat/pub hols 9-5 Sun 10-3 at Diemersdal ▪ Closed Good Fri, Dec 25 & Jan 1 ▪ Xamarin Guest

House & Restaurant ▪ BYO picnic ▪ Conference & function venue (up to 250 people) ▪ Game drives ▪ Golf course ▪ Tour groups ▪ Conservation area ▪ 4x4 trail ▪ Facilities for children ▪ Owner(s) John Hayes, Johan Teubes & Thys Louw ▪ Winemaker(s) Thys Louw & Mari Branders ▪ Viticulturist(s) Johan Teubes (2004) ▪ 10ha (shiraz, sauv) ▪ 60t/6,000cs own label 10% red 90% white ▪ PO Box 27 Durbanville 7551 ▪ info@ sirlambert.co.za ▪ www.sirlambert.co.za ▪ S 32° 5' 52.40" E 018° 18' 19.50" ▪ F +27 (0)21-979-1802 ▪ **T +27 (0)21-976-3361**

☐ **Sir Robert Stanford Estate** *see* Robert Stanford Estate
☐ **Six Hats** *see* Piekenierskloof Wine Company
☐ **Sixpence** *see* Opstal Estate
☐ **1685** *see* Boschendal Wines
☐ **Sixty 40** *see* Boland Kelder

Sizanani Wines ⓠ

Owned by employees of Stellenbosch estate Bellevue, the Sizanani brand portfolio has had a makeover and now features two interesting and fashionable blends: the red based on cinsaut and shiraz, the wooded white with verdelho and roussanne as components. Export markets are being developed.

Location: Stellenbosch ▪ Est 2005 ▪ 1stB 2006 ▪ Tasting & sales at Bellevue Estate Stellenbosch ▪ Owner(s) Stellenbosch Wine & Logistics (Pty) Ltd ▪ CEO Annelize Tities ▪ Winemaker(s) Wilhelm Kritzinger & Anneke Potgieter (both 2005, Bellevue) ▪ Viticulturist(s) Dirkie Morkel (Feb 2005, Bellevue) ▪ 4,000cs own label 40% red 40% white 20% rosé ▪ PO Box 33 Koelenhof 7605 ▪ annelizepebbles@ gmail.com ▪ www.sizanani-wines.co.za ▪ F +27 (0)21-865-2899 ▪ **T +27 (0)21-865-2055/+27 (0)72-511-8899**

Skaap Wines 🍴 🏠 ◎ ⓑ

'We hope that our wines will help bring people together,' says owner Thierry Schaap, who bought a prime mountain site aiming to make wines that not only 'give enjoyment' but also 'give back to the local community'. His Children's Foodure foundation does exactly that: feeding, clothing and educating youngsters in the Helderberg.

★★★★ **Skaap 42 Shiraz** Subtler than **12** (★★★★), violet-scented **13** is soft & juicy, with smoky plums, black berries & understated hints of black pepper & clove spice.

★★★★ **Skaap 43 Sauvignon Blanc** Elegant **14** from own & Durbanville fruit is dry with mouthwatering lime & riper pineapple fruit, textured (from some skin contact) with clean mineral finish.
Not tasted: **Méthode Cap Classique Brut**. — JG

Location: Sir Lowry's Pass ▪ Map: Helderberg ▪ WO: Coastal ▪ Est/1stB 2011 ▪ Private functions/dinner by appt ▪ Tour groups ▪ Local art on display & for sale ▪ Conferences (up to 18 pax) ▪ Walks/hikes ▪ MTB trail ▪ Conservation area ▪ 5-bedroom guest house, dining room with chef & 2 self-catering lodges ▪ Swimming pool ▪ Owner(s) Thierry Schaap ▪ Cellarmaster(s)/winemaker(s) Riaan Oosthuizen (Jan 2011) ▪ 17ha/4ha (shiraz, sauv) ▪ 1,100cs own label 30% red 70% white ▪ BWI, IPW ▪ PO Box 3794 Somerset West 7130 ▪ info@skaapwines.com ▪ www.skaapwines.com ▪ S 34° 06' 11.35" E 018° 55' 05.87" ▪ **T +27 (0)21-858-1982**

Skilpadvlei Wines ⓠ 🍴 🏠 ◎ ⓑ ♿

A multifaceted offering at the 4th-generation Joubert family property in Polkadraai Hills, overlooking Stellenbosch. Olives, tomatoes and wine all flow from the site where turtles were found in the 1800s, giving the farm its name. The cellardoor pool has been paved over, creating an al fresco tasting area.

Cabernet Sauvignon-Shiraz ★★★★ **14** equal blend has appealingly sweet, ripe berry fruit, supple structure & commendable length. **Skilpaddop Rosé** ★★★★ Returns from extended sabbatical with pretty, tinsel pink, off-dry **15** from grenache, showing elegant red berry fruit, pleasant leesy texture. WO W Cape. Also tasted: **ML Joubert 12** ★★★★ **Skilpaddop Dry Red 12** ★★★ **Chenin Blanc 15** ★★☆ **Sauvignon Blanc 15** ★★★ — GdB

Location/map: Stellenbosch ▪ Map grid reference: C6 ▪ WO: Stellenbosch/Western Cape ▪ Est 2004 ▪ 1stB 2001 ▪ Tasting & sales Mon-Sat 8-5 Sun 8-4 ▪ Fee R25 ▪ Closed Dec 25/26 & Jan 1/2 ▪ Restaurant Mon-Sat 8-late Sun 8-4 ▪ Facilities for children ▪ Gift/decor shop ▪ Conferences ▪ Weddings & functions ▪ B&B guest house & self-catering cottages ▪ Owner(s) WD Joubert ▪ Cellarmaster(s) Kowie du Toit (consultant) ▪ Viticulturist(s) Johan Pienaar & Eben Archer (consultants) ▪ 78ha/55ha (cab, merlot, ptage, shiraz, chenin, sauv) ▪ 652t/12,000cs own label 80% red 20% white ▪ PO Box 17 Vlottenburg 7604 ▪ info@skilpadvlei.co.za ▪ www.skilpadvlei.co.za ▪ S 33° 57' 31.5" E 018° 45' 52.4" ▪ F +27 (0)21-881-3538 ▪ **T +27 (0)21-881-3237**

Skinny Legs   (NEW)

Currently assisting at AA Badenhorst Family Wines, Kyle Dunn has been making wine in Swartland for a decade. This, his own brand, debuted in 2010, a year after he graduated from Cape Peninsula University of Technology as one its first oenology majors. A fan of 'the interesting and unique', such as skin-fermented whites, he currently has a '14 Semillon and '14 Grenache Gris from Swartland in bottle, and a '13 Pinot Noir from McGregor on the market. He's inspired by thinking about how the wines from the lost city of Atlantis tasted. He also says the greatest of a man's follies is taking himself too seriously!

Location: Malmesbury ▪ Est/1stB 2010 ▪ Owner(s) Skinny Legs Wine Company ▪ Winemaker(s) Kyle Dunn ▪ 500cs own label ▪ PO Box 1177 Malmesbury 7299 ▪ sales@skinnylegs.co.za ▪ www.skinnylegs.co.za

☐ **Skipper's** *see* New Beginnings Wines
☐ **Skoon Vallei** *see* Eerste Hoop Wine Cellar

Slaley   (Ⓣ) (Ⓨ) (ⓞ)

The Hunting family's scenic Stellenbosch cellardoor is one of few where you can taste and buy older vintages across a range of reds, rosés and whites, all at peak drinking age. Besides its popular bistro and function/conference venue, the winery now includes clay pigeon shooting among its amenities.

Hunting Family range

★★★★ **Merlot** Ⓐ Dark chocolate & meat extract add complexity to **07**'s rich dark fruit, while the serious oak regime (28 months, 40% new) provides spice & deep muscle tone for further cellaring.

★★★★ **Shiraz** Ⓐ Luscious berries & spice array, touch of wintergreen, doesn't quite cloak **06**'s (★★★★) dry tannins, less seductive than **04**. No **05**.

★★★★ **Reserve Noble Late Harvest Chardonnay** Ⓐ Last was **07**, decadent & irresistible, concentrated honey/raisin character (from vine-dried grapes) perfect match for strong cheeses.

Not retasted: **Pinotage 07** ★★★☆ **Cabernet Sauvignon-Merlot 07** ★★★ **Chardonnay 10** ★★★☆

Broken Stone range

★★★★ **Pinotage** Ⓐ Vanilla from 70% American barrels enriches **06**'s mulberry fruit while leaving the supple juiciness intact. Admirable intensity yet elegant (13% alcohol), polished. No **05**.

Not retasted: **Shiraz 07** ★★★ **Sauvignon Blanc 13** ★★★ Not tasted: **Cabernet Sauvignon, Cabernet Sauvignon-Shiraz-Pinotage**.

Social range

Lindsay's Whimsy Rosé Ⓐ ★★★☆ Dry **13** from pinotage, full bodied & packed with strawberry fruit. Weightier style is deliberate, says team, so wine will 'stay wine as opposed to water if you add ice'! Not tasted: **Lindsay's Whimsy Cape Blend**. — GdB

Location/map: Stellenbosch ▪ Map grid reference: E2 ▪ WO: Simonsberg–Stellenbosch ▪ Est 1957 ▪ 1stB 1997 ▪ Tasting & sales Tue-Sun 10–4 ▪ Fee R20, waived on purchase ▪ Closed Good Fri, Dec 25/26 & Jan 1 ▪ Cellar tours by appt ▪ Bistro: light meals during tasting hours ▪ Farm produce ▪ Venue & conference facility with AV capacity ▪ Clay pigeon shooting ▪ Owner(s) Hunting family ▪ 240ha/51ha (cab, merlot, ptage, shiraz, chard, sauv) ▪ 320t/24–30,000cs own label 90% red 9% white 1% rosé ▪ IPW ▪ PO Box 119 Koelenhof 7605 ▪ info@slaley.co.za ▪ www.slaley.co.za ▪ S 33° 51' 53.7'' E 018° 50' 51.1'' ▪ F +27 (0)86-529-2347 ▪ **T +27 (0)21-865-2123**

Slanghoek Winery   (Ⓠ) (◎) (ⓐ)

A truly breathtaking curtain of mountains rising near-vertically from the valley floor is reason enough to make the (slight) detour to Slanghoek's efficient and modern grower-owned winery, a vigorous 65 this year. Do bring your mountain bike — there are rides of varying difficulty on offer, with pre-booked cellar tours and of course tasting of the portfolio, slightly rearranged but still offering tasty, well-priced drops.

Private Selection

★★★★ **Crème de Chenin** ⊘ Delicious dried pears & apricots on classy **14** Natural Sweet, seasoned with splash hanepoot. Fine acid balance cuts through 88 g/l sugar. Heady spice & honey finish. Bargain.

★★★★ **Noble Late Harvest** (ⓧ) Rich, honeyed **13**, first since **07**, has commendable concentration & focus. Delicious. From chenin with 10% muscat d'Alexandrie, 9 months in new French oak.

> **Chardonnay** (ⓦ) ★★★ Honeyed sweet fruit on part-oaked **15** with appealing buttery citrus flavours. Likeable, easy-drinking, pocket friendly.

Pinotage ★★★ Genteel **14** has bright red-cherry fruit, a light body & appealing juiciness. **Shiraz** ★★★ Characterful, lightweight **11** has chalky tannins supporting spicy plum & cherry fruit touched with sweetness. **Sauvignon Blanc** ★★★ Brisk, cheerful **15** has ripe but attractively understated fruit. Light & bright. Also tasted: **Cabernet Sauvignon** 13 ★★☆ **Merlot** 13 ★★☆ **Camerca** 13 ★★☆ **Chenin Blanc** 15 ★★☆ **Special Late Harvest** 15 ★★★

Slanghoek range

Vin Doux ★★☆ Overtly sweet but characterful & tasty muscat-scented **NV** bubbles from hanepoot. **Red Muscadel** ★★★★ Intensely sweet (264 g/l) **15** fortified muscat de Frontignan shows authentic raisin fruit with pleasant texture. Likeable midwinter warmer. **Cape Ruby** ⊘ ★★★★ Solid & wholesome 'port' from touriga, **14** convincing cherry fruit & refined spirit grip. Reduced sugar adds to appeal. Also tasted: **Cuvée Brut** NV ★★☆ **Hanepoot Jerepigo** 15 ★★★★ **Red Jerepigo** 15 ★★☆

Vinay range

Crispy White ★★ Entry-level **NV** from sauvignon, chenin & colombard, just-dry, with forward guava fruit. Also tasted: **Smooth Blended Red NV** ★★ **Natural Sweet Rosé NV** ★★ — GdB

Location: Rawsonville • Map: Breedekloof • WO: Slanghoek • Est 1951 • 1stB 1970 • Tasting & sales Mon-Fri 9–5 Sat 10–1 • Closed Easter Fri/Sun, Dec 25 & Jan 1 • Cellar tours by appt • Slanghoek MTB Route, fee R20: 13km ride with optional extra, more challenging 4km • Owner(s) 25 producers • Cellarmaster(s) Pieter Carstens (Aug 2002) • Winemaker(s) Nico Grundling (Dec 2002) & Werner du Plessis (Aug 2014), with Jacques de Goede (Dec 2001) & Mathilda Viljoen (Aug 2014) • Viticulturist(s) Callie Coetzee (Nov 2010) • 1,830ha • 30,000t/80,000cs own label 25% red 55% white 10% rosé 10% fortified • Other export brand: Zonneweelde • ISO 22000, BWI, IPW • PO Box 75 Rawsonville 6845 • info@slanghoek.co.za • www.slanghoek.co.za • S 33° 39' 1.1" E 019° 13' 49.0" • F +27 (0)23-344-3157 • **T +27 (0)23-344-3026**

☐ **Slent** see Ayama Wines

Slowine   (Ⓠ) (♉) (ⓐ)

Slowine's label reminds us that 'quality takes time', by featuring the Common Padloper Tortoise, whose folkloric cousin famously beat the hare, with a percentage of sales going towards conservation. The wines are made at recently revamped Villiersdorp Cellar in collaboration with Luddite and Beaumont, all growing vines around Groenland Mountain.

Cabernet Sauvignon ★★★ **14** bursts with blackberry fruit & dark chocolate, sweetness balanced by firm tannins & fresh acidity. Calls for BBQ ribs! **Merlot** ★★★★ A step up on **13** (& some more ambitious examples), **14** has no green notes, only ripe plum/berry fruit & hints of milk chocolate, soft tannins adding pleasing richness. **Chenin Blanc-Sauvignon Blanc** ⊘ ★★★★ Perfect spring day in a bottle, **15** combines blossoms with freshly mown grass on nose, leading to peaches & lime flavours, zesty & refreshing. Also tasted: **Pinotage** 14 ★★★ **Shiraz** 14 ★★★ **Chenin Blanc** 15 ★★★ **Sauvignon Blanc** 15 ★★☆ Not retasted: **Rosé** 14 ★★☆ — JG

Location: Villiersdorp ▪ WO: Western Cape/Cape South Coast ▪ Est/1stB 2005 ▪ Tasting & sales at Villiersdorp Cellar ▪ Owner(s) Villiersdorp Cellar ▪ Shareholders Beaumont Wines & Luddite Wines ▪ Technical team: Sebastian Beaumont & Niels Verburg ▪ Winemaker(s)/viticulturist(s) Christo Versfeld ▪ 300ha (merlot, chenin, sauv) ▪ 3,600t/40,000cs own label 40% red 40% white 20% rosé ▪ BWI, IPW ▪ PO Box 14 Villiersdorp 6848 ▪ marketing@slowine.co.za ▪ www.slowine.co.za ▪ F +27 (0)28-840-0957 ▪ **T +27 (0)28-840-0083**

☐ **Sneeukop** *see* Rogge Cloof
☐ **Snowfield Boutique Winery** *see* Rogge Cloof

Snow Mountain Wines

Previously listed under Nabygelegen, Snow Mountain is a small-batch project by that winery's owner-cellarmaster James McKenzie centered on high-altitude vineyards managed and vinified by him in selected cellars. A new Artisan Collection from unique/interesting sites was being finalised at press time.

★★★★ Syrah 13's spicy intensity reprised on **14** (**★★★★**), similar clove, juniper, cured meat & dark fruit complexities but delivered with shade less suavity, finesse; some obvious stalky notes.

Pinot Noir ★★★ 14 very different style to previous' restraint: liqueur top notes hint at generous alcohol (15%), Christmas cake & prune notes with subtle leather & oak spice. Appears to be evolving fast – drink soon. **Chardonnay-Pinot Noir ★★★** Elegantly packaged fashionable blend combines fresh citrus fruit & savouriness in a light straw glassful. Bit more opulent than previous, **15** finishes dry, slightly pithy. Not tasted: **The Mistress**, **Chardonnay**. — HJ

Location: Wellington ▪ WO: Western Cape ▪ Est/1stB 2009 ▪ Closed to public ▪ Owner(s) Snow Mountain CC ▪ Cellarmaster(s)/winemaker(s) James McKenzie (2009) ▪ 60t ▪ Own label 50% red 50% white ▪ PO Box 302 Wellington 7654 ▪ avalonwines@icon.co.za ▪ www.snowmountainwines.com ▪ **T +27 (0)82-829-1189**

☐ **Social** *see* Slaley
☐ **Soek Die Geluk** *see* Goedverwacht Wine Estate

SoetKaroo Wine Estate   ⓆⓈ

Herman and Susan Perold's 'hobby that got out of hand' is focused on fortified dessert wines, hand-crafted with 'meticulous/neurotic quality control' from a tiny vineyard in Prince Albert village. Susan aims for lower sugar and alcohol on her muscats, and says the maturing touriga and petit verdot vines are producing ever-greater fruit intensity, causing a style progression from Cape Ruby to Cape Vintage.

Red Muscat d'Alexandrie ★★★★ 14 pink-hued fortified dessert with trademark hanepoot grapiness. Syrupy sweet, delicious. **Cape Vintage Petit Verdot ★★★** Blueberries & violets, opulent **14** 'port' has enough fruit/oak backing for a good future. Nice spirit grip. Not tasted: **Red Muscat de Frontignan**, **Cape Vintage Touriga Nacional**. — CR

Location: Prince Albert ▪ Map: Klein Karoo & Garden Route ▪ WO: Western Cape ▪ Est 2000 ▪ 1stB 2004 ▪ Tasting & sales Mon-Sat 9-1; afternoons by appt ▪ Closed Dec 25 ▪ Owner(s) Herman & Susan Perold ▪ Cellarmaster(s)/winemaker(s) Susan Perold (Jan 2007) ▪ 2t ▪ 56 Church Str Prince Albert 6930 ▪ perold@netactive.co.za ▪ www.soetkaroo.co.za ▪ S 33° 13' 21.9" E 022° 1' 48.0" ▪ F +27 (0)86-524-3801 ▪ **T +27 (0)23-541-1768**

Solara   Ⓠ ⓄⒾ ⓃⒺⓦ

Octogenarian and former entrepreneur Pat Werdmuller Von Elgg and son Otto bought McGregor spread Houtbaai in 2003 as a haven for animals needing rehabilitation. At first the grapes were sold off, but a lot of nurturing turned the agriculture organic (certified in 2005), and wines were produced for Woolworths – now they're made by Rooiberg for this own label, named for Pat's first company. In keeping with the ethical, natural spirit, much of the farm is under natural fynbos, with teeming wildlife safely wandering the vineyards at will.

Organic Sauvignon Blanc Ⓥ **★★★** Organic & from a single-vineyard, **14**'s perfume has wet pebble minerality, suggestion of nettles, fruit coming to fore in the flavours, citrus & greengage. — CR, CvZ

Location: McGregor ▪ Map/WO: Robertson ▪ Est 2005 ▪ 1stB 2014 ▪ Tasting by appt ▪ Farm tour by prior arrangement ▪ Owner(s) Pat & Otto Werdmuller Von Elgg ▪ Winemaker(s) André van Dyk & André Scriven (both Rooiberg Winery) ▪ 27.556ha/10.52ha (ptage, cbard, sauv) ▪ 8-10t/ha 1,100cs own label 100% white ▪ BWI, IPW, SGS/Lacon Organic ▪ PO Box 181 McGregor 6708 ▪ houtbaai@breede.co.za ▪ S 33° 57' 37.17 E 019° 48' 57.79 ▪ **T +27 (0)23-625-1867**

☐ **Soleil de Karusa** *see* Karusa Vineyards
☐ **Solidus** *see* Claime d'Or
☐ **Solms-Astor** *see* Solms-Delta

Solms-Delta $(Ⓨ)(Ⓨ)(ⓒ)(Ⓐ)(Ⓖ)

The personal interests of the Solms and Astor families, co-owners of this venerable Franschhoek estate, have long been an important part of what happens here — music, history and social sustainability. Thus early on, the third ownership leg went to staff family members. The result is a unique combination of museums (including a new one dedicated to music), workshops, popular harvest and music festivals, plus an indigenous garden and traditional-food restaurant, now set in the renovated stables. All combine to give one of the best living expressions of Cape history and culture for visiting tourists. That same culture is reflected in many of the evocative wine names, traditional vineyard practices, such as vine-drying of grapes, and newly enlarged Wijn van de Caab tasting area, with old-style veranda and lawns.

Premium range

★★★★☆ **Africana** From grapes desiccated on the vine, a speciality here. Old-World-styled shiraz, **12** (★★★★) has tealeaves, underlying prunes, some scrub. More austere than **11**, its savoury dryness promising a long life.

★★★★ **Hiervandaan** Grenache, vine-dried shiraz, mourvèdre, dab cinsaut, well-tried blending partners don't disappoint in **12**. Beef extract, liquorice & scrub, a delicious juicy liveliness. Can age.

★★★★☆ **Amalie** (Ⓨ) **13** grenache blanc-led white blend with widely sourced chenin, roussanne & viognier, partly barrel fermented. Aromas of pear, apricot blossom & nut. The dry, broad palate is ripe but with refreshing acidity, subtle oak not obscuring the fruit.

★★★★ **Koloni** Muscat de Frontignan with 17% vine-dried muscat d'Alexandrie, oak matured 9 months, distinctive **13** has preserved melon & pineapple richness, tastes almost dry despite 13.5 g/l sugar. Also tasted: **Gemoedsrus 12** ★★★★ Not retasted: **Cape Jazz Shiraz NV** ★★☆

Lifestyle range (ⓃⓔⓌ)

Shiraz ★★★ Trademark red fruit & spice in **14**, tannins providing structure & a savoury food-friendly finish. **Rosé** ★★★ From grenache, elegant dry **15** shows red berries but the flavours are more earthy, mineral. This is ideally a food wine, almost savoury. **Chenin Blanc** ★★★ Attractive mix citrus & melon in dry **15**, finishing softly fruity. — CR

Location/map: Franschhoek ▪ WO: Western Cape/Franschhoek ▪ Est 1690 ▪ 1stB 2004 ▪ Tasting & sales daily 9–5 ▪ Fee R20pp ▪ Closed Dec 25 & Jan 1 ▪ Cellar tours by appt ▪ Wijn van de Caab tasting room (cheese platters, picnics & set menus for tour groups) ▪ Child friendly ▪ Fyndraai Restaurant ▪ Conferences ▪ Weddings/functions ▪ Walking farm tours ▪ Dik Delta fynbos culinary garden ▪ Cape music museum, social history museum & archaeological sites ▪ Harvest festival (Mar) ▪ Summer music concerts (Jan/Feb) ▪ Owner(s) Solms & Astor Family Trusts and Wijn de Caab Workers' Trust ▪ Winemaker(s) Hagen Viljoen (Nov 2012), with Joan Heatlie (Aug 2012) ▪ Viticulturist(s) Rosa Kruger (Jul 2011) ▪ 78ha/33ha (grenache n/b, mourv, ptage, shiraz, chenin, macabeo, muscat d'A, muscat de F, rouss, viog) ▪ 370t/80,000cs own label 63% red 33% white 4% rosé ▪ BWI, IPW, WIETA ▪ PO Box 123 Groot Drakenstein 7680 ▪ info@solms-delta.co.za ▪ www.solms-delta.co.za ▪ S 33° 51' 51.0" E 018° 59' 23.8" ▪ F +27 (0)21-874-1852 ▪ **T +27 (0)21-874-3937**

Somerbosch Wines $(Ⓨ)(Ⓨ)(ⓒ)(Ⓐ)(Ⓖ)

The laid-back lifestyle of which brothers Marius, Japie and Wrensch Roux are proponents is reflected in their Helderberg winery's wines and welcome (further enhanced by decadent red wine and ice-cream pairings). Equally representative is the name of their flagship, Kylix, an ancient Greek earthenware drinking vessel, broad-based and shallow for sipping supine.

Somerbosch range

★★★★ **Kylix** Merlot's lead role in previewed **12** evident in ripe black cherry & plum notes, 25% cab providing firm structure, 35% shiraz violet whiffs, spicy conclusion. Deftly oaked (30% new) to reward cellaring 3+ years. No **11**.

Merlot ★★★☆ Smooth & elegant **13**'s ripe red fruit concentration framed by downy tannins, accented by dark chocolate & vanilla spice. Satisfying & juicy stalwart of the range. **Rosé** (NEW) ★★★ Pleasant sipping, solo or with summer salads, dry rosepetal-scented **14** is from shiraz. **Chardonnay** ★★★ Pear, tangerine flavours & limy acidity ensure unwooded **15** delivers satisfying everyday drinking. **Sauvignon Blanc-Semillon** (NEW) ⊘ ★★★☆ **15** bouncy 50/50 partnership to enjoy anytime, anywhere. Granny Smith apple & kiwifruit, lingering farewell has interesting greengage nuance. **Méthode Cap Classique Brut** ★★★☆ Chardonnay plus pinots meunier & noir in commendable **NV** sparkler. Lovely onion skin hue, racy bead & subtle red scents on fine mousse, earthy touch in dry conclusion. Also tasted: **Cabernet Sauvignon 12** ★★★ **Shiraz 11** ★★★ **Shiraz-Merlot 14** ★★★ **Chenin Blanc 15** ★★★ **Sauvignon Blanc 15** ★★★ Not retasted: **Pinotage 12** ★★★ Not tasted: **Late Bottled Vintage Port**.

Poker Hill range

Not tasted: **Shiraz-Merlot**. — GM

Location/WO: Stellenbosch ▪ Map: Helderberg ▪ Est 1950 ▪ 1stB 1995 ▪ Tasting & sales daily 9-5 ▪ Fee R20/6 wines, waived on purchase of any 3 btls; R40pp/ice cream & red wine tasting ▪ Closed Dec 25 & Jan 1 ▪ Cellar tours by appt ▪ Somerbosch Bistro: b'fast & lunch daily ▪ Facilities for children ▪ Farm produce ▪ Conferences ▪ Owner(s) Somerbosch Wines cc ▪ Cellarmaster(s)/winemaker(s)/viticulturist(s) Marius & Japie Roux (both 1995) ▪ 55ha/43ha (cab, merlot, shiraz, sauv) ▪ 350t 55% red 45% white ▪ PO Box 12181 Die Boord 7613 ▪ enquiries@somerbosch.co.za, sales@somerbosch.co.za ▪ www.somerbosch.co.za ▪ S 34° 0' 28.6" E 018° 49' 6.9" ▪ F +27 (0)21-855-4457 ▪ **T +27 (0)21-855-3615**

Somerset Wines   ⓘ

This national sales, marketing and distribution company, with over 40 years of experience, bottles its own value-for-money wines, sourced now from Breedekloof's Bergsig and named for Lord Somerset, British governor at the Cape from 1814 to 1826, and his wife Elizabeth. A portion of sales goes to charity.

Lord Somerset range

Sauvignon Blanc ⊕ ⊘ ★★★ **15** is frankly rather yummy with ripe apple & pear notes, nicely rounded with decent length.

Cabernet Sauvignon ⊘ ★★★ Displaying good varietal character with its ripe blackcurrant fruit, almost Ribena-like on the nose, medium-bodied **13** is very pleasant. **Chenin Blanc** (NEW) ★★☆ Crisp & uncomplicated **15** has crunchy green apple & tart pineapple notes, dry & refreshing, finishing a little sour. Also tasted: **Shiraz** ⊘ 13 ★★★ **Merlot-Cabernet Sauvignon** ⊘ 13 ★★☆ **Soft Smooth Red NV** ★★ Not retasted: **Chenin Blanc Bushvine 13** ★★★

Lady Somerset range

Stylish Elegant Red (Ⓧ) ★★★ Pick of the latest red crop, plump **NV** has soft stewed plums from merlot, hints of smoke & pepper from shiraz. **Natural Sweet Rosé** (Ⓧ) ★★★ Shy at first, flirtatious **NV** is all strawberries & cream. Not retasted: **Crisp Dry White NV** ★★ **Sparkling Blush NV** ★★★ **Natural Sweet Red NV** ★★★ **Natural Sweet White NV** ★★★ — JG

Location: Somerset West ▪ Map: Helderberg ▪ WO: Western Cape ▪ Est 2010 ▪ 1stB 2011 ▪ Tasting & sales Mon-Fri 8.30-5 Sat 9-1 ▪ Closed all pub hols ▪ Tour groups ▪ Wine shop ▪ Owner(s) Boetie Rietoff, Greig Rietoff ▪ Cellarmaster(s) De Wet Lategan (Bergsig) ▪ Winemaker(s) Chris du Toit (Bergsig), with Jeff Wedgwood (consultant) ▪ 200,000cs 80% red 20% white ▪ PO Box 2240 Somerset West 7129 ▪ info@ somersetbeverages.co.za ▪ www.somersetwines.com ▪ F +27 (0)21-852-9563 ▪ **T +27 (0)21-851-8188**

Somfula Wines ⓘ

Swartland-based Bongi Somfula developed a love of wine while working as a wine label designer in Cape Town. Her goal is to become a recognised brand locally and overseas, and build a network of agents. So far so good: retail giant Pick n Pay now stocks her wines in the Western Cape (and hopefully further afield in the future), and she's 'in communication with other supermarkets and with restaurants'.

Location: Riebeek West ▪ Est/1stB 2009 ▪ Tasting by appt ▪ Closed Easter Fri/Sun/Mon, Dec 25/26 & Jan 1 ▪ Owner(s) Nokubonga Somfula ▪ 60% red 20% white 20% rosé ▪ c/o PO Box 1 Riebeek West 7306 ▪ info@somfulawine.co.za ▪ www.somfulawine.co.za ▪ F +27 (0)86-293-3443 ▪ **T +27 (0)79-464-0204**

Sonklip Wine ⓘ

Engineer Frik Kirsten's later-in-life winemaking was inspired by a garagiste course and the 'thinking-out-the-box' approach of star vintner Eben Sadie (whose vaunted Mev. Kirsten old-vine chenin comes from Frik's Stellenbosch family farm, Westridge). Current Sonklip releases include a '13 malbec-cab and '14 shiraz-mourvèdre blend. He hopes to produce a chardonnay this year.

Location/map: Stellenbosch ▪ Map grid reference: G5 ▪ 1stB 2009 ▪ Tasting & cellar tours for groups only, by appt ▪ Owner(s)/winemaker(s) Frik Kirsten ▪ 200cs own label 100% red ▪ PO Box 6198 Uniedal 7612 ▪ frik.kirsten@gmail.com ▪ S 33° 56' 3.55" E 018° 53' 44.95" ▪ F +27 (0)21-887-5869 ▪ **T +27 (0)21-887-5869**

☐ **Sonop Organic** *see* Jacques Germanier

Sophie & Mr P

The vernacular name for sauvignon blanc, Sophie Te'blanche, is the inspiration for this nattily packaged and affordably priced Iona Vineyards brand. Stable mates Le Rouge and Le Rosé have retired, leaving popular Mr P and Ms S to benefit from the infusion of fruit from a recently acquired Elgin property.

Mr P Pinot Noir ★★ Fruit on **14** dimmed by toasty oak (all older), short on flesh, freshness. Not quite the seductive Mr P of the label. **Sophie Te'blanche ★★★** Vitality & tropical fruit abundance in **15**, with dash semillon, balanced, dry. Discontinued: **Sophie Le Rouge, Sophie Le Rosé**. — AL

Location: Elgin ▪ WO: Elgin/Cape South Coast ▪ Est/1stB 2009 ▪ Closed to public ▪ Owner(s) Andrew Gunn ▪ Cellarmaster(s) Werner Muller (May 2011) ▪ (cab, merlot, pinot, shiraz, sauv) ▪ 150t/20,000cs own label 10% red 85% white 5% rosé ▪ PO Box 527 Grabouw 7160 ▪ orders@sophie.co.za ▪ www.sophie.co.za ▪ F +27 (0)28-284-9078 ▪ **T +27 (0)28-284-9678**

☐ **Southern Cape Vineyards** *see* Barrydale Winery & Distillery

Southern Right ⓘ ⓒ ♿

This Hemel-en-Aarde Valley vintners' pinotage celebrates its 20th release with the 2014 vintage, a landmark co-owner Anthony Hamilton-Russell is happy to note: 'When pinotage is experiencing a new wave of local and international interest; it's become "cool to like pinotage". About time!' Greater use of untoasted and larger-format barrels is helping their stylistic goal of clean, pristine fruit, uninfluenced by oak aroma or flavour. The sauvignon blanc's success continues in the US, where it's a regular Wine Spectator Wine of the Day. Both wines now bear neck labels stating 'Naturum esse omne' – Nature is everything – reflecting the team's efforts to conserve the Southern Right whales found in local waters.

★★★★ Pinotage 14 reverts to 100% pinotage. Mint-laced with usual cool-climate vitality, there's also nice breadth to the cherry-rich flavours. Fine tannins provide form without hindering current drinkability.

★★★★☆ Sauvignon Blanc ⊘ Breathtaking **15** offers effusion of tangy tropical fruits. Lees-ageing brings greater breadth but doesn't disturb overall intensity, persistence. Bone-dry & beautifully balanced – a lovely wine. **14 (★★★★)** was overly bracing. Walker Bay WO. — AL

Location: Hermanus ▪ Map: Elgin, Walker Bay & Bot River ▪ WO: Hemel-en-Aarde Valley/Walker Bay ▪ Est 1994 ▪ 1stB 1995 ▪ Tasting, sales & cellar tours Mon-Fri 9-5 Sat 9-1 ▪ Closed Easter Fri/Mon, Dec 25/26 & Jan 1 ▪ Fynbos reserve, renosterveld reserve & 3 wetlands ▪ Quad bike route ▪ Owner(s) Mark Willcox, Mikki Xayiya & Anthony Hamilton Russell ▪ Winemaker(s) Emul Ross (2014) ▪ Viticulturist(s) Johan

Montgomery (2005) ▪ 447ha/±36ha (ptage, sauv) ▪ 225-280t/30-40,000cs own label 20% red 80% white ▪ PO Box 158 Hermanus 7200 ▪ hrv@hermanus.co.za ▪ www.southernright.co.za ▪ S 34° 24' 3.2" E 019° 13' 0.4" ▪ F +27 (0)28-312-1797 ▪ **T +27 (0)28-312-3595**

Southern Sky Wines ⓦ

Experience in advertising, events and marketing aids Andrew Milne in his Paarl-based wine negociant business. He intends balancing an established southeast Asian export market with local sales growth, now offering clients a bespoke label design service. New is the Tara Hill Reserve range. Other labels include Signature Selection, Almara, Imagine, Marimba and Ready Steady, untasted by us.

Location: Paarl ▪ Map: Paarl & Wellington ▪ Map grid reference: E5 ▪ Est/1stB 2002 ▪ Tasting & sales by appt ▪ Owner(s) Andrew Milne ▪ Winemaker(s) Andrew Milne (Jan 2003) ▪ 10,000cs own label 95% red 5% white ▪ Other export brands: Golden Chalice, Hawk's Head, Les Fleurs, Rowlands ▪ PO Box 1312 Paarl 7624 ▪ andrew@ssw.co.za ▪ www.ssw.co.za ▪ S 33° 45' 8.78" E 018° 57' 42.55" ▪ F +27 (0)21-863-0444 ▪ **T +27 (0)21-863-4440**

South Hill Vineyards ⓦ ⓗ ⓐ ⓒ ⓔ

This farm was one of those in Elgin converted from neglected apple and pear orchards to grapes, after it was bought in 2001 by winelovers. So vineyards were planted on the various slopes, while rehabilitating natural fynbos has long been a concern. Other than wine, attractions include art gallery, function venue, guest house and restaurant. The Kevin King label is named for South Hill's owner.

Kevin King range

★★★★ Bazza ⓦ **12** pinot noir shows mouthwatering blackberry, tar, ink & violets. Approachable, with sweet ripe tannin, balance & depth. Seasoned oak; just 13.2% alcohol.

★★★★ Micah Older-oak-matured shiraz-led blend with 25% each mourvèdre & barbera. Pepper & raspberry-tinged **13** delicious glassful: focused & precise with spicy fruit, dry tail.

★★★★ Bassey ⓝⓔⓦ Older-oaked semillon, 37% unwooded sauvignon in impressive **14** debut. Latter provides green mango, crushed stones, tropical fruit & cut grass complexity, the former enigmatic combo plushness & energy. Versatile dinner companion, structure for some ageing.

South Hill range

★★★★ Cabernet Sauvignon Fine bouquet of cassis, earth & cherries grace ripe yet fresh **12**. Soft & elegant, with tannin cradling intense fruit unobstructed by tiny (7%) new oak component.

★★★★ Sauvignon Blanc Appealing **15** has attractive herbal notes, mineral tones & a vibrant palate that is concentration but remains balanced, refreshing. Also-tasted **14** less intense but as zingy; grass, lime, granadilla & nettle complexity.

Also tasted: **Cabernet Sauvignon Rosé 14 ★★★☆** Not tasted: **Blanc de Blancs Méthode Cap Classique.** — JPf

Location/WO: Elgin ▪ Map: Elgin, Walker Bay & Bot River ▪ Est 2001 ▪ 1stB 2006 ▪ Tasting Mon-Sun 10-4 ▪ The Gallery @ South Hill (original artworks) ▪ Gallery Restaurant open Wed-Sun for lunch ▪ The Guest House and Pumphouse Cottage ▪ Function venue for conferences & weddings ▪ Conservation area ▪ Owner(s) South Hill Vineyards (Pty) Ltd ▪ Winemaker(s) Sean Skibbe (Jun 2005) ▪ Viticulturist(s) Kevin Watt (Jun 2015, consultant) ▪ 57ha/28ha (cab, pinot, shiraz, chard, riesling, sauv, sem, viog) ▪ 130t/7,000cs own label 20% red 80% white ▪ PO Box 120 Elgin 7180 ▪ info@southhill.co.za ▪ www.southhill.co.za ▪ S 34° 14' 6.22" E 019° 6' 32.77" ▪ F +27 (0)86-530-4065 ▪ **T +27 (0)21-844-0888**

Spekulasie Landgoed ⓦ ⓗ ⓐ ⓒ ⓔ

Jan Pieterzoon was an early Dutch settler in the Cape and progenitor of the Louw family, and a descendant now has this large Swartland estate. Johan and Linza Louw celebrate Jan in a blend made by Linza in traditional hands-on fashion in her 'petite' cellar, but most of the grapes go to Darling Cellars.

De Beatrix ★★★ Big, ripe **13** shiraz with a dollop pinotage. Flavoursome, but heavy & a touch too sweet in effect. **De Pieterzoon ★★★** Lightly perfumed aromas on rustic, solid **13** dominated by pinotage (blend with 30% shiraz). Rich & ripe, rather less sweet than Beatrix. Not tasted: **The Elizabeth**. — TJ

Location: Malmesbury ▪ Map/WO: Swartland ▪ Est 2008 ▪ 1stB 2010 ▪ Tasting, sales & cellar tours Mon-Sat/pub hols by appt ▪ Fee R20pp ▪ Light meals & refreshments by appt only ▪ Facilities for children ▪ Conferences/weddings ▪ Hiking trails ▪ Conservation area ▪ Accommodation ▪ Owner(s)/cellarmaster(s)/viticulturist(s) Johan & Linza Louw ▪ Winemaker(s) Linza Louw ▪ 220ha/27ha (cab, merlot, ptage, shiraz) ▪ ±120t/200cs own label 75% red 25% rosé ▪ PO Box 173 Malmesbury 7299 ▪ spekulasie@cornergate.com ▪ www.spekulasie-estate.co.za ▪ S 33° 23' 23.43" E 018° 35' 7.58" ▪ **T +27 (0)82-559-6066/+27 (0)72-375-7078**

☐ **Spencer Bay** *see* Namaqua Wines

Spice Route Winery

Ever the pragmatist, Spice Route owner Charles Back believes 'wine on its own is not a strong enough drawcard to appeal to the average tourist'. Hence the creation of Spice Route Destination, a 'pluri-agricultural farm' and brand home in Paarl with a kaleidoscopic offering, including 'bean-to-bar' chocolate maker, microbrewery, distillery and glass blowing studio. Naturally also a venue for tasting the all-Fairtrade wines, made the past 15 vintages by Charl du Plessis on Klein Amoskuil farm, acquired by Charles in the late 1990s out of the conviction of that the Swartland was under-utilised. The vines there are 'coming of age', the team say, and as they do mourvèdre is 'showing the most profound expression of the deep ferricrete soils'. Also flourishing are pinotage and grenache, hence more plantings.

★★★★ **Grenache** Generous yet well-composed **13** (★★★★☆) takes step up on earthy, savoury **12**, with plum, cherry & olive tapenade complexity, fine tannin structure. Accessible now thanks to bountiful fruit, unobtrusive oak (15 months, mainly used) but with staying power for good few years.

★★★★ **Mourvèdre** Well-composed **13** very satisfying sipper; typical blue berry & blackcurrant aromas, oak-derived nutmeg, approachable & will keep few years. Last-tasted **10** (★★★★) was also delicious.

★★★★ **Terra de Bron Swartland Mourvèdre** ② Now recognises fruit source in name. Dusty mulberry fruit on previewed **12**, great integration of supple tannins already, with touches of cured meat & lavender to add to complexity. Finishes dry & long.

★★★★ **Pinotage** Two vintages rated. **14**, **13** similar in many ways: profusion of blackberry & plum fruit, vibrant enlivening acidity, robust tannins & vanilla courtesy 18 months American oak (40% new). Both fine expressions of SA's own grape.

★★★★ **Terra de Bron Darling Syrah** **12**, previewed previous edition, more complex after year in bottle – dark chocolate, meat & game, dark fruits & dried flower notes – & now more authoritative with commanding tannin structure, striking balance, long blueberry-spice farewell.

★★★★☆ **Terra de Bron Swartland Syrah** Luscious **12**, elevated in older French barrels, is built to age for a decade or more, like **09** (listed last time without 'Swartland' in name). Spiced with black pepper, it has a grippy tannin structure, great fruit depth, incipient complexity & refinement.

★★★★ **Chakalaka** Gregarious melange of 6 varieties, mainly syrah/shiraz & mourvèdre, plus rare-in-Cape petite sirah & tannat. **13** (★★★★☆) more satisfying even than **12**, with white pepper, wild scrub & red berries, intriguing slate-like minerality. Full bodied, with tannin frame.

★★★★ **Malabar** ② **09** is opulent & ripe but more restrained than **07** (★★★★). Rich, with a berry liqueur character, supported by smooth tannins. Neither up to lofty standard of **06** (★★★★★). No **08**.

★★★★☆ **Chenin Blanc 14** well executed to offer lovely fruit intensity, integrated oak (old French) & tangy acidity. Fresh & vibrant, as pleasing as lush & silky **13**.

★★★★ **Sauvignon Blanc** Summer sipper **15**, preview from Darling vines, flush with typical gooseberry, greengage & grass; brisk acidity enlivens the tropical fruit palate, extends the finish.

★★★★☆ **The Amos Block Sauvignon Blanc** ② Excellent varietal expression from oldest sauvignon vineyard in SA, planted 1965, hand-picked **14** is complex, intense, shows wonderful concentrated flavours of citrus & greenpepper. Elegant, never-ending finish.

★★★★ **Terra de Bron Darling Semillon** ⑬ Jasmine- & lime-infused **14** impresses now & shows great ageing potential with intense fruit character, well-managed oak, silky texture & endless finish.

★★★★ **Viognier 14** generous perfumed apricot, dried mango whiffs, smooth textured with older oak in support. Like spicy **13**, broad & rich, with invigorating acid seam. — GM

Location: Malmesbury/Paarl ▪ Map: Paarl & Wellington ▪ Map grid reference: D6 ▪ WO: Swartland/Darling ▪ Est/1stB 1998 ▪ Tasting & sales Mon-Sun 9-5, last tasting 30min before closing ▪ Closed Good Fri, Dec 25 & Jan 1 ▪ Spice Route Restaurant ▪ Tour groups by appt ▪ Red Hot Glass Studio ▪ DV Artisan Chocolate Roastery & Espresso Bar ▪ Cape Brewing Company ▪ Barley & Biltong Emporium ▪ Wilderer's Distillery & La Grapperia Restaurant ▪ Owner(s) Charles Back ▪ Winemaker(s) Charl du Plessis (Dec 2001), with Licia Solomons (Jan 2006) ▪ 90ha (barbera, carignan, grenache, mourv, petite sirah, ptage, sangio, shiraz, tannat, chenin, rouss, sauv, sem, viog) ▪ 60% red 40% white ▪ Fairtrade, IPW, WIETA ▪ PO Box 583 Suider-Paarl 7624 ▪ info@spiceroute.co.za ▪ www.spiceroutewines.co.za ▪ S 33° 45' 50.5" E 018° 55' 9.7" ▪ F +27 (0)21-863-3797 ▪ **T +27 (0)21-863-5200**

Spier

Since acquiring this historic Stellenbosch wine property straddling the Eerste River in 1993, the Enthoven family has transformed it into a hospitality and business centre, wine tourism destination, hub of creative community endeavours, model for sustainable farming practices, and producer of an extensive range of highly rated wines. The latter is courtesy of dynamic, long-serving cellarmaster Frans Smit and talented young guns like 2014 Diners Club Young Winemaker of the Year Jacques Erasmus Now comes the restoration of Spier's historic core, The Werf, with a boutique wine cellar due in 2016 dedicated to estate-grown, organically certified wine. Aspiring to recreate traditional 18th-century farmyard activities and communal life are an artisan bakery, biodynamic vegetable garden and farmers' market. Not forgetting the Living Arts Foundation and contemporary pop-up wine and food events.

Frans K. Smit range

★★★★☆ **CWG Auction Reserve Frans K. Smit** Trio of cab, merlot & cab franc, from Helderberg, two years oak, slightly longer than **10**. Exceptional **11** (★★★★★) has a 'feminine' side, with alluring spice & savoury notes to dark berry fruit, packed in a dense, muscular frame; deserves time.

★★★★☆ **Frans K. Smit** Generous flagship Cape Blend (cab & merlot plus shiraz, pinotage) honours the cellarmaster. Inky **09** from brilliant harvest has suave bramble fruit nestling in savoury tannins, 31 months 100% new oak & over 15% alcohol just settling. A blockbuster from any angle. WO Stellenbosch.

21 Gables range

★★★★ **Cabernet Sauvignon** Serious Stellenbosch fruit treated accordingly. Very svelte **12** lavished 2 years 70% new French oak, which guards sleeping cassis/blackberry fruit in youth; one for the long haul.

★★★★☆ **Pinotage** Singular expression of the variety; woodsmoke-kissed **13** (★★★★★) exceptional; a clove-nuanced baked plum core has freshness & finesse; enough substance to handle 14.7% alcohol but fine structure & dry finish keep it from being a fruit bomb. Home grapes, as for **12**.

★★★★ **Chenin Blanc** Big & bold **14** is showy but risks losing nuance of the grape. Loads of new oak & oodles of summer fruits provide days of flavour & touch of sugar. From Tygerberg vines.

★★★★ **Sauvignon Blanc 13** we said was like a dip in an icy lake — refreshing, to say the least. **14** (★★★★★) even more bracing! Lancing grassy attack to tangy asparagus/canned pea fruit, with penetrating flavour delivered by Tygerberg vines.

Creative Block range

★★★★ **5** Cabernet & merlot lead 5-way Bordeaux blend. Forest floor, cigarbox & cedar tones swirl in **13**; beautifully integrated medium body with a fresh underlying minerality. Most satisfying. WO Coastal.

★★★★ **3** Shiraz & mourvèdre seasoned by splash viognier; half new oak, some American. **13** whiffs of meat spice, dense but sleek & smooth with a savoury green olive flourish. Stellenbosch & Darling grapes.

★★★★☆ **2** ⊘ Stunning **14** (★★★★★) leaps back to form — & onto the podium (including Diners Young Winemaker 2014). Strident grassy muscularity of dominant sauvignon gets width & balance from 15% semillon (5% barrel fermented); deeply flavoured, incisive, enduring. WO Coastal. **13** (★★★★) less mineral than this & **12**.

Also tasted: **8 13** ★★★★

Collaborative Series

★★★★☆ **Noble Late Harvest** ⓐ Joint project between Spier & activist-poet Breyten Breytenbach's Pirouge Collective. Amber **09** folds apricot, tangerine & candied lemon into sweet, mellow whole. Mere 500 x 375 ml bottles from Stellenbosch chenin, 3 years in older wood.

Ideology

Weisser Riesling ★★★☆ Fascinating exhibition of floral, quince & stonefruit interest; **14** semi-dry, lightly oaked, for jaded palates. Tygerberg vines. In abeyance: **Wild Ferment Pinotage**, **'Rhône-Style Blend'**, **Chardonnay-Pinot Noir**, **Wild Ferment Sauvignon Blanc**.

Signature range

Merlot ★★★ Unmistakably minty, **14** is supple & ready for conviviality. **Cabernet Sauvignon-Merlot-Shiraz** ★★★ Lithe tannins allow cassis fruit to flourish in **14**, nicely poised, alcohol just in check. **Chardonnay-Pinot Noir** ★★★ **15** onion skin hue leads out strawberry features, clean & fresh rosé for al fresco meals. **Chenin Blanc** ★★★ Sunshine in a glass; **15** packed with succulent peach & melon, difficult to resist. **Sauvignon Blanc** ★★★ Summer-streaked **15**, nettles & grass, zesty acidity enlivens tropical tail. Also tasted: **Cabernet Sauvignon 14** ★★★ **Pinotage 14** ★★★ **Shiraz 14** ★★★ **Chardonnay 15** ★★★ Not retasted: **Méthode Cap Classique 12** ★★★☆ — DS

Location/map: Stellenbosch ▪ Map grid reference: C7 ▪ WO: Western Cape/Stellenbosch/Coastal/ Tygerberg ▪ Est 1692 ▪ 1stB 1770 ▪ Tasting 10–4.30 & sales 9–5 daily ▪ Tasting from R35 ▪ Facilities for children ▪ Tour groups ▪ Farm produce ▪ Conferences ▪ Manor House & Heritage Walk ▪ Conservation area ▪ 4-star Spier Hotel ▪ Eight Restaurant, Eight to Go & Spier Hotel Restaurant ▪ Craft bakery & café ▪ Farmer's market every Sat ▪ Spier Secret Festival, an annual food & wine event ▪ Owner(s) Enthoven family ▪ Cellarmaster(s) Frans Smit (Dec 1995) ▪ Winemaker(s) Johan Jordaan (reds, Jul 2007) & Jacques Erasmus (whites, Apr 2007) ▪ Wine procurement/winemaker(s) Johan de Villiers, Anton Swarts & Lizanne Jordaan ▪ Viticulturist(s) Johann Smit (Dec 1999) ▪ 650ha (barbera, cabs s/f, malbec, merlot, mourv, p verdot, ptage, shiraz, chard, chenin, sauv, sem, viog) ▪ 3,850t own label 65% red 31% white 3% rosé 1% MCC ▪ ISO 22000:2005, BWI, Fairtrade, IPW, Organic, WIETA ▪ PO Box 99 Lynedoch 7603 ▪ info@spier.co.za ▪ www.spier.co.za ▪ S 33° 58' 24.63" E 018° 47' 2.23" ▪ F +27 (0)21-809-1930 ▪ **T +27 (0)21-809-1100 (wine tasting)**

Spioenkop Wines   ⓛ

To make great wine, so the saying goes, you have to know great wine. Who would know great wine better than a Master Sommelier, a qualification Spioenkop cellarmaster and viticulturist Koen Roose-Vandenbroucke doesn't shout about but surely plays a role in the quality of wine achieved to date. Koen and wife Hannelore's current focus is on getting their Elgin estate better known. Their by-appointment tastings are to give visitors personal attention. 'We can explain to create a terroir wine, vines can't look like a model on a catwalk.' This is a family affair, and the next generation is already involved. Ypke, aged 8, impresses with her wine knowledge while Thor, just 3, is happiest in the vineyards with his father.

1900 range

★★★★☆ **Pinotage** Charming **14** again leans towards variety's pinot noir parentage. Its notably brilliant hue is matched by floral, cherry & raspberry aromatic exuberance & dainty fresh feel, owing as much to the fine ripe tannins as acidity. If not as long lived as **13**, it should give equal enjoyment. WO W Cape.

★★★★ **Chenin Blanc** ⓐ **13**'s riveting acidity, concentration & length tempered by tropical juicy appeal, botrytis & oxidative hints. Partly barrel fermented for structure. Good few years potential.

★★★★ **Sauvignon Blanc** ⓐ Elegant yet steely **13** returns to form after less composed **12** (★★★★). Refreshing winter melon notes gain juiciness from splash semillon. Incisively dry, long.

Spioenkop range

★★★★ **Pinotage** ⓐ Pinot noir-like **13**, fresh, with pure cherry raspberry flavours; nice grippy tannins on dry finish. Subtle oaking (40% new). Just 12% alcohol, ideal lunchtime red.

★★★★☆ **Chenin Blanc** ⓐ Austere yet compelling **13** from young Elgin vines. Tighter than '1900' version with purity & precision in its orange pith character. Palate tension, finishing tannic grip suggest this is a long runner & worth the wait. Portion oaked; natural ferment (as are all).

★★★★ **Riesling 14** ticks all varietal fruit boxes – pepper, lime, spice – delivered in lightish body with gentle verve rather than racy tension. Few grams sugar prolongs flavours on this enjoyable summer sundowner. **13** (★★★★★) poised, elegant.

★★★★☆ **Sauvignon Blanc 14** (★★★★) lighter vintage, toned-down version of rich, zesty **13**. Well handled to display best of quiet winter melon, lime notes & easygoing liveliness. Best over next year/2.

Pinot Noir (NEW) ★★★★ **13** made with usual attention to detail. Fruit purity (darker berry spectrum, some undergrowth), freshness, careful tannin extraction & oaking (20% new French) all honest portrayal of Elgin pinot. Modest 12.6% alcohol. — AL

Location: Elgin ▪ Map: Elgin, Walker Bay & Bot River ▪ WO: Elgin/Western Cape ▪ Est 2008 ▪ 1stB 2010 ▪ Tasting, sales & cellar tours by appt only ▪ Fee R20, waived on purchase (case of wine) ▪ Closed all pub hols ▪ Owner(s) Valuline 119 (Pty) Ltd, 5 shareholders ▪ Cellarmaster(s)/winemaker(s)/viticulturist(s) Koen Roose-Vandenbroucke (2008) ▪ ±47ha/10ha (ptage, pinot, chenin, riesling, sauv) ▪ 40t/5,000cs own label 20% red 80% white ▪ PO Box 340 Grabouw 7160 ▪ info@spioenkopwines.co.za ▪ www.spioenkopwines.co.za ▪ S 34° 14' 14" E 019° 3' 50" ▪ **T +27 (0)21-859-1458/+27 (0)79-491-6613/+27 (0)72-440-2944**

☐ **Splattered Toad** *see* Cape Point Vineyards

Spookfontein Wines   (♀) (🍴) (🏠) (📷)

Vines and olive trees account for a small part of this family-owned Upper Hemel-en-Aarde farm, with over 250 ha of fynbos stretching up the mountainside and providing a home to a rich birdlife. Aside from a new regime in the cellar, recent changes include a sauvignon blanc joining the range, and a restaurant offering 'ethical eating' lunches and valley vistas.

★★★★ **Phantom** (♀) Merlot-led (with cab & cab franc) **08** raises the bar on **07** (★★★★). Poised & lengthy, but greater grip & just the right amount of flavour without seeming worked.

Rosé ★★☆ Dry, fresh & pleasantly easygoing **15** from merlot, with sweet fruit & a light tannic twist.
Sauvignon Blanc (NEW) ★★☆ Dry, pleasantly fruity **15** with unchallenging soft texture. Hemel-en-Aarde WO. Not retasted: **Cabernet Sauvignon 09** ★★☆ **Cabernet Franc 09** ★★★ **Merlot 09** ★★★★ **Late Bottled Vintage NV** ★★★★ Not tasted: **Pinot Noir**, **Méthode Cap Classique**. — TJ

Location: Hermanus ▪ Map: Elgin, Walker Bay & Bot River ▪ WO: Upper Hemel-en-Aarde Valley/Hemel-en-Aarde Valley ▪ Est 2000 ▪ 1stB 2004 ▪ Tasting & sales Tue-Sun 10.30-4.30 ▪ Closed Dec 25/26 & Jan 1 ▪ Restaurant open for lunch ▪ Functions T +27 (0)73-067-7936 Norah ▪ Two self-catering guest cottages ▪ Conservation area ▪ Owner(s) Spookfontein Wines cc (Mike Davis) ▪ Viticulturist(s) Andries Gotze (Jan 2000) ▪ 313ha/±12ha (cabs s/f, merlot, pinot) ▪ 50t/2,000cs own label 85% red 5% white 10% rosé ▪ PO Box 12031 Mill Street Cape Town 8010 ▪ jani@dragons.co.za ▪ S 34° 21' 19.5" E 019° 17' 20.8" ▪ **T +27 (0)21-461-6053/+27 (0)72-199-8774**

Spotswood Wines   (♀)

Bill Spotswood, enviably a chocolate production engineer in a former life, and son Nick came south from Polokwane in 2007 to this boutique property on Stellenbosch's Blaauwklippen Road. They've now added a chardonnay to the range off their small vineyard – vinified by Guy Webber (at Stellenzicht) and Gunther Schultz (at Tamboerskloof), while Bill takes care of the vines.

> **Durif** (♀) ★★★☆ From the variety also known as petite sirah. Deep-coloured **13** adds subtle coffee & tobacco notes to dark fruit. Juicy, but with savoury firm structure that only adds to drinkability. Good for a few years.

Chardonnay (NEW) ★★★ Easygoing, nicely rounded & clean-cut **15** made for early, undemanding pleasure; true varietal citrusy flavours. Also tasted: **Shiraz 13** ★★★★ **Dry Rosé 15** ★★★ **Viognier 15** ★★★★ Occasional release: **Shiraz Reserve**. — TJ

Location/map/WO: Stellenbosch ▪ Map grid reference: F7 ▪ Est 2007 ▪ 1stB 2008 ▪ Tasting & sales by appt ▪ Owner(s) Spotswood family ▪ Winemaker(s) Guy Webber (Jan 2012, consultant) & Gunther Schultz (consultant) ▪ Viticulturist(s) Bill Spotswood (Sep 2007) ▪ 7.05ha/3ha (durif, shiraz, chard, viog)

- 28t/3,000cs own label 56% red 19% white 25% rosé ▪ Suite 200 Private Bag X4 Die Boord 7613 ▪ spotswoodwines@gmail.com ▪ www.spotswoodwines.com ▪ S 33° 59' 2.0" E 018° 51' 35.0" ▪ F +27 (0)21-880-2893 ▪ **T +27 (0)21-880-2893**

Springfield Estate   ⓘ ⓐ

Abrie Bruwer celebrated 20 Springfield vintages in 2015, having steered the family farm from wholesale supply to own-label bottling in 1995. He was a regional pioneer of independent fine-wine making from such classics as sauvignon blanc and cabernet, then uncommon to the area; a risk taker in re-establishing vines in new soils, different row directions; an early advocate of now on-trend traditional winemaking methods aptly described by individualistic wine names. A reputation for quality and style consistency seems set to be cemented by the next generation: Jenna handles marketing and the logistics of the Cape Town warehouse, while Emma and Pieter 'Boy Boy' are studying winemaking at Stellenbosch and Elsenburg respectively.

★★★★☆ **Méthode Ancienne Cabernet Sauvignon** Dense dark fruit coaxed from rugged 2.8 ha single-vineyard planted 1979. **09**'s new oak effortlessly subsumed into clean fruit purity, from whole berries, naturally fermented (as all the reds). Bottle ageing (4 years) enhances balance; elegant but insistent.

★★★★ **The Work of Time** Aptly named cab franc, merlot, cab & petit verdot (39/34/17/10) from old vineyards. Similar unhurried winemaking to Méthode Ancienne; patience rewarded in fruit purity & intensity. **09** (★★★★★) balanced & complex, an elegant step up on muscular & brooding **08**.

★★★★ **Wild Yeast Chardonnay** Naturally crafted unwooded **13**, ripe, rounded & more tropical tone than flamboyant **12** (★★★★☆); balanced, creamy & contemplative, at a more demure 13.2% alcohol.

★★★★ **Life From Stone Sauvignon Blanc** Older vines in sparse soil & high density planting show flinty minerality & tangy grapefruit intensity, leavened by creamy lees undertone. **15** step up on **14** (★★★☆). Friendly 12.5% alcohol. Also in 500 ml.

★★★★ **Special Cuvée Sauvignon Blanc** Riverine soils & different clone yield more open-textured richness than sibling (neither oaked). **15** old vine quality & lees enhance nettle, passionfruit & citrus.

★★★★ **Miss Lucy** (NEW) Sprightly sauvignon, pinot gris & semillon (41/30/29) blend, spotlights Red Stumpnose & other endangered marine species. **15** crisp pomelo, beeswax & starfruit flavours with a creamy lees & light oak underpin.

Also tasted: **Whole Berry Cabernet Sauvignon 13** ★★★★ Not tasted: **Méthode Ancienne Chardonnay**. Occasional release: **Pinot Noir**. — MW

Location/map/WO: Robertson ▪ Est/1stB 1995 ▪ Tasting & sales Mon-Fri 8—5 Sat 9—4 ▪ Closed Easter Fri/Sun, Dec 25 & Jan 1 ▪ Cellar tours by appt ▪ BYO picnic ▪ Owner(s) Bruwer family ▪ Cellarmaster(s)/viticulturist(s) Abrie Bruwer ▪ Winemaker(s) Abrie Bruwer, with Johan van Zyl ▪ 150ha (cabs s/f, merlot, p verdot, chard, sauv) ▪ IPW ▪ PO Box 770 Robertson 6705 ▪ admin@springfieldestate.com ▪ www.springfieldestate.com ▪ S 33° 50' 12.1" E 019° 54' 54.0" ▪ F +27 (0)23-626-3664 ▪ **T +27 (0)23-626-3661**

Springfontein Wine Estate   ⓘ ⓝ ⓗ ⓞ

The focus on chenin and pinotage continues to grow at this family-owned winery near Stanford. Bushvine plantings, some ungrafted, should all be in production by 2018 and winemaker Tariro Masayiti is positive about the increased breadth and range the new blocks will give him. A wine bar has opened, and the expanded tasting facility now offers sundowner snacks and drinks, overseen by award-winning chef and part-owner Jürgen Schneider. As founder members, the team at press time were looking forward to the official opening of the Stanford Wine Route.

Single Vineyard range

★★★★ **Jonathan's Ridge Pinotage** Soft & appealing nose on **12** leads to fresh raspberry & cherry fruit, integrated tannins & solid finish. Nicely oaked (French, American & Hungarian), a delicious drop.

★★★★ **Jil's Dune Chenin Blanc** Rich & lavish **13**, now bottled, packs a hefty punch of ripe stonefruit laced with caramel, toffee & cream. Would benefit from a tad more acidity (though no malo) to spice up slightly hollow tail.

Discontinued: **Jonathan's Ridge Mendocino Pinotage**.

Estate Wines

★★★★ Ikhalezi Noble Late Harvest ⓐ From chenin. **07** (★★★★★) is one of a kind. Astonishingly rich, it's so refreshed by racy acidity that it drinks beautifully; syrupy, tangy apricot with an added savoury roasted almond tone from new oak. 375 ml. Even better than gorgeous **06** preview.

Ulumbaza White of Springfontein ★★★ Very pleasant **14** steps up on previous but maintains tradition of splash blanc de noir pinotage in semillon/chardonnay blend (so each Ulumbaza wine contains pinotage). Fresh fruity sipper with flavours of pears, nectarines & cream. Not retasted: **Ulumbaza Red of Springfontein 11 ★★★★ Ulumbaza Pink of Springfontein 13 ★★** Occasional release: **Special Red**.

Terroir Selection

★★★★ Chenin Blanc 13 continuing quality of previous with a pretty pear & peach nose overlayed with orange & yellow citrus. Plenty of depth & richness from 60% oak (20% new) & some botrytised fruit.

Also tasted: **Pinotage 11 ★★ Sauvignon Blanc 14 ★★★★** Not retasted: **Blanc de Pinotage 13 ★★★★** Discontinued: **Cabernet Sauvignon**, **Petit Verdot**, **Chardonnay**.

Limestone Rocks range

★★★★ Gadda da Vida From pinotage, 16 months new American oak for **10** (★★★) shows through strongly with charry/BBQ sauce notes masking chewy dark fruit. Lacks opulence of **09**. Drink with food.

Whole Lotta Love ⓝⓔⓦ **★★★** Unusual blend of pinotage, petit verdot & shiraz **11** shows raisined character, dried fruit but carries 26 months oak off well, with integrated tannins & firm finish. — CM

Location: Stanford ▪ Map: Elgin, Walker Bay & Bot River ▪ WO: Walker Bay ▪ Est 1996 ▪ 1stB 2004 ▪ Tasting & sales daily ▪ Wine Bar(n) for wine tasting, snacks & coffee — see website for opening hours, or call to make a booking for Springfontein Eats Restaurant ▪ Tour groups ▪ Cellar tours ▪ Farm produce ▪ Walking/hiking trail ▪ Springfontein Sleeps Lodging ▪ Owner(s) Johst & Jennifer Weber, with Jürgen & Susanne Schneider, family & friends ▪ Cellarmaster(s)/winemaker(s) Tariro Masayiti (Jan 2013) ▪ Viticulturist(s) Hildegard Witbooi (Oct 2013), with Vusumzi Rigala (Jul 2014) ▪ 500ha/25ha (cab, p verdot, ptage, chard, chenin) ▪ 145t/20,000cs own label 76% red 22% white 2% rosé ▪ PO Box 71 Stanford 7210 ▪ info@springfontein.co.za ▪ www.springfontein.co.za ▪ S 34° 25' 38.5" E 019° 24' 32.7" ▪ F +27 (0)28-341-0112 ▪ **T +27 (0)28-341-0651/+27 (0)72-371-7546**

Spring Grove Wines ⓐ

Banhoek's Spring Grove, originally part of the Zorgvliet property, was purchased by David Parodi and family 11 years ago. After uprooting the vineyards, their Italian heritage encouraged them to include sangiovese and pinot grigio in the replant. The wines are made at Zorgvliet by Bernard le Roux.

★★★★ Sangiovese ⓐ Preview **13** fragrant & appealing; like last-tasted **10** (★★★★), fruit almost leaps from glass except it's varietally correct sour cherries, not berries, tailored & toned in older oak to lengthy dry conclusion.

Not retasted: **Pinot Grigio 14 ★★★** Not tasted: **Shiraz**, **Sauvignon Blanc**, **Viognier**. — CvZ

Location/map: Stellenbosch ▪ Map grid reference: H4 ▪ WO: Banghoek ▪ 1stB 2005 ▪ Tasting & sales by appt ▪ Owner(s) Parodi family ▪ Winemaker(s) Bernard le Roux (Dec 2013) ▪ Viticulturist(s) Hannes Jansen van Vuuren (Mar 2008) ▪ 10ha/6.4ha (sangio, shiraz, pinot gris, sauv, viog) ▪ 41t/25,200L bulk ▪ PO Box 670 Vereeniging 1930 ▪ hannes@zorgvliet.com ▪ S 33° 54' 46.50" E 018° 56' 13.6" ▪ F +27 (0)86-697-3938 ▪ **T +27 (0)82-856-8717**

☐ **Springvalley** see Old Vines Cellars
☐ **Spruitdrift** see Namaqua Wines
☐ **Stablemate** see Excelsior Estate

Stanford Hills Winery ⓐ ⓟ ⓐ ⓞ ⓑ

As well as growing indigenous flowers for export, roses for the local market and olives, Peter and Jami Kastner continue to live their Walker Bay wine dream. Their expanding range (MCC bubbly on the way) can be tasted at their 100-seat restaurant with views of the farm dam and unspoilt Stanford Valley.

Jacksons Pinotage (symbol) ★★★☆ **14** is nicely balanced despite almost 15% alcohol, French & Hungarian oak adding hint of aniseed to ripe blackberry fruit & mocha, quite gritty tannins should soften.

Veldfire Cape Blend (new) ★★★☆ **14**'s whole is greater than the sum of its parts (65% shiraz, 35% pinotage) with ripe red & black berries lifted by hints of fynbos, pepper & spice. **Rosé** (new) ★★☆ Candyfloss pink **15** from shiraz has ripe red cherry aroma, dry on palate with red berry fruit, especially cranberry. Also tasted: **Veldfire Pinotage 14** ★★★ **Shiraz 14** ★★★ **Sauvignon Blanc 15** ★★★☆ Not tasted: **Chardonnay**. Discontinued: **Veldfire Shiraz**. — JG

Location: Stanford ▪ Map: Elgin, Walker Bay & Bot River ▪ WO: Walker Bay ▪ Est 1856 ▪ 1stB 2002 ▪ Tasting, sales & restaurant Thu-Mon/pub hols 9-5 Tue/Wed by appt only ▪ Grappa, preserves ▪ Restaurant: breakfast & lunch, chalkboard menu changes daily ▪ Functions & events (up to 100 pax) ▪ Hiking/MTB trails ▪ Horse riding ▪ Fishing ▪ Whale watching flights from own airfield ▪ 5 self-catering cottages & main farmhouse (sleeps up to 32 pax) ▪ Owner(s) Stanford Hills Estate (Pty) Ltd ▪ Cellarmaster(s)/winemaker(s) Peter Kastner (Apr 2005) ▪ Viticulturist(s) Peter Kastner ▪ 131ha/12ha (ptage, shiraz, chard, sauv) ▪ 60t/4,000cs own label 66% red 34% white ▪ PO Box 1052 Stanford 7210 ▪ info@ stanfordhills.co.za ▪ www.stanfordhills.co.za ▪ S 34° 25' 21.4" E 019° 28' 25.7" ▪ F +27 (0)28-341-0286 ▪ T +27 (0)28-341-0841

Star Hill

(icons)

Owners and financial services practitioners Grant Hatch and Christopher Palmer Tomkinson are clearly intrepid, given that their vineyards are 723m up the Langeberg Mountains (earning the rare Wine of Origin appellation, Tradouw Highlands)! The continental climate is ideally suited to quality production, and because there is no cellar, the wines are made off-site by a consultant.

★★★★ **Shiraz** (symbol) Single-vineyard **11** is meaty, peppery, shows scrub nuances, the fruit a dark-toned underpin. Tannin grip adds definition, ensures longevity.

★★★★ **Chenin Blanc** Wild ferment, lightly oaked, some age, so expect something different in **13** from Montagu single-vineyard. Almonds, dried orange peel, body plumped by a dab of sugar. Tangy, delicious, more impressive than **12** (★★★☆).

★★★★ **Sauvignon Blanc** Quite individual, **14**'s perfume has a thatch & mineral character, a suggestion of sage, citrus & melon flavours. Beautifully balanced, elegant, stylish. **13** sold out untasted.

Blanc de Noir (new) ★★ From shiraz, hence the red berry notes, but **14** is bone-dry, light textured & perfect patio fare. Not retasted: **Viognier 12** ★★★★ Not tasted: **Fountainhead**. — CR

Location: Montagu ▪ Map: Klein Karoo & Garden Route ▪ WO: Tradouw Highlands/Montagu ▪ Est 2005 ▪ 1stB 2009 ▪ Tasting & sales daily 9-3 ▪ Closed Dec 25 ▪ Akkerboom farmstall & restaurant ▪ Facilities for children ▪ Gifts ▪ Farm produce ▪ Conference facilities on Killarney Farm ▪ Walks/hikes ▪ Mountain biking ▪ Akkerboom self-catering cottages (www.akkerboomcountrycottages.com) ▪ Owner(s) Grant Hatch & Christopher Palmer Tomkinson ▪ Winemaker(s)/viticulturist(s) Lourens van der Westhuizen (consultant) ▪ 15ha (shiraz, chenin, sauv, viog) ▪ 1,000cs own label 40% red 60% white ▪ PO Box 342 Montagu 6720 ▪ starhill@tradouw.co.za ▪ www.starhillwines.com ▪ S 33° 54' 46.86" E 020° 29' 32.31" ▪ F +27 (0)28-572-1644 ▪ T +27 (0)28-572-1610

Stark-Condé Wines

(icons)

'I am getting too old for this!' says graphic designer-turned-winemaker José Conde of the latest frenetic harvest, having taken in 50% of the crop in one week! At the recently enlarged cellar in the heart of Stellenbosch's beautiful Jonkershoek Valley, after 15 vintages in boutique-sized premises , the creative pulse remains strong, however. Not only with this wine venture but also wife Marie's Postcard Café, renowned for cuisine with Japanese flair. It hasn't all been plain sailing since yachtsman and retired father-in-law Hans-Peter Schröder bought the Oude Nektar home farm in the 1980s, with Jonkershoek experiencing many a forest fire. Fortunately the 2015 blaze that ravaged the valley missed the farm (narrowly), with the crop safely brought in the day before. Accolades continue to roll in, most recently the trophy (for the second time) for best cabernet sauvignon at the Six Nations Challenge.

Three Pines range

★★★★★ **Cabernet Sauvignon** From the best cab vineyard, & similar components (splashes petit verdot & merlot) to predecessor but **13**'s (★★★★) fruit profile leaner & leafier, in more tightly coiled framework than superlative & more densely fruited **12**. Unyielding in youth, needs cellaring.

★★★★☆ **Syrah** Smallest crop ever from elevated syrah/shiraz vineyard yields **13**'s concentrated dark fruit, infused with scented violets, in streamlined, fine-grained tannin structure. Complex, intense, well groomed & suave. Confident rebound after **12** (★★★★), recalling **11** (★★★★★).

Stark-Condé range

★★★★ **Cabernet Sauvignon** Same vineyard source & make-up as **12** (★★★★☆) but **13** not quite as intense, authoritative. Bright fruit framed by sappy dry tannins; well crafted with good length & prospects. 4 own-farm blocks; dashes merlot, petit verdot, cab franc & malbec. Stellenbosch WO, like Syrah.

★★★★ **Syrah** Two vineyards at different altitudes yield muscular, dry tannin structure & opulent dark fruit in **13** (★★★★☆). Authoritative & confident, all elements in place with Rhône-style peppery farewell. Already tempts but richer rewards in time. Trumps **12**.

Also tasted: **The Field Blend 14** ★★★ Discontinued: **Oude Nektar**.

Postcard Series

★★★★☆ **Round Mountain Pinot Noir** Organically grown single Overberg block yields perfumed berry fruits with smoky undertone; firm, sappy tannin structure, fresh & bright, but **14** (★★★★) shade less intense & balanced in youth than maiden **13**. Deserves time – future treasures in store.

★★★★ **Sauvignon Blanc** From Elgin, **14** raises bar on **13** (★★★) with flinty grapefruit flavours & racy acidity; lovely purity, texture (from lees ageing & partial oaking) & length at moderate 12.7% alcohol.

Also tasted: **Chenin Blanc 14** ★★★★☆ Not retasted: **Pinot Noir 13** ★★★☆ In abeyance: **Rowey Vineyards Pinot Noir**. — MW

Location/map: Stellenbosch ▪ Map grid reference: G6 ▪ WO: Jonkershoek Valley/Stellenbosch/Elgin/Overberg ▪ Est/1stB 1998 ▪ Tasting & sales Mon-Sun 9.30–4 ▪ Fee R30pp ▪ Closed most pub hols (please call to confirm) ▪ Postcard Café open Wed-Sun 9.30-4 ▪ Owner(s) Jonkershoek Cellars (Pty) Ltd ▪ Cellarmaster(s) José Conde (1998) ▪ Winemaker(s) José Conde (1998), with Elizma van Wyngaard (2012) ▪ Viticulturist(s) Andrew Klinck, with Kevin Watt ▪ 250ha/40ha (cabs s/f, merlot, p verdot, shiraz) ▪ 250t/12,000cs own label 80% red 20% white ▪ PO Box 389 Stellenbosch 7599 ▪ info@stark-conde.co.za ▪ www.stark-conde.co.za, www.postcardcafe.co.za ▪ S 33° 57' 13.83" E 018° 54' 37.59" ▪ F +27 (0)21-887-4340 ▪ **T +27 (0)21-861-7700/+27 (0)21-887-3665**

☐ **Starlette** see Allée Bleue Wines
☐ **Star Tree** see Orange River Cellars

Steenberg Vineyards

On prime, cool-climate, mountainside Constantia land, boasting a history as vaunted as its vinous Cape Dutch neighbours, Steenberg has emerged as a contemporary classic. While still offering the 'lifestyle' package of luxury residential golf estate, boutique hotel and restaurants developed by former corporate owners from 1990, it's now guided by 'wine people'. The Graham Beck family business, owners since 2005, honed its winegrowing skills at the eponymous Robertson property; former cellarmaster John Loubser is MD; and well-versed winemaker JD Pretorius will soon see replanted specialities sauvignon blanc and semillon take already elegant wines (alongside fine reds, a rare nebbiolo and new ultra-premium MCC) to the next level. Informal elegance are watchwords in the tasting room, expanded Bistro Sixteen82, reconceptualised Catharina's Restaurant and natural indigenous surrounds too.

Icon range

★★★★☆ **Magna Carta** Sauvignon's pristine flinty scrub-nuanced fruit, layered with semillon's richness, combine perfectly with steely acidity & stony minerality of fine **13**. Eerily quiet at first — & in youth — eminently drinkable on release, but rewards ageing. Semillon (36%) barrel fermented (40% new); blend 9 months older oak.

Ultra Premium range

★★★★☆ **Nebbiolo** Perfect foil after a few steely sauvignons! Grape perfectly matched to cool climes too. Deceptively pale **13** unfurls aromatic violets to show savoury sour cherry brightness amongst the suave smoky depth of flavour, all defined by firm tannin & acidity of the variety. Only seasoned oak.

★★★★ **Catharina** Selection of best of vintage; perfumed eucalyptus in powerful yet lithe blend. Deft **13**'s merlot fruit lifted by 33% cab (plus splash shiraz). 73% new oak well integrated in 'cool' package.

★★★★ **The Black Swan Sauvignon Blanc** Includes low yields of old Block 28, giving spine & heft to grassy fruit from maturing vines; **14**'s thrilling cool-climate tension filled out by 10% semillon.

★★★★ **Semillon** Intense minerality & savoury acidity keep the focus as always, but textured **13** – like **12** – not as rich, complex & weighty as previous. 9 months in oak, 35% new.

★★★★ **1682 Pinot Noir MCC** Fragrant, beautifully weighted & textured dry rosé bubbly. **12** yeasty (on lees ±30 months) but firm, bright & assertive with steely grip. Widely sourced grapes.

★★★★☆ **Lady R MCC** (NEW) Impressive new standard-bearing sparkling fills gap in range: classic blend pinot noir & chardonnay (60/40, latter oak fermented), long (54 months) on lees. **10** altogether fuller, toastier & more dense than stablemates, complex & enduring. WO W Cape.

Super Premium range

★★★★ **Merlot** Diners Club Young Winemaker award for JD Pretorius in 2014. Overt minty character permeates medium structure, but **12** graceful & more refined than **11** (★★★★). Style loved by many.

★★★★ **Shiraz** Elegant & expressive **13** has plenty of meat spice & earthiness in its smooth texture. Mediumweight, there's no threat of taste fatigue. 15 months in oak, 45% new.

★★★★ **1682 Chardonnay MCC** Crisp blanc de blancs sparkler now **NV**; citrus zing tempered a year on lees; gets breadth from 12% oak-aged reserve wine & splash pinot noir. A super aperitif. WO W Cape.

Sauvignon Blanc ★★★★ Sauvignon's fresh minerality, with gravitas derived from lees-ageing & partially oak-fermented 14% semillon component; **15** steely, stylish. **Sparkling Sauvignon Blanc** ★★★ Funky fizz in orange finery; **NV** tastes of, well, bubbly sauvignon! Bottle fermentation too brief to qualify as MCC, or to mask grassy fruit. Hugely popular. Also tasted: **Echo Red Blend 13** ★★★★ **Sphynx Chardonnay 15** ★★★★ **Rattlesnake Sauvignon Blanc 14** ★★★★

Klein Steenberg range

Cabernet Sauvignon ★★★☆ Brambly fruit in firm frame, **13** easy albeit uncomplex. WO W Cape, as all these. Also tasted: **Cabernet Sauvignon-Merlot-Cabernet Franc 13** ★★★ **Rosé 15** ★★ **Sauvignon Blanc 15** ★★ — DS

Location: Constantia ▪ Map: Cape Peninsula ▪ WO: Constantia/Western Cape/Coastal ▪ Est 1990 ▪ 1stB 1996 ▪ Tasting & sales Mon-Sun 10–6 ▪ Tasting R20pp/R40pp for flagship range, waived on purchase ▪ Closed Good Fri & Dec 25 ▪ Cellar tours Mon-Fri 11 & 3 ▪ Bistro Sixteen82; Catharina's at Steenberg ▪ Steenberg Hotel & Spa; conferences; world-class golf course, walking trail ▪ Extensive merchandising area ▪ Annual festivals: Constantia Fresh (Feb), Constantia Food & Wine (Apr) ▪ Conservation area ▪ Owner(s) Graham Beck Enterprises ▪ Cellarmaster(s) JD Pretorius (Mar 2009) ▪ 60ha (cab, merlot, nebbiolo, shiraz, sauv, sem) ▪ 312t/70,000cs own label 40% red 60% white ▪ WIETA ▪ PO Box 224 Steenberg 7947 ▪ info@steenbergfarm.com ▪ www.steenbergfarm.com ▪ S 34° 4' 17.0" E 018° 25' 31.1" ▪ F +27 (0)21-713-2201 ▪ **T +27 (0)21-713-2211**

☐ **Steenbok** *see* Riebeek Cellars
☐ **Steenhuis** *see* Wine-of-the-Month Club
☐ **STELL** *see* Stellenrust

Stellar Winery   ⓘ

It started in the early 2000s as a Vredendal winery, with tanks 'beneath the stars', vinifying some 1,000 tons of grapes to internationally recognised organic specs. Today, Stellar Winery is SA's largest producer of organic Fairtrade wines, handling nearly 12,000 tons from over 200 ha. Currently the world's largest producer of no-sulphur-added wines, its 12.5 million bottles-a-year total output is absorbed by a rapidly expanding global market. New to the range is Dig This!, a collaboration with Greenpop, a community development organisation encouraging 'green' living on the continent. Increased demand for organic bag-in-box wines in Scandinavia has prompted the installation of a BIB filling line, which will also facilitate the launch of the first organic BIBs locally.

River's End range

★★★★ **Chenin Blanc** (NEW) ⊘ Poised **14**'s subtle vanilla & butter notes from 6 months in new barrels in harmony with its thatchy white peach fruit tones; persistent & quietly confident dinner companion. WO Koekenaap, like Pinot.

Pinot Noir (🐘) ★★★☆ Gentle cherry & raspberry appeal, balanced 12.5% alcohol & form-giving tannin on step-up **14**, one of new wave of budget-priced pinot bottlings. Order with confidence.

Sensory Collection

★★★★ **Shiraz** (NEW) Liquorice, fragrant oak spice (all-new wood), plum & lily notes on polished **13** from Swartland. Moderate 13.5% alcohol, sweet fruit & few grams sugar are easy to drink solo, also work well with spicy food.

Pinotage (NEW) ⊘ ★★★★ Fragrant oak detail (18 months new French), opulent dark fruits, smooth entry & enlivening bitter nip: modern **13** from Swartland makes a pleasing debut. Not retasted: **Chardonnay 13** ★★

Running Duck range

Cabernet Sauvignon-Pinotage (🐘) ⊘ ★★★★ **13** marriage 48% cab, pinotage, dash shiraz the complete package: complex fruit profile, well-managed oak, undaunting 13.4% alcohol.

Also tasted: **Sauvignon Blanc** ⊘ 15 ★★☆ **Sauvignon Blanc-Semillon** ⊘ 15 ★★★ Note: range was 'Stellar Organic Reserve'.

Stellar Organics range

Pinotage ⊘ ★★★ Improved **15** sympathetically oaked to let succulent strawberry fruit shine. Drinks easily. Olifants River WO. **Shiraz** ⊘ ★★★ Toasty oak character on **15** balanced by bouncy red plum fruit & few grams sugar. **Rosé** ⊘ ★★ **15** from colombard, dash pinotage, is dry, faintly aromatic & best enjoyed young, well chilled. **Chenin Blanc** ★★★ **15**'s thatch & lemon broadened by tropical notes of melon & papaya; zesty acidity & pithy grip well support the ripe fruit. Also tasted: **Chenin Blanc-Sauvignon Blanc** ⊘ 15 ★★★ Not retasted: **Cabernet Sauvignon 13** ★★★ **Merlot 13** ★★ **Chardonnay 14** ★★☆ **Chardonnay-Pinot Noir Sparkling 13** ★★☆ Not tasted: **Sparkling Extra Dry**.

Dig This! range (NEW)

Shiraz-Cabernet Sauvignon ⊘ ★★★ Early-drinking everyday **NV** red with juicy flavours & rustic but mild tannins. **Chenin Blanc-Sauvignon Blanc** ⊘ ★★★ Touch oak adds subtle vanilla & butter to lemon-fresh **NV** from Koekenaap, few grams sugar give roundness, length. Good match for fish.

Stellar Organics No-Sulphur-Added

Cabernet Sauvignon ⊘ ★★★ Roasted nuts, lively red berries on **15**, somewhat atypical fruit profile but tasty, rounded. Genteel solo sipper. Olifants River WO. **Rosé** ⊘ ★★★ Rather frivolous pink colour belies the punchy flavours, **15** packed with berries in a bone-dry body, with moderate 12% alcohol. **Limited Release Blanc de Blanc** ★★★ Was 'White'. Restrained nose of melon & white pepper, **15** an atypical colombard but not unattractive, with pick-me-up liveliness. Olifants River WO. Also tasted: **Merlot** ⊘ 15 ★★ **Pinotage** ⊘ 15 ★★ **Shiraz** ⊘ 15 ★★

Live-A-Little range

Wildly Wicked White ⊘ ★★★ Tropical styling, zesty acidity & pithy conclusion: latest **NV** from chenin delivers good everyday drinking. **Somewhat Sweet & Soulful** ★★ **NV** from pinotage is not obviously sweet, has sufficient grip to lift & lengthen the palate, make it pizza/pasta compatible. Also tasted: **Really Ravishing Red** ⊘ NV ★★★ **Rather Revealing Rosé** ⊘ NV ★★ **Slightly Sweet & Shameless** ⊘ NV ★★☆ Not retasted: **Slightly Sweet & Sassy Sparkling NV** ★☆

Heaven on Earth range

Natural Sweet ⊘ ★★★☆ Stylish dessert from air-dried muscat d'Alexandrie, unwooded. Latest **NV** (**14**) shows delicate sweetness & some complexity in its muscat, citrus zest & melon nuances; pleasingly low 10% alcohol. Misses the spark, gravitas of previous. — CvZ

Location: Vredendal ▪ Map: Olifants River ▪ WO: Western Cape/Koekenaap/Olifants River/Swartland ▪ Est 2000 ▪ 1stB 2001 ▪ Tasting & sales Mon-Fri 8–5 ▪ Closed all pub hols ▪ Cellar tours by appt ▪ Owner(s) Rossouw family, Stellar Empowerment Trust & others ▪ Winemaker(s) Klaas Coetzee (Aug 2010) & Mauritius Naude ▪ Viticulturist(s) Klaas Coetzee ▪ ±68ha/Stellar Farming & ±149ha/Independent organic producers (cab, merlot, ptage, pinot, ruby cab, shiraz, chenin, chard, muscat d'A, sauv) ▪ 11,900t ▪ Other export brands: African Star, Firefly, Ithemba, Moonlight Organics, Natural Star, Running Duck, Sunshine ▪ PO Box 4 Klawer 8145 ▪ info@stellarorganics.com ▪ www.stellarorganics.com ▪ S 31° 42' 24.70" E 018° 33' 33.70" ▪ F +27 (0)86-635-1968 ▪ **T +27 (0)27-216-1310**

Stellekaya Winery ⓠ ⑪

Stellekaya's home ('kaya' in isiXhosa) is a shared wine centre at Stellenbosch's Bosman's Crossing, conceptualised over a decade ago by entrepreneurial vintners Dave and Jane Lello. Equally pioneering is winemaker Ntsiki Biyela, reared in KwaZulu-Natal, trained in the Cape, seasoned in Bordeaux and Tuscany. Grapes, previously bought in, increasingly are from the Lellos' young Blaauwklippen vines.

Fusion Collection

★★★★ **Aquarius** ⊘ Bordeaux blend, equal split cab, merlot & cab franc. Tealeaf & violet nuanced **14** improves on plump & pleasantly firm **13** (★★★★) with greater vibrancy, complexity.

★★★★ **Orion** ⓠ Flagship cab-led Bordeaux blend. Heaps of concentration in **08**, intense blackcurrants & cigarbox, yet the palate remains juicy, streamlined, with supple tannins.

Not retasted: **Cape Cross 09** ★★★☆ **Hercules 09** ★★★☆

Premium Eclipse Collection

★★★★ **Cabernet Sauvignon** Like **09**, **11** has dash cab franc; shows wild mint, plum, blue berry & cassis, smart oaking. Full bodied & poised, with tannin structure for food or long-term cellaring. No **10**.

★★★★ **Merlot 10** recalls **08**'s dark-fruited profile with oak in careful support, mainly older barrels, to retain the supple sleekness. No **09**.

★★★★ **Shiraz** Rich & spicy **11** has prune, clove & beef bouillon tones, long velvet finish for immediate appeal yet, like similarly youthful **09**, structure to improve with few years.

Not retasted: **Pinotage 11** ★★★☆ Not tasted: **Pinot Noir, Pinot Grigio**.

Boschetto range

White ⓠ ★★★ Mouthwatering zestiness on **14** chenin gives way to exuberant pineapple, apple & pear. Delicious solo or with summer salads. Not tasted: **Red**. — GM

Location/map: Stellenbosch ▪ Map grid reference: E5 ▪ WO: Stellenbosch/Western Cape ▪ Est 1998 ▪1stB 1999 ▪ Tasting, sales & cellar tours Mon-Fri 10–4 ▪ Closed all pub hols & Dec 16 to 3rd week of Jan ▪ Private luncheon & wine tasting with winemaker by arrangement (min 6 pax) ▪ Vineyard tours for groups of 10+ with tasting, cheese & biscuits – booking essential ▪ Owner(s) Dave & Jane Lello ▪ Winemaker(s) Ntsiki Biyela (Feb 2004) ▪ Viticulturist(s) Paul Wallace (Jan 2005, consultant) ▪ 23ha/15ha under vine ▪ 12,000cs own label ▪ Brands for clients: The Grand Beach Café ▪ IPW ▪ PO Box 12426 Die Boord Stellenbosch 7613 ▪ info@stellekaya.co.za ▪ www.stellekaya.co.za ▪ S 33° 56' 27.6" E 018° 50' 47.3" ▪ F +27 (0)21-883-2536 ▪ **T +27 (0)21-883-3873**

Stellenbosch Family Wines ⓠ

De Vries, Van Wyk and Truter are the families behind this young boutique brand. Sterling Koelenhof Winery provides the grapes and facilities, and that cellar's winemaker/GM, Andrew de Vries, assists, but the actual vinification is by his son Carlo, aged 11! Michelle-Lize van Wyk designs the front labels (a new one is on the way) and marketer Christel Truter sent the wines to China, to an enthusiastic reception.

Pinotage ⓝⒺⓦ ★★★☆ Oaky notes of chocolate, tar & char on **13**, cushioned by plush dark berry fruit, supple tannins. **CMP Legacy Red** ★★★ **13** mainly cab with merlot & pinot noir, has improved since last time, shows character & some distinction. Savoury, with fruitier notes of red berry, sappy tannin conclusion. **Chardonnay ★★★** Revisited **13** restrained lemon & lemongrass notes, gravelly acidity, lightly oaked to allow fruit to take the lead. Also tasted: **Cabernet Sauvignon 13 ★★☆ Merlot 14 ★★☆ Pinot Noir 13 ★★★ Family Blend 13 ★★☆** — CvZ

Location/map/WO: Stellenbosch ▪ Map grid reference: D1 ▪ Est/1stB 2013 ▪ Tasting by appt ▪ Fee R20/6 wines ▪ Sales Mon-Sat 8-6 by appt ▪ Owner(s) Renata de Vries, Michelle-Lize van Wyk & Christel Truter ▪ Winemaker(s) Carlo de Vries, with Andrew de Vries (both Jan 2013, consultants) ▪ 2,900cs own label 90% red 10% white ▪ c/o PO Box 1 Koelenhof 7605 ▪ info@stellenboschfamilywines.co.za ▪ www.stellenboschfamilywines.co.za ▪ S 33° 50' 5.2" E 018° 47' 52.7" ▪ **T +27 (0)82-835-7107**

Stellenbosch Hills Wines   ⑨ ⑥ ⑥

Situated in the Vlottenburg area, at the foot of the Polkadraai Hills, Stellenbosch Hills has stood the test of time and socio-economic changes, successfully converting from a co-operative to a company of growers with a thriving own brand and cellardoor. The enterprise's 70th anniversary is being celebrated with, among others, a limited release of its signature dessert wine, from the rare muscat de Hambourg grape, fortified with seven-year-old potstill brandy and packaged to match the momentous occasion.

1707 Reserve range
White ★★★☆ Tropical notes in seriously styled (& packaged), oaked (all-new barrels) **13** blend chardonnay, semillon, viognier, with lovely textured palate. Also tasted: **Red 12 ★★★☆**

Stellenbosch Hills Cultivar Collection
★★★★ Muscat de Hambourg ⑨ **12** (**★★★**) engagingly sweet & grapey but misses depth & complexity of **10**, which took the jerepiko-style desert to a new level. No **11**.
Shiraz ★★★ Succulently fruity but nice & dry **13**, softly spicy, appealing, with hints of mocha & vanilla.
Chenin Blanc ★★★ Delightful, well-made **15** delivers crisp apple flavours & appetising acidity for everyday enjoyment. **Sauvignon Blanc ★★☆** Crisply dry **15** gratifies with uncomplicated flavourful tropical fruitiness. Also tasted: **Cabernet Sauvignon 12 ★★★ Merlot 12 ★★☆ Pinotage 13 ★★★**

Polkadraai range
Merlot-Shiraz ★★ Fresh, spice- & mocha-imbued **14**, unpretentious dry red in 3L pack. Polkadraai Hills WO, like all these. **Chenin Blanc-Sauvignon Blanc ★★** Tasty, dry & fruity **15** 70/30 blend for carefree summer sipping. Also tasted: **Pinotage-Merlot 14 ★★★ Sauvignon Blanc 15 ★★★** Not retasted: **Pinot Noir Rosé Sparkling 14 ★★☆** — IM

Location/map: Stellenbosch ▪ Map grid reference: D6 ▪ WO: Stellenbosch/Polkadraai Hills ▪ Est 1945 ▪ 1stB 1972 ▪ Tasting & sales Mon-Fri 9–5 Sat 10–3 ▪ Fee R15; R50 wine, biltong & droëwors tasting ▪ Closed Sun & all pub hols ▪ The Tank art gallery ▪ Owner(s) 16 members ▪ Cellarmaster(s) PG Slabbert (Jan 1997) ▪ Winemaker(s) Juan Slabbert (Jan 2009) ▪ Viticulturist(s) Johan Pienaar & Eben Archer (consultants) ▪ 715ha (cab, merlot, ptage, shiraz, chard, chenin, muscat de Hambourg, sauv) ▪ 8,000t/ 20,000cs own label 68% red 30% white 2% other ▪ IPW ▪ PO Box 40 Vlottenburg 7604 ▪ info@ stellenbosch-hills.co.za ▪ www.stellenbosch-hills.co.za ▪ S 33° 57' 38.2" E 018° 48' 1.8" ▪ F +27 (0)21-881-3357 ▪ **T +27 (0)21-881-3828**

Stellenbosch Reserve   ⑨

These sophisticated wines are Rust en Vrede proprietor Jean Engelbrecht's homage to Stellenbosch, 'a unique town [and] birthplace, and home to many of South Africa's greatest leaders, intellectuals, artists, scientists, sportsmen and winemakers'.

★★★★ Ou Hoofgebou Cabernet Sauvignon ⑭ᴱ Classic cab nose on **13**, with cassis, vanilla & black cherries vying with spicy cedarwood. More elegant than powerful, with firm ripe tannins & a strong finish. Needs time.

★★★★ Kweekskool Merlot ⑭ᴱ Very accomplished **13** makes promising debut with black berries, polish & chocolate leading to dense dark fruit & well-balanced tannins, good acidity. Gentle oak (20% new) adds backbone.

★★★★☆ **Vanderstel** ⓠ Was 'Stellenbosch Reserve'. Restraint & gentility mark polished **12** 4-way Bordeaux blend. Taut & chiselled, it deserves time.

★★★★ **Moederkerk Chardonnay** (NEW) Makes a classy entry with toasted yellow stonefruit wrapped in honey & toffee cream. **14** good fruit/oak balance although latter surprisingly assertive (only 50% oaked, 15% new); should come round soon though. — CM

Location/WO: Stellenbosch ▪ Est 2004 ▪ 1stB 2005 ▪ Tasting & sales at Guardian Peak ▪ Owner(s) Jean Engelbrecht ▪ Winemaker(s) Roelof Lotriet (Sep 2014) ▪ Viticulturist(s) Dirkie Mouton (Jan 2010) ▪ 14t/ 3,000cs own label 70% red 30% white ▪ IPW ▪ PO Box 473 Stellenbosch 7599 ▪ info@ thestellenboschreserve.com ▪ www.thestellenboschreserve.com ▪ F +27 (0)21-881-3000 ▪ **T +27 (0)21-881-3881**

Stellenbosch University Welgevallen Cellar ⓠ

In the premises where Abraham Perold crossed pinot noir and hermitage (cinsaut) to create pinotage in the 1920s, Stellenbosch University oenology students today still learn their winecraft. Maker of the own label, Riaan Wassüng, says five new wines are lining up to graduate to the commercial arena.

Die Laan range
Cabernet Sauvignon (NEW) ★★★ Typical varietal blackcurrant with a hint of tobacco on well-oaked (no new barrels) **11** with 10% petit verdot. Ripe flavours, yet the finish shows more herbaceous character & firm tannins. **Cape Fortified** (NEW) ★★★ Ripe fruitcake notes on **05** 'port' from tintas barocca & roriz in old oak barrels for 8 years. Pretty simple & unlingering, neither too sweet nor fiery, the tannins softened & easygoing. Also tasted: **Pinotage 12** ★★★★ **Cape Blend 12** ★★★ **Sauvignon Blanc 15** ★★☆ **Viognier 14** ★★★ Occasional release: **Rector's Reserve**.

Maties range
Rooiplein ★★★ Ripe, well-fruited, subtly oaked **NV** blend is softly textured, tasty & relaxed, but with a little grip to hold it together. — TJ

Location/map/WO: Stellenbosch ▪ Map grid reference: F6 ▪ Est 2001 ▪ 1stB 2009 ▪ Tasting Mon-Fri 9-4 ▪ Fee R10pp ▪ Closed all pub hols & Dec 15-Jan 10 ▪ Owner(s) Stellenbosch University ▪ Cellarmaster(s)/ winemaker(s) Riaan Wassüng (Jan 2004) ▪ Viticulturist(s) Vaatjie Jacobs (Jan 1973) ▪ 11ha/10ha (cab, ptage, shiraz, chard, sauv) ▪ 4,600cs own label 68% red 32% white ▪ Department of Viticulture & Oenology, Private Bag X1 Matieland 7602 ▪ winesales@sun.ac.za, rfw@sun.ac.za ▪ http://academic.sun.ac.za/viti_oenol/ ▪ S 33° 56' 22.38" E 018° 52' 1.92" ▪ **T +27 (0)21-808-2925/+27 (0)83-622-6394**

Stellenbosch Vineyards ⓠ 🍴 🏛 ♿

The public face of this large and progressive global wine business, based at 17th-century Stellenbosch farm Welmoed, is a stylish food-and-wine destination combining a convivial tasting lounge where visitors can enjoy the diverse wine portfolio listed below, and family-friendly restaurant Bistro 13, helmed by celebrity chef Nic van Wyk. Mostly exported labels Arniston Bay and Versus not tasted this edition.

The Flagship range
★★★★★ **Petit Verdot** ⓠ Enticing black berry, dark chocolate & exotic spice aromas on flagship **10** from Groenekloof vines. Lush, with acid & tannin backbone to give shape to concentrated fruit flavours. Seamless, velvety texture & unflagging sappy finish.

Infiniti range
★★★★ **Brut Methodé Cap Classique** (NEW) Delightful **08** sparkling is rich, dry & biscuity, with fine slowly spiralling strings of bubbles. Lovely lemon freshness after 6 years on the lees. Mostly chardonnay (56%) with pinot noir, splash pinot meunier.

★★★★ **Noble Late Harvest** (NEW) Luscious sweet dessert **12** is mostly chenin with a drop of muscat; fragrant honey, rosepetal aromas with intense dried fruit flavours; long & uncloying, intriguing touch of dried herbs in the aftertaste. WO W Cape.

Credo range
★★★★ **Chenin Blanc** ⓠ Extensive oaking (2 years, 50% new) noticeable on awarded **10** but smartly handled, integrated. Complex, concentrated Granny Smith/Golden Delicious aromas & flavours.

Chardonnay ★★★ Barrel-fermented **14** is fruit-shy, oaky, with a brisk lemon twist to finish. Also tasted: **Shiraz 12** ★★★ **Shiraz-Merlot-Viognier 12** ★★★☆

Stellenbosch Vineyards range

★★★★ **Hayden's Red** Classy Bordeaux blend is mostly cab & merlot, **13** mouthfilling flavour on supportive tannins, a smooth, creamy texture & polished French oak, 18 months.

Cabernet Sauvignon (NEW) ★★★★ Bright red-berry fruit, hints of graphite & pencil shavings on **12**, underpinned by still-taut tannins. Seriously conceived wine (2 years in oak), for fine-dining rather than quaffing. **Shiraz** (NEW) ★★★★ Savoury & spicy **13** is bouncy, full of life, fresh fruitiness layered with oak that is integrated well. **Sauvignon Blanc** (NEW) ★★★★ Pungent **14** shows asparagus, sweet peas & a savoury nuance; good balance & smooth mouthfeel. Also tasted: **Bushvine Pinotage 13** ★★★★ **Bushvine Chenin Blanc 15** ★★★★ **Hayden's White 14** ★★★★

Four Secrets range

Sparkling Shiraz (🏆) ★★★ Among tiny handful of shiraz sparklers in SA. Characterful carbonated **NV** has firm, ever so slightly sweet lavender & blackberry bubbles. Not retasted: **Shiraz NV** ★★★

Welmoed range

> **Chardonnay** (🌿) ★★★ **15** citrus-toned & oak-brushed sipper, effortless, gains vivacity from bouncy acidity. WO W Cape. **Sauvignon Blanc** (✓) (🌿) ★★★★ Dependable well-priced label, perfect al fresco partner **15** is green-fruited, characterful & smooth.

Rosé ★★ Undemanding dry **15** pink from shiraz is fruity, with strawberry & spice flavours. **Pinot Grigio** (NEW) ★★★ Floral & light, with seductive perfume on easy-to-drink **15**. Some depth & length. **Sparkling Brut** ★★★ Eye-catching packaging, with intense Granny Smith apple appeal on frothy **NV** dry fizz from chenin with dollops chardonnay, sauvignon. WO W Cape. Also tasted: **Cabernet Sauvignon 14** ★★ **Viognier 15** ★★★ — WB

Location/map: Stellenbosch ▪ Map grid reference: C7 ▪ WO: Stellenbosch/Western Cape/Groenekloof ▪ Est 2004 ▪ Tasting & sales Mon–Fri 9–6 Sat 9–5 Sun 10–5 ▪ Fee R30pp ▪ Closed Dec 25 & Jan 1 ▪ Bistro 13 ▪ Facilities for children ▪ Owner(s) 200+ shareholders ▪ Winemaker(s) Abraham de Villiers (Dec 2004) & Bernard Claassen (Feb 2005), with Petri de Beer (Jan 2015) & Stefan Erwee (Feb 2014) ▪ Viticulturist(s) Francois de Villiers (1998) ▪ 5,500t ▪ 55% red 35% white 10% rosé ▪ ISO 22000, Fairtrade, IPW, WIETA ▪ PO Box 465 Stellenbosch 7599 ▪ info@stellvine.co.za ▪ www.stellenboschvineyards.co.za ▪ S 33° 59' 26.06" E 018° 46' 2.21" ▪ F +27 (0)21-881-3102 ▪ **T +27 (0)21-881-3870**

Stellendrift – SHZ Cilliers/Kuün Wyne   (🏆)

Wine's in Stellenbosch-based Fanie Cilliers' blood – his forebears were French vignerons before they fled to the Cape in 1700; by 1709 they had 8,000 vines under cultivation. His portfolio includes wines made by himself as well as joint-venture bottlings with other cellars. Regular ranges include Stellendrift, Cilliers Cellars or De Oude Opstal, none ready for review. 'Good sales are being maintained,' Fanie reports.

Location/map: Stellenbosch ▪ Map grid reference: C7 ▪ Est 1995 ▪ 1stB 1996 ▪ Tasting, sales & cellar tours by appt ▪ Owner(s) Fanie Cilliers (SHZ Cilliers/Kuün Wines) ▪ Winemaker(s)/viticulturist(s) Fanie Cilliers (Nov 1995) ▪ 2,200cs own label 90% red 10% white ▪ PO Box 6340 Uniedal 7612 ▪ fcilliers@ vodamail.co.za ▪ www.stellendrift.co.za ▪ S 33° 58' 54.92" E 018° 46' 15.91" ▪ F +27 (0)21-887-6561 ▪ **T +27 (0)21-887-6561/+27 (0)82-372-5180**

Stellenrust   (🏆) (🍴) (🛒) (📷)

This large family estate has some 200 hectares under vines in Stellenbosch, divided pretty equally between holdings on the Bottelary Hills and at the home farm in the 'Golden Triangle'. Winemaking, functions and tastings happen in the multi-pillared headquarters at the latter. Some of the vineyards are fairly venerable – including a cinsaut block featuring in a varietal bottling (and in a blend to come), which testifies to the alertness to current trends of the team of winemaker Tertius Boshoff and viticulturist Kobie van der Westhuizen. Underlining this, Tertius remarks that 'the focus in the cellar is increasingly on getting the naked grape into the bottle'.

Super Premium range

★★★★☆ **Cabernet Franc 12** characteristic dried-leaf fragrance mingling with ripe berries & tobacco, cedarwood notes. Supple, light-feeling & fresh (though over 14% alcohol), with dry grape tannins, it is elegant & understated — even a touch aloof. Will reward the patient. Good value, like many here.

★★★★ **Old Bushvine Cinsaut** Charming aromas on **13** — not as floral & red-fruited as some less-ripe examples, but more depth. Unobviously serious, & should develop, though lovely now.

★★★★ **Peppergrinder's Shiraz** Spicy nutmeg & floral perfume on **12**. Seriously built, & with a light touch to the slight fleshiness, sweet fruit & dry but succulent tannins. Leave 5+ years.

★★★★☆ **Timeless 12** the usual blend of cab with merlot & cab franc. Herbal touch to the aromatics leads to thoroughly well balanced palate: full fruit flavour alongside savoury, spice element. Ripe & rich, yet with freshness & real finesse. Give it many years.

★★★★ **JJ Handmade Picalót** Tasty **12** blend pinotage (56%) with cab, merlot. Cedary oak & perfume, red/black fruit juiciness. No great depth, but not trivial though approachable. Well oaked, like all.

★★★★ **Barrel Fermented Chardonnay** ⓥ Butterscotch & toast on **13**, then citrus & stonefruit on generous palate, mouthwatering acidity focusing the flavours; green-lime finish. Judicious oaking.

★★★★☆ **49 Barrel Fermented Chenin Blanc** ⓥ Changing number gives vine age. Natural ferment & time in oak (some new) on **13**. Botrytised portion adds sweet honeyed note, but lemony acid vitalises the lusciousness. Glamorous, elegant & complex. The long finish also noted on **12** (★★★★★).

Not tasted: **Cornerstone Pinotage, Chenin d'Muscat Noble Late Harvest**.

Premium range

Chardonnay ⓥ ★★★☆ Mild but interesting aromas on lightly oaked **15**, with stonefruit & citrus — though almond is dominant on the finish. Creamy texture, good acid. Should get even better over a few years. **Chenin Blanc** ⓥ ★★★☆ **15** most appealing & fresh, offering apple & pear & dusty thatch notes. Gently rich, flavourful & succulent with a firm underpinning of ripe acidity. Minimally oaked. **Sauvignon Blanc** ⓥ ★★★★ Beautifully forward, brightly tropical **15**. Full flavours, lively, & with lingering sweet fruit on a firm dry base. Also in 375 ml.

Not retasted: **Pinotage 13** ★★★★ **Simplicity 13** ★★★ Not tasted: **Cabernet Sauvignon, Merlot, Shiraz**.

Kleine Rust range

Chenin Blanc-Sauvignon Blanc ★★☆ Fruity, extrovert **15** packed with flavour. Some sweetness, but stiffened by balanced acidity. Also in 375 ml. Also tasted: **Pinotage Rosé 15** ★★☆ **Semi-Sweet 15** ★★★ Not retasted: **Pinotage-Shiraz 13** ★★★ — TJ

Location/map/WO: Stellenbosch ▪ Map grid reference: E7, C3 ▪ Est/1stB 1928 ▪ Tasting & sales (Hberg & Btlry) Mon-Fri 10–5 Sat 10-3 ▪ Closed Ash Wed, Easter Fri-Mon, Ascension Day, Dec 25/26 & Jan 1 ▪ Cellar tours by appt ▪ Farm-style platters & pre-arranged lunches/dinners ▪ BYO picnic ▪ Tour groups ▪ Grape 'stompings' ▪ Gifts ▪ Conferences ▪ Weddings/functions (300+ pax) ▪ Walking/hiking & MTB trails ▪ Art exhibition ▪ Owner(s) Stellenrust Family Trust ▪ Cellarmaster(s) Tertius Boshoff (Jan 2004) ▪ Winemaker(s) Herman du Preez (2014) & Nelius Swart (2013) ▪ Viticulturist(s) Kobie van der Westhuizen (Jan 2000) ▪ 200ha (cabs s/f, cinsaut, merlot, ptage, shiraz, chard, chenin, muscat d'A, sauv) ▪ 2,000t/300,000cs own label 50% red 40% white 10% rosé + 40,000cs for clients ▪ Other export brands: Pillar & Post, STELL, Steynsrust, Xaro ▪ Brands for clients: Embrace, Lion's Pride, Ruyter's Bin, Sabi Sabi private game lodge ▪ Fairtrade, HACCP ▪ PO Box 26 Koelenhof 7605 ▪ info@stellenrust.co.za ▪ www.stellenrust.co.za ▪ S 33° 59' 18.0" E 018° 50' 57.9" (Helderberg) S 33° 51' 44.41" E 018° 46' 34.11" (Bottelary) ▪ F +27 (0)21-880-2284 ▪ **T +27 (0)21-880-2283**

Stellenview Premium Wines ⓥ (NEW)

Entrepreneurial winemaker Reino Kruger has established this new company, based at Devon View Winery in Stellenbosch's Devon Valley. 'The vision,' Reino says, 'is to establish new brands in premium and super-premium categories over the next five years. The 450-ton cellar is ideally suited for this.'

Location/map: Stellenbosch ▪ Map grid reference: D4 ▪ Est/1stB 2015 ▪ Tasting, sales & cellar tours Mon-Fri 8-5 Sat/Sun by appt ▪ Closed all pub hols ▪ Owner(s) Reino Kruger ▪ Cellarmaster(s) Reino Kruger (Apr 2015) ▪ 12ha (cabs s/f, merlot, p verdot) ▪ 450t/50,000cs own label 90% red 10% white ▪ Export brands: Cape Star, Kruger Family Reserve, Stellenview Reserve, Sunkloof, The Great Five Collection, The Great Five Reserve ▪ PO Box 3220 Somerset West 7129 ▪ info@stellenviewwines.com ▪ www.stellenviewwines.com ▪ S 33° 54' 0.61" E 018° 48' 23.49" ▪ F +27 (0)86-240-7394 ▪ **T +27 (0)21-852-4711**

Stellenzicht Vineyards   (♀)(⌂)(◎)

Lusan-owned Stellenzicht takes its name from the remarkable vista from its location on the northern slopes of the Helderberg towards Stellenbosch town. More views – of the cellar interior and the mountain spires – have been created by updates of the tasting venue, now with a spacious al fresco deck area. Newly planted is a block of material propagated from a single vine in the Plum Pudding Hill vineyard, renowned for producing the Syrah that topped Penfolds Grange in the 1995 SAA Shield taste-off.

Stellenzicht Specialities

★★★★ Plum Pudding Hill Syrah 09 reminiscent of woodland mushrooms, dark spice & tobacco lifted by sweet oak (100% new). Supple entry but finishes briskly dry. Ready to uncork & enjoy. No **08**.

Rhapsody ★★★ 09, retasted, equal parts shiraz & pinotage displaying evolved tones of sweet plum jam. Bracing, short tail.

Golden Triangle range

Pinotage ★★★ 13 bold & boldly oaked, sweet coconut notes currently suppress ripe mulberry fruit flavours though lacks complementary texture of **12** (★★★★). May benefit from short-term ageing. **Shiraz ★★★ 12** brightly spiced from both oak & fruit; dark berry notes too. Full-bodied & still edgily fresh. Should benefit from year/2 settling. Mix French, American, Hungarian oak, 34% new. Also in 1.5/3/5L. Also tasted: **Cabernet Sauvignon 12 ★★★☆ Sauvignon Blanc 15 ★★** — AL

Location/map/WO: Stellenbosch ▪ Map grid reference: F8 ▪ Est 1982 ▪ 1stB 1989 ▪ Tasting & sales Mon-Fri 9–5 Sat/Sun 10–4 ▪ Fee R25 ▪ Closed Good Fri & Dec 25 ▪ Cellar tours by appt ▪ BYO picnic ▪ Summer music concerts ▪ Owner(s) Lusan Premium Wines ▪ Winemaker(s) Guy Webber (Oct 1998), with Nataleé Botha (Aug 2010) ▪ Viticulturist(s) Quintus van Wyk ▪ 228ha/99ha (cabs s/f, malbec, merlot, p verdot, ptage, shiraz, chard, sauv, sem, viog) ▪ 1,000t/40,000cs own label 85% red 15% white ▪ BRC, HACCP, WIETA ▪ PO Box 104 Stellenbosch 7599 ▪ info@stellenzicht.co.za ▪ www.stellenzicht.co.za ▪ S 33° 59' 50.0" E 018° 51' 59.8" ▪ F +27 (0)21-880-1107 ▪ **T +27 (0)21-880-1103**

Sterhuis   (♀)(◎)(⁂)(♿)

The name 'Star House', early Cape colonists' nickname for the original Bottelary Hills farmhouse topped by a rising Venus, now describes the vertiginous vineyards established by lawyer André Kruger for elegant, understated wines made by supercharged son Johan. A special 2014 vintage 'gifted' them their first Reserve Chardonnay from block C4, 'explosive stuff' slated for release this year. And botrytis on some 2015 viognier provided his first 'sticky', whose 200 g/l sugar 'I hope will fit into the bottle!'

★★★★☆ Merlot Accomplished **10** different league to more austere **09** (★★★★); exudes minty freshness & bright red-berry fruit in a lithe & balanced body that renders the alcohol unobtrusive. Elegant, with a good core of clean berry flavours & supportive oak.

★★★★★ Chardonnay Barrel Selection 13 shows hallmark refined quality & complexity, from low-yield (4t) fruit, naturally vinified. 100% oaked (40% new wood) but well integrated. Perhaps not as expressive in youth as **12**, but all elements in harmony; fine & ageworthy, with a long limy farewell.

★★★★ Chenin Blanc Barrel Selection 14 (★★★★★) older vines (15-45 years) yield rich glacé pineapple, apple & almond flavours, enhanced by natural fermentation & old oak. Beautifully balanced & fresh, more self-assured in youth than **13**, already showing polished opulence.

★★★★ Sauvignon Blanc Vivacious expression of the variety. **15** rich melange of stonefruit focused by racy acidity; balanced & fresh, with creamy substrate courtesy 4 months on lees. WO Stellenbosch.

★★★★☆ **Astra White** ⓦ A third each of best barrels chenin, sauvignon & chardonnay. Oak spice & white chocolate lead to toasty, sweet-fruited & vanilla-rich **09**. Bold in flavour & aroma with loads of oak tones needing to meld. Palate cleansed by tart orange peel & fresh lemon/lime zing.

★★★★ **Blanc de Blancs Méthode Cap Classique 11** sparkling from chardonnay is refined, long & creamy, with similar citrus & honey flavours to **10**. Extra-dry but ample richness & texture from old-oak-fermented base wine, 36 months on lees & year bottle maturation.

Also tasted: **Chenin Blanc 14 ★★★☆** Not retasted: **Elgin Pinot Noir 13 ★★★★ Merlot-Cabernet Sauvignon 12 ★★★★** Not tasted: **Unwooded Chardonnay**. Discontinued: **Cabernet Sauvignon**. — MW

Location/map: Stellenbosch ▪ Map grid reference: C4 ▪ WO: Bottelary/Stellenbosch/Elgin ▪ Est 1980 ▪ 1stB 2002 ▪ Tasting, sales & cellar tours by appt ▪ Closed Christian hols ▪ Facilities for children ▪ Conservation area ▪ Owner(s) Kruger family ▪ Winemaker(s) Johan Kruger ▪ 100ha/40ha under vine ▪ 300t/12,000cs own label 25% red 75% white ▪ PO Box 131 Koelenhof 7605 ▪ johan@sterhuis.co.za ▪ www.sterhuis.co.za ▪ S 33° 54' 43.1" E 018° 46' 4.2" ▪ F +27 (0)21-906-1195 ▪ **T +27 (0)83-411-0757**

Stettyn Cellar ⓠ ⓐ ⓞ ⓑ ⓖ

A handful of grape-growing Klein Drakenstein foothill farms – including 18th-century Stettyn, home to eight generations of the Botha family – feed this cellar, given multi-million rand upgrades in recent years after becoming a supplier to, among others, FirstCape, South African 'superbrand' in the UK, and exporting to Germany and China.

Stettyn range

Reserve Shiraz-Cabernet Sauvignon ⓦ **★★★★** More serious styling than other ranges, **11** enticing bacon, smoke & pepper from shiraz (65%), cab's leafy notes; restrained oak detail from 22 months older barrels. Not retasted: **Reserve Straw Wine NV ★★★☆ Reserve Cape Vintage 08 ★★★**

Griffin range

Cabernet Sauvignon ★★★ Oak-spiced blackcurrants & cherries, **13**'s fruitiness giving the smoothly rounded body added appeal, length. **Chardonnay** ⓝⓔⓦ **★★★** Equal French/Hungarian oak gives sweet spice overlay to **15**'s tropical fruit, ending gently savoury. **Sauvignon Blanc ★★★** Dab oak, still rare for sauvignon in SA, adds interest to **15**'s green fig & sage character. Also tasted: **Merlot 14 ★★★** Not retasted: **Shiraz 13 ★★★ Pinot Grigio 13 ★★★**

Stone range

Red ⓥ **★★★ 14**'s smoky fruit flavours & light-textured appeal all thanks to its shiraz, petit verdot & merlot blend combo. Also tasted: **White 14 ★★★** — CR

Location: Villiersdorp ▪ Map: Worcester ▪ WO: Western Cape/Worcester ▪ Est 1964 ▪ 1stB 1984 ▪ Tasting & sales Mon-Thu 9–5 Fri 9-4.30 Sat (Oct-Mar) 10-1 ▪ Closed all pub hols ▪ Cellar tours from 1.30-4 by appt ▪ BYO picnic ▪ Facilities for children ▪ Vineyard tours R200pp ▪ Owner(s) 4 major producers (3 family owned) ▪ Cellarmaster(s) Albie Treurnicht (Nov 2000) ▪ Winemaker(s) Albie Treurnicht (Nov 2000), with JM Crafford (Nov 2012) ▪ Viticulturist(s) Pierre Snyman (Vinpro) ▪ 400ha (cab, merlot, ptage, shiraz, chard, chenin, sauv) ▪ 7,500t/19,000cs own label 25% red 75% white + 6.1m L bulk ▪ Brands for clients: FirstCape, Felicité, The Griffin Range ▪ ARA, BEE, HACCP, IPW, WIETA ▪ PO Box 1520 Worcester 6849 ▪ info@stettyncellar.co.za ▪ www.stettyncellar.co.za ▪ S 33° 52' 14.8" E 019° 22' 2.3" ▪ F +27 (0)86-771-3568 ▪ **T +27 (0)23-340-4220**

☐ **Steynsrust** *see* Stellenrust
☐ **Steytler** *see* Kaapzicht Wine Estate
☐ **Stilfontein** *see* Eerste Hoop Wine Cellar

Stoep ⓠ

Owned by SA asset manager Gerrit Mars and two Swiss partners, this garagiste label formerly part of Paarl Main Street Winery's portfolio is now intermittently vinified and bottled by André Liebenberg at his Helderberg winery Romond.

Red ★★★ Cab-led with cab franc & merlot, **09** shows the fruit expression of a good vintage, but despite an elegant palate, the firm tannin base (30 months oaking) requires further maturation, or matching with rich food. — CR, CvZ

Location/WO: Stellenbosch ▪ Est/1stB 2001 ▪ Tasting, sales & tours by appt ▪ Owner(s) Zelpy 1023 (Pty) Ltd: 3 shareholders Gerrit Mars (SA), Sven Haefner (Swiss) & Daniel Hofer (Swiss) ▪ Cellarmaster(s)/winemaker(s) André Liebenberg (Romond) & Gerrit Mars ▪ 50% red 50% white ▪ gerritmars@mweb.co.za ▪ **T +27 (0)82-352-5583**

Stofberg Family Vineyards ⓠ

On a large grape-farm in Breedekloof is this boutique winery, using just a fraction of the chenin blanc growing all around. Winemaker Mariëtte Coetzee was born a Stofberg and makes her wines in the family farm's old distillery. The wines are named after daugher Mia, 'to symbolise new and small beginnings that will grow year by year'.

★★★★ Mia Shiraz Big, burly **13** (★★★★) has ripe fruit aromas & flavours well counterpointed by smoky tobacco oak influence. Seriously structured, with a pleasingly dry finish despite a few grams of sugar & a big 14.6% alc. Touch less polished than **12**. WO W Cape.

Mia Chenin Blanc ★★★ Gently, ripely fruity aromas on soft & easygoing **15**, with some rather unintegrated acidity for backbone. — TJ

Location: Rawsonville ▪ Map: Breedekloof ▪ WO: Western Cape/Breedekloof ▪ Est 2011 ▪ 1stB 2012 ▪ Tasting, sales & cellar tours Mon-Fri 7.30-5.30 Sat/Sun by appt only ▪ Closed all pub hols ▪ Owner(s) PJD Stofberg, M Coetzee & GJN Coetzee ▪ Cellarmaster(s)/winemaker(s) Mariëtte Coetzee (Nov 2011) ▪ Viticulturist(s) Pieter Jacobus Daniël Stofberg (Jan 1981), Andries de Wet (Jun 2002, consultant) & Gideon Jacobus Nicolaas Coetzee (Nov 2011) ▪ ±102ha (chenin) ▪ 11t/1,205cs own label 8% red 51% white 41% MCC ▪ PO Box 298 Rawsonville 6845 ▪ mariette@stofbergfamilyvineyards.co.za ▪ www.stofbergfamilyvineyards.co.za ▪ S 33° 40' 17.24" E 019° 18' 37.27" ▪ F +27 (0)86-770-5138 ▪ **T +27 (0)82-867-6958**

☐ **Stonedale** *see* Rietvallei Wine Estate
☐ **Stonehaven** *see* Cape Point Vineyards

Stonehill

Tucked away in Stellenbosch's Devon Valley is Lorna Hughes' small vineyard, where, with husband Dave (an adviser to this guide), she indulges her passions for wine, rescue dogs and hiking. Lorna tends the vines and Mark Carmichael-Green makes the wines to spec in boutique volumes.

Bristle Red ★★★ Modestly oaked **09** cab/shiraz with red & black fruit & a little spice; soft, easy tannins for drinkability. Nicely ready. **Bristle White** ⓠ **★★★★** Generous, appealing oaked viognier, **11**'s peach tones prevail over lees creaminess & oak spices. Discontinued: **Dry Cabernet Sauvignon Rosé.** — TJ

Location/WO: Stellenbosch ▪ Est 1990 ▪ 1stB 2003 ▪ Closed to public ▪ Owner(s)/vineyard manager(s) Lorna Hughes ▪ Winemaker(s) Mark Carmichael-Green ▪ 4ha/3.2ha (cab, shiraz) ▪ 70% red 30% white ▪ PO Box 612 Stellenbosch 7599 ▪ lhughes@telkomsa.net ▪ F +27 (0)21-865-2740 ▪ **T +27 (0)73-420-3300**

Stone Ridge Wines ⓠ

The Eksteen family have been growing wine grapes on their 300-ha Voor Paardeberg property for 6 generations. Viticulturist Jan Eksteen keeps back parcels of prime red and white grapes to craft just 2,400 cases for the family label with advisers Bernard Smuts and JD Rossouw. None reviewed this edition.

Location: Paarl ▪ Map: Paarl & Wellington ▪ Map grid reference: D1 ▪ Est 2002 ▪ 1stB 2003 ▪ Tasting by appt only ▪ Winemaker(s) Bernard Smuts & JD Rossouw (both consultants) ▪ Viticulturist(s) Jan Eksteen (2002) ▪ 300ha (cab, ptage, shiraz, chard, chenin, sauv) ▪ 20t/2,400cs own label 50% red 50% white ▪ PO Box 7046 Northern Paarl 7623 ▪ stoneridge@uitkijk.co.za ▪ S 33° 34' 19.72" E 018° 52' 45.48" ▪ F +27 (0)21-869-8071 ▪ **T +27 (0)82-324-8372**

☐ **Stone Road** *see* Louisvale Wines
☐ **Stones in the Sun** *see* Dunstone Winery

Stonewall Wines

The handsome white-gabled cellar on this substantial Helderberg estate is not far short of 200 years old, and here, appropriately, owner-winegrower De Waal Koch makes his boutique-size range of wines (other grapes from the farm are sold off) in a classically modest style. To join them ('we are very excited about it!') is a maiden MCC bubbly from chardonnay.

★★★★ **Rubér** As usual, appropriately oaked merlot, cab franc & cab is more complex & impressive than the Cab, but with same drinkability, restraint & elegance. **13** should keep & improve good few years.

Cabernet Sauvignon ★★★★ In house's typical honest, unshowy style, **13**, with its pleasing herbal note, neatly balances fruit & gently firm structure. Not retasted: **Chardonnay 13** ★★★★ Not tasted: **Valle Felice**. — TJ

Location: Stellenbosch ▪ Map: Helderberg ▪ WO: Stellenbosch/Western Cape ▪ Est 1828 ▪ 1stB 1997 ▪ Tasting & sales by appt Mon-Fri 10–5 Sat 10–1 ▪ Closed Easter Fri-Sun, Dec 25/26 & Jan 1 ▪ Refreshments by appt ▪ Helderberg Wine Festival ▪ Owner(s) De Waal Koch ▪ Cellarmaster(s) Ronell Wiid (Jan 2000, consultant) ▪ Winemaker(s) De Waal Koch (Jan 2000) ▪ Viticulturist(s) De Waal Koch (Jun 1984) ▪ 90ha/70ha (cabs s/f, merlot, ptage, shiraz, chard, pinot gris, sauv) ▪ 300t/4,000cs own label 80% red 20% white ▪ PO Box 5145 Helderberg 7135 ▪ stonewall@mweb.co.za ▪ S 34° 1' 59.0" E 018° 49' 14.6" ▪ F +27 (0)21-855-2206 ▪ **T +27 (0)21-855-3675**

StoneyCroft

Home to the Stone family since 2000, this tiny property in Devon Valley produces quality shiraz, so much is expected from the young cabernet vines. Wines are made for businessman John Stone and his two daughters' own label by the Steytlers of nearby Kaapzicht.

★★★★ **Shiraz** ⓢ **09** (★★★★) sweet vanilla bouquet & plump berry palate well controlled by sappy grip & bitter-choc tail; ±15% alcohol perhaps just a little less balanced than **08** & previous. — CvZ

Location/map/WO: Stellenbosch ▪ Map grid reference: D3 ▪ Est 2000 ▪ 1stB 2001 ▪ Tasting by appt ▪ Owner(s) John Stone ▪ Winemaker(s) Danie Steytler (2001), with Danie Steytler jnr (both Kaapzicht) ▪ Viticulturist(s) Gary Probert (Jan 2010, consultant) ▪ 4ha/3.5ha (cab, shiraz) ▪ 20t/3,000cs own label 100% red ▪ PO Box 239 Koelenhof 7605 ▪ john@stoneycroft.co.za ▪ www.stoneycroft.co.za ▪ S 33° 53' 24.41" E 018° 48' 19.78" ▪ F +27 (0)21-865-2360 ▪ **T +27 (0)21-865-2301/+27 (0)82-801-1804**

Stony Brook

This well-established family winery in Franschhoek, founded by Nigel and Joy McNaught a few decades back, not long ago underlined both family and continuity when son Craig moved into the chief winemaker position. The vineyards are not very extensive, but include a wide range of varieties. Testifying to the dynamism here, more tempranillo, cabernet and petit verdot have recently been planted, and a new cellar was built 'just in time' for harvest 2015.

★★★★★ **Ghost Gum** Commanding **11** single vineyard cabernet (with splash merlot) spent 32 months in all-new oak, which is well assimilated & further structures the ripe, dense & deliciously compact blackcurrant fruit. Broachable now, with food, but will reward cellaring.

★★★★☆ **Syrah Reserve 12** back on track after **11**'s (★★★★) slight dip. Opaque & youthful, big & bold – not for the faint-hearted. Vibrant mulberry fruit & roasted spices checked by seamless tannins (no new oak this vintage), finishing with a lightly warm glow.

★★★★☆ **Ovidius** (NEW) Maiden tempranillo **13** is beautifully perfumed, with densely plush fruit. Fine acidity & tannins from half-new oak (26 months) structure & balance ripe, velvet richness. Deserves time to reveal its full charms.

★★★★ **The Max** Classic, harmonious **12** blend all 5 Bordeaux varieties (cab-led) is gorgeously aromatic with seamlessly integrated oak plushness checking succulent dark berry fruit. No **11**.

★★★★ **SMV** Distinctive floral & spice appeal in appealingly juicy **12** shiraz-led blend, with mourvèdre & tiny dollop viognier. Softly round, sweet red fruit flavours given a spicy boost.

★★★★ **Sauvignon Blanc** Strikingly aromatic, pithy textured **14** equal blend Franschhoek & zippy, mineral Elgin fruit, portion fermented in barrel with lees contact imparting breadth & complexity.

★★★★ **Ghost Gum White** Switch from sauvignon blend to chardonnay & semillon, playing to area's strengths. Regal barrel-fermented **14** structured throughout by lovely acidity & persistent, textured citrus.

★★★★ **Lyle** Seriously fabulous **09** MCC sparkling, blend own chardonnay & Stellenbosch pinot noir. Brioche complexity & textural breadth from 60 months on lees & oak-fermented portion.

★★★★ **V on A** Unctuously sweet (328 g/l sugar) & pretty **12** barrel-fermented, dessert-style viognier. Low 7% alcohol appeals, touch more acidity would be welcome. Could enjoy on its own as a dessert.

Also tasted: **The 'J' 14** ★★★★ Not retasted: **Pinot Noir 09** ★★★★ **Shiraz 12** ★★★★ Occasional release: **Camissa**, **Snow Gum**, **Rosé**. — IM

Location/map: Franschhoek • WO: Franschhoek/Coastal/Western Cape • Est 1995 • 1stB 1996 • Tasting by appt • Fee R50 • Sales Mon-Fri 10—5 Sat 10-1; enquire about pub hols • Self-catering cottages • Owner(s) Nigel & Joy McNaught • Winemaker(s) Craig McNaught (2011), with Michael Blaauw (Jan 2008) • Viticulturist(s) Paul Wallace (consultant) • 23ha/14ha (cab, malbec, merlot, mourv, p verdot, pinot, shiraz, tempranillo, chard, sem, viog) • 100t/6,500cs own label 65% red 35% white • ISO 14001:2003 • PO Box 22 Franschhoek 7690 • info@stonybrook.co.za • www.stonybrook.co.za • S 33° 56' 28.7" E 019° 7' 4.1" • F +27 (0)86-664-2794 • **T +27 (0)21-876-2182**

Stormborn Wines ⓃⒺⓌ

Believing that too many uninteresting wines are made from interesting vineyards, Konrad Raubenheimer is working (latterly in Swartland's Antebellum cellar, alongside other small-scale vintners renting space) to change that. He rationalised — correctly — that if he could find a few remarkable blocks and make wines he wanted to drink, others would want to, too. His current releases are 2014s from Swartland, grenache noir Die Stilte and skin-macerated chenin Firstborn; in the wings are a 2014 Swartland syrah/shiraz; and 2015 pinot noir and riesling (both Elgin) and Bordeaux blend (Stellenbosch).

Location: Riebeek-Kasteel • konrad@stormborn.co.za • www.stormborn.co.za

Storm Wines Ⓠ

Production has much more than doubled for this Hemel-en-Aarde area-based pinot noir specialist, from its (admittedly tiny) 2012 beginnings — unsurprisingly, given the local and foreign acclaim for Hannes Storm's wines, expanding the reputation gained from his lengthy winemaking stint at Hamilton Russell. 'Site-specific wines with personality and character' is Hannes's motto, and a third pinot was due for its maiden harvest in 2016 off his own steep, stony vineyard in the Valley. Further possible expansion: experimenting on a small scale with chardonnay.

Storm range

★★★★☆ **Moya's Pinot Noir** Tiny Upper Hemel-en-Aarde Valley single-vineyard, tiny 2.1 t/ha yield. Medley of berries, violets in sophisticated, restrained **13**; perfectly balanced with persistent peacock-tail finish. Like older-barrel-matured **12**, silky smooth, 20% new oak fully integrated.

★★★★ **Vrede Pinot Noir** Different site (Hemel-en-Aarde Valley single-vineyard), 30% new oak, make **13** (★★★★☆) sturdier than Moya but equally fine, complex. Meaty, peppery red fruit aromas, flavours. Characterful, with enlivening acidity & minerality, similar admirable focus to streamlined **12**. — JPf

Location: Hermanus • WO: Upper Hemel-en-Aarde Valley/Hemel-en-Aarde Valley • Est 2011 • 1stB 2012 • Tasting by appt • Closed Easter Fri/Sun, Ascension day, Dec 25/26 & Jan 1 • Owner(s) Hannes Storm • Winemaker(s)/viticulturist(s) Hannes Storm (Dec 2011) • 3ha (pinot) • 9t/1,400cs own label 100% red • BWI, IPW • PO Box 431 Hermanus 7200 • hannes@stormwines.co.za • www.stormwines.co.za • **T +27 (0)82-325-4517**

Stoumann's Wines ⓠ ⓟ ⓐ

Facilities are being upgraded at the winery of conservation-minded Napoleon 'Nappies' Stoumann and wife Annalise to create easier visitor access and a coffee shop. Though unready for review, red wines have been bottled (and labelled with their endangered Cape Geometric Tortoise logo) and are available for tasting/sale from the cellardoor near Vredendal.

Location: Vredendal ▪ Map: Olifants River ▪ Est 1998 ▪ 1stB 2008 ▪ Tasting, sales & cellar tours Mon-Fri 8-5 Sat by appt ▪ Closed all pub hols ▪ Cheese platters/meals/braai available on request ▪ Tour groups ▪ Farm produce ▪ Conferences ▪ Owner(s)/cellarmaster(s)/winemaker(s) Napoleon Stoumann ▪ Viticulturist(s) CG Stoumann (Jan 2010) ▪ 100ha (cab, merlot, muscadel r/w, ptage, ruby cab, shiraz, chard, chenin, cbard, hanepoot) ▪ 1,040t/4,000cs own label 50% red 40% white 10% rosé + 800,000L bulk ▪ IPW ▪ PO Box 307 Vredendal 8160 ▪ stoumanns@cybersmart.co.za ▪ www.stoumanns.co.za ▪ S 31° 41' 20.5" E 018° 30' 23.3" ▪ F +27 (0)27-213-1448 ▪ **T +27 (0)27-213-2323/+27 (0)83-236-2794**

Strandveld Wines ⓠ ⓒ ⓐ ⓐ

This is a viticultural collaboration between private investors and Elim's Albertyn family, primarily sheep and wheat farmers within the Nuwejaars Wetland Special Management Area. The winery is named for the endangered Cape coastal vegetation fringing the vineyards, Africa's most southerly. The wine labels reflect the colourful maritime and natural history of the area, and the two ranges, with some occasional releases, currently include a follow-up to the Anders Sparrman Pinot Noir which debuted with the '09.

Strandveld range

★★★★ Anders Sparrman Pinot Noir Herbaceous & piquant red fruit & savoury, earthy tone to youthful **14**. Tight, brooding, fruit just emerging from 11 months in oak, 42% new. Shows serious intent but unyielding in youth, more so than last **09**; give plenty of time.

★★★★ Pinot Noir Perfumed white pepper & red fruits on fine **12**. More 'feminine' than Sparrman, new oak (42%) in harmony; lithe tannins enhanced by 42 months bottle ageing. Less restrained than **11**, same intensity & potential to develop.

★★★★☆ Syrah With 15 % viognier, **12** raises the bar on **11** (**★★★★**). Dense, richly textured layers of flavour, pepper, plums & polished leather. Youthful, but showing innate balance & complexity, enhanced by deft oaking. Will age with distinction. Also in magnum.

★★★★☆ The Navigator ⓠ Shiraz & grenache (59/25) blend with mourvèdre & viognier, honouring Henry the Navigator. Fruit tightly woven into firm, muscular structure from cooler **12** vintage. A treasure chest for the future, currently best decanted. WO Cape South Coast.

★★★★ Sauvignon Blanc Pofadderbos From the 'Puff Adder Bush' single-vineyard. **14** lovely minerality & some tropical hints; less stern than **13** still taut & racy; quiet intensity, one for the table.

★★★★☆ Adamastor **13** sauvignon & semillon (52/48), latter oaked providing creamy underpin for stonefruit, scented lime & greengage. Vivacious fruit/acid balance, delicate scented nuance mid-palate & finish. Elegant table & cellar mate.

First Sighting range

Shiraz-Grenache Rosé ★★★ Now bottled, **14** sunset-hued savoury sipper with tangy cranberry tone, light crisp & dry al fresco partner. WO Cape South Coast. **Sauvignon Blanc ★★★★** Distinct stony minerality to **14** with 12% semillon, which adds a waxy texture; well-behaved, almost smooth-textured summer seafood wine. Also tasted: **Pinot Noir 13 ★★★ Shiraz 13 ★★★★** — MW

Location: Elim ▪ Map: Southern Cape ▪ WO: Elim/Cape South Coast ▪ Est 2002 ▪ 1stB 2003 ▪ Tasting, sales & cellar tours Mon-Thu 8–5 Fri 8-4 Sat 10-3 ▪ Closed Good Fri & Dec 25 ▪ Farm produce ▪ BYO picnic ▪ Walks/hikes ▪ Mountain biking ▪ Conservation area ▪ Two self-catering cottages ▪ Owner(s) Strandveld Vineyards & Rietfontein Trust ▪ Winemaker(s) Conrad Vlok (Dec 2004), with Donovan Ackermann (Aug 2012) ▪ Viticulturist(s) Tienie Wentzel (Oct 2009) ▪ 66ha (pinot, shiraz, sauv, sem) ▪ 246t/28,000cs own label 43% red 57% white ▪ BWI, IPW ▪ PO Box 1020 Bredasdorp 7280 ▪ info@strandveld.co.za ▪ www.strandveld.co.za ▪ S 34° 39' 59.2" E 019° 47' 26.8" ▪ F +27 (0)28-482-1902/6 ▪ **T +27 (0)28-482-1902/6**

☐ **String of Pearls** see Francois La Garde

Strydom Vintners

This is an own label by leading husband-and-wife winemakers Louis and Rianie Strydom, both CWG members and involved independently with 5 star-lauded Helderberg properties Ernie Els and Haskell/Dombeya respectively. Since 2012, the Strydom wines have been made from mostly their own small Simonsberg farm's fruit, Rianie being especially pleased about the first prestige CWG auction wine ('12) from own grapes (last year's auction debut was from Napier). On shale and deep red clay, the Strydom vines allow for a somewhat drier, more restrained style compared with Helderberg's sweet-fruited opulence. In Strydom hands, both terroirs are expressed with great flair.

★★★★☆ Cabernet Sauvignon ⓔ **12** has all hallmarks of quality cab from warmer part of Stellenbosch: generously structured, with muscle, grip & rich, dark fruit filling. Appealing freshness & complementary oak (20%). Cellaring will deliver more pleasures.

★★★★ Syrah ⓔ **12** bit forbidding at present with its dark spice richness & full body, though nicely structured with fine, supple tannins, careful oaking (20% new) to benefit from cellaring.

★★★★☆ CWG Auction Reserve Paradigm (ⓝⓔⓦ) Classic Bordeaux blend from excellent **12** vintage. Headed by cab's luxurious dark berry scents, commanding grip. Merlot, petit verdot, cab franc & oak (70% new) provide further aromatic, textural dimension; harmonious, precise & lengthy. Deserves cellaring.

★★★★ Retro ⓥ Vintage blend; cab, shiraz & cinsaut in **13**. Older oak only focuses on rich, savoury flavours, delicious juicy grape tannins. Ripe but totally dry. A most superior country-style wine. No **12**.

★★★★ The Freshman ⓥ **15** straight sauvignon blanc, brimming with ripe lemongrass, greengage concentration & balanced vivacity. Immensely likeable, drinkable. Big step up from **14** (★★★). — AL

Location/WO: Stellenbosch ▪ Est 2012 ▪ 1stB 2009 ▪ Closed to public ▪ Owner(s) Louis & Rianie Strydom ▪ Cellarmaster(s) Rianie Strydom ▪ 8.5ha/6.5ha (cab, merlot, shiraz, sauv, sem) ▪ ±30t/1,000cs own label 50% red 50% white ▪ IPW ▪ PO Box 1290 Stellenbosch 7599 ▪ rianie@strydomvineyards.com ▪ **T +27 (0)21-889-8553/+27 (0)82-290-6399**

☐ **Stubborn Man** see Pearl Mountain
☐ **Stumble Vineyards** see Flagstone Winery
☐ **Suikerbosch** see Zidela Wines
☐ **Suikerbossie Ek Wil Jou Hê** see Boer & Brit

Sumaridge Wines ⓟ ⓜ ⓐ ⓞ ⓑ ⓖ

This significant Hemel-en-Aarde producer was a relatively early player, and remains an important one, in the development of the area's reputation this century. Winemaker and director Gavin Patterson last year celebrated a decade here, learning 'the peculiarities of this region' – his concern to express them in his wines is behind names like Epitome and Maritimus. Sustainable farming remains a focus, as does staff welfare (Sumaridge was 'the first producer in the Walker Bay district' to get WIETA ethical accreditation). 'We remain,' says Gavin, 'on our path of holistic sustainability throughout the business, with a view to ensuring the integrity of our site, the land and our people through our wines.'

★★★★ Merlot Perfumed **14** (★★★★☆) handsome red fruit & blackcurrant combo with genteel vanilla & cinnamon, dash mocha. Full bodied, with masterly oaking (35% new, 15 months). Step up on also-tasted **13**, showing more blue fruit, athletic tannins cosseted by generous plum palate. No **12**.

★★★★☆ Pinot Noir ⓔ Elegant yet powerful **12** (★★★★★) shows dark, spicy fruit interwoven with violets. Fruit is energetic, with finely grained tannin, shows a seamless oak integration (30% new). Like **11**, it needs time to open up. Also in 1.5 & 4.5L, next like.

★★★★ Epitome ⓔ Crème de cassis, black pepper & plum notes emerge from densely packed **10** (★★★★★) from pinotage & shiraz (**08** also included merlot). Partly naturally fermented & raised in 50% seamlessly integrated new oak. Concentrated flavours, yet with great lift & vigour, finishing long.

★★★★☆ Chardonnay Alluring **13** (★★★★★) carefully detailed & precise barrel ferment/ageing 10 months, mostly 2nd fill oak. There's yellow stonefruits, kumquats, quince & roasted almonds, a flinty nuance & bright citrus finish. Even more impressive than **12**. Also in magnum.

★★★★ Sauvignon Blanc Classic green & mineral notes interwoven with citrus on elegant **15**; restrained flavours enlivened by zippy acidity.

★★★★ Maritimus ⓐ **12** (★★★★☆) similar interesting blend to **11**, with sauvignon, chardonnay, semillon & drop viognier. Complex, broad yet focused, revealing extended fine lees-ageing & sensitive light oaking. Natural fermentation all round. In magnum too.

Not retasted: **Rosé 14 ★★★★** Not tasted: **The Wayfarer**. — GM

Location: Hermanus ▪ Map: Elgin, Walker Bay & Bot River ▪ WO: Upper Hemel-en-Aarde Valley ▪ Est 1997 ▪ 1stB 2000 ▪ Tasting & sales daily 10–3 ▪ Tasting fee R25, redeemable on purchase ▪ Closed Easter Fri/Sun, Dec 25/26 & Jan 1 ▪ Seasonal tasting platter options plus kiddies platter ▪ Facilities for children ▪ Tour groups ▪ Conferences ▪ Weddings/functions ▪ Luxury self-catering lodge ▪ Conservation area ▪ Extensive nature trails ▪ Mountain biking ▪ Bass & fly fishing by arrangement ▪ Owner(s) Holly & Simon Bellingham-Turner ▪ Winemaker(s) Gavin Patterson (Jun 2005), with Reginald Maphumulo (Jun 2000) & Walter Pretorius (Jul 2013) ▪ 210ha/42ha (cab f, malbec, merlot, ptage, pinot, shiraz, chard, sauv, sem) ▪ 150t/20,000cs own label 45% red 50% white 5% rosé ▪ IPW, WIETA ▪ PO Box 1413 Hermanus 7200 ▪ info@sumaridge.co.za ▪ www.sumaridge.co.za ▪ S 34° 22' 1.6" E 019° 15' 18.6" ▪ F +27 (0)86-623-4248 ▪ **T +27 (0)28-312-1097**

☐ **Sumerton** *see* Zidela Wines

Summerhill Wines ⓠ ⓞ

The craft beer 'revolution' sweeping SA is in full ferment on Charles Hunting and wife Ingrid's estate near Stellenbosch, after Sir Thomas Brewing Co recently transplanted itself here. Brewmaster Marius Malan is also a Cape Wine Master, and he oversees Summerhill's reds, so official permission is being sought to vinify on-site. Meanwhile pre-booked private (wine) tastings in the manor house are a big hit.

Chenin Blanc ⊘ ⓣ **★★★★** Expressive tropical fruit in **15**, the delicious limy acidity perking up the flavours, giving length & appetite appeal.

Not retasted: **Shiraz-Merlot 12 ★★★** — CR

Location/map: Stellenbosch ▪ Map grid reference: E3 ▪ WO: Western Cape ▪ 1stB 2008 ▪ Tasting & sales Mon-Thu 9-4.30 Fri 9-2 ▪ Private tastings in manor house by appt ▪ Closed all pub hols ▪ Amenities: see intro ▪ Owner(s) Summerhill Wines cc, Charles R Hunting ▪ Winemaker(s) Hannes Meyer (whites, Simonsig) & Marius Malan (reds, Malanot Wines) ▪ Viticulturist(s) Paul Wallace (consultant) ▪ 15ha/3.5ha (merlot, shiraz, chenin) ▪ 24t/2,500cs own label 40% red 60% white ▪ PO Box 12448 Die Boord 7613 ▪ charles@summerhillwines.co.za, manager@summerhillwines.co.za ▪ www.summerhillwines.co.za ▪ S 33° 52' 57.71" E 018° 50' 49.39" ▪ F +27 (0)86-621-8047 ▪ **T +27 (0)21-889-5015**

Sumsaré Wines ⓠ ⓗ ⓞ ⓘ

Spell 'Sumsaré' backwards, and you get 'Erasmus', the Robertson family behind the brand. Patriarch Danie had an aha moment back in 2007 to bottle a commemorative wine for the home farm's 200th anniversary. The quixotic idea has since blossomed into a boutique wine and brandy business run by the 7th generation, daughters Francèl, Danielle and Janine, and son Johannes.

Location/map: Robertson ▪ Est 2008 ▪ 1stB 2007 ▪ Tasting, sales & tours by appt Mon-Fri 9–5 Sat 9–1 ▪ Closed Easter Fri-Mon, May 13, Pentecost, Dec 25/26 & Jan 1 ▪ Tour groups ▪ Facilities for children ▪ Farm produce ▪ BYO picnic ▪ Weddings ▪ Owner(s) Francèl Rabie, Johannes Erasmus, Danielle Jackson & Janine Joubert ▪ Winemaker(s) Lourens van der Westhuizen (Arendsig) ▪ Viticulturist(s) Briaan Stipp (Robertson Winery) ▪ 45ha/40ha (cab, ptage, ruby cab, shiraz, chard, chenin, cbard, muscadel w) ▪ 700t/±260cs own label 40% red 60% white ▪ PO Box 402 Robertson 6705 ▪ sumsare.wines@barvallei.co.za ▪ www.sumsarewines.co.za ▪ S 33° 54' 14.66" E 019° 40' 4.75" ▪ F +27 (0)86-505-8590 ▪ **T +27 (0)23-626-2152/+27 (0)82-221-6653**

☐ **Sunkissed** *see* Douglas Green
☐ **Sunkloof** *see* Stellenview Premium Wines
☐ **Sunning Hill** *see* Vinopoly Wines
☐ **Sunshine** *see* Stellar Winery

Super Single Vineyards ⓘ

The name of Daniël de Waal's wine business (based at the old Cannetevallei family farm in Stellenboschkloof) signifies a search for specific vineyard sites – often small ones, usually meaning small volumes. This remains the basis for the Pella range – all with Coastal origins, mostly Stellenbosch; but the Mount Sutherland wines come from Danie's remarkable venture in the Sutherland-Karoo district of the Northern Cape: 'the highest and coldest winegrowing region in Africa,' he says. Vinification is in the DeWaal Wines cellar.

Mount Sutherland Continental Wines

★★★★☆ **Syrah** Alluring & complex **13** true to its extreme high-altitude vineyard: is ripe & packed with flavour but boasts cool blackberry, iron & black pepper notes. Sympathetically aged in older oak; like **12**, will reward the patient.

★★★★☆ **Tempranillo** ⓃⒺⓌ Intensely fruity, well-defined **13** from vines 1,500m above sea level. Reasonably extracted, pure, ripe with fine tannin & well-judged oak; successfully straddles modern & traditional styling to finish dry.

Also tasted: **Riesling 14** ★★★★ Discontinued: **Sauvignon Blanc**.

Pella Coastal Wines

★★★★ **Cabernet Sauvignon** Ⓠ After focused **08** (★★★★★), **09** has noble, dark & earthy Bordeaux overtones with rich ripeness & lovely dry finish. Slightly gawky oak spices should integrate with time.

★★★★ **Merlot** Ⓠ Velvety yet structured **12** with dollop petit verdot; classic ripe berry & choc aromas lead to firm well-oaked palate – tight, but promising development. **11** (★★★★) was simpler.

★★★★ **Thomas Se Dolland Pinotage** From a north-facing, low-yielding site planted in 1960, sleek & nimble **13** aromatic & rich; exudes brambles & clean leather, density lifted by pleasant orange zest acidity & spicy undertones from 18 months older oak.

Also tasted: **Sauvignon Blanc 14** ★★★★ Not retasted: **Malbec 12** ★★★☆ **Petit Verdot 12** ★★★★ Discontinued: **The Vanilla**. — JPf

Location/map: Stellenbosch ▪ Map grid reference: C5 ▪ WO: Stellenbosch/Sutherland-Karoo/Coastal ▪ Est/1stB 2004 ▪ Tasting Mon-Fri 10-5; Sat 10-5 (Sep 1-Apr 30)/by appt (May 1-Aug 31) ▪ Closed all pub hols ▪ Owner(s)/viticulturist(s) Daniël de Waal ▪ Winemaker(s) Daniël de Waal, with Kyle Zulch ▪ 60ha Canettevallei farm ▪ (cab, malbec, nebbiolo, p verdot, pinot, shiraz, tempranillo, riesling, sauv) ▪ 2,000cs own label 80% red 20% white ▪ PO Box 89 Vlottenburg 7604 ▪ marketing@ssvineyards.co.za ▪ www.supersinglevineyards.co.za ▪ S 33° 56′ 29.73″ E 018° 45′ 15.20″ ▪ F +27 (0)21-881-3026 ▪ **T +27 (0)72-200-5552 (Daniël)/+27 (0)82-556-0205 (Kyle)**

Surfing Vintners ⓃⒺⓌ

Annually for the past 16 years, a group of surfing wine people have taken part in the Vintners Surf Classic, entry fee for which is 5L of (their best) red wine. Blended and bottled under the label Big Red, some of the resulting ±100 magnums (1.5L) over the years have been employed for benevolent causes. Now the 25 Surfing Vintners have decided to 'take Big Red commercial' in support of Surf4Life, a charity founded by a fellow surfer, the late Taryn Pratt. Each vintner is donating 50L of wine, allowing 800 magnums (shepherded into bottle at Grangehurst) to be offered for sale in the course of this year.

★★★★ **Big Red** Equal shiraz, cab, pinotage & a dab of grenache in barrel sample **14**. Plush & fruit-filled but true to its name, broad shouldered, with the eventual tannin structure (oaking still in progress, rating tentative) giving musculature for a future. — CR, CvZ

Location: Stellenbosch ▪ WO: Coastal ▪ Est/1stB 2000 ▪ Closed to public ▪ Winemaker(s) various; led by Jeremy Walker, Gunter Schultz & Miles Mossop ▪ 800 magnum btls own label 100% red ▪ PO Box 206 Stellenbosch 7599 ▪ jeremy@grangehurst.co.za ▪ F +27 (0)86-710-6067 ▪ **T +27 (0)21-855-3625**

☐ **Survivor** see Overhex Wines International
☐ **Sutherland** see Thelema Mountain Vineyards
☐ **Sutherland Continental** see Super Single Vineyards
☐ **Swallow** see Natte Valleij Wines, TCB Wines

Swallow Hill Winery (Ⓥ) (🏠)

Among a tiny handful of vineyards in Greyton, this 2-ha parcel is farmed and wines handcrafted with minimal intervention by Britons Di and Brian Dawes. Unreviewed, their current range includes two '14 blends, with an oaked viognier and a tempranillo envisaged. Tasting/sales are available by appointment, along with guest accommodation for those wishing to explore the picturesque little town and surrounds.

Location: Greyton ▪ Map: Southern Cape ▪ Est 2009 ▪ 1stB 2013 ▪ Tasting, sales & cellar tours by prior arrangement ▪ Conservation area ▪ Farm stay: en-suite guest room (2 pax) ▪ Owner(s) Di & Brian Dawes ▪ Cellarmaster(s) John Brian Dawes ▪ Winemaker(s) Di Dawes, with John Brian Dawes ▪ Viticulturist(s) Di Dawes & John Brian Dawes ▪ 21ha/2ha (tempranillo, viog) ▪ 2t own label 50% red 50% white ▪ IPW, SAWIS ▪ PO Box 299 Greyton 7233 ▪ wine@swallowhill.co.za ▪ www.swallowhill.co.za ▪ S 34° 6' 10.10" E 019° 36' 35.46" ▪ **T +27 (0)82-423-9634**

☐ **Swartland Stories** *see* Pulpit Rock Winery

Swartland Winery (Ⓥ) (📷) (👤) (♿)

The crop of thousands of hectares of Swartland vineyards, many unirrigated bushvines, are delivered to this large-scale producer east of the rolling wheatfields and sheep pastures of Malmesbury. Founded as a multi-member co-operative in 1948, it is now a diversified business, the cellar leased to up-and-coming Leeuwenkuil. Swartland offers laboratory and bottling services to external customers while retaining its focus on marketing its wines, made under contract by Leeuwenkuil under the watchful eye of wine coordinator Christo Koch. The emphasis is on retaining defined quality tiers by vinifying special batches separately and thus expressing unique regional character.

Idelia range

★★★★ **Cape Blend** (🍇) Label suggests pinotage content, but undisclosed blend in barrel-matured **10** (★★★☆) offers intense fruit beneath acetone whiff. Last-tasted **08** was better. Swartland WO.

Swartland Bushvine range

★★★★ **Cabernet Sauvignon** Savoury palate of **10**, retasted, shows texture, balance & harmony of ripe fruit & supportive oak with a spicy fynbos nuance adding complexity.

★★★★ **Shiraz** Richly berried with spicy grip, **13** (★★★★) is a tad less substantial than **10**. No **11**, **12**.

Also tasted: **Chenin Blanc 14** ★★★ Not retasted: **Pinotage 13** ★★★☆

Reserve range

Cabernet Sauvignon-Merlot (NEW) ★★★ Friendly brightness to unfussy **14** blend with neither grape dominating in mix of equal parts. Not retasted: **Pinotage 13** ★★★ Not tasted: **Limited Selection Cabernet Sauvignon-Merlot**.

Swartland Winemakers Collection

★★★★ **Cape Vintage** Lithe **09** (★★★☆) 'port' a shade less impressive than rich **08**. Spicy, with nutty edge to berry fruit flavours of tinta & shiraz with splash touriga.

Cabernet Sauvignon ★★★ Generous, bold & juicy **14** has bags of appeal. Light but with good length & body, & a spicy tail. **Merlot** ★★★ **14** keeps up standard in easy red-fruit succulence & light appeal. WO W Cape. **Tinta Barocca** ★★★ Gentle grip of light **13** is grape derived as it's unwooded, as all these except Cape Vintage. **Bukettraube** ★★★ Fresh, flavourful **15** offers tangy sweetness & ease. **Sauvignon Blanc** (✓) ★★★ Grapefruit tang with flint backing on improved **15**, vibrantly juicy & lively. WO W Cape as next. **Red Muscadel** (NEW) ★★★ Muscat simplicity on maiden bottling of **NV** jerepiko. **White Jerepigo** ★★★ Peachy chenin notes show on **NV** fortified with syrupy concentration balanced by tangy appeal. **Cape Ruby** ★★★ Floral spice hints on port-style tinta & shiraz **NV**. Restraint evident in appealing sweetness & gentle spirit glow. Also tasted: **Pinotage 14** ★★★ **Shiraz 14** ★★★ **Chardonnay 15** ★★★ **Chenin Blanc 15** ★★★ **Hanepoot NV** ★★★ **Red Jerepigo NV** ★★★ Not retasted: **Dry Red NV** ★★ **Blanc de Noir 14** ★★★ **Sparkling Rosè NV** ★★★ **Cuvée Brut NV** ★★★ — FM

Location: Malmesbury ▪ Map: Swartland ▪ WO: Swartland/Western Cape ▪ Est/1stB 1948 ▪ Tasting & sales Mon-Fri 9–5 Sat 9–2 ▪ Closed Mar 21, Easter Fri/Sun, Dec 25/26 & Jan 1 ▪ Facilities for children ▪ Tour groups ▪ Farm produce ▪ Owner(s) 60 producers ▪ Wine coordinator Christo Koch (Feb 2014) ▪ Viti-culturist(s) Claude Uren (Nov 2010) ▪ 2,689ha (cab, malbec, merlot, ptage, shiraz, chard, chenin, sauv) ▪ 20,000t 38% red 55% white 5% rosé 2% sparkling ▪ BRC, IFS, IPW, WIETA ▪ PO Box 95 Malmesbury 7299 ▪ susan@swwines.co.za ▪ www.swwines.co.za ▪ S 33° 27' 12,7" E 018° 45' 17.7" ▪ F ı 27 (0)22-487-1750 ▪ **T ı 27 (0)22-482-1134**

☐ **Swartrivier** *see* Stellenrust
☐ **Sweet Darling** *see* Darling Cellars
☐ **Swepie Selection** *see* Domein Doornkraal
☐ **Swerwer** *see* JC Wickens Wines

SylvanVale Vineyards

Planted in the 1960s, vineyards around the Devon Valley Hotel near Stellenbosch have been rejuvenated by viticulturist Lorna Hughes to produce the own-label SylvanVale range for upmarket hotel owner Louis Group. This year, grapes from chenin bushvines will 'hopefully' join wines vinified to spec by seasoned consultant Mark Carmichael-Green.

SylvanVale range

★★★★ **Pinotage Reserve** Ⓥ Best decanted to remove sediment, **06** has matured beautifully, acquir-ing leather & star anise complexity while retaining bold fruit. Medium bodied yet rich, soft tannins.

Dry Cabernet Sauvignon Rosé ★★★ Not quite as dry as name or indeed analysis suggests, **14** is characterised by red cherry & strawberry flavours, pleasantly smooth rather than crisp & refreshing. Not retasted: **Cabernet Sauvignon 05 ★★★★ Pinotage 06 ★★★**

Ghost Tree range

Three Colours Red (NEW) ★★★★ Appealing **13** cab-merlot brims with ripe plums & black cherries, a velvety wine finishing on raspberry-studded dark choc note. **Bristle White** (NEW) ★★★★ **11** viognier ageing gracefully, peach & tangy apricot flavours mellowing into creamy texture as oak-derived vanilla spice & hints of toasted nuts prevail. Drink soon. Not retasted: **Three Colours White 14 ★★★** — JG

Location/map: Stellenbosch ▪ Map grid reference: D4 ▪ WO: Stellenbosch/Devon Valley ▪ Est 1997 ▪ 1stB 1998 ▪ Tasting & sales daily 11–7 ▪ Fee R25 ▪ Open pub hols ▪ Flavours Restaurant: 120 seater; Vineyard Terrace; Cedarwood Bar & Lounge ▪ The Devon Valley Hotel: 50 rooms ▪ Facilities for children ▪ Tour groups ▪ Conferences ▪ 6 banqueting venues (max capacity 98 pax) ▪ Walking/hiking trails ▪ Owner(s) Louis Group Hotels, Spas & Vineyards ▪ Winemaker(s) Mark Carmichael-Green (Sep 2003, consultant) ▪ Viticulturist(s) Lorna Hughes (1997, consultant) ▪ 8ha/4.3ha (cab, ptage, chenin) ▪ 6t/1,050cs own label 100% rosé ▪ PO Box 68 Stellenbosch 7599 ▪ info@sylvanvale.com ▪ www.sylvanvale.com ▪ S 33° 54' 12.5" E 018° 48' 57.7" ▪ F +27 (0)21-865-2610 ▪ **T +27 (0)21-865-2012**

☐ **Tabiso** *see* Darling Cellars
☐ **Table Bay** *see* Ultra Liquors

Taillard Family Wines

The wine names of this Voor Paardeberg winery refer to relevant mining terms, that of the winery itself to the heritage of co-proprietor Pieter Taljaard, a financial director in the mining industry and owner of the home farm, Kersfontein. The cellar dates back to 1790, and is the domain of eminent winemaker Teddy Hall. 'Vineyard renewal and new plantings are our focus right now,' he says.

★★★★ **Pinotage Reserve** (NEW) A touch of raspberry fragrance lifts **14**'s dark fruit. Fairly understated but balanced, good presence of sweet fruit on a firm tannic structure – though a few years will benefit.

Watershed (NEW) ★★★★ Clean berry & herbal aromas with tobacco & cedar hints on **14** blend cab franc, merlot, cab. Unshowy, well structured & fresh, though neither complex nor concentrated, & with a touch of sweetness showing on the finish. Not retasted: **The Bullion 13 ★★★ Deep Level 10 ★★ The Miner 12 ★★★ Prospector's Cape Late Bottled Vintage 09 ★★★★** — TJ

Location/WO: Paarl ▪ Map: Paarl & Wellington ▪ Map grid reference: D1 ▪ Tasting, sales & tours by appt ▪ Closed all pub hols ▪ Owner(s) Pacas Winery (Pty) Ltd (Pieter Taljaard, Hermann Helmbold, Anelise Taljaard) ▪ Cellarmaster(s)/winemaker(s) Teddy Hall ▪ Viticulturist(s) Morné van Greunen (Feb 2009) ▪ ±44ha (cabs s/f, merlot, p verdot, ptage, shiraz, chenin) ▪ 1,000cs own label 80% red 20% white ▪ BWI, IPW ▪ PO Box 7274 Noorder-Paarl 7623 ▪ lynette@taillardwines.com ▪ www.taillardwines.com ▪ S 33° 35' 22.5" E 018° 52' 45.0" (VP) ▪ F +27 (0)21-869-8365 ▪ **T +27 (0)21-869-8384**

Tall Horse

Cheery labels and easy, fruit-forward style of this giraffe-themed DGB brand have clearly captured consumer tastes locally and overseas. Website Tallhorsewines.com continues the quirky brand persona.

Tamboerskloof Wine – Kleinood Farm   Ⓟ

Born with the millennium, this winery was established by Gerard de Villiers and wife Libby on the farm Kleinood in Stellenbosch's Blaauklippen Valley. 'Small, cherished' is what the farm's Afrikaans name appropriately signifies; the label's name comes from the Cape Town suburb where the owners resided. Gerard, most usefully, is an engineer with a serious involvement in many important winery designs behind him. Wine-and-vine man Gunter Schultz has a dual eminence: he's also arguably the Cape's leading winemaker-surfer. The second edition of his single-vineyard syrah, John Spicer, was due for release as we went to press.

★★★★ John Spicer Syrah Ⓟ Deeper fruit than on standard Syrah, but **09** masked by oak (75% new) in youth – harmony might yet come. Ripe tannins; slightly warm finish, though alcohol just 14%.

★★★★ Syrah Gently savoury (not simply fruity) aromas on ripe **11**, with subtle oak spice as well as sweet fruit. Well built; 14.5% alcohol not obvious. Good length but no real complexity. **12** also tasted: feels bigger all round, with more fruit intensity too. Both with dollops mourvèdre & viognier. Magnums too.

★★★★ Viognier Older oak influence helps give **14** more interest & complexity. More restrained in expression than some gushing examples, but variety-true peach-pip fully present. Silky & lingering.

Also tasted: **Katharien Syrah Rosé 15 ★★★★** — TJ

Location/map/WO: Stellenbosch ▪ Map grid reference: F7 ▪ Est 2000 ▪ 1stB 2002 ▪ Tasting, sales & cellar tours Mon-Fri by appt ▪ Closed all pub hols ▪ Owner(s) Gerard & Libby de Villiers ▪ Winemaker(s) Gunter Schultz (Sep 2007), with Julio Engelbrecht (Jan 2008) ▪ Viticulturist(s) Gunter Schultz (Sep 2007) ▪ 22ha/10ha (mourv, shiraz, rouss, viog) ▪ 80t/6,000cs own label 76% red 10% white 14% rosé ▪ BWI, IPW ▪ PO Box 12584 Die Boord 7613 ▪ office@kleinood.com ▪ www.kleinood.com ▪ S 33° 59' 42.6" E 018° 52' 14.8" ▪ F +27 (0)21-880-2884 ▪ **T +27 (0)21-880-2527**

Tanagra Winery & Distillery   Ⓟ ⌂ 📷

Visitors to Tanagra's guest cottages near McGregor can enjoy not only the small range of husk spirits and eaux de vie distilled on-site by German co-owner Robert Rosenbach, but also red wines (Cabernet Sauvignon, Shiraz, Carah and Heavenly Chaos) and Blanc de Noir vinified nearby with an adviser.

Location: McGregor ▪ Map: Robertson ▪ Est/1stB 2003 ▪ Tasting (wine/grappa), sales & cellar/distillery tours daily by appt ▪ Farm produce ▪ Boutique distillery ▪ Luxury farm accommodation in 6 cottages (self-catering/B&B) ▪ Adjoining Vrolijkheid Nature Reserve ▪ Owner(s) Robert & Anette Rosenbach ▪ Cellarmaster(s) Robert Rosenbach & Lourens van der Westhuizen ▪ Winemaker(s) Robert Rosenbach & Lourens van der Westhuizen ▪ Distiller(s) Robert Rosenbach ▪ Viticulturist(s) Lourens van der Westhuizen ▪ 78ha/12.5ha (cabs s/f, merlot, ptage, shiraz, cbard) ▪ 120t/1,600cs own label 90% red 10% blanc de noir ▪ BWI, IPW ▪ PO Box 92 McGregor 6708 ▪ tanagra@tanagra-wines.co.za ▪ www.tanagra-wines.co.za ▪ S 33° 55' 29.6" E 019° 52' 15.9" ▪ F +27 (0)23-625-1847 ▪ **T +27 (0)23-625-1780**

Tangled Tree

This eco-friendly range has two entwined Karee trees on its label, symbols of the bond between Van Loveren founders and passionate gardeners Hennie and Jean Retief. Packaged in light, robust, recyclable, low-carbon PET (plastic) bottles, it's perfect for active and outdoorsy winelovers. Off Robertson vines.

Spicy Shiraz ★★ Advertised pepper & some red plum whiffs, **14** waft of vanilla for everyday appeal. **Rose Petal Moscato Rosé** ★★ Was 'Moscato Rosé'. New name perfectly describes **15**, with delicate rose notes to red muscadel's sweet, intensely grapey flavour. Also tasted: **Chocolate Cabernet Sauvignon 14** ★★ **Tropical Sauvignon Blanc 15** ★★ Not retasted: **Butterscotch Chardonnay 14** ★★ — CvZ

Tanja Beutler Wine Collection

Battling with red tape gave winemaker, marketer and garagiste front-woman Tanja Beutler the idea for her Merlot and now her only headache is not having enough wine to sell. 'There was no MCC made this year and last year's Merlot sold out within a few months.' Cocking a different snook at bureaucracy, Tanja now offers a red tape consulting service for smaller producers — see under Make Your Own Wine.

Red Tape range

★★★★☆ **Merlot** Excellent modern **13** balances ripe black & red berries, plenty of spice & good ripe tannins in attractive mouthful. Well-judged alcohol lurks behind the fruit, suggesting full-flavoured food may make for ideal combination.

Juliet Méthode Cap Classique range

Not tasted: **Brut**. — CM

Location: Somerset West ▪ WO: Elgin ▪ Est 2007 ▪ 1stB 2010 ▪ Sales by prior arrangement ▪ Owner(s) Tanja Beutler ▪ 650cs own label 87% red 13% MCC ▪ PO Box 804 Somerset Mall 7137 ▪ tanja@ hiddengems.co.za ▪ F +27 (0)86-612-6118 ▪ **T +27 (0)21-855-4275**

Tanzanite Wines   ⓘ

As the name suggests, Wentzel and Melanie van der Merwe's Worcester-based venture is a rare gem, focusing exclusively on handcrafting small parcels of méthode cap classique sparkling. Also rare and gem-like is the first of their long-awaited, even longer-gestated (7 years) larger-format releases, taking an already tiny production to a new level of exclusivity: just ±500 bottles, individually numbered. We tasted No. 2, and now can't wait to sample the promised vintage-dated bubbles...

Limited Editions (NEW)

★★★★☆ **Méthode Cap Classique Limited Edition** Superb NV (**07**) sparkling only in numbered magnums (±500 made). Chardonnay, pinot noir (85/15) nurtured 7 years before disgorgement. More refined, contemplative than Brut. Subtle brioche, toasted nuts & honey nuances, with clean lemony tone.

Tanzanite range

★★★★☆ **Méthode Cap Classique Brut** Always-excellent sparkler, engaging & flavoursome. Newest **NV** is chardonnay-led with 20% pinot noir. Richer & more of a toasty, creamy impression than rosé, despite same 60 months on lees. Clean & crisp green-fruited elegance. Also in magnum.

Méthode Cap Classique Brut Rosé ★★★★ NV bubbly reprises 60/40 pinot noir/chardonnay composition & savoury cranberry tone of previous in lighter, aperitif style, without the intensity, depth. — MW

Location: Worcester ▪ WO: Western Cape ▪ Est 2006 ▪ Tasting Mon-Sat by appt ▪ Owner(s) Wentzel & Melanie van der Merwe ▪ Cellarmaster(s) Melanie van der Merwe (Apr 2006) ▪ 800cs own label ▪ PO Box 5102 Worcester 6850 ▪ melanie@tanzanitewines.co.za ▪ www.tanzanitewines.co.za ▪ F +27 (0)86-694-0654 ▪ **T +27 (0)23-347-0018**

Tassenberg

Dry red affectionately known as 'Tassies'. Launched in 1936, the blend has varied over the years but not the affable persona. 750ml, 2L & 5L. By Distell.

Tassenberg ⓥ ★★★ Unoaked & easygoing pizza & pasta mate from widely sourced cab & cinsaut. Latest **NV** is soft, round & fruity, as ever. — JPf

Taverna Rouge

Big-selling budget-priced red blend by Distell; available in 750ml bottles and 2L packs.

Taverna Rouge ⓥ ★★ Off-dry **NV** quaffer, earthy/spicy red berries, appealingly structured. — JPf

TCB Wines

Theunis Christoffel Basson (TCB), the 6th generation to farm the Rawsonville property, focuses on exports of bulk wine but bottles around 30% of production locally. Own labels include Swallow, Cape Sparrow and Wolfenberg. The Cabernet, Merlot, Classic Red and Sauvignon Blanc missed our deadline.

Location: Rawsonville ▪ Map: Breedekloof ▪ Est 2002 ▪ 1stB 2008 ▪ Tasting, sales & cellar tours Mon-Fri 8-5 ▪ Fee R10pp ▪ Closed all pub hols ▪ Tour groups by appt only ▪ BYO picnic ▪ Conferences ▪ Self-catering units ▪ Owner(s) / manager TC Botha ▪ Cellarmaster(s)/winemaker(s) Christo Basson (Oct 2008) ▪ Viticulturist(s) Johan Slabber (Feb 1999) ▪ 190ha (cab, merlot, ptage, ruby cab, shiraz, chenin cbard, nouvelle, sauv, sem) ▪ 1,800t/600cs own label 70% red 30% white + 200cs for clients ▪ IPW ▪ PO Box 56 Rawsonville 6845 ▪ basson.christo8@gmail.com ▪ S 33° 42' 5.63" E 019° 18' 21.92" ▪ F +27 (0)23-349-1325 ▪ **T +27 (0)23-349-1748**

☐ **Tea Leaf** *see* Boutinot South Africa

Teddy Hall Wines

In the early 1990s Teddy Hall moved from financial services to winemaking and soon reached eminence, with an enviable reputation especially for chenin blanc (winning numerous important awards, including being 2001 Diners Club Winemaker of the Year). He left Rudera, the prestigious winery he had founded, and established this eponymous brand in 2006, making his wines in rented cellar space in Stellenbosch – an appropriate location for his premium labels, whose names are borrowed from interesting (somewhat disreputable) characters of the early days of the Cape. Teddy somehow also finds time to consult.

Premium range

★★★★☆ **Hercùles van Loon Cabernet Sauvignon** Ⓥ Dense & brooding **09** includes 10% merlot. Rich & full but balanced, pleasantly austere on the finish.

★★★★☆ **Dr Jan Cats Chenin Blanc Reserve** Ⓥ Refined **11** showing complexity & just enough texture to ensure that the acidity is nicely coated while the finish is long & dry.

★★★★ **Brut Méthode Cap Classique** Ⓥ Pure & precise bottle-fermented sparkling from chardonnay. **NV** lemon & subtle brioche character, zippy acidity & lots of fine, long-lasting bubbles.

Sybrand Mankadan Chenin Blanc ★★★★ Tropical fruit, peach & an interesting earthy note on lightly oaked **14**. Not at all showy, but lingering finish reveals character & a quiet intensity. **Brut Rosé Méthode Cap Classique** Ⓝⓔⓦ ★★★ Fresh, lean **NV** sparkling from pinotage offers light red fruit & bone-dry conclusion. Not retasted: **Jan Blanx Super White Cuvée 13** ★★★☆ **Blanc de Blancs Méthode Cap Classique 08** ★★★★☆

Doreen range

Shiraz Ⓝⓔⓦ ★★★ Some charm on **13**, with smoky aromas leading to dark-fruited palate, though the tannic structure is fairly forceful – a year or two in bottle would help here. Also tasted: **Sauvignon Blanc 14** ★★★☆

Moments Collection

Winter Moments Shiraz-Cabernet Sauvignon ★★★ Shiraz-led **13** blend has ripe plummy aromas leading to nicely fruity palate with firm tannic structure ensuring that the bright easiness doesn't turn trivial. Also tasted: **Summer Moments Chenin Blanc 14** ★★★ — TJ

Location/WO: Stellenbosch ▪ Closed to public ▪ Owner(s)/cellarmaster(s)/winemaker(s)/viticulturist(s) Teddy Hall ▪ PO Box 2868 Somerset West 7129 ▪ teddy@teddyhallwines.com ▪ www.teddyhallwines.com ▪ F +27 (0)86-504-8178 ▪ **T +27 (0)83-461-8111**

☐ **Tembana Valley** *see* Rooiberg Winery

Tempel Wines

Tempel Wines' Scandinavian owner Alf Ljungqvist says unwavering focus on discerning customers in home territory is paying dividends. A tasting tour there last year generated 'massive interest and appreciation', and further events are planned. Key to success is the structure of the portfolio, offering 'a one stop shop for loyal aficionados' and piquing consumers' interest at shows. Direct-to-customer marketing/ sales give creative freedom and help make the wines '"handcrafted" in the true sense of the word'.

★★★★ **3D** (NEW) Malbec-led 3-way Bordeaux blend in **14**, espresso savoury richness, black plum under-pin throughout the perfume, flavours. Just enough tannin for food but no hard edges, tasty & accessible.

★★★★ **Six Senses** (NEW) Six red varieties, including rare sangiovese and zinfandel but not one dominates in dark & brooding **13**. Plush, with pliable tannins giving form to bountiful fruit, a delicious cherry tone to the flavours. Well-crafted tannins, with hidden depth & grip.

Opus 5 Pinotage (NEW) ★★★★ Concentration already evident in the inky colour, **14** is still far off its peak. Loganberries & cedar, some white pepper, the tannins firm but ripe, well matched to the fruit. Also tasted: **Evidence Pinotage 13** ★★★☆ — CR, CvZ

Location/WO: Paarl ▪ Map: Paarl & Wellington ▪ Map grid reference: E3 ▪ Est 2000 ▪ 1stB 2003 ▪ Tasting, sales & cellar tours by appt ▪ Fee R25 ▪ Guest lodge (B&B), with 5 cottages ▪ Owner(s)/winemaker(s) Alf Ljungqvist ▪ 6ha/4.2ha (ptage) ▪ 24t/1,700cs own label 85% red 15% white ▪ PO Box 7295 Noorder-Paarl 7623 ▪ sales@tempelwines.co.za ▪ www.tempelwines.co.za ▪ S 33° 40' 34.0" E 018° 58' 32.2" ▪ F +27 (0)21-872-3883 ▪ **T +27 (0)21-872-4065**

☐ **Terra Del Capo** *see* Anthonij Rupert Wyne
☐ **Terra Madre** *see* High Constantia Wine Cellar
☐ **Terre de Papillon** *see* Baratok Wines

Teubes Family Wines   Ⓠ Ⓜ Ⓐ Ⓖ Ⓞ Ⓩ Ⓖ

Viticultural consultant Johan Teubes and wife Ella recently received WIETA accreditation for their ethically and sustainably grown Houmoed farm grapes. Their boutique range welcomes a shiraz and two wood-kissed chenins (the more serious Teubes Family version not ready for tasting). And cellarmaster son Sybrand, betrothed to a 'dynamic' damsel, adds another winemaker to the family.

Teubes Family Collection

★★★★ **Sauvignon Blanc** Both big & racy, generous tropical tones, richness reflective of its 15% alcohol. Previewed mid-July, oak-brushed **15** needs more 'sauvage' edges smoothed; better with food.

Shiraz (NEW) ★★☆ Tasty if uncomplicated **12** carries its 14% alcohol well; new French oak (20%) & few grams sugar lift its spicy, chocolate features. Olifants River WO, as for Sauvignon. Not tasted: **Pinotage Reserve**.

Lambert's Bay's Finest range

★★★★ **Sauvignon Blanc** Interesting, almost saline quality on part-oaked, lively **15**. Pre-bottling, seems more flinty, pebbly than fruity, though engaging ripe juicy acids linger on the agreeably dry tail.

Limited Releases
Not tasted: **Cabernet Sauvignon**.

Malkopbaai range

Chenin Blanc (NEW) (ⓥ) ★★★ Luscious tropical fruit salad flavours on **14** enhanced by French-oak-fermented portion. Quaffable 12.5% alcohol, fruitily dry.

Also tasted: **Pinotage 13** ★★ **Sauvignon Blanc 15** ★★★ Not retasted: **Rosé 14** ★★ — AL

Location: Vredendal ▪ Map: Olifants River ▪ WO: Western Cape/Olifants River/Lamberts Bay ▪ Est 2010 ▪ 1stB 2011 ▪ Tasting & sales Mon-Fri 8-5 Sat 9.30-5 ▪ Fee R20 ▪ Closed Easter Sat/Sun, Dec 25 & Jan 1 ▪ Cellar tours by appt ▪ Tour groups (up to 40 pax) ▪ Facilities for children ▪ Farm produce ▪ Cheese platters & pizza ▪ BYO picnic ▪ Conferences ▪ Walks/hikes ▪ Bergkraal 4x4 trail ▪ Mountain biking ▪ Conservation area ▪ Guest cottages ▪ Owner(s) Johan & Ella Teubes ▪ Cellarmaster(s) Sybrand Teubes ▪ Winemaker(s) Sybrand Teubes & Elaine Conradie ▪ Viticulturist(s) Johan Teubes ▪ (cab, ptage, shiraz, chard, sauv) ▪ 300t ▪ WIETA ▪ PO Box 791 Vredendal 8160 ▪ sybrand@teubeswines.co.za ▪ www.teubeswines.co.za ▪ S 31° 43' 19.1" E 018° 30' 14.5" ▪ F +27 (0)27-213-3773 ▪ **T +27 (0)27-213-2377**

Thabani Wines

Jabulani Ntshangase started out in wine as a store assistant in New York City almost 4 decades ago, going on to co-found seminal Spice Route Winery, and mentoring young black winemakers. His own brand, Thabani, is made to spec mostly for the on-trade. Highberry, listed separately, is a newer venture with vinegrower Andre Parker and ex-Waterkloof winemaker Werner Engelbrecht.

Location: Cape Town ▪ Closed to public ▪ Owner(s) Jabulani Ntshangase ▪ PO Box 1381 Stellenbosch 7599 ▪ jntshangase@aol.com ▪ www.thabani.co.za ▪ F +27 (0)86-648-3676 ▪ **T +27 (0)82-734-9409**

Thandi Wines ⓠ

With HQ in Stellenbosch's Eersterivier cellar, Thandi is one of SA's original agricultural empowerment ventures (1999) and the world's first Fairtrade-accredited wine label (2003). The vision of being socially and ethically responsible has remained steadfast, and all profits go towards upliftment initiatives.

Premium Selections

Merlot (NEW) ★★★ Savoury-tinged ripe berry flavours on **13** still integrating mid-2015, creamy undertone should afford succulent drinkability in year/2. **Chardonnay** (NEW) ★★★ Oatmeal & lime throughout **14**, light & creamy, brush of oak for attractive easy drinking. Also tasted: **Sauvignon Blanc 15** ★★☆

Thandi Single Varietal range

Shiraz Rosé ★★☆ Light candyfloss tone to tangy & dry **15**. For carefree sipping. Also tasted: **Cabernet Sauvignon 12** ★★★ **Shiraz Rosé Sparkling 14** ★★☆ Discontinued: **Shiraz**.

Thandi Dual Varietal range

Shiraz-Cabernet Sauvignon ★★★ **14** spicy red fruit in juicy blend, cab adding freshness & supple structure. Balanced & satisfying now & for few years. WO W Cape. Not retasted: **Chardonnay-Chenin Blanc 14** ★★★★ Discontinued: **Cabernet Sauvignon-Merlot, Sauvignon Blanc-Semillon**. — MW

Location/map: Stellenbosch ▪ Map grid reference: D6 ▪ WO: Stellenbosch/Western Cape ▪ Est 1995 ▪ Tasting & sales Mon-Thu 10-4 Fri 10-3 ▪ Fee R20pp ▪ Closed all pub hols ▪ Tour groups ▪ Owner(s) Thandi Wines (Pty) Ltd ▪ Fairtrade ▪ PO Box 597 Stellenbosch 7599 ▪ info@thandiwines.co.za ▪ www.thandiwines.com ▪ S 33°57' 47.66" E 018°47' 38.51" ▪ F +27 (0)86-561-0152 ▪ **T +27 (0)21-881-3290**

☐ **The 19th Wines** see 19th Wines

The Ahrens Family ⓠ (NEW)

Young gun Albert Ahrens aims to make wines with the distinctive characteristics, not just of a specific variety, but of its 'address' – the area of origin. 'Just like Karoo lamb tastes different to Namaqua lamb, address gives identity to a wine (assuming well-suited variety/ies).' Extensive Swartland experience (at Lammershoek and partnering BLANKbottle's Pieter Walser) informs the Black and White Black labels. He's also collaborated with growers in Bottelary and Elgin, hoping to eventually help create and define each area's DNA for local and international palate recognition.

★★★★ **Bottelary Seventy** Athletic cab takes supple cinsaut to the dark side, & we love it! **13** lulls with sweet cassis & red fruits, judicious oak seasoning; reasserts authority with no-nonsense grip. Stellenbosch fruit, 18 months older French oak.

★★★★ **The White Black** Voor Paardeberg & Swartland grapes star in textural **13**, equal parts roussanne, marsanne, blancs grenache & clairette. Glides seamlessly across the palate, its smoothness enlivened by bright acidity, lifted by subtle tannic end. Fermented/aged year in older, larger French oak.

Elgin Pinot Noir ★★★★ Pretty pale cherry hue & fruit aromatics, flavours on satiny **14**. Well-balanced, delicate feel despite 14.5% alcohol; fades a tad quickly. 14 months, older French oak. **Black** ★★★☆ Shiraz (59%) with equal portions carignan & grenache, 7% cinsaut in raspberry-toned **14** Swartland blend. Spice, garrigue scrub & modest oak (10% new, 14 months) add to the attraction & length. **Bottelary OVC (Old Vine Chenin)** ★★★☆ Barrel-fermented/aged **14** Stellenbosch vines has rich lemon, pear & white peach aromas & tastes juxtaposed with a fresh finish thanks to 3 different picking dates, easy drinkability courtesy well-balanced 6 g/l sugar. — TJ, CvZ

Location: Somerset West ▪ Map: Paarl & Wellington ▪ Map grid reference: G6 ▪ WO: Bottelary/Swartland/
Western Cape/Elgin ▪ Est/1stB 2008 ▪ Tasting & sales by appt only ▪ Owner(s) Albert Ahrens ▪ Cellar-
master(s)/winemaker(s)/viticulturist(s) Albert Ahrens (2008) ▪ 15t/2,000 cs own label 65% red 35%
white ▪ albert@theahrensfamily.com ▪ S 33° 45' 11.30" E 019° 1' 48.19" ▪ **T +27 (0)79-196-6887**

☐ **The Artisan Collection** see Snow Mountain Wines
☐ **Theater of Wine** see Val du Charron
☐ **The Auction Crossing** see Auction Crossing Private Cellar
☐ **The Back Roads** see Black Elephant Vintners
☐ **The Bernard Series** see Bellingham

The Berrio Wines ⓠ

This Elim winery started as a project between winegrower Francis Pratt and winemaker Bruce Jack of
Flagstone (more recently of Accolade too). But after 2008, winemaking returned to the home farm near
the tip of Africa, with Francis taking prime responsibility for wines as well as vines. More recently he has
entrusted the winemaking to Cederberg cellarmaster David Nieuwoudt (who also has vines in the area).
Sauvignon blanc is the big grape in this windswept area, but reds are making a forceful entrance, and
now there's a promising addition to The Berrio's range – a shiraz.

★★★★ **Shiraz** (NEW) 13 ripe but refined, appealing perfumed aromas: spicy, peppery, with red & black
berries. The flavours not intense, a touch sweet, supported by sensitive oaking (40% new) & soft tannins.

★★★★☆ **Sauvignon Blanc** ⊘ Ripe but fresh 15 has blackcurrant note a salient feature, also tropical
& green elements. Poised & elegant, with the same silky richness on the intense palate as last-tasted 13,
but less bracing, more serene in its balance. Subtle salinity on the long finish.

★★★★☆ **Weather Girl** 15 same successful unoaked 60:40 blend sauvignon & semillon as last-tasted
13, equally featuring pear & citrus, with a tangy note of salt. The ripe, textured richness well balanced by
enlivening acidity leading to a sweet-fruited lingering conclusion.

Discontinued: **Cabernet Sauvignon**. — TJ

Location/WO: Elim ▪ Map: Southern Cape ▪ Est 1997 ▪ 1stB 2002 ▪ Tasting & sales by appt; see website
for opening hours from Dec 2015 ▪ Closed Sun, Easter Fri/Sun, Dec 25/26 & Jan 1 ▪ Owner(s)/viticultur-
ist(s) Francis Pratt ▪ Cellarmaster(s) David Nieuwoudt (Cederberg) ▪ Winemaker(s) David Nieuwoudt
(2013, Cederberg) ▪ 2,276ha/±30ha (pinot, shiraz, sauv, sem) ▪ ±30t/3,000cs own label 20% red 80%
white ▪ PO Box 622 Bredasdorp 7280 ▪ wine@theberrio.co.za ▪ www.theberrio.co.za ▪ S 34° 37' 17.0" E
019° 48' 32.3" ▪ F +27 (0)86-603-2894 ▪ **T +27 (0)28-482-1880**

☐ **The Big 5** see Jacques Germanier

The Blacksmith (NEW)

Elsenburg graduate Tremayne Smith found his varietal inspiration – grenache, cinsaut and carignan – in
Spain during one of three vintages there. He'd cut his teeth at De Trafford and Sijnn before joining
Mullineux & Leeu, making just 1,120 bottles of maiden-vintage '14 Vin Blanc from Swartland chenin,
and 600 of Vin Noir (Paarl cinsaut, Swartland carignan), most snapped up after Wine Cellar's Young Guns
showcase. Both are naturally fermented, with no additives besides a little sulphur, and bottled unfil-
tered/unfined. For harvest 2016, Tremayne plans on doubling production; longer term, he has his heart
set on a small cellar out of which he can grow the brand and work with varieties he loves to drink.

Location: Riebeek-Kasteel ▪ 1stB 2014 ▪ Closed to public ▪ Owner(s)/winemaker(s) Tremayne Smith ▪
3.5t/187cs own label 54% red 46% white ▪ tremayne@theblacksmithwines.co.za

☐ **The Bridge Wines** see Bridge Wines

The Butcher Shop & Grill 🍴

Alan Pick, proprietor of Butcher Shop & Grill in Sandton and Cape Town, has long been a prolific, high-
profile Cape Winemakers Guild customer, and has built good relationships with its members. Some (as
well as other producers) provide bottlings for his various ranges.

Limited Editions

★★★★ **Hartenberg The Snuffbox Merlot** ⓥ 07 a fruit-filled mouthful of cassis, black plums, rum-soaked raisins, embraced by youthfully sturdy tannins which since should have integrated.

★★★★☆ **Morgenster** ⓥ Master-crafted Bordeaux blend dominated by cabs (sauvignon, franc 70%) in 03, should be spectacular now. Followed merlot-driven 01. No 02.

★★★★ **Vergelegen The Dani** ⓥ Labelled for the restaurant, 04 a fully mature, meaty & firm, ready to drink Bordeaux-styled red blend from this famous Stellenbosch estate.

★★★★☆ **Niels Verburg Cabernet Sauvignon-Shiraz-Mourvèdre** Bold 12 (★★★★★) blend (see Luddite Saboteur). Textured, bright, succulent, rounded black fruit, fynbos & dried herbs. Firm oak back-bone yet silky, fine tannins & spicy cured meat lift on long finish. 11 (★★★★) less handsome than 09.

★★★★ **Vergelegen The Carine** ⓥ Ingratiatingly fruity 11 sauvignon blanc is softer, less steely & bracing than the property's usual style.

Pick's Pick Gold Label range

★★★★☆ **Cabernet Sauvignon** (NEW) Bold & statuesque 12 merges deep, dark blackcurrants with mineral-iodine, cloaked with chalky ripe tannins; New World strut with classic structure. By Ernie Els.

★★★★ **Reserve Pinot Noir** ⓥ Expressive 11 from The Winery of Good Hope. Fresh acidity & earthiness combine with body & structure in elegant & harmonious wine.

Not retasted: **Blend Twelve** 12 ★★★☆ Not tasted: **Pinotage**.

Pick's Pick range

★★★★ **Merlot** ⓥ Step up from last-tasted 09 (★★★☆), 11 from Jordan offers ageing potential coupled with current enjoyment, its sleekly curvaceous body ends dry & food friendly.

★★★★ **Shiraz-Cabernet Sauvignon** 13 has family resemblance to 12 (★★★★), but plumper, riper fruit on still-rigid tannins. By Ernie Els.

★★★★ **Sauvignon Blanc** 14 generous ripeness, purity & focus, with vibrant crispness underpinning sweet passionfruit. Good intensity & length, showing variety's most appealing characteristics. By Jordan.

⁝ **Unoaked Chardonnay** (NEW) ⓥ ★★★☆ Rich leesy texture on 14, with overtly ripe citrus fruit. Very appealing, good length. Substance without attitude. By Jordan. ⁝

Pinotage (NEW) ★★★★ Fruit driven, juicy & smooth, Beyerskloof's 13 is a ripe plummy mouthful. **Shiraz** ★★★☆ Peppers & spice on 14 bring joy & happiness, with ripe berried fruit & succulent finish. From Guardian Peak. **Chardonnay** ★★★ Restrained & eminently drinkable, unwooded 13 from The Winery of Good Hope has pleasant citrus tang, some light richness & a good dry finish. Also tasted: **Shiraz 11** ★★★☆ **Rosé 14** ★★★★ Not retasted: **Protea Merlot 12** ★★★ **Classic French Blend 12** ★★★★ **Bubbly NV** ★★★★ Not tasted: **Cabernet Sauvignon, Protea Sauvignon Blanc**. Discontinued: **Cape White Blend**. — FM

Location: Cape Town/Sandton ▪ WO: Various ▪ Owner(s) Alan Pick ▪ Beach Road Mouille Point (opposite lighthouse) Cape Town 8005; Shop 30 Nelson Mandela Square Sandton 2196 ▪ thebutchershop@mweb.co.za ▪ F +27 (0)11-784-8674 ▪ **T +27 (0)11-784-8676/7**

☐ **The Cirrus Wine Company** *see* Cirrus Wines
☐ **The Collection** *see* Mooiplaas Estate & Private Nature Reserve
☐ **The Cooperative** *see* Bosman Family Vineyards
☐ **The Crags** *see* Bramon Wines
☐ **The Cross Collection** *see* Dieu Donné Vineyards
☐ **The Den** *see* Painted Wolf Wines

The Drift

Involved with wine brands for half his life, Bruce Jack (Flagstone founder/winemaker and SA chief vintner for global big-brand owner Accolade Wines) is carefully exploring 'what lies beyond' in growing wine (including foundation blocks for trialling varieties), as well as herbs, olives and organic vegetables on isolated Overberg mountainside land, family-owned since 1994. It's a highly personal, deeply philosophical project, in consultation with creative wife Penny (the label graphics are hers). Following initial bottlings from bought-in grapes, smidgens of the farm's first pinot noir, touriga franca rosé, barbera and multi-variety red blend (none available for tasting here yet) are a passion in progress.

Location: Napier ▪ 1stB 2005 ▪ Wine sales Mon-Fri 8.30-4 ▪ Owner(s) Jack family ▪ Winemaker(s) Bruce Jack ▪ Viticulturist(s) Chris Keet (consultant) ▪ 204ha/12ha (barbera, malbec, pinot, shiraz, tannat, tinta, touriga franca, touriga, chard) ▪ WIETA ▪ PO Box 55 Napier 7270 ▪ info@thedrift.co.za ▪ www.thedrift.co.za ▪ F +27 (0)86-563-9533 ▪ **T +27 (0)86-150-2025**

Theescombe Estate Wine   Ⓠ Ⓜ Ⓞ Ⓝ

In peri-urban Port Elizabeth, the Futter family's tiny wine venture is basically a hobby but clearly a great deal of passion goes into it, and there's much enthusiasm for welcoming visitors wanting to 'taste, eat and party'. The vineyard was first planted in 2006 and gradually augmented. Roger, viticulturist, today keeps 3,500 vines 'happy'. Wife Sandra crafts the wines, and conducts tours and tutored tastings. Children Craig, Tamlin and Nigel too are involved in the 'wonderful journey'.

Pinotage ★★★ Pleasing spicy fruitcake perfume on **13**, but woody character of staves (over-)used in maturation dominates the fruit – though not unpleasantly. Big 14.5% alcohol not obvious. — TJ, CvZ

Location: Port Elizabeth ▪ Map/WO: Eastern Cape ▪ Est/1stB 2010 ▪ Tasting, sales & cellar tours by appt ▪ Fee R10 ▪ Closed Dec 19 to Jan 7 ▪ Meals/platters (cheese, olives & biltong) to be pre-booked ▪ Functions ▪ No card facilities ▪ Owner(s) Futter family ▪ Winemaker(s) Sandra Futter (Oct 2007) ▪ Viticulturist(s) Roger Futter (Jun 2006) ▪ 1.94ha/1ha (cab, ptage, chenin, sem, white muscadel) ▪ 1-4t ▪ PO Box 28642 Sunridge Park Port Elizabeth 6008 ▪ theescombewines@hotmail.co.za ▪ www.theescombewines.wix.com/theescombewines ▪ S 33° 58' 44.82" E 025° 28' 27.46" ▪ **T +27 (0)41-379-4035/+27(0)73-889-6663**

☐ **The Flagship** *see* Stellenbosch Vineyards
☐ **The Fledge & Co** *see* Fledge & Co

The Foundry   Ⓠ

This collaboration between Chris Williams (Meerlust cellarmaster) and wine partner James Reid (Accolade Wines SA operations director and Voor Paardeberg grower) set all agog from their first ('01) releases. The Syrah was a five-star wine in the 2004 edition of this guide and had UK winewriter Jancis Robinson highlighting The Foundry as 'one to watch'. Since then, Chris has succeeded admirably in his quest to find 'pockets of viticultural excellence, allow the grapes to ripen optimally and coax them into great wine'. The release of a maiden grenache noir from a 'meticulous' grower completes their stable of Rhône wines, 'a vindication of our commitment to these varieties in the Cape'.

★★★★ **Grenache Noir** Ⓝ Spicy **14** has supple grape tannin platform to showcase pristine fruit, provide structure & layered texture; succeeds in delivering great presence & interest without obvious power. Partial stem & whole-berry ferment, combo older oak & concrete.

★★★★☆ **Syrah** Ⓐ Always a class act, Stellenbosch's Faure area the source of **09**, well crafted, multi-layered & smooth, with dark fruit, generous spice & violets. 10% new oak provides support, & 30% whole berry (with stems) ferment lends structure to a rich, round, complex palate.

★★★★★ **Grenache Blanc** A local benchmark for the variety, from Voor Paardeberg. **14** (★★★★☆) refined white peach & ginger aromas; precise & tangy with hallmark mineral undertones; shade less intensity than **13**, which had 5% roussanne.

★★★★ **Roussanne** Ⓐ Standout **13** (★★★★☆) expressive yet delicate nose of peach blossom with slight melon & mineral undertones; bone-dry, succulent, with refreshing pebbly flavour & a peacock finish showing more complexity than **12**. Seasoned oak & partial malo, as for Grenache Blanc. .

★★★★☆ **Viognier** Expressive but well-controlled **14** (★★★★★) has wonderful lift & complexity; apricot blossom, lemon curd & lemongrass scents subtly supported by older oak ferment, same well-judged freshness as **13**. — JPf

Location/map: Stellenbosch ▪ Map grid reference: C8 ▪ WO: Stellenbosch/Voor Paardeberg ▪ Est 2000 ▪ 1stB 2001 ▪ Tasting, sales & cellar tours by appt ▪ Closed all pub hols ▪ Owner(s) Chris Williams & James

Reid ▪ Cellarmaster(s)/winemaker(s) Chris Williams (Nov 2000) ▪ Viticulturist(s) Chris Williams (Nov 2000), with growers ▪ 11ha (grenache, shiraz, rouss, viog) ▪ ±30t/4,000cs own label 40% red 60% white ▪ PO Box 12423 Die Boord 7613 ▪ thefoundry@mweb.co.za ▪ www.thefoundry.co.za ▪ S 34° 1' 1.7" E 018° 45' 24.7" ▪ F +27 (0)21-843-3274 ▪ **T +27 (0)82-577-0491**

☐ **The Full Fifteen Africans** *see* New Beginnings Wines
☐ **The Game Reserve** *see* Graham Beck Wines

The Garajeest   (NEW)

The name is to be pronounced 'garage-east', says Zimbabwe-born, Elsenburg-trained Callan Williams, 'director, founder, winemaker and driver' of this small family business. Dreamer too, this garagiste with an overt sense of humour also to be reflected in the labels. 'No dream too big,' she says of her plan to acquire land and cellar of her own (and qualify as a Master of Wine). Meanwhile, 'we source grapes from Elgin and rent cellar space in the Helderberg.' A '15 cabernet franc quietly matures in barrel.

★★★★ **Semillon** Work in progress when tasted, so rating provisional, but **15** looks promising: enticing with lemon & lanolin, with focused acid & flavours; firm, well textured. The lemony finish a touch short. — TJ, CvZ

Location/WO: Elgin ▪ Est 2014 ▪ 1stB 2015 ▪ Closed to public ▪ Owner(s) Callan Williams ▪ Cellarmaster(s)/winemaker(s) Callan Williams (May 2014) ▪ (cab, sem) ▪ 11t/±1,800cs own label 70% red 30% white ▪ IPW ▪ PO Box 141 Grabouw 7160 ▪ callan@thegarajeest.co.za ▪ www.thegarajeest.co.za ▪ **T +27 (0)72-524-2921**

The Giant Periwinkle   (logo)

Pierre Rabie is a Cape Town lawyer, but winemaking in his genes led to this garagiste venture based on grapes from, mostly, cool-climate Elim. To complete a geographical triangle leading to a lot of travelling, he now makes his wines at Leipzig Winery near Worcester (where they can be tasted). Minimal intervention is central to Pierre's pure, characterful wines: no additives, fining or filtration, only older oak, and from 2015 only wild-yeast fermentation.

★★★★ **Old Lady On The Corner Pinot Noir** (NEW) **14** offers a fairly subdued red fruit character, with undertones of forest floor. Fresh & rather charming, structured by soft tannins & acidity in pleasing harmony.

★★★★ **Kelp Forest Syrah 13** more impressive & finer than chunky **12** (★★★). Spicy, dark fruit still quite tightly held – a few years might advance on the dry, velvety, balanced palate; older oak well integrated.

★★★★☆ **Blanc Fumé** Finely structured & fresh **14** (★★★★) sauvignon blanc a shade off **13** in expressive complexity. But as balanced & elegantly harmonious, with room for development. Fermented/matured in older barrels.

Coenraad de Buys (NEW) ★★★ Undisclosed red blend in ripe, fruity **13**. Friendly (a braai – BBQ – wine suggests 'wine facilitator' Rabie), but as nicely structured as it is tasty. Not tasted: **Sea Witch Pinot Noir**. Discontinued: **21 Degrees Sauvignon Blanc**. — TJ

Location: Nuy ▪ WO: Elim ▪ Est 2009 ▪ 1stB 2012 ▪ Tasting at Leipzig Winery ▪ Owner(s)/winemaker(s) Pierre Jacques Rabie jnr ▪ 0.06ha (sauv, pinot) ▪ ±300cs own label 60% red 40% white ▪ PO Box 415 Bredasdorp 7280 ▪ pjrabie@capebar.co.za ▪ F +27 (0)21-422-2142 ▪ **T +27 (0)21-426-2653**

☐ **The Goats do Roam Wine Company** *see* Goats do Roam Wine Company

The Goose Wines   (logo) (logo)

Professional golfer Retief Goosen (aka 'The Goose') and friend and business partner Werner Roux bought the serendipitously named Ganzekraal ('goose pen') in the Outeniqua mountains in 2005. The centuries-old farm falls within the Upper Langkloof wine ward, where average growing season temperatures hover around a beneficially low 17°C. A pinot noir joins a still compact range, vinified off-site, that maintains a quiet yet assured global presence (much like its namesake).

★★★★ **Expression** ⓥ Plush, ripe-styled **09** from cab & shiraz. Dark plummy fruit has vibrant acid support, soft supple tannins. 30% new French oak.

Pinot Noir ⓝ ★★★★ Loganberries, salty liquorice, a suggestion of scrub in atypical but attractive **13**, with lots to offer, including a good future, the tannins forming a firm backbone. Stellenbosch & Walker Bay grapes. **Sauvignon Blanc** ★★★ Vibrating with zinging freshness, **15** has lovely lemongrass perfume, flavours. Also tasted: **Cabernet Sauvignon 13** ★★★★ **Shiraz 12** ★★★ In abeyance: **T-Box Sauvignon Blanc**. — CR

Location: George ▪ Map: Klein Karoo & Garden Route ▪ WO: Upper Langkloof/Western Cape ▪ Est 2005 ▪ Tasting by appt ▪ Meals/refreshments by appt ▪ Owner(s) Retief Goosen & Werner Roux ▪ Winemaker(s) Alwyn Liebenberg (Jan 2007, consultant) ▪ Viticulturist(s) Bennie Botha (Jan 2009) ▪ 500ha/21ha (cab, shiraz, sauv) ▪ 120t/18,666cs own label 66% red 34% white + 140cs for clients ▪ Brands for clients: Reuben's (Franschhoek & Robertson) ▪ HACCP ▪ PO Box 2053 George 6530 ▪ michele@ thegoosewines.com ▪ www.thegoosewines.com ▪ S 33° 47' 25.72" E 022° 41' 45.36" ▪ F +27 (0)86-543-1808 ▪ **T +27 (0)82-610-2276**

☐ **The Grand Beach Café** *see* Stellekaya Winery

The Grape Grinder

Innovating, staying lean and negotiating the best deal is the secret to success for Paarl-based negociants Oliver Kirsten and Johan du Toit, who co-founded The Grape Grinder after cutting their teeth at Juno Wines. They're unveiling two rosés this edition, and doubtless hoping these emulate the funky labelled, mocha-toned pinotage, which has proved to be 'catnip for wine consumers'.

Grinder range
Shiraz ⓥ ★★★★ Seductively bold, peppery & structured **13** a notable notch better than previous. **Cinsault Rosé** ⓝ ★★☆ Primary raspberry appeal to unfussy, juicy dry **14** charmer. Swartland WO. **Chenin Blanc** ★★★ Fresh stonefruit tang on textured **14** shows improvement on predecessor. Not retasted: **Pinotage 13** ★★★

Milkwood range
Shiraz-Viognier ★★★ Ripely fruited, spicy **13** less expressive than last. WO W Cape.

Wild Olive range
Rosé ⓝ ★★☆ Ripe cherry vibrancy on medium-bodied **14** from cab & merlot. Nice dry finish. **Old Vines Chenin Blanc** ★★★ Peppery succulence to **14** from old Swartland vines, honeyed richness unaided by wood. — FM

Location: Paarl ▪ WO: Coastal/Western Cape/Swartland ▪ Est/1stB 2010 ▪ Closed to public ▪ Owner(s) Oliver Kirsten & Johan du Toit ▪ Cellarmaster(s) Pieter Carstens (Dec 2010, consultant) ▪ Winemaker(s) Pieter Carstens (Dec 2010, consultant) & Johan Gerber (consultant) ▪ 70,000cs own label 80% red 20% white ▪ ISO 2009, BRC, WIETA ▪ PO Box 606 Paarl 7624 ▪ oliver@grapegrinder.com ▪ www.grapegrinder.com ▪ F +27 (0)86-588-4338 ▪ **T +27 (0)21-863-3943**

☐ **The Great Five** *see* Stellenview Premium Wines
☐ **The Green House** *see* Bon Cap Organic Winery
☐ **The Griffin** *see* Stettyn Cellar

The High Road   ⓥ ⓞ ⓑ

Former insurance practitioners and wine hobbyists Les Sweidan and Mike Church made wine, Bordeaux varieties especially, their business more than a decade ago. They share space, recently refurbished, at Stellenbosch winemaking precinct Bosman's Crossing, where visitors can try the first limited-edition varietal cabernet, untasted by us but also available to club members and selected retailers.

★★★★ **Classique** Ingratiatingly ripe, smooth-textured **11** cab-led Bordeaux blend achieves seriousness of style in 'softer' vintage, improves on friendly **10** (★★★☆).

★★★★ **Director's Reserve** Bold, powerful **11** cab-led Bordeaux blend makes a statement with abundant intensely rich, sweet dark fruit flavours, underpinned by seamless tannin's savoury grip. Polished
showstopper. Also in magnum. — IM

Location/map/WO: Stellenbosch ▪ Map grid reference: E5 ▪ Est/1stB 2003 ▪ Tasting by appt only ▪ Closed
all pub hols ▪ Boardroom facilities ▪ Owner(s) Les Sweidan & Mike Church ▪ Winemaker(s) Mark
Carmichael-Green (2004, consultant) ▪ Viticulturist(s) Paul Wallace (2004, consultant) ▪ 26t/2,000cs
own label 100% red ▪ 7D Lower Dorp Street, Bosman's Crossing, Stellenbosch 7600 ▪ wine@
thehighroad.co.za ▪ www.thehighroad.co.za ▪ S 33° 56' 27.1" E 018° 50' 49.1" ▪ F +27 (0)21-886-4288
▪ T +27 (0)76-044-5020

The Hills   (℗)

Chimanimani is a smallholding in Stellenbosch's prime Devon Valley where Vic Hills, whose family has
owned the property since 1964, grows 5 ha of noble reds and a block of old chenin. Grapes are mostly
sold but since 2006 a soupçon is made for the own label by celebrated neighbour Martin Meinert.

Cabernet Sauvignon ★★★☆ **11** same tobacco, cedarwood & spice nuances from lengthy 36 months
in 33% new oak, but more serious intent, concentration, than previous. Nudges next level. **10** & **09** also
available ex farm. **Dry Red** (NEW) ★★★ Pleasing **11** shiraz has ripe mulberry, prune & menthol aromas,
graceful tannins courtesy extended ageing in 33% new oak. Also tasted: **Ensemble 11** ★★★ Not
retasted: **Shiraz 10** ★★★ **Chenin Blanc 14** ★★ Not tasted: **Pinot Noir** — GM

Location/map: Stellenbosch ▪ Map grid reference: D4 ▪ WO: Devon Valley ▪ Est/1stB 2006 ▪ Tasting & sales by
appt ▪ Owner(s) The Victor Hills Family Trust ▪ Winemaker(s) Martin Meinert (Feb 2006, consultant) ▪ Viticul-
turist(s) Vic Hills (Jan 1998) ▪ 6ha/5ha (cab, pinot, shiraz, chenin, sauv) ▪ 40t/600cs own label 80% red 20%
white ▪ PO Box 12012 Die Boord Stellenbosch 7613 ▪ vwhills@iafrica.com ▪ www.thehills-wine.co.za ▪ S 33°
55' 04.1" E 018° 48' 47.1" ▪ T +27 (0)21-865-2939/+27 (0)82-493-6837

The House of GM&AHRENS   (℗) (⑪)

Lawyer Gerrit Maritz excavated beneath his Franschhoek home to house a barrel and bottle fermentation
cellar for this MCC sparkling focused venture with winemaker Albert Ahrens (The Ahrens Family). The
quality more than matches the classy packaging (a five-bottle 'bubbly hatbox'), exclusive availability
(via 'the list' on their website) and special Spring Day sunrise breakfast celebrating each new vintage.

★★★★★ **Vintage Cuvée** Classically styled, creamy **11** MCC, premium priced. Chardonnay, pinot noir
blend from 7 sites; year in older barrels before bottling & 42 months on lees. Seamlessly elegant & luxuriously textured style matched by glamorous packaging. — IM

Location/map: Franschhoek ▪ WO: Western Cape ▪ Est 2007 ▪ 1stB 2008 ▪ Tasting, sales & cellar tours by
appt ▪ Closed all pub hols ▪ Meals/refreshments by appt ▪ Owner(s) Albert Ahrens & Gerrit Maritz ▪
Cellarmaster(s)/viticulturist(s) Albert Ahrens (Jan 2007) ▪ 10t/400 x 5-btl cs own label 100% MCC ▪ P O
Box 5619 Helderberg 7135 ▪ info@gmahrens.com ▪ www.gmahrens.co.za ▪ S 33° 54' 14" E 019° 07' 08"
▪ T +27 (0)79-196-6887 (Albert)/+27 (0)83-348-1230 (Gerrit)

The House of JC le Roux   (℗) (⑪) (◎) (♿)

Adopting the French 'champagne house' concept, this destination Devon Valley cellar owned by Distell is
dedicated to the production of sparkling wine and the edification of visitors through bubbly's varied
styles and charms. JC le Roux has been well known and much loved since the 1980s, particularly for its
best-selling carbonated semi-sweet pink sparklers. But its premium bottle-fermented MCCs earn equal
kudos, a fact perhaps better known since 'coming home' in the late 1990s, the modern cellar being on
part of the original property owned by French Huguenot winegrower and namesake Jean le Roux.

Méthode Cap Classique range
★★★★ **Pinot Noir** (℗) Appealing strawberry & shortbread on **09**, with crisply precise acidity. Rounder,
more generous than **08** (★★★☆), the perfect summertime aperitif.

★★★★ **Scintilla** (℗) Jump to **08** vintage, first since **03** shows change to leaner, more focused sparkling
style. Creamy mousse with soft acid. Chardonnay/pinot noir 70/30 is complex & integrated.

Brut ⊘ ★★★☆ Competent but not all that exciting **NV** from pinot noir & chardonnay, pleasant creamy mouthfeel but rather neutral fruit. Also tasted: **La Vallée Rosé** ⊘ NV ★★★ **La Vallée NV ★★☆** Not retasted: **Pinot Noir Rosé 09 ★★★☆**

Sparkling range
Sauvignon Blanc ★★★ Varietal character shows through in **15** off-dry carbonated bubbly. Straightforward but pleasant. 10% colombard. Also tasted: **La Chanson NV ★★ La Fleurette NV ★★** **Le Domaine NV ★★** — GdB

Location/map: Stellenbosch ▪ Map grid reference: D4 ▪ WO: Western Cape ▪ 1stB 1983 ▪ Tasting & sales Mon-Fri 9—4 Sat/pub hols 10—3 Sun 10—2 ▪ Fee R40-R85 ▪ Self tour available during opening hrs ▪ Closed Good Fri, Dec 25 & Jan 1 ▪ Tour groups ▪ Gifts ▪ Le Venue restaurant ▪ Owner(s) Distell ▪ Cellarmaster(s) Elunda Basson ▪ Winemaker(s) Elunda Basson (2007), with John November (2011) ▪ Farm manager Graham Daniels (2015) ▪ Viticulturist(s) Bennie Liebenberg (Jan 2000) ▪ 27ha own vyds ▪ 20% red 80% white ▪ ISO 9200 ▪ PO Box 184 Stellenbosch 7599 ▪ info@jcleroux.co.za ▪ www.jcleroux.co.za ▪ S 33° 54' 16.6" E 018° 48' 37.4" ▪ **T +27 (0)21-865-8200**

☐ **The House of Krone** see Twee Jonge Gezellen Estate-House of Krone
☐ **The House of Mandela** see House of Mandela
☐ **The Hughes Family** see Hughes Family Wines
☐ **The Juno Wine Company** see Juno Wine Company

Thelema Mountain Vineyards   ⓘ ♿

Little stands still at prestigious family-run Thelema farm and winery on the crest of Stellenbosch's Helshoogte Pass. Winemaker Rudi Schultz is experimenting in the vineyards, trying new ways of pruning and planting different cover crops, and new wines make their appearance this edition, adding to the portfolio of premium labels which perfectly express their terroir. The newer arm of their business, the cool-climate Elgin vineyards feeding the Sutherland label, continues to fascinate and excite cellarmaster and co-owner Gyles Webb. 'Elgin is still embryonic with regard to viticulture and we don't know with any certainty what will do best there. My view is that chardonnay shows a lot of promise and is likely to be the best grape variety for the area.' The excellent debut unoaked bottling certainly supports this view.

Thelema range
★★★★☆ Cabernet Sauvignon Concentrated mouthful of ripe black fruit, **11** (**★★★★**) is fresh & supple, well integrated tannins giving pleasing gritty grip. Fraction shorter than stellar **10** but lots to like.

★★★★ The Mint Cabernet Sauvignon Signature mint & dark chocolate notes on **12** combine nicely with fresh black plums & cherries. Lovely ripe tannins & a savoury tweak at finish suggest endless food-matching possibilities. Also in magnum.

★★★★ Merlot Improving on **11** (**★★★☆**), **12** gives plenty of dark fruits & overlay of violets & chocolate. Upfront tannins shield the full potential but long, spicy finish suggests patience will be rewarded.

★★★★☆ Merlot Reserve Occasional release is easily warranted in **12** with lots of spice, leather, cooked plums & dried meat providing intriguing & concentrated core. Soft tannins add structure while oak (18 months, almost all new) asserts with fresh aniseed finish.

★★★★ Shiraz Fragrant & enticing **12** mixes smoke, spice, leather & cherries with velvet-smooth tannins. Quite forthright & powerful now, definitely enough intensity to settle & improve.

★★★★★ Rabelais Already appetising **11** (**★★★★★**) continues success of **10** with heady & powerful combination of cab with 10% petit verdot. Warm, spicy aromas of liquorice, dark chocolate, cardamom spice lead to dense, dark berries with firm tannins & lengthy finish. For the long term.

★★★★ Chardonnay Back-on-song **14** dances to a delicious tune of citrus & melon fruit beautifully balanced with a creamy core & toasty, ginger-biscuit spice. 10 months in oak, 30% new. **13** (**★★★☆**) slightly overdone.

★★★★ Ed's Reserve Dry White From unusual 'muscat' clone of chardonnay, **14** exhibits signature flowers, perfume, litchis & spice given body by ripe yellow stonefruit, all edged with good balancing acidity. **13** (**★★★★☆**) was exceptional.

★★★★ **Riesling** Excellent example **13** already showing development (plenty of petrol, lilies & perfume) with crunchy green apple freshness & crisp acidic bite. Few grams sugar add richness & body, balance out acidity to perfection. Notch above **12** (★★★★).

★★★★☆ **Sauvignon Blanc** ⊘ Appetising **15** continues quality of **14** & delights with classic Pouilly-Fumé-like flintiness, English gooseberries & grass. Brisk acidity, already well integrated, carries thrilling flavours through to an intense & persistent finish.

★★★★☆ **Sauvignon Blanc Reserve** (NEW) From a single block, **15** bursts with tropical fruit (pineapples & guavas) with orange citrus freshness from well-integrated acidity. 4 months on lees add creamy richness, leading to satisfying lengthy finish.

★★★★ **Blanc de Blancs Méthode Cap Classique** Crisp Granny Smith apple notes on nose of fresher **12** are given definition & richness by creamy core, with hints of sweet/savoury biscuits & curd. Beautifully balanced, 28 months on lees. Elgin grapes.

> **Mountain Red** ⊛ ★★★★ Thoroughly enjoyable **13** has fresh, appetising black & red fruit with soft, supportive tannins for cut-above everyday drinking. 2,800 magnums made. WO W Cape.

Verdelho (NEW) ★★★★ **15** tank sample makes pleasing entry with confected orange & lemon peel nose, good palate weight & balancing acidity. Fresh & appetising version of this Portuguese white grape. **Semillon Late Harvest** (NEW) ★★★★ Fresh appetising nose on low-alcohol **13**, with creamy apricots & nectarines. Yeasty creaminess persists on the palate before satisfying finish. Also tasted: **Muscat de Frontignan 15** ★★★ **Vin de Hel Muscat Late Harvest 13** ★★★★ Discontinued: **Riesling Late Harvest**.

Sutherland range

★★★★ **Syrah** Step-up **11** is a serious player with more chops than **10** (★★★★). Handles 15.5% alcohol well, wrapping it up in velvety black plums & cherries with ripe tannins asserting at finish. Elgin fruit, as all this range.

★★★★ **Chardonnay** ⊗ Breakfast notes on **12** of honey, oatmeal, creamy citrus. Well-integrated oak mixes happily with cooked apples & pears for harmonious, all-day everyday wine.

★★★★ **Unoaked Chardonnay** (NEW) **15** achieves wonderful balance between fruit, acid & alcohol. Fresh, zesty citrus with a touch of cream from lees-ageing, pears & melons all taking a turn at the finish.

★★★★ **Sauvignon Blanc** Pungent, vegetal **15** pre-bottling leads on to plenty of tinned guavas & grapefruits. Intense citrus core, zesty acidity & good length suggest improvements on way.

★★★★ **Viognier-Roussanne** Continuous improvement visible on **13** (★★★★☆) stepping up on lovely **12** (also tasted) with poise & grace. Delicious melange of stonefruit (peaches, nectarines & more) with added interest of fresh almonds, ginger & nutmeg spice. 10 months in oak, none new.

Also tasted: **Pinot Noir 13** ★★★ **Grenache Rosé 15** ★★★ **Riesling 15** ★★★★ Not retasted: **Cabernet Sauvignon-Petit Verdot 10** ★★★ — CM

Location/map: Stellenbosch ▪ Map grid reference: G4 ▪ WO: Stellenbosch/Elgin/Western Cape ▪ Est 1983 ▪ 1stB 1988 ▪ Tasting & sales Mon-Fri 9–5 Sat 10–3 ▪ Fee R25/6 wines, waived on purchase ▪ Owner(s) McLean & Webb Family Trusts ▪ Cellarmaster(s) Gyles Webb (1983) ▪ Winemaker(s) Rudi Schultz (Dec 2000), with Duncan Clarke (Jan 2009) ▪ 257ha/90ha (cab, grenache, merlot, p verdot, pinot, shiraz, chard, muscat d'F, riesling, rouss, sauv, viog) ▪ 1,000t/60,000cs own label 40% red 60% white ▪ BWI ▪ PO Box 2234 Dennesig Stellenbosch 7601 ▪ info@thelema.co.za ▪ www.thelema.co.za ▪ S 33° 54' 30.0" E 018° 55' 23.4" ▪ F +27 (0)21-885-1800 ▪ **T +27 (0)21-885-1924**

The Liberator

Rick the Cape Crusader, aka UK-based Richard Kelley MW, who lived and worked in the SA winelands for several years, returns regularly to 'liberate' hidden wine gems for export markets. Each wine is an 'Episode' with its own story told on the witty label and the website.

★★★★ **An Arrogance of Sommeliers** (NEW) Cab-led Bordeaux blend with merlot, malbec, petit verdot, cab franc (47/20/16/15/2). **13** tad aloof, brusque in youth, tightly knit dark fruit enveloped in dry chalky tannins mid-2015, but everything in place for harmony & approachability given time.

★★★★☆ **Special Edition Blood Brothers 'Blue'** ⓃⒺⓌ Elegant **12** merlot-led Bordeaux blend with cab, cab franc, petit verdot & malbec (59/26/6/5/4). Piquant minted fruit tone, supple dry tannins. Oak (40% new) well integrated, sappy & fresh with understated intensity & good length.

★★★★ **Special Edition Blood Brothers 'Red'** ⓃⒺⓌ Mostly syrah/shiraz (70%) with grenache, mourvèdre & splash zinfandel. **11** densely packed ripe fruit, dark & savoury, almost brooding; dry tannins temper 14.6% alcohol. Ageworthy, like 'Blue'.

★★★★ **Doctor Melck and the Spiders from SARS** ⓃⒺⓌ Well-assembled chenin, sauvignon, verdelho, viognier, semillon (46/23/19/8/4). Rich, tangy peach & lime flavours, partly polished in oak. Fresh, aromatic & appealing **14** is perfect with fusion food.

Swartland Evolution ⓃⒺⓌ Ⓥ ★★★ Light-footed & -hearted, smooth & juicy **14** has just enough of cab's cool leafy freshness to temper cinsaut's open-textured fruitiness. Unwooded & ready to savour.
Adventure Edition Midnight Bakkie ⓃⒺⓌ Ⓥ ★★★☆ Silky, rich & flavoursome **14** chenin with splash roussanne giving alluring scented white peach & lime, buffed by oak. Ready now but no rush. WO W Cape.

Special Edition Trample Dance ⓃⒺⓌ ★★★★ Kaleidoscopic 5-way blend pinotage, touriga, shiraz, grenache & mourvèdre. Quite gutsy **12**, ripe & spicy red fruits in lithe tannin structure. Well crafted, balanced, for smooth & lively drinkability. WO W Cape. Also tasted: **The Francophile Syrah 14** ★★☆ **The Francophile Chenin Blanc 15** ★★★ — MW

WO: Stellenbosch/Western Cape/Swartland ▪ Est 2010 ▪ 1stB 2008 ▪ Closed to public ▪ Owner(s) Richard Kelley MW & Eduard Haumann ▪ 50% red 50% white ▪ loirelover@hotmail.com ▪ www.theliberatorwine.com ▪ T +44 (0)1476-870717

☐ **The Marais Family** see Wonderfontein
☐ **The Mason's Winery** see Mason's Winery

Thembi & Co   Ⓠ

Medical nursing assistant turned entrepreneur and vintner Thembi Tobie for now is based in Paarl but working towards a permanent home for her eponymous brand. Her wines are unpretentious and companionable, perfect after-work unwinders and casual meal or picnic partners.

Shiraz ★★★ Last tasted ex tank, since bottled, **14** shows a scrub nuance in its dark plum character. Remains smooth & easy. **Chardonnay** ★★ Toasty thread in **14**'s gentle citrus flavours, soft & round drinkability. Also tasted: **Chenin Blanc 14** ★★★ Not retasted: **Pinotage 14** ★★★ — CR

Location: Paarl ▪ WO: Swartland ▪ Est/1stB 2009 ▪ Tasting by appt ▪ Owner(s) Thembi Tobie ▪ PO Box 3511 Paarl 7120 ▪ thembi@thembiwines.co.za ▪ www.thembiwines.co.za ▪ T +27 (0)83-277-5117

☐ **Thembu** see House of Mandela
☐ **The Mentors** see KWV

Themika   ⌂ ⃞ ⓃⒺⓌ

When Cape Town doctors Paul and Dagmar Whitaker bought a fruit farm in Tulbagh (named for daughters Kim and Thea), they were delighted to find old chenin vines. The grapes have gone into the illustrious straw wines made for Tulbagh Mountain Vineyards (now Fable) and Mullineux, but are now vinified for the Themika label by Paul at Antebellum near Riebeek-Kasteel, with owner Herman Redelinghuys and consultant JH Meyer – something of a specialist in the hands-off style the Whitakers seek.

★★★★☆ **Barrel Select Chenin Blanc 14** from low-yielding vines, spontaneous ferment/maturation in mostly older oak, unfined & unfiltered. Very fragrant, flavoursome with white peach, almonds & fynbos; oak is only a background murmur, & 'light' drinkability achieved at just over 13% alcohol. — TJ, CvZ

Location/WO: Tulbagh ▪ 1stB 2013 ▪ Themika guest house T +27 (0)83-373-5818 (farm house & 3 self-catering cottages) ▪ MTB routes ▪ Owner(s) Paul & Dagmar Whitaker ▪ Winemaker(s) Paul Whitaker & Herman Redelinghuys/Johan Meyer (consultants) ▪ Viticulturist(s) Paul Whitaker ▪ 56ha/3ha (chenin) ▪ 4,5t/220cs own label 100% white ▪ ansec166@docswhitaker.co.za ▪ www.themika.com

☐ **The Naked Truth** *see* PicardiRebel

The Observatory Cellar 💡

The Observatory was among the first with a 'natural and green' philosophy, and high-end wines expressive of the prime north Perdeberg terroir. Looking to restore past form, recent co-owner and cellarmaster (with advisers) Joe van der Westhuizen is 'increasing the extent of rejuvenated old bushvines', some planted around 1950, to create a bigger pool of quality grapes for harvest 2016 and beyond.

Dark Matter Red Blend (NEW) ★★ Al fresco wine from shiraz & pinotage, suitably dark colour & black (berry) aromas lighten & get tangy on palate with piquant berry juice character. Enjoy **14** this summer, lightly chilled. Not retasted: **Chardonnay 14** ★★ **Chenin Blanc 14** ★★★★ — MW

Location: Malmesbury ▪ Map/WO: Swartland ▪ Est 2011 ▪ 1stB 2014 ▪ Tasting, sales & cellar tours by appt ▪ Owner(s) Joe van der Westhuizen & Mechtild Braxmaier ▪ Cellarmaster(s) Joe van der Westhuizen, assisted by consultants ▪ Winemaker(s) Joe van der Westhuizen (Nov 2011) ▪ Viticulturist(s) various ▪ 71ha/20ha (ptage, shiraz, chard, chenin) ▪ 8t/±580-600cs own label 40% red 60% white ▪ PO Box 16306 Vlaeberg 8018 ▪ wine@theobservatorycellar.com ▪ www.theobservatorycellar.com ▪ S 33° 31' 17.4" E 018° 46' 59.7" ▪ **T +27 (0)62-071-4258/+27 (0)83-628-9313**

☐ **The Old Man's Blend** *see* Groote Post Vineyards
☐ **The Old School** *see* Alkmaar Boutique Vineyard
☐ **The Pavillion** *see* Boschendal Wines
☐ **The Point** *see* Cape Point Vineyards

The Rhino of Linton Park 💡

UK-owned Wellington producer Linton Park invites you to 'taste the nature of Africa' in these easy-drinking wines, showing environmental and social concern by helping protect the endangered rhino, using eco-friendly lightweight glass and bottling in Africa – 'fairer for Africa'.

Red Rhino range

Cabernet Sauvignon ★★★ Sweet fruitcake ease to light **14**. Unoaked, as all Rhinos, with few grams flattering sugar, as all the reds. **Cape Red** ⊘ ★★★ Fynbos edge to mulberry fruit of **13**, 60/40 merlot & shiraz melange. Soft tannin hug on finish. Also tasted: **Merlot 14** ★★★ **Pinotage 13** ★★★ Not retasted: **Shiraz 13** ★★★

Pink Rhino range

Rosé (🍷) ★★★ Tangy, juicy, light red berries on sweetish yet fresh **NV** from two white grapes & shiraz. Not retasted: **Natural Sweet NV** ★★

White Rhino range

> **Chardonnay** ⊘ 🍇 ★★★ Tangy lemon-lime succulence to **14**, a most attractive, fruit-filled dry sipper. Modest 12.5% alcohol for lunching.

Cape White ⊘ ★★★ **15** ably manages awkward union of spiky sauvignon & broader chardonnay. Also tasted: **Chenin Blanc** ⊘ **15** ★★★ **Sauvignon Blanc 15** ★★ — DS

Location: Wellington ▪ WO: Western Cape/Wellington ▪ Tasting & sales by appt at Linton Park ▪ Owner(s) Camellia PLC UK ▪ Winemaker(s) JG Auret (2007) ▪ Viticulturist(s) Rudolf Jansen van Vuuren (2012) & Johan Viljoen (consultant) ▪ PO Box 1234 Wellington 7654 ▪ sales@lintonparkwines.co.za, info@lintonparkwines.co.za ▪ www.rhinowines.com, www.lintonparkwines.co.za ▪ F +27 (0)21-873-0851 ▪ **T +27 (0)21-873-1625**

☐ **The Royal** *see* Valley Vineyards Wine Company
☐ **The Ruins** *see* Bon Cap Organic Winery
☐ **The Rustler** *see* Flagstone Winery
☐ **The Sadie Family** *see* Sadie Family Wines
☐ **The Saints** *see* DGB

☐ **The Spice Route Winery** *see* Spice Route Winery
☐ **The Stellenbosch Reserve** *see* Stellenbosch Reserve

The Three Foxes

They couldn't resist! Having settled on a single-variety old-vines clairette blanche bottling as their white wine going forward, the three pushovers, er, foxes – Mullineux & Leeu cellarmaster Chris Mullineux and brothers Pascal and Olivier Schildt – succumbed to the charms of a 55-year-old semillon block, which they've blended, rather deliciously, with the clairette and given the charming/apropos name Gnarly White. Doubtless it will help keep sales in London and New York ticking over 'quietly but nicely'.

Gnarly White ⓝ ⓦ ★★★ Fashionably skin-fermented (3 months) clairette blanche & old-oaked semillon (63/37) **14** blend is tailormade for summer tapas: dry, inherently fresh & creamy, with subtle lanolin, apple cider & marzipan flavours. Bonus of modest 12% alcohol. Also in magnum.

Occasional release: **Carignan**, **Mourvèdre**, **Castillo Syrah**, **Clairette Blanche**. — MW

Location: Riebeek-Kasteel ▪ WO: Coastal ▪ Est/1stB 2004 ▪ Closed to public ▪ Owner(s) Pascal Schildt, Olivier Schildt, Mullineux & Leeu Family Wines ▪ Winemaker(s)/viticulturist(s) Chris Mullineux (Jan 2004) ▪ 1.2ha (carignan, clairette, sem) ▪ 4t/400cs own label 20% red 80% white ▪ PO Box 369 Riebeek-Kasteel 7307 ▪ pascal.schildt@gmail.com ▪ www.the-three-foxes.com ▪ F +27 (0)86-720-1541 ▪ **T +27 (0)82-333-6888**

☐ **The Tin Mine** *see* Zevenwacht
☐ **The Township Winery** *see* Township Winery
☐ **The Tree Series** *see* Bellingham

Theuniskraal   ⓠ ⓰

Named for a son of one of the earliest families to settle in Tulbagh Valley (circa 1699), Theuniskraal has been farmed by the Jordaans since 1927. Their Cape Riesling, from the variety also known as crouchen blanc, is something of a Cape institution, having been made since 1948.

Moscato Rosé ★★ Shocking pink **15** has matching unsubtle sweetness & red berry flavour, less extrovert alcohol (10%). From rare muscat ottonel, splash shiraz. **Bouquet Blanc** ★★☆ Natural Sweet ex gewürztraminer & muscadel, **15** delightful grapey raisin flavours, light hearted (10% alcohol) & balanced. Also tasted: **Cape Riesling 15** ★★★ **Semillon-Chardonnay 15** ★★★ Not retasted: **Prestige 13** ★★★ — GdB

Location/map/WO: Tulbagh ▪ Est 1705 ▪ 1stB 1947 ▪ Tasting & sales Mon-Fri 9–12 & 1–4, Sat 10–1 ▪ Closed Easter Sat/Sun, Dec 25 & Jan 1 ▪ Owner(s)/viticulturist(s) Jordaan family ▪ Cellarmaster(s) Andries Jordaan (1991) ▪ Winemaker(s) Andries Jordaan (1991) & Wagner Jordaan ▪ 140ha wine ▪ BWI ▪ PO Box 34 Tulbagh 6820 ▪ tkraal@lando.co.za ▪ www.theuniskraal.co.za ▪ S 33° 13' 41.3" E 019° 8' 7.1" ▪ F +27 (0)23-230-2284 ▪ **T +27 (0)23-230-0687/89**

☐ **The Village Walk** *see* Franschhoek Cellar
☐ **The Wine Fusion** *see* Wine Fusion

The Winery of Good Hope   ⓠ

'The Winery of Good Hope is more than just a winery,' says founder and MD Alex Dale. 'It's an approach. An alternative way of thinking, being and doing.' The aim at this Helderberg cellar, he says, is to make 'quality wine with a conscience' using increasingly non-interventionist techniques including carbonic maceration, cluster pressing, natural fermentation, no filtration and low sulphur. Following critical acclaim for the additive-free Radford Dale wines, Alex says he has been inundated with requests for the fresher, lower-alcohol wines that his team has been developing across each range in recent years. He also points out that the Good Hope/Land of Hope names are more than vague geographical reference: 'They reflect that we're fully accredited for environmental, ethical and social-upliftment practices.'

Radford Dale range

★★★★ **Thirst Cinsault** (NEW) Best served chilled, **15** defies red wine rules with modest alcohol (11.5%), barely discernible tannins & core of fresh but concentrated red cherry & cranberry fruit for easy drinking.

★★★★ **Thirst Gamay Noir** (NEW) An even lighter red for chilled refreshment, juicy **15** with floral nose is packed with red cherry & strawberry fruit, fresh & bright but not simple thanks to herby, savoury notes. Coastal WO.

★★★★☆ **Freedom Pinot Noir** Already charming **14** should go the distance with its depth of flavour & complexity, violet perfume & sour cherry/red berry with some earthiness; finely structured, with poised acidity & taut tannins. Natural ferment. WO Elgin.

★★★★☆ **Pinot Noir AD** Only made in best vintages when deemed capable of ageing 'for a good number of years', **13** from Elgin has more intense red cherry & raspberry fruit than Freedom sibling, tangy & quite tannic with seductive hint of smoke.

★★★★ **Pinot Noir EL** (NEW) Sporting its Rhône-based maker's initials, **13** bursts with red cherry/berry fruit at modest 12.5% alcohol; light bodied but smooth with fine, nicely knit tannins. Also-tasted **14** (slightly higher alcohol) promises similar development. Both WO Elgin.

★★★★ **Frankenstein Pinotage** Pure berry fruit abounds in lightly wooded **14** (★★★★☆), prof Perold's 'monster' showing gentle side with fynbos perfume, restraint with soft tannins, elegance with fresh acidity, real character with clove spice – even more than in **13**.

★★★★ **Nudity** 'Natural wine' (no added sulphur, yeasts or additives) from organic Voor Paardeberg vines, **14** (★★★★☆) has red plum, raspberry & redcurrant fruit with hints of fynbos & smoked meat, no spice derived from old barrels, as used in **13** & before.

★★★★☆ **Syrah** Denser, darker, weightier than 'nude' sibling, **13** ex Stellenbosch is nonetheless fresh & elegant, with pinch of black pepper, also Chinese five spice, nicely knit with berry fruit after 19 months in French oak (20% new).

★★★★ **Black Rock** Brilliant **13** (★★★★★), medium-bodied blend of co-fermented Swartland syrah/ shiraz, cinsaut, carignan, grenache, mourvèdre & viognier has delicate lavender perfume, juicy bramble/ wild berry fruits & savoury spice, immediately accessible like **12** but built to age.

★★★★☆ **Gravity** (②) Forceful, forward **10** from shiraz, cab, merlot offering spice & bright red & black berries on a firmly structured base. Successfully balances the claims of fresh fruitiness & savoury depths to give some early complexity supported by good oaking. Will benefit from cellaring.

★★★★☆ **Chardonnay** (②) A little toast accompanies the refined cool citrus on **13** in youth, though mostly older barrels used. Stony minerality & subtlety ensure big distance from fat, caricatured chards. A satisfying, silky glide all the way to lingering, mouthwatering finish. Bone-dry & just 12.5% alcohol.

★★★★☆ **Renaissance Chenin Blanc** (②) Another wine with stony, understated intensity & finesse. The oak on **13** from old, unirrigated bushvines broadens & adds to the texture, supporting the clean fruit flavours. The elegant, serene highpoint from this chenin specialist.

★★★★ **Thirst Clairette Blanche-Chenin Blanc-Verdelho** (NEW) Boundaries are pushed in new 'natural wine' Thirst label, unusual **15** white blend is refreshing with just 12% alcohol, high natural acidity & distinctly salty minerality that somehow enhances apple, pear, peach sweetness.

★★★★ **Vine Dried Chenin Blanc** Lusciously sweet but lively **13**, rich, with Golden Delicious & yellow sultana flavours from Stellenbosch grapes desiccated on the vine, also boosting balancing acidity. 375 ml.

Discontinued: **Merlot**, **Shiraz-Merlot**, **Vine Dried Viognier**.

Land of Hope range

★★★★ **Cabernet Sauvignon** From two vineyards on the Helderberg, **12** has intense blueberry & dark cherry fruit with slight herby note, nicely rounded with grippy but supple tannins.

★★★★☆ **Reserve Cabernet Sauvignon** More plush & complex than cab sibling above, **13** has almost Ribena-like black fruit concentration & a hint of earthiness, as did last **11** (★★★★), yet is also fresh & elegant with delicate oak spice, nicely balanced with fine, smooth tannins.

★★★★ **Reserve Pinot Noir** **12** from Elgin & Stellenbosch has lovely red berry purity & hint of savoury minerality, less intense than Radford Dales but also less pricey & therefore great value for money.

★★★★ **Chardonnay** (NEW) Elegant & approachable **14** from Stellenbosch & Robertson has orange citrus tang, rich & rounded from nine months on lees, subtle oak spice from barrel-fermented portion.

★★★★ **Reserve Chenin Blanc** Single-vineyard, barrel-fermented **14** from Helderberg has floral nose & crisp red apple flavours, bright acidity cutting through creamy texture, appealing hints of vanilla.

Vinum range

★★★★ **Cabernet Sauvignon** There's a slight leafiness to **13**, acidic freshness also lifting blackcurrant intensity, while firm but supple tannins as well as cigarbox spice hint at graceful ageing potential.

★★★★ **Chenin Blanc** (②) Perhaps the most forthcoming of the chenins. **13** sweet melony flavours & notes of tropical ripeness, but less concentrated than **12** (★★★★☆) & showing its oaking a little more.

Winery of Good Hope range

★★★★ **Granite Ridge Reserve** (②) Varying blend with shiraz. **12** (★★★★) has pinotage & 3 others. Big & bold, less easygoing than previous **09**. Tannic power, juicy fruit, solid dry finish.

Mountainside Shiraz (✓) (🍷) ★★★★ Fermented naturally then half barrel-matured in older oak 6 months, accessible **13** is mostly about ripe red berry fruit as well as fynbos aromatics with hint of smoke.

Bush Vine Chenin Blanc ★★★★ From old Helderberg bushvines, **14** is dry but intensely fruity, peach blossom nose leading to peach fruit & Granny Smith apple sweet-sour acidity, 9 months on lees adding weight. Also tasted: **Oceanside Cabernet Sauvignon-Merlot 13** ★★★ **Unoaked Chardonnay 14** ★★★ Not retasted: **Bush Vine Pinotage 12** ★★★★ Not tasted: **Pinot Noir Reserve**. — JG

Location: Stellenbosch ▪ Map: Helderberg ▪ WO: Stellenbosch/Swartland/Western Cape/Elgin/Stellenbosch ▪ Est/1stB 1998 ▪ Tasting & sales Mon-Fri 9-5 by appt ▪ Closed all pub hols ▪ Owner(s) Alex Dale, Andy Openshaw, Yalumba, Edouard Labeye, Cliff Roberson, Ben Radford & Heather Whitman ▪ Cellarmaster(s) Edouard Labeye (1998) ▪ Winemaker(s) Jacques de Klerk (Oct 2009), with Bernhard Bredell (2013) ▪ Viticulturist(s) Edouard Labeye, Jacques de Klerk, Gus Dale & Bernhard Bredell ▪ ±100ha (cab, carignan, cinsaut, gamay, grenache, mourv, ptage, pinot, syrah, chard, chenin, clairette, verdelho) ▪ 600t/40,000cs own label 50% red 50% white ▪ Brands for clients: Pick's Pick ▪ Level 2 BEE, IPW, WIETA ▪ Postnet Suite 124 Private Bag X15 Somerset West 7129 ▪ thewineryofgoodhope@thewineryofgoodhope.co.za ▪ www.thewineryofgoodhope.com ▪ S 34° 0' 57.5" E 018° 49' 2.6" ▪ F +27 (0)21-855-5529 ▪ **T +27 (0)21-855-5528**

☐ **The Wingnut** see Chateau Naudé Wine Creation

The Wolftrap

This range of modestly priced wines (and over-delivering, it's generally conceded) is made by eminent Boekenhoutskloof, from widely sourced fruit. And is hugely successful. 'It's just gone crazy!' says Boekenhoutskloof technical director Marc Kent happily. He points out that one reason for the quality is that the overflow from the smart and expensively made Chocolate Block ends up in these bottles.

★★★★ **The Wolftrap White** (✓) **14** raises bar on **13** (★★★☆) in grip & concentration. Viognier (48%) leads chenin, dab grenache blanc. Broad, juicy & vibrant stonefruit flavour balanced by oak.

The Wolftrap (✓) (🍷) ★★★★ Ripe cherry, plum & spice indicative of the syrah/shiraz, mourvèdre, viognier grapes in **14**. Lithe & supple yet well defined by oaked portion. Also in magnum. WO W Cape as all. **The Wolftrap Rosé** (🍷) ★★★ Dry **15** has almost equal parts shiraz, grenache with light (14%) cinsaut seasoning. Ample berry/cherry vibrancy, light yet lingering. — FM

☐ **The Zahir** see Lateganskop Winery
☐ **Thierry & Guy** see Fat Bastard

Thokozani Wines

(②) (🍴) (🏠) (◎)

Now into its second decade, Wellington's Thokozani is mostly owned by Diemersfontein Wines employees, with Diemersfontein and external investors providing a gentle wind beneath their spreading wings.

This empowerment venture has become as much a hospitality and event organisation (with conference facilities) as a wine company, with export markets on four continents.

SMV ★★★★ Cocoa edge to soft-textured plum fruit on **14** shiraz, mourvèdre & viognier mix. Light oak frame (combo American & French barrels). **CCV ★★★ 13** blend of chenin, chardonnay & viognier offers stonefruit & melon succulence. Unwooded, light & easy. Not retasted: **Rosé 14 ★★** — FM

Location/WO: Wellington ▪ Map: Paarl & Wellington ▪ Map grid reference: F2 ▪ Est/1stB 2005 ▪ Tasting & sales daily 10-5 ▪ Closed Dec 25 ▪ Cellar tours by appt ▪ Seasons Restaurant ▪ Tour groups ▪ Conferences ▪ Walks/hikes ▪ 4-star Thokozani Cottages ▪ Owner(s) Diemersfontein employees, external investors & Diemersfontein Wines ▪ Cellarmaster(s) Francois Roode (Sep 2003) ▪ Winemaker(s) Francois Roode (Sep 2003), with Lauren Hulsman (Nov 2011) ▪ Viticulturist(s) Waldo Kellerman (Aug 2007) ▪ 180ha/60ha (cabs s/f, grenache, malbec, mourv, p verdot, ptage, roobernet, shiraz, chenin, viog) ▪ 60t/8,000cs own label 40% red 40% white 20% rosé ▪ WIETA ▪ PO Box 41 Wellington 7654 ▪ info@thokozani.co.za ▪ www.thokozani.co.za ▪ S 33° 39' 41.1" E 019° 0' 31.1" ▪ F +27 (0)21-864-2095 ▪ **T +27 (0)21-864-5050**

Thorne & Daughters Wines

Seeking out 'great parcels of vineyard' and vinifying their fruit simply, honestly and gently is the approach of 'ridiculously passionate' boutique vintners John Thorne Seccombe and wife Tasha. The couple launched their vintage-toy-themed wines mid-2014 to immediate critical acclaim and commercial success, locally and in several export markets. They've since moved cellar operations to Gabriëlskloof (home to a number of other young guns, who are 'a constant source of energy and inspiration'), continued their search for exceptional blocks and 'really started to refine our vision of Cape wines'.

★★★★☆ Zoetrope Chardonnay (NEW) From old Overberg dryland bushvines, native yeast fermented in old French oak. **14** great delicacy & intensity achieved with just 12.4% alcohol. Pure lemon & lime fruits delivered with dash, zest & pithy grip. Very long. Needs time to settle; good to ±2020, possibly beyond.

★★★★☆ Rocking Horse Chenin in lead role in **14** multi-region blend. Fresher, less oxidative than roussanne-based **13**, throwing focus on the many intriguing layers of flavour — almonds, citrus & spice — & creamy yet firm texture, like white wine in red wine's skin; should age accordingly. Fascinating & fabulous.

Not tasted: **Tin Soldier Semillon**. — AL

Location: Bot River ▪ WO: Western Cape/Overberg ▪ Est 2012 ▪ 1stB 2013 ▪ Closed to public ▪ Owner(s) John & Tasha Seccombe ▪ Cellarmaster(s)/winemaker(s)/viticulturist(s) John Seccombe (Dec 2012) ▪ 20t/1,000cs own label 5% red 95% white ▪ PO Box 96 Elgin 7180 ▪ john@thorneanddaughters.com ▪ www.thorneanddaughters.com ▪ F +27 (0)86-246-2923 ▪ **T +27 (0)76-036-7116**

Thunderchild

Bearing the motto 'In Aid of Humanity', Thunderchild is made pro bono by sympathetic Robertson wineries and sold from their cellardoors. After audited costs, all proceeds are ploughed into the education of the children of Die Herberg, a shelter founded in 1918 in the wake of the influenza pandemic.

Thunderchild ★★★★ Behind the lovely label is ripely attractive, modestly oaked **13** blend merlot, cab franc & cab. Balanced & ready for early drinking, with nice texture & gentle grip. — TJ

Location/WO: Robertson ▪ Est 2003 ▪ 1stB 2008 ▪ Wines available from Rooiberg Winery, Ashton Cellar, Bon Courage, Robertson Winery, Ashton Wine Boutique, Affie Plaas Farmstall, Platform 62, Tanagra Winery, De Wetshof Winery & La Verne Wine Boutique — see individual cellars for opening times ▪ Owner(s) Thunderchild Wingerd Trust ▪ Cellarmaster(s) Various Robertson winegrowers ▪ 5ha (cabs s/f, merlot) ▪

PO Box 770 Robertson 6705 ▪ info@thunderchild.co.za ▪ www.thunderchild.co.za ▪ F +27 (0)23-626-3664 ▪ **T +27 (0)23-626-3661**

Tierhoek　　　　　　　　　　　　　　　　　　　　　　　⚲ 🍷 🏠 ◎

Picturesque, remote and challenging, but the results have justified the effort at this Piekenierskloof property bought by the Sandells in 2001. Old vineyards were part of the attraction, 60-year-old ungrafted grenache and 40-year-old chenin, rare assets in the winelands, and still delivering desirable quality, but new planting involved the removal of massive boulders. Respecting the environment, the wines are made as naturally as possible, starting with no pesticides or herbicides in the vineyards. From the old plantings comes a single-vineyard chenin blanc, while a varietal mourvèdre also joins the range.

Tierhoek range

★★★★☆ **Grenache** ⊘ Terroir expressive with fynbos, dried herbs, **13**'s wild berries brushed with salty liquorice, prosciutto tones from small French barrel oaking. Succulent, smoothly curvaceous & delicious. Includes dab of shiraz.

★★★★ **Mourvèdre** (NEW) Plush & opulent, dark-fruited **13** has mocha, tarry notes, a touch of wildness hiding in its depths. A firm tannin backbone from 18 months French barriques, bodes well for the future.

★★★★ **Syrah-Mourvèdre-Grenache** Mainly syrah/shiraz but others make their presence felt in dark & brooding **14**, smoked meat, cloves & allspice, some fynbos, with black plums at core. Succulent, already appealing, can age.

★★★★ **Chardonnay** Last a preview, **14**'s extra year added richness, settled the flavours. Natural ferment, light oaking, but buttered toast adds layers to the citrus, silky elegance. Fresh mineral notes at the end.

★★★★ **Chenin Blanc** From 37 year old vines. Tropical, with small oaked portion lending a toasted almond note, **14** is smooth textured, curvaceous, a fine acid thread carrying the flavours to a dry finish.

★★★★☆ **Chenin Blanc Reserve** (NEW) ⊘ From a single-vineyard & differently vinified to its sibling, 100% oak treatment in 300L barrels, **14** is svelte, tightly knit. Cedar tones vie with stonefruit, savoury end made for fine-dining. Sophisticated, impressive.

★★★★ **Sauvignon Blanc** Intense gooseberries & passionfruit greet you in **15**, but the cool climate comes through on the palate, mineral, flinty notes making an appearance.

★★★★☆ **Straw Wine** Powerhouse of flavours & sweetness from 30 year old hillside chenin vines, grapes air-dried & vinified in a solera, barrel aged 1-6 years. Sherry-like perfume in **NV**, dried fruit, then surprisingly luscious & mouthfilling, long apricot richness. In 375 ml.

Sandveld range

★★★★ **Sauvignon Blanc** ⊘ **15** (★★★★☆) differs from its sibling in its pithy grapefruit, green fig styling, more prominent minerality. Lovely, tightly focused, ends on a lemongrass note. Improves on **13**. **14** sold out untasted.

Piekeniers range

White ★★★★ Blend chenin, chardonnay, sauvignon in previewed **15**, already expressive. Stonefruit throughout, tangy acidity giving lipsmacking freshness. Occasional release: **Red**. — CR

Location: Citrusdal ▪ Map: Olifants River ▪ WO: Piekenierskloof ▪ Est 2001 ▪ 1stB 2003 ▪ Tasting, sales & cellar tours on the farm Mon-Fri 8.30-4.30 by appt ▪ Fee R20, waived on purchase ▪ Closed all pub hols ▪ BYO picnic ▪ Walks/hikes ▪ Conservation area ▪ Guest house (sleeps 9) ▪ Owner(s) Shelley Sandell ▪ Winemaker(s) Carla Nieuwoudt (Jan 2014), with Basie Snyers (Oct 2006) ▪ Viticulturist(s) Ryno Kellerman (Aug 2006) ▪ 700ha/16ha (grenache, mourv, shiraz, chard, chenin, sauv) ▪ 70t/6,000cs own label 40% red 60% white ▪ BWI, IPW ▪ PO Box 53372 Kenilworth 7745 ▪ info@tierhoek.com ▪ www.tierhoek.com ▪ S 32° 23' 27.49" E 018° 51' 24.14" ▪ F +27 (0)86-731-6351 ▪ **T +27 (0)21-674-3041/+27 (0)82-536-7132**

☐ **Tiger Horse** *see* Boutinot South Africa
☐ **Time Manner Place** *see* Flagstone Winery

Tim Martin Wines   ⓘ NEW

Tim Martin has established a rare thing – a wholly urban winery, in converted warehouse space in gritty Salt River near central Cape Town. Here he ferments his reds in open-top wooden fermenters and whites in large oak barrels or foudres, without yeast inoculation. If his winemaking philosophy demands minimal intervention, his overall aim is also simple: drinkability. 'I would much rather,' he says, 'that the bottle be finished easily than that it scores well in a blind line-up.'

★★★★ **Chad** Sensitively older-oaked **14** chenin fresher, less assertive than Mothership. Clean, pure, characterful & complex – from fennel hint on aroma to long lemon-tinged finish. Gentle acid, silky texture.

★★★★ **Mothership** Appley, slightly oxidative, wild-ferment character on **14** chenin, not at expense of fruit depth. Gently rich, fine acidity, good pithy finish. Ex Paarl; fermented/aged in new 1,500L foudre.

Qaisar ★★★☆ **14** from mourvèdre refreshing & fairly light; some sweet fruit flavours but perhaps a touch dilute. Strong tannins need time – which might much improve the wine & its rating. — TJ, CvZ

Location: Cape Town ▪ Map: Cape Peninsula ▪ WO: Swartland/Paarl ▪ Est 2012 ▪ 1stB 2014 ▪ Tasting Sat by appt ▪ Closed all pub hols ▪ Owner(s)/cellarmaster(s)/winemaker(s)/viticulturist(s) Tim Martin ▪ 1,100cs own label 33% red 67% white ▪ Unit 3 Spencer Square, Spencer Road, Salt River, Cape Town 7925 ▪ tim@tmwines.co.za ▪ www.tmwines.co.za ▪ S 33° 55' 45.10" E 018° 27' 54.30"

☐ **Tin Cups** see Wineways Marketing

☐ **Tin Hill** see Signal Gun Wines

☐ **Tin Mine** see Zevenwacht

☐ **Titanic** see Louis

☐ **Title Deed** see Croydon Vineyard Residential Estate

☐ **Tobias** see Bryan MacRobert Wines

Tokara   ⓘ ⚟ ◎ ⚇ ♿

The early 2000s editions of this guide were marked by continually disappointed expectations of a wine bearing the label of this ambitious winery founded by banker GT Ferreira on the crest of Helshoogte Pass, just outside Stellenbosch town (a few had appeared as Zondernaam wines). It was the 2006 edition that announced, with clusters of stars, the maiden releases. Miles Mossop was now getting into his stride (having had the benefit of consulting eminent Thelema neighbour Gyles Webb). He and viticulturist Aidan Morton have in the succeeding decade shown themselves to be a formidable (and unusually lengthy) partnership, taking Tokara into the top league of Cape wine. Ferreira-owned farms in Elgin and Hemel-en-Aarde supplement the home-grown crop with grapes from cooler terroir.

Reserve Collection

★★★★☆ **Pinotage** Swaggeringly bold & ripe **13** (★★★). Ample fruit, bright acidity & spicy all-new oak still negotiating roles, warm-hearted 15.5% alcohol the smoothing mediator. Departure from balanced **12** & previous.

★★★★ **Syrah** Achieves elegant balance after lighter **11** (★★★★), **12** clean-fruited intensity with subtle white pepper nuance; oak well integrated into firm, fresh structure. Still an infant, deserves cellaring.

★★★★☆ **Director's Reserve Red 12** follows familiar classic styling. Now a 4-way Bordeaux blend of cab, merlot, petit verdot, cab franc (72/15/10/3), no malbec as in **11**. Structured, seamless & already elegantly poised albeit still very youthful – will age with distinction. Larger bottle formats available.

★★★★☆ **Stellenbosch Chardonnay 14** trumps **13** (★★★★) in piquant fruit/acid balance, supple & rich framework & very good length; shows more toasty oak than Tokara sibling but has depth of flavour to carry it. Already tempting but plenty of life & future rewards in store.

★★★★☆ **Elgin Sauvignon Blanc** Unoaked, as for Tokara sibling, but with more intensity. **15** subtle white peach, a mineral touch & leesy breadth; shows real presence & concentration from cooler Elgin site, with a long grapefruit farewell. Elegant fine-dining partner.

★★★★☆ **Director's Reserve White** Classy **14** sauvignon/semillon (71/29) blend. Quite tight-knit & bracing but leavened by polished lanolin, beeswax nuance & generous 14.2% alcohol. Similar 27% new oak but more understated than previous, with structure & pedigree to age elegantly.

★★★★☆ **Noble Late Harvest** ⊗ Oak-fermented/aged **13** from Elgin sauvignon. Unctuously rich & viscous elixir, laced with glacé pineapple, barley sugar & lime. Focused intensity at 10.67% alcohol.

Discontinued: **Walker Bay Chardonnay**, **Walker Bay Sauvignon Blanc**.

Tokara range

★★★★ **Cabernet Sauvignon** Now pure cab, **13** (★★★★) is leaner & more herbaceous than more intense, finer **12**. Supple tannin structure, smooth & warm courtesy 14.6% alcohol.

★★★★ **Chardonnay** Balanced & fresh, zesty flourish of lime enhanced by brush of new oak; **14** medium bodied with some mid-palate creaminess. Equally good solo or with food. WO W Cape, like next.

★★★★ **Sauvignon Blanc 15** without semillon of previous but in similar bright style. Tangy passionfruit in piquant balance, light footed with life for good few years.

Also tasted: **Grenache Rosé 15** ★★★ Not retasted: **Grenache 12** ★★★☆ **Shiraz 11** ★★★☆

Brandy range

★★★★ **5 Year Potstill** Current release **07** shows attractive youthful mix dried fruit & floral notes, with nutty, clean oak support & a hint of sweetness. Light, smooth & bright. — WB, MW

Location/map: Stellenbosch ▪ Map grid reference: G4 ▪ WO: Stellenbosch/Elgin/Walker Bay/Western Cape ▪ 1stB 2001 ▪ Tasting & sales Mon-Fri 9—5 Sat/Sun 10—3 ▪ Closed Easter Fri/Mon & Dec 25 ▪ Tokara Restaurant Tue-Sun lunch 12.30-2.30 & dinner 7-9.30 ▪ Delicatessen Tue-Sun 10-4 ▪ Facilities for children ▪ Gift shop ▪ Art exhibitions ▪ Owner(s) GT & Anne-Marie Ferreira ▪ Winemaker(s) Miles Mossop (Jan 2000), with Dumisani Mathonsi (Jan 2004) ▪ Viticulturist(s) Aidan Morton (Nov 2000) ▪ 104ha (cabs s/f, grenache, malbec, merlot, mourv, p verdot, ptage, shiraz, chard, chenin, sauv, sem) ▪ 705t/100,000cs own label 40% red 59% white 1% rosé ▪ PO Box 662 Stellenbosch 7599 ▪ wine@tokara.com ▪ www.tokara.com ▪ S 33° 55' 2.9" E 018° 55' 13.7" ▪ F +27 (0)21-808-5911 ▪ **T +27 (0)21-808-5900**

☐ **Tooverberg** *see* Klein Parys Vineyards

Topaz Wine   ⓛ ♿

This winemaking collaboration among friends, started in 2000 from half a hectare of garden-grown pinot noir, continues to expand its offering, with a Custom Crush White now complementing the Red. The Topaz team, though down to just two, now offer all-year tastings and report 'enthusiastic and positive feedback' on their online beginners wine course (see their website).

★★★★ **Pinot Noir** Clean-cut **13** from Elgin shows cherry, wood spice & cured meat complexity, moderate tannin grip for now or 3-5 years. Lightly chill in summer.

★★★★ **Shiraz** ⊗ Last tasted (as 'Syrah') was elegant **07**. Smoothly textured spicy **12** (★★★★) exhibits Elgin's cool-climate pepperiness & finishes with appetising savoury acidity.

★★★★ **Viognier** Handsome old-barrel-matured **14** from Franschhoek vines. Enticing yellow stonefruit, almond whiffs, enlivening acidity delivers step up on lightly oxidative **12** (★★★★).

Custom Crush White ⓝⓔⓦ ★★★☆ Equal parts sauvignon, semillon. Floral nose, palate that bursts with lime, greengage & tropical fruit, feisty acidity; **15** is the perfect seafood companion. Also tasted: **Custom Crush Red NV** ★★★★ In abeyance: **Shiraz-Mourvèdre**. — GM

Location/map: Stellenbosch ▪ Map grid reference: F2 ▪ WO: Elgin/Simonsberg-Paarl/Franschhoek/Stellenbosch ▪ Est 2000 ▪ 1stB 2001 ▪ Tasting & sales Sat 10-2, or by prior arrangement ▪ Owner(s) Topaz Wine Company (Pty) Ltd, shareholders Tanja Beutler & Anthony Hill ▪ Winemaker(s) Topaz winemaking team ▪ 1,200cs own label 80% red 20% white ▪ IPW ▪ PO Box 804 Somerset Mall 7137 ▪ tanja@topazwines.co.za ▪ www.topazwineco.com ▪ S 33° 50' 55.67" E 018° 51' 26.19" ▪ F +27 (0)86-612-6118 ▪ **T +27 (0)21-855-4275**

Topiary Wines   ⓛ ⓨ⅃ ⌂ ⌂ ◉ ♿

The name Franschhoek takes on added significance at this boutique winery in the foothills of the Wemmershoek mountains, for it's owned by two Frenchmen with long wine experience. Philippe Colin, as a vigneron in Burgundy's Chassagne-Montrachet, knows a thing or two about producing chardonnay and will release his maiden Cape version to high expectations. Accommodation in self-catering cottages and the manor house, all with stunning views, is now offered too.

★★★★ **Shiraz** Modern-styled **11** (★★★☆) not as elegant or intense as last-tasted **13** unoaked preview. Lively acidity only just keeps ample ripe fruit & full 14.4% alcohol in check.

★★★★★ **Blanc de Blancs Brut** ② Méthode cap classique sparkling **11** (★★★★☆) in a richer, more contemplative style than last-tasted, stellar **09**, which showcased chardonnay's zesty freshness. 30 months on lees, with fine lime undertone & long, clean finish.

Cabernet Sauvignon ★★★★ Oaked **11**, out of vintage sequence, better balanced than **13** unwooded preview. Ample ripe fruit & approachable tannins, ready to be savoured. Not tasted: **Rosé**. — MW

Location/map/WO: Franschhoek ▪ Est 2005 ▪ 1stB 2006 ▪ Tasting & sales Tue-Sat 9-5 Sun & Mon by appt only ▪ Fee R20, waived on purchase ▪ Closed Easter Sun, Dec 24/25 & Jan 1 ▪ Meals/refreshments & cellar tours on special request ▪ BYO picnic ▪ Small tour groups ▪ 1.7km fynbos hiking trail ▪ Conservation area ▪ B&B plus 2 self-catering cottages ▪ Owner(s) Philippe Colin & Serge Jaczynski ▪ Cellarmaster(s)/winemaker(s) Philippe Colin (Aug 2014) ▪ Viticulturist(s) Dirk Wouter van der Merwe (Jan 2013) ▪ 63ha/20ha (cab, shiraz, chard) ▪ 44t/8,000cs own label 90% red 10% white ▪ IPW ▪ PO Box 108 La Motte 7691 ▪ topiarysales@telkomsa.net ▪ www.topiarywines.com ▪ S 33° 51' 52.2" E 019° 2' 39.0" ▪ F +27 (0)86-750-1742 ▪ **T +27 (0)21-867-0258**

☐ **Top Secret** see Ultra Liquors

☐ **Tormentoso** see MAN Family Wines

☐ **Torres Claude** see Crows Nest

☐ **Totus** see Trajan Wines

☐ **Touch of Oak** see Rijk's

Township Winery ⓘ

This innovative community winegrowing project encourages householders in the economically challenged areas of Philippi, Nyanga and Crossroads to plant backyard vines and supply grapes to a small Philippi Village winery, where Township wines can also be tasted and bought. Original impetus for the venture came from low-income housing developer Kate Jambela, supported by Wellington-based wine entrepreneur Graham Knox, who oversees winemaking together with consultant winemaker Roger Burton, with administrative help from Nomhle Zondani.

Township Winery range

★★★★ **Philippi Merlot** ② **12** preview has ripeness & focus, with mulberry notes & creamy tannins. Impressive poise, weight & balance. Shows potential once settled.

The Flats Pinotage ② ★★★ Soundly crafted, with wild berry fruit, **12** delivers pure varietal character in a light, spicy package. Not retasted: **Philippi Sauvignon Blanc 10** ★★★☆ **The Flats Viognier 12** ★★☆ Not tasted: **Philippi Shiraz**.

Dido range

The Storm Mourvèdre-Shiraz ② ★★★ Light-bodied **09** previously showed feisty cherry fruit, hints of pepper & spices. Not retasted: **Pinot Grigio 10** ★★★★ Not tasted: **Pinotage**. — IM

Location: Philippi ▪ Map: Cape Peninsula ▪ WO: Western Cape ▪ Est 2009 ▪ 1stB 2010 ▪ Tasting Mon-Fri 10-4 ▪ Owner(s) The Township Winery cc ▪ Cellarmaster(s) Roger Burton (2014, consultant) & Graham Knox ▪ 800cs own label 50% red 50% white ▪ PO Box 63 Philippi 7781 ▪ nomhle@townshipwinery.com ▪ S 34° 0' 1.02" E 018° 35' 37.71" ▪ F +27 (0)21-447-4476 ▪ **T +27 (0)73-450-9516**

Trajan Wines

Established in 2005 by wine enthusiasts with dreams of an own brand and community service, Stellenbosch's Trajan latterly has focused on its premium range Totus. Fairtrade accredited, the brand funds a crèche/daycare school and helps fight child abductions by supporting Missing Children SA.

Totus range

Shiraz ⓐ ★★★★ Swartland & Paarl grapes for **10**; high-toned berries, cherries, even some liquorice, to accompany the tobacco notes. Tannins evident in the flavours, savoury rather than harsh, this is a wine that would age well. **Chenin Blanc** ⓐ ★★★★ Appealing **10** shows sunny ripeness, deftly handled oak lends body & form without dominating. Not retasted: **Cabernet Sauvignon 09** ★★★★
Pinotage 09 ★★★ **Shiraz-Mourvèdre 08** ★★★★ **Sauvignon Blanc 13** ★★★★ — CR

Location: Stellenbosch ▪ WO: Coastal/Western Cape ▪ Est 2005 ▪ 1stB 2008 ▪ Closed to public ▪ Owner(s) Trajan Wines (Pty) Ltd ▪ Winemaker(s) Mark van Schalkwyk (Sep 2005) ▪ Viticulturist(s) Mark van Schalkwyk ▪ 10,000c's own label 70% red 30% white ▪ Fairtrade ▪ PO Box 1498 Stellenbosch 7599 ▪ info@trajanwines.co.za ▪ www.trajanwines.co.za ▪ F +27 (0)86-299-4281 ▪ **T +27 (0)83-505-2681**

☐ **Trans-Karoo** *see* Boer & Brit
☐ **Travino** *see* Klawer Wine Cellars

Tread Lightly by Backsberg   ⓐ

Sustainability is in the Backsberg DNA and this range reflects the Back family's ethos in name as well as nature. Eco-friendly, lightweight and shatterproof 1-litre PET (plastic) bottles are the packaging of choice here — understood to be a Cape first for certified wine — for early, easy drinking with a conscience.

PET range

Sauvignon Blanc ⓐ ★★★ **15** crisp & forthright, with hints of passionfruit, dust & herbaceousness. Light, likeable & well priced.

Merlot ★★★ Sound & unpretentious **14**, juicy, medium bodied, fresh & plummy. Comes with 2-year 'sell-by date', as for all these, enjoy accordingly. Also tasted: **Rosé 15** ★★★ Discontinued: **Cabernet Sauvignon**, **Chenin Blanc**. — GdB

Location: Paarl ▪ WO: Western Cape/Paarl ▪ Est/1stB 2010 ▪ Tasting, sales & cellar tours at Backsberg Estate (see entry) ▪ Owner(s) Michael Back & Simon Back ▪ Winemaker(s) Alicia Rechner (Jun 2012) ▪ Viticulturist(s) Clive Trent (Jul 1992) ▪ PO Box 537 Suider-Paarl 7624 ▪ info@backsberg.co.za ▪ www.backsberg.co.za ▪ F +27 (0)21-875-5144 ▪ **T +27 (0)21-875-5141**

☐ **Tree Series** *see* Bellingham
☐ **Trees of Knowledge** *see* Diners Club Bartho Eksteen Academy
☐ **Tres Estrellas** *see* Santa Cecilia
☐ **Tribal** *see* Jacques Germanier

Trizanne Signature Wines

With her Stellenbosch degree in viticulture and oenology behind her, Trizanne Barnard worked vintages in Australia, France and Portugal before returning home to take up significant winemaking positions, notably at prestigious Anwilka. This led to her own label emerging in 2009 and her increasing concentration on this — though various consultancies have also happened. Trizanne does a lot of harvest-time driving, making her wines at Cape Point Vineyards, from fruit sourced in cool Elim and warm Swartland.

Trizanne Signature Wines range

★★★★ **Syrah-Grenache** ⓐ Dark, savoury, bright fruit on juicily fresh Swartland blend. **13** balanced, with firm but gentle tannic grip, & (above all) delicious. Only older oak used, to keep fruit purity.

★★★★ **Elim Sauvignon Blanc** Aromatic **14** has notes of pineapple, fynbos, peach & citrus making it as interesting & individual as usual. Full flavoured, harmonious, well textured & pleasing, with no rough edges.

★★★★ **Reserve Sauvignon Blanc-Semillon** Gently oaked **14** near-equal blend. Broader, less fowardly fruity than Sauvignon, richer, rounder (& longer-lived). Fresh lemony acid guides to a succulent conclusion.

Not tasted: **Elim Syrah**.

Clearsprings Wines

Not tasted: **Sauvignon Blanc**. — TJ

Location: Cape Town ▪ WO: Elim/Swartland ▪ Est 2008 ▪ 1stB 2009 ▪ Closed to public ▪ Wine sales via website ▪ Owner(s)/winemaker(s) Trizanne Barnard ▪ 19,000cs own label 45% red 65% white + 2.5m L bulk wine export ▪ 14 Van der Horst Avenue Kommetjie 7975 ▪ info@trizanne.co.za ▪ www.trizanne.co.za ▪ F +27 (0)86-669-0913 ▪ **T +27 (0)21-783-0617/+27 (0)82-383-6664**

Truter Family Wines

Small quantities of wine are made under the Agaat ('Agate') label of Wellington-based Hugo and Celeste Truter, both trained winemakers, who always wanted to produce handcrafted wines focusing on blends rather than 'boring' single cultivars.

Agaat range

★★★★ Christina ⓥ Forthright sauvignon aromas in light-footed **14** (★★★★) blend with chenin, nouvelle & dash viognier. Immediate charm, with less weight than **12**. No **13**.

John David ★★★★ Abundant pinotage bright red fruit bolstered by cab's tannins & shiraz spiciness. Year in almost all-new oak signals **14**'s serious intentions. — IM

Location: Wellington ▪ WO: Western Cape ▪ Est 2008 ▪ 1stB 2010 ▪ Closed to public ▪ Owner(s) Hugo & Celeste Truter ▪ Winemaker(s) Hugo Truter ▪ 1,000cs own label 50% red 50% white ▪ hugo@truterfamilywines.co.za ▪ www.truterfamilywines.co.za ▪ **T +27 (0)83-639-6288**

TTT Cellar Calitzdorp   ⓥ ⓐ ⓒ ⓓ

Port Elizabeth electrical contractor Ashley Mason's hobby, assisting late 'port' supremo Tony Mossop at his Calitzdorp quinta, Axe Hill, has evolved into a full-fledged winery on the Mason family farm nearby. Still commuting, but with resident help, Ashley elected to skip harvest 2014 ('too much rain'); the in-tank/barrel 2015 wines too young for tasting – another gentle reminder that 'TTT' (things take time).

Location: Calitzdorp ▪ Map: Klein Karoo & Garden Route ▪ 1stB 2003 ▪ Tasting, sales & tours Mon-Fri 8-4 Sat 8-2 Sun by appt ▪ Closed Easter Fri-Mon, Apr 27, May 1, Dec 25 & Jan 1 ▪ Honey & olive oil ▪ BYO picnic ▪ Owner(s) Ashley & Pat Mason ▪ Cellarmaster(s)/viticulturist(s) Ashley Mason ▪ Winemaker(s) Ashley Mason, with Johan Julies ▪ 0.5ha (souzão, tinta, touriga, hanepoot) ▪ 4t/600cs own label 100% red ▪ PO Box 7067 Newton Park 6055 ▪ tttcellars@iafrica.com ▪ S 33° 31' 50.94" E 021° 41' 44.88" ▪ F +27 (0)44-213-3114 ▪ **T +27 (0)44-213-3114**

Tulbagh Winery   ⓥ ⓐ ⓒ ⓓ

This busy grower-owned winery, operating two cellars (in Tulbagh and Porterville), maintains steady overseas growth feeding German, UK and French brands. This is balanced with an extensive own portfolio, exported with special focus recently on China and Africa, and listed locally by retail giants like Pick n Pay. Yet new wines keep coming: a port-style Cape Vintage, Bordeaux red, additions to the irreverently named Flippenice line-up (including a trendy lite Natural Sweet rosé) and easy-drinking iLike label.

Klein Tulbagh Reserve range

Port ⓝⓔⓦ ★★★★ Fruitcake richness in **02**, from pinotage, shows good oak/spirit balance. In perfect drinking condition for winter, around a fire with friends. Not retasted: **Merlot 13 ★★★★ Pinotage 13 ★★★** Not tasted: **Cabernet Sauvignon**, **Shiraz**.

Tulbagh range

Cabernet Sauvignon ★★★ Mocha tones, black plums lead you in to **12**'s savoury flavours, juicy texture. **Pinotage ★★★** Mixed red berries, elegantly structured **13** has good food-friendly tannin dryness. **Chenin Blanc ★★★** Perfume of freshly sliced pear, **15**'s crisp mineral dryness is ideal for food. **Pinotage Doux ★★** Bright-fruited red berries sweetly captured in a **NV** bubbly. Also tasted: **Syrah 14 ★★★ Pinotage Rosé 15 ★★ Sauvignon Blanc Brut NV ★★★ Sauvignon NV ★★** Not retasted: **Merlot 13 ★★ Shiraz-Pinotage 13 ★★★ Chardonnay 14 ★★★ Sauvignon Blanc 14 ★★ Colombard-Chenin Blanc 14 ★★★ Muscat Ottonel Doux NV ★★**

Paddagang range

CCM (NEW) ★★★ Cab-dominant Bordeaux-style blend. **13**'s fruitcake character, touch of mint, drink smoothly, well. Also tasted: **Sopkoppie Rooi Muskadel NV** ★★★ Not retasted: **Paddapoot Hanepoot 12** ★★ Not tasted: **Brulpadda Port**.

Flippenice range

Xtra Lite ★★ As promised, bone-dry, just 9% alcohol in greengage-flavoured **NV** fernão pires dominant blend. **XLite Natural Sweet Rosé** (NEW) ★★ Low alcohol (9%) **NV** from pinotage is a red berry flavoured party goer. Also tasted: **Cabernet Sauvignon-Merlot NV** ★★ **Chenin Blanc-Sauvignon Blanc NV** ★★

iLike range (NEW)

Chenin Blanc ★★ Apple & pear fruitiness in light & dry **NV**.   — CR

Location: Tulbagh/Porterville ▪ Map: Tulbagh ▪ WO: Tulbagh/Coastal ▪ Est 1906/2006 ▪ 1stB 1910 ▪ Tulbagh Cellar: Tasting & sales Mon-Fri 9–5 Sat & pub hols 9–1 Sun at Paddagang Wine Shop 11-3 ▪ Porterville Cellar: Tasting & sales Mon-Fri 9–5 ▪ Closed Easter Fri-Sun, Dec 25/26 & Jan 1 ▪ Cellar tours by appt ▪ Gifts ▪ Farm produce ▪ BYO picnic ▪ Conferences ▪ Walks/hikes ▪ Mountain biking in the area ▪ Owner(s) 86 members ▪ Cellarmaster(s) / Production manager(s) Naude Bruwer (Jan 2010) ▪ Winemaker(s) Porterville: Lara Loubser (Oct 2014); Tulbagh: Helena Neethling (Jun 2010) ▪ Viticulturist(s) Carl Allen (Aug 2003) ▪ 740ha (cab, merlot, ptage, shiraz, chenin, chard, sauv) ▪ 9,600t own label 65% red 30% white 5% rosé & 8m L bulk + 40,000cs for clients ▪ Brands for clients: Grimont (Germany), Millberg (UK/France) ▪ IPW ▪ PO Box 85 Tulbagh 6820; PO Box 52 Porterville 6810 ▪ info@tulbaghwine.co.za ▪ www.tulbaghwine.co.za ▪ S 33° 15' 8.8" E 019° 8' 36.5" ▪ F +27 (0)23-230-1358; +27 (0)22-931-2171 ▪ **T +27 (0)23-230-1001 (Tulbagh); +27 (0)22-931-2170 (Porterville)**

☐ **Tullie Family Vineyards** see Lanner Hill

☐ **Tunnel** see Du Toitskloof Winery

Twee Jonge Gezellen Estate-House of Krone   (♀) (◎)

It's a story of renovation (a cellar being further upgraded) and expansion (20 hectares of chardonnay and pinot noir planted under the guidance of eminent viticulturist Rosa Kruger) at the historic 'Two Young Companions' estate in Tulbagh, bought by major wine company Vinimark in 2012. And giving everything a facelift, says winemaker Stephan de Beer: 'Making it beautiful again!' The House of Krone brand, though, still honours the family which had been here since 1710 and more latterly established it as an important producer of serious sparkling wine — something which the ambitious new owners plan on taking to a higher (and much more expansive) level.

Krone range

★★★★ **Rosé Cuvée Brut** Pinot noir/chardonnay (60/40) MCC sparkling offering fresh cranberry & savoury brioche flavours. **13** tangy & tingling, with a fine, creamy mousse. Delicate, flavoursome, with good length. Also in magnum, like Borealis.

★★★★ **Borealis Cuvée Brut** Nutty sourdough & apple flavours in **13** chardonnay/pinot (65/35) MCC bubbly. Tightly knit, brisk, food-friendly style. Perhaps less refined in texture than Rosé though both 22 months on lees.

★★★★ **The Phoenix** (NEW) After 9 years maturation, elegant **NV** chardonnay/pinot (50/50) MCC sparkler rises from the lees deliciously fresh & vibrant. Clean-cut acidity with refined & lingering lime & almond flavours. Tulbagh WO.

Chardonnay-Pinot Noir (♥) ★★★ Versatile non-sparkling rosé (53/48 blend) exuding drinkability & freshness. **14** appealing hint of brioche & berries; balanced, friendly, with delicate onion skin hue.

Also tasted: **Night Nectar 13** ★★★ Not tasted: **Nicolas Charles Krone Marque 1**.   — MW

Location/map: Tulbagh ▪ WO: Western Cape/Tulbagh ▪ Est 1710 ▪ 1stB 1937 ▪ Tasting & sales Mon-Fri 10–4 Sat 10–2 ▪ Closed all pub hols ▪ Cellar tours Mon-Sat at 11 ▪ Annual festival: Christmas in Winter (Jun) ▪ Owner(s) TJG Estate (Pty) Ltd ▪ Winemaker(s) Stephan de Beer (2008) ▪ Viticulturist(s) Rosa

Kruger ▪ PO Box 16 Tulbagh 6820 ▪ info@tjg.co.za ▪ www.houseofkrone.co.za ▪ S 33° 14' 18.1" E 019° 6' 51.8" ▪ F +27 (0)23-230-0686 ▪ **T +27 (0)23-230-0680**

Twelve Apostles Winery   ⓦ

Civil engineer and online wine marketer by day, Cape Town father-and-son team Chris and Charles Lourens say they are 'garagiste winemakers in the true sense of the word... with a passion for the art of small-scale winemaking'. Their hand-sorted, basket-pressed wines not available for review this edition.

Location: Cape Town ▪ Est/1stB 2009 ▪ Tasting by appt only ▪ Owner(s)/winemaker(s) Chris & Charles Lourens ▪ 3-5t/±650cs own label 50% red 50% white ▪ Brands for clients: Kanah Winery ▪ SAWIS ▪ PO Box 16007 Panorama 7506 ▪ info@twelveapostleswinery.co.za ▪ www.twelveapostleswinery.co.za ▪ F +27 (0)86-510-2431 ▪ **T +27 (0)82-375-2884**

- ☐ **24 Rivers** see Valley Vineyards Wine Company
- ☐ **21 Gables** see Spier
- ☐ **Twins** see Lateganskop Winery
- ☐ **II Centuries** see Nederburg Wines
- ☐ **Two Cubs** see Knorhoek Wines

Two Oceans

Distell's Two Oceans wines have been flowing into some 80 countries since the early 1990s, matching easy drinking with modern, bright and breezy livery on sustainability-driven lightweight bottles. Led in the local popularity stakes by the sauvignon blanc and cab-merlot blend, the brand recently focused on widespread marketing of the shiraz (the deal sweetened with shiraz-infused chocolate). More innovations are promised by new global marketer Thandi Ntuli, particularly pleased with growth in Canada.

Cabernet Sauvignon-Merlot ★★★ Braai-friendly **14** has a dash of petit verdot, delivers characterful, medium-bodied mouthful of cherries & berries. **Shiraz Rosé** ⓦ ★★☆ Pretty pink **14** is floral & dryish, with cherry & strawberry attractions that are hard to resist. **Pinot Grigio** ⓦ ★★★ Light & floral **14**, pleasant poolside refreshment with 15% colombard, dash sweetness for extra happiness. **Sauvignon Blanc** ★★★ Capsicum, passionfruit & citrus tones on **15**, well pitched for anytime uncomplicated sipping. Not retasted: **Pinot Noir 14** ★★★☆ **Pinotage 14** ★★★ **Shiraz 14** ★★★☆ **Soft & Fruity Red 13** ★★★ **Chardonnay 14** ★★★ **Semillon-Chardonnay 13** ★★★ **Fresh & Fruity White 14** ★★☆ Not tasted: **Shiraz-Cabernet Sauvignon.** — GM

Location: Stellenbosch ▪ WO: Western Cape ▪ Owner(s) Distell ▪ Cellarmaster(s) Elize Coetzee & Wim Truter ▪ Winemaker(s) Kristin Basson, Pieter Badenhorst, Bonny van Niekerk & John November ▪ Viticulturist(s) Bennie Liebenberg, Annelie Viljoen & Henk van Graan ▪ Distell PO Box 184 Stellenbosch 7599 ▪ info@distell.co.za ▪ www.twooceanswines.co.za ▪ **T +27 (0)21-809-7000**

- ☐ **Two Tunns** see Valley Vineyards Wine Company
- ☐ **Tygerberg** see Altydgedacht Estate
- ☐ **Uiterwyk Estate** see DeWaal Wines

Uitkyk Estate   ⓦ ⓘ ⓒ ⓐ ⓖ

Established in 1929 by Prussian nobleman Hans von Carlowitz, the elegant Lusan-owned Uitkyk Estate on prime Simonsberg slopes combines the 18th-century manor house's history with modern winemaking, eco-mindedness and varied family-friendly tourist attractions including pre-booked gourmet picnics on the lawns (boule or croquet optional). See also Flat Roof Manor entry.

Uitkyk Estate range

★★★★ **Carlonet** Venerable label (now established as cab with a dash of shiraz) in impressive modern guise: forceful & intense, with sweet fruit, rich & ripe, but well balanced & hiding their big alcohols (over 14.5%); oak well handled. Both **11** & **12** tasted. **12** (★★★★★) has purer, more concentrated, sweet fruit, & is likely to develop over a decade. Both vintages also in larger formats.

Chardonnay ★★★☆ Quietly true aromas on well-oaked **14** (which has 14% chenin), with some nuttiness & orange peel. Lightly rich, with the citrus more pickled lime on the palate. **Sauvignon Blanc** ★★★☆ Forward ripe, tropical fruit notes – especially guava – on previewed **15**. Flavourful, balanced & quite fresh, finishes with a succulent green flourish. Also tasted: **Pinotage 13** ★★★☆ **Chenin Blanc 13** ★★★☆ Not retasted: **Shiraz 10** ★★★☆ **Shiraz-Cabernet Sauvignon 09** ★★★

Brandy range

★★★★ **10 Year Grand Reserve Brandy** Ⓖ Smart 10-year-matured pure postill estate brandy, unusually from clairette, cinsaut & chenin grapes. Plenty of oak vanilla & spice to accompany the fruit, though not great complexity. Smooth, rich, round & balanced. — WB, TJ

Location/map: Stellenbosch ▪ Map grid reference: F2 ▪ WO: Stellenbosch/Simonsberg–Stellenbosch ▪ Est 1712 ▪ 1stB 1957 ▪ Tasting & sales Mon-Fri 9–5 Sat/Sun 10–4 ▪ Tasting R25/5 wines; R25 brandy tasting; R50 brandy & chocolate experience ▪ Closed Good Fri & Dec 25 ▪ Facilities for children ▪ Manor House tours ▪ Tour groups ▪ Cheese platters ▪ Picnics, to be booked 24hrs in advance ▪ Conferences ▪ Conservation area ▪ Owner(s) Lusan Premium Wines ▪ Brandy master Estelle Lourens (Jan 2000) ▪ Cellarmaster(s)/winemaker(s) Estelle Lourens (Oct 2000) ▪ Viticulturist(s) Rudi Buys (2001) ▪ 591ha/140ha (cab, shiraz, chard, pinot grigio, sauv) ▪ 772t/18,400cs 55% red 45% white (Uitkyk) & 71,000cs 53% red 45% white 2% rosé (Flat Roof Manor) ▪ BWI champion, WIETA ▪ PO Box 104 Stellenbosch 7599 ▪ info@uitkyk.co.za ▪ www.uitkyk.co.za ▪ S 33° 51' 24.8" E 018° 51' 50.7" ▪ F +27 (0)21-884-4717 ▪ **T +27 (0)21-884-4416**

☐ **Ukuzala** *see* Mountain River Wines

Ultra Liquors

This nationwide drinks retail chain has a particularly dynamic wine division under general manager Mark Norrish, a man deeply experienced in the wine world, with a well-honed palate. As well as third-party brands, it offers various ranges of its own labels, with the good-value Secret Cellar and comparatively pricey (but perhaps even better value) Top Secret bottlings allowing farms to sell off excess stock anonymously. Numerous show awards testify to the benefit of this to the fussy and price-conscious consumer – including a gold medal and trophy for 'Discovery of the Year' at the 2015 Trophy Wine Show.

Top Secret range

★★★★ **Sauvignon Blanc-Semillon** ⊘ Pungent nettle & grapefruit intensity to **14**. Lean, taut & precise, 36% semillon a palate lengthening presence in the persistent flinty mouthful. Coastal WO.

Merlot ⊘ ★★★ **11** offers ample Christmas cake flavour & ripe juiciness with poised dusty tannin grip. **Pinot Noir** ★★★★ Smoky edge to typical forest fruit notes of light yet pleasingly savoury **13** from Elgin, with earthy depth too. **Brut Rosé** ⊘ ★★★★ Tangy raspberry verve to delicate salmon pink **NV** méthode cap classique sparkling. Light & enjoyable. Note: the wines in this established range all ⓃⒺⓌ this edition, as for Secret Cellar range.

Secret Cellar range

★★★★ **Pinotage 211** ⊘ With splash cinsaut, unwooded **14** offers vibrant, sweet ripe red fruit with enough acid to freshen. Deep & dense, with cocoa nuance at end. Cheery & very drinkable. Darling WO.

★★★★ **Big Five 273** ⊘ Rich **13** Bordeaux-style red from Constantia. Inky graphite depth & concentration, focused, long & smooth. 2 years older French oak provides fine dry tannin & defined structure.

★★★★ **Syrah-Mourvèdre-Grenache 303** ⊘ Soft-textured shiraz-led three-way mix. **14** spicy, intense yet bright, clean, balanced & harmonious, with distinct pepper tail. Stellenbosch WO.

★★★★ **Sauvignon Blanc 527** ⊘ Crisp cool-climate nettle & flint character from Darling fruit on **14**. Very typical, lively zip to end. WO Coastal.

Cabernet Sauvignon 259 ⊘ ★★★★ Herbal edge to black fruit & tealeaf notes of **13**. Pure & intense, with good integration of fruit & oak (15% new French). Coastal WO. **Merlot-Cabernet Sauvignon 143** ⊘ ★★★ Merlot leads boldly fruited, very ripe palate with light tannin grip on **13**. **Chardonnay-Pinot Noir 955** ★★★★ Pale onion skin hue to **14**. Equilibrium of bold berry notes & succulence, light bodied. WO Robertson. **Rosé 658** ★★★ Wispy floral hints balance tangy berry vibrancy on **14** delicate salmon-hued dry sipper. Robertson grapes. **Chenin Blanc 235** ⊘ ★★★★ Fresh **15** offers stonefruit vivacity & apple crunch with juicy acidity & medium length. Coastal WO. **Sauvignon Blanc 689** ★★☆ Tropical varietal notes lighten zesty typicity on **14. Sauvignon Blanc-Semillon 105** ⊘ ★★★ Crunchy green apple & grapefruit vibrancy on **14**, clean, precise finish. Coastal WO. **Blanc de Blanc 428** ⊘ ★★★☆ All-chardonnay **NV** méthode cap classique is taut & zesty, with chalky mouthfeel, light lime/apple vibrancy & clean dry finish. **Brut 558** ⊘ ★★★★ Citrus & apple fruit with honeyed biscuit breadth & some complexity on long, creamy palate of **NV** méthode cap classique bubbly from chardonnay & pinot noir. Crisp acidity keeps it fresh.

Table Bay range

★★★★ **Brut** (NEW) ⊘ Ripe apple & biscuit tones to **NV** méthode cap classique sparkler from chardonnay/pinot noir. Tangy & vibrant. From Robertson.

What A Mouthful range (NEW)

Red ★★ Easy, soft plum simplicity to **NV** sipper from mainly shiraz. **White** ★★ Cheerful peach tropicality to **NV** zesty summer sipper from chenin. — WB, FM

Location: Cape Town ▪ WO: Western Cape/Coastal/Robertson/Darling/Elgin/Constantia/Stellenbosch ▪ Owner(s) Colin Robinson ▪ Winemaker(s) Various ▪ 426 Main Road Wynberg Cape Town 7800 ▪ marknorrish@ultraliquors.co.za, dale@ultraliquors.co.za ▪ F +27 (0)21-797-4351 ▪ **T +27 (0)21-797-4340**

Under Oaks ⓥ ⓐ

The Britz family cellar on Paarl Mountain's flanks was extensively renovated for the 2015 harvest, and from it in due course will flow a number of blends produced by winemaker Bertus Fourie from 'many pockets of interesting cultivars'. Visitor amenity wise, the well-established eatery continues to serve 'the best pizza south of Italy', and a newer country house offers luxury accommodation and lovely views.

Cabernet Sauvignon Reserve (NEW) ★★★ Plump & round, with supple tannins underpinning the fruit-cake flavours, **12** already drinks well. Also tasted, **10** (★★) shows more liquorice & spice, juicy but quite zesty. Paarl WO, like next. **Shiraz Reserve** (NEW) ★★★★ Opulent, accessible **10** has a serious side, a firm tannin backbone from 24 months in barrel, 50% new, to promise a future. **Sauvignon Blanc** ★★★ Sparks with lively freshness, a leafy nuance, **15**'s greengage & melon flavours adding to the appeal. Malmesbury grapes. Also tasted: **Cabernet Sauvignon-Syrah** (NEW) **10** ★★★ **Lightly Wooded Chardonnay 14** ★★★ **Chenin Blanc 15** ★★☆ Not tasted: **Merlot, Pinotage, Shiraz.** — CR, CvZ

Location: Paarl ▪ Map: Paarl & Wellington ▪ Map grid reference: E3 ▪ WO: Coastal/Paarl ▪ 1stB 2003 ▪ Tasting Tue-Sun 11-4 ▪ Fee R25 standard tasting, various pairings @ R50 ▪ Cellar tours/private tastings by appt only ▪ Pizzeria Tue-Sat 11-9 Sun 11-3 ▪ 4-star country house ▪ info@underoaks.co.za ▪ www.underoaks.co.za ▪ S 33° 40' 30.0" E 018° 56' 32.2" ▪ F +27 (0)86-649-9307 ▪ **T +27 (0)21-872-6070**

United Nations of Wine

United Nations of Wine is the catch-all for the Fairtrade, WIETA and CarbonNeutral brands Frisky Zebras and Luscious Hippos, intended as 'fun, friendly and affordable' by creator, Canadian-born, locally resident David John Bate. His other label, the separately listed Leopard Frog, is aimed at appreciators of classic, long-lived (though by no means conventional) wines. Neither tasted for this edition.

Location: Sandton ▪ Est/1stB 2005 ▪ Closed to public ▪ Owner(s) Dogwood Trust ▪ Cellarmaster(s)/winemaker(s) David John Bate (Jun 2005) ▪ 60,000cs own label 50% red 50% white ▪ Fairtrade, CarbonNeutral, WIETA ▪ 8 Royal Ascot Lane Sandown Sandton 2196 ▪ info@unitednationsofwine.com ▪ www.unitednationsofwine.com ▪ F +27 (0)11-883-0426 ▪ **T +27 (0)11-884-3304**

uniWines Vineyards ⓥ ⓐ ⓐ ⓑ

Diversity, ethical trade and innovation are key values of the 50 producer-shareholders contributing to this large winery, with three production cellars — Groot Eiland, Nuwehoop and Daschbosch — processing 45,000 tons. The Breedekloof 'uni' bottles a significant quantity for its own labels -100,000 cases — much of it accredited by Fairtrade and all (including the husk spirit) intended 'to match consumer needs'.

Daschbosch range

Plicatilis ★★★ Flagship **13** Rhône blend is nicely ripe & spicy shiraz, with splashes mourvèdre & viognier, brisk acidity lending some elegance. **Steen** (NEW) ★★★ Dry, oaked **14** chenin has oily texture & ripe yellow apple flavours with obvious acidity. Also tasted: **Procavia Cabernet Sauvignon-Merlot 12** ★★★ **Exanimo 14** ★★★

Ankerman range

Cabernet Sauvignon-Merlot (NEW) ★★★ Chocolatey **14** preview pleasantly flavoured for unpretentious drinking. **Shiraz-Pinotage** (NEW) ★★ Mocha-laced **14**'s fresh acidity offers some structure to previewed easy-drinking blend. **Chenin Blanc-Chardonnay** (NEW) ★★ Preview of **15** simple, crisp pleasant enough sipper. Not retasted: **The Foothold 13** ★★★ **The Referee 13** ★★★ **The Whistle 14** ★★★ **Nectar de Provision Red NV** ★★★ **Nectar de Provision White NV** ★★★☆

Meander range

Moscato Rosé (NEW) ★★ Sweet, pink **14** in delightful 'soda pop' style with light fizz & low alcohol. For celebration & casual libation. Also in 340 ml. Not retasted: **Merlot-Shiraz 13** ★★★ **Moscato 14** ★★☆ **Chenin Blanc-Sauvignon Blanc 14** ★★

Palesa Fairtrade range

Shiraz Pouch ★★ Attractively spicy, simple **14** pre-bottling sample for easy, early consumption. In 1.5L. **Chenin Blanc** ★★☆ Summery, crisply dry **15** appealingly tropical & fresh. **Husk Spirit** (Ⓩ) ★★★☆ From cab, perfumed & smooth, easy & gentle. A fusion of sweet berry perfume & integrated spirit. Also tasted: **Merlot 14** ★★★ **Pinotage 14** ★★ **Chenin Blanc Pouch 15** ★★★ **Sauvignon Blanc 15** ★★ Not retasted: **Moscato NV** ★★★

Discontinued: **Groot Eiland range**. — WB, IM

Location: Rawsonville ▪ Map/WO: Breedekloof ▪ Est/1stB 2007 ▪ Tasting & sales Mon-Thu 8–5 Fri 8-4 Sat/pub hols 10–2 ▪ Closed Easter Fri-Mon, Dec 25/26 & Jan 1 ▪ Cellar tours Mon-Fri & by appt Sat/during harvest ▪ Tour groups ▪ BYO picnic ▪ Conferences ▪ Soetes & Soup festival (Jul) ▪ Owner(s) 50 shareholders ▪ Cellarmaster(s) Nicolaas Rust (Oct 2008) ▪ Winemaker(s) WS Visagie (Nov 2010), Stefan Niemand (Jul 2014), Schalk van der Merwe (Dec 2007), Paul Burger (Dec 2013), Christo Smit (Jan 2001) & Madre Kotze (Apr 2013) ▪ Viticulturist(s) Nicholas Bruyns (Jul 2013) ▪ 6,000+ha/2,050ha (cab, cinsaut, merlot, ptage, shiraz, chard, chenin, cbard, sauv) ▪ 45,000t/100,000cs own label 50% red 50% white + 50,000cs for clients ▪ Brands for clients: Cape Promise, Fairtrade Original ▪ ISO 22000:2008, BWI, Fairtrade, IPW, WIETA ▪ PO Box 174 Rawsonville 6845 ▪ info@uniwines.co.za ▪ www.uniwines.co.za ▪ S 33° 43' 16.7" E 019° 21' 0.0" ▪ F +27 (0)86-529-1392 ▪ **T +27 (0)23-349-1110**

☐ **Upington** see Orange River Cellars

Upland Organic Estate (Ⓘ) (Ⓞ)

Wellington-based veterinarian and small-scale winemaker Edmund Oettlé has never shied from challenges. He's farmed sustainably (certified organic in 1994) and used re-tooled, recycled equipment long before eco-friendliness became a local winelands mantra. Now he's made a pinot noir and at press time was adding this finicky grape to his range of minimal sulphur and animal-product-free wines and spirits.

Upland Estate range

Cabernet Sauvignon (Ⓥ) ★★★☆ Another year in the bottle has benefitted **09**, with suppler structure, mature dark-berry fruit. Not retasted: **Tandem Cape Ruby 07** ★★★

Brandy range

★★★★ **Pure Potstill Brandy** (Ⓩ) (Ⓥ) Pure amber colour on 10 year old from chenin & crouchen blanc. Complex layers of dried pineapple, peach, citrus rind & vanilla mingle with hint of smoke. Full bodied, with a smooth richness & elegance, long-lingering aftertaste.

★★★★ **Undiluted Cask Strength Potstill Brandy** (Ⓩ) (Ⓥ) 100% potstill, 13 years in oak. The only local brandy in this undiluted style (62% alcohol). Intense perfumed, fruit-rich nose; lovely, long flavours. Smooth despite the power. For small sips!

Husk Spirit range

★★★★ Grapé ⓥ ♥ Another rare organic spirit. From pinot noir; teases with fragrant fynbos, nutty aromas; fresh herb & strawberry flavours combine for a smooth, understated mouthful. — WB

Location/WO: Wellington ▪ Map: Paarl & Wellington ▪ Map grid reference: G3 ▪ Est 1990 ▪ 1stB 1996 ▪ Tasting, sales & tours by appt ▪ Closed Easter Fri-Mon & Dec 25 ▪ Distillery: brandy & grappa ▪ Organic olives, olive oil, dried fruit & nuts ▪ Craft workshop ▪ Owner(s) Edmund & Elsie Oettlé ▪ Cellarmaster(s) / brandy master(s) Edmund Oettlé ▪ Winemaker(s)/viticulturist(s) Edmund Oettlé ▪ 46ha/10ha (cab, pinot, chenin, cbard, crouchen) ▪ 20t/1,200cs own label 100% red & 2,000L brandy ▪ QCS organic certification ▪ PO Box 152 Wellington 7654 ▪ info@organicwine.co.za ▪ www.organicwine.co.za ▪ S 33° 40' 19.9" E 019° 2' 40.0" ▪ F +27 (0)21-873-5724 ▪ **T +27 (0)82-731-4774**

Usana   ⓛ ⓞ

Winshaw is an important name in the history of Cape wine, and brothers JP and Pierre Winshaw will have taken the Xhosa meaning of Usana ('new beginning') seriously. Moving towards spontaneous fermentation is the latest move in the Stellenbosch cellar. As for bricks and mortar, the tasting room and deli was expected to open in 2016, alongside an upgraded function venue.

★★★★ The Fox Cabernet Sauvignon Alluring brambly blackcurrant, plum & tobacco intro, **13**'s fine tannic structure firms up the juicy fruit, its super, long-lingering flavours supported by 18% new oak.

★★★★ Sauvignon Blanc 15 (★★★☆) same lees creaminess as **13**, smoothing the brisk acidity, but the new vintage is quieter than previous, its tropical fruit more food styled. No **14**.

Also tasted: **Barrel Fermented Chenin Blanc 14** ★★★☆ **Pinot Gris 15** ★★★★ — DS

Location/map: Stellenbosch ▪ Map grid reference: C5 ▪ WO: Stellenbosch/Elgin ▪ Est/1stB 2003 ▪ Tasting & sales by appt; tasting room & deli to open during 2016 — see website for trading hours ▪ Farm produce ▪ Weddings & functions ▪ Owner(s) JP & Pierre Winshaw ▪ Winemaker(s) Jasper Raats (2012, consultant), with Hendrien de Munck (2010, consultant) ▪ Viticulturist(s) Pierre Winshaw, Deon Joubert & Nikki Joubert ▪ 300ha/45ha (cabs s/f, malbec, merlot, chard, pinot gris, sauv) ▪ 29t/4,000cs own label 30% red 70% white ▪ PO Box 68 Lynedoch 7603 ▪ jp@usana.co.za, pierre@usana.co.za ▪ www.usana.co.za ▪ S 34° 0' 14.42" E 018° 45' 36.97" ▪ **T +27 (0)83-650-9528**

Uva Mira Mountain Vineyards   ⓛ ⓕ ⓞ ⓖ

The home of the 'wonderful grape' (the meaning of the Latin name) is still on those high Helderberg slopes commanding marvellous views. But recent years have seen important changes, apart from the farm's 2014 acquisition by Toby Venter, CEO of Porsche South Africa. Winemaker Christiaan Coetzee arrived in 2012 and his reds now feature among the expanded, reconceived ranges — all the wines in smart new livery, but some available only in very small volumes. Christiaan's been joined in the immaculately micro-managed, breeze- and altitude-cooled vineyards by Christo Crous, who's doing quite a bit of tweaking there, and inaugurating a new planting programme.

★★★★ The Mira Cabernet Sauvignon ⓝⓔⓦ Gorgeous explosion of bright berry fruit (red & black) on the palate of **13**. The strong tannins are ripe & supportive, the oaking good, the whole well balanced — though still tight. Promises well.

★★★★☆ Cabernet Franc ⓝⓔⓦ Still in the tight coils of youth (decant now — but rather leave 5+ years), impressive **13** has variety's dry-leaf fragrance with lovely berry fruit. Fine-toned & silky; elegant but formidable musculature. Long-lingering, dry finish points to intensity & to future development.

★★★★ The Mira Merlot ⓝⓔⓦ Dark-fruited, herbal **13** with mocha & chocolate is flavourful & structured with big tannins that, though succulent, need a few years to tame (decant in youth). A serious wine.

★★★★ DW Syrah ⓝⓔⓦ Ripe, fragrant aromas with tobacco & spice from generous oaking (83% new) on **13**. Not as strongly structured as less pricey Mira version, but more breadth & depth of sweet fruit.

★★★★ OTV ⓝⓔⓦ Named with initials of Toby Venter's father. **13** cab-based Bordeaux blend the most fulsome of these, with ultra-ripe fruit & only mildly intrusive all-new oak. Lightly flavoursome, quite easygoing; the finish a little weak. Made in limited quantities, like other top reds.

★★★★☆ **Chardonnay** The grandest, most complex & complete of the 3 chards. **14** offers pure-fruited aromas, nothing obtruding except a touch of mellow, nutty oak (65% new). Lovely creamy texture & richness not impinging on the elegance. Characterful & persistent, with good citric fresh bite. Tiny quantities.

★★★★ **The Single Tree Chardonnay** Forward citrus & stonefruit on single-vineyard **14**, rounder than Mira version; balanced spicy oaking (80% new) adds to complexity. Crisp & vigorous lime-lemon conclusion.

★★★★☆ **Sing-a-Wing Sauvignon Blanc** Was 'Sauvignon Blanc Limited Release'. **14** more intensity, weight & ripe depth than The Mira version, with appealing blackcurrant hints. Forceful, with a bracing freshness tinged with green notes, but not brash or aggressive.

★★★★ **The Mira Sauvignon Blanc** Adds prefix for **14**. Tropical exuberance, with citrus & green grace-notes. Finely textured, a serious acidity in vibrant balance; just a trifle short on length & intensity. WO W Cape.

The Mira Shiraz (NEW) ★★★★ The fruit lighter on this **13** than DW, but adding a gentle fragrance & a sweet core, along with spicy notes. Serious oaking (60% new) adds to tannic power. A few years should help harmonise. **The Mira Chardonnay** (NEW) ★★★★ Gently spicy, nutty & toasty **14** with a good vein of lemony acidity. Good flavours & very satisfying, but lighter & shorter than other versions here. Discontinued: **Syrah**, **Merlot-Cabernet Sauvignon**, **Red Blend**. — TJ

Location/map: Stellenbosch ▪ Map grid reference: F8 ▪ WO: Stellenbosch/Western Cape ▪ Est 1997 ▪ 1stB 1998 ▪ Tasting & sales Mon-Sun 10-6 ▪ Fee R45-R75 ▪ Closed Easter Fri/Sun, Dec 25/26 & Jan 1 ▪ Artisan cheese platters & savoury meat platters ▪ Olive oil, honey ▪ Conservation area ▪ Owner(s) Toby & Jessica Venter ▪ Winemaker(s) Christiaan Coetzee (2012) ▪ Viticulturist(s) Christo Crous (2014) ▪ 140ha/30ha (cabs s/f, merlot, shiraz, chard, sauv) ▪ 100t/14,000cs ▪ Off Annandale Road Stellenbosch 7600 ▪ info@uvamira.co.za ▪ www.uvamira.co.za ▪ S 34° 1' 31.3" E 018° 51' 26.1" ▪ F +27 (0)21-880-1682 ▪ **T +27 (0)21-880-1683**

Vaalvlei Wines

(icons)

Stanford conservationist and winemaker/viticulturist Naas Terblanche, advised by Raka's Josef Dreyer and Charl van Teijlingen CWM, says his team continue to spend 'lots of time and effort' optimally managing the vineyards and tweaking cellar techniques. A Vintage 'port' from shiraz missed our deadline.

Shiraz ★★ Less new oak (25%) than Reserve, **12** slightly leaner, drier, an earthy farmyard nuance to cool-climate fruit. Pair with hearty food. **Shiraz Reserve** ★★★ All-new oak shows on **12**'s dark & spicy tone but fruit, acid & tannins in balance; tight knit though, allow year/2 to unwind. Not tasted: **Sauvignon Blanc**. — MW

Location: Stanford ▪ Map: Elgin, Walker Bay & Bot River ▪ WO: Walker Bay ▪ Est 2005 ▪ 1stB 2008 ▪ Tasting & sales Mon-Sat 11-5 by appt ▪ Closed Good Fri & Dec 25 ▪ 2 self-catering cottages ▪ Fly-fishing ▪ Owner(s) Terblanche family ▪ Cellarmaster(s)/viticulturist(s) Naas Terblanche (Mar 2005) ▪ Winemaker(s) Naas Terblanche (Mar 2005) & Josef Dreyer (Aug 2005, Raka), advised by Charl van Teijlingen CWM (Mar 2008) ▪ 50ha/3ha (shiraz, sauv) ▪ 19t/650cs own label 40% red 60% white ▪ PO Box 92 Stanford 7210 ▪ info@vaalvlei.co.za ▪ www.vaalvlei.co.za ▪ S 34° 26' 56.11" E 019° 33' 07.05" ▪ **T +27 (0)28-341-0170/+27 (0)72-782-3431**

Val de Vie Wines

(icons)

Part of a Huguenot descendent's 1783 land grant, Paarl's Val de Vie luxury residential and polo estate celebrates its French heritage and attendant wine culture. Vines line the avenues and fringe the residences, and a modern cellar produces a boutique range of mostly Rhône varieties and blends, and a champagne-style bubbly. This being SA, the pinotage rosé is as apropos as it is delicious.

Val de Vie range

★★★★ **Shiraz** (icon) **08**'s smoky mulberry & plum appeal follows similar **07**. Rounded yet muscled & firm. Dark char depth & density. Oak shows restraint, 70% new for 11 months. Long finish. WO Coastal.

★★★★ **Ryk Neethling** (icon) Honouring the Olympic swimming gold medallist. Taut & toned **10** from shiraz, mourvèdre, carignan, grenache & cinsaut. Rich & savoury, with restrained black fruit wrapped around a firm body of tannin.

★★★★☆ **1783** ⓥ Premium-priced flagship, mainly mourvèdre, shiraz & dabs grenache, carignan & cinsaut. Stunning **09** is rich, smooth, oozes ripe berry fruit, cured meat: concentrated yet elegant, with an earthy, savoury goodbye. No **08**.

★★★★ **GVC** ⓥ **11** (★★★) blend of grenache blanc, viognier & clairette blanche misses vivacity of **08**. Soft fruit, some oaky vanilla, fleeting flavours.

Not retasted: **Cuvée de Vie NV** ★★★☆

Polo Club range

Craftsman ⓥ ★★★★ **12** Rhône-style red blend is full-flavoured, earthy & spicy, with succulent black fruit & a refreshing acid counterweight. Not retasted: **Filly Rosé 14** ★★★ Not tasted: **Cabernet Franc**, **Chenin Blanc**, **Sauvignon Blanc**. — DS

Location: Paarl • Map: Franschhoek • WO: Western Cape/Coastal • Est 2003 • 1stB 2004 • Tasting & sales Tue-Sun 11-4 • Closed Good Fri, Dec 25 & Jan 1 • Polo Club Restaurant • Conservation area • Owner(s) Val de Vie Wines (Pty) Ltd • PO Box 6223 Paarl 7620 • wine@valdevie.co.za • www.valdevie.co.za • S 33° 48' 15.0" E 018° 58' 4.0" • F +27 (0)21-863-2741 • **T +27 (0)21-863-6100**

Val du Charron   ⓥ 🍴 🏠 ◎ ♿

The Entwistle family have completely transformed this former fruit farm in Wellington into a multifacted lifestyle destination including luxury accommodation – the new Coach House is graded five stars – a spa, new steakhouse-style restaurant and varied activities. Wine is no afterthought however: their 'winetasting like no other', named Theater of Wine, last year won Drinks International's award for world's most innovative wine tourism experience. And their mourvèdre block, manicured by farm manager Dial Fransman, placed third in Vinpro's nationwide Vineyard of the Year competition.

Estate Reserve range

Cabernet Sauvignon ★★★☆ Asphalt nuance to partly bunch-fermented **13**'s blackcurrant, fruit ripeness creates sweet impression while technically dry. **Pinot Gris** ★★★☆ 5% oaked portion adds breadth to **14**'s greengage fruit; a medium-bodied, friendly drop. Also tasted: **Syrah 13** ★★★☆ Not retasted: **Chardonnay 14** ★★★☆

Theater of Wine range

Black Countess ★★★☆ Shiraz-led 5-way blend including pinotage, **13** smouldering tarry aromas, obvious oak which somewhat masks the juicy fruit. Not retasted: **Erasmus 12** ★★★☆ Discontinued: **Four White Legs**. — DS

Location/WO: Wellington • Map: Paarl & Wellington • Map grid reference: H1 • Est 2007 • 1stB 2009 • Tasting daily 10-4 • Sales Mon-Fri 8-5 Sat/Sun 10-4 • Cellar tours during tasting hours • Restaurant • Tour groups • Conferences/functions (100 pax) • Walks/hikes • Mountain biking trail • Spa • 4 and 5 star guest house (stay@vdcwines.com) • Owner(s) Val du Charron Wines (Pty) Ltd • Winemaker(s) Bertus Fourie (Apr 2010, consultant) • Viticulturist(s) Heinie Nel (Apr 2010, consultant) • 43ha/21ha (cab, ptage, shiraz, chard, chenin) • ±300t • Other export brands: Girlfriends Wine, Goldcoast 3L BIB • IPW • PO Box 890 Wellington 7654 • ce@vdcwines.com • www.vdcwines.com • S 33° 37' 28.14" E 019° 2' 55.32" • F +27 (0)86-509-4865 • **T +27 (0)21-873-1256**

☐ **Valley Green** see Hannay Wines

Valley Vineyards Wine Company

Wine partners Richard James and Richard Addison, specialists in Argentina and South Africa respectively, combine their knowledge and long experience to select wines from mainly those countries for their UK merchant house. Their SA brands include Lion Ridge, Millbrook, Mischief Maker, Post Tree, The Royal, 24 Rivers, Two Tunns and, reviewed for the first time this edition, Short Street blends from Swartland.

Short Street range ⓝⓔⓦ

SGM ★★☆ Shiraz dominates but grenache, mourvèdre (& splash viognier) play a role in **14**'s dusty, cocoa-imbued dark fruit styling. Savoury, with tannin grip that seeks creamy dishes. **CGV** ★★★☆ Half chenin with grenache, dab viognier, unwooded **14** has appealing minerality, gentle stonefruit underpin. Finishes fruity-fresh. — CR, CvZ

Location: Riebeek-Kasteel ▪ WO: Swartland ▪ Est/1stB 2009 ▪ Closed to public ▪ Owner(s) Richard Addison & Richard James ▪ ±100,000cs own label 40% red 40% white 15% rosé 5% other ▪ Other export brands: see intro ▪ PO Box 2175 Riebeek-Kasteel 7307 ▪ raddison@valleyvineyardswine.com ▪ www.valleyvineyardswine.com ▪ **T +27 (0)71-238-6765**

Van Biljon Wines ⓠ ⓗ

Anton and Julia van Biljon's farm Tarentaal, on a southerly slope of Stellenbosch's Polkadraai Hills, is devoted to the five traditional red Bordeaux varieties alluded to in the wine's name – as is their boutique winery. And devoted to the vineyards (which the van Biljons started replanting a decade back), and to their vinification, is eminent consultant Chris Keet, who also makes his own wine in the cellar.

★★★★☆ **Cinq** Five red Bordeaux varieties, including 50% cab in fine modern, ripe & rich (but not overplush) **13**, which wears its power gracefully. Modestly oaked (20% new), leaving sweet fruit to dominate, but subdued by savoury, spicy succulence. More harmony than **12** (★★★★). — TJ

Location/map/WO: Stellenbosch ▪ Map grid reference: B6 ▪ Est 2004 ▪ 1stB 2013 ▪ Tasting, sales & cellar tours Mon-Sat by appt ▪ Closed all pub hols ▪ Self-catering Tarentaal Cottage ▪ Owner(s) Anton & Julia van Biljon ▪ Winemaker(s) Christopher Keet (Oct 2008, consultant), with Anton van Biljon (Jan 2011) ▪ Viticulturist(s) Christopher Keet (Oct 2008, consultant) ▪ 7ha/3ha (cabs s/f, malbec, merlot, p verdot) ▪ 15t/500cs own label 100% red ▪ IPW ▪ PO Box 1292 Hermanus 7200 ▪ info@vanbiljonwines.co.za ▪ www.vanbiljonwines.co.za ▪ S 33° 58' 4.98" E 018° 45' 8.39" ▪ F +27 (0)28-313-0435 ▪ **T +27 (0)21-882-8445**

Van Eck, Family & Friends ⓠ ⓡ ⓐ ⓞ ⓢ ⓝⓔⓦ

Medical practitioner and secretary of the Garagiste Movement, Johann van Eck, his family and friends in 2010 decided to make their own wine in the boutique cellar at The Barn on Worcester's Church Street, revelling in the conviviality of the process but with an underlying seriousness of purpose, namely to make 'astounding quality wine, as true ambassadors of the respective terroirs'. They see wine as 'art on the palate', and hands-off winemaking as the means to capture 'nature in the bottle'.

★★★★ **Die Petrus Johannes** Malbec-led, with petit verdot, a dash of cabs franc & sauvignon, plus mourvèdre, giving **10** black cherry richness, some fynbos. Full ripe, with pleasing succulence, smoothness. **The Third Opinion** ★★★ Shiraz with 3% viognier, 24 months barrel aged, as all these, giving **10** a bold dark-fruited profile, voluptuous curves from high-alcohol ripeness. **Dweller By The Oak** ★★★★ Classic 5-part Bordeaux blend showing cab's herbaceous nuances within the cassis core. Oaking (small portion American) translates **10** into a smooth, streamlined palate. **Spice of the South** ★★★★ Shiraz-led with mourvèdre, dab viognier, **10** is opulent, with full-ripe plums/prunes, café au lait seasoning. Drink now till 2020. **Catherina** ★★★ Subtitled 'Pure Innocence'. From Elim sauvignon blanc, barrel-fermented/aged – skillfully done in **14**, allowing the fruit to shine. Green fig, nice cool-climate mineral notes but zesty acidity alters the balance. — CR, CvZ

Location/map: Worcester ▪ WO: Coastal/Elim ▪ Est 2010 ▪ 1stB 2012 ▪ Tasting, sales & cellar tours by appt Mon-Sat 10-7 Sun 10-6 ▪ Tasting R100pp ▪ Closed Easter Fri/Mon, Ascension Day & Dec 25 ▪ The Barn restaurant open for b'fast & lunch ▪ Facilities for children ▪ Glass blowing ▪ Art gallery ▪ Farm produce ▪ BYO picnic ▪ Owner(s) Van Eck family & friends ▪ Cellarmaster(s)/winemaker(s) Johann van Eck (Jan 2010) ▪ 8t/512cs own label 87% red 13% white ▪ PO Box 7021 Worcester Waterfront, Worcester 6864 ▪ winery@winethebarn.co.za ▪ www.winethebarn.co.za ▪ S 33° 38' 47.73" E 019° 26' 5.63" ▪ F +27 (0)21-413-0650 ▪ **T +27 (0)23-347-2255**

Van Loveren Family Vineyards ⓠ ⓡ ⓗ ⓞ ⓖ

Just one wine made up this dynamic Robertson family business' range when brothers Nico and Wynand Retief launched their Premier Grand Cru in 1980. Today, its offerings span reserve wines available only from the tasting room and select wine shops; everyday drinking wines marketed nationwide (and overseas); Weigh-Less-approved low-alcohol options; sparklings; and the innovative PET (plastic) bottle range, Tangled Tree, listed separately. Four Cousins, South Africa's biggest-selling bottled wine brand, is the heart of the business and, recently, Van Loveren entered the ready-to-drink (RTD) market with the low-alcohol, fruit-flavoured, wine-based range, Four Cousins FIVER. But there's always something brand-new here: on the cards at press time were a cider and whisky. See also Vinopoly Wines.

Pater range (NEW)

★★★★ Die Hoeksteenwyn One-off release to honour Retief brothers & founders Nico & Wynand. 100% cab, only from cellardoor. Unforced **11** plum & prune nose, clean leather nuance. Firm tannin structure from 2 years in new French oak cushioned by ample fruit, ends dry & long.

Christina Van Loveren Limited Releases

★★★★ Shiraz 13 continues on upward track launched by savoury **12**, sees oak regime change from 100% new to just 30%. Pepper, red plum notes accentuated by sweetness from 10% American wood component; will improve ±5 years. Some Durbanville grapes.

★★★★ Chardonnay Classy oak (5 months, 100% new French) distinguishes this bottling from the VL version. **14** more effusive than **13** (★★★★), packed with lively lemon fruit, toast & nut detail.

★★★★ Sauvignon Blanc From Darling grapes, green pea & white asparagus-toned **14** offers satisfying vinosity, lipsmacking acidity & creamy length for solo or dinner table enjoyment. Drier, higher alcohol than standard bottling.

★★★★ Méthode Cap Classique Brut Traditional-method sparkling. Latest **NV** 9 months on gross lees in tank, 17 on fine lees in bottle hence more expressive brioche notes than previous. Racy bubbles, lemon freshness ex chardonnay, weight from pinot noir to entice, satisfy.

> **Noble Late Harvest Chenin Blanc** (NEW) (♥) **★★★☆** Rich but not-too-sweet **13**, unwooded, with notes of honey nougat, hazelnuts & watermelon jam. Perfect match for blue cheese. 375 ml.

Méthode Cap Classique Brut Rosé (NEW) **★★★☆** Pinot noir & chardonnay blush MCC sparkling only available from cellardoor. **NV** berry toned, with creamy texture from 22 months lees-ageing, though not as well knit as sibling. Also tasted: **Cabernet Sauvignon 13 ★★★☆** Discontinued: **Noble Late Harvest Rhine Riesling**.

Van Loveren range

River Red ★★☆ Perennial favourite unfettered by oak. **14** juicy combo ruby cabernet (80%) & merlot perfect for solo sipping. Also in 1.5L & 500ml. **Daydream Chardonnay-Pinot Noir** (NEW) **★★☆** De rigueur blend with pretty blush & perfume of pink musk sweets from 6% pinot noir, weight from 14% alcohol. Off-dry **15** for chilled enjoyment. **Chardonnay ★★★** Lightly oaked, lemony **14** has vanilla whiffs, buttery texture for extra appeal, subtle grassy hint for lift. **Chenin No. 5 ★★ 15** perfumed with Granny Smith apple characters, is very quaffable. **Pinot Grigio ★★☆** True-to-variety **15** has pear drop aroma (overlain with guava ferment character mid-2015), telltale texture. Bone-dry, yet with good vinosity for casual enjoyment. **Blanc de Blanc ★★☆ 15** much improved poolside sipper from colombard (80%), appealing spice, grass & pear drop bouquet, zingy palate ex sauvignon component. Also in 500 ml. **Special Late Harvest Gewürztraminer ★★★☆** Floral, spice & all things nice... plus melon, white peach & nougat on light-hearted **14**. Sweetness cut, appeal upped by gentle tannic tug, variety's bitter grip. Also tasted: **Merlot 14 ★★☆ African Java Pinotage 15 ★★☆ Blackberry Cabernet Sauvignon-Shiraz 14 ★★ Neil's Pick Colombar 15 ★★☆ Sauvignon Blanc 15 ★★ Cape Ruby NV ★★☆** Not retasted: **Blue Velvet Pinot Noir 13 ★★★ Blanc de Noir Red Muscadel Blush 14 ★★ Blanc de Noir Shiraz 14 ★ Red Muscadel 14 ★★★☆** Not tasted: **Cramond Cabernet Sauvignon-Merlot**. Discontinued: **Cramond Sauvignon Blanc-Chardonnay**.

Four Cousins range

Dry Red ★★☆ Characterful **NV** braai companion from unoaked ruby cab & merlot. In 1 & 3L. **Dry White ★★** Spice attraction on easygoing colombard & sauvignon **NV**, now conquering Belgium. In 1.5L & 3L. **Sweet Rosé ★★** Grapey refreshment delivered by low-alcohol (8%), strawberry-toned **NV**. Also in 1.5 & 3L. Also tasted: **Natural Sweet Red NV ★★ Natural Sweet White NV ★★** Discontinued: **Extra Light White, Light Natural Sweet Rosé**.

Four Cousins Singles Collection (NEW)
Cocoa Cabernet Sauvignon ★★ Easy, berry-packed **14**, more blood & iron than cocoa character.
Mulberry Merlot ★★☆ Pleasant drink-now **14** offers the advertised aromas & flavours.

Four Cousins Skinny range (NEW)
Red ★★ Weigh-Less-endorsed low-calorie option (as all these), berries & dust on **NV** from merlot, low 9.5% alcohol. **Sweet Rosé** ★★ **NV** from red muscadel is surprisingly gutsy, with spice & tannin frame around sweet fruit core. 9% alcohol. **White** ★★ Slimmer's friend from semillon, **NV**'s attractive khaki bush aroma let down by dilute finish.

Four Cousins Sparkling range
Red Sweet Sparkling ★ Carbonated **NV** from ruby cab, frothy fun with sweet tail. **Sauvignon Blanc Brut** ★★ Latest **NV** (**14**) from sauvignon joyful & invigorating, with 'wet beach' minerality, 'seaweed' salinity & zesty dry tail. Also tasted: **Blush Sparkling NV** ★★ **White Sweet Sparkling NV** ★

Five's Reserve range
Pinotage (Ⓖ) ★★ Some tar, coffee wafts on lightly oaked **13** BBQ companion (previous vintages unwooded.) Not retasted: **Cabernet Sauvignon 13** ★★ **Merlot Rosé 14** ★★ **Chenin Blanc 14** ★☆

Papillon Sparkling range
Brut ★★☆ Latest **NV** from colombard (80%) & sauvignon easy & charming celebratory sparkler, with apple & honey notes. Also tasted: **Vin Doux Rosé NV** ★★ **Demi-Sec NV** ★★

Brandy range
Brandy (Ⓖ) ★★★ 5 year old blended brandy (50% potstill) from chenin & colombard. Peaches, caramel & fresh fruit flavours – cheerful & charming, some dry elegance. Good on the rocks. — WB, CvZ

Location/map: Robertson ▪ WO: Robertson/Western Cape ▪ Est 1937 ▪ 1stB 1980 ▪ Tasting & sales Mon-Fri 8.30-5 Sat 9.30-3 Sun 11-2 ▪ Closed Easter Fri/Sun, Dec 25 & Jan 1 ▪ Cellar tours by appt ▪ Garden tours ▪ Food & wine tasting platters ▪ Fish Eagle hiking trail ▪ MTB trails (bike rental available) ▪ Self-catering farm cottage ▪ Christina's @ Van Loveren bistro open daily ▪ Owner(s) Nico, Wynand, Phillip, Hennie, Bussell & Neil Retief ▪ Cellarmaster(s) Bussell Retief ▪ Winemaker(s) Danelle Conradie (Jan 2007), Malcolm Human (Jan 2012) & Chris Crafford (Nov 2014), with Jonas Cupido ▪ Viticulturist(s) Neil & Hennie Retief ▪ 650ha (cab, merlot, mourv, muscadel r/w, ptage, pinot noir/gris, ruby cab, shiraz, touriga nacional, chard, chenin, cbard, gewürz, morio muscat, nouvelle, sauv, sem, viog) ▪ 10,000t/2.5m cs own label 33% red 33% white 34% rosé ▪ Brands for clients: Woolworths ▪ BWI, Fairtrade, IPW ▪ PO Box 19 Klaasvoogds 6707 ▪ info@vanloveren.co.za ▪ www.vanloveren.co.za ▪ S 33° 52' 31.3" E 020° 0' 9.1" ▪ F +27 (0)23-615-1336 ▪ **T +27 (0)23-615-1505**

Van Ryn
(Ⓠ) (Ⓐ)

Named for its Dutch immigrant founder, Distell's flagship brandy range continues to garner global praise. Besides regularly winning the Worldwide Best Brandy award at a leading wine and spirit show with one or other of its premium potstill products, Van Ryn's century-old, visitor-friendly premises (with on-site cooperage), offering tours and inspired food-and-brandy pairings, has recently also been recognised on the international wine tourism front.

★★★★★ **Au.Ra** (Ⓖ) Among SA's longest-matured, rarest & priciest brandies: 30 year minimum maturation. Even smoother, more sumptuously mouthfilling than others in range, but retaining elegance. Full spicy, dried fruit complexity splendidly supported by oak. Sets a local standard for excellence.

★★★★★ **20 Year Collectors Reserve** (Ⓖ) Concentrated nose of dark berries, dried fruit & spice. Spice, especially, repeated on the palate along with apricot & prune amidst the complexity. Reminiscences of oak but never intrusive. Mellow, silky & very rich, with forthright finish.

★★★★★ **15 Year Fine Cask Reserve** Irresistible notes of fragrant flowers, orange zest & dark chocolate just part of the ethereal complexity of this exquisite glassful of sniffing & sipping pleasure. Tasting of slightly tweaked blend (with new components) confirms this as worthy of the highest rating. Like others, from chenin & colombard, widely sourced.

★★★★★ 12 Year Distillers Reserve Ⓟ 100% potstill brandy, like all below. Deep colour, with mahogany gleam. Fragrant, delicate aromas of fruit, herbs, flowers lead to full, richly powerful but gentle palate, then a long, sustained finish. Complete, balanced, triumphant.

★★★★☆ Vintage 10 Year Ⓟ Testimony to the quality possible for a vintage brandy – that is, with a component of matured (not potstill) spirit. Youthful, with a showy array of fruit aromas, plus some sandalwood & vanilla from oak. The mature & fruity parts marry appealingly. Assertive, rich, lively. — WB, TJ

Location/map: Stellenbosch ▪ Map grid reference: D6 ▪ Est 1905 ▪ Tasting & sales Mon-Fri 9-5 (May-Sep) 9-6 (Oct-Apr) Sat 9-4 Sun (Oct-Apr only) 11-4 ▪ Van Ryn's tasting; brandy, coffee & chocolate pairing; Van Ryn's Florentine Collection Reserve tasting ▪ Closed Good Fri, Dec 25 & Jan 1 ▪ Cellar tours Mon-Fri 10, 11.30 & 3 Sat 10, 11.30 & 1 ▪ Tour groups ▪ Gift shop ▪ Conference & boardroom facilities ▪ Exhibitions & special events ▪ Museum collection of historical brandies on display ▪ Owner(s) Distell ▪ Brandy master(s) Marlene Bester (Jul 2009) ▪ ISO 9001:1995 ▪ Van Ryn Road Vlottenburg Stellenbosch 7604 ▪ info@vanryns.co.za ▪ www.vanryn.co.za ▪ S 33° 57' 43.26" E 018° 48' 4.87" ▪ F +27 (0)21-881-3127 ▪ **T +27 (0)21-881-3875**

☐ **Van Zijls Family Vintners** *see* Imbuko Wines

Van Zylshof Estate   Ⓟ

The Bonnievale estate has been in Van Zyl hands for three generations. Oupa Andries built the cellar in 1940, and son Chris and grandson Andri have bottled wines under their label since 1994. From viticulture to marketing, all aspects of the winery are managed by family members.

> **Chenin Blanc** ⑦ **★★★ 15**'s floral slightly fruit-shy nose leads to fresh peach on the palate, tropical guava with fresh lemony finish. **Sauvignon Blanc** ⑦ **★★★** Whiffs of freshly mowed grass on **15**, crisply dry yet fruity with crunchy green apples.

Riverain Unwooded Chardonnay ★★★ Nudging higher rating, zesty **15** refreshes with juicy orange & pineapple fruit; dry, with good length. Not retasted: **Cabernet Sauvignon-Merlot 12 ★★☆ Rosé 14 ★★☆** Discontinued: **Chardonnay**. — JG

Location: Bonnievale ▪ Map/WO: Robertson ▪ Est 1940 ▪ 1stB 1994 ▪ Tasting & sales Mon-Fri 9–5 Sat 9–1 ▪ Closed Good Fri, Ascension Day, Dec 25 & Jan 1 ▪ Cellar tours by appt ▪ Owner(s) Van Zylshof Trust ▪ Cellarmaster(s)/winemaker(s)/viticulturist(s) Andri van Zyl (Mar 1993) ▪ 37ha/32ha under vine ▪ 450t/ ±8,000cs own label 15% red 80% white 5% rosé ▪ PO Box 64 Bonnievale 6730 ▪ vanzylshof@ lando.co.za ▪ www.vanzylshof.co.za ▪ S 33° 56' 18.5" E 020° 6' 23.4" ▪ F +27 (0)23-616-3503 ▪ **T +27 (0)23-616-2401**

Varkenskraal   Ⓟ

André and Gail Cockcroft bought Varkenskraal in Klein Karoo in 2011, determined to improve the neglected vineyards and make their own wine – the grapes were going to the co-op. Many problems needed facing: above all it's difficult, they say, to make affordable wines on a small scale. Especially with the depredations of birds and baboons – chardonnay vines suffered particularly, while floods and hail in early 2014 didn't help! But here they are, and hoping to have a tasting facility by the time you read this.

Merlot ★★★ Mint chocolate intro to youthful **14**, tannins needing another year/2 to meld. For earlier drinking, match with rich creamy dishes. **Chenin Blanc ★★★** Lime & apple, becoming more tropical on the palate, but still with an appealing hint of green. **14** light textured & softly round. — CR, CvZ

Location: De Rust ▪ Map: Klein Karoo & Garden Route ▪ WO: Klein Karoo ▪ Est 1995 ▪ 1stB 2014 ▪ Tasting by appt ▪ Guest house ▪ Owner(s) André & Gail Cockcroft ▪ Cellarmaster(s) Jacques Kruger (Feb 2014, Bergwater) ▪ Viticulturist(s) Vinpro (Mar 2014, consultant) ▪ 82ha/7.18ha (merlot, chard, chenin) ▪ 28t/ 1,200cs own label 53% red 47% white ▪ PO Box 20 De Rust 6651 ▪ andre@varkenskraal.co.za ▪ www.varkenskraal.co.za ▪ S 33° 27' 19.21" E 022° 33' 29.70" ▪ **T +27 (0)44-241-2352**

Vaughan Johnson's Wine & Cigar Shop

Cape Town doyen Vaughan Johnson, into his 4th decade of purveying wine, says foreign tourists popping in at his shop in the V&A Waterfront are enjoying the benefits of the weak rand. 'Nevertheless, the whole world is in recession (or short of disposable income) so overpriced SA wines aren't selling. Three times the price isn't equal to three times the quality.' Hence his own modestly priced range.

Good Everyday Cape White ★★★ **NV** sauvignon & chenin offers dry, fruity, uncomplicated quaffing, with nice texture from brief lees-ageing. Not retasted: **Good Everyday Cape Red NV** ★★★ — JG

Location: Cape Town ▪ Map: Cape Peninsula ▪ WO: Paarl/Wellington ▪ Est/1stB 1985 ▪ Sales Mon-Fri 9–6 Sat 9–5 Sun 10–5 ▪ Open pub hols ▪ Gifts, souvenirs, spirits & beer available ▪ Owner(s) Vaughan Johnson ▪ PO Box 50012 Waterfront 8002 ▪ vjohnson@mweb.co.za ▪ www.vaughanjohnson.co.za ▪ S 33° 54' 19.15" E 018° 25' 10.68" ▪ F +27 (0)86-509-6401 ▪ **T +27 (0)21-419-2121**

Veenwouden Private Cellar

This small Paarl estate was acquired by international opera star Deon van der Walt in 1989, and named for the Netherlands home of the first Van der Walt to come to the Cape (in 1727). Deon died tragically in 2006, but the family presence continues in the person of his brother Marcel, winemaker here from nearly the beginning. No new wines this year, and there is the whiff of some sort of change in the air.

Reserve Collection

★★★★ **Merlot** 🕐 **12**, with splash cab franc, shows refinement despite 14.5% alcohol. Cool red fruit & mint, deftly oaked. Balanced, silky tannins already tempting, with charm for 4-6 years.

★★★★ **Syrah** 🕐 Similar fresh spicy tone to **11**, but preview of **12** (★★★★) shows less fruit intensity. Bright & sappy, with supple tannins.

★★★★ **Classic** 🕐 Cab-led quintet of Bordeaux varieties, **10** more restrained than **09**. Tart savoury fruit sheathed in chalky tannins. Refined, all elements in place, just needs time's smoothing hand.

Not retasted: **Chardonnay 11** ★★★★

Hugh Masekela Collection

★★★★ **Hugh Masekela** 🕐 Harmonious merlot-based **10** blend with cab, shiraz. Invitingly rich, savoury with caressing velvet feel, gentle grip.

Premium Collection

Pinot Noir 🕐 ★★★★ **12** elegant, but taut & introverted in youth. Time & decanting will reveal greater charm. Not tasted: **Chardonnay**.

Vivat Bacchus Collection

Red 🕐 ★★★★ Approachable merlot-based **11** with a little shiraz; spicy flavours polished with French oak. WO Coastal, as next. Not retasted: **Sauvignon Blanc-Chenin Blanc 12** ★★★ — MW

Location: Paarl ▪ Map: Paarl & Wellington ▪ Map grid reference: E3 ▪ WO: Paarl/Coastal ▪ Est 1989 ▪ 1stB 1993 ▪ Tasting, sales & cellar tours by appt ▪ Fee R100, waived on purchase ▪ Owner(s) 5 W Wineries (Pty) Ltd, t/a Veenwouden ▪ Cellarmaster(s) Marcel van der Walt ▪ Winemaker(s) Marcel van der Walt, with Faried Williams ▪ Viticulturist(s) Marcel van der Walt, with Sias Louw ▪ 14ha/12.5ha (cabs s/f, malbec, merlot, p verdot, pinot) ▪ ±100t/11,000cs own label 90% red 10% white ▪ PO Box 7086 Northern Paarl 7623 ▪ admin@veenwouden.com ▪ www.veenwouden.com ▪ S 33° 41' 7.0" E 018° 57' 52.4" ▪ F +27 (0)21-872-1384 ▪ **T +27 (0)21-872-6806**

☐ **Veldt** *see* Robertson Wide River Export Company
☐ **Velo** *see* Wildehurst Wines

Vendôme

Farmed by the Le Roux family for 10 generations, Vendôme on the Berg River banks in Paarl was named for their Huguenot heritage and ancestral home in central France. The Le Rouxs recently joined forces with the De Waals (Oude Denneboom) and Loubsers (Kuypers Kraal) in a marketing venture, Kaapse Familie Wingerde (see separate entries).

Sans Barrique ★★ Light herbal brush to **13** sauvignon blanc/semillon mix, lees-aged in tank 12 months. Discontinued: **Classique**, **Merlot-Cabernet Sauvignon**. — WB, FM

Location/WO: Paarl ▪ Map: Paarl & Wellington ▪ Map grid reference: E6 ▪ Est 1692 ▪ 1stB 1999 ▪ Tasting & sales by appt ▪ Closed all pub hols ▪ Restaurant Mon-Fri 8-5 Sat 8-2 ▪ Functions ▪ Owner(s)/winemaker(s)/ viticulturist(s) Jannie le Roux ▪ 20ha (cab, merlot, shiraz, chard, chenin, cbard, sauv, sem) ▪ 5t/600cs own label 50% red 50% white ▪ PO Box 36 Paarl 7645 ▪ lerouxjg@icon.co.za ▪ www.vendome.co.za ▪ S 33° 45' 27.8" E 018° 58' 42.4" ▪ F +27 (0)21-863-0094 ▪ **T +27 (0)21-863-3905**

☐ **Vera Cruz Estate** see Delheim Wines

Vergelegen Wines   (⚲) (🍴) (◎) (⚑) (⚬)

Only an owner with the deep pockets of global mining company Anglo American could have preserved this historic 3,000-ha property in the manner fitting its status as the 18th-century estate and model farm of Cape governor Willem Adriaan van der Stel. Much has been preserved, besides buildings, including 300+ year old camphor trees, national monuments since 1942, 17 heritage gardens, and all without losing sight of environmental conservation or social upliftment needs. But this is also a wine business. The French-designed largely underground octagonal cellar is perched on a hill with spectacular views of False Bay; winemaker André van Rensburg works closely with renowned French consultant oenologist Michel Rolland to bring a further dimension to the award-winning wines; and cool-climate terroir is creatively expressed in the wine range.

Flagship range

★★★★★ **Vergelegen V** (⚲) Premium-priced flagship, 100% cab with 23 months all-new oak, **11** is more savoury than Reserve Cab, tightly knit, made for the long haul. Cigarbox & blackcurrants, lead pencils, firm but ripe tannin as foundation. Accessible but still an infant. No **10**.

★★★★★ **Vergelegen GVB Red** Masterly Bordeaux blend. Cab led, 24 months new French barriques yet **11** already hinting at its potential. Plush blackcurrants, cedar/cigar box spicing, has latent power, will reward cellaring. Also tasted **10**, similar styling & excellence. Give them both time. Winemaker recommends decanting.

★★★★★ **Vergelegen GVB White** (⚲) Pioneering barrel-fermented/aged semillon & sauvignon blend. Toasted almond & gentle lemon bouquet in **13**, but flavours richer, dried fig & preserved citrus peel, mouthfilling, hedonistic, back to **11**'s styling. Would reward cellaring.

Reserve range

★★★★★ **Cabernet Sauvignon** (⚲) **09** is seamless, has such integration of fruit & oak that it's difficult to pick out a single flavour element. Plush silky tones, sleek musculature for a long distinguished future. With a dash merlot, cab franc.

★★★★★ **Merlot** Consistently one of the Cape's finest. Plums & Belgian chocolate, an intriguing violet nuance, **12** is streamlined, beautifully balanced with suave tannins, elegance; & a future to count on.

★★★★★ **Shiraz** Intense red berries, espresso nuances & black pepper, complex **13** strikes an impressive balance between fruit & savoury. The tannins are supple, polished, the wine already delicious but as all these, the ability to age well.

★★★★★ **DNA** Cab franc leads in 4-part serious nod to Bordeaux. Finesse & fine crafting show in **11**'s perfect balance between oak & fruit, cedar & red berries, a whiff of fennel. Streamlined, with deep muscle tone, a long future ahead.

★★★★ **Chardonnay** Upping the ante over **12** with better oak/fruit balance, **13** (★★★★★) is svelte & polished, a mouthwatering freshness extending the tangerine & hazelnut flavours. Most serious of the chardonnays, no New World showiness, 40% new small oak. Very fine.

★★★★★ **Sauvignon Blanc Schaapenberg** Named for 25 year old hillside single-vineyard overlooking False Bay. Always with oystershell minerality, **15** also has leafy fennel tones, a tight-knit tension & revitalising acidity to live a long time. Individual & classy.

★★★★★ **Semillon** From 26 year old vines. Part barrel ferment/aged, so fruit has the final say. A gentle savoury seam through the lime & green apple flavours, impressive **14** crackles with health & vitality, promising a rewarding future. Follows standout **13** (★★★★★).

★★★★☆ **Semillon Straw Wine** ⓥ Shimmering gold dessert from vine- & pallet-dried grapes, fermented on skins/stems, aged 14 months older barrels. Nuts, glacé pineapple & varietal lanolin on hedonistic **11**. Bolt of tangy lime cuts sweetness for a clean, lingering finish. 375 ml.

Not tasted: **MMV**.

Premium range

★★★★ **Shiraz** Accessible & attractive, with spiced plums, pepper & scrub, smooth textured & succulent, **12**'s well-judged tannins a hidden asset, promising a future. WO W Cape.

★★★★ **Cabernet Sauvignon-Merlot** For relatively earlier drinking than other reds, well crafted **11** is a cab/merlot-led 5-part Bordeaux blend. Boasts cassis & tobacco, smooth curves & nice fresh length.

★★★★ **Chardonnay** ⓥ Only part-oaked to showcase the fruit flavours, **13**'s orange/lemon & buttered toast styling puts it back on track after **12** (★★★★). Elegant, with a lifting freshness.

★★★★ **Sauvignon Blanc** Green fig & nettles, pure & focused **15** reflects its cool-climate origin in the vibrant limy acidity, extended length. Good ageing potential. — CR

Location: Somerset West ▪ Map: Helderberg ▪ WO: Stellenbosch/Western Cape ▪ Est 1987 ▪ 1stB 1991 ▪ Tasting & sales daily 9.30–4.30 (gate closes at 4) ▪ Estate closed Good Fri, May 1 & Dec 25 ▪ Daily heritage & gardens tour at 10; cellar tours at 11.30 & 3 ▪ All tours R20pp (reservations advised) ▪ Tasting R30/6 wines (excl flagship wines), R10 each for flagship wines ▪ Camphors Restaurant, Stables Restaurant & Forest Picnic ▪ Facilities for children ▪ Gift shop ▪ Historic Cape Dutch homestead ▪ Library ▪ Exhibition corridor ▪ 316 year old camphor trees (National Monuments since 1942) ▪ Conservation area ▪ 17 gardens including Camellia garden of excellence & children's adventure garden & maze ▪ Owner(s) Anglo American plc ▪ Winemaker(s) André van Rensburg (Jan 1998) ▪ Viticulturist(s) Dwayne Lottering (Nov 2003) ▪ 3,000ha/158ha (cab, merlot, sauv) ▪ 900t/120,000cs own label 58% red 42% white ▪ ISO 9001, ISO 14001, ISO 22000, OSHAS 18000, BWI champion, WIETA ▪ PO Box 17 Somerset West 7129 ▪ info@vergelegen.co.za ▪ www.vergelegen.co.za ▪ S 34° 4' 38.33" E 018° 53' 30.03" ▪ **T +27 (0)21-847-2100**

Vergenoegd Wine Estate   ⓠ ⑭ ⑩ ⑧ ⑥

There are new owners at Stellenbosch estate Vergenoegd for the first time in almost 200 years. Former proprietor and the sixth generation here, John Faure, stays on as cellarmaster and custodian of a tradition stretching back to the 17th century, and of the house style, focused on red wine and 'port'. Passionate about birds since childhood, John's vision for a project to strengthen indigenous waterbird populations and improve the hydrology and water quality of the Cape's agricultural landscape continues.

Vintage Collection

★★★★ **Cabernet Sauvignon** ⓥ Rich, robust **03** on review was still very youthful, best broached in few years. Should keep ±10. On track after lighter **02** (★★★★).

★★★★ **Shiraz** ⓥ **01**, tasted for 2014 edition, more winning than **00**, with ripe black cherries, notes of herb, olive, mocha; fruit generally more apparent. Still in restrained but richly savoury house style.

★★★★☆ **Estate Blend** ⓥ **01** will also benefit from maturation, we noted some years back; already grand & imposing but not lacking delight. Balanced, finishing satisfyingly dry.

Classic range

★★★★ **Cabernet Sauvignon** Distinctive, stalwart SA cab with emphasis on grape's fine astringency & structure, reined-in fruit. **09** loses **08**'s dab cab franc, needs year/2 to gain more complexity.

★★★★ **Merlot** Forthright **09** (★★★★) riper, meatier & less refined than elegant **08** but satisfying dry conclusion, enlivening herbal nuance. ±20 months in oak, 80% new; 13% malbec for extra punch.

★★★★ **Shiraz** 07 (★★★★★), with smidgens cab & touriga, has **06**'s game, truffle & leather undertones plus its intensity & weight but is better knit, with crunchy texture, still lively & dry. Also in magnum.

★★★★ **Estate Blend** Like **06**, cab-led Bordeaux red bucks the trend for early consumption. Step-up **07** (★★★★★) beguiles with complex oak spice & red/black fruit but its taut tannin frame will reward cellaring many years. Also in magnum.

★★★★☆ **Old Cape Colony Cape Vintage** ⓥ **07** (★★★☆) tinta, touriga offering less convincing than powerful & elegant **06**. Has Xmas cake richness, fiery conclusion, oxidative headiness.

Not retasted: **Terrace Bay 07** ★★★

Runner Duck range

White ★★★ Sauvignon (90%) provides the grassiness & zip, splash semillon the engaging lemon tones in lively **15**. Just enough creamy breadth from 3 months lees-ageing to pair with oysters. WO W Cape. Also tasted: **Red 13** ★★★ Discontinued: **Rosé**.

Limited Edition range

Tawny Port ⊘ ★★★ Sweetly rich & rustic once-off **99** from tinta tasted a few years back. — CvZ

Location/map: Stellenbosch ▪ Map grid reference: B8 ▪ WO: Stellenbosch/Western Cape ▪ Est 1696 ▪ 1stB 1972 ▪ Tasting & sales Mon-Fri 9–5 Sat/Sun 9.30–4 ▪ Fee R35 ▪ Closed Good Fri, Dec 25 & Jan 1 ▪ Cellar tours by appt ▪ Facilities for children ▪ Tour groups ▪ Wine-related gifts ▪ Fresh duck eggs in spring ▪ 6 boule courts ▪ Guided historical walks & duck tours by appt ▪ Waterbird habitat project ▪ Bird hides ▪ Conservation area ▪ Pomegranate Restaurant open for lunch Tue-Sun, dinner by appt ▪ Owner(s) Vergenoegd Trust ▪ Cellarmaster(s) John Faure (Nov 1983) ▪ Winemaker(s) Marlize Jacobs (Dec 2007) ▪ Viticulturist(s) Marlize Jacobs (Dec 2007), advised by Drikus van der Westhuizen (2004) ▪ 300ha/66ha (cabs s/f, malbec, merlot, p verdot, shiraz, tinta, touriga) ▪ 500t ▪ 94% red 3% white 3% rosé ▪ BWI, IPW, WIETA ▪ PO Box 1 Faure 7131 ▪ info@vergenoegd.co.za ▪ www.vergenoegd.co.za ▪ S 34° 2' 2.8" E 018° 44' 20.1" ▪ F +27 (0)21-843-3118 ▪ **T +27 (0)21-843-3248**

Verlieft Wines ⓠ

Dirk Roos of this Stellenbosch boutique family brand believes that terroir is best expressed through one or two wines — their core red Bordeaux-style wine was due to be supplemented, around our going-to-press time, by a well-matured muscat de Frontignan, and there's also, says Dirk, 'a very good possibility of a 2016 white Bordeaux blend'.

Location: Stellenbosch ▪ Est 2010 ▪ Tasting & sales by appt ▪ Closed Easter Fri-Mon, Dec 25/26 & Jan 1 ▪ Owner(s) Roos Family Wines ▪ Cellarmaster(s) Dirk Roos ▪ PO Box 104 Stellenbosch 7605 ▪ kirsten@verlieft.co.za, dirk@mooiplaas.co.za ▪ www.verlieft.co.za ▪ **T +27 (0)82-904-6886**

Versailles ⓠ ⓞ

Owner Annareen de Reuck is the scion of the Malan family which helped establish the Wellington grower-owned cellars now merged into Wellington Wines. Small parcels of her Versailles grapes are vinified in the old estate cellar. Current releases '15 Merlot and '15 Sauvignon Blanc untasted.

Location: Wellington ▪ Map: Paarl & Wellington ▪ Map grid reference: E1 ▪ Est/1stB 2004 ▪ Tasting, sales & tours by appt ▪ Conservation area ▪ Owner(s) Annareen de Reuck (Malan) ▪ Vineyard manager(s) M Joseph ▪ 100ha (cab, cinsaut, merlot, shiraz, chenin, cbard, riesling) ▪ ±1,200t ▪ PO Box 597 Wellington 7654 ▪ adereuck@ezinet.co.za, orders@versailleswines.co.za ▪ www.versailles.co.za ▪ S 33° 37' 34.98" E 018° 59' 37.11" ▪ F +27 (0)86-502-1482 ▪ **T +27 (0)21-873-2618/+27 (0)82-898-9314**

☐ **Versus** see Stellenbosch Vineyards
☐ **Vet Rooi Olifant** see Kaapzicht Wine Estate

Viceroy

Among SA's most enduring blended brandies, with mid-1800s ties to the Van Ryn Wine & Spirit Company (both brands now owned by Distell). Today Viceroy, with five years' barrel maturation upping the ante in its category, is sold throughout Africa and fast becoming one of the biggest export labels there.

5 Year ⊘ ★★★★ A more serious blended brandy. Tweaked blend more complex than 5 year category would imply; though touch obviously fiery & sweet on the finish, still sippable unmixed. — WB

☐ **Victoria Bay** see Darling Cellars

Vierkoppen ⓠ

As planned, Britons David and Daphne Briscoe have completed a boutique cellar on the Klaasvoogds vineyard holding they bought in 2008, and taken over the reins from contract winemakers. The 2,500L they made (doubtless with lots of pride and satisfaction) last harvest with sage advice from near-neighbour Newald Marais (Kranskop) will be matured in French oak and 'not released until it's ready!'

★★★★☆ Cabernet Sauvignon Ⓠ With dash cab franc. Cassis & coconut spicing from 2 years French oak but **11** has other layers of interest as well, a bit of scrub, forest floor. Polished, silky, with aristocratic elegance, outclasses jammy, less complex **10** (★★★☆). labelled 'Weavers Nest'.

Weavers Nest Reserve 🆕 ★★★☆ Classic cab & merlot blend (60/40) launches the Reserve label; **13** brambly cassis, tobacco & cedar lead out a soft & supple ensemble, easy to drink but worthy of contemplation too. Not tasted: **Pinotage**, **Sauvignon Blanc**. — DS

Location/map/WO: Robertson ▪ Est 2008 ▪ 1stB 2009 ▪ Tasting & sales by appt ▪ Fee R50pp ▪ Closed Dec 25 & Jan 1 ▪ Owner(s) David & Daphne Briscoe ▪ Cellarmaster(s) David Briscoe (Mar 2008) ▪ Winemaker(s) David Briscoe & Alkie van der Merwe (2014, consultant) ▪ Viticulturist(s) Philip Swart (Apr 2013, consultant) ▪ 32ha/10ha (cab, durif, merlot, ptage, ruby cab, sauv) ▪ 100t/1,700cs own label 80% red 20% white ▪ PO Box 950 Robertson 6705 ▪ vierkoppen@gmail.com ▪ www.vierkoppen.com ▪ S 33° 48' 1.52" E 019° 58' 55.76" ▪ **T +27 (0)78-413-1733**

Vierlanden Boutique Family Cellar　　　　　　　Ⓠ ◎

Garagistes Danel van Tonder, wife Esther, younger brother Marius and winemaker friend PJ Geyer vinify small parcels from selected sites in a thatched cellar in Durbanville's Vierlanden area.

Chardonnay Ⓠ ★★★ Pleasant **12** ex Franschhoek, with nut & lime notes; juicy, with a loose structure & strong hint of sweetness. Not retasted: **ThatchRoof 11** ★★★ **Sauvignon Blanc 14** ★★★★ — TJ

Location: Durbanville ▪ Map: Durbanville, Philadelphia & Darling ▪ WO: Swartland/Franschhoek/Elgin ▪ Est 2009 ▪ 1stB 2010 ▪ Tasting, sales & cellar tours Mon-Sat by appt ▪ Fee R55 ▪ Closed all pub hols ▪ Conferences ▪ Owner(s) Vierlanden Boutique Wines cc ▪ Cellarmaster(s) Esther van Tonder (Jan 2009) ▪ Winemaker(s) Esther van Tonder (Jan 2009), Marius van Tonder & PJ Geyer ▪ 1ha/0.25ha (cab) ▪ 4t/±650cs own label 60% red 40% white ▪ Le Petit Jem, 137 on Murray, Vierlanden Heights, Durbanville 7550 ▪ vierlandencellar@gmail.com ▪ www.vierlandencellar.com ▪ S 33° 48' 21.44" E 018° 39' 35.36" ▪ F +27 (0)21-975-7286 ▪ **T +27 (0)21-975-7286**

Vilafonté　　　　　　　　　　　　　　　　　　　Ⓠ

The establishment of Vilafonté in the mid 1990s, with two eminent US wine people investing, represented a signal mark of confidence in Cape terroir. Phil Freese, who consults to some of California's grand wineries (and some SA ones), designed and continues to direct their Paarl vineyards while Zelma Long, listed in Decanter's latest Top 30 Winemakers Worldwide, is in charge of the cellar on the outskirts of Stellenbosch town. Both are frequent visitors and fully involved, with the help of Martin Smith as resident winemaker and Mike Ratcliffe (also of Warwick) the managing partner. The '12 wines tasted this edition are a milestone for the venture, being the 10th vintage and almost 20 years since Phil identified 'the unique vilafontes soils on our expressive parcel of Simonsberg bench-land'.

★★★★☆ Series C Cab-based blend, as name hints, with malbec & merlot, & 7% cab franc in **12** versus none in **11** (★★★★★). Classic aromas & flavours – blackcurrant, graphite & cedarwood spice. Balanced, for early drinking after decanting hour/2; will also reward decade+ cellaring.

★★★★☆ Series M M is for merlot & malbec, which typically dominate this Bordeaux blend with cab. **12**'s (48/45/17) opulent berry fruits, dark chocolate nuances give way to earthy, spicy notes, grippy structure, hint of minerality. Like perfumed **11**, satisfying now, even better in 5+ years. — GM

Location/map: Stellenbosch ▪ Map grid reference: E5 ▪ WO: Paarl ▪ Est 1996 ▪ 1stB 2003 ▪ Tasting, sales & tours by appt only ▪ Owner(s) Mike Ratcliffe, Zelma Long & Phil Freese ▪ Winemaker(s) Zelma Long & Martin Smith (May 2010) ▪ Viticulturist(s) Phil Freese & Edward Pietersen (2006) ▪ 17ha (cabs s/f, malbec, merlot) ▪ 60t/4,000cs own label 100% red ▪ Unit 7C Lower Dorp Street Bosman's Crossing Stellenbosch 7600 ▪ info@vilafonte.com ▪ www.vilafonte.com ▪ S 33° 56' 26.8" E 018° 50' 49.8" ▪ F +27 (0)21-883-8231 ▪ **T +27 (0)21-886-4083**

Viljoensdrift Fine Wines & Cruises

The 5th generation to grow and make wine here in Robertson (historically for sale in bulk), the incumbent Viljoen brothers started bottling under their own label in 1998. Still producing wine for clients, they have steadily increased own-label bottling over the years. This edition there's a promising single-vineyard pinotage off vines planted when Manie and Fred used their knowledge of the different soil types and slopes – 'and instinct', they quip – to meticulously lay out a bespoke block.

River Grandeur range

Pinotage Single Vineyard ★★★☆ Was just 'Pinotage'. Step-up **14** same big alcohol as previous but it's deftly balanced by juicy strawberry fruit & enlivening bitter lift. Could show even better year/2. **Sauvignon Blanc** ★★ Water-white **15** faint blackcurrant fragrance, understated flavours, perky acidity. Try with salmon-wrapped asparagus & zingy Hollandaise sauce, say team. Also tasted: **Cabernet Sauvignon 14** ★★★☆ **Cape Blend 14** ★★★ Not retasted: **Merlot 12** ★★★ **Shiraz 12** ★★★ Not tasted: **Chardonnay**.

Viljoensdrift range

★★★★ **Villion** 🅐 Much-improved méthode cap classique sparkling from chardonnay, 5 years on lees; **08** golden patina, lovely lightness to fresh-bread profile, svelte extra-dry finish. Last was **NV** (★★★).
Cape Vintage Reserve ★★★ **13**'s succulent fruit, maraschino cherry & chocolate tones make it a dessert in its own right. From souzão. Also tasted: **Muskapino Sweet Sparkling Rosé 15** ★★

Anchor Drift range

Dry White ★★ Green pea, faint florals & brisk entry on modest, fleeting **NV** mouthful from sauvignon. Not retasted: **Dry Red NV** ★★ — CvZ

Location/map/WO: Robertson ▪ Est/1stB 1998 ▪ Tasting, sales & river cruises at Riverside venue Mon-Fri 10–5 Sat 10-4 & 1st Sun/month 10-3; open 7 days/week during Dec/Jan ▪ Closed Good Fri, Dec 25 & Jan 1 ▪ Self-help deli – create your own picnic basket ▪ Tour groups ▪ Conferences ▪ Owner(s) Fred & Manie Viljoen ▪ Winemaker(s) Fred Viljoen, with Zonia Lategan ▪ Viticulturist(s) Manie Viljoen ▪ 240ha/120ha (cab, ptage, shiraz, chard, chenin, sauv) ▪ 2,000t/±160,000cs own label 55% red 40% white 4% rosé 1% port + 15,000L for clients ▪ Other export brands: Elandsberg, Riverscape, Vuurgloed ▪ BWI, IPW, WIETA ▪ PO Box 653 Robertson 6705 ▪ rivercruises@viljoensdrift.co.za ▪ www.viljoensdrift.co.za ▪ S 33° 52' 8.4" E 019° 59' 13.6" ▪ F +27 (0)23-615-3417 ▪ **T +27 (0)23-615-1901 (cellar)/+27 (0)23-615-1017 (tasting/cruises)**

☐ **Village Walk** *see* Franschhoek Cellar

Villiera Wines

There's always been more to the wine business than just wine at Stellenbosch's Grier family estate since it was founded by cousins Jeff and Simon over 30 years ago. Good value to go with the quality, for a start. But Villiera also has long been known for its sustainability initiatives, eco and social, and their better-communicated efforts (through updated packaging) in this arena have been well received. In the same spirit, fewer additives – and in some cases zero sulphur – are added during vinification. Trendy Jasmine, the aromatic, slightly sweeter white launched last edition, is a hit, and Domaine Grier, their venture in Roussillon, southern France, is 'showing great promise'.

Villiera Wines range

★★★★ **Cabernet Sauvignon 13** continues on path set by generous **12**. Classic cab dark berry, iodine & violet notes, with herbal lift from splash cab franc, harmonious tannins from year in mostly French oak.

★★★★ **Traditional Barrel Fermented Chenin Blanc** Barrel-fermented (50% new) **15** (★★★★★) more complex & rich than **14**. Full bodied but bone-dry, with enlivening acidity & spicy farewell, depth from low-yielding dryland bushvines, apricot nuance from 3% botrytised portion.

★★★★ **Traditional Bush Vine Sauvignon Blanc** Old favourite off low-yielding bushvine single vineyard, portion oaked. Complex **15** entices with grass, capsicum, basil & asparagus, delivers lipsmacking satisfaction with vibrant acidity, toned body – all at just 12.6% alcohol.

Pinotage ⓦ ★★★☆ Spicy stews or cassoulet the Griers' suggestion to accompany ebullient **13**, its dark fruit, savoury spiciness & smoky finish the perfect match.

Merlot ★★★ **13** vanilla-infused plum, blue berry & dark chocolate appeal; soft tannins, berry persistence. Great with roasted duck, lamb or seared tuna. **Chenin Blanc** ★★★☆ Pear & tropical fruit toned **15**, lightly oaked, enlivened with zesty acidity for freshness, summer appeal. Also tasted: **Sauvignon Blanc 15** ★★★☆ **Jasmine 15** ★★★ Not tasted: **Monro, Inspiration**.

Méthode Cap Classique range
★★★★ **Brut Natural** ⓐ Quiet charm in delicate **10** sparkler from chardonnay. Bone-dry, 3 years on lees for refined mousse, subtle weight & aroma. Soft, smooth & seamless. No dosage or added sulphur.

★★★★☆ **Monro Brut** House's impressive flagship bubbly, consistent performer & household favourite. **09** includes old-barrel-fermented chardonnay portion, plus pinot noir & pinot meunier for fruitiness, palate weight. Plush yet focused, with toasted almond, brioche dimension from 5 years on lees.

★★★★ **Tradition Brut** Latest delicious **NV** adds pinot meunier to usual mix chardonnay, pinot noir & pinotage. Fine bubbles, creamy mousse, enlivening citrus freshness. Also in 375 ml & 1.5L.

Also tasted: **Tradition Brut Rosé NV** ★★★☆ **Starlight Brut NV** ★★★

Down to Earth range
White ★★★ Mostly sauvignon with 27% semillon for extra zing, **15** is lean, lime-fresh, laced with gooseberry & apple. For food or sunsets. Also tasted: **Red 14** ★★★ — GM

Location/map: Stellenbosch ▪ Map grid reference: D1 ▪ WO: Stellenbosch/Western Cape ▪ Est/1stB 1983 ▪ Tasting, sales & self-guided cellar tours Mon-Fri 9–5 Sat 9–3 ▪ Closed Good Fri, Dec 25 & Jan 1 ▪ MCC & nougat pairing; cheese platters & soft drinks ▪ Wildlife sanctuary ▪ Game drive safaris & birding R180pp (R90 for children under 15) incl tasting (valid until 31 Jan 2016) & self-guided tour of cellar, book ahead ▪ Owner(s) Grier family ▪ Cellarmaster(s) Jeff Grier (1983) ▪ Winemaker(s) Christiaan Visser (Dec 2008) ▪ Viticulturist(s) Simon Grier ▪ 180ha (cab, merlot, ptage, pinot, shiraz, chard, chenin, sauv) ▪ 1,800t/120,000cs own label 28% red 37% white 35% MCC ▪ Brands for clients: Woolworths (local); Marks & Spencer (export) ▪ B-BBEE, HACCP, WIETA ▪ PO Box 66 Koelenhof 7605 ▪ wine@villiera.com ▪ www.villiera.com ▪ S 33° 50' 14.4" E 018° 47' 34.4" ▪ F +27 (0)21-865-2314 ▪ **T +27 (0)21-865-2002/3**

Villiersdorp Cellar　　　　　　　　　　　　ⓐ ⓜ ⓖ ⓐ
The farms of Villiersdorp Cellar's 40 grower-owners are situated in four distinct geographical regions around Villiersdorp town, and these terroirs are highlighted, along with the winery's founding date, in the Since 1922 brand. With winemaker Christo Versfeld adding the vines to his purview, new offices and recently re-decorated tasting facilities, the team is upbeat about the year ahead.

Since 1922 range
Van Der Stel Sauvignon Blanc-Semillon ★★★ Forthcoming 70/30 combo billows grass & chilli pepper, tastes of ripe green figs; lively **15** is summer in a bottle. Cape South Coast WO. Also tasted: **Bossieveld Cabernet Sauvignon-Merlot 14** ★★★☆

Villiersdorp Cellar range
Treintjiewyn Hanepoot Jerepiko ★★★ 'Little Tractor' **NV** fortified muscat dessert's orange rind, watermelon perfumes leap out the glass, deliciously suffuse the balanced palate. Not retasted: **Cape Ruby NV** ★★ — CvZ

Location/map: Villiersdorp ▪ WO: Western Cape/Cape South Coast ▪ Est 1922 ▪ 1stB 1974 ▪ Tasting & sales Mon-Fri 8–5 Sat 9-1 ▪ Fee R10 for groups of 7+ ▪ Closed Easter Fri-Mon & Dec 25/26 ▪ Cellar tours by appt ▪ Kelkiewyn Restaurant ▪ Farm produce ▪ Walks/hikes ▪ MTB & 4x4 trails ▪ Tractor museum open on request ▪ Owner(s) 40 growers ▪ Winemaker(s)/viticulturist(s) Christo Versfeld ▪ 300ha (merlot, chenin, sauv) ▪ 3,600t/19,000cs own label 30% red 30% white 30% rosé 10% fortified ▪ BWI, IPW ▪ PO Box 14 Villiersdorp 6848 ▪ marketing@villiersdorpcellar.co.za ▪ www.villiersdorpcellar.co.za ▪ S 33° 59' 11.2" E 019° 17' 48.5" ▪ F +27 (0)28-840-0957 ▪ **T +27 (0)28-840-0083**

☐ **Vinay** see Slanghoek Winery

Vin du Cap International ⓘ

Based on Stellenbosch's Vrede farm, wine trading house Vin du Cap has been export focused since its inception in 2011 but has recently gained ground locally due to growing demand. Christa Calitz and her co-owners are planning 'new and exciting wines', and pleased to report expanded shipments to China.

Vrede Vineyard Select range

Cape Blend (NEW) ★★★☆ **10** mostly cab, with pinotage & petit verdot. Seductive & full bodied, with plum & bramble fruit, cedarwood spice, solid tannin structure from 20 months oak. Not retasted: **Cabernet Sauvignon 13** ★★ Not tasted: **Syrah**. Discontinued: **Lourentius van Andringa**, **Andrea**.

Charmé range

> **Pinotage** (NEW) (ⓦ) ★★★ French & American barrels give **14** its vanilla attraction. There's plum, mulberry, malleable tannins & oak char, too. All add to the enjoyment.

Cabernet Sauvignon (✓) ★★★☆ Pocket-friendly **13** raises the bar with generous fruit expression (blue & red berries, blackcurrant), form-giving tannins, cigarbox oak whisper in the farewell. Also tasted: **Shiraz 14** ★★★ **Sauvignon Blanc 15** ★★☆

Jabari range

Not tasted: **Shiraz**, **Cape Red**. — GM

Location/map/WO: Stellenbosch ▪ Map grid reference: D1 ▪ Est 2011 ▪ Tasting & sales strictly by appt ▪ Owner(s) LvA Bellingan, Andrea Lubbe & Christa Calitz ▪ 90% red 10% white ▪ PO Box 7271 Stellenbosch 7599 ▪ christa@vinducap.com ▪ www.vinducap.com ▪ S 33° 50' 37.8" E 018° 48' 31.4" ▪ F +27 (0)21-851-8475 ▪ **T +27 (0)82-929-2894**

☐ **Vinehugger** see Reyneke Wines

VinGlo Wines (NEW)

Cape Town-based VinGlo selects, produces, blends and exports its own wines as well as bespoke labels for clients. 8th Wonder was originally created for a US distributor of organic and sustainable beef looking to diversify its portfolio. First exported in 2013, the brand now also goes to Switzerland and Zimbabwe.

8th Wonder range

★★★★ **Good Hope Chardonnay** Attractive nut & lemon fragrance, creamy citrus fruit, (older) oak adding support not flavour: **12** appealing glassful for solo or with food.

Cape Cauldron ★★★☆ 100% cab from Simonsberg vines. Coffee nuance, red fruit whiffs & flavours on **12** atypical of variety; firm tannin structure, refreshing astringency not. Deftly handled oak (30% new) ups the enjoyment quotient. **Lively Grove Pinotage** ★★★ Intense mulberry & strawberry bouquet dusted with oak vanilla spice; **11** supple & fruitful so could be broached now but possibly better in year/2 once oak tannins knit. **Silver Tree Reserve** ★★★★ Subtitled 'Meritage', the name coined by the Californians to designate red or white Bordeaux-style blends. **13** merlot-led (58%) plus 4 others permitted in that region of France. Spicier than sibling (ex 10% new oak component, some American), more elegant; graceful dinner companion. **Silver Tree Red** ★★★ Merlot & cab franc (49/38) dominate Bordeaux-style red **13**, labelled 'Meritage' in the Californian tradition. Homely & easygoing with plum fruit, malleable tannin from 4 years in older, mainly French with soupçon American wood. — TJ, CvZ

Location: Cape Town ▪ WO: Stellenbosch ▪ Est/1stB 2012 ▪ Closed to public ▪ Winemaker(s) Therese de Beer (2012, consultant) ▪ 7-10t/ha ▪ 8,000cs own label 80% red 20% white ▪ 50 Esme Road Newlands Cape Town 7700 ▪ grant@vinglo.co.za ▪ www.vinglowines.co.za, www.8thwonderwines.com ▪ F +27 (0)86-548-3343 ▪ **T +27 (0)21-671-7905**

Vinimark

Wine merchants marketing, selling and distributing various ranges with local partners, including Robertson Winery, Kleindal, Long Beach and Silversands, some listed separately.

Stellenbosch ▪ Closed to public ▪ Directors Tim Rands, Cindy Jordaan, Geoff Harvey, Gys Naudé, Rudiger Gretschel & Guy Pause ▪ Exports: Geoff Harvey ▪ geoff@vinimark.co.za ▪ PO Box 441 Stellenbosch 7599 ▪ www.vinimark.co.za ▪ F +27 (0)21-886-4708 ▪ **T +27 (0)21-883-8043/4**

Vinopoly Wines

Bonnievale-based Vinopoly is a negociant and brand owner established in 2013 by the Retief family of Van Loveren to access the value-for-money seekers among the wineloving public. Supplying house brands to Pick n Pay (SunningHill), Spar (Cape Auction) and Food Lover's Market (Wine Lover's), it also owns the Bakenskop and Es La Vida brands, the latter also now available in Namibia.

Bakenskop range

Shiraz ⓥ ★ Smoky-savoury **11** for game dishes, reflects house's moderate alcohol levels. **Sauvignon Blanc** ★ Fresh grass, greenpepper nuances on easy-drinking **15** summer sipper. **White Muscadel** ★★★ Grapey sweetness, zingy acidity & good spirit management on **15** fortified, with litchi & orange flavours. Winter sipper or with ice-cream in summer. Not retasted: **Cabernet Sauvignon 12 ★★ Merlot 12 ★★ Pinotage 12 ★★★☆ Es La Vida Rosa NV ★★ Chardonnay 14 ★★ Es la Vida Blanca NV ★★ Red Muscadel 14 ★★★**

Cape Auction range

Red ⓥ ★★ Plummy **NV** crowd pleaser. Not retasted: **Rosé NV ★★ White NV ★★**

SunningHill range

Rosé ⓥ ★★ Pretty pink **NV**, fragrant strawberry aromas & flavours. Semi-sweet but with a nice zip. Not retasted: **Red NV ★★ White NV ★★** — CvZ

Location: Bonnievale ▪ WO: Western Cape/Robertson ▪ Closed to public ▪ Owner(s) Van Loveren Vineyards ▪ PO Box 92 Bonnievale 6730 ▪ info@vinopoly.co.za ▪ www.vinopoly.co.za ▪ F +27 (0)23-616-3146 ▪ **T +27 (0)23-616-2137/8/9**

☐ **Vino Pronto** *see* Hirst Wines
☐ **Vinum** *see* The Winery of Good Hope

Virgin Earth

The Virgin Earth home farm is situated on the foothills of the Langeberg. Most of the 13,000 ha estate is a pristine game park where wild antelope roam. The 25 ha of vines were established in ancient virgin soils, and are organic in conversion (the winery also officially Fairtrade). Contributing to the character and quality of the wines, winemaker Piet Kleinhans says, is the extreme weather, ranging from 'clouds from heaven to winds from hell'.

★★★★ **Cabernet Franc** (NEW) Aromatic, cool-toned **12** offers appetising pure red-fruit & roasted spice aromas, fresh flavours plumped out by touch sugar & underpinned by almost half new oak. Fairtrade certified, like several of these.

★★★★ **Lost Barrel Shiraz** Named for barrel lost during maturation underwater. Spicy **10** from home fruit has beautifully ripened pure red fruit; judicious oaking provides some grip, as in last-made **07** (★★★★) from Overberg.

★★★★ **Pepper Tree Sauvignon Blanc** ⊘ Pungent, vibrant **15** lean, herbaceous cool-climate profile. Zesty lime & green apple fruit delivered with pleasing texture from maturation on lees.

★★★★ **Succulent** Beguilingly floral, juicy-dry **14** semillon, viognier, chardonnay blend flaunts seductive marzipan, peaches & oak spice, structured for food by all-new oak.

★★★★ **Noble Late Harvest** ⓥ From semillon, last **08** ticked all the boxes: deeply rich & full-flavoured; apricot, pineapple, good length. Deliciously easy to drink. 30% in seasoned barrels. 500 ml.

Pinot Noir 🍇 ★★★☆ Light-footed, savoury **13** from Philadelphia grapes shows lovely fruit/oak balance. Cherry, plum flavours in a charming body. Wallet friendly for a pinot. **High 5** 🍇 ★★★★ All 5 Bordeaux varieties in cab-led **13** blend. Touch sweetness plumps flavours, underpinned by nicely firm tannins. **Shiraz-Viognier** ★★★★ Berry-laden **13** with dollop viognier adding floral hint to spicy roasted herbs.

Also tasted: **Pinotage 13** ★★★★ Not retasted: **Sauvignon Blanc-Semillon 14** ★★★☆ **Viognier MCC 08** ★★★ Not tasted: **Chenin Blanc**. — IM

Location: Riversdale ▪ WO: Langeberg-Garcia/Philadelphia/Coastal/Overberg ▪ Est 2002 ▪ 1stB 2003 ▪ Closed to public ▪ Owner(s) Kobus du Plessis ▪ Winemaker(s) Piet Kleinhans (Sep 2008) & Joseph Gertse (Jan 2000) ▪ Viticulturist(s) Rudi Benn (Jan 2001) & Hendrik Otto (2004) ▪ 13,000ha/25ha (cabs s/f, merlot, p verdot, pinot, shiraz, chard, chenin, sauv, sem, verdelho, viog) ▪ 70,000cs own label 40% red 45% white 15% rosé ▪ Fairtrade, organic in conversion, WIETA ▪ PO Box 451 Melkbosstrand 7437 ▪ sales@havanahills.co.za ▪ www.havanahills.co.za ▪ F +27 (0)21-972-1105 ▪ **T +27 (0)21-972-1110**

Virginia

For over 4 decades, a consistent semi-sweet white, widely sourced, by Distell. 2 & 5L.

Virginia ★ Familiar label, familiar **NV** sweetish fruity character ensure perennial popularity. — AL

☐ **Vivat Bacchus** see Veenwouden Private Cellar

Vleiland Wines $(\mathbb{Q})$ (⌣) (◎)

While winemaking remains a passion for Vredendal-based Nico Laubscher jnr, he hasn't found time for much beyond a small cab-shiraz bottling (latest '12 untasted). He and father Nico grow grapes for Namaqua Wines and have bought more land for vines, as well as squashes, cucumbers and tomatoes.

Location: Vredendal ▪ Map: Olifants River ▪ Est 2004 ▪ 1stB 2005 ▪ Tasting & sales by appt Mon-Fri 8-5 Sat 8-12 ▪ Closed Easter Fri-Mon, Dec 25 & Jan 1 ▪ BYO picnic ▪ Walks/hikes ▪ 4x4 & mountain bike trails ▪ Owner(s) Nico Laubscher snr, Alette Laubscher, Nico Laubscher jnr ▪ Winemaker(s)/viticulturist(s) Nico Laubscher ▪ 60ha (cab, ptage, shiraz, chenin, cbard, sauv) ▪ 790t/560cs own label 100% red ▪ PO Box 627 Vredendal 8160 ▪ alzanne@mylan.co.za ▪ S 31° 44' 42.24" E 018° 32' 8.16" ▪ F +27 (0)27-213-2825 ▪ **T +27 (0)27-213-2525/+27 (0)82-905-1640**

☐ **Voetspore** see Arendskloof

Vondeling $(\mathbb{Q})$ (◎) (♿)

A progressive and eco-conscious British-owned property. There are few Cape farms that employ a full-time botanist, as Vondeling does, to geo-tag, catalogue and DNA fingerprint endangered fynbos on its biodiverse Voor Paardeberg land. Taking it further, this is also home base for the area's Fire Protection Association and the Voor Paardeberg Sustainability Initiative. On the wine front, the second méthode ancestrale sparkling vintage was due for release at press time, the first having sold out within weeks. There's an organic pinotage rosé to come, and the young grenache blanc block has come on-stream.

Flagship Wines

★★★★ **Erica** (NEW) ⊘ Previously 'Erica Shiraz'. Rhône-style blend, shiraz-led, **12** (★★★★★) is hedonistic & layered, Belgian chocolate, cloves & allspice, brambleberries, the list goes on. Fine-grained tannins assure a good future, but already delicious. Also tasted, less special **11**, similar flavours, firmer tannins; give 1-2 years before opening.

★★★★☆ **Babiana** Single vineyard chenin leads in **13**, with 3 others, bunch pressed, partial natural ferment/ageing in barrel. Lots on offer, toasted hazelnuts, melon preserve, with freshness to spare, so drinking pleasure is assured. Bold, distinctive, with a future.

★★★★☆ **Sweet Carolyn** Occasional release, ambrosial vine-dried muscat de Frontignan. Fermented on the skins, giving **12** astonishingly pure aromas, orange blossom, pineapple, a hint of spice. And then come the flavours, threaded through with racy acidity, making the 109 g/l sweetness tangy, irresistible.

Vondeling range

★★★★ **Cabernet Sauvignon** Supple, packed with fruit, **13** is the best of both worlds, offering luscious immediate pleasure but with the deep muscle tone to age, evolve & offer additional insights over time.

★★★★ **Chardonnay** Bunch pressed, wild yeast barrel fermented/aged year, portion unwooded & **14** shows the care lavished. Svelte, with buttered toast & citrus preserve flavours, brightened by limy acidity.

★★★★ **Sauvignon Blanc** Nice combo oystershell minerality & limy fruit in **15**, elegant, with resonating freshness & length. Mouthwateringly delicious now, can also age.

★★★★ **Rurale Méthode Ancestral** Ⓓ Ancient method where fermenting juice is bottled & conversion to bubbly takes place in it, in one process. **13** from chardonnay, great lemony intensity, long zesty finish, can age.

Also tasted: **Petit Rouge 14** ★★★ **Rosé 15** ★★☆ Not retasted: **Baldrick Shiraz 13** ★★★☆ **Petit Blanc 14** ★★★ — CR

Location: Paarl ▪ Map: Paarl & Wellington ▪ Map grid reference: C1 ▪ WO: Voor Paardeberg ▪ Est 2001 ▪ 1stB 2005 ▪ Tasting & sales Mon-Fri 10-5 Sat/pub hols by appt ▪ Wedding/function/conference venue ▪ St Clement's Chapel ▪ Owner(s) Richard Gower, Julian Johnsen & Anthony Ward ▪ Winemaker(s) Matthew Copeland (Jul 2007), with Emile van der Merwe (Dec 2011) ▪ Viticulturist(s) Magnus Joubert (Jul 2012) ▪ 115ha (cabs s/f, carignan, grenache r/w, malbec, merlot, mourv, p verdot, shiraz, chard, chenin, muscat de F, sauv, viog) ▪ 1,100t/100,000cs own label 40% red 40% white 20% rosé ▪ Other export brand: Signal Cannon ▪ BWI champion ▪ PO Box 57 Wellington 7654 ▪ admin@vondelingwines.co.za ▪ www.vondelingwines.co.za ▪ S 33° 35' 22.50" E 018° 52' 45.00" ▪ F +27 (0)21-869-8219 ▪ **T +27 (0)21-869-8595**

☐ **Vrede** see Vin du Cap International

Vrede en Lust Wine Farm   Ⓓ Ⓜ Ⓗ Ⓞ Ⓐ Ⓖ

Buys family vines in Simonsberg-Paarl, and more recent Casey's Ridge blocks in Elgin are the source of the wide Vrede en Lust wine range. Pétanque courts on the elegant cellardoor's menu of attractions hint at the European nuance here, the 1688 founder being Flemish merchant Jacques de Savoye.

Location: Paarl ▪ Map: Franschhoek ▪ Est 1688 ▪ 1stB 2002 ▪ Tasting & sales daily 10—5 ▪ Closed Good Fri & Dec 25 ▪ Tours 10—4 by appt ▪ Lust Bistro & Bakery ▪ Guest accommodation in deluxe suites & manor house ▪ Tour groups by appt ▪ Conferences, functions & weddings ▪ Play area for children ▪ Pétanque courts ▪ Owner(s) Buys family ▪ Winemaker(s) Susan Erasmus (2006), with Karlin Nel ▪ Viticulturist(s) Etienne Buys (Jun 1998) ▪ 275ha total ▪ Vrede en Lust: 66ha (cab, grenache, malbec, merlot, p verdot, shiraz, chard, viog); Casey's Ridge, Elgin: 88.9ha (cabs s/f, merlot, shiraz, chard, chenin, pinots g/n, riesling, sauv, sem, viog); Ricton: 127ha (cab, cinsaut, ptage, shiraz, chard) ▪ 800t/45,000cs own label ▪ WIETA ▪ PO Box 171 Groot Drakenstein 7680 ▪ info@vnl.co.za ▪ www.vnl.co.za ▪ S 33° 50' 15.9" E 018° 57' 13.4" ▪ F +27 (0)21-874-1859 ▪ **T +27 (0)21-874-1611**

☐ **Vredehoek** see Koopmanskloof Wingerde

Vredenheim Wines   Ⓓ Ⓜ Ⓗ Ⓞ Ⓖ

Plans are on the drawing board at family-owned Vredenheim for a new tasting room but there'll be no changes to its trademark antelope enclosure or popular African Big Cats Park. The wine range is led by a red blend dedicated to matriarch and 'gracious lady' Rikie Bezuidenhout and a chardonnay honouring late husband 'M'Lord' Coen. The couple moved here from a KwaZulu-Natal game farm in 1986.

Gracious Lady ★★★ High-toned **13** is mainly cab (85%) with drops shiraz, merlot. Fruity, with soft tannins & vanilla finish, brisk acidity for food partnering. WO W Cape. **Rosé** ★★ NV (**15**) mostly sauvignon blanc with dab cab for colour; faint berries, semi-sweet farewell. **Sauvignon Blanc** ★★★ Appealing blackcurrant, some papaya & well-managed acidity; **15** delivers pleasant refreshment solo or with the meal. Also tasted: **Sparkling Wine Off-Dry NV** ★★ Not retasted: **Cabernet Sauvignon 10** ★★★ **Merlot 11** ★★☆ **Pinotage 13** ★★★ **Shiraz 11** ★★★ **M'Lord Chardonnay 12** ★★★ — CvZ

Location/map: Stellenbosch ▪ Map grid reference: D6 ▪ WO: Stellenbosch/Western Cape ▪ Tasting & sales Mon-Sat 9-4.45 ▪ Closed Good Fri, Dec 25 & Jan 1 ▪ Restaurant Barrique T +27 (0)21-881-3001 ▪ Hudson's Coffee Shop T +27 (0)21-881-3590 ▪ Conferences/functions ▪ Vredenheim Angus Stud ▪ Big Cats

Park ▪ Jaguar cars for hire ▪ Curio shop ▪ Guest house ▪ Owner(s) Bezuidenhout family ▪ Winemaker(s) Kowie du Toit ▪ Viticulturist(s) Kalie Kirsten ▪ 80ha under vine ▪ 20,000cs own label 60% red 40% white ▪ PO Box 369 Stellenbosch 7599 ▪ wine@vredenheim.co.za ▪ www.vredenheim.co.za ▪ S 33° 57' 38.2" E 018° 48' 29.4" ▪ F +27 (0)21-881-3296 ▪ **T +27 (0)21-881-3637**

Vredevol Private Wine Cellar

After Johan and Anne-Mari le Hanie bought their farm in Klawer (Olifants River), the intention was to establish a boutique cellar for an 'Out of Region' range. A Merlot-Cab was, in fact, made from Coastal fruit and vinified in Stellenbosch. The '11 was the last we tasted.

Location: Klawer ▪ Est 2007 ▪ 1stB 2008 ▪ Closed to public ▪ Owner(s) Johan & Anne-Mari le Hanie ▪ Cellarmaster(s)/winemaker(s) Johan van Wyk (Jul 2010) ▪ 30ha ▪ 1,000cs own label 50% red 50% white ▪ PO Box 12695 Die Boord 7613 ▪ vredevol.wines@vodamail.co.za ▪ F +27 (0)21-887-1288 ▪ **T +27 (0)21-887-1277**

Vriesenhof Vineyards   ⓘ

There's a discernable transition towards a less traditional winemaking style at this gracious Cape Dutch winery in the Stellenbosch Mountain foothills. With rugby legend and stalwart cellarmaster Jan Coetzee as mentor the past eight years, Nicky Claasens is not going to compromise on quality, however, and changes are gradual and considered, like using less new oak and lighter-toasted barrels, and planting a few more hectares of grenache. Having cut his teeth on fine old Kanonkop vintages and aspiring to Corton-like elegance and delicacy on their chardonnays, Nicky is the man to watch.

Vriesenhof range

★★★★ **Cabernet Sauvignon** ⓘ Estate's best cab bottled in magnum, just 980 of **10** available. More fruit intensity than muted & savoury **09** (★★★☆). Still tightly coiled & brooding, with a dense fruit core & firm tealeaf tannins. Deserves cellar time.

★★★★☆ **Grenache** ⓘ Limited bottling from Piekenierskloof. **12** supremely elegant, silky & balanced. Initially understated, grows in savoury & perfumed red-fruited intensity. A real sophisticated beauty. Also-tasted **13** more overt fruit & perfume, more vivacious, outgoing. Same pedigree & good structure but not as balanced, needs more time to harmonise. Both also sold in magnum.

★★★★ **Pinot Noir** Persistent, gently scented wild mushrooms & damp leaves framed by dry chalky tannins, **13** is refined though still tight, needs time to unfurl. More intense than **11** (★★★☆). No **12**.

★★★★ **Kallista** Dark berries, leather & leafy notes on **10** Bordeaux blend (cab, merlot, cab franc & malbec); extended oaking restrains fruit but there's enough freshness for good few years drinking pleasure. Step up on **09** (★★★★). Also in magnum.

★★★★ **Chardonnay** Rich but understated **14**, genteel baked apple & spice, toasted hazelnut flavours unfurling. Classically styled & contemplative, inherent balance with good intensity & length.

Also tasted: **Pinotage 11** ★★★

Paradyskloof range

Grenache 🆕 ★★★☆ Savoury & scented berry notes, **13** dry supple tannins & creamy texture from 15 months older oak. Satisfying; ready to enjoy now & for a few years. **Pinot Noir** ★★★★ Pale & perfumed **14**, raspberry, cherry fruit with supple tannins & sappy freshness. Lighter style to enjoy while Vriesenhof sibling matures. Also tasted: **Pinotage 13** ★★★ **Grenache Rosé 15** ★★☆ **Chardonnay 14** ★★☆ Not retasted: **Cabernet Sauvignon 10** ★★ **Pinot Noir Blend 11** ★★★☆ — MW

Location/map: Stellenbosch ▪ Map grid reference: F7 ▪ WO: Stellenbosch/Piekenierskloof ▪ Est 1980 ▪ 1stB 1981 ▪ Tasting & sales Mon-Thu 10–4 Fri 10–3.30 Sat by appt ▪ Fee R25 ▪ Closed all pub hols ▪ Cellar tours by appt ▪ Owner(s) Landgoed Vriesenhof (Pty) Ltd ▪ Cellarmaster(s) Jan Coetzee ▪ Winemaker(s) Nicky Claasens (2008), with Richard Phillips (2001) ▪ Viticulturist(s) Coetzee Ehlers ▪ 60ha/45ha (cabs s/f, grenache, merlot, pinot, ptage, chard) ▪ 300t/34,000cs own label 90% red 10% white ▪ PO Box 155 Stellenbosch 7599 ▪ info@vriesenhof.co.za ▪ www.vriesenhof.co.za ▪ S 33° 58' 16.7" E 018° 52' 2.8" ▪ F +27 (0)21-880-1503 ▪ **T +27 (0)21-880-0284**

☐ **Vry Burger** *see* Group CDV

☐ **Vusani** *see* House of Mandela

Vuurberg ⓠ

Surely a label to watch, we said last edition, of the Banhoek property bought by Netherlands-born Sebastiaan Klaassen while visiting on a kite surfing holiday in 2000. Slowly and carefully, Sebastiaan since has built a solid reputation for handcrafted boutique wines, and this year he breaks into the elite 5 star ranks with a brilliant Bordeaux-shiraz blend. Its creator, Donovan Rall (with a stellar reputation under his own, eponymous label), has been winemaker here the past six years, and his deft touch is also evident in the fine, intricate Vuurberg White. Both wines speak of great care taken from vine to bottle.

★★★★ **Vuurberg Reserve** ⊘ **12** (★★★★★) ratchets quality on **10**, in turn up on **09** (★★★☆). Genteel yet powerful blend of petit verdot, cab, merlot (from Elgin), malbec & shiraz. Textured, rich, layered & dense. Ripe yet restrained, with cedary oak (50% new French) contrast with graphite, fruitcake & spice. Complex & long. **11** untasted.

★★★★ **White** Chenin still the hero in broad, rich **14** (★★★★☆) six-part blend of semillon, viognier, roussanne, grenache blanc & verdelho. Vivacious lime counters stonefruit & creamy lees notes. Like **13**, spontaneous ferment & mainly older oak. Powerful yet refined. — FM

Location/map: Stellenbosch ▪ Map grid reference: H4 ▪ WO: Western Cape ▪ Tasting, sales & cellar tours by appt ▪ Closed all pub hols ▪ Owner(s)/cellarmaster(s) Sebastiaan Klaassen ▪ Winemaker(s) Donovan Rall (Oct 2010) ▪ 8ha (cabs s/f, malbec, merlot, p verdot, chenin, viog) ▪ 2,000cs own label 50% red 50% white ▪ PO Box 449 Stellenbosch 7599 ▪ info@vuurberg.com ▪ www.vuurberg.com ▪ S 33° 54' 28.9" E 018° 56' 52.7" ▪ **T +27 (0)72-182-7571**

☐ **Vuurgloed** *see* Viljoensdrift Fine Wines & Cruises

Waboomsrivier Wine Cellar ⓠ

Grower-owned Waboomsrivier has a new winemaking assistant, Pieter van Wyk. Originally from Cavinia, Northern Cape, he trained and worked in Wellington, Wolseley and at Adam Trautwein in Germany before joining this 20,000 tons-a-year Breedekloof cellar. Not new, but noteworthy, is the Cape Vintage, back in the bottled-wine line-up after a sabbatical.

Wagenboom range

Arborea ⓣ ★★★ Intense crème de cassis & sweet vanilla oak (from American oak), **12** characterful blend cab, pinotage & shiraz, with lively acidity, perky tannins.

Cape Vintage ★★★ Returns with **14**, more Ruby than Vintage style, with fairly low alcohol, highish sugar. Attractive Xmas cake & tangerine nuances; very drinkable, like all in this wallet-friendly range. Also tasted: **Chenin Blanc 15** ★★★ **Sauvignon Blanc 15** ★★ **Hanepoot 13** ★★★★ Discontinued: **Pinotage**. — WB, CvZ

Location: Worcester ▪ Map/WO: Breedekloof ▪ Est 1949 ▪ Tasting & sales Mon-Fri 8-5 ▪ Closed all pub hols ▪ Cellar tours by appt during harvest ▪ Cellarmaster(s) Bennie Wannenburg (Sep 2005) ▪ Winemaker(s) Wim Viljoen (Sep 1991), with André Landman (Jan 2013) & Pieter van Wyk (Jan 2015) ▪ Viticulturist(s) Pierre Snyman (Vinpro) ▪ ±1,106ha ▪ 20,467t ▪ ISO 22000:2011 ▪ PO Box 24 Breërivier 6858 ▪ sales@wabooms.co.za ▪ www.waboomsrivier.com ▪ S 33° 31' 43.08" E 019° 12' 35.24" ▪ F +27 (0)23-355-1731 ▪ **T +27 (0)23-355-1730**

☐ **Wade Bales Winemaker Selection** *see* Wade Bales Wine Society

Wade Bales Wine Society ⓠ

Long-established Wade Bales Wine Society is a specialist merchant sourcing fine-wine from producers and selling directly to private clients based on their individual needs and preferences. The Society is also a negociant, bottling and marketing exclusive and limited-release wines to its customers under the Bales Choice and Wade Bales Winemaker Selection labels.

Location: Constantia ▪ Map: Cape Peninsula ▪ Est 1992 ▪ Tasting & sales Mon-Fri 8.30-5 ▪ Closed all pub hols ▪ Owner(s) Wade Bales ▪ 10,000cs own label ▪ Private Bag X2 Constantia 7848 ▪ info@ thewinesociety.co.za ▪ www.wadebaleswinesociety.co.za ▪ S 34° 2' 5.43" E018° 25' 32.98" ▪ F +27 (0)21-794-2821 ▪ **T +27 (0)21-794-2151**

☐ **Wagenboom** see Waboomsrivier Wine Cellar

Waka Waka Wines   ⓠ

Swahili for 'Let's Get Started!', Waka Waka is a joint venture between Perdeberg Winery and REH Kendermann in Germany, intended to create 'a new and vibrant wine style' offering quality and value.

Sauvignon Blanc-Chenin Blanc ★★★ 14 50/50 blend is a real crowd pleaser: smooth tropical fruit flavours, zippy Lemon Twist finish, moderate alcohol bonus. Also tasted: **Shiraz-Cabernet Sauvignon 13 ★★★** Not tasted: **Sauvignon Blanc**. — WB

Location/WO: Paarl ▪ Tasting & sales at Perdeberg Winery ▪ Owner(s) 33 shareholders ▪ Cellarmaster(s) Albertus Louw (Oct 2008) ▪ Winemaker(s) Riaan Möller (Dec 2006) & Dylan Dowell-Ellis (Sep 2014) ▪ Viticulturist(s) Heinie Nel (Jul 2013) ▪ PO Box 214 Paarl 7620 ▪ info@perdeberg.co.za ▪ www.perdeberg.co.za ▪ F +27 (0)21-869-8245 ▪ **T +27 (0)21-869-8244**

Walker Bay Vineyards   ⓠ ⓜ 🍴 📷 ⓐ ♿

Lovers of wine, beer, spring water and food are all catered for at this family-cordial estate outside Stanford, with a cellar, Birkenhead micro-brewery, water-bottling plant and restaurant on the premises. Wine wise, there's a new (untasted) Merlot, and a focus on expanding their export market.

Cabernet Sauvignon ⓥ **★★★** Charry oak & austere acidity dominate **11**'s savoury fruit. Not tasted: **Amesteca, Rosé, Chardonnay, Chardonnay Unoaked, Sauvignon Blanc**. — AL

Location: Stanford ▪ Map: Elgin, Walker Bay & Bot River ▪ WO: Walker Bay ▪ Est 1997 ▪ 1stB 2007 ▪ Tasting & sales Mon-Sat 10-5 Sun 11-4 ▪ Tasting fee R20/wine & R60/beer ▪ Closed Good Fri & Dec 25 ▪ Cellar tours by appt ▪ Micro brewery ▪ Restaurant ▪ BYO picnic ▪ Facilities for children ▪ Tour groups ▪ Owner(s) Birkenhead Holdings Ltd (Isle of Man) ▪ GM Reinhard Odendaal ▪ Winemaker(s)/viticulturist(s) Reinhard Odendaal ▪ 300ha/24ha (cab, merlot, p verdot, pinot, shiraz, chard, sauv, sem) ▪ 100t/14,000cs own label 40% red 60% white ▪ PO Box 530 Stanford 7210 ▪ info@birkenhead.co.za ▪ www.walkerbayestate.co.za ▪ S 34° 26' 30.5" E 019° 27' 40.5" ▪ F +27 (0)28-341-0196 ▪ **T +27 (0)28-341-0183**

☐ **Wandering Beeste** see Boutinot South Africa

Wandsbeck Wyne Koöp Bpk   ⓠ ⓐ ♿

Picturesquely sited on a rise above Robertson's Agterkliphoogte Valley ('so remember to bring your camera!'), grower-owned Wandsbeck continues to upgrade and extend its cellar facilities, the better to produce 6 million litres for its bulk-wine customers. The 4,000 cases bottled for the own label clearly is a drop in the ocean, but it's a tasty, unpretentious and well-priced drop.

Shiraz **★★★** Early-drinking **13** has French oak spice, American wood sweetness; fruity, vibrant & styled for year-round enjoyment. **Sauvignon Blanc ★★☆** Pineapple, ruby grapefruit & sweet fresh-cut grass, lightish 12.5% alcohol make **15** an easy al fresco companion. Really wallet friendly, too. Not retasted: **Cabernet Sauvignon 13 ★★☆ Revelation Red 12 ★★★ Symphony 13 ★★ Revelation White 13 ★★★ Muscadel 13 ★★★** — CvZ

Location/map/WO: Robertson ▪ Est 1965 ▪ 1stB 1986 ▪ Tasting & sales Mon-Fri 8–5 Sat/Sun by appt ▪ Closed all pub hols ▪ Cellar tours by appt ▪ Facilities for children ▪ Owner(s) 21 members ▪ Cellarmaster(s) Jacques du Toit (Jun 2008) ▪ Winemaker(s) Hugo Conradie (Aug 2013) ▪ Viticulturist(s) Hennie Visser ▪ 516ha (cab, cinsaut, merlot, ruby cab, shiraz, chenin, chard, cbard, sauv) ▪ 8,500t/ 4,000cs own label 43% red 29% white 14% rosé 14% other + 6m L bulk ▪ IPW ▪ PO Box 267 Robertson 6705 ▪ info@wandsbeckwyne.co.za ▪ www.wandsbeckwyne.co.za ▪ S 33° 55' 60.0" E 019° 36' 34.4" ▪ F +27 (0)23-626-3329 ▪ **T +27 (0)23-626-1103**

Warwick Estate   ⚥ 🍽 📷 👤 ♿

Stan Ratcliffe was the visionary over 50 years ago when he bought this property in the Stellenbosch-Simonsberg foothills, planting cabernet which still forms the backbone of its reds. Wife Norma, pioneer woman winemaker and Cape Winemakers Guild member and former chair, was the driving force. For her achievements and contributions to the industry, she was the first female recipient of the 1659 Wine Icon of the Year Award for 2015, an accolade previously bestowed on the late Nelson Mandela. Son and 2nd-generation head of the family business, Mike, has notched up a good few achievements of his own, like using his local and international connections to help the Cape Wine Auction, which supports 13 charities actively working for education from infant to adult, raise in excess of R17 million to date.

★★★★☆ The Blue Lady Cabernet Sauvignon Single-vineyard & barrel selection **12** back on track. Fine yet firm tannin structure, opulent blackcurrant fruit, serious 26 months French oak for decade or more cellaring. More monarch than **11** (**★★★★**) regent.

★★★★★ Cabernet Franc One of the Cape's best; typically supple, complex & generous with the promise of development. Like precise **11**, **12** (**★★★★★**) from a single-vineyard, has persistent poise, French oak (27 months, 28% new) no more than a background note.

★★★★ The Black Lady Syrah Step-up **13** (**★★★★★**) sleek, polished but in no way forced. Forthcoming mulberry & black plum aromas & tastes, subtle oak dusting. Unlike earlier-drinking **12**, needs 5+ years to show at best.

★★★★☆ Trilogy Classic Cape expression of cab-led Bordeaux-style red, marrying cassis fruit, exotic spice & fine tannins. **12** (**★★★★**) shade broader, more leathery than modern, focused **11**; as seriously wooded (2+ years French barrels, 56% new). Also in 1.5, 5 & 12L.

★★★★ Three Cape Ladies (⚥) Cape Blend with pinotage (40%), equal cab & shiraz working well together in **12**, as in **11**. Creamy dark fruit, touch of liquorice & well structured palate.

★★★★☆ The White Lady Chardonnay In tune with the times, naturally vinified **14** (**★★★★★**) is our prestigious White Wine of the Year 2016. Thrilling lime-seamed vibrancy, stony minerality & exceptional length of flavour make a stunning package for now & good few years. Even more seductive than **13**. Own grapes wild yeast fermented, 10 months aged in perfectly judged 33% new French oak.

The First Lady Cabernet Sauvignon ★★★ 13's sweet cassis & leafy notes spiced with cardamom from 8% shiraz. Smooth fruit & vanilla oak interplay, fresh mouthful for now & 3+ years. WO W Cape. Also in magnum. **The First Lady Dry Rosé** (ℕ) **★★★** Delicate **15** welcome addition to Cape's growing rosé category with ginger & watermelon nuances, bone-dry finish. From pinotage. WO W Cape. Also tasted: **Old Bush Vines Pinotage 13 ★★★★ The First Lady Unoaked Chardonnay 14 ★★★☆ Professor Black Sauvignon Blanc 14 ★★★★** — CvZ

Location/map: Stellenbosch ▪ Map grid reference: F1 ▪ WO: Simonsberg–Stellenbosch/Western Cape/Coastal ▪ Est 1964 ▪ 1stB 1983 ▪ Tasting & sales daily 9–5 ▪ Cellar tours by appt ▪ 'Big 5' vineyard safari ▪ Gourmet picnics in summer; tapas-inspired winter menu ▪ Facilities for children ▪ Gifts ▪ Conferences ▪ Weddings ▪ Owner(s) Ratcliffe family ▪ Winemaker(s) Nic van Aarde (May 2011), Carami van der Merwe (Jun 2015) ▪ Viticulturist(s) Ronald Spies (Nov 2001) ▪ 110ha/70ha (cabs s/f, merlot, ptage, shiraz, chard, sauv) ▪ 400t/46,380cs own label 60% red 40% white ▪ BWI, WIETA ▪ PO Box 2 Elsenburg 7607 ▪ info@warwickwine.com ▪ www.warwickwine.com ▪ S 33° 50′ 27″ E 018° 51′ 54.0″ ▪ **T +27 (0)21-884-4410**

Waterford Estate   ⚥ 📷 ♿

The Jem flagship blend, occasionally showcasing up to 11 red varieties, is indicative of careful thought and planning that's standard operating procedure at this stylish estate belonging to IT magnate Jeremy Ord and wife Leigh. Cellarmaster and partner Kevin Arnold has been at the helm since day one, retaining venerable vineyards on this portion of the old Stellenrust farm in Stellenbosch's Blaauwklippen Valley and planting innovative grape varieties best suited to the soils, aspects and climate. The cellardoor experience also sets Waterford apart, with wine walks and a tailored vineyard safari drive great ways for visitors to taste the neatly delineated range — including the Library Collection of small parcels or one-offs which express the team's constant experimentation.

Waterford Estate range

★★★★☆ **Cabernet Sauvignon** Complex yet subtle & superbly defined **12** has ample Christmas cake flavour, with fynbos & cocoa depth. Ripe yet elegant & supple with silky mouthfeel. Includes usual drops merlot & cab franc, new oak boosted to 35%. Also in larger formats.

★★★★☆ **The Jem** ② Intricate 8-way cab-led blend, with melange of rich dark fruit taut, textured & modern in style. **10** ample succulence tempered by firm dry tannin & oak spice (40% new). Balanced & lissom, it keeps on giving. Will reward patient cellaring. Also in magnum.

★★★★ **Chardonnay** Typically elegant, broad & toasty **14** from oak — just 28% new — but balanced by lively citrus fruit & acid tang (no malo). Rich, textured & long. Also in 1.5L.

★★★★ **Sauvignon Blanc 14** (★★★★), previewed last time, still is juicy, crisp & lively if a touch lean. Tasty, but a tad less impressive than last-tasted **11**. Single-vineyard bottling, as for Chardonnay.

Also tasted: **Rose Mary 15** ★★★ Discontinued: **Reserve Chardonnay**.

Library Collection

★★★★☆ **Edition: 3BB** ② Cab-based **09** with cab franc & merlot is serious, even stern. Forthright tannins should soften & harmonise in 5+ years. Decant now & drink with food.

Not retasted: **Edition: MB 04** ★★★★ **Edition: Riesling 13** ★★★★ **Edition: VRC 13** ★★★★ **Edition: VSBC 13** ★★★ Not tasted: **Edition: BW**.

Waterford range

★★★★ **Elgin Pinot Noir 13** raises the bar on **12** (★★★★) with its lithe suppleness & leashed power. Beautiful integration of vivid cherry fruit & oak (10% new). Juicy & bright but with depth & concentration.

★★★★☆ **Kevin Arnold Shiraz** Earthy depth & concentration on sleek yet ripe & rich **11**. Spicy pepper lift to plush black fruit. Squeeze of dry tannin from older oak & drop mourvèdre (8%). Layered & sexy with a long finish. Also in larger format bottles.

★★★★ **Elgin Sauvignon Blanc** Grapefruit verve to nettly **15** (★★★★). Bright succulence & typicity but a touch shorter, less intense than **14**.

★★★★ **Méthode Cap Classique Brut 07** sparkling ups the ante on **06** (★★★★) in its crisp yet creamy, taut & focused mousse. Equal chardonnay (50% fermented in old oak), pinot noir make for full, leesy precision & rich, long aftertaste.

★★★★ **Heatherleigh Family Reserve** Seville orange marmalade appeal to **NV** Natural Sweet dessert from mostly muscat d'Alexandrie, chardonnay & chenin. Solera aged (just 5% new oak), it is floral, light & delicate with ample acid balance, leaving it clean & dry at end. 375 ml.

Pecan Stream range

Chenin Blanc ⊕ ★★★★ Delightful, invisibly oaked **15** steps up a notch. Light grip to tropical melon, pear & stonefruit flavour, leesy edge too. Textured & rounded.

Also tasted: **Pebble Hill 12** ★★★★ **Sauvignon Blanc 15** ★★★ — FM

Location/map: Stellenbosch ▪ Map grid reference: F7 ▪ WO: Stellenbosch/Western Cape/Elgin ▪ Est/1stB 1998 ▪ Tasting, sales & cellar tours Mon-Fri 9–5 Sat 10–5 ▪ Tasting fees: R50/standard; R55/chocolate; R55/The Jem (current vintage only); R150/Library; R200/reserve; R250/wine walk & R550/wine drive, pre-booking essential ▪ Closed Good Fri, Dec 25 & Jan 1 ▪ Tea/coffee/soft drinks & chocolates ▪ 14ha BWI conserved land ▪ Owner(s) Jeremy & Leigh Ord; Kevin Arnold (partner) ▪ Cellarmaster(s) Kevin Arnold (1998) ▪ Winemaker(s) Mark le Roux (Jul 2009) ▪ Viticulturist(s) David van Schalkwyk (Jun 2014) ▪ 120ha/60ha (barbera, cabs s/f, grenache, malbec, merlot, mourv, p verdot, sangio, shiraz, tempranillo, chard, sauv) ▪ 498t/54,000cs own label 51% red 45% white 3% rosé 1% other ▪ PO Box 635 Stellenbosch 7599 ▪ info@waterfordestate.co.za ▪ www.waterfordestate.co.za ▪ S 33° 59' 54.6" E 018° 52' 12.7" ▪ F +27 (0)21-880-1007 ▪ **T +27 (0)21-880-5300**

Waterkloof

This breathtaking property on the Schapenberg near Somerset West was acquired by British wine importer Paul Boutinot in 2003 after a decade-long search to find a new classic area capable of producing truly fine wine with a defining sense of origin. It's now over a decade since the property's 'hidden amphitheatre of potential' produced its maiden vintage in 2005, with half the estate set aside to pre-serve its natural vegetation, the other half farmed biodynamically (Demeter certification as well as Ceres organic certification achieved in 2015). Winemaker Nadia Barnard arrived in 2009, the maiden vintage for the state-of-the-art gravitational cellar. In this ultra-modern facility, however, she adheres to tradi-tional, non-interventionist methods (such as no inoculation or acidification) to produce 'honest' wines.

Waterkloof range

★★★★☆ **Sauvignon Blanc** Bunch pressed, naturally barrel-fermented & bottled without fining (as all below), layered **14** is beautifully integrated, with whiffs of fynbos & a flinty finish framing intense goose-berry & lime fruit, acid zinging through creamy texture. No **13**.

Circle of Life range

★★★★ **Red** Rhône crashes Bordeaux party in **12** as syrah/shiraz brings cassis & spice to soft plums & fruitcake sweetness of 51% merlot, 19% petit verdot. Excellent, if not quite the stellar success of **10** (★★★★☆).

★★★★ **White** From 60% sauvignon & 33% chenin, mostly co-fermented (half in barrel), with dashes chardonnay & semillon, **13** (★★★★★) deserves even more serious contemplation than **12**. Tangy apricot & kumquat, mineral stone & smoke, long savoury finish.

Seriously Cool range

★★★★☆ **Cinsault** ⓥ Made for serving 'cool', **14** (★★★★) is slightly less complex than **13** but still a 'serious' take on SA's old workhorse red with with blossom, black cherry & plum notes, lively acidity com-bining with spice & meatiness on the palate.

Chenin Blanc ⓝ ★★★★ Actually quite fun, partly barrel-fermented **14** calls for 'serious chilling' to tone down, ever so slightly, its sweet fynbos honey & peach flavours, almost (somehow not quite) bal-anced by its 4.1 g/l acidity.

Circumstance range

★★★★ **Cabernet Sauvignon** Only bottled when good enough, lithe **13** is best yet, blackberry & dark chocolate notes lifted by herbs/tobacco, fine tannins & fresh acidity. Level up on last **10** (★★★☆).

★★★★ **Cabernet Franc** **13** (★★★☆) seems slightly less polished than maiden **12**, a rustic earthiness underpinning ripe raspberries & other red fruit, with hints of thyme, black pepper & aniseed.

★★★★☆ **Syrah** Already smooth & silky, integrated & elegant, **12** will benefit from a few more years to allow black pepper & intriguing rosemary & thyme notes to develop while succulent dark fruit softens. No **11**.

★★★★ **Sauvignon Blanc** Less intellectual than some of its counterparts, peachy **14** has more than a twist of lime to enliven sweet stonefruit, rich texture & leesy intensity.

Cape Coral Mourvèdre Rosé ★★★★ Salmon-pink **15** calls for tapas, its crisp acidity countering soft ripe raspberry & cherry fruit with a hint of spice, leaving palate refreshed for next bite (or sip). Also tasted: **Merlot 12** ★★★★ **Viognier 13** ★★★★ Not retasted: **Chenin Blanc 13** ★★★★ Not tasted: **Chardonnay**. — JG

Location: Somerset West ▪ Map: Helderberg ▪ WO: Stellenbosch ▪ Est 2004 ▪ 1stB 2005 ▪ Tasting & sales daily 10-5 ▪ Fee: standard R30/6 wines, premium R40/6 wines ▪ Closed Dec 25 & Jan 1 ▪ Healey's cheese tasting ▪ Waterkloof platters R130 with selection of cheese, olives, meat terrine, gherkins, pickles, chut-ney & bread ▪ Cellar tours by appt ▪ The Restaurant at Waterkloof ▪ Walking/hiking/horse riding trails ▪ Conservation area ▪ Art collection on display ▪ Tutored horse riding & biodynamic walking tours with ploughman's platter & wine tasting ▪ Owner(s) Paul Boutinot ▪ Cellarmaster(s)/winemaker(s) Nadia Barnard (Jan 2013) ▪ Viticulturist(s) Christiaan Loots (Jan 2010) ▪ 149ha/56ha (cabs s/f, grenache, mer-lot, mourv, p verdot, shiraz, chard, chenin, sauv, sem, viog) ▪ 450t/20,000cs own label 50% red 45% white 5% rosé ▪ WWF-SA Conservation Champion, Ceres organic, Demeter biodynamic, IPW, WIETA ▪ PO Box 2093 Somerset West 7129 ▪ info@waterkloofwines.co.za ▪ www.waterkloofwines.co.za ▪ S 34° 5' 55.4" E 018° 53' 22.8" ▪ F +27 (0)21-858-1293 ▪ **T +27 (0)21-858-1292**

☐ **Waterlilly** *see* Bloemendal Estate

Waverley Hills Organic Wines & Olives ⓨ ⓟ ⓒ ⓐ ⓖ

'Business as usual' reports Johan Delport, cellarmaster at this Tulbagh farm where the Du Toit family owners of parent company Brenn-O-Kem (recycler of winery waste) have adopted an eco-friendly model. Said business includes the coming into full production of young pinotage vines this year, and launch of a No Sulphites Added Merlot, building on the sell-out success of the NSA Cabernet Sauvignon.

Premium range

★★★★ CW Reserve Shiraz ⓥ From tiny parcel yielding unusually small grapes & bunches. **12** a pretty smart package: beguiling cassis & vanilla aromas, red berry flavours; vivacious & poised despite 15.5% alcohol.

★★★★ Shiraz-Mourvèdre-Viognier ⓥ Year in bottle has served **11** well; now more knit, complex. Drop viognier a deft touch, sufficient to lift red fruit melange without detracting from delicate fynbos & lily notes, savoury conclusion. Preview **12** similar, more refreshment.

Méthode Cap Classique Brut ⓥ ★★★☆ **12** celebratory blanc de blancs sparkler shows intense brioche character, creamy mousse from 2 years lees-ageing, chardonnay's lemon in the lengthy aftertaste. Also tasted: **Viognier-Semillon-Chardonnay** ⓥ **14** ★★★★

Estate range

★★★★ Grenache ⓥ ⓥ Step-up **14** is 100% grenache (**13** (★★★) had smidgens shiraz & viognier), punches above its weight. Lovely limpid fruit given extra appeal by fynbos seasoning, texture by faintly bitter tannins; all enlivened by fresh but balanced acidity. Enjoy soon.

Shiraz ⓥ ★★★ Producer's signature fynbos whiffs mingle with forthcoming pepper notes on **12**'s crunchy red fruit. Vibrant, with long tarry finish. **Cabernet Sauvignon-Merlot** ⓥ ★★★ Near-equal parts cab & merlot with 7% chardonnay ringing the changes; **14** ex-tank plummy with reined-in oak, subtle fynbos nuance. Also tasted: **Cabernet Sauvignon** ⓥ **14** ★★★ **Cabernet Sauvignon-Shiraz** ⓥ **14** ★★★ Not retasted: **Rooi Jerepigo 13** ★★★ Not tasted: **Merlot, Rosé, Pinot Grigio, Light, Sauvignon Blanc-Semillon**.

No Sulphites Added range

Not tasted: **Cabernet Sauvignon No Added Sulphites, Merlot No Added Sulphites**. — CvZ

Location/map/WO: Tulbagh ▪ Est 2006 ▪ 1stB 2004 ▪ Tasting, sales & cellar tours Mon-Fri 8-5 Sat 10-4 Sun 11-3 ▪ Closed Easter Fri/Mon & Dec 25 ▪ Restaurant Tue-Sat 10-4 Sun 11-3 & Wed/Fri evenings ▪ Picnic baskets by appt ▪ Facilities for children ▪ Tour groups ▪ Farm produce ▪ Conferences ▪ Wedding venue & chapel ▪ Walks/hikes ▪ Conservation area ▪ Fynbos nursery ▪ Owner(s) Brenn-O-Kem (Pty) Ltd ▪ Cellarmaster(s) Johan Delport (Oct 2008) ▪ Winemaker(s) Andre Ewerts (Jul 2008) ▪ Viticulturist(s) Johan Greeff (May 2012) ▪ 80ha/30ha (cab, grenache, merlot, mourv, ptage, shiraz, chard, pinot gris, sauv, sem, viog) ▪ 230t/20,000cs own label 75% red 15% white 5% rosé 5% MCC ▪ Other export brand: Dixon's Peak ▪ BWI champion, WIETA ▪ PO Box 71 Wolseley 6830 ▪ info@waverleyhills.co.za ▪ www.waverleyhills.co.za ▪ S 33° 24' 21.2" E 019° 14' 19.6" ▪ F +27 (0)23-231-0004 ▪ **T +27 (0)23-231-0002**

Wavescape Wines

A joint venture between Jeremy Walker of Grangehurst (who handles the wines at his Stellenbosch cellar) and surf reporter Steve Pike, the aim is to create 'vibrant blends of surfing and winemaking', as expressed in the names of the wines: a White Curl chenin-sauvignon (untasted by us) joining Red Barrel.

Red Barrel ★★★☆ Nothing pretentious or boring about well-balanced, open-knit **09**, revisited as bottled wine. Cab-shiraz & drop mourvèdre unobstructed by oak, with good fruit complexity, it's serious fun! Not tasted: **White Curl**. — JPf

Location: Stellenbosch ▪ WO: Coastal ▪ Est 2014 ▪ 1stB 2009 ▪ Closed to public ▪ Sales by telephone or websites ▪ Owner(s) Grangehurst Winery (Jeremy Walker) & Wavescape (Steve Pike) ▪ Cellarmaster(s) Jeremy Walker ▪ 1,700cs own label 70% red 30% white ▪ PO Box 206 Stellenbosch 7599 ▪ jeremy@grangehurst.co.za, spike@wavescape.co.za ▪ www.wavescape.co.za, www.grangehurst.co.za ▪ F +27 (0)86-710-6067 ▪ **T +27 (0)21-855-3625**

☐ **Weathered Hands** see Dewaldt Heyns Family Wines

Webersburg Wines

This small, classically styled wine collection, partly from a tiny home vineyard and vinified initially by consultant Giorgio Dalla Cia and latterly by Matthew van Heerden, forms part of local businessman Fred Weber's overhaul of 18th-century Cape Dutch property Groenerivier against the Helderberg slopes. Luxury accommodation, function venue and restaurant complete the picture.

★★★★☆ **Cabernet Sauvignon** Restrained **13** with aromas of mocha, pencil shavings, red- & blackcurrant & integrated 70% new toasty oak. Finely structured palate with ripe yet fresh flavours framed by beautiful fine tannin, moderate alcohol. A Stellenbosch classic! Larger formats too.

★★★★ **Webersburg** ⓧ Cab-based blend with merlot & petit verdot true to restrained house style. **11** underlying tomato & redpepper notes; a touch mouth drying & angular – allow few years to harmonise. Last tasted was **05**. Also in magnum. Stellenbosch WO.

★★★★ **Sauvignon Blanc** Subtle **14** (★★★★☆) offers the usual nettle gooseberry aromas, crisp & crunchy mineral flavours which persist but miss the complexity of last-tasted **12**.

★★★★ **Webersburg MCC Brut** ⓧ 3-variety **NV** sparkler with intense citrus & honey biscuit styling, seam of acidity giving freshness. Elegant & lengthy.

Not retasted: **Webersburg MCC Brut Rosé NV** ★★★★ — JPf

Location/map: Stellenbosch ▪ Map grid reference: E8 ▪ WO: Western Cape/Stellenbosch ▪ Est 1995 ▪ 1stB 1996 ▪ Tasting, sales & cellar tours Mon-Fri 10–5 Sat/Sun 10-4 ▪ Fee R40 ▪ Closed Dec 25/26 & Jan 1 ▪ Bistro ▪ Tour groups ▪ Historic buildings: manor house 1786; cellar & jonkershuis 1796 ▪ 5-star Cape Dutch guest house ▪ Conferences ▪ Weddings/functions ▪ Owner(s) Fred Weber ▪ Winemaker(s)/viticulturist(s) Matthew van Heerden ▪ 20ha/5ha under vine ▪ 30t/4,000cs own label 80% red 20% white ▪ PO Box 3428 Somerset West 7129 ▪ info@webersburg.co.za ▪ www.webersburg.co.za ▪ S 34° 0' 22.1" E 018° 50' 34.5" ▪ F +27 (0)21-881-3217 ▪ **T +27 (0)21-881-3636**

Wederom Boutique Winery

Robertson's Du Toit family believe wine is a necessity in the home, so their boutique red (honouring the Italian POWs who tended the vines here in the 1940s) is priced accordingly, their customer service is as attentive as possible, and there's a personal greeting for cellardoor visitors and stay-over guests alike.

Giovanni Salvadori Shiraz ★★★ Espresso overlay to vibrant red fruit, **12** partly wooded honest easy-sipper with friendly grip. Includes 10% petit verdot. — CvZ

Location/map/WO: Robertson ▪ Est 2002 ▪ 1stB 2003 ▪ Tasting, sales & cellar tours by appt ▪ Fee R20pp tasting/tour ▪ Closed Good Fri & Dec 25 ▪ Meals by appt ▪ Tour groups ▪ Gifts ▪ Farm produce ▪ Conferences ▪ Weddings/functions ▪ Hikes ▪ Conservation area ▪ Italian prisoner of war museum ▪ Hanepoot Huisies guest house ▪ Owner(s) Philip & Almien du Toit ▪ Cellarmaster(s)/winemaker(s)/viticulturist(s) Philip du Toit ▪ 3ha (merlot, shiraz) ▪ IPW ▪ PO Box 60 Robertson 6705 ▪ wederom@myisp.co.za ▪ www.wederom.co.za ▪ S 33° 49' 5.5" E 019° 47' 15.8" ▪ **T +27 (0)23-626-4139**

☐ **Wedgewood** see Nordic Wines

Welbedacht Wine Estate

Excelling in rugby, or sport generally, seems to be a requirement (or an attraction?) for all key staff at the Burger family's Wellington estate. Scion Schalk jnr at press time was set to play for SA in his 4th Rugby World Cup, while recently appointed winemaker Hardus van Heerden has the position of lock on Wellington's first team. And the new financial manager has provincial colours as a Bisley shooter. All are united around a serious and large wine property (two farms joined together in the 1990s), widely planted to white and red grapes, including noteworthy old-vine chenin, pinotage and cinsaut. There are two ranges, with some evocative names paying homage to the family's sporting prowess.

Schalk Burger & Sons Proprietors Reserve range

★★★★ **No. 6** ⓧ Striking shiraz-led 6-way mix. **06** (★★★★☆) plush fruitcake & plum spice, big & bold but harmonious, lithe as a flank brushing off a tackler. 2 years older French oak. Step up on **05**.

★★★★ **Myra** ⓧ Last tasted was **07** viognier, chenin, chardonnay blend. Oxidative, rich & satiny.

Mon René ★★★★ Chardonnay MCC sparkling named for Burger daughter. Latest **NV** spent 18 months on lees, has ginger biscuit & citrus preserve styling, attractively rich development. Finishes freshly dry.

Welbedacht Estate range

★★★★ **Bohemian Syrah** ⓖ **10** illustrates viability of variety with these Wellington vineyards. Big but supple, rich & savoury with well-integrated fine tannin. **09** sold out untasted.

★★★★ **Cricket Pitch** ⓖ Cab-based Bordeaux quintet; **10** retains freshness, lightness of touch, allowing focus on well-layered fruit, gentle rounded grip. **09** sold out untasted.

★★★★ **Hat Trick** Changing blend, pinotage, merlot & shiraz in **12**, with 24 months oak. Liquorice & glossy dark berries, aromatic spices; streamlined, the tannin grip promising a future. No **11**.

★★★★ **Old Bush Vine Chenin Blanc** ⓖ Vines into their 5th decade; tentatively rated tank sample **12** as sun-rich in colour as in its tempting ripe fruit; a gentle oxidative richness adds to its individuality. Used 300L French oak. **10** (★★★★) was promising. **11** untasted.

Merlot Barrique Select ★★★★ Opulent dark plums, vanilla & sweet spicing from 18 months in French/Hungarian oak, **12** is out to win a popularity contest. Fleshy, with supple tannins making it soft & smooth, oh so easy to drink. Also tasted: **Chardonnay Barrel Fermented 14** ★★★★ Not retasted: **Cabernet Sauvignon Barrique Select 12** ★★★★ Not tasted: **Pinotage**, **Patriot**. Discontinued: **Sauvignon Blanc**.

Meerkat range

Chenin Blanc ⓥ ★★★ Small yield from bushvines gives **15** lovely thatch & stonefruit typicity, a curvaceous body. **Sauvignon Blanc** ⓥ ★★★ Green melon & lemongrass flavours bolstered by lively acidity, **15** is freshness personified.

Burrow Blend ★★★ Lightly oaked 6-part blend includes pinotage, shiraz, cinsaut. **15** for drinking not keeping, but enough firmness for creamy dishes. Also tasted: **Pinotage 15** ★★★ **Pinotage Rosé 15** ★★★ **Sun Angel Semi-Sweet NV** ★★ **Unwooded Chardonnay 15** ★★★ — CR

Location/WO: Wellington ▪ Map: Tulbagh ▪ Est/1stB 2005 ▪ Tasting, sales & cellar tours Mon-Fri 9–5 Sat 10–2 Sun (summer only) 10-2 ▪ Fee R15 ▪ Closed Easter Fri & Mon, Dec 25 & Jan 1 ▪ No. 6 Restaurant @ Welbedacht ▪ Picnics ▪ Facilities for children ▪ Tour groups ▪ Gifts ▪ Conferences ▪ Functions ▪ Welbedacht cricket oval ▪ Bradgate manor house ▪ Owner(s) Schalk Burger Family Trust ▪ Winemaker(s) Hardus van Heerden (Jan 2015) ▪ 140ha/130ha (19 varieties r/w) ▪ 1,300t ▪ 75% red 20% white 5% rosé ▪ BWI, CVC, IPW, WIETA ▪ PO Box 51 Wellington 7654 ▪ tiaan@welbedacht.co.za ▪ www.meerkatwines.co.za, www.schalkburgerandsons.co.za ▪ S 33° 34′ 39.8″ E 019° 1′ 12.8″ ▪ F +27 (0)86-669-5641 ▪ **T +27 (0)21-873-1877**

Welgegund Wines

An arm-long list of developments since taking ownership in 2014 attests to the Brimacombe family's efforts in transforming venerable Wellington estate Welgegund. No vine is left uninspected (or planted), no structure unrenovated, no sprig of fynbos uncoddled (or planted) as part of 'a green approach'. The wine side, naturally, is being recast under ex-Doolhof wine/vine man Friedrich Kühne, with innovations, experiments and new bottlings all happening. And an estate extra-virgin olive oil debuting soon.

Location: Wellington ▪ Map: Paarl & Wellington ▪ Map grid reference: G2 ▪ Est 1800 ▪ 1stB 1997 ▪ Tasting & sales by appt ▪ Carignan B&B cottages with pool, tennis court & amens ▪ Owner(s) Brimacombe family ▪ Winemaker(s)/vineyard manager(s) Friedrich Kühne ▪ 35ha/15ha (carignan, cinsaut, grenache, shiraz, chard, chenin, viog) ▪ 1,000cs 75% red 25% white ▪ PO Box 683 Wellington 7654 ▪ sales@welgegund.co.za ▪ www.welgegund.co.za ▪ S 33° 39′ 38.3″ E 019° 2′ 13.6″ ▪ **T +27 (0)21-873-2123**

Welgeleë Boutique Wedding & Wine Farm

Chris and Lidea Meyer ceased circumnavigating the world's oceans to settle on Paarl wine estate Welgeleë, tapping into the market for winelands weddings, country conferences and, latterly, team building programmes. Contributing to the farm's charm are a handmade cab and pair of shirazes.

Location: Paarl ▪ Map: Paarl & Wellington ▪ Map grid reference: D7 ▪ Est 1999 ▪ 1stB 2003 ▪ Tasting & sales daily 9–5 ▪ Picnics by appt ▪ Function venues (±45 & 160 pax): weddings, conferences & team building ▪ Owner(s) Liris Trust (Chris & Lidea Meyer) ▪ Winemaker(s) Chris Meyer ▪ Viticulturist(s) Chris & Lidea Meyer ▪ 26ha/3ha (shiraz) ▪ 600cs own label 100% red ▪ PO Box 439 Klapmuts 7625 ▪ chris@ welgelee.com ▪ www.welgelee.com ▪ S 33° 47' 45.3" E 018° 53' 35.4" ▪ F +27 (0)86-590-4632 ▪ **T +27 (0)21-875-5726**

Welgemeend Estate

This small Paarl farm has an important history: the late Billy Hofmeyr here made the Cape's first Bordeaux blend and Rhône-style pinotage blend. The enthusiastic team owning and running Welgemeend these days buy in many grapes and have greatly expanded the range (now a brand-new rosé, sauvignon blanc and bubbly) while aiming to retain the estate's reputation for restraint and elegance.

Estate Reserve ★★★★ Bordeaux blend led by merlot (52%) with cab, cab franc, stylistically Old World inclined; savoury **11** with house's firm tannins & modest fruit intensity. Laudable dryness & subtle oaking, like all the reds. **Private Cellar Rosé** (NEW) ★★☆ From cab franc, bone-dry & crisp, faintly berry toned, **14** perfect for sushi. **Sauvignon Blanc** (NEW) ★★☆ Tropical-toned **14** an amiable summer companion. WO Paarl. **Sparkling Symphony** (NEW) ★★ Carbonated celebratory bubbly mostly sauvignon with dash shiraz. **14** lots of sweetish berry fruit, big energetic bubbles. WO W Cape. Also tasted: **Douelle 11** ★★★ **Soopjeshoogte 11** ★★ **Amadé 13** ★★★ **Chenin Blanc 14** ★★★ — JPf

Location: Paarl ▪ Map: Paarl & Wellington ▪ Map grid reference: C7 ▪ WO: Coastal/Paarl/Stellenbosch/ Western Cape ▪ Est 1974 ▪ 1stB 1979 ▪ Tasting, sales & cellar tours Mon-Fri 10–4 Sat 10–2/by appt in winter ▪ Closed all pub hols ▪ Owner(s) Welgemeend Estate (Pty) Ltd ▪ Winemaker(s) Lizette Steyn-James (Mar 2007), advised by Louis Nel ▪ Viticulturist(s) Lizette Steyn-James (Mar 2007) ▪ 16ha/11ha (cabs s/f, grenache, malbec, merlot, ptage, shiraz) ▪ 27t own label 50% red 50% white ▪ PO Box 1408 Suider-Paarl 7624 ▪ info@welgemeend.co.za ▪ www.welgemeend.co.za ▪ S 33° 47' 50.8" E 018° 53' 8.5" ▪ F +27 (0)86-654-3806 ▪ **T +27 (0)21-875-5210**

☐ **Welgevallen Cellar-Stellenbosch University** *see* Stellenbosch University Welgevallen Cellar

Welgevallen Wines (Ⓠ)

Named for the farm on which Stellenbosch's prestigious Paul Roos Gymnasium was built in 1866, Welgevallen wines are donated by old boys who are now winemakers and estate owners. Sales generate funds enabling talented youngsters from economically disadvantaged families to attend the school.

Pinotage (Ⓠ) ★★★☆ **09** succulent, smooth, worth seeking out as much for palate appeal as for noble (fund-raising) intentions. Not tasted: **Cabernet Sauvignon-Merlot**, **Sauvignon Blanc**. — CvZ

Location/map/WO: Stellenbosch ▪ Map grid reference: F5 ▪ Est/1stB 2000 ▪ Visits Mon-Fri 10–2 ▪ Closed pub & school hols ▪ Owner(s) Paul Roos Gymnasium Old Boys Union ▪ Winemaker(s)/viticulturist(s) Wouter Pienaar & Tinnie Momberg (consultants) ▪ 800cs own label 75% red 25% white ▪ c/o Paul Roos Gymnasium Old Boys Union Suidwal Stellenbosch 7600 ▪ oldboys@prg.wcape.school.za ▪ www.paulroos.co.za ▪ S 33° 56' 31.2" E 018° 51' 41.1" ▪ F +27 (0)21-883-8627 ▪ **T +27 (0)21-883-8627**

Wellington VO (NEW)

'The brandy for the regular South African guy', according to brand owner Edward Snell & Co. A blend of 3- and 5-year-old barrel-matured brandies, distilled in 1,000L copper potstills at Oude Molen in Elgin by consultant brandy master Kobus Gelderblom, Wellington VO boasts of being one of the few 'natural' local blended brandies: without bonificateurs, natural flavouring agents allowed by law.

Closed to public ▪ Owner(s) Edward Snell & Co. ▪ Brandy master(s) Kobus Gelderblom (Oude Molen) ▪ riaanv@esnell.co.za ▪ **T +27 (0)21-506-2600**

Wellington Wines (Ⓠ)(⌂)(♿)

Wellington Wines was formed in 2011 with the amalgamation of long-time neighbour cellars Wamakersvallei and Wellington Wynkelder. Latterly the union was joined by Bovlei Cellar, one of SA's oldest wineries. Today, under new production manager Francois van Niekerk, Wellington Wines produces an extensive range of own labels but also markets itself as 'a very attractive proposition for big contracts' because of its 'potential to make high volumes of excellent quality wine'. It also acts as a wine designer, providing 'a one-stop production solution to many wine-distributors, -buyers and –lovers'.

La Cave range

★★★★ **Méthode Cap Classique** A new bottling of maiden **11** sparkling shows the advantage of further ageing: the aromas show a lovely developed baked apple & brioche character, the tasty palate marked with a fresh, focused & dry citrus grip.

Chenin Blanc (NEW) ★★★★ Toasty oak with citrus & dried peach notes on **13** & **14** (both tasted). **13** nicely juicy & succulent, though flavours marred by the oaking regime, with creamy texture. Equally rich **14** fresher & livelier, the oak again obvious but more attractive in the balance. Also tasted: **Cabernet Sauvignon 14** ★★★☆ **Pinotage 14** ★★★★ **Shiraz 14** ★★★★ **Cape Blend 13** ★★★★

Wellington Wines range

Chenin Blanc ⊘ 🏆 ★★★ Light tropical flavours on **15**. Balanced, rounded & juicily fresh, with a peachy charm.

Pinotage 10.5% Alcohol (NEW) ★★ Fruity aromas on very simple **13**; a little grip & finishing sweet.
Chenin Blanc 10% Alcohol (NEW) ★★ A touch insipid, the 10% alcohol making for obvious lightness; **15** notes of green boiled sweets plus some earthiness. **Sauvignon Blanc** (NEW) ★★★ Lively & dry, **15** is lightly flavoursome, with grassy & citrus notes. Also tasted: **Shiraz 13** ★★ **Chardonnay 14** ★★★ Not retasted: **Cabernet Sauvignon 12** ★★★ **Pinotage 12** ★★★ **Moscato Frizzante NV** ★★

Bovlei Vineyard Selected range

Merlot ⊘ ★★★★ Focused, richly fruity **10** offers elegance, balance & good varietal character. Laudable effort at the price. Not retasted: **Cabernet Sauvignon 10** ★★★★ **Pinotage 10** ★★★★ **Shiraz 10** ★★★★ Discontinued: **Shiraz-Mourvèdre**.

Bovlei Winemakers Selection

Chardonnay ⊘ 🏆 ★★★ Unwooded **14** shows more depth & character than Wellington version, from first sniff to the good dry, lime finish. One of many bargains in this range.

Shiraz ★★★ Smoky & spicy aromas on **13**, leading to palate richer & softer than others in the range, but still quite seriously built (none of them present as dumbed-down). **Sauvignon Blanc** ⊘ ★★★ As usual, **15** neatly blends greener notes into the ripe tropical flavours, in a nicely rounded, unassertive package, touch more intensity than previous. **Brut** ★★★ Discontinued we said, but happily not! Latest **NV** sparkler from sauvignon & chenin at the sweeter end of the brut category, but very quaffable, with crisp appley character. Also tasted: **Cabernet Sauvignon 13** ★★★ **Merlot 13** ★★★ **Pinotage 12** ★★★ **Rosé NV** ★★ **Chenin Blanc 15** ★★★ Not retasted: **Beaukett NV** ★★ **Special Late Harvest 13** ★★ **Cape Ruby NV** ★★★ Discontinued: **Vin Rouge, Gewürztraminer, Vin Blanc**. — TJ

Location: Wellington ▪ Map: Paarl & Wellington ▪ Map grid reference: E2 ▪ WO: Wellington/Western Cape ▪ Est 1941 ▪ Tasting & sales Mon-Fri 9–5; Sat 9-1/pub hols 9-5 (only Bovlei tasting room) ▪ Fee R25/5 wines ▪ Cellar tours by appt ▪ BYO picnic ▪ Owner(s) 70 shareholders ▪ Production manager Francois van Niekerk (Sep 2014) ▪ Winemaker(s) Chris Smit (Nov 2005) & Daniel Slabber (Nov 2014), with Reon Richter (Oct 2013) & Erik van Wyk (Jan 2015) ▪ Viticulturist(s) Marko Roux (Nov 2008) ▪ 2,400ha ▪ 27,000t 60% red 40% white ▪ Export brand: Bain's Way ▪ BWI, BRC, Fairtrade, IPW, WIETA ▪ PO Box 509 Wellington 7654 ▪ sales@wellingtonwines.com ▪ www.wellingtonwines.com ▪ S 33° 38' 17.7" E 018° 59' 20.6" (Wellington), S 33° 38' 18.4" E 019° 1' 54.2" (Bovlei) ▪ F +27 (0)21-873-3194/+27 (0)21-864-1483 ▪ T +27 (0)21-873-1582

☐ **Welmoed** see Stellenbosch Vineyards

Weltevrede Estate

With over a century of winemaking history and more than 21 vintages of MCC bubbly under his belt, 4th-generation winemaker Philip Jonker and family have plenty to celebrate. He is, however, a humble and compassionate man involved in a number of community empowerment ventures. Ever mindful of the positive role played by staff in the farm's success, he embarked on a project to honour all the permanent workers on the farm, creating a new 1912 range, featuring each of their names on the classically styled labels. A private tasting in their candle-lit underground cellars is one of the special ways to enjoy the wines at the estate near Bonnievale.

Weltevrede 1912 range ⓃⒺⓌ

★★★★ **Malbec** Youthful **13** from Stellenbosch is brooding & savoury; firm chalky tannin structure courtesy 18 months in all-new oak doesn't diminish fruit's intensity; all elements in place – deserves cellaring.

★★★★ **Pinotage** Poised **13** shows perfumed red fruit finely balanced with full complement of new oak, lithe texture, medium body. Already tempting but will continue to improve with time. WO W Cape

Cabernet Sauvignon ★★★☆ Lighter styled than longer-lived Hardrock sibling, **13** delicate leafy cassis fruit, very fresh & supple, finishes on a clean scented note. **Chardonnay** ★★★ 100% new oak gives **14** its golden colour & pervasive butterscotch/caramel tone, ripe pear & peach fruit peeping out & hoping to emerge fully with time (& justify rating).

Terroir range ⓃⒺⓌ

★★★★ **Hardrock Cab** Plush-textured **13** cabernet sauvignon has a dense fruit core & pliable firm tannins; new oak adds sweet spice to intense & deep fruit. Already tempting but worth ageing.

Estate range

Bedrock Black Syrah Ⓥ ★★★☆ Noticeable oak on perfumed **12** seamlessly integrated with the peppery fruit, elegant & fine conclusion. Not retasted: **Place of Rocks Chardonnay 13** ★★★☆ Not tasted: **Poet's Prayer Chardonnay**.

Simplicity range

Cigarbox Shiraz ★★★ Unsubtle but charming **14** offers spicy red fruit in an outdoorsy/barbecuesy package. WO W Cape, as all here. Also tasted: **Cherrychoc Merlot 14** ★★★☆ **Vanilla Chardonnay 14** ★★★ **Trop!co Sauvignon Blanc 14** ★★

Philip Jonker Brut Cap Classique Collection

★★★★ **Entheos** Fine mousse & oystershell nuance to **NV** sparkling from chardonnay (60%), pinot noir. Crisp, crunchy apple flavours, lovely freshness & creamy undertone from 18-24 months lees-ageing.

★★★★ **The Ring** Some minerality, crisp apple, lime & brioche on intense, clean & refined **10** (★★★★☆) sparkling. Tight-knit, courtesy lower sugar, chardonnay-only & longer lees-ageing (42 months) than **09** & two siblings. Romantic backstory on the label explains the name.

Also tasted: **Lindelize NV** ★★★☆

Heritage range

★★★★ **Ouma se Wyn** 'Granny's Wine' a deliciously sweet yet uncloying fortified from old-vine white muscat de Frontignan. **14** a combo of ouma's warm embrace & her decadent dessert, with clean limy finish. Better than **12** (★★★☆); no **13**.

Not retasted: **Oupa se Wyn 12** ★★★☆ — MW

Location: Bonnievale ▪ Map: Robertson ▪ WO: Robertson/Western Cape ▪ Est 1912 ▪ 1stB 1945 ▪ Tasting & sales Mon-Fri 8—5 Sat 9—3.30 ▪ Closed Easter Fri/Sun, Dec 25/26 & Jan 1 ▪ Cellar tours & underground tasting by appt ▪ Walks/hikes ▪ Conservation area ▪ Weddings/functions ▪ 4 self-catering guest cottages ▪ Owner(s) Lourens Jonker ▪ Cellarmaster(s) Philip Jonker (Jan 1997) ▪ Viticulturist(s) Francois Viljoen (consultant) ▪ 360ha/106ha (cab, merlot, pinot, shiraz, chard, cbard, gewürz, sauv) ▪ 1,300t/50,000cs own label 15% red 75% white 10% other ▪ Brands for clients: Woolworths ▪ BWI ▪ PO Box 6 Bonnievale 6730 ▪ info@weltevrede.com ▪ www.weltevrede.com ▪ S 33° 56' 30.9" E 020° 3' 4.4" ▪ F +27 (0)23-616-2460 ▪ **T +27 (0)23-616-2141**

Welvanpas

Like so many, Welvanpas owner and cellarmaster Dan Retief is upbeat about 'balanced' harvest 2015. A scion of Great Trek leader Piet Retief, it's fitting that his Wellington wine estate offers pre-booked 'history packages' featuring interesting chats about local lore over lunch at on-site Die Ou Meul coffee shop.

Pinotage ⊘ ★★ **12** gentle plummy, mulberry flavours, rounded plump palate, balanced easy-drinking style with a brush of oak (from staves) & smoky farewell. Not retasted: **De Krakeelhoek Rood 12** ★★ **Revival Red 12** ★★★ **Chardonnay 12** ★★ Not tasted: **Amity**. — MW

Location/WO: Wellington ▪ Map: Paarl & Wellington ▪ Map grid reference: H1 ▪ Est 1704 ▪ 1stB 1994 ▪ Tasting & sales Tue-Fri 8–5 Sat/Sun 8–3 ▪ Fee R10pp ▪ Closed Easter Fri-Mon, Dec 16-Jan 2 ▪ Die Ou Meul coffee shop open daily ▪ Facilities for children ▪ Tour groups ▪ History package incl lunch & talk on Piet Retief family, booking required ▪ Farm produce ▪ BYO picnic (day permit R20pp) ▪ Walks/hikes ▪ Bains MTB trails ▪ Owner(s)/viticulturist(s) Dan Retief ▪ Cellarmaster(s) Dan Retief (Jan 1993) ▪ Winemaker(s) Dan Retief (Jan 1990), with Neels Kruger (Jan 1999) ▪ 260ha/50ha (11 varieties r/w) ▪ 25t own label 80% red 15% white 5% rosé ▪ PO Box 75 Wellington 7654 ▪ welvanpas@gmail.com ▪ S 33° 37' 59.9" E 019° 4' 12.5" ▪ F +27 (0)21-864-1239 ▪ **T +27 (0)21-864-1239**

☐ **Weskus** *see* Winkelshoek Wine Cellar

Whalehaven Wines

Under the auspices of the Bottega family owners (also of Idiom Collection) much work has been done to improve quality at their winery in Hemel-en-Aarde. Awards from a variety of competitions, local and overseas, have given winemaker Reino Thiart much satisfaction, while the wines have been reorganised into clearly defined tiers, all of which can be tasted (often in exciting food-and-wine combinations) at the friendly cellardoor in Hermanus.

Classic range
★★★★ **Merlot** Ripe & forthright **12** continues on from step-up **11**. Concentrated berries & cherries backed up by warm alcohol, leading to interesting & complex finish. Good food wine.

★★★★ **Pinotage** Quiet entry to **12** builds up through savoury notes, ripe black cherries, leathery hints to a juicy, ripe & pleasurable finish. Distinctly pinotage, thoroughly enjoyable too. **11** (★★★) shade less so. Also tasted: **Cabernet Franc 10** ★★★ **Sauvignon Blanc 15** ★★★★ Not tasted: **Viognier**.

Conservation Coast range
Pinot Noir ★★★★ Savoury, leathery **13** handles sweet vanilla oak well but finishes warmer & less elegantly than **12** (★★★★). Upper Hemel-en-Aarde WO. Also tasted: **Chardonnay 13** ★★★★

Abalone range
Not tasted: **Pinotage-Merlot**, **Chenin Blanc-Viognier**.

Old Harbour range
Red ⊘ ★★★ Accessible merlot-led **12** is a crowd-pleasing mix of spiced red & black berries. Sweetly fruited, pleasant stuff.

Pinotage Rosé ★★★ Fresh strawberries & hints of spice on pretty **14**. Slightly confected but enjoyable dry summer drinking. — CM

Location: Hermanus ▪ Map: Elgin, Walker Bay & Bot River ▪ WO: Coastal/Upper Hemel-en-Aarde Valley/Cape South Coast ▪ Est/1stB 1995 ▪ Tasting & sales Mon-Fri 9.30–5 Sat/Sun 10.30–2.30 ▪ Wine tasting R30pp/R60pp for paired tastings with fine floral chocolates & aromatic jams ▪ Tours by appt ▪ Tour groups (up to 40 pax) ▪ Private tasting room can be booked for small functions/corporate events (up to 12 pax) ▪ Owner(s) Bottega family ▪ Winemaker(s) Reino Thiart ▪ 120t capacity ▪ Private Bag X14 Hermanus 7200 ▪ wine@whalehaven.co.za, experience@whalehaven.co.za, info@bottegafamilywine.co.za ▪ www.whalehaven.co.za, www.bottegafamilywine.co.za ▪ S 34° 24' 36.9" E 019° 11' 60.0" ▪ F +27 (0)28-316-1640 ▪ **T +27 (0)28-316-1633**

☐ **What A Mouthful** *see* Ultra Liquors

☐ **Whispering Jack** *see* Flagstone Winery
☐ **White River** *see* Bergsig Estate
☐ **Wijnskool** *see* Diners Club Bartho Eksteen Academy

Wilde Haf Wines   ⓠ

Last listed under 'Carmel', and originating from that Elgin farm, 'Wilde Haf' is the Hiemstra family's trib-ute to their roots in the Netherlands province of Friesland, buffeted by a 'Wild Ocean'. The young pinot noir and riesling blocks are overseen by viticultural adviser and neighbour Paul Wallace, and vinified by Luddite's Niels Verburg. Marketing through select merchants has begun, and a tasting centre is planned.

Pinot Noir ★★★ Forthcoming spice, macerated cherry features on **14** enhanced by complementary oak. Would rate higher with little more concentration, verve. **Riesling ★★★** Year on, retasted **14** shows clean, punchy pepper & lime aromas, let down by disjointed acid/sugar which leaves sweet 'n sour con-clusion. — AL

Location/WO: Elgin ▪ Map: Elgin, Walker Bay & Bot River ▪ Est/1stB 2013 ▪ Tasting & sales by appt only ▪ Owner(s) Tak & Cecilia Hiemstra ▪ Cellarmaster(s)/winemaker(s) Niels Verburg (Luddite Wines) ▪ Viticul-turist(s) Paul Wallace (Jul 2010, consultant) ▪ 19ha/1.3ha (pinot, riesling) ▪ 7t/531cs own label 30% red 70% white ▪ PO Box 2 Elgin 7180 ▪ voyabiz@hotmail.co.za ▪ S 34° 12' 44.03" E 019° 3' 8.67" ▪ F +27 (0)21-859-3031 ▪ **T +27 (0)79-359-5583**

Wildehurst Wines   ⓠ ⌂

Joanne Hurst has been expanding her shiraz & viognier 'garden' at the foot of the rugged Koringberg, in the heart of the wheat-dominated Swartland: grenache and mourvèdre have been planted next to the tiny cellar. Other interesting varieties, both white and red, are brought in for the growing range (MCCs on the way) of Swartland Independent Producer wines.

Wildehurst range

★★★★ Red Earthy, spicy & slightly wild shiraz, mourvèdre & drop viognier; unhampered by oak, **12**'s palate is rich but with good lift & fine structure; perfect for venison stew. No **11**.

★★★★ Chenin Blanc From 30 year old bushvines, lightly oaked, as was **12**. **13** (★★★★) richly tex-tured with appealing rusticity, offering pear & ginger notes; emphasises weight over intensity.

Velo range

Rosé ★★★☆ Mostly grenache & 3 others, part-oaked **14** has crunchy red fruit & earthy undertones, not terribly complex but a lot of fun to drink. Also tasted: **Red 13 ★★★★ Blanc 14 ★★★★** — JPf

Location: Koringberg ▪ Map/WO: Swartland ▪ Est 2006 ▪ 1stB 2009 ▪ Tasting & sales daily at The Wine Kollective, Riebeek-Kasteel ▪ Closed Dec 25 & Jan 1 ▪ Cellar tours & tasting by appt at 1 Main Road, Koringberg ▪ Guest accommodation ▪ Owner(s) Chris & Joanne Hurst ▪ Winemaker(s) Sheree Nothnagel (Dec 2013) ▪ Viticulturist(s) John Loxton (2006, consultant) ▪ ±0.5ha (grenache, mourv, shiraz, viog) ▪ 16t ▪ own label 45% red 45% white 10% rosé ▪ PO Box 103 Koringberg 7312 ▪ wildehurst@gmail.com ▪ www.wildehurst.co.za ▪ S 33° 01' 10.10" E 018° 40' 26.42" ▪ F +27 (0)22-423-8396 ▪ **T +27 (0)22-423-8396 (winery)/+27 (0)60-374-9267**

Wildekrans Wine Estate   ⓠ ⑪ ⌂ ⓞ ⓐ

Vine-growing dates back over a century at this large Bot River farm. Significant rebirth – a new vineyard programme and a new cellar – started nearly two decades back, together with fruit orchards and olive groves. Restoring old buildings was also a priority, as was responsible farming. There's plenty more that's new: plantings of tempranillo and grenache; a tasting room at the original old cellar and a restaurant in the old barn; and a grappa and brandy still. The carefully crafted wines show a prevailing aesthetic: ripe, forthright and easily, sweetly approachable.

Barrel Selection Reserve range

★★★★ Pinotage Enticing spicy aromas on **13**, with hints of tobacco complementing varietal red fruit & banana notes. Very ripe, like **12** (★★★★) but a touch firmer, less overtly sweet, with soft, firm tannins.

★★★★ **Cape Blend** More complex blend on **13** than **12** (★★★☆): 48% pinotage with shiraz, cab & pinot noir. Delightful aromas of red/black spicy fruit carry on to rich velvety palate with smooth tannins. Fine subtle oaking, well integrated, is a feature of these otherwise anti-classic reds, as is softness, big alcohols & near off-dry levels of residual sugar – making for a clear stylistic choice.

Chenin Blanc ★★★☆ Richly sweet fruit (fresh apricot even) on ingratiating, just-dry **14**, but there's a lightness at its centre. Clever oaking (30% new) adds breadth & interest. Also tasted: **Shiraz 13** ★★★☆ Not tasted: **Sauvignon Blanc**.

Estate range

Cabernet Franc-Merlot ⊘ ★★★☆ Characteristic herbal, dry-leaf aromas of cab franc alongside obviously ripe fruit on **13**, seems drier & leaner & more modest than most here, with a little savoury dry tannin. **Sauvignon Blanc** ★★★ Nicely balanced, friendly **15** has tropical character cut with some green freshness. By a long way the driest & least alcoholic wine in the entire range! Also tasted: **Pinotage 13** ★★★ **Shiraz 13** ★★★

Méthode Cap Classique range

Brut Rosé ★★★☆ Lovely pale partridge-eye colour on bright, creamy **12** from pinot noir (giving a red berry zing) & chardonnay. Certainly not steely, but tasty, quite fresh, & well balanced. Also tasted: **MCC Chenin Blanc 12** ★★★ — TJ

Location/WO: Bot River ▪ Map: Elgin, Walker Bay & Bot River ▪ Est/1stB 1993 ▪ Tasting, sales & cellar tours Mon-Fri 8.30–5 Sat 11-5 Sun 11-4 ▪ Closed Dec 25 ▪ Restaurant ▪ Tour groups ▪ Picnics to order ▪ Conferences/functions ▪ Walks/hikes ▪ Mountain biking ▪ Birding ▪ Conservation area ▪ Grappa & brandy still ▪ Self-catering cottages ▪ Owner(s) Gary & Amanda Harlow ▪ Winemaker(s) William Wilkinson (2006) ▪ Viticulturist(s) Braam Gericke (2008) ▪ 1,015ha/71.8ha (ptage, pinot, tempranillo, chard, chenin, grenache blanc) ▪ 350t own label 55% red 40% white 5% rosé; ±13,200cs for clients ▪ WIETA ▪ PO Box 31 Botrivier 7185 ▪ wines@wildekrans.com ▪ www.wildekrans.com ▪ S 34° 9' 42.6" E 019° 0' 36.0" ▪ F +27 (0)21-413-0967 ▪ **T +27 (0)28-284-9902**

☐ **Wild Olive** *see* The Grape Grinder

William Everson Wines   ⓠ ⌂

With a cellar in his Grabouw home, William Everson is a literal garagiste albeit occupied full-time in recent vintages by his artisan apple and pear ciders. Previous releases of his wines are available on-site by appointment and at several farmstalls and restaurants around Elgin, Hermanus and Cape Town.

Elgin Shiraz ⓠ ★★★ Smoky **09** more elegant, subtle & crisp than previous. **Shiraz-Mourvèdre** ⓠ ★★★ **10** offers leathery dark chocolate & a pleasant firmness. Not retasted: **Stellenbosch Cabernet Sauvignon 09** ★★☆ **Paarl Shiraz 08** ★★★★ Not tasted: **Poplar Overberg Cabernet Sauvignon**, **Poplar Overberg Shiraz**, **One Barrel Chardonnay**. — GM

Location: Grabouw ▪ Map: Elgin, Walker Bay & Bot River ▪ WO: Elgin/Stellenbosch/Paarl ▪ Est/1stB 2001 ▪ Tasting, sales & tours by appt ▪ Self-catering accommodation (www.mentmor.co.za) ▪ Owner(s)/winemaker(s) William Everson ▪ 4t/800cs own label 60% red 40% white ▪ 2281 Essenhout Avenue Klipkop Grabouw 7160 ▪ william@eversonwine.co.za, william@eversonscider.com ▪ www.eversonwine.co.za, www.eversonscider.com ▪ S 34° 8' 44.01" E 019° 1' 1.21" ▪ F +27 (0)86-662-4045 ▪ **T +27 (0)82-554-6357**

☐ **Willowbrook** *see* Wine-of-the-Month Club
☐ **Windfall** *see* Boutinot South Africa

Windfall Wine Farm   ⓠ ⓦ ⌂ ⌂

This Agterkliphoogte Valley wine and guest farm, rejuvenated by KwaZulu-Natal property developer Robert Alexander with co-owner/farm manager/viticulturist Jaco de Wet and daughters Bianca Weingartz and Sarah Alexander, is going great guns. A bumper 2015 included doubled-up production, release of their first rosé and potstill brandy, and the birth of Bianca's second son, Hunter.

Windfall Wine range

Barrel 41 ★★★ 13 same blend as Kibali, similarly light textured but smoother, less bright, spicy fruit, finishes sweeter. Both French oaked, 19 months, none new. **Grenache Rosé** ⓝ **★★☆ Semi-sweet 15** pearly pink with juicy wild strawberry, spicy cream flavours. Balanced, lightish quaffer. **Sauvignon Blanc ★★★** Juicy tropical fruit, lengthened by gentle, balanced freshness in pleasantly sippable **15**, lightly oaked. Also tasted: **Shiraz 13 ★★★ Kibali 13 ★★★ Chenin Blanc 15 ★★☆** Not retasted: **Cabernet Sauvignon 13 ★★★ Mendola 08 ★★★**

Brandy range ⓝ

★★★★ Potstill Brandy Turn up Mozart & enjoy the bright gold hues, sweet peach, apricot & pear drop tones, vibrant floral & spice finish. A delight from chenin in 500 ml. — WB, AL

Location/map/WO: Robertson ▪ Est 1998 ▪ 1stB 2006 ▪ Tasting, sales & tours by appt ▪ Closed all pub hols ▪ Picnics by appt; or BYO picnic ▪ 5 self-catering cottages (sleeps between 2 & 4 people) R330pppn ▪ Owner(s) Bianca Weingartz, Sarah Alexander & Jaco de Wet ▪ Cellarmaster(s) Kobus van der Merwe (Jan 2006, consultant) & Jaco de Wet ▪ Winemaker(s) Kobus van der Merwe (Jan 2006, consultant), with Van Zyl de Wet (Jan 2009, consultant) ▪ Viticulturist(s) Jaco de Wet (Jan 2003) ▪ 300ha/49ha (cab, merlot, pinot, ruby cab, chard, chenin, sauv) ▪ 840t/1,250cs own label 75% red 25% white ▪ PO Box 22 Robertson 6705 ▪ info@windfallwine.co.za ▪ www.windfallwine.co.za ▪ S 33° 56' 33.37'' E 019° 38' 42.98'' ▪ F +27 (0)86-743-4162 ▪ **T +27 (0)83-320-8473**

Windmeul Cellar ⓠ ⓞ ⓑ

Now in its 72nd year, grower-owned Windmeul was named after Blake's Mill, an engineering wonder of its day, built in the late 1890s and central to the grain industry of the Agter Paarl area. Don't be prejudiced by the 13,000+ ton production; this is winemaking of a high order. Under cellarmaster Danie Marais, the winery delivers remarkable value, too. Look out for a very special potstill brandy, and a farmstall/deli, currently in the works.

Reserve range

★★★★ Cabernet Sauvignon Pure, focused varietal character, vibrant fruit & finely structured tannins on **12** reflect care & finessed winemaking. Remarkable value too.

★★★★☆ Pinotage ⓥ **14 (★★★★★)** promises big things, with intricate flavour combination of berry compote, vanilla custard, wild herbs & cinnamon, borne on robust but silky tannin structure. Already approachable but will benefit from cellaring. Benchmark pinotage, as we said of **13** too.

★★★★ Shiraz Big, savoury **12** exudes ripeness & intensity. Black cherries sprinkled with currants, spiced with garrigue scrub & white pepper. Hefty tannin platform needs time to soften.

★★★★☆ The Legend Classy Bordeaux-style blend of mainly cab with petit verdot & merlot, **13** flagship label has weighty, brooding presence. Black fruit laced with liquorice & iodine, wrapped in satin tannins.

★★★★☆ Cape Blend ⓖ Voluptuous **13** only a shade off spectacular **12 (★★★★★)**, with ripe & rich black plum fruit, fleshy body & dense, strapping tannins. Mostly pinotage (55%), supported by cab, merlot & dollop petit verdot.

★★★★ Chardonnay ⓖ Concentrated citrus & buttered toast on **12**. Though mouthfilling & rich, bright acid balances the overall structure & fresh, zesty finish. Will reward ageing few years. Paarl WO.

★★★★ Chenin Blanc ⓥ Impressively rounded & stately **14** ex-barrel easily handles 12 months in oak. Ripe, rich fruit, elegantly spiced, with texture & body to match. Extraordinary value.

Windmeul range

★★★★ White Muscadel ⓖ Fragrant, vibrant orange peel on fresh **10** fortified dessert. Slippery, dense & concentrated, with a delicious alcohol grip balancing sweetness.

Cabernet Sauvignon-Merlot ⓥ ⓣ **★★★☆ Impressive varietal fruit profile, solid & substantial, 13** is also bargain priced. **Chenin Blanc** ⓥ ⓣ **★★★ Unusual herbaceous aromas, but 15** is pure bottled refreshment. Hints of white stonefruit, pineapple. Very pocket friendly too.

Also tasted: **Cabernet Sauvignon 13 ★★★ Merlot 13 ★★★ Sauvignon Blanc 15 ★★** Not retasted: **Pinotage 12 ★★★ Port 10 ★★★** Not tasted: **Shiraz, Chardonnay.** — GdB

Location: Paarl ▪ Map: Paarl & Wellington ▪ Map grid reference: D3 ▪ WO: Coastal/Paarl ▪ Est 1944 ▪ 1stB 1945 ▪ Tasting & sales Mon-Fri 9—5 Sat 9—3 ▪ Closed all pub hols ▪ Cellar tours by appt ▪ Farmers' market every 1st Sat of each month, with fresh produce & meals ▪ Function/tasting area ▪ Owner(s) 42 members ▪ Cellarmaster(s) Danie Marais (Oct 1999) ▪ Winemaker(s) Abraham van Heerden (Nov 2014), with Andri le Roux (Sep 2014) ▪ Viticulturist(s) Anton Laas (Oct 2007) ▪ 1,700ha ▪ 13,500t/12,000cs own label 54% red 44% white 1% rosé 1% fortified + 800cs for clients ▪ Suite 179, Private Bag X3041, Paarl 7620 ▪ windmeul@iafrica.com ▪ www.windmeulwinery.co.za ▪ S 33° 40' 18.1" E 018° 54' 30.6" ▪ F +27 (0)21-869-8614 ▪ **T +27 (0)21-869-8100/8043**

☐ **Winds of Change** *see* Jacques Germanier

Wine Concepts   ⓠ

There have been several changes to the Wine Concepts specialist wine shops' offering recently. Chief is that, responding to changing consumer shopping habits, the Johannesburg store has closed to become an online emporium. In Cape Town, the two stores will continue to create and stock own brands. Their pinot noir, Black Block, has proven so successful, it has taken on a commercial life of its own and is now listed separately.

Location: Cape Town ▪ Tasting & sales Mon-Fri 9—7 Sat 9—4 ▪ Owner(s) Newlands: Michael Bampfield-Duggan; Kloof Street: Neil & Sue Proudfoot ▪ Wine consultant Michael Bampfield-Duggan ▪ Cardiff Castle cnr Kildare & Main St Newlands 7700 ▪ newlandshop@wineconcepts.co.za ▪ www.wineconcepts.co.za ▪ F +27 (0)21-671-9031/+27 (0)88-021-426-4401 ▪ **T +27 (0)21-671-9030 (Newlands)/+27 (0)21-426-4401 (Gardens)**

Wine Fusion

In an innovative take on entrepreneurial wine-selling, Wellington-based Graham Knox gathers a team of winemakers to produce singular and evocatively named wines, bottled offshore.

Location: Wellington ▪ Est 2007 ▪ Closed to public ▪ Cellarmaster(s) Graham Knox (Dec 2007) ▪ Winemaker(s) various ▪ 1.5m L bulk 60% red 40% white ▪ c/o Wine Masterpieces (Pty) Ltd PO Box 1209 Wellington 7654; TWF 90 London Rd London SE16LN UK T +44 2077171569 ▪ graham@ thewinefusion.com ▪ F +27 (0)21-447-4476 ▪ **T +27 (0)21-447-4476/+27 (0)83-625-2865**

☐ **Wine Lover's** *see* Vinopoly Wines
☐ **Winemaster's Reserve** *see* Nederburg Wines

Wine-of-the-Month Club

Wine-of-the-Month Club, South Africa's original and still leading wine mail-order business, distributes third-party wines selected by its expert panel as well as its own labels such as Berg en Dal, Boschenheuwel, Giant's Peak, Montebello, Semara, Sentinel, Steenhuis and Willowbrook.

Location: Cape Town ▪ Est 1986 ▪ MD Gis Collard ▪ Private Bag X2 Glosderry 7702 ▪ wineclub@ wineofthemonth.co.za ▪ www.wineofthemonth.co.za ▪ F +27 (0)86-674-4690 ▪ **T +27 (0)21-709-6300**

☐ **Winery of Good Hope** *see* The Winery of Good Hope

Wines of Cape Town   ⓠ

A negociant business based in Bellville, Wines of Cape Town specialises in mainly red private-label wines for clients in Asia and Africa. It also exports its own brand of 'good-value, well-made wines', Dolphin Sands, available in 6L packaging with branded dispenser which chills the contents optimally.

Location: Bellville ▪ Map: Durbanville, Philadelphia & Darling ▪ Est 2007 ▪ Tasting by appt ▪ Owner(s) DS Sarnia (Pty) Ltd ▪ 80% red 20% white ▪ Brands for clients: Bushman's Creek, Diamond Creek, Dolphin Bay ▪ 71 Sonneblom Street Stellenridge Bellville 7530 ▪ sales@winesofcapetown.com ▪ www.winesofcapetown.com ▪ F +27 (0)21-876-3486 ▪ **T +27 (0)21-876-2129**

Wine Village-Hermanus   Ⓠ Ⓖ

Wine Village at the entrance to Hemel-en-Aarde Valley is the realisation of Paul and Cathy du Toit's dream to bring together the fine wines of South Africa under one roof. Daughter Ulla manages events and the popular annual Hermanus Wine & Food Festival. Are We Having Fun Yet? is their house brand.

Are We Having Fun Yet? range

Red ★★☆ Vintage rings varietal changes in this easy-drinker. Shiraz & merlot combo in plummy **14** with just enough tannin bite for food. **White** (NEW) ★★☆ From sauvignon, with attractive Turkish delight & marzipan bottle-age on nose, **14** palate still vibrant & bouncy, uncomplicated & quaffable. — CvZ

Location: Hermanus ▪ Map: Elgin, Walker Bay & Bot River ▪ WO: Walker Bay ▪ Est 1998 ▪ 1stB 2004 ▪ Open Mon–Fri 9–6 Sat 9–5 Sun 10–3 ▪ Closed Good Fri & Dec 25 ▪ Owner(s) Paul & Cathy du Toit ▪ ±2,000cs 50% red 50% white ▪ PO Box 465 Hermanus 7200 ▪ winevillage@hermanus.co.za ▪ www.winevillage.co.za ▪ S 34° 24' 40.7" E 019° 12' 1.9" ▪ F +27 (0)86-509-4931 ▪ **T +27 (0)28-316-3988**

Wineways Marketing

Negociant business Wineways Marketing buys grapes from Stellenbosch, Swartland and elsewhere for vinification at Leeuwenkuil and Stellenbosch Vineyards, and marketing under brand names Black Box, Black Tie, Coral Reef, De Villiers, Leipoldt 1880, Mountain Dawn, Tin Cups and Mountain Shadows. They're available locally as well as throughout Africa, the Indian Ocean islands and Middle East.

Location: Kuils River ▪ Est 2000 ▪ Closed to public ▪ Owner(s) Carl Schmidt, Stephen Vermeulen & Fanie Marais ▪ Winemaker(s) Pieter Carstens (Leeuwenkuil) & Bernard Claassen (Stellenbosch Vineyards) ▪ 400,000cs own label 60% red 40% white ▪ Plot 689, Zinfandel Street, Saxenburg Park 2, Blackheath 7580 ▪ info@wine-ways.co.za ▪ www.wine-ways.co.za ▪ F +27 (0)86-509-9587 ▪ **T +27 (0)21-905-7713/6/9**

☐ **Wingnut** see Chateau Naudé Wine Creation

Winkelshoek Wine Cellar

The visitor centre at Piketberg on the West Coast has closed, but Winkelshoek's own labels (and that of sibling Schenkfontein, listed separately) remain available in the trade. Winkelshoek's Weskus brand has been repackaged and slightly pruned, and now includes Dry Red, Blanc de Blanc, Sweet Rosé and Natural Sweet. The Winkelshoek 5L Classic line-up is Red, White, Sweet Rosé, Johannisberger and Extra Lite; the Cap Vino range includes Red (now wooded) and White (chenin). For post-prandial pleasure, there's also the full-sweet wine below.

White Jerepigo ⊘ ★★☆ Raisiny, tasty but simple **15** fortified sweetie, the alcohol nicely in balance with the fruit. — TJ

Location: Piketberg ▪ WO: Swartland ▪ Closed to public ▪ Owner(s) Hennie Hanekom & Jurgens Brand ▪ Cellarmaster(s) Hennie Hanekom ▪ Winemaker(s) Hendrik Hanekom (2011) ▪ PO Box 395 Piketberg 7320 ▪ info@winkelshoek.co.za ▪ F +27 (0)22-913-1095 ▪ **T +27 (0)22-913-1092**

Winters Drift   Ⓠ Ⓨ ⓞ Ⓐ Ⓖ

Warm smiles welcome visitors to Winters Drift, elegantly and nostalgically housed in the renovated Elgin train station, where the new 51 Miles wines are exclusively available, along with restaurant, facilities for children and a boule court, ensuring a pleasant visit for families of all ages.

Winters Drift range

Pinot Noir ★★★☆ Lots of interest on **14**, sweet red-berried fruit, spice & leather, but wood & smoke slightly dominate. Fresh acid may keep it together till oak settles down. Also tasted: **Chardonnay 14** ★★★☆ Not retasted: **Shiraz 12** ★★★ Discontinued: **Rosé**, **Sauvignon Blanc**.

51 Miles range (NEW)

Unwooded Chardonnay ★★★ **14** has plenty of juicy orange/lemon citrus notes with nicely managed alcohol. Exclusive to the tasting room, like next. **Sauvignon Blanc** ★★★ Lively & fresh **14** shows lots of lemons & limes with some green figs & good acidity. — CM

Location/WO: Elgin ▪ Map: Elgin, Walker Bay & Bot River ▪ Est 2004 ▪ 1stB 2010 ▪ Tasting Tue-Fri 9-4 Sat 10-4 ▪ Fred & Max restaurant ▪ Facilities for children ▪ Boule court ▪ Conservation area ▪ Owner(s) Fruitways (Pty) Ltd ▪ Cellarmaster(s) Koen Roose (Spioenkop) ▪ Viticulturist(s) Gerhard Bruwer (2015) & Francois Viljoen (Vinpro) ▪ 1,600ha/±54ha (cab, grenache, merlot, mourv, pinot, shiraz, chard, sauv, sem) ▪ 460t/7,000cs own label 40% red 60% white ▪ PO Box 155 Somerset West 7137 ▪ gerhard@wintersdrift.com, emy@wintersdrift.com ▪ www.wintersdrift.com ▪ S 34° 08' 59.42" E 019° 02' 22.61" ▪ F +27 (0)21-859-4893 ▪ **T +27 (0)21-859-3354**

☐ **Witch** *see* Mother Rock Wines

Withington

Wine marketing doyen Charles Withington's own labels, available from his Darling wine shop, among others, aim at 'drinkers' rather than 'thinkers'. Ever varying, the line-up includes a red blend which manifests his fondness for cinsaut, dating from the days of selling Rustenberg Dry Red. To follow is a chenin blanc from old Darling vines, reflecting the belief that 'the future of great wine lies in the past'.

Withington range

Roan Ranger (NEW) ★★★ Fashionable cinsaut with grenache & mourvèdre in fresh, fruity & low-tannin **13** blend, harmonised in older oak. **NBC Chardonnay** ★★★☆ Unwooded **15** echoes generous pineapple & citrus of **13**. Zestily fresh, lingering & dry. No **14**. Also tasted: **Malbec 14** ★★★ Not retasted: **Shiraz-Cabernet Sauvignon 09** ★★★

Darlington range

Chardonnay (Ⓥ) ★★★ **12** has tropical-styled citrus lightness & easy-drinking appeal. Seamless & rounded to dry end. Not retasted: **Malbec 12** ★★★ Discontinued: **Pinotage**.

Greendale range

In abeyance: **Chenin Blanc-Chardonnay**.

Living Rock range

In abeyance: **Cinsaut-Ruby Cabernet**, **Chenin Blanc-Chardonnay**.

Brandy range

★★★★ **Voorkamer** (Ⓥ) Literally 'Living Room', & intended for convivial occasions there, 7-year potstilled colombard is genteel, with a smooth creamy texture, spiced orchard fruit & a lingering balanced citrus conclusion. A delight. Also in 50 ml 'miniatures'. — WB, AL

Location: Darling ▪ Map: Durbanville, Philadelphia & Darling ▪ WO: Darling/Paarl ▪ Est 2001 ▪ 1stB 2003 ▪ Tasting & sales at Darling Wine Shop Mon-Sat 10-6 (10-7 in summer) Sun 11-2 ▪ Closed Mar 21, Easter Fri/Sun & Dec 25/26 ▪ Fresh West Coast oysters served when available ▪ Owner(s) Withington family ▪ 6,000cs own label 70% red 30% white + 8,000cs for clients ▪ Brands for clients: Cape Diversity, Greendale ▪ PO Box 236 Darling 7345 ▪ mail@withington.co.za ▪ www.withington.co.za ▪ S 33° 22' 28" E 018° 22' 38" ▪ **T +27 (0)22-492-3971/+27 (0)74-194-1711**

Withoek (Ⓥ) (🏠) (📷)

In the red hills on the fringe of Calitzdorp village, the Geyser family vineyards share space with fruit orchards, self-catering cottages and a cellar dating from the 1940s, where Fanie Geyser makes his boutique wines, keeping things simple and traditional. His new vintages unready for review.

Location: Calitzdorp ▪ Map: Klein Karoo & Garden Route ▪ Est/1stB 1996 ▪ Tasting, sales & cellar tours by appt ▪ Self-catering cottages ▪ Walks ▪ Conservation area ▪ Owner(s) Geyser family ▪ Winemaker(s) Fanie Geyser ▪ Viticulturist(s) Johannes Mellet ▪ 454ha/30ha (cab, p verdot, ruby cab, shiraz, tinta, touriga, chenin, cbard, hanepoot, muscadel) ▪ ±300t/800cs own label 50% red 50% fortified ▪ PO Box 181 Calitzdorp 6660 ▪ withoek@telkomsa.net ▪ www.withoek.blogspot.com ▪ S 33° 32' 24.1" E 021° 40' 59.8" ▪ F +27 (0)86-628-7853 ▪ **T +27 (0)44-213-3639**

☐ **Witklip** *see* Eerste Hoop Wine Cellar

Woestkloof Estate ⌂

Longtime Wellington vine nurseryman Ben Hoogenhout, daughter Celia and her German husband Simon Obholzer (their names combined form the Simelia brand name) collaborate on these two wines. From old vines on the family's Groenberg Mountain farm, they're vinified by Louis Nel. The 2014 vintage was still in barrel at time of going to press.

Simelia range

Merlot ⓧ ★★★☆ Blackcurrants, a whiff of mint resting on a bed of firm tannin, **13** an ideal food match or give it a few years. **Syrah** ⓧ ★★★ Deep dark fruit, liquorice & spice, the tannins still brusque; give **13** time to meld or serve with rich casseroles. — CR, CvZ

Location/WO: Wellington ▪ Est farm circa 1837/wine brand 2012 ▪ 1stB 2013 ▪ Closed to public ▪ Casa Simelia luxury self-catering house ▪ Hiking/walking trails ▪ Owner(s) BM Hoogenhout Trust (farm); Simon A Obholzer & Celia Hoogenhout-Obholzer (wine brand) ▪ Winemaker(s) Louis Nel (Nov 2012, consultant) ▪ 42ha/2.2ha (merlot, syrah) ▪ 8t/±1,016cs plus ±100 magnum btls own label 100% red ▪ info@simelia.co.za ▪ www.simelia.co.za ▪ F +27 (0)86-637-2920 ▪ **T +27 (0)21-424-7261**

☐ **Wolfenberg** see TCB Wines

Wolfkloof ⓧ ⓗ 🛒 ⓞ

Robertson-based Jan Kannemeyer's boutique vintning began in 2004 when he concluded he couldn't call himself a vinegrower and not make wine. Merlot — all of one barrel — was his first attempt and the variety is still his favourite. Current releases under his JC Kannemeyer label are Handcrafted Merlot '12, White Merlot '15, Light Barrel Fermented Chardonnay '12 and Thin Lizzy Chardonnay '15 (unwooded).

Location/map: Robertson ▪ Est 1883 ▪ 1stB 2004 ▪ Tasting, sales & cellar tours by appt ▪ Meals by appt; or BYO picnic ▪ Tour groups ▪ Conferences (40 pax) ▪ Weddings/functions (100 pax) ▪ Hiking trail ▪ Owner(s)/cellarmaster(s)/winemaker(s) Jan Kannemeyer ▪ Viticulturist(s) Hennie Visser (consultant) ▪ 360ha/4ha (merlot, chard) ▪ 10t/1,000cs own label 40% red 40% white 20% rosé + 180cs for clients ▪ PO Box 40 Robertson 6705 ▪ info@wolfkloof.co.za ▪ www.wolfkloof.co.za ▪ S 33° 47' 28.1" E 019° 52' 1.4" ▪ F +27 (0)86-554-4894 ▪ **T +27 (0)74-339-5008**

☐ **Wolftrap** see The Wolftrap

Wolvendrift Private Cellar ⓧ ⓗ ⓞ Ⓐ ♿

This Robertson farm has been in the Klue family for more than 100 years, and 4 generations have made wine in its cellar. Hospitality is a particular focus, and the child-friendly facilities and attractions include a vineyard deck with mountain views, pre-booked meals on the lawns, and weddings in the cellar itself.

Location/map: Robertson ▪ Est 1903 ▪ Tasting & sales Mon-Fri 8.30–4.30 Sat 11–2 ▪ Closed Easter Fri-Mon, May 1, Dec 25/26 & Jan 1 ▪ Cellar tours by appt ▪ Refreshments/meals by pre-booking ▪ Facilities for children ▪ Tour groups ▪ Walking/hiking trails ▪ Conservation area ▪ Weddings & functions ▪ Owner(s) Michael Klue ▪ Winemaker(s) Jan Klue (Jan 2003) ▪ Viticulturist(s) Jan Swart (Jan 2000) ▪ 120ha (cab, merlot, chard, chenin, cbard, sauv) ▪ 45% red 45% white 10% fortified ▪ PO Box 24 Robertson 6705 ▪ info@wolvendriftwines.co.za ▪ www.wolvendriftwines.co.za ▪ S 33° 55' 0.1" E 020° 0' 9.0" ▪ F +27 (0)23-616-2396 ▪ **T +27 (0)23-616-2890**

Women in Wine

Women in Wine was established by a group of black female professionals inspired by quality wines and the empowerment of women in the winelands. Their portfolio consists of two labels — Three Graces Reserve (Euphrosyne Cabernet, Thalia Merlot and Aglaia Chardonnay) and Women in Wine (Cabernet, Chardonnay and Sauvignon) — neither available for review.

Location: Paarl ▪ Closed to public ▪ PO Box 12869 Die Boord Stellenbosch 7613 ▪ info@ womeninwine.co.za ▪ www.womeninwine.co.za ▪ F +27 (0)21-872-8967 ▪ **T +27 (0)21-872-8967**

Wonderfontein

$(\mathbb{Q})\ (\boxdot)\ (\textcircled{})$

Appropriately for an estate hosting weddings and functions, Wonderfontein's 5th-generation Marais family is focusing on MCC sparkling and at press time readying a Brut Rosé to join the ever-improving and fetchingly packaged Paul René Brut.

★★★★ **Paul René MCC Brut** Chardonnay-based **NV (12)** has myriad tiny bubbles, luxurious brioche notes & broad creamy palate from 20 months on lees. Refreshing, satisfying & certainly worth seeking out.

★★★★ **Wonderfontein Red Muscadel** Revisited & improved **11** lovely example of this fortified dessert style: genteel potpourri fragrance of rosepetals, tangerine, ginger & blossoms; intense raisin & fig flavours, fresh spirit tail.

La Bonne Vigne Sauvignon Blanc ★★★ Gentle cassis & fig tones, **15** flavoursome palate & long grassy tail for summer enjoyment. Also tasted: **La Bonne Vigne Merlot 12** ★★ **Wonderfontein White Muscadel 12** ★★★☆ Not retasted: **La Bonne Vigne Shiraz 11** ★★★ Not tasted: **La Bonne Vigne Rosé**. Discontinued: **The Marais Family Merlot**. — CvZ

Location/map/WO: Robertson ▪ Est ca 1884 ▪ Tasting by appt only ▪ Sales Mon-Fri 9–5.30 Sat 9–1 ▪ Tour groups ▪ Conferences/events (40-80 guests), picnic facilities, 4×4 trail & other attractions ▪ Owner(s) Paul René Marais ▪ Winemaker(s) Stefan Bruwer ▪ Viticulturist(s) Gert Visser & Gerald Stemmet ▪ 310ha (cab, merlot, ptage, pinot, ruby cab, shiraz, chard, chenin, sauv) ▪ 5,500t/6,000cs own label 10% red 80% white 1% rosé 9% fortified ▪ PO Box 4 Robertson 6705 ▪ henk@wonderfonteinestate.co.za ▪ www.wonderfonteinestate.co.za ▪ S 33° 49' 3.5" E 019° 52' 2.1" ▪ F +27 (0)23-626-2669 ▪ **T +27 (0)23-626-2212**

Woolworths

The cornucopia of quality wines covering classic and on-trend varieties and styles at SA's top-end retail giant Woolworths is testament to the expertise and unflagging passion of wine selector Allan Mullins, a Cape Wine Master, and long-time colleague and buying manager Ivan Oertle. Their enduring reputation enables sourcing from and collaboration with SA's leading vintners, the Woolworths team's reach now extended by experienced wine buyer Carolyn Barton. Their 'more listings, more exclusivity' mantra is echoed in two new premium ranges, Fine Wines and Craft Wines, introduced at select stores (too late for inclusion here), and a host of fresh bottlings including an ultra-premium, mature MCC. And their 'value with a difference' Italian, Spanish and South American offerings are to be extended by other international areas of origin.

Cabernet Sauvignon range

★★★★ **Cabernet Sauvignon** (NEW) **13** classic dark berry, iodine & violet notes, with herbal lift from splash cab franc, harmonious tannins from year in oak (90% French, American). By Villiera.

★★★★ **Cabernet Sauvignon Reserve** Gentle fynbos brush to richly fruited, lithe **13**. Complex & layered with harmonious oak, 70% new. Lovely integration & depth as befits Diemersfontein origin.

★★★★ **Exclusive Cabernet** From Grangehurst, **10** offers subtle aromas of cassis, earth & blackcurrant. As usual, in unshowy, classic food-friendly style with well-judged refreshing acidity.

★★★★ **Private Collection Cabernet Sauvignon** (✓) Was 'Cabernet Sauvignon Reserve'. Mintseamed & intense, Spier's **13** is dark & brooding in youth but already has a lovely texture; decanting or cellaring will help it unfold, reveal its hidden charms.

★★★★ **Single Vineyard The Hutton Cabernet Sauvignon** Named for vineyard soil type, Spier's **13** is tight & tannic in youth, but packed with ripe cassis fruit, promising much more in a year/2.

DD Cabernet Sauvignon (NEW) ★★★ Stalky influence on red & black berries with sweet bellpepper nuance, **14** slight rhubarb note too, with milk choc coating. Easy casual sipper by Diemersdal. **NSA Organic Running Duck Cabernet Sauvignon** (✓) ★★★ **15**'s luscious fruit melds with genteel oak tannins in everyday dinner companion. From Stellar Winery, Fairtrade certified. Also tasted: **Blackberry Cabernet Sauvignon 14** ★★★ **Vintage Selection Cabernet Sauvignon 14** ★★★☆ Not retasted: **House Cabernet Sauvignon 12** ★★★ **Longmarket Cabernet Sauvignon 12** ★★★

Merlot range

★★★★ **Merlot Reserve** ⓡ Firmly structured **09** from Morgenhof shows dark cherries, blackberries, & slight herbaceous note. Powerful, with integrated acidity but warmish finish ex 14.8% alcohol.

★★★★ **Organic Merlot** ⓥ With dabs of cab franc & malbec, **14** minted red fruit in firm but juicy structure with piquant freshness. Perfect with lamb. From Laibach.

★★★★ **Reserve Collection** Delightfully drinkable **12** from Jordan is juicy, cassis driven & supple. Bright New World varietal expression with vigour & deft balance. Ready to go – don't bother cellaring.

★★★★ **Shannon Merlot** Voluptuous **13** with hint of oak char, sufficient tannic grip to extend the finish, as in **12**. Very drinkable now but should improve ±5 years.

★★★★ **Single Vineyard Koffie Klip Merlot** Named for vineyard soil type, succulent **13** improves on **12** (★★★☆) with cherry & cranberry fruit cosseted by 60% new French oak, all subtly balanced. Ex Spier. **Merlot** ⓝ ★★★ By Villiera. **13** has vanilla-infused plum, blue berry & dark choc appeal, soft tannins, berry persistence. Great with roasted duck, lamb or seared tuna. **NSA Merlot** ⓝ ★★★ Balanced **13** leafy aromas, dark chocolate & plummy fruit, also a more serious tarry thread. By Jordan. **NSA Organic Swooping Falcon Merlot** ⓥ ★★ **15** by Stellar Winery is perfect for country-style food, with fresh acidity & robust tannins. **Oakleaf Merlot** ★★★ From Delheim. Good red berry aromas with a touch of choc & mint on **13**. Nicely oaked; firmly built but ready for good drinking. **Vinehugger Merlot** ⓝ ⓥ ★★★ Bright, spicy red plums on unfussy **13** by Reyneke. Oak rounded, but has nip of fresh lively tannins, balanced for current drinking. Also tasted: **Blackcherry Merlot 14** ★★ **Light Merlot 14** ★☆ **Longmarket Merlot 14** ★★ Not retasted: **House Merlot 14** ★★☆ **Platinum Merlot 13** ★★★

Pinot Noir range

★★★★ **Limited Release CM Pinot Noir** From Catherine Marshall, **14** shows perfumed wild berries & ferrous/savoury nuance. Dry but very supple, with signature freshness & elegance. Already appealing but will continue to develop gracefully.

★★★★ **Pinot Noir Reserve** From Paul Cluver, **14** fresh earth & savoury strawberry tones with smooth tannins; polished, elegant & balanced; tempting now, could age few years. **13** untasted.

DMZ Pinot Noir ★★★★ Delightfully fresh, earthy **14**'s silky charm has sufficient weight & interest to ensure agreeably savoury sipping. By DeMorgenzon. **Unwooded Pinot Noir** ⓝ ★★★ A 'red white wine' best served lightly chilled, friendly **15** from Haute Cabrière has light tannins, sweet red berries & a hint of spice. Also tasted: **Single Vineyard Le Petit Shannon Pinot Noir 14** ★★★☆

Pinotage range

★★★★ **Pinotage Reserve 13** by Diemersfontein ups the ante on **12** (★★★☆) while toning down the oak (just 50% new). Ample ripe black berries with good grip, concentration & depth. Integrated & serious. **Coffee Pinotage** ★★★ Wake up & smell the java! **14** soft, sweet mocha-choc appeal to rounded & light Diemersfontein offering. **Simonsig Pinotage** ★★★☆ Attractive combo blueberry fruit & spicing, **13** (★★★★) finishes firm & dry. Match with rich, creamy dishes; has good ageing potential. Also tasted: **House Pinotage** ⓥ **14** ★★★☆ **Light Pinotage 14** ★☆ **NSA Organic Glowing Firefly Pinotage** ⓥ **15** ★★ Not retasted: **Exclusive Selection Pinotage 13** ★★★ **Longmarket Pinotage 14** ★★★

Shiraz range

★★★★ **Syrah Reserve** From The Winery of Good Hope, naturally fermented **13** has a delicate floral/fynbos nose, fresh acidity, gentle tannins & lightest oak touch highlighting dark plum & berry fruit. **Chocolate Shiraz** ★★★ Choccywoccydoodah! Big, berried cocoa bang for your buck. **14** soft, bright, juicy & cheerful, from Diemersfontein. **Longmarket Redstone Shiraz** ⓥ ★★★★ Step-up **13** from Rooiberg has smoky bacon wafts, sour cherry & mulberry flavour, savoury finish with a flick of tannin; characterful solo or BBQ sipper. Also tasted: **House Shiraz 14** ★★★ Not retasted: **NSA Organic Diving Hawk Shiraz 14** ★★☆

Niche Red Cultivars

★★★★ **Ferricrete Cabernet Franc** Was 'Cabernet Franc Reserve'. **13** trumps **12** (★★★★) with lifted mint & coriander wafts mingling with bright black berries, supple, integrated tannins. Ex Paul Cluver.

★★★★ **Granite Blocks Cabernet Franc** ⓡ Pungent & powerful **12** shows plushy black berries & soft tannins. Satisfying depth of flavour, soft & balanced. No **11**. By cab franc specialists Raats Family.

★★★★ **Winemaster's Reserve Grenache** ⊘ Was 'Nederburg Grenache'. Earthy & rich but with bright mulberry, fynbos & sprinkling of nutmeg, **14** from Nederburg ticks all the drinkability boxes. Dollop carignan for complexity.

★★★★ **Limited Release Malbec** By Bellevue, **13**'s vibrant cherry & plum nuances merge with dried herb & spice in elegant & perfectly poised glassful.

★★★★ **Malbec Reserve** Seductive **13** is silky smooth, packed with choc/blueberry richness. Firm yet gentle frame from 14 months in 60% new oak. By Diemersfontein.

Red Blends

★★★★ **Cabernet Sauvignon-Merlot Reserve** Delicious Neil Ellis **13** from Stellenbosch with some cab franc too, as usual. Succulent, dry & well balanced; firm structure. Accessible, but will keep.

★★★★☆ **Cobblers Hill** Big-bodied, dense & assertive Bordeaux-style blend from Jordan, **12** perfect balance of ripeness, fruit intensity & subtle spicing, with toned-down tannins, muscular litheness & resonating, harmonious finish.

★★★★ **Organic Ladybird Red** ⓝ ♡ Mostly merlot & cab, with cab franc, petit verdot & malbec. **13** from Laibach lively, supple & structured, both ripe & savoury. Cellaring potential. Also in magnum.

★★★★ **Vinehugger Cabernet Sauvignon-Merlot** ⓝ ⊘ ♡ Richly flavoursome 50/50 blend. **14** is dense but unheavy, softly rounded but not without form or freshness. Properly dry, the conclusion is long & savoury. A bargain not to be missed! From Reyneke Wines.

★★★★ **Warwick Cape Lady** Sugared plum & candyfloss, sweet vanilla oak on **13** (★★★☆) blend shiraz (60%), pinotage & cab from Warwick. Lively dinner companion now & for few years. Shade less hedonistic than **11**. No **12**.

★★★★ **Shiraz-Grenache-Mourvèdre** ⊘ Made by Ken Forrester, shiraz-led **12** with 38% grenache & 22% mourvèdre has black pepper, clove, leather & tar adding intrigue to intense red & black berry fruit.

> **Grand Rouge** ♡ ★★★ **14** strikes right chord of approachability with sound structure; focus on rich, juicy flavours of **14**'s cab-led Bordeaux blend. By La Motte.

Danie de Wet Merlot-Cabernet Sauvignon ⓝ ★★★★ Sweet fruitcake & spice flavours on **14**, slightly dusty robust tannins with dark chocolate on the finish. By De Wetshof. **Reserve Collection Merlot-Malbec** ⓝ ★★★★ Modern, juicy **14** red blend showing the lush fruit-forward seamlessness of these varieties (22% malbec). By Diemersdal. **Alchemy Syrah-Cabernet Sauvignon** ⓝ ★★★☆ Instantly engaging squishy black fruit appeal to **13**. Light easy-drinker with bright plum & pepper notes. From Hartenberg. **DMZ Concerto Red** ⓝ ★★★★ From DeMorgenzon. Overtly spicy, appealingly sleek **13** shiraz, mourvèdre, grenache blend flaunts dark wild berry fruit. **Cabernet Sauvignon-Shiraz** ⓝ ★★★ Peppery nuance to light fruitcake & plum vibrancy of maiden **14**, approachable blend by Diemersfontein. **Platinum Cabernet Sauvignon-Shiraz Reserve** ★★★☆ Gets 'Platinum' prefix this edition. Firm build, rich savoury fruit buffed with 10% new oak, La Motte's **14** provides perfect partner to steak or casseroles. Also tasted: **Cabernet Sauvignon-Merlot 13** ★★★★ **Longmarket Cabernet Sauvignon-Merlot 14** ★★ **Longmarket Shiraz-Pinotage 14** ★★★ **His** ⓝ NV ★★ **Juicy Red** ⊘ NV ★★★ **The Portuguese Connection** ⊘ **14** ★★★★ **Natural Sweet Red 15** ★ Not retasted: **Longmarket Syrah-Mourvèdre-Viognier 13** ★★★★ Discontinued: **Bel Rosso**.

Rosé Wines

Chardonnay-Pinot Noir ⓝ ★★★★ Haute Cabrière first in SA with this trending style; latest **15** has character if not sweetness of pears & litchi, red berry hints & rich, rounded mouthfeel contributing to food versatility. **Light Rosé** ⓝ ★★★ By Villiera, **15** dry & zesty, delivers loads of flavour at just 9% alcohol. Mainly pinot noir with gamay. **Longmarket Pinotage Rosé** ⓝ ★★ Softly dry **15**, light & fruity; slightly chill for extra enjoyment. From Villiera. **Organic Ladybird Rosé** ⓝ ♡ ★★★ **15** from Laibach is savoury & piquant with cab, merlot & cab franc in the mix. Lightish (12.5% alcohol) yet feisty, dry & smooth, perfect for picnics or sundowners. **Pinot Noir Rosé** ⓝ ★★★ Lightish **15** from Villiera perfumed with cherry & cinnamon spice; zesty acidity, dry tail for seafood or creamy dishes. **Tranquille Blush** ⓝ ★★★★ Copper-tinged pinot noir & chardonnay **NV** has a mere 11.5% alcohol; refreshing, tangy & mouth-tingling as red berries combine with peach & citrus. By Haute Cabrière. Also tasted: **Her** ⓝ NV ★★ **Pinotage-Shiraz Rosé 15**

★★★ **Simonsig Chenin Blanc-Pinotage 15** ★★★ **Cape Rosé NV** ★☆ **Natural Sweet Rosé 15** ★★ Discontinued: **Light Pinot Noir Rosé**, **Longmarket Rosé**.

Chardonnay range

★★★★☆ **Barrel Fermented Elgin Chardonnay** (NEW) **14** from Neil Ellis, with this showing a touch more oak than the estate's own version — but well integrated, & a little tighter & more intense. Ripe fruit (pear, citrus) charm deliciously complements firm, racy succulence.

★★★★ **Danie de Wet Chardonnay** Was 'Chardonnay Reserve'. Blooms in glass to reveal well-knit & poised **14**, citrus curd & white flower flavours, delicate oak spicing & extended lees-contact. Shows De Wetshof's mastery of variety.

★★★★ **Single Vineyard Block 2A Chardonnay** Lime, baked apple & oak spice on rich & mouthfilling **14** from a Paul Cluver single-vineyard. Generous texture streamlined by clean citrus-toned acidity. Good weight for food pairing.

★★★★ **Danie de Wet Limestone Hill Chardonnay** Was 'De Wetshof Unwooded Chardonnay', still made by that producer. Improving on **13** (★★★☆), unwooded **15** is rounded & shows clean lime zest aromas, citrus curd flavours, elegant minerality & a long moreish goodbye. No **14**.

★★★★ **Reserve Collection** Was 'Exclusive Selection'. Indistinguishable from Jordan's own brand, unoaked **14** (★★★☆) has lees richness, bright citrus fruit, extended finish. Shade lighter than **13**.

★★★★ **Wild Yeast Chardonnay** (NEW) Naturally crafted, unwooded **13** from Springfield reveals a gentle, ripe tropical-toned persona; balanced, creamy & contemplative at a demure 13.3% alcohol.

> **Vinehugger Chardonnay** (NEW) (symbol) (symbol) ★★★☆ Attractive citrus, creamy features on **14** gain extra bounce, flesh from 30% old-oaked portion. Satisfying, if not overly complex. By Reyneke.

Private Collection Chardonnay (NEW) ★★★☆ Citrus, nut & vanilla jostle in open-faced **14** from Spier. Barrelled, 40% new for one year; just-dry. Also tasted: **Longmarket Chardonnay 15** ★★★ **The Ladybird Chardonnay** (symbol) **14** ★★★☆ **Light Chardonnay 15** ★☆ **Vanilla Chardonnay 14** ★★★ Not retasted: **Organic Feeding Duck Chardonnay 14** ★★★ **House Chardonnay 14** ★★★

Chenin Blanc range

★★★★ **Chenin Blanc Reserve** Made by 'Chenin King' Ken Forrester, as was **13** (★★★★), improved **14** has a creamy texture with leesy sourdough hints & turmeric on the finish, framing core of tangy apricot & zesty lime fruit.

★★★★ **Granite Blocks Chenin Blanc** Subtle & delicate unwooded **14** improves on fragrant **13** (★★★★) with greater concentration on the palate, a peacock tail flourish. Similar green honey melon & lemongrass. By Raats Family.

★★★★ **Simonsig Chenin Blanc Unwooded** (symbol) Was 'Exclusive Collection Chenin Blanc Sur Lie'. Classy unwooded **14** celebrates tropical fruit, with lovely citrus zestiness making it spark with life. Lees-ageing, dab of sugar give satisfying palate weight.

Private Collection Chenin Blanc ★★★☆ Was just 'Private Collection'. A glossy show stealer! Spier's **14** is big & bold, with nutty tropical fruit flavours, oodles of oak & flattering touch of sweetness. Will find many fans. **Longmarket Chenin Blanc** (symbol) ★★★ Tropical unwooded **15** from Ken Forrester has intense guava, pear & tangy pineapple fruit, zesty acidity to offset sweetness, very refreshing. **Peachy Chenin Blanc** (NEW) ★★★ Full frontal apricot — oh, & peach — profile to off-dry **15** from Spier. Also tasted: **House Chenin Blanc** (symbol) **15** ★★★ **Light Chenin Blanc 15** ★☆ Not tasted: **Noble Late Harvest Chenin Blanc**. Discontinued: **Chenin Blanc**.

Sauvignon Blanc range

★★★★☆ **Shannon Sauvignon Blanc** (NEW) Water-white **14** has intense grass & citrus notes, form-giving acidity, long conclusion plus breadth & toasty elements from portion barrel fermented semillon (11%). Lovely now but structured to improve ±5 years in bottle.

★★★★ **DD Sauvignon Blanc** (NEW) Vibrant, balanced & fresh **15** shows typical Durbanville capsicum & nettle along with attractive appley peach notes; appetising finish. By Diemersdal, in magnum.

★★★★ Durbanville Sauvignon Blanc ⊘ Sound sense of place, showing typical Durbanville capsicum & nettle along with attractive fresh apple & peach notes on **15**, vibrant, balanced & fresh. Step up on maiden **14** (★★★★), also from Diemersdal.

★★★★☆ Elgin Sauvignon Blanc (NEW) ⊘ Impressive floral & citric complexity on **15** from Neil Ellis. Harmonious, with fine presence, fresh but gentle in effect – though not without power. Lingering grapefruit finish.

★★★★ Exclusive Selection Nitida Sauvignon Blanc As previously, **15** has 7% semillon for silky texture, with high proportion of Darling sauvignon 'sweetening' perception of peach & naartjie fruit despite being completely dry.

★★★★ Exclusive Selection Sauvignon Blanc Big-boned, wildly aromatic **14** from Cape Point Vineyards is exuberant & enticing; racy yet balanced, with fine focus. Cape Peninsula vines.

★★★★ Sauvignon Blanc (NEW) Dash semillon adds gravitas, breadth to cool, South Cape Coast-sourced **14**. Though quietly persuasive, the tangerine & honey flavours are led by creamy, viscous structure & lengthened by an urgent zesty tang. Great food style from La Motte.

Vinehugger Sauvignon Blanc (NEW) ⊘ ★★★ From Reyneke Wines, fresh, gently lively **14** with pure yet unshowy varietal figgy fruit. Dry, with digestible 12.5% alcohol. Also tasted: **White Rock 15** ★★★★ **Light Sauvignon Blanc 15** ★★ **Longmarket Sauvignon Blanc 15** ★★ **Organic Swooping Swallow Sauvignon Blanc** ⊘ **15** ★★★ Not retasted: **House Sauvignon Blanc 13** ★★★ Not tasted: **Single Vineyard Windy Peak**.

Niche White Cultivars

★★★★ Ferricrete Gewürztraminer ⊘ Was 'Exclusive Selection Gewürztraminer'. Intense & perfumed **14** (★★★★★) from Paul Cluver. Delicate intensity effortlessly achieved on semi-dry palate, with delightful interplay between rose & litchi flavours & zingy fresh balancing acidity. Improves on **13**.

★★★★ Ferricrete Riesling ⊘ Grown on ferricrete soils by Paul Cluver, **13** is clean & creamy, with perfumed lime & kiwi. Tangy fruit & acid (masking 19 grams sugar), appealing low 10.6% alcohol, but shade off the thrilling tension & intensity of **12** (★★★★★).

Exclusive Selection Viognier ★★★★ Ken Forrester's barrel-fermented **13** has reined-in floral perfume, ripe peach & apricot flavours enlivened by crisp acidity, with savoury oak spice to finish. Also tasted: **Longmarket Pinot Grigio 15** ★★☆ **Moscato Light 15** ★★★

White Blends

★★★★☆ DMZ Concerto White Was 'DMZ White'. Textured viognier/roussanne-led 5-way **14** (★★★★) blend not quite as impressive as last-tasted **12** but still over-delivers, with full-flavoured yellow peaches & spice. From DeMorgenzon.

★★★★ Nitida Cellars Sauvignon Blanc-Semillon Reserve Graceful **15** Bordeaux-style white has delicious roundedness from 29% semillon, toning down fresh acidity of sauvignon with herbaceous as well as tropical gooseberry notes.

Longmarket Chardonnay-Viognier ★★★ Uncluttered everyday enjoyment from Spier. Brush of oak gives some sophistication to **14**, with upbeat cling peach aftertaste. **Longmarket Sauvignon Blanc-Semillon** ★★★ Grassy **15**'s slight sweet impression nicely balanced by brisk acidity. Unwooded blend by Spier. **Natural White** ★★★ By Villiera, unusual blend riesling & chardonnay, naturally fermented. Citrus blossom **15** dry, light & lively; perfect foil for salmon salads, sushi. Also tasted: **Cape White NV** ★★ **Longmarket Sauvignon Blanc-Chenin Blanc 15** ★★★ **Zesty White NV** ★★ **Bianca Light 15** ★★ **Natural Sweet White 15** ★★ Not retasted: **Cape Sweet Wine NV** ★★ Discontinued: **NSA Organic Fluttering Butterfly White**.

Méthode Cap Classique Sparkling range

★★★★ Exclusive Selection Pinot Noir Rosé NSA No sulphur added pale blush MCC from Simonsig; strawberry-scented **14** has delicacy, finesse, is finely drawn. Bone-dry, its silky structure carries the fruit & gentle minerality to a satisfying conclusion.

★★★★ Brut ⊘ Adds pinot meunier to usual mix chardonnay, pinot noir & pinotage. Fine dry bubbles, some creaminess to the texture, lively citrus aromas & fresh acidity. **NV** by Villiera. Also in 375ml & 1.5L.

★★★★ **Brut Natural** From chardonnay, extra-dry & aperitif-styled **NV** from Villiera has engaging brioche & lemon peel notes, refined balance with refreshing & persistent mousse, complexity from over 3 years on lees. No dosage or added sulphur.

★★★★☆ **Vintage Reserve Brut** ⓃⒺⓌ Impressive & delicious **09** from bubbly exponents par excellence, Villiera. Includes older-barrel-fermented chardonnay portion, plus pinot noir & pinot meunier for fruitiness, palate weight. Plush yet focused, with toasted almond, brioche dimension from 5 years on lees.

Also tasted: **Ladybird Brut Méthode Cap Classique** ⓥ **13** ★★★ **Brut Rosé** ⓥ **NV** ★★★☆

Sparkling Wines

Organic Sauvignon Blanc Brut ⓥ ★★★ Latest **NV** clean & dry sparkling with some sophistication in its tiny bubbles, biscuity notes & some ripe pear on palate. By Rooiberg. **Spumante Doux** ★★☆ Honey & peaches in a happy, frothy **NV** party bubbly. Easy & unpretentious fun from Rooiberg. Also tasted: **Spumante Rosé NV** ★★ **Spumante Brut NV** ★★

1L Box range

Dry Red ★ Despite name, sweetish, fruity **NV** quaffer. By Simonsvlei, as all these. **Sweet White** ⓃⒺⓌ ★ Plain **NV** sweet with few rough edges. Mostly chenin. **Sweet Red** ⓃⒺⓌ ★ Fresh but straightforward & very sweet **NV**. Drink chilled. Also tasted: **Natural Sweet Rosé NV** ★★ **Crisp White NV** ★★ **Light White NV** ★ Discontinued: **Semi-Sweet**.

2L Box range

Longmarket Cabernet Sauvignon-Merlot ★★★ Happy 60/40 marriage **14** has vibrant red & black berries, friendly tannins. Ready for just about anything. Ex Simonsvlei. Also tasted: **Longmarket Merlot 14** ★★ **Longmarket Chardonnay 15** ★★★ **Longmarket Sauvignon Blanc 15** ★★☆

3L Box range

Light Red ★★ Sound red-berry flavours on dryish **NV**. Low 9% alcohol. From Simonsvlei, as are all. **Natural Sweet Rosé** ⓃⒺⓌ ★★ Juicy sweet strawberries on fresh **NV**. Just 8% alcohol. Also tasted: **Dry Red NV** ★ **Crisp White NV** ★★ **Light White NV** ★ Discontinued: **Light Rosé**.

5L Box range

Dry Red ★ Plain **NV**, roughish edge smoothed by few grams sugar. By Simonsvlei, as all these. **Sweet White** ⓃⒺⓌ ★★ **NV** offers balanced fruity sweetness, zesty tail. Also tasted: **Crisp White NV** ★★ Discontinued: **Semi Sweet**. — Various tasters

WO: Various ▪ Selector Allan Mullins T +27 (0)21-407-2777 AllanMullins@woolworths.co.za ▪ Buying manager Ivan Oertle T +27 (0)21-407-2762 IvanOertle@woolworths.co.za ▪ Wine product developer Rebecca Constable T +27 (0)21-407-3162 RebeccaConstable@woolworths.co.za ▪ Owner(s) Woolworths Holdings ▪ Woolworths House 93 Longmarket Street Cape Town 8000 ▪ www.woolworths.co.za ▪ F +27 (0)21-407-3958 ▪ **T +27 (0)21-407-9111**

☐ **Workhorse (Marks & Spencer)** *see* Ken Forrester Wines
☐ **Xaro** *see* Stellenrust
☐ **Xenna** *see* Annex Kloof Wines
☐ **Y** *see* Yonder Hill

Yardstick Wines   ⓛ

Winemaker Adam Mason focuses on identifying unique, characterful sites of SA's 'varietal heroes', including chenin blanc, cinsaut and syrah/shiraz, and styling them specifically to be food compatible. Vinification, kept as traditional as possible, saw the introduction of concrete fermentation tanks in 2015. 'Back to the future!' beams Adam. His partner-in-wine, appropriately, is a chef – Peter Tempelhoff from The McGrath Collection; no surprise a Marvelous Burger filled with Wagyu beef is now on the menu.

Yardstick range

★★★★ **Pinot Noir** A pinot of great delicacy & freshness, pure fruit being the focus. **14** perfectly achieves this balancing act: gorgeous floral notes, cherries with spice accessory balanced by fine tannin from older oak.

★★★★ **Chardonnay** Unshowy yet expressive, **14** has similar citrus energy & silky breadth as **13**. Ferment/aged in older oak to gain maximum benefit of time sur lie without diminishing fruit purity, freshness.

Marvelous range

★★★★ **Blue** **13** Bordeaux-style quintet, cab franc's dainty leafy spice in lead, adding lift, distinction to overall supple, creamy feel. Seamless partnership, seasoned in older oak only. Cab-based **14** also tasted; some minty austerity needs time to settle.

★★★★ **Yellow** Delicious creamy breadth, firm texture & concentration on chenin-led **14**. More vinous & savoury than fruity, just concluding spicy tang from muscat d'Alexandrie/viognier components. Older oak.

Also tasted: **Red 14** ★★★★ — AL

Location/map: Stellenbosch ▪ Map grid reference: C6 ▪ WO: Western Cape ▪ Est/1stB 2009 ▪ Tasting by appt ▪ Owner(s) Peter Tempelhoff, Charles Banks & Adam Mason ▪ Winemaker(s) Adam Mason ▪ Yardstick 3,400cs & Marvelous 8,000cs ▪ 70% red 30% white ▪ adam@marvelouswines.com, peter@marvelouswines.com ▪ www.yardstickwines.com, www.marvelouswines.com ▪ S 33° 53' 22.8" E 018° 49' 8.3" ▪ F +27 (0)21-881-3372 ▪ **T +27 (0)82-924-3286 (Adam)/+27 (0)82-578-5320 (Peter)**

Yonder Hill   (Ⓨ) (◎) (⅙)

Well- and widely seasoned Abé Beukes has added viticulturist to his cellarmaster and winemaker roles at the Naudé family estate in the Helderberg foothills. He oversees a mostly red-wine range focused on Bordeaux varieties, from a combination of own young blocks and selected parcels further afield (the Y-range wines tasted this edition are partly from Abé's most recent residency, Darling Cellars).

Premium range

★★★★ **Merlot** (Ⓨ) Chunky, solid **12** has herbal notes with sweet berry fruit. Grippy, dry tannins, partly from oaking with a generous new component, needed time to settle mid-2014.

★★★★ **Nicola** (Ⓨ) Cab-led Bordeaux blend in blockbuster style, **10** intense fruit & all-new oak to match. Well balanced, apart from the oak, & should develop well – needs 5+ years to show its best.

Also tasted: **Inanda 13** ★★★★

Y range

Merlot ★★★ Soft Christmas cake flavours with smooth balanced tannins, **14** is an irresistible easy-drinker. WO W Cape, as all these. **Sauvignon Blanc** (⊘) ★★★★ Floral & crisp **15** ups the appeal with good balance & depth of flavour. Long lemon zest finish. Not retasted: **Shiraz 13** ★★★ — WB

Location: Stellenbosch ▪ Map: Helderberg ▪ WO: Stellenbosch/Western Cape ▪ Est 1989 ▪ 1stB 1993 ▪ Tasting & sales Mon-Fri 9—4 Sat (Nov-Feb) 10-4 ▪ Closed all pub hols ▪ Tour groups ▪ Gift shop ▪ Olives & olive oil tasting ▪ Owner(s) Naudé family ▪ Cellarmaster(s)/winemaker(s) Abé Beukes (2014) ▪ Viticulturist(s) Abé Beukes ▪ 14ha/6ha (cabs s/f, merlot, p verdot) ▪ 50t/15,000cs own label 95% red 5% white ▪ PO Box 914 Stellenbosch 7599 ▪ wines@yonderhill.co.za ▪ www.yonderhill.co.za ▪ S 34° 2' 22.5" E 018° 49' 40.2" ▪ F +27 (0)21-855-1006 ▪ **T +27 (0)21-855-1008**

☐ **You Raise Me Up** see La Chaumiere Estate
☐ **Zahir** see Lateganskop Winery
☐ **Zalze** see Kleine Zalze Wines

Zanddrift Vineyards – Chapel Cellar   (Ⓨ) (♈) (◎) (Ⓐ)

Owned by retired Singapore architect Koh Seow Chuan, Zanddrift boutique winery's mostly exported Chapel Cellar range – Cabernet Sauvignon, Shiraz, Myrna (cab-shiraz), semi-sweet Rosé and Lost (unwooded sauvignon, chenin and chardonnay) – is named for the chapel-like visitor locale, newly upgraded to cater for all members of the family.

Location: Paarl ▪ Map: Paarl & Wellington ▪ Map grid reference: E6 ▪ Est 1995 ▪ Tasting & sales Mon-Fri 9-5 ▪ Restaurant & function venue T +27 (0)60-802-2933 (Hennie) ▪ Kids play area with jungle gym ▪ Special menu for kids ▪ Small weddings (70-80 pax) ▪ Private functions ▪ Live entertainment ▪ Owner(s) Windsharp Trading 23, Koh Seow Chuan (Singapore) ▪ Winemaker(s)/viticulturist(s) Christo Jacobs ▪

8.5ha (cab, shiraz) ▪ PO Box 1302 Suider-Paarl 7624 ▪ zanddrift@telkomsa.net ▪ S 33° 45' 39.20" E 018° 59' 11.41" ▪ F +27 (0)86-530-1892 ▪ **T +27 (0)21-863-2076/+27 (0)82-256-5006**

Zandvliet Wine Estate   Ⓠ Ⓖ

De Wet family ownership came to an end last year when 4th-generation siblings Paul and Dan sold this venerable Robertson estate. Continuity is assured, however, in winemaker Jacques Cilliers, in his 5th vintage, now with added responsibility of general manager. He and the new owners have hit the ground running: already there is restructuring of the ranges, new barrels have arrived and additional plantings of chardonnay and shiraz are on track. A large property, 148 hectares under vines, with a particular focus on shiraz plus widespread exports, the new energy is expressed in Jacques' words: 'Zandvliet's back!'

Hill of Enon range

★★★★ **Small Berry Pick Shiraz** Like its sibling, 100% new oak, here American for 30 months, gives **12** heaps of spice, perfectly matched to dark plum, Morello cherry flavours. Smoothly curvaceous, drinking beautifully, & with a future ahead.

★★★★ **Terroir Chardonnay** Was 'Kalkveld Chardonnay'. 100% new French barrels fermented/aged, giving oatmeal & raw almonds, earthiness, a citrus core. Not showing its age, **11** has elegance, sophisticated restraint.

Kalkveld range

Shiraz Ⓠ ★★★★☆ **09** vintage ripeness shows in plum & black cherry perfume, flavours, given an appealing cigarbox tone by well-judged oaking. A food-friendly savoury ending, with touch of scrub adding interest.

Zandvliet Estate range

Shiraz ★★★ Ticks the shiraz boxes without going over the top, appealing **13** has dark fruit & cocoa, some smokiness, is juicy & streamlined. Available in various bottle sizes – 375 ml to 18L. **Chardonnay** ★★★ Sympathetic oaking allows the melon & nectarine fruit flavours to shine, **14** has pleasing elegance, fresh length. Not retasted: **VLW Cape Vintage Shiraz 12** ★★★★☆

My Best Friend range

Cape Red ★★ Cab with 10% shiraz, unwooded & just off-dry, **13** is about drinkability, enjoying the smooth plummy flavours with friends. **Cape Muscat** ★★★ Natural Sweet, canned pineapple & litchi perfume leaping out the glass, **15** from muscat d'Frontignan is a sweet delight. Packed with flavour yet alcohol is friendly, only 7.5%. Not retasted: **Cape White 14** ★★ Discontinued: **Shiraz Rosé**, **Sauvignon Blanc**.

Discontinued: **Le Bistro range**. — CR

Location: Ashton ▪ Map/WO: Robertson ▪ Est 1867 ▪ 1stB 1975 ▪ Tasting & sales Mon-Fri 9—5 Sat 10-2 ▪ Closed Easter Fri/Sun, Dec 25/26 & Jan 1 ▪ Tour groups ▪ Private tastings by appt ▪ Winemaker(s) / GM Jacques Cilliers (Dec 2011) ▪ PO Box 36 Ashton 6715 ▪ info@zandvliet.co.za ▪ www.zandvliet.co.za ▪ S 33° 50' 50.7" E 020° 2' 13.7" ▪ F +27 (0)23-615-1327 ▪ **T +27 (0)23-615-1146**

☐ **Zandwijk** see Kleine Draken
☐ **Zantsi** see Darling Cellars
☐ **Zaràfa** see Mountain River Wines
☐ **Z-Collection** see Zevenwacht
☐ **Zebra Collection** see Rooiberg Winery
☐ **Zellerhof** see Huguenot Wine Farmers
☐ **Zenith** see Kumala

Zevenwacht   Ⓠ Ⓨ Ⓐ Ⓞ Ⓐ Ⓖ

One would think that having built up a highly regarded wine brand and a multifaceted tourist mecca over two decades would entitle this family-run Stellenbosch estate to rest on its laurels. The Johnsons and their winegrowing team's work ethic, however, is as unstinting and dedicated as ever. The focus is on precision viticulture, with a full assessment of each vineyard throughout the year. To ensure that the fruits of these labours are optimised in the cellar, there has been a major gearing up in mechanisation, from harvesting machines to selective sorting tables. The quality is already evident in their classy Bordeaux red blend and 360° Sauvignon Blanc.

Flagship range

★★★★ **Syrah** Savoury **12** is well composed but tightly knit, its pliable but firm fruit & oak tannins (16 months 20% new) just need time's smoothing hand. Rung above **11** (★★★★).

★★★★ **Chardonnay** Zesty & bright **14** shows great fruit purity; well-judged oak creates a rich, nutty platform for lime, pear flavours; balanced & elegant step up on **13** (★★★).

★★★★ **Sauvignon Blanc** Both **14** (★★★★) & **15** tasted. **14**, with 4% semillon, riper & softer with more tropical tones, mouthfilling succulence courtesy lees-ageing; **15** fresher & livelier, more herbaceous verve (& more semillon) to the fruit profile. Long, food-friendly farewell. Also in 375 ml.

Also tasted: **Merlot 12** ★★★ **Chenin Blanc 14** ★★★ Not retasted: **Cabernet Sauvignon 12** ★★★★

Z-Collection

★★★★ **Reserve** Classically styled Bordeaux blend merlot, petit verdot, malbec, cab franc (59/27/5/5/4) in **12** (★★★★★). Lovely fruit intensity, seamless structure with fine-grained tannins; so balanced & elegant, it's already tempting but will handsomely reward ageing. No **11**. **10** was 'CMC'.

★★★★ **SG Rhône Style** Ⓥ Seamless mix of shiraz & grenache (60/40) ex 4 blocks. **11** appealing layers of dark & spicy flavour in a balanced oak framework, easily carries 14.5% alcohol. Ageworthy.

★★★★ **Gewürztraminer** From 28 year old gnarled vines, unusual & characterful barrel-fermented dry **14**; charming rosepetal, litchi & Turkish delight nuances, tad more subdued than **13** (★★★★★) by rich texture from lees-ageing in oak, yet still fresh.

★★★★★ **360° Sauvignon Blanc** From elevated sea-facing vineyards. 15% semillon & partial oak fermentation add appealing palate weight, richness, to fig & lime flavours. **14** zesty & fresh step up on **13** (★★★★) with good intensity & length.

Not tasted: **Grenache**. Discontinued: **CMC**.

Tin Mine Collection

★★★★ **Red** Ⓥ Smooth, generous & approachable **13**, shiraz, grenache & mourvèdre (46/39/15) ample savoury & smoky berry fruit in supple oak frame. Sufficient structure to age a few years. Also in 1.5L.

Also tasted: **White 14** ★★★★

7even range

Rosé ★★★ Tangy, crisp & dry **15** with plenty of light berry, savoury appeal from cab. Popular (production doubled!) al fresco sipper. **Bouquet** ★★★ Aromatic, spicy-food partner from muscat de Fontignan, viognier & gewürztraminer. Latter's perfumed presence takes centre stage in **14**, semi-dry but fresh, lively, smooth. Also tasted: **Pinotage 14** ★★ **Rood 13** ★★★ **Sauvignon Blanc 15** ★★★ — MW

Location: Kuils River ▪ Map/WO: Stellenbosch ▪ Map grid reference: B5 ▪ Est 1980 ▪ 1stB 1983 ▪ Tasting & sales Mon-Fri 8.30–5 Sat/Sun 9.30–5 ▪ Fee R35 incl glass ▪ Closed Dec 25 ▪ Cellar tours by appt ▪ Restaurant ▪ Picnics in summer ▪ Facilities for children ▪ Gift shop ▪ Conferences ▪ Weddings/banqueting ▪ Walking & MTB trails ▪ 4x4 trail by appt ▪ Conservation area ▪ Mangwanani spa ▪ 4-star country inn ▪ Owner(s) Harold Johnson ▪ Winemaker(s) Jacques Viljoen (May 2005), with Charles Lourens (Jun 2014) ▪ Viticulturist(s) Eduard van den Berg (Jan 2001) ▪ 473ha/100ha (cabs s/f, grenache, merlot, mourv, ptage, primitivo, shiraz, chard, chenin, gewürz, muscat de F, rouss, sauv, sem, viog) ▪ 657t/100,000cs own label 48% red 48% white 4% rosé ▪ BWI, IPW ▪ PO Box 387 Kuils River 7579 ▪ info@ zevenwacht.co.za ▪ www.zevenwacht.co.za ▪ S 33° 55' 46.0" E 018° 43' 38.2" ▪ F +27 (0)21-903-3373 ▪ T +27 (0)21-900-5700

Zidela Wines

Stellenbosch family negociant Zidela, its owners well versed in wine buying, production and marketing, provides bulk and bottled wine for buyers' own brands and the proprietary brands below, to Europe, the US, China and Russia, among others. Some labels also available locally.

Mooiberg range

Cabernet Sauvignon Ⓥ ★★★ **13** with walnut & olive notes. Mild fruitiness held in firm tannic & acid grip. Not retasted: **Sauvignon Blanc 14** ★★★

New World Collection

Pinotage ⓥ ★★ Berried aromas on **13** lead quickly, via a slightly severe palate, to a tart, red-fruited conclusion. Unwooded, as for all ranges. Not retasted: **Sauvignon Blanc 14 ★★**

Suikerbosch range

Shiraz-Merlot ⓥ ★★ Some smooth roundness on **13**, but still with grippy & tart finish. As frequently in all these ranges, a few grams of sugar aims to add a little richness. Not retasted: **Cabernet Sauvignon 14 ★★☆ Merlot 13 ★★ Rosé 14 ★★ Chardonnay 14 ★★ Chenin Blanc 14 ★★ Golden Muscat 14 ★**

Sumerton range

Sauvignon Blanc ⓥ ★★ Pleasant tropical notes on **14**, with short, sweetish finish. Not retasted: **Cabernet Sauvignon-Pinotage 13 ★★**

Zidela range

Rosé ⓥ ★★ Unassuming red-berry fragrance on lowish-alcohol, off-dry **14**. Not retasted: **Chenin Blanc 14 ★★☆** Not tasted: **Cabernet Sauvignon, Merlot, Pinotage, Shiraz, Bouquet Blanc, Sauvignon Blanc**. — TJ

Location: Stellenbosch = WO: Western Cape = Est 2001 = 1stB 2002 = Closed to public = Owner(s) Danie Kritzinger, Herman Nell, Jaco Kritzinger & Erik Kritzinger = 60% red 30% white 10% rosé = 11 million litres for clients = PO Box 3021 Matieland 7602 = info@zidelawines.co.za = www.zidelawines.co.za, www.privatewinelabel.co.za = F +27 (0)21-880-2937 = **T +27 (0)21-880-2936**

Zonnebloem

This enduring Distell brand draws from a long-standing network of grape growers for its Limited Editions and core Zonnebloem ranges, some 3rd- and 4th-generation suppliers. Even the more recent Fairtrade wines, Place in the Sun (listed separately), are sourced from longtime partners. Youth and experience combine from vintage 2016 with Elize Coetzee as new chief of the venerable Adam Tas cellar in Stellenbosch and Bennie Liebenberg (ex Fleur du Cap) overseeing the vineyards.

Limited Editions

★★★★ **Pinotage** ⓥ Very lovely **10** is a welcome return after absence. Perfumed nose, moist plumcake flavours, chewy pliable tannins. Plenty of elegance & polish. All-new oak.

★★★★ **Shiraz** Sleek **12** beguiles with pepper & macerated fruit, leather & spice courtesy new French/American oak. Flavourful & fresh, also grippy with attractive green walnut lift; a good food wine.

★★★★ **Sauvignon Blanc** ⓥ Waxy lemons & herbal honey notes on **13**. Showing some age but great fruit intensity & good levels of acidity ensuring pleasant drinking for a further few years. Coastal WO.

★★★★ **Semillon** ⓥ Pungent pine needles, peppers & limes on the nose of elegant, unwooded **13**. From a Malmesbury single vineyard, racy citrus acidity is balanced by creamy intensity. Good potential.

★★★★ **Sauvignon Blanc-Semillon** ⓥ Delicious drinking on **12**, showing some development mid-2013 but should be more to come as layered, complex finish hints. Coastal WO.

Not retasted: **Cabernet Sauvignon 11 ★★★** Not tasted: **Chenin Blanc**.

Zonnebloem range

★★★★ **Shiraz-Mourvèdre-Viognier** Expressive **13** leaps out the glass with scrub, pepper & black olive notes, dark fruit & Asian spice. Tannins touch rustic but enlivened by fresh acidity, crunchy fruit, new/2nd fill oak well melded. A really good drink. **12** untasted.

★★★★ **Lauréat** Stylish **12** follows successful recipe 5% each shiraz, mourvèdre & petit verdot to add spice, leather & chewy black fruit to cab/merlot blend; polished tannins, sleek finish. For special occasions.

Blanc de Blanc ⓣ ★★★ Effusive & charming chenin & sauvignon, **15** delivers good concentration, flavour, in the form of lime, papaya & ripe apples. Perennial summer favourite. WO W Cape.

Shiraz ★★★☆ Spiced plum & smoky bacon on **13**, well composed & showing restraint; satisfying & unpretentious aperitif or supper wine. **Chardonnay ★★☆** Uncomplicated enjoyment from pleasant fruit medley, subtly supported by oak in **14**. WO Western Cape. Also tasted: **Cabernet Sauvignon 13** ★★★ **Merlot 13** ★★★ **Pinotage 13** ★★★★ **Sauvignon Blanc 15** ★★★★ — JPf

Location: Stellenbosch ▪ WO: Stellenbosch/Coastal/Western Cape ▪ Est 1893 ▪ Wine sales at Die Bergkelder Wine Centre ▪ Owner(s) Distell ▪ Cellarmaster(s) Elize Coetzee (Nov 2015) ▪ Winemaker(s) Bonny van Niekerk (reds, Oct 2007) & John November (whites, Nov 2015), with Bradley van Niekerk, Praisy Dlamini, Michelle Louw & James Ochse ▪ Viticulturist(s) Bennie Lieberberg (Jan 2016) ▪ (cab, merlot, shiraz, chard, sauv, sem) ▪ 9,000t/±440,000cs own label 59% red 41% white ▪ ISO 9002, Fairtrade ▪ PO Box 184 Stellenbosch 7599 ▪ info@zonnebloem.co.za ▪ www.zonnebloem.co.za ▪ F +27 (0)21-886-4879 ▪ **T +27 (0)21-809-7000**

☐ **Zonneweelde** *see* Slanghoek Winery

Zorgvliet Wines   ⓪ ⑪ ⌂ ⓞ Ⓐ Ⓖ

The Van der Merwe family, versed in hospitality (patriarch and mining man Mac's investments include a bushveld lodge), has cannily unearthed the many riches of this prime property in Stellenbosch's mountain-ringed Banhoek Valley. The renovated 17th-century farm buildings, supplemented by new Cape Dutch vernacular constructions (including modern cellar) offer both elegant and rustic venues for weddings, conferences, overnight stays, spa pampering and picnics. The surrounding slopes provide an array of aspects and elevations for a fine selection of wines. New blood taking Zorgvliet forward includes son Stephen and wife Izelle, the flagship red named for their daughter.

Zorgvliet range

★★★★ **Cabernet Sauvignon** Ⓐ All-new French oak makes **10** spicier than velvety soft **09**, more grippy from 18 months ageing too. Vibrant fruitcake appeal to ripe fruit.

★★★★ **Cabernet Franc** Fragrant herbs on delicate **13**, shows a supple structure, sensitive oaking that makes the fruit shine. A cranberry uplift on finish.

★★★★ **Petit Verdot** Inky ruby with perfumed polished leather aromas on **12**. Intense dark cherry fruit gripped by firm tannins. Will reward the patient. Last-tasted **10** (★★★★) for the shorter term.

★★★★ **Richelle** Red flagship is a 4-way Bordeaux blend offering mint, tealeaf & cassis flavour in **12**, with rich plum succulence around lithe tannin core. Balanced & restrained; has a good future. No **11**.

★★★★ **Single Vineyard Sauvignon Blanc 14**, now bottled, oozes sweet tropical granadilla & fig ripeness rather than typical zest, bit too soft for higher rating. **13** was structured & taut.

★★★★ **Simoné** Back-to-form **13** is bright & delicate, semillon still leads sauvignon in flagship wooded white blend. Butterscotch, lemon meringue & soft spice delight on harmonious palate. Follows lighter **12** (★★★★).

Not retasted: **Blanc de Blancs 10** ★★★★ Not tasted: **Natural Sweet Sauvignon Blanc**.

Silver Myn range

> **Argentum** Ⓣ ★★★★ Younger sibling to Richelle Bordeaux red; improved **13** displays spicy plum pudding notes, soft approachable tannins.

Also tasted: **Cabernet Franc Rosé 15** ★★★ **Sauvignon Blanc 15** ★★★ — WB

Location/map: Stellenbosch ▪ Map grid reference: H4 ▪ WO: Banghoek ▪ Est/1stB 2000 ▪ Tasting & sales Mon-Fri 9–5 Sat/Sun 10–5 pub hols 10–4 ▪ Closed Good Fri, Dec 25 & Jan 1 ▪ Fee R30pp, waived on purchase ▪ Cellar tours by appt ▪ Zorgvliet picnic Sep-Apr ▪ Facilities for children ▪ Tour groups ▪ Gifts ▪ Conferences ▪ Walks/hikes ▪ Zorgvliet Country Lodge (17 rooms) ▪ Owner(s) Van der Merwe family ▪ Winemaker(s) Bernard le Roux (Dec 2013), with Ruben Adams ▪ Viticulturist(s) Hannes Jansen van Vuuren ▪ 131ha/46ha (cabs s/f, merlot, p verdot, shiraz, tannat, chard, chenin, sauv, sem, viog) ▪ 300t/30,000cs own label 25% red 45% white 27% rosé 3% MCC + 200t for clients ▪ Other export brand: Enigma by Zorgvliet ▪ PO Box 1595 Stellenbosch 7599 ▪ cellar@zorgvliet.com ▪ www.zorgvlietwines.com ▪ S 33° 54' 41.7" E 018° 56' 32.0" ▪ F +27 (0)21-885-1318 ▪ **T +27 (0)21-885-1399**

This Year's Ratings Summarised

Here we summarise the wines featured in the A–Z section, with their ratings, sorted first by wine style, in alphabetical order, and then by producer or brand. New wines in **bolder type**. **NS** = no star; **NT** = not tasted; **NR** = tasted but not rated; **D** = discontinued. Where wineries produce more than one version of a particular style, the number of versions is indicated in brackets after the name. A number of wines were tasted as pre-bottling barrel or tank samples, and therefore ratings are provisional. Refer to the A-Z for details.

Barbarossa

★★★★☆ AA Badenhorst

Barbera

★★★★ Fairview, Merwida

★★★☆ Altydgedacht, Hofstraat, Idiom

Biodynamic

★★★★★ Reyneke (Shiraz/syrah)

★★★★☆ Reyneke (3) (Shiraz/syrah, Chenin blanc wooded, dry, Sauvignon blanc wooded)

★★★★ Reyneke (3) (Pinotage, Red blends, Cape Bordeaux, Sauvignon blanc wooded)

Blanc de noir

★★★★ Aaldering, Mellasat, Olifantsberg

★★★☆ Blaauwklippen, Meinert, Springfontein

★★★ Boschendal, Buitenverwachting, Eaglevlei, Groot Constantia, Lemberg, Lovane, Lynx, Nieuwedrift, Peter Falke ★★★ Altydgedacht, Deux Frères, Swartland ★★ Asara, Flagstone, Landskroon (2), **Star Hill**, Van Loveren ★☆ Ameera ★ Van Loveren **NT** Arra, Boucheron, **Brenaissance**, De Redley, **Esona**, Lovane, Maison, Montpellier, Tanagra **D** Aan de Doorns, Signal Hill

Brandy

★★★★★ Boplaas, KWV Brandies (5), Oude Meester, Van Ryn (4)

★★★★☆ Blaauwklippen, Boplaas (2), Elsenburg, Klipdrift , KWV Brandies, Oude Meester (2), Oude Molen, Van Ryn

★★★★ Avontuur, Backsberg (3), Barrydale, Blaauwklippen, Boplaas, Flight of the Fish Eagle, Gentleman Spirits (2), **Kaapzicht**, **Kingna Distillery**, KWV Brandies (2), Mimosa, Mons Ruber, Napier, Oude Molen (2), Richelieu, **Robertson**, Tokara, Uitkyk, Upland (2) (Organic), **Windfall**, Withington

★★★☆ Barrydale (2), **Bezalel**, Collisons, Die Mas, Grundheim, Klipdrift (2), KWV Brandies, Oude Meester, Oude Molen, Viceroy ★★★ Bezalel, Chateau, Die Mas, Grundheim (2), Kingna Distillery, Limosin, Louiesenhof (2), Olof Bergh, Richelieu, Robertson, Van Loveren ★★★ D'Aria, Grundheim, Mons Ruber, **Robertson NT Anthonij Rupert**,

Aufwaerts, Huguenot (2), Mimosa, Mooiuitsig (2), **Wellington VO**, **Wonderfontein** (2) **D** Boplaas, Kaapzicht, Nederburg

Bukettraube

★★★☆ Cederberg ★★★ Swartland ★★ Darling Cellars ★★ Seven Sisters

Cabernet franc

★★★★★ Cape Chamonix

★★★★☆ De Trafford, Hannay, Hermanuspietersfontein, Holden Manz, Lynx, **Mitre's Edge**, Môreson, Nelson, Raats, Rainbow's End, Raka, Stellenrust, **Uva Mira**, Warwick

★★★★ Camberley, CK Wines, Doolhof, **Edgebaston**, **Glen Carlou**, Hillcrest, Knorhoek, Mont du Toit, Oldenburg, Ormonde, Raats, Ridgeback, **Virgin Earth**, Woolworths (2), Zorgvliet

★★★☆ **Botanica**, Claime d'Or, Druk My Niet, **Hawksmoor**, **Joubert-Tradauw**, **Morgenster**, Rainbow's End, **Romond**, Russo, Waterkloof ★★★ Avontuur, **Blaauwklippen**, Bushmanspad, Haut Espoir, Lynx, **Nomada**, **Onderkloof**, Osbloed, Spookfontein , Whalehaven **NT** Anthonij Rupert, Benguela Cove, Brugman, Buitenverwachting, High Constantia, Idiom, Lovane, My Wyn, Onderkloof , Rietvallei, Signal Hill, Val de Vie **NR** The Garajeest **D** Audacia

Cabernet sauvignon

★★★★★ Delaire, Guardian Peak, Kleine Zalze

★★★★☆ Bartinney (2), Bilton, Boekenhoutskloof, **Camberley**, Cederberg, Darling Cellars, **De Trafford** (2), Delaire, Delheim, **Edgebaston** (2), Eikendal, Elgin Vintners, Ernie Els, Fleur du Cap, Glen Carlou, Glenelly, Graham Beck, Grangehurst, Groot Constantia, House of Mandela, Jordan, Kanonkop, Kleine Zalze, Laibach, Le Bonheur, Le Riche (2), Meerlust, Mitre's Edge, Nederburg (2), Neil Ellis, Oldenburg, PaardenKloof, Raka, Rickety Bridge, Rudera (2), Rust en Vrede (2), Rustenberg, **Simonsig**, Springfield, Stony Brook, Strydom, Teddy Hall, **The Butcher Shop**, The Winery of Good Hope, Uitkyk, Vergelegen (2), Vierkoppen, Warwick, Waterford, Webersburg

★★★★ Alto, Annandale, Anura, Arra, Asara, Backsberg, Bayede!, Belfield, Bergsig, Bilton, **BLANKbottle**, Boland, Bon Courage (2), Boschkloof, Bosman, Brenaissance, Brugman, Buitenverwachting, Capelands, Cederberg, Chateau Naudé, Dalla Cia, De Wetshof, Delheim, Devonvale, DeWaal, Diemersfontein, **Dragonridge**, Druk My Niet, Edgebaston, Eerste Hoop, Ernie Els, Excelsior, Fairview, Flagstone, Glen Carlou, Glenelly, Goedverwacht, Groenland, Guardian Peak, Hartenberg, Holden Manz, Jakob's Vineyards, Journey's End, Kaapzicht, Katbakkies, Kloovenburg, Knorhoek, La Bri, La Motte, La Petite Ferme, Landskroon, Lanzerac, Le Riche, Louis, Lutzville, Lynx, M'hudi, Marianne, McGregor, Meerendal, Meinert, Mooiplaas (2), Morgenhof, Muratie, Napier, Neil Ellis, New Beginnings, Niel Joubert, Nitida, Nuy, Oldenburg, Org de Rac (Organic), Osbloed, Overgaauw, Perdeberg, Post House, Rainbow's End, Rannoch, Restless River, Ridgeback, Robertson, **Rustenberg**, Savanha, Saxenburg, **Scrucap**, Sijnn, South Hill, Spier, Stark-Condé (2), Stellakaya, **Stellenbosch Reserve**, Super Single Vineyards, Swartland, The Winery of Good Hope (2), Thelema (2), Usana, **Uva Mira**, **Van Loveren**, Vergenoegd (2), Villiera, Vondeling, Vriesenhof, Waterkloof, **Weltevrede**, Windmeul, **Woolworths** (5), Zorgvliet

★★★★ AlexKia, Allesverloren, Amani, Ameera, **Arendskloof**, Arra, BABISA, Beau Joubert, Benguela Cove, Bloemendal, Blue Crane, Bon Terroir, Bonnievale, Boschheim, Botanica, **Botha**, **Brothers**, Chennells, Claime d'Or, Cloof, Conviction, De Meye, Devonair, Domaine Coutelier, Doolhof, Dormershire (2), Eaglevlei, False Bay, Fat Bastard, Feiteiras, Fleur du Cap, Fort Simon, Graham Beck, Grande Provence, Groenland, Haut Espoir, Jacques Smit, Klein Roosboom , Knorhoek, Koopmanskloof (Fairtrade), Kyburg, L'Avenir, La Petite Ferme, **Laibach**, Linton Park (2), Longridge, Lourensford, **Lovane** (2), Lyngrove, MAN Family, Marklew, Middelvlei, Mimosa, Miravel, Mitre's Edge, MolenVliet, Mont du Toit, Mont Rochelle, Morgenster, Mountain Ridge, Nederburg, Neethlingshof, Noble Hill, Opstal, Ormonde (2), Overhex, Peter Falke, Plaisir, Porcupine Ridge, Rickety Bridge, Rooiberg, **Rookiewino.com**, Sauvignon.com, Simonsig, Simonsvlei, Springfield, **Stellenbosch Vineyards**, Stellenzicht, Stonewall, SylvanVale, Teubes, The Goose, The Hills, Tokara, Topiary, Trajan, **Ultra Liquors**, Upland (Organic), Val du Charron, Van Loveren, Viljoensdrift, Vin du Cap, **VinGlo**, Warwick, Welbedacht, Wellington

Winery (2), **Weltevrede**, Woolworths, Zevenwacht

★★★ Altydgedacht, **Audacia** (2), Ayama, Baccarat, Bellingham, Bergwater, **Blaauwklippen** (2), Bonview, Boplaas, Boschheim, Botha, Brampton, Breëland, Bushmanspad, Cape Dreams, Carisbrooke, Conradie, Darling Cellars, De Krans, De Meye, De Wet, Desert Rose, Die Mas, Domaine Brahms, Drostdy-Hof, Du Toitskloof (Fairtrade), Durbanville Hills, Earthbound (Organic, Fairtrade), Eikehof, Excelsior, Fairview, Flagstone, Goede Hoop, Hildenbrand, Hoopenburg, Hunneyball, Jacobsdal, Jakkalsvlei, Jason's Hill, Juno, **Kaapse Familie Wingerde**, **Ken Forrester**, Klawer, Klein Parys, Kleine Zalze, Kranskop, L'Olivier, La Chaumiere, La Petite Provence, Landskroon, Le Manoir de Brendel, Leipzig, Linton Park, Louis, Lovane, Maastricht, MAN Family, Merwida, Mostertsdrift, Mount Rozier, Mountain Ridge, **Nabygelegen**, Namaqua, Napier, Nederburg (2), Niel Joubert, Obikwa, **Olsen**, Orange River, Org de Rac (Organic), Painted Wolf, Pearl Mountain, Perdeberg, Phizante Kraal, Pulpit Rock (2), Riebeek (2), Robertson (4), Roodezandt, Rooiberg, Rosendal, Seal Breeze, Simonsvlei, Slowine, Somerbosch, Somerset Wines, Stellar (Organic, Fairtrade), Stellenbosch Hills, **Stellenbosch University**, Stettyn, Swartland, Thandi (Fairtrade), **Under Oaks**, Vredenheim, Waverley Hills (Organic), Wellington Winery (2), Windfall, Windmeul, **Woolworths** (4) (Organic, Fairtrade), Zonnebloem (2) ★★★ **Aan de Doorns**, Alexanderfontein, Alvi's Drift, **Barnardt Boyes**, Bayede!, Beau Joubert, Bergsig, Boschrivier, Brandvlei, Calitzdorp, Cape Dreams, Clairvaux, David Frost, De Bos (Fairtrade), Desert Rose, Douglas Green, Du Preez (2), Dusty Heath, Eagle's Cliff, Entre Nous, Fairvalley (Fairtrade), Franschhoek Cellar, Goudini, Group CDV, Hofstraat, House of Mandela (2) (Fairtrade), **Imbuko**, Kanu, Kleine Draken (Kosher), Landzicht, Leopard's Leap, Libby's Pride, Linton Park, Montagu Wine Cellar, Namaqua, **Neil Patterson**, Piekenierskloof, Place in the Sun (Fairtrade), Seven Sisters, Slanghoek, Spier, Spookfontein , Steenberg, Stellar (Organic, Fairtrade), Stellenbosch Family Wines, The Rhino of Linton Park, Tulbagh Winery, Walker Bay Vineyards, Wandsbeck, William Everson, Woolworths, Zidela (2) ★★ Asara, Avontuur, Bergwater, Blomendahl, De Breede (Organic), Hathersage, Het Vlock Casteel, Hoopenburg, Imbuko, Kleine Draken (Sacramental, Light & low-alcohol, Kosher), **La Residence**, Long Mountain, Lutzville, M'hudi, Mountain River (2), Namaqua, **Nicholson Smith**, Oude Compagnies Post, Schalkenbosch,

Schenkfontein, Stellenbosch Vineyards, Tangled Tree, Van Loveren (Fairtrade), Vin du Cap, Vriesenhof ★★ Ashton, Landzicht, Long Mountain, Simonsvlei, **Van Loveren**, Vinopoly **NT** Abbottshill, Akkerdraai, Anthonij Rupert (2), **Arendsig**, Arra, Blomendahl, Camberley, Cameradi, Cape Hutton, Cape Point, Cape Rock, Clive Torr, Clovelly, Cranefields, Crows Nest, De Doorns, De Villiers (3), Devonair, Dieu Donné, DuVon, Esau, Fernskloof (Organic), Goedvertrouw, **Govert** (2), Graceland, Havana Hills (Fairtrade), Herold, High Constantia (2), Huguenot, La Kavayan, La Petite Vigne, Langverwacht, Le Pommier, Louisvale, Lovane (3), Major's Hill, Manley, Maske, Melkboomsdrift, Miravel, Mont Rochelle, Montpellier, Mooi Bly, Mount Vernon, Nederburg (2) (Fairtrade), Nietvoorbij, Nuweland, Nuy, Onderkloof , Oneiric, Rico Suter, Rietvallei, **RiverGold**, Ruitersvlei, Saam, Sarah's, Savanha, Silvermist, Slaley, Southern Sky (3), Stellendrift (3), Stellenrust, Stone Ridge, Stoumann's, Tall Horse, Tanagra, TCB Wines, **The Butcher Shop**, **The High Road**, TTT Cellar, Tulbagh Winery, Waverley Hills (Organic), Welgeleë, William Everson, Wineways (4), Withoek, Women in Wine (2), Zanddrift, Zidela **NR** Hildenbrand **D** Annex Kloof, Boplaas, Dornier, Hout Bay, Olifantsberg, Remhoogte, Springfontein, Stark-Condé, Sterhuis, The Berrio, Tread Lightly, uniWines (Light & low-alcohol), Zandvliet

Cape Riesling
★★★ Theuniskraal **NT** Calais **NR Hildenbrand**

Carignan
★★★★☆ Blackwater

★★★★ Fairview

NT The Three Foxes

Chardonnay unwooded
★★★★ De Wetshof (2), Eikendal, Glen Carlou, GlenWood, Groote Post, Springfield, **Thelema**, **Woolworths** (2)

★★★☆ Alexanderfontein, Bellpost, **Blue Owl**, Bouchard Finlayson, Brunia, Claime d'Or, De Wetshof, Diemersdal, False Bay, Glenelly, Goudini, Jordan, La Petite Ferme, Lourensford, Meerendal, Môreson, Seven Springs , Signal Gun, **The Butcher Shop**, Warwick, Withington, Woolworths

★★★ AlexKia, Alkmaar, Ayama, Boland, Cape Dreams, Constantia Uitsig, De Meye, De Wetshof, Doolhof, Eaglevlei, Franschhoek Cellar, Hildenbrand, Hoopenburg, **Ken Forrester**, Kleine Zalze, Kloovenburg, Landskroon, McGregor, Middelvlei, Neethlingshof, Org de Rac (Organic),

Perdeberg, Plettenvale, Riebeek, Rooiberg, The Butcher Shop, The Rhino of Linton Park, The Winery of Good Hope, Van Zylshof, Wellington Winery, **Winters Drift**, Woolworths ★★★ **Asara**, Ashton, Backsberg (Kosher), Blomendahl, Brampton, Cloof, Cloverfield, Darling Cellars, Die Mas, **Dragonridge**, Felicité, Graham Beck, Koopmanskloof (Fairtrade), Louisvale, Lutzville, Obikwa, Place in the Sun (Fairtrade), Somersbos, Swartland, Tulbagh Winery, Vriesenhof , Welbedacht, Wellington Winery, Weltevrede, Woolworths ★★ Bon Courage, Calais, Leopard's Leap, Long Mountain, The Observatory, Vinopoly, Welbedacht ★★ Group CDV (3), Libby's Pride, Woolworths (Light & low-alcohol), Zidela ★ **Schenkfontein NT** Boucheron, Buffalo Creek, De Villiers, Dieu Donné, Jean Daneel, Karusa, La Couronne, Oneiric, Pearl Mountain, Rietvallei, Savanha, Sterhuis, Stone Ridge, Tall Horse, Walker Bay Vineyards, Women in Wine **NR** De Krans **D** Delheim, Leeuwenberg, Mont Rochelle, Zandvliet

Chardonnay wooded
★★★★★ Buitenverwachting, Dorrance, GlenWood, Graham Beck, Haskell, **MVH Signature Wines**, Newton Johnson, **Paul Cluver**, Sterhuis, Sumaridge, Warwick

★★★★☆ Backsberg, Bartinney, Boschendal (2), Bouchard Finlayson (3), Cape Chamonix (2), Cape Point, **Creation** (2), Crystallum (2), De Grendel, De Wetshof (2), **Delaire**, DeMorgenzon, Eikendal, Fleur du Cap, GlenWood, Groot Constantia, Hamilton Russell, **Hannay**, Hartenberg, Iona, Jordan (3), **Julien Schaal** (2), Koelfontein, Lanzerac, **Longridge**, Lourensford, **Malanot**, Môreson, Mulderbosch, **Muratie**, Oak Valley, Paul Cluver (2), Restless River, Richard Kershaw, Saxenburg, The Winery of Good Hope, **Thorne & Daughters**, Tokara, Uva Mira, Vergelegen, **Woolworths**

★★★★ Anura, Ashton, Ataraxia, **B Vintners**, Babylonstoren, Badsberg, Bloemendal, Cape Chamonix, Capelands, **Capensis**, **Clouds**, Constantia Uitsig, Corder, Dalla Cia, De Wetshof, Delaire, Delheim, DeMorgenzon, Domaine Coutelier, Doolhof, Durbanville Hills, Edgebaston, Elgin Vintners, **False Bay**, Glen Carlou (2), Glenelly, Goudini, Grande Provence, Groote Post, Hartenberg, Haskell, **Highlands Road**, JH Meyer, Joubert-Tradauw, Journey's End (2), Kleine Zalze, La Couronne, La Motte, La Petite Ferme, Lanzerac, Longridge, Lord's, Maison, Marklew, Meerlust, Migliarina, Mimosa, Mulderbosch, Muratie, Napier, **Neil Ellis**, Nelson, Newton Johnson, Oldenburg, Ormonde, Paserene, **Pearl Mountain**, Plaisir, Pulpit Rock, Rhebokskloof, Rickety Bridge, **Robertson** (2), Rooiberg, Rosendal,

Rustenberg (2), Scrucap, Seven Springs , **Stellenbosch Reserve**, Stellenrust, **The Winery of Good Hope**, Thelema (3), Tierhoek, Tokara, Uva Mira, Van Loveren, Vergelegen, **VinGlo**, Vondeling, Vriesenhof , Waterford, Windmeul, Woolworths (2), Yardstick, Zandvliet, Zevenwacht

★★★★ Aaldering, Amani, Anura, Arendskloof, Bayede!, Bergsig, Bon Courage, Bridge, Brothers, Claime d'Or, Clayton, **Clive Torr**, Clos Malverne, De Wet, Diemersdal, Domaine des Dieux, Eerste Hoop, Entre Nous, Ernst Gouws, Fairview, Fort Simon, Four Paws, Fram, Freedom Iill, Goedverwacht, Haut Espoir, Havana Hills, Holden Manz, Hoopenburg, House of Mandela, Journey's End, Klein Constantia, Kloovenburg, Kranskop, La Bri, La Vierge, Le Bonheur, **Lieben**, Linton Park, Louisvale, Lourensford, Lyngrove, Mellasat, Merwida, Mont Rochelle, Morgenhof, Mountain River, **Namaqua**, Nederburg, Niel Joubert, **Nuy** (2), **Org de Rac** (Organic), Ormonde, Overgaauw, Rhebokskloof, Riebeek, Simonsig (2), Slaley, Steenberg, Stellenrust, Stonewall, Uitkyk, **Uva Mira**, Val du Charron, Veenwouden, Welbedacht, Weltevrede, Whalehaven, Winters Drift, **Woolworths** (3) (Organic) **★★★** Avontuur, Backsberg, Barista, **Benguela Cove**, Boschendal, Boschkloof , **Botha**, Brandvlei, Calitzdorp, Cape Classics, Douglas Green, Drostdy-Hof, Du Toitskloof (Fairtrade), Durbanville Hills, Eerste Hoop, Fairvalley (Fairtrade), Fat Bastard, Flagstone, Fleur du Cap, **Fröhlich**, Goede Hoop, Goedvertrouw, Graham Beck, **Groot Parys** (Organic), Hildenbrand, Hill & Dale, Kanu, Klawer, **Kumala** (2), La Chaumiere, Linton Park, Lothian, Louiesenhof, Louisvale, Mount Rozier, Nederburg, New Beginnings, Newstead, Noble Hill, Orange River, Org de Rac (Organic), Passages, **Porcupine Ridge**, Robertson (4), Simonsvlei, Slanghoek, Spier, **Spotswood**, Stellenbosch Family Wines, Stellenbosch Vineyards (2), **Stettyn**, **Thandi**, Two Oceans, Van Loveren, Vierlanden, Vredenheim, **Weltevrede**, Withington, Zandvliet **★★★** Asara, Barrydale, Bellingham, Burgershof, De Bos (Fairtrade), **Die Mas**, Excelsior, Goedverwacht, Groot Parys (Organic), House of Mandela (Fairtrade), Klein Parys, L'Olivier, Leipzig, Niel Joubert, Osbloed, Piekenierskloof, Pulpit Rock, Re'Mogo (Organic, Fairtrade), Schalkenbosch, Stellar (Organic, Fairtrade), Under Oaks, Woolworths (3) (Organic), Zonnebloem **★★** Bonnievale, Cloverfield, Hathersage, Long Mountain, Lorraine, Mostertsdrift, Stellar (Organic, Fairtrade), Tangled Tree, Thembi & Co **★☆** Kleine

Draken (Kosher), Welvanpas **NT** Almenkerk, Altydgedacht, Alvi's Drift, Anthonij Rupert (2), **Arendsig**, Avondrood, Baleia, Brenaissance, Chateau Naudé, Clovelly, Crows Nest, Dieu Donné (2), Eikehof, Elgin Heights, **Esona** (Organic), Fairview, Fernskloof (Organic), Hermit on the Hill, Hillock, Imbuko, Kloovenburg, Ladera, Langverwacht, Lazanou (Organic), Le Riche, **Lismore**, Lutzville, Major's Hill, MAN Family, Meinert, Mont Rochelle, Montpellier, Mooi Bly, Mount Vernon, Mountain Oaks (Organic), **My Wyn**, Nederburg, Nietvoorbij, Nitida, Olifantsberg, Olsen, Onderkloof , Oneiric, Overhex, Quoin Rock, Rietvallei (2), **RiverGold**, Rupert & Rothschild, Savanha, Snow Mountain, Springfield, Stanford Hills, Stoumann's, Veenwouden, Viljoensdrift, Vrede en Lust, Walker Bay Vineyards, Waterkloof, Weltevrede, William Everson, Windmeul, Women in Wine **D** De Zoete Inval, Du Preez, Meerendal, Neil Ellis, Springfontein, Tokara, Van Zylshof, Waterford

Chenin blanc off-dry/semi-sweet (w & u/w)

★★★★☆ Bergsig, DewaldtHeyns, Ken Forrester, **Longridge**, Overhex

★★★★ Beaumont, Hazendal, Kanu, Katbakkies, Knorhoek, Slanghoek

★★★☆ Trajan **★★★** Flagstone, Ken Forrester, Nederburg, Woolworths **★★☆** Cloof (Fairtrade), Kanu, Landskroon, Mountain Ridge, Nuweland **★★** Ashton (Perlé), Bottelary, Fleur du Cap **★☆** Bonnievale (Perlé, Light & low-alcohol), Kupferberger Auslese, Robertson, Seven Sisters (Perlé, Light & low-alcohol), Woolworths **★** Landzicht **NT** Hillock, Huguenot, Ken Forrester, Landskroon, Valley Vineyards **D** Breëland, Kanu, Tread Lightly, Woolworths (3)

Chenin blanc unwooded dry

★★★★☆ Bayede!, Fledge & Co

★★★★ Babylon's Peak, Beaumont, Black Pearl, Blackwater, **Boland**, **Fledge & Co**, Maison, Mooiplaas, Neethlingshof, Old Vines, Perdeberg, Raats, Woolworths (2)

★★★☆ Alvi's Drift, Annex Kloof, Ayama, Babylonstoren, Blaauwklippen, Boschendal, Cederberg, Chateau Naudé, **Cloof**, De Meye, De Wet, Delaire, Ernie Els, Fairview, False Bay, Glen Carlou, Groot Parys (Organic), Groote Post, Kaapzicht, Ken Forrester, Kleine Zalze, La Chataigne, Lazanou (Organic), Napier, Olsen, Oude Denneboom, Overhex, Phizante Kraal, Scrucap, Simonsig, Summerhill, The Winery of Good Hope, **Ultra Liquors** **★★★** Alexanderfontein, Ashton (2), Backsberg, Badsberg, Bellingham, Bergsig,

Boutinot, Cape Dreams, Cloof, Darling Cellars, Diemersfontein, Domaine Brahms, Doolhof, Dornier, Drostdy-Hof, Du'SwaRoo, Eagle's Cliff, Eaglevlei, Earthbound (Organic, Fairtrade), Fairview, False Bay, Fish Hoek, Freedom Hill, Goudini, Groenland, Groot Parys (Organic), Hawksmoor, **Imbuko**, Jordan, Kleine Zalze (2), Knorhoek, Kumala, **Laibach**, Lanzerac, Leeuwenkuil, Leopard's Leap, Lyngrove, M'hudi, Namaqua, Nederburg, Nieuwedrift, Perdeberg, **Perdeberg Vineyard Collection**, Piekenierskloof, **Porcupine Ridge**, Rhebokskloof, Rickety Bridge, Rooiberg, Ruitersvlei, Simonsvlei, Slowine, Somersbosch, Spier, Stellar (2) (Organic, Fairtrade), Stellekaya, Stellenbosch Hills, Stellenbosch Vineyards, Teddy Hall, The Grape Grinder (2), The Liberator, The Rhino of Linton Park, Van Zylshof, **Varkenskraal**, Welbedacht, Welgemeend, Wellington Winery, Windmeul, Woolworths (2) ★★★ Aan de Doorns, Ayama, Baccarat, Barrydale, Barton, Bon Courage, Botha (2), Bottelary, **Boutinot**, Brandvlei, Cloverfield, De Bos (Fairtrade), De Krans, DeWaal, Douglas Green, Du Toitskloof (Fairtrade), Fairvalley (Fairtrade), Franschhoek Cellar, **Fröhlich**, Goede Hoop, Hildenbrand, Hoopenburg, **iKapa Jazz** (Organic, Fairtrade), Klawer, Klein Parys, Knorhoek, Koopmanskloof (Fairtrade), Landskroon, MAN Family, Monterosso, Nederburg, Nelson, New Beginnings, Niel Joubert, Nuy, Obikwa, Onderkloof, Orange River, **Piekenierskloof**, Re'Mogo (Organic, Fairtrade), Robert Stanford, Robertson (2), Roodezandt, Rosendal, Schenkfontein, Simonsvlei, Skilpadvlei, Slanghoek, **Somerset Wines**, Stofberg, Swartland, Thembi & Co, Tulbagh Winery, Under Oaks, uniWines (2) (Fairtrade), Waboomsrivier, Wellington Winery, Zidela ★★ **Asara**, Bayede!, Croydon, Domein Doornkraal, Imbuko, Jacaranda, Leipzig, Long Mountain (2), Lutzville, McGregor, Montagu Wine Cellar, Pulpit Rock, Riebeek, The Hills, **Tulbagh Winery**, **Ultra Liquors**, Van Loveren, **Wellington Winery** ★★ House of Mandela (Fairtrade), Van Loveren (Fairtrade), Zidela **NT** Anthonij Rupert, **Arendsig**, Arra, Blomendahl, Calais, Catch Of The Day, Cavalli, **Clive Torr**, De Villiers, DuVon, Eagle's Cliff, Huguenot, Klein Parys, **Kyburg**, Langverwacht, MAN Family, Maske, Montpellier, Mooi Bly, Mountain River, Nuy, Ormonde, Rietvallei, **RiverGold**, Saam, Savanha, **Scali**, Stoumann's, Swartland, Tall Horse, TTT Cellar, Valley Vineyards (2), Virgin Earth, Vrede en Lust, Wineways, Zonnebloem **NR Boutinot D** Bayede!,

Darling Cellars, La Petite Ferme, Laibach, Le Pommier, Mason's Winery, Mellasat

Chenin blanc wooded, dry
★★★★★ Botanica, **David & Nadia Sadie**, Eenzaamheid, Kaapzicht, Keermont, Ken Forrester, **Mullineux**

★★★★☆ **Adoro**, Alheit (2), Beaumont, Bosman (Fairtrade), **Botanica**, Cederberg, **David & Nadia Sadie** (2), De Trafford, **DeMorgenzon**, Donkiesbaai, Doran, Dornier, Dorrance, Edgebaston, Fram, **Hogan**, Intellego, Jean Daneel, Kleine Zalze, Mulderbosch (2), Mullineux (2), Nederburg, Opstal, **Patatsfontein**, Raats, Reverie, Reyneke (Biodynamic), Rijk's (2), Rudera, Sadie (2), Spice Route (Fairtrade), Spioenkop, Stellenrust, Sterhuis, Teddy Hall, The Winery of Good Hope, **Themika**, **Tierhoek**, Villiera

★★★★ AA Badenhorst, Allée Bleue, Alvi's Drift, Avondale (Organic), Bellingham, BLANKbottle, Boland, **Boutinot**, **Bryan MacRobert**, Catherine Marshall, **Cloof**, **Clouds**, DeanDavid, Delaire, Delheim, DeMorgenzon, Diemersfontein, Domaine Brahms, **Fleur du Cap**, **Foxwood**, Graham Beck, Grande Provence, Groot Parys (2) (Organic), **Hermit on the Hill**, **Hirst**, Intellego, Jordan, Kleine Zalze, L'Avenir (2), **Le Sueur**, Leeuwenkuil, Leopard's Leap, Longridge, Luddite, Lutzville, Maison, Migliarina, Miles Mossop, Mooiplaas, Mount Abora, Mulderbosch (2), **Neil Patterson**, Old Vines, Oldenburg, **Olifantsberg**, Paardebosch, Perdeberg, Post House, Remhoogte (2), Ridgeback, Rijk's, Rudera, Saam, Saltare (2), Signal Hill, Simonsig, Spier, Spioenkop, Springfontein (2), Star Hill, **Stellar** (Organic, Fairtrade), Stellenbosch Vineyards, The Winery of Good Hope (2), Tierhoek, **Tim Martin** (2), Welbedacht, Windmeul, Woolworths

★★★☆ Antebellum, Anura, Beau Joubert, Bellevue, **Breëland**, Crios Bríde, Damarakloof, Fort Simon, **Goudini**, Groot Parys (Organic), Hazendal, Kleine Zalze, L'Avenir, **Landskroon**, **Lateganskop**, Malanot, MAN Family, **Merwida**, Morgenhof, Mount Pleasant, Nabygelegen, Painted Wolf (2), **Phizante Kraal**, **Piekenierskloof**, Rudera, Stark-Condé, Stellenbosch Vineyards, Stellenrust, Sterhuis, Teddy Hall, **The Ahrens Family**, The Observatory, Uitkyk, Usana, Villiera, Waterford, **Waterkloof** (2), **Wellington Winery**, Wildehurst, Wildekrans, Woolworths ★★★ Andy Mitchell, **Barton**, **BLANKbottle**, **Blue Crane**, Cape Classics, **De Wet**, Dragonridge, Fleur du Cap, Graham Beck, Hofstraat, **Joostenberg** (2) (Organic), Orange River, Raka, **Solms-Delta**, Swartland, **Teubes**, uniWines, Zevenwacht ★★★ Asara, **Botha**,

Koelenhof, **Pulpit Rock**, Windfall ★★ Jacaranda **NT** Aeternitas, Andy Mitchell, Anthonij Rupert, Beaumont, Boer & Brit, Bryan MacRobert (2), Chateau Naudé, Dagbreek, Druk My Niet, **Glen Heatlie**, Groot Parys (Organic), **Hornbill** , Jean Daneel, Kulsen, Linton Park, Mimosa, Mullineux, **My Wyn**, Rickety Bridge, Riebeek, Rietvallei, Robert Stanford, **Santa Cecilia** (2), Stone Ridge, Val de Vie **D** Super Single Vineyards

Cinsaut

★★★★★★ AA Badenhorst

★★★★★☆ **Adoro**, Mount Abora, Sadie

★★★★ **AD Wines**, **Eenzaamheid**, **Neil Ellis**, **Signal Hill**, Stellenrust, **The Winery of Good Hope**, Waterkloof

★★★☆ Elsenburg, **Leeuwenkuil**, MAN Family, Osbloed, Rico Suter ★★★ **Bellevue**, **Boutinot** (2) ★★ Landskroon **NT** Natte Valleij, Wineways

Clairette blanche

★★★★ **Craven** (2)

NT The Three Foxes

Colombard

★★★ Cape Dreams, McGregor, Orange River, Rooiberg ★★★ Bon Courage, Goedverwacht, Stellar, Stettyn, Van Loveren ★★ Aan de Doorns, Bezalel ★☆ Hartswater (2), Montagu Wine Cellar ★ Schenkfontein **NT** Langverwacht, Nuy **D** Woolworths

Fairtrade

★★★★★☆ Du Toitskloof (Red blends, Cape Bordeaux), The Winery of Good Hope (Shiraz/syrah), Bosman (Chenin blanc wooded, dry), Spice Route (4) (Grenache noir, Shiraz/syrah, Red blends, shiraz/syrah-based, Chenin blanc wooded, dry)

★★★★ **Stellar** (Chenin blanc wooded, dry, Organic), Du Toitskloof (Red blends, shiraz/syrah-based), Bosman (2) (Red blends, shiraz/syrah-based, White blends, wooded, dry), Fairview (Pinotage), Goats do Roam (Red blends, shiraz/syrah-based), Rivendell (Sauvignon blanc unwooded), **Spice Route** (6) (Mourvèdre, Mourvèdre, Pinotage, Shiraz/syrah, Semillon wooded, Viognier), Township Winery (Merlot), Virgin Earth (Sauvignon blanc unwooded)

★★★☆ Stellar (2) (Pinot noir, Pinotage, Organic), Du Toitskloof (2) (Nebbiolo, Hanepoot fortified), Havana Hills (Shiraz/syrah, Sauvignon blanc unwooded), Stellar (Vin de paille, Organic), Bosman (Pinotage), Thandi (White blends, unwooded, dry), De Bos (Sauvignon blanc unwooded), Fairvalley (2) (Pinotage, Sauvignon

blanc unwooded), Goats do Roam (3) (Red blends, shiraz/syrah-based, Rosé dry, White blends, unwooded, dry), Koopmanskloof (2) (Cabernet sauvignon, Shiraz/syrah), **Jacques Germanier** (Red blends, other, Organic), uniWines (Husk spirit/grappa-styles), Rivendell (Rosé dry), Spice Route (Sauvignon blanc unwooded), Virgin Earth (2) (Pinot noir, Red blends, Cape Bordeaux) ★★★ Woolworths (Cabernet sauvignon, Organic), Stellar (White blends, unwooded, dry, Organic), Nederburg (Sauvignon blanc unwooded), Du Toitskloof (Red blends, other), **Stellar** (2) (Pinotage, White blends, wooded, dry, Organic), Du Toitskloof (6) (Cabernet sauvignon, Pinotage, Shiraz/syrah, Red blends, other, Chardonnay wooded, Sauvignon blanc unwooded), Stellar (2) (Cabernet sauvignon, Rosé dry, Organic), Du Toitskloof (2) (Muscadel, red, fortified, Port-style, red), Stellar (Chenin blanc unwooded dry, Organic), Thandi (Cabernet sauvignon), Havana Hills (Sangiovese), Thandi (Red blends, shiraz/syrah-based), Earthbound (4) (Cabernet sauvignon, Pinotage, Chenin blanc unwooded dry, Sauvignon blanc unwooded, Organic), Fairvalley (Chardonnay wooded), Koopmanskloof (3) (Merlot, Pinotage, Sauvignon blanc unwooded), **Havana Hills** (3) (Red blends, shiraz/syrah-based, Rosé dry, Sauvignon blanc unwooded), **Jacques Germanier** (Red blends, Cape Bordeaux, Organic), Place in the Sun (3) (Merlot, Shiraz/syrah, Sauvignon blanc unwooded), Township Winery (Pinotage) ★★★☆ Woolworths (2) (Shiraz/syrah, Sauvignon blanc unwooded, Organic), **Stellar** (6) (Sauvignon blanc unwooded, Cabernet sauvignon, Shiraz/syrah, Chardonnay wooded, White blends, unwooded, dry, Red blends, shiraz/syrah-based, Organic), Du Toitskloof (6) (Merlot, Red blends, with pinotage, Chenin blanc unwooded dry, White blends, off-dry/semi-sweet (w & u/w), Sparkling, Non-MCC, red, off-dry/semi-sweet, Sparkling, Non-MCC, white, dry, Light & low-alcohol), Thandi (Sauvignon blanc unwooded), Du Toitskloof (Hanepoot unfortified), Cloof (Chenin blanc off-dry/semi-sweet (w & u/w)), Stellar (2) (Red blends, shiraz/syrah-based, White blends, off-dry/semi-sweet (w & u/w), Organic), Thandi (2) (Rosé dry, Sparkling, Non-MCC, rosé, dry), Stellenrust (3) (Red blends, with pinotage, Rosé dry, White blends, unwooded, dry), House of Mandela (6) (Cabernet sauvignon, Merlot, Pinotage, Shiraz/syrah, Chardonnay wooded, Sauvignon blanc unwooded), De Bos (3) (Cabernet sauvignon, Chardonnay wooded, Chenin blanc unwooded dry), Earthbound (Pinot noir,

Organic), Fairvalley (2) (Cabernet sauvignon, Chenin blanc unwooded dry), **iKapa Jazz (4)** (Pinotage, Red blends, with pinotage, Chenin blanc unwooded dry, Sparkling, Méthode cap classique, white, dry, Organic), Koopmanskloof (3) (Rosé dry, Chardonnay unwooded, Chenin blanc unwooded dry), Havana Hills (Red blends, Cape Bordeaux), **Jacques Germanier** (2) (White blends, unwooded, dry, White blends, unwooded, dry, Organic), uniWines (4) (Merlot, Chenin blanc unwooded dry, Chenin blanc unwooded dry, Hanepoot unfortified, Perlé, Light & low-alcohol), Place in the Sun (2) (Cabernet sauvignon, Chardonnay unwooded), Re'Mogo (5) (Pinotage, Red blends, with pinotage, Chardonnay wooded, Chenin blanc unwooded dry, Sparkling, Méthode cap classique, white, dry, Organic), Township Winery (Viognier) ★★ Woolworths (2) (Merlot, Pinotage, Organic), Stellar (3) (Chardonnay wooded, Merlot, Rosé dry, Organic), Van Loveren (2) (Cabernet sauvignon, Rosé dry, Organic), Stellar (3) (Merlot, Pinotage, Shiraz/syrah, Organic), Du Toitskloof (3) (Red blends, with pinotage, Rosé off-dry/semi-sweet, Sweet red, Light & low-alcohol), Stellar (2) (Rosé dry, Sweet red, Organic), **iKapa Jazz** (2) (Rosé dry, Sparkling, Non-MCC, rosé, off-dry/semi-sweet, Organic), uniWines (2) (Shiraz/syrah, Sauvignon blanc unwooded dry), **Re'Mogo** (2) (Rosé dry, Sparkling, Non-MCC, rosé, off-dry/semi-sweet, Organic) ★★ Van Loveren (2) (Pinotage, Chenin blanc unwooded dry), Du Toitskloof (White blends, unwooded, dry), Stellar (Sparkling, Non-MCC, rosé, off-dry/semi-sweet), House of Mandela (Chenin blanc unwooded dry), uniWines (Pinotage) **NT** Nederburg (2) (Cabernet sauvignon, Pinotage), Havana Hills (Cabernet sauvignon), De Bos (Pinot noir), Township Winery (Shiraz/syrah) **D** Nederburg (Red blends, shiraz/syrah-based), Woolworths (Colombard, Organic), Du Toitskloof (White blends, wooded, dry), Thandi (3) (Shiraz/syrah, Red blends, Cape Bordeaux, White blends, unwooded, dry)

Fernão pires
★★★☆ BLANKbottle

Gamay noir
★★★★ The Winery of Good Hope
★★★ Kleine Zalze ★★ Asara

Gewürztraminer
★★★★☆ Paul Cluver, Woolworths
★★★★ Nederburg, Neethlingshof, Zevenwacht

★★★☆ Altydgedacht, Simonsig ★★★ Bergsig, Delheim ★★★ Bon Courage ★★ Koelenhof **NT** Montpellier **D** Wellington Winery

Grenache blanc
★★★★☆ The Foundry
★★★★ Bosman, Signal Hill

Grenache noir
★★★★★ David & Nadia Sadie

★★★★☆ Momento, Neil Ellis, Sadie, Spice Route (Fairtrade), Tierhoek, Vriesenhof

★★★★ Black Elephant, Diemersdal, Painted Wolf (Organic), Signal Hill, **The Foundry**, Waverley Hills (Organic), Woolworths

★★★☆ Four Paws, Fraai Uitzicht 1798, **Piekenierskloof** (2), Saronsberg, Tokara, **Vriesenhof** ★★★ Franki's ★★★ Lynx **NT** AA Badenhorst, Arendsig, Esau, Hermit on the Hill (2), **Migliarina**, Nederburg, **Oude Compagnies Post**, Zevenwacht

Grüner veltliner
★★★★☆ Diemersdal

Hanepoot fortified
★★★★☆ Goudini, Muratie, Signal Hill

★★★★ Aan de Doorns, Boplaas, Calitzdorp, Constantia Uitsig, Klawer, Nuweland, Opstal, Orange River

★★★☆ Badsberg, De Wet, Du Toitskloof (Fairtrade), Goudini, Jakkalsvlei, Kaapzicht, Slanghoek, Waboomsrivier ★★★ Boplaas, Clairvaux, Die Mas, Domein Doornkraal, Koelenhof, **Robert Stanford**, Swartland, Villiersdorp ★★☆ Grande Provence ★★ Bergwater, Tulbagh Winery **NT** Aufwaerts, Calitzdorp, Du Preez, Huguenot (2) (Sacramental), Landzicht, Mooiuitsig, Stoumann's, TTT Cellar

Hanepoot unfortified
★★★☆ Hofstraat ★★★ Du Toitskloof (Fairtrade), uniWines (2) (Perlé, Light & low-alcohol, Fairtrade) ★★ Cape Classics (Light & low-alcohol), Overhex, Riebeek (Perlé, Light & low-alcohol), Wellington Winery ★ Zidela **NT** Natte Valleij, Swartland

Hárslevelü
★★★★ Lemberg

Husk spirit/grappa-styles
★★★★★ Dalla Cia

★★★★ Dalla Cia (3) (Organic), Gentleman Spirits (4), Mont Destin, Org de Rac (Organic), Upland

★★★☆ Dalla Cia, Gentleman Spirits, **Kaapzicht**, **Simonsig**, uniWines ★★★ Iona, Klein Constantia **NT** Dalla Cia

Icewine
★★☆ Kaapzicht

Jerepigo red
★★★★ Badsberg, Blaauwklippen

★★★☆ Avontuur, Domein Doornkraal, Orange River, Solms-Delta ★★★ Domein Doornkraal, Grundheim, **Jakkalsvlei**, **Reiersvlei**, Simonsvlei, Swartland, uniWines ★★☆ Botha, Hartswater, Mons Ruber, Slanghoek, Waverley Hills ★★ Die Mas **NT** Camberley, Feiteiras, Huguenot, Landzicht, Stonewall, Stoumann's

Jerepigo white
★★★★☆ Signal Hill

★★★★ Botha, Calitzdorp

★★★☆ Backsberg, Lateganskop, Niel Joubert, Opstal, Orange River, Riebeek, uniWines ★★★ Die Mas, Mons Ruber, Sedgwick's Old Brown, Swartland ★★☆ Chateau Naudé, Namaqua, Winkelshoek ★★ Brandvlei, Hartswater **NT** Feiteiras, Huguenot

Kosher
★★★ Backsberg (2) (Merlot, Pinotage) ★★★☆ Backsberg (2) (Chardonnay unwooded, Sparkling, Méthode cap classique, white, dry), Kleine Draken (Cabernet sauvignon) ★★★ Backsberg (Sweet red, Sacramental), Kleine Draken (5) (Cabernet sauvignon, Merlot, Sauvignon blanc unwooded, Sparkling, Non-MCC, white, off-dry/semi-sweet, Natural Sweet, white, Sacramental, Light & low-alcohol) ★★ Kleine Draken (2) (Chardonnay wooded, Natural Sweet, red, Light & low-alcohol) **NT** Kleine Draken (Rosé off-dry/semi-sweet) **D** Kleine Draken (Red blends, Cape Bordeaux)

Late Harvest
★★★★ Bergsig, **Thelema** (2) (Light & low-alcohol) ★★★ **Roodezandt** ★★ Overmeer Cellars ★★☆ Drostdy-Hof, Kellerprinz, Robertson **NT** Landau du Val, Mooiuitsig **D** Montagu Wine Cellar, Nederburg, Thelema

Light & low-alcohol
★★★★☆ Fairview (2) (Vin de paille, Shiraz/syrah), Fleur du Cap (Noble Late Harvest), Bon Courage (Noble Late Harvest), De Wetshof (Noble Late Harvest)

★★★★ Paul Cluver (Riesling), Laibach (Natural Sweet, white), Stony Brook (Natural Sweet, white) ★★★☆ De Grendel (Noble Late Harvest), Hofstraat (Hanepoot unfortified), **Thelema** (Late Harvest) ★★★ Woolworths (White blends, off-dry/semi-sweet (w & u/w)), Namaqua (Noble Late Harvest), Villiera (Sparkling, Méthode cap classique, white, dry), Zandvliet (Natural Sweet, white), Orange River (Natural Sweet, rosé), Perdeberg (Sparkling, Non-MCC, rosé, off-dry/semi-sweet), **Highlands Road** (Special Late Harvest), Somerset Wines (Natural Sweet, white), Quando (Natural Sweet, white) ★★☆ **Woolworths** (2) (Rosé dry, Sparkling, Non-MCC, white, off-dry/semi-sweet), Du Toitskloof (Sparkling, Non-MCC, red, off-dry/semi-sweet, Fairtrade), Overhex (Rosé off-dry/semi-sweet), Solms-Delta (Sparkling, Non-MCC, red, off-dry/semi-sweet), Imbuko (Muscadel, white, unfortified, Perlé), Orange River (Sparkling, Non-MCC, white, off-dry/semi-sweet), Badsberg (Sparkling, Non-MCC, white, off-dry/semi-sweet), Cold Duck (5th Avenue) (Sparkling, Non-MCC, rosé, off-dry/semi-sweet), Grünberger (Natural Sweet, white), Klawer (Sparkling, Non-MCC, rosé, off-dry/semi-sweet), Somerset Wines (3) (Sparkling, Non-MCC, rosé, dry, Natural Sweet, red, Natural Sweet, rosé), uniWines (2) (Hanepoot unfortified, Hanepoot unfortified, Perlé, Fairtrade) ★★ **Robertson** (5) (Natural Sweet, rosé, Sweet red, Natural Sweet, red, Sparkling, Non-MCC, red, off-dry/semi-sweet, Natural Sweet, red), Van Loveren (Natural Sweet, rosé), Woolworths (Rosé off-dry/semi-sweet), Van Loveren (Sparkling, Non-MCC, rosé, off-dry/semi-sweet), **Simonsvlei** (Natural Sweet, rosé), Overhex (2) (White blends, off-dry/semi-sweet (w & u/w), Sweet red), Du Toitskloof (2) (Rosé off-dry/semi-sweet, Sweet red, Fairtrade), **Woolworths** (Natural Sweet, rosé), Overhex (Sparkling, Non-MCC, white, off-dry/semi-sweet), **Nicholson Smith** (3) (Rosé off-dry/semi-sweet, White blends, off-dry/semi-sweet (w & u/w), Sweet red), **Tulbagh Winery** (2) (White blends, unwooded, dry, Natural Sweet, rosé), 4th Street (2) (Natural Sweet, red, Natural Sweet, rosé, Perlé), Douglas Green (Natural Sweet, white), Viljoensdrift (Sparkling, Non-MCC, rosé, off-dry/semi-sweet), **Wellington Winery** (2) (Pinotage, Chenin blanc unwooded dry), 4th Street (Natural Sweet, white), Eaglevlei (Sauvignon blanc unwooded), **Lourensford** (Rosé dry), **Fleur du Cap** (2) (Rosé off-dry/semi-sweet, Chenin blanc off-dry/semi-sweet (w & u/w)), Riebeek (Hanepoot unfortified, Perlé), Long Mountain (Sparkling, Non-MCC, rosé, off-dry/semi-sweet), Badsberg (Muscadel, white, unfortified, Perlé), De Krans (Muscadel, white, unfortified, Perlé), De Wet (Muscadel, white, unfortified, Perlé), Grünberger (Natural Sweet, rosé), Cape Classics (Hanepoot unfortified), Kleine Draken (3) (Cabernet sauvignon, Sparkling, Non-MCC, white, off-dry/semi-sweet, Natural Sweet, white, Sacramental, Kosher), **uniWines** (Rosé off-dry/semi-sweet), Drostdy-Hof (3) (Natural Sweet, red, Natural Sweet, rosé, Natural Sweet, white), Alvi's Drift (2) (Sparkling, Non-MCC, rosé, off-dry/semi-sweet, Sparkling, Non-MCC, white, off-dry/semi-sweet), The House of JC le Roux (2) (Sparkling, Non-MCC, red, dry, Sparkling, Non-MCC, white, off-dry/semi-sweet) ★★ Robertson (12) (White blends, unwooded, dry, Natural Sweet, rosé, Natural Sweet, white, Rosé off-dry/semi-sweet, Sparkling, Non-MCC, rosé, off-dry/semi-sweet, Sparkling, Non-MCC, white, off-dry/semi-sweet, Sauvignon blanc unwooded, Natural Sweet, red, Natural Sweet, white, Natural Sweet, white, White blends, unwooded, dry, Natural Sweet, rosé), Woolworths (6) (Merlot, Pinotage, Natural Sweet, rosé, Chardonnay unwooded, Chenin blanc off-dry/semi-sweet (w & u/w), Sauvignon blanc unwooded), Van Loveren (2) (Natural Sweet, red, Natural Sweet, white), Woolworths (2) (White blends, off-dry/semi-sweet (w & u/w), Natural Sweet, white), **Van Loveren** (3) (Merlot, Rosé off-dry/semi-sweet, Semillon unwooded), Group CDV (Natural Sweet, white), Woolworths (Red blends, other), Overhex (Sparkling, Non-MCC, rosé, off-dry/semi-sweet), Conradie (Rosé off-dry/semi-sweet, Perlé), 4th Street (Natural Sweet, white, Perlé), Douglas Green (Natural Sweet, rosé), 4th Street (2) (Natural Sweet, red, Natural Sweet, rosé), Botha (White blends, off-dry/semi-sweet (w & u/w)), Bonnievale (Chenin blanc off-dry/semi-sweet (w & u/w), Perlé), Vinopoly (2) (Rosé off-dry/semi-sweet, Muscadel, white, unfortified, Perlé), Kleine Draken (Natural Sweet, red, Kosher), Landzicht (2) (Natural Sweet, rosé, Natural Sweet, white), Rooiberg (Sauvignon blanc unwooded), Seven Sisters (Chenin blanc off-dry/semi-sweet (w & u/w), Perlé), The House of JC le Roux (Sparkling, Non-MCC, red, off-dry/semi-sweet), Slanghoek (Natural Sweet, rosé) ★ **Woolworths** (2) (White blends, unwooded, dry, Sweet red), Van Loveren (2) (Sparkling, Non-MCC, red, off-dry/semi-sweet, Sparkling, Non-MCC, white, off-dry/semi-sweet), Simonsvlei (Natural Sweet, rosé), Woolworths (White blends, other, unwooded, dry), **Douglas Green** (Natural Sweet, red), Riebeek (Sweet red, Perlé), Bonnievale (Ruby cabernet) ★ Woolworths (Natural Sweet, red), Riebeek (Rosé off-dry/semi-sweet, Perlé), Drostdy-Hof (White blends, unwooded, dry) **NT** Waverley Hills (Semillon unwooded), Lutzville (3) (Natural Sweet, red, Natural Sweet, rosé, Natural Sweet, white), Swartland (Hanepoot

unfortified), Neethlingshof (Noble Late Harvest), Swartland (Rosé off-dry/semi-sweet) **D** Woolworths (Rosé dry), Van Loveren (2) (White blends, unwooded, dry, Natural Sweet, rosé), Woolworths (Rosé off-dry/semi-sweet), Flat Roof Manor (Rosé off-dry/semi-sweet), uniWines (Cabernet sauvignon), Obikwa (Muscadel, white, unfortified), Altydgedacht (Noble Late Harvest), Thelema (Late Harvest)

Malbec

★★★★ Annex Kloof, Anura, Bellevue, Diemersfontein, Druk My Niet, Mooi Bly, Paul Wallace, **Plaisir**, Signal Hill, **Weltevrede**, Woolworths (2)

★★★☆ Bloemendal, **Buitenverwachting**, Doolhof, Fairview, Glen Carlou, Hildenbrand, Hillcrest, **Kumala**, Le Pommier, **Nederburg**, Neethlingshof, Super Single Vineyards ★★★ Bushmanspad, Dornier, **Fish Hoek**, Flagstone, **Flat Roof Manor**, La Couronne, Raka, Withington (2) ★★☆ Blaauwklippen, **Maison de Teijger** ★★ Kleine Zalze **NT** Black Elephant, Mount Vernon, Ormonde, Vrede en Lust

Marsanne

★★★★☆ Bellingham

★★★★ **Leeuwenkuil**

Merlot

★★★★★ Bein (2), Eagles' Nest, Groot Constantia, **Hartenberg**, Laibach (Organic), Lourensford, Meerlust, Mitre's Edge, Nederburg, Remhoogte, Shannon, Sterhuis, Sumaridge, Tanja Beutler, Thelema, Vergelegen

★★★★ Amani, Barton, Bayede!, Bein, Buitenverwachting, Catherine Marshall, **Creation** (2), De Trafford, De Wetshof, Delaire, DeWaal, Eikendal, Elgin Vintners, Fleur du Cap, Glenelly, GlenWood, Hartenberg, Haskell, Hazendal, Hillcrest, Jordan, Journey's End, La Bri, La Petite Ferme, Laibach, Landskroon, Lanzerac, Linton Park, Marianne, Noble Hill, Overgaauw, Rainbow's End, Raka, Rickety Bridge, Rust en Vrede, Rustenberg, Saxenburg, Slaley, Steenberg, Stellekaya, **Stellenbosch Reserve**, Super Single Vineyards, The Butcher Shop (2), Thelema, Township Winery (Fairtrade), **Uva Mira**, Veenwouden, Whalehaven, Woolworths (5) (Organic), Yonder Hill

★★★☆ Akkerdal, AlexKia, Altydgedacht, Annandale, Anura, Ayama, **Benguela Cove**, Bilton, Blaauwklippen (2), Bloemendal, **Blue Owl**, Boland, Boschkloof, Botanica, **Botha**, **Boutinot**, Cloof, Clos Malverne, Darling Cellars, De Breede (Organic), De Grendel, Doolhof, Durbanville Hills, Eaglevlei, Ernie

Els, Ernst Gouws, Excelsior, Fairview, False Bay, Fraai Uitzicht 1798, Graham Beck, Groenland, Groote Post, Hout Bay, Jordan, Kaapzicht, Ken Forrester, Klein Roosboom , Kloovenburg, Knorhoek, Kyburg, L'Avenir, Lanner Hill, **Leeuwenberg**, Linton Park, Longridge, Lyngrove, **Meerendal** (3), Meinert, Miravel, Morgenhof, Morgenster, Mount Rozier, Muratie, Nabygelegen, Neethlingshof, **New Beginnings**, Niel Joubert (2), Oldenburg, Ormonde, Plaisir, Porcupine Ridge, Post House, **Romond**, **Rosendal**, Scrucap, Seal Breeze, Signal Gun, Slowine, Somerbosch, Spookfontein , Tulbagh Winery, Vergenoegd, Waterkloof, Welbedacht, Wellington Winery, Woestkloof ★★★ Alexanderfontein, **Alte Neffen**, Anura, Asara, Audacia (2), Backsberg (2) (Kosher), Bellpost, Botha, Brenaissance, Cape Classics, D'Aria, De Meye, Delheim, DeWaal, Die Mas, Diemersdal, Dornier, Durbanville Hills, Excelsior, Fairview, Flagstone, Flat Roof Manor, Fleur du Cap, Fort Simon, Glen Carlou, Goede Hoop, Group CDV, Guardian Peak, Hathersage, Hofstraat, Holden Manz, **Hornbill** , House of Mandela, Jason's Hill, Klein Parys, Koelenhof, Koopmanskloof (Fairtrade), Leeuwenberg, Lievland, Marklew, **MolenVliet**, Mont du Toit, **Nederburg** (2), Nico van der Merwe, Nuweland, **Olsen**, Org de Rac (2) (Organic), Ormonde, Passages, Pearl Mountain, Perdeberg, Place in the Sun (Fairtrade), Pulpit Rock, Ridgeback, Riebeek, Robertson (4), Rosendal, Tread Lightly, **Ultra Liquors**, Viljoensdrift, Villiera, Wellington Winery, **Woolworths** (5) (Organic), Yonder Hill, Zevenwacht, Zonnebloem ★★★ Alvi's Drift, Arra, Badsberg (2), Bellingham (2), Blomendahl, Bonnievale, Boplaas, Boschendal, Burgershof, Calitzdorp, Cape Dreams, Desert Rose, Drostdy-Hof, Du Preez, Du Toitskloof (Fairtrade), **Fat Bastard**, Fish Hoek, Flagstone, Fort Simon, Franschhoek Cellar, Goede Hoop, Goedverwacht, Group CDV, Havana Hills, Het Vlock Casteel, Hill & Dale, Hoopenburg, House of Mandela (Fairtrade), Kanu, Kleine Zalze, Kranskop, Landskroon, Le Manoir de Brendel, Libby's Pride, Louisvale, Lourensford, MAN Family, Namaqua, Riebeek, Simonsvlei, Slanghoek, Spier, Stellenbosch Family Wines, Stellenbosch Hills, Stellenbosch Vineyards, Stettyn, Swartland, **Thandi**, The Butcher Shop, The Rhino of Linton Park, uniWines (Fairtrade), **Van Loveren** (2), **Varkenskraal**, Vredenheim, Wandsbeck, Weltevrede, Windmeul, Woolworths ★★ **Asara**, Bayede!, Bergwater, Bonview, Bottelary, Bridge, Douglas Green, Fort Simon,

Glenview, Goudini, Group CDV, Klawer, Kleine Draken (Kosher), La Petite Province, **Landzicht** (2), Leopard's Leap, Lomond, Lutzville, **Mountain Ridge**, Nicholson Smith, Obikwa, Robertson, Rooiberg, **Schenkfontein**, Seven Sisters, Stellar (2) (Organic, Fairtrade), Tulbagh Winery, Viljoensdrift, Woolworths (4) (Organic, Fairtrade) ★★ De Bos (Fairtrade), Hoopenburg, Long Mountain, **Simonsvlei**, **Van Loveren** (Light & low-alcohol), Vinopoly, Wonderfontein, Woolworths (Light & low-alcohol), Zidela **NT** Anthonij Rupert (2), Bergwater, Buffalo Creek, Calais, Camberley, Catherine Marshall, Cranefields, De Villiers (2), Dieu Donné, Domaine Brahms, Domaine Coutelier, Du Preez, Dunstone, Eikehof, Fernskloof (Organic), Graceland, Herold, High Constantia (2), Kirabo, **Klein Dauphine**, Klein Parys, Kleinhoekkloof, La Couronne, Linton Park, Major's Hill, Manley, Maske, Mont Rochelle, My Wyn, Nederburg, Nietvoorbij, Old Vines, Oude Compagnies Post, Overhex, Painted Wolf, Rietvallei, **RiverGold**, Ruitersvlei, Sarah's, Savanha, Stellendrift (2), Stellenrust, Stone Ridge, Swartland, Tall Horse, TCB Wines, **Under Oaks**, Versailles, Vrede en Lust, **Walker Bay Vineyards**, **Waverley Hills** (2), Wineways (5), Women in Wine, Zidela **D** Blue Crane, Durbanville Hills, Rooiberg, Schalkenbosch, The Winery of Good Hope, uniWines, Wonderfontein

Mourvèdre

★★★★ **Black Pearl**, Fairview, Grangehurst, **Hirst**, Raka, Signal Hill, Spice Route (2) (Fairtrade), **Tierhoek**

★★★☆ Arra, Beaumont, Boschheim, Hawksmoor, Hermit on the Hill, MAN Family, **Tim Martin** ★★☆ Arra **NT** Almenkerk, Idiom, Oude Compagnies Post, The Three Foxes

Muscadel, red, fortified

★★★★★ Rooiberg

★★★★☆ Nuy (2)

★★★★ Allesverloren, Badsberg, Bon Courage, Boplaas, De Wet, Montagu Wine Cellar, Nuweland, Orange River, Wonderfontein

★★★☆ Aan de Doorns, Boplaas, Clairvaux, Excelsior Vlakteplaas, Klawer (2), Namaqua, Reiersvlei, Slanghoek, Van Loveren ★★★ Boplaas, Du Toitskloof (Fairtrade), Jakkalsvlei, Klein Parys, Landzicht, Roodezandt, Tulbagh Winery ★★★☆ Conradie, Die Mas, Grundheim, McGregor, **Swartland**, Vinopoly, Wandsbeck **NT** Ashton, Boplaas, Calitzdorp, Karusa, Mooiuitsig, Rietvallei (2), Robertson, SoetKaroo, TTT Cellar, Wolvendrift

Muscadel, red, unfortified
NT Landzicht

Muscadel, white, fortified
★★★★★ Alvi's Drift, Boplaas, La Couronne

★★★★☆ Boplaas, Calitzdorp, De Krans, Domein Doornkraal, Monis, Nuy, Orange River

★★★★ Bon Courage, De Wet, Graham Beck, Lutzville, Weltevrede, Windmeul

★★★☆ Clairvaux, Klawer, Merwida, Namaqua, Wonderfontein ★★★ Boplaas, Die Mas, Excelsior Vlakteplaas, Landzicht, McGregor, Robertson, Vinopoly ★★ Grundheim **NT** Montagu Wine Cellar, Mooiuitsig, Mostertsdrift, Withoek **D** De Wetshof

Muscadel, white, unfortified
★★★★☆ AA Badenhorst

★★★★ Elsenburg

★★★ Leopard's Leap ★★☆ Imbuko (Perlé, Light & low-alcohol), Thelema ★★ Badsberg (Perlé, Light & low-alcohol), De Krans (Perlé, Light & low-alcohol), De Wet ★☆ Vinopoly **NT** Fledge & Co, Karusa (2) **D** Obikwa

Muscat de Hambourg fortified
★★★★ Weltevrede ★★★ Stellenbosch Hills

Muscat Ottonel unfortified
NT Zidela

Natural Sweet, red
★★★★☆ Adoro

★★☆ Cape Dreams, Goudini, Somerset Wines ★★ 4th Street (Perlé, Light & low-alcohol), **Bonnievale**, Drostdy-Hof (Light & low-alcohol), Robertson (2) (Light & low-alcohol), Rooiberg ★☆ 4th Street (Light & low-alcohol), Kleine Draken (Light & low-alcohol, Kosher), Van Loveren ★ **Douglas Green** (Light & low-alcohol), Kanu ☆ Woolworths **NT** Arra, Blomendahl (2), Bosman, Cape Hutton, Lutzville

Natural Sweet, rosé
★★★★☆ Groot Constantia

★★★ Orange River ★★★ Nelson, Seven Sisters, Somerset Wines ★★ 4th Street (Perlé, Light & low-alcohol), Drostdy-Hof (Light & low-alcohol), Grünberger (2) (Perlé, Light & low-alcohol), Robertson (Light & low-alcohol), Rooiberg, **Simonsvlei** (Light & low-alcohol), The Rhino of Linton Park, **Tulbagh Winery** (Light & low-alcohol), Van Loveren (Light & low-alcohol), **Woolworths** ★☆ 4th Street (Light & low-alcohol), Douglas Green (Light & low-alcohol), Landzicht (Light & low-alcohol), Robertson (3) (Light & low-alcohol), Slanghoek (Light & low-

alcohol), Woolworths ★ Simonsvlei **NT** Lutzville **D** Van Loveren

Natural Sweet, white
★★★★★ Klein Constantia

★★★★☆ Badsberg, **Bartho Eksteen**, Dornier, Perdeberg

★★★★ Laibach (Light & low-alcohol), **Mimosa**, Ridgeback, Stony Brook (Light & low-alcohol), Waterford

★★★☆ Delheim, Glen Carlou ★★★ **Lynx**, Quando (Light & low-alcohol), Rooiberg, Somerset Wines (Light & low-alcohol), Zandvliet ★★★ Arra, Domein Doornkraal, Grünberger (Light & low-alcohol), Theuniskraal ★★ 4th Street (Light & low-alcohol), Douglas Green (Light & low-alcohol), Drostdy-Hof (Light & low-alcohol), Goudini, Kleine Draken (Light & low-alcohol, Kosher), Orange River ★★ 4th Street (Perlé, Light & low-alcohol), Group CDV (Light & low-alcohol), Landzicht (Light & low-alcohol), Robertson (3) (Light & low-alcohol), Van Loveren (Light & low-alcohol), Woolworths **NT** Edgebaston, Jordan, Lord's, Lutzville (Light & low-alcohol), Nederburg, Quoin Rock, Zorgvliet **D** Le Pommier, Meerendal, Rickety Bridge

Nebbiolo
★★★★☆ Steenberg

★★★★ Idiom, Morgenster

★★★☆ Du Toitskloof ★★★ Hofstraat **NT** Dagbreek

Noble Late Harvest
★★★★★ Miles Mossop, Nederburg, Signal Hill

★★★★☆ **Benguela Cove**, Boekenhoutskloof, Bon Courage (Light & low-alcohol), Boschendal, Buitenverwachting, De Wetshof (Light & low-alcohol), Delheim, Fleur du Cap (Light & low-alcohol), Ken Forrester, Lourensford, Lutzville, Nederburg, Paul Cluver, **Paul Wallace**, Post House, Rudera, Spier, Springfontein, Tokara

★★★★ Asara, Badsberg, Beaumont, Blaauwklippen (2), Bloemendal, Darling Cellars, Durbanville Hills, Fort Simon, **Fryer's Cove**, Gabriëlskloof, Joostenberg, Kanu, Kranskop, Longridge, Mulderbosch, Shannon, Signal Hill, Simonsig, Slaley, Slanghoek, **Stellenbosch Vineyards**, Virgin Earth

★★★☆ Blaauwklippen, De Grendel (Light & low-alcohol), **Highlands Road**, Nelson, **Rickety Bridge**, **Van Loveren** ★★★ Hildenbrand, Namaqua **NT** Avontuur, Badsberg, Cape Point, D'Aria, Delaire, Hartenberg, L'illa, Morgenhof, Neethlingshof, Nitida, Stellenrust, Villiera,

Woolworths **D** Altydgedacht (Light & low-alcohol), Du Toitskloof , Hermanuspietersfontein, Van Loveren

Non-muscat, white, fortified
★★★★ Haute Cabrière

Nouveau
★★★ Groot Parys (Pinotage) ★★ Asara (Gamay noir)

Organic
★★★★☆ Avondale (Sparkling, Méthode cap classique, white, dry), **Klein Constantia** (Sauvignon blanc unwooded), Laibach (Merlot), Hughes Family (White blends, wooded, dry), Porseleinberg (Shiraz/syrah), Silvermist (Sauvignon blanc unwooded)

★★★★ **Woolworths** (3) (Merlot, Red blends, Cape Bordeaux, Red blends, Cape Bordeaux), **Stellar** (Chenin blanc wooded, dry, Fairtrade), Avondale (3) (Red blends, shiraz/syrah-based, Chenin blanc wooded, dry, White blends, wooded, dry), Bellingham (Shiraz/syrah), Org de Rac (3) (Cabernet sauvignon, Shiraz/syrah, Sparkling, Méthode cap classique, white, dry), Painted Wolf (Grenache noir), Waverley Hills (3) (Shiraz/syrah, Red blends, shiraz/syrah-based, Grenache noir), Org de Rac (Husk spirit/grappa-styles), Upland (2) (Brandy, Brandy), Dalla Cia (Husk spirit/grappa-styles), De Breede (Shiraz/syrah), Groot Parys (2) (Chenin blanc wooded, dry, Vin de paille), Elgin Ridge (Sauvignon blanc unwooded), Upland (Husk spirit/grappa-styles), Laibach (Red blends, Cape Bordeaux), Lazanou (White blends, unwooded, dry), Joostenberg (Shiraz/syrah)

★★★★☆ **Woolworths** (2) (Chardonnay wooded, Chardonnay wooded), Avondale (3) (Shiraz/syrah, Red blends, Cape Bordeaux, Rosé dry), **Stellar** (2) (Pinotage, Red blends, with pinotage, Fairtrade), **Org de Rac** (2) (Chardonnay wooded, Red blends, shiraz/syrah-based), Waverley Hills (2) (White blends, wooded, dry, Sparkling, Méthode cap classique, white, dry), Org de Rac (Red blends, other), Stellar (Vin de paille, Fairtrade), De Breede (Merlot), Groot Parys (3) (Chenin blanc wooded, dry, Chenin blanc unwooded dry, Sparkling, Méthode cap classique, white, off-dry/semi-sweet), Elgin Ridge (Pinot noir), Laibach (White blends, wooded, dry), Lazanou (3) (Shiraz/syrah, Red blends, shiraz/syrah-based, Chenin blanc unwooded dry), Matzikama (Pinot noir), Mountain Oaks (Pinotage), **Jacques Germanier** (Red blends, other, Fairtrade), Joostenberg (2) (Red blends, shiraz/syrah-based, Red blends, other),

Upland (Cabernet sauvignon) ★★★ **Woolworths** (4) (Cabernet sauvignon, Merlot, Rosé dry, Sauvignon blanc unwooded, Fairtrade), Stellar (White blends, unwooded, dry, Fairtrade), Woolworths (Sparkling, Méthode cap classique, red, dry), Org de Rac (Merlot), **Stellar** (2) (Pinotage, White blends, wooded, dry, Fairtrade), **Org de Rac** (6) (Cabernet sauvignon, Merlot, Chardonnay wooded, Chardonnay unwooded, White blends, unwooded, dry, Port-style, red), Waverley Hills (4) (Cabernet sauvignon, Shiraz/syrah, Red blends, other, Red blends, other), Org de Rac (Red blends, Cape Bordeaux), **Stellar** (3) (Cabernet sauvignon, Rosé dry, Chenin blanc unwooded dry, Fairtrade), **Groot Parys** (4) (Pinotage, Rosé dry, Chardonnay wooded, Chenin blanc unwooded dry, Nouveau), Earthbound (4) (Cabernet sauvignon, Pinotage, Chenin blanc unwooded dry, Sauvignon blanc unwooded, Fairtrade), Matzikama (Shiraz/syrah), Mountain Oaks (Red blends, Cape Bordeaux), **Jacques Germanier** (Red blends, Cape Bordeaux, Fairtrade), Reyneke (2) (Red blends, shiraz/syrah-based, White blends, unwooded, dry), **Joostenberg** (3) (Chenin blanc wooded, dry, Chenin blanc wooded, dry, White blends, wooded, dry), **Solara** (Sauvignon blanc unwooded), Groot Parys (Red blends, with pinotage) ★★☆ Woolworths (3) (Shiraz/syrah, Chardonnay wooded, Sauvignon blanc unwooded, Fairtrade), Stellar (Sauvignon blanc unwooded, Fairtrade), Woolworths (Sparkling, Non-MCC, white, dry), **Stellar** (5) (Cabernet sauvignon, Shiraz/syrah, Chardonnay wooded, White blends, unwooded, dry, Red blends, shiraz/syrah-based, Fairtrade), Org de Rac (3) (Shiraz/syrah, Red blends, shiraz/syrah-based, Rosé dry), Waverley Hills (Jerepigo red), Org de Rac (Red blends, Cape Bordeaux), Stellar (2) (Red blends, shiraz/syrah-based, White blends, off-dry/semi-sweet (w & u/w), Fairtrade), De Breede (2) (Red blends, Cape Bordeaux, Red blends, Cape Bordeaux), Groot Parys (Chardonnay wooded), Earthbound (Pinot noir, Fairtrade), **iKapa Jazz** (4) (Pinotage, Red blends, with pinotage, Chenin blanc unwooded dry, Sparkling, Méthode cap classique, white, dry, Fairtrade), **Jacques Germanier** (2) (White blends, unwooded, dry, White blends, unwooded, dry, Fairtrade), Re'Mogo (5) (Pinotage, Red blends, with pinotage, Chardonnay wooded, Chenin blanc unwooded dry, Sparkling, Méthode cap classique, white, dry, Fairtrade), Upland (Port-style, red) ★★ Woolworths (2) (Merlot, Pinotage, Fairtrade), Stellar (7) (Chardonnay wooded, Merlot, Rosé dry,

Merlot, Pinotage, Shiraz/syrah, Rosé dry, Fairtrade), De Breede (Cabernet sauvignon), **iKapa Jazz** (2) (Rosé dry, Sparkling, Non-MCC, rosé, off-dry/semi-sweet, Fairtrade), Mountain Oaks (Red blends, with pinotage), **Re'Mogo** (2) (Rosé dry, Sparkling, Non-MCC, rosé, off-dry/semi-sweet, Fairtrade) ★★ De Breede (Red blends, Cape Bordeaux) **NT** Stellar (Sparkling, Non-MCC, white, dry), Waverley Hills (4) (Rosé dry, Pinot gris/grigio, White blends, unwooded, dry, Cabernet sauvignon), Groot Parys (Chenin blanc wooded, dry), Fernskloof (6) (Cabernet sauvignon, Merlot, Pinotage, Red blends, shiraz/syrah-based, Rosé dry, Chardonnay wooded), Lazanou (Chardonnay wooded), Mountain Oaks (3) (Rosé dry, Chardonnay wooded, White blends, unwooded, dry), Scali (2) (White blends, wooded, dry, Sparkling, Méthode ancestrale), Silvermist (Red blends, other), Scali (Pinotage) **NR** Lazanou (Viognier) **D** Woolworths (Colombard, Fairtrade), Joostenberg (2) (Rosé dry, White blends, unwooded, dry)

Perlé Wines

★★★ **Louiesenhof** (Rosé off-dry/semi-sweet) ★★★ **Robertson** (Sauvignon blanc unwooded, Perlé), Group CDV (White blends, off-dry/semi-sweet (w & u/w), Perlé), Imbuko (Muscadel, white, unfortified, Perlé, Light & low-alcohol), Autumn Harvest Crackling (Rosé off-dry/semi-sweet, Perlé), De Wet (Rosé off-dry/semi-sweet, Perlé), Grünberger (White blends, off-dry/semi-sweet (w & u/w), Perlé), uniWines (2) (Hanepoot unfortified, Hanepoot unfortified, Perlé, Light & low-alcohol, Fairtrade) ★★ Asara (Gamay noir, Perlé, Nouveau), 4th Street (2) (Natural Sweet, red, Natural Sweet, rosé, Perlé, Light & low-alcohol), Wellington Winery (Hanepoot unfortified, Perlé), Ashton (Chenin blanc off-dry/semi-sweet (w & u/w), Perlé), Riebeek (Hanepoot unfortified, Perlé, Light & low-alcohol), Badsberg (Muscadel, white, unfortified, Perlé, Light & low-alcohol), Capenheimer (White blends, off-dry/semi-sweet (w & u/w), Perlé), De Krans (Muscadel, white, unfortified, Perlé, Light & low-alcohol), De Wet (Muscadel, white, unfortified, Perlé, Light & low-alcohol), Grünberger (Natural Sweet, rosé, Perlé), Jakkalsvlei (Rosé off-dry/semi-sweet, Perlé), Wandsbeck (Rosé off-dry/semi-sweet) ★☆ Conradie (Rosé off-dry/semi-sweet, Perlé, Light & low-alcohol), 4th Street (Natural Sweet, white, Perlé, Light & low-alcohol), Bonnievale (Chenin blanc off-dry/semi-sweet (w & u/w), Perlé, Light & low-alcohol), Autumn Harvest Crackling (White blends, off-dry/semi-sweet (w & u/w), Perlé),

Vinopoly (2) (Rosé off-dry/semi-sweet, Muscadel, white, unfortified, Perlé, Light & low-alcohol), Seven Sisters (Chenin blanc off-dry/semi-sweet (w & u/w)) ★ Riebeek (Sweet red, Perlé, Light & low-alcohol), Bonnievale (Ruby cabernet, Perlé, Light & low-alcohol), Autumn Harvest Crackling (Sweet red) ☆ Riebeek (Rosé off-dry/semi-sweet) **NT** Bergsig (White blends, off-dry/semi-sweet (w & u/w), Perlé), Calitzdorp (White blends, off-dry/semi-sweet (w & u/w))

Petit verdot

★★★★★ Stellenbosch Vineyards

★★★★ Anura, **Mitre's Edge**, Raka, Zorgvliet

★★★☆ **Botanica**, Doolhof, Hillcrest, **Leeuwenberg**, Pulpit Rock, Super Single Vineyards ★★★ Asara, Bellevue, **Die Mas**, Maison de Teijger **NT** Almenkerk, Calais, Definitum, Du Preez, High Constantia, Kirabo, Kleinhoekkloof, Lovane, My Wyn, Nederburg, Rico Suter, TTT Cellar **D** Havana Hills, Springfontein

Petite sirah/durif

★★★★☆ Fairview

★★★★ Black Elephant

★★★☆ Spotswood **NT** Karusa

Pinot gris/grigio

★★★★ Arendskloof

★★★☆ **Craven**, Idiom, Nederburg, Township Winery, Usana, Val du Charron ★★★ Fairview, Flat Roof Manor, Hill & Dale, **Nederburg**, Overhex, **Stellenbosch Vineyards**, Stettyn ★★★ **Merwida**, Spring Grove, Two Oceans, Van Loveren, Woolworths ★★ Obikwa, Robertson **NT** Anthonij Rupert, De Grendel, Stellekaya, Waverley Hills

Pinot noir

★★★★★ Bouchard Finlayson, Newton Johnson, Sumaridge

★★★★☆ Bouchard Finlayson, **Buitenverwachting**, Cape Chamonix, Cederberg, Clouds, **Creation** (2), Crystallum (4), Dalla Cia, De Grendel, Donkiesbaai, Driehoek, Elgin Vintners, **Euphoria**, Hamilton Russell, Litigo, Paul Cluver (2), Shannon, Storm (2), The Winery of Good Hope (2)

★★★★ Arendskloof, **Black Block**, Blackwater, Boschendal, Brunia, Cape Chamonix, Catherine Marshall (2), Clive Torr, Craven, Creation, De Wetshof, Edgebaston (2), **Fledge & Co**, Groote Post, Haute Cabrière, **Herold**, Iona, Jasper Raats, **JH Meyer** (2), **Joubert-Tradauw**, La Chaumiere, La Vierge, Meerlust, Meinert, Muratie, Nederburg, Newton Johnson, **Nitida**, Oak Valley, Paul Cluver, Seven Springs , Signal Hill, South Hill, Stark-Condé,

Strandveld (2), The Butcher Shop, **The Giant Periwinkle**, **The Winery of Good Hope** (2), Topaz, Vriesenhof, Waterford, Woolworths (2), Yardstick

★★★★ Altydgedacht, Andy Mitchell, **B Vintners**, Boschheim, Claime d'Or, Dâbar, **DeMorgenzon**, Elgin Ridge (Organic), Fat Bastard, Flagstone, Fryer's Cove, Glen Carlou, Grande Provence, Herold, Highlands Road, Hoopenburg, **JH Meyer**, Kleine Zalze, La Vierge (2), Laibach, Lieben, Lomond, **Lynx**, Maison de Teijger (3), Matzikama (Organic), Meerendal, Paul Cluver, Paul Wallace, **Robert Stanford**, Scrucap, **Spioenkop**, Stark-Condé, Stellar (Fairtrade), Sterhuis, Stony Brook, **The Ahrens Family**, **The Goose**, Two Oceans, **Ultra Liquors**, Veenwouden, Virgin Earth (Fairtrade), Vriesenhof, Whalehaven, Winters Drift, Woolworths (2) ★★★ Andy Mitchell, Avontuur, **Bellevue**, Bon Courage, **Corder**, De Wetshof, Domaine des Dieux, **Eerste Hoop**, Ernst Gouws, Haute Cabrière, **Hazendal**, JH Meyer, **Kaapzicht**, **Klein Constantia**, Kranskop, Lemberg, Lord's, Lothian, Maastricht, Maison de Teijger, Namaqua, **Nederburg**, Packwood, Peter Falke, Quando, Robertson, **Stellenbosch Vineyards**, Strandveld, Thelema, Van Loveren, Wilde Haf, **Woolworths** ★★★ **Benguela Cove**, Earthbound (Organic, Fairtrade), Maison de Teijger (2), Osbloed, Overhex, Snow Mountain, Stellenbosch Family Wines ★★ Goedvertrouw, Sophie & Mr P **NT** AntHill, Baleia, Botanica, Clive Torr, De Bos (Fairtrade), Elemental Bob, Felicité, Glen Carlou, Herold, Karusa, Kleinhoekkloof, Longbarn, **Lord's**, **MVH Signature Wines**, **My Wyn**, Newton Johnson (3), Ormonde (2), Snow Mountain, Spookfontein, Springfield, Stark-Condé, Stellekaya, The Giant Periwinkle, The Hills, The Winery of Good Hope, Wine Fusion **D** Backsberg, Blackwater

Pinotage

★★★★★ Beeslaar, Rijk's, Spier, Windmeul

★★★★☆ Bellingham, **Beyerskloof** (2), Cape Chamonix, Cecilia, Chateau Naudé, Delheim, DeWaal, Diemersfontein, Flagstone, Grangehurst, Groot Constantia, Kaapzicht (2), Kanonkop (2), L'Avenir, Lemberg, Meerendal, Môreson, Paardebosch, Pulpit Rock, Simonsig, Spioenkop, The Winery of Good Hope

★★★★ Aaldering, Alkmaar, Allée Bleue, Altydgedacht, Anura, Arendskloof, **B Vintners**, Bayede!, Beaumont, Bellevue, Beyerskloof, **Black Elephant**, Clos Malverne, Conradie, DeWaal, Diemersdal, Durbanville Hills, Eaglevlei, Eenzaamheid, Eikendal, Escapades, Fairview (2)

(Fairtrade), Flagstone, **Fleur du Cap**, Four Paws, Fram, Kanonkop, Kleine Zalze, L'Avenir, Lanzerac, Longridge, Lyngrove, M'hudi, Neethlingshof, Nuy, **Overhex**, Painted Wolf (2), Perdeberg, Remhoogte, Reyneke (Biodynamic), Rijk's, Rooiberg, Slaley, Southern Right, Spice Route (Fairtrade), Spioenkop, Springfontein, Super Single Vineyards, SylvanVale, **Taillard**, **Ultra Liquors**, **Weltevrede**, Whalehaven, Wildekrans, Woolworths, Zonnebloem

★★★★ Anura, **Arendskloof**, Badsberg, Bellevue, Bergsig, Beyerskloof, Bloemendal, Boland, Bosman (Fairtrade), Brampton, Camberley, Cape Dreams, Clos Malverne, DeanDavid, Delheim, DewaldtHeyns, Die Mas, Diemersdal, Diemersfontein, Doolhof, Dornier, **Dragonridge**, Eagle's Cliff, Ernst Gouws, Fairvalley (Fairtrade), False Bay, Fleur du Cap, Franschhoek Cellar, Freedom Hill, Graham Beck, Hidden Valley, Hofstraat, Hoopenburg, Hornbill, Imbuko, Ken Forrester, Kleine Zalze, Knorhoek, Laibach, **Louiesenhof**, Lutzville, M'hudi, Maastricht, Malanot, MAN Family, Marianne, Marklew, Meerendal, Meinert, Middelvlei, Mooiplaas, Mountain Oaks (Organic), Mountain River, Neethlingshof, Niel Joubert, Olifantsberg, Olsen, Onderkloof, Passages, Perdeberg, Raka, Rhebokskloof, Rico Suter, Rijk's, Robertson, Romond, Saxenburg, Schalkenbosch, Silkbush, Slaley, Stanford Hills, **Stellar** (Organic, Fairtrade), Stellekaya, **Stellenbosch Family Wines**, Stellenbosch University, Stellenbosch Vineyards, Stellenrust, Swartland, **Tempel** (2), **The Butcher Shop**, The Winery of Good Hope, Uitkyk, Viljoensdrift, Villiera, Vinopoly, Virgin Earth, Warwick, Welgevallen, Wellington Winery (2), Woolworths (2), Zonnebloem ★★★ Aaldering, Alvi's Drift, Amani, Ayama, Backsberg (2) (Kosher), Barista, Barnardt Boyes, Bayede!, Bellingham (2), Bergsig, Blomendahl, Boplaas, Calitzdorp, Cape Dreams, Chateau Naudé, Cloof, Darling Cellars (3), David Frost, De Zoete Inval, DeWaal, Doran (2), Drostdy-Hof, Du Toitskloof (Fairtrade), Durbanville Hills, Earthbound (Organic, Fairtrade), Fairview, **Flagstone**, Fort Simon, Goede Hoop, Groot Parys (Organic, Nouveau), Hill & Dale, House of Mandela, **Imbuko**, Jacobsdal, Klein Parys (2), Koelenhof, Koopmanskloof (Fairtrade), Lanzerac, Lemberg, Louiesenhof, Lyngrove, M'hudi, McGregor, Merwida, Miravel, Morgenhof, Namaqua, **Nederburg** (2), New Beginnings, Obikwa, Orange River, Painted Wolf, **Perdeberg Vineyard Collection**, Piekenierskloof, Pulpit Rock, Rickety Bridge, Riebeek, Rooiberg, Signal Gun, Simonsig, Simonsvlei, Slanghoek, Slowine, Somerbosch,

Springfontein, Stanford Hills, Stellar (Organic, Fairtrade), Stellenbosch Hills, Stellenzicht, Swartland, SylvanVale, Taillard, The Grape Grinder, **Theescombe**, Thembi & Co, Tokara, Township Winery (Fairtrade), Trajan, Tulbagh Winery, Two Oceans, **Vin du Cap**, **VinGlo**, Vriesenhof (2), Wellington Winery (2), Wildekrans, Windmeul, Woolworths (3) ★★★ Aan de Doorns, Allée Bleue, Arra, Avontuur, Ayama, Bon Courage, Botha, Devon Rocks, Douglas Green, Fat Bastard, Fish Hoek, Flagstone, Graham Beck, Hawksmoor, House of Mandela (Fairtrade), **iKapa Jazz** (Organic, Fairtrade), Jason's Hill, **Juno**, Klawer, Kleine Zalze, Koelenhof, Le Manoir de Brendel, Leipzig, Namaqua (2), Re'Mogo (Organic, Fairtrade), **Reiersvlei**, Riebeek, Rooiberg, Simonsvlei, Spier, Stellenbosch Vineyards, Swartland, The Rhino of Linton Park, Tulbagh Winery, Van Loveren, Vredenheim, Welbedacht ★★ Ashton, Bergheim, Breëland, Group CDV (2), Landskroon, Lutzville, Reiersvlei, Robertson, **Schenkfontein**, Simonsvlei, Springfontein, Stellar (Organic, Fairtrade), Teubes, **Wellington Winery** (Light & low-alcohol), Welvanpas, Woolworths (Organic, Fairtrade), Zevenwacht, Zidela ★★ Long Mountain (2), Mountain River, uniWines (Fairtrade), Van Loveren (Fairtrade), Woolworths **NT** Anthonij Rupert, Arra, Avondrood, Black Elephant, Blomendahl, Boer & Brit, Buffalo Creek, Calais, Croydon, De Villiers, Domaine Brahms, Fernskloof (Organic), Freedom Hill, Govert, Group CDV, Imbuko, Jakkalsvlei, Karusa, Klein Parys, Knorhoek, L'Avenir, La Couronne, Major's Hill, MAN Family, Manley, Mount Vernon, Nederburg (3) (Fairtrade), Neil Ellis (2), Nietvoorbij, Nuweland, **Nuy**, Old Vines, Oude Compagnies Post (2), Overhex, Rosendal, Ruitersvlei, Saam, Scali (2) (Organic), Spier, Stellenbosch University, Stellendrift, Stellenrust, Tall Horse, Teubes, **The Butcher Shop**, Township Winery, **Under Oaks**, **Valley Vineyards**, Vierkoppen, Welbedacht, Welgegund, Wine Fusion, Wineways (5), Zidela **NR** Mountain River **D** Annex Kloof, Anura, Burgershof, De Zoete Inval, Goudini, Lateganskop, Long Mountain, Rhebokskloof, Springfontein, uniWines, Waboomsrivier, Wellington Winery, Withington

Port-style, pink
★★★ Boplaas ★★★ De Krans **NT** Peter Bayly

Port-style, red
★★★★★ Boplaas (2), De Krans

★★★★☆ Axe Hill, Boplaas (3), De Krans (3), Groot Constantia

★★★★ Allesverloren, Anura, Beaumont, Bergsig, Boplaas (3), De Wet (2), Delaire, **Hout Bay**, Kloovenburg, Landskroon, Lieben, Monis, Muratie (2), Overgaauw, Peter Bayly, **Rosendal**, Simonsig ★★★☆ Aan de Doorns, Alto, Annandale, Axe Hill, Backsberg, Beau Joubert, Bergsig (2), Beyerskloof, Calitzdorp, **Dagbreek**, De Krans, Domein Doornkraal (2), Douglas Green, Du'SwaRoo, Elsenburg, Flagstone, Grundheim, Jacques Smit, Kaapzicht, Louiesenhof, Monis, Rooiberg, Slanghoek, Spookfontein , Swartland, Taillard, **Tulbagh Winery**, Vergenoegd, Zandvliet ★★★ Anura, Axe Hill, Badsberg, Bon Courage, Botha, Catherine Marshall, Clairvaux, Die Mas, Druk My Niet, Du Toitskloof (Fairtrade), Fairview, Holden Manz, Koelenhof, Louiesenhof, **Lovane**, **Org de Rac** (Organic), Riebeek, Robertson, SoetKaroo, **Stellenbosch University**, Stettyn, Swartland, Vergenoegd, Viljoensdrift, Waboomsrivier, Windmeul ★★☆ Grundheim, Hofstraat, Orange River, Peter Bayly, Upland (Organic), Van Loveren, Wellington Winery ★★ Allée Bleue, **Entre Nous**, Klawer, Namaqua, Reiersvlei, Villiersdorp ★☆ Bergwater, **Reiersvlei** ★ McGregor **NT** Anthonij Rupert, Boplaas, Calitzdorp, Goede Hoop, Grundheim, Karusa, Landzicht, Lieben, Lovane, Montpellier, Morgenhof, My Wyn, Nietvoorbij, SoetKaroo, Somersbosch, TTT Cellar (2), Tulbagh Winery, Withoek (3) **D** De Zoete Inval (2), Highlands Road, Maison

Port-style, white
★★★☆ Axe Hill ★★★ Boplaas, Grundheim, Peter Bayly **NT** My Wyn, TTT Cellar

Red blends, Cape Bordeaux
★★★★★ Delaire, Meerlust, Miles Mossop, Mulderbosch, Mvemve Raats, Spier

★★★★☆ Allée Bleue, Backsberg, Bartinney, Barton, Beaumont, Boschkloof , Buitenverwachting, Cape Chamonix, Constantia Glen (2), De Toren (2), DeMorgenzon, Diemersdal, Dornier, Druk My Niet, Du Toitskloof (Fairtrade), Eikendal, Epicurean, Ernie Els, Grande Provence, Grangehurst (2), Groot Constantia, Hartenberg, Hermanuspietersfontein, Hillcrest, Jordan (2), Journey's End, Kaapzicht, Kanonkop, Keet, Klein Constantia, Laibach, Le Bonheur, Longridge, Lourensford, **Mitre's Edge**, Môreson, Morgenster (2), Muratie, Nabygelegen, Nederburg, Neethlingshof, Nitida, Oak Valley, Ormonde, Overgaauw, Raats, Rainbow's End, Raka, Remhoogte, Romond, Rustenberg, Simonsig,

Springfield, Stellenbosch Reserve, Stellenrust, **Strydom**, The Butcher Shop, **The Liberator**, Thelema, Tokara, Van Biljon, Vergelegen (2), Vergenoegd (2), Vilafonté (2), Waterford, Windmeul, Woolworths, **Zevenwacht**

★★★★ Akkerdraai, Arra, Asara, BABISA, **Babylonstoren**, Backsberg, Beau Joubert, Belfield, Bellevue, Beyerskloof, Bilton, **Botanica**, Brothers, **Buitenverwachting**, Camberley, CK Wines, Cloof, Conspirare, Constantia Uitsig, Creation, Croydon, Dalla Cia, Damarakloof, Darling Cellars, De Grendel, De Toren, Deux Frères, Diemersdal, Dornier, Elgin Vintners, Gabriëlskloof, Glen Carlou, Grangehurst, Haskell, Hermanuspietersfontein, Hidden Valley, Holden Manz, Kanu, Knorhoek, La Bri, La Motte, La Petite Ferme, Laibach (Organic), Le Riche, Leopard's Leap, Lovane, Lynx, Marklew, Miravel, Mooiplaas, Morgenhof (2), Namaqua, Napier, Nederburg, Neil Ellis, Nelson, Nico van der Merwe, Nico Vermeulen, Noble Hill, **Overhex**, **Paul Wallace**, Peter Falke, Raka, Reyneke (Biodynamic), Ridgeback, Robert Stanford, **Rosendal**, Russo, Saltare, Saronsberg, Spier, Spookfontein , Stellekaya (2), Stellenbosch Vineyards, Stonewall, Stony Brook, **Tempel**, The Butcher Shop, The High Road (2), **The Liberator**, **Ultra Liquors**, Uva Mira, Veenwouden, Vergelegen, Vriesenhof , Warwick, Webersburg, Welbedacht, **Woolworths** (3) (Organic), Yardstick, Yonder Hill, Zorgvliet

★★★½ Aaldering, Amani, Anura, Ashton, Avondale (Organic), Avontuur, Babylon's Peak, Beau Constantia, Black Oystercatcher, **BLANKbottle**, Boschkloof , Buitenverwachting, Cape Chamonix, Capelands, Claime d'Or, Cloof, Clos Malverne, D'Aria, Delavia, DeWaal, Domaine Brahms, Doolhof (2), Dornier, Edgebaston, Equitania, Gabriëlskloof, Goudini, Havana Hills, Hillcrest, Idiom, Ken Forrester, Klein Constantia, Klein Roosboom , L'Avenir, Louisvale, Marianne, **Miles Mossop**, Mimosa, **MolenVliet**, Monterosso, Neethlingshof, Nelson, Nick & Forti's, Noble Savage, Oldenburg, Passages, Rogge Cloof, **Russo**, Saronsberg, Schalkenbosch, Scrucap, Skilpadvlei, Steenberg, Sterhuis, **SylvanVale**, **Taillard**, The Butcher Shop, Thunderchild, **Van Eck**, **Vierkoppen**, **VinGlo**, Virgin Earth (Fairtrade), Welgemeend, Wildekrans, Windmeul, **Woolworths** (3), Yonder Hill, Zorgvliet

★★★ Akkerdal, Alkmaar, Allée Bleue, Audacia, Avontuur, Barry Gould, Bayede!, Beyerskloof, Blomendahl, Bonnievale, Brenaissance, Camberley, Cape Classics, De Wet, **De Zoete Inval**, Diemersdal, Diemersfontein, Doolhof (2), Eagle's Cliff, Eagles' Nest, Fort Simon (2), Goedverwacht,

Hartenberg, Herold, Jacaranda, **Jacques Germanier** (Organic, Fairtrade), Jason's Hill, Journey's End, Landskroon, **Le Pommier**, Louiesenhof, Lourensford, **MolenVliet** (2), Morgenhof, Mostertsdrift, Mountain Oaks (Organic), Opstal, Org de Rac (Organic), Overhex, Perdeberg, Rooiberg, Signal Gun, Simonsvlei, Slaley, Steenberg, Stoep, **Swartland**, The Winery of Good Hope, Thelema, **Tulbagh Winery**, Two Oceans, **Ultra Liquors**, uniWines (2), **VinGlo**, Vondeling, Welgemeend, Woolworths **★★★** Akkerdal, AntHill, Asara, Ayama, Beau Joubert, Darling Cellars, De Breede (2) (Organic), Doran, Douglas Green, Dusty Heath, Fort Simon (2), Havana Hills (Fairtrade), **Jacaranda**, La Petite Provence, McGregor, Nicholson Smith, Org de Rac (Organic), Overgaauw, Riebeek, Simonsig, Slanghoek, Somerset Wines, Stellenbosch Family Wines, Taillard, **uniWines**, Van Zylshof, Vaughan Johnson, Vierlanden, Villiersdorp, Woolworths **★★** **Asara**, Bon Courage, Boschendal, Doran, Dusty Heath, Glen Carlou, **Hathersage**, La Couronne, Mountain Ridge, Saxenburg, Schalkenbosch, Tulbagh Winery, Welgemeend, Woolworths **★★** De Breede (Organic), Leopard's Leap **NT** Alto, Amani, Anthonij Rupert (2), Beau Constantia, Boer & Brit, Camberley, Crows Nest, Diemersfontein, Dieu Donné, Equitania, Fernskloof, **Govert**, Hathersage (2), High Constantia, Hillock, Hoopenburg, Jordan (2), Lathithá, Malanot, Meerlust, Montpellier, Môreson (2), Natte Valleij, Nederburg, Nietvoorbij (2), Nomada, Old Vines, Oneiric, Rietvallei, Rosendal, Ruitersvlei, Rupert & Rothschild, Southern Sky, Springfontein, Star Hill, Stellendrift (3), Swartland (3), Van Loveren, Villiera, Vrede en Lust, Vredevol, Walker Bay Vineyards, Welgevallen, Wineways (4), Wolvendrift **D** Anura, Darling Cellars, Durbanville Hills, Entre Nous, Kleine Draken (Kosher), Kleine Zalze, Louis, Rhebokskloof, Thandi (Fairtrade), Uva Mira, Vendôme (2), Vin du Cap, Wineways, Zevenwacht

Red blends, other

★★★★★ Ernie Els, Fleur du Cap, Haskell, **Savage**, The Butcher Shop, Vuurberg

★★★★½ Adoro, Arendskloof, Bergsig, Black Pearl, **Boplaas**, Bouchard Finlayson, **Cape Wine** , Dalla Cia, De Trafford, Druk My Niet, Ernie Els, Fairview (2), **Fledge & Co**, Graham Beck, Ken Forrester, Mont du Toit (2), Nederburg (3), Paserene, Plaisir, Rust en Vrede, **Savage**, The Winery of Good Hope, Val de Vie, Waterford

★★★★ Akkerdal, Allesverloren, Amani (2), Annandale (2), Babylonstoren, Blaauwklippen, Boplaas, Bramon, Capaïa (2), De Krans, De Meye,

Eikendal, Fairview, **Flagstone**, Glen Carlou, Graceland, Groenland, Keermont, Klein Gustrouw, Lingen, Marianne, Mellasat, Mont du Toit, Morgenster, Nabygelegen, Nietgegund, Osbloed, Solms-Delta, Somerbosch, Steenberg, Strydom, **Tempel**, **The Ahrens Family**, The Goose, **Van Eck**, Veenwouden, Waterkloof, Zonnebloem

★★★★☆ Akkerdal, Arumdale, Ataraxia, Axe Hill (2), Badsberg, **BLANKbottle** (2), Blue Crane, Boplaas, Boschheim (2), Capaia, Cederberg, Cloof, Desert Rose, Dormershire, Escapades, **Four Paws**, GlenWood, Goats do Roam, Hartenberg, Haut Espoir, Havana Hills, Hill & Dale, Holden Manz (2), Idiom, **Jacques Germanier** (Organic, Fairtrade), Jacques Smit, Joostenberg (Organic), Joubert-Tradauw, Kanu, **Kyburg** (2), **La Chaumiere**, La Vierge, **Leeuwenberg** (2), Linton Park, Mary Le Bow, Micu Narunsky, Mont Rochelle, Nederburg, Neil Ellis, Org de Rac (Organic), Osbloed, **Owl & Vine**, Peter Falke, Plaisir, Rainbow's End, Remhoogte, Rhebokskloof (2), Rico Suter, Schalkenbosch, Skilpadvlei, Stellekaya, Swartland, Thelema, Topaz, Veenwouden, Wavescape, Wildehurst, Woolworths (2) ★★★ Allée Bleue, Allesverloren, Arra, Audacia, Backsberg, Blaauwklippen, **BLANKbottle**, Blomendahl, Bonnievale, Botha, Bushmanspad, Calitzdorp, Chateau Libertas, Chennells, Clos Malverne, Delheim, Dornier, Du Preez, Du Toitskloof (2) (Fairtrade), Du'SwaRoo, Esau, Franki's, Groote Post, Hermanuspietersfontein, Keermont, Koelenhof, Kumala, La Kavayan, Micu Narunsky, Mont Destin, Napier, Nuweland, Onderkloof, Peter Bayly, Raka, Robertson, RobinHood, Saxenburg, Simonsig, Somerset Wines, Spier, Stellenbosch Family Wines, Stonehill, **The Giant Periwinkle**, The Hills, **The Liberator**, The Rhino of Linton Park, Township Winery, Vergenoegd (2), Villiera, Vredenheim, Waverley Hills (2) (Organic), Windfall, **Withington**, **Woolworths** ★★★☆ Barnardt Boyes, Barton, Blaauwklippen, Bon Courage, Brandvlei, Burgershof, Esau, Goudini, Graceland, Hazendal, Kumala (2), Landskroon (2), M'hudi, Mitre's Edge, Robertson, Tassenberg, Theuniskraal, **Under Oaks**, uniWines, Van Loveren, Welvanpas, Whalehaven, Woolworths (2) ★★ Aan de Doorns, Bergwater (2), Blouvlei, Bonnievale, Du'SwaRoo, Grande Provence, Kanu, Landskroon, Montagu Wine Cellar, Nicholson Smith, Overmeer Cellars, Robertson (2), Stellenbosch Hills, Swartland, Taverna Rouge, Van Loveren, Zandvliet ★☆ Simonsvlei, Van Loveren, Vinopoly, Welvanpas, **Woolworths** (2) (Light & low-alcohol) ★ Kumala (2), Leopard's Leap,

Woolworths (3) **NT** 4G Wines (2), Abbottshill, Akkerdal, Almenkerk, Ameera, Anthonij Rupert, Avondrood, Beaumont, Boer & Brit, Boucheron, Buffalo Creek, Calais (2), Camberley, Cape Rock, Casa Mori, Cranefields, Crows Nest (2), Dieu Donné, Gilga, Glen Heatlie, Govert (2), Hermit on the Hill, Huguenot (2), Idiom, Jean Daneel, Karusa, Ken Forrester, Kirabo (2), Klein Parys, Kumala, La Vierge, Le Bonheur, **Leeuwenberg**, Mont du Toit, Mooiuitsig, Mount Vernon, Mountain River, Natte Valleij, Nederburg (2), Oneiric, Osbloed, Oude Compagnies Post, **Piekenierskloof**, Rietvallei, Silvermist (Organic), **Sizanani**, Southern Sky, Spier, Stony Brook (2), Stoumann's, Tanagra (2), TCB Wines, Tierhoek, TTT Cellar (2), Vin du Cap, Vleiland, Wineways, Withington, Zanddrift **D** Backsberg, Bayede!, Boplaas, Darling Cellars (2), De Zoete Inval, Guardian Peak, Leeuwenberg, Sophie & Mr P, Uva Mira

Red blends, shiraz/syrah-based

★★★★★ Luddite, Nico van der Merwe, The Winery of Good Hope, **Vondeling**

★★★★☆ AA Badenhorst, Anwilka, Arra, **Bartho Eksteen**, Bellingham, Boekenhoutskloof, Cape Rock, David & Nadia Sadie, **De Grendel**, Fable, Glenelly, Haskell, Hermanuspietersfontein, Ken Forrester, Mount Abora, Newton Johnson, Paradisum, Rall, Ridgeback, Rust en Vrede, Sadie, Saronsberg, Savage, Spice Route (Fairtrade), Strandveld, Sumaridge, Welbedacht

★★★★ AA Badenhorst, Akkerdal, Alto, Annex Kloof, **Anura**, Anwilka, Avondale (Organic), Babylon's Peak, **Bartho Eksteen**, Barton, Black Oystercatcher, Black Pearl, Blackwater, Blake, Boschendal, Bosman (Fairtrade), **Bryan MacRobert**, Bushmanspad, **Clayton**, **Cloof**, Creation, Crios Bride, Deux Frères, Du Toitskloof (Fairtrade), Eenzaamheid, Ernie Els, Goats do Roam (Fairtrade), Graham Beck, Grangehurst, Guardian Peak, Hawksmoor, Hidden Valley, Highlands Road, Hoopenburg, Hout Bay, Hughes Family, Iona, Kaapzicht, Kleine Zalze, Kloovenburg, Landskroon, Lazanou, Lemberg, Leopard's Leap, Lomond, **MAN Family**, Mont Destin, Neil Ellis, Newton Johnson, **Olifantsberg**, Painted Wolf, Pearl Mountain, Perdeberg, Post House, Remhoogte, Rogge Cloof, **Rosendal**, Rustenberg, Scrucap, Sijnn, Simonsvlei, South Hill, Spice Route, Spier, Stony Brook, **Surfing Vintners**, The Butcher Shop, **The Liberator**, Tierhoek, Trizanne, **Ultra Liquors**, Val de Vie, Waverley Hills (Organic), Wildehurst, Woolworths, Zevenwacht (2), Zonnebloem

★★★★ Alkmaar, Antebellum, Ayama, Babylon's Peak, Beau Constantia, **Benguela Cove**, Bilton, Black Elephant, **Blue Crane**, Boschendal, Brampton, Bryan MacRobert, **Clayton**, D'Aria, Darling Cellars, DeMorgenzon, Diemersfontein, Dorrance, Esau, Feiteiras, Flat Roof Manor, Four Paws, Freedom Hill, Goats do Roam (Fairtrade), Groenland, **Hartenberg**, Hawksmoor, Hazendal, Hermanuspietersfontein, **Hunneyball**, Idiom, Joostenberg (Organic), Journey's End, Kronendal, La Chataigne, Lazanou (Organic), Leeuwenkuil, Longridge, Louis, Lourensford, Lyngrove, Lynx (2), Mullineux, Naughton's, Nico van der Merwe, Old Vines, **Org de Rac** (Organic), Ormonde, Oude Compagnies Post, Painted Wolf, Post House, Rickety Bridge, Rico Suter, Rosendal, Saam, Schalkenbosch, Sijnn, Simonsig, **Stanford Hills**, Stellenbosch Hills, Stellenbosch Vineyards, Stettyn, The Ahrens Family, The Butcher Shop, The Wolftrap, Thokozani, Trajan, Val de Vie, **Van Eck**, Virgin Earth, Waterford (2), **Woolworths** (3), Yardstick ★★★ Arra, Beau Joubert, Beaumont, **Blaauwklippen**, Boschendal (2), Bryan MacRobert, **Cape Classics**, **De Zoete Inval**, Domaine des Dieux, Drostdy-Hof, Eagle's Cliff, Edgebaston, Graham Beck, **Hartenberg** **Havana Hills** (Fairtrade), **Hildenbrand**, **Imbuko**, Jacaranda, Klein Parys, Kleine Zalze (2), **Konkelberg**, Lievland, Lourensford, MAN Family, Marianne, **Metzer**, Muratie, Nederburg, Noble Hill, Oude Compagnies Post, Reyneke (Organic), Saam, Somersbosch, Stellenrust, Teddy Hall, Thandi (Fairtrade), The Grape Grinder, Uitkyk, uniWines, Waka Waka, William Everson, Windfall, Withington ★★☆ Andy Mitchell, Bayede!, Bellingham, Boschendal, Boutinot, D'Aria, Drostdy-Hof, Excelsior, Flagstone, Groenland, Juno, Kaapzicht, Klawer, Kleine Zalze, Knorhoek, **Koelenhof**, Kumala, Leopard's Leap, Maske, Org de Rac (Organic), Ridgeback, Riebeek, Robert Stanford, **Rosendal**, Simonsvlei, **Stellar** (2) (Organic, Fairtrade), Stellenbosch University, Stettyn, Summerhill, Tulbagh Winery, **Valley Vineyards**, Wine Village-Hermanus, Zevenwacht ★★ Domaine Brahms, Pulpit Rock, **Ultra Liquors**, Zidela ★☆ Group CDV **NT** Abbottshill, AntHill, Auction Crossing, BABISA, Barnardt Boyes, Brenaissance, Cape Rock, Cecilia, **De Kleine Wijn Koöp**, De Villiers, DeMorgenzon, Dieu Donné, Elemental Bob, Fernskloof (Organic), Graceland, Hermit on the Hill, Heron Ridge, **Hirst**, Hoopenburg, Jean Daneel (3), Joostenberg, Kanu, Karusa (2), Manley, Melkboomsdrift, My Wyn, Nederburg,

Orangerie, Oude Compagnies Post (2), Oude Denneboom, Perdeberg, Porcupine Ridge, Post House, Rietvallei, **Santa Cecilia**, Somersbosch, Topaz, TTT Cellar, Two Oceans, **Valley Vineyards** (3), Vrede en Lust (3), Welgegund **D** Beaumont, Cowlin, Darling Cellars (2), La Motte, Mount Babylon, Nederburg (Fairtrade), Overhex, The Winery of Good Hope, uniWines, Wellington Winery

Red blends, with pinotage

★★★★★ Kaapzicht

★★★★☆ Alvi's Drift, **Beaumont** (2), Beyerskloof, Clos Malverne (2), Grangehurst (2), Meinert, **Opstal**, Rhebokskloof, Spier, Windmeul

★★★★ Anura, Ashbourne, Ashton, Beyerskloof, **Boland**, Bosman, Doolhof (2), Goede Hoop, Groot Constantia, Idiom, Klein Parys, Lanzerac, Middelvlei, **Nuy**, **Paul Roos**, Post House, Raka, Rogge Cloof, Simonsig, Stellenrust, Warwick, Welbedacht, Wildekrans

★★★☆ Asara, Carrol Boyes, Doolhof, Eaglevlei, Esau, Flagstone, Hawksmoor (2), Kaapzicht, Lateganskop, Lemberg, Lorraine, Lutzville, **Meerendal**, **Olsen**, Orange River, **Painted Wolf**, Pulpit Rock, **Romond**, Rooiberg, Spier, Springfontein, Stellar (Organic), Stellekaya, **The Liberator**, The Winery of Good Hope, Truter Family, Val du Charron (2), **Vin du Cap**, Vriesenhof, Wellington Winery, Woolworths ★★★ Anura, Asara, Ayama, Bellevue, Bergsig, Cloof, Die Mas, Goats do Roam, Groot Parys (Organic), Hornbill, Kanonkop, Knorhoek, L'Avenir, Leipzig, **Marianne**, Meinert, Mellasat, Middelvlei, Mostertsdrift, **Rhebokskloof**, Skilpadvlei, Spekulasie, **Springfontein**, Stellenbosch University, Stellenzicht, Two Oceans, Viljoensdrift, Waboomsrivier, Welgemeend, Woolworths ★★☆ Ashton, **Boutinot**, Cloof, Conradie, D'Aria, Definitum, Douglas Green,, Dragonridge, Du Toitskloof (Fairtrade), **iKapa Jazz** (Organic, Fairtrade), Jakkalsvlei, Koelenhof, Kumala (2), Louiesenhof, Namaqua, New Beginnings, Nuy, Re'Mogo (Organic, Fairtrade), Seven Sisters, Spekulasie, Stellenbosch Hills, Stellenrust (Fairtrade), uniWines, Welbedacht ★★ **Cape Dreams**, Clairvaux, Domein Doornkraal, Douglas Green, Drostdy-Hof, Du Toitskloof (Fairtrade), Flagstone, Kumala, Mooiplaas, Mountain Oaks (Organic), Roodezandt, Rooiberg, **Silkbush**, **The Observatory**, uniWines, Vinopoly, Zidela ★☆ Slanghoek ★ Reiersvlei **NT** Altydgedacht, Arra, Boer & Brit, **Cavalli**, Clos Malverne, Clovelly, Croydon, De Doorns, Fernskloof, Freedom Hill (2), Govert, Hillock, Lyngrove, Maske, Meerendal,

Mellasat, Mount Vernon, My Wyn, Oude Compagnies Post, Overhex, Rupert & Rothschild, **Santa Cecilia**, Savanha, Slaley (2), Stellekaya, Stellendrift (2), **Valley Vineyards**, Welbedacht, Whalehaven, Wine Fusion, Wineways **D** Vin du Cap

Red muscat d'Alexandrie, fortified
★★★☆ SoetKaroo

Riesling
★★★★☆ Oak Valley

★★★★ De Wetshof, Groote Post, Jordan, Nitida, Paul Cluver (2) (Light & low-alcohol), Scrucap, Spioenkop, Thelema, Woolworths

★★★☆ Altydgedacht, **Bergsig**, BLANKbottle, Fairview, Hartenberg, **Highlands Road**, Klein Constantia, Lothian, **Meinert**, Spier, Super Single Vineyards, Thelema, Waterford ★★★ La Vierge, Meinert, Nederburg, Osbloed, Wilde Haf **NT** Hartenberg, Rietvallei, Vrede en Lust **D** Darling Cellars

Rosé dry
★★★★ Bartho Eksteen, Bramon, **Fable**, Paardebosch

★★★☆ AA Badenhorst, Aaldering, Allée Bleue, Avondale (Organic), Brampton, Cape Dreams, Cloof, Clouds, Delaire, Desert Rose, **Dornier**, Eagles' Nest, Foothills, Goats do Roam (Fairtrade), Grangehurst, Haute Cabrière (2), Hermanuspietersfontein, Jordan, Morgenster, Opstal, Perdeberg, Rivendell (Fairtrade), Romond, Signal Gun, Sijnn, South Hill, Sumaridge, Tamboerskloof, The Butcher Shop, **Ultra Liquors**, Waterkloof, Wildehurst, **Woolworths** (2) ★★★ Allesverloren, **Andy Mitchell**, Antebellum, **Arendskloof**, Arumdale, Asara (2), Babylonstoren, **Barton** (2), Beaumont, Bein, Beyerskloof, Bloemendal, Boschendal, Cederberg, **Cowlin**, Croydon, De Grendel, De Krans, De Meye, DeMorgenzon, Dornier, **Dorrance**, Durbanville Hills, Elgin Vintners, Ernie Els, False Bay, Feiteiras, **Fish Hoek**, Fort Simon, **Four Paws**, Franki's, Gabriëlskloof, Grande Provence, Groot Parys (Organic), **Groote Post**, **Guardian Peak**, Havana Hills (2) (Fairtrade), Hawksmoor, Herold, Highlands Road, Holden Manz, Hout Bay, Jacaranda, Kanonkop, Ken Forrester, Klein Constantia, Kleine Zalze, La Chataigne, La Petite Ferme, **La Residence**, Lanzerac, Leopard's Leap, **Longridge**, Lourensford, Muldersbosch, Nederburg, Nelson, Noble Savage, Painted Wolf, Quando, Rainbow's End, Raka, Robert Stanford, **Ruitersvlei**, Rustenberg, Schalkenbosch, **Simonsvlei**, Solms-

Delta, Stellar (Organic, Fairtrade), SylvanVale, The Wolftrap, Thelema, Tokara, Twee Jonge/Krone, Val de Vie, **Warwick**, Waterford, Whalehaven, **Woolworths** (3) (Organic), Zorgvliet ★★★ Anura, Avontuur, Baccarat, Bellingham, Benguela Cove, Blaauwklippen, Black Oystercatcher, Boschendal, **Cloof** (2), **De Bos**, **Delavia**, Delheim, Diemersdal, Du'SwaRoo, Eagle's Cliff, Eerste Hoop, Escapades, **Fat Bastard**, Felicité, Franschhoek Cellar, **Fröhlich**, Goedverwacht, Graham Beck, Hill & Dale, **Klein Roosboom**, Kleine Zalze, Kloovenburg, Koopmanskloof (Fairtrade), L'Avenir, Le Pommier, Leeuwenkuil, **Lothian**, Louisvale, Marianne, Mellasat, Merwida, Morgenhof, Mountain River, Niel Joubert, Noble Hill, Obikwa, Org de Rac (Organic), Overhex, Painted Wolf, Plettenvale, Rickety Bridge, Riebeek, Scrucap, Slaley, Slowine, **Somerbosch**, Spier, Spookfontein, Spotswood, **Stanford Hills**, Stellenrust (Fairtrade), Strandveld, Thandi (Fairtrade), **The Grape Grinder** (2), Two Oceans, **Ultra Liquors**, Van Zylshof, Vondeling, Vriesenhof, **Welgemeend**, **Woolworths** (2) (Light & low-alcohol), Zevenwacht ★★ Bushmanspad, Darling Cellars, Doolhof, Doran, Douglas Green, Dragonridge, Drostdy-Hof, Hoopenburg, **iKapa Jazz** (Organic, Fairtrade), **Leopard's Leap** (2), Lord's, **Lourensford** (Light & low-alcohol), Mitre's Edge, **Muratie**, Oude Compagnies Post, Piekenierskloof (Fairtrade), **Re'Mogo** (Organic, Fairtrade), Rooiberg, Saronsberg, **Schenkfontein**, Springfontein, Steenberg, Stellar (2) (Organic, Fairtrade), Stellenbosch Vineyards, Van Loveren (Fairtrade), **Woolworths** ★★ Hildenbrand, Mooiplaas, **Woolworths NT** Abbottshill, Almenkerk, Anthonij Rupert, Avondrood, **Baccarat**, Beau Joubert, Blomendahl (2), Bryan MacRobert, Cape Rock, Cavalli, Claime d'Or, De Villiers, Dormershire, Dunstone, Excelsior, Fernskloof (Organic), Group CDV, Hillcrest, Klein Dauphine, Kleinhoekkloof, La Couronne, Leeuwenberg, Mount Vernon, Mountain Oaks (Organic), Muratie, New Beginnings (2), Perdeberg, Rietvallei, Savanha, Spekulasie, Spier, Stony Brook, Tall Horse, Topiary, Vrede en Lust, Walker Bay Vineyards, Waverley Hills **NR Packwood D** Andy Mitchell, Bosman, Fairview, Fish Hoek, Joostenberg (Organic), La Petite Vigne, Mont Rochelle, Rhebokskloof (2), Sophie & Mr P, Stonehill, Vergenoegd, Woolworths (Light & low-alcohol), Zandvliet

Rosé off-dry/semi-sweet
★★★★ Botanica, Skilpadvlei ★★★ Devon Rocks, Grande Provence, **Louiesenhof** ★★☆ Autumn Harvest Crackling (Perlé), Backsberg, **BLANKbottle**,

Cloverfield, D'Aria, De Wet (Perlé), Hazendal, Knorhoek, Kumala, Lorraine, Lutzville, Meerendal, Mostertsdrift, Nederburg, Overhex (Light & low-alcohol), The Rhino of Linton Park, Tread Lightly, **Van Loveren**, Welbedacht, **Windfall ★★ Alvi's Drift**, Amani, Bergsig, Bergwater, Botha, Bottelary, Brandvlei, Calitzdorp, Du Toitskloof (Light & low-alcohol, Fairtrade), **Fleur du Cap** (Light & low-alcohol), Goudini, Graça, Imbuko, Jakkalsvlei (Perlé), Kanu (2), Kleine Draken, Koelenhof, Kumala, **Nicholson Smith** (Light & low-alcohol), Overmeer Cellars, Pulpit Rock, RobinHood, Teubes, Theuniskraal, Thokozani, Tulbagh Winery, **uniWines** (Light & low-alcohol), Vinopoly, Wandsbeck (Perlé), Woolworths **★★** Ashton, Bon Courage, Cellar Cask, Conradie (Perlé, Light & low-alcohol), Darling Cellars, Hartswater, **Kumala** (2), Robertson (Light & low-alcohol), **Simonsvlei**, Tangled Tree, **Van Loveren** (Light & low-alcohol), Vinopoly (2) (Perlé, Light & low-alcohol), Vredenheim, Wellington Winery, Woolworths, Zidela (2) **★** Long Mountain **☆** Riebeek **NT** Blomendahl, Buffalo Creek, Dieu Donné, Hillock, Karusa, Kleine Draken (Kosher), Lathithá, Mooiuitsig, Nietvoorbij, Onderkloof , Overhex, Rietvallei, Saxenburg, Stoumann's, Swartland (Light & low-alcohol), Tall Horse, Wineways (2), Wonderfontein, Zanddrift **D** Badsberg, Flat Roof Manor (Light & low-alcohol), Kanu, McGregor, Winters Drift, Woolworths (2) (Light & low-alcohol)

Roussanne

★★★★★ Bellingham

★★★★☆ Hermit on the Hill, Ken Forrester, The Foundry

★★★★ Fairview, Painted Wolf, Simonsig

★★★☆ Rustenberg

Ruby cabernet

★★★☆ Bellpost **★★★** Orange River, Robertson (2) **★★** Barrydale, Long Mountain **★☆** Hartswater **★** Bonnievale **NT** Langverwacht, Lutzville, Nuweland **D** McGregor

Sacramental Wines

★★ Backsberg (Sweet red, Sacramental, Kosher), Kleine Draken (Cabernet sauvignon) **NT** Huguenot (Hanepoot fortified, Sacramental), Landzicht (Muscadel, red, unfortified)

Sangiovese

★★★★ Anura, Spring Grove

★★★☆ Dragonridge, Idiom, Monterosso, Morgenster, Raka **★★★** Havana Hills (Fairtrade),

Kleine Zalze **★★** Koelenhof **NT** Anthonij Rupert, Fairview, Idiom

Sauvignon blanc unwooded

★★★★★ Cederberg, Neil Ellis, Spier

★★★★☆ Bartinney, Bramon, Buitenverwachting, Constantia Glen, De Grendel, Diemersdal, Driehoek, Flagstone, Fleur du Cap, Graham Beck, Groote Post, Hillcrest, Jean Daneel, **Klein Constantia** (2) (Organic), Kleine Zalze, Silvermist (Organic), Southern Right, Spice Route, The Berrio, **Thelema** (2), Tierhoek, Tokara, Uva Mira, Vergelegen, Woolworths

★★★★ Aaldering, Altydgedacht, Ataraxia, Boplaas, Boschendal (2), Bouchard Finlayson (2), Brunia, Buitenverwachting, Cape Point, Cederberg, Constantia Mist, Constantia Uitsig, Corder, Darling Cellars, De Grendel, De Wetshof, Diemersdal (2), Diners Club Bartho Eksteen , Durbanville Hills, Elgin Ridge (Organic), Fryer's Cove (2), Gabriëlskloof, Garden Route, Groote Post, Hermanuspietersfontein, Hidden Valley, Izak van der Vyver, Jasper Raats, Jordan, Ken Forrester, Klein Constantia, Klein Gustrouw, La Motte (2), Lanner Hill, Lomond, Maastricht, Merwida, Nederburg, Neethlingshof, Nitida, Noble Savage, **Nova Zonnestraal**, Ormonde (2), PaardenKloof, Packwood, Phizante Kraal, Plaisir, Rivendell (Fairtrade), Rosendal, Saxenburg, Scrucap, Seven Springs , Signal Gun, Sir Lambert, Skaap, South Hill, Spioenkop (2), Springfield (2), Star Hill, Steenberg, Sterhuis, Strandveld, Strydom, Sumaridge, Teubes, The Butcher Shop, Thelema, Tierhoek, Tokara, Trizanne, **Ultra Liquors**, Uva Mira, Van Loveren, Vergelegen, Virgin Earth (Fairtrade), Vondeling, Waterkloof, **Woolworths** (5), Zevenwacht, Zonnebloem

★★★☆ Adoro, Alexanderfontein, Allée Bleue, Alvi's Drift, Andersons, AntHill, Ashton, Bayede!, Benguela Cove, Bergsig, Black Oystercatcher, Bonnievale, Boschendal, **Boutinot**, Brothers, Brugman, Bushmanspad, Capaia, **Cloof**, Clos Malverne, Clouds, Conradie, Creation, Crios Bríde, D'Aria, Dalla Cia, De Bos (Fairtrade), Delaire, Doolhof, Dornier, Durbanville Hills, Eagles' Nest, Edgebaston, Elgin Vintners, Elsenburg, Ernie Els, Escapades, Excelsior, Fairvalley (Fairtrade), Fairview, False Bay, Fort Simon, Freedom Hill, Goede Hoop, Graham Beck, Groenland, Hartenberg, Haskell, Havana Hills (Fairtrade), Herold, Hout Bay, Imbuko, Journey's End, Kaapzicht, Ken Forrester, Klein Constantia, Kleine Zalze, Kloovenburg, Kranskop, **Kuypers**, La Petite Ferme, Land's End, Le Bonheur, Le Pommier, **Leeuwenberg**, Lemberg, Lievland, Lomond (2), Longbarn, Lutzville,

Meerendal, Mimosa, Mooiplaas, Morgenhof, Mount Rozier, Mountain River (2), Mulderbosch, Neethlingshof, Newstead, Nico Vermeulen, Niel Joubert, **Nomada**, Ormonde, Perdeberg, Quando, Raka, Robert Stanford, Rustenberg, Scrucap, Signal Gun (2), Silvermist, Simonsig (2), Simonsvlei, Spice Route (Fairtrade), Springfontein, Stanford Hills, **Stellenbosch Vineyards** (2), Stellenrust, Strandveld, Super Single Vineyards, Township Winery, Trajan, Uitkyk, Usana, Vierlanden, Villiera, Warwick, Waterford (2), Webersburg, Whalehaven, Yonder Hill, Zonnebloem, Zorgvliet ★★★ Anura, Arumdale, Avontuur, Backsberg, Barton, Bellingham, **Benguela Cove**, Bilton, Blaauwklippen, Boland, Bon Courage, Boplaas, Boschkloof , Boschrivier, Brampton, Breëland, Cape Point, Claime d'Or, Clairvaux, **Cowlin**, Dâbar, David Frost, De Wetshof, Delheim, DeWaal, **Die Mas**, Du Preez, Du Toitskloof (Fairtrade), Durbanville Hills, Earthbound (Organic, Fairtrade), Ernst Gouws, Excelsior, Fairview, False Bay, Fish Hoek, Fleur du Cap, Foothills, Fort Simon, Four Paws, Franschhoek Cellar, **Fröhlich**, Gantouw, Glen Carlou, Glenview, GlenWood, Goedverwacht, Guardian Peak, Havana Hills (Fairtrade), Highlands Road, Hill & Dale, Hoopenburg, Jakkalsvlei, Juno, Kleine Zalze, Knorhoek, **Konkelberg**, Koopmanskloof (Fairtrade), L'Avenir, La Chataigne, Lanzerac, Linton Park, Lord's, Louis, Louisvale, LuKa, Lutzville, Lyngrove, **Maison de Teijger**, Marklew, **Midgard**, Miravel, Misty Mountains, Monterosso, Morgenster, Nabygelegen, Namaqua, **Nederburg** (4) (Fairtrade), **Neil Patterson**, Nelson, **Nico van der Merwe**, Old Vines, Onderkloof , Overgaauw, Overhex, PaardenKloof, Paul Wallace, Perdeberg, Peter Falke, Place in the Sun (Fairtrade), Porcupine Ridge, Rickety Bridge, Ridgeback, Robertson, Roodezandt, **Rosendal**, Saronsberg, Seal Breeze, Skilpadvlei, Slanghoek, **Solara** (Organic), Somersbosch, Somerset Wines, Sophie & Mr P, Spier, Swartland, Teubes, The Goose, Tread Lightly, Under Oaks, Van Zylshof, Vredenheim, Waterford, Welbedacht, Wellington Winery, Wildekrans, **Winters Drift**, Wonderfontein, **Woolworths** (2) (Organic), Zorgvliet ★★★ Aan de Doorns, Arendskloof, Asara, Ayama, Badsberg, **Barrydale**, Beau Joubert, **Bezalel**, Botha, Burgershof, Calitzdorp, Cape Classics, Cloverfield, D'Aria, Darling Cellars, De Wet, Die Mas, Diemersdal, Domaine des Dieux, Douglas Green, Fort Simon, Fryer's Cove, Goede Hoop, Goedvertrouw, Grande Provence, Hathersage, House of Mandela (Fairtrade), **Imbuko**, Kanu, Klein Parys, Klein

Roosboom , Knorhoek, L'Olivier, Landskroon, Lateganskop, Le Manoir de Brendel, Leipzig, Libby's Pride, Louisenhof, Lourensford, M'hudi, Misty Mountains, Muratie, Nuweland, Nuy, Obikwa, Piekenierskloof, Rhebokskloof, **Robertson** (5) (Perlé), Ruitersvlei, Saam, Sauvignon.com, Seven Sisters, Slaley, Slowine, **Spookfontein** , **St Francis Point**, Stellar (Organic, Fairtrade), Stellenbosch Hills (2), Stellenbosch University, Teddy Hall, Thandi (Fairtrade), Two Oceans, **Ultra Liquors**, Vin du Cap, Wandsbeck, **Welgemeend**, **Wellington Winery**, **Wine Village-Hermanus**, Woolworths (2) (Organic, Fairtrade), Zevenwacht, Zidela ★★ Bayede!, Brandvlei, Calais, Cape Dreams, Domein Doornkraal, Douglas Green, Drostdy-Hof, Du Preez, Eagle's Cliff (2), Eaglevlei (Light & low-alcohol), Fat Bastard, Flagstone, Flat Roof Manor, Goudini, Grande Provence, Hoopenburg, **Jacaranda**, Klawer, Kleine Draken (Kosher), Koelenhof (2), Leopard's Leap, Long Mountain, Lorraine, McGregor, Mountain Ridge, Nicholson Smith, Noble Hill, Riebeek, Rooiberg, Schalkenbosch, **Simonsvlei** (2), Steenberg, Stellenzicht, Tangled Tree, The Rhino of Linton Park, Tulbagh Winery, uniWines (Fairtrade), Van Loveren, Viljoensdrift (2), Waboomsrivier, Weltevrede, Windmeul, Woolworths, Zidela (2) ★★ Asara, Bergwater (2), Imbuko, Robertson (3) (Light & low-alcohol), Rooiberg (Light & low-alcohol), **Schenkfontein**, Woolworths ★ Vinopoly **NT** Akkerdal, Almenkerk (2), **Ameera**, Anthonij Rupert (2), **Arendsig**, Avondrood, Baleia, Barnardt Boyes, Bayede!, Bellevue, **Black Oystercatcher**, Blomendahl, Blouvlei, Blue Crane, Boer & Brit, Brenaissance, Buffalo Creek, Camberley, Cape Hutton, Catch Of The Day, Clive Torr, De Doorns, **Devonvale**, Dieu Donné, Dormershire, Dunstone, DuVon, Eikehof, Elgin Heights, **Esona**, Flagstone, Groot Constantia, Het Vlock Casteel, High Constantia (2), Hillcrest, Hillock (2), **Kaapse Familie Wingerde**, Karusa, Klein Roosboom , Kleinhoekkloof, Langverwacht, Le Bonheur, Linton Park, Major's Hill, MAN Family, Manley, Montpellier, Mooiuitsig, Môreson, Mount Vernon, Nederburg, Nitida, Nomada, Oneiric, Rare Earth, Reiersvlei, Rietvallei (3), **RiverGold**, Rosendal, Sarah's, Savanha, Spring Grove, Stellendrift, Stoumann's, Tall Horse, TCB Wines, The Butcher Shop, Trizanne, Vaalvlei, Val de Vie, **Valley Vineyards**, Versailles, Vierkoppen, Vrede en Lust, Waka Waka, Walker Bay Vineyards, Welgevallen, Wineways, Withoek, Wolvendrift, Women in Wine, Woolworths, Zidela **D** Boplaas, Cloof, Hermanuspietersfontein, La Couronne, Nederburg, Super Single Vineyards, The

Giant Periwinkle, Tokara, uniWines, Welbedacht, Winters Drift, Zandvliet

Sauvignon blanc wooded

★★★★★ Nederburg

★★★★☆ Bloemendal, Buitenverwachting, Cape Point, Cederberg, Delaire, Hermanuspietersfontein, **Hermit on the Hill**, Iona, Klein Constantia, Mulderbosch, **Nederburg**, Oak Valley, Reyneke (Biodynamic), Shannon, Waterkloof, **Woolworths** Zevenwacht

★★★★ Anura, Backsberg, **Bartho Eksteen** (2), Black Oystercatcher, Boutinot, Cape Chamonix, Catherine Marshall, D'Aria, DeMorgenzon, Diemersdal, **Fledge & Co**, **Fryer's Cove**, Jordan, **Klein Constantia**, La Petite Ferme, La Vierge, Louis, Meinert, Neil Ellis, Newton Johnson, **Overhex**, Reyneke (Biodynamic), Stark-Condé, Stony Brook, Teubes, The Butcher Shop, The Giant Periwinkle, Villiera

★★★☆ Asara, Black Elephant, Bloemendal, Eikendal, Lourensford, Marianne, Miravel, Môreson, **Namaqua**, Steenberg (2), Woolworths ★★★ Amani, Avontuur, Hazendal, **Maison de Teijger**, Mont Rochelle, Opstal, Painted Wolf, Stettyn, **Van Eck**, Windfall ★★☆ Orange River **NT** Hannay, Hermit on the Hill (2), High Constantia, Klein Constantia, **Lismore**, Meerendal, Paul Cluver, Quoin Rock (2), Rickety Bridge, Spier, Stone Ridge, Swartland, The Goose, Wildekrans **D** Le Pommier, Lourensford

Semillon unwooded

★★★★ Zonnebloem

★★★☆ Brunia, Ormonde ★★ Van Loveren **NT** Lutzville, **Waverley Hills D** Nederburg

Semillon wooded

★★★★★ Constantia Uitsig, Mullineux

★★★★☆ **Adoro**, **Alheit**, Bloemendal, Boekenhoutskloof, Cederberg, **David & Nadia Sadie**, **Opstal**, **Rickety Bridge**, Sadie, Shannon, **Signal Hill**, Vergelegen

★★★★ BLANKbottle, Boutinot, Cape Point, **Escapades** (2), Fairview, Fleur du Cap, Franschhoek Cellar, Haut Espoir, La Chataigne, Landau du Val, Nitida, **Oak Valley**, Rickety Bridge, **Spice Route** (Fairtrade), Steenberg, **The Garajeest**

★★★☆ Dornier, Eaglevlei, Hathersage ★★★ Hildenbrand **NT** Anthonij Rupert, GlenWood, My Wyn, Thorne & Daughters, Vrede en Lust

Sherry-style wines

★★★★ KWV Sherry-Style Wines (2), Monis

★★★☆ Douglas Green (3), Monis (2) **NT** Huguenot, Karusa, Landzicht, Mooiuitsig (4)

Shiraz/syrah

★★★★★ Bellingham, Eagles' Nest, Leeuwenkuil, Mullineux, Reyneke (Biodynamic), Richard Kershaw

★★★★☆ Annandale, Arra, **Beau Constantia**, **Boekenhoutskloof** (2), Boschendal, **Boschkloof** (2), Cederberg, Cirrus, D'Aria, De Grendel, **De Trafford** (3), Delheim, DeMorgenzon, Dorrance, Driehoek, Fable, Fairview (4) (Light & low-alcohol), GlenWood, Graham Beck, Groot Constantia, Hartenberg (3), Haskell (2), Hilton, Keermont, Kleine Zalze, La Motte (2), Linton Park, Lomond, Luddite, Mont Destin, Mullineux (2), Muratie, Nederburg, Nico van der Merwe, Oldenburg, Porseleinberg (Organic), Raka, Reyneke (Biodynamic), Rijk's, Rust en Vrede (2), Rustenberg, Saltare, Saronsberg, **Savage**, Saxenburg (2), Signal Hill, Sijnn, Simonsig (2), Spice Route (Fairtrade), Stark-Condé (2), Stony Brook, Strandveld, Super Single Vineyards, The Foundry, The Winery of Good Hope (2) (Fairtrade), Vergelegen, Vergenoegd, Warwick, Waterford, Waterkloof

★★★★ Aeternitas, Akkerdal, Alto, Andreas, Anura (2), Arra, Babylonstoren, Backsberg, Beau Belle, Bellingham (Organic), Bilton, Bizoe, Blaauwklippen, Bloemendal (2), Boland, Bonnievale, Boschendal, Camberley, Cederberg, Cloof, **Craven**, Creation, De Breede (Organic), Delheim, DeMorgenzon, DewaldtHeyns, Diners Club Bartho Eksteen , Domaine Brahms, Doran, Dunstone, Edgebaston, Ernie Els, Fairview, Flagstone, Fort Simon, Franschhoek Cellar, Gabriëlskloof, Glenelly, GlenWood, Groenland, Groote Post, Hartenberg, Haskell, Hermit on the Hill, Heron Ridge, Hilton, Holden Manz, House of Mandela, **Jasper Raats**, Joostenberg (Organic), Jordan, Journey's End (2), Katbakkies, Keermont, Kleine Zalze, Kloovenburg, La Petite Ferme, Land's End, Landskroon, Lomond (2), Longridge, Lyngrove, Lynx, M'hudi, Maison, Malanot, Migliarina, Mimosa, Mont Rochelle, Mooiplaas, **Moya Meaker**, Nederburg, Nelson, Nico van der Merwe, Nico Vermeulen, Niel Joubert (2), Nitida, Noble Hill, Nuy, Olifantsberg, Org de Rac (Organic), Ormonde, PaardenKloof, Perdeberg, Peter Falke, Rainbow's End, Rhebokskloof, Rickety Bridge, Ridgeback, Riebeek, Rijk's, Robert Stanford, Robertson (2), Rooiberg, Rosendal, Rudera, Schultz Family, **Scrucap**, Skaap, Solms-Delta, Spice Route (Fairtrade), Star Hill, Steenberg, **Stellar**, Stellekaya, Stellenrust, Stellenzicht, Strydom, Tamboerskloof (2), **The Berrio**, The Giant Periwinkle, Thelema (2), Tokara, **Uva Mira**, Val de Vie, Van Loveren,

Vergelegen, Vergenoegd, Virgin Earth, Waverley Hills (Organic), Welbedacht, Windmeul, Woolworths, Zandvliet, Zevenwacht, Zonnebloem ★★★☆ Aaldering, Allée Bleue, Allegria, Allesverloren, **Ameera**, Andy Mitchell, Annex Kloof, Antebellum, **Arendskloof**, Asara, Auction Crossing, Audacia, Avondale (Organic), Avontuur, Ayama, Backsberg, Beau Belle, **Beaumont**, Belfield, Bellpost, Benguela Cove, Black Elephant, Blackwater, **BLANKbottle**, **Blomendahl**, Bon Courage (2), Boschheim, **Boutinot**, Brenaissance, Cape Dreams, Cloof, **Corder**, Crows Nest, **Dâbar**, Darling Cellars (2), De Meye, DeanDavid, Delaire, Devonvale, Diemersdal, Diemersfontein, Doolhof, Drostdy-Hof, Eagle's Cliff, Eerste Hoop, Elana, **Enfin**, Ernst Gouws, Excelsior, False Bay, Fleur du Cap, Foothills, **Foxwood**, Fram, **Fryer's Cove**, Gabriëlskloof, Garden Route, Glen Carlou, Goedverwacht, Grande Provence, Guardian Peak, Hartenberg, Havana Hills (Fairtrade), Hawksmoor, Hazendal, **Herold**, Heron Ridge, Hildenbrand, Hofstraat, Holden Manz, Hout Bay, Intellego (2), Jacques Smit, Joubert-Tradauw, Kaapzicht, Katbakkies, Klein Parys, Koelfontein, Koopmanskloof (Fairtrade), Kyburg, La Bri, La Chaumiere, La Vierge, Landskroon, Lazanou (Organic), Leeuwenberg, Linton Park, Louiesenhof, Lourensford, Lutzville, Maastricht, MAN Family, Marianne, Meerendal (2), Metzer (2), Middelvlei, Mitre's Edge, Mont du Toit, Mount Pleasant, Mountain Ridge, Namaqua, Naughton's, Neethlingshof, Neil Ellis, Nick & Forti's, Oak Valley, Olsen, Onderkloof, **Orange River**, Oude Denneboom, Perdeberg, Phizante Kraal, Plaisir, Porcupine Ridge, Post House, Rhebokskloof (2), Riebeek, Rijk's, Rivendell, Rooiberg, Rustenberg, Saronsberg, Scrucap, Seal Breeze, Seven Springs, Signal Gun (2), Simonsig, Slaley, Snow Mountain, Spotswood, **Stellenbosch Vineyards**, Stofberg, StoneyCroft, Stony Brook, Strandveld, Swartland, The Butcher Shop (2), The Grape Grinder, The Winery of Good Hope, Tokara, Topaz, Topiary, Trajan, Two Oceans, Uitkyk, **Under Oaks**, **Uva Mira**, Val du Charron, Veenwouden, Vondeling, Wellington Winery (2), Weltevrede, Wildekrans, William Everson, Woolworths, Zandvliet, Zonnebloem ★★★ Alexanderfontein, Alte Neffen, Alvi's Drift, Amani, **Audacia**, Axe Hill, Bayede!, Beau Joubert, Bellevue, Bellingham, **Bemind**, Bergheim, **Bezalel**, **Blaauwklippen** (2), Blue Crane, Boplaas, Boschendal, Boschrivier, Botha, Brampton, Bridge, Bushmanspad, Cape Dreams, Cape Point, Carrol Boyes, Chateau Naudé, Chennells, Claime d'Or,

Clive Torr, David Frost, **Delavia**, Desert Rose, Dormershire (2), **Dornier**, Du Toitskloof (Fairtrade), Du'SwaRoo, Durbanville Hills (2), Elgin Vintners, Fairview, False Bay, Fat Bastard, Fort Simon (2), Four Paws, Fraai Uitzicht 1798, Franschhoek Cellar, Freedom Hill, Goede Hoop, Graceland, Graham Beck, Groenland, Haut Espoir, Hawksmoor, Imbuko, Jason's Hill, Juno, Kanu, Klein Roosboom , Knorhoek, Kranskop, Kumala, La Couronne, **La Residence**, Ladera, Lanzerac, Le Fût, Le Manoir de Brendel, Leeuwenkuil, Lemberg, Lievland, Londinium, Lord's, Lutzville, Lyngrove, M'hudi, MAN Family, Marianne, Matzikama (Organic), Misty Mountains, Mount Rozier, Mountain Ridge, **Nederburg**, Nelson, Nieuwedrift, Nuweland, Orange River, Ormonde, **Painted Wolf**, **Perdeberg Vineyard Collection**, Pfeifer's, Place in the Sun (Fairtrade), Pulpit Rock, Rogge Cloof, **Ruitersvlei**, **Saxenburg**, Silkbush, Simonsvlei (3), Slaley, Slanghoek, Slowine, **Solms-Delta**, Somerbosch, Spier, Stanford Hills, Stellenbosch Hills, Stellenbosch Vineyards, Stellenzicht, Stettyn, **Teddy Hall**, The Goose, **The Hills** (2), The Rhino of Linton Park, Thembi & Co, Tulbagh Winery, Vaalvlei, **Van Eck**, Viljoensdrift, Vin du Cap, Vredenheim, **Wandsbeck**, Waverley Hills (Organic), Wederom, Wildekrans, William Everson, Windfall, Winters Drift, Woestkloof, Woolworths (2), Yonder Hill, Zandvliet ★★★ Arra, Ashton, Ayama, **Barnardt Boyes**, Barrydale, Bayede!, Bergwater, Bonview, Cloverfield, De Meye, De Wet, **De Zoete Inval**, DeWaal, Die Mas, Doran, Douglas Green, Du Preez, Eerste Hoop, Excelsior, Fish Hoek, Goudini, Het Vlock Casteel, Hill & Dale, House of Mandela (2) (Fairtrade), Koelenhof, Le Manoir de Brendel, Leopard's Leap, **Louisvale**, **Marianne**, Mellasat, Mountain River, Nicholson Smith, Org de Rac (Organic), Piekenierskloof, Riebeek, Robertson (3), Roodezandt, Schenkfontein, Simonsvlei, Somerset Wines, Stellar (Organic, Fairtrade), Stellenbosch Vineyards (2), Swartland, **Teubes**, The Liberator, Wellington Winery, Weltevrede, Wonderfontein, Woolworths ★★ Bergwater, Blomendahl, Bonnievale, Brandvlei, Calitzdorp, Clairvaux, Clive Torr, Devonvale, Eikehof, Hoopenburg, Klawer, Kumala, Leipzig, Libby's Pride, Mountain River, Namaqua, Obikwa, Oude Compagnies Post, Pulpit Rock, Reiersvlei, Stellar (Organic, Fairtrade), Taillard, Tangled Tree, uniWines (Fairtrade), Vaalvlei, Wellington Winery ★☆ **Hildenbrand**, Libby's Pride, Schalkenbosch ★ Long Mountain, McGregor, Vinopoly **NT** Abbottshill, Almenkerk, Altydgedacht, AntHill, Anthonij Rupert (2),

Arendsig, Arumdale, Avondrood, Axe Hill, Baleia, Bergheim, Blaauwklippen, Blomendahl, Brothers, Brunia, Calais, Cameradi, Cape Rock, Catch Of The Day, Cavalli, Cloof, Clovelly, Cranefields, **De Kleine Wijn Koöp**, De Villiers, Dieu Donné, Du Preez, Du'SwaRoo, Dunstone, DuVon, Elgin Heights, **Esona**, Fernskloof, Freedom Hill, Gilga, Havana Hills, Hermit on the Hill (2), High Constantia, Hillock, Jordan, Karusa, Keermont, Kirabo, Kleinhoekkloof, La Terre La Mer, Langverwacht (2), Linton Park, **Lismore**, Lorraine, Major's Hill, Manley, Mason's Winery (2), Melkboomsdrift, Montpellier, Mooi Bly, Mullineux, My Wyn, Nederburg (2), New Beginnings, Nietvoorbij, **Nuy**, Oneiric (2), Overhex, Painted Wolf, Quoin Rock (2), Rietvallei, **RiverGold**, Rosendal (2), Ruitersvlei, Saam (2), **Santa Cecilia**, Savanna, Scali, Schultz Family, Southern Sky, Spotswood, Spring Grove, Stellendrift, Stellenrust, Stone Ridge (2), Stoumann's, Tall Horse, Tanagra, The Three Foxes, Township Winery (Fairtrade), Trizanne, TTT Cellar, Tulbagh Winery, Under Oaks, **Valley Vineyards**, Vin du Cap (2), Vrede en Lust (2), Welgeleë (2), William Everson, Windmeul, Wine Fusion, Wineways (3), Withoek, Zanddrift, Zidela **D** Andy Mitchell, Annex Kloof, Asara, Babylon's Peak, Boplaas, Conradie, Corder, Hidden Valley, Hoopenburg, Julien Schaal, Lourensford, Metzer, Neil Ellis, Remhoogte, Rhebokskloof, Sir Lambert, Stanford Hills, Thandi (Fairtrade), uniWines, Uva Mira

Sparkling, Méthode ancestrale

★★★★ Vondeling

★★★☆ Groot Parys ★★ Dragonridge NT AA Badenhorst, Scali

Sparkling, Méthode cap classique, red, dry

★★★ Nitida, Woolworths **NT** Camberley

Sparkling, Méthode cap classique, rosé, dry

★★★★☆ Ambeloui, CharlesFox

★★★★ Bon Courage, Chabivin, Chateau Naudé, Clos Malverne, Colmant, De Wetshof, Fairview, Graham Beck (2), **Kleine Zalze**, Lourensford, Perdeberg, Rickety Bridge, Saltare, Silverthorn, Simonsig, Steenberg, Twee Jonge/Krone, Woolworths

★★★☆ Allée Bleue, Arendskloof, Ayama, Barrydale, Boplaas, Boschendal, **Francois La Garde**, Haute Cabrière, Klein Optenhorst, L'Avenir, Longridge, Môreson, **Newstead**, Plettenvale, **Scrucap**, Signal Gun, Tanzanite, The House of JC le Roux, **Ultra Liquors**, **Van Loveren**, Villiera, Webersburg, Weltevrede, Wildekrans, Woolworths

★★★ Domaine des Dieux, Groote Post, Koelenhof, Pongrácz, The House of JC le Roux ★★★☆ Namaqua, **Teddy Hall** ★★ Louisvale **NT** Anthonij Rupert, **Black Oystercatcher**, Dieu Donné, Du Preez, Francois La Garde, Karusa, **Le Lude**, **Lord's**, Montpellier, Môreson, Mount Babylon, Packwood, Ross Gower, Sumaridge, **Wonderfontein**

Sparkling, Méthode cap classique, rosé, off-dry/semi-sweet

★★ Tulbagh Winery

Sparkling, Méthode cap classique, white, dry

★★★★★ Anura, Cederberg

★★★★☆ Ambeloui, Avondale (Organic), **Black Elephant**, Boschendal (2), **CharlesFox** (2), Colmant (2), Graham Beck (3), Longridge, Pongrácz, **Rijk's**, Saltare (2), **Silverthorn** (3), Simonsig, **Steenberg**, **Tanzanite** (2), TheHouse of GM&AHRENS, Topiary, Villiera, Weltevrede, **Woolworths**

★★★★ Allée Bleue, Alvi's Drift, Ayama, **Bartho Eksteen**, Bon Courage (2), Boschendal, **Bosman**, Bramon, **Chabivin**, **Conradie**, Constantia Uitsig, Darling Cellars, De Grendel, De Wet, De Wetshof, **Delaire**, Domaine des Dieux, Genevieve, **Grande Provence**, Hildenbrand, Hoopenburg, House of Mandela, **Huis van Chevallerie** (2), Klein Constantia, **Kleine Zalze** (2), L'Avenir, La Motte, Lourensford, **Meerendal**, Mooiplaas, Môreson, Morgenhof, Muratie, Nico van der Merwe, Niel Joubert, Nitida, Org de Rac (Organic), Perdeberg, Pongrácz, Rhebokskloof, Roodezandt, Saltare, Saronsberg, Saxenburg, Scrucap, Signal Hill, Simonsig, Steenberg, **Stellenbosch Vineyards**, Sterhuis, Stony Brook, Teddy Hall, The House of JC le Roux (2), Thelema, **Twee Jonge/Krone** (2), **Ultra Liquors**, Van Loveren, Viljoensdrift, Villiera (2), Waterford, Webersburg, Wellington Winery, Weltevrede, Wonderfontein, Woolworths (2)

★★★☆ Altydgedacht, Andy Mitchell, **Aurelia**, Ayama, Backsberg, **Blaauwklippen**, **Bloemendal**, Bramon, Crios Bríde, **De Krans**, DeMorgenzon, Graham Beck, Hazendal, Klein Parys, **Lanzerac**, Lateganskop, Leopard's Leap, Longridge, Lord's, Plaisir, Ross Gower, Somerbosch, Spier, Teddy Hall, The Butcher Shop, The House of JC le Roux, **Ultra Liquors** (2), Val de Vie, Waverley Hills (Organic), Welbedacht, Zorgvliet ★★★ Avontuur, **Bemind**, Chabivin, Francois La Garde, Haute Cabrière, Hout Bay, Klein Parys, La Chaumiere, Maison, **MAN Family**, Riebeek, Robertson, Villiera (Light & low-alcohol), Virgin Earth, Wildekrans, Windfall ★★★☆

Backsberg (Kosher), **Dâbar**, Du Preez, Glen Carlou, **iKapa Jazz** (Organic, Fairtrade), Nieuwedrift, Re'Mogo ★★ **Jacaranda**, **Louisvale**, Schalkenbosch **NT Anthonij Rupert** (2), Boer & Brit, Buitenverwachting, Cape Chamonix, Dieu Donné, Domaine Coutelier, Elgin Heights, Francois La Garde, Groot Constantia, High Constantia, Highlands Road, Kanu, Karusa, Ken Forrester, Klein Roosboom , **Le Lude**, Lovane, Meerendal, Mimosa , Montpellier, Môreson, My Wyn, Newstead, **Noble Savage**, **Nuy**, Old Vines, Perdeberg, Quoin Rock, Rare Earth, Rickety Bridge, Saxenburg, Skaap, Spookfontein , Tanja Beutler, Twee Jonge/ Krone, Vergelegen **D** Chabivin (3), De Zoete Inval, Diners Club Bartho Eksteen , L'Avenir

Sparkling, Méthode cap classique, white, off-dry/semi-sweet

★★★★ Colmant

★★★☆ Graham Beck, Groot Parys ★★★ The House of JC le Roux **NT** South Hill

Sparkling, Non-MCC, red, dry

★★ The House of JC le Roux

Sparkling, Non-MCC, red, off-dry/semi-sweet

★★★ Stellenbosch Vineyards ★★★ Du Toitskloof (Light & low-alcohol, Fairtrade), Solms-Delta ★★ Robertson ★★ The House of JC le Roux ★ Van Loveren

Sparkling, Non-MCC, rosé, dry

★★★ Boplaas, **Huis van Chevallerie**, Kloovenburg ★★★ **Blaauwklippen**, Somerset Wines (Light & low-alcohol), Stellar, Thandi **NT** Knorhoek

Sparkling, Non-MCC, rosé, off-dry/semi-sweet

★★★ Perdeberg (Light & low-alcohol), Rhebokskloof, Swartland ★★★ Aan de Doorns, Bergwater, Cold Duck (5th Avenue) (Light & low-alcohol), Domein Doornkraal, Klawer (Light & low-alcohol), **Nuy**, Orange River, Stellenbosch Hills ★★ Alvi's Drift (Light & low-alcohol), Bon Courage, **iKapa Jazz** (Organic, Fairtrade), Koelenhof, Long Mountain (Light & low-alcohol), **Re'Mogo** (Organic, Fairtrade), Rooiberg, Van Loveren (2) (Light & low-alcohol), Viljoensdrift (Light & low-alcohol), Vredenheim, **Welgemeend**, Woolworths ★★ Goedverwacht, Mountain Ridge, Overhex (Light & low-alcohol), Robertson (Light & low-alcohol), Stellar **NT** Ashton, Bayede!, Rietvallei

Sparkling, Non-MCC, white, dry

★★★ Clos Malverne, **Klein Parys**, Nederburg, Orange River, Steenberg, Stellenbosch Vineyards, Swartland, The House of JC le Roux ★★★ Bergwater, Botha, Du Toitskloof (Fairtrade), **Lyngrove**, Obikwa, Riebeek, Slanghoek, Tulbagh Winery, Van Loveren, Wellington Winery, Woolworths ★★ Alvi's Drift, Bonnievale, Goudini, Merwida, Overhex, Rooiberg, Van Loveren, Woolworths ★★ Robertson **NT** Hermit on the Hill, Rietvallei, Stellar **D** Bergsig

Sparkling, Non-MCC, white, off-dry/semi-sweet

★★★ Nuy, Twee Jonge/Krone ★★★ Badsberg (Light & low-alcohol), D'Aria, Eaglevlei, Koelenhof, Opstal, Orange River (Light & low-alcohol), Slanghoek, Woolworths ★★ Alvi's Drift (Light & low-alcohol), Kleine Draken (Light & low-alcohol, Kosher), Overhex (Light & low-alcohol), Rooiberg, The House of JC le Roux (Light & low-alcohol), Tulbagh Winery ★★ Grand Mousseux, Robertson (Light & low-alcohol), Van Loveren ★ Van Loveren **NT** De Doorns

Special Late Harvest

★★★★ Backsberg, Drostdy-Hof, Van Loveren ★★★ Badsberg, Fairview, **Highlands Road** (Light & low-alcohol), Robertson, Slanghoek ★★★ Bon Courage ★★ Wellington Winery **NT** Bergsig, Nederburg **D** Roodezandt

Sweet red

★★★★ Dormershire ★★★ Simonsig ★★ Backsberg (Sacramental, Kosher), Bottelary, Cape Classics, Du Toitskloof (Light & low-alcohol, Fairtrade), Louiesenhof, **Nicholson Smith** (Light & low-alcohol), Overhex (Light & low-alcohol), **Robertson** (Light & low-alcohol), RobinHood, Somerset Wines, Stellar ★★ Cellar Cask, Hartswater, Imbuko, RED ESCape, Robertson (2), Tulbagh Winery ★ Autumn Harvest Crackling (Perlé), Darling Cellars, Kumala (2), Riebeek (Perlé, Light & low-alcohol), **Woolworths NT** Lynx, Mooiuitsig, Perdeberg, Wineways **D** Woolworths

Sylvaner

★★★★ Overgaauw

Tannat

★★★★ Mooi Bly

★★★★ Fairview, Glen Carlou, **Lowerland** ★★ Kranskop

Tempranillo/tinta roriz

★★★★☆ Stony Brook, Super Single Vineyards ★★★★ De Krans ★★★ Dornier **NT** Baleia

Tinta barocca

★★★★☆ Sadie

★★★★ De Krans, Momento

★★★☆ Allesverloren, Boplaas ★★★ BLANKbottle, Boplaas, Jeu ★★☆ Swartland ★★ Reiersvlei **NT** Nuweland

Touriga franca

★★★★ Boplaas

Touriga nacional

★★★★☆ Boplaas, Sijnn

★★★★ Allesverloren, De Krans

★★★☆ Dagbreek, MAN Family, Overgaauw ★★★ Bergsig, Boplaas ★★☆ Calitzdorp **NT** Reiersvlei

Trincadeira/tinta amarela

★★★★ Dagbreek

Verdelho

★★★★ Fairview

★★★☆ BLANKbottle, Feiteiras, **Thelema** ★★★ Owl & Vine ★★☆ Flagstone

Vin de paille

★★★★★ Mullineux (2)

★★★★☆ Boplaas, Brugman, De Trafford, Donkiesbaai, Fairview (Light & low-alcohol), La Motte, Meinert, Nuweland, Tierhoek, Vergelegen, Vondeling

★★★★ Boplaas, Goede Hoop, Groot Parys (Organic), Hazendal, Keermont, Lemberg, Môreson, Orange River, Rustenberg, Saronsberg, The Winery of Good Hope

★★★☆ Asara, Maison, Simonsig, Stellar (Organic, Fairtrade), Stettyn ★★★ Mellasat, Naughton's **NT** Druk My Niet, Fairview, Fledge & Co, Signal Hill **D** The Winery of Good Hope

Viognier

★★★★★ The Foundry

★★★★☆ Hilton, Lourensford

★★★★ Alvi's Drift, Babylonstoren, Beau Constantia, Bellingham, Buitenverwachting, Creation, De Grendel, Diemersfontein, Eagles' Nest, Fairview, Flagstone, **Glen Carlou**, Grande Provence, **Hilton**, Idiom, Kanu, La Petite Ferme, Mellasat, Painted Wolf, Ridgeback, Spice Route (Fairtrade), Tamboerskloof, Topaz

★★★☆ Anura, Arra (2), Backsberg, Chennells, Cloof, Elgin Vintners, Elsenburg, **Franki's**, Gabriëlskloof, **Hidden Valley**, Klawer, Kranskop, La Bri, Lynx, Mitre's Edge, Rhebokskloof, Riebeek, Saronsberg, Spotswood, Star Hill, Stonehill, **SylvanVale**, Waterkloof, Woolworths ★★★ Auction Crossing, Calais, Chennells, Clive Torr, Eerste

Hoop, Excelsior, Fort Simon, Fraai Uitzicht 1798, **Fröhlich**, Katbakkies, **Lowerland**, Lynx, Maison, Noble Hill, Robertson, Silkbush, Stellenbosch University, Stellenbosch Vineyards ★★★ Ayama, Township Winery ★★ Leipzig **NT Arendsig**, Arra, Avondrood, Black Elephant, Dieu Donné, Fairview, Hermit on the Hill, Karusa, Katbakkies, **Lismore**, Lorraine, **Miles Mossop**, Montpellier, My Wyn, Naughton's, Schalkenbosch, Spring Grove, TTT Cellar, Vrede en Lust, Whalehaven **NR** Lazanou **D** Bilton, Corder, Graham Beck, Hilton, Lutzville, Nederburg, Nick & Forti's, Niel Joubert

White blends, off-dry/semi-sweet (w & u/w)

★★★★ Four Paws, Kaapzicht, Solms-Delta

★★★☆ Amani, BLANKbottle, Bramon, Virgin Earth ★★★ Altydgedacht, Bellpost, De Wetshof, Edgebaston, Onderkloof, Opstal, Robertson, Saxenburg, Signal Gun, Villiera, Waka Waka, Woolworths (Light & low-alcohol), Zevenwacht ★★☆ Boschendal, Drostdy-Hof, Du Toitskloof (Fairtrade), Grande Provence, Group CDV (Perlé), Grünberger (Perlé), Kanu, RobinHood, Stellar (Organic, Fairtrade), Stellenrust, Tulbagh Winery, Two Oceans ★★ Bonnievale, Capenheimer (Perlé), Graça, Leopard's Leap, **Nicholson Smith** (Light & low-alcohol) Overhex (Light & low-alcohol), Overmeer Cellars, **Rhebokskloof**, Tulbagh Winery, Vinopoly ★★☆ Autumn Harvest Crackling (Perlé), Botha (Light & low-alcohol), Cellar Cask, Drostdy-Hof, Landzicht, Robertson (3), Vinopoly, Wellington Winery, **Woolworths** (3) (Light & low-alcohol) ★ Kumala (2), Virginia ☆ **Woolworths NT** Bergsig (Perlé), Calitzdorp (Perlé), Imbuko, Mooiuitsig (2), Overhex, Painted Wolf, Swartland, TTT Cellar, Wine Fusion **D** Montpellier, The Butcher Shop

White blends, unwooded, dry

★★★★☆ Ashbourne, The Berrio

★★★★ B Vintners, Barton, Boplaas, Bouchard Finlayson, Elgin Vintners, Grande Provence, Groote Post, Jean Daneel, Lazanou (Organic), **Rosendal**, Woolworths, Zonnebloem

★★★☆ Allée Bleue, Ayama, Beaumont, **Benguela Cove**, Creation, Goats do Roam (Fairtrade), **Hartenberg**, Lynx, Neil Ellis, Overhex, Quando, Slowine, **Somersbosch**, Teddy Hall, Thandi (Fairtrade), Tierhoek, **Topaz**, Truter Family, **Valley Vineyards** ★★★ Ashbourne, Boschendal, **Boutinot**, Buitenverwachting, Darling Cellars, Dorrance, Foothills, Four Paws, **Imbuko** (2), Jakkalsvlei, Kumala, Longridge, Mellasat, Mooiplaas, Nabygelegen, Napier, Nederburg, Old

Vines, Opstal, **Org de Rac** (Organic), Post House, Reyneke (Organic), Saronsberg, Saxenburg, Snow Mountain, Springfontein, Stellar (Organic, Fairtrade), SylvanVale, Thokozani, uniWines, Vergenoegd, Villiera, Vondeling, Wandsbeck, Woolworths, Zonnebloem ★★★ **Asara** (2), Ayama, Barton, Bayede!, Beau Joubert, Beyerskloof, Bon Courage, Boschendal, Boutinot, Brandvlei, Cloof, Darling Cellars, **De Zoete Inval**, Diemersfontein (2), Flagstone, Group CDV, **Hathersage**, Hazendal, **Jacques Germanier** (2) (Organic, Fairtrade), Klein Parys, Kumala, Landskroon, Morgenhof, Namaqua, **Niel Joubert**, Stellar (Organic, Fairtrade), Stellenrust (Fairtrade), The Rhino of Linton Park, Theuniskraal, Van Loveren, Vaughan Johnson, Veenwouden, Villiersdorp, Woolworths (2) ★★ Bellingham, Douglas Green, Glen Carlou, Kumala, Leopard's Leap, Nicholson Smith, Noble Hill, Pulpit Rock, Robertson (3), **Silkbush**, Simonsvlei, Slanghoek, Somerset Wines, Stellenbosch Hills, Tulbagh Winery (Light & low-alcohol), uniWines, Van Loveren, Vendôme, Woolworths, Zandvliet ★★ Bonnievale, Drostdy-Hof, Du Toitskloof (Fairtrade), Knorhoek, Kumala, Nuy, Overmeer Cellars, Robertson (2) (Light & low-alcohol), Simonsvlei, **uniWines**, Woolworths (4) ★ Kumala (2), Woolworths (2) ☆ Drostdy-Hof (Light & low-alcohol), Oom Tas **NT** Boer & Brit, Eikehof, Groot Constantia, Group CDV, Hathersage, Joostenberg, Jordan, Kanu, Karusa, Môreson, Mount Vernon, Mountain Oaks (Organic), Mountain River, **New Beginnings**, Nico Vermeulen, Oude Denneboom, Somersbosch, Stellendrift, Vrede en Lust (2), Waterford, Waverley Hills (Organic), Wavescape, Welvanpas, Whalehaven, Wine Fusion, Withington, Zanddrift **D** De Zoete Inval, Doolhof, Joostenberg (Organic), Leeuwenberg, Nederburg, Schalkenbosch, Thandi (Fairtrade), Van Loveren (2) (Light & low-alcohol), Wellington Winery

White blends, wooded, dry

★★★★★ Bloemendal, Cape Point, Constantia Glen, Constantia Uitsig, David & Nadia Sadie, Mullineux, Newton Johnson, Nitida, Oak Valley, Sadie, Spier, Waterkloof

★★★★☆ AA Badenhorst (2), Alheit, **B Vintners**, Backsberg, Bizoe, Cape Chamonix, Cape Point, Cederberg, Delaire, DeMorgenzon, Fable, Fairview, Flagstone, Groot Constantia,

Hermanuspietersfontein, Hughes Family (Organic), Keermont, Lemberg, Lourensford, Miles Mossop, Momento, Môreson, Morgenster, Nederburg, **Nitida**, Olifantsberg, Rall, Sadie (2), Savage, Sijnn, Solms-Delta, Steenberg, Sterhuis, Strandveld, Sumaridge, Thelema, Thorne & Daughters, Tokara, Vergelegen, Vondeling, Vuurberg

★★★★ AA Badenhorst, Allée Bleue, Altydgedacht, Alvi's Drift, Avondale (Organic), Babylon's Peak, Bellingham, Bergsig, Black Oystercatcher, **Blackwater**, BLANKbottle, Bosman (Fairtrade), Celestina, Darling Cellars, DeMorgenzon, Dornier, Eerste Hoop, Ernst Gouws, Escapades, Fledge & Co, Gabriëlskloof, Grande Provence, Highlands Road, **Kanu**, Leeuwenkuil, Lomond (2), Mulderbosch, Muratie, Nabygelegen, Neethlingshof, Nico van der Merwe, **Painted Wolf**, **Paul Roos**, Rickety Bridge, **Sijnn**, **South Hill**, **Springfield**, Stony Brook, The Ahrens Family, **The Liberator**, **The Winery of Good Hope**, The Wolftrap, Trizanne, **Ultra Liquors**, Virgin Earth, Welbedacht, Woolworths, Yardstick, Zorgvliet

★★★☆ Adoro, **Beau Constantia**, Bergheim, Black Elephant, Blake, BLANKbottle, **Boland**, Hildenbrand, Idiom, Laibach (Organic), **Le Pommier**, Micu Narunsky, **Mont Rochelle**, Nuweland, Porcupine Ridge, Stellenbosch Hills, Stellenbosch Vineyards, Stony Brook, **The Liberator**, Waterford, Waverley Hills (Organic), Wildehurst, Zevenwacht

★★★ Doolhof, Hildenbrand, Joostenberg (Organic), Kumala, **Leeuwenberg**, Leipzig, Nederburg, **Piekenierskloof**, Stark-Condé, **Stellar** (Organic, Fairtrade), **The Three Foxes**, Two Oceans, **Ultra Liquors**, uniWines, Val de Vie, Waterford, Woolworths ★★☆ Doran, Kumala, Namaqua (2) ★★ Kumala ★ Kumala **NT** Alvi's Drift, AntHill, Beau Constantia, Bergheim, Cape Rock, Cavalli, D'Aria, **De Kleine Wijn Koöp**, Elemental Bob, Fijndraai, Gilga, Hermit on the Hill, Hillock, Jean Daneel, Karusa, Klein Parys, Malanot, Mountain Oaks, My Wyn, Nomada, **Nuy**, Orangerie, Osbloed, Perdeberg, Rietvallei, Scali (Organic), **Sizanani**, Vrede en Lust, Welgegund, Withington **D** Anura, Du Toitskloof (Fairtrade), Metzer, Nederburg (2), Val du Charron

Zinfandel/Primitivo

★★★★ Idiom

★★★☆ Blaauwklippen, Grande Provence **NT** Blaauwklippen **D** Glen Carlou

The Industry

Overview

According to the latest available data (2014), South Africa is the 7th largest wine-producing nation by volume. France, with 16.7% of global production, is the new number one producer, followed by Italy (16%), Spain (14.9%) and the US (8%). South Africa, with ±1,13m litres (excluding grape juice and grape juice concentrate), in 2014 slightly raised its contribution to global volume, to 4.1%, despite the number of wine-grape growers in the country continuing to decline (3,314 compared with 3,323 the previous year).

The overall number of wine cellars crushing grapes also continued to dip, to 559, as did the number of private cellars, from 493 in 2013 to 485. (Producing wholesalers crushing grapes were slightly up, to 25, while co-operatives — 'producer cellars' in officialese — went down a notch to 49.) Though their number continued to decline in 2014, to 225, micro-cellars vinifying less than 100 tons still constituted ±40% of all producers and thus remained a potent force in the industry.

Vineyards

Adjusted official figures show that new vineyard establishment slumped to a new low of 2,164 ha in 2014, versus 6,007 in 2004 (the average annual rate of uprooting remained fairly steady at ±4,000 ha over the past decade).

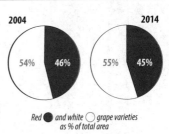

2004 54% 46%

2014 55% 45%

Red ● and white ○ grape varieties as % of total area

In 2014, planting for white wine significantly outstripped that for red (1,369 ha vs 795), and white-wine grape chenin retained its entrenched position as most-planted variety (519 ha added). Colombard remained the second most-planted white-wine variety, with 403 ha, followed by sauvignon (120) and chardonnay (87). Pinotage, with 212 ha, again outpaced cab (123), shiraz (120) and ruby cab (94) as most-planted red-wine variety.

As ever, much more chenin was uprooted than planted, but the variety still led the overall hectareage table, with 18% of the total 99,463 ha under vine. Cab, with 11%, remained the leading red. The percentage of very young vines (under 4 years) decreased fractionally in 2014 to 7.5%, while the portion older than 20 years rose slightly to 20%.

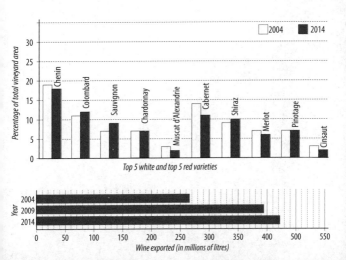

Top 5 white and top 5 red varieties

Wine exported (in millions of litres)

South African Wine Industry — Ten-year Overview

	2005	2006	2007	2008	2009	2010	2011	2012	2013	2014
Number of wineries	581	576	560	585	604	573	582	582	564	559
Total vine area (excl sultana) (hectares)	101 607	102 146	101 957	101 325	101 259	101 016	100 568	100 093	99 680	99 463
Producing area 4 yrs & older (excl sultana) (hectares)	87 284	89 426	91 326	92 503	93 285	93 198	92 621	91 867	91 972	92 047
Avg yield (tons/hectare)	13.42	14.55	14.80	15.41	14.45	13.53	14.06	15.40	16.30	16.52
Grapes crushed (millions of tons)	1.17	1.30	1.35	1.43	1.35	1.26	1.30	1.41	1.50	1.52
Total production (millions of litres)	905.2	1 013.0	1 043.5	1 089.0	1 033.4	984.8	1 012.8	1 097.0	1 156.9	1 181.1
Domestic sales (millions of litres)	334.2	337.4	355.5	355.8	338.3	346.4	353.3	361.2	368	394.6
Consumption per capita (litres SA wine)	7.13	7.12	7.43	7.31	6.86	6.93	6.98	6.98	6.95	7.31
Export volume (millions of litres)	281.1	271.7	312.5	411.7	395.6	378.5	357.4	417.2	525.6	422.7
Stock : sales ratio	0.55:1	0.66:1	0.64:1	0.47:1	0.49:1	0.48:1	0.59:1	0.55:1	0.45:1	0.60:1

Exports

Exports of 422,7 m litres, or ±46% of South Africa's total wine production, in 2014 were substantially lower than 2013's ten-year high of 525,6 m litres. Chenin, sauvignon and chardonnay topped the list of most-exported varietal wines (bottled and bulk), with in-vogue pinks, cab, shiraz, pinotage and merlot also in demand. The UK, Germany, Russia, Sweden and France were the top five markets for SA wine (packaged and bulk) in 2014. For packaged wine only, the UK, Sweden, Germany, the Netherlands and the US were the five biggest outlets.

Local wine consumption

South African domestic per-capita wine consumption rose to 7.31L in 2014, the highest since 2008.

While wine's combined market share (natural, fortified and sparkling) continued to increase slightly to 17.1% in 2014, it remained substantially lower than beer (55.7%). Brandy's 5% share continued to decline, while whisky's 6.7% represented steady incremental growth.

Of natural wine sold in South Africa during 2014 (including locally bottled imports), ±50% was in glass, and of that 60% was in the standard 750 ml bottle. Wine in bag-in-box accounted for a slightly higher ±29% of total sales, plastic containers ±19% and Tetra packs ±2%. Foil bags — the notorious papsakke, now carefully regulated — represented a minuscule 0.3%.

Note

Statistical data was provided by SA Wine Industry Information & Systems.

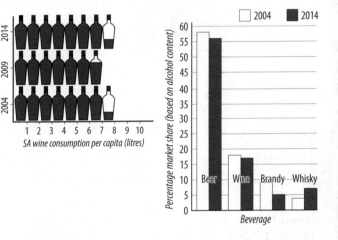

SA wine consumption per capita (litres)

Percentage market share (based on alcohol content) — Beer, Wine, Brandy, Whisky — Beverage — 2004 / 2014

Wine Industry Organisations

African Vintners Alliance See Black Own Brands

Agricultural Ethical Trade Initiative (WIETA) See Wine & Agricultural Ethical Trade Association

ARC Infruitec-Nietvoorbij Senior research manager: prof Bongani Ndimba ▪ Public relations officer: Derusha Crank ▪ **T +27 (0)21-809-3100** ▪ F +27 (0)21-809-3400 ▪ infocape@arc.agric.za ▪ www.arc.agric.za Internationally regarded one-stop research institute, committed to provide sustainable technologies to the developing and commercial agricultural sectors in South Africa, through leading and dynamic research, technology development and technology transfer on deciduous fruit, viticulture, alternative crops and indigenous herbal teas. Nietvoorbij, research farm of the ARC, is synonymous with quality research in oenology and viticulture. Annually, 1,000 different small-batch wines are made for research purposes, along with commercial wines for sale to the public.

Black Own Brands Marketing: Vivian Kleynhans ▪ **T +27 (0)71-049-4109** ▪ bob@ africanrootswines.com

Established to create an enabling environment for emerging black-owned wineries.

Cape Port Producers' Association (CAPPA) Chair: Carel Nel ▪ **T +27 (0)44-213-3326** ▪ F +27 (0)44-213-3750 ▪ boplaas@mweb.co.za

Cape Vintner Classification (CVC) CEO Charl Theron ▪ **T +27(0)83-269-0577** ▪ F +27(0)86-275-8887 ▪ info@cvc1659.co.za ▪ www.cvc1659.co.za

Independent body committed to the accreditation, governance, representation and promotion of distinctive site-specific wines produced by registered 'estates'. Through a system of certification and classification, CVC endorsement underscores its members' commitment to terroir-specific winemaking as well as excellence in cellar practices, environmental championing and cellardoor experience.

Cape Winemakers Guild (CWG) Chair: Andries Burger ▪ General Manager: Kate Jonker ▪ **T +27 (0)21-852-0408** ▪ F +27 (0)21-852-0409 ▪ info@capewinemakersguild.com ▪ www. capewinemakersguild.com

Independent, invitation-only association, founded in 1982 to promote winemaking excellence among its members. Since 1985, the CWG has held a highly regarded annual public auction. Established in 1999, the Nedbank CWG Development Trust supports social development in the winelands through its Protégé Programme, which plays an active role in transformation of the wine industry, ensuring its long-term health and sustainability. The Guild also offers Billy Hofmeyr AGRI Seta bursaries to final year Viticulture & Oenology students.

Chardonnay Forum of South Africa Chair: Johann de Wet ▪ johanndewet@dewetshof.com ▪ **T +27 (0)23-615-1853** ▪ F +27 (0)23-615-1915

Chenin Blanc Association (CBA) Chair: Ken Forrester ▪ **T +27 (0)21-855-2374 / +27 (0)82-783-7203** ▪ F +27 (0)21-855-2373 ▪ ken@kenforresterwines.com ▪ www.chenin.co. za ▪ Manager: Ina Smith ▪ **T +27 (0)82-467-4331** ▪ F +27 (0)86-672-8549 ▪ ina.smith@ iafrica.com ▪ @CheninBlancAsso

Fairtrade Africa - Southern Africa Network (FTA-SAN) Regional head: Faith Muisyo ▪ **T +27 (0)21-447-3486** ▪ f.muisyo@ fairtradeafrica.net ▪ www.fairtradeafrica.net Fairtrade Africa (FTA) is the umbrella organisation representing Fairtrade-certified producers in Africa. FTA aims to effectively represent and provide services to producers within the International Fairtrade system and to contribute to livelihood improvement of African producers by increasing access to markets. FTA-Southern Africa Network (SAN) is FTA's regional network, representing southern African Fairtrade producers in the global Fairtrade system on issues related to governance, new price setting, standards consultation and making standards more relevant to local farming practices. FTA-SAN supports producers with their development program, market access and promotes south-south trade and intra-Africa trade.

Fairtrade Label South Africa (FLSA) Executive director: Arianna Baldo ▪ **T +27 (0)21-448-8911** ▪ info@fairtrade.org.za ▪ www.fairtrade. org.za

FLSA was established in 2009 to create a Fairtrade market in South Africa, and increase awareness about Fairtrade and ethical farming practices among local businesses and consumers. Wine is one of the key Fairtrade products, and an increasing number of local farms and wineries choose Fairtrade as endorsement for their sound ethical and environmental practices.

Garagiste Movement of South Africa See under Make Your Own Wine

Institute of Cape Wine Masters National chair: Winifred Bowman ▪ **T +27 (0)83-702-3665** ▪ National vice-chair: Mary-Lou Nash +27 (0)83-297-9796 ▪ Secretary: Debi van Flymen **T +27 (0)82-493-2549** ▪ info@icwm.co.za ▪ www. icwm.co.za

Successful completion of examinations set since 1983 by the Cape Wine & Spirit Education Trust and, latterly, the Cape Wine Academy, have qualified 93 Cape Wine Masters. The Institute runs tastings and other wine events, and provides membership services to members worldwide, along with information and access to specialist advice for the wine industry in general.

Integrated Production of Wine (IPW) Manager: Daniël Schietekat ▪ **T +27 (0)21-889-6555** ▪ F +27 (0)866-903-224 ▪ daniel@ipw.co. za ▪ www.ipw.co.za

Innovative, widely supported initiative aimed at producing wine in an environmentally sustainable, profitable way by means of guidelines for both farm and cellar, embracing all aspects of grape production, winemaking and biodiversity conservation. See also Sustainable Wine South Africa.

Méthode Cap Classique Producers' Association Chair: Peter Ferreira ▪ bubblesferreira@gmail.com ▪ Admin: Elsabe Ferreira ▪ **T +27(0)21-863-1599** ▪ F +27 (0)21-863-1552 ▪ info@capclassique.co.za

Muscadel SA Chair: Henri Swiegers ▪ **T +27 (0)23-344-3021** ▪ F +27 (0)86-617-9443 ▪ winemaker@badsberg.co.za ▪ Vice-chair: André Scriven ▪ **T +27 (0)23-626-1664** ▪ andres@rooiberg.co.za

Pinotage Association Chair: Beyers Truter ▪ **T +27(0)21-865-1235** ▪ F +27 ()21-865-2683 ▪ reception@beyerskloof.co.za ▪ Manager: Elsabe Ferreira **T +27 (0)21-863-1599** ▪ F +27 (0)21-863-1552 ▪ admin@pinotage.co.za ▪ www.pinotage.co.za

Sauvignon Blanc Interest Group of South Africa (SBIG) Admin: Elsabe Ferreira ▪ **T +27 (0)21-863-1599** ▪ F +27 (0)21-863-1552 ▪ elsabe@efpromosies.co.za

Shiraz South Africa Chair: Edmund Terblanche ▪ **T +27 (0)82-770-2929** ▪ F +27 (0)21-876-3446 ▪ et.cellar@la-motte.co.za ▪ Secretary: Sandra Lotz ▪ **T +27 (0)82-924-7254** ▪ F +27 (0)86-267-4333 ▪ info@shirazsa.co.za

South African Black Vintners Alliance See Black Own Brands

South African Sommelier Association (SASA) Chair: Neil Grant ▪ Vice-chair: David Clarke ▪ info@sommeliers.org.za ▪ www.sommeliers.org.za

Membership-driven, non-profit, voluntary private organisation established in 2012 to promote a culture of fine wine, food and service excellence in South Africa; formalise the profession of sommelier; and provide a forum for dialogue, exchange of ideas, knowledge and skills.

South African Wine Industry Information & Systems (SAWIS) Executive Manager: Yvette van der Merwe ▪ **T +27 (0)21-807-5703** ▪ F +27 (0)86-559-0274 ▪ info@sawis.co.za

Responsible for the collection, processing and dissemination of industry information. Administers the Wine of Origin (WO) system and manages the Information Centre, a comprehensive information resource base for the SA wine and brandy industry.

South African Wine Industry Trust (SAWIT) Chair: Sharron Marco-Thyse ▪ CEO: Charles Erasmus ▪ **T +27(0)21-889-8101** ▪ F +27 (0)86-503-6222 ▪ sawit@live.co.za ▪ www.sawit.co.za

The vision of SAWIT is the creation of a transformed wine industry that is sustainable and

vibrant, populated by an empowered worker community that shares equitably in growth and prosperity.

Southern Africa Fairtrade Network (SAFN) See Fairtrade Africa - Southern Africa Network

Sustainable Wine South Africa (SWSA) www.swsa.co.za ▪ Contact details as for individual organisations.

Alliance between the Wine & Spirit Board (WSB), Integrated Production of Wine (IPW), WWF-SA Conservation Champion programme and Wines of South Africa (WOSA), driving the industry's commitment to sustainable, eco-friendly production.

Wine & Agricultural Ethical Trade Association (WIETA) CEO: Linda Lipparoni ▪ **T +27 (0)21-880-0580** ▪ F +27 (0)21-880-0580 ▪ linda@wieta.org.za, info@wieta.org.za ▪ www.wieta.org.za

Multi-stakeholder, non-profit, voluntary organisation established in 2002 to promote ethical trade in wine, fruit, cut flowers and general agriculture. WIETA has adopted a code of labour standards for the wine industry, and its main task is to support, enhance and promote members' ethical performance and best practice through training, technical assessments and ethical inspections to assess compliance. WIETA recently adopted an ethical seal which has been endorsed by the wine industry in recognition of wine supply chains' ethical commitment to good working conditions on farms and in cellars.

Wine & Spirit Board Chair: Matome Mbatha ▪ Secretary: Hugo van der Merwe ▪ **T +27 (0)21-889-6555** ▪ F +27 (0)21-889-5823 ▪ hugo@wsb.org.za

Mainly administers the Wine of Origin, Estate Brandy and Integrated Production of Wine (IPW) schemes.

Wines of South Africa (WOSA) CEO: Siobhan Thompson ▪ Non-executive chair: Michael Jordaan ▪ info@wosa.co.za ▪ **T +27 (0)21-883-3860** ▪ F +27 (0)21-883-3861 ▪ www.wosa.co.za

Generic marketing organisation, responsible for raising the profile of SA wine in key export markets.

Wine Industry Development Association (WIDA) Executive manager: Henry Petersen ▪ **T +27 (0)21-872-9181** ▪ F +27 (0)2-872-4560 ▪ henry@wida.co.za ▪ www.wida.co.za

Promotes transformation through social development, human resource development and training, economic empowerment, and industrial relations, and protects the interests of vulnerable communities in the industry.

Wine Industry Network of Expertise & Technology (WINETECH) Executive manager: Gerard Martin ▪ **T +27 (0)21-276 0498** ▪ F +27 (0)86-611-7846 ▪ marting@winetech.co.za

Coordinates the research, training and technology transfer programmes of participating institutions and individuals, to improve the competitiveness of the wine industry.

WWF-SA Biodiversity & Wine Initiative (BWI) See WWF-SA Conservation Champion Programme

WWF-SA Conservation Champion Programme manager: Shelly Fuller ▪ **T +27 (0)21-882-9085** ▪ sfuller@wwf.org.za ▪ Head of extension: Joan Isham ▪ **T +27 (0)21-882-9085** ▪ jisham@wwf.org.za

In 2005 the Biodiversity & Wine Initiative (BWI) started as a world-leading partnership between the SA wine industry and the conservation sector to minimise further loss of threatened natural habitat within the Cape Floral Kingdom (CFK), and contribute to sustainable wine production through better environmental management practices on farm and in the cellar. After 10 years of successful implementation, the results illustrate the project's achieved impact: for every 1 ha under vine, 1.4 ha of conservation land are under better management and almost 90% of the industry is using the Integrated Production of Wine (IPW) accreditation scheme. The needs of the membership base are now shifting to a more holistic approach of managing environmental risk and thus the programme is moving into a new phase of focus. Going forward the BWI name will fall away and consumers can support WWF-SA Conservation Champions by buying wines displaying the colourful sugarbird and protea logo, recognising industry leaders who are committed to continual improvement of production practices and biodiversity conservation. The WWF-SA Conservation Champion works closely with IPW and supports the sustainability seal of Sustainable Wine South Africa (SWSA).

Winegrowing Areas

From modest beginnings in the Dutch East India Company's 17th-century gardens below Table Mountain, South Africa's vineyards now cover 99,463 ha and more than 100 official appellations. Changes to the Wine of Origin (WO) scheme of 1972/3 saw 'geographical units' incorporated into the WO classification alongside 'regions', 'districts' and 'wards' (the latter have the smallest footprint of the WO areas, following earlier amendments to the 'estate' legislation). Below are brief notes on the most important grape cultivation zones. Information supplied by Wines of South Africa (WOSA) and

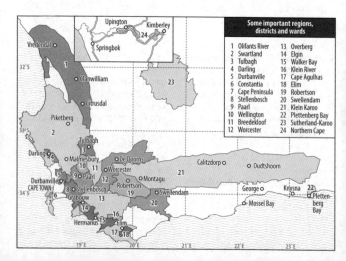

	Some important regions, districts and wards	
1 Olifants River	13 Overberg	
2 Swartland	14 Elgin	
3 Tulbagh	15 Walker Bay	
4 Darling	16 Klein River	
5 Durbanville	17 Cape Agulhas	
6 Constantia	18 Elim	
7 Cape Peninsula	19 Robertson	
8 Stellenbosch	20 Swellendam	
9 Paarl	21 Klein Karoo	
10 Wellington	22 Plettenberg Bay	
11 Breedekloof	23 Sutherland-Karoo	
12 Worcester	24 Northern Cape	

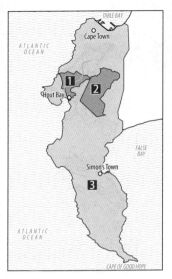

1 Hout Bay   2 Constantia   3 Cape Peninsula

SA Wine Industry Information & Systems (SAWIS), and reflects 2014 data for the WO areas. Note: Area maps are not to the same scale.

Breedekloof Large (13,015 ha) Breede River Valley district producing mainly for brandy industry and merchant trade, but also featuring some quality-focused boutiques and family estates with reputations for pinotage, chenin, chardonnay and semillon. Major varieties (ha): chenin (2,784), colombard (1,945), sauvignon (998), pinotage (964), chardonnay (933). See under Robertson for climate, geology etc.

Cape Peninsula Cool-climate district (441 ha) with wards Hout Bay and Constantia. Vineyards mainly on western and eastern mountain slopes, and inner-city Cape Town. Recognised for sauvignon and semillon. Sauvignon (197), merlot (37), cab (32), shiraz (31), chardonnay (26).

Cape South Coast 'Umbrella' region (2,719 ha) for Cape Agulhas, Elgin, Overberg, Plettenberg Bay, Swellendam and Walker Bay districts, and Herbertsdale, Napier and Stilbaai East wards.

Cederberg 72-ha ward in the Cederberg Mountain range, with some of SA's remotest and highest vineyards (950-1,100 m). Best known for shiraz (15 ha) and sauvignon (11). Also chenin (9) chardonnay (9), cab (7).

Central Orange River This ward along the Orange River (Gariep) is a production zone within the Northern Cape Geographical Unit. Altitude: 500-1,000 m; temp 25.3℃; rain: 250/208 mm; geology: granite, dolorite, shale, alluvial. Overwhelmingly a white-grape area but red plantings are increasing. Sultana (6,561), colombard (2,286), chenin (961), villard blanc (212), muscat d'Alexandrie (147).

Constantia Premium viticultural ward on the eastern flank of the Cape Peninsula, cooled by south-easterly sea breezes. Recognised for whites generally, notably sauvignon, semillon and muscat. Altitude: 100-300 m; temp (Mean February

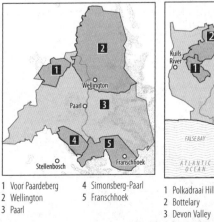

1 Voor Paardeberg   4 Simonsberg-Paarl
2 Wellington   5 Franschhoek
3 Paarl

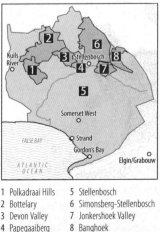

1 Polkadraai Hills   5 Stellenbosch
2 Bottelary   6 Simonsberg-Stellenbosch
3 Devon Valley   7 Jonkershoek Valley
4 Papegaaiberg   8 Banghoek

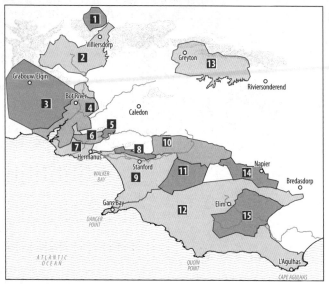

1 Elandskloof
2 Theewater
3 Elgin
4 Bot River
5 Hemel-en-Aarde Ridge
6 Upper Hemel-en-Aarde
7 Hemel-en-Aarde Valley
8 Stanford Foothills
9 Walker Bay
10 Klein River
11 Sunday's Glen
12 Cape Agulhas
13 Greyton
14 Napier
15 Elim

Temperature, MFT) 20.6°C; rain: total/summer 1,056/335 mm; geology: granite (sandstone). Major varieties: sauvignon (180), merlot (36), cab (29), shiraz (27), chardonnay (22).

Darling District (2,715 ha) encircling the eponymous West Coast town, best known for the wines from its higher-lying ward, Groenekloof, long the source of top sauvignon; growing reputation for reds, especially shiraz. Groenekloof: cab (470), shiraz (349), sauvignon (312), pinotage (183), merlot (175).

Durbanville Ward within the Tygerberg district, with reputation for striking merlot and sauvignon. The latter (435) is the dominant variety, followed by cab (240), merlot (224), shiraz (202) and chardonnay (91). Altitude: 150-350 m; temp 22.4°C; rain: 481/140 mm; geology: shale.

Elgin Cool upland district (827 ha) within the Cape South Coast region, yielding aromatic whites and elegant reds. Altitude: 200-250 m; temp 19. 7°C; rain: 1,011/366 mm; geology: shale (

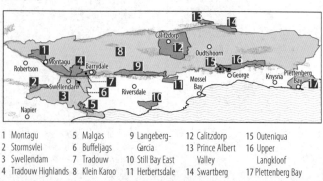

1 Montagu
2 Stormsvlei
3 Swellendam
4 Tradouw Highlands
5 Malgas
6 Buffeljags
7 Tradouw
8 Klein Karoo
9 Langeberg-Garcia
10 Still Bay East
11 Herbertsdale
12 Calitzdorp
13 Prince Albert Valley
14 Swartberg
15 Outeniqua
16 Upper Langkloof
17 Plettenberg Bay

sandstone). Sauvignon (328), pinot noir (115), chardonnay (105), shiraz (75), cab (54).

Elim Maritime ward within the Cape Agulhas district, its 139 ha of vineyards are arrayed around the old mission village of Elim near Africa's most southerly point. Sauvignon (78), shiraz (31), semillon (11), pinot noir (10), cab (3).

Franschhoek Valley A district with 1,245 ha under vine, recognised for cab and semillon. Sauvignon (194), chardonnay (189), cab (180), shiraz (168), merlot (116).

Hemel-en-Aarde See Walker Bay

Klein Karoo Scrubby semi-arid region (2,499 ha), reliant on irrigation. Recognised for excellent 'ports' and fortifieds generally. Calitzdorp district: muscat d'Alexandrie (85), colombard (74), chenin (36), cab (22), touriga (16). Tradouw ward: chardonnay (13), shiraz (10), merlot (9), sauvignon (8), colombard (8). Interesting stirrings in Langeberg-Garcia district (44), and Upper Langkloof (48) and Tradouw Highlands (10) wards.

Northern Cape See Central Orange River

Olifants River Quality moves are afoot in this north-westerly Cape grape-growing region (9,990 ha), particularly in the Bamboes Bay 'micro-ward' (just 6 ha), Citrusdal Mountain district (600) and, near the coast, Lutzville Valley district (3,067), as

well as the cool upland ward of Piekenierskloof (482). Inland, a climate conducive to organic cultivation is being exploited to that end. Altitude: 20-100 m; temp 23°C; rain: 139/47 mm; geology: mainly schist and alluvial deposits. Koekenaap ward (Lutzville Valley): chenin (305), colombard (222), sauvignon (163), pinotage (40), cab (65). Piekenierskloof: pinotage (68), chenin (51), palomino (49), grenache noir (47), sauvignon (38). Citrusdal Mountain: chenin (93), pinotage (78), palomino (49), grenache noir (47) sauvignon (46).

Orange River See Central Orange River

Paarl This district has many mesoclimates, soils and aspects, and thus succeeds with a variety of styles and grapes. Altitude: 100-300 m; temp 23.2°C; rain: 945/273 mm; geology: granite and shale. Paarl proper is recognised for shiraz and, more recently, viognier and mourvèdre grown on warmer slopes. Chenin (1,423), shiraz (910), cab (895), pinotage (580), cinsaut (388). The following are wards: Simonsberg-Paarl, on the warmer slopes of the Simonsberg, recognised for red blends, shiraz and chardonnay. Cab (278), chardonnay (191), sauvignon (186), shiraz (180), merlot (114); and Voor Paardeberg, long an uncredited source of top-quality grapes, now becoming a star in own right. Cab (381), shiraz (321), chenin (235), merlot (214), pinotage (191).

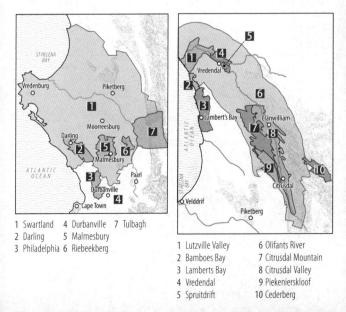

1 Swartland	4 Durbanville	7 Tulbagh
2 Darling	5 Malmesbury	
3 Philadelphia	6 Riebeekberg	

1 Lutzville Valley	6 Olifants River
2 Bamboes Bay	7 Citrusdal Mountain
3 Lamberts Bay	8 Citrusdal Valley
4 Vredendal	9 Piekenierskloof
5 Spruitdrift	10 Cederberg

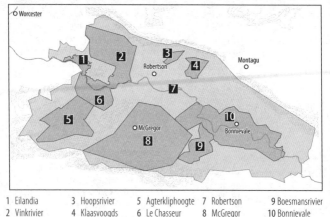

| 1 Eilandia | 3 Hoopsrivier | 5 Agterkliphoogte | 7 Robertson | 9 Boesmansrivier |
| 2 Vinkrivier | 4 Klaasvoogds | 6 Le Chasseur | 8 McGregor | 10 Bonnievale |

Robertson Traditionally a white-wine district (14,094), increasingly recognised for shiraz and cab. Chardonnay, sauvignon and sparkling remain standouts. Altitude: 150-250 m; temp 23°C; rain: 280/116 mm; geology: shale and alluvial. Colombard (2,173), chardonnay (1,930), chenin (1,665), sauvignon (1,509), cab (1,508).

Stellenbosch To many, this intensively farmed district (13,196) is the wine capital of SA. Key contributors to quality are the cooler mountain slopes, varied soil types and breezes off False Bay which moderate summer temperatures. Altitude: 200-400 m; temp 21.5°C; rain: 713/229 mm; geology: granite (sandstone). Jonkershoek Valley,

a ward east of Stellenbosch town, is recognised for cab and cab blends. Cab (60), merlot (23), chardonnay (22), shiraz (18), sauvignon (15). Simonsberg-Stellenbosch, in the south-western foothills of the Simonsberg Mountain, is especially recognised for cab, cab blends and pinotage, and reds generally. Cab (304), sauvignon (186), merlot (170), shiraz (147), chardonnay (130). North-west of Stellenbosch town are four adjoining wards: Papegaaiberg - chardonnay (28), sauvignon (22), chenin (21), pinot gris (12), pinotage (11); Devon Valley, recognised mainly for red blends - merlot (131), sauvignon (112), cab (108), shiraz (65), pinotage (59); Bottelary, noted for pinotage, shiraz

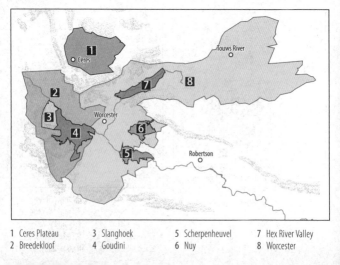

| 1 Ceres Plateau | 3 Slanghoek | 5 Scherpenheuvel | 7 Hex River Valley |
| 2 Breedekloof | 4 Goudini | 6 Nuy | 8 Worcester |

and warm-blooded blends - chenin (415), cab (363), sauvignon (286), shiraz (278), pinotage (253); the most westerly ward, Polkadraai Hills - sauvignon (163), cab (153), shiraz (131), merlot (90), chenin (69); and Banghoek, the mountain amphitheatre above the village of Pniel - cab (75), shiraz (42), merlot (31), sauvignon (28), chardonnay (24). The remainder of the Stellenbosch district, as yet officially undemarcated, includes Stellenboschberg, Helderberg and Faure, recognised for red blends, chenin and sauvignon. Cab (1,609), shiraz (1,208), sauvignon (1,009), merlot (896), chenin (697).

Sutherland-Karoo High-altitude (1,450 m) semi-arid district around SA's coldest town, Sutherland, in the Northern Cape. Currently with only 4 ha under vine (mainly pinot noir, shiraz, chardonnay) but showing potential.

Swartland Traditionally associated with full-bodied reds, but latterly also with chenin and Mediterranean-style red and white blends, this fashionable district (10,854) north of Cape Town has three wards, Malmesbury, Riebeekberg and newer St Helena Bay, plus a large unappellated area. Riebeekberg: chenin (213), pinotage (185), shiraz (176), chardonnay (106), cab (95); Malmesbury: cab (708), shiraz (570), pinotage (499), chenin (469), sauvignon (316); St Helena Bay: sauvignon (13), chenin (6), semillon (4), shiraz (3), pinotage (2). 'Swartland': chenin (1,772), shiraz (888), pinotage (767), cab (740),

chardonnay (364). Altitude: 100-300 m; temp 23.3°C; rain: 523/154 mm; geology: granite and shale.

Tulbagh Inland district (1,097) traditionally known for sparkling and lightish whites, acquiring reputation for quality reds and serious white blends. Altitude: 160-400 m; temp 24°C; rain: 551/175 mm; geology: sandstone boulderbeds and shale. Chenin (222), colombard (149), shiraz (126), cab (112), chardonnay (69).

Walker Bay Highly regarded maritime district (979) south-east of Cape Town, recognised for pinot noir, pinotage, sauvignon and chardonnay. Altitude: 100-250 m; temp 20.3°C; rain: 722/322 mm; geology: shale, granite and sandstone. Sauvignon (264), shiraz (135), pinot noir (132), chardonnay (105), cab (77). Bot River, Hemel-en-Aarde Ridge, Hemel-en-Aarde Valley, Stanford Foothills, Sunday's Glen and Upper Hemel-en-Aarde Valley are wards.

Wellington District (4,340) in the Coastal region increasingly reputed for shiraz and gutsy red blends. Chenin (929), cab (739), shiraz (624), pinotage (445), chardonnay (302).

Worcester District (6,609) producing chiefly for the brandy industry and merchant trade, but small quantities bottled under own labels often represent good quality/value. Recognised for everyday reds/whites and fortifieds. Chenin (1,968), colombard (1,193), chardonnay (460), shiraz (416), pinotage (392). See under Robertson for climate, geology etc.

Wine of Origin-defined production areas
(New appellation/s in **bold**.)

Geographical Unit	Region	District	Ward
Eastern Cape	—	—	St Francis Bay
KwaZulu-Natal	—	—	—
Limpopo	—	—	—
Northern Cape	—	Douglas	—
		—	Central Orange River
		—	Hartswater
		—	Rietrivier (Free State)
		Sutherland-Karoo	—
Western Cape	Breede River Valley	Breedekloof	Goudini
			Slanghoek
		Robertson	Agterkliphoogte
			Boesmansrivier
			Bonnievale
			Eilandia
			Hoopsrivier
			Klaasvoogds
			Le Chasseur
			McGregor
			Vinkrivier
		Worcester	Hex River Valley
			Nuy
			Scherpenheuvel
	Cape South Coast	Cape Agulhas	Elim
		Elgin	—
		Overberg	Elandskloof
			Greyton
			Klein River
			Theewater
		Plettenberg Bay	—
		Swellendam	Buffeljags
			Malgas
			Stormsvlei
		Walker Bay	Bot River
			Hemel-en-Aarde Ridge
			Hemel-en-Aarde Valley
			Stanford Foothills
			Sunday's Glen
			Upper Hemel-en-Aarde Valley
		—	Herbertsdale
		—	Napier
		—	Stilbaai East
	Coastal	Cape Peninsula	Constantia
			Hout Bay
		Darling	Groenekloof
		Franschhoek Valley	—

Geographical Unit	Region	District	Ward
Western Cape (*continued*)	Coastal (*continued*)	Paarl	Simonsberg-Paarl
			Voor Paardeberg
		Stellenbosch	Banghoek
			Bottelary
			Devon Valley
			Jonkershoek Valley
		Stellenbosch (*continued*)	Papegaaiberg
			Polkadraai Hills
			Simonsberg–Stellenbosch
		Swartland	Malmesbury
			Riebeekberg
			St Helena Bay
		Tulbagh	—
		Tygerberg	Durbanville
			Philadelphia
		Wellington	—
	Klein Karoo	Calitzdorp	—
		Langeberg-Garcia	—
		—	Montagu
		—	Outeniqua
		—	Tradouw
		—	Tradouw Highlands
		—	Upper Langkloof
	Olifants River	Citrusdal Mountain	Piekenierskloof
		Citrusdal Valley	—
		Lutzville Valley	Koekenaap
		—	Bamboes Bay
		—	Spruitdrift
		—	Vredendal
	—	—	Cederberg
	—	Ceres Plateau	Ceres
	—	—	Lamberts Bay
	—	—	Prince Albert Valley
	—	—	Swartberg
Source: SAWIS			

Grape Varieties

Below are brief notes on some of the grape varieties mentioned in the guide, and their contribution to the national vineyard (statistics from SA Wine Industry Information & Systems — SAWIS). See under Winegrowing Areas for details of the most widely planted and best-performing varieties in the major vine cultivation zones.

Red-wine varieties

Barbera Piedmont's second grape (after nebbiolo), its natural high acidity suiting warm climates; sought after, too, for low tannins, good colour. Tiny footprint in SA.

Cabernet sauvignon Adaptable and internationally planted black grape making some of the world's finest and longest-lasting wines. And retaining some of its inherent qualities even when overcropped in less suitable soils and climates. Can stand alone triumphantly, but frequently blended with a wide range of other varieties: traditionally, as in Bordeaux, with cab franc, merlot and a few minor others, but also in SA sometimes partnering varieties such as shiraz and pinotage. Number of different clones, with differing characteristics. ±12% of total vineyard area.

Cabernet franc Like its descendant cabernet sauvignon, with which it is often partnered, a classic part of the Bordeaux blend, but in SA and elsewhere — particularly in the Loire — also used for varietal wines. Tiny, stable vineyard area (±1%).

Carignan Hugely planted in the south of France, where it is not much respected. But there, as in SA, older, low-yielding vines can produce pleasant surprises. Insignificant vineyard area.

Cinsaut (noir) Aka 'Cinsault'. Another of the mass, undistinguished plantings of southern France, which only occasionally comes up trumps. Used to be known locally as hermitage, the name reflected in its offspring (with pinot noir), pinotage. About 2% of vineyard area.

Durif See petite sirah/durif

Gamay noir Although it produces some serious long-lived wines in Beaujolais, its use for (mainly) early- and easy-drinking 'nouveau' wines there, often using carbonic maceration, is the model mostly copied in SA. Insignificant vineyard area.

Grenache (noir) The international (ie French) name for the Spanish grape garnacha. Widespread in Spain and southern France, generally used in blends (as in Rioja and Châteauneuf), but occasionally solo. A favourite for rosés. When vigour restrained, capable of greatness, but this is rare. Tiny plantings here. (White/pink versions also occur.)

Malbec Once a significant part of Bordeaux's blend, now most important in Cahors in western France (where it is known as cot), and as Argentina's signature variety. In SA a few varietal and blended examples; very small plantings.

Merlot Classic blending partner (as in Bordeaux) for cabernet, fashionable around the world, where it tends to be seen as an 'easier' version of cab — although this is perhaps because it is often made in a less ambitious manner. Merlot varietal wines increasingly common in SA too. ±6% of vineyard area.

Mourvèdre Internationally known by its French name, though originally Spanish (monastrell). In Australia and California also called mataro. Particularly successful in some serious southern French blends, and increasingly modish internationally. Minuscule plantings here.

Nebbiolo Perhaps the greatest red grape to have scarcely ventured from its home — Piedmont in this case, where it makes massive, tannic, long-lived wines. Minute plantings here.

Petite sirah/durif Originally from southern France, a cross of peloursin and syrah/shiraz. Produces tannic, densely fruited wines. Boutique-scale plantings/vinifications in SA.

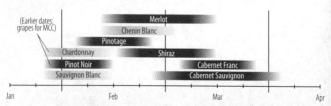

Approximate ripening dates in the Stellenbosch area for some important grape varieties

Petit verdot Use of this excellent variety in the Médoc limited by its late ripening. Now appearing in some local blends, and a few varietals. 0.8% of vineyard area.

Pinotage A 1920s cross between pinot noir and cinsaut ('hermitage'). Made in a range of styles, from simply fruity to ambitious, well-oaked examples. 7.4% of vineyard area, increasing.

Pinot noir
Notoriously difficult grape to succeed with outside its native Burgundy, but SA, along with the rest of the New World, now produces some excellent examples. Just over 1% of the vineyard.

Ruby cabernet US cross between cabernet sauvignon and carignan, designed for heat tolerance. Rather rustic, used mostly in cheaper blends. ±2% of vineyard area.

Sangiovese Tuscany's signature black grape, producing light or big wines, depending on how it is grown. Can be unacceptably acidic and tannic with little colour unless well-managed in the vineyard.

Shiraz Better known as syrah outside SA and Australia (and on some local labels too). Internationally increasing in popularity, with northern Rhône and now also Australia as its major domiciles. Made here in a variety of styles — generally wooded. ±10.5% of vineyard area.

Tannat From France's Basque region, recently Uruguay's calling card but still little more than a curiosity in SA. Known for deep colour and high tannin.

Tempranillo Aka tinta roriz. The soul of Spain's storied Rioja and Ribera del Duero. Low tannin, balanced acidity and plush fruit; suited to warm climates but hardly on the SA radar – yet.

Tinta amarela See Trincadeira

Tinta barocca Elsewhere spelt 'barroca'. One of the important Portuguese port-making grapes, which is now its primary role in SA, usually blended. Also used for some varietal unfortified wines, and namelessly in some 'dry reds'. 0.2% of vineyard area.

Touriga nacional Important Portuguese port-making grape, now usefully grown here for similar ends, along with tinta bacrocca, tinta roriz (tempranillo) and souzão. Tiny plantings.

Trincadeira Also 'tinta amarela'; from Portugal, deep coloured with good black fruit and big tannins. Very limited plantings in SA.

Zinfandel The quintessential Californian grape (of European origin, and the same as Italy's primitivo), used here in a small way for some big wines. Tiny plantings.

White-wine varieties

Bukettraube Light and acidic variety, to add zing to white blends.

Chardonnay In SA, as elsewhere, many new vineyards of this grape have come on-stream, with wines showing a wide range of styles, quality and price. Generally used varietally, but also in blends, and for sparkling. (Heavily) wooded in more ambitious wines. ±7.5% of vineyard area.

Chenin blanc SA has more chenin (locally also called steen) than even France's Loire Valley, the variety's home. Used here for everything from generic 'dry white' to ambitious sweet wines, to brandy. Increasing numbers of table-wine successes in recent years, as well as inexpensive but flavoursome easy drinkers. ±18% of vineyard area.

Clairette blanche High alcohol, low acid, musky component of southern Rhône white blends; bottled as single variety only off superior sites. In SA, also mainly used in blends.

Colombar(d) One of the mainstays of brandy production in SA, colombard (usually without the 'd' in SA) is also used for numerous varietal and blended wines, ranging from dry to sweet — seldom wooded. Steady ±12% of vineyard area.

Fernão pires Aromatic workhorse from Portugal; can be used for wide range of wine styles. Insignificant footprint in SA.

Gewürztraminer Readily identifiable from its rosepetal fragrance, best known in its Alsatian guise. In SA usually made off-dry. Insignificant vineyard area.

Grenache blanc Staple of Rhône white blends, finding adherents in SA, particularly when given skin contact, oak fermentation/ageing. Needs careful handling.

Hanepoot Traditional Afrikaans name for muscat d'Alexandrie, SA's most planted muscat variety (see also muscadel below). ±2% of vineyard area (some for raisins and table grapes), slowly declining.

Hárslevelü From Tokaj, Hungary; delicate when fermented dry, fat and smoky in sweeter styles. Only 24 ha in SA.

Marsanne Rhône grape, more widely planted than 'twin' roussanne. Dependable, but flabby in too-warm terroir, bland in too-cool.

Muscadel Name used here for both muscat de Frontignan and muscat blanc à petits grains (both red and white versions). The grape associated with the famous Constantia dessert wines of the 18th century today is used chiefly for dessert and fortified wines and for touching up blends. Red and white versions total about 1% of vineyard area.

Muscat See Hanepoot and Muscadel.

Nouvelle Local crossing of semillon and neutral ugni blanc/trebbiano, produces intense grass and greenpepper characters. Tiny quantities typically blended.

Pinot blanc Import from north-east Italy; no serious examples locally.

Pinot gris/grigio In north-east Italy prized for acidity, France's Alsace for plump richness. Tiny quantities in SA, named 'gris' or 'grigio' depending on style.

Riesling The name by itself now refers to the great German grape (as it does in this guide). Previously, the grape had to carry the prefix 'Rhine' or 'weisser', and the 'riesling' was an official SA synonym for the inferior crouchen blanc, also known as Cape riesling and mostly used anonymously in blends, occasionally varietally. Rhine riesling often off-dry here, in blends or varietally, some excellent botrytised dessert examples. Crouchen: less

than 0.5% of vineyard area, steady; Rhine: small but steady 0.2%.

Roussanne Like frequent blending partner marsanne, from the northern Rhône. Also aromatic component of Châteauneuf du Pape. Gaining a following in SA.

Sauvignon blanc Prestigious vine most associated with eastern Loire regions, Bordeaux and New Zealand — whose wines have helped restore fashionability to the grape. The SA version no longer a poor relation of these. Usually dry, but some sweet wines; sometimes wooded, more often not (former sometimes called fumé blanc/blanc fumé). ±9% of vineyard area.

Semillon Spelt sémillon in French. Sometimes heavily wooded, sometimes sweet, more often in blends. ±1% of vineyard area, including rare red version.

Sylvaner Native of Germany's Franken, more about style and texture than flavour. Still only one varietal bottling in SA.

Verdelho From Portugal (not to be confused with Spain's verdejo). Both a grape and a (sweet) fortified style in Madeira; mostly dry in the southern hemisphere.

Viognier Increasingly fashionable variety internationally, spreading out from its home in the northern Rhône, now showing promise here. Usually wooded. Still less than 1% of the total.

Competitions, Challenges & Awards

An increasing number of wine competitions, awards and challenges are run by liquor industry bodies, independent companies, publishing houses and individuals. Below are the main national events:

Absa Top Ten Pinotage Competition Run annually by the Pinotage Association and a major financial institution to help set international quality targets for growers of pinotage. Local/overseas judges. See under Industry Organisations for contact details.

Amorim Cap Classique Challenge Annual competition to appoint SA's top bottle-fermented sparkling wines. Mostly local judges. ▪ admin@ capclassique.co.za ▪ www.capclassique.co.za ▪ **T** +27 (0)21-863-1599 ▪ F +27 (0)21-863-1552

CAPPA Cape Port & Wine Challenge Organised by the Cape Port Producers' Association to award best in class and gold medals in each of the port categories, and select the Top 10 Portuguese-

style wines. Local judges. ▪ info@boplaas.co.za ▪ www.capeportproducers.co.za ▪ **T +27 (0)44-213-3326** ▪ F +27 (0)44-213-3750

Diners Club Winemaker of the Year Inaugurated in 1981, this prestigious competition features a different category each year. The Young Winemaker of the Year recognises the winning entrant aged 30 years or younger. Local panel with some overseas representation. ▪ winemaker@ dinersclub.co.za ▪ www.dinersclub.co.za ▪ **T +27 (0)21- 795-5400** ▪ F +27 (0)21-794-8185

Gold Wine Awards Consumers, identified as suitably qualified by the Cape Wine Academy, award gold medals to excellent wines below a yearly predetermined price. Results are then processed to determine whether the winners offer real value for money. The top 5 Excellent Wine at the Price (EWP) brands are also announced. ▪ enquiries@goldwineawards.com ▪ www. goldwineawards.com

Michelangelo International Wine & Spirits Awards sponsored by Collotype Labels

Well-established competition (1997) of which judging panels consist of 18 internationally accredited experts from around the globe and two experienced, well-known local judges. Foreign as well as SA wines, brandies and liqueurs compete under OIV rules for 16 trophies as well as Platinum awards and Gran d'Or, gold and silver medals. The Liqueur Awards were introduced in 2014 and a panel of liqueur specialists brought from Europe to judge the inaugural entries. ▪ lorraine@michelangeloawards. com ▪ www.michelangeloawards.com ▪ T +27 (0)82-556-8679 / +27 (0)21-856-0059 ▪ F +27 (0)86-555-8061

Muscadel Award for Excellence

Annual competition aimed at raising consumer awareness and recognising quality in the creation, packaging and promotion of SA's muscadel wines. Local judges. ▪ winemaker@badsberg.co.za, andres@rooiberg.co. za ▪ T +27 (0)23-344-3021 / +27 (0)23-626-1664 ▪ F +27 (0)23-344-3023

Nedbank Green Wine Awards

A three-part competition, recognising the best wine made from certified organically grown grapes, wines made from IPW-certified farms and the producer with the best environmental practices. Results are published in the Nedbank Green Wine Awards booklet. Local judges. ▪ kathryn.frew@ramsaymedia.co. za ▪ www.greenwineawards.com ▪ T +27 (0)21-530-3308

Old Mutual Trophy Wine Show

Convened by Michael Fridjhon and sponsored by Old Mutual. Seeks to identify the best wines in SA and award trophies to the top gold medal winner in the major classes, as well as the top producer overall. Local and international judges. ▪ alex@ outsorceress.co.za ▪ www.trophywineshow.co.za ▪ T +27 (0)11-482-5936 ▪ F +27 (0)86-532-5177

Perold Absa Cape Blend Competition

Launched in 2011 and aimed at creating a signature style for Cape Blends (see SA Wine Styles section). Local judges. Contacts as for Absa Top Ten Pinotage.

Shiraz SA Wine Challenge

Recent (2013) annual competition to identify the 12 best varietal shirazes and 3 best shiraz blends across all regions and styles. Local/international judges. ▪ info@ shirazsa.co.za ▪ www.shirazsa.co.za ▪ T +27 (0)82 924 7254 ▪ F +27 (0)86-267 4333

South African Airways (SAA) Wine Awards

Annual selection of wines to fly with the national carrier (drinkability in flight conditions an important consideration). The top red, white, bubbly and port each receive a trophy. Local and overseas palates. ▪ UnathiNotununu@flysaa.com, YolandeSchutte@flysaa.com ▪ T +27 (0)11-978-9301 / +27 (0))11-978-3982 ▪ F +27 (0)86-641-4479

SA National Bottled Wine Show See Veritas

South African Terroir Wine Awards

Only wines that truly portray a specific terroir can enter, making this a highly exclusive competition. The best wines certified as from single vineyards, units registered for the production of estate wine, wards in SA's officially recognised winegrowing areas, as well as small districts that are not divided into wards, are awarded. SA's top 5 estate wines are also honoured. Novare Trophies for SA Terroir Top Wine Area, Top Wine Estate and Top Producer are also awarded. Seven local judges. ▪ mlab@iafrica. com ▪ www.terroirwineawards.co.za ▪ T +27 (0)21-975-8166

South African Wine Tasting Championship (SAWTC)

In the spirit of ongoing education, and in an attempt to encourage new converts to wine, the South African Wine Tasting Championship (SAWTC) offers all winelovers the chance to put their talents to the test and be the centre of a local wine event, with an opportunity to compete internationally. ▪ ridon@iafrica.com ▪ www.sawtc.co.za ▪ T +27 (0)21-422-5206 ▪ F +27 (0)21-422-5238

South African Young Wine Show

Inaugurated 1975 to gauge the quality of embryo wines, prior to finishing and bottling, thereby also recognising wineries which sell their products in bulk. The grand champion receives the General Smuts Trophy. Local judges. ▪ information@veritas.co.za ▪ www.youngwineshow.co.za ▪ T +27 (0)21-863-1599 ▪ F +27 (0)21-863-1552

TAJ Classic Wine Trophy

Established in 1998 to recognise ageworthy, elegant and well-made SA wines. Staged in partnership with the TAJ Cape Town and La Revue du Vin de France. Overseas judges. ▪ info@classicwinetrophy.co.za ▪ www. classicwinetrophy.co.za ▪ T +27 (0)21-683-7479 ▪ F +27 (0)86-588-2989

Top 100 South African Wines National fine-wine challenge that aims to identify the best 100 wines of SA using mainly Master of Wine (MW) qualified judges. The winning wines are showcased via an international app, available free for Android and iOS devices from www.top100sawines.com Winning wines can tasted at events around the world. ▪ info@top100sawines.com ▪ www.top100sawines.com

Trophy Wine Show See Old Mutual Trophy Wine Show

Ultra Value Wines New, innovative price-point judged competition, focusing on wines retailing for less than R100/bottle. An algorithm adjusts the score of each wine to arrive at an 'Ultra Value Wine' result, with winners awarded double gold, gold or silver medals. ▪ info@ buybetterwine.com ▪ www.buybetterwine.com, www.ultravaluewines.com

Veritas SA's biggest competition for market-ready wines, awarding double-gold, gold, silver and bronze medals across a wide range of categories. Local palates with some overseas input. ▪ information@veritas.co.za ▪ www.veritas.co.za ▪ **T +27 (0)21-863 1599** ▪ F +27 (0)21-863-1552

Wine Education

Cape Wine Ambassador Thought to be only fully online course on SA wines, Cape Wine Ambassador is a beginner's programme focusing on edutainment and learning about wine in a fun way in the comfort of your own home. Aspects covered include how to taste, viticulture and winemaking, wine styles and wine appreciation. ▪ anthony@topazwineco.com ▪ www.topazwineco.com

Cape Wine Academy Founded by the wine industry in 1979, CWA is the wine education body for the industry, tertiary colleges, hospitality, corporate and the public in SA. Offices in Stellenbosch and Johannesburg with satellites in Durban, Pretoria, Bloemfontein, Kenya, Zimbabwe and London. Runs wine theory and tasting educational courses with examinations, from the South African Wine Course (level 1) through to Cape Wine Master's programme as well as the registered Cape Sommelier program. Also fun, edutainment and team building with Wine & Food, Wine & Cheese and corporate tastings. Stellenbosch: **T +27 (0)21-889-8844** ▪ F +27 (0)21-889-7391 ▪ Johannesburg: **T +27 (0)11-024-3616** ▪ F +27 (0)86-559-7329 ▪ info@

capewineacademy.co.za ▪ www.capewineacademy.co.za

University of Stellenbosch Garagiste Winemaking Course See under Make Your Own Wine

Wine Judging Academy Run by Michael Fridjhon in association with the University of Cape Town's Graduate School of Business, this intensive 3-day tasting and wine judging course aims to increase the number of competent wine judges at work in the local industry. ▪ crossley@reciprocal.co.za

WSET in South Africa with the International Wine Education Centre Founded in 1969 and the industry standard for wine education in 63 countries, the UK-based Wine & Spirit Education Trust's (WSET) courses are offered by the IWEC, catering for enthusiastic amateurs and wine industry professionals alike. WSET are the only internationally recognised wine courses available and offered throughout Africa, in-situ training for front-of-house staff is also offered and for those wanting to take their wine education to the highest level, WSET is the direct path to the Master of Wine (MW) qualification. Standalone spirits courses also available. ▪ info@thewinecentre.co.za ▪ www.thewinecentre.co.za ▪ **T +27 (0)72-390-9166**

Make Your Own Wine

BuytheBarrel at Hildenbrand Wine, Olive & Art Estate
Sign up and buy a barrel, choose your grapes and decide which style of wine you want to make. Either pick and press the grapes – the hard part – or fast-forward to taste and blend your wine with the help of the qualified resident winemaker. Then design your label, bottle your wine (you get 300 bottles!) and sip, ship, sell or share it as you see fit. ▪ alex@

buythebarrel.co.za ▪ www.buythebarrel.co.za ▪ **T +27 (0)84-582-6376**

Garagiste Movement of South Africa Chair: Clive Torr ▪ clive@garagistemovement.co.za ▪ PRO: Tanja Beutler ▪ tanja@garagistemovement.co.za ▪ **T +27 (0)21-855-4275** ▪ F +27 (0)86-612-6118

Now formally constituted as an association, the

Garagiste Movement provides a platform for small-scale winegrowers to connect with like-minded producers, obtain advice and market their wines.

Make Your Winemaking Dreams Come True Clive Torr, chair of the Garagiste Movement, and the committee can facilitate the making of your own wine. Prof Wessel du Toit of Stellenbosch University (see entry below) teaches the theory and Clive directs you to make a barrel. ▪ clivetorrwines@mweb.co.za ▪ www.clivetorrwines.co.za ▪ **T +27 (0)82-557-0836** ▪ F +27 (0)86-513-4034

Sign Your Name in Wine at Stellenrust/JJ Handmade Wines Stellenrust wine farm near Stellenbosch offers groups of 20 or more the opportunity to pick grapes, crush them in 3-ton open-tank fermenters and put a personal signature on their very own wine. Packages include a full-day excursion followed by traditional braai lunch and bottles of participants' handcrafted wine (after proper barrel maturation in the JJ Handmade Wines boutique cellar). info@stellenrust.co.za ▪ www.stellenrust.co.za ▪ **T +27 (0)21-880-2283** ▪ F +27 (0)21-880-2284

Topaz Hands-On Winemaking Course In Topaz Wine's one-day harvest workshop for aspiring garagistes, you pick your own grapes, destem and crush, mix and add yeast and do the first punch-down. A year later you return to bottle your wine from barrel and take your very own 12 bottles home with you. The course includes lunch, the 'Less is More' garagiste handbook, two tasting glasses and a tasting of garagiste wines. ▪ tanja@topazwines.co.za ▪ **T +27(0)21-855-4275**

Topaz 'Red Tape' Consulting For smaller producers who don't want to employ someone fulltime, Tanja Beutler takes the headache out of the red tape in wine. With over 20 years' industry experience, Tanja handles SAWIS and Excise monthly returns and annual audits, export logistics, wine bottling and labelling logistics, packaging, as well as Pastel accounts up to trial balance. ▪ tanja@topazwines.co.za ▪ **T +27 (0)21-855-4275**

University of Stellenbosch Garagiste Winemaking Course The premium short course for people interested in producing quality small-scale wines at home or simply expanding their wine knowledge. Attendees receive a set of notes; observe the use of garagiste winemaking equipment; taste different vinifications; bottle their own wine; and receive a certificate from Stellenbosch University. ▪ wdutoit@sun.ac.za ▪ **T +27 (0)21-808-2022** ▪ F +27 (0)21-808-4781

A-Code Numbers & Codes

Many wines appear on the market under brand names, with, at first glance, no reference to their producers or purveyors. However, consumers need not buy 'blind', and may trace a wine's provenance by checking the official 'A-number' which appears on the bottle or pack. This identity code tells you either who produced the wine, or who sourced it for resale. In the latter case, an enquiry to the merchant should elicit the source. The list keeps growing and being revised, and is too lengthy to reproduce in this guide. Via the SAWIS web page **www.sawis.co.za/sealsearch.php**, it is possible however to search the list of A-codes, as well as the certification codes issued for each wine by the Wine & Spirit Board, for details about the production area, variety and vintage.

Styles & Vintages

Recent South African Vintages

South African wines do not exhibit the major vintage variations seen in some winegrowing areas. There are, nevertheless, perceptible differences from year to year. Dry, hot summers are the norm but a variety of factors make generalisations difficult and possibly misleading.

2015 Near-perfect conditions produced a smaller but pristine crop displaying exceptional quality across the style spectrum. One of the great vintages, possibly surpassing 2009.

2014 Later, slightly smaller and unusually cool, among wettest pre-seasons in years. Seemingly lighter, less powerful wines; potential for fine concentration and elegance if picked judiciously.

2013 Biggest crop to date; moderate conditions yielded good to very good reds and whites, lighter alcohol levels.

2012 Unusually dry, hot January strained unirrigated vineyards; otherwise good to very good vintage for both reds and whites; moderate alcohol levels.

2011 Yet more variable than the last, impossible to generalise. As in 2010, producer's track record should guide the buying/cellaring decision.

2010 A real test of the winegrower's savvy, and one of the toughest recent harvests to call. Be guided by producer's track record.

2009 Perhaps one of the greatest vintages. Late, gruelling, but whites and reds both stellar.

2008 Long, wet, late and challenging but also unusually cool, favouring elegance in reds and whites.

2007 Elegant, structured whites; smaller red-grape berries gave intense colour and fruit concentration.

2006 Perhaps the best white-wine vintage in a decade — particularly expressive sauvignon and chenin. Fleshy, mild-tannined reds, with lower alcohols.

2005 Particularly challenging. Concentrated if alcoholic reds; mostly average whites, some exceptions.

2004 Cooler dry conditions yielded elegant, often ageworthy wines with lower alcohols, softer tannins.

Older Vintages

2003 Outstanding, especially for reds — concentrated and structured, and often slow to show their best. **2002** Challenging and patchy, but top producers show fine concentration and moderate alcohols. **2001** Some excellent reds — fruity and concentrated, best are long lived. Flavourful if alcoholic whites. **2000** Powerful, concentrated reds, befitting a hot year; the best have kept very well. Whites generally less impressive, not for long ageing. **1999** Fat, alcoholic reds with ripe fruit for earlier drinking. Generally not too much excitement among the whites. **1998** Excellent red vintage with enough fruit for extended cellaring; whites generally not for keeping. **1997** Among coolest and latest vintages on record. Supple, elegant reds; some excellent and stylish whites. **1996** Generally awkward reds, not for keeping; whites, except for top NLHs, best drunk up. **1995** For many, the vintage of the 90s. Concentrated reds, some still maturing spectacularly. **1994** Hottest, driest vintage in decades; variable quality; new-clone cabs and early ripening reds fared well. **1993** Without serious mishaps; some excellent sauvignons; above-average reds. **1992** Coolish season, favouring whites, especially sauvignon; the reds (notably pinotage) very good; **1991** Dry, warm to hot, favouring early to mid-season ripeners; some long-lasting reds. **1990** Uneven year, alternately cool and warm; average whites and reds; not for further ageing. **1980s**: even years ('82, '84, '86) usually more favourable for reds; uneven years, marginally cooler, favoured whites, but 'white' years '87 and, especially, '89 produced remarkable reds. **1970s**: again, even years generally favoured reds. Best was '74; but top wines from some other vintages are still delicious. **1960**s and earlier yielded some astonishingly long-lived wines.

South African Wine Styles

Blanc de blancs White wine made from white grapes only; also used for champagne and méthode cap classique.

Blanc fumé or **fumé blanc** Dry white from sauvignon, usually but not necessarily wooded (nor smoked, smoky).

Blanc de noir A pink wine (shades range from off-white through peach to pink) made from red grapes. See also Rosé.

Blend See Varietal wine and Cape Blend.

Brut See Sugar or sweetness, and Sparkling wine.

Cap classique See Sparkling wine.

Cape Blend Evolving term, increasingly used to denote a (red) blend with pinotage, the 'local' grape making up a significant part of the assemblage; sometimes simply a blend showing a distinct 'Cape' character; occasionally used for chenin-based blends.

Carbonated See Sparkling wine.

Cultivar Grape variety (a contraction of 'cultivated variety').

Cuvée French term for the blend of a wine.

Demi-sec See Sugar or sweetness.

Dessert wine A sweet wine, often to accompany the dessert but sometimes pleasurably prior, as in the famous Sauternes/foie gras combo.

Dry to sweet See Sugar or sweetness.

Estate wine Term now reserved for wine originating from an officially registered 'unit for the production of estate wine' (see www.sawis.co.za for current list).

Fortified wines Increased in alcoholic strength by the addition of spirit, by SA law to minimum 15% alcohol by volume.

Grand cru See Premier Grand Cru.

Jerepiko or **jerepigo** Red or white wine, produced without fermentation; grape juice is fortified with grape spirit, preventing fermentation; very sweet, with considerable unfermented grape flavours.

Kosher See Winemaking terms section.

Late Harvest Sweet wine from late-harvested and therefore sweeter grapes. See Sugar or sweetness.

Méthode ancestrale See Sparkling wine

Méthode cap classique(MCC) See Sparkling wine.

Noble Late Harvest (NLH) Sweet dessert wine (still, perlé or sparkling) exhibiting a noble rot (botrytis) character, from grapes infected by the *botrytis cinerea* fungus. This mould, in warm, misty autumn weather, attacks the skins of ripe grapes, causing much of the juice to evaporate. As the berries wither, their sweetness and flavour become powerfully concentrated. SA law dictates that grapes for NLH must be harvested at a minimum of 28° Balling and residual sugar must exceed 50g/L.

Nouveau Term originated in Beaujolais for fruity young and light red, usually from gamay and made by the carbonic maceration method. Bottled soon after vintage to capture the youthful, fresh flavour of fruit and yeasty fermentation.

Orange wine Unofficial name for fashionable style of white-wine making using extended skin contact (see under Winemaking Terms), as for red wine, resulting in darker hues and greater flavour/aroma intensity, sometimes with an (attractive) oxidative character and/or noticeable tannins.

Perlant, perlé, pétillant Lightly sparkling, usually carbonated wine.

Port Fortified dessert with excellent quality record in South Africa since late 1980s, partly through efforts of Cape Port Producers' Association which has adopted 'Cape' to identify the local product. Following are CAPPA-defined styles: **Cape White**: non-muscat grapes, wood-aged min 6 months, any size vessel; **Cape Pink**: non-muscat varieties, pink hue, barrel/tank-aged min 6 months; **Cape Ruby**: full bodied, fruity; min 50% barrel/tank-aged 6-36 months; **Cape Vintage**: fruit of one harvest; dark, full-bodied; tank/cask-aged min 1 year; must be certified, sold in glass, vintage dated; **Cape Vintage Reserve**: as for Vintage, but 'superior quality'; **Cape Late Bottled Vintage** (LBV): fruit of single year, full-bodied, slightly tawny colour, barrel/bottle aged min 3 years (of which min 2 years in oak); **Cape Tawny**: min 80% wood matured, amber-orange (tawny) colour, smooth, slightly nutty taste; **Cape Dated Tawny**: single-vintage tawny.

Premier Grand Cru Unlike in France, not a quality rating in SA — usually an austerely dry white.

Residual sugar See Sugar or sweetness.

Rosé Pink wine, made from red or a blend of red and white grapes. The red grape skins are removed before the wine takes up too much colour.

Single-vineyard wine Classification for wines from officially registered vineyards, no larger than 6ha in size and planted with a single variety.

Sparkling wine Bubbly, or 'champagne', usually white but sometimes rosé and even red, given its effervescence by carbon dioxide — allowed to escape in the normal winemaking process. **Champagne** undergoes its second fermentation in the bottle. Under an agreement with France, SA does not use the term, which describes the sparkling wines from the Champagne area. Instead, **méthode cap classique** (MCC) is the SA term to describe sparkling wines made by the classic method. **Méthode ancestrale** results from a spontaneous ferment initiated in tank and completed in bottle. **Charmat** undergoes its second, bubble-forming fermentation in a tank and is bottled under pressure. **Carbonated** sparklers are made by the injection of carbon dioxide bubbles (as in fizzy soft drinks). See also Sugar or sweetness.

Special Late Harvest (SLH) SA designation for a lighter dessert-style wine. There is no legal stipulation for residual sugar content, but if the RS is below 20g/L, the label must state 'extra dry', 'dry', 'semi-dry' or 'sweet', as the case may be. The minimum alcohol content is 11% by volume.

Stein Semi-sweet white wine, usually a blend and often confused with steen, a grape variety (chenin blanc), though most steins are at least made partly from steen grapes.

Sugar or sweetness In still wines: extra-dry or bone-dry wines have less than 2.5g/L residual sugar, undetectable to the taster. A wine legally is dry up to 5g/L. Taste buds will begin picking up a slight sweetness, or softness, in a wine — depending on its acidity — at about 6g/L, when it is still off-dry. By about 8–9g/L a definite sweetness can usually be noticed.

However, an acidity of 8–9g/L can render a sweet wine fairly crisp even with a sugar content of 20g/L plus. Official sweetness levels in SA wine are listed in the table opposite. (* Recent amendments allow for higher sugar levels for dry (9g/L) and semi-dry (18g/L) if the total acidity is within 2g/L or 10g/L respectively of the sugar level.

Varietal wine From a single variety of grape. Legislation requires the presence in the wine of 85% of the stated variety or vintage. Blends may name component parts only if those components were vinified separately, prior to blending; then they are listed with the larger contributor(s) named first. If any one of the blend partners is less than 20%, percentages for all the varieties must be given. Blends may be vinified separately in any recognised WO area; component areas may be named, as above except the threshold is 30%.

Vintage In SA primarily used to denote year of harvest. Not a quality classification (a 'vintage' port in Europe means one from an officially declared great port-grape year).

Wine	Sugar (g/l)
Still wines	
Extra-dry	≤ 2.5
Dry*	≤ 5
Semi-dry*	5 ≤ 12
Semi-sweet	> 5 < 30
Late Harvest	≥ 20
Special Late Harvest (SLH)	—
Natural Sweet (or Sweet Natural)	> 20
Noble Late Harvest (NLH)	> 50
Naturally dried grape wine (straw wine)	> 30

Brandy, Husk Spirit & Sherry-styles

Brandy and Husk Spirit

South African brandy is distilled mostly from chenin blanc and colombard, and divided into three main stylistic categories. Put simply and reductively these are as follows:

- **Blended Brandy** must by law contain at least 30% brandy distilled in a potstill and aged for at least three years in oak barrels. The remaining component will be of wine spirit (made in a continuous still). More often than not, these brandies are intended to partner mixers or to play a role in cocktails. The alcohol by volume (ABV) must be at least 43% (in practice it usually is 43%).

- **Vintage Brandy** (a small category) must have at least 30% potstill brandy aged minimum eight years. Up to 70% wine spirit is permitted but it too must be matured at least eight years.

- **Potstill Brandy** is doubled distilled in copper pots. It is 100% potstilled (neutral wine spirit no longer allowed) and aged at least three years in oak barrels smaller than 340L. The ABV is minimum 38%, as for Vintage brandy.

Estate Brandy is brandy in any of the above categories in which all stages of production, from vineyard to maturation, took place on one property (as for 'estate' wine).

Not (yet) regulated locally, these official French (cognac) designations are increasingly used here:

- **VS (Very Special)** – In SA, youngest component is at least 3 years old (2 years in the EU)
- **VSOP (Very Superior Old Pale)** - youngest component is at least 5 years old (4 years)

- **XO (Extra Old)** – youngest component is at least 10 years old (6 years)

Husk Spirit will have an ABV level of at least 43% and not be matured; Premium Husk Spirit must be at least 40% ABV, and be matured in oak for between three and six months.

Sherry-Style Fortified Wines

There are eight classes of sherry-style wines described in South Africa's Liquor Products Act.

The colour of these wines must range – depending on the class – from pale straw to amber. Their aromas and flavours must be 'nutty' and 'woody'.

Five of the eight classes must have a discernible flor yeast and/or wood character. In addition, these classes should:

- In the case of **Fino**, the residual sugar shall not exceed 20 g/l, and the alcohol content must not exceed 16%. It should have an almond flavour.
- The alcohol content of an **Amontillado** must be at least 16%, and it should have a flavour of hazelnuts.
- **Oloroso** must have rich, nutty flavours; a minimum of 50 g/l residual sugar, and at least 16% alcohol by volume.
- The residual sugar content of a **Pale Dry** wine cannot exceed 30 g/l, and its alcohol content should exceed 16%.

- Similarly, the alcohol content of a **Pale Cream** must exceed 16%, but its residual sugar can only range between 30 g/l and 80 g/l.
- The remaining three classes need only exhibit a discernable wood character.
- In addition, the residual sugar and alcohol content of a **Medium Cream** must be between 80■ g/l and 115■ g/l, and above 16% respectively.
- A **Full Cream** wine must have at least 115 g/l residual sugar, and an alcohol content above 16%.
- A muscat character and an aldehyde content of at least 80 mg/l, a residual sugar content of at least 100 g/l, and at least 16% alcohol by volume is necessary for an **Old Brown**. This may also only be sweetened with concentrated must, or with fortified wine with a residual sugar content of at least 180 g/l.

Words & Phrases

Winetasting Terms

Short of a ready description? Here are a few frequently-used words, phrases and explanations that may be helpful. See also Winemaking terms; SA wine■ styles.

Accessible, approachable Flavours and feel of the wine are harmonious, easily recognised; it is ready to drink.

Aftertaste The lingering flavours and impressions of a wine; its persistence — the longer, the better.

Alcoholic 'Hot' or, in excess, burning character caused by imbalanced or excessive alcohol. Also simply spirituous.

Astringent Mouth-puckering sensation, associated with high tannin (and sometimes acid); also bitter, sharp.

Aroma Smells in the bouquet, or nose, especially the odours associated with the grape rather than the winemaking process.

Attack First sensations on palate/nose — pungent, aggressive, quiet etc.

Austere Usually meaning unyielding, sometimes harsh. Sometimes, more favourably, to imply a notable restraint/refinement.

Backbone The wine is well formed, firm, not flabby or insipid.

Baked 'Hot', earthy quality. Usually from scorched/shrivelled grapes which have been exposed too long to the sun, or from too warm a barrel fermentation, especially in some whites.

Balance Desirable attribute. The wine's chief constituents — alcohol, acid, tannin, fruit and wood (where used) — are in harmony.

Bead Bubbles in sparkling wine; a fine, long-lasting bead is the most desirable. See also Mousse.

Big Expansive in the mouth, weighty, full-bodied, as a result of high alcohol or fruit concentration.

Bite or **grip** Imparted by tannin, acid and/or alcohol, important in young wines designed for ageing. If overdone can impart undesirable bitterness, harshness or spiry 'glow'.

Bitter Sensation perceived mainly on the back of the tongue, and in the finish of the wine. Usually unpleasant, though an accepted if not immediately admired character of certain Italian wines. Sometimes more positively associated with the taste of a specific fruit or nut, such as cherry-kernel or almond.

Body Fullness on the palate.

Botrytis/ed Exhibits a noble rot/botrytis character, from grapes infected by the *botrytis cinerea* fungus.

Bottle-age Negative or positive, depending on context. Positively describes development of aromas/flavours (ie complexity) as wine moves from youth to maturity. Much-prized attribute in fine whites and reds. Negatively, bottle age results in a wine with stale, empty or even off odours.

Buttery Flavour and texture associated with barrel-fermented white wines, especially chardonnays; rich, creamy smoothness.

Claret Another name for a dry red Bordeaux or Bordeaux-like red.

Classic Showing characteristics of the classics of Bordeaux, Burgundy etc; usually implying balance, elegance, subtlety.

Coarse Rough, unbalanced tannins, acid, alcohol or oak.

Complexity Strong recommendation. A complex wine has several layers of flavour, usually developing with age/maturation. See Bottle age.

Concentration See Intensity.

Confected Over-elaborately constructed, artificial, forced; sometimes overly sweet.

Corked, **corky** Wine is faulty; its flavours have been tainted by yeast, fungal or bacterial infections, often but not necessarily from the cork. It smells damp and mouldy in its worst stages — but sometimes it's barely detectable. In a restaurant, a corked wine should be rejected and returned immediately; producers are honour-bound to replace corked wine.

Creamy Not literally creamy, of course; more a silky, buttery feel and texture.

Crisp Refers to acidity. Positively, means fresh, clean; negatively, too tart, sharp.

Deep and **depth** Having many layers; intense; also descriptive of a serious wine.

Dense Well-padded texture, flavour packed.

Deposits (also sediment or crust) Tasteless and harmless tartrates, acid crystals or tannin in older red wines. Evidence that wine has not been harshly fined, filtered or cold-stabilised.

Dried out Bereft of fruit, harder constituents remaining; tired.

Earthy Usually positive, wine showing its origins from soil, minerals, damp leaves, mushrooms etc.

Easy Undemanding (and hopefully inexpensive).

Elegant Stylish, refined, 'classic'.

Esters Scents and smells usually generated by alcohols and acids in wine. A wine may be 'estery' when these characteristics are prominent.

Extract An indication of the 'substance' of a wine, expressed as sugar-free or total extract (which would include some sugars). 18g/L would be low, light; anything much above 23g/L in whites is significant; the corresponding threshold for reds is around 30g/L.

Fat Big, full, ample in the mouth.

Finesse Graceful, polished. Nothing excessive.

Finish The residual sensations — tastes and textures — after swallowing. Should be pleasant (crisp, lively) and enduring, not short, dull or flat. See also Length.

Firm Compact, has good backbone.

Flabby Usually, lacking backbone, especially acid.

Flat Characterless, unexciting, lacks acid. Or bubbly which has lost its fizz.

Fleshy Very positive, meaning a wine is well fleshed out with texture and grape flavours.

Flowery, floral Flower-like (ie the smell of rose, honeysuckle, jasmine etc). Distinct from 'fruity' (ie smell/taste of papaya, cantaloupe, grape! etc).

Forward rather than shy; advancing in age too; mature.

Fresh Lively, youthful, invigorating. Closely related to the amount of acid in the wine and absence of oxidative character: a big, intensely sweet dessert without a backbone of acidity will taste flat and sickly; enough acid and the taste is fresh and uncloying.

Fruity See Flowery.

Full High in alcohol and extract.

Gamey Overripe, decadent, not universally unattractive; also meaty, 'wild'.

Gravel/ly With suggestions of mineral, earthy quality; also firm texture.

Green Usually unripe, sour; also herbaceous; sometimes simply youthful.

Grip Gripping, firm on palate, in finish. Acid, tannin, alcohol are contributors.

Heady Usually refers to the smell of a wine. High in alcohol; intense, high-toned.

Herbaceous Grassy, hay-like, heathery; can also indicate under-ripeness.

Hollow Lacking substance, flavours.

Honey or **honeyed** Sometimes literally a honey/ beeswax taste or flavour; a sign of developing maturity in some varieties or more generally a sign of bottle-age.

Hot Burning sensation of alcohol in finish.

Intensity No flab, plenty of driving flavour; also deep colour.

Lean Thin, mean, lacking charm of ample fruit; also, more positively, compact, sinewy.

Lees/leesy Taste-imparting dead yeast cells (with grape skins and other solid matter) remaining with wine in tank/barrel (or bottle in the case of *méthode champenoise* sparkling wines) after fermentation. The longer the wine is 'on its lees' (*sur lie*) the more richness and flavour it should absorb.

Light/lite Officially wines under 10% alcohol by volume; also light in body (and often short on taste); a health-conscious trend in both reds and whites.

Lively Bouncy, fresh flavours.

Long or **length** Enduring; wine's flavours reverberate on the palate long after swallowing.

Maderised Oxidised and flat; colour is often brownish. Over-mature.

Meaty Sometimes suggesting a general savouriness; but also literally the aroma of meat — raw, smoked etc.

Mousse Fizz in sparkling wines; usually refers also to quality, size and effervescence of the bubbles. See also Bead.

Mouthfeel, mouthfilling Texture, feel; racy, crispness (fine with appropriate dishes) or generous, supple, smooth.

Neutral What it says, neither here nor there.

New World Generally implies accessible, bold, often extrovert (in terms of fruit and use of oak). **Old World** embraces terms like subtle, complex, less oaky, more varied and generally more vinous (than fruity). See also Classic.

Oaky Having exaggerated oak aromas/flavours (vanilla, spice, char, woodsmoke etc). Oak balanced by fruit in young wines may lessen with age, but over-oaked young wines (where fruit is not in balance) will become over-oaked old wines.

Palate Combination of flavour, taste and texture of a wine.

Pebbly See Gravelly.

Perfumed or **scented** Strong fragrances (fruity, flowery, animal etc)

Phenolic Astringency or bitterness, usually in white wine, attributed to excessive phenolic compounds.

Plump Well fleshed in a charming, cherubic way.

Porty Heavy, over-ripe, stewed; a negative in unfortified wine.

Rich Flavourful, intense, generous. Not necessarily sweet.

Robust Strapping, full-bodied (but not aggressive).

Rough Bull-in-a-china-shop wine, or throat sand-papering quality.

Round Well balanced, without gawkiness or jagged edges.

Sharp or **tart** All about acid, usually unbalanced. But occasionally sharpish, fresh wine is right for the occasion.

Short or **quick** Insubstantial wine, leaving little impression.

Simple One-dimensional or no flavour excitement.

Stalky Unripe, bitter, stemmy.

Stewed Over-ripe, cooked, soft, soggy fruit.

Structure Vague word, usually refers to the wine's make up (acid, tannin, alcohol) in relation to its ageing ability; if a wine is deemed to have 'the structure to age' it suggests these principal preservatives are in place.

Stylish Classy, distinguished; also voguish.

Supple Very desirable (not necessarily subtle), yielding, refined texture and flavours. See also Mouthfeel.

Tannic Tannins are prominent in the wine, imparting, positively, a mouth-puckering, grippy, tangy quality; negatively, a harsh, unyielding character.

Tension Racy, nervous fruity-acid play on the palate.

Terpene(s)/terpenoid Strong, floral compounds influencing the aromas of especially riesling, gewürztraminer and the muscats; with bottle-age, terpenes often develop a pungent resinous oiliness.

Texture Tactile 'feel' in the mouth: hard, acidic, coarse and alcoholic; or, smooth, velvety, 'warm'.

Toasty Often used for barrel-fermented or -aged wines showing a pleasant biscuity, charry character.

Vegetal Grassy, leafy, herby — in contrast to fruity, flowery, oaky. Overdone, a no-no.

Yeasty Warm bakery smells, often evident in barrel-fermented whites and *méthode champenoise* sparkling wines, where yeasts stay in contact with the wine after fermentation.

Winemaking Terms

A few brief reference explanations. See also sections Winetasting Terms, SA Wine Styles.

Acid and **acidity** The fresh — or, in excess, sharp or tart — taste of wine. Too little acid and the wine tastes dull and flat. In SA, winemakers are permitted to adjust acidity either by adding acid — at any stage before bottling — or by lowering the acid level with a de-acidifier. See also Volatile acid and Malolactic.

Alcohol Essential component of wine, providing fullness, richness and, at higher levels, sometimes an impression of sweetness. Also a preservative, helping keep wines in good condition. Produced by yeasts fermenting the sugars in the grape. Measured by volume of the total liquid. Most unfortified table wines in SA have between 11% and 14.5% alc by vol; fortifieds range from ±16% to 21%. A variation of up to 1% between the strength stated on the label and the laboratory analysis is permitted by local law. Various techniques (such as reverse osmosis and 'spinning cone', also the addition of water) exist to address the increasingly important issue of high alcohol levels in wine, and some are legal in SA (though not for export to, eg, Europe).

Barrels (**barrel-aged**; **barrel-fermented**) Wines are transferred into barrels to age, pick up oaky flavours etc. When must or fermenting must is put into barrels, the resulting wine is called barrel-fermented. A barrel or cask is generally a 225–500L oak container; *barrique* is a French word for a 225L barrel; a pipe, adapted from the Portuguese *pipa*, usually indicates a vessel of 530–630L; vat is a term generally used for larger wooden vessels (foudre is the fashionable synonym).

Batonnage See Lees.

Biodynamic See Organic.

Blend A wine made from two or more different grape varieties, vintages, vineyards or containers. Some of the world's finest wines are blends.

Bottles While the 750ml (75cl) bottle is now the most widely used size of container for wine, it is by no means the only one. Smaller bottles (375 & 500ml) are popular with restaurants and airlines, and larger sizes are prized by collectors because of their novelty value and/or their tendency to promote slower wine ageing. The following are the larger bottle sizes (note: some no longer in production):

Capacity		Bordeaux	Champagne/Burgundy
litres	bottles		
1.5	2	Magnum	Magnum
3	4	Double magnum	Jéroboam
4.5	6	Jéroboam	Rehoboam
6	8	Impériale	Methuselah
9	12	—	Salmanazar
12	16	—	Balthazar
15	20	—	Nebuchadnezzar

Brettanomyces or **'brett'** Naturally occurring yeast, usually associated with red wine and regarded as a spoilage factor, because its growth triggers the formation of volatile acids, phenols and other compounds which, in sufficient concentration, impart a range of unpleasant characters, from barnyard to sweat to cheese. At low concentrations, can enhance complexity and character.

Carbonic maceration or **maceration carbonique** Method of fermenting wine without first crushing the grapes. Whole clusters with stalks etc are put into closed vat; intracellular fermentation occurs within the grape berries, which then burst.

Chaptalisation Originally French term for the addition of sugar to grape must to raise the alcohol of a wine. Selectively legal in northern Europe, where acid adjustments are not allowed as they are in SA. Winemakers in both hemispheres bend the rules.

Charmat Method of making sparkling wine in a sealed tank (*cuvée close*) under pressure. Easier, cheaper than *méthode champenoise*.

Chips See Oak chips.

Cold ferment 'Cold' is a relative term; applied to fermentation of mainly white wines in temperature-controlled tanks, it refers to a temperature around usually 13–16°C. The benefits, especially important in a warm country, include conserving the primary fruit aromas and ensuring fermentation is carried out steadily and thoroughly.

Cold soak or **cold maceration**. Red-wine making method carried out prior to fermentation. Skins and juice are held, usually for a few days, at a sufficiently cool temperature to prevent fermentation. The theory is that this extracts more favourable colour and aromas than after fermentation.

Cold stabilisation Keeping a wine at about −4°C for a week or more to precipitate tartaric acid and 'clean up' the wine, preventing later formation of (harmless) tartrate crystals in bottle. Some winemakers believe this process damages flavour and prefer to avoid it.

Disgorgement (*dégorgement* in French) Important stage in the production of traditionally fermented sparkling where accumulated sediment (or lees), which could cloud the finished wine, is removed from the neck of the bottle.

Dosage The sugar added to sparkling wine after the second fermentation.

Fermentation The conversion of sugar in grapes into alcohol and carbon dioxide, a function of enzymes secreted by yeasts. Wild yeasts occur in vineyards and wineries, but in modern Cape winemaking cultured yeasts are normally added to secure the process. Beyond about 15% of alcohol, yeasts are overwhelmed and fermentation ceases, although it usually is stopped (for instance by cooling, filtration or the addition of alcohol) before this stage. See also Malolactic.

Filtration Removes last impurities including **yeast** cells. Done excessively, can thin a wine. Some traditionalists bottle without cold- or protein-stabilisation or filtration.

Fining and **protein stabilisation** Fining is ridding wine of suspended particles by adding substances that attract and draw the particles from the wine.

Flash-pasteurisation See Kosher.

Foudre See Barrels.

Free run After grapes have been de-stalked and crushed, juice runs freely.

Garage wine Generic term for wine made in minuscule quantities, sometimes literally in a garage; a grower of such wine is sometimes called a *garagiste*.

Glycerol Minor product of alcoholic fermentation; from the Greek for sweet. Has an apparent sweetening effect on even dry wines and also gives a viscous, mouthfilling character.

Icewine Sweet, concentrated wine from grapes picked and pressed while frozen. Not a recognised category for SA wine production.

Kosher Wine made 'correctly', i.e. under rabbinical supervision, to be suitable for use by religious Jews. Vinification and any initial movement of the wine must be done by an observant Jew. Flash-pasteurisation, increasingly by means of new flavour-preserving processes such as Thermoflash, renders the resulting *meshuval* wine (literally 'boiled' or 'cooked') fit for handling by non-Jews.

Leafroll virus Virus (or complex of viruses), widespread throughout the winegrowing world, which causes the vine to perform below its potential and thereby produce wine which is lower in colour, body and flavour than that derived from virus-free or 'cleaned-up' plants.

Lees Spent yeast cells and other matter which collect at the bottom of any container in winemaking. Yeast autolysis, or decomposition, can impart richness and flavour to a wine, sometimes referred to as leesy. Lees stirring or *batonnage* involves mixing the bed of lees in a barrel or tank through the wine, which is said to be *sur lie*; it is employed primarily on barrel-fermented white wines. The main effects of mixing lees and wine are to prevent off-odours developing from lack of oxygen, to limit the amount of wood tannin and oak character extracted, and to increase flavour.

Malolactic fermentation (malo) Occurs when bacteria convert malic into lactic acids. This reduces the acidity of a wine, a normal and healthy process, especially in reds — provided, of course, it occurs before bottling.

Maturation Ageing properties are closely related to tannin and/or fixed acid content of a wine. A relatively full red wine with tannin has lasting power. With age, it may develop complexity, subtlety and smooth mellowness. Lighter wines with lower tannins are drinkable sooner but probably will not reach the same level of complexity. A number of Cape whites mature well over several years, but most are best drunk in their fruity youth, up to 18 months.

Méthode champenoise Classic method of making champagne by inducing secondary fermentation in the bottle and producing fine bubbles. Due to French restrictions on terminology, Cape sparkling wines made in this way are called méthode cap classique (MCC).

Micro-oxygenation Technique enabling introduction of precise, controlled doses of oxygen to must/wine. Advocates claim softer tannins, more stable colours and other advantages.

Oak chips, either in older barrels or stainless steel tanks, are widely used in SA, as are oak **staves**. Still frowned on by some purists, the 'additives' approximate the flavour effects of a new barrel, far more cheaply, more easily handled.

Oak-matured See Barrels.

Organic viticulture/winemaking Increasingly popular alternative to 'conventional' or 'industrialised' winegrowing, emphasising natural and sustainable farming methods and cellar techniques. A variant is biodynamic viticulture, influenced by anthroposophy, focused on improving wine quality through harmony with nature and its rhythms.

Oxidation Change (usually for the worse) due to exposure to air, in whites often producing dark yellow or yellowish colour (called maderisation), altering, 'ageing' the taste. Controlled oxidation can be used to produce positive development in wine (see next entry).

Oxidative winemaking Intentional exposure to oxygen during vinification, imparting in a nutty/biscuity quality to the wine. Contrast with protective winemaking, where contact with oxygen is avoided as much as possible.

Pasteurisation See Kosher.

pH A chemical notation, used in winemaking and evaluation. The pH of a wine is its effective, active acidity — not in volume but by strength or degree. The reading provides a guide to a wine's keepability. The optimum pH in a wine is somewhere between 3.1 and 3.4 — which significantly improves a wine's protection from bacterial spoilage, so permitting it to mature and develop if properly stored.

Racking Drawing or pumping wine off from one cask or tank to another, to leave behind the deposit or lees.

Reductive Wine in an unevolved, unoxidised state is said to be 'reductive'; usually with a tight, sometimes unyielding character. The absence of air (in a bottled wine) or the presence of substantial sulphur dioxide (anti-oxidant) levels, will inhibit both oxidation and reduction processes, which are linked and complementary.

Reverse osmosis A specialised filtration technique, permitted in SA for various purposes, including the removal of water from wine. See also Alcohol.

Skin contact After crushing and de-stemming, white grapes may be left for a period with the juice, remaining in contact with skins (before being moved into the press, from which the grape juice is squeezed). Some winemakers believe the colours and flavours in and under the grape skins should be maximised in this way; others believe extended (or any) contact can lead to coarseness, even bitterness.

Spinning cone See Alcohol.

Sulphur dioxide (SO$_2$) Sterilising agent and pre-servative, near-ubiquitous in winemaking since antiquity, now strictly controlled. In SA, max total SO$_2$ level for dry wines is 150–160mg/L; for wines with 5+ g/L sugar it is 200mg/L; and botrytis-style wines 300▪ mg/L. Any wine with more than 10mg/L total SO$_2$ must carry the warning 'Contains sulphites' (or 'sulfites') on the label.

Sur lie See Lees.

Tannin Vital preservative in wine, derives primar-ily from the grape skins. Necessary for a red wine's longevity. A young wine's raw tannin can give it a harshness, but no red wine matures into a great one without tannin, which itself under-goes change, combines with other substances and mellows. Tannin leaves a mouth-puckering dryness about the gums, gives 'grip' to a wine. A wooded wine will usually also contain some wood tannin.

Tartrates Harmless crystals formed by tartaric acid precipitating in non-cold-stabilised wine. Because of lack of public acceptance, usually avoided through cold stabilisation.

Terroir Important, controversial (and in SA over-used) French term embracing soil, climate, topography and other elements which constitute the natural environment of a vineyard site and give it a unique character.

Thermovinification/Thermoflash See Kosher.

Unfiltered See Filtration.

Virus or **virused** See Leafroll.

Volatile acid (VA) The part of the acidity which can become volatile. A high reading indicates a wine is prone to spoilage. Recognised at high levels by a sharp, 'hot', vinegary smell. In SA, most wines must by law be below 1.2g/L of VA; in practice, the majority are well below 1g/L.

Whole-bunch pressing or **cluster pressing** Some SA cellars use this age-old process of plac-ing whole bunches directly in the press and gently squeezing. The more usual method is to de-stem and crush the berries before pressing. Whole-bunch pressing is said to yield fresher, cleaner must, and wine lower in polyphenols which, in excess, tend to age wines faster and render them coarser.

Wood-fermented/matured See Barrels.

Yeasts Micro-organisms that secrete enzymes which convert or ferment sugar into alcohol. See fermentation.

Touring Wine Country

Wine Routes, Trusts & Associations

For localised information about regional official wine routes and wineries, contact these organisations:

Breedekloof Wine & Tourism ▪ T +27 (0)23-349-1791 ▪ F +27 (0)23-349-1720 ▪ info@breedekloof.com ▪ www.breedekloof.com

Constantia Valley Wine Route ▪ T +27 (0)83-679-4495 (Carryn Wiltshire) ▪ info@constantiafoodandwine.co.za ▪ www.constantiawineroute.com

The Darling Wine & Art Experience ▪ +27 (0)22-492-3971 ▪ taste@darlingwine.co.za ▪ www.darlingtourism.co.za

Durbanville Wine Valley Association ▪ T +27 (0)83-310-1228 (Angela Fourie) ▪ info@durbanvillewine.co.za, angela@durbanvillewine.co.za ▪ www.durbanvillewine.co.za

Elgin Valley Wine Guild ▪ T +27 (0)71-267-9785 ▪ info@elginwine.co.za ▪ www.elginwine.co.za

Elim Winegrowers ▪ T +27 (0)28-482-1902/ +27 (0)82-328-3824 (Conrad Vlok) ▪ conrad@strandveld.co.za

Franschhoek See Vignerons de Franschhoek

Green Mountain Eco Route (Elgin/Bot River) ▪ T +27 (0)28-284-9827 ▪ info@groenlandberg.co.za ▪ www. groenlandberg.co.za

Helderberg See Stellenbosch

Hermanus Wine Route & Hemel-en-Aarde Winegrowers Association ▪ T +27 (0)83-305-7319 (Frieda Lloyd) ▪ frieda@hermanuswineroute.com ▪ T +27 (0)28-312-3862 (Bevan Newton Johnson) ▪ bevan@newtonjohnson.com ▪ www.hermanuswineroute.com

Klein Karoo Wine Route ▪ T +27(0)44-272-7492 / +27 (0)82-214-5910 ▪ F +27 (0)86-528-4055 (Ellen Marais) ▪ info@kleinkaroowines.co.za ▪ www.kleinkaroowines.co.za

Northern Cape Wine Association See Orange River Wine Route

Olifants River Vodacom Wine Route See West Coast Wine Route

Orange River Wine Route ▪ T +27 (0)54-337-8800 (Marlé Strauss) ▪ F +27 (0)54-332-4408 ▪ info@orangeriverwines.com

Paarl Wine Route ▪ T +27 (0) 21-872-4842 / +27 (0) 72-654-6017 ▪ info@paarlwine.co.za ▪ www.paarlwine.co.za

Robertson Wine Valley ▪ T +27 (0)23-626-3167 / +27 (0)83-701-5404 ▪ F +27 (0)23-626-1054 ▪ manager@robertsonwinevalley.com ▪ www.robertsonwinevalley.com

Stellenbosch Wine Routes ▪ T +27 (0)21-886-4310 ▪ info@wineroute.co.za ▪ www.wineroute.co.za

Santam Swartland Wine & Olive Route ▪ T +27 (0)22-487-1133 ▪ F +27 (0)22-487-2063 ▪ swartlandinfo@westc.co.za ▪ www.swartlandwineandolives.co.za

Tulbagh Wine Route ▪ T/F +27 (0)23-230-1348/75 ▪ tulbaghinfo@lando.co.za ▪ www.tulbaghwineroute.com ▪ www.tulbaghtourism.co.za

Vignerons de Franschhoek ▪ T +27 (0)21-876-2861 ▪ F +27 (0)21-876-2768 ▪ marketing@franschhoek.org.za, office@franschhoek.org.za ▪ www.franschhoek.org.za

Walker Bay Wine Wander ▪ T +27 (0)28-316-3988 ▪ F +27 (0)86-509-4931 ▪ wine@hermanus.co.za

Wellington Wine Route ▪ T +27 (0)21-864-1378 ▪ wine@wellington.co.za ▪ www.wellington.co.za

West Coast Wine Route ▪ T +27 (0)82-611-3999 / +27 (0)27-201-3376 / F +27 (0)27-213-4819 ▪ monika@namaquawestcoast.com ▪ www.namaquawestcoast.com

Worcester Wine Route ▪ T +27 (0)23-342-8710 ▪ F +27 (0)86-771-4468 ▪ info@worcesterwineroute.co.za ▪ www.worcesterwineroute.co.za

Winelands Tourism Offices

For additional accommodation options, brochures and local advice, contact the information offices and/or publicity associations of the wine areas you plan to visit.

Breedekloof Wine & Tourism ▪ T +27 (0)23-349-1791 ▪ F +27 (0)23-349-1720 ▪ info@breedekloof.com ▪ www.breedekloof.com

Calitzdorp Tourism ▪ T +27 (0)44-213-3775 ▪ F +27 (0)86-569-1447 ▪ tourism@calitzdorp.org.za ▪ www.calitzdorp.org.za

Cape Town Tourism ▪ Contact Centre: T +27 (0)86-132-2223

Cape Town Tourism (Head-Office) ▪ T +27 (0)21-487-6800 ▪ F +27 (0)21-487-6859 ▪ capetown@capetown.travel, info@capetown.travel

Somerset West ▪ T +27 (0)21-840-1400 ▪ F +27 (0)21-840-1410 ▪ somersetwest@capetown.travel

Elgin Valley Tourism ▪ T +27 (0)21-848-9838 ▪ F +27 (0)86-660-0398 ▪ info@elginvalley.co.za ▪ www.elginvalley.co.za

Franschhoek Wine Valley ▪ T +27 (0)21-876-2861 ▪ F +27 (0)21-876-2768 ▪ info@franschhoek.org.za, office@franschhoek.org.za ▪ www.franschhoek.org.za

Hermanus Tourism Bureau ▪ T +27 (0)28-312-2629 ▪ F +27 (0)28-313-0305 ▪ hermanustourism@hermanus.co.za ▪ www.hermanustourism.info

McGregor Tourism ▪ T +27 (0)23-625-1954 ▪ info@tourismmcgregor.co.za ▪ www.tourismmcgregor.co.za

Northern Cape Tourism ▪ T +27 (0)53-832-2657 ▪ F +27 (0)53-831-2937 ▪ reception@experiencenortherncape.com ▪ www.experiencenortherncape.com

Paarl Tourism ▪ T +27 (0)21-872-4842 ▪ paarlinfo@dlta.co.za ▪ www.paarlonline.com

Paarl Tourist Information Centre ▪ T +27 (0)21-872-4842 ▪ paarlinfo@dlta.co.za ▪ www.paarlonline.com

Robertson Tourism Association ▪ T +27 (0)23-626-4437 / +27 (0)23-626-6248 ▪ F +27 (0)23-626-4290 ▪ info@robertson.org.za ▪ www.robertsontourism.co.za

Route 62 ▪ T +27 (0)82-871-9730 ▪ info@route62.co.za ▪ www.route62.co.za

Saldanha Bay Tourism Organisation ▪ marketing@sbto.co.za, tourismmanager@sbto.co.za ▪ www.capewestcoastpeninsula.co.za

Saldanha: T +27 (0)22-715-1142 ▪ saldanha@sbto.co.z

Hopefield: T/F +27 (0)22-723-1720 ▪ hopefield@sbto.co.za

Langebaan: T +27 (0)22-772-1515 ▪ F +27 (0)22-772-1531 ▪ langebaan@sbto.co.z

Vredenburg: T +27 (0)22-715-1142 ▪ F +27 (0)22-715-1141 ▪ vredenburg@sbto.co.za

Paternoster: T/F +27 (0)22-752-2323 ▪ paternoster@sbto.co.z

St Helena Bay: T +27 (0)22-736-2374 ▪ sthelena@sbto.co.za

Jacobs Bay: +27 (0)22-715-1142 ▪ saldanha@sbto.co.za

Stellenbosch 360 ▪ T +27 (0)21-883-3584 ▪ F +27 (0)21-882-9550 ▪ info@stellenbosch360.co.za ▪ www.stellenbosch.travel

Wellington Tourism ▪ T +27 (0)21-864-1378 ▪ anne-ghrett@dlta.co.za, info@wellingtontourism.co.za ▪ www.wellington.co.za

West Coast Peninsula Tourism Bureau See Saldanha Bay Tourism Organisation

Worcester Tourism Association ▪ +27 (0)23-342-6244 /+27 (0)76-200-8742 ▪ info@worcestertourism.com ▪ www.worcestertourism.com

Specialist Wine Tours

Adamastor & Bacchus Cape Gourmet Wine & Culinary Tours ▪ English, Afrikaans, Dutch, Norwegian, German ▪ www.adamastorbacchus.com ▪ johnford@iafrica.com, jarche@iafrica.com ▪ T +27 (0)21-439-3169 / +27 (0)83-229-1172

African Story Wine Tours ▪ English ▪ info@africanstorytours.com ▪ www.africanstorytours.com ▪ T +27 (0)73-755-0444 / +27 (0)79-694-7915

African Trax Tours ▪ English ▪ africantrax@telkomsa.net ▪ www.africantrax.co.za ▪ T +27 (0)83-692-8873

African Wonder Tours ▪ Afrikaans, English ▪ info@africanwonder.co.za ▪ www.africanwonder.co.za ▪ T +27 (0)82-325-1485

Amber Tours ▪ English ▪ lesley@ambertours.co.za ▪ www.ambertours.co.za ▪ T +27 (0)83-448-7016

Bizoe Wine Tours ▪ Afrikaans, English ▪ info@bizoe.co.za ▪ www.bizoe.co.za ▪ T +27 (0)21-843-3307 / +27 (0)83-709-3957 ▪ F +27 (0)86-653-8186

Boutique Winery Tours ▪ English ▪ info@boutiquewinerytours.com ▪ www.boutiquewinerytours.com ▪ T +27 (0)72-562-9863 / +27 (0)21-555-1147

Cape Fusion Tours ▪ English ▪ cazcape@mweb.co.za, info@capefusion.co.za ▪ www.capefusiontours.com ▪ T +27 (0)21-461-2437 / +27 (0)83-235-9777 ▪ F +27 (0)86-672-5877

'C' the Cape Tours ▪ English, Afrikaans ▪ cherylscott@ballmail.co.za, cheryl.dawnscott@gmail.com ▪ www.cthecapetours.co.za ▪ T +27 (0)21-433-2545 / +27 (0)83-698-5483 ▪ F +27 (0)86-654-5989

Double Gold Wineland Tours ▪ English • throughkimseyes210@gmail.com • T +27 (0)82-293-3176

D'Vine Wine & Dine ▪ pauline.nel@dvinewinedine.co.za ▪ www.dvinewineanddine.co.za ▪ +27 (0)73-972-7830 / +27 (0)21-975-4851 ▪ +27 (0)86-601-1238

Exclusively African Tours ▪ English, Dutch (German, Swedish, French on request) ▪ ian@travelxa.com ▪ www.holidaystosouthafrica.co.uk ▪ T +27 (0)21-5314887 ▪ F +27 (0)86-609-0896

Franschhoek Wine Tours ▪ English, Afrikaans ▪ info@winelandstours.com ▪ www.franschhoekwinetours.com ▪ +27 (0)83-301-6774

Go Cape Tourism Services Private Wine Tours ▪ English, Afrikaans & German on request ▪ john@gocape.co.za ▪ www.gocape.co.za ▪ T +27 (0)72-630-7907

Go! Shuttles & Tours ▪ English, German, Afrikaans, French and Italian ▪ info@goshuttle.co.za, nic@gotours.co.za ▪ www.gotours.co.za ▪ T +27 (0)72-368-3455 ▪ F +27 (0)86-548-2375

Gourmet Travels ▪ English, German ▪ rainer@gourmettravels.co.za ▪ www.gourmettravels.co.za ▪ T +27 (0)82-449-7666 ▪ F +27 (0)86-542-0542

Gourmet Wine Tours ▪ English ▪ sflesch@iafrica.com ▪ www.gourmetwinetours.co.za ▪ T +27 (0)21-705-4317 / +27 (0)83-229-3581 ▪ F +27 (0)86-241-1685

Greatest Africa • English, French ▪ richard@greatestafrica.com ▪ www.greatestafrica.com ▪ T +27 (0)21-855-5244 / +27 (0)83-650-5661

Hunneyball Tours ▪ English, Swedish ▪ jim.hunneyball@gmail.com, marie@hunneyballhouse.com ▪ www.hunneyballhouse.com/tours ▪ T +27(0)71-674-9379 / +27(0)21-882-8083

Janet Malherbe ▪ English, German, French & Flemish ▪ janetm@mweb.co.za ▪ www.janetmalherbe.webs.com ▪ T +27 (0)82-553-8928 ▪ T/F +27 (0)21-862-1484

Judy Krohn Personal Itineraries & International Wine Experience ▪ English, German ▪ judithk@lantic.net ▪ www.judykrohn.co.za ▪ T +27 (0)84-500-1941 / +27 (0)21-851-7009

Klaus Schindler See Schindler's Africa

Luhambo Tours ▪ English, Afrikaans, German ▪ bookings@luhambotours.com ▪ www.luhambotours.com ▪ T +27 (0)21-551-0467 / +27 (0)82-306-4141

Ocean & Vine Adventures & Tours ▪ English, translator on request ▪ wayne@wine.co.za, oceanv@netactive.co.za ▪ www.prowinetours.co.za ▪ T +27 (0)21-559-6906 / +27 (0)82-900-6999 ▪ F +27 (0)21-559-6906

Percy Tours, Hermanus ▪ English, Afrikaans & some French ▪ travel@percytours.com ▪ www.percytours.com, www.hermanuswinetours.com ▪ T +27 (0)72-062-8500 / +27 (0)28-316-4871

Redwood Tours ▪ English, Afrikaans ▪ info@redwoodtours.co.za ▪ www.redwoodtours.co.za ▪ T +27 (0)21-886-8138 / +27 (0)82-443-6480

Schindler's Africa ▪ German, English ▪ schindler@kapstadt.de ▪ www.kapstadt.de/schindlers-africa ▪ T +27 (0)83-270-3449

Southern Destinations ▪ English ▪ info@southerndestinations.com, vanessa@southerndestinations.com ▪ www.southerndestinations.com ▪ T +27 (0)21-671-3090 ▪ F +27 (0)21-674-7481

Sunswept Tours ▪ English, Afrikaans ▪ glynis@hermanus.co.za, glynis@thewineguides.co.za ▪ www.sunswepttours.com ▪ T +27 (0)82-775-8843

Taste The Cape Travel & Tours ▪ English, other languages upon request ▪ info@tastethecape.co.za ▪ www.tastethecape.co.za ▪ T +27 (0)21-788-1649 / +27 (0)79-812-0220

Tri Active Events Management (Green Mountain Eco Route) ▪ English, Afrikaans ▪ info@triactive.co.za, lodge@triactive.co.za, natasha@triactive.co.za ▪ www.triactive.co.za ▪ T +27 (0)21-844-0975 / +27 (0)83-456-2181 ▪ F +27 (0)86-607-3650

Tsiba Tsiba Wine Tours & Travel ▪ Dutch, English, French, German, Spanish ▪ info@tsibatsiba.

co.za ▪ www.tsibatsiba.co.za ▪ T +27 (0)82-956-8104

Vineyard Ventures (Glen Christie) English, Afrikaans, German; other languages on request ▪ vinven@iafrica.com ▪ www.vineyardventures. co.za ▪ T +27 (0)21-434-8888 / +27 (0)82-920-2825 ▪ F +27 (0)86-579-9430

Walker Bay Wine Wander ▪ English, Afrikaans, French, German ▪ wine@hermanus.co.za, travel@percytours.com ▪ T +27 (0)28-316-3988 / +27 (0)72-062-8500 ▪ F +27 (0)86-509-4931

Wanderer Wines ▪ English, German, French, Italian ▪ wines@wanderer.co.za ▪ www.wanderer. co.za ▪ T +27 (0)82-878-1176 ▪ F +27 (0)86-648-0352

Wellington Wine Walk ▪ English, Afrikaans ▪ info@winewalk.co.za ▪ www.winewalk.co.za ▪ T +27 (0)82-335-8132 / +27 (0)83-235-5570

Wine Desk ▪ Scheduled (small group) and private day tours led by specialist wine guides. Available in most languages for private tours ▪ info@ winedesk.co.za, ligia@winedesk.co.za ▪ www. winedesk.co.za ▪ T +27 (0)21-424-6364 / +27 (0)82-822-6127 ▪ F +27 (0)86-607-2980

Wine Escapes ▪ info@wineescapes.co.za ▪ www. wineescapes.co.za ▪ T +27 (0)83-453-2670

WineFairy ▪ English ▪ info@winefairy.co.za, katie@winefairy.co.za ▪ www.winefairy.co.za ▪ T +27 (0)79-892-2859

Wine & Whales Tours ▪ English ▪ wineandwhales@telkomsa.net ▪ T +27 (0)72-019-4456 / +27 (0)21-852-6545

Winemaker-led Tasting Tours ▪ English; translators on request with sufficient notice ▪ vitis@ mweb.co.za ▪ www.winetastingtours.co.za ▪ T +27 (0)82-322-3733

Restaurants in the Winelands and Cape Town

Below are some dining out options in Cape Town and the winelands. These are paid entries. The venues supplied information on their cuisine, menus and attractions, which was then edited for consistency of style. For more restaurants among the vines, consult the A–Z section of the guide for wineries that offer light lunches, picnics etc. Look for the ⑪ symbol beside the individual entries. Unless stated to the contrary, all allow you to bring your own (BYO) wine — the corkage fee is indicated at the start of each entry. Should you wish to know about wheelchair access, please discuss with the relevant restaurant.

INDEX OF RESTAURANTS

BREDASDORP

Black Oystercatcher Restaurant Moddervlei Farm, Bredasdorp ▪ Farm-style gourmet ▪ Open Tues-Sun 11am-2.30pm and Mon - cheese platters available ▪ Closed Good Fri, Dec 24/25 and on private functions ▪ Booking advised ▪ Children welcome ▪ Visa and MasterCard accepted ▪ No BYO ▪ Owner Dirk Human ▪ venue@ blackoystercatcher.co.za ▪ www. blackoystercatcher.co.za ▪ **+27 (0)28-482-1618** ▪ F +27 (0)28-666-7954

At the Black Oystercatcher Restaurant, we live by the season. We serve fresh produce that grows in our own garden as the seasons dictate. As a result, we offer a relaxed dining experience in a country atmosphere. Here fresh food, complementing our boutique wines, is prepared to order and enjoyed at leisure. The seasons also determine the mood at Black Oystercatcher Restaurant: the refreshing sea breeze will cool you down in summer, or enjoy our cosy log fires in the winter months. (See also Accommodation and A-Z sections)

CAMPS BAY

Azure The Twelve Apostles Hotel and Spa, Victoria Road, Camps Bay, Cape Town ▪ South African with a French style ▪ Open daily for breakfast 7am-10.30am, lunch 12.30pm-3.30pm and dinner 6pm-10pm ▪ Booking advised ▪ Children welcome ▪ No BYO ▪ Major credit cards accepted ▪ Owners Tollman Family ▪ Executive chef Christo Pretorius ▪ restaurants@12apostles.co.za ▪ www.12apostleshotel.com ▪ **T +27 (0)21-437-9000** ▪ F +27 (0)21-437-9062

Azure is the nautical-themed cliffside restaurant at Cape Town's Twelve Apostles Hotel and Spa, where mesmerising ocean views vie for attention with executive chef Christo Pretorius's creations, some of them taken from internationally honoured owner Bea Tollman's cookbook. Azure offers leisurely English breakfasts, à la carte lunches or dinners, and weekend buffet lunches on the Atlantic-facing terrace – the perfect spot for spectacular sunsets and cocktails. (See also Accommodation)

CAPE TOWN

Aubergine Restaurant 39 Barnet Street, Gardens, Cape Town ▪ Classical cuisine with innovative twists and Asian influence ▪ Outdoor terrace ▪ Lunch Wed-Fri 12pm-2pm in summer, dinner Mon-Sat 6pm-10pm ▪ Closed Sun and alternate Mon ▪ Booking advised ▪ Children 5+ welcome ▪ Major credit cards accepted ▪ No BYO ▪ Owner/ chef Harald Bresselschmidt ▪ info@aubergine.co.za ▪ www.aubergine.co.za ▪ **T +27 (0)21-465-0000** ▪ F +27 (0)86-671-0835

At this warmly sophisticated restaurant revolving around wine-pairing, a 15,000-bottle cellar gives chef/patron Harald Bresselschmidt's keen palate and culinary skills free rein to accent flavour, aroma and texture, whether preparing seafood, prime aged meat or produce from the restaurant's own garden. Degustation menu taste-teasers include sautéed calamari and chorizo with tomato risotto, ostrich tartare and seared scallop, lamb and aubergine strudel and nectarine tarte tatin.

Auslese Function Venue 115 Hope Street, Gardens, Cape Town ▪ Wines paired with sophisticated menus in classic yet innovative style ▪ Booking advised ▪ Open for pre-booked functions only ▪ Closed Sun ▪ Children welcome ▪ Major credit cards accepted ▪ BYO by arrangement ▪ Owner/chef Harald Bresselschmidt ▪ info@auslese.co.za ▪ www.auslese.co.za ▪ **T +27 (0)21-461-9727 (reservations and enquiries 021-465-0000)** ▪ F +27 (0)86-671-0835

At this sister venue to elegant Aubergine, chef/ patron Harald Bresselschmidt can tailor any occasion for you, from a private birthday party to a corporate event – or simply when you want the perfect pairing for your wine gems but don't feel like cooking. Custom-designed for functions, whether cocktail events with canapés and tapas or sit-down wine-pairing dinners, Auslese also hosts regular music evenings and winemaker events.

Burrata The Old Biscuit Mill, 373–375 Albert Road, Woodstock, Cape Town ▪ Contemporary Italian ▪ Open Tue-Sat and selected public holidays ▪ Booking advised ▪ Children welcome ▪ Major credit cards accepted ▪ Corkage R65 (1 bottle per table) ▪ Owners Neil Grant and Barry Engelbrecht ▪ Head chef Stephen du Bruyn ▪ info@burrata.co.za ▪ www.burrata.co.za ▪ **T +27 (0)21-447-6505** ▪ F +27 (0)86-528-6209

Well known for its authentic, wood-fired, Neapolitan-style pizzas, Burrata is Italian in broad strokes but head chef Stephen du Bruyn likes to add his own unique flair to everything he creates in his open-plan kitchen. From the cosy restaurant, watch him and his team weave their magic while browsing the winelist with its broad and varied selection of unique hidden gems as well as firm favourites.

Savoy Cabbage Restaurant & Champagne Bar 101 Hout Street, Cape Town ▪ Contemporary cuisine ▪ Lunch Mon-Fri 12pm-2.30pm, dinner Mon-Sat 7pm-10.30pm ▪ Closed Sun ▪ Booking advised ▪ Major credit cards accepted ▪ Air-conditioned ▪ Corkage R45 ▪ Owner Caroline Bagley ▪ info@savoycabbage.co.za ▪ www.savoycabbage.co.za ▪ **T +27 (0)21-424-2626** ▪ F +27 (0)21-424-3366

Well into its second decade and as popular as ever, this city-centre venue boasts a string of accolades and plaudits from international critics. Expect exposed brick and high ceilings, evergreen favourites as menu fixtures, and daily-changing taste treats like Three Little Pigs with pan-fried loin, smoked fillet and sticky glazed belly; or house-smoked Norwegian salmon on buckwheat crêpe with grapefruit jelly and Keta caviar. Intelligent boutique winelist.

Sotano 121 Beach Road, Mouille Point, Cape Town ▪ Mediterranean, classic tapas ▪ Open daily 7am-10.30pm ▪ Booking advised ▪ Children welcome ▪ Major credit cards accepted ▪ No BYO ▪ Owner Brendon Crew ▪ Executive chef Russell Jalil ▪ info@sotano.co.za ▪ www.sotano.co.za ▪ **T +27 (0)21-433-1757**

Mediterranean-inspired food stars at this vibey seaside eatery. Sip bubbly watching the sunset from the outside deck and nibble an array of tapas like lamb koftas, halloumi and patatas bravas. Hearty mains feature signature paella; tempting lighter options include salads and flat breads with creative toppings. Try spicy Lebanese shakshouka for something different, and don't miss yummy Eggs Benedict at brunch. The winelist is well-curated.

Towers Restaurant African Pride Crystal Towers Hotel & Spa, Corner Century Boulevard and Rialto Road, Century City, Cape Town ▪ Internationally-inspired cuisine ▪ Open daily from 6.30am-10.30pm ▪ Booking advised ▪ Children welcome ▪ Major credit cards accepted ▪ Corkage R65 ▪ Executive chef Terrence Ford ▪ events@crystaltowershotel.com ▪ www.africanpridehotels.com/crystaltowers ▪ **T +27 (0)21-525-3888** ▪ F +27 (0)21-525-3889

Towers Restaurant at the African Pride Crystal Towers Hotel & Spa, Century City, offers an opulent dining experience designed to excite the senses. The spacious fine-dining area overlooks a display kitchen with world-class chefs in action. The à la carte menu promises something for every palate, made from a selection of ingredients from around the world, but with an emphasis on local and sustainable produce. (See also Accommodation)

CONSTANTIA

Buitenverwachting Restaurant, Courtyard & Coffee Bloc Buitenverwachting Wine Farm, Klein Constantia Road, Constantia, Cape Town ▪ High-end bistro ▪ Breakfast Mon-Sat 9am-11am, lunch Mon-Sat 12pm-3pm and dinner Mon-Sat 7pm-9pm ▪ Closed public holidays ▪ Closed Sun (Nov-Mar) and Sun/Mon (Apr-Oct) ▪ Booking advised ▪ Children welcome for lunch only ▪ Major credit cards accepted ▪ Corkage R55 ▪ Executive chef Edgar Osojnik ▪ restaurant@buitenverwachting.com ▪ www.buitenverwachting.com ▪ **T +27 (0)21-794-3522** ▪ F +27 (0)21-794-1351

Buitenverwachting Restaurant, Courtyard and Coffee Bloc seamlessly combines al fresco farm-style with inspired dining. The newly refurbished glass enclosed terrace offers spectacular views to compliment innovative menus from chef Edgar. The menu combines rustic favourites with a contemporary fine food selection – ideal for light lunches and sophisticated dinners. (See also A-Z sections)

Jonkershuis Constantia Groot Constantia Wine Estate, Groot Constantia Road, Constantia, Cape Town ▪ Cape Malay/Global cuisine ▪ Summer trading (Sept-April) Mon-Sat 9am-9pm and Sun 9am-5pm ▪ Reduced winter trading hours ▪ Breakfast daily 9am-11.30am ▪ Booking advised ▪ Children welcome ▪ Function facilities ▪ Major credit cards and Zapper accepted ▪ Corkage R50/750ml bottle ▪ Owners Chris Coetzee and Tammy Botbyl ▪ Executive chef Stefan Marais ▪ info@jonkershuisconstantia.co.za ▪ www.jonkershuisconstantia.co.za ▪ **T +27 (0)21-794-6255** ▪ F +27 (0)86-532-6961

Nestled in the historic core with sweeping views over the oldest wine producing vineyards in SA and across the coastline of False Bay. Intimate fireside dining, alfresco gathering on the front lawns or in the covered courtyard. Our menu reflects sustainability and a rich Cape Malay heritage. (See also A-Z sections)

DURBANVILLE

Ke-Monate @ Signal Gun Signal Gun Wine Farm, Vissershok Road, Durbanville, Cape Town ▪ Continental cuisine ▪ Tues-Fri 9am-10pm (summer) and 11.30am-10pm (winter), Sat 9am-10pm, Sun 9am-4pm and public holidays 9am-5pm ▪ Closed on Mon ▪ Booking advised ▪ Children welcome (play area outside) ▪ No BYO ▪ Major credit cards accepted ▪ Owners MJ and Estani de Wit ▪ manager@signalgun.com ▪ www.signalgun.com ▪ **T +27 (0)21-976-7343**

Walking into the restaurant at Signal Gun Wine Farm, Ke-Monate @ Signal Gun, feels almost like walking into your friends' home for dinner. With its relaxed atmosphere, it's all about enjoying great food, in particular the speciality chicken roulade and best-selling pizzas whilst choosing from a selection of superb wines that are sure to satisfy all tastes. (See also A-Z sections)

ELGIN

The Pool Room at Oak Valley Oak Valley Estate, R321, Oak Avenue, Elgin ▪ Mediterranean/Country cuisine ▪ Breakfast Tues-Sun 9am-11am, lunch Tues–Sun 12pm–3.30pm, dinner Fri 6.30pm-10pm ▪ Picnics available by pre-order from Nov 01 to Apr 30 ▪ Closed on Mon, Easter Mon, Dec 26 and Jun 15-Aug 15 ▪ Booking advised ▪ Children welcome ▪ Wheelchair-friendly ▪ Major credit cards accepted (no Amex) ▪ No BYO ▪ No pets ▪ Owners AG Rawbone-Viljoen ▪ poolroom@oak-valley.co.za ▪ www.oakvalley.co.za ▪ **T +27 (0)21-859-4111** ▪ F +27 (0)21-859-3405

When visiting Oak Valley Estate in Elgin, relax on The Pool Room terrace relishing country-inspired cuisine, made using ingredients sourced from the farm where possible. Feast on free-range beef, acorn-fed pork, charcuterie platters, naturally grown vegetables and freshly baked artisanal breads from the wood-burning oven. Wagyu beef, known for its intense marbling, is on offer from time to time, depending on availability. (See also A-Z sections)

South Hill South Hill Vineyards, 113 The Valley Road, Elgin ▪ Contemporary, bistro, country-style cuisine ▪ Open Wed-Sun for breakfast 8.30am-11am and lunch 12pm-3pm ▪ Open public holidays (except if it falls on a Mon or Tues) ▪ Closed Mon and Tues, Christmas Day, Boxing Day and New Year's Day ▪ Wine Tastings Mon-Sun 10am-4pm ▪ Booking advised ▪ Children welcome ▪ BYO allowed but not encouraged ▪ Corkage R50/bottle ▪ Visa and MasterCard accepted ▪ Owners Kevin and Sandra King ▪ Executive chef Fleur van den Hoogen ▪ info@southhill.co.za ▪ www.southhill.co.za ▪ **T +27 (0)21-844-0888/0033** ▪ F +27 (0)86-509-3433

The Gallery Restaurant at South Hill situated in our gallery space serves breakfast and lunches from Wednesday to Sunday. Our chef serves a bistro-

style menu using locally sourced produce. The Gallery and Sculpture Garden offers a variety of artworks that include paintings, small and large scale sculptures, photography, ceramics and mixed medium works as well as conceptual work. (See also Accommodation and A-Z sections)

FRANSCHHOEK

Fyndraai Restaurant Solms-Delta Wine Estate, Delta Road, off R45, Groot Drakenstein, Franschhoek Valley ▪ Traditional African cuisine with indigenous influence ▪ Open daily 10am-5pm ▪ Closed Dec 25 and Jan 01 ▪ Booking advised ▪ Children welcome ▪ Major credit cards accepted ▪ Corkage R35 ▪ Executive chef Shaun Schoeman ▪ restaurant@solms-delta.co.za ▪ www.solms-delta.co.za ▪ **T +27 (0)21-874-3937**

The Cape's diverse culinary traditions are celebrated at Fyndraai Restaurant on Franschhoek wine farm Solms-Delta, where chef Shaun Schoeman's main food influences are Afrikaner/Dutch, Cape Malay and indigenous Khoe. Enjoy dishes such as the best-selling sticky glazed pork belly with spekboom and buttered kapok aartappels while seated under the oak trees, on the lawn or inside a beautiful, contemporary, air-conditioned glass room with vineyard views. (See also A-Z sections)

Haute Cabrière Restaurant & Terrace Haute Cabrière, Franschhoek Pass (R45), Franschhoek ▪ Contemporary South African cuisine ▪ Open Tues-Sat lunch, dinner and snacks throughout the day, Sun lunch (Oct-Apr), and Tues-Sat lunch and snacks throughout the day, and Sun lunch (May-Sept) ▪ Closed Mon, Dec 25 and 26 and Jan 01 ▪ Booking advised ▪ Children welcome ▪ Major credit cards accepted ▪ No BYO ▪ Owner Clos Cabrière (Pty) Ltd ▪ restaurant@cabriere.co.za ▪ www.cabriere.co.za ▪ **T +27 (0)21-876-3688**

Set into the side of Franschhoek Mountain, Haute Cabrière Restaurant offers a unique atmosphere and promises a memorable dining experience. The contemporary South African farm-to-table menu revolves around seasonal availability of produce, which is mostly sourced locally or even grown on Haute Cabrière. Vegetarian dishes play a starring role and the estate's famous wines and cap classiques perfectly round off the experience. (See also A-Z sections)

Monneaux Restaurant Main Road, Franschhoek ▪ Contemporary cuisine ▪ Open daily for breakfast, lunch and dinner ▪ Booking advised ▪ Children welcome ▪ Major credit cards accepted ▪ Corkage R50 ▪ Executive chef Louis Jansen ▪ info@

fch.co.za ▪ www.monneaux.co.za ▪ **T +27 (0)21-876-3386** ▪ F +27 (0)21-876-2744

A restaurant ranked among Franschhoek's top, offering a contemporary take on the classics. Enjoy lunch on the fountain terrace under a spreading Pepper tree and dinner in the elegantly relaxed dining room in the manor house. Set on the site of Franschhoek's first *parfumerie*, enjoy dishes such as pistachio crusted lamb rack and our Franschhoek salmon trout tataki. (See also Accommodation and A-Z sections)

Orangerie @ Le Lude Le Lude Méthode Cap Classique, Bowling Green Avenue (Lamprechts Road), Franschhoek ▪ Contemporary cuisine ▪ Open daily for breakfast, lunch, tea and dinner ▪ Closed Sun evenings ▪ Booking advised ▪ Children welcome ▪ Major credit cards accepted ▪ Owners Nic and Ferda Barrow ▪ Chef Westley Muller ▪ info@lelude.co.za ▪ www.lelude.co.za ▪ **T +27 (0)87-754-9927**

Brand new Orangerie @ Le Lude is a grape throwaway from the iconic Huguenot Monument. The interior is spacious and light with a French flair whilst outdoors there is a gorgeous terrace with a magnificent view of the Franschhoek Mountains. Fresh herbs and vegetables from the kitchen garden are transformed into dishes that reflect the seasonal abundance. Enjoy breakfast daily or a lazy lunch/dinner, or try the carefully paired canapés with the Le Lude MCC. (See also Accommodation and A-Z Sections)

GRABOUW

FRESH at Paul Cluver Paul Cluver Wines, De Rust Estate, Kromco turnoff N2, Grabouw ▪ Contemporary country cuisine ▪ Open for lunch Wed-Sun 12pm-3.30pm ▪ Open public holidays unless it falls on a Mon and Tues ▪ Closed for the month of July, Christmas Day, Boxing Day and the Easter weekend ▪ Booking advised ▪ Children welcome ▪ No BYO ▪ Major credit cards accepted (no Diners Club and Amex) ▪ Owner Nicola (Niki) Hall-Jones ▪ Executive chef Damian Dearlove ▪ niki@freshatpaulcluver.co.za ▪ www.freshatpaulcluver.co.za ▪ **T +27 (0)21-844-0014** ▪ C +27 (0)71-563-6020

An ever-changing menu which is led by the best of what is available from our magnificent garden and trusted suppliers. We strive to offer beautiful food which is simply prepared in an informal and relaxed environment, affording a dining experience that is warm and uncomplicated, yet unforgettable. (See also A-Z sections)

HERMANUS

B's Steakhouse No.5 Hemel-en-Aarde Village, Hermanus ▪ Classic South African steakhouse ▪ Open for dinner Tue-Sun 6pm till late ▪ Open on Mon during school holidays and public holidays ▪ Booking advised ▪ Children welcome (preferably early) ▪ Major credit cards accepted ▪ Corkage R40 ▪ Owner/chef Bruce Henderson ▪ bssteakhouse@absamail.co.za ▪ www.diningout.co.za ▪ **T +27 (0)28-316-3625**

Celebrating two decades in business this year, B's Steakhouse is the oldest single owner-run restaurant in Hermanus. 'We specialise in South Africa's finest beef on offer,' says owner Bruce Henderson whose speciality is the best-selling fillet mignon. Seafood lovers and vegetarians are also catered for, while the restaurant has achieved Diamond status no fewer than three times in the annual Diners Club Wine List Awards.

Fusion Restaurant Village Square, Waterfront Piazza, Marine Drive, Hermanus ▪ Fusion ▪ Open Mon-Sun 9am-9pm ▪ Bookings advised for dinner ▪ Children welcome ▪ Major credit cards accepted ▪ BYO allowed ▪ Corkage fee R30 ▪ Owners Estelle & Petrus Hendriksz ▪ hendriksz@telkomsa.net ▪ www.fusioncafe-hermanus.co.za ▪ **T +27 (0)28-312-4277**

Fusion (blending of different styles and tastes) is a family owned business. Overlooking Walker Bay, Fusion is known as the best land-based whale watching spot in the world. The menu includes dishes inspired by the sea, cattle ranch, chicken coup, vegetable garden and the sandwich bar. Petri uses his inspiration, initiative and flair to create meals that are truly unique. Local wines from Hemel-en-Aarde Valley, craft beers, spirits and cocktails.

HOUT BAY

Pure Restaurant Hout Bay Manor, Baviaanskloof Road, off Main Road, Hout Bay, Cape Town ▪ Continental cuisine ▪ Open daily for breakfast 6.30am-11am, lunch 12pm-5pm and dinner 6.30pm-9.30pm ▪ Closed Jun 23 to Aug 03 ▪ Booking advised ▪ Children welcome ▪ Major credit cards accepted ▪ Corkage R90 for wine and R105 for champagne ▪ Owner Susan Struengmann ▪ Head chef Philip Botes ▪ sales@houtbaymanor.co.za ▪ www.pure-restaurant.co.za ▪ **T +27 (0)21-791-9393** ▪ F +27 (0)21-790-0118

At the heart of Hout Bay Manor in the picturesque fishing village of Hout Bay is Pure, a rustic family restaurant where head chef Philip Botes offers flavourful dishes made from only the freshest ingredients sourced locally. In addition to his best-selling burgers and steaks, he offers daily venison and seafood specials, with wine and dine evenings taking place once a month throughout the year. (See also Accommodation)

PAARL

Bosman's Restaurant Plantasie Street, Paarl ▪ Global cuisine ▪ Open daily for breakfast 7am-10.30am, lunch 12pm-2pm, High Tea 3pm-5pm and dinner 7pm-9.30pm ▪ Booking advised ▪ Children welcome ▪ No BYO ▪ All major credit cards accepted ▪ christine@granderoche.co.za ▪ www.granderoche.co.za ▪ **T +27 (0)21-863-5100** ▪ F +27 (0)21-863-2220

Take your taste buds on a journey of culinary delight at Bosman's, the Grande Roche Hotel's award-winning restaurant. Here, award-winning, Michelin-trained executive head chef Roland Gorgosilich infuses classic cuisine with imagination and innovation. His inspired menus and the freshest of ingredients are the hallmarks of this restaurant. Dine on the terrace and enjoy the views that make the setting of this hotel so spectacular. (See also Accommodation)

PHILADELPHIA

Mariella's Restaurant Capaia Wine Estate, Botterberg Road, Philadelphia, Cape Town ▪ Fine dining ▪ Open Tues and Thurs 11am-3pm, Wed, Fri and Sat 11am-10pm and Sun 11am-5pm ▪ Open public holidays ▪ Closed on Mon ▪ Booking advised ▪ Children welcome ▪ Major credit cards accepted ▪ BYO allowed ▪ Corkage fee R40 ▪ Executive chef Mark Hartlief ▪ mariellas@capaia.co.za ▪ www.capaia.co.za ▪ **T +27 (0)21-972-1103**

Situated on Capaia Wine Estate just outside Philadelphia, 30 minutes from Cape Town, this restaurant is named after the owners' daughter and headed up by executive chef Mark Hartlief, whose dishes incorporate tastes from East and West (though desserts are true French indulgence!). While grown-ups relax on the deck, overlooking the rolling hills of the Swartland, children can play on the lawn and jungle gym. (See also A-Z sections)

RIEBEEK-KASTEEL

Union Restaurant 33 Main Street, Riebeek Kasteel ▪ Modern South African cuisine ▪ Open 7 days a week from 7.30am-9.30pm ▪ Booking advised ▪ Children welcome ▪ BYO allowed ▪ Corkage R50 for wine and R75 for sparkling ▪ Major

credit cards and EFT accepted ▪ info@royalinriebeek.com ▪ www.royalinriebeek.com ▪ **T +27 (0)22-448-1378** ▪ F +27 (0)86-545-3559

'More than anything food should satisfy'... At Union Restaurant, Swartland Revolution wines meet Swartland Evolution cooking. Award-winning chef Mike Bassett and his team take locally sourced produce from its raw form into exciting modern dishes. While using the latest techniques, Union Restaurant stays faithful to the rich and diverse heritage of so many different influences through the ages. Enjoy the Swartland with a lunch or dinner at Union Restaurant, paired with some of the country's best wines in the setting of the oldest hotel in the Cape. Life doesn't get much better than this. (See also Accommodation)

ROBERTSON

Rosendal Restaurant Rosendal Winery & Wellness Retreat, Klaas Voogds West, Robertson ▪ Continental/African cuisine ▪ Open daily for breakfast 8am-10am, lunch 12pm-1.30pm and dinner 6.30pm-9pm ▪ Booking advised ▪ Children welcome ▪ No BYO ▪ Executive chef Roald Marais (Vaaitjie) ▪ info@rosendalwinery.com ▪ www.rosendalwinery.com ▪ **T +27 (0)23-626-1570** ▪ F +27 (0)23-626-1571

Rosendal Restaurant invites our international and local guests to explore our 'Traditional & Today' menu! The menu revolves around locally sourced or grown produce. Our flavours and textures are specifically designed for the 'home cooked hungry' or the 'spa/healthy enriched craver'. On sunny days, guests can enjoy the beautiful mountain views from the terrace, while on cool days a roaring fire creates a cosy atmosphere. Our talented culinary staff will overwhelm you with their beautiful mouth-watering dishes. (See also Accommodation and A-Z sections)

SOMERSET WEST

The Restaurant at Waterkloof Waterkloof Estate, Sir Lowry's Pass Village Road, Somerset West ▪ Classic French cuisine with a modern twist ▪ Open daily Mon-Sat 12pm-2pm and 7pm-9pm, and Sun 12pm-2pm ▪ Closed on Mon and Tues during winter months ▪ Closed for winter break mid-Jun to mid-July, Dec 25 and Jan 01 ▪ Booking advised ▪ Major credit cards accepted ▪ No BYO ▪ Owner Paul Boutinot ▪ Executive chef Grégory Czarnecki ▪ restaurant@waterkloofwines.co.za ▪ www.waterkloofwines.co.za ▪ **T +27 (0)21-858-1491** ▪ F +27 (0)21-858-1293

Waterkloof Estate's signature 'restaurant in the sky', perched high on the Schapenberg overlooking False Bay, is stylishly appointed in a 10m-high glass promontory flowing from the slick tasting lounge and gravitational cellar. The restaurant has an open-plan kitchen, in keeping with the Waterkloof winemaking philosophy of honesty and transparency, where chef Gregory Czarnecki gives classic French cuisine a whimsical, creative edge in an eco-conscious way. (See also A-Z sections)

Vergelegen Vergelegen Wine Estate, Lourensford Road, Somerset West ▪ **Camphors at Vergelegen** (à la carte/contemporary/global) lunch Wed-Sun 12pm-3pm, dinner Fri and Sat 6.30pm-9pm, **Stables at Vergelegen** (bistro) open Mon-Sun for breakfast 9.45am-11.30am, lunch 11.30am-3.30pm, tea/coffee and cakes 9.45am-4pm; **Picnic at Vergelegen** (luxury/elegant picnic) pre-booked baskets available Nov-Apr between 12.15pm-1.30pm ▪ Estate closed Good Fri, May 01 and Dec 25 ▪ Booking advised ▪ Picnic and Stables specifically child-friendly ▪ Major credit cards accepted ▪ No BYO ▪ Owners Anglo American plc ▪ info@vergelegen.co.za ▪ www.vergelegen.co.za ▪ Camphors Restaurant/Picnic at Vergelegen **T +27 (0)21-847-2131** ▪ Stables Bistro **T +27 (0)21-847-2156**

Experience the world of Vergelegen first-hand – from spectacular gardens to arts and culture, historic homestead and ancient camphor trees, wine tasting and cellar tours and restaurants to suit all tastes. The Camphors at Vergelegen signature restaurant, Stables at Vergelegen bistro restaurant and the seasonal luxury Picnic at Vergelegen are only a few of a myriad of enjoyable activities at Vergelegen. (See also A-Z sections)

STANFORD

Springfontein Eats & Wine Barn Wortelgat Road, Stanford ▪ **Springfontein Eats** ▪ Global cuisine ▪ Daily changing menu ▪ Open Tues and Wed lunch, Thurs-Sat lunch and dinner, Sun lunch only ▪ Open for lunch on public holidays ▪ Closed on Mon and Sun evenings ▪ **Wine Barn** ▪ German country kitchen ▪ Open Fri-Tues 12pm-9pm ▪ Closed Wed and Thurs ▪ Weekly changing menu ▪ Booking advised ▪ Children welcome ▪ Major credit cards accepted (no Amex) ▪ No BYO ▪ Executive chef Jurgen Schneider ▪ hospitality@springfontein.co.za ▪ www.springfontein.co.za ▪ **T +27 (0)28-341-0651** ▪ F +27 (0)28-341-0112

Springfontein Eats is set on our working wine farm where we keep things down to earth! Home-grown and foraged herbs and veggies, locally sourced fish and meats. Look for locavore food, with a hint of molecular gastronomy. The Wine Barn offers more rustic dishes and a favourite is German sausages and homemade bread. Wine tastings also available. (See also Accommodation and A-Z sections)

STELLENBOSCH

Chez Shiraz Devonvale Golf & Wine Estate, Bottelary Road, Koelenhof, Stellenbosch ▪ African/International cuisine ▪ Open daily 7am-9pm ▪ Booking advised ▪ Children welcome ▪ Major credit cards accepted ▪ No BYO ▪ Owner JJ. Provoyeur, D. Abromowitz, B. Gutkin and R. Tanur ▪ Executive chef William Farmer ▪ marketing@devonvale.co.za ▪ www.devonvale.co.za ▪ **T +27 (0)21-888-4731** ▪ F +27 (0)21-865-2113

As the main à la carte restaurant at Devonvale Golf & Wine Estate, Chez Shiraz is decorated in a typically French style, with a French menu adding to the atmosphere while friendly staff provide genuine hospitable warmth. In addition to offering a stately fine-dining experience for lunch and dinner, the restaurant serves a buffet-style breakfast every morning, with casual al fresco meals available on The Terrace. (See also Accommodation and A-Z sections)

Cucina di Giovanni's Eikendal Vineyards, R44 between Somerset West and Stellenbosch ▪ Italian ▪ Open Tues-Sat 12pm-10pm and Sun 12pm-4pm ▪ Closed on Mon ▪ Open on public holidays unless it falls on a Mon ▪ Booking advised ▪ Children welcome ▪ No BYO ▪ Owner Dino Koutsis ▪ info@giovannicapetown.co.za ▪ www.giovannicapetown.co.za ▪ **T +27 (0)21-855-5033** ▪ F +27 (0)21-855-0470

After almost a decade as one of Somerset West's most popular eateries, Cucina di Giovanni has opened a second restaurant closer to Stellenbosch at Eikendal Vineyards. Giovanni's has an Italian theme and specialises in authentic thin-based pizzas and pasta dishes, but its international menu also includes such dishes as eisbein, in honour of the farm's Swiss owners, all created to go with Eikendal's award-winning wines. (See also Accommodation and A-Z sections)

Delaire Graff Restaurant Delaire Graff Estate, R310 Helshoogte Pass, Banhoek Valley, Stellenbosch ▪ Bistro-chic cuisine ▪ Open daily (times change according to the season) ▪ Booking advised ▪ Children welcome during lunch only ▪ Major credit cards accepted ▪ Corkage fee (limit of 4 bottles of wine per party) ▪ Owner Laurence Graff ▪ Head chef Michael Deg ▪ reservations@ delaire.co.za ▪ www.delaire.co.za ▪ **T +27 (0)21-885-8160**

Offering an expression of the seasons, Delaire Graff Restaurant is where favourite bistro classics are served with the finest South African touches following chef Michael Deg's philosophy that the best food begins with the finest local ingredients. Enjoy dishes including the best-selling braised Karoo lamb neck or coconut Namelaka dessert on the terrace with vineyard and Simonsberg Mountain views, or within the artfully designed interiors. (See also A-Z sections)

EIGHT Spier Wine Farm, R310, Baden Powell Rd, Stellenbosch ▪ Farm-to-table South African fare ▪ Open Tues-Sun 10am-4pm, dinner Thurs-Sat 6. 30pm-10pm ▪ Closed for dinner in winter ▪ Booking advised ▪ Children welcome ▪ Major credit cards accepted ▪ No BYO ▪ eight@spier.co.za ▪ www.spier.co.za ▪ **T +27 (0)21-809-1188** ▪ F +27 (0)21-881-3087

Eight is Spier's farm-to-table eating experience. Like its name, the restaurant is an expression of balance, cycles, harmony, infinity and abundance. The produce used at Eight is either grown on the farm or sourced from nearby farmers. Natural and organic ingredients are preferred and combined to create nourishing, healthy, and delicious food. (See also Accommodation and A-Z sections)

Flavours Restaurant The Devon Valley Hotel, Devon Valley Road, Devon Valley, Stellenbosch ▪ Contemporary Cape cuisine ▪ Open daily 7am-9pm ▪ Booking advised ▪ Children welcome ▪ Corkage R35 ▪ Major credit cards accepted ▪ Executive chef Markus Schwemberger ▪ Owner HS&V Hospitality ▪ info@devonvalleyhotel.com ▪ www. devonvalleyhotel.com ▪ **T +27 (0)21-865-2012**

Flavours Restaurant at the Devon Valley Hotel offers an elegant dining experience in a picturesque setting. Offering breakfast, lunch and dinner daily, the restaurant's focus is on contemporary Cape cuisine: classic dishes with bold flavours and fresh, clean tastes, perfectly paired with wines from an award-winning winelist. Flavour always comes first, with a gentle and homely ambience adding understated elegance to any special occasion. (See also Accommodation)

Guardian Peak Winery & Grill Guardian Peak Wines, Annandale Road, Stellenbosch ▪ Grill house

▪ Open Mon-Sun 12pm-3.30pm and Wed-Sat 6pm-10pm ▪ Closed Good Friday and Dec 25 ▪ Booking advised ▪ Children welcome ▪ Major credit cards accepted ▪ No BYO ▪ Owner Jean Engelbrecht ▪ Executive chef Steffan Boshoff ▪ info@ guardianpeak.com ▪ www.guardianpeak.com ▪ **T +27 (0)21-881-3899** ▪ F +27 (0)21-881-3388

For a true Stellenbosch winelands experience, relax at tables on a wide veranda with vineyard vistas. Wine-inspired lunches and dinners match hearty, wholesome dishes (including tasty vegetarian options), but focus is on prime-quality steak and venison: choices from the grill include fillet, rump, and rib-eye, with tempting sauces. Treat yourself to a 'Portfolio Tasting' with wines from Guardian Peak's greater portfolio, sold under separate brands. (See also A-Z sections)

Indochine Restaurant Delaire Graff Estate, R310 Helshoogte Pass, Banhoek Valley, Stellenbosch ▪ Asian-influenced cuisine ▪ Open daily for lunch 12pm-2.30pm and dinner 6.30pm-9pm ▪ Booking advised ▪ Children welcome ▪ Major credit cards accepted ▪ Corkage fee (limit of 4 bottles of wine per party) ▪ Owner Laurence Graff ▪ Head chef Virgil Kahn ▪ guest.relations@delaire.co.za ▪ www. delaire.co.za ▪ **T +27 (0)21-885-8160**

Delaire Graff Estate's Asian-influenced restaurant, Indochine, is an intimate and evocative food theatre, designed to provide an all-sensory dining experience. From the best-selling Vietnamese Duck to the Seafood Geng-Gati Curry, each of chef Virgil Kahn's dishes are synonymous with vitality, wellness and healthy living. Beneath the Swallows in Flight art installation, the blue and copper palette is calming, with views stretching across to Table Mountain. (See also A-Z sections)

Lanzerac Wine Estate - Dining Lanzerac Hotel & Spa, No.1 Lanzerac Road, Stellenbosch ▪ French Contemporary cuisine ▪ Open daily from 7am-midnight ▪ Booking advised ▪ Children welcome ▪ Corkage R45 ▪ Major credit cards accepted ▪ Executive chef Stephen Fraser ▪ fandb@lanzerac.co.za ▪ www.lanzerac.co.za ▪ **T +27 (0)21-887-1132** ▪ F +27 (0)21-887-2310

The Governors Hall, the main à la carte restaurant at Lanzerac Hotel & Spa, opens its impressive wood-panelled doors daily to welcome guests to a gastronomic explosion of international and local cuisine, served with the estate's own award-winning wines. Generous buffet-style breakfasts and appetising lunches are also served daily, with alfresco meals offered at the Terrace Restaurant, overlooking the historic Manor House, and at the Lanzerac Deli. (See also Accommodation and A-Z sections)

Rust en Vrede Restaurant Rust en Vrede Wine Estate, Annandale Road (off R44), Stellenbosch ▪ Fine dining, contemporary take on the classics ▪ Mon-Sat Winemakers lunch 12pm-3pm, Tues-Sat dinner 6pm till late ▪ Closed Sun, Good Fri and Dec 25 ▪ Booking advised ▪ Major credit cards accepted ▪ No BYO ▪ Owner Jean Engelbrecht ▪ Executive chef John Shuttleworth ▪ info@rustenvrede.com ▪ www.rustenvrede.com ▪ **T +27 (0)21-881-3881** ▪ F +27 (0)21-881-3000

Dine in sought-after style in the wine estate's historic cellar, where décor and a see-it-all open plan kitchen, plus the finest glasses and custom-designed tableware, enhance creative four and six-course gourmet menus. Executive chef John Shuttleworth brings original touches to a range of perfectly-plated dishes, while sommelier Barry Scholfield adds his expertise to the innovative wine-matching experience; not all of the wines are South African. (See also A-Z sections)

The Big Easy Restaurant & Wine Bar 95 Dorp Street, Stellenbosch ▪ Up-market and contemporary ▪ Open daily ▪ Closed Dec 25 ▪ Booking advised ▪ Children welcome ▪ Major credit cards accepted ▪ No BYO ▪ info@thebigeasy.co.za ▪ www.thebigeasyrestaurant.co.za ▪ **T +27 (0)21-887-3462/464/468** ▪ F +27 (0)21-887-3470

The Big Easy Restaurant and Wine Bar in Stellenbosch offers a taste of laidback luxury served with a hint of history. In a building known as 'The Grand Old Lady' with its Cape Dutch/Georgian/Victorian architecture, the restaurant specialities are venison loin, succulent beef steaks and wild mushroom risotto, complemented by over 170 wines, many from the restaurant owners' cellars: Rupert Wines, Rust en Vrede Wines, Guardian Peak Wines, Ernie Els Wines and Audacia Wines. All are invited to come and enjoy this sophisticated yet easy dining experience.

The Restaurant @ Clos Malverne Devon Valley Road, Devon Valley, Stellenbosch ▪ Global cuisine ▪ Tues-Sun 12pm-5pm (kitchen closes at 3pm) ▪ Closed on Mon, Christmas and Good Friday ▪ Booking advised ▪ Children welcome ▪ Major credit cards accepted ▪ No BYO ▪ Owners Seymour and Sophia Pritchard ▪ Executive chef Nadia Louw Smith ▪ info@closmalverne.co.za ▪ www.closmalverne.co.za ▪ **T +27 (0)21-865-2022** ▪ F +27 (0)86-618-9352

Since opening in 2009, this popular winelands destination has acquired a devoted following for chef Nadia Louw Smith's fresh, seasonal and contemporary 'world-inspired' cuisine, which is best enjoyed on the wraparound balcony, overlooking Clos Malverne's prized vineyards. 'We have all the right ingredients, including award-winning wines, a diverse menu and priceless views, to help you get your groove back for the week that lies ahead.' (See also A-Z sections)

Tokara Restaurant Tokara Farm, Helshoogte Rd, R310, Stellenbosch ▪ South African modern cuisine ▪ Open Tues-Sat for lunch and dinner, Sun lunch ▪ Open public holidays ▪ Closed Sun evenings and Mon ▪ Booking advised ▪ Children welcome ▪ No BYO ▪ Major credit cards accepted (no Amex) ▪ Owners Wilhelm Kühn, Johan Terblanche, Jaap-Henk Koelewijn ▪ Executive chef Richard Carstens ▪ reservations@tokara.com ▪ www.tokararestaurant.co.za ▪ **T +27 (0)21-885-2550**

Tokara Restaurant, situated on top of the Helshoogte Pass outside Stellenbosch, offers seasonal terroir-focused contemporary cuisine, award-winning wines and dramatic views over Stellenbosch and False Bay. The restaurant interior underwent a 'refresh' during 2015 and a fire pit was added to the kitchen. Chef Richard Carstens has launched a further evolutionary iteration of his celebration of local sustainable cuisine in line with these changes. (See also A-Z sections)

Warwick Wine Estate - Gourmet Picnics On the R44 between Stellenbosch and Paarl ▪ Gourmet Picnics ▪ Open Mon-Fri 12pm-4pm, Sat 11am-5pm, Sun and public holidays 12pm-4pm ▪ Booking advised ▪ Children welcome ▪ Major credit cards accepted ▪ No BYO ▪ Owners Mike and Norma Ratcliffe ▪ Executive chef Melanie Shepherd ▪ visit@warwickwine.com ▪ www.warwickwine.com ▪ **T +27 (0)21-884-4410**

Warwick has a well-deserved reputation for our Gourmet Picnics. Our Executive chef combines the highest quality ingredients from locally sourced artisanal suppliers. Our delicious picnics are perfect for that special occasion, or just for a lazy-day-out in wine country. Gourmands rave about our picnics and keep coming back — you will too. For families, we create delicious children's picnics that are designed by parents who 'get it'. (See also A-Z section)

Zevenwacht Restaurant Zevenwacht Wine Estate, Langverwacht Road, Kuils River, Cape Town ▪ Contemporary country cuisine ▪ Breakfast Mon-

Fri 7am-10am, Sat/Sun and public holidays 8am-11am, lunch 12pm-3pm and dinner 6pm-10pm daily ▪ Booking advised ▪ Children welcome ▪ Major credit cards accepted ▪ No BYO ▪ Executive chef Henna Von Wielligh ▪ restaurant@zevenwacht.co.za ▪ www.zevenwacht.co.za ▪ **T +27 (0)21-900-5800** ▪ F +27 (0)21-903-5257

Decorated with finesse and charm, Zevenwacht Restaurant is located within a turn-of-the-19th century Cape Dutch manor house with views of a tranquil lake and park-like gardens. Open for breakfast, lunch and dinner seven days a week, the restaurant offers contemporary continental cuisine, perfectly prepared, as well as a range of picnic baskets (including a braai basket) served on tree-shaded lawns sloping down to the lake. (See also Accommodation and A-Z sections)

TULBAGH

Readers Restaurant 12 Church Street, Tulbagh ▪ Global contemporary, fusion of flavours ▪ Open Wed-Mon 9am-10pm ▪ Closed Tues ▪ Booking advised ▪ Children welcome ▪ Major credit cards and Snap Scan accepted (no Amex) ▪ Corkage R25 ▪ Owner Carol Collins ▪ readers@iafrica.com ▪ www.readersrestaurant.co.za ▪ **T +27 (0)23-230-0087** ▪ C +27 (0)82-894-0932

Built in 1754, the oldest house in Tulbagh's historic Church Street was revitalised in 1997 as this charming restaurant under Silwood-trained chef Carol Collins. Since then she has maintained her excellent reputation for 'home-cooked meals with a difference', from game steak served with gooseberry and Amarula sauce to homemade ice cream in unusual flavours. The menu changes daily depending on the availability of fresh produce. (See also Accommodation)

Accommodation in the Winelands and Cape Town

INDEX OF ACCOMMODATION

BREDASDORP

Black Oystercatcher Cottages Moddervlei Farm, Bredasdorp ▪ 4 cottages ▪ R450pps, single R650 ▪ Visa and MasterCard accepted ▪ Restaurant ▪ Weddings/functions ▪ Pool ▪ Cycling ▪ Walking trails ▪ Canoeing ▪ Birding ▪ Wine tasting ▪ Secure parking ▪ Fireplace (in some cottages) ▪ Free WiFi ▪ Owner Dirk Human ▪ stay@blackoystercatcher.co.za ▪ www.blackoystercatcher.co.za ▪ **T +27 (0)28-482-1618** ▪ F +27 (0)86-666-7954

Overlooking the rich biodiversity of the Agulhas Plain, each of Black Oystercatcher's four cottages is beautifully furnished with a king-size bed or two singles plus a kitchenette, lounge area and patio – perfect for sipping a glass of wine in summer. There is an on-site restaurant and activities include mountain biking, hiking, birdwatching and swimming. Linen and towels are provided, and there is free WiFi access. (See also Restaurants and A-Z sections)

CALITZDORP

The Retreat at Groenfontein Groenfontein Road, District Calitzdorp (20km from Calitzdorp, off Route 62) ▪ TGCSA 3 & 4-star guest house; AA Quality Assured highly recommended ▪ Rates on request ▪ Visa and MasterCard accepted ▪ Restaurant (problem diets catered for - advise when booking) ▪ Weddings/functions ▪ Pool ▪ Children and pets welcome ▪ Mountain biking ▪ Walking trails ▪ Birding ▪ River with rock pools ▪ Secure parking ▪ Laundry service ▪ Safe ▪ WiFi and TV in lounge ▪ French, German, Italian and Swedish spoken ▪ Owner Marie Holstensson ▪ info@groenfontein.com ▪ www.groenfontein.com ▪ **T +27 (0)44-213-3880** ▪ F +27 (0)86-271-5373

A consistent award-winner, this welcoming, personally run, 3- and 4-star Victorian farmhouse offers both standard and garden rooms. You'll enjoy personal pampering, hearty breakfasts and tasty dinners. The inviting lounge and dining room overlook sweeping lawns and the majestic Swartberg. Take leisurely walks, challenging trails, explore the rock pools in the bird-rich river, or simply laze at the pool, soaking up the peace and silence.

CAMPS BAY

The Twelve Apostles Hotel and Spa Victoria Road, Camps Bay, Cape Town ▪ TGCSA 5-star hotel ▪ 70 rooms ▪ Seasonal rates from R5480 to R6770 per room B&B ▪ Major credit cards accepted ▪ Azure Restaurant ▪ Conferences ▪ Weddings/functions ▪ Spa ▪ Sauna ▪ Gym ▪ Pool ▪ Walks/hikes ▪ Birding ▪ Wine tasting ▪ Secure parking ▪ Shuttle service ▪ Laundry service ▪ Air-conditioning ▪ Ceiling fans ▪ Underfloor heating ▪ TV ▪ DSTV ▪ DVD player ▪ WiFi ▪ Safe ▪ Japanese, Spanish and German spoken ▪ Owners Tollman Family ▪ reservations1@12apostles.co.za ▪ www.12apostleshotel.com ▪ **T +27 (0)21-437-9000** ▪ F +27 (0)21-437-9062

The award-winning Twelve Apostles Hotel and Spa is situated on Cape Town's most scenic route, flanking Table Mountain National Park and overlooking the Atlantic Ocean. Part of the family-run Red Carnation Hotel Collection, it offers 55 deluxe guest rooms and 15 luxurious suites, not to mention a holistic spa and private cinema, with Azure Restaurant serving up breathtaking views in addition to legendary local cuisine. (See also Restaurants)

CAPE TOWN

African Pride Crystal Towers Hotel & Spa Corner Century Boulevard and Rialto Road, Century City, Cape Town ▪ 180 rooms ▪ Best available rates ▪ Major credit cards accepted ▪ Towers Restaurant ▪ Conferences ▪ Weddings/functions ▪ Spa ▪ Gym and sauna ▪ Pool ▪ Air-conditioning ▪ TV and DVD player ▪ DSTV ▪ Safe ▪ WiFi ▪ Secure parking ▪ Shuttle service ▪ Laundry service ▪ English, Afrikaans and Xhosa spoken ▪ reservations@crystaltowershotel.com ▪ www.africanpridehotels.com/crystaltowers ▪ **T +27 (0)21-525-3888** ▪ F +27 (0)21-525-3889

The African Pride Crystal Towers Hotel & Spa, situated in Century City, just 10 minutes from the CBD and the Durbanville winelands, has become one of Cape Town's most favoured executive destinations thanks to its first-rate conferencing facilities. However, leisure guests also enjoy its intimate ambiance and five-star amenities – the lavish Crystal life! – as well as convenient pedestrian connectivity to Canal Walk Shopping Centre. (See also Restaurants)

Brooklands Guest House 3 Surbiton Road, Rosebank, Cape Town ▪ TGCSA 4-star guest house ▪ 6 rooms ▪ Low season from R650pps B&B, high season from R750pps B&B ▪ Major credit cards accepted ▪ Restaurant open 7am-9pm daily ▪ Children welcome ▪ Booking advised ▪ No Conferences ▪ Weddings/functions ▪ Pool ▪ Fireplace ▪ Safe ▪ TV ▪ DSTV ▪ DVD player ▪ Mini bar fridge ▪ WiFi ▪ Owners Philip and Sandra Engelen ▪ brooklands@mweb.co.za ▪ www.brooklands-guesthouse.co.za ▪ **T/F +27 (0)21-689-3594**

Charming Victorian villa, within walking distance of some seven restaurants, near Newlands rugby and cricket grounds, and less than 15 mins drive from Cape Town International Airport. Breakfast in the sunroom overlooking the garden; dine by prior arrangement; in winter relax beside the drawing room fire. If you're planning winelands excursions, consult your hosts, wine enthusiasts who planted a petit shiraz vineyard beside the boule court.

CEDERBERG

Sanddrif Holiday Resort Dwarsrivier Farm, Cederberg ▪ TGCSA 3-star self-catering (exclusive caravan and camping) ▪ 16 Self-catering chalets and 40 campsites ▪ Rates on request ▪ Mountain biking ▪ Walks/hikes ▪ Birding ▪ Fishing ▪ Wine tasting ▪ Secure parking ▪ Fireplace ▪ Dutch spoken ▪ Owner Nieuwoudt family ▪ sanddrif@cederbergwine.com ▪ www.cederbergwine.com/sanddrif ▪ **T +27 (0)27-482-2825** ▪ F +27 (0)86-509-1683

Located in the heart of the Cederberg, Sanddrif is Cederberg Private Cellar's holiday resort, established in the late 1950s when trailblazing hikers and rock climbers started asking the Nieuwoudt family whether they could overnight on the farm.

Now more accessible while retaining an air of remoteness, Sanddrif offers four well-known day hikes, rock climbing, bird watching, swimming, mountain biking, rock art and a unique observatory. (See also A-Z sections)

ELGIN

South Hill South Hill Vineyards, 113 The Valley Road, Elgin ▪ TGCSA 4-star self-catering (Exclusive Category) ▪ Rates from R845 per room B&B, exclusive use of the Guest House (6 rooms, self-catering) from R4730 per night, Pumphouse Cottage (sleeps 2, self-catering) from R930 per night ▪ Major credit cards accepted ▪ Restaurant ▪ Conferences ▪ Weddings/functions ▪ Jacuzzi (Pumphouse Cottage) ▪ Pool (Guest House) ▪ Fireplace ▪ Mountain biking ▪ Walks/hikes ▪ Birding ▪ Fishing ▪ Boule court ▪ Wine tasting ▪ TV (Guest House) ▪ DSTV and DVD Player ▪ iPod docking station ▪ WiFi ▪ info@southhill.co.za ▪ www.southhill.co.za ▪ **T +27 (0)21-844-0888/0033** ▪ F +27 (0)86-509-3433

South Hill Guesthouse is a six-bedroom, en-suite luxury villa with full guest amenities. Our Pumphouse Honeymoon Cottage is situated in the seclusion of an indigenous fynbos garden on the banks of our middle dam surrounded by shiraz vineyards. So, whether you are coming for a wedding, a weekend, a holiday or just a complete chill out in the week - South Hill has much to offer! (See also Restaurants and A-Z sections)

FRANSCHHOEK

Franschhoek Country House & Villas Main Road, Franschhoek ▪ TGCSA 5-star country house ▪ 26 rooms ▪ Low season from R1890 per room B&B ▪ High season from R2700 per room B&B ▪ Major credit cards accepted ▪ Monneaux Restaurant ▪ Conferences ▪ Weddings/functions ▪ Spa ▪ Two pools (one heated) ▪ Close by mountain biking, golf course, horse riding, walks/hikes, fishing, cellar tours and wine tasting ▪ Secure parking ▪ Shuttle service ▪ Laundry service ▪ Air-conditioning ▪ Fireplace ▪ Under-floor heating ▪ TV ▪ DSTV and DVD player ▪ WiFi ▪ Safe ▪ info@fch.co.za ▪ www.fch.co.za ▪ **T +27 (0)21-876-3386** ▪ F +27 (0)21-876-2744

Five-star boutique hotel with top-rated Monneaux Restaurant on the outskirts of the village, surrounded by vineyards and majestic mountains. Offering a selection of rooms and exclusive suites, guests can laze at one of the two pools (one heated), enjoy a massage, visit the boutique wine farms in Franschhoek, or take a complimentary shuttle service to the charming town. (See also Restaurants)

La Providence Guest House & Wine Farm Middagkrans Road, Franschhoek ▪ Luxury guest house ▪ Accredited member of GHAA ▪ Rates from R2700 per room B&B ▪ Major credit cards accepted ▪ Bar ▪ Pool ▪ Secure parking ▪ Air-conditioning ▪ Under-floor heating ▪ Safe ▪ Coffee/tea making facility with Nespresso machine ▪ Hairdryer ▪ WiFi ▪ German and English spoken ▪ ellen.rose@laprovidence.co.za ▪ www.laprovidence.co.za ▪ **T +27 (0)21-876-4790**

One of Franschhoek's newest destinations for visitors is La Providence, a small and luxurious guesthouse and wine farm located only five minutes behind the famous Huguenot Monument. Here visitors are able to experience the atmosphere of tradition permeating this historic valley, while a thoughtful modern interior design has managed to blend the past with the future into a memorable fusion of comfort, peace and pleasure. (See also A-Z sections)

Lily Pond House Le Lude Méthode Cap Classique, Bowling Green Avenue (Lamprechts Road), Franschhoek ▪ Luxury guest house ▪ 2 en-suite rooms ▪ Rates R1750pps ▪ Major credit cards accepted ▪ Restaurant ▪ Pool ▪ Cellar tours ▪ Cap Classique tasting ▪ Under-floor heating ▪ Secure parking ▪ Fully equipped kitchen ▪ Catered breakfast available ▪ Braai area ▪ TV ▪ DSTV ▪ Safe ▪ WiFi ▪ Owners Nic and Ferda Barrow ▪ www.lelude.co.za ▪ info@lelude.co.za ▪ **T +27 (0)87-754-9927**

Your own private cottage with 5 star luxury is situated between vineyards and lily ponds... The Lily Pond House is fully equipped with a modern kitchen, dining/sitting room, private pool and sheltered braai area. Maximum of 4 persons. (See also Restaurants and A-Z sections)

HOUT BAY

Hout Bay Manor Baviaanskloof Road, off Main Road, Hout Bay ▪ TGCSA 5-star boutique hotel ▪ 16 rooms ▪ Seasonal rates from R1800-R4200 per room B&B ▪ Major credit cards accepted ▪ Pure Restaurant ▪ Conferences ▪ Weddings/functions ▪ Spa ▪ Pool ▪ Secure parking ▪ Shuttle service ▪ Laundry service ▪ Air-conditioning ▪ Under-floor heating ▪ TV ▪ DSTV ▪ iPod docking station ▪ WiFi ▪ Safe ▪ Owner Susan Struengmann ▪ sales@houtbaymanor.co.za ▪ www.houtbaymanor.com ▪ **T +27 (0)21-790-0116** ▪ F +27 (0)21-790-0118

On the gentle slopes of Hout Bay lies Hout Bay Manor, a sparkling yet hidden gem of luxury and indulgence. Built in 1871 by Jacob Trautmann, it was originally known as the Royal Hotel and became a popular romantic destination for honeymooners. In recent years, it has been completely restored in Cape colonial style to recapture the tranquillity, charm and grace of a bygone era. (See also Restaurants)

PAARL

Druk My Niet Wine Estate and Guest Cottages Bodal Road, Daljosafat, Paarl ▪ 3 self-catering cottages ▪ Rates per cottage per night: Protea R1000 (sleeps two), Guava R1500 (sleeps four), Fynbos R2600 (sleeps six) ▪ Major credit cards accepted ▪ Pool ▪ Walks/hikes ▪ Cellar tours ▪ Wine tasting ▪ Air-conditioning ▪ Fireplace ▪ TV ▪ DSTV and DVD player ▪ WiFi ▪ Safe ▪ German spoken ▪ Owners Georg and Dorothee Kirchner ▪ carlien@dmnwines.co.za ▪ www.dmnwines.co.za ▪ **T +27 (0)21-868-2393**

Stay at Druk My Niet's beautiful self-catering cottages, set amid vines with spectacular Paarl valley views. Relax and unwind over the farm's own wines in cosy Protea Cottage, sleeping two in a bedroom with a large en-suite bathroom; beautiful Guava Cottage, sleeping four in two bedrooms, each with its own bathroom; or fully fitted Fynbos Cottage, sleeping six in three double rooms (two bathrooms). (See also A-Z sections)

Grande Roche Hotel Plantasie Street, Paarl ▪ TGCSA 5-star hotel ▪ 28 rooms ▪ Rates on request ▪ Major credit cards accepted ▪ Bosman's Restaurant ▪ Conferences ▪ Weddings/functions ▪ Gym ▪ Pools ▪ Tennis court ▪ Wine tasting ▪ Secure parking ▪ Shuttle service ▪ Laundry service ▪ Air-conditioning ▪ Under-floor heating ▪ TV ▪ DSTV ▪ WiFi ▪ Safe ▪ German spoken ▪ reserve@granderoche.co.za ▪ www.granderoche.co.za ▪ **T +27 (0)21-863-5100** ▪ F +27 (0)21-863-2220

Nestled at the foot of the magnificent Paarl Rock is a small luxury hotel like no other. The Grande Roche Hotel is a place where the atmosphere of a bygone era brings a sense of gracious, unhurried living, but it's also where history interacts with modern comforts. After staying in their choice of 28 stylishly appointed suites, guests visiting the Grande Roche Hotel are guaranteed a reluctant departure. (See also Restaurants)

RIEBEEK-KASTEEL

The Royal Hotel 33 Main Street, Riebeek Kasteel ▪ AA Superior Hotel ▪ 10 rooms ▪ Low season R795pps B&B, high season R895pps B&B ▪ Major credit cards and EFT accepted ▪ Union Restaurant ▪ Conferences ▪ Weddings/functions ▪ Pool ▪ Laundry service ▪ Air-conditioning ▪ Under-floor heating ▪ Safe ▪ TV ▪ DSTV ▪ DVD player ▪ WiFi ▪ Owner Robert Brendel ▪ info@royalinriebeek.com ▪ www.royalinriebeek.com ▪ **T +27 (0)22-448-1378** ▪ F +27 (0)86-545-3559

Located in Riebeek-Kasteel, the Royal Hotel is the Western Cape's oldest and most colonial hotel. It offers beautiful and luxurious accommodation with great valley and Kasteelberg views from the garden, swimming pool and pool deck. Listed in 2006 among the government's 50 most fabulous places to visit in South Africa, the hotel boasts a 150-year-old bar and the longest stoep south of the Limpopo. (See also Restaurants)

ROBERTSON

Rosendal Guest House Rosendal Winery & Wellness Retreat, Klaas Voogds West, Robertson ▪ 4-star guest house ▪ Tripadvisor Certificate of Excellence 2014 ▪ 8 rooms ▪ Seasonal rates from R550-R1134pps B&B ▪ Major credit cards, EFT and cash accepted ▪ Restaurant ▪ Weddings/functions ▪ Spa ▪ Pool ▪ Mountain biking ▪ Walks/hikes ▪ Wine tasting ▪ Secure parking ▪ Laundry service ▪ WiFi ▪ Owners Geir and Sissel Tellefsen ▪ Executive chef Roald Marais (Vaaitjie) ▪ info@rosendalwinery.com ▪ www.rosendalwinery.com ▪ **T +27 (0)23-626-1570** ▪ F +27 (0)23-626-1571

Need a relaxing getaway? Head for the serenity of Klaasvoogds, to this four-star guest house with revitalising spa, where qualified therapists offer traditional treatments using products made from wine grapes, enriched with antioxidants. Elegant colonial-style accommodation in the original manor and farmhouse ranges from luxury spa rooms to farm rooms and also interlinking family rooms, all en-suite and overlooking vineyards, pond, pool or picturesque garden. (See also Restaurants and A-Z sections)

STANFORD

Springfontein Sleeps Wortelgat Road, Stanford ▪ 5 rooms ▪ Rates from R1200 per room B&B ▪ Major credit cards accepted (no Amex) ▪ Restaurant ▪ Weddings/functions ▪ Pool ▪ Tennis court ▪ Mountain biking ▪ Walks/hikes ▪ Birding ▪ Cellar tours ▪ Wine tasting ▪ Laundry service ▪ Fireplace ▪

Under-floor heating ▪ WiFi ▪ Mini-bar, coffee/tea making facilities ▪ Owners Jurgen Schneider and Johst Weber ▪ hospitality@springfontein.co.za ▪ www.springfontein.co.za ▪ **T** +27 (0)28-341-**0651** ▪ C +27 (0)73-553-0676 ▪ F +27 (0)28-341-0112

Riverside Suites offers three new suites featuring bedroom with lounge area, under-floor heating, large bathrooms and swimming pool with views onto the Klein River Mountains. Sleeps two guests per suite. **Milkwood Cottage** offers a large en suite bedroom, open-plan living area, fireplace and outside patio. Sleeps two guests. **Fisherman Cottage** offers a modern, romantic one-room unit with double bed and fireplace. Sleeps two guests. (See also Restaurants and A-Z sections)

STELLENBOSCH

Aaldering Luxury Lodges Aaldering Vineyards & Wines, Devon Valley Road, Stellenbosch ▪ TGCSA 5-star guest house ▪ 3 rooms ▪ Rates R2500 per room B&B ▪ Major credit cards accepted ▪ Spa treatments (by arrangement) ▪ Walks/hikes ▪ Birding ▪ Fishing ▪ Cellar tours ▪ Wine tasting ▪ Laundry service ▪ Secure parking ▪ Shuttle service ▪ Air-conditioning ▪ Fireplace ▪ Safe ▪ TV ▪ DSTV ▪ CD Player ▪ iPad ▪ WiFi ▪ Owners Fons and Marianne Aaldering ▪ estate@aaldering.co.za ▪ www.aaldering.co.za ▪ **T** +27 (0)21-865-2495

Indulge yourself Cape Dutch-style at one of Aaldering Estate's three five-star luxury lodges, each offering a king-size bedroom, designer bathroom with bath and shower, spacious living room with romantic fireplace, antiques, and kitchenette with Nespresso coffee machine (full hot breakfast served daily). Included in the price are three bottles of wine, to enjoy during your stay, and a personal cellar tasting with the winemaker. (See also A-Z sections)

Caledon Villa 7 Neethling Street, Stellenbosch ▪ TGCSA 3-star guest house ▪ National monument ▪ 15 rooms ▪ Low season R525-R600pps B&B, high season R625-R750pps B&B ▪ Visa & MasterCard accepted ▪ Conferences ▪ Pool ▪ Secure parking ▪ Shuttle service ▪ Air-conditioning and fireplaces in some rooms ▪ DSTV selection ▪ WiFi ▪ Safe deposit ▪ German and Dutch also spoken ▪ Owners Johan & Ode Krige ▪ info@caledonvilla.co.za ▪ www.caledonvilla.co.za ▪ **T/ F** +27 (0)21-883-8912

Explore the historic heart of Stellenbosch with its restaurants, shops and art galleries on foot from this splendid Edwardian house. The owner's in-depth research into history, culture, genealogy,

wine and art is reflected in the character and ambience of Caledon Villa. Enjoy the colour play of sunset on the mountains from our roof terrace and expect expert assistance in the planning of any outings and tours!

Devonvale Golf & Wine Estate Bottelary Road, Koelenhof, Stellenbosch ▪ TGCSA 4-star hotel ▪ 29 hotel rooms (Petit rooms, one-bedroom self-catering apartment and two-bedroom self-catering apartments) ▪ 7 holiday houses ▪ Seasonal rates ▪ Major credit cards accepted ▪ Restaurant ▪ Conferences ▪ Weddings/functions ▪ Spa ▪ Exercise room ▪ Pool ▪ Golf course ▪ Mountain biking ▪ Walks/hikes ▪ Birding ▪ Wine tasting ▪ Outdoor kids play area ▪ Secure parking ▪ Shuttle service ▪ Laundry service ▪ Air-conditioning ▪ TV ▪ DSTV ▪ WiFi ▪ Safe ▪ German spoken ▪ Hairdryer ▪ Telephone ▪ Mini fridge and kitchenette in apartments ▪ Fully equipped kitchen with fridge and washing machine in holiday houses ▪ Owners JJ Provoyeur, D. Abromowitz, B. Gutkin & R. Tanur ▪ Executive chef William Farmer ▪ marketing@devonvale.co.za ▪ www.devonvale.co.za ▪ **T** +27 (0)21-865-2080 ▪ F +27 (0)21-865-2113

Devonvale Golf & Wine Estate is a world-class championship golf course, working wine farm and residential estate located just outside Stellenbosch. Offering upmarket accommodation and conferencing/event opportunities, it boasts a lovely spa as well as the Chez Shiraz restaurant, which is open seven days a week from 7am until 9pm. Chef William Farmer specialises in African/international dishes and his three-course set menu is most popular. (See also Restaurants and A-Z sections)

Eikendal Lodge Eikendal Vineyards, R44 between Somerset West & Stellenbosch ▪ TGCSA 4-star country house; AA Superior country style retreat ▪ 2014 Award of Excellence (9.2/10 Booking.com) ▪ 9 rooms ▪ Low season R735-R785pps B&B, high season R1220-R1270 pps B&B ▪ Major credit cards accepted ▪ Restaurant ▪ Conferences ▪ Weddings/functions ▪ Pool ▪ Mountain biking ▪ Walks/hikes ▪ Birding ▪ Fishing ▪ Cellar tours ▪ Wine tasting ▪ Secure parking ▪ Laundry service ▪ Air-conditioning ▪ TV ▪ DSTV ▪ WiFi ▪ Safe ▪ Fridge ▪ Owner Prof. Rudolf Saager ▪ info@eikendallodge.co.za ▪ www.eikendallodge.co.za ▪ **T** +27 (0)21-855-3617 ▪ F +27 (0)21-855-3862

Nestled among lush vineyards on a working winery, Eikendal Lodge is a country-style retreat offering bed-and-breakfast accommodation in nine beautifully appointed en-suite rooms, each with a private terrace boasting spectacular views. In addition to daily wine tastings, activities include fly fishing (with lessons offered by experts), hiking and jogging. Attention to detail, personalised service and a homely atmosphere give each guest a sense of ownership. (See also A-Z sections)

Hunneyball House 32 Herold Rd, central Stellenbosch ▪ 8 rooms ▪ Rates on request ▪ Most major credit cards accepted ▪ Pool ▪ Cellar tours ▪ Wine and regional tours ▪ Shuttle ▪ Ceiling fans ▪ Fireplace ▪ Safe ▪ TV, DSTV and DVD Player available in certain rooms ▪ WiFi ▪ Owners Marie and Jim Hunneyball ▪ marie@hunneyballhouse.com ▪ www.hunneyballhouse.com ▪ **T +27 (0)21-882-8083**

Hunneyball House is located in the centre of bustling Stellenbosch, within strolling distance of museums, tourist attractions and some of the finest restaurants in the country. The garden is an oasis of beautifully landscaped shady areas with several fountains and a solar-heated swimming pool. Particularly renowned for their speciality breakfasts, the owners are happy to arrange wine tasting tours covering one or several wine farms.

Laibach Vineyards Lodge Laibach Vineyards, R44, Klapmuts Road, Stellenbosch ▪ TGCSA 4-star self-catering ▪ 5 apartments ▪ R590pps, single R1000 ▪ Major credit cards accepted ▪ Pool ▪ Walks/hikes ▪ Wine tasting ▪ Secure parking ▪ Ceiling fans ▪ TV ▪ DSTV ▪ WiFi ▪ Safe ▪ Owners The Laibach Family from Germany ▪ info@laibachwines.com ▪ www.laibachwines.com ▪ **T +27 (0)21-884-4511** ▪ F +27 (0)86-665-2839

Laibach Vineyards invites you to its lodge in the middle of a sea of organic vines. At this 50-hectare working wine farm, just a few kilometres north of Stellenbosch, five spacious and comfortable self-catering apartments are offered, each with a private en suite bathroom, a small but fully furnished kitchen, LCD satellite TV and WiFi, and a deck with magnificent Table Mountain views. (See also A-Z sections)

Lanzerac Hotel & Spa No.1 Lanzerac Road, Stellenbosch ▪ TGCSA 5-star boutique hotel ▪ 48 rooms and suites ▪ Seasonal rates on request ▪ Major credit cards accepted ▪ Governors Hall and The Terrace Restaurants ▪ Conferences ▪ Weddings/functions ▪ Spa and Wellness Centre ▪ Sauna ▪ Gym ▪ Pool ▪ Jacuzzi ▪ Horse riding ▪ Mountain biking ▪ Walks/hikes ▪ Birding ▪ Cellar tours ▪ Wine tasting ▪ Secure parking ▪ Shuttle service ▪

Laundry service ▪ Air-conditioning ▪ Under-floor heating ▪ TV ▪ DSTV ▪ WiFi ▪ In-room tea & coffee facilities ▪ Safe ▪ info@lanzerac.co.za ▪ www.lanzerac.co.za ▪ **T +27 (0)21-887-1132** ▪ F +27 (0)21-887-2310

Steeped in history dating back to 1692 and nestled in the idyllic Jonkershoek Valley of Stellenbosch, 300-year-old Lanzerac is synonymous with old-world charm and rich Cape heritage. Staying in exquisitely styled rooms and suites, blending period grandeur with contemporary style, guests are indulged with warm and passionate service and the finest wine and cuisine – in short, the finest hospitality the Cape winelands has to offer. (See also Restaurants and A-Z sections)

Saxenburg Estate Polkadraai Road, Kuils River ▪ 4 self-catering apartments ▪ Seasonal rates R700-R950 per room ▪ Major credit cards or EFT accepted ▪ Conferences ▪ Pool ▪ Wine tasting ▪ Secure parking ▪ TV ▪ DSTV ▪ WiFi ▪ Safe ▪ Owners Bührer Family ▪ info@saxenburg.co.za ▪ www.saxenburg.co.za ▪ **T +27 (0)21-903-6113** ▪ F +27 (0)21-903-3129

Escape the rush of the city and enjoy the tranquil ambience of one of the Cape's oldest wine farms. Saxenburg Estate is centrally located just 10 minutes away from Stellenbosch and offers various self-catering accommodation options, with breakfast available by prior arrangement. Whether travelling solo or with friends, for business or pleasure, consider the apartments at Saxenburg Estate: secure and comfortable. (See also A-Z sections)

Spier Hotel R310, Baden Powell Rd, Stellenbosch ▪ 4-star hotel ▪ 153 rooms ▪ From R1450 per room B&B ▪ Major credit cards accepted ▪ Eight Restaurant ▪ Conferences ▪ Weddings/functions ▪ Spa ▪ Pool ▪ Mountain biking ▪ Walks/hikes ▪ Segway tours, Eagle encounters and Audio walks ▪ Birding ▪ Cellar Tours ▪ Wine tasting ▪ Secure parking ▪ Shuttle service ▪ Laundry service ▪ Air-conditioning ▪ Ceiling fans ▪ TV ▪ DSTV ▪ WiFi ▪ Safe ▪ Tripadvisor Hall of Fame ▪ Dutch and French spoken ▪ info@spier.co.za ▪ www.spier.co.za ▪ **T +27 (0)21-809-1100** ▪ F +27 (0)21-881-3087

Village-style buildings, lush green lawns and spacious rooms situated next to the calming Eerste River are the defining characteristics of the 4 star Spier Hotel. Our rooms are clustered around six courtyards, each with its own swimming pool. The design is reminiscent of the Bo-Kaap or Mediterranean villages where pedestrians have right of way. The Spier Hotel is situated on the historic Spier wine farm in the heart of the Stellenbosch winelands, just 20 minutes from Cape Town International Airport. (See also Restaurants and A-Z sections)

The Devon Valley Hotel   Devon Valley Road, Devon Valley, Stellenbosch ▪ TGCSA 4-star hotel ▪ 50 suites ▪ Seasonal rates from R695-R975pps B&B ▪ Major credit cards accepted ▪ Flavours Restaurant ▪ Conferences ▪ Weddings/functions ▪ 2 Pools ▪ Mountain biking ▪ Walks/hikes ▪ Birding ▪ Boule court ▪ Wine tasting ▪ Secure parking ▪ Shuttle service ▪ Laundry service ▪ Air-conditioning ▪ Fireplaces (some) ▪ TV ▪ DSTV and DVD Player ▪ WiFi ▪ Safe ▪ German spoken ▪ Owner HS&V Hospitality ▪ info@devonvalleyhotel.com ▪ www.devonvalleyhotel.com ▪ **T +27 (0)21-865-2012**

The award-winning Devon Valley Hotel is hidden away in a shady, green and peaceful corner of the Stellenbosch winelands. Nestling in its own SylvanVale vineyards, the hotel showcases breath-taking views of the olive groves, vineyards and majestic Helderberg Mountains, while offering the finest in authentic handmade hospitality. The hotel offers 50 stylishly furnished bedrooms and six air-conditioned conference venues with an abundance of natural light. (See also Restaurants)

Zevenwacht Country Inn   Zevenwacht Wine Farm, Langverwacht Road, Kuils River ▪ TGCSA 4-star country house (country inn honeymoon and luxury suites only) ▪ Total 38 rooms: 1 honeymoon suite (deluxe), 12 country inn luxury suites, 7 x 3-bedroom cottages, 1 x 4-bedroom self-catering chalet ▪ Low season from R670pps B&B, high season from R880pps B&B ▪ Major credit cards accepted ▪ Restaurant ▪ Conferences ▪ Weddings/functions ▪ Mangwanani Spa ▪ Sauna ▪ Pool ▪ Tennis court ▪ Mountain biking ▪ Walks/hikes ▪

Birding ▪ Cellar tours ▪ Wine tasting ▪ Secure parking ▪ Shuttle service ▪ Laundry service ▪ Air-conditioning ▪ TV ▪ DSTV ▪ WiFi ▪ Safe ▪ Owner Harold & Denise Johnson ▪ info@zevenwacht.co.za ▪ www.zevenwacht.co.za ▪ **T +27 (0)21-900-5700** ▪ F +27 (0)21-903-337303

Meaning 'Seven Expectations', the name Zevenwacht encapsulates several delights that await visitors at this historic estate. A leader in wine tourism, Zevenwacht was among the first farms to establish its own restaurant, hotel and conference facility, since joined by a spa. Choose between the Country Inn, offering four-star accommodation in luxuriously appointed, air-conditioned suites, the three-bedroom Vineyard Cottages, or the self-catering four-bedroom Chalet. (See also Restaurants and A-Z sections)

TULBAGH

Wittedrift Art Manor House   Vos Street, Tulbagh ▪ 3 self-catering suites ▪ Seasonal rates from R1000-R1250 per suite ▪ Nearby restaurant ▪ Conferences ▪ Weddings/functions ▪ Pool ▪ Secure parking ▪ Laundry service ▪ TV, DSTV and DVD player located in living room, as well as a fireplace ▪ WiFi ▪ Safe ▪ Owner Carol Collins ▪ readers@iafrica.com ▪ www.wittedriftmanorhouse.co.za ▪ **C +27 (0)82-894-0932**

Boasting an incredible art collection, majestic Wittedrift is a fully equipped, self-catering manor house that comfortably accommodates up to 12 in three large wings. Each consists of a large king room, separate twin room and private bathroom with bath and shower. The large dining room is ideal for private parties, soirees and small conferences, while the large stoep leads to beautiful gardens with a pool. (See also Restaurants)

Disabled Access in SA Wineries

The Accessibility for All initiative, launched in conjunction with Guy Davies' Disability Solutions team in the 2002 guide, has been funded by Platter's in the interests of inclusive wine tourism.

The aim is to verify that venues which are open to the public at set times, and claim to be disabled friendly, are in fact accessible. Accessibility for All means that any person with a special need, not only wheelchair users (as the international wheelchair icon seems to suggest) is provided safe access at venues where the icon is displayed in the guide.

The special needs community is broad and accounts for about 15% of the population. It includes people who are visually impaired, hearing impaired, elderly, mothers with prams and others.

The 2002 book featured 104 wineries that had been assessed and shown as accessible. That number now stands at 208, illustrating the willingness of the wine industry to make the effort to be inclusive of a wider audience.

We believe the right attitude to accommodating visitors at venues is very important, with 'friendly' being the key word. Wine tourism is an integral part of South Africa's tourism offering, in which service is king. Accessibility should be seen as a core service.

The assessments in brief:

- Jeremy Hazell, Disability Solutions' leg-man, visits only wineries that consider their facilities to be disabled friendly. The evaluations cover both new and recently upgraded venues, and the results are incorporated into the relevant producer entries in the A-Z section of the book, in the form of the universally recognisable 'wheelchair' icon, as well as in the look-up tables which accompany the maps.

- Wineries open only by appointment are excluded, as it is felt that in these cases visitors can ascertain their individual requirements when making an appointment.

- The assessments cover four aspects: parking, the tasting area, toilet facilities and cellar tours, if offered. The focus is on the tasting area, however, and in the A-Z we display the icon for wineries whose tasting area is considered accessible.

- All assessments are concluded with suggestions to wineries on how to improve access, where necessary, in all four of the above aspects.

- Many wineries have perfectly accessible toilet facilities but others have toilets that are either in the process of renovation or not spacious enough for all wheelchair users. We suggest that wineries are phoned in advance to determine if their toilet facilities are adequate.

- Bear in mind that wineries which are not flagged as accessible in the A-Z or the maps table do not necessarily have deficient or non-existent facilities for people with disabilities; it might simply be that we are not yet in a position to comment on them.

- With Jeremy criss-crossing the winelands with his wheelchair and hand-controlled car, assessments are a work in progress. So we invite readers who have any comments and suggestions about the project to please contact him through our offices or directly on his mobile phone +27 (0)82-377-3498 or email jeremy@disabilitysolutions.co.za.

- While Guy and Jeremy base their assessments on the principles of Universal Design (making things safer, easier and more convenient for everyone), they try to be sensitive to the practical implications for each winery. In agricultural, rural and historical settings it is often a real challenge for wineries to ensure that access conforms to international standards.

Winelands Maps

The maps in this section show locales where wine is available for tasting/sale either at set times or by appointment. The larger-scale map below shows the areas covered by the maps, and the table starting on the next page lists some details for prospective visitors.

Areas covered by the maps

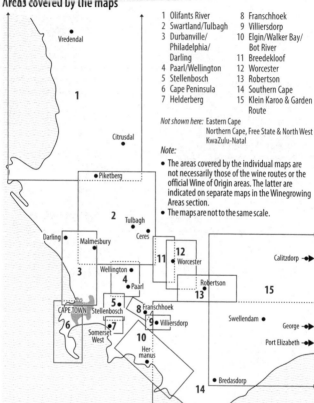

1 Olifants River
2 Swartland/Tulbagh
3 Durbanville/
   Philadelphia/
   Darling
4 Paarl/Wellington
5 Stellenbosch
6 Cape Peninsula
7 Helderberg
8 Franschhoek
9 Villiersdorp
10 Elgin/Walker Bay/
   Bot River
11 Breedekloof
12 Worcester
13 Robertson
14 Southern Cape
15 Klein Karoo & Garden
   Route

Not shown here: Eastern Cape
Northern Cape, Free State & North West
KwaZulu-Natal

Note:

• The areas covered by the individual maps are not necessarily those of the wine routes or the official Wine of Origin areas. The latter are indicated on separate maps in the Winegrowing Areas section.
• The maps are not to the same scale.

Some distances from Cape Town (kilometres)

Calitzdorp	370	Paarl	60	Tulbagh	120
Franschhoek	75	Robertson	160	Vredendal	300
Hermanus	120	Stellenbosch	45	Worcester	110

Key for maps

═══ Main access roads	R62 R60 ═ Road numbers	
── Roads	⬤ ● Towns	
······· Gravel roads		

Details of Locales Shown on Maps

The tables below are intended to facilitate winery visits by providing summary information about all the winetasting venues which are open to the public, either at set times or by appointment, and appear on our winelands maps. Venues are listed by region, and details provided include a **map grid-reference**, if applicable; whether the particular venue is **open only by appointment** (T); **open on Saturdays and/or Sundays** (✓ = at set times; T = by appointment); **open on public holidays** (✗ = closed all public holidays; otherwise assume open all or some holidays); and whether **meals/refreshments are available** (BYO = bring your own picnic). Other details include availability of **accommodation**, **cellar tours** and **facilities for children**.

Venues which have tasting facilities **friendly to individuals with reduced mobility**, as audited by our disability consultants, are highlighted. **Other languages spoken** (besides English and Afrikaans) are also noted (Danish = da, Dutch/Flemish = nl, French = fr, German = de, Hebrew = he, Hungarian = hu, Italian = it, Japanese = ja, Mandarin = mdr, Norwegian = nn, Portuguese = pt, Romanian = ro, Russian = ru, Setswana = tn, Spanish = sp, Swedish = sv, Swiss = gsw, isiXhosa = xh, isiZulu = zu). For more information, **particularly items marked with an asterisk**, see the A–Z and Restaurants/ Accommodation sections. For **GPS coordinates**, where known, for wineries open to the public, see the relevant A-Z entries.

	Grid reference	Open by appt. only	Open Saturdays	Open Sundays	Open public holidays	Meals/refreshments	Accommodation	Cellar tours	Disabled friendly	Child friendly	Languages spoken
Breedekloof Map											
Aufwaerts		T									
Avondrood			T			T/BYO*	✓	✓		1	
Badsberg			✓		✗	BYO		T	✓	1	
Bergsig			✓			✓		T	✓	1	
Botha			✓			BYO		T	✓		
Breëland		T*				T/BYO*	✓	T			
Dagbreek		T			✗	BYO		T			
De Breede		T									
Du Preez			✓		✗	BYO		T*	✓		
Du Toitskloof			✓			✓		T	✓		de
Goudini			✓			✓*		T			
Jason's Hill			✓			✓		T	✓	1	
Kirabo		T			✗	T/BYO		✓		1	
Ladera		T*				T*		T			sp
Lateganskop								T			
Lorraine		T			✗	T/BYO*		T			
Merwida			✓				✓		✓		
Mountain Oaks		T						T			
Mountain Ridge					✗	BYO			✓		
Olifantsberg		T*									

	Grid reference	Open by appt. only	Open Saturdays	Open Sundays	Open public holidays	Meals/refreshments	Accommodation	Cellar tours	Disabled friendly	Child friendly	Languages spoken
Opstal			✓	T		✓*		✓*	✓	1	
Rico Suter		T					✓				de/fr/it
Slanghoek			✓					T	✓		
Stofberg			T	T	×			✓*			
TCB Wines					×	BYO	✓	✓			
uniWines			✓			BYO		✓*	✓		
Waboomsrivier					×			T*			
Cape Peninsula Map											
Ambeloui		T									
Beau Constantia			✓	✓		✓*					
Buitenverwachting			✓		×	✓		T	✓		
Cape Point			✓	✓		✓*			✓	1	
Constantia Glen			✓	✓		✓*					
Constantia Mist		T					✓				
Constantia Uitsig			✓	✓		✓					
Dorrance						✓					fr
Eagles' Nest			✓	✓		✓			✓		
Groot Constantia			✓	✓		✓		✓	✓	1	de/fr/nl
High Constantia			✓			T/BYO		✓			
Hout Bay		T						T		1	de
Klein Constantia			✓	✓*					✓		fr/sv
New Beginnings		T									fr
Nova Zonnestraal		T			×						
Signal Hill			✓*		×	✓*		✓			fr
Silvermist			✓	✓		✓*	✓				
Steenberg			✓	✓		✓	✓	✓	✓		
Tim Martin		T*			×						fr
Township Winery											
Vaughan Johnson											
Wade Bales Wine Society					×						
Durbanville, Philadelphia & Darling Map											
Altydgedacht			✓	✓		✓		T		1	
Bloemendal			✓	✓		✓			✓		
Capaia			✓*	✓*		✓		✓		1	de
Cloof			✓			✓*		T	✓	1	
D'Aria			✓	✓		✓	✓			1	nl
Darling Cellars			✓			✓*		T	✓	1	xh

	Grid reference	Open by appt. only	Open Saturdays	Open Sundays	Open public holidays	Meals/refreshments	Accommodation	Cellar tours	Disabled friendly	Child friendly	Languages spoken
De Grendel			✓	✓		✓		T	✓		
Diemersdal			✓	✓		✓		T			
Durbanville Hills			✓	✓		✓*		✓*	✓	1	
Groote Post			✓	✓		✓*		✓	✓	1	
Hillcrest			✓	✓		✓		T			
Klein Roosboom			✓	✓		✓*		✓	✓	1	
Kronendal		T				✓*		T	✓		
Lanner Hill		T*									
Maastricht		T									
Maison de Teijger		T									
Meerendal			✓	✓		✓	✓	T	✓	1	xh/zu
Nitida			✓	✓		✓			✓	1	
Nomada		T									
Nuweland			✓	✓		✓		T	✓	1	
Ormonde			✓							1	
Phizante Kraal			✓			✓					
Russo		T			X			T			
Signal Gun			✓	✓		✓					
Vierlanden		T*			X			T*			
Wines of Cape Town		T									
Withington			✓	✓					✓		
Eastern Cape Map											
Harrison		T					✓	T			
La Terre La Mer		T						T			
St Francis Point		T									
Theescombe		T				T*		T			
Elgin, Walker Bay & Bot River Map											
Alheit		T									
Almenkerk			✓	✓		✓/BYO*		✓*			nl/fr
Arumdale			✓	✓							
Ataraxia			✓	✓*							
Barry Gould		T				T*	✓			1	
Bartho Eksteen			✓			✓*		✓		1	fr/xh
Barton			✓				✓	✓	✓		
Beaumont			✓	✓		✓*	✓	✓	✓		
Belfield		T					✓	T			
Benguela Cove			✓	✓					✓		

	Grid reference	Open by appt. only	Open Saturdays	Open Sundays	Open public holidays	Meals/refreshments	Accommodation	Cellar tours	Disabled friendly	Child friendly	Languages spoken
Blomendahl		T									de
Boschrivier			✓			✓/BYO	✓		✓		
Bouchard Finlayson			✓		×	✓/BYO*		✓	✓		de/fr
Catherine Marshall		T				T		T			
Charles Fox			✓	✓				✓		1	
Corder			T	T	×						
Creation			✓	✓		✓		✓	✓	1	de/fr
Dispore Kamma		T						T			
Domaine des Dieux			✓	✓							
Eerste Hoop		T*					✓	T			
Elgin Ridge		T*				✓/BYO*		T*			fr
Elgin Vintners			✓	✓			*				
Feiteiras		T									
Gabriëlskloof			✓			✓		T	✓	1	
Goedvertrouw		T				T	T			1	
Hamilton Russell			✓					T			tn/xh
Hannay		T				T/BYO		T			
Hermanuspietersfontein			✓	✓*		✓*	✓	T	✓		
Highlands Road			✓	✓		✓		✓	✓	1	
Hornbill			✓			✓	✓	✓			
Iona		T		×				✓			
Jakob's Vineyards		T									
La Vierge			✓	✓		✓		T	✓		fr
Lothian		T					✓				sp
Luddite		T				T*		T	✓		nl
Misty Mountains			✓			✓*		T			
Mount Babylon		T						T			
Newton Johnson			✓		×	✓			✓		
Oak Valley			✓	✓		✓	✓		✓		it/fr
Oneiric		T				BYO					
Oude Molen			T*		×			✓*			
PaardenKloof		T*						T			xh
Paul Cluver			✓	✓*		✓*			✓		
Paul Wallace		T*	✓								
Raka			✓			BYO		T	✓		
Restless River		T			×	T/BYO*		T			
Richard Kershaw		T									fr

	Grid reference	Open by appt. only	Open Saturdays	Open Sundays	Open public holidays	Meals/refreshments	Accommodation	Cellar tours	Disabled friendly	Child friendly	Languages spoken
Rivendell			✓	✓		✓*				1	
Robert Stanford			✓	✓		✓*				1	
Ross Gower		T					✓				fr/de
Shannon		T							✓		de/sp
South Hill			✓	✓		✓*	✓		✓		
Southern Right			✓					✓	✓		
Spioenkop		T			×			T			fr/nl
Spookfontein			✓	✓		✓	✓				
Springfontein			✓	✓		✓*	✓	✓			
Stanford Hills			✓	✓		✓*	✓		✓		
Sumaridge			✓	✓		✓*	✓		✓	1	
Vaalvlei		T*					✓				
Walker Bay Vineyards			✓	✓		✓/BYO		T	✓	1	
Whalehaven			✓	✓				T			
Wilde Haf		T									
Wildekrans			✓	✓		✓	✓	✓	✓		
William Everson		T					✓	T			
Wine Village-Hermanus			✓	✓					✓		
Winters Drift			✓			✓			✓	1	
Franschhoek Map											
Akkerdal					×		✓				
Allée Bleue			✓	✓		✓	✓	T	✓	1	de
Anthonij Rupert			✓	✓*		✓			✓		
Babylonstoren			✓	✓		✓*	✓	✓	✓		
Backsberg			✓	✓		✓/BYO		T*	✓	1	
Bellingham			✓	✓		✓*				1	
Black Elephant		T						T			
Boekenhoutskloof		T			×				✓		xh
Boschendal			✓	✓		✓	✓	✓	✓	1	
Cape Chamonix			✓	✓		✓	✓	T			
Colmant								✓*	✓		fr
Dieu Donné			✓	✓		✓		T*			
Eikehof			✓	✓		✓*					
Four Paws		T									
Franschhoek Cellar			✓	✓		✓*			✓	1	
Freedom Hill			✓		T	T*			✓	1	
GlenWood			✓*	✓*		✓*		✓*	✓		

	Grid reference	Open by appt. only	Open Saturdays	Open Sundays	Open public holidays	Meals/refreshments	Accommodation	Cellar tours	Disabled friendly	Child friendly	Languages spoken
Grande Provence			✓	✓		✓	✓	✓*	✓	1	
Haut Espoir		T			×			T	✓		
Haute Cabrière			✓	✓		✓		✓*	✓		fr/de
Holden Manz			✓	✓		✓	✓	✓	✓		de
La Bri			✓			✓*		✓			
La Chataigne			✓	✓	×		✓		✓		sv
La Chaumiere		T						T			
La Couronne			✓	✓		✓*	✓			1	
La Motte			✓			✓			✓	1	xh
La Petite Ferme		T*				✓	✓	✓			
La Petite Vigne		T						T			
Landau du Val		T									
Le Lude			✓	✓		✓	✓	✓			
Le Manoir de Brendel			✓	✓			✓			1	
Leopard's Leap			✓	✓		✓				1	
Lynx			✓	T	T			✓			de/sp
Maison			✓	✓		✓					
Mont Rochelle			✓	✓		✓	✓	✓*			
Môreson			✓	✓		✓		✓			
My Wyn			T	T	T	T*		✓			
Noble Hill			✓	✓		✓		T	✓	1	fr
Plaisir			✓	✓*		✓*	*	✓	✓	1	de
Rickety Bridge			✓	✓		✓	✓	✓	✓	1	
Rupert & Rothschild			✓			✓*			✓		
Solms-Delta			✓	✓		✓*		T	✓	1	
Stony Brook		T*					✓		✓		
The House of GM&AHRENS		T			×	T		T			
Topiary			✓	T		T/BYO	✓	T	✓		fr
Val de Vie			✓	✓		✓			✓		
Vrede en Lust			✓	✓		✓	✓	T*	✓	1	
Helderberg Map											
Aeternitas		T			×						
Avontuur			✓	✓		✓		T	✓		de/pt
BLANKbottle		T*									
Cape Classics		T									
Cavalli			✓	✓		✓*			✓		
Chennells		T*			×			T			de/sp

	Grid reference	Open by appt. only	Open Saturdays	Open Sundays	Open public holidays	Meals/refreshments	Accommodation	Cellar tours	Disabled friendly	Child friendly	Languages spoken
Clive Torr		T									
Conspirare		T									
Croydon			✓					T	✓	1	
Eikendal			✓	✓		✓*	✓	✓	✓	1	de
Equitania		T			X	BYO					
Flagstone			✓					T	✓		
Foothills		T				T	✓				
Grangehurst			✓*	✓*			✓				
Hathersage		T*			X						
Heron Ridge		T			X			T			
Highberry		T									
Idiom			✓*			✓*					it
Jasper Raats		T									
Journey's End		T*				T/BYO*					
Ken Forrester			✓	✓*		✓*			✓		
Le Riche			T		X			✓			de
Lithos		T*			X			T			
Longridge			✓			✓		T	✓		
Lourensford			✓	✓		✓		✓	✓		
Lyngrove		T*	✓	✓		✓*	✓				
Miravel		T			T	T	✓				nl/fr
Morgenster			✓	✓		✓					
Mount Rozier											
Onderkloof		T					✓	T			
Osbloed		T*						T*			
Paul Roos		T						T			fr
Pfeifer's		T									gsw/de
Post House			T		X	BYO	✓	✓	✓		
Romond		T*					✓	T*			
Skaap						T*	✓			1	nl
Somerbosch			✓	✓		✓		T	✓	1	
Somerset Wines			✓		X						
Stonewall		T*				T					
The Winery of Good Hope		T*			X						fr/sv
Vergelegen			✓	✓		✓		✓*	✓	1	
Waterkloof			✓	✓		✓*		T	✓		
Yonder Hill			✓*		X				✓		

	Grid reference	Open by appt. only	Open Saturdays	Open Sundays	Open public holidays	Meals/refreshments	Accommodation	Cellar tours	Disabled friendly	Child friendly	Languages spoken
Klein Karoo & Garden Route Map											
Andersons		T			×						
Axe Hill		T						T			
Baleia			✓					T			
Barrydale			✓								
Bergwater			✓	✓		T/BYO	✓	T	✓		
Boplaas			✓	✓				T		1	
Bramon			✓	✓		✓		T	✓	1	
Calitzdorp			✓			T/BYO		T	✓		
De Krans			✓			✓/BYO*			✓	1	
Domein Doornkraal			✓			✓*	✓				
Du'SwaRoo		T*			×						
Excelsior Vlakteplaas		T									
Fernskloof			✓	T*		BYO	✓			1	sp
Garden Route			✓*						✓		
Grundheim			✓					✓			
Herold			✓			✓*	✓	✓	✓	1	
Hillock			✓	✓		✓	✓	✓			
Jakkalsvlei			✓			✓				1	
Joubert-Tradauw			✓			✓	✓	✓	✓	1	
Karusa			✓			✓			✓		
Kingna Distillery			T	T				✓*			de
Lieben		T									
LuKa		T									
Mimosa			✓	✓		✓	✓		✓		de/gsw
Mons Ruber			✓		×	BYO					
Montagu Wine Cellar					×				✓		
Newstead			✓			T*		T			zu
Packwood			T	T	T	T*	✓				
Peter Bayly		T						T			
Plettenvale		T				✓	✓				
Rare Earth			✓	✓			✓				
Reiersvlei		T*						✓			
SoetKaroo			✓						✓		de
Star Hill			✓	✓		✓	✓			1	
The Goose		T				T					
TTT Cellar			✓	T		BYO		✓	✓		

	Grid reference	Open by appt. only	Open Saturdays	Open Sundays	Open public holidays	Meals/refreshments	Accommodation	Cellar tours	Disabled friendly	Child friendly	Languages spoken
Varkenskraal		T					✓				
Withoek		T					✓	T			
KwaZulu-Natal Map											
Abingdon		T*	✓	✓		✓*		T			
Highgate		T				✓		T		1	de
Northern Cape, Free State & North West Map											
Bezalel			✓			✓*		✓		1	nl
Die Mas			✓			T/BYO*	✓	✓*		1	
Douglas					×			T			
Hartswater								T			
Landzicht					×						
Lowerland		T						T			
Orange River			✓		×			✓*	✓		
Olifants River Map											
Bellpost		T						T			
Cape Rock		T				BYO		T			
Cecilia		T									
Cederberg			✓	✓*		BYO	✓				
Desert Rose		T									
Driehoek			✓			BYO	✓			1	
Fryer's Cove			✓			✓*		✓	✓		
Klawer			✓			BYO			✓	1	
Lutzville			✓			✓		✓	✓		de
Matzikama		T									
Melkboomsdrift						✓*	✓				
Namaqua			✓			✓*		✓*		1	
Seal Breeze			✓			T/BYO		✓	✓	1	
Sir Lambert		T*				✓/BYO*	✓			1	
Stellar					×			T			
Stoumann's			T		×	T		✓			
Teubes			✓			✓/BYO*	✓	T	✓	1	
Tierhoek		T*			×	BYO	✓	T*			
Vleiland		T*				BYO					
Paarl & Wellington Map											
Alkmaar	G2		✓					T			
Andreas	G1	T*			×		✓	T			sv
Anura	C7		✓	✓		✓*		✓	✓		de

	Grid reference	Open by appt. only	Open Saturdays	Open Sundays	Open public holidays	Meals/refreshments	Accommodation	Cellar tours	Disabled friendly	Child friendly	Languages spoken
Arra	C8		✓	✓							
Avondale	F6	T*						T	✓	1	
Ayama	B2	T*				T/BYO				1	it
Baratok Wines	G2	T			×						
Bayede!	E6		T	T	×						
Bergheim	E6	T									
Black Pearl	D5	T*					✓	T*	✓		
Blouvlei	G2		T		×			✓*	✓		de
Boland	E4		✓	✓		✓		T			
Bosman	G1	T*						T			
Calais	F4	T*					✓				
Cape Wine	E5		✓			✓					
Crows Nest	D3		T	T	T	T/BYO		✓*		1	
Damarakloof	A7	T*									
David Frost	E5		✓								
De Villiers	E6	T									
De Zoete Inval	E6	T									
Diemersfontein	F2		✓	✓		✓	✓	T			
Diners Club Bartho Eksteen	C3	T						T			
Domaine Brahms	C3	T			T			T			
Doolhof	H1		✓	✓		✓*	✓	T	✓		
Doran	D1	T*	✓	✓					✓		
Druk My Niet	F4	T			×	T/BYO	✓	T			de
Dunstone	H1		✓	✓		✓	✓	✓*	✓	1	
Eenzaamheid	B5	T									
Esau	E6	T									
Fairview	D6		✓	✓		✓			✓		
Glen Carlou	D7		✓	✓		✓		T	✓	1	de
Groot Parys	E5	T									nl
Hawksmoor	A7	T*				T*	✓				fr/de/ja
Hildenbrand	G2		✓	T*		T*	✓		✓		de
Imbuko	F4		✓		×	T*		T			
Jacaranda	F1		✓			T*	✓				fr/de/mdr
Jacques Germanier	C1		✓		×	✓*	✓	✓			fr
Jacques Smit	F2	T						T		1	
Joostenberg	A7	T*				✓	✓	T	✓	1	
Juno	E5		✓			✓					

	Grid reference	Open by appt. only	Open Saturdays	Open Sundays	Open public holidays	Meals/refreshments	Accommodation	Cellar tours	Disabled friendly	Child friendly	Languages spoken
Klein Optenhorst	H1	T									
Klein Parys	E5		✓			✓		✓	✓	1	
Kleine Draken	D6				×	T*		T	✓		
KWV	E6		✓	✓		✓*		✓	✓		de
La Ferme Derik	D3	T						T			
Laborie	E6		✓	✓		✓	✓		✓		de
Landskroon	D6		✓*			BYO	✓	T*		1	
Lazanou	F1	T*				T*	✓				
Le Fût	F5	T									
Linton Park	G1	T*			×	T		T*			
Maske	G2	T				BYO					de
Mason's Winery	E6	T				✓*					
Mellasat	G5		✓	✓		T*		T	✓		
Mitre's Edge	C8	T*					✓	T			
Mont du Toit	G2		T		×	BYO*	✓	✓*	✓		de
Mooi Bly	F4	T				BYO	✓	T			nl
Nabygelegen	H1		✓		×		✓	✓			
Napier	G2		✓			✓*		✓	✓		
Nederburg	F5		✓	✓*		✓*		✓	✓		de
Nelson	D3	T			×		✓	T	✓	1	
Niel Joubert	C8	T*			×						
Olsen	G5	T									
Oude Denneboom	C2	T					✓				
Painted Wolf	E6	T*									fr
Pearl Mountain	E4		✓	✓		✓					
Perdeberg	B3		✓			T/BYO*		T*			xh
Rhebokskloof	D3		✓	✓		✓		T	✓	1	
Ridgeback	D3		✓	✓		✓	✓	T	✓	1	
Ruitersvlei	D6		✓	✓		✓	✓		✓		
Scali	C1	T*			×		✓	T			
Simonshoogte	D7	T						T		1	fr/de
Simonsvlei	D7		✓	✓*		✓		T	✓	1	
Southern Sky	E5	T									
Spice Route	D6		✓	✓		✓			✓		
Stone Ridge	D1	T									
Taillard	D1	T			×			T	✓		
Tempel	E3	T					✓	T			de/fr/sv

	Grid reference	Open by appt. only	Open Saturdays	Open Sundays	Open public holidays	Meals/refreshments	Accommodation	Cellar tours	Disabled friendly	Child friendly	Languages spoken
The Ahrens Family	G0	T									
Thokozani	F2		✓	✓		✓	✓	T			
Under Oaks	E3		✓	✓				✓	T		
Upland	G3	T			T			T			de
Val du Charron	H1		✓	✓		✓	✓	✓	✓		
Veenwouden	E3	T						T			
Vendôme	E6	T			×	✓			✓		
Versailles	E1	T						T			
Vondeling	C1		T		T				✓		
Welgegund	G2	T					✓				
Welgeleë	D7		✓	✓		T					
Welgemeend	C7		✓*		×				✓	✓	
Wellington Winery	E2		✓*			BYO		T	✓		
Welvanpas	H1		✓	✓		T/BYO*				1	nl
Windmeul	D3		✓		×·			T	✓		
Zanddrift	E6					✓				1	
Robertson Map											
Arendsig		T				T/BYO	✓	T			
Ashton			✓					T	✓	1	
Bemind			✓					✓			
Bon Courage			✓			✓			✓	1	
Bonnievale			✓						✓	1	
Buffalo Creek			✓	T				✓*			
Bushmanspad						BYO	✓				nl
Cape Dreams		T						T			
Clairvaux					×	BYO		T	✓		
Cloverfield									✓		
De Wetshof			✓					T*	✓		
DuVon		T					✓	T			
Esona			✓			✓*					
Excelsior			✓			✓/BYO*	✓			1	
Fraai Uitzicht 1798			✓	✓		✓*	✓				de
Fröhlich		T									
Goedverwacht			✓			✓/BYO*		✓			
Graham Beck			✓	✓					✓		
Kleinhoekkloof		T*									
Klipdrift			✓	✓		✓		✓*			

	Grid reference	Open by appt. only	Open Saturdays	Open Sundays	Open public holidays	Meals/refreshments	Accommodation	Cellar tours	Disabled friendly	Child friendly	Languages spoken
Kranskop			✓			BYO		✓			de
Langverwacht					×			✓	✓		
Le Grand Chasseur		T			×			✓			
Lord's			✓	T	T	✓*		✓			
Major's Hill			✓				✓	T		1	
McGregor			✓			BYO		T	✓		
Quando		T			×						de
Rietvallei			✓			✓*		T	✓		
RiverGold		T				BYO					
Robertson			✓	✓				T	✓		
Roodezandt					×			T*	✓	1	
Rooiberg			✓			✓			✓	1	
Rosendal			✓	✓		✓	✓	✓	✓		nn
Solara		T									
Springfield			✓			BYO		T			
Sumsaré		T*				BYO		T*		1	
Tanagra		T*					✓	T			de
Van Loveren			✓	✓		✓	✓	T	✓		
Van Zylshof			✓					T	✓		
Vierkoppen		T									
Viljoensdrift			✓	✓*		✓*					fr
Wandsbeck			T	T	×			T	✓	1	de
Wederom		T			T	T	✓	T			de
Weltevrede			✓				✓	T	✓		
Windfall		T			×	T/BYO*	✓	T			
Wolfkloof		T				T/BYO		T			
Wolvendrift			✓			T		T	✓	1	
Wonderfontein		T*									
Zandvliet			✓						✓		
Southern Cape Map											
Andy Mitchell		T						T			
Black Oystercatcher			✓	✓		✓*	✓	✓	✓	1	
Brunia		T*				✓*					
Jean Daneel		T				✓		T			de
Lismore		T								1	
Lomond		T*			×	✓	✓				
Sijnn			✓*		×	✓*		✓*			

	Grid reference	Open by appt. only	Open Saturdays	Open Sundays	Open public holidays	Meals/refreshments	Accommodation	Cellar tours	Disabled friendly	Child friendly	Languages spoken
Strandveld			✓			BYO	✓	✓			
Swallow Hill		T						✓	T			de/fr/sp
The Berrio		T*									
Stellenbosch Map											
Aaldering	D4		✓*		×		✓	T	✓		
Akkerdraai	E8		✓								de
Allegria	B6	T					✓				nl/de/gsw
Alto	E8		✓	✓							
Amani	B6	T							✓		
Ameera	D7	T									nl/fr/de
Annandale	E8		✓			BYO		✓	✓		
Asara	D6		✓	✓		✓	✓	T		1	de
Audacia	E7		✓	✓	×	✓*			✓	1	
B Vintners	B6	T*			×						
Bartinney	H5				×	✓*		T	✓		
Beau Belle	C7	T*				T/BYO*	✓	T*			
Beau Joubert	B6		T		×	BYO	✓	T			
Bein	B6	T						T			de/fr
Bellevue	C3		✓								
Beyerskloof	E3		✓			✓		T	✓		
Bilton	E8		✓	✓				T*	✓	1	
Blaauwklippen	E6		✓	✓		✓		✓*	✓	1	de
Boschheim	E5	T									de
Boschkloof	C6		✓			✓/BYO		✓			
Botanica	D4	T*				✓*	✓				
Boutinot	H4	T			×			T			
Brampton	F5		✓			✓*					
Brenaissance	D4		✓	✓		✓	✓			1	
Camberley	H4		✓	✓		T/BYO*	✓	T			
Cape Hutton	E7	T						T			
Carisbrooke	C6				×						
Casa Mori	D3	T					✓	T			it/fr
Chabivin	E7		✓	✓							fr
Clos Malverne	D4		✓	✓		✓		✓*	✓		
Clouds	G5		✓			✓*	✓				
Clovelly	D4	T						T			
Dalla Cia	E5		✓			✓			✓		it

	Grid reference	Open by appt. only	Open Saturdays	Open Sundays	Open public holidays	Meals/refreshments	Accommodation	Cellar tours	Disabled friendly	Child friendly	Languages spoken
De Meye	E1	T*	√	√		√*		T*	√		
De Toren	B6	T						T			
De Trafford	G8		√		×			√*			
Delaire	G5		√	√		√	√	T*	√		
Delheim	F2		√	√		√		√	√		de
DeMorgenzon	C5		√	√				T			
Deux Frères	E3	T*				BYO					
Devon Rocks	D3	T					√	T			de/sv
Devonair	D3	T			×		√				
Devonvale	D3	T*				√	√		√		de/fr
DeWaal	C5		√			√					de
Die Bergkelder	E5		√					√	√		
Domaine Coutelier	D4	T			×			T			fr
Dormershire	A5	T			×			T			
Dornier	F7		√	√		√*	√	T	√	1	
Eaglevlei	E1		√	√		√*			√	1	
Edgebaston	F3	T									
Elgin Heights	C6	T									
Elsenburg	E2	T									
Entre Nous	H5	T			T	BYO		T			
Ernie Els	F8		√			√*		√	√		
Ernst Gouws	D1		√						√	1	de
Escapades	B4	T									
Fort Simon	C4		√		×		√	T	√		
Francois La Garde	E5	T									
Gentleman Spirits	E7		√*	√*				T			de
Gilga	D5	T					√				
Glenelly	F4	T*						T	√		de/fr
Goede Hoop	C3		√			T/BYO*		√			
Graceland	E7	T*			×						
Groenland	B3		√			BYO*		T	√	1	
Guardian Peak	E8		√	√		√			√		
Hartenberg	C4		√	√*		√*		T	√	1	de
Haskell	E8		√	√		√*	√	T	√	1	
Hazendal	B3		√	√		√		√	√	1	de/ru
Hidden Valley	F8		√	√		√*		T	√		
Hogan Wines	H5	T									

	Grid reference	Open by appt. only	Open Saturdays	Open Sundays	Open public holidays	Meals/refreshments	Accommodation	Cellar tours	Disabled friendly	Child friendly	Languages spoken
Hoopenburg	E1				×	BYO	✓	✓			
Hunneyball	F5	T					✓				
Jacobsdal	B6	T*									
Jordan	C5		✓	✓		✓*	✓	T*	✓		
Kaapzicht	B4		✓				✓	T			de
Kanonkop	F2		✓			T/BYO*			✓		
Kanu	E3		✓		×				✓		
Katbakkies	D5	T*			×						
Keermont	F8	T*						T			
Klein DasBosch	F7	T*				✓					
Kleine Zalze	E6		✓	✓		✓	✓		✓		
Knorhoek	F3		✓	✓		✓*	✓	✓	✓	1	
Koelenhof	D1		✓			BYO			✓	1	de
Kyburg	D4	T					✓				fr/de
Laibach	F1		✓*				✓	T			
Lanzerac	G5		✓	✓		✓	✓	✓	✓		
L'Avenir	E3		✓				✓	T	✓	1	fr
Le Bonheur	F1		✓	✓		✓*					
Le Pommier	H4		✓	✓		✓	✓			1	
Lievland	F1	T				T*	✓	T	✓		
L'Olivier	D5	T					✓				
Louiesenhof	E4		✓	✓		✓*	✓		✓	1	de
Louisvale	D4				×	BYO		✓	✓		
Lovane	D6		✓	✓	×	✓	✓	✓			
Malanot	E3	T						T*	✓		
Marianne	G1		✓	✓		✓	✓	✓	✓		de/fr
Marklew	F1	T						T			
Meerlust	B8		✓		×			T			
Meinert	D4	T*			×						de
Middelvlei	E4		✓	✓		✓*	✓	T	✓	1	
MolenVliet	H4	T					✓				
Mont Destin	G1		T		×		✓	✓*			de/fr
Monterosso	E4	T			T			T			it/zu
Mooiplaas	B4		✓	✓		T*	✓			1	
Morgenhof	F3		✓	✓		✓	✓	T	✓	1	de/fr
Mostertsdrift	E4	T				T*		T		1	
Mulderbosch	C6		✓	✓		✓*			✓		fr

	Grid reference	Open by appt. only	Open Saturdays	Open Sundays	Open public holidays	Meals/refreshments	Accommodation	Cellar tours	Disabled friendly	Child friendly	Languages spoken
Muratie	F2		✓	✓		✓*	✓	T			
Mvemve Raats	B6	T			✗						
Natte Valleij	F1	T*			✗		✓	T*		1	
Neethlingshof	D5		✓	✓		✓*		T	✓	1	de
Neil Ellis	G5		✓			✓*			✓		
Neil Patterson	E5	T						T			
Nico van der Merwe	B6	T									fr/de
Nietvoorbij	F4				✗						
Noble Savage	F5		✓								
Oldenburg	H5		✓*			✓*	*		✓		
Origin	D3	T									fr/de
Overgaauw	D5		✓			✓*					
Peter Falke	E8		✓	✓		✓*					
Quoin Rock	F3	T									
Raats	B6	T			✗						
Rainbow's End	H5	T						T			
Remhoogte	E3		✓			✓*	✓	T	✓		
Re'Mogo	E4		T*						✓		
Reyneke	B6	T*						T	✓		
Rudera	G6	T									
Rust en Vrede	E8		✓			✓*			✓		
Rustenberg	G4		✓	✓					✓		
Saltare	F5	T*						T			
Saxenburg	A5		✓	✓		✓*	✓				
Seven Sisters	D7	T									
Simonsig	E2		✓	✓		✓		✓*	✓	1	
Skilpadvlei	C6		✓	✓		✓	✓		✓	1	
Slaley	E2		✓	✓		✓		T			
Sonklip	G5	T*						T			
Spier	C7		✓	✓		✓	✓		✓	1	de/xh
Spotswood	F7	T									
Spring Grove	H4	T									
Stark-Condé	G6		✓	✓		✓			✓		ja
Stellekaya	E5				✗	T*		✓			zu
Stellenbosch Family Wines	D1	T									
Stellenbosch Hills	D6		✓		✗				✓		
Stellenbosch University	F6				✗						

	Grid reference	Open by appt. only	Open Saturdays	Open Sundays	Open public holidays	Meals/refreshments	Accommodation	Cellar tours	Disabled friendly	Child friendly	Languages spoken
Stellenbosch Vineyards	C7		✓	✓		✓			✓	1	xh
Stellendrift	C7	T						T			
Stellenrust	E7, C3		✓			✓/BYO*		T			xh
Stellenview	D4		T	T	x			✓*			
Stellenzicht	F8		✓	✓		BYO		T			
Sterhuis	C4	T						T	✓	1	
StoneyCroft	D3	T									
Summerhill	E3				x						
Super Single Vineyards	C5		✓*		x						
SylvanVale	D4		✓	✓		✓	✓		✓	1	de/xh
Tamboerskloof	F7	T*			x			T*			de/fr
Thandi	D6				x						
The Foundry	C8	T			x			T			
The High Road	E5	T			x				✓		
The Hills	D4	T									
The House of JC le Roux	D4		✓	✓		✓		✓*	✓		
Thelema	G4		✓						✓		
Tokara	G4		✓	✓		✓			✓	1	
Topaz	F2		✓*						✓		de
Uitkyk	F2		✓	✓		✓*			✓	1	
Usana	C5	T*									
Uva Mira	F8		✓	✓		✓*			✓		
Van Biljon	B6	T			x		✓	T			
Van Ryn	D6		✓	✓*				✓*			
Vergenoegd	B8		✓	✓		✓*		T	✓	1	xh
Vilafonté	E5	T						T			
Villiera	D1		✓			✓*		✓	✓		fr
Vin du Cap	D1	T									
Vredenheim	D6		✓			✓	✓		✓		
Vriesenhof	F7		T		x			T			
Vuurberg	H4	T			x			T			
Warwick	F1		✓	✓		✓*		T	✓	1	
Waterford	F7		✓					✓	✓		
Webersburg	E8		✓	✓		✓	✓	✓	✓		
Welgevallen	F5				x			✓			
Yardstick	C6	T									
Zevenwacht	B5		✓	✓		✓	✓	T	✓	1	xh

	Grid reference	Open by appt. only	Open Saturdays	Open Sundays	Open public holidays	Meals/refreshments	Accommodation	Cellar tours	Disabled friendly	Child friendly	Languages spoken
Zorgvliet	H4		✓	✓		T*	✓	T	✓	1	
Swartland Map											
AA Badenhorst		T			×		T	T			
Abbottshill		T				BYO		T			
Allesverloren			✓			✓*		T	✓	1	
Annex Kloof			✓	✓		BYO		T	✓		
Antebellum		T						T			
Babylon's Peak		T				T*	✓		✓		
Bryan MacRobert		T			×						
David & Nadia Sadie		T									
Dragonridge		T				T/BYO*	✓	T		1	
Franki's		T*			×	BYO*	✓	T*			
Het Vlock Casteel			✓			T*			✓		
Hofstraat		T						T			
Hughes Family		T									sp
Huis van Chevallerie		T									de/fr/it
Kloovenburg			✓	✓*		BYO	✓	✓*	✓		
Lammershoek		T				T/BYO		T			
Mullineux		T*						T			
Nieuwedrift			✓			T/BYO		✓		1	
Orangerie		T						T			
Org de Rac			✓			T/BYO*		✓	✓		de
Paardebosch		T									
Pulpit Rock			✓			BYO	✓	T	✓		
Riebeek			✓	✓		BYO		T	✓		
Sadie		T*									
Santa Cecilia			✓	✓		✓*	✓				
Spekulasie		T			T	T	✓	T		1	
Swartland			✓						✓	1	
The Observatory		T						T			de
Wildehurst			✓	✓			✓	T*			
Tulbagh Map											
Drostdy-Hof			✓						✓		
Fable		T						T			
Koelfontein			✓		×	BYO	✓				
Lemberg			✓	✓		T/BYO*	✓	✓	✓		
Longbarn								T			

	Grid reference	Open by appt. only	Open Saturdays	Open Sundays	Open public holidays	Meals/refreshments	Accommodation	Cellar tours	Disabled friendly	Child friendly	Languages spoken
Manley			✓			✓	✓	T			
Montpellier			✓	✓		✓*	✓	✓		1	
Oude Compagnies Post		T						T			
Rijk's			✓				✓	T	✓		
Saronsberg			✓			BYO	✓	T			
Schalkenbosch		T			×		✓	T			de
Theuniskraal			✓						✓		
Tulbagh Winery			✓*	✓*		BYO		T	✓		
Twee Jonge/Krone			✓		×			✓			de
Waverley Hills			✓	✓		✓		✓	✓	1	
Welbedacht			✓	✓*		✓	✓	✓	✓	1	de
Villiersdorp Map											
Cranefields		T									
Villiersdorp			✓			✓		T	✓		
Worcester Map											
Aan de Doorns			✓		×			T*	✓		
Alvi's Drift		T			×			T			
Auction Crossing			✓		×	✓		T		1	
Brandvlei			✓		×			T	✓		
Conradie			✓	✓		✓/BYO	✓	✓		1	
De Doorns			✓						✓		
De Wet			✓		×	BYO		T	✓		
Eagle's Cliff					×	✓*			✓	1	
Leipzig			✓			✓*	✓	✓*		1	ru
Nuy			✓			✓			✓		
Overhex			✓	✓		✓*		T	✓	1	
Stettyn			✓*		×	BYO		T*	✓	1	
Van Eck		T*				✓/BYO		✓*		1	de/xh

Northern Cape, Free State & North West

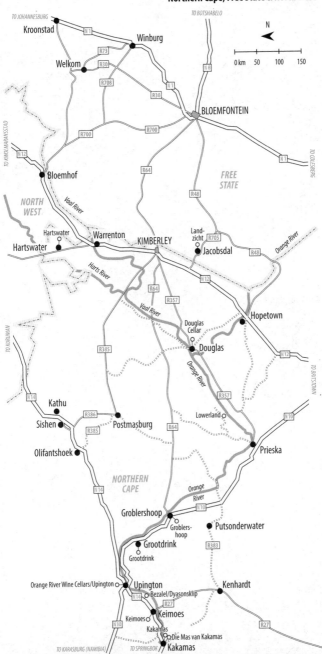

Southern Cape

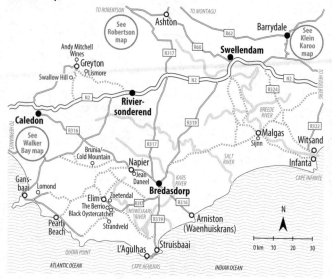

KwaZulu-Natal

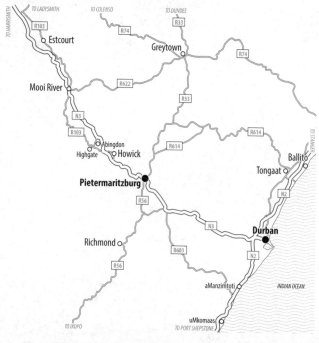

Olifants River & West Coast

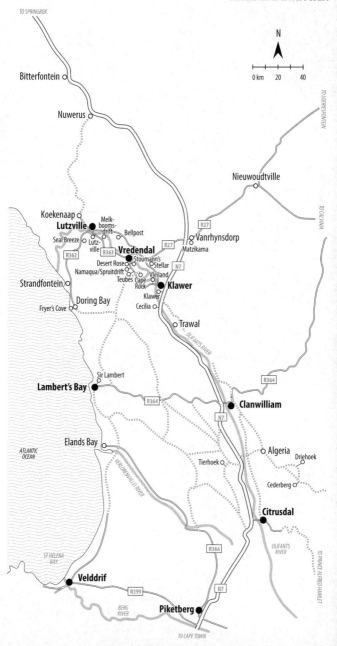

Eastern Cape

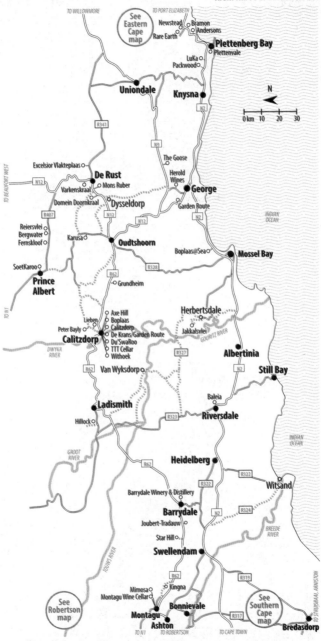

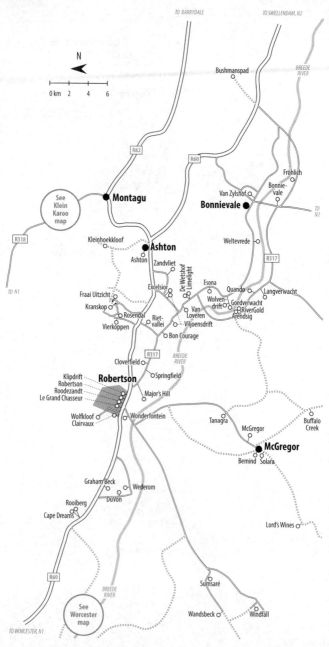

Breedekloof

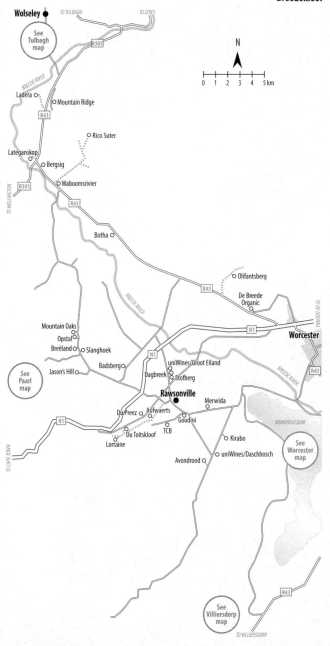

N

0 1 2 3 4 5 km

Wolseley

TO TULBAGH   *TO CERES*

See Tulbagh map

R303

BREEDE RIVER

Ladera

Mountain Ridge

R43

Rico Suter

Lateganskop

Bergsig

TO WELLINGTON

R301

Waboomsrivier

R43

Botha

BREEDE RIVER

Olifantsberg

R43

De Breede Organic

TO DE DOORNS

Mountain Oaks

Opstal

N1

Worcester

Breëland

Slanghoek

BREEDE RIVER

R43

Jason's Hill

Badsberg

N1

uniWines/Groot Eiland

Dagbreek

Stofberg

See Paarl map

Rawsonville

Merwida

Du Preez

Aufwaerts

BRANDVLEI DAM

N1

Goudini

TCB

TO CAPE TOWN

Du Toitskloof

Lorraine

Kirabo

See Worcester map

Avondrood

uniWines/Daschbosch

See Villiersdorp map

R43

TO VILLIERSDORP

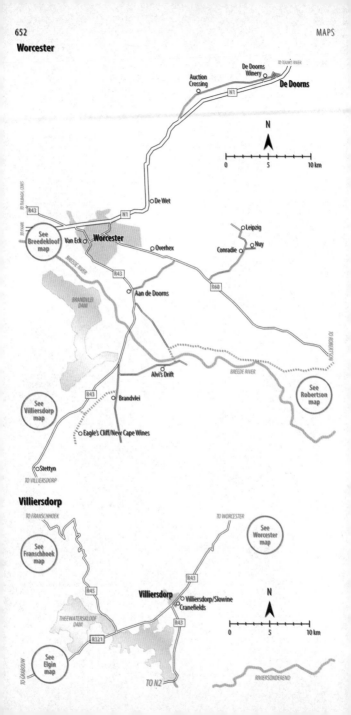

Worcester

TO TULBAGH
Auction Crossing
De Doorns Winery
De Doorns
N1
TO CERES
R43
TO PAARL
De Wet
N1
See Breedekloof map
Van Eck
Worcester
Leipzig
Overhex
Conradie
Nuy
BREEDE RIVER
R43
R60
TO ROBERTSON
BRANDVLEI DAM
Aan de Doorns
Alvi's Drift
BREEDE RIVER
See Robertson map
See Villiersdorp map
R43
Brandvlei
Eagle's Cliff/New Cape Wines
Stettyn
TO VILLIERSDORP

N
0　　5　　10 km

Villiersdorp

TO FRANSCHHOEK
TO WORCESTER
See Franschhoek map
See Worcester map
R45
R43
Villiersdorp
Villiersdorp/Slowine
Cranefields
THEEWATERSKLOOF DAM
R43
R321
See Elgin map
TO GRABOUW
TO N2
RIVIERSONDEREND

N
0　　5　　10 km

Elgin, Walker Bay & Bot River

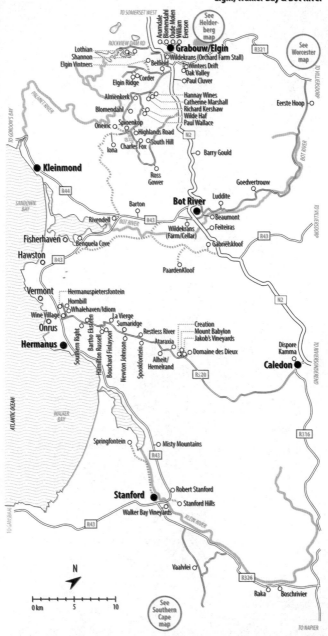

Swartland

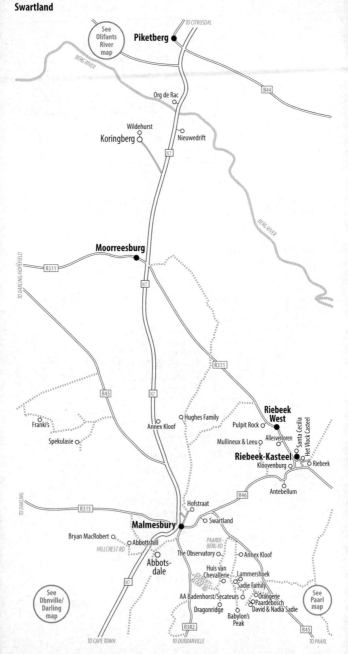

TO CITRUSDAL

See Olifants River map

Piketberg

BERG RIVER

R44

Org de Rac

Wildehurst
Koringberg
Nieuwedrift

N7

BERG RIVER

Moorreesburg

R311

R311

TO DARLING/HOPEFIELD

R45

N7

Hughes Family

Riebeek West

Franki's
Annex Kloof
Pulpit Rock

Santa Cecilia
Het Vlock Casteel

Spekulasie
Mullineux & Leeu
Allesverloren

Riebeek-Kasteel

Klóovenburg
Riebeek

Antebellum

R46

TO DARLING

R315

Hofstraat

Malmesbury

Swartland

Bryan MacRobert
Abbottshill

PAARDE-BERG RD

HILLCREST RD

The Observatory
Annex Kloof

Abbots-dale

Huis van Chevallerie
Lammershoek

N7

Sadie Family

Orangerie
Paardebosch

AA Badenhorst/Secateurs
David & Nadia Sadie

See Dbnville/ Darling map

Dragonridge
Babylon's Peak

See Paarl map

R302

TO CAPE TOWN

TO DURBANVILLE

R45

TO PAARL

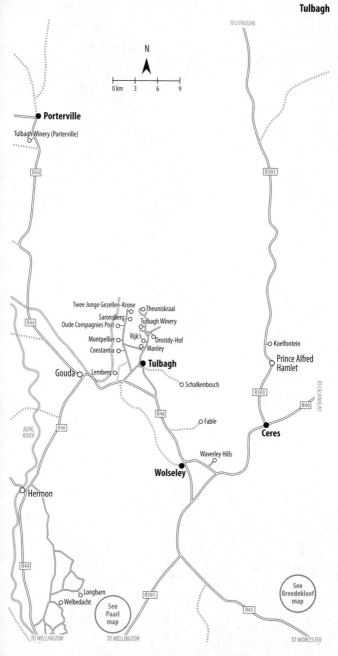

Franschhoek

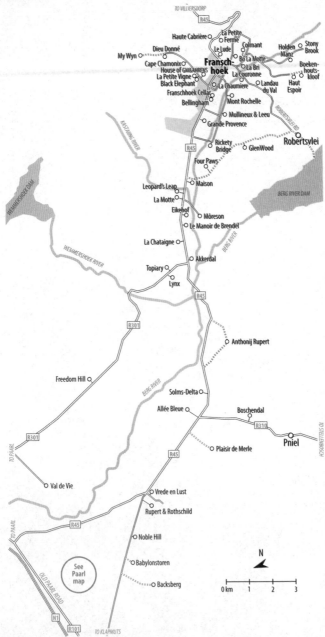

Durbanville, Philadelphia & Darling

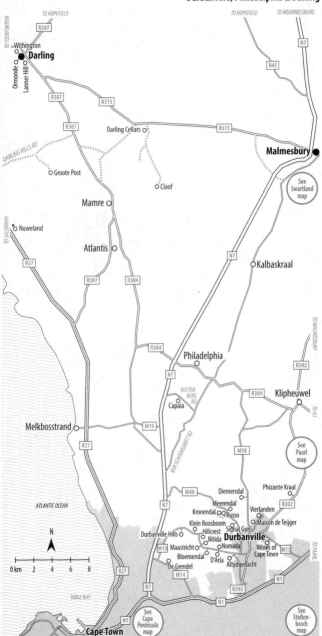

Helderberg

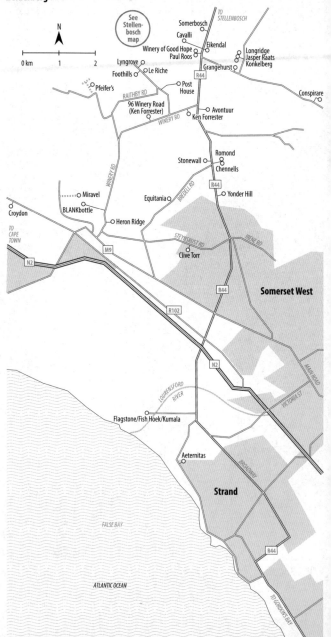

N

0 km   1   2

See Stellenbosch map

TO STELLENBOSCH

Somerbosch

Cavalli

Eikendal

Winery of Good Hope
Paul Roos

Longridge
Jasper Raats
Konkelberg

Lyngrove

Grangehurst

Foothills

Le Riche

R44

Conspirare

Pfeifer's

RAJTHBY RD

Post House

96 Winery Road
(Ken Forrester)

WINERY RD

Avontuur

Ken Forrester

WINERY RD

Romond

Stonewall

Chennells

Miravel

Equitania

R44

Yonder Hill

Croydon

BLANKbottle

BREDELL RD

Heron Ridge

TO CAPE TOWN

STEYNSRUST RD

IRENE RD

N2

M9

Clive Torr

R44

Somerset West

R102

N2

MAIN ROAD

LOURENSFORD RIVER

VICTORIA ST

Flagstone/Fish Hoek/Kumala

Aeternitas

Strand

BROADWAY

FALSE BAY

R44

ATLANTIC OCEAN

TO GORDON'S BAY

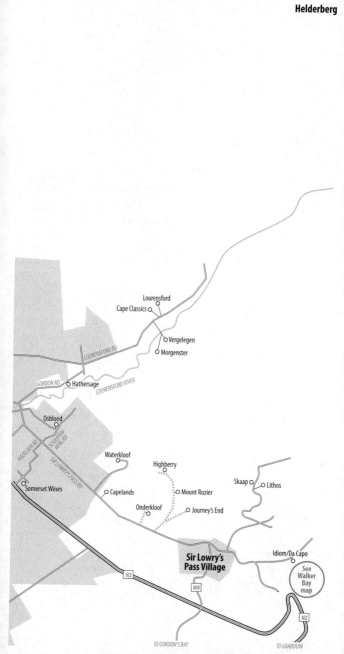

Lourensford

Cape Classics

Vergelegen

Morgenster

LOURENSFORD RD

GORDON RD   Hathersage

LOURENSFORD RIVER

Osbloed

HAZELDEN RD

SCHAPENBERG RD

SIR LOWRY'S PASS RD

Waterkloof

Highberry

Skaap   Lithos

Somerset Wines

Capelands

Mount Rozier

Onderkloof

Journey's End

Sir Lowry's Pass Village

Idiom/Da Capo

See Walker Bay map

N2

M9

N2

TO GORDON'S BAY

TO GRABOUW

Paarl & Wellington

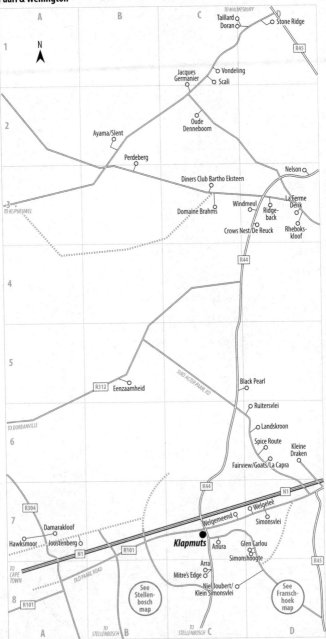

N

A　　　　B　　　　C　　　　D

TO MALMESBURY

Taillard
Doran
Stone Ridge
R45

Vondeling
Jacques
Germanier
Scali

Oude
Denneboom

Ayama/Slent

Perdeberg

Nelson

Diners Club Bartho Eksteen

La Ferme
Derik

Windmeul
Ridge-
back

Rheboks-
kloof

TO KLIPHEUWEL

Domaine Brahms

Crows Nest/De Reuck

R44

R312
Eenzaamheid

SUID AGTER PAARL RD

Black Pearl

Ruitersvlei

Landskroon

TO DURBANVILLE

Spice Route

Kleine
Draken

Fairview/Goats/La Capra

R44
N1

R304
Welgemeend
Welgeleë
Simonsvlei

Damarakloof

Hawksmoor
Joostenberg

Klapmuts

Anura
Glen Carlou

Simonshoogte

N1
R101
OLD PAARL ROAD

TO
CAPE
TOWN

Arra

Mitre's Edge

Niel Joubert/
Klein Simonsvlei

See
Stellen-
bosch
map

See
Fransch-
hoek
map

R45

R101

TO
STELLENBOSCH

TO
STELLENBOSCH

A　　　　B　　　　C　　　　D

Paarl & Wellington

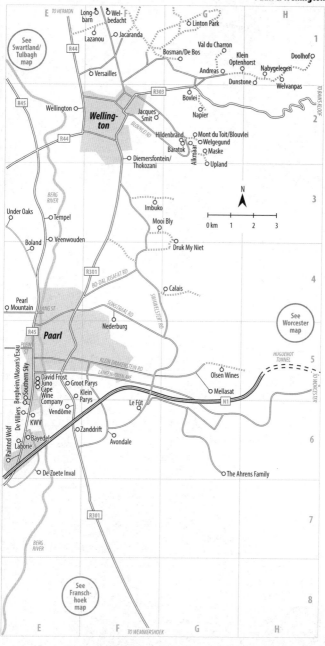

Stellenbosch

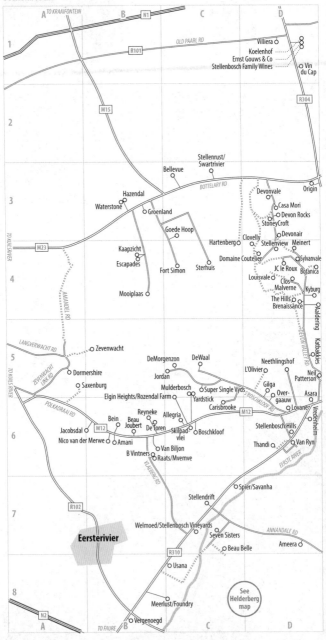

See Helderberg map

Eersterivier

Stellenbosch

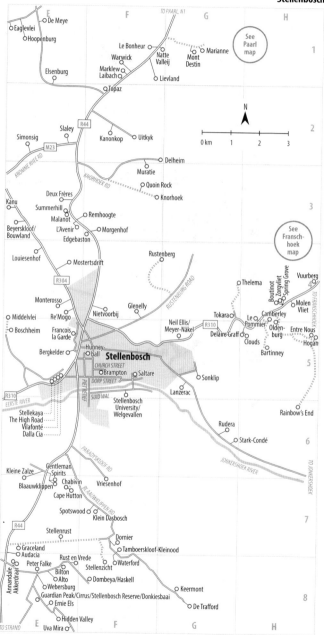

See Paarl map

See Franschhoek map

TO PAARL N1

E
F
G
H

De Meye
Eaglevlei
Hoopenburg

Le Bonheur
Warwick
Marklew
Laibach
Elsenburg
Topaz
Natte
Valleij
Mont
Destin
Marianne
Lievland

N

0 km   1   2   3

R44
Slaley
Simonsig
M23
Kanonkop
Uitkyk
KROMME RIVIER RD

Delheim
Muratie
Quoin Rock
Deux Frères
Summerhill
Malanot
L'Avenir
Edgebaston
Remhoogte
Morgenhof
Knorhoek
KNORHOEK RD

Kanu
Beyerskloof/
Bouwland
Louiesenhof
Mostertsdrift
Rustenberg

R304
Monterosso
Re'Mogo
Nietvoorbij
Glenelly
RUSTENBURG ROAD
Thelema
Boutinot
Zorgvliet
Spring Grove
Vuurberg
Molen
Vliet

Middelvlei
Boschheim
Francois
la Garde
Neil Ellis/
Meyer-Näkel
Tokara
R310
Le
Pommier
Camberley
Oldenburg
Entre Nous
Hogan

Bergkelder
Hunney-
ball
Stellenbosch
Delaire Graff
Clouds
Bartinney

CHURCH STREET
Brampton
Saltare
Sonklip
DORP STREET
SUID WAL
Stellenbosch
University/
Welgevallen
Lanzerac

Stellekaya
The High Road
Vilafonté
Dalla Cia
Rudera
Stark-Condé
Rainbow's End

R310
EERSTE RIVIER

PIET RETIEF

PARADYSKLOOF RD
JONKERSHOEK RIVER

TO JONKERSHOEK

Kleine Zalze
Gentleman
Spirits
Chabivin
Blaauwklippen
Cape Hutton
Vriesenhof

Spotswood
Klein Dasbosch

R44
Stellenrust
Dornier

Graceland
Audacia
Peter Falke
Bilton
Alto
Webersburg
Guardian Peak/Cirrus/Stellenbosch Reserve/Donkiesbaai
Ernie Els
Hidden Valley
Uva Mira

Rust en Vrede
Stellenzicht
Dombeya/Haskell
Tamboerskloof-Kleinood
Waterford
Keermont
De Trafford

BLAAUWKLIPPEN RD
Annandale
Akkerdraai

TO STRAND

E
F
G
H

1
2
3
4
5
6
7
8

TO FRANSCHHOEK